THE ROUTLEDGE READER OF AFRICAN AMERICAN RHETORIC

The Routledge Reader of African American Rhetoric is a comprehensive compendium of primary texts that is designed for use by students, teachers, and scholars of rhetoric and for the general public interested in the history of African American communication. The volume and its accompanying electronic resources include dialogues, creative works, essays, folklore, music, interviews, news stories, raps, videos, and speeches that are performed or written by African Americans. Both the book as a whole and the various selections in it speak directly to the artistic, cultural, economic, gendered, social, and political condition of African Americans from the enslavement period in America to the present, as well as to the Black Diaspora.

Vershawn Ashanti Young works in the following areas of Africana studies: language, gender, performance studies, and rhetoric. He is on faculty in the Department of Drama and Speech Communication at the University of Waterloo in Canada. He has published in such journals as *PMLA, African American Review, College Communication and Composition, JAC: A Journal of Rhetoric, Politics, and Society,* and *Present Tense: A Journal of Rhetoric in Society.*

Michelle Bachelor Robinson is the director of the Comprehensive Writing Program and a professor of African American Rhetoric at Spelman College. Her research and teaching focus on community engagement, historiography, African American rhetoric and literacy, composition pedagogy and theory, and student and program assessment. She is actively involved in community research, oral history collection, and community writing and serves as a university partner and consultant for the Historic Black Towns and Settlements Alliance, Inc.

THE ROUTLEDGE READER OF AFRICAN AMERICAN RHETORIC

The Longue Durée of Black Voices

Edited by
Vershawn Ashanti Young and
Michelle Bachelor Robinson

Routledge
Taylor & Francis Group

NEW YORK AND LONDON

First published 2018
by Routledge
711 Third Avenue, New York, NY 10017

and by Routledge
2 Park Square, Milton Park, Abingdon, Oxon OX14 4RN

Routledge is an imprint of the Taylor & Francis Group, an informa business

Library of Congress Cataloging in Publication Data
Names: Young, Vershawn Ashanti, editor. | Robinson, Michelle Bachelor, editor.
Title: The Routledge reader of African American rhetoric : the Longue Duree
    of Black voices / edited by Vershawn Ashanti Young and Michelle Bachelor
    Robinson.
Description: First edition. | London ; New York : Routledge / Taylor & Francis
    Group, [2017]
Identifiers: LCCN 2017037189 | ISBN 9780415731058 (hardcover) | ISBN
    9780415731065 (softcover)
Subjects: LCSH: African Americans—Communication. | African Americans—
    Intellectual life. | Black English. | Oratory—United States. | English
    language—United States—Rhetoric. | Readers—African Americans.
Classification: LCC P94.5.A372 U569 2017 | DDC 302.23089/96073—dc23
LC record available at https://lccn.loc.gov/2017037189

ISBN: 978-0-415-73105-8 (hbk)
ISBN: 978-0-415-73106-5 (pbk)

Typeset in Minion
by Apex CoVantage, LLC

Visit the eResources: www.routledge.com/9780415731065

Not reverie, nor nostalgia, nor melancholia, nor that most misused term, déjà vu, none of these explain from where the voices within me hail.

—*Divine Days* by Leon Forest (1992)

I dedicate this book to Ari Zhah Young—African American rhetoric is your heritage, your culture, your powerful resource for agency, authority and authenticity. May you keep it close and use it wisely.

I dedicate this book to black voices from histories past, voices we still hear—voices paving the road to a brighter future. To black voices here now—that call and respond to me—that spur me to action, to stillness, to introspection, to persuasion. To those black voices that are to come—may the legacy left for you fill your voice with cadence and candor on behalf of black people everywhere.

—VAY

This text is dedicated to all the Black rhetors of the Diaspora who have historically employed their voices to enrich the lives of their people.

—MICHELLE

CONTENTS

ABOUT THE SECTION EDITORS

Dara N. Byrne is Associate Provost and Dean of Undergraduate Studies at John Jay College of the City University of New York. She is also an Associate Professor in the Department of Communication and Theater Arts and is a specialist in critical language studies, intercultural communication, and digital media. Her publications include contributions to volumes such as *Brown v. Board of Education: Its Impact on Public Education 1954–2004* (2005, Word for Word); *Learning Race and Ethnicity: Youth and Digital Media* (2008, MIT Press); and *The Unfinished Agenda of the Selma-Montgomery Voting Rights March* (2005, Wiley), among others. Dara's current research project examines vigilante justice in online social-networking sites.

Kermit E. Campbell is Associate Professor and Chair of the Department of Writing & Rhetoric at Colgate University in Upstate New York. He has published a book (*"Gettin' Our Groove On"*) and several essays on African American rhetoric, hip-hop, and writing pedagogy. Since 2012, he has served as an associate editor of *African Journal of Rhetoric* (*AJR*) and is a member of the Executive Council of the organization that publishes the journal, the African Association for Rhetoric based in Cape Town, South Africa.

Khirsten L. Echols is Assistant Professor of English at the University of Pittsburgh. Khirsten's scholarly commitments live at the intersections of cultural rhetorics, material history, and digital humanities. Specifically, her work is centered on HBCU communities and the rhetorical affordances of institutional narratives for revisionist presentations of HBCU histories.

Yanique Hume holds a PhD in interdisciplinary studies from Emory University and is a Lecturer in Cultural Studies at the University of the West Indies, Cave Hill Campus (Barbados). She specializes in the multidisciplinary field of Caribbean Cultural Studies with a focus on Cuba and Haiti. Her research and teaching areas include: religious and performance cultures of the African diaspora, Caribbean thought, popular culture, migration, and diasporic identities. She is the coeditor of two anthologies, *Caribbean Cultural Thought: From Plantation to Diaspora* (2013) and *Caribbean Popular Culture: Power, Politics and Performance* (2016). Yanique is the recipient of grants from the Social Science Research Council, the International Development Research Centre, the Ford Foundation, and the Wenner Gren Foundation for Anthropological Research.

Joy James is F.C. Oakley 3rd Century Professor at Williams College. James is author of Shadowboxing: Representations of Black Feminist Politics; Transcending the Talented Tenth: Black

Leaders and American Intellectuals; Resisting State Violence: Radicalism, Gender and Race in U.S. Culture. Her edited books include Warfare in the American Homeland; The New Abolitionists: (Neo) Slave Narratives and Contemporary Prison Writings; Imprisoned Intellectuals; States of Confinement; The Black Feminist Reader (co-edited with TD Sharpley-Whiting); The Angela Y. Davis Reader; and numerous chapters and articles addressing feminist and critical race theory, democracy, and social justice.

Aaron Kamugisha is Senior Lecturer in Cultural Studies at the University of the West Indies, Cave Hill Campus. His current work is a study of coloniality and freedom in the contemporary Anglophone Caribbean, mediated through the thought of C.L.R. James and Sylvia Wynter. He is the editor of four edited collections on Caribbean thought: *Caribbean Political Thought: The Colonial State to Caribbean Internationalisms* (2013), *Caribbean Political Thought: Theories of the Post-Colonial State* (2013), and, with Yanique Hume, *Caribbean Cultural Thought: From Plantation to Diaspora* (2013) and *Caribbean Popular Culture: Power, Politics and Performance* (2016). He is a member of the editorial working committee for the journals *Social and Economic Studies, Journal of West Indian Literature*, and *Small Axe: A Caribbean Journal of Criticism*.

Valerie Kinloch is the Renée and Richard Goldman Dean of the University of Pittsburgh School of Education. She previously served as a professor of literacy studies and the associate dean of diversity, inclusion, and community engagement in the College of Education and Human Ecology at The Ohio State University. Her scholarship examines the literacies and community engagements of youth and adults inside and outside schools. Author of numerous publications on race, place, literacy, and diversity, her books include: *Still Seeking an Attitude: Critical Reflections on the Work of June Jordan* (2004), *June Jordan: Her Life and Letters* (2006), *Harlem on Our Minds: Place, Race, and the Literacies of Urban Youth* (2010), *Urban Literacies: Critical Perspectives on Language, Learning, and Community* (2011), *Crossing Boundaries: Teaching and Learning With Urban Youth* (2012), and *Service-Learning in Literacy Education: Possibilities for Teaching and Learning* (2015). She is working on projects on literacy, justice, race and community engagement.

Kameelah Martin is a scholar of African Diaspora literatures and cultures of North America, with special focus on folklore and spirituality. She is author of two monographs, *Conjuring Moments in African American Literature: Women, Spirit Work & Other Such Hoodoo* (2012) and *Envisioning Black Feminist Voodoo Aesthetics: African Spirituality in American Cinema* (2016). She is book review editor for the *College Language Association Journal* and currently serves as Professor of African American Studies and English at the College of Charleston (Virginia).

Jeffrey McCune is an Associate Professor of African & African American Studies and Women, Gender, and Sexuality Studies at Washington University in St. Louis. He is the Director of the Mellon Mays Undergraduate Fellowship Program. Dr. McCune is the author of the award-winning book *Sexual Discretion: Black Masculinity and the Politics of Passing* (University of Chicago, 2014). This manuscript was awarded The National Communication Association's 2015 GLBTQ Book Award and several other book honors. For his service in scholarship and to the field, Dr. McCune was awarded the 2015 Modern Language Association's GL/Q Caucus Michael Lynch Service Award. He is presently working on two book projects. The first, a full-length manuscript, is titled *Read!: An Experiment in Seeing Black*, and the other is titled *On Kanye: A Philosophy of Black Genius*. In addition to these works, Dr. McCune is in the process of collecting ethnographic and archival material to complete a second play, *AFTERLIFE: An Archive of Violence*, which explores the day-to-day impact of state-sanctioned violence on individuals within Black and Brown communities.

Vorris L. Nunley's investments are in rhetorical history and theory, African American Studies, civility/incivility, public pedagogies and composition, and neoliberalism. His work addresses the intersections of rhetoric, spatiality, affect, and neoliberalism. Informed by work in literature, rhetoric (traditional/ethnic/gendered), visceral theory, and critical, feminist theory, Professor Nunley argues for the existence of a strand of African American rhetoric and philosophy he refers to as African American Hush Harbor Rhetoric (AAHHR). Recently, his work engages in the nature of reality as a trope, neoliberalism as a public pedagogy and how it commodifies, produces, and mediates the construction and reception of masculinity/femininity, blackness, and excess. Professor Nunley also writes articles and editorials for the *Los Angeles Review of Books* and a variety of local, national, and international papers.

Michelle Bachelor Robinson is the director of the Comprehensive Writing Program and a professor of African American Rhetoric at Spelman College. Her research and teaching focus on community engagement, historiography, African American rhetoric and literacy, composition pedagogy and theory, and student and program assessment. She is actively involved in community research, oral history collection, and community writing and serves as a university partner and consultant for the Historic Black Towns and Settlements Alliance, Inc.

Donja Thomas holds a PhD in cultural and critical literacies from the College of Education and Human Ecology at The Ohio State University. She is a veteran secondary English educator, Black studies curriculum developer, activist, and scholar who has been engaged in creating classroom curriculums that center the use of critical conscious literacies and the importance of employing curricular practices rooted in the Black experience, in order to advance Black Studies in K-12 schooling. Her work explores how curricular practices rooted in the Black experience, can challenge understandings of achievement, identity, and critical consciousness for racially diverse students. Her extensive experience as an educator and researcher seeks to develop a model for infusing Black cultural studies into public school curricula.

Greg Thomas is teaching global Black Studies texts out of the English Department at Tufts University in the Boston area of Massachusetts. The founding editor of *PROUD FLESH*, an e-journal, he is the author of *The Sexual Demon of Colonial Power: Pan-African Embodiment and Erotic Schemes of Empire* (Indiana UP, 2007) as well as *Hip-Hop Revolution in the Flesh: Power, Knowledge and Pleasure in Lil' Kim's Lyricism* (Palgrave Macmillan, 2009). He is also a coeditor with L. H. Stallings of *Word Hustle: Critical Essays and Reflections on the Works of Donald Goines* (Black Classic Press, 2011). Currently, he is at work on a critical study of George L. Jackson, "The Dragon."

Elizabeth West is a Professor of English at Georgia State University. She focuses on spirituality and gender in early African American and Women's Literature, and African Diaspora Literatures of the Americas. She coedits the Roman & Littlefield book series, Black Diasporic Worlds: Origins and Evolutions from New World Slaving. She is the author of *African Spirituality in Black Women's Fiction* (Lexington Books, 2011) and coeditor of *Literary Expressions of African Spirituality* (Lexington Books, 2013). She is Treasurer of the College Language Association and Executive Director of the South Atlantic Modern Language Association, and serves on the Advisory Board of The Obama Institute for Transnational Studies.

Vershawn Ashanti Young works in the following areas of Africana studies: language, gender, performance studies, and rhetoric. He is on faculty in the Department of Drama and Speech Communication at the University of Waterloo in Canada. He has published in such journals as *PMLA, African American Review, College Communication and Composition, JAC: A Journal of Rhetoric, Politics*, and *Society*, and *Present Tense: A Journal of Rhetoric in Society*.

ILLUSTRATIONS

PREFACE

Routledge Reader of African American Rhetoric

The Routledge Reader of African American Rhetoric is composed of two parts, this print text and an online companion, that together feature dialogues, creative works, critical articles, essays, folklore, interviews, news clips, visual images, music videos, media links, raps, and speeches that are performed or written by Black people, primarily African Americans. Thus, unlike other readers of rhetoric that focus sometimes on essays but mainly on the oral traditions of African American culture (e.g., sermons or "playing the dozens"), our reader is a comprehensive compendium of primary texts that speak directly to the artistic, cultural, economic, religious, social, and political condition of African Americans from the enslavement period in America to our present era, as well as to the Black Diaspora.

The purpose of our anthology is to provide students, teachers, scholars, and general readers with an anthology of texts that are unequivocally rhetorical in that they seek to influence American culture, ideologies, laws, policies, individuals, and society, with African American life and culture in view. Along with the traditional focus on works of nonfiction within rhetorical studies, we have also included creative and imaginative texts that are educative, didactic, argumentative, and/or persuasive in nature. This textual diversity underscores our particular view of rhetoric as the pervasive means for engaging conversations, controversies, and ideas that, in this case, affect and pertain to all Americans, but especially to African Americans. Thus, to gloss the point, from our perspective, rhetoric, and therefore our reader, is not limited to speech making, essays, or the oral/vernacular traditions, but is enormously expansive, existing in various, if not all, forms of media. Our aim then in producing this collection is not only to produce a comprehensive reader of African American rhetoric but also to illustrate through the selections that African American rhetoric is found in every genre of art and literature and in every form of communication, and is, in short, all around us.

As scholars and teachers of rhetoric ourselves, we have produced the kind of text that we use in our courses and in our own research. We have produced this text because, in our experience, there is currently no other compendium of mostly primary texts that traverses various social sciences, arts, and media and is dedicated to the presentation and study of African American rhetoric. Therefore we hope our book is also useful to many others. In this regard, we would like readers to understand how our book complements some existing texts and stands importantly apart from others. For example, readers familiar with the two well-known anthologies of

African American literature (Norton and Riverside) and two books devoted to African American studies (*Call and Response* and *Let Nobody Turn Us Around*) know that the former set includes some rhetorical texts, particularly from the vernacular tradition, but privileges imaginative literature, such as fiction, drama, and poetry, and foregoes a close examination of rhetorical principles operating in the texts.

In fact, anthologies devoted to literary study often do not include much explicit discussion of how writers and speakers are engaged in rhetorical acts that seek to change and alter, often for the better, their own and other Black peoples' lived experience. This tendency may help explain why in many rhetoric courses the study of imaginative literature is frowned upon. We, however, do not frown upon literature, but instead find the lack of rhetorical attention given to the study of literature to be quite limiting. The other two books we name, *Call* and *Nobody Turn*, are admittedly closer to the conceptual framework of our project. However, these books present the opposite issue as the literary anthologies in that they do not include much imaginative media. They also have a different scope from our book in that they revolve around disciplinary issues in the field of African American studies. There are, to be sure, other readers like ours that include a blend of imaginative and nonfiction selections (e.g., Gilyard and Wardi, *African American Literature*, 2004). But again, the focus here is primarily on the aesthetic study of literature without a strong emphasis on how aesthetics and literature are deeply rhetorical.

Our reader also stands apart but is deeply influenced by some legacy texts that feature analyses of African American language and rhetoric. These include collections that focus on sociolinguistics and literacy (e.g., Bentley and Crawford, *Black Language Reader*, 1973), and others that present academic analyses in the form of scholarly essays on African American rhetoric (e.g., Jackson and Richardson, *Understanding African American Rhetoric*, 2003; Richardson and Jackson, *African American Rhetoric(s)*, 2007).

With our book, we are proud to be joining the rich legacy of interest in and understanding of African American rhetoric that the aforementioned books represent. We are even more proud, however, to present a decidedly unique text that has several useful features: primary material, original theoretical analyses, discussion questions, a list of further readings, and a companion website that contains a list of iTunes and weblinks for each section that provide audio and visual presentations of African American rhetoric. Taking all of these components together, our book not only presents African American rhetoric as an important historical and everyday cultural performance but also shows how this practice is pedagogically rich and reaches across themes and disciplines.

Given the scope of African American rhetoric and the ambitions of our project, we have organized this reader into four parts. Each of these parts includes three or four sections (except for Part I, which has only one section) and each of the sections has its own expert editor(s). Each part offers its own introduction, written by one of the two general editors—that is, written by either Vershawn Ashanti Young or Michelle Bachelor Robinson. Then the expert editors that we invited to develop a section of readings from a particular thematic perspective share their vision in a short but substantial statement that opens their own sections. All of these original, theoretical writings address such critical questions as: What are the cultural and philosophical principles operating in the works, individually as well as a unit? What do these works indicate and represent in terms of the arc of an African American rhetoric? And what are the rhetorical principles operating in the texts, and why are these texts important?

In addition, each individual selection of primary texts in this reader is preceded by a contextualizing annotation. This comment serves to put the reading in both its contemporaneous cultural context and to show its relevance to the African American rhetorical tradition. These comments, as well as the opening section statements, constitute one of the most important and unique features of this book. Since all of the editors are experts in the fields they represent, they show how important rhetoric is to a vast array of disciplines, such as Africana, Caribbean, and Black Diasporic Studies, communication studies, creative writing, digital and technocultural communications, English language and literature, feminism and women's studies, gender and sexuality studies, hip-hop, political science, education, literacy studies, and performance studies. They also underscore how the study of each of these disciplines is important to understanding African American rhetoric.

Further, each separate section offers discussion questions that are written by each section editor. These questions invite readers to ruminate on, examine, and discuss the rhetorical principles operating in the selections as a group, as well as how the sections come together to illustrate the rhetoricity of the themes they represent. Allow us to offer a glimpse into the four parts and into the individual sections they contain with the following descriptions:

Part I, "African American Rhetoric—Definitions and Understanding," provides a framing introduction—"African American Rhetoric: What It Be, What It Do"—written by the two general editors, Vershawn Ashanti Young and Michelle Bachelor Robinson. This introduction is followed by the section "African American Rhetorical Theory," which contains three selections that provide theoretical foundations of African American rhetoric.

Part II, "The Blackest Hours: Origins and Histories of African American Rhetoric," is divided into four sections: "Nobody Knows Our Name: African Orature in the American Diaspora" (Campbell); "Religion and Spirituality/ Transportations and Transformations of Spirituality and Identity in the New World" (Martin and West); "Language, Literacy, and Education" (Kinloch and Thomas); and "Black Presence—African American Political Rhetoric" (Robinson, Nunley, and Echols). This unit explores the roots of African American rhetoric and how these roots constitute routes into cultural conversations about church, education, politics, and oral traditions and practices.

Part III, "Discourses on Black Bodies," presents selections that all work together as a way to engage relevant conversations and intersections among gender, race, sexuality, and performance. It is divided into three sections: "Race Women and Black Feminisms" (James); "Motions of Manhood" (Young); and "The Quare of Queer" (McCune).

Part IV, "The New Blackness: Multiple Cultures, Multiple Modes," is divided into four thematic sections: "Caribbean Thought and Its Critique of Subjugation" (Kamugisha and Hume); "Black Technocultural Expressivity" (Byrne); "Beat Rebels *Corrupting Youth* Against Babylon" (Thomas); and "Black Art: Black Argument" (Robinson and Young). This unit expands the purview of African American rhetoric into the diasporic traditions of Black cultural thought by connecting the rhetorics of Black people in America to those in the Caribbean. The unit further forges new ground and respects the legacy of rhetorics in creative media in the sections on digital and visual technology and on arts and music.

While the selections within each section are arranged chronologically by order of historical publication or first presentation in order to give readers a sense of African American rhetorical history as it has developed, we are also interested in the context of the works in order to ascertain "the available means of persuasion"—that is, how and why rhetors construct their views and arguments in the way that they do. Thus, while the twelve sections in this book are more porous than what might be evident in the section headings that group them (e.g., some selections could appear in more than one unit), these twelve sections offer a comprehensive examination of the many social, political, cultural, religious, and aesthetic facets that make up African American rhetoric.

In the end, we hope our reader presents African American rhetoric as an enduring and essential legacy within both American history and the Black Diaspora that is worthy of the most inclusive and serious consideration.

Vershawn A. Young
University of Waterloo

Michelle Bachelor Robinson
Spellman College

Works Cited

Bentley, R.H., and S.D. Crawford. *Black Language Reader*. Glenview, IL: Scott Foresman, (1973).
Gilyard, K., and A. Wardi. *Anthology of African American Literature*. New York: Pearson/Longman, 2004.
Jackson, R., and E. Richardson. *Understanding African American Rhetoric: Classical Origins to Contemporary Innovations*. New York: Routledge, 2003.
Richardson, E., and R. Jackson. *African American Rhetoric: Interdisciplinary Perspective(s)*. Carbondale: Southern Illinois University Press, 2007.

ACKNOWLEDGEMENTS

Every book has a story behind it. This one is no different. This was a labor. A labor that had to be of commitment, if not of love. Since the time this book was first conceived to print, I got married, had a child (who is now five), went back to law school, got a J.D., took the bar exam, published four other books, had two sabbaticals, got a divorce, ran two major conferences—for the College Language Association and the Conference on College Communication and Composition—and have remained steadfast to the first of its kind volume on African American Rhetoric. For those people who stood beside me and infused energy and inspiration into me, I wish to thank you. You know who you are, but I do wish to highlight a special few:

My mom, Dorothy

My pops, Richard

My bruhs, Robert, Wolf, James, Curtis

My Sis's, Bell, Latonya, Cookie, Baby Shanda, and Kia

Friends for life, Frankie, Asao, Cornell, Johnny, Angelo R., Eliz W., Angie, Corliss, Monica, Neisha-Anne, Hecktor F., Greg R., Mike M. and fill in the blank with your name _____

My Routledge crew, Linda, Laura, Nicole, Ryan, Stephanie, Kristen, and Autumn at Apex CoVantage

I also acknowledge all the beautiful black voices that provide me with so much, so much: Phillis, Jupiter, Olaudah, Linda, Countee, Charles, Audre, James, Ralph, W.E.B, Cornel, Lorraine, August, Suzan, Leon, Nikki, Nikky F., and so on and so on. . . .

Cover art thanks to Alvin E. Miller, Jr. (Nashville, TN) and photography credit goes to Joel Brouwer (University of Alabama).

—VAY

I am grateful for Vershawn Ashanti Young's reaching out in February 2011 for me to meet him for coffee and then extending an invitation for me to join him on this journey. These many years have been a roller coaster ride, but I am pleased and excited for what emerged, a solid tool for the teaching of African American rhetoric. I am also grateful for all the ways that my village contributed to the shaping of this text. My Mom, Beverly Bachelor Moss, and her parents, Jacob and Mildred Bachelor, were the first to teach me that my words were important. My husband Michael A. Robinson has been a quiet encourager and sounding board through the developmental rough spots. My sons have indulged me in inspirational discussions as the text evolved:

Caleb J. Miller for his iTunes suggestions; Joshua A. Miller for his expertise on what music to include in the Black Arts Media Section; and Alvin E. Miller, Jr. (my oldest) for the beautiful mixed media piece that he designed and sculpted from my ramblings over how the cover of this text needed to be everything, plus fly! The original piece dons a wall in my Spelman office, and I am so proud when I tell people that my son is the artist and the piece is the cover of our book. I am also grateful to my research assistants: Carolyn "Allie" Sockwell for her mad skills for researching, logging, and tracking permissions; Kelsey Worsham who picked up where Allie left off; and Khirsten Echols for combing through libraries to locate texts and researching blurbs. A special thanks is sent to Kevin Browne for being my friend in all things academic and reminding me to go be great! And finally, Carmen Kynard whose voice is still so much a part of this text, even though circumstances led her to other projects.

—MICHELLE

PART I

AFRICAN AMERICAN RHETORIC—DEFINITIONS AND UNDERSTANDING

INTRODUCTION: AFRICAN AMERICAN RHETORIC: WHAT IT BE, WHAT IT DO

Volume editors: Vershawn Ashanti Young and Michelle Bachelor Robinson

---

What It Be

The late dramatist, essayist, poet, theater director, and overall rhetorician LeRoi Jones (later Amiri Baraka) contends in *Blues People* (1963), his influential study of the African American experience through music, that "When a man looked up in some anonymous field and shouted, 'Oh, Ahm tired a dis mess,/Oh, yes, Ahm so tired a dis mess,' you can be sure he was an American" (xii). Baraka uses this scenario to establish the angle he pursues in his study—an angle we adopt in this introduction to explain the method of reading African American rhetoric that we, as the general editors, advance in this volume.

The context of Baraka's anecdote reveals that "the man" in question is an African who is enslaved in America. The enslaved African recognizes, assesses, and speaks against his status and situation in America. It is at this point in "the man's" experience, Baraka argues, that "the man" ceases to be a captured African and begins the journey from slave to citizen. Using this image, Baraka states the purpose of his study: "the Negro as slave is one thing, The Negro as American is quite another. But the path the slave took to 'citizenship' is what I want to look at" (emphasis in original, ix).

While we too are interested in the African American journey from slave to citizenship, we are primarily interested, in this volume, in presenting and evaluating the rhetorics that African Americans have engaged, deployed, and employed since the first importation of slaves in 1619 to Barack Obama's two terms as the first elected U.S. president of African descent (circa 2008–2016). For our particular rhetorical purposes then, Amiri Baraka's scenario helps us pinpoint six elements that constitute African American rhetoric as a general category, and helps us argue the case for considering, as we do, some of the varied discourses that have occupied African Americans over the past four hundred years.

The first element of African American rhetoric we wish to consider is language, which is why we begin the first full part after the introduction with an assessment of the rhetorics of language and literacy. In Baraka's image, the "man" speaks ("Oh, Ahm tired a dis mess") in a way that is distinct from but certainly influenced by and related to other common Englishes of the time. His dialect is not quite the same as an imagined "master" might speak. However, it is certainly intelligible to the master and others. Thus we can call this first element, the language from and of the African American experience, a language that shares similarities to other Englishes and is used to communicate across Englishes. However, from a linguistic perspective, this language has its own identifiable patterns of grammar, phonology, morphology, and syntax (Young et al.).

The various ways that this language gets used and deployed leads to a discussion of style, the second element of African American rhetoric.

Culturally speaking, African American style is not only the manner or flair with which African Americans use language but is also expressive of particular viewpoints or perspectives. Linguist and rhetorical theorist Geneva Smitherman (1977) helps us understand the relationship between these first two elements when she advises readers to:

> Think of black speech as having two dimensions: language and style. Though we will separate the two for purposes of analysis, they are often overlapping. This is an important point, frequently overlooked in the discussions of Black English. Consider two examples. Nina Simone sing: "It bees dat way sometime." Here the language aspect is the use of the verb be to indicate a recurring event or habitual condition, rather than a one-time-only occurrence. But the total expression—"It bees dat way sometime"—also reflects Black English style, for the statement suggests a point of view, a way of looking at life, and a method of adapting to life's realities. To live by the philosophy of "It bees dat way sometime" is to come to grips with the changes that life bees puttin us through, and to accept the changes and bad times as a constant, ever-present reality.
>
> Reverend Jesse Jackson preach: "Africa would if Africa could. America could if America would. But Africa cain't and America ain't." Now here Reverend Jesse is using the language of Black Dialect when he says "ain't" and when he pronounces can't as "cain't." But the total expression, using black rhythmic speech, is the more powerful because the Reb has plugged into the style of Black Dialect. The statement thus depends for full communication on what black poet Eugene Redmond calls "songified" pattern and on an Afro-American cultural belief set. That belief holds that White America has always failed blacks and will continues to do so; and that going back to Africa or getting any help from African countries is neither feasible nor realistic because newly emerging African nations must grapple first with problems of independence (economic and otherwise) inherited from centuries of European colonization.
>
> (*Talkin and Testifyin*, 3)

It is important to note that Smitherman describes "black speech" here in two interconnected ways. The first is "speech as language," or as the ability to express thoughts and feelings by articulate sounds, when she describes, for example, "the use of the verb be to indicate a recurring event or habitual condition." The second is "speech as an address or discourse delivered to an audience," when she says that "Nina Simone sing" or "Reverend Jesse Jackson preach," they are singing and preaching to others, to all onlookers and hearers. The point here is that "speech as language" and "speech as discourse" are inherently and intimately intertwined. And that often Black speech as language is used to express a point or make a case by the very way the words themselves are performed (Jackson's "cain't" for instance). That is to say that the words themselves convey arguments that exist in tandem with the overall discursive perspective being offered.

Smitherman's analysis further helps us to appreciate that African American rhetoric is expressed in multifarious media—that is to say, any medium through which African American language and style can be conveyed. So as Smitherman shows by using the examples of a singer and a preacher, African American rhetoric is just as likely to be expressed through art and music as through lecture or oratory, as we will explain further later. But for now, Smitherman's explanation of Black speech helps detail the third and fourth elements of African American rhetoric: discourse and perspective. In this context, discourse is an expression on some particular aspect of African American life and experience. In other words, discourse is a set of exchanges on a topic or area, like slavery as a topic, or politics as an area, or arts and aesthetics as ideas. In the case of "the man" in Baraka's illustration, the discourse would be the problem of slavery, and his perspective is uttered in the words "Oh, Ahm tired a dis mess," and further underscored in the repetition and intensification: "Oh, yes, Ahm so tired a dis mess." So, in short, the perspective is what the man thinks and feels about the topic, the arguments he makes to start, intervene into, and participate in an ongoing discussion.

These four elements—language, style, discourse, and perspective—are folded into what literary critics Henry Louis Gates Jr. and Nellie Y. McKay call the enduring "trope of the talking book." For Gates and McKay, this trope began in 1770 when "African American slaves, remarkably, sought to write themselves out of slavery by mastering the Anglo-belletristic tradition" as represented in the "first full-length black autobiography, *A Narrative of the most remarkable particulars in the life of James Albert Ukawsaw Gronniosaw, an African Prince* (1770)" (emphasis in original, Gates and McKay 2004, xxxviii). In this first published slave narrative, Gronniosaw describes a scene wherein he observes an eighteenth-century reading practice, where his master is reading a book in an undertone, with his lips moving and uttering sounds as his eyes move along the pages. Upon witnessing this, Gronniosaw says, "I was never so surprised in my life, as when I saw the book talk to my master" (quoted in Gates and McKay 2004, xxxviii). He continues:

> As soon as my master had done reading, I followed him to the place where he put the book, being mightily delighted with it, and when nobody saw me, I opened it, and put my ear down close upon it, in great hopes that it would say something to me; but I was sorry, and greatly disappointed, when I found that it would not speak. This thought immediately presented itself to me, that every body and every thing dispised me because I was black.
>
> (Quoted in Gates and McKay 2004, xxxviii)

Gates and McKay reasons that "the text of Western letters refused to speak to the person of African descent; paradoxically, we read about that refusal in a text created by that very person of African descent." So, "with Gronniosaw's An African Prince, a distinctively 'African' voice registered its presence in the republic of letters; it was a text that both talked 'black,' and through its unrelenting indictment of the institution of slavery, talked back" (Gates and McKay 2004, xxxviii). Although Gates and McKay are perhaps too committed to discussing African American print culture to the exclusion of the long history of speech and spoken discourses that most assuredly must have influenced any writing by Gronniosaw and others, the point they make about the trope of the talking book is important because the trope highlights the elements of rhetoric. As Gates and McKay observe, Gronniosaw and other early African American writers were both "talking black and talking back." They talked Black by using Black language and style, even if that language was not a precise African American dialect, but looked more like the "Anglo-belletristic tradition" of the time. But the distinctive language elements could be observed in the revision of tropes and images common to Anglo-belletristic tradition, a revision that included the African American experience and sensibilities. Further, there was the creation of new tropes and ideas unique to the African American experience. And both these revisions and new linguistic strategies of communication were adopted by others, creating and establishing a Black speech community among African American writers. As Gates and McKay write,

> Making a text "speak" in the full range of timbres that the African enslaved in England and America brought to the process of writing became a dominate urge of the ex-slave authors.

So compelling did Gronniosaw's trope of the talking book prove to be that between 1770 and 1815, no fewer than five authors of slave narratives used the same metaphor.

(Gates and McKay 2004, xxxviii)

Here, Gates and McKay underscore the fifth and sixth elements of African American rhetoric, community and suasion. Here community should not be confused with unity, but represents the connection among a group of people who experience the same circumstances by the fact of some identity or status category they share. And further, the group draws upon the language and styles developed within the African American experience. In the example provided by Gates and McKay, we see how writers of slave autobiographies shared the image and metaphor of the talking book.

Further, community can be observed among Black artists in early America, such as the first critic of African American literature, Jupiter Hammon, a Black poet, who wrote a poem to Phillis Wheatley, "An Address to Miss Phillis Wheatley" (1778). In his poem to Wheatley, Hammon adheres to the principles of rhetoric as he engages in what might be the first act of African American rhetorical and literary analysis of a Black writer's work. And further, Scipio Moorhead, an enslaved African artist, drew the now famous portrait of Phillis Wheatley that became the frontispiece for her book of poems in 1773. Wheatley herself wrote a poem, an homage, to Scipio in her book.[1] What should by now be very clear is that from the beginning, African Americans, whether visual artists, creative writers, or speech makers, used principles of rhetoric even as they were creating them. Community is one principle that African American rhetors exemplified through acknowledgment of and communication with each other through various media. The other element, suasion, is the act of influencing or persuading, and further trying to improve interpersonal and intercultural relationships. So to recap, the six elements are (1) language; (2) style; (3) discourse; (4) perspective; (5) community; and (6) suasion.

By identifying and discussing these six elements together, we are establishing a certain kind of rhetorical reading. These elements come together to form a method of reading that understands rhetoric as "the particular arguments on a subject" (Scott and Brockriede 1969, 3). This is the method that Scott and Brockriede promote in their influential collection of essays in *The Rhetoric of Black Power*. They write, "The concept of rhetoric invites a fundamental ambiguity in the focusing on verbal discourse. At times it seems to refer to the means of persuasion, as contrasted with specific ends a persuader may seek and with particular materials he may use" (2). This "would include verbal patternings that could be abstracted from the stuff of arguments and shared with arguments on other subjects far different" (Scott and Brockriede 1969, 3). This analysis could be a useful framework whereby one observes one strategy used in one song or sermon, like the songified pattern that Smitherman says Jesse Jackson employed in the foregoing examples. On the other hand, "rhetoric refers to the particular arguments on a subject and to the special interaction of people in a situation." Here rhetoric comes to include "the tendencies to shape lines of argument favorable or unfavorable to that subject and to influence kinds of interpersonal relationships" (Scott and Brockriede 1969, 3).

This latter take on rhetoric is the one we promote by encouraging readers to consider our six elements in aggregate rather than separately. This is why Consequently, we have divided the book into topics and categorized the rhetorics according to particular discourses and situations. By doing this we are following the advice of Scott and Brockriede, who write, "seeing rhetoric as situational is to guard against some common dangers. Critics are too prone to see persons involved in persuasion as grand actors without taking due account of the scenes in which they act" (1969, 3). For, as they further put it, "speaking and audience influence each other within a social context. For many black Americans the situation is the terribly frustrating one of working for goals of equal opportunity in a country that is predominantly white" (4).[2]

What It Do

We have already described the organizational structure, theoretical impulse, and pedagogical design of this book in the preface. We refer readers there as well as to the complete table of contents for more on these elements. In this concluding section to the introduction, we will not repeat much of that here. Instead we will embellish a bit further how African American rhetoric acts, reacts, and exists differently than what we might refer to as European rhetorical traditions. We also underscore why any serious study of African American rhetoric must include a consideration of creative arts, literature, visuality, nonfiction, and developing forms of media. Here, we draw on two important points from the reading we include in this section from one of the pioneering scholars of African American rhetoric, Molefi Asante (Arthur Smith). In his seminal essay, "Markings of an African Concept of Rhetoric," Asante opens with the claim that "any interpretation of African rhetoric must begin at once to dispense with the notion that in all things Europe is teacher and African is pupil" (Smith [Asante] 1972, 363). It goes without saying that Asante's anti-colonial impulse applies to African Americans, as well as to Africans in a traditional, ethnic sense. Thus in this volume we present African American rhetoric with its own set of legacies, debates, and performances, and not as a subgenre of American rhetoric. This understanding has led to the way this book has been conceived and constructed, seeing African American rhetoric as fundamentally community-oriented and persuasive, as well as inclusive of all areas of arts, humanities, and social sciences. It is also expansive in its influence of and representation in new and developing forms of media. We appeal to Asante in these regards as well.

He writes, "By the nature of traditional African philosophy, rhetoric in African society is an architectonic functioning art continuously fashioning the lives and attitudes of the people" (369). In other words, rhetoric is a fundamental, inherent, ongoing aspect of African American life and culture. It is everywhere all the time where Black people exist and is expressed in their various perspectives and views of the world. This sentiment means precisely that African American rhetoric is powerfully seen and heard in artistic as well as social and political acts. And this should come as no surprise, since Asante explains,

> What I am suggesting is that the African speaker means to be poet, not lecturer; indeed, the equipment of the two will always be different. So now it is possible to say that traditional African public discourse is given to concrete images capable of producing compulsive relationships and invoking the inner needs of audiences because of the inherent power of the images and not because of syllogistic reasoning. Additionally, the more powerful the speaker, the more fascinated the audiences will be.
>
> (372)

Asante is not suggesting that syllogistic reasoning, which is a classic element in the study of American and European rhetoric, is completely absent in African or African American rhetoric. What he is saying is that it is not the fundamental nor driving element of Black people's rhetoric. Poetic language, artistic impulses, and powerful imagery form the bases of Black rhetoric. This argument, in short, underscores our reasons for compiling this comprehensive reader with selections from various media, with a tendency toward the artistic—because, given the foundations of African American rhetoric, it is not only the right thing to do but also the Black thing to do.

Notes

1. See Wheatley's poem "To S.M., a Young African Painter, on Seeing His Works" in this volume.
2. Framing, understanding, and analyzing African American rhetoric can be ascertained from a long list of sources. Some of the ones that have shaped the method of reading and analyzing African American

rhetoric that we advance in this book are appended to this introduction and offered as pedagogical and theoretical frameworks for reading the parts of this book.

Works Cited

Gates Jr, Henry, L., and Nellie Y. McKay. *Norton Anthology of African American Literature*. Second Edition. New York: Norton, 2004.

Jones, LeRoi. *Blues People*. New York: William Morrow and Company, 1963. Print.

Hammon, Jupiter. "An Address to Miss Phillis Wheatley." (1778). In *Norton Anthology of African American Literature*. Second Edition. Eds. Henry L. Gates Jr. and Nellie Y. McKay. New York: Norton, 2004, p. 165.

Scott, Robert and Wayne Brockriede, eds. *The Rhetoric of Black Power*. New York, Evanston, and London: Harper and Row, 1969. Print.

Smith, Arthur (Molefi Asanti). *Language, Communication and Rhetoric in Black America*. New York: Harper & Row, 1972. Print.

Smitherman, Geneva. *Talkin and Testifyin: The Language of Black America*. Detroit: Wayne State University Press, 1977. Print.

1

AFRICAN AMERICAN RHETORICAL THEORY

Edited by Vershawn Ashanti Young and Michelle Bachelor Robinson

———⚬≋⚬———

Arthur L. Smith (Molefi Asante)

There was no shortage of African American rhetoric during the modern civil rights movement of the 1950s and 1960s. In fact, one might say that there was a renaissance of African American public address during this time, comparable to the late abolitionist period circa 1850–1870. However, there are only a handful of studies dedicated to understanding and promoting African American rhetoric, and very few of scholars analyzing Black rhetoric were actually African American themselves. The following selection is taken from an essay by Arthur L. Smith, who has become known as Molefi Asante. Asante is currently a scholar of African and African American studies, but was trained as and become an influential figure of communication studies, focusing on African American rhetoric. In this excerpt, as the essay title pinpoints, the topic is looking at the influence of Africa in the language, communication, and rhetoric of African Americans. Just as African American English is influenced by the languages of Africa that both free and enslaved Africans brought with them to America, so it must be that African American rhetoric bears out semblances and connections to the linguistic and rhetorical practices of Africa, as Asante explains.

Markings of an African Concept of Rhetoric

Arthur L. Smith (Molefi Asante)[1]

Any interpretation of African rhetoric must begin at once to dispense with the notion that in all things Europe is teacher and Africa is pupil. To raise the question of an imperialism of the rhetorical tradition is to ask a most meaningful question as we pursue the basic concepts of African rhetoric, because Western theorists have too often tended to generalize from an ethnocentric base. Clearly, what will have to be argued in this paper is the existence of an African concept of communication. Elsewhere I have given attention to broad outlines in the traditional African background.[2] In this paper I hope to discuss some concrete propositions that might conceivably be drawn from traditional African philosophy. Obviously, such a task is not easy because of the absence of systematic guidelines to follow, but it is not impossible, inasmuch as anthropologists and sociologists studying some of the basic phenomena have left their research notes for us to investigate.[3] And furthermore, the details of African philosophy are being placed in focus for Western minds by many African writers, popular and scholarly.[4] Conceivably, from these sources it can be established that rhetorical differences within cultures rest upon the different emphases of similar phenomena rather than on purely biological differences among peoples.

Admittedly, nothing of the stature of Aristotle's *Rhetoric* appears in African cultural history, but long before there was a system of rhetoric, men engaged in speechmaking. It is generally agreed that the practice of public speaking predates the development of systematic treatises. Furthermore, what is in essence the Western appreciation of the written word is not historically shared by Africans, and such a statement does not imply cultural superiority or inferiority but cultural difference. Perhaps the question to be raised in this connection is: What is the purpose of the written word? The answer to this question speaks of the complex problem of cultural evaluation. Put simply, writing is used for communication and historical preservation. In traditional African society those two ends were admirably satisfied by the drum. Communication was swift and the range was great; in the event the first drummer was unable to reach all of the persons he wanted to, another at the outer fringes would take up the message for further transmission. And too, the drummer along with the village sage became a repository of all the necessary historical data relating to the village. Thus, while African culture did not produce a written treatise on rhetoric, it is, nevertheless, perhaps more so than Western society, an expressive society.[5] In a discussion on the difference between physique and culture, Sidney Mintz attempted to explore behavioral patterns of Afro-Americans by noting that seemingly minor behavioral patterns are tied to the expressive media, such as music, dance, drama, voice, and the like.[6] Mintz further notes: "it is reasonable to view these expressions as continuities with the African past, and as some evidence of the success of Afro-Americans in conserving cultural materials that could not be conserved in other aspects of life."[7] What is of importance to us is that Africans maintained an expressive sense that manifested itself as life-force in dance, music, and speech. Expression, therefore, is not the captive of the written word; it is revealed in life.

What if there had been a major African treatise on rhetoric emanating from the university at Timbuktu? Rhetoric, in fact, was later taught by several Islamic scholars, among them, Uthman Dan Fodio of Nigeria. But be that as it may, we cannot seek to find in African society values that correspond exactly to European standards. On the other hand, we must not attempt to fit European values into African society. There exist no universal measures for rhetorical standards. In a short recommendation to the second conference of the National Developmental Project on Rhetoric, I contended that we must ask ourselves this question: "Is rhetorical theory concerned only with speaking in a democracy?" That question can be extended to include another dimension: Is rhetoric strictly Western?

Unquestionably, in some senses it is, and it would be foolish to argue any other way. But to contend that as conventionally perceived it is universal in theory, practice, and evaluation as measured in Western society would be to argue for cultural imperialism. *De Inventione*, the *Arte of Speaking, Select British Eloquence,* and our most contemporary works are, for the most part, products of the Western mind. We should not generalize for all audiences in all cultures. This is perhaps as it should be in our scholarship. Despite the state of research in the field, rhetoric as often defined can be found in African culture. Man interacting vocally with another man for the purpose of getting him to act cooperatively has existed in Ghana as long as it has in Greece.

Yet man interacting in African society proceeds from different bases than man interacting in European society. The reason is simple. People respond to the ideal that is concealed in every fact of their existence, and this ideal is determined for them according to different views of life. Whatever approach to the universe, values, neighbors, and other relationships, however complex, people come to accept comprise the philosophical base of their culture. Although anthropologists and Africanists have given few discussions of symbolic interaction among Africans (in reality, speech-communication scholars have argued that this is their purview), they have provided significant data on the nature of African society. Abstracted from this knowledge are possible suggestions for a system of African rhetoric.

First, let us establish the dimensions of public speaking in any society. To stimulate one's fellow to cooperative action through the use of language is no mean task; it requires skill, knowledge of human nature, and the necessary physical organs to utter sounds. Skill implies a certain technical proficiency, an ability to use one's knowledge effectively. Thus the interrelationship of skill and knowledge of human nature is clearly the basis of any meaningful venture in public speaking. What we argue, then, is what rhetoricians have argued before, that public discourse is an art. Thonssen and Baird made much ado about the foundations of the art of speaking.[8] But art is that which is produced by a systematic application of skill in effecting a given result; of course, we could extend that to include the craft, occupation, or activity requiring such skill. Suffice it to say, while it has been made plain by rhetoricians that rhetoric is concerned with the systematic observation and classification of facts and the establishment of verifiable general principles, no one has denied that public discourse is an art.

African art is never *l'art pour l'art;* it is always functional. This is true whether we are speaking of music, sculpture, or public speaking. There can be no art without a functional objective within the mind of the artist; his work must do something, perform something, or say something. Public discourse as an art form can only be complete when it is productive, and hence functional. Now it might be thought that this is neo-Aristotelianism with an African cast. However, the difference is most important. Where neo-Aristotelian rhetoricians placed emphasis on the observer as far as judgment of discourse was concerned, Africans highlight the creative process of the artist. To be an observer is to be primarily interested in the product, but to be an artist means that the creation and its function in society are uppermost. Thus, the African sees the discourse as the creative manifestation of what is *called to be.* That which is *called to be* because of the mores and values of the society becomes the created thing; and the artist, or speaker, satisfies the demands of the society by calling into being that which is functional. Functionality in this case refers to the object (sculpture, music, poem, speech, etc.) possessing a meaning within the speaker and audience's world view.

In such a view of art public discourse becomes a power, and the fundament of rhetoric is not the discourse object but the creative attitude of the speaker. To say that public discourse becomes a power is only to emphasize the activity aspect of the discourse in African thought. One cannot speak of a speech as an object but of speech as an attitude. The power of effective action is the force of the public discourse; and the speaker who makes a speech never completes a discourse as object because completeness is to be found in action.

Now that we have said African art is never *l'art pour l'art*, it is possible to say a few words about the relationship between society and the public discourse. What is the meaning of the speech in traditional African society? In what sense can the speech be said to fit into the tribal cosmogony? These are not easy questions to answer, and yet it seems that the answers lie somewhere in the realms of African personality theory and African culture. Several scholars have recently attempted exploration of conceptual systems, theories of personality, and culture related to Africa. They have found that it is as impossible to speak of an "African mind" as it is to speak of an "Oriental temperament," and for some of the same reasons. When we speak of Africans we are talking about a multitude of attitudes, peoples, and philosophies, and in this circumstance to speak of an African mind is to speak foolishly. Thus we speak broadly of traditional African society.

African society is essentially a society of harmonies, inasmuch as the coherence or compatibility of persons, things, and modalities is at the root of traditional African philosophy. Several scholars have commented on the nature of traditional African law as being concerned with the restoration of equilibrium.[9] In customary African law not establishment of guilt but rather the smooth and peaceful running of the community is the primary consideration.[10] In fact, Adesanya, a Nigerian writer, declares "this is not simply a coherence of fact or faith, nor of reason and traditional beliefs, nor of reason and contingent facts, but a coherence of compatibility among all disciplines."[11] The concatenation of everything exists so tightly that to subtract one item is to paralyze the system.

The public discourse, therefore, cannot exist apart from the mutual compatibility of the entire traditional world-view. In force, for force is active form and content operating harmoniously, the speech is logically linked to the society. Obviously, this type of society appears rigid and constricting to most Western peoples, but, on the other hand, in customary African society the possibilities are plentiful. Clearly the difference lies in two varied conceptions of the speech and the speaker. Merriam has written that "In Euro-American Society there is a tendency to compartmentalize the arts and to divorce them from aspects of everyday life; thus we have 'pure' as opposed to 'applied' art as well as the 'artist' and 'commercial artist' or 'craftsmen,' who are also differentiated both in role and in function."[12] The speech is a functioning and integral part of the society and cannot be separated from the entire world-view because the word power is indeed the generative power of the community.[13] Additionally, traditional African philosophy cannot make the distinction of "speaker" and "audience" to the degree found in rhetorical traditions of Euro-American society. Separateness of speaker or artist from audience in Euro-American society is based upon the degree of participation. But in African society the coherence among persons and things accord so that music, dance, or *Nommo* must be a collective activity.[14] Melville Herskovits observed that distinctions of artist and audience are foreign to traditional African culture, "Art is a part of life, not separated from it."[15] This does not mean that there are no individual speakers or artists but rather that their performance becomes a collective experience. In Neo-African culture, particularly as expressed in North and South America, one gets the feel of this group performance in religious meetings and, indeed, in some secular gatherings. What are conventionally labeled reactions and responses of the audience might conceivably be better understood if we spoke of these phenomena as collective actions of participants. Afro-Americans viewing the movie *Cotton Comes to Harlem* are participating in the events of that movie not in the oral interpretation sense of "fulfilling the potential" but in creating the potential. The potential does not exist apart from the participants; thus when Godfrey Cambridge is "being seen" on the movie screen, the "audience" is being seen.

But African rhetoric is not only distinguished in its concern for coherence and participation but also in its relationship to the stability of the traditional society. Mutual compatibility of the several aspects of a philosophical perspective is only one benefit of coherence; another is the smooth operation of the village or tribe. In instances of conflict or disagreement among members of the society, public discourse must function to restore the stability that conflict creates. And too, within the speech the speaker is constantly restoring the internal harmony of the discourse through tone, volume, and rhythm. Delivery becomes, for the traditional African speaker, an opportunity to engage in a textual as well as a contextual search for harmony. The stability of the community is essential, and public speaking, when used in connection with conflict solution, must be directed toward maintaining community harmony. As a microcosmic example of the traditional African society's base in the harmony of all parts, the meaningful public discourse manifests rhetorical agreeableness in all its parts.

By the nature of traditional African philosophy, rhetoric in African society is an architectonic functioning art continuously fashioning the lives and attitudes of the people. The *word* is productive and imperative, calling forth and commanding. Its power derives from the traditional emphasis on the spoken word in African society. Words as spoken by the chief or village physician may be effective because of the station, assigned or inherited, of the speaker, even though power inheres in vocal communication. The centrality of the word has existed for a long time in African communities. Jahn explains that " . . . the central significance of the word in African culture is not a phenomenon of one particular time."[16] Furthermore,

> If there were no word, all forces would be frozen, there would be no procreation, no change, no life. "There is nothing that there is not; whatever we have a name for, that is," so speaks the wisdom of the Yoruba priests. The proverb signifies that the naming, the enunciation produces what it names. Naming is an incantation, a creative act. What we cannot conceive of is unreal; it does not exist. But every human thought, once expressed, becomes reality. For the world holds the course of things in train and changes and transform them. And since the word has this power, every word is an effective word, every word is binding.[17]

Thus because the word is imperative, it is the fundament as well as the fashioning instrument of traditional African society. All religion, music, medicine, and dance is produced by vocal expression, inasmuch as creativity is called into existence by man speaking. There is also a correlation between the effectiveness of the word and the power of the speaker as expressed by his personality and status. The more powerful the priest, the stronger his incantations and invocations. But no priest can exist apart from the word, indeed without the word, nothing can be, for the word creates reality.

The overwhelming importance of expression in African culture has been referred to by several scholars.[18] Expression possesses this place of significance in speech as well as in music in African society, and the interrelationship of the two expressive genres is well established. All study of African music requires verbal emphasis as well as demonstration because of the power of the expressive word.[19] Furthermore, the commonality of pitch, rate, volume, duration, and message content makes speech and music parts of the same expressive pattern. Wachsmann contends that "In Africa a useful working hypothesis is that there is little music that does not have some affinity with words."[20] Since the word principle is behind all production and generation, it is possible to consider it as an architectonic system that gives existence to all things. Transformation is accomplished when a speaker employs words in any social situation in an attempt to bring about harmonious relationships within the traditional society. Whether the specific situation is an interpersonal conflict mediated by a chief or village elder, a natural disaster, or an attempt to persuade villagers to follow a certain course of action, transformation is sought through the expressive word. In this sense we can speak of an African architecton that influences communal behavior, in fact is the source and origin of that behavior.

I have discussed the place of the spoken word, the function of speaker, and the character of the audiences in an African concept of rhetoric. But one will ask: What is the substance of African public discourse? The questioner posing these queries would be exercising the contextual criteria provided by Western thought. To ask what is the *substance* is to see a dichotomy between form and substance, and this query does not plague African thought. Since form and content are *activity*, then *force* unifies what is called form and content in creative expression. The speech is meant to be alive and moving in all of its aspects so that separation of the members becomes impossible because the creative production is "an experience" or a happening occurring within and outside the speaker's soul. Thus, unlike the Euro-American, the African seeks the totality of an experience, concept, or system. Traditional African society looks for unity of the whole rather than specifics of the whole; such a concentration, which also emphasizes synthesis more than analysis, contributes to community stability because considerations in the whole are more productive than considerations in detail. Now it is clear that this has a very real bearing upon the making of a public discourse.

The public discourse convinces not through attention to logical substance but through the power to fascinate. Yet this does not preclude the materials of composition or the arrangement and structure of those materials; it simply expresses a belief that when images are arranged according to their power and chosen because of their power, the speaker's ability to convince is greater than if he attempted to employ syllogisms. The syllogism is a Western concept; *Nommo* is an African concept. When a speaker possesses visionary ecstasy, vivid but controlled, his audience's participation is more assured than if he exercised only syllogistic reasoning. Perhaps that is drawing the choices too clearly, inasmuch as few neo-Aristotelians would argue for a dichotomy of emotion and logic. However, it is necessary to state the polar positions to illustrate the emphasis of the traditional African speaker. What I am suggesting is that the African speaker means to be poet, not lecturer; indeed, the equipment of the two will always be different. So now it is possible to say that traditional African public discourse is given to concrete images capable of producing compulsive relationships and invoking the inner needs of audiences because of the inherent power of the images and not because of syllogistic reasoning. Additionally, the more powerful the speaker, the more fascinated the audiences will be.

We have discussed some concrete rhetorical ideas drawn from traditional African philosophy. Yet our work can only be heuristic until we can establish more explicitly the parameters of traditional African philosophy; this means that the universals within several systems must be identified, because one cannot speak of African philosophy with any real degree of accuracy. There are philosophies; but as a growing number of Africanists are discovering, there are concepts that transcend the boundaries of tribe or village. Furthermore, the implications for systems of African rhetoric might emerge once African philosophies are explored; but this will take a whole new school of scholars. Meanwhile the markings that I have discussed here should provide serious students of the field with a launching pad.

Notes

1. Arthur L. Smith. "Markings of an African Concept of Rhetoric," in *Language, Communication and Rhetoric in Black America*, ed. Arthur L. Smith (Molefi Asante) (New York: Harper and Row, 1972).
2. See Arthur L. Smith, "Socio-Historical Perspectives of Black Oratory," *The Quarterly Journal of Speech* (October 1970).
3. See Noel O. King, *Religions of Africa* (New York: Harper & Row, 1970); John Paden and Edward Soja, eds., *The African Experience* (Evanston: Northwestern Press, 1970); Robert LeVine, *Dream and Deeds: Achievement Motivation in Nigeria* (Chicago: University of Chicago Press, 1966); Jean Vansina, *Kingdoms of the Savanna* (Madison: University of Wisconsin Press, 1968); B. N. Colby, "Ethnographic Semantics," *Current Anthropology*, VII (1966), pp. 3–32; A. K. Romney and R. G. D'Andrade, eds., *Transcultural Studies in Cognition*, special issue of the *American Anthropologist*, LXVI (June 1964); Jack Berry and Joseph Greenberg, "Sociolinguistic Research in Africa," *African Studies Bulletin* IX (September 1966), pp. 1–9; and Arthur Tuden and Leonard Plotnicov, eds., *Social Stratification in Africa* (New York: Free Press, 1970).
4. Among the leading West African writers are Wole Soyinka, Sembene Ousmane, Chinua Achebe, Leopold Senghor, Sekou Toure, Amos Tutuola, and Cyprian Ekwensi. While all of these writers, with the exception of one or two, have concentrated on popular writing, there are strong signs of a serious investigation of African life and thought at both the African Studies Center at the University of Ibadan in Nigeria and the Institute of African Studies at the University of Ghana.
5. Joseph White, "Toward a Black Psychology," *Ebony* (September 1970), pp. 45–52.
6. Sidney Mintz, Foreword in Norman Whitten, Jr., and John F. Szwed, *Afro-American Anthropology* (New York: Free Press, 1970), p. 5.
7. Ibid.
8. Lester Thonssen and A. Craig Baird, *Speech Criticism* (New York: Ronald Press, 1948), Chapter 2.
9. See Hilda Kuper and Leo Kuper, eds., *African Law: Adaptation and Development* (Los Angeles: University of California Press, 1965)
10. Paul Bohannan, *Justice and Judgment Among the Tiv* (London: Oxford Press, 1957), p. 6.

11. Adebayo Adesanya, "Yoruba Metaphysical Thinking," *ODU*, 5 (Ibadan, 1958), p. 39.
12. Alan Merriam, "African Music," in William Bascom and Melville Herskovits, *Continuity and Change in African Culture* (Chicago: University of Chicago Press, 1958), p. 49.
13. Smith, "Socio-Historical Perspectives of Black Oratory."
14. I have used the term *Nommo* elsewhere in my writings. It is a term borrowed first from the Dogon tribe by Janheinz Jahn to express the complexities and dimensions of communication in African society.
15. Melville Herskovits, *Man and His Works* (New York: Knopf, 1948), p. 379.
16. Janheinz Jahn, *Muntu: The New African Culture* (New York: Grove Press, 1961), p. 134.
17. Ibid., p. 133.
18. For instance, Leopold Senghor, "Der Geist der Negro Afrikanischen Kultur," *Schwarze Ballade*, Janheinz Jahn, ed. (Frankfurt: Verlag, 1965), pp. 203–227.
19. Klaus Wachsmann, "Ethnomusicology in Africa," *The African Experience*, John Paden and Edward Soja, eds. (Evanston: Northwestern Press, 1970), p. 135.
20. Ibid.

Geneva Smitherman

Geneva Smitherman is a linguist who has dedicated her life to studying and promoting the social and educational dimensions of what is now known as African American language. Her early book, *Talkin and Testifyin: The Language of Black America*, from which the following selection is taken, is written in African American language, demonstrating that the language is just as viable for academic uses as it is for rapping and jiving on the streets. *Talkin and Testifyin* was published first in 1977 and then again in 1986, and is still in print and widely taught and cited. The excerpt here outlines how African American language is an important component of African American rhetoric.

Talkin and Testifyin: The Language of Black America

Geneva Smitherman[1]

The first major force was the social change movements (or upheavals—depending on where you comin from) of the sixties, spearheaded by the 1954 Supreme Court school desegregation decision, followed by the 1955 refusal of black Rosa Parks to move to the back of the bus, and the emergence of Martin Luther King, Jr., and the civil rights thrust, followed by black power and the black cultural consciousness movement. The second major force was embodied in White America's attempt to deal with this newly released black energy by the implementation of poverty programs, educational and linguistic remediation projects, sociolinguistic research programs, and various other up-from-the-ghetto and "Great Society" efforts. As we all know, these two forces have not acted in concert. While blacks were shouting "I'm black and I'm proud," Anglos were admonishing them to "be like us" and enter the mainstream. While you had black orators, creative artists, and yes, even scholars rappin in the Black Thang, educators (some of them black, to be sure) were preaching the Gospel that Black English speakers must learn to talk like White English speakers in order to "make it."

Much that you hear nowadays about Black Dialect tends to be general and to focus on global concerns over social policy and political matters, with insufficient attention to elements of the language itself and the historical background and sociocultural development of that language (aside from the special academics mentioned earlier). That has been unfortunate because we need much more knowledge about the language and the way it functions in the communication system of blacks. Therefore, let us get off this global trip and get down to the nitty-gritty of answering the questions, just what *is* Black English, where did it come from and what are the implications for black-white interaction and teaching black children?

In a nutshell: Black Dialect is an Africanized form of English reflecting Black America's linguistic-cultural African heritage and the conditions of servitude, oppression and life in America. Black Language is Euro-American speech with an Afro-American meaning, nuance, tone, and gesture. The Black Idiom is used by 80 to 90 percent of American blacks, at least some of the time. It has allowed blacks to create a culture of survival in an alien land, and as a by-product has served to enrich the language of all Americans.

Think of black speech as having two dimensions: language and style. Though we will separate the two for purposes of analysis, they are often overlapping. This is an important point, frequently overlooked in discussions of Black English. Consider two examples. Nina Simone sing: "It bees dat way sometime." Here the language aspect is the use of the verb *be* to indicate a recurring event or habitual condition, rather than a one-time-only occurrence. But the total expression—"It bees dat way sometime"—also reflects Black English style, for the statement suggests a point of view, a way of looking at life, and a method of adapting to life's realities. To live by the philosophy of "It bees dat way sometime" is to come to grips with the changes that life bees puttin us through, and to accept the changes and bad times as a constant, ever-present reality.

Reverend Jesse Jackson preach: "Africa would if Africa could. America could if America would. But Africa cain't and America ain't." Now here Reverend Jesse is using the language of Black Dialect when he says "ain't" and when he pronounces *can't* as "cain't." But the total expression, using black rhythmic speech, is the more powerful because the Reb has plugged into the style of Black Dialect. The statement thus depends for full communication on what black poet Eugene Redmond calls "songified" pattern and on an Afro-American cultural belief set. That belief holds that White America has always failed blacks and will continue to do so; and that going back to Africa or getting any help from African countries is neither feasible nor realistic because newly emerging African nations must grapple first with problems of independence (economic and otherwise) inherited from centuries of European colonization.

These two very eloquent examples of Black English illustrate that the beauty and power of the idiom lies in its succinctness: saying the same thing in standard written English has taken more than ten times as many words. Black English, then, is a language mixture, adapted to the conditions of slavery and discrimination, a combination of language and style interwoven with and inextricable from Afro-American culture.

Where did this black language and style come from? To answer this question, we have to begin at least as far back as 1619 when a Dutch vessel landed in Jamestown with a cargo of twenty Africans. The arrival of this slaveship marked the beginning of slavery in Colonial America. What kind of language did these and immediately succeeding generations of slaves speak? Was it Ibo, Yoruba, Hausa, some other West African language, Pidgin English? We know that these "new Negroes" (as they were often described in Colonial America) did not jump fresh off the boat doing the Bump and speaking White English! Yet we don't have any tape or phono recordings, nor any other actual direct speech samples of early Black American English. Thus we have to rely on reconstructions of black talk based on indirect evidence, such as representations of Black Dialect in White and Black American literature, written reproductions of the dialect in journals, letters, and diaries by whites, and generalized commentary about slave speech, usually also from whites. Another important source of evidence is based on analogies of Black American speech characteristics with those of other English-based pidgins and creoles found in the Caribbean and in parts of Africa. Language systems such as Jamaican Creole or Nigerian Pidgin English are still in active use today and provide a kind of linguistic mirror image of Black American (Pidgin and Creole) English in its early stages of development.

What this image suggests is as follows. African slaves in America initially developed a pidgin, a language of transaction, that was used in communication between themselves and whites. Over the years, the pidgin gradually became widespread among slaves and evolved into a creole. Developed without benefit of any formal instruction (not even a language lab!), this lingo involved the substitution of English for West African words, but within the same basic structure and idiom that characterized West African language patterns. For example, West African languages allow for the construction of sentences without a form of the verb *to be*. Thus we get a typical African-English Pidgin sentence such as "He tell me he God," used by Tituba, a slave from the island of Barbados in the British West Indies, and recorded by Justice Hathorne at the Salem witch trial in 1692. In Tituba's *he God* statement, the words are English, but the grammar or structure is West African. Such sentence patterns, without any form of the verb *be*, can frequently be heard in virtually any modern-day black community.

Now, as anyone learning a foreign tongue knows, the vocabulary of the new language is fairly easy to master; to some extent, sounds are also. But syntactical structure and idiomatic rules require considerable time and practice to master. Moreover, the one item of a language that remains relatively rigid and fixed over time is its structure. The formation of this Black

American English Pidgin demonstrates, then, simply what any learner of a new language does. They[2] attempt to fit the words and sounds of the new language into the basic idiomatic mold and structure of their native tongue. For example, when I used to teach English to foreign students at the university, I once had a German student render Patrick Henry's famous motto as "Give me the liberty or the death." He was generalizing from the German rule which dictates that definite articles must accompany nouns. Similarly, when I used to teach high school Latin, I'd get native English speakers (whites) who would insist on using the apostrophe rather than the proper case ending to indicate possession, producing, for instance, *agricola's filia* (or sometimes even worse, *agricolae's filia*) for *the farmer's daughter*. And then there is the typical error of the English speaker learning French who forms the compound *paille-chapeau* on the model of *straw hat*.

Below are a few of the West African language rules that were grafted onto early Black English, and which still operate in Black English today.

The slave's application of his or her intuitive knowledge of West African rules to English helped bridge the communications gap between slave and master. However, the slaves also had the problem of communicating with each other. It was the practice of slavers to mix up Africans from different tribes, so in any slave community there would be various tribal languages such as Ibo, Yoruba, Hausa. Even though these African language systems shared general structural commonalities, still they differed in vocabulary. Thus the same English-African language mixture that was used between slave and master had also to be used between slave and slave. All this notwithstanding, it is only logical to assume that the newly arrived Africans were, for a time at least, bilingual, having command of both their native African tongue and the English pidgin as well. However, there was no opportunity to speak and thus reinforce their native language, and as new generations of slaves were born in the New World, the native African speech was heard and used less and less, and the English pidgin and creole varieties more and more. Needless to say, didn't nobody sit down and decide, consciously and deliberately, that this was the way it was gon be—languages, pidgins, creoles, dialects was all like Topsy: they jes grew.

Unfortunately, we have little empirical record of this growth in what we may call its incubation period, that is, for the period from the arrival of the first slaves in 1619 up until the Revolutionary War in 1776. In point of fact, not until 1771 do we get an actual recorded sample of Black American speech *from a black*. (Slightly before this time, there are a few recorded instances of *whites* trying to speak "Negro" in addressing both slaves and Indians.) In the comedy *Trial of*

Table 1.1

Grammar and structure rule in West African languages	Black English
Repetition of noun subject with pronoun	My father, he work there.
Question patterns without *do*	What it come to?
Same form of noun for singular and plural	one boy; five boy
No tense indicated in verb; emphasis on manner or character of action	I know it good when he ask me
Same verb form for all subjects	I know; you know; he know; we know; they know
SOUND RULE IN WEST AFRICAN LANGUAGES	BLACK ENGLISH
No consonant pairs	*jus* (for *just*); *men* (for *mend*)
Few long vowels or two-part vowels (diphthongs)	*rat* or *raht* (for *right*); *tahm* (for *time*)
No /r/ sound	*mow* (for *more*)
No /th/ sound	Black English speaker substitutes /d/ or /f/ for /th/; thus *souf* (for *south*) and *dis* (for *this*)

Atticus Before Justice Beau, for a Rape, written in 1771, a Massachusetts Negro named Caesar is given a bit part in the play—two short lines—in which he says:

> Yesa, Master, he tell me that Atticus he went to bus [kiss] 'em one day, and a shilde [child] cry, and so he let 'em alone . . . Cause, Master, I bus him myself.

Though scant, this speech sample is striking for its parallel to modern-day black speech forms. For example, note the lack of *-s* on the verb in *he tell* and the repetition of the subject in *Atticus he*. Contemporary Black English examples are found in sentences like "The teacher, he say I can't go" and "My brother, he know how to fix it."

As mentioned, if we broaden our scope to encompass African slaves in English-speaking communities outside the United States, we can pick up some additional cogent examples of early Black Dialect that parallel the structure of many sentences heard in contemporary Black America. For instance, there is the seventeenth-century statement of Tituba, "He tell me he God," which was alluded to earlier, and there is a 1718 representation of black speech from the colony of Surinam in South America: "Me bella well" (I am very well). Both sentences parallel contemporary Black English structures like *My momma do that all the time* (no *-s* on verb *do*), and *They rowdy* (no form of verb *to be* in the sentence). Toby, a Barbadian slave in 1715, used plural forms like "There lives white mans, white womans, negree mans, negree womans . . ." These forms are similar to today's Black English plurals in phrases like *five womens* and *these mens*. A possible explanation for the derivation of this kind of plural is the process of "hypercorrection." That is, in trying to appropriate White English without the aid of specified grammatical rules (or teachers to teach the rules), the African speaker took the initiative and made some rather sensible deductions and analogies about English speech forms. Thus, if in English an *-s* is used to indicate the plural, then logically you should put an *-s* on all words in the plural—we have *one boy, two boys*, and *one book, two books*, so why not *one man, two mans* (or *two mens*), and *one child, two childrens*? Another kind of hypercorrection is in the use of *-s* in certain verb forms. Not being exactly sure where the *-s* goes, the speaker chooses the *-s* with many subject-verb combinations (just to make sure!). Since English requires us to say *he does*, why not *I does*? (And is it *he do* and *they does*, or *he does*, and *they do*?)

Though hypercorrection accounts for a small number of Black Dialect patterns, Black English's main structural components are, of course, the adaptations based on African language rules. The historical development we are reconstructing here is the continuity of Africanisms in Black English throughout time and space. We can possibly get a firmer grasp of the total historic picture by considering just one aspect of Black English structure from the early days to the present and from within as well as outside of the United States. Note, then, the following summary illustration of "zero copula" in Black English (that is, sentence patterns with no form of the verb *to be*).

He tell me he God. *Barbados*, 1692
Me bella well (I am very well.) *Surinam*, 1718
Me massa name Cunney Tomsee. (My master's name is Colonel Thompson.) *U.S.*, 1776
Me den very grad. (I am then very glad.) *U.S.*, 1784
You da deble. (You are the devil.) *U.S.*, 1792
He worse than ebber now. *U.S.*, 1821
What dis in heah? (What is this in here?) *U.S.*, 1859
But what de matter with Jasper? (But what is the matter with Jasper?) *U.S.*, 1882
Don't kere, he somethin' t'other wif dis here Draftin' Bo'd. (I don't care, he is something or other [signifying person of authority] with this Draft Board.) *U.S.*, 1926

'E mean tid' dat. (He is mean to do that.) *Gullah Creole, from the Sea Islands, U.S.,* 1949
Di kaafi kuol. (The coffee is cold.) *Jamaica,* 1966
They some rowdy kids. *U.S.,* 1968
A siki. (He sick.) *Surinam,* 1972
This my mother. *U.S.,* 1975

It is true that a number of early Black American English forms have survived until the present day, but it is also true that the distance between contemporary Black and White American English is not as great as it once was. And certainly it is not as great as the distance between, say, contemporary Jamaican Creole English and the English of White America and Britain. How have time and circumstance affected the African element in Black American English? The answer to this question lies in the impact of mainstream American language and culture on Black America, and in the sheer fact of the smaller ratio of blacks to whites in this country (as compared to overwhelmingly huge black populations in the Caribbean and in Africa). With such close linguistic-cultural contact, the influence of the majority culture and language on its minorities is powerful indeed, and there is great pressure on the minorities to assimilate and adopt the culture and language of the majority.

In the early period of American history, the African experience was very immediate and real to the slaves and many yearned to escape back to Africa. As time progressed, though, the African slave became rather firmly entrenched in the New World, and hopes of returning to the motherland began to seem more like unattainable fantasies. Having thus resigned themselves to a future in the New World, many slaves began to take on what Langston Hughes has termed the "ways of white folks"—their religion, culture, customs, and, of course, language. At the same time, though, there were strong resistance movements against enslavement and the oppressive ways of white folks. Thus, from the very beginning, we have the "push-pull" syndrome in Black America, that is, *pushing* toward White American culture while simultaneously *pulling* away from it. (W.E.B. DuBois used the term "double consciousness" to refer to this ambivalence among blacks.) A striking example of the phenomenon is the case of the ex-slave Absalom Jones, founder of one of the first separate black church movements within white Protestant denominations. Jones took on the white man's religion, and proceeded to practice it. (The "push.") Yet when he attempted to pray in a white church in Philadelphia in 1787, an usher pulled him from his knees and ousted him from the church. Thereupon, Jones, along with another ex-slave, Richard Allen, established the African Methodist Episcopal Church. (The "pull.")

The "push-pull" momentum is evidenced in the historical development of Black English in the push toward Americanization of Black English counterbalanced by the pull of retaining its Africanization. We may use the term "de-creolization" to refer to the push toward Americanizing of the language. As slaves became more American and less African, the Black English Creole also became less Africanized. It began to be leveled out in the direction of White English and to lose its distinctive African structural features—that is, the Black English Creole became de-creolized. This process was undoubtedly quite intense and extensive during the Abolitionist period and certainly following Emancipation. It was a primary tactic of Abolitionists (and, traditionally, all fighters for the black cause) to prove blacks equal to whites and therefore worthy of freedom and equality. How could blacks claim American equality if they were not speaking American lingo? Ay, but here we come to the rub or the pull. For blacks have never really been viewed or treated as equals, thus their rejection of White American culture and English—and hence today the process of de-creolization remains unfinished (not to mention various undercurrent and sporadic efforts at re-creolization, such as that among writers, artists, and black intellectuals of the 1960s, who deliberately wrote and rapped in the Black Idiom and sought to preserve its distinctiveness in the literature of the period).

The dynamics of push-pull can help to illuminate the complex sociolinguistic situation that continues to exist in Black America. That is, while some blacks speak very Black English, there are others who speak very White English, and still others who are competent in both linguistic systems. Historically, black speech has been demanded of those who wish to retain close affinities with the black community, and intrusions of White English are likely to be frowned upon and any black users thereof promptly ostracized by the group. Talkin proper (trying to sound white) just ain considered cool. On the other hand, White America has insisted upon White English as the price of admission into its economic and social mainstream. Moreover, there is a psychological factor operating here: people tend to feel more comfortable when they can relax and rap within the linguistic framework that has been the dialect of their nurture, childhood, identity, and style. Hence, even when there is no compelling social pressure to use Black English, there may be an inner compulsion to "talk black."

Let us return to history for a minute to gain a broader understanding of these dynamics. Slaves continued to be imported into America at least up to 1808 when the African slave trade was outlawed by federal legislation. In a sense, we can extend the date even further since the Slave Trade Act was not rigidly enforced. (As late as 1858, just three years before the Civil War, over 400 slaves were brought direct from Africa to Georgia.) This constant influx of slaves made the black community one where there were always numbers of slaves who could speak no English at all. Some idea of the linguistic situation in Black America can be gleaned from newspaper advertisements about runaway slaves. These ads generally cited the slave's degree of competence in English as a method of identification. Judging from the advertisements, there were, linguistically speaking, three groups of African slaves in Colonial times.

The recent arrivals ("new" Negroes) knew practically no English at all. An ad in the *New York Evening Post* in 1774 read: "Ran away . . . a new Negro Fellow named Prince, he can't scarce speak a Word of English."

Then there were slaves who were not born in the U.S. but had been here some time and were still in the process of learning English; some of these were referred to as speakers of either "bad" English or only "tolerable" English. In 1760 the *North-Carolina Gazette* ran this ad: "Ran away from the Subscriber, living near Salisbury, North Carolina . . . a negro fellow named JACK, African born . . . came from Pennsylvania about two years since . . . He is about 30 years of age, and about 5 feet high, speaks bad English."

Those slaves who had successfully mastered English, most of whom, according to the ads, had been born and brought up in America, were referred to as speakers of "good" or "exceptional" English. In 1734 this ad appeared in the Philadelphia *American Weekly Mercury*: "Run away . . . a Negro Man named *Jo Cuffy*, about 20 Years of age . . . ; he's *Pennsylvania* born and speaks good *English*."

Recall that not all blacks in early America were slaves; many either were freed by their masters or bought themselves out of servitude. An important mark of the free person of color, and thus a survival necessity for runaway slaves, was linguistic competence in White English. Moreover, early black writers such as Phillis Wheatley, Jupiter Hammon, Frederick Douglass, and others wrote in the current White English dialect of their respective times. Clearly, from these very early years, there seemed to be one variety of English prevalent among unlettered blacks and those still bound to the plantation way of life, and another variety, quite like that of whites, used and acquired by those few blacks who were literate and free, as well as by those who were more closely associated with Ole Massa. Furthermore, it is highly probable that the black speakers of White English, because of proximity and necessity, commanded the Black English Creole as well. In Beverly Tucker's 1836 novel, *The Partisan Leader*, this white Southerner distinguished two types of slave speech: field and house. Tucker asserted that the dialect of the house slave was highly similar to that of Ole Massa. Moreover, in the novel, the house slave Tom switches from the dialect acquired from his master to field speech to mislead Yankee invaders.

In short, there was a social pattern in early Black America where status—and even survival as a freeman—depended to a great extent on competence in White English (the "push"). Yet, then as now, the linguistic situation was complicated by other forces—the oppression and slavery associated with White English speakers, and the simple fact that there were more black speakers of Black English than black speakers of White English. Hence, both circumstance and psychology would propel blacks toward Black English (the "pull") and require that any black speaker of White English be fluent in Black English as well ("push" and "pull").

Our look at the history of Black English would be incomplete without attention to the special case of Gullah Creole. This dialect, also known as Geechee speech, is spoken by rural and urban blacks who live in the areas along the Atlantic coastal region of South Carolina and Georgia. While some Geechees inhabit the Sea Islands along the coast, many also live around Charleston and Beaufort. Most of the ancestors of these blacks were brought direct from Nigeria, Liberia, Gambia, Sierra Leone, and other places in West Africa where Ibo, Yoruba, Mandingo, Wolof, and other West African languages were and still are spoken. Today, Gullah people form a special Black American community because they have retained considerable African language and cultural patterns. Even the names Gullah and Geechee are African in origin—they refer to languages and tribes in Liberia. For decades, these people have lived in physical and cultural isolation from both mainstream Black and White America, and they bear living witness to the language and way of life that other American blacks have long since lost. (However, the African purity of the Geechee community has recently been threatened by the advent of American tourism attempting to capitalize on the "exotic, Old World charm" of the folk. Hotels, night spots, and other modern-day conveniences and tourist attractions are being constructed on the Sea Islands, thereby uprooting large numbers of blacks and disrupting their traditional African way of life.)

Despite a twentieth-century white writer's reference to Gullah speech as a "slovenly" approximation of English, issuing forth from "clumsy, jungle tongues and thick lips," anybody knowledgeable about African-English language mixtures can readily discern the systematic African element in Gullah Creole. In black linguist Lorenzo Turner's fifteen-year study of this dialect, he found not only fundamental African survivals in sound and syntax, but nearly 6,000 West African words used in personal names and nicknames, in songs and stories, as well as in everyday conversation. It is important for our understanding of Black English to recognize that black speech outside of Geechee areas was undoubtedly once highly similar to Gullah and is now simply at a later stage in the de-creolization process. For example, both Gullah and non-Gullah blacks still use the West African pattern of introducing the subject and repeating it with a personal pronoun. Thus, the Gullah speaker says, "De man an his wif hang to de tree, they lik to pieces." (The man and his wife hanging to the tree, they were licked to pieces.) The non-Gullah speaker handles the subject in the same way: "Yesterday, the whole family, they move to the West Side." On the other hand, only Gullah blacks still use the West African pattern of placing the adjective after the noun: "day clean broad." Other speakers of Black English follow the same pattern as White English speakers: "broad daylight."

We can say, then, that contemporary Black English looks back to an African linguistic tradition which was modified on American soil. While historical records and documents reveal a good deal about the development and change of this Africanized English, there is much that the records don't tell us. As a former slave said, "Everything I tells you am the truth, but they's plenty I can't tell you."

Notes

1. Geneva Smitherman, *Talking and Testifyin: The Language of Black America* (Detroit: Wayne State University Press, 1986 [1977]).
2. In traditional usage, this sentence would have begun with the masculine pronoun "he," since it refers to "any learner," which is singular. However, due to the public's increased awareness of sexist uses of the English language, plural pronouns have now become acceptable substitutes for the masculine singular. I will continue to follow this procedure throughout, along with using "his or her." For an excellent set of guidelines for avoiding sexist language use, see "Guideline for Nonsexist Use of Language in NCTE Publications," National Council of Teachers of English.

Keith Gilyard

In this selection, Gilyard provides a historical and comprehensive look at the various studies of African American rhetoric that were conducted and published in different periods. Gilyard argues that, given the consistent attention paid to the both the rhetorical practices of African Americans and to African American persuasion and argumentation, there can be no doubt that African American rhetoric is not only distinct—although related—in its origins and purposes from its counterpart, American rhetoric, but must also be a recognized area of study and research, a disciplinary field as it were. This excerpt is a goldmine of citations on African American rhetorical theory. Although Gilyard primarily focuses on works that privilege oratory, speech, and spoken language, what he uncovers can be applied to African American rhetoric writ large.

Introduction: Aspects of African American Rhetoric as a Field

Keith Gilyard[1]

To encapsulate all the various efforts in the scholarly study of African American rhetoric would be a task virtually as daunting as if the object were to summarize all reportage and analysis of the Black experience overall. Voluminous attention has been devoted to Black discourses because such discourses have been the major means by which people of African descent in the American colonies and subsequent republic have asserted their collective humanity in the face of an enduring White supremacy and tried to persuade, cajole, and gain acceptance for ideas relative to Black survival and Black liberation. So immediately one recognizes the impracticality of trying to write definitively about such a vast network of activities in such limited space. What I attempt, therefore, is a meaningful historical sketch of a particular body of rhetorical scholarship, a choice that necessarily implies certain critical sacrifices. For example, I will forgo formal discussion of linguistics and the creative arts, although I possess impressive arguments why such truncation of rhetorical inquiry should not be carried too far. The very existence of African American Vernacular English (AAVE) inscribes a significant rhetorical situation, and the prevailing functional character of African American artistic expression renders problematic any move to divorce its production and any criticism thereof from the realm of rhetorical inquiry. Nonetheless, I maintain that it is useful, in order to actually get through one essay, to focus on what there is to say about Black persuasive or associative verbal practices beyond the specific linguistic items of AAVE, or Standard English for that matter, or on what is left to say of public discourse if one agrees to bracket texts that are literary or musical. What is left to say of strategy and method? The answer comprises the terrain that this essay explores. The focus is on what scholars working taxonomically and employing rhetorical perspectives ranging from Aristotelian principles to Afrocentric conceptions have made of oratory by those of African descent in the United States. Of course, this approach also ignores what normally would be regarded as interpersonal communication. I am aware, too, how ultimately indefensible that decision is in the long run given that even one-on-one verbal interaction designed to elicit cooperation is surely rhetoric as well. However, some of the collections I mention, such as *Language, Communication, and Rhetoric in Black America* (A. Smith, 1972), do include such work that extends beyond the scope of this project. In addition, I recommend Thomas Kochman's *Rappin' and Stylin' Out* (1972) and Michael Hecht's *African American Communication* (1993).

Serious analysis of African American oratory dates back to the nineteenth century. In the 1850s and 1860s, speeches by the likes of Frederick Douglass and Charles Langston were published and commented on in publications such as the *Liberator* and the *Anglo American Magazine*. By 1890, anthologies such as E. M. Brawley's *The Negro Baptist Pulpit* were being produced. However, the first standard reference work on African American rhetoric, *Negro Orators and*

Their Orations, was compiled by Carter G. Woodson in 1925. Woodson reveals himself to be of a classical bent methodologically. He liberally invokes such authorities as Demosthenes, Quintillian, and Cicero. He employs Aristotelian classifications, categorizing speeches as judicial, deliberative, or epideictic. Nonetheless, Woodson does move beyond the classical by positing Christian pulpit oratory as a fourth major category. Of course, Black orators did not get much practice with speeches of the judicial type, or the deliberative when *deliberative* is narrowly defined as being before legislative bodies. But by Woodson's reckoning, Blacks excelled at the epideictic, or the occasional speech, and in the pulpit.

By use of chapter headings, Woodson traces a movement from "The First Protest" to "Progressive Oratory," with stops along the way that signal "More Forceful Attacks," "Further Efforts for a Hearing," "The Oratory of the Crisis," "The Oratory of Defiance," "Deliberative Oratory—Speeches of Negro Congressmen," "Speeches of Negro Congressman Outside of Congress," "Oratory in the Solution of the Race Problem," "The Panegyric," "Optimistic Oratory," and "Occasional Oratory." He cites as first examples of public protest against enslavement two speeches: one titled "Negro Slavery" by "Othello," which was subsequently printed in 1787, and a second titled "Slavery," which was signed "By a Free Negro" and printed in 1788. For more forceful appeals, he offers such examples as Peter Williams's 1808 "Oration on the Abolition of the Slave Trade" and James Forten's 1813 "A Late Bill Before the State of Pennsylvania," in which Forten argued against a proposed bill to bar free people of color from entering the state. The chapter "Further Efforts" includes James McCune Smith's 1838 "The Abolition of Slavery and the Slave Trade in the French and British Colonies," which was celebratory of the political event and designed to spur hope and further the cause of abolition in the United States. As abolitionist activity gathered force, Charles Lenox Remond and then Frederick Douglass became the most famous Black orators, and a dozen or so speeches by the two between 1841 and 1863 are Woodson's main examples of those who spoke to the "crisis" and to the issue of "defiance." Speeches by congressmen during the Reconstruction era include, in session, John Willis Menard's 1868 "The Negro's First Speech in Congress, Made by John Willis Menard in Defense of His Election to Congress when His Seat Was Contested and Won by His Political Opponent" and, out of session, James Mercer Langston's 1874 "Equality before the Law." Douglass's 1879 "The Negro Exodus from the Gulf States" is noted as an example of "solution" rhetoric; Bishop Reverdy Ransom's 1905 centennial oration in appreciation of William Lloyd Garrison is included among examples of the panegyric. Optimistic oratory is most closely associated with Booker T. Washington. C. V. Roman at various times delivered "A Knowledge of History Conducive to Racial Solidarity," which is presented as an excellent example of the occasional address. Progressive oratory, to Woodson, is symbolized by the likes of Ida B. Wells-Barnett, William Monroe Trotter, James Weldon Johnson, Mordecai Johnson, Archibald Grimké, Francis Grimké, and William Pickens, who delivered at several venues the notable address "The Kind of Democracy the Negro Race Expects."

Woodson was a historian by training; thus, he attempts little in the way of technical or structural analysis of the speeches themselves. His emphasis is on documenting and cataloging, a tendency that is again evident in *The Mind of the Negro* (1926), which includes more than 250 letters, most of which had been published in the *Journal of Negro History*, of which Woodson was editor. The letters, in Woodson's view, help to round out a conception of the Black mindset. But he views the letters as shapers of perspective, not merely as reflective. Authors include several who were known for their oratory as well, such as Richard Allen, Absalom Jones, Douglass, Remond, Henry Highland Garnet, and William Wells Brown.

Religious oratory, as Woodson affirms, has been central to the African American rhetorical tradition from the outset and was the primary channel by which millions of Blacks came to comprehend and speculate about the social world of which they were part. Richard Allen,

Absalom Jones, Henry Highland Garnet, and Francis Grimké, for example, were all preachers. Therefore, the study of Black pulpit oratory as well as scholarly treatment of the Black church in general are necessary components of research in African American public discourse. As early as 1890, anthologies like E. M. Brawley's *The Negro Baptist Pulpit* were published, and W. E. B. Du Bois wrote about Black religious practices in *The Negro Church* (1903) and *The Souls of Black Folk* (1903/1989). James Weldon Johnson's 1927 *God's Trombones* is based on the "stereotyped sermon" he identified that moves formulaically from creation to judgment day. However, the first thorough treatment of Black preaching is William Pipes's *Say Amen, Brother! Old-Time Negro Preaching: A Study in American Frustration* (1951/1992). In this work, based on seven sermons recorded in Macon County, Georgia, Pipes classifies such preaching according to the following scheme derived from classical rhetoric:

Invention

A. Purposes

To persuade the sinner to "take up the new life" according to the Bible, the real world of God.

To impress the audience, so that there will be an outburst (escape) of emotion in shouting and frenzy.

To give religious instruction, according to the Bible.

B. Subject Matter

The Bible is the source of all ideas, information, and truths: God is good; "the more we suffer in this world, the greater will be our reward after death"; morality, social obligations, and religious fidelity are to be emphasized; there are evidences of fear and superstition.

C. Modes of Persuasion

Personal Appeal: the minister is uneducated but is "called" by God; his word is the word of God; the preacher is usually an impressive person, has a dramatic bearing and a melodious voice.

Emotional Appeal: by means of rhythm, sensationalism, rhetorical figures, imagery, suggestion, etc., the minister puts the audience into a mood to accept his ideas; this is the greatest appeal.

Logical Argument: not as important as emotional appeal; the best argument is that "it's true because the Bible said so."

Disposition

There is no logical organization because there is little preparation. The emotions determine everything.

Style

Familiar, concrete, narrative, ungrammatical language; Biblical; humor; deals with *things* rather than with *ideas*.

Delivery

Awkward, spectacular, dramatic, bombastic; musical voice; rhythmical and emotional; enthusiastic; sincere.

(p. 72)

Pipes's work remains significant for the rigor with which he treats Black sermons and for his insights about the continuing importance of old-time preachers to the African American struggle for equality. However, he bases much of his analysis of Black religious practices on an acceptance of stereotypes about "primitive" Africans who, restricted to the "jungles of Africa," lacked opportunities to develop sophistication. Given his perspective, Pipes sees early

Black religion as primarily an escapist adaptation to servitude. He ignores its rebellious, in some cases multilayered, meanings. Other scholars avoid this mistake, most notably Henry H. Mitchell, whose *Black Preaching* (1970) now arguably stands as the best book on Black religious oratory.

General historical treatments of Black oratory include Lowell Moseberry's *An Historical Study of Negro Oratory in the United States to 1915* (1955) and Marcus Boulware's *The Oratory of Negro Leaders: 1900–1968* (1969). Moseberry, trained in a department of speech, brings a broader array of rhetorical methods to his task than does Woodson. Like Woodson, he regards his primary objective to be "a historical report on the platform activities of the Negro" (p. iv). However, differing in method, he seeks to "discover areas in the eloquence of the Negro that seemed to deviate from standard oratorical practice" (p. iv). After painting the familiar social, political, and economic backdrop against which African American oratory up until the death of Booker T. Washington took place, he turns his attention to what he perceives to be a Black expressive and signifying difference. He argues that while Black orators used the same degree of induction, deduction, and causal reasoning employed by White rhetors of similar training and educational levels, they made a distinct departure from Anglo-Saxon patterns of oratory in terms of pathetic proof and style (p. 147). Black orators relied on keen invective, humor, and distinct—what Moseberry was willing to call African—brands of rhythmic phrasing. These observations are similar to those made by Pipes about Black sermons—evidence that sacred and secular African American rhetorical practices are interpenetrating. According to Moseberry, the most striking display of Black form is what we may call a jubilee rhetoric. As he explains:

> A stylistic device of the Negro orators that, perhaps, was contrived as much for its appeal to the emotions as for its rhetorical value was an antithetical refrain that strongly resembles the "jubilee" tones of the Negro spirituals. This "jubilee" consists of a series of ideas containing a major undertone of tragedy, alternating with a contrasting jubilant response. The pathetic appeal of the "jubilee" builds in emotional intensity until it explodes climactically in an exultant "shout" of challenge.
>
> (1955, p. 150)

As Moseberry further indicates, Douglass's 1852 "Fifth of July Oration" is a clear example, one in which the optimistic notes precede the tragic:

Jubilee
> The sunlight that brought life and healing to you

Tragic Undertone
> Has brought stripes and death to me.

Jubilee
> The Fourth of July is yours,

Tragic Undertone
> Not mine.

Jubilee
> You may rejoice

Tragic Undertone
> I must mourn. To drag a man in fetters into the grand illumined temple of liberty and call upon him to join you in joyous anthems, were inhuman mockery and sacrilegious irony.
>
> (pp. 151–152)

The same technique, in reverse pattern, is demonstrated by Francis Grimké:

Tragic Undertone
The way is certainly very dark. There are many things to discourage us.
Jubilee
But there is a brighter side to the picture, and it is of this side that I desire especially to speak.
Tragic Undertone
Before doing so, however, it may be well for us to notice in passing some of the things which seem to indicate the approach of a still deeper darkness . . . and first, lawlessness is increasing in the South.
Jubilee
After thirty-three years of freedom.
Tragic Undertone
Our civil and political rights are still denied us. The Fourteenth and Fifteenth Amendments to the Constitution are still a dead letter. The spirit of opposition, of oppression, of injustice is not diminishing but increasing.

(Moseberry, 1955, p. 152)

Boulware's study is the first major historical treatment of African American rhetoric devoted exclusively to texts of the twentieth century. He takes as his major tasks a chronicling of Black oratorical output and the creation of classification schemes. For Boulware, the mission of the Black orator invariably revolved around six goals: (1) to protest grievances, (2) to state complaints, (3) to demand rights, (4) to advocate racial cooperation, (5) to mold racial consciousness, and (6) to stimulate racial pride. He sets the pursuit of this mission in the twentieth century against the backdrop of, in his view, the century's six great American presidents—Theodore Roosevelt, Woodrow Wilson, Franklin D. Roosevelt, Harry Truman, John F. Kennedy, and Lyndon B. Johnson—and their presidencies as popularly labeled, that is, the Rooseveltian Era, 1901–1909; the New Freedom Period, 1913–1921; the New Deal, 1933–1945; the Fair Deal, 1945–1953; the New Frontier, 1961–1965;[2] and the Great Society, 1965–1969. Guided by his typologies, Boulware spins a history of African American oratory that begins in 1900, when Booker T. Washington was the dominant African American figure and orator in the country, up until the summer of 1968. He traces or alludes to such public careers as those of Washington, Mary Church Terrell, W. E. B. Du Bois, Mordecai Johnson, Marcus Garvey, Sadie Mossell Alexander, James Weldon Johnson, Nannie Helen Burroughs, Langston Hughes, Charlotte Hawkins Brown, Paul Robeson, Mary McLeod Bethune, A. Philip Randolph, Zora Neale Hurston, Adam Clayton Powell Jr., Benjamin Mays, Gardner Taylor, Walter White, Roy Wilkins, Father Divine, Daddy Grace, Roy Wilkins, Malcolm X, James Baldwin, and Martin Luther King Jr.

By the time Boulware's study appeared, African American political and cultural expressions had reached a high point in terms of their impact on the national consciousness. Major civil rights protests had been featured prominently for more than a decade on television, as were, more recently, the inner-city rebellions and Black Power pronouncements. It was also evident that civil progress, ongoing demands, and violent civil unrest by African Americans were driven largely by passions and rhetoric little known or understood by the nation at large. Of course, some folks never cared to know or understand, but public and academic gatherings relative to African American issues, including artistic and overall communication issues, attracted significant audiences. From this context stemmed a large wave of books on the Black experience. Among that wave were several major works of rhetorical scholarship such as Haig Bosmajian and Hamida Bosmajian's *The Rhetoric of the Civil Rights Movement* (1969), Robert Scott and

Wayne Brockriede's *The Rhetoric of Black Power* (1969), Arthur Smith's *Rhetoric of Black Revolution* (1969), and James Golden and Richard Rieke's *The Rhetoric of Black Americans* (1971).

The Bosmajians' work is intended for use as a textbook; they refrain from offering rhetorical analyses of the individual pieces in the collection because they planned to leave those tasks to prospective students. However, they impressively frame their volume with rhetorical and historical commentary. In particular, they describe how African Americans and their allies mounted a massive persuasion campaign aimed at securing equality and justice on the heels of the Supreme Court desegregation decision and the Montgomery bus boycott. Actions themselves were decidedly rhetorical in that campaign; the sit-ins, freedom rides, picketing, marches, wade-ins, read-ins, and jail-ins were perhaps the more effective forms of persuasion. Yet the speeches, songs, and pamphlets were indispensable in terms of, as the Bosmajians term it, "a rhetorical or suasory function" (1969, p. 5). The authors also indicate a continual situation with which the activists were confronted:

> The civil-rights leaders faced a formidable rhetorical problem; several questions about their persuasion had to be answered: To whom was their persuasion to be directed? Segregationists? Moderate whites? Negroes? What form should the protest take? What effect would the persuasion have on the audience? For example, on one hand the Montgomery bus boycott was directed against city authorities and the bus company with their segregation policies; yet, on the other hand, the boycott, with the accompanying mass meetings, speeches, songs, and demonstrations, had a persuasive effect upon the thousands of Negroes who had to become united participants in the boycott; unless the Negroes of Montgomery could be persuaded to stop riding the buses, the boycott was doomed to failure. Further, because the nation and the entire world had their attention focused on Montgomery and the actions of the civil-rights leaders, this larger audience also had to be considered, for they too were watching and being persuaded.
>
> (p. 5)

The Bosmajians highlight the words of Martin Luther King Jr., James Farmer, and Roy Wilkins as examples of the mainstream, integrationist civil rights campaign. But because the editors' view of the Civil Rights Movement allows for a certain indeterminacy, they show how those speakers were in dialogue with competing and challenging rhetorics, that of conservative Alabama clergy on the one hand and Black power advocates on the other. Thus King's April 16, 1963, "Letter from Birmingham Jail" is reprinted as is the April 12, 1963, "Public Statement by Eight Alabama Clergymen." Also included are the transcript of the debate between Farmer and Malcolm X that took place at Cornell University on March 7, 1962; Wilkins's July 5, 1966, "Keynote Address to the NAACP Annual Convention," in which he condemned the idea of Black power; and Floyd McKissick's July 1967 "Speech at the National Conference on Black Power," in which he advocated the concept.

Two selections by Stokely Carmichael are presented: a pamphlet, *Power and Racism*, which was distributed by the Student Nonviolent Coordinating Committee, and his January 16, 1967, "Speech at Morgan State College." Carmichael is the person most associated perhaps with both the Student Nonviolent Coordinating Committee (SNCC) and the slogan "Black Power." *Newsweek* reported in its May 15, 1967, issue that he was speaking at various campuses and "soaking whites $1,000 for a rather tame exposition of black power, charging Negro colleges $500 for the gloves-off treatment" ("Which Way for the Negro?" 1967, p. 28). The pamphlet is intended to illustrate the former approach; the speech at Morgan State College is meant to indicate the latter.

Scott and Brockriede also present civil rights and Black power discourses as integrally connected. Just as the statements of Black power advocates constitute much of the Bosmajians's "civil rights" book, the arguments of King, and even Hubert Humphrey, and accompanying critical perspectives by the editors constitute a sizable portion of the "Black power" book. In particular, the editors/authors detail Humphrey's technique as he denounced Black power at the NAACP Annual Convention in 1966 one day after Roy Wilkins had done so. But they feel that while Humphrey managed to establish great ethos with the 1,500 delegates, mainly by parroting Wilkins's address, in doing so he missed an opportunity to complicate and enrich a discussion of Black power. It is an opportunity that King himself never missed. Although he never embraced the slogan, he was never simplistically antagonistic toward it and always considered carefully its rhetorical effects and the premises behind it. This is illustrated by the selection "Martin Luther King, Jr. Writes about the Birth of the Black Power Slogan," which is a reprint of the second chapter of his *Where Do We Go from Here: Chaos or Community?* (1968). The complexity of King's thinking and the influence of Black power proponents upon him is also evident in his last speech to the Southern Christian Leadership Conference (SCLC) on August 16, 1967, "The President's Address to the Tenth Anniversary Convention of the Southern Christian Leadership Conference."

Contrasting speeches by Carmichael are included in the text; in this case they represent a talk given before an African American audience in Detroit and one given before a White audience in Whitewater, Wisconsin. Background essays on Black power are provided by James Comer and Charles V. Hamilton.

Smith's book, along with two subsequent works, *The Voice of Black Rhetoric* (1971), edited with Stephen Robb, and *Language, Communication, and Rhetoric in Black America* (1972), represent some of the most in-depth work in the area of African American rhetoric. Smith, now known as Molefi Asante, developed a specialty in agitational rhetoric as part of his doctoral studies at UCLA. He was well equipped and positioned, as a theorist and a witness, to assess the agitational Black rhetoric of the 1960s. He sees Black nationalist and Black power rhetorics to be essentially aggressive (toward Whites) and unifying (toward African Americans). To move the Black masses, the Black rhetor must, as Boulware suggests, posit grievances. Of course, given America's treatment of Black folks, that is the easiest part of the job. The harder task is to fulfill the requirement that the rhetoric be consistent with or overcome an audience's mythology. King, for example, could always count on a large audience, particularly in the South, to hear an appeal based on Christian love. Malcolm X, on the other hand, had to overcome Christian beliefs to attract disciples to the Nation of Islam.

Smith employs several classification schemes regarding strategies, themes, and audiences to enhance his descriptions. Particularly useful is the four-part strategic structure that appears as part of all long-term agitation campaigns: (1) vilification, (2) objectification, (3) mythication, and (4) legitimation. *Vilification* is to create an antihero by attacking the ideas, actions, and being of a conspicuous member of the opposition, mainly by charging that the person is a key agent of domination. *Objectification* is to blame a specific but ill-defined group, such as the White power structure or, simply, Whitey for the audience's suffering. This gives the rhetor more flexibility to denounce, tap into his or her audience's mythology, and arouse them. *Mythication* is the suggestion that "suprarational" forces support the audience's struggle; this often means using religious symbolism to convey a sense that triumph has been ordained. This is exemplified by King speaking of the "coming of the Lord"; Malcolm asserting that the government, that which oppresses, is against God; or numerous speakers' likening the Black struggle to the story of Exodus. *Legitimation* is the attempt to justify one's own actions or those of fellow activists, usually by reversing blame and citing the oppressor's "original sin." It is generally the only defensive strategy employed by revolutionists, who characteristically remain on the offensive.

Smith also identifies a four-part thematic structure that is basic to Black secular, agitational rhetors: (1) all Blacks face a common enemy, (2) there is a conspiracy to violate Black manhood,

(3) there is pervasive American hypocrisy, and (4) Black unity is requisite for Black liberation. With respect to the nature of the Black audience, Smith (1969, p. 67) proposes the following table:

Table 1.2 Audience composition

Characteristics	Type of audience
Age	
Adults	Religious
Youth	Secular
Sex	
Female	Religious
Male	Secular
Education	
Less	Religious
More	Secular

Adult audiences, then, are seen to favor and be more apt to respond to religious oratory than would Black youth. Females are seen as more religious than males, and those less formally educated are seen as more religious than those with more education. Broad tendencies, of course, can always be complicated. There have always been old, secular, informally educated radicals around in the 'hood, some of them women. Smith, however, feels that the table is an accurate indicator of where audible support is likely to emanate from during a speech.

In *The Voice of Black Rhetoric*, Smith and Robb describe the general characteristics of African American rhetoric considered historically. Twenty speakers are offered as exemplary, ranging from David Walker, who keynoted a meeting of the First General Colored Association in Boston in 1828, to H. Rap Brown, who spoke on colonialism and revolution in Detroit in 1967. An interesting methodological development involved the editors' discussion of Nommo, the African belief in the pervasive, mystical, transformative, even life-giving power of the Word. As they articulate:

> It is a cardinal mistake of our society to operate on the basis that language functions of whites are everywhere reproducible in black societies in terms of influences and ends. With an African heritage steeped in oral traditions and the acceptance of transforming vocal communication, the Afro-American developed, consciously or subconsciously, a consummate skill in using language to produce his own alternate communication patterns to those employed by whites in the American situation. Communication between different ethnic and linguistic groups was difficult, but the almost universal African regard for the power of the spoken word contributed to the development of alternate communication patterns in the work songs, Black English, sermons, and Spirituals, with their dual meanings, one for the body and one for the soul. It is precisely the power of the word in today's black society that authentically speaks of an African past. Thus, to omit black rhetoric as manifest in speeches and songs from any investigation of black history is to ignore the essential ingredient in the making of black drama.
>
> (1972, p. 2)

The concern with African influences would become a more prominent component of Smith's evolving rhetorical theory. Among the twenty-nine essays in *Language, Communication, and*

Rhetoric in Black America, which were on by that time predictable topics or subjects, Smith includes six of his own, including "Markings of an African Concept of Rhetoric." As the title suggests, he begins to rely more heavily on Afrocentric concepts of rhetoric, posing Nommo, for example, as opposite Western persuasive technique:

> The public discourse convinces not through attention to logical substance but through the power to fascinate. Yet this does not preclude the materials of composition or the arrangement and structure of those materials; it simply expresses a belief that when images are arranged according to their power and chosen because of their power, the speaker's ability to convince is greater than if he attempted to employ syllogisms. The syllogism is a Western concept; *Nommo* is an African concept . . . . Perhaps that is drawing the choices too clearly, inasmuch as few neo-Aristotelians would argue for a dichotomy of emotion and logic. However, it is necessary to state the polar positions to illustrate the emphasis of the traditional African speaker.
>
> (1972, pp. 371–372)

Of course, the African concept of rhetoric is to be used to explicate oratory in the United States as well. In fact, Smith's essay addresses in a sense the peculiar qualities of African American oratory noted by the likes of Moseberry. Elaboration of Smith's ideas can be found in subsequent works, most notably the numerous passages on rhetoric in *The Afrocentric Idea* (Asante, 1998).

Golden and Rieke's anthology is fairly duplicative, including texts by speakers such as Walker, Remond, Douglass, Garvey, King, and Malcolm X. The distinguishing and lasting quality of the collection is the lengthy introduction, which is an insightful discussion of various political goals and rhetorical issues. As Golden and Rieke explain, they are suggesting that "some of the separatist rhetoric includes the possibility that once black men have gotten together and established some political, economic and cultural identity and power, they might be able to join other ethnic groups forming a kind of assimilated United States society" (1971, p. 44).

An additional issue addressed by Golden and Rieke is the very worth of large-scale rhetorical intervention. Are the problems faced by the nation with respect to racialized inequality open to amelioration through what we generally regard as persuasive means? Or, given some of the deep-rootedness of racism, are coercive means, such as the physical force that ended enslavement or influenced legislation in the 1960s, more appropriate? These questions point to a possible "crisis of faith," particularly for Black rhetors and scholars, and are queries that must be confronted seriously.

Geneva Smitherman's widely acclaimed book, *Talkin and Testifyin: The Language of Black America* (1977/1986) also was conceived in the late 1960s. Although primarily considered a linguist, Smitherman is perhaps most responsible for popularizing the "Black Modes of Discourse," vernacular conceptions that are invaluable with respect to rhetorical analysis. The modes are (1) call-response, a series of spontaneous interactions between speaker and listener; (2) signification, the art of humorous put downs, usually through verbal indirection; (3) tonal semantics, the conveying of meanings in Black discourse through specifically ethnic kinds of voice rhythms and vocal inflections; and (4) narrative sequencing, the habitual use of stories to explain and/or persuade. Smitherman (1995) alternately conceptualizes an African American Verbal Tradition (AAVT) that encompasses (1) signification, (2) personalization, (3) tonal semantics, and (4) sermonic tone. The latter framework enables her to make sense of Black discourse that is not generally regarded as AAVE. She theorizes, for example, that the use of AAVT made Clarence Thomas a more sympathetic figure than Anita Hill in the African American community. While the syntax they both used during the confirmation hearings was unquestionably standard, Thomas made the matter personal and emotional, signifying along the way. Hill, on the other hand, seemed without passion or anger, emotions she had a right to feel and if displayed would have cast her inside AAVT and probably garnered her more support, particularly among African American women. Smitherman, therefore, seemingly in response to Golden and Rieke, points clearly to the value of rhetorical study as a mode of activist intervention. Because Hill did not resolve her rhetorical dilemma in the most socially productive way, she missed, according to Smitherman, an important moment to deliver more incisive and powerful commentary on sexual harassment, which is certainly a Black as well as larger issue. Smitherman concludes that Black women seeking to develop effective voices as part of the freedom struggle need a "head and heart rhetoric" to provide leadership for African Americans and the nation (2000, p. 265).

Significant post-1970s treatments of African American rhetoric include David Howard-Pitney's *The Afro-American Jeremiad: Appeals for Justice in America* (1990); Keith Miller's *Voice of Deliverance: The Language of Martin Luther King, Jr., and Its Sources* (1992); Shirley Wilson Logan's *With Pen and Voice: A Critical Anthology of Nineteenth-Century African-American Women* (1995) and *"We Are Coming": The Persuasive Discourse of Nineteenth-Century Black Women* (1999); Bradford Stull's *Amid the Fall, Dreaming of Eden: Du Bois, King, Malcolm X, and Emancipatory Composition* (1999); and Jacqueline Jones Royster's *Traces of a Stream: Literacy and Social Change among African American Women* (2000).

Howard-Pitney identifies the African American jeremiad to be an appropriation of the American jeremiad, which itself consists of statements of or references to the popular doctrine of America's divine promise, chastisement because of present moral decline, and prophecy that the nation will soon overcome its faults and emerge transcendent. The African American version posits Blacks as a chosen people within the parameters of the nation's archetypal civil myth. Howard-Pitney describes and discusses thoroughly the successes and failures of six leaders—Douglass, Washington, Wells, Du Bois, Bethune, and King—who utilized the form extensively. King and Du Bois, along with Malcolm X, are the subjects of Stull's study; Stull suggests that their composing processes, broadly and deeply construed, could serve as a model for liberatory composition classrooms. And King is obviously the sole subject of Miller's book, which locates King firmly within the tradition of Black religious oratory while exploring his borrowings from the writings of Whites.

Logan's first book, an important anthology that represents the frequently neglected tradition of Black woman rhetors, mainly features speeches by seven women—Maria Stewart, Sojourner Truth, Frances Ellen Watkins Harper, Anna Julia Haywood Cooper, Ida B. Wells, Fannie Barrier Williams, and Victoria Earle Matthews. Her second is an in-depth study in which most of these women are seen in the context of a particular trope—Maria Stewart in connection with the idea of "Ethiopia Rising," for example, or Ida B. Wells in relation to the "Presence of Lynching." Directly connected to Logan's project is Royster's book, which focuses on the essays of elite nineteenth-century African American women such as Stewart, Cooper, and Wells. Royster also posits an Afrafeminist ideology and argues its relevance for rhetorical studies.

Despite the recent impressive work in the field, which includes, by the way, Philip Foner and Robert James Branham's compilation of older speeches, *Lift Every Voice: African American Oratory, 1787–1900* (1998), many of the earlier volumes have gone out of print. In 1995, citing the lack of a sufficiently comprehensive text as well as a decline in African American rhetoric course offerings, Lyndrey Niles edited *African American Rhetoric: A Reader*. Approximately half the volume consists of reprinted material (mentioned above) by Asante, Golden, and Rieke. The most interesting additions for these purposes are Melbourne Cummings and Jack L. Daniel's "A Comprehensive Assessment of Scholarly Writings in Black Rhetoric" and Ronald Jackson's "Toward an Afrocentric Methodology for the Critical Assessment of Rhetoric." These scholars, affirming work by the likes of Asante and Smitherman, consider traditional academic models and limited notions such as "persuasion" to be too static to account for the richness, dynamism, and cultural content relative to speaker-audience interactions in African-derived contexts. As Cummings and Daniel assert, "Black rhetoric, with its concentration on Nommo, rhythmical patterns, audience assertiveness, and so on, cannot be dealt with by simply applying the conventional Euro-American tools of rhetorical criticism" (p. 100). In line with this thinking, Jackson proffers an Afrocentric model in which Nommo is graphically posited as the center around which eight elements—rhythm, soundin', stylin', improvisation, storytelling, lyrical code, image making, and call and response—revolve (see fig. 2; R. Jackson, 1995, p. 154). As Jackson elaborates:

> Rhythm is similar to polyrhythm in that it suggests that the energy of the rhetor must be one with the energy of the audience . . . . The rhythm must coincide with the mystical and magical power of the word, so that the speaker, the word, and audience are all on one accord . . . . Soundin' is the idea of wolfin' or signifyin' within the African American tradition . . . . Stylin' is the notion that a speaker has combined rhythm, excitement, and enthusiasm which propel a message and the audience . . . . Improvisation is a stylistic device which is a verbal interplay, and strategic catharsis often resulting from the hostility and frustration of a white-dominated society. It is spontaneity . . . . Storytelling . . . is often used by a rhetor to arouse epic memory . . . . Lyrical Code is the preservation of the word through a highly codified system of lexicality. It is the very dynamic lyrical quality which provides youth to the community usage of standard and Black English. It is often used by speakers to appear communalistic, commonplace, and not so convoluted in diction . . . . Image making is the element which considers legends, myths, and heroes in a given culture . . . . Call and response is the final element which offers a culmination of all these elements into an interactive discourse atypical of European communities. It is the idea that one should affirm by clapping, saying "amen," or responding in some way.
>
> (p. 154)

At this point, I hope to have amply demonstrated the richness of African American rhetoric as a field of inquiry while indicating, if only implicitly, what future work needs to be done. Numerous studies are required that will allow us to understand the import of current and emerging Black discourses. This is not to project an insular sense but to suggest that an understanding of continued Black articulations for a better society form a central question to be confronted by all if we are to bring a better society into existence. Nor do I mean to imply, by emphasizing contemporary subject matter, that we halt historical investigations. In fact, it is crucial that we uncover and remain aware of some of the questions our forerunners posed because some of them remain unanswered. Will optimists, which all rhetoricians are at heart, remain prone, as both Woodson and Boulware suggest, to losing whatever hold they have on the public because of the inability to deliver tangible results? Will Black leadership that emerges from the working classes become more important, as Pipes envisions it might, than that which stems from the academy? There is yet much to witness.

Notes

1. Keith Gilyard, "Introduction: Aspects of African American Rhetoric as a Field," in *African American Rhetoric(s): Interdisciplinary Perspective*, eds. Elaine B. Richardson and Ronald L. Jackson II (Carbondale: Southern Illinois University Press, 2007).
2. Although Kennedy was assassinated in 1963, I have used the dates of his elected term as the period of the New Frontier.

Section 1: Further Reading

Cummings, Melbourne S. "Teaching the African American Rhetoric Course." In *African American Communications: An Anthology in Traditional and Contemporary Studies*, 1993. Dubuque, IA: Kendall Hunt. (p. 241).

Cummings, Melbourne, and Jack Daniel. "The Study of African American Rhetoric." In *The Rhetoric of Western Thought*. Dubuque, IA: Kendall Hunt, 1997. (pp. 360–385).

Jackson II, Ronald L. and Elaine B. Richardson. *Understanding African American Rhetoric: Classical Origins to Contemporary Innovations*. Abingdon, UK: Routledge, 2003.

Niles, Lyndrey A., ed. *African American Rhetoric: A Reader*. Dubuque, IA: Kendall Hunt, 1995.

Scott, Robert Lee and Wayne Brockriede, eds. *The Rhetoric of Black Power*. New York: Harper & Row, 1969.

Smith, Arthur Lee. *The Voice of Black Rhetoric: Selections*. Ed. Stephen Robb. Boston: Allyn and Bacon, 1971.

Section 1: Discussion Questions

1. Although some African Americans predominantly use Standard English, which linguists link closely with Midwestern middle- and upper-class Whites, describe how African Americans might still employ "the language of Black experience" when engaged in African American rhetoric.

2. Explain how the theoretical readings that follow the introduction—that is, the selections from Asante, Smitherman, and Gilyard—enhance one another. Choose at least two readings and illustrate how they work together to explain what African American rhetoric is.

3. The introduction lists six principles of African American rhetoric. What are those six principles? While each principle can be used as a separate framework for rhetorical analysis, explain why and how these principles are inextricably linked in African American rhetorical practice. Pick a couple of principles to focus on for your response to this question.

PART II

THE BLACKEST HOURS— ORIGINS AND HISTORIES OF AFRICAN AMERICAN RHETORIC

INTRODUCTION: "COMING OUT OF THE DARK": THE BEGINNINGS OF AFRICAN AMERICAN RHETORIC

Edited and with an introduction by Michelle Bachelor Robinson

———— ⊰≈⊱ ————

"The Blackest Hours" is a unit comprising rhetoric that gets at the very core of African American culture and heritage. Given the circumstances under which Africans' American trajectory began, the rhetorical engagement of this unit is a natural beginning for a text historically and thematically organized. The thematic sections here center around initial issues in which African Americans began to publicly and privately engage, make argument, and make meaning of their circumstances and their lives. The Orature section marks the ways in which narrative, our narratives, began to define our culture and heritage in this strange and foreign land. The Spirituality, Education, and Politics sections account for the areas and issues of concern when African Americans began engagement in public discourse. All of the sections in this unit begin with excerpts, either whole or in part, from rhetoric asserted before or during chattel slavery in America and move into the twentieth and twenty-first centuries.

In order to thoroughly understand the nature of our original and historical rhetoric, it is necessary to provide context by giving careful consideration to the psychological, sociological, and cultural circumstances under which Africans' American experiences began. In her book *Post Traumatic Slave Syndrome: America's Legacy of Enduring Injury and Healing*, Dr. Joy DeGruy offers a compelling look into the cultural aftermath of slavery and the generational impact the institution has had on our people. DeGruy tells a story in a recorded talk that she delivered at the Building Bridges Conference at Gustavus Adolphus College in St. Peter, Minnesota. I share a summary of this narrative here but offer the caveat that DeGruy's oral delivery (in its best griot tradition) is far more compelling and convincing, and I encourage readers to watch, in its entirety, the talk listed in the works cited below.

In this story DeGruy describes a scenario of two moms having a chat at a school function—one Black, one White—their sons are best friends. In this conversation, the Black mom congratulates and compliments the White mom on her son's recent accomplishments. The White mom responds by expressing her pride with her son. The Black mom agrees and cosigns on the young man's recent success. The White mom then shifts the conversation, as is the polite thing to do, and begins to compliment the Black mom on her son's recent success and accomplishments as well, which are equally, if not more, compelling than his White counterpart and best friend. The Black mom responds by saying, "Girl, yeah, you think so, but ooh Lawd that boy works my nerves." And so goes the narrative.

DeGruy offers an analysis of this scenario. She explains that the White mom's visceral reaction to this scenario is to think that Black people are so negative, but DeGruy argues that we as Black people know that this Black mother is equally as proud of her son as the White mom. DeGruy describes the Black mom's response as learned, post-slavery behavior. Though she acknowledges that the Black mom's behavior is "not healthy," she offers a context by asking the audience to move the narrative back three hundred years. A White slaveholder walks up to an enslaved mom and says, "That boy of yours is sho' comin' along." The enslaved mom responds, "No, no suh. He's stupid and lazy." She does not want to highlight her son's best features, which would make him stand out as exceptional, because she does not want her boy to be sold away for his attributes. DeGruy offers an analysis of this episode of denigration as a mechanism for protection. And I offer DeGruy's description of post-traumatic slave disorder as a context for understanding the origins of the rhetoric that this unit will explore through the oral, spiritual, educational, and political situatedness of American chattel slavery, Jim Crow, and other forms of systematic oppression, and ultimately through messages and movements that affect change and forward mobility.

In the first section of this unit, Kermit Campbell engages the scholarly conversation of naming and classifying African American oral culture. After offering a context for oral traditions and the African traditions from which they evolve, Campbell settles on using the term "orature," borrowed from Pio Zirimu and employed as a way of understanding the connections between African and African American oral traditions (see Campbell's introduction). It seems appropriate to begin this unit with a section on orature since Campbell's first excerpt is taken from the epic tale of Sundiata, set in the motherland, and predates American chattel slavery. Immediately following, Elizabeth West and Kameelah Martin begin their section titled "Religion and Spirituality/Transportations and Transformations," with excerpts from Olaudah Equiano, David Walker, and Omar Said. Their section ends with the words of Minister Louis Farrakhan and includes all manner of spirituality that exist in between. West and Martin argue that despite the "denigrating rhetoric of Black spirituality, Blacks in the new world would articulate a spiritual cosmology born out of their own cultural carryovers and those they adopted and transformed." Their section explores Black rhetoric that engages the multiple religious traditions of the enslaved, and later free, Africans in America and African Americans.

Paired hand in hand with religious rhetoric is the rhetoric of education. Blacks have historically viewed literacy learning as a vehicle for upward sociopolitical mobility. In "Language, Literacy, and Education," Valerie Kinloch and Donja Thomas offer Black rhetorical excerpts that engage issues of education and language and thus begin with excerpts from Frederick Douglass, offer Booker T. Washington, W.E.B. Du Bois, and Carter G. Woodson, and ultimately end with Keith Gilyard. Many of these texts are theoretical edicts on the role education plays in the lives of Black folks, and others are personal narratives about one's educational experiences. In all texts offered here, it is clear that the message of the educational narrative has been an intrinsic part of the African American rhetorical tradition from the onset.

In the final section in this unit, "Black Presence," Robinson, Nunley, and Echols offer excerpts from texts categorized as political discourse. These texts were selected and have been included because their purpose is to affect political change. This section spans the range of human rights issues. Because many of these texts draw upon movements of the current age, this section boasts a robust media section with both audio and video recordings. Giving voice to and witnessing the delivery of these texts allow readers to connect the rhetorical prowess back to African American orature, as well as other sections in this book.

The African American rhetorical experience evolves under a unique set of historical circumstances, one of threat, vulnerability, danger, and oppression, and yet we survive, even thrive. These circumstances and unusual trajectory require consideration as readers explore texts in these thematic sections, and thus, the Origins and Histories unit offers a lens for understanding how griots, moms, dads, ministers, teachers, politicians, and a host of other activists use rhetoric to protect, instruct, prepare, train, guide, uplift, and advocate for their people.

Works Cited

DeGruy, Joy. Building Bridges Conference at Gustavus Adolphus College. Online video clip. YouTube. 11 Feb. 2012. Web. Retrieved 15 Jul. 2015. www.youtube.com/watch?v=MH7tpAK8APY

———. *Post Traumatic Slave Syndrome: America's Legacy of Enduring Injury and Healing*. Portland: Uptone Press, 2005.

2

NOBODY KNOWS OUR NAME: AFRICAN ORATURE IN THE AMERICAN DIASPORA

Edited and with an introduction by Kermit E. Campbell

Negroes in the North are right when they refer to the South as the Old Country. A Negro born in the North who finds himself in the South is in a position similar to that of the son of the Italian emigrant who finds himself in Italy, near the village where his father first saw the light of day. Both are in countries they have never seen, but which they cannot fail to recognize. The landscape has always been familiar; the speech is archaic, but it rings a bell; and so do the ways of the people, though their ways are not his ways. Everywhere he turns, the revenant finds himself reflected. He sees himself as he was before he was born, perhaps; or as the man he would have become, had he actually been born in this place. He sees the world, from an angle odd indeed, in which his fathers awaited his arrival, perhaps in the very house in which he narrowly avoided being born. He sees, in effect, his ancestors, who, in everything they do and are, proclaim his inescapable identity.

—James Baldwin, *Nobody Knows My Name*

Trying to settle on a name for what people of African descent do so well verbally is a bit like trying to identify African peoples themselves. We are all African or descended from that grand signifier Africa, yes, but that truth or purported truth hardly settles the matter, for across the continent and throughout the diaspora the marker of our African-ness, beyond mere physicality, is not always clear or universally accepted. Some have, in fact, vigorously rejected the rather commonsensical notion that the languages and discursive practices of people of the African diaspora derive in large part from Africa. The British (see John McWhorter) or Southern Rednecks (descendants of the less cultured Brits of the slave era, like the Scottish, Welsh, and Irish immigrants, according to Thomas Sowell) are responsible, they say, for the cultures of the African diaspora (particularly, in their case, African American vernacular language and culture).

Of course, no one can deny the influence of Europe on Africans in the American diaspora; the English language (not to mention the French and Spanish languages in certain parts of the United States) alone bears witness to that influence. But to deny any influence whatsoever from Africa, or rather from African oral traditions, seems patently absurd. The ancestral links Henry Louis Gates Jr. draws between African and African diaspora trickster figures (see the second selection ahead) are reason enough to trust that there is, say, an African American vernacular tradition rooted in an earlier African (or at least West African) oral tradition, however impure, however fragmented that tradition may be. And yet, what do we call this tradition that, at least in part, defines us? Anthropologists tend to call it *folklore*, and, alternatively with reference to folklore's broader history, *oral tradition*. Literary scholars, not surprisingly, opt for a corollary

41

to literature, and so *oral* literature tends to be their preferred term, which, in the case of Ruth Finnegan's *Oral Literature in Africa*, would likely include many of the pieces in this section of the present book. Africans themselves, not all but a highly select group of them, have opted for the term "orature," which has gradually gained currency since coined by Ugandan linguist Pio Zirimu in the 1960s. Zirimu defined the term simply as "the use of an utterance as an aesthetic means of expression" (quoted in Ngugi Wa Thiong'o's *Penpoints, Gunpoints, and Dreams*, p. 111). Thiong'o explains that Zirimu used the term "to connote a system of aesthetics, an oral narrative system, for instance, which could be differentiated from the system of visual narratives" (p. 111). For his own part, Kenyan novelist and literary critic Ngugi Wa Thiong'o sees orature as "all those works of imagination produced through word of mouth" (p. 105). The closest Thiong'o comes to detailing what those works of imagination could be is when he states that "[p]erformance was what made the oral imaginative product so very powerful, be it a riddle, a proverb, a story, a poem, myth, or legend" (p. 109). While it is tempting to take this list of verbal expressive products as definitive of orature, Thiong'o appears to be far more interested in abiding principles like performance. As he puts it plainly, "[t]he audience-performer relationship is one of the most important elements of orature" (p. 121).

The audience-performer relationship is also quite important for African American orature, for African American rhetoric, but rhetoric or the rhetorical is missing from Thiong'o's conception of the term. Hence, we have to turn elsewhere for a conception of orature that takes into account verbal expressions that bear on rhetoric. The scholar who has perhaps written the most on the subject is Temple University professor of African American studies Molefi Kete Asante (formerly Arthur Smith). While a comprehensive treatment of Asante's conception of the term orature is beyond the scope of this introduction, a look at portions of one of his major works, *The Afrocentric Idea*, will provide, I think, a critical frame for reading and interpreting the various selections included here.

It is unclear when precisely Asante began using the term orature and synthesizing it with his ideas about rhetoric and afrocentricity. Twice in *The Afrocentric Idea* he mentions Thiong'o, but not with regard to his use of the term orature. In the course of discussing African public discourse, he simply states that "I use the term orature to refer to this phenomenon [an expressive sense manifested by African Americans] as the sum total of oral tradition, which includes vocality, drumming, storytelling, praise singing, and naming" (p. 72). Elsewhere Asante links the word orature to oratory. He claims that "[o]rature is the comprehensive body of oral discourse on every subject and in every genre of expression produced by a people. It includes sermons, lectures, raps, the dozen, poetry, and humor" (p. 96). He then goes on to define oratory, saying, "[o]ratory refers to the practice of eloquent public speaking" (p. 96). Presumably, the two terms are linked by virtue of the fact that the one (oratory) is subsumed by the other (orature). Orature is quite broad here, encompassing perhaps all of the selections presented in this section, from griot speech to the singing of Moms Mabley and Ray Charles, but whether it is an equivalent term to *rhetoric* or a subgenre of rhetoric is unclear. Asante follows the definitions of orature and oratory with this rather sweeping statement:

> The study of black speeches, then, emphatically imposes itself upon any true investigation into our history and orature. Since the Africans brought to America a fertile oral tradition augmented by the pervasiveness of *nommo*, the generating and sustaining powers of the spoken word, orature permeated every department of African American life.
>
> (p. 96)

Admittedly, this statement does not clear up much of the confusion. However, it does represent the complexity of the subject and explains why orature is an apt signifier for the great variety of excerpts presented here. The examples of music and song (e.g., the soulful singing of Aretha

Franklin and the rather whimsical songs of Shirley Ellis), classic sermons, signifying (signifying from supposedly happy-go-lucky slaves and a mischievous monkey), badman toasts, rapping deejays, mother wit from mamas and sisters, and griots traditional (as in the *Sundiata* epic of Mali) and modern (spoken word artists like the Last Poets and Gil Scot-Heron) are but a sampling of the African orature that, as Asante says, "permeate[s] every department of African American life" (p. 96). And with that, I suppose, some folks will know our name.

D. T. Niane

One major strand of African orature is the epic poetry of civilizations as old as the Kingdom of Ghana or Wagadu to epic poems of kingdoms, villages, or a people as modern as the Fulbe or Macina. Much like epics in the Western world, these narrative poems recount the mythic tale of a heroic figure who is instrumental in the founding or restoration of a nation to a condition of great prominence. West Africa has several of these historic narratives, one of the more popular being the thirteenth-century epic *Sundiata*. The transmission of these epics orally from generation to generation is a feat of rhetorical artistry and performance in and of itself. However, certain forms of rhetoric or discourse are on display in the context of narrative. Two of these forms appear in the portion of the text excerpted here. The first is an example of the ritual of verbal insults and boasting before commencing battle. The second is the griot's or bard's exhortation to the epic's hero Sundiata to be "a man of action" (p. 63), which exhortation is, according to Medieval Arab observer Ibn Battuta, a kind of preaching.

The Epic of Old Mali

D. T. Niane[1]

Sundiata went and pitched camp at Dayala in the valley of the Niger. Now it was he who was blocking Soumaoro's road to the south. Up till that time, Sundiata and Soumaoro had fought each other without a declaration of war. One does not wage war without saying why it is being waged. Those fighting should make a declaration of their grievances to begin with. Just as a sorcerer ought not to attack someone without taking him to task for some evil deed, so a king should not wage war without saying why he is taking up arms.

Soumaoro advanced as far as Krina, near the village of Dayala on the Niger and decided to assert his rights before joining battle. Soumaoro knew that Sundiata also was a sorcerer, so, instead of sending an embassy, he committed his words to one of his owls. The night bird came and perched on the roof of Djata's tent and spoke. The son of Sogolon in his turn sent his owl to Soumaoro. Here is the dialogue of the sorcerer kings:

'Stop, young man. Henceforth I am the king of Mali. If you want peace, return to where you came from,' said Soumaoro.

'I am coming back, Soumaoro, to recapture my kingdom. If you want peace you will make amends to my allies and return to Sosso where you are the king.'

'I am king of Mali by force of arms. My rights have been established by conquest.'

'Then I will take Mali from you by force of arms and chase you from my kingdom.'

'Know, then, that I am the wild yam of the rocks; nothing will make me leave Mali.'

'Know, also that I have in my camp seven master smiths who will shatter the rocks. Then, yam, I will eat you.'

'I am the poisonous mushroom that makes the fearless vomit.'

'As for me, I am the ravenous cock, the poison does not matter to me.'

'Behave yourself, little boy, or you will burn your foot, for I am the red-hot cinder.'

'But me, I am the rain that extinguishes the cinder; I am the boisterous torrent that will carry you off.'

'I am the mighty silk-cotton tree that looks from on high on the tops of other trees.'

'And I, I am the strangling creeper that climbs to the top of the forest giant.'

'Enough of this argument. You shall not have Mali.'

'Know that there is not room for two kings on the same skin, Soumaoro; you will let me have your place.'

'Very well, since you want war I will wage war against you, but I would have you know that I have killed nine kings whose heads adorn my room. What a pity, indeed, that your head should take its place beside those of your fellow madcaps.'

'Prepare yourself, Soumaoro, for it will be long before the calamity that is going to crash down upon you and yours comes to an end.'

Thus Sundiata and Soumaoro spoke together. After the war of mouths, swords had to decide the issue. Sogolon's son was in his tent when someone came to announce to him the arrival of Fakoli, Soumaoro's insurgent nephew. All the men stood to arms and the war chiefs drew up their men. When everything was in order in the camp, Djata and the Mandingo leaders received Fakoli followed by his warriors. Fakoli halted before Sundiata and spoke thus:

'I salute you, Sundiata. I am Fakoli Koroma, king of the tribe of Koroma smiths. Soumaoro is the brother of my mother Kassia. I have taken up arms against my uncle because he has outraged me. Without fearing incest he has pushed his effrontery to the lengths of robbing me of my wife Keleya. As for you, you are coming to reconquer the kingdom of your fathers, you are fighting Soumaoro. We have the same goal and therefore I come to place myself under your orders. I bring you my strong-armed smiths, I bring you sofas who do not know what fear is. Sundiata, I and my men are yours.'

Balla, Sundiata's griot, said, 'Fakoli, come and sit among your brothers whom Soumaoro's injustice has smitten, the judge folds you to his bosom. You could not do better than entrust your cause to the son of Sogolon.'

Sundiata made a sign indicating that the griot had spoken well, but he added, 'I defend the weak, I defend the innocent, Fakoli. You have suffered an injustice so I will render you justice, but I have my lieutenants about me and I would like to know their opinions.'

All the war chiefs agreed. Fakoli's cause became Sundiata's cause. Justice had to be granted to the man who came to implore justice. Thus Sundiata accepted Fakoli Da-Ba, Large-Mouthed Fakoli, among his war chiefs.

Sundiata wanted to have done with Soumaoro before the rainy season, so he struck camp and marched on Krina where Soumaoro was encamped. The latter realized that the decisive battle had come. Sundiata deployed his men on the little hill that dominates the plain. The great battle was for the next day.

In the evening, to raise the men's spirits, Djata gave a great feast, for he was anxious that his men should wake up happy in the morning. Several oxen were slaughtered and that evening Balla Fasséké, in front of the whole army, called to mind the history of old Mali. He praised Sundiata, seated amidst his lieutenants, in this manner:

'Now I address myself to you, Maghan Sundiata, I speak to you king of Mali, to whom dethroned monarchs flock. The time foretold to you by the jinn is now coming. Sundiata, kingdoms and empires are in the likeness of man; like him they are born, they grow and disappear. Each sovereign embodies one moment of that life. Formerly, the kings of Ghana extended their kingdom over all the lands inhabited by the black man, but the circle has closed and the Cissés of Wagadou are nothing more than petty princes in a desolate land. Today, another kingdom looms up, powerful, the kingdom of Sosso. Humbled kings have borne their tribute to Sosso, Soumaoro's arrogance knows no more bounds and his cruelty is equal to his ambition. But will Soumaoro dominate the world? Are we, the griots of Mali, condemned to pass on to future generations the humiliations which the king of Sosso cares to inflict on our country? No, you may be glad, children of the "Bright Country", for the kingship of Sosso is but the growth of yesterday, whereas that of Mali dates from the time of Bilali. Each kingdom has its childhood, but Soumaoro wants to force the pace, and so Sosso will collapse under him like a horse worn out beneath its rider.

'You, Maghan, you are Mali. It has had a long and difficult childhood like you. Sixteen kings have preceded you on the throne of Niani, sixteen kings have reigned with varying fortunes, but from being village chiefs the Keitas have become tribal chiefs and then kings. Sixteen generations have consolidated their power. You are the outgrowth of Mali just as the silk-cotton tree is the growth of the earth, born of deep and mighty roots. To face the tempest the tree must have long roots and gnarled branches. Maghan Sundiata, has not the tree grown?

'I would have you know, son of Sogolon, that there is not room for two kings around the same calabash of rice. When a new cock comes to the poultry run the old cock picks a quarrel with him and the docile hens wait to see if the new arrival asserts himself or yields. You have come to Mali. Very well, then, assert yourself. Strength makes a law of its own self and power allows no division.

'But listen to what your ancestors did, so that you will know what you have to do.

'Bilali, the second of the name, conquered old Mali. Latal Kalabi conquered the country between the Niger and the Sankarani. By going to Mecca, Lahibatoul Kalabi, of illustrious memory, brought divine blessing upon Mali. Mamadi Kani made warriors out of hunters and bestowed armed strength upon Mali. His son Bamari Tagnokelin, the vindictive king, terrorized Mali with this army, but Maghan Kon Fatta, also called Naré Maghan, to whom you owe your being, made peace prevail and happy mothers yielded Mali a populous youth.

'You are the son of Naré Maghan, but you are also the son of your mother Sogolon, the buffalo-woman, before whom powerless sorcerers shrank in fear. You have the strength and majesty of the lion, you have the might of the buffalo.

'I have told you what future generations will learn about your ancestors, but what will we be able to relate to our sons so that your memory will stay alive, what will we have to teach our sons about you? What unprecedented exploits, what unheard-of feats? By what distinguished actions will our sons be brought to regret not having lived in the time of Sundiata?

'Griots are men of the spoken word, and by the spoken word we give life to the gestures of kings. But words are nothing but words; power lies in deeds. Be a man of action; do not answer me any more with your mouth, but tomorrow, on the plain of Krina, show me what you would have me recount to coming generations. Tomorrow allow me to sing the "Song of the Vultures" over the bodies of the thousands of Sossos whom your sword will have laid low before evening.'

It was on the eve of Krina. In this way Balla Fasséké reminded Sundiata of the history of Mali so that, in the morning, he would show himself worthy of his ancestors.

Note

1. D. T. Niane, *Sundiata: An Epic of Old Mali*, trans. G. D. Pickett, revised edition (Essex, England: Pearson Education, 2006), pp. 59–63.

S. Belcher

Another major strand of African orature that arguably also survived the middle passage and proved quite suited to the condition of slavery throughout the African diaspora (i.e., the Caribbean, South America, and the American South) is the tale of the trickster. Ananse of the Ashanti, Eshu of the Yoruba, and Legba of the Fon are a few of the more internationally recognized trickster figures in Africa, particularly West Africa. While Eshu and Legba have direct descendants (albeit variants) in places such as Cuba and Haiti, according to Henry Louis Gates Jr. in his seminal work *The Signifying Monkey: A Theory of African American Literary Criticism*, the premiere trickster in Black America is the Signifying Monkey. The Signifying Monkey is the subject of traditional African American folklore as well as the quintessential American music forms of jazz and blues. Most often the Signifying Monkey appears in a narrative poem that is referred to in African American culture as a toast. Unlike other toasts (e.g., Shine and Stag-O-Lee), however, the Signifying Monkey not only represents the rhetorical artistry of the toast teller (e.g., Rudy Ray Moore or any number of young African American men who would perform toasts publicly) but also puts on display the verbal prowess of the Monkey—that is, his uncanny ability to signify. The Monkey's ability to use language to insult and deceive his brawnier adversary, the Lion, is symbolic of the power of rhetoric to resist dominant forces and overcome disadvantages.

Eshu of the Yoruba

S. Belcher[1]

Eshu is only one of the Yoruba tricksters; there is also the tortoise Ajapa. But Eshu, or Eshu-Elegbara, as his fuller name goes, occupies a special place because of his association with Orunmila, the god or orisha *of Ifa divination (see also Chapter 49). Eshu himself is also an* orisha. *Like the Fon Legba (see Chapters 18 and 51), to whom he is closely related, Eshu works to introduce the unpredictable into an orderly system; this can cause trouble at times, but it also can help (as in the second story below, when Eshu helps Orunmila escape a destined death). The following stories were all recorded around 1960.*

Eshu's Knowledge

At the time of creation, the various *orisha* went to their Father's house to receive their powers. At that time, Eshu had no possessions or farm to delay him, and so he arrived first. He stayed and helped the Father as he carved the various beings that would fill the world; he did not get impatient, but he stayed and stayed for sixteen years, helping the Father. Other *orisha* would come and stay for four or eight days, waiting until the Father assigned them a post and duties, then they left and returned to their homes or farms. Eshu did not leave. He learned how the Father shaped humans: how he made hands and feet and eyes. Eshu learned everything. So finally the Father told him to go and take his place at the crossroads. He said that everyone coming to see him should give Eshu a gift, and everyone leaving should give him a gift. So Eshu became wealthy, and he said, 'Lazy men live by their wisdom; only fools do not know how to manage their affairs.'

Eshu, Orunmila and the Servant of Death

Agbigbo became a servant of Death; his task was to carry the coffins in which Death placed those he had killed to their houses. One night, Orunmila, the *orisha* of Ifa divination, dreamed of death. The next day, he consulted the Ifa oracle and was told what offerings to prepare. He collected the materials for the sacrifice and carried them to the shrine of Eshu.

Agbigbo was sent with a coffin to the home of Orunmila. Along the way, he met Eshu sitting outside his shrine. Eshu asked him what he was doing with the coffin and Agbigbo told him it was intended for Orunmila. Eshu asked him what he would take to leave Orunmila alone, and Agbigbo said that he could be persuaded by the gift of a rat, a bird and some other bush-meat. Eshu said that he had all these things, for they had been included in the sacrifice Orunmila had left with him. He gave them to Agbigbo, who put the coffin on his head and went his way. As he left, Eshu commanded that he should never be able to put the coffin down. And this is the mark of Agbigbo to this day: he is a bird with a large tuft of feathers on his head, indicating the coffin he carries.

Eshu Parts Two Friends

Two men were very close friends and had sworn that nothing would part them. Their compounds were next to each other, their fields lay on opposite sides of the road out of the village; they were always together. At one time, they consulted the Ifa oracle, and were told to make a sacrifice to Eshu, but they did not. And so Eshu punished them.

One day, he came walking down the road between their fields. His hat was red on one side, white on the other. After he had gone, one friend spoke to the other and mentioned the white hat. The other corrected him: the hat had been red. The first was sure the hat was white. The second knew it was red. They argued about it and finally began to fight. When they stopped, they went back to work in the fields.

Eshu came walking back in the other direction. This time, the man who had seen the white side saw the red and the man who had seen the red saw the white. Each went to apologize to the other. But when the first said the hat had been red, the second thought he was mocking him. Again, the discussion led to blows, and their families had to come and help them back to their compounds.

The families spoke to the men, and reminded them how close they had been, and asked why they had come to fight in this way. They said there must be an underlying cause, and so the two friends consulted Ifa again. They learned how Eshu had set them against each other, and so this time they made the prescribed sacrifice to Eshu and appeased him. They remained friends after that.

Legba of the Fon

The Fon of Benin (formerly Dahomey) established the kingdom of Abomey in the seventeenth century (see Chapter 51); they later came under the domination of the Yoruba state of Oyo at the end of the eighteenth century, and from them they took a number of ritual elements, and particularly the practice of Ifa (Fa) divination. Legba, the trickster figure, is similar to the Yoruba Eshu; he has also become important in the Caribbean practice of vodun, *because, as the intermediary of humans and gods, it is he who enables believers to be possessed by their divinities. This story is retold from a version collected in the 1930s.*

Many stories are told of Legba, and he serves many purposes in the complex Fon pantheon. It is said that he was the youngest born of Mawu, goddess of the sun, and so she favoured him and gave him the gift of all languages, so that he serves as the linguist or spokesman for the gods; all who would approach a god must do so through Legba. Another story says that he was given this post because he, alone of the gods, was able to play a gong, a bell, a drum and a flute, all at the same time and while dancing. Legba is also the servant of Fa, the deity of divination, although the representations of this situation vary. One story says that Fa is personified by the female

Gbadu, who has sixteen eyes around her head and sits atop a palm tree looking out over the world; each morning, Legba climbs the tree and opens her eyes according to her instructions. Children of Gbadu were the first Fa diviners in the world, by a dispensation of Mawu. Legba is also said to have caused the war between the sky and the earth at the beginning of time, and then to have effected the settlement by which the people on earth may request rainfall from the sky.

One complex story illustrates Legba's qualities. At one time, he and his siblings Minona, a female deity who protects women, and Aovi, a god who punishes those humans who disrespect the gods, formed a funeral band and went about the country playing music for funerals. They heard of a funeral for a great man, and so they went there to perform. At the funeral they encountered several other persons. King Metonofi (it is said he ruled the land of the dead) was there, displeased because he had married his daughter to the king of Adja and he had proved impotent with her. The king of Adja's son was there, because he had come to consult Fa, the spirit of divination who was also Legba's master. And Fa himself was there, because he was needed. Fa could not speak by himself; he required Legba's assistance to express himself.

The king of Adja's son came and told Fa about his father's troubles with Metonofi's daughter, and Fa told him he could supply a powder that would enable his father to consummate his marriage. He then told Legba to give the prince some of the white powder which he kept in his sack. But Legba gave the prince a red powder instead, that removed potency, rather than the white one which restored it. Then the funeral went on, and Legba's band played its music so that the mourners could dance.

The three siblings were paid in cowrie-shells, the currency of the time, and they left the town and stopped at a crossroads to divide the shells. But the shells would not divide evenly: there was always one left over, and the three could not decide what to do with the remaining shell, or who should get it. Finally, a woman came by and they asked her what to do. The woman answered that she thought the eldest child should receive the last cowrie, and so Minona should have it. But Legba and Aovi were furious at this answer, and so they killed the woman and threw her body in the bush. Legba, always lecherous, then slipped off and lay with the corpse.

Another woman came by, and she said that the middle child should receive the extra cowrie. She was killed by Minona and Legba, and again Legba lay with the corpse. A third woman came by, and she was killed when she said the cowrie should go to the youngest. Legba lay with her body too.

Then Legba created the figure of a dog, and made it move and speak, and sent it to the three siblings. They asked it what to do with the cowrie, and the dog answered that they should give it to the ancestors. The dog dug a hole and buried the cowrie, and the three siblings were satisfied. They went home. Since that time, the dog is respected among humans.

Meanwhile, people began to complain to King Metonofi and to Fa: women had been killed, and the powder Legba had given the prince, which was supposed to restore potency, had instead made men impotent. The king sent for Legba, and he ran away to the home of his in-laws. As it happened, his father-in-law was away at the time, and so Legba slept next to his mother-in-law and in the middle of the night they lay together.

The next morning, the king's men caught him and brought him to face his accusers and their charges, among whom he could now also count his father-in-law who accused him of adultery. First they asked about the three women who had been killed, and Legba explained that it was always a pair of siblings who killed them, not he. He also explained how he had solved the problem by creating the dog, and he produced the figure of the dog.

King Metonofi was very impressed by Legba's ingenuity, and so he declared that Legba would be given a special responsibility to watch over people. Minona he ordered to go become a guardian of women, and because Aovi was so violent, Metonofi charged him with enforcing respect for the gods.

Then Legba's father-in-law spoke his complaint, and Legba had to admit that he had slept with the woman, but explained that it was a mistake because she had been lying where his wife normally lay. But Metonofi and the other people were not satisfied with this explanation, and so they ordered that Legba was not to live in houses with people, but must always be found in the open spaces such as crossroads, and this is why shrines to Legba are generally placed at crossroads.

Finally, they heard the case of the king of Adja and the complaint that Legba had given men the red powder instead of the white. Legba simply denied this. He said the red powder was perfectly good. But he had changed the colours of the powders: he mixed the white powder with blood, so that it became red, and he mixed the red powder with white clay, so that it became white. When the people said Legba had given them the red powder, Metonofi ordered Legba to take some of it himself.

Then came the question of the marriage of Metonofi's daughter. Metonofi built a hut and placed his daughter inside it, and then said the men of Adja should attempt intercourse with her. One by one they tried, but none succeeded. Then Legba said that he would accomplish this task. He asked for drums to play when he entered the hut, and then he danced in and lay with the daughter, who was a virgin. Then, still erect and with blood on his penis, he danced out of the hut and showed everyone what he had accomplished.

Metonofi then said that Legba should marry his daughter, but Legba said that instead she should marry his master, Fa, and he gave her the name Adje, which means cowries. At the wedding, Legba mixed the good powder in with the palm wine which was served to all the guests, and so the men of the country recovered their potency.

Note

1. S. Belcher, "Eshu of the Yoruba & Legba of the Fon," in *African Myths of Origin* (New York, NY: Penguin Books, 2005), pp. 97–103.

Alex Haley

Since author Alex Haley draws quite extensively on the griot tradition to corroborate what he was told about his ancestry during his childhood, it seems to me appropriate to include excerpts about the griot from Haley's epic novel. The first of these excerpts illustrates the role of the griot in Gambian society. It is through the griot that young boys, including Haley's ancestor, could know about the great deeds of ancient kings and warriors. The second excerpt from *Roots* shows how the griot, one Kebba Kanji Fofana, related to Haley the history of the Kinte clan and by doing so then demonstrated his style of oratory, as D. T. Niane calls it in the introduction to *Sundiata*. Although it is not the kind of preaching or exhortation style we see in the selection from *Sundiata*, it is another example of the griot's repertoire.

Roots

Alex Haley[1]

"You are ceasing to be children. You are experiencing rebirth as men," the kintango said one morning to the assembled kafo. This was the first time the kintango had used the word "men" except to tell them what they weren't. After moons of learning together, working together, being beaten together, he told them, each of them was finally beginning to discover that he had two selves—one within him, and the other, larger self in all those whose blood and lives he shared. Not until they learned that lesson could they undertake the next phase of manhood training: how to be warriors. "You know already that Mandinkas fight only if others are warlike," said the kintango. "But we are the finest warriors if driven to fight."

For the next half moon, Kunta and his mates learned how to make war. Famous Mandinka battle strategies were drawn in the dust by the kintango or his assistants, and then the boys were told to re-enact the strategies in mock battles. "Never completely encircle your enemy," counseled the kintango. "Leave him some escape, for he will fight even more desperately if trapped." The boys learned also that battles should start in late afternoon, so that any enemy, seeing defeat, could save face by retreating in the darkness. And they were taught that during any wars, neither enemy should never do harm to any traveling marabouts, griots, or blacksmiths, for an angered marabout could bring down the displeasure of Allah; an angered griot could use his eloquent tongue to stir the enemy army to greater savagery; and an angered blacksmith could make or repair weapons for the enemy.

Under the direction of the kintango's assistants, Kunta and the others carved out barbed spears and made barbed arrows of the kind used only in battle, and practiced with them on smaller and smaller targets. When a boy could hit a bamboo cane twenty-five steps away, he was cheered and praised. Tramping into the woods, the boys found some koona shrub, whose leaves they picked to be boiled back at the jujuo. Into the resulting thick, black juice they would dip a cotton thread, and they were shown how that thread, wound around an arrow's barbs, would seep a deadly poison into whatever wound the arrow made.

At the end of the war-training period, the kintango told them more than they had ever known before—and told them more excitingly than they had ever heard it—about that greatest of all Mandinka wars and warriors—the time when the army of the fabled ex-slave general Sundiata, son of Sogolon, the Buffalo Woman, conquered the forces of the Boure country's King Soumaoro, a king so cruel that he wore human-skin robes and adorned his palace walls with enemy's bleached skulls.

Kunta and his mates held their breaths, hearing how both armies suffered thousands of wounded or dead. But the archers of the Mandinkas closed in on Soumaoro's forces like a giant trap, raining down arrows from both sides and moving in steadily until Soumaoro's terrified army finally fled in rout. For days and nights, said the kintango—and it was the first time the boys ever had seen him smile—the talking drums of every village followed the marching progress of the victorious Mandinka forces, laden with enemy booty and driving thousands of captives before them. In every village, happy crowds jeered and kicked the prisoners, whose shaved heads were bowed and whose hands were tied behind their backs. Finally General Sundiata called a huge meeting of the people, and he brought before them the chiefs of all the villages he had defeated and gave them back their spears of chiefhood's rank, and then he established among those chiefs the bonds of peace, which would last among them for the next one hundred rains. Kunta and his mates went dreamily to their beds, never prouder to be Mandinkas.

As the next moon of training began, drumtalk reached the jujuo telling of new visitors to be expected within the next two days. The excitement with which the news of *any* visitors would have been received, after so long since the fathers and brothers had come to see them, was doubled when the boys learned that the sender of the message was the drummer of Juffure's champion wrestling team, which was coming to conduct special lessons for the trainees.

Late in the afternoon of the next day, the drums announced their arrival even earlier than expected. But the boys' pleasure at seeing all the familiar faces again was forgotten when, without a word, the wrestlers grabbed them and began to flip them onto the ground harder than they had ever been thrown in their lives. And every boy was bruised and hurting when the wrestlers divided them into smaller groups to grapple one another, as the champions supervised. Kunta had never imagined there were so many wrestling holds, nor how effectively they could work if used correctly. And the champions kept drumming into the boys' ears that it was knowledge and expertness and not strength that made the difference between being an ordinary wrestler and a champion. Still, as they demonstrated the holds for their pupils, the boys couldn't help admiring their bulging muscles as much as their skill in using them. Around the fire that night, the drummer from Juffure chanted the names and the feats of great Mandinka wrestling champions of even a hundred rains in the past, and when it was the boys' time for bed, the wrestlers left the jujuo to return to Juffure.

Two days later came news of another visitor. This time the message was brought by a runner from Juffure—a young man of the fourth kafo whom Kunta and his mates knew well, though in his own new manhood, he acted as if he never had seen these third-kafo children. Without so much as a glance at them, he ran up to the kintango and announced, between deep breaths, that Kujali N'jai, a griot well known throughout The Gambia, would soon spend one full day at the jujuo.

In three days he arrived, accompanied by several young men of his family. He was much older than any of the griots Kunta had seen before—so old, in fact, that he made the kintango seem young. After gesturing for the boys to squat in a semicircle about him, the old man began to talk of how he became what he was. He told them how, over years of study from young manhood, every griot had buried deep in his mind the records of the ancestors. "How else could you know of the great deeds of the ancient kings, holy men, hunters, and warriors who came hundreds of rains before us? Have you met them?" asked the old man. "No! The history of our people is carried to the future in here." And he tapped his gray head.

The question in the mind of every boy was answered by the old griot: Only the sons of griots could become griots. Indeed, it was their solemn *duty* to become griots. Upon finishing their manhood training, these boys—like those grandsons of his own who sat beside him here today—would begin studying and traveling with selected elders, hearing over and over again the historical names and stories as they had been passed down. And in due time, each young man would know that special part of the forefathers' history in the finest and fullest detail, just as it had been told to his father and his father's father. And the day would come when that boy would become a man and have sons to whom *he* would tell those stories, so that the events of the distant past would forever live.

When the awed boys had wolfed down their evening meal and rushed back to gather again around the old griot, he thrilled them until late into the night with stories his own father had passed down to him—about the great black empires that had ruled Africa hundreds of rains before.

"Long before toubob ever put his foot in Africa," the old griot said, there was the Empire of Benin, ruled by an all-powerful King called the Oba, whose every wish was obeyed instantly. But the actual governing of Benin was done by trusted counselors of the Oba, whose full time was needed just for making the necessary sacrifices to appease the forces of evil and for his proper attentions to a harem of more than a hundred wives. But even before Benin was a yet richer kingdom called Songhai, said the griot. Songhai's capital city was Gao, filled with fine houses for black princes and rich merchants who lavishly entertained traveling tradesmen who brought much gold to buy goods.

"Nor was that the richest kingdom," said the old man. And he told the boys of ancestral Ghana, in which an entire town was populated with only the King's court. And King Kanissaai had a thousand horses, each of which had three servants and its own urinal made of copper. Kunta could hardly believe his ears. "And each evening," said the griot, "When King Kanissaai would emerge from his palace, a thousand fires would be lit, lighting up all between the heavens and the earth. And the servants of the great King would bring forth food enough to serve the ten thousand people who gathered there each evening."

Here he paused, and exclamations of wonder could not be restrained by the boys, who knew well that no sound should be made as a griot talked, but neither he nor even the kintango himself seemed to notice their rudeness. Putting into his mouth half of a kola nut and offering the other half to the kintango, who accepted it with pleasure, the griot drew the skirt of his robe closer about his legs against the chill of the early night and resumed his stories.

"But even Ghana was not the richest black kingdom!" he exclaimed. "The very richest, the very oldest of them all was the kingdom of ancient Mali!" Like the other empires, Mali had its cities, its farmers, its artisans, its blacksmiths, tanners, dyers, and weavers, said the old griot. But Mali's enormous wealth came from its far-flung trade routes in salt and gold and copper. "Altogether Mali was four months of travel long and four months of travel wide," said the griot, "and the greatest of all its cities was the fabled Timbuktu!" The major center of learning in all Africa, it was populated by thousands of scholars, made even more numerous by a steady parade of visiting wise men seeking to increase their knowledge—so many that some of the biggest merchants sold nothing but parchments and books. "There is not a marabout, not a teacher in the smallest village, whose knowledge has not come at least in part from Timbuktu," said the griot.

When finally the kintango stood up and thanked the griot for the generosity with which he had shared with them the treasures of his mind, Kunta and the others—for the first time since they came to the jujuo—actually dared to voice their displeasure, for the time had come for them to go to bed. The kintango chose to ignore this impertinence, at least for the time being, and sternly commanded them to their huts—but not before they had a chance to beg him to urge the griot to come back and visit them again.

They were still thinking and talking of the wondrous tales the griot had told them when—six days later—word came that a famous moro would soon be visiting the camp. The moro was the highest grade of teacher in The Gambia; indeed, there were only a few of them, and so wise were they—after many rains of study—that their job was to teach not schoolboys but other teachers, such as the arafang of Juffure.

Even the kintango showed unusual concern about this visitor, ordering the entire jujuo to be thoroughly cleaned, with the dirt raked and then brushed with leafy branches to a smoothness that would capture the honor of the fresh footprints of the moro when he arrived. Then the kintango assembled the boys in the compound and told them, "The advice and the blessings of this man who will be with us is sought not only by ordinary people but also by village chiefs and even by kings."

When the moro arrived the next morning, five of his students were with him, each carrying headbundles that Kunta knew would contain treasured Arabic books and parchment manuscripts such as those from ancient Timbuktu. As the old man passed through the gate, Kunta and his mates joined the kintango and his assistants on their knees, with their foreheads touching the ground. When the moro had blessed them and their jujuo, they rose and seated themselves respectfully around him as he opened his books and began to read—first from the Koran, then from such unheard-of books as the Taureta La Musa, the Zabora Dawidi and the Lingeeli la Isa, which he said were known to "Christians" as The Pentateuch of Moses, The Psalms of David and The Book of Isaiah. Each time the moro would open or close a book, roll or unroll a manuscript, he would press it to his forehead and mutter, "Amen!"

When he had finished reading, the old man put his books aside and spoke to them of great events and people from the Christian Koran, which was known as the Holy Bible. He spoke of Adam and Eve, of Joseph and his brethren; of Moses, David, and Solomon; of the death of Abel. And he spoke to them of great men of more recent history, such as Djoulou Kara Naini, known to the toubob as Alexander the Great, a mighty King of gold and silver whose sun had shown over half of the world.

Before the moro finally rose to leave that night, he reviewed what they already knew of the five daily prayers to Allah, and he instructed them thoroughly in how to conduct themselves inside the sacred mosque of their village, which they would enter for their first time when they returned home as men. Then he and his students had to hurry in or nearly three hours. Shortly afterward, a letter told me that the *Reader's Digest* would provide me with a three-hundred-dollar monthly check for one year, and plus that—my really vital need—"reasonable necessary travel expenses."

I again visited Cousin Georgia in Kansas City—something had urged me to do so, and I found her quite ill. But she was thrilled to hear both what I had learned and what I hoped to learn. She wished me Godspeed, and I flew then to Africa.

The same men with whom I had previously talked told me now in a rather matter-of-fact manner that they had caused word to be put out in the back country, and that a *griot* very knowledgeable of the Kinte clan had indeed been found—his name, they said, was "Kebba Kanji Fofana." I was ready to have a fit. "Where *is* he?" They looked at me oddly: "He's in his village."

I discovered that if I intended to see this *griot*, I was going to have to do something I'd never have dreamed I'd ever be doing—organizing what seemed, at least to me then, a kind of minisafari! It took me three days of negotiating through unaccustomed endless African palaver finally to hire a launch to get upriver; to rent a lorry and a Land-Rover to take supplies by a roundabout land route; to hire finally a total of fourteen people, including three interpreters and four musicians, who had told me that the old *griots* in the back country wouldn't talk without music in the background.

In the launch *Baddibu*, vibrating up the wide, swift "Kamby Bolongo," I felt queasily, uncomfortably alien. Did they all have me appraised as merely another pith helmet? Finally ahead was James Island, for two centuries the site of a fort over which England and France waged war back and forth for the ideal vantage point to trade in slaves. Asking if we might land there awhile, I trudged amid the crumbling ruins yet guarded by ghostly cannon. Picturing in my mind the kinds of atrocities that would have happened there, I felt as if I would like to go flailing an ax back through that facet of black Africa's history. Without luck I tried to find for myself some symbol remnant of an ancient chain, but I took a chunk of mortar and a brick. In the next minutes before we returned to the *Baddibu*, I just gazed up and down that river that my ancestor had named for his daughter far across the Atlantic Ocean in Spotsylvania County, Virginia. Then we went on, and upon arriving at a little village called Albreda, we put ashore, our destination now on foot the yet smaller village of Juffure, where the men had been told that this *griot* lived.

There is an expression called "the peak experience"—that which emotionally, nothing in your life ever transcends. I've had mine, that first day in the back country of black West Africa.

When we got within sight of Juffure, the children who were playing outside gave the alert, and the people came flocking from their huts. It's a village of only about seventy people. Like most back-country villages, it was still very much as it was two hundred years ago, with its circular mud houses and their conical thatched roofs. Among the people as they gathered was a small man wearing an off-white robe, a pillbox hat over an aquiline-featured black face, and about him was an aura of "somebodiness" until I knew he was the man we had come to see and hear.

As the three interpreters left our party to converge upon him, the seventy-odd other villagers gathered closely around me, in a kind of horseshoe pattern, three or four deep all around; had I stuck out my arms, my fingers would have touched the nearest ones on either side. They were all staring at me. The eyes just raked me. Their foreheads were furrowed with their very intensity of staring. A kind of visceral surging or a churning sensation started up deep inside me; bewildered, I was wondering what on earth was this . . . then in a little while it was rather as if some full-gale force of realization rolled in on me: Many times in my life I had been among crowds of people, but never where *every one was jet black!*

Rocked emotionally, my eyes dropped downward as we tend to do when we're uncertain, insecure, and my glance fell upon my own hands' brown complexion. This time more quickly than before, and even harder, another gale-force emotion hit me: I felt myself some variety of a hybrid . . . I felt somehow impure among the pure; it was a terribly shaming feeling. About then, abruptly the old man left the interpreters. The people immediately also left me now to go crowding about him.

One of my interpreters came up quickly and whispered in my ear, "They stare at you so much because they have never here seen a black American." When I grasped the significance, I believe that hit me harder than what had already happened. They hadn't been looking at me as an individual, but I represented in their eyes a symbol of the twenty-five millions of us black people whom they had never seen, who lived beyond an ocean.

The people were clustered thickly about the old man, all of them intermittently flicking glances toward me as they talked animatedly in their Mandinka tongue. After a while, the old man turned, walked briskly through the people, past my three interpreters, and right up to me. His eyes piercing into mine, seeming to feel I should understand his Mandinka, he expressed what they had all decided they *felt* concerning those unseen millions of us who lived in those places that had been slave ships' destinations—and the translation came: "We have been told by the forefathers that there are many of us from this place who are in exile in that place called America—and in other places."

The old man sat down, facing me, as the people hurriedly gathered behind him. Then he began to recite for me the ancestral history of the Kinte clan, as it had been passed along orally down across centuries from the forefathers' time. It was not merely conversational, but more as if a scroll were being read; for the still, silent villagers, it was clearly a formal occasion. The *griot* would speak, bending forward from the waist, his body rigid, his neck cords standing out, his words seeming almost physical objects. After a sentence or two, seeming to go limp, he would lean back, listening to an interpreter's translation. Spilling from the *griot's* head came an incredibly complex Kinte clan lineage that reached back across many generations: who married whom; who had what children; what children then married whom; then their offspring. It was all just unbelievable. I was struck not only by the profusion of details, but also by the narrative's biblical style, something like: "—and so-and-so took as a wife so-and-so, and begat . . . and begat . . . and begat . . . " He would next name each begat's eventual spouse, or spouses, and their averagely numerous offspring, and so on. To date things the *griot* linked them to events, such as "—in the year of the big water"—a flood—"he slew a water buffalo." To determine the calendar date, you'd have to find out when that particular flood occurred.

Simplifying to its essence the encyclopedic saga that I was told, the *griot* said that the Kinte clan had begun in the country called Old Mali. Then the Kinte men traditionally were black-smiths, "who had conquered fire," and the women mostly were potters and weavers. In time, one branch of the clan moved into the country called Mauretania; and it was from Mauretania that one son of this clan, whose name was Kairaba Kunta Kinte—a *marabout*, or holy man of the Moslem faith—journeyed down into the country called The Gambia. He went first to a village called Pakali N'Ding, stayed there for a while, then went to a village called Jiffarong, and then to the village of Juffure.

In Juffure, Kairaba Kunta Kinte took his first wife, a Mandinka maiden whose name was Sireng. And by her he begot two sons, whose names were Janneh and Saloum. Then he took a second wife; her name was Yaisa. And by Yaisa, he begot a son named Omoro.

Those three sons grew up in Juffure until they became of age. Then the elder two, Janneh and Saloum, went away and founded a new village called Kinte-Kundah Janneh-Ya. The youngest son, Omoro, stayed on in Juffure village until he had thirty rains—years—of age, then he took as his wife a Mandinka maiden named Binta Kebba. And by Binta Kebba, roughly between the years 1750 and 1760, Omoro Kinte begat four sons, whose names were, in the order of their birth, Kunta, Lamin, Suwadu, and Madi.

The old *griot* had talked for nearly two hours up to then, and perhaps fifty times the narrative had included some detail about someone whom he had named. Now after he had just named those four sons, again he appended a detail, and the interpreter translated—"About the time the King's soldiers came"—another of the *griot's* time-fixing references—"the oldest of these four sons, Kunta, went away from his village to chop wood . . . and he was never seen again . . . ." And the *griot* went on with his narrative.

I sat as if I were carved of stone. My blood seemed to have congealed. This man whose life-time had been in this back-country African village had no way in the world to know that he had just echoed what I had heard all through my boyhood years on my grandma's front porch in Henning, Tennessee . . . of an African who always had insisted that his name was "Kin-tay"; who had called a guitar a "*ko*," and a river within the state of Virginia, "Kamby Bolongo"; and who had been kidnaped into slavery while not far from his village, chopping wood, to make himself a drum.

I managed to fumble from my duffelbag my basic notebook, whose first pages containing grandma's story I showed to an interpreter. After briefly reading, clearly astounded, he spoke rapidly while showing it to the old *griot*, who became agitated; he got up, exclaiming to the people, gesturing at my notebook in the interpreter's hands, and *they* all got agitated.

I don't remember hearing anyone giving an order, I only recall becoming aware that those seventy-odd people had formed a wide human ring around me, moving counterclockwise, chanting softly, loudly, softly; their bodies close together, they were lifting their knees high, stamping up reddish puffs of the dust. . . .

The woman who broke from the moving circle was one of about a dozen whose infant chil-dren were within cloth slings across their backs. Her jet-black face deeply contorting, the woman came charging toward me, her bare feet slapping the earth, and snatching her baby free, she thrust it at me almost roughly, the gesture saying "Take it!" . . . and I did, clasping the baby to me. Then she snatched away her baby; and another woman was thrusting her baby, then another, and another . . . until I had embraced probably a dozen babies. I wouldn't learn until maybe a year later, from a Harvard University professor, Dr. Jerome Bruner, a scholar of such matters, "You didn't know you were participating in one of the oldest ceremonies of humankind, called

'The laying on of hands'! In their way, they were telling you 'Through this flesh, which is us, we are you, and you are us!'"

Later the men of Juffure took me into their mosque built of bamboo and thatch, and they prayed around me in Arabic. I remember thinking, down on my knees, "After I've found out where I came from, I can't understand a word they're saying." Later the crux of their prayer was translated for me: "Praise be to Allah for one long lost from us whom Allah has returned."

Since we had come by the river, I wanted to return by land. As I sat beside the wiry young Mandingo driver who was leaving dust pluming behind us on the hot, rough, pitted, back-country road toward Banjul, there came from somewhere into my head a staggering awareness . . . that *if* any black American could be so blessed as I had been to know only a few ancestral clues—could he or she know *who* was either the paternal or maternal African ancestor or ancestors, and about *where* that ancestor lived when taken, and finally about *when* the ancestor was taken—then only those few clues might well see that black American able to locate some wizened old black *griot* whose narrative could reveal the black American's ancestral clan, perhaps even the very village.

In my mind's eye, rather as if it were mistily being projected on a screen, I began envisioning descriptions I had read of how collectively millions of our ancestors had been enslaved. Many thousands were individually kidnaped, as my own forebear Kunta had been, but into the millions had come awake screaming in the night, dashing out into the bedlam of raided villages, which were often in flames. The captured able survivors were linked neck-by-neck with thongs into processions called "coffles," which were sometimes as much as a mile in length. I envisioned the many dying, or left to die when they were too weak to continue the torturous march toward the coast, and those who made it to the beach were greased, shaved, probed in every orifice, often branded with sizzling irons; I envisioned them being lashed and dragged toward the longboats; their spasms of screaming and clawing with their hands into the beach, biting up great choking mouthfuls of the sand in their desperation efforts for one last hold on the Africa that had been their home; I envisioned them shoved, beaten, jerked down into slave ships' stinking holds and chained onto shelves, often packed so tightly that they had to lie on their sides like spoons in a drawer . . . .

My mind reeled with it all as we approached another, much larger village. Staring ahead, I realized that word of what had happened in Juffure must have left there well before I did. The driver slowing down, I could see this village's people thronging the road ahead; they were weaving, amid their cacophony of crying out something; I stood up in the Land-Rover, waving back as they seemed grudging to open a path for the Land-Rover.

I guess we had moved a third of the way through the village when it suddenly registered in my brain what they were all crying out . . . the wizened, robed elders and younger men, the mothers and the naked tar-black children, they were all waving up at me, their expressions buoyant, beaming, all were crying out together, "Meester Kinte! Meester Kinte!"

Note

1. Alex Haley, *Roots: The Saga of an American Family* (New York, NY: Dell Publishing, 1976), pp. 114–118; 716–721.

James Weldon Johnson

Because of the sermonizing public oratory of Dr. Martin Luther King Jr., Americans generally recognize the sermon as a staple of the African American oral tradition and, therefore, African American rhetoric. Fewer, however, realize just how old is the practice of preaching sermons or, more importantly, what the earliest sermons might have looked (or sounded) like. The sermons collected in James Weldon Johnson's *God's Trombones* are representative of those early sermons, what Johnson calls folk sermons, that may have descended from slave preachers. In the last quarter of the nineteenth century, as a boy, Johnson heard these classic sermons and was moved to preserve them in this collection published in 1927. In the preface to *God's Trombones*, Johnson himself remarks on the rhetoricalness of the sermons. He states that

[t]he old-time Negro preacher of parts was above all an orator, and in good measure an actor. He knew the secret of oratory, that at bottom it is a progression of rhythmic words more than it is anything else . . . At such times his language was not prose but poetry.

(5)

The Creation

James Weldon Johnson[1]

And God stepped out on space,
And he looked around and said:
I'm lonely—
I'll make me a world.

And far as the eye of God could see
Darkness covered everything,
Blacker than a hundred midnights
Down in a cypress swamp.

Then God smiled,
And the light broke,
And the darkness rolled up on one side,
And the light stood shining on the other,
And God said: That's good!

Then God reached out and took the light in his hands,
And God rolled the light around in his hands
Until he made the sun;
And he set that sun a-blazing in the heavens.
And the light that was left from making the sun
God gathered it up in a shining ball
And flung it against the darkness,
Spangling the night with the moon and stars.
Then down between
The darkness and the light
He hurled the world;
And God said: That's good!

Then God himself stepped down—
And the sun was on his right hand,
And the moon was on his left;
The stars were clustered about his head,
And the earth was under his feet.
And God walked, and where he trod
His footsteps hollowed the valleys out
And bulged the mountains up.

Then he stopped and looked and saw
That the earth was hot and barren.
So God stepped over to the edge of the world
And he spat out the seven seas—
He batted his eyes, and the lightnings flashed—
He clapped his hands, and the thunders rolled—
And the waters above the earth came down,
The cooling waters came down.

Then the green grass sprouted,
And the little red flowers blossomed,
The pine tree pointed his finger to the sky,
And the oak spread out his arms,
The lakes cuddled down in the hollows of the ground,
And the rivers ran down to the sea;
And God smiled again,
And the rainbow appeared,
And curled itself around his shoulder.

Then God raised his arm and he waved his hand
Over the sea and over the land,
And he said: Bring forth! Bring forth!
And quicker than God could drop his hand,
Fishes and fowls
And beasts and birds
Swam the rivers and the seas,
Roamed the forests and the woods,
And split the air with their wings.
And God said: That's good!

Then God walked around,
And God looked around
On all that he had made.
He looked at his sun,
And he looked at his moon,
And he looked at his little stars;
He looked on his world
With all its living things,
And God said: I'm lonely still.

Then God sat down—
On the side of a hill where he could think;
By a deep, wide river he sat down;
With his head in his hands,
God thought and thought,
Till he thought: I'll make me a man!

Up from the bed of the river
God scooped the clay;
And by the bank of the river
He kneeled him down;
And there the great God Almighty
Who lit the sun and fixed it in the sky,
Who flung the stars to the most far corner of the night,
Who rounded the earth in the middle of his hand;
This Great God,
Like a mammy bending over her baby,
Kneeled down in the dust
Toiling over a lump of clay
Till he shaped it in his own image;

Then into it he blew the breath of life,
And man became a living soul.
Amen. Amen.

The Prodigal Son

Young man—
Young man—
Your arm's too short to box with God.

But Jesus spake in a parable, and he said:
A certain man had two sons.
Jesus didn't give this man a name,
But his name is God Almighty.
And Jesus didn't call these sons by name,
But ev'ry young man,
Ev'rywhere,
Is one of these two sons.

And the younger son said to his father,
He said: Father, divide up the property,
And give me my portion now.
And the father with tears in his eyes said: Son,
Don't leave your father's house.
But the boy was stubborn in his head,
And haughty in his heart,
And he took his share of his father's goods,
And went into a far-off country.

There comes a time,
There comes a time
When ev'ry young man looks out from his father's house,
Longing for that far-off country.

And the young man journeyed on his way,
And he said to himself as he travelled along:
This sure is an easy road,
Nothing like the rough furrows behind my father's plow.

Young man—
Young man—
Smooth and easy is the road
That leads to hell and destruction.
Down grade all the way,
The further you travel, the faster you go.
No need to trudge and sweat and toil,
Just slip and slide and slip and slide
Till you bang up against hell's iron gate.

And the younger son kept travelling along,
Till at night-time he came to a city.
And the city was bright in the night-time like day,
The streets all crowded with people,
Brass bands and string bands a-playing,
And ev'rywhere the young man turned
There was singing and laughing and dancing.
And he stopped a passer-by and he said:
Tell me what city is this?
And the passer-by laughed and said: Don't you know?
This is Babylon, Babylon,
That great city of Babylon.
Come on, my friend, and go along with me.
And the young man joined the crowd.

Young man—
Young man—
You're never lonesome in Babylon.
You can always join a crowd in Babylon.
Young man—
Young man—
You can never be alone in Babylon,
Alone with your Jesus in Babylon.
You can never find a place, a lonesome place,
A lonesome place to go down on your knees,
And talk with your God, in Babylon.
You're always in a crowd in Babylon.

And the young man went with his new-found friend,
And bought himself some brand new clothes,

And he spent his days in the drinking dens,
Swallowing the fires of hell.
And he spent his nights in the gambling dens,

Throwing dice with the devil for his soul.
And he met up with the women of Babylon.
Oh, the women of Babylon!
Dressed in yellow and purple and scarlet,
Loaded with rings and earrings and bracelets,
Their lips like a honeycomb dripping with honey,
Perfumed and sweet-smelling like a jasmine flower;
And the jasmine smell of the Babylon women
Got in his nostrils and went to his head,
And he wasted his substance in riotous living,
In the evening, in the black and dark of night,
With the sweet-sinning women of Babylon.
And they stripped him of his money,
And they stripped him of his clothes,
And they left him broke and ragged
In the streets of Babylon.

Then the young man joined another crowd—
The beggars and lepers of Babylon.
And he went to feeding swine,
And he was hungrier than the hogs;
He got down on his belly in the mire and mud
And ate the husks with the hogs.
And not a hog was too low to turn up his nose
At the man in the mire of Babylon.

Then the young man came to himself—
He came to himself and said:
In my father's house are many mansions,
Ev'ry servant in his house has bread to eat,
Ev'ry servant in his house has a place to sleep;
I will arise and go to my father.

And his father saw him afar off,
And he ran up the road to meet him.
He put clean clothes upon his back,
And a golden chain around his neck,
He made a feast and killed the fatted calf,
And invited the neighbors in.

Oh-o-oh, sinner,
When you're mingling with the crowd in Babylon—
Drinking the wine of Babylon—
Running with the women of Babylon—
You forget about God, and you laugh at Death.
Today you've got the strength of a bull in your neck

And the strength of a bear in your arms,
But some o' these days, some o' these days,
You'll have a hand-to-hand struggle with bony Death,
And Death is bound to win.

Young man, come away from Babylon,
That hell-border city of Babylon.
Leave the dancing and gambling of Babylon,
The wine and whiskey of Babylon,
The hot-mouthed women of Babylon;
Fall down on your knees,
And say in your heart:
I will arise and go to my Father.

Note

1. J. W. Johnson, "The Creation & The Prodigal Son," in *God's Trombones: Seven Negro Sermons in Verse* (New York, NY: Penguin Books, 1990 [1927]), pp. 17–25.

Zora Neale Hurston

The tales in folklorist Zora Neale Hurston's *Mules and Men* were collected primarily in 1927–28. Much like those in Roger Abrahams's *Singing the Master*, Hurston's tales, such as "Ole Massa and John," reflect aspects of slave life, often how the slave outsmarts and gets over on his White master. These are again examples of the signifying practices that were commonplace in African American culture. "Why Negroes Are Black" is one of many creation myths or variations on the biblical creation story. These tales are often humorous, meant to poke fun at the inexplicable in God's creation.

Why Negroes Are Black and Ole Massa and John Who Wanted to Go to Heaven

Zora Neale Hurston[1]

"Uh, hunh!" Gold gloated. "Ah knowed you didn't know whut you was talkin' about. Now Ah'm goin' ter tell you how come we so black: Long before they got thru makin' de Atlantic Ocean and haulin' de rocks for de mountains, God was makin' up de people. But He didn't finish 'em all at one time. Ah'm compelled to say dat some folks is walkin' 'round dis town right now ain't finished yet and never will be.

Well, He give out eyes one day. All de nations come up and got they eyes. Then He give out teeth and so on. Then He set a day to give out color. So seven o'clock dat mornin' everybody was due to git they color except de niggers. So God give everybody they color and they went on off. Then He set there for three hours and one-half and no niggers. It was gettin' hot and God wanted to git His work done and go set in de cool. So He sent de angels. Rayfield and Gab'ull[2] to go git 'em so He could 'tend some mo' business.

They hunted all over Heben till dey found de colored folks. All stretched out sleep on de grass under de tree of life. So Rayfield woke 'em up and tole 'em God wanted 'em.

They all jumped up and run on up to de th'one and they was so skeered they might miss sumpin' they begin to push and shove one 'nother, bumpin' against all de angels and turnin' over foot-stools. They even had de th'one all pushed one-sided.

So God hollered "Git back! Git back!" And they misunderstood Him and thought He said, "Git black," and they been black ever since.

Ulmer says: "Joe Wiley, youse as big a liar as you is a man! Whoo-wee. Boy, you molds 'em. But lemme tell y'all a sho nuff tale 'bout Ole Massa."

"Go 'head and tell it, Cliff," shouted Eugene Oliver. "Ah love to hear tales about Ole Massa and John. John sho was one smart nigger."

So Cliff Ulmer went on.

You know befo' surrender Ole Massa had a nigger name John and John always prayed every night befo' he went to bed and his prayer was for God to come git him and take him to Heaven right away. He didn't even want to take time to die. He wanted de Lawd to come git him just like he was—boot, sock and all. He'd git down on his knees and say: "O Lawd, it's once more and again yo' humble servant is knee-bent and body-bowed—my heart beneath my knees and my knees in some lonesome valley, crying for mercy while mercy kin be found. O Lawd, Ah'm astin' you in de humblest way I know how to be *so* pleased as to come in yo' fiery chariot and take me to yo' Heben and its immortal glory. Come Lawd, you know Ah have such a hard time. Old Massa works me *so* hard, and don't gimme no time to rest. So come, Lawd, wid peace in one hand and pardon in de other and take me away from this sin-sorrowing world. Ah'm tired and Ah want to go home."

So one night Ole Massa passed by John's shack and heard him beggin' de Lawd to come git him in his fiery chariot and take him away; so he made up his mind to find out if John meant dat thing. So he goes on up to de big house and got hisself a bed sheet and come on back. He throwed de sheet over his head and knocked on de door.

John quit prayin' and ast: "Who dat?"

Ole Massa say: "It's me, John, de Lawd, done come wid my fiery chariot to take you away from this sin-sick world."

Right under de bed John had business. He told his wife: "Tell Him Ah ain't here, Liza."

At first Liza didn't say nothin' at all, but de Lawd kept right on callin' John: "Come on, John, and go to Heben wid me where you won't have to plough no mo' furrows and hoe no mo' corn. Come on, John."

Liza says: "John ain't here, Lawd, you hafta come back another time."

Lawd says: "Well, then Liza, you'll do."

Liza whispers and says: "John, come out from underneath dat bed and g'wan wid de Lawd. You been beggin' him to come git you. Now g'wan wid him."

John back under de bed not saying a mumblin' word. De Lawd out on de door step kept on callin'.

Liza says: "John, Ah thought you was so anxious to get to Heben. Come out and go on wid God."

John says: "Don't you hear him say 'You'll do'? Why don't you go wid him?"

"Ah ain't a goin' nowhere. Youse de one been whoopin' and hollerin' for him to come git you and if you don't come out from under dat bed Ah'm gointer tell God youse here."

Ole Massa makin' out he's God, says: "Come on, Liza, you'll do."

Liza says: "O, Lawd, John is right here underneath de bed."

"Come on John, and go to Heben wid me and its immortal glory."

John crept out from under de bed and went to de door and cracked it and when he seen all dat white standin' on de doorsteps he jumped back. He says: "O, Lawd, Ah can't go to Heben wid you in yo' fiery chariot in dese ole dirty britches; gimme time to put on my Sunday pants."

"All right, John, put on yo' Sunday pants."

John fooled around just as long as he could, changing them pants, but when he went back to de door, de big white glory was still standin' there. So he says agin: "O, Lawd, de Good Book says in Heben no filth is found and I got on his dirty sweaty shirt. Ah can't go wid you in dis old nasty shirt. Gimme time to put on my Sunday shirt!"

"All right, John, go put on yo' Sunday shirt."

John took and fumbled around a long time changing his shirt, and den he went back to de door, but Ole Massa was still on de door step. John didn't had nothin' else to change so he opened de door a little piece and says:

"O, Lawd, Ah'm ready to go to Heben wid you in yo' fiery chariot, but de radiance of yo' countenance is *so* bright, Ah can't come out by you. Stand back jus' a li'l way please."

Ole Massa stepped back a li'l bit.

John looked out agin and says: "O, Lawd, you know dat po' humble me is less than de dust beneath yo' shoe soles. And de radiance of yo' countenance is so bright Ah can't come out by you. Please, please, Lawd, in yo' tender mercy, stand back a li'l bit further."

Ole Massa stepped back a li'l bit mo'.

John looked out agin and he says: "O, Lawd, Heben is so high and wese so low; youse so great and Ah'm so weak and yo' strength is too much for us poor sufferin' sinners. So once mo' and agin yo' humber servant is knee-bent and body-bowed askin' you one mo' favor befo' Ah step into yo' fiery chariot to go to Heben wid you and wash in yo' glory—be so pleased in yo' tender mercy as to stand back jus' a li'l bit further."

Ole Massa stepped back a step or two mo' and out dat door John come like a streak of lightning. All across de punkin patch, thru de cotton over de pasture—John wid Ole Massa right behind him. By de time dey hit de cornfield John was way ahead of Ole Massa.

Back in de shack one of de children was cryin' and she ast Liza: "Mama, you reckon God's gointer ketch papa and carry him to Heben wid him?"

"Shet yo' mouf, talkin' foolishness!" Liza clashed at de chile. "You know de Lawd can't outrun yo' pappy—specially when he's barefooted at dat."

Notes

1. Zora Neale Hurston, "Why Negroes Are Black and Ole Massa and John Who Wanted to Go to Heaven," in *Mules and Men* (New York, NY: Quality Paperback Books, 1963 [1935]), pp. 29–30; 69–72.
2. The angels Raphael and Gabriel.

Elijah Wald

Often for the sociolinguist and scholar of African American folklore, the dozens (alternatively, the dirty dozens, sounding, or snaps) are simply a game, a ritualistic form of verbal insult performed by African American adolescent males in America's inner cities. However, musician and writer Elijah Wald cites examples of the dozens that were rendered by grown men and at a time (the early twentieth century) that predates the existence of the modern inner city. The examples drawn from this source illustrate some important characteristics of the dozens that are often overlooked because observers tend to focus on the ribaldry of jokes about mamas. In the first excerpt, Wald quotes H. Rap Brown's well-known quip about the dozens and the poetry lessons taught in school. From his perspective, the streets are a kind of grammar school for many African Americans, teaching pupils the nuances of wordplay. The second excerpt illustrates a dozens exchange between two adult men in Wichita, Kansas. Originally observed and recorded by poet and journalist Frank Marshall Davis in *Livin' the Blues*, we can see that another major characteristic of the dozens is that it is a public performance or display. The dozens works, that is, only when there is an audience, onlookers with whom one can gauge the force of one's jibes.

The Dozens: A History of Rap's Mama

Elijah Wald[1]

I learned how to talk in the street, not from reading about Dick and Jane going to the zoo and all that simple shit. The teacher would test our vocabulary each week, but we knew the vocabulary we needed. They'd give us arithmetic to exercise our minds. Hell, we exercised our minds by playing the Dozens.

> I fucked your mama
> Till she went blind.
> Her breath smells bad,
> But she sure can grind.

> I fucked your mama
> For a solid hour.
> Baby came out
> Screaming, Black Power . . .

And the teacher expected me to sit up in class and study poetry after I could run down shit like that. If anybody needed to study poetry, she needed to study mine. We played the Dozens for recreation, like white folks played Scrabble.

When Davis was seventeen he moved to Wichita to take a job as a busboy and was startled to find the grown-up waiters indulging in a rougher, unrhymed version of the game during their afternoon lunch break. It started with the same seemingly innocent phrase that sparked Danny Barker's anecdote:

> A short waiter "spotted a thin, mournful undertaker type, grinned, and asked pleasantly, 'How's yo mammy today?'"
> "Uh-oh," said another waiter laughing. "Right straight in the dozens!"
> "Soon's these jokers git together, they're 12th Street bound," commented another.

"I hear yo' baby sister's in jail again," came back the undertaker type. "She was runnin' a service station with a great big sign, 'Oil an' Ass for Sale.'"

The first threw up his hands in mock supplication. "I was jus' being polite, askin' 'bout your ma, an' you insults me. Jus' for that, nex' time your mother comes aroun' offering me a ten-cent trick, I'll turn her down."

"You ungrateful motherfucker," the other shot back. "If it don't be for me, you wouldn't be alive today. Yo' ma was all set to drown you 'til I step in an' say no. Soon's you was born, you ran up a chandelier. Yo' ma not only couldn't tell whose you was, she couldn't even tell *what* you was."

"Listen at this grannydodger," said the first. "When you was born, you was las' in a litter of three. The fust two out grabbed yo' ma's titties an' started sucking. That meant they wasn't but one thing left fo' you to eat on. So you ain't no motherfucker, you's a mothersucker."

Note

1. Elijah Wald, *The Dozens: A History of Rap's Mama* (New York: Oxford University Press, 2012), pp. 8; 15–16; 32.

B. Jackson

The trickster and badman tales are commonplace in African American vernacular culture. The tales are often called toasts, a rather peculiar referent given that standard English discourse has a few of its own uses of the word "toast." But in the Black vernacular toasts are narrative poems about the exploits of a hero or antihero, one who personifies the Black man or woman who is (or acts) bad (as in good) or uses trickery (trickeration in the vernacular) to get over on the man or whoever gets in the hero's way. "Stackolee" (or "Stag-O-Lee") is the classic badman toast, but there are others, like Dolemite, who in the 1970s was portrayed by comedian Rudy Ray Moore in a series of blaxploitation films. "The Signifying Monkey" is about the quintessential trickster by that name whose antics are, at times, destructive but ultimately amoral given the perverted environment he is obliged to operate in. "Titanic" or "Shine" centers on a character who technically is neither badman or trickster but rather a bit of both. In a sense, he is the ultimate heroic figure because he signifies (e.g., colorfully spurns offers of sex and money to save himself) and takes action (e.g., not expecting to be rescued, he takes matters into his own hands and swims to shore).

Stackolee

B. Jackson[1]

It was back in the time of nineteen hundred and two,
I had a fucked-up deck a cards and I didn't know what to do.
My woman was leavin', she was puttin' me out in the cold.
I said, "Why you leavin' me, baby?" She said, "Our love has grown cold."
So she kept packin' the bags, so I said, "Fuck it," you know.
So I waded through water and I waded through mud
and I came to this town called the Bucket of Blood.
And I asked the bartender for something to eat,
he give me a dirty glass a water and a tough-assed piece a meat.
I said, "Bartender, bartender, don't you know who I am?"
He said, "Frankly, my man, I don't give a goddam."
I said, "My name is Stackolee." He said, "Oh, yes, I heard about you up this way,
but I feed you hungry motherfuckers each and every day."
'Bout this time the poor bartender had gone to rest—
I pumped six a my rockets [bullets] in his motherfucken chest.
A woman run out the back screamin' real loud, said, "I know my son ain't dead!"
I said, "You just check that hole in the ugly motherfucker's head."
She say, "You may be bad, your name may be Stack,
but you better not be here when Billy Lions get back."
So I walked around the room and I seen this trick,
and we went upstairs and we started real soon.
Now me and this broad we started to tussle
and I drove twelve inches a dick through her ass before she could move a muscle.
We went downstairs where we were before,
we fucked on the table and all over the floor.
'Bout that time you could hear the drop of a pin—
that bad motherfucker Billy Lions had just walked in.
He walked behind the counter, he seen the bartender dead,

he say, "Who put this hole in this ugly motherfucker's head."
Say, "Who can this man's murderer be?"
One motherfucker say, "You better speak soft, his name is Stackolee."
He say, "Stack, I'm gonna give you a chance to run before I draw my gun."
Bitch jumped up and said, "Billy, please."
He shot that whore through both her knees.
A pimp eased up and turned out the lights
and I had him dead in both my sights.
When the lights came back on poor Billy had gone to rest,
I had pumped nine a my rockets in his motherfucken chest.
The next day about half-past ten
I was standin' before the judge and twelve other good men.
They say, "What can this man's charges be?"
One sonofabitch say, "Murder in the first degree."
Another say, "What can this man's penalty be?"
One say, "Hang him," another say, "Give him gas."
A snaggle-tooth bitch jumped up and say, "Run that twister through his jivin' ass!"
My woman jumped up and said, "Let him go free,
'cause there ain't nobody in the world can fuck like Stackolee."

The Signifying Monkey

Deep down in the jungle in the coconut grove
lived the most Signifying Monkey that the world ever knowed.
His eyes were red and his ass was sore,
and everytime he dozed that Lion'd roar.
The Monkey told the Lion one bright summer day,
"There's a bad motherfucker heading your way.
He talked about your brother, put your sister in the shelf,
the way he talked about your mother I wouldn't say to myself."
Now the Lion let out a ferocious rage
just like a young jitterbug blowin' his cage.
Went through the jungle at a terrible pace,
like a young sixteen-year-old with a cunt in his face.
Went through the jungle 'tween coconut trees,
knocking down giraffes to their motherfucken knees.
Then he spied the Elephant under a sycamore tree,
said, "Come on, bad motherfucker, it's just you and me."
The Elephant got up and was in the groove,
said, "You must be constipated and want your bowels removed."
The Lion let out a ferocious roar
and his tail shot out like a forty-four.
He made a pass at the Elephant's back,
the Elephant sidestepped and knocked him dead on his hairy ass.
He broke six ribs, fucked up his face,
jumped on his stomach, and knocked his ass out of place.
They fought all day, and they fought all night,
the Lion begin to wonder if he gonna win this fight.

They fought all night and they fought all day,
the Lion begin to wonder if he gonna get away.
They fought and they fought till the Lion said "Quits,"
'cause he swore he'd get the sonofabitch start this signifying shit.
So back through the jungle more dead than alive,
and that's when the Monkey start his signifying jive.
Said, "Oh, Mr. Lion, you don't look so well,
why it looks like you caught natural hell.
When you left, this old jungle rung,
now you come back damn near hung.
King of the Jungle, why ain't you a bitch?
You look more like a whore with the seven-year itch.
Said, "Now, you sonofabitch, don't you roar,
'cause I'll get down out of this tree and kick your hairy ass some more."
Said, "Every time me and my wife try to get a little bit,
you come around with this 'hi-ho' shit."
Now the Lion looked up to the Monkey, "You know I didn't get beat."
He said, "You're a lyin' motherfucker, I had a ringside seat."
The Lion looked up out of his one good eye,
said, "Lord, let that skinny little bastard fall out of that tree before I die."
The Monkey got frantic, jumped up and down,
his left foot missed, his skinny ass hit the ground.
Like a streak of bolt and a flash of heat,
the Lion was on him with all four feet.
He beat the Monkey till his nose bleed,
that's when the Monkey started his plead.
He said, "Oh, Mr. Lion, almighty friend,
don't you remember the other night we got drunk on gin?"
"Old Kangaroo Kate with the slick-lining jive
gave us some trim for your eighty-five."
Said, "Now, I got a wife with thirteen kids.
What the hell would they do if they found me dead?"
Said, "Monkey, I'm not kicking your ass for lyin',
I'm kicking your hairy ass for signifyin.'"
Little by little and bit by bit,
I'm gonna put a stop to all this signifyin' shit."
The Monkey looked up with tears in his eyes,
said, "Mr. Lion, I apologize."
Lion said, "I've heard that shit before,
Monkey, I'm not letting your ass go no more."
The Monkey said, "Let me get my teeth out of the grit and balls out of the sand,
and I'll fight your ass like a *real* he-man."
So the Lion stepped back to the end of the curve,
'cause that was the boldest challenge he'd ever heard.
But faster than the hand or the human eye could see,
the Monkey was back in the coconut tree.
Said, "Now, you better be on your way, you hairy slut,
before I split your fucken hair with a coconut."

Titanic (A)

All the old folks say the fourth a May was a hell of a day.
I was in a little seaport town and the great *Titanic* was goin' down.
Now the sergeant and captain was havin' some words
when they hit that big iceberg.
Up come Shine from down below,
he said, "Captain, captain," say, "you don't know,"
say, "we got nine feet of water over the boiler-room floor."
And the captain said, "Go on back and start stackin' sacks,
we got nine water pumps to keep the water back."
Up come Shine from down below,
he said, "Captain, captain," says, "You don't know,
we got forty feet of water over the boiler-room floor."
He said, "Go on back and start stackin' sacks,
we got nine water pumps to keep the water back."
Shine said, "Your shittin' is good and your shittin' is fine,"
say, "but there's one time you white folks ain't gonna shit on Shine."
Now a thousand millionaires was lookin' at him
when he jumped in the ocean and he begin to swim.
Rich man's daughter came up on deck
with her drawers around her knees and underskirt around her neck.
Like a noonday clock Shine stopped
and his eyes fell dead on that cock.
She says, "Shine, oh, Shine," says, "save me please,"
say, "I give you all the pussy that your eyes may see."
He said, "I know you got your pussy and that's true,
but there's some girls on land got good a pussy as you."
She said, "Shine, oh, Shine," say, "please save my life,"
say, "I'll make you a lawfully wedded wife."
He said, "Your shittin' is good and your shittin' is fine,
but first I got to save this black ass of mine."
Now was another fella by the name of Jim,
he jumped in the ocean and he begin to swim.
Another girl ran up on deck
with her drawers around her knees and underskirt around *her* neck.
Like a noonday clock Jim stopped
and his eyes fell dead on that cock.
Now she had long black hair that hang from the crown of her head to the nape of her belly,
she had a twenty-pound pussy that shook like jelly.
Say, "Shine, oh, Shine," says, "save me please,
I'll give you everything that your eyes may see."
And before the last word could fall from her lip,
Jim climbed his black ass back up on that ship.
Up come a shark from the bottom of the sea,
said, "Look what godalmighty done sent to me."
Shine bowed his neck and showed his ass,
"Get out the way, let a *big* shark pass."
And after old shark seen that Shine had him beat,

he said, "Swim, black motherfucker, 'cause I don't like black meat."
About four-thirty when the *Titanic* was sinkin',
Shine done swimmed on over in Los Angeles and started drinkin'.
But now when he heard the *Titanic* had sunk
he was in New York damn near drunk.
He said, "Ladies and gentlemen," say, "when I die don't ya'll bury me at all,
soak my balls in alcohol and lay my old rod up across my breast,
and tell all the peoples old Shine has gone to rest."

Titanic (B)

It was sad indeed, it was sad in mind,
April the 14th of 1912 was a hell of a time,
when the news reached a seaport town
that the great *Titanic* was a sinking down.
Up popped Shine from the deck below,
says, "Captain, captain," says, "you don't know."
Says, "There's about forty feet of water on the boiler-room floor."
He said, "Never mind, Shine, you go on back, and keep stackin' them sacks,
I got forty-eight pumps to keep the water back."
Shine said, "Well, that seems damned funny, it may be damned fine,
but I'm gonna try to save this black ass of mine."
So Shine jumped overboard and bagin to swim,
and all the people standin' on the deck watchin' him.
Captain's daughter ran on the deck with her dress above her head and her titties below her
    knees,
and said, "Shine, Shine, won't you save poor me?"
Say, "I'll make you as rich as any chine can be."
Shine said, "Miss, I know you is pretty and that is true,
but there's women on the shore can make a ass out a you."
So Shine turned over and began to swim,
people on the deck were still watchin' him.
A whale jumped up in the middle of the sea,
said, "Put a 'special delivery' on his black ass for me."
Shine said, "Your eyes may roll and your teeth may grit,
but if you're figurin' on eatin' me you can can that shit."
Shine continued to swim, he looked back, he ducked his head, he showed his ass,
"Look out sharks and fishes let me pass."
He swimmed on till he came to New York town,
and people asked had the *Titanic* gone down.
Shine said, "Hell yeah." They said, "How do you know?"
He said, "I left the big motherfucker sinkin' about thirty minutes ago."

Note

1. B. Jackson, "Stackolee," "The Signifying Monkey," and "*Titanic*," in *Get Your Ass in the Water and Swim Like Me: African American Narrative Poetry From Oral Tradition* (New York, NY: Routledge, 2004 [1974]), pp. 46–47; 171–172; 184–185.

Daryl Cumber

While many of the more popular or more widely publicized elements of the African American oral tradition (e.g., toasts, the dozens, rapping) tend to be dominated by men, anyone who has any familiarity at all with Black culture knows that African American women have a legacy of orature all their own. Or rather, they have a legacy of orature that is the wellspring of all orature, what we traditionally refer to as Mother Wit. Rare is the African American boy or girl who has not received a healthy dose of Mother Wit. The "Mama Sez" sections of Daryl Cumber Dance's anthology *Honey, Hush!* is a perfect example. There she lists a wide variety of expressions one might hear mamas say. The expressions illustrate Black female humor, to be sure, but in an actual situation when such utterances are used (depending on the nature of the utterance) ain't a damned thing funny. Thus, rhetorically speaking, expressions like "A hard head makes a soft behind" or "There's more than one way of skinning a cat" function as aphorisms, as they impart communal wisdom for daily living in the world. The excerpts from "Sister to Sister" function much the same, only at the level of female peers and not always with the purpose of instruction or correction. Some are retorts ("Put that in your pipe and smoke it"), some are congratulatory ("You go, girl"), and some instructive ("It's a poor dog that won't switch its own tail"). Used appropriately, of course, all of these expressions tend to elicit a response (or at least acknowledgment) from the receiver.

Mama Sez

Daryl Cumber[1]

Her tongue knows no Sunday.
A whistling woman and a crowing hen never come to a good end.
A pullet always tells where she lays her first egg.
You ever see a fish what kept his mouth shut caught on anybody's hook?
Shut mouth don't catch no flies.
We can all sing together, but we can't all talk together.
The empty barrel makes the most noise.
A tattler keeps the pot boiling.
What eyes don't see, mouth can't talk about.
Never let your right hand know what your left hand is doing.
See and be blind; hear and be deaf.
Believe half of what you see and nothing that you hear.
Every shut eye ain't sleep; every good-bye ain't gone.
The bush has ears and the wall has a mouth.
You kin hide the fire, but what you gon' do with the smoke?
Chile, don't you raise yo' voice at me. Don't you ever forget, I brought you into this world
    and I'll take you out.
Chile, you kin cloud up, just so you don't rain.
Gal, don't roll your eyes at me!
No she didn't cut eye/suck teeth!
I raised her since she was knee high to a duck!
Dr. Brown ain't yo' mother. [reminder that the final authority whose advice is to be followed
    is always the mother—often said after a child has quoted a teacher or a doctor or even a
    minister]
You talk back to me, gal, I'll knock you into next week!

God don't like ugly!

Old Lady Know-it-all died last year.

A hard head makes a soft behind.

You got to crawl before you can walk.

A po' dog is glad of a whippin'.

There are three kinds of people in this world: those who make things happen, those who watch things happen, and those who wonder, "What happened?"

When you're down and out, raise your head high and shout, "I'm out o' here!"

What you don't have in your head, you got to have in your feet.

The chickens come home to roost.

When trouble sleeps, don't wake 'im up.

Feed the devil wit' a *long* spoon.

Heep a good cotton stalks get chopped up from 'sociatin' wid de weeds.

If you don't want to trade with the devil, keep out of his shop.

If you make yourself an ass, folks will ride you.

If you live with dogs, you learn to howl.

If you play with dogs, you get bitten.

You run with dogs, you get fleas.

A dog that will bring a bone will carry one.

Don't put the cart before the horse.

Don't swap the Devil for a witch.

An open door admits many visitors.

You made your bed, now lie in it.

If you make your bed hard, it's you gon' have to lie on it.

If you can't stand the heat, you better git outta the kitchen.

If you're wearing rags, stay away from the fire.

Live by the sword, you die by the sword.

Where there's smoke, there's fire.

Every tub must sit on its own bottom.

Look before you leap.

You have to take the fat with the lean.

Any poor dog will tuck his tail sometimes.

Even the biggest brook runs dry sometimes.

I don't keep nothin' hidden in the closet.

Don't ever forget on what side yo' bread is buttered.

One hand washes the other.

You scratch my back, I'll scratch yours.

We've got to all stand together or we will fall together. It's a whole lot easier to break a single stick than a bundle of sticks.

Nothing ventured, nothing gained.

A seldom visitor makes the best friend.

You can't hurry up good times by waitin' for 'em.

The first one to the spring gets the clearest water.

Naught from naught leaves naught.

Don't cry over spilt milk.

Don't worry. A dog wants a bone more than once.

You never miss your water till your well runs dry.

The sun ain't gon' shine in your door always.

It's six in one hand and a half-dozen in the other.

Robbing Peter to pay Paul.

The rich get richer and the poor get chirren.

He's not gon' buy the cow if he can get the milk for free.

You be safe long as you remember to keep your dress down and your drawers up.

Keep your drawers up and your knees shut

If you give an inch, they'll take a foot.

He's a chip off the old block, and the chip don't fall too far from the block the leaves don't fall too far from the tree.

Chip off the old block tastes like timber.

The gourd will follow the vine.

Where there's smoke, there's fire.

Pity the bee that don't make no mo' honey than she want.

The bird can't fly with one wing.

The littlest snow flakes make the deepest snow.

There's more than one way of skinning a cat.

It's a mighty bad wind that never shifts.

It don't rain every time the clouds gather.

Be careful what you pray for, cause you just might get it.

It takes two birds to make a nest.

It's many a slip between the cup and the lip.

Don't worry that the right man hasn't come along yet. Remember, there's a lid for every pot.

"If it don't fit don't force it." [Mother Love, *Listen Up*, 55]

Take what you can get until you get what you want.

Walk with a crooked stick until you can find a straight one.

Don't cut up more than you can eat.

Monkey see, monkey do.

Crow and corn can't grow in the same field.

If you gon' dig a hole for someone, you better dig two.

Gal, you can't spit in my face and call it rain. [spoken to one who is trying to deceive]

Boy, you can't piss on me and tell me it's raining.

Who the cap fit, wear it.

Don't shout before the spirit rises.

The dead man can't hire his own gravedigger.

The graveyard is the cheapest boarding house.

Sister to Sister

You may not get all you pay for, but you will damn sho pay for all you get.

I keep my money in my bra cause they're the only two suckers I can trust.

Don't let your mouth write a check your ass can't cash.

You got to play big to win big.

Whatever you do, be sure to C-Y-O. [cover your ass]

You run your mouth; I'll run my business.

Friends are few and far between.

Just cause you paranoid don't mean somebody is not after you.

Wait for you! I don't wait! Weight broke the mule's back/Weight broke the wagon down.

If you not gon' shit, git off the pot.

Girl, don't pay no tention to what dey call you. Labels are for canned goods and you sho don't sit aroun' on nobody's grocery shelf.

Girl, when you gonna wake up and smell the coffee!

All he's looking for is a one-night stand.

Don't let him tell you to play like Jack and Jill and go up the hill for no *water*. Water don't run up hill.

Remember what one strawberry said to the other: "If we hadn't gone to bed together we wouldn't be in this *jam* today."

[Speaking to women thinking of cheating] "You think the grass is greener somewhere else? If your grass is brown it's because you haven't been waterin it, tending to it." [Mother Love, *Listen Up*, 127]

Note

1. Daryl Cumber Dance and N. Giovanni, "Mama Sez" and "Sister to Sister," in *Honey, Hush! An Anthology of African American Women's Humor* (New York, NY: W.W. Norton, 1998), pp. 83–97.

W. Barlow

After the minstrel tradition and Black vaudeville, Black radio then entered the commercial marketplace. The excerpts here focus on the Black radio disc jockeys, or DJs, who by the 1940s, 1950s, and 1960s came to be known as personality jocks for their larger-than-life personalities on air. Much of this was due to their speech on the radio, rapping and rhyming while cueing up a record or at the start of playing a record. In 1948, Doctor Hep Cat (Lavada Durst) began his foray into this kind of disc jockeying at KVET in Austin, Texas. Among the more celebrated Black disc jockeys of this mold was also Douglas "Jocko" Henderson, who, beginning in the 1950s, worked at radio stations in Baltimore, Philadelphia, and eventually New York. Like Durst, Henderson would also craft his own unique rhymes in a kind of jive talk or rap similar to the rhyming that appeared many years later in the first rap record.

The Rise of Black Appeal Radio

W. Barlow[1]

The coming of a new and growing wave of African American disc jockeys on the nation's airwaves was linked to a chain of events that ultimately led to the emergence of the first "black appeal" stations in the country. Instead of earmarking a percentage of their airtime for black-oriented shows, these local outlets committed their entire broadcast schedules to programming by and for African Americans. For the most part, this transition—unthinkable prior to World War II—was economically driven. During the postwar years, the radio industry's control over national programming, advertising, and listenership collapsed when the major networks focused on television. Radio again became a local and laissez-faire enterprise, in which stations had to fend for themselves amid increasingly cutthroat competition. In these circumstances, the black radio consumer could no longer be ignored—especially in urban markets, where African Americans constituted a substantial percentage of the total population. Ironically, the first radio stations to switch over to black appeal formats were located in the South, and all but one were white owned. As with programs like *King Biscuit Time*, the dictates of the local Southern marketplace prevailed over the customs of segregation.

A Black Appeal Beacon: WDIA

The first major breakthrough for a black appeal station took place in Memphis, Tennessee, where African Americans made up 40 percent of the population in the postwar era. Like most large industrial and commercial centers in the South, Memphis prospered and grew considerably during the war years; business was profitable and jobs plentiful. At the same time, the city continued to maintain a rigid color line and tolerate a corrupt political machine, run by E. H. "Boss" Crump, a wily segregationist who lorded over local politics and vice from the 1910s to the 1940s. In spite of the backward machine politics, however, the economic climate in Memphis remained bullish in the postwar period, especially in the field of broadcasting. Television was still out of most families' reach, and radio prevailed as the most popular, profitable, and ubiquitous broadcast medium. While the networks were preoccupied with bringing TV on line, in Memphis, radio again was becoming accessible to entrepreneurs and open to format innovations.

In the middle of 1947, two white Memphis business associates, John Pepper and Bert Ferguson, launched WDIA—a low-power, 250 watt daytime operation. It was the city's sixth AM radio station. Pepper was the scion of a wealthy Memphis family with extensive business interests in the Mississippi Delta. A graduate of Duke University, he had owned a radio station downriver, at Greenville, Mississippi. After serving as a naval pilot during World War II, he returned to his hometown ready to start another radio station. He recruited an old friend and fellow radio enthusiast, Bert Ferguson, as a partner in the project. Ferguson, another Memphis native and a college graduate who served in the navy during the war, had worked for Pepper at the Greenville station. Pepper put up most of the $48,000 to start WDIA, while Ferguson applied for the FCC license and then managed the station's day-to-day operations. WDIA signed on the air June 7 with a country-and-western music format; but business was slow, and within a year the struggling newcomer switched to a classical music format. Late in 1948, with the station still in the red and on the auction block, Ferguson convinced his reluctant partner to try black appeal.

While an announcer and engineer for WBHQ in Memphis in the late 1930s, Ferguson had engineered the late-night remote broadcasts of the city's traditional *Midnight Ramble*, a local African American vaudeville review staged exclusively for white folks at a Beale Street theater every Thursday evening. These broadcasts were hosted by the master of ceremonies of the *Midnight Ramble*, Nat D. Williams, one of Beale Street's favorite sons. Ferguson was impressed by Williams's rapport with the white audience and by the unique crossover appeal of the weekly broadcast. Not only was it popular among white listeners, but as he learned from Williams, the *Midnight Ramble* show was also a source of pride in the local black community. Almost ten years later, Williams was Ferguson's first choice for hosting a daily show on WDIA. It was a brilliant stroke that changed the station's fortunes and established a formidable black community institution.

Ferguson and Pepper were aware of the political and economic risks in their venture. As Ferguson later recalled: "The atmosphere was such, with Crump running everything, and we could see him saying, 'Look, we don't want any nigger radio station in town.'" To avoid opposition from the city's hard-line segregationists, WDIA moved gradually and without fanfare toward an all-black format, in the hope that the changes would go undetected.

"Product identification" was their major economic worry. At the time, the rule of thumb in the advertising end of the radio business was that black appeal shows imposed an undesirable racial image on the sponsor's product; the products thus identified with Africans Americans would be shunned by whites. Conventional wisdom dictated that only advertising for products and services sold exclusively to the black population made sense on black appeal shows. Ferguson and Pepper couldn't afford to lose the few regular white sponsors they had on WDIA, but they also saw great potential in the untapped African American market. As Ferguson put it: "The Negro market has become too important to be overlooked or ignored any longer in this day of strong competition for the consumer dollar—and the Negro's money has the same golden color as anyone's!" Applying the same strategy they used with the politicians, WDIA's owners proceeded cautiously, saying nothing to the sponsors about the format changes taking place. The station produced its first black appeal program and began to cultivate a new audience among African Americans. The hope was that once the ratings were up, the advertisers would go along with the changes.

The Radio Genius of Nat D.

WDIA's first African American disc jockey, Nat D. Williams, was short in stature and almost blind; nonetheless, he was a towering visionary in the Memphis black community—a virtual Renaissance man. His remarkable career as an educator, newspaper columnist, showman, promoter, producer, and radio broadcaster spanned four decades, from the 1930s to the 1960s, and was full of pioneering achievements. Born in 1909 in a house on Beale Street—the fabled hub of African American cultural and social life in Memphis—Williams was raised by his mother, a dancer in local vaudeville revues, and his grandmother, who nurtured his lifelong love of learning. Throughout his life, Nat D. was plagued by terrible eyesight and wore thick glasses; friends gave him the nickname "3-D" in the 1950s. Yet, despite his poor vision, Williams graduated from high school with honors and earned a degree in history at Tennessee Agricultural and Industrial (A & I) College, a black college in nearby Nashville. He worked a short time as a journalist in New York City, then returned to Memphis in the early 1930s and took a job teaching history at Booker T. Washington High School. Long before the standard high school texts had any mention of it, he was including material on African Americans and Native Americans in his U.S. history classes. His popular lectures on famous black and American Indian historical figures who were in the forefront of their people struggles against white domination were memorable eye-openers to the legions of students who passed through his classes.

Williams was a formidable newspaper essayist. His weekly column in the *Memphis World*, called "Down on Beale Street," belongs to a tradition in American journalism that dates back to Frederick Douglass and even Tom Paine. The columns were outspoken in their advocacy of political rights, economic opportunity, and racial pride for African Americans. Williams was particularly concerned with the color line in American society and wrote some of his most elegant and provocative columns condemning it. He published the following in 1946:

> Too long and too deeply has consciousness of color pervaded our lives. It sinks into the souls of our saints, tainting their saintliness. It seeps into the minds of our children, making them old before their time. It rides into the consciousness of our young men, warping their dreams. It shackles the minds of our scholars, making them intellectual eunuchs. Too long has it been drummed into my ears and seared on my consciousness that the Negro woman's bed is the playground of the world. The Negro press, stage and screen glorify only the Negro woman who has white features. The nation's press and movies portray the typical Negro woman as Aunt Jemima, despite the counteracting refinement of a Madame Bethune or Marian Anderson. I hope to see the day, black as I am, when men will not be afraid to be fair, when they can welcome justice in their courts; allow truth a real hearing in their schools, churches and homes; and make the lust for gold and power secondary to the urge for service and human welfare. I hope I can live to see the day, black as I am, when colored folks here in the United States will have a common ideal rather than a common misery.

In another column, written early the same year, Williams wrote candidly about his color: "I'm black, Jack, black as a hundred midnights in a cypress swamp. But may I remind you, I ain't mad about it. This black is all right with me, it hasn't cost me a dime. I pay only for ignorance—not my blackness." Over the years, Williams's columns in the *Memphis World* were periodically reprinted in the *Pittsburgh Courier* and the *Chicago Defender;* as a consequence, he gained a national reputation as a champion of racial justice.

In his role as a Beale Street impresario, Williams emceed the *Midnight Ramble* and was also the driving force behind the legendary Amateur Night at the Palace Theater, initiated in the late 1930s. Every Tuesday evening, aspiring musicians, dancers, comics, vocalists, and fans from Memphis and the surrounding rural counties would converge on the Palace Theater on Beale Street, to compete for the amateur title or to cheer for their favorite contestants. Among those who won the coveted title over the years were future R & B luminaries B. B. King, Bobby "Blue" Bland, Al Hibler, Johnny Ace, Rufus Thomas—and a young, white farm boy named Elvis Presley. Nat D. was involved in producing an entertainment extravaganza and parade for the popular "Memphis Cotton Makers' Jubilee," a yearly event held simultaneously on both sides of the city's color line—whites called it the "Memphis Cotton Carnival"—which was similar to Mardi Gras in New Orleans. He also produced and hosted an annual musical fund-raiser for Booker T.

Washington High School, using student talent. These local entertainment ventures increased Williams's stature in the city and provided him with an unexpected bridge to radio broadcasting.

Tan Town Jamboree, Williams's original show on WDIA, premiered on October 25, 1948, at 3 P.M. At the start of the broadcast, the novice radio host made a gaffe that became his trademark on the air; as he recalled, "When he [the cue man] pointed his finger at me, I forgot everything I was supposed to say. So I just did what became typical of me. I laid out for dead. I just started laughing 'cause I was laughing my way out. And the man said, 'The people seem to like that,' and we made it standard. So ever since then, Nat has started his program laughing and closed his program laughing."

Williams's booming baritone laugh, along with his folksy rapport with his listeners, became the focal point of his DJ personality. He would open his show with his raucous laugh and then the rhyme "Well, yes siree, its Nat D. on the Jamboree, comin' at three on AM seventy-three. Now whatchu bet?" In a similar vein, he sprinkled his radio discourse with folk witticisms: "Worryin' is just like a rockin' chair, lots of movement, but you ain't getting nowhere." Like Daddy-O Daylie and Doctor Hep Cat, Nat D. was one of the early black disc jockeys in the country who incorporated rhyming and signifying into his style of broadcasting. In spite of his educational position, he chose to speak like a Beale Street sage.

The musical format that Williams pioneered on WDIA was a dramatic shift from the classical music it replaced. He described the transition as follows: "We came up with the idea of giving them some blues. Only thing is, the only black record the station had was 'Stomping at the Savoy'—which became my first theme song—and it was by a white writer. We started scrounging around and finally got some records by blues artists like Fats Waller and Ivory Joe Hunter and then we had to clean them up. Some of these records were—well—suggestive. And the way I cleaned them up was, when it got to be suggestive, I'd just start laughing and talking. First thing you know, it caught on. The listeners were ready for a different sound."

Initially, however, white listeners were hostile. Outraged callers demanded: "Get that nigger off the air!" There were even a few bomb threats. One irate woman admonished: "If John Pepper's grandfather could see what's going on here now, he would turn over in his grave!" (Pepper's grandfather was a Delta plantation and slave owner during the Civil War.) Black listeners, by contrast, were elated and flooded the station with letters praising the show. The African American response was so overwhelming that in a matter of weeks, Williams was doing two additional shows: *Tan Town Coffee Club* in the mornings and *Nat D.'s Supper Club* in the evenings. The station was becoming a black appeal outlet.

Williams had no illusions about his employers' motives. In his *Memphis World* column, he openly discussed the proposition with his readers: "They are businessmen. They don't necessarily love Negroes. They make that clear. But they do love progress and are willing to pay the price to make progress. One of the most neglected markets in the Mid South is the Negro market. And that's true because so many white businessmen take the Negro for granted." In a different literary vein, Williams's column forecast the financial breakdown of the color line:

'Mongst all this talk
'Bout integration
As collud folks balk
'Gainst segregation
Looms one bodacious tho't:
It's called dollar-gration!

Yet, while Nat D. clearly recognized the untapped potential of the African American market, at no time in his radio career did he make any effort to exploit it as an entrepreneur. Instead, he approached the endeavor as a race activist, much as he approached his entertainment projects. Unlike Jack Cooper and Al Benson, Williams did not make a fortune in radio broadcasting; for the most part, he and his family continued to live on his modest teacher's salary. Nevertheless, his impact on the development of black appeal radio would be as far-reaching as that of Cooper and Benson.

WDIA's transition to an all-black format, which took a little less than a year, was orchestrated by Nat D. Williams with the advice and consent of General Manager Bert Ferguson. Williams was the mastermind behind most of the new programs that debuted on the station in the wake of *Tan Town Jamboree*'s surprising breakthrough. Shows included religious broadcasts, public-affairs offerings, women's programming, gospel music shows, and more R & B shows. In addition, Williams was the major conduit for most of the African Americans who came to be employed by WDIA as on-air staff. Ferguson was more than willing to go along with these recommendations after he discovered the station's ratings were skyrocketing. In the spring of 1949, WDIA jumped from last to second in the Memphis radio market, attracting 17 percent of the local listening audience; by the fall of 1949, it was number one in the market, with 28 percent of listeners regularly tuning in. Simultaneously, WDIA completed its transition to a totally black format.

WDIA's Sunday broadcast schedule converted to black appeal programming early in the transition period. Most of the day was given over to a variety of religious offerings. Three live fifteen-minute segments featured the city's most acclaimed African American gospel quartets: the Spirit of Memphis, the Southern Wonders, and the all-female Songbirds of the South. In addition, a series of remote broadcasts of religious services featured prominent black churches, including the Baptist congregation of Dr. Herbert Brewster, the city's leading African American minister and one of the country's foremost gospel composers. Finally, Nat D. hosted a Sunday-morning Bible class for WDIA's younger listeners, as well as a roundup of local church news and community affairs announcements.

Williams's most ambitious and controversial public-affairs show was *Brown America Speaks*. The thirty-minute Sunday-afternoon roundtable forum, featuring some of the city's leading black citizens and hosted by a more somber Nat D. Williams than appeared on the blues programs, premiered on September 11, 1949, at 4:30 p.m. It quickly became known for candid discussions of racially charged subjects, such as the segregation of the city's public facilities, job and wage discrimination in the workforce, and police brutality in the black community. *Brown America Speaks* won an award for public-service excellence in 1950 from Ohio State's Institute for Education in Radio and Television. It also generated a good deal of hate mail. Williams's daughter recalled that her father would receive a regular barrage of these letters on the Tuesday after the Sunday broadcasts, regardless of the topic, and that many were routinely written by the same irate white listeners. Nat D. also had a hand in initiating such WDIA public-affairs offerings as *Good Neighbors*, a thirty-minute Sunday-evening program that weekly highlighted a "good neighbor" who was making a positive contribution to the black community, and *Workers Wanted*, a biweekly listing of local employment opportunities for African Americans.

A Woman's Place Is on the Air

Another dimension of WDIA's unique black appeal format were the programs by and for African American women. The first, *Tan Town Homemakers*, aimed at middle-class black housewives, debuted in August 1949. *Homemakers* was broadcast from 9 to 10 A.M. on weekdays and hosted by Willa Monroe, the reigning diva of Memphis's African American social elite. Monroe's lover, Robert Wright—a wealthy bandleader and show business entrepreneur who owned the city's premier black nightclub, the Brown Derby—had given her a twenty-room mansion, where she lavishly entertained their many friends. One of those in Monroe's social set was Nat D. Williams, and her guest appearances on his shows led directly to her being hired at WDIA. *Tan Town Homemakers* was a mix of soft ballads by such female artists as Eartha Kitt, Sarah Vaughan, and Dinah Washington; Willa's favorite recipes and homemaker hints; "women's news" from the society pages of the local black newspaper; and interviews with other local African American women of prominence. Monroe was an overnight sensation on WDIA. According to the spring 1950 ratings, 40 percent of the Memphis listening audience tuned in to her show. She was in such great demand among her female fans that she held office hours to accommodate their requests for homemaker counseling. The startling success of the *Homemakers* show paved the way for more women's programming on the station.

The next wave of African American women heard on WDIA in the early 1950s included two teaching colleagues of Nat D. Williams, Gerry Brown and Carlotta Stewart Watson, as well as Star McKinney and Martha Jean Steinberg. Gerry Brown won the station's first female disc-jockey contest in 1950 and was hired as hostess for a ballad-dominated R & B show called *Nite Spot*, on weeknights from 9 to 10 P.M. Brown ended her radio career when she married nearly a year later. Carlotta Stewart Watson, who used the name Aunt Carrie on the airwaves, produced and hosted *Spotlight*, a fifteen-minute weekday-morning call-in show that focused on advice for love and family problems. Star McKinney, hired as the station's "society editor" in 1950, soon started hosting a weekend society news segment. The reigning beauty queen of the Cotton Makers' Jubilee, McKinney also teamed up with Robert "Honeyboy" Thomas for the Saturday-morning show *Boy Meets Girl*, which featured the romantic ballads of black crooners and chanteuses, such as Nat King Cole and Dinah Washington.

By far the most successful and popular black female DJ to emerge on WDIA in the 1950s was Martha Jean Steinberg, who took on the radio name "Martha Jean the Queen." The Memphis native was married to a local musician, trumpeter Luther Steinberg, and was active in the local African American community as a fashion show producer before joining the station. After placing second in WDIA's disc-jockey contest, Martha Jean was recruited to cohost a Sunday-evening show with Nat D. Williams. He was the "old-timer" who preferred the swing-era recordings of Duke Ellington, Fats Waller, Ella Fitzgerald, and Jimmy Lunceford, whereas she was the "new-timer" who favored such R & B artists as Laverne Baker, the Clovers, Ruth Brown, and the Drifters. On the air, the regal Martha Jean exuded feminine savvy and sex appeal; her sultry voice was equally attractive to male and female listeners. Before long, she replaced Gerry Brown as the disc jockey on *Nite Spot*, then took over as the hostess of *Tan Town Homemaker* when ill health forced Willa Monroe to retire from radio. Steinberg also replaced Star McKinney as cohost of *Boy Meets Girl*, and she launched her own Saturday-afternoon show, *Premium Stuff*, which showcased the week's hottest R & B discs. By the end of the decade, Martha Jean truly was WDIA's queen of the airwaves. Her hard work and perseverance had won for her a privileged place in the station's male-dominated pantheon of radio personalities. As such, she was an important female broadcast pioneer, not just in Memphis but throughout the country.

Spin Doctors of the Postwar Era

Sponsor's groundbreaking series on "Negro Radio" showcased African American disc jockeys, recognizing them as the driving force behind the emergence and profitability of the black appeal stations. Their pivotal position in the post–World War II radio industry enabled African American DJs to fill the coffers of their white employers even as they gave voice to the aspirations, concerns, and sensibilities of their own people. In the words of Martha Jean "the Queen" Steinberg, the mid-South's premier black female disc jockey in the the 1950s.

We were the mayors back then. At that particular time, you have to understand that you didn't have any black politicians, no black judges, very few black lawyers . . . you didn't have any so-called black leaders. So we were the ones who spoke out. We were considered the mayors of the cities. . . . We were shaping the minds and hearts of the people, and we did a good job. We encouraged them to go to school, to get degrees, to be educated. Told them about racial pride. We talked to young girls about not having babies. We kept our communities intact.

For the most part, the black disc jockeys who rose to prominence in the postwar years were inspired by the Al Benson, not the Jack Cooper, school of broadcasting. In their desire to celebrate and extend the black oral tradition, rather than emulate the white cultural mainstream, they relied on verbal strategies of African American folklore—especially rhyming and signifying. These traditional modes of expression were meant to be entertaining, but they also masked the messages going out over the air. Steinberg explains: "We were bright people—independent thinkers . . . even philosophers. But we had to act like clowns to get our point across and not upset anything, or let anyone know we were upsetting anything." This "double-voiced" discourse, embedded in the DJs' speech and the musical messages, was the key to their appeal as African American broadcasters. Yet, ironically, it marked a return to the wellspring of the black oral tradition and an inversion of the blackface ventriloquy that had dominated the airwaves in the previous era.

The Travels of "Jack the Rapper": Jack Gibson

One of the most successful graduates of the Al Benson school of broadcasting was Jack Gibson, the man who would later be known as "Jack the Rapper" throughout the world of black entertainment. Gibson, a native of Chicago, was a graduate of Lincoln University, a black college located in Jefferson City, Missouri. In the early 1940s, he studied drama at Lincoln and led the student jazz orchestra. Degree in hand, he returned to his hometown seeking a job as a film actor; but after being rejected as "too light to play a Negro and too dark to pass for white," he ventured into radio. His first broadcasting job was in 1945 as a character actor in Richard Durham's pioneering black soap opera Here Comes Tomorrow. Within a year, he was also hosting a nightly thirty-minute music show on WJJD, the same station that sponsored the soap opera.

In 1948, Al Benson took note of Gibson's music show and took the fledgling DJ under his wing, as an assistant on Benson's morning R & B show. According to Gibson:

I would go and pick him up every morning at his house. He always insisted that I stop at the local liquor store and get a bottle of Hennessy—quart bottles. I took that and the 78 records that we had with us in to the studio. I would set up his quart bottle of Hennessy with a glass and give his stack of 78s to the engineer. Al would sit there and take a sip, then signal his engineer to play a record or open the mike. I sat in the corner and watched, sometimes waiting for him to nod off so I could take over. But he never missed a cue. So I just watched him and answered the phones, which were always ringing off the hook.

During his apprenticeship with Benson, Gibson heard and saw first-hand how his mentor was able to attract and hold such a huge audience: "He was very flamboyant and very outspoken and very earthy, and then I guess maybe the people at that time from Chicago—you know, they came from Louisiana and Mississippi—they were used to hearing people mess up the King's English. So Al was their man. And that taught me to break up a few verbs myself, and I found out that it worked!" Having grown up in Chicago, Gibson was familiar with Jack Cooper's efforts on the local airwaves, as well as with the stylistic and language differences between the professional-sounding Cooper and Benson: "Jack Cooper, he was a straight announcer, so he'd say, 'Look here, I hope you all go to Aunt Mami's Beauty Saloon, because she has a new special.' Al Benson would probably say, 'Y'all need yo' hair fried? Better get on down to Auntie Mami's, she gotta thing goin' on. Tell her Ole Swingmaster send yal' See, that was the difference, that was a personality against what we called a straight announcer."

Jack Gibson worked for Al Benson until the fall of 1949, when an old college friend made a tempting offer. J. B. Blayton Jr.'s father had just purchased radio station WERD in Atlanta. Blayton was leaving Chicago for Atlanta to manage the outlet and wanted Gibson to come with him and be his program director. Gibson jumped at the chance to work for the first black-owned radio station in the country. As WERD's program director, charged with switching the station over to a black appeal format, he had a difficult first year; but with the support of the Blaytons, he changed the programming and replaced most of the all-white on-air personnel with African Americans. Gibson also worked as a regular disc jockey on WERD, putting to good use what he had learned from Al Benson. By 1951, WERD had become Atlanta's leading black appeal station, and Jack Gibson was the city's most popular DJ.

Later in 1951, Gibson moved on to WLOU in Louisville, Kentucky, home of the Kentucky Derby, where he became known on the airwaves as "Jockey Jack." Resplendent in a silk jockey outfit and carrying a leather riding crop for publicity, he liked to open his show with the traditional Derby bugle call and the following incantation:

My father wasn't a jockey, but he sure taught me to ride. He sat right in the middle, then rocked from side to side. Ride, Jockey Jack, Ride!

Two years later, Gibson was on the move again—this time to WMDM in Miami, where he hosted the station's afternoon R & B show and worked as program director. It was at WMBM that Jack Gibson made national headlines for his ill-fated Ballantine beer giveaway, when the police arrested him and his station manager for disturbing the peace. The Miami police assumed that Gibson, like the WMDM general manager, was white; both were held in a cell reserved for white lawbreakers, where the press photographed them peering out from behind bars. When Jockey Jack returned to his hotel in Miami's black business district, the manager, having seen the photo in the local press, concluded that Gibson was a white man trying to pass for black and demanded that he vacate his room. It took the bemused DJ a while to convince the manager otherwise.

Late in 1954, Gibson returned to WERD in Atlanta, resuming his duties as program director and disc jockey and honing his skills as a broadcaster and community activist. In 1958, he accepted a similar position and the challenge of creating a black appeal format for WCIN in Cincinnati. Dudley Riley, a former DJ who grew up in Cincinnati, recalled the transition: "Well, CIN did not exist . . . as a black station in the city prior to Jack's coming. . . . I think Jack got to the people first, he related to the music they wanted to hear, and he himself was a dynamic type of individual. He brought that over onto the air, and then he got out and met the people. He brought the black businessmen into CIN for advertising and things of that nature, so then the blacks actually participated in CIN. Before it was practically all white."

Early in 1962, the founder of Motown Records, Berry Gordy, lured Jockey Jack away from radio broadcasting and hired him as the fledgling labels' national director of Promotions and Public Relations. For the next five years, Gibson visited black appeal radio outlets around the country, promoting Motown's latest releases. He was also involved in producing the legendary Motown Revue concert tours, becoming a "big brother" figure to many of the label's young stars (like Diana Ross and Stevie Wonder).

Although he left his disc-jockey career behind when he went to work for Motown, Jack Gibson never lost interest in black appeal radio. Over the years, as the industry changed, he became increasingly concerned with what he viewed as the decline of the community and personality style of broadcasting that he had helped pioneer in the 1950s. By 1976, this concern led to the founding of Jack the Rapper, a monthly trade publication that targeted black radio and music enterprises. Under Gibson's guidance, the magazine became an advocate for African American personality jocks and black appeal programming in an era of "urban contemporary" crossover formats. As an extension of his trade publication, he also launched the annual Jack the Rapper Black Family Affair Convention in 1977. Initially held in Atlanta, the three-day music and radio convention quickly grew into the largest regular gathering of African Americans working in these industries. Both endeavors catapulted Gibson back to the forefront of the black entertainment world, where he remains to this day.

Journeyman Jock: "Joltin'" Joe Howard

African American disc jockeys such as Gibson moved frequently from job to job because of low wages, lack of job security, and changing fortunes in the radio industry. As more black appeal stations went on the air, new and usually more lucrative employment opportunities opened up. "Joltin'" Joe Howard was just such a journeyman in black appeal radio during the postwar years. A native of Galveston, Texas, his earliest broadcast influence was George Prater, a local product who hosted the city's first R & B show, Harlem Echo, on KGBC beginning in 1949. Prater, who had been paralyzed in an auto accident, broadcast out of a makeshift bedroom studio; his show was the most popular black appeal program in the market throughout the 1950s. Howard broke into broadcasting as a DJ in nearby Houston on KNUZ, the city's pioneering black appeal station. KNUZ's nightly R & B show, begun in the late 1940s, was called The Beehive. Howard got the job because of his excellent diction and his natural ability to read commercial copy.

In 1952, Howard moved across town to a better-paying job with KYOK, a station that had just been taken over by the New Orleans–based OK Group. Once again, his ability to read copy was the deciding factor in his being hired. According to Howard: "It was a funny thing at KYOK. This was shortly after the OK chain had bought the station, and they brought in their format from New Orleans. All of their air personnel had names which made their identities unmistakable . . . or so the owners thought. Hotsy Totsy, Zing Zang, Dizzy Lizzy. So when I went over, they wanted to know what to name me . . . but I held out for my own name. The reason I held out and prevailed was because they really needed somebody who could read." Like many other black DJs, male and female, on the air-waves during the postwar era, Howard resisted this type of stereotyping by white management.

In 1954, Joe Howard made a brief foray into mainstream white radio as an announcer and a DJ. He was hired, with a substantial salary increase, by WAKE in Atlanta to be the voice behind their commercial spots and to host an evening pop-music show. But the crossover venture was short-lived. When a major sponsor discovered that the voice in his radio ads belonged to a black man, he demanded that the station owners get rid of Howard. Ironically, the sponsor had initially sought Howard out to congratulate him on his job performance. As Howard recalled: "So I got fired. They called me in and told me as gingerly as they could. . . . I got fired because I sounded too much like a white man is the way they put it." During this period, the black announcers who managed to cross over to mainstream white stations were hired because they were able to sound like the white announcers on the air; it was only when their racial ventriloquy was discovered, as in Howard's case, that problems arose.

WAKE's loss was WERD's gain. Howard was soon hired by J. B. Blayton Jr. to host the station's morning R & B show, even though Blayton was somewhat apprehensive about how Howard would get along with his "number-one cat," Jockey Jack Gibson. As it turned out, the two men became good friends; they often spent time together on Auburn Avenue, the hub of Atlanta's black community, and they sat in on each other's shows. Along with two of the station's other veteran disc jockeys, Roosevelt Johnson and Jimmy Winnington, they became known as the "four horsemen" of WERD. In the process, and under the tutelage of Jack Gibson, Joe Howard was finding his own voice and developing his own style as a personality jock.

In 1956, both Howard and Gibson were offered disc-jockey positions at a new black-owned radio station in Inkster, Michigan, by Larry Dean Faulkner, the outlet's first program director. Faulkner, the son of a Chicago minister, had attended Fisk University in Nashville, where he helped launch that city's first black appeal station, WSOK; he was then hired by the owner of WCHB, Dr. Haley Bell, to do the same thing for Bell's Inkster operation. Faulkner's recruiting trip to Atlanta was only partially successful: Joe Howard accepted the offer, but Jack Gibson chose to stay with WERD for the time being. WCHB was located on the edge of the Detroit radio market, facing stiff competition from WJLB, the city's reigning black appeal outlet. At the time, WJLB featured an all-star lineup of black personality jocks: "Rockin'" Leroy White, "Frantic" Ernie Durham, "Senator" Bristow Bryant, and Miss Susie Strother—all of whom had large followings. Nevertheless, within a year of signing on the air, WCHB was challenging WJLB for the leadership position in the black appeal segment of the market, and "Joltin'" Joe Howard was the hottest new DJ on the Detroit airwaves.

Faulkner borrowed Howard's nickname from "Joltin'" Joe DiMaggio, the baseball star; it fit nicely with Howard's animated, rapid-fire style of broadcasting. As Howard recalled:

> What happened was when I went in, my style was new. The thing that was different about my style was that it was fast-paced. I talked faster than any other human being on radio, yet I was articulate and understandable. I used a lot of slang because that was the order of the day, but I used it in a cutesy way, rather than really getting down. Of course . . . I stole a lot of Jack's stuff. He was still in Atlanta. I stole a lot of it and went up to Detroit. I used the theme song he used to use by Big Jay McNeely called "The Goose." The record came on and was fast-paced with a break. When the break came, I would say something like—"It ain't the Lone Ranger and Tonto!" Every morning I would say something different. People around town got to betting on what I'd say. "I bet he says Little Red Riding Hood! No, I bet five dollars he says Dick Tracy!" Little gimmicks like that caught on.

Over the next two decades, Joltin' Joe Howard was a popular fixture on black appeal radio in the Detroit market. He worked for WCHB until 1960, then switched over to WJLB for a seven-year run as their top DJ. In the late 1960s, Howard was involved in launching WGPR, Detroit's premier progressive black FM station.

Space Commander: Douglas "Jocko" Henderson

Perhaps the most celebrated black disc jockey to emerge in the 1950s was Douglas "Jocko" Henderson, the space-age commander of the legendary Rocket Ship shows, broadcast in a number of key urban markets throughout the country:

> Once again it's rocket ship time.
> And those not on board must be outta their mind.
> The rocketeers are lined up side by side,
> ready to take their most exciting ride.
> From earth to the moon you gotta go,

with your rocket ship commander—Jocko.
We'll be on the moon if the fuel will last.
So let's leave the earth with a big bad blast.
[Sound effect: rocket ship blasting off]
Way up here in the stratosphere,
gonna holler mighty loud and clear.

Eeeh, tiddley-tock,
Yo! This is the Jock.
Back on the scene,
with my record machine.
Saying oo-poppa-do,
How do you do?
Dy-no-mite!
Now on with the flight.

Douglas Henderson grew up in segregated Baltimore, Maryland. His mother was a teacher, and his father, who had a doctorate in education, was the superintendent of the city's black schools. At the urging of his father, who had a strong desire that his son follow in his footsteps, Henderson attended the Tuskegee Institute in Alabama from 1949 to 1952. But even while in college, his interests were gravitating toward radio; in particular, he was fascinated by the rhyming hipster Maurice "Hot Rod" Hulbert, who had reigned as the hottest black DJ in Baltimore since the debut of his Rocket Ship show on WITH late in 1950. While home on vacation in the summer of 1952, Henderson auditioned for a job as a DJ, and much to his father's dismay, he was hired. His original program, The Doug Henderson Show, debuted on WSID in June; it was a two-hour weekday afternoon time slot and paid him only $12 a week. Luckily, the novice disc jockey was able to supplement his meager radio salary by selling cars on the air until a better offer came along—which happened rather quickly.

Late in 1952, WHAT in Philadelphia offered Henderson an afternoon show for $50 a week; he played hard to get until the offer reached $120 a week, then agreed to it. Henderson used the move to Philadelphia as an opportunity to create an new radio persona for himself—one that owed a great deal to his Baltimore idol, Hot Rod Hulbert. As he recalled:

Anyway, I began to stop using Doug Henderson and just picked up . . . formed the name Jocko because Jocko rhymed with Daddy-O and Mommy-O, and the hottest show on radio. And instead of just having a regular show, we had a rocket-ship show. . . . I borrowed the rocket-ship show from Hot Rod, who was in Baltimore during that time. That's what he called his show. And we began to rhyme up everything—"Yo tiddley yock, this is the Jock, back on the scene in my record machine, sing oop bop a-doo, how do you do." All kinds of rhyme. And the kids picked up on this.

The practice of rhyming, part of the black oral tradition, was especially appealing to Henderson's African American audience.

"Jocko" Henderson reached overnight celebrity status in the Philadelphia radio market with his weekday afternoon Rocket Ship show. Within a matter of months, he was lured away from WHAT to rival WDAS for a $350 a week salary. Then, in 1954, he was hired by WLIB in New York City to host their morning show, and he began a daily commute between the two locations to do the broadcasts. In the mid-1950s, both WDAS and WLIB were highly rated black appeal outlets in their respective locales, and those two markets alone showcased many of the most popular and powerful R & B DJs in the country. In Philadelphia, the WDAS lineup included Jocko, the veteran Kai Williams, and the debonair John Bandy, known on the air as "Lord Fauntleroy." Bandy, whose family was from Jamaica, spoke with a British accent and wore an ascot as his trademark. Henderson was especially impressed with his demeanor on the air: "He used to rhyme up everything. . . . He was fantastic! Unbelievable!" (In the late 1950s, Lord Fauntleroy retired to a country estate outside Philadelphia, after a much-publicized interracial marriage to Gulf Oil heiress Roberta Pew.) WDAS's major competition came from WHAT, the station that initially brought Henderson to Philadelphia, whose lineup featured the city's original R & B DJ, Ramon Bruce (Ravin' with Ramon), as well as Larry Dixon and Georgie Woods—the "Man with the Goods." Woods would become the city's best-known African American disc jockey by the end of the decade, surpassing even Jocko in listenership and notoriety.

Although Jocko Henderson continued to reside in Philadelphia, his broadcasting career was increasingly centered in New York City. At WLIB, he joined an impressive roster of personality jocks, including Washington, D.C., veteran Hal Jackson; Jack Walker, the "Pear-Shaped Talker"; Phil "Doctor Jive" Gordon; comic Nipsy Russell; and jazz pianist Billy Taylor. The other leading black appeal disc jockeys in the market during the mid-1950s were Willie Bryant, the "Mayor of Harlem," on WHOM; and Tommy Smalls, the city's second "Doctor Jive," who broadcast in the afternoons on WWRL. Smalls's career in radio scripted like a classic American tragedy. The young, bush-league DJ from Savannah, Georgia, became an overnight sensation in the New York market. At the height of his career on WWRL, he not only hosted the city's top-rated afternoon R & B show but promoted local R & B concerts that rivaled those of rock-and-roll kingpin Alan Freed. He was a talent scout for Ed Sullivan's famous Toast of the Town TV variety show and appeared in person on the nationally televised CBS program to introduce the R & B acts. He was also the co-owner of a popular Harlem nightclub, Smalls Paradise. Then, in 1960, the bottom fell out: Tommy Smalls became a target of a New York City "payola" investigation. At age thirty-four, he was indicted for accepting over $13,000 in bribes from eighteen different record companies and subsequently was banished from the radio industry. A decade later, he died in poverty, a forgotten man.

Like Tommy Smalls, Jocko Henderson used his fame on the airwaves as a springboard to allied ventures in television and concert production. In the late 1950s, he launched Jocko's Rocket Ship Show on WNTA-TV, an independent Newark, New Jersey, television outlet. After hosting the live after-school dance party for black teenagers for about a year, Henderson abandoned the TV show. His inability to attract national sponsorship and network interest, despite excellent local ratings, left him angry and frustrated. As he later recalled: "The television industry, like radio before it, was very racist back then. Sponsors would not buy time, for example, on Nat King Cole's television show, even though he was popular among whites and blacks. If I had been a little further ahead in time, things might have been different for me. If I hadn't been black, American Bandstand [Dick Clark's popular ABC television show] might have been mine."

Henderson's R & B concert productions fared much better than his short-lived TV show. When he began staging R & B revues at the Apollo Theater in the mid-1950s, he faced stiff competition from Tommy Smalls, who used the Apollo as a venue for his own concerts. But when Smalls's various enterprises were shut down after the payola investigations, the Apollo Theater became, in effect, the house that Jocko built. His much-ballyhooed concerts there showcased the latest R & B luminaries: Sam Cooke, the Coasters, Clyde McPhatter, Smokey Robinson, the Supremes, Marvin Gaye, and Stevie Wonder. Like Al Benson, Jocko Henderson was a star attraction himself, and his appearances at the Apollo concerts were as eagerly received as the R & B acts he introduced. In fact, his Apollo Theater entrances were legendary; in his own words: "The guys at the Apollo built a rocket . . . wired it up in the air . . . and when the show started, they would turn it loose and it would glide down with the smoke and the lights . . . rocket sounds . . . and everything. It would glide to the center of the stage and I'd get out in my space suit saying,

'Yo tiddley-yock, this the the Jock . . . your ace from outta space!' And this killed the people. They fell out . . . couldn't believe it!" For these rocket-ship openings, Henderson wore an authentic U.S. Air Force space suit that had been donated to him as a publicity stunt by the Pentagon's space program.

During his Apollo Theater reign, the radio rocket man made international headlines for his most fabled space-age caper. In 1959, when Soviet cosmonaut Yuri Gagarin became the first man to orbit the Earth, one of Henderson's coworkers at WDAS in Philadelphia sent the Russian space pioneer the following telegram: "Congratulations! I'm really glad you made it. Now it's not so lonely up here." It was signed "Jocko Henderson, American Rocket Ship Commander." A few years later, a U.S. correspondent discovered that an enlarged copy of the telegram had been enshrined in a newly opened Moscow space museum. Apparently, the Russians thought Jocko was one of Yuri's American counterparts. Henderson was as surprised and bemused by the incident as everyone else: "Oh man, it was amazing. . . . You know, the Russians blew it up and encased it in plastic, first thing you see when you walk into the museum . . . and as far as I know, it's still there, even with the New York Times story saying, you know, Jocko ain't no rocket-ship man. He's a DJ. Yes, yes, yes, that's funny . . . that is really, really funny."

At the height of his career on the airwaves, Jocko Henderson had a large and devoted following not only in New York and Philadelphia but also in Boston, Washington, D.C., Miami, Detroit, and St. Louis, where tailor-made tapes of his Rocket Ship show were broadcast regularly. His "Rocketeers" fan club at the time claimed to have fifty thousand members. Henderson was so well known that when his idol and mentor, Hot Rod Hulbert, tried to break into the Philadelphia and New York radio markets in the late 1950s, he was invariably accused of imitating Jocko! Offended but undeterred, Hulbert tried in vain to set the record straight:

> All right Big Mommy-O and Big Daddy-O,
> keen teens in your blue jeans,
> ladies and Gentlemen everywhere:
> Commander Hot Rod is in place,
> the high priest of outer space.
> Not the imitator,
> I am the originator, the creator.
> Not the flower, not the root,
> but the seed, sometimes called the herb.

In this instance, however, the teacher proved no match for the student; outside of Baltimore, Hot Rod was never able to overcome the stigma of being a Jocko imitator.

The 1950s were the glory days for the signifying spin doctors, who seemed to be on the air everywhere. There was Doctor Hep Cat in Austin, Texas; two Doctor Jives in New York City and another one in Durham, North Carolina; Doctor Daddy-O in New Orleans and Houston; Doctor Jazzmo in Shreveport, Louisiana; Doctor Bop in Columbus, Ohio; and Doctor Feelgood in Atlanta. In addition, the country's black appeal outlets were the launching pads for Jocko and Hot Rod, Jocky Jack and Joltin' Joe, Moohah and Gatemouth, Honeyboy and King Bee, Butterball and Spiderman, Sugar Daddy, Daddy Deep Throat, and Daddy Rabbit, Satellite Poppa and Poppa Stoppa, Ravin' Ramon and Rockin' Leroy, Alley Cat and King Kong, the Black Pope and Prince Omar, Lord Fauntleroy and Sir Walter Raleigh, Genial Gene and Frantic Ernie, Jive Master Kolb, and Jack Walker the Pear-Shaped Talker. Behind these radio pseudonyms were the voices of the country's premier "personality jocks," as they came to call themselves—African American DJs who used their wits, guile, and imagination to break down Jim Crow in the radio industry and reshape the soundscape of the nation's airwaves. In the words of historian Portia Maultsby: "We can best describe African American DJs as performers. They connected with the community. They shucked and jived with the community. In spite of the microphones, DJs were committed to having a personal conversation with their audiences . . . which they did. So the oral tradition of storytelling, speaking in rhythm and rhyme, speaking in an improvised style, as well as an animated delivery, is a cultural expression that was familiar to the masses. Which is why so many people enjoyed personality radio."

Note

1. W. Barlow, *Voice Over: The Making of Black Radio* (Philadelphia: Temple University Press, 1999), pp. 106; 141–142.

⎯⎯⎯⎯◦◦◦◦⎯⎯⎯⎯

Section 2: Further Reading

Dolemite. Dir. D'urville Martin. Perf. Rudy Ray Moore, D'urville Martin, Jerry Jones, and Lady Reed. Dimension Pictures. 1975. Film. (Scenes of Moore telling toasts before a variety of audiences.)
Gaunt, Kyra. "Excerpts of 'Jumprope Songs'." In *The Games Black Girls Play*. New York: New York University Press, 2006.
McNeil, Dee Dee. "There's a Difference between a Black Man and a Nigger." In *Things Gonna Get Better: The Watts Prophets 1969–71*. LP. Water Music Records, 2005.
Ray. Dir. Taylor Hackford. Universal Studios. 2004. Film. (Music scenes demonstrating experimentation with crossing genres).
Talk to Me. Dir. Kasi Lemmons. Focus Features. 2007. Film. (Scenes demonstrating talk radio).
Womack, Bobby and J. J. Johnson. "Across 110th Street." Soundtrack. United Artists, 1972.

Section 2: Discussion Questions

1. Choose one of the theoretical readings in this section and identify and describe how the six elements of African American rhetoric, are either performed or demonstrated. To refresh, the six elements are (1) language; (2) style; (3) discourse; (4) perspective; (5) community; and (6) suasion.
2. Based on the theoretical readings in this section, identify and explain other elements of African American rhetoric that are different from the six above.
3. Based on the theoretical readings in this section, explain in your own words what African American rhetoric do?
4. Based on the theoretical readings in this section, explain in your own words how African American rhetoric lives?

3

RELIGION AND SPIRITUALITY/ TRANSPORTATIONS AND TRANSFORMATIONS OF SPIRITUALITY AND IDENTITY IN THE NEW WORLD

Edited and with an introduction by Kameelah Martin and Elizabeth West

Introduction

New World slavery issued in a race discourse that equated slavery with two interchangeable terms: Black and African. The populations captured and transported to fuel the plantation machine of the Americas were transformed into a monolithic people situated outside the boundaries of nationhood and humanity. By the close of the eighteenth century, colonial statesmen and intellectuals had led the way to cementing a view of Africans as having no human qualities worthy of serious consideration—and this included the matter of Black religiosity. The question of African religion was presumed answerable with a single and presumably obvious determination: that there was no such thing. Unacknowledged as legitimate faith systems, African supernatural beliefs were subjected to such reductive terms as "witchcraft," "black magic," and "superstition." This dismissal rested in the assertion that while religion originates in divine inspiration, its legitimacy is confirmed by specific markers: written texts, highly stylized writing and language, institutionalized practices and doctrines, and designated man-made structures for worship and management. Black spirituality was deemed mere emotion or impulse, arising out of whimsical beliefs that connected to no meditative reflection or divine inspiration. Within this ethnocentric and racialized view, if Blacks could be transformed into humanity at all, their primitive and pagan sensibilities would have to be exchanged for Anglo Christianity and its civilizing influence.

Despite this denigrating rhetoric of Black spirituality, Blacks in the New World would articulate a spiritual cosmology born out of their own cultural carryovers and those they adopted and transformed. The pre–Middle Passage ethoi of Africans enslaved in the Americas were as varied as their population group origins, and thus the origins of African American spiritual expressions are at least as varied. We find evidence of this in the early writings of Blacks who recalled their pre-American existence. Early to present-day African American authors reveal how New World Black identities and worldviews are shaped through ongoing negotiations of imposed Anglo Christian precepts and Black ways of knowing that originate outside White-fashioned religiosity. The works included in this section on African American spirituality show the beginnings and ongoing variations of Black spiritual expressions born out of this dynamic. In the early works of Olaudah Equiano and Omar ibn Said we find discourses of identity mergence that speak African humanity and history into existence: both articulate Christian conversion language that seemingly signals Black acquiescence. However, they connect their native Africa to symbols and discourses of

Christianity that ironically suggest similitude and possible common origins between Christianity and Africans. With his critique of flawed White Christians contrastingly cast against his recollection of the ideals and practices of Igbos (which ironically seem more Christian), Equiano clearly signifies on Whites and their presumptions of cultural and physical superiority.

Many of the works selected for this section illustrate the African oral tradition and especially its reliance on storytelling as a medium to explore and convey abstract and cultural ideas. Sojourner Truth's transcribed narrative exemplifies the integral legacy of this oral tradition: most striking in this regard are the recurring moments in her story that read like the African American spiritual practice of testifyin'. Similarly, as she recounts how she learned to balance the influences of Islam and Christianity as a resident on Sapelo Island, Cornelia Walker Bailey illustrates the folktale tradition of what has been named "sampling" in the hip-hop world. While not included in this section of the current volume, in "An Antebellum Sermon," Paul Lawrence Dunbar undermines White theological and sermonic tradition through the poem's spirited and clever poet-preacher. Dunbar captures the African American sermonic tradition that borrows from oral practices, such as improvisation, rhythm and rhyme, and call-and-response. A Black preacherly tradition is also established in the interpretation of Christianity and the Bible to articulate Black identity and to proclaim a liberation theology. This appropriation of scripture would vary in form and delivery: for example, in a dispassionate and controlled voice reminiscent of the Western classical tradition, Anna Julia Cooper's essay "The Gain From a Belief " (though not included in this volume) clearly contrasts the passionate, evocative voice of Dunbar's antebellum Black preacher. The voice of Jamaican native Marcus Garvey arguably represents a bridging of the classical influence in Cooper's text and the more folk-rooted expression of Dunbar's poetic voice. Ethiopianism serves as theological and ideological anchor in the Pan-Africanist vision of Garvey, and this discourse also exemplifies the politics of scriptural exegesis at work in countless African American sermons.

Martin Luther King Jr.'s "Eulogy for the Martyred Children" (though not included in this volume) highlights a classic example of religious posturing that has become indicative of the Black church, while Malcolm X used the foundational teachings of the Nation of Islam to wage battle against the impossible politics of 1960s America. The sacred, however, is not always distinct from the secular expressions of Black folk. Nowhere is this more evident than in Joseph Lowery's benediction at the first inauguration of President Barack Obama in 2009. Signifyin' on James Weldon Johnson's immortalized lyrics to "Lift Every Voice and Sing," Lowery's prayer also relies on the rhythmic cadence of Black southern dialect, the call and response of the congregation, and the acrobatics common in African American vernacular speech.

While the civil rights generation borrowed from biblical scripture and the Qu'ran to masterfully turn a phrase, the Black Arts movement reclaimed their Africanity and privileged cultural forms that acknowledged that African past. African cosmologies and spiritual retentions that had gone underground were revived in the explosion of written and oral literature that followed. Ishmael Reed infamously demonstrates how African cosmologies can be wielded as a powerful rhetorical tool against the hegemony of Western cultural supremacy. Reed's literary corpus also entreats the *visual* rhetoric of Vodou to convey meaning for his readers and as well as his political leanings. The various ways that African-centered spirituality continues to sustain and nourish the children of the African Diaspora is particularly evident in the discursive practices of women of color. Academia and spirituality find an unlikely pairing in bell hooks's "Walking in the Spirit," in which she addresses how being in touch with the divine—through routes such as dream life, ancestor worship, solitude, and spirit writing—can and should be the first avenue toward healing from depression, abuse, and the other traumas of life for Black women. Black women's prayers reveal the intimacy with the Divine that hooks is advocating. Removing the hierarchy of organized religion from Black women's spiritual praxis, Iyanla Vanzant's "A

Mother's Prayer for Her Unborn Child" revitalizes the language and point of view of traditional prayers to make both the idea and meaning of spirit work accessible for Black women to practice *any* and *every* where; with or *without* the pastor. Yet, Louis Farrakhan's oration on the divinity of Black women (though not included in this volume) raises many concerns about the use of religion to demean Black women in the same breath in which it calls upon their divinity.

It is commonly expressed that Black folk take their religion, their God with them at every turn. This sentiment finds validity in the way that African Americans openly and boldly cross their spiritual inclinations over into forums once thought antithetical to religion in mainstream belief: religion and politics; scripture and comedy act; Islam and gender rights; and even hip-hop has found God. There is arguably no larger influence on the linguistic sophistication and conveyance of African American speech than the religious and spiritual dispositions of that group.

Olaudah Equiano

These excerpts from the narrative of eighteenth-century ex-slave and seaman Olaudah Equiano (1745–1797) cover the period of his youth in his native Igbo society through his early experience and Christian conversion in captivity in the New World. Although he recounts his personal experiences, Equiano assumes a commonplace Western narrative voice for this time—that of the objective, outsider spectator. It is a voice that goes light on the emotional appeal, relying instead on the authority assumed in the neoclassical gaze and position of observation and fact finding. In large part, it is a comparative analysis of African and European ethoi and traditions. Without directly claiming the African's equal humanity and civil development to that of Europeans, Equiano infers this through his comparisons, along with his occasional criticisms of Europeans and their culture and concurrent praise of his native Igbo people and their society. The trick of Equiano's language play is his ironic appropriation of Western paradigms of civilization and humanity to illustrate European failings and Igbo endowments. Readers are drawn to his story, ironically, through the tempered, balanced voice he employs to convey unimaginable atrocities—in particular, the account of his initial captivity and the deadly transatlantic voyage to New World slavery.

The Interesting Narrative of the Life of Olaudah Equiano, or Gustavus Vassa, the African

Olaudah Equiano[1]

As to religion, the natives believe that there is one Creator of all things, and that he lives in the sun, and is girted round with a belt; that he may never eat or drink, but, according to some, he smokes a pipe, which is our own favorite luxury. They believe he governs events, especially our deaths or captivity; but, as for the doctrine of eternity, I do not remember to have ever heard of it; some, however, believe in the transmigration of souls in a certain degree. Those spirits which were not transmigrated, such as their dear friends or relations, they believe always attend them, and guard them from the bad spirits or their foes. For this reason they always, before eating, as I have observed, put some small portion of the meat, and pour some of their drink, on the ground for them; and they often make oblations of the blood of beasts or fowls at their graves. I was very fond of my mother, and almost constantly with her. When she went to make these oblations at her mother's tomb, which was a kind of small solitary thatched house, I sometimes attended her. There she made her libations, and spent most of the night in cries and lamentations. I have been often extremely terrified on these occasions. The loneliness of the place, the darkness of the night, and the ceremony of libation, naturally awful and gloomy, were heightened by my mother's lamentations; and these concurring with the doleful cries of birds, by which these places were frequented, gave an inexpressible terror to the scene.

We compute the year from the day on which the sun crosses the line, and on its setting that evening, there is a general shout throughout the land; at least, I can speak from my own knowledge, throughout our vicinity. The people at the same time make a great noise with rattles, not unlike the basket rattles used by children here, though much larger, and hold up their hands to heaven for a blessing. It is then the greatest offerings are made; and those children whom our wise men foretell will be fortunate are then presented to different people. I remember many used to come to see me, and I was carried about to others for that purpose. They have many offerings, particularly at full moons; generally two, at harvest, before the fruits are taken out of the ground; and when any young animals are killed, sometimes they offer up part of them as a sacrifice. These offerings, when made by one of the heads of a family, serve for the whole. I remember we often had them at my father's and my uncle's, and their families have been present. Some of our offerings are eaten with bitter herbs. We had a saying among us to anyone of a cross temper, "That if they were to be eaten, they should be eaten with bitter herbs."

We practised circumcision like the Jews, and made offerings and feasts on that occasion, in the same manner as they did. Like them also, our children were named from some event, some circumstance, or fancied foreboding, at the time of their birth. I was named *Olaudah*, which in our language signifies vicissitude, or fortunate; also, one favored, and having a loud voice and well spoken.[2] I remember we never polluted the name of the object of our adoration; on the contrary, it was always mentioned with the greatest reverence; and we were totally unacquainted with swearing, and all those terms of abuse and reproach which find their way so readily and copiously into the language of more civilized people. The only expressions of that kind I remember were, "May you rot, or may you swell, or may a beast take you."

I have before remarked that the natives of this part of Africa are extremely cleanly. This necessary habit of decency was with us a part of religion, and therefore we had many purifications and washings; indeed almost as many, and used on the same occasions, if my recollection does not fail me, as the Jews. Those that touched the dead at any time were obliged to wash and purify themselves before they could enter a dwelling-house. Every woman, too, at certain times was forbidden to come into a dwelling-house, or touch any person, or anything we eat. I was so fond of my mother I could not keep from her, or avoid touching her at some of those periods, in consequence of which I was obliged to be kept out with her, in a little house made for that purpose, till offering was made, and then we were purified.

Though we had no places of public worship, we had priests and magicians, or wise men. I do not remember whether they had different offices, or whether they were united in the same persons, but they were held in great reverence by the people. They calculated our time, and foretold events, as their name imported, for we called them *Ah-affoe-way-cah*, which signifies calculators or yearly men, our year being called *Ah-affoe*.[3] They wore their beards, and when they died, they were succeeded by their sons. Most of their implements and things of value were interred along with them. Pipes and tobacco were also put into the grave with the corpse, which was always perfumed and ornamented, and animals were offered in sacrifice to them. None accompanied their funerals, but those of the same profession or tribe. They buried them after sunset, and always returned from the grave by a different way from that which they went.

These magicians were also our doctors or physicians. They practised bleeding by cupping, and were very successful in healing wounds and expelling poisons. They had likewise some extraordinary method of discovering jealousy, theft, poisoning, the success of which, no doubt, they derived from the unbounded influence over the credulity and superstition of the people. I do not remember what those methods were, except that as to poisoning; I recollect an instance or two, which I hope it will not be deemed impertinent here to insert, as it may serve as a kind of specimen of the rest, as is still used by the Negroes in the West Indies. A young woman had been poisoned, but it was not known by whom; the doctors ordered the corpse to be taken up by some persons, and carried to the grave. As soon as the bearers had raised it on their shoulders, they seemed seized with some[4] sudden impulse, and ran to and fro, unable to stop themselves. At last, after having passed through a number of thorns and prickly bushes unhurt, the corpse fell from them close to a house, and defaced it in the fall; and the owner being taken up, he immediately confessed the poisoning.[5]

The natives are extremely cautious about poison. When they buy any eatables, the seller kisses it all round before the buyer, to shew him it is not poisoned; and the same is done when any meat or drink is presented, particularly to a stranger. We have serpents of different kinds, some of which are esteemed ominous when they appear in our houses, and these we never molest. I remember two of those ominous snakes, each of which was as thick as the calf of a man's leg, and in color resembling a dolphin in the water, crept at different times into my mother's night house, where I always lay with her, and coiled themselves into folds, and each time they crowed like a cock. I was desired by some of our wise men to touch these, that I might be interested in the good omens, which I did, for they were quite harmless, and would tamely suffer themselves to be handled; and then they were put into a large earthen pan, and set on one side of the highway. Some of our snakes, however, were poisonous; one of them crossed the road one day as I was standing on it, and passed between my feet without offering to touch me, to the great surprise of many who saw it; and these incidents were accounted by the wise men, and likewise by my mother and the rest of the people, as remarkable omens in my favor.

Such is the imperfect sketch my memory has furnished me with, of the manners and customs of a people among whom I first drew my breath. And here I cannot forbear suggesting what has long struck me very forcibly, namely, the strong analogy which even by this sketch, imperfect as it is, appears to prevail in the manners and customs of my countrymen and those of the Jews, before they reached the land of promise, and particularly the patriarchs while they were yet in that pastoral state which is described in Genesis—an analogy, which alone would induce me to think that the one people had sprung from the other. Indeed, this is the opinion of Dr. Gill, who, in his commentary on Genesis, very ably deduces the pedigree of the Africans from Afer and Afra, the descendents of Abraham by Keturah his wife and concubine (for both these titles are applied to her). It is also conformable to the sentiments of Dr. John Clarke, formerly Dean of Sarum, in his truth of the Christian religion; both these authors concur in ascribing to us this original.[6] The reasonings of those gentlemen are still further confirmed by the scripture chronology; and if any further corroboration were required, this resemblance in so many respects, is a strong evidence in support of the opinion. Like the Israelites in their primitive state, our government was conducted by our chiefs or judges, our wise men and elders; and the head of a family with us enjoyed a similar authority over his household, with that which is ascribed to Abraham and the other patriarchs. The law of retaliation obtained almost universally with us as with them: and even their religion appeared to have shed upon us a ray of its glory, though broken and spent in its passage, or eclipsed by the cloud with which time, tradition, and ignorance might have enveloped it; for we had our circumcision (a rule, I believe, peculiar to that, people), we had also our sacrifices and burnt-offerings, our washings and purifications, and on the same occasions as they did.

As to the difference of color between the Eboan Africans and the modern Jews, I shall not presume to account for it. It is a subject which has engaged the pens of men of both genius and learning, and is far above my strength. The most able and Reverend Mr. T. Clarkson, however, in his much admired *Essay on the Slavery and Commerce of the Human Species*,[7] has ascertained the cause in a manner that at once solves every objection on that account, and, on my mind at least, has produced the fullest conviction. I shall therefore refer to that performance for the theory,[8] contenting myself with extracting a fact as related by Dr. Mitchel.[9] "The Spaniards, who have inhabited America, under the torrid zone, for any time, are become as dark colored as our native Indians of Virginia; of which *I myself have been a witness.*" There is also another instance[10] of a Portuguese settlement at Mitomba, a river in Sierra Leone, where the inhabitants are bred from a mixture of the first Portuguese discoverers with the natives, and are now become in their complexion, and in the woolly quality of their hair, *perfect Negroes*, retaining however a smattering of the Portuguese language.[11]

* * *

One morning, when I got upon deck, I saw it covered all over with the snow that fell over night. As I had never seen anything of the kind before, I thought it was salt: so I immediately ran down to the mate, and desired him, as well as I could, to come and see how somebody in the night had thrown salt all over the deck. He, knowing what it was, desired me to bring some of it down to him. Accordingly I took up a handful of it, which I found very cold indeed; and when I brought it to him he desired me to taste it. I did so, and I was surprised beyond measure. I then asked him what it was; he told me it was snow, but I could not in anywise understand him. He asked me, if we had no such thing in my country; I told him, No. I then asked him the use of it, and who made it; he told me a great man in the heavens, called God. But here again I was to all intents and purposes at a loss to understand him; and the more so, when a little after I saw the air filled with it, in a heavy shower, which fell down on the same day.

After this I went to church; and having never been at such a place before, I was again amazed at seeing and hearing the service. I asked all I could about it, and they gave me to understand it was worshipping God, who made us and all things. I was still at a great loss, and soon got into an endless field of inquiries, as well as I was able to speak and ask about things. However, my little friend Dick used to be my best interpreter; for I could make free with him, and he always instructed me with pleasure. And from what I could understand by him of this God, and in seeing these white people did not sell one another as we did, I was much pleased; and in this I thought they were much happier than we Africans. I was astonished at the wisdom of the white people in all things I saw; but was amazed at their not sacrificing, or making any offerings, and eating with unwashed hands, and touching the dead. I likewise could not help remarking the particular slenderness of their women, which I did not at first like; and I thought they were not so modest and shame-faced as the African women.

I had often seen my master and Dick employed in reading; and I had a great curiosity to talk to the books as I thought they did, and so to learn how all things had a beginning. For that purpose I have often taken up a book, and have talked to it, and then put my ears to it, when alone, in hopes it would answer me; and I have been very much concerned when I found it remained silent.

My master lodged at the house of a gentleman in Falmouth, who had a fine little daughter about six or seven years of age, and she grew prodigiously fond of me, insomuch that we used to eat together, and had servants to wait on us. I was so much caressed by this family that it often reminded me of the treatment I had received from my little noble African master. After I had been here a few days, I was sent on board of the ship; but the child cried so much after me that nothing could pacify her till I was sent for again. It is ludicrous enough, that I began to fear I should be betrothed to this young lady; and when my master asked me if I would stay there with her behind him, as he was going away with the ship, which had taken in the tobacco again, I cried immediately, and said I would not leave him. At last, by stealth, one night I was sent on board the ship again; and in a little time we sailed for Guernsey, where she was in part owned by a merchant, one Nicholas Doberry.

Chapter 4

The author is baptized—Narrowly escapes drowning—Goes on an expedition to the Mediterranean—Incidents he met with there—Is witness to an engagement between some English and French ships—A particular account of the celebrated engagement between Admiral Boscawen and Monsieur Le Clue, off Cape Logas, in August 1759—Dreadful explosion of a French ship—The author sails for England—His master appointed to the command of a fire ship—Meets a Negro boy, from whom he experiences much benevolence—Prepares for an expedition against Belle Isle—A remarkable story of a disaster which befell his ship—Arrives at Belle Isle—Operations of the landing and siege—The author's danger and distress, with his manner of extricating himself—Surrender of Belle Isle—Transactions afterwards on the coast of France—Remarkable instance of kidnapping—The author returns to England—Hears a talk of peace, and expects his freedom—His ship sails for Deptford to be paid off, and when he arrives there he is suddenly seized by his master and carried forcibly on board a West India ship and sold.

It was now between two and three years since I first came to England, a great part of which I had spent at sea; so that I became inured to that service, and began to consider myself as happily situated, for my master treated me always extremely well; and my attachment and gratitude to him were very great. From the various scenes I had beheld on shipboard, I soon grew a stranger to terror of every kind, and was, in that respect at least, almost an Englishman. I have often reflected with surprise that I never felt half the alarm at any of the numerous dangers I have been in, that I was filled with at the first sight of the Europeans, and at every act of theirs, even the most trifling, when I first came among them, and for some time afterwards. That fear, however, which was the effect of my ignorance, wore away as I began to know them. I could now speak English tolerably well, and I perfectly understood everything that was said. I not only felt myself quite easy with these new countrymen, but relished their society and manners. I no longer looked upon them as spirits, but as men superior to us; and therefore I had the stronger desire to resemble them, to imbibe their spirit, and imitate their manners. I therefore embraced every occasion of improvement, and every new thing that I observed I treasured up in my memory. I had long wished to be able to read and write; and for this purpose I took every opportunity to gain instruction, but had made as yet very little progress. However, when I went to London with my master, I had soon an opportunity of improving myself, which I gladly embraced. Shortly after my arrival, he sent me to wait upon the Miss Guerins, who had treated me with much kindness when I was there before; and they sent me to school.

While I was attending these ladies, their servants told me I could not go to Heaven unless I was baptized. This made me very uneasy, for I had now some faint idea of a future state: accordingly I communicated my anxiety to the eldest Miss Guerin, with whom I was become a favorite, and pressed her to have me baptized; when to my great joy, she told me I should. She had formerly asked my master to let me be baptized, but he had refused. However she now insisted on it; and he being under some obligation to her brother, complied with her request. So I was baptized in St. Margaret's church, Westminster, in February 1759, by my present name. The clergyman at the same time, gave me a book, called *A Guide to the Indians,* written by the Bishop of Sodor and Man.[12] On this occasion, Miss Guerin did me the honor to stand as god-mother, and afterwards gave me a treat.

I used to attend these ladies about the town, in which service I was extremely happy; as I had thus many opportunities of seeing London, which I desired of all things. I was sometimes, however, with my master at his rendezvous house, which was at the foot of Westminster bridge. Here I used to enjoy myself in playing about the bridge stairs, and often in the waterman's wherries,[13] with other boys. On one of these occasions there was another boy with me in a wherry, and we went out into the current of the river; while we were there, two more stout boys came to us in another wherry, and abusing us for taking the boat, desired me to get into the other wherry-boat. Accordingly, I went to get out of the wherry I was in, but just as I had got one of my feet into the other boat, the boys shoved it off, so that I fell into the Thames; and, not being able to swim, I should unavoidably have been drowned, but for the assistance of some watermen who providentially came to my relief.

The *Namur* being again got ready for sea, my master, with his gang, was ordered on board; and, to my no small grief, I was obliged to leave my school-master, whom I liked very much, and always attended while I stayed in London, to repair on board with my master. Nor did I leave my kind patronesses, the Miss Guerins, without uneasiness and regret. They often used to teach me to read, and took great pains to instruct me in the principles of religion and the knowledge of God. I therefore parted from those amiable ladies with reluctance, after receiving from them many friendly cautions how to conduct myself, and some valuable presents.

Notes

1. Olaudah Equiano, *Interesting Narrative of the Life of Olaudah Equiano*, ed. Robert J. Allison (Boston: Bedford Books, 1995 [1788]), pp. 41–45; 63–64; 71–73.

2. *Ola*, or ring, is a symbol of good fortune to the Ibo. *Ude* means "pleasing sound." (Acholonu, *Igbo Roots*, 42–43.)

3. *Ofo-nwanchi* were traveling men who calculated the years. Often dwarfs, they were sometimes called *afo-nwa-ika*, or "funny monkeys," by children in the villages they visited. Local priests were *nze nzu*. (Acholonu, *Igbo Roots*, 18–19.)

4. See also Lieutenant Matthew's Voyage, p. 123. [Equiano's note.] John Matthews, *A Voyage to the River Sierra Leone . . . with a Letter on the . . . African Slave Trade* (London, 1788).

5. An instance of this kind happened at Montserrat, in the West Indies, in the year 1763. I then belonged to the *Charming Sally*, Capt. Doran. The chief mate, Mr. Mansfield, and some of the crew being one day on shore, were present at the burying of a poisoned Negro girl. Though they had often heard of the circumstance of the running in such cases, and had even seen it, they imagined it to be a trick of the corpse bearers. The mate therefore desired two of the sailors to take up the coffin, and carry it to the grave. The sailors, who were all of the same opinion, readily obeyed, but they had scarcely raised it to their shoulders before they began to run furiously about, quite unable to direct themselves, till at last, without intention, they came to the hut of him who had poisoned the girl. The coffin then immediately fell from their shoulders against the hut, and damaged part of the wall. The owner of the hut was taken into custody on this, and confessed the poisoning. I give this story as it was related by the mate and crew on their return to the ship. The credit which is due to it, I leave with the reader. [Equiano's note.]

6. Dr. John Gill (1697–1771), a Baptist divine, published his multivolume *Exposition of the Holy Scriptures* in 1766. John Clarke's *Truth of the Christian Religion, in Six Books* (1711) is a translation of Hugo Grotius (1583–1645), *De veritatus religionis christianae* (1627).

7. Thomas Clarkson, *Essay on the Slavery and Commerce of the Human Species, Particularly the African* (London, 1786). Clarkson (1760–1846) wrote this essay for an academic competition at Cambridge in 1785. He won the contest and became a lifelong abolitionist. His documentation of the horrors of the slave trade became a foundation for antislavery activity. His brother John, a Royal Navy officer, helped to found the Sierra Leone colony.

8. Pages 178 to 216. [Equiano's note.]

9. Philos. Trans. No. 476, Sec. 4, cited by Mr. Clarkson, p. 205. [Equiano's note.] John Mitchell, "An Essay upon the Causes of the Different Colours of People in Different Climates," *Philosophical Transactions of the Royal Society* 43 (1746).

10. Same page. [Equiano's note.]

11. The Portuguese established a trading post at Mitombe, Sierra Leone, in the 1460s.

12. Thomas Wilson (1697–1755), bishop of Sodor and Man, wrote *The Knowledge and Practice of Christianity Made Easy for the Meanest Mental Capacities; or, an Essay towards an Instruction for the Indians* (London, 1740) in the form of a dialogue between an Indian and a Christian.

13. Long, light rowboats.

David Walker

With the publication of his *Appeal* in 1829, David Walker (1785–1830) delivered what is now one of the most recognized publications of early Black nationalism. The *Appeal* is notable for its direct call for African American rebellion—it foretells Malcolm X's cry for Black liberation "by any means necessary." Its tone is confrontational, accusatory, provocative, angry, yet humorous. It is a cry for Black liberation that does not ask for the compassion or sympathy of Whites—in fact, Walker subtitles his work to clarify that he is addressing Blacks. Cleary, given the mixed readership of Black publications in early nineteenth-century America, Walker knows that Whites will read his text. It is this indirect address to Whites that makes the work so provocative—Walker's audacity to invisibilize or marginalize White readers while he simultaneously critiques whiteness was alarming to southern Whites in particular, as they lived with the ongoing fear of slave insurrections. The *Appeal* is clearly a satirical work in the tradition of Western rhetoric, but it is more salient for its illustration of African American oral conventions. In particular, Walker engages in signifying and playing the dozens to bring front and center the flawed U.S. national body/family and its leadership/parents (particularly highlighted through reoccurring taunts directed to founding father Thomas Jefferson). In Article I and throughout the *Appeal*, Walker employs the Bible as his reference text, and he articulates what might be called a tradition of the Christian soldier in Black race rhetoric. Walker orients his call to arms on the premise that God sanctions the battle of men to be free. As with the biblical typology that informed Puritan rhetoric, Walker invokes biblical figures and accounts to foretell the inevitable rise of enslaved Blacks.

Article I. Our Wretchedness in Consequence of Slavery

David Walker[1]

MY BELOVED BRETHREN:—The Indians of North and of South America—the Greeks—the Irish, subjected under the king of Great Britain—the Jews, that ancient people of the Lord—the inhabitants of the islands of the sea—in fine, all the inhabitants of the earth, (except however, the sons of Africa) are called *men*, and of course are, and ought to be free. But we, (coloured people) and our children are *brutes!!* and of course are, and *ought to be* SLAVES to the American people and their children forever!! to dig their mines and work their farms; and thus go on enriching them, from one generation to another with our *blood* and our *tears!!!!*

I promised in a preceding page to demonstrate to the satisfaction of the most incredulous, that we, (coloured people of these United States of America) are the *most wretched, degraded* and *abject* set of beings that *ever lived* since the world began, and that the white Americans having reduced us to the wretched state of *slavery*, treat us in that condition *more cruel* (they being an enlightened and Christian people,) than any heathen nation did any people whom it had reduced to our condition. These affirmations are so well confirmed in the minds of all unprejudiced men, who have taken the trouble to read histories, that they need no elucidation from me. But to put them beyond all doubt, I refer you in the first place to the children of Jacob, or of Israel in Egypt, under Pharaoh and his people. Some of my brethren do not know who Pharaoh and the Egyptians were—I know it to be a fact, that some of them take the Egyptians to have been a gang of *devils*, not knowing any better, and that they (Egyptians) having got possession of the Lord's people, treated them *nearly* as cruel as *Christian Americans* do us, at the present day. For the information of such, I would only mention that the Egyptians, were Africans or coloured people, such as we are—some of them yellow and others dark—a mixture of Ethiopians and the natives of Egypt—about the same as you see the coloured people of the United States at the present day.—I say, I call your attention then, to the children of Jacob, while I point out particularly to you his son Joseph, among the rest, in Egypt.

"And Pharaoh, said unto Joseph, thou shalt be over my house, and according unto thy word shall all my people be ruled: only in the throne will I be greater than thou."[2]

"And Pharaoh said unto Joseph, see, I have set thee over all the land of Egypt."[3]

"And Pharaoh said unto Joseph, I am Pharaoh, and without thee shall no man lift up his hand or foot in all the land of Egypt."[4]

Now I appeal to heaven and to earth, and particularly to the American people themselves, who cease not to declare that our condition is not *hard*, and that we are comparatively satisfied to rest in wretchedness and misery, under them and their children. Not, indeed, to show me a coloured President, a Governor, a Legislator, a Senator, a Mayor, or an Attorney at the Bar.—But to show me a man of colour, who holds the low office of a Constable, or one who sits in a Juror Box, even on a case of one of his wretched brethren, throughout this great Republic!!—But let us pass Joseph the son of Israel a little farther in review, as he existed with that heathen nation.

"And Pharaoh called Joseph's name Zaphnathpaaneah; and he gave him to wife Asenath the daughter of Potipherah priest of On. And Joseph went out over all the land of Egypt."[5]

Compare the above, with the American institutions. Do they not institute laws to prohibit us from marrying among the whites? I would wish, candidly, however, before the Lord, to be understood, that I would not give a *pinch of snuff* to be married to any white person I ever saw in all the days of my life. And I do say it, that the black man, or man of colour, who will leave his own colour (provided he can get one, who is good for any thing) and marry a white woman, to be a double slave to her, just because she is *white*, ought to be treated by her as he surely will be, viz: as a NIGER!!!! It is not, indeed, what I care about intermarriages with the whites, which induced me to pass this subject in review; for the Lord knows, that there is a day coming when they will be glad enough to get into the company of the blacks, notwithstanding, we are, in this generation, levelled by them, almost on a level with the brute creation: and some of us they treat even worse than they do the brutes that perish. I only made this extract to show how much lower we are held, and how much more cruel we are treated by the Americans, than were the children of Jacob, by the Egyptians.—We will notice the sufferings of Israel some further, under *heathen Pharaoh*, compared with ours under the *enlightened Christians of America*.

"And Pharaoh spake unto Joseph, saying, thy father and thy brethren are come unto thee:"

"The land of Egypt is before thee: in the best of the land make thy father and brethren to dwell; in the land of Goshen let them dwell: and if thou knowest any men of activity among them, then make them rulers over my cattle."[6]

I ask those people who treat us so *well*, Oh! I ask them, where is the most barren spot of land which they have given unto us? Israel had the most fertile land in all Egypt. Need I mention the very notorious fact, that I have known a poor man of colour, who laboured night and day, to acquire a little money, and having acquired it, he vested it in a small piece of land, and got him a house erected thereon, and having paid for the whole, he moved his family into it, where he was suffered to remain but nine months, when he was cheated out of his property by a white man, and driven out of door! And is not this the case generally? Can a man of colour buy a piece of land and keep it peaceably? Will not some white man try to get it from him, even if it is in a *mud hole*? I need not comment any farther on a subject, which all, both black and white, will readily admit. But I must, really, observe that in this very city, when a man of colour dies, if he owned any real estate it most generally falls into the hands of some white person. The wife and children of the deceased may weep and lament if they please, but the estate will be kept snug enough by its white possessor.

But to prove farther that the condition of the Israelites was better under the Egyptians than ours is under the whites, I call upon the professing Christians, I call upon the philanthropist,

I call upon the very tyrant himself, to show me a page of history, either sacred or profane, on which a verse can be found, which maintains, that the Egyptians heaped the *insupportable insult* upon the children of Israel, by telling them that they were not of the *human family*. Can the whites deny this charge? Have they not, after having reduced us to the deplorable condition of slaves under their feet, held us up as descending originally from the tribes of *Monkeys* or *Orang-Outangs?* O! my God! I appeal to every man of feeling—is not this insupportable? Is it not heaping the most gross insult upon our miseries, because they have got us under their feet and we cannot help ourselves? Oh! pity us we pray thee, Lord Jesus, Master.—Has Mr. Jefferson declared to the world, that we are inferior to the whites, both in the endowments of our bodies and of minds? It is indeed surprising, that a man of such great learning, combined with such excellent natural parts, should speak so of a set of men in chains. I do not know what to compare it to, unless, like putting one wild deer in an iron cage, where it will be secured, and hold another by the side of the same, then let it go, and expect the one in the cage to run as fast as the one at liberty. So far, my brethren, were the Egyptians from heaping these insults upon their slaves, that Pharaoh's daughter took Moses, a son of Israel for her own, as will appear by the following.

"And Pharaoh's daughter said unto her, [Moses' mother] take this child away, and nurse it for me, and I will pay thee thy wages. And the woman took the child [Moses] and nursed it.

"And the child grew, and she brought him unto Pharaoh's daughter and he became her son. And she called his name Moses: and she said because I drew him out of the water."[7]

In all probability, Moses would have become Prince Regent to the throne, and no doubt, in process of time but he would have been seated on the throne of Egypt. But he had rather suffer shame, with the people of God, than to enjoy pleasures with that wicked people for a season. O! that the coloured people were long since of Moses' excellent disposition, instead of courting favour with, and telling news and lies to our *natural enemies*, against each other—aiding them to keep their hellish chains of slavery upon us. Would we not long before this time, have been respectable men, instead of such wretched victims of oppression as we are? Would they be able to drag our mothers, our fathers, our wives, our children and ourselves, around the world in chains and handcuffs as they do, to dig up gold and silver for them and theirs? This question, my brethren, I leave for you to digest; and may God Almighty force it home to your hearts. Remember that unless you are united, keeping your tongues within your teeth, you will be afraid to trust your secrets to each other, and thus perpetuate our miseries under the *Christians!!!!!* Addition.—Remember, also to lay humble at the feet of our Lord and Master Jesus Christ, with prayers and fastings. Let our enemies go on with their butcheries, and at once fill up their cup. Never make an attempt to gain our freedom or *natural right*, from under our cruel oppressors and murderers, until you see your way clear[8]—when that hour arrives and you move, be not afraid or dismayed; for be you assured that Jesus Christ the King of heaven and of earth who is the God of justice and of armies, will surely go before you. And those enemies who have for hundreds of years stolen our *rights*, and kept us ignorant of Him and His divine worship, he will remove. Millions of whom, are this day, so ignorant and avaricious, that they cannot conceive how God can have an attribute of justice, and show mercy to us because it pleased Him to make us black—which colour, Mr. Jefferson calls unfortunate!!!!!! As though we are not as thankful to our God, for having made us as it pleased himself, as they (the whites,) are for having made them white. They think because they hold us in their infernal chains of slavery, that we wish to be white or of their color—but they are dreadfully deceived—we wish to be just as it pleased our Creator to have made us, and no avaricious and unmerciful wretches, have any business to make slaves of, or hold us in slavery. How would they like for us to make slaves of, and hold them in cruel slavery, and murder them as they do us?—But is Mr. Jefferson's assertions true? viz. "that it is unfortunate for us that our Creator has been pleased to make us *black*." We will not take his say so, for the fact. The world will have an opportunity to see whether it is unfortunate for us, that our Creator *has made us* darker than the *whites.*

Fear not the number and education of our *enemies,* against whom we shall have to contend for our lawful right; guaranteed to us by our Maker; for why should we be afraid, when God is, and will continue, (if we continue humble) to be on our side?

The man who would not fight under our Lord and Master Jesus Christ, in the glorious and heavenly cause of freedom and of God—to be delivered from the most wretched, abject and servile slavery, that ever a people was afflicted with since the foundation of the world, to the present day—ought to be kept with all of his children or family, in slavery, or in chains, to be butchered by his *cruel enemies.*

I saw a paragraph, a few years since, in a South Carolina paper, which, speaking of the barbarity of the Turks, it said: "The Turks are the most barbarous people in the world—they treat the Greeks more like *brutes* than human beings." And in the same paper was an advertisement, which said: "Eight well built Virginia and Maryland *Negro fellows* and four *wenches* will positively be *sold* this day, *to the highest bidder!*" And what astonished me still more was, to see in this same *humane* paper!! the cuts of three men, with clubs and budgets on their backs, and an advertisement offering a considerable sum of money for their apprehension and delivery. I declare, it is really so amusing to hear the Southerners and Westerners of this country talk about *barbarity,* that it is positively, enough to make a man *smile.*

The sufferings of the Helots among the Spartans, were somewhat severe, it is true, but to say that theirs, were as severe as ours among the Americans, I do most strenuously deny—for instance, can any man show me an article on a page of ancient history which specifies, that, the Spartans chained, and handcuffed the Helots, and dragged them from their wives and children, children from their parents, mothers from their suckling babes, wives from their husbands, driving them from one end of the country to the other? Notice the Spartans were heathens, who lived long before our Divine Master made his appearance in the flesh.

Can Christian Americans deny these barbarous cruelties? Have you not, Americans, having subjected us under you, added to these miseries, by insulting us in telling us to our face, because we are helpless, that we are not of the human family? I ask you, O! Americans, I ask you, in the name of the Lord, can you deny these charges? Some perhaps may deny, by saying, that they never thought or said that we were not men. But do not actions speak louder than *words?*—have they not made provisions for the Greeks, and Irish? Nations who have never done the least thing for them, while *we,* who have enriched their country with our blood and tears—have dug up gold and silver for them and their children, from generation to generation, and are in more miseries than any other people under heaven, are not seen, but by comparatively, a handful of the American people? There are indeed, more ways to kill a dog, besides choking it to death with butter. Further—The Spartans or Lacedemonians, had some frivolous pretext, for enslaving the Helots, for they (Helots) while being free inhabitants of Sparta, stirred up an intestine commotion, and were, by the Spartans subdued, and made prisoners of war. Consequently they and their children were condemned to perpetual slavery.[9]

I have been for years troubling the pages of historians, to find out what our fathers have done to the *white Christians of America,* to merit such condign punishment as they have inflicted on them, and do continue to inflict on us their children. But I must aver, that my researches have hitherto been to no effect. I have therefore, come to the immoveable conclusion, that they (Americans) have, and do continue to punish us for nothing else, but for enriching them and their country. For I cannot conceive of any thing else. Nor will I ever believe otherwise, until the Lord shall convince me.

The world knows, that slavery as it existed among the Romans, (which was the primary cause of their destruction) was, comparatively speaking, no more than a *cypher,* when compared with ours under the Americans. Indeed I should not have noticed the Roman slaves, had not the very learned and penetrating Mr. Jefferson said, "when a master was murdered, all his slaves in the same house, or within hearing, were condemned to death."[10]—Here let me ask Mr. Jefferson, (but he is gone to answer at the bar of God, for the deeds done in his body while living,) I therefore ask the whole American people, had I not rather die, or be put to death, than to be a slave to any tyrant, who takes not only my own, but my wife and children's lives by the inches? Yea, would I meet death with avidity far! far!! in preference to such *servile submission* to the murderous hands of tyrants. Mr. Jefferson's very severe remarks on us have been so extensively argued upon by men whose attainments in literature, I shall never be able to reach, that I would not have meddled with it, were it not to solicit each of my brethren, who has the spirit of a man, to buy a copy of Mr. Jefferson's *Notes on Virginia*, and put it in the hand of his son. For let no one of us suppose that the refutations which have been written by our white friends are enough—they are *whites*—we are *blacks*.

We, and the world wish to see the charges of Mr. Jefferson refuted by the blacks *themselves*, according to their chance; for we must remember that what the whites have written respecting this subject, is other men's labours, and did not emanate from the blacks. I know well, that there are some talents and learning among the coloured people of this country, which we have not a chance to develop, in consequence of oppression; but our oppression ought not to hinder us from acquiring all we can. For we will have a chance to develop them by and by. God will not suffer us, always to be oppressed. Our sufferings will come to an *end*, in spite of all the Americans this side of *eternity*. Then we will want all the learning and talents among ourselves, and perhaps more, to govern ourselves.—"Every dog must have its day," the American's is coming to an end.

But let us review Mr. Jefferson's remarks respecting us some further. Comparing our miserable fathers, with the learned philosophers of Greece, he says:

> Yet notwithstanding these and other discouraging circumstances among the Romans, their slaves were often their rarest artists. They excelled too, in science, insomuch as to be usually employed as tutors to their master's children; Epictetus, Terence and Phaedrus, were slaves,—but they were of the race of whites. It is not their *condition* then, but *nature*, which has produced the distinction.[11]

See this, my brethren!! Do you believe that this assertion is swallowed by millions of the whites? Do you know that Mr. Jefferson was one of as great characters as ever lived among the whites? See his writings for the world, and public labours for the United States of America. Do you believe that the assertions of such a man, will pass away into oblivion unobserved by this people and the world? If you do you are much mistaken—See how the American people treat us—have we souls in our bodies? Are we men who have any spirits at all? I know that there are many *swell-bellied* fellows among us, whose greatest object is to fill their stomachs. Such I do not mean—I am after those who know and feel, that we are MEN, as well as other people, to them, I say, that unless we try to refute Mr. Jefferson's arguments respecting us, we will only establish them.

But the slaves among the Romans. Every body who has read history, knows, that as soon as a slave among the Romans obtained his freedom, he could rise to the greatest eminence in the State, and there was no law instituted to hinder a slave from buying his freedom. Have not the Americans instituted laws to hinder us from obtaining our freedom? Do any deny this charge? Read the laws of Virginia, North Carolina, &c. Further: have not the Americans instituted laws to prohibit a man of colour from obtaining and holding any office whatever, under the government of the United States of America? Now, Mr. Jefferson tells us, that our condition is not so hard, as the slaves were under the Romans!!!!!!

It is time for me to bring this article to a close. But before I close it, I must observe to my brethren that at the close of the first Revolution in this country, with Great Britain, there were but thirteen States in the Union, now there are twenty-four, most of which are slaveholding States, and the whites are dragging us around in chains and in handcuffs, to their new States and Territories to work their mines and farms, to enrich them and their children—and millions of them believing firmly that we being a little darker than they, were made by our Creator to be an inheritance to them and their children for ever—the same as a parcel of *brutes.*

Are we MEN!!—I ask you, O my brethren! are we MEN? Did our Creator make us to be slaves to dust and ashes like ourselves? Are they not dying worms as well as we? Have they not to make their appearance before the tribunal of Heaven, to answer for the deeds done in the body, as well as we? Have we any other Master but Jesus Christ alone? Is he not their Master as well as ours?— What right then, have we to obey and call any other Master, but Himself? How we could be so *submissive* to a gang of men, whom we cannot tell whether they are *as good* as ourselves or not, I never could conceive. However, this is shut up with the Lord, and we cannot precisely tell—but I declare, we judge men by their works.

The whites have always been an unjust, jealous, unmerciful, avaricious and bloodthirsty set of beings, always seeking after power and authority.—We view them all over the confederacy of Greece, where they were first known to be any thing, (in consequence of education) we see them there, cutting each other's throats—trying to subject each other to wretchedness and misery— to effect which, they used all kinds of deceitful, unfair, and unmerciful means. We view them next in Rome, where the spirit of tyranny and deceit raged still higher. We view them in Gaul, Spain, and in Britain.—In fine, we view them all over Europe, together with what were scattered about in Asia and Africa, as heathens, and we see them acting more like devils than accountable men. But some may ask, did not the blacks of Africa, and the mulattoes of Asia, go on in the same way as did the whites of Europe. I answer, no—they never were half so avaricious, deceitful and unmerciful as the whites, according to their knowledge.

But we will leave the whites or Europeans as heathens, and take a view of them as Christians, in which capacity we see them as cruel, if not more so than ever. In fact, take them as a body, they are ten times more cruel, avaricious and unmerciful than ever they were; for while they were heathens, they were bad enough it is true, but it is positively a fact that they were not quite so audacious as to go and take vessel loads of men, women and children, and in cold blood, and through devilishness, throw them into the sea, and murder them in all kind of ways. While they were heathens, they were too ignorant for such barbarity. But being Christians, enlightened and sensible, they are completely prepared for such hellish cruelties.

Now suppose God were to give them more sense, what would they do? If it were possible, would they not *dethrone* Jehovah and seat themselves upon his throne? I therefore, in the name and fear of the Lord God of Heaven and of earth, divested of prejudice either on the side of my colour or that of the whites, advance my suspicion of them, whether they are *as good by nature* as we are or not. Their actions, since they were known as a people, have been the reverse, I do indeed suspect them, but this, as I before observed, is shut up with the Lord, we cannot exactly tell, it will be proved in succeeding generations.—The whites have had the essence of the gospel as it was preached by my master and his apostles—the Ethiopians have not, who are to have it in its meridian splendor—the Lord will give it to them to their satisfaction. I hope and pray my God, that they will make good use of it, that it may be well with them.[12]

Notes

1. David Walker, "Article I," in *David Walker's Appeal*, introd. James Turner (Baltimore, MD: Black Classic Press, 1993 [1829]), pp. 27–38.
2. See Genesis, chap. xli.
3. xli. 44.

4. xli. 44.

5. xli. 45.

6. Genesis, chap. xlvii, 5, 6.

7. See Exodus, chap. ii. 9, 10.

8. It is not to be understood here, that I mean for us to wait until God shall take us by the hair of our heads and drag us out of abject wretchedness and slavery, nor do I mean to convey the idea for us to wait until our enemies shall make preparations, and call us to seize those preparations, take it away from them, and put every thing before us to death, in order to gain our freedom which God has given us. For you must remember that we are men as well as they. God has been pleased to give us two eyes, two hands, two feet, and some sense in our heads as well as they. They have no more right to hold us in slavery than we have to hold them, we have just as much right, in the sight of God, to hold them and their children in slavery and wretchedness, as they have to hold us, and no more.

9. See Dr. Goldsmith's *History of Greece*—page 9. See also, Plutarch's Lives. The Helots subdued by Agis, king of *Sparta*.

10. See his *Notes on Virginia*, page 210.

11. See his *Notes on Virginia*, page 211.

12. It is my solemn belief, that if ever the world becomes Christianized, (which must certainly take place before long) it will be through the means, under God of the *Blacks*, who are now held in wretchedness, and degradation, by the white *Christians* of the world, who before they learn to do justice to us before our Maker—and be reconciled to us, and reconcile us to them, and by that means have clear consciences before God and man.—Send out Missionaries to convert the Heathens, many of whom after they cease to worship gods, which neither see nor hear, become ten times more the children of Hell, then ever they were, why what is the reason? Why the reason is obvious, they must learn to do justice at home, before they go into distant lands, to display their charity, Christianity, and benevolence; when they learn to do justice, God will accept their offering, (no man may think that I am against Missionaries for I am not, my object is to see justice done at home, before we go to convert the heathens.)

Omar ibn Said

Omar ibn Said (1770?–1863) represents the ethnic and religious diversity of Africans transported to the Americas during the centuries of the transatlantic slave trade. A practicing Muslim and Arabic scholar, he reminds us of the significant population of African Muslims who were among the millions captured and transported to New World slavery. Said was born in present-day Senegal in 1770 and died in North Carolina after nearly sixty years of semi-free slave status granted by his White benefactor, Jim Owen. Said reports in his autobiography that Owen and a number of local North Carolina Whites were impressed with his literacy in Arabic and his devotion to Muslim rituals. Also sympathetic to Said's small physical stature and lack of experience and exposure to harsh physical labor, Owen saved him from being purchased by a harsh slave master. Said's claim to have converted from Islam to Christianity is unconvincing from the start of his narrative: he foregrounds the narrative with conventional prayers from the Koran, even as he apologizes for his ineptness in both Arabic and English. Rather than calling Owen's rescue a purchase, Said reports that after he "came into the hand of Owen" he was treated with great consideration. Said's narrative is rooted in this kind of euphemistic or deceptive discourse, with Said clearly appealing to his White Christian benefactors. Thus, Said reports that he was a devout Muslim but was converted to Christianity. While he pronounces himself Christian, his discourse is rooted in the Muslim holy text—the Koran. The overwhelming memory of his encounter with slavery is not anchored in the Black-White race binary but rather the Christian-Muslim binary. Said's narrative illustrates the discourse manipulation employed in the shaping of Black New World spirituality: Said melds his Africanized version of Islam with the Christianity of his captors. The result is a spiritual cosmology derived from a practice that has become familiar today through its application in the contemporary African American music world, where it has become known as sampling.

"Oh Ye Americans": The Autobiography of Omar ibn Said

Omar ibn Said[1]

In the name of God, the merciful the gracious.[2]—God grant his blessing upon our Prophet Mohammed. Blessed be He in whose hands is the Kingdom and who is Almighty; who created death and life that he might test you; for he is exalted; he is the forgiver (of sins), who created seven heavens one above the other. Do you discern anything trifling in creation? Bring back your thoughts. Do you see anything worthless? Recall your vision in earnest. Turn your eye inward for it is diseased. God has adorned the heavens and the world with lamps, and has made us missiles for the devils, and given us for them a grievous punishment, and to those who have disbelieved their Lord, the punishment of hell and pains of body. Whoever associates with them shall hear a boiling caldron, and what is cast therein may fitly represent those who suffer under the anger of God.—Ask them if a prophet has not been sent unto them. They say, "Yes; a prophet has come to us, but we have lied to him." We said, "God has not sent us down anything, and you are in grievous error." They say, "If we had listened and been wise we should not now have been suffering the punishment of the Omniscient." So they confess they have sinned in destroying the followers of the Omniscient. Those who fear their Lord and profess his name, they receive pardon and great honor. Guard your words, (ye wicked), make it known that God is all-wise in all his manifestations. Do you not know from the creation that God is full of skill? that He has made for you the way of error, and you have walked therein, and have chosen to live upon what your God Nasur has furnished you? Believe on Him who dwells in Heaven, who has fitted the earth to be your support and it shall give you food. Believe on Him who dwells in Heaven, who has sent you a prophet, and you shall understand what a teacher (He has sent you). Those that were before them deceived them (in regard to their prophet). And how came they to reject him? Did they not see in the heavens above them, how the fowls of the air receive with pleasure that which is sent them? God looks after all. Believe ye: it is He who supplies your wants, that you may take his gifts and enjoy them, and take great pleasure in them. And now will you go on in error, or walk in the path of righteousness. Say to them, "He who regards you with care, and has made for you the heavens and the earth and gives you prosperity, Him you think little of. This is He that planted you in the earth, and to whom you are soon to be gathered." But they say, "If you are men of truth, tell us when shall this promise be fulfilled?" Say to them, "Does not God know? and am not I an evident Prophet?" When those who disbelieve shall see the things draw near before their faces, it shall then be told them, "These are the things about which you made inquiry." Have you seen that God has destroyed me or those with me? or rather that He has shewn us mercy? And who will defend the unbeliever from a miserable punishment? Say, "Knowledge is from God." Say; "Have you not seen that your water has become impure? Who will bring you fresh water from the fountain?"

O Sheikh Hunter,[3] I cannot write my life because I have forgotten much of my own language,[4] as well as of the Arabic. Do not be hard upon me, my brother.—To God let many thanks be paid for his great mercy and goodness.

In the name of God, the Gracious, the Merciful.—Thanks be to God, supreme in goodness and kindness and grace, and who is worthy of all honor, who created all things for his service, even man's power of action and of speech.

From Omar to Sheikh Hunter

You asked me to write my life. I am not able to do this because I have much forgotten my own, as well as the Arabic language. Neither can I write very grammatically or according to the true idiom. And so, my brother, I beg you, in God's name, not to blame me, for I am a man of weak eyes, and of a weak body.

My name is Omar ibn Seid. My birthplace was Fut Tûr, between the two rivers.[5] I sought knowledge under the instruction of a Sheikh called Mohammed Seid, my own brother, and Sheikh Soleiman Kembeh, and Sheikh Gabriel Abdal. I continued my studies twenty-five years. Then there came to our place a large army, who killed many men, and took me, and brought me to the great sea, and sold me into the hands of the Christians, who bound me and sent me on board great ship and we sailed upon the great sea a month and a half, when we came to a place called

Charleston in the Christian language. There they sold me to a small, weak, and wicked man, called Johnson, a complete infidel, who had no fear of God at all. Now I am a small man, and unable to do hard work so I fled from the hand of Johnson and after a month came to a place called Fayd-il.[6] There I saw some great houses (churches). On the new moon I went into a church to pray. A lad saw me and rode off to the place of his father and informed him that he had seen a black man in the church. A man named Handah (Hunter?) and another man with him on horseback, came attended by a troop of dogs. They took me and made me go with them twelve miles to a place called Fayd-il, where they put me into a great house from which I could not go out. I continued in the great house (which, in the Christian language, they called *jail*) sixteen days and nights. One Friday the jailor came and opened the door of the house and I saw a great many men, all Christians, some of whom called out to me, "What is your name? Is it Omar or Seid?" I did not understand their Christian language. A man called Bob Mumford[7] took me and led me out of the jail, and I was very well pleased to go with them to their place. I stayed at Mumford's four days and nights, and then a man named Jim Owen, son-in-law of Mumford, having married his daughter Betsey, asked me if I was willing to go to a place called Bladen. I said, Yes, I was willing. I went with them and have remained in the place of Jim Owen until now.

Before [after?] I came into the hand of Gen. Owen a man by the name of Mitchell came to buy me. He asked me if I were willing to go to Charleston City. I said "*No, no, no, no, no, no, no, I am not willing to go to Charleston. I stay in the hand of Jim Owen.*"

O ye people of North Carolina, O ye people of S. Carolina, O ye people of America all of you; have you among you any two such men as Jim Owen and John Owen? These men are good men. What food they eat they give to me to eat. As they clothe themselves they clothe me. They permit me to read the gospel of God, our Lord, and Saviour, and King; who regulates all our circumstances, our health and wealth, and who bestows his mercies willingly, not by constraint. According to power I open my heart, as to a great light, to receive the true way, the way of the Lord Jesus the Messiah.

Before I came to the Christian country, my religion was the religion of "Mohammed, the Apostle of God—may God have mercy upon him and give him peace." I walked to mosque before day-break, washed my face and head and hands and feet. I prayed at noon, prayed in the afternoon, prayed at sunset, prayed in the evening. I gave alms every year, gold, silver, seeds, cattle, sheep, goats, rice, wheat, and barley. I gave tithes of all the above-named things. I went every year to the holy war against the infidels. I went on pilgrimage to Mecca, as all did who were able.—My father had six sons and five daughters, and my mother had three sons and one daughter. When I left my country I was thirty-seven years old; I have been in the country of the Christians twenty-four years.—Written A.D. 1831.

O ye people of North Carolina, O ye people of South Carolina, O all ye people of America—

The first son of Jim Owen is called Thomas, and his sister is called Masa-jein (Martha Jane?). This is an excellent family.

Tom Owen and Nell Owen have two sons and a daughter. The first son is called Jim and the second John. The daughter is named Melissa.

Seid Jim Owen and his wife Betsey have two sons and five daughters. Their names are Tom, and John, and Mercy, Miriam, Sophia, Margaret and Eliza. This family is a very nice family. The wife of John Owen is called Lucy and an excellent wife she is. She had five children. Three of them died and two are still living.

O ye Americans, ye people of North Carolina—have you, have you, have you, have you, have you among you a family like this family, having so much love to God as they?

Formerly I, Omar, loved to read the book of the Koran the famous. General Jim Owen and his wife used to read the gospel, and they read it to me very much,—the gospel of God, our Lord, our Creator, our King, He that orders all our circumstances, health and wealth, willingly, not constrainedly according to his power.—Open thou my heart to the gospel, to the way of uprightness.—Thanks to the Lord of all worlds, thanks in abundance. He is plenteous in mercy and abundant in goodness.

For the law was given by Moses but grace and truth were by Jesus the Messiah.

When I was a Mohammedan I prayed thus: "Thanks be to God, Lord of all worlds, the merciful the gracious, Lord of the day of Judgment, thee we serve, on thee we call for help. Direct us in the right way, the way of those on whom thou has had mercy, with whom thou hast not been angry and who walk not in error. Amen."—But now I pray "Our Father", etc., in the words of our Lord Jesus the Messiah.

I reside in this our country by reason of great necessity. Wicked men took me by violence and sold me to the Christians. We sailed a month and a half on the great sea to the place called Charleston in the Christian land. I fell into the hands of a small, weak and wicked man, who feared not God at all, nor did he read (the gospel) at all nor pray. I was afraid to remain with a man so depraved and who committed so many crimes and I ran away. After a month our Lord God brought me forward to the hand of a good man, who fears God, and loves to do good, and whose name is Jim Owen and whose brother is called Col. John Owen. These are two excellent men—I am residing in Bladen County.

I continue in the hand of Jim Owen who never beats me, nor scolds me. I neither go hungry nor naked, and I have no hard work to do. I am not able to do hard work for I am a small man and feeble. During the last twenty years I have known no want in the hand of Jim Owen.

Notes

1. Omar ibn Said [Sayyid], "Autobiography of Omar ibn Said, Slave in North Carolina," (1831), ed. John Franklin Jameson, *The American Historical Review*, 30.4 (July 1925), 787–795; reprinted in Allan D. Austin, ed., *African Muslims in Antebellum America: A Sourcebook* (New York: Garland, 1984).
2. "The opening sermon is from the Quran [Koran], Surah 67, complete." [Austin footnote, p. 517]
3. "'Sheikh Hunter' may have been the man who brought him to jail and who apparently protected Omar." [Austin footnote, p. 517]
4. I.e., his native African language spoken in Futa Toro. Omar apparently learned Arabic from Islamic scholars in Futa Toro.
5. Senegal River and Gambia River.
6. Fayetteville, North Carolina. [Austin footnote, p. 517]
7. Identified by 20th-century scholars as the county sheriff or the clerk of court. [Austin footnote, p. 518]
8. See "Omar Ibn Sayyid," entry in Davidson Encyclopedia, Davidson College Library, at library.davidson. edu/archives/ency/Omars.asp.
9. Austin footnote no. 37, p. 519.

Richard Allen

Richard Allen (1760–1831) begins his short autobiographical sketch foregrounding it as a document that might reveal to posterity events of his life that connect to his religious works. Allen's autobiographical sketch arguably represents the early melding of African American Christianity and life narrative in African American letters. In this respect Allen echoes the premise established in countless early American autobiographical accounts. But Allen's connection to an Anglo-American Puritan tradition coexists with an African-rooted rhetorical tradition that does not confine itself to premises of historical accounting. He confesses at the start that he will give accounts of his life that may be out of order but that nonetheless convey the essence of his life story. He underscores a difference in the preacherly or sermonic tradition of African Americans and their White counterparts who, influenced by the Age of Enlightenment, felt compelled to tie their narratives of religion and faith to a discourse of fact and history. He gives the account of his religious conversion in the familiar format of his day—the Puritan conversion narrative that charts the transition of the fallen Adam from his state of unacknowledged sinner to confessed and redeemed follower of Christ. He attributes favorable outcomes to the providence of God. Allen reveals a priority for orality over written tradition: "Sure am I that reading sermons will never prove so beneficial to the coloured people as spiritual or extempore preaching." He also shows a skill for African American signifying, particularly illustrated in his recollection of the founding of the AME Church. He highlights the divine mission of this founding by contrasting it with the institution they are fleeing. Without directly calling names, Allen's contrast leaves a scathing picture of those White church officials who had attempted to undermine the establishment of a church for Blacks.

The Life, Experience, and Gospel Labours of the Rt. Rev. Richard Allen. To Which Is Annexed the Rise and Progress of the African Methodist Episcopal Church in the United States of America. Containing a Narrative of the Yellow Fever in the Year of Our Lord 1793: With an Address to the People of Colour in the United States

Richard Allen[1]

Preface

A GREAT part of this work having been written many years after events actually took place; and as my memory could not exactly point out the exact time of many occurrences; they are, however, (as many as I can recollect) pointed out; some without day or date, which, I presume, will be of no material consequence, so that they are confined to the truth.

Could I but recollect the half of my trials and sufferings in this life, with the many meetings I have held, and the various occurrences that have taken place in my travelling to and fro, preaching the Gospel of our Lord and Saviour Jesus Christ to Adam's lost race, they would swell this little book far beyond my inclination, and weary perhaps those into whose hands it may chance to come; and as I have been earnestly solicited by many of my friends to leave a small detail of my life and proceedings, I have thought proper, for the satisfaction of those who (after I am dead and in the grave) may feel an inclination to learn the commencement of my life, to leave behind me this short account for their perusal.

Life, &c.

I was born in the year of our Lord 1760, on February 14th, a slave to Benjamin Chew, of Philadelphia. My mother and father and four children of us were sold into Delaware State, near Dover, and I was a child and lived with him until I was upwards of twenty years of age, during which time I was awakened and brought to see myself poor, wretched and undone, and without the mercy of God must be lost. Shortly after I obtained mercy through the blood of Christ, and was constrained to exhort my old companions to seek the Lord. I went rejoicing for several days, and was happy in the Lord, in conversing with many old experienced Christians. I was brought under doubts, and was tempted to believe I was deceived, and was constrained to seek the Lord afresh. I went with my head bowed down for many days. My sins were a heavy burden. I was tempted to believe there was no mercy for me. I cried to the Lord both night and day. One night I thought hell would be my portion. I cried unto Him who delighteth to hear the prayers of a poor sinner; and all of a sudden my dungeon shook, my chains flew off, and glory to God, I cried. My soul was filled. I cried, enough for me—the Saviour died. Now my confidence was strengthened that the Lord, for Christ's sake, had heard my prayers, and pardoned all my sins. I was constrained to go from house to house, exhorting my old companions, and telling to all around what a dear Saviour I had found. I joined the Methodist society, and met in class at Benjamin Wells's, in the forest, Delaware State. John Gray was the class-leader. I met in his class for several years.

My master was an unconverted man, and all the family; but he was what the world called a good master. He was more like a father to his slaves than any thing else. He was a very tender, humane man. My mother and father lived with him for many years. He was brought into difficulty, not being able to pay for us; and mother having several children after he had bought us, he sold my mother and three children. My mother sought the Lord and found favour with him, and became a very pious woman. There were three children of us remained with our old master. My oldest brother embraced religion, and my sister. Our neighbours, seeing that our master indulged us with the privilege of attending meeting once in two weeks, said that Stokeley's negroes would soon ruin him; and so my brother and myself held a council together that we would attend more faithfully to our master's business, so that it should not be said that religion made us worse servants, we would work night and day to get our crops forward, so that they should be disappointed. We frequently went to meeting on every other Thursday; but if we were likely to be backward with our crops we would refrain from going to meeting. When our master found we were making no provision to go to meeting, he would frequently ask us if it was not our meeting day, and if we were not going. We would frequently tell him, "no, sir, we would rather stay at home and get our work done." He would tell us, "Boys, I would rather you would go to your meeting: if I am not good myself, I like to see you striving yourselves to be good." Our reply would be, "Thank you, sir; but we would rather stay and get our crops forward." So we always continued to keep our crops more forward than our neighbours; and we would attend public preaching once in two weeks, and class meeting once a week. At length our master said he was convinced that religion made slaves better and not worse, and often boasted of his slaves for their honesty and industry. Some time after I asked him if I might ask the preachers to come and preach at his house. He being old and infirm, my master and mistress cheerfully agreed for me to ask some of the Methodist preachers to come and preach at his house. I asked him for a note. He replied, if my word was not sufficient, he should send no note. I accordingly asked the preacher. He seemed somewhat backward at first, as my master did not send a written request; but the class-leader (John Gray) observed that my word was sufficient; so he preached at my old master's house on the next Wednesday. Preaching continued for some months; at length Freeborn Garrison preached from these words, "Thou art weighed in the balance, and art found wanting." In pointing out and weighing the different characters, and among the rest weighed the slave-holders, my master believed himself to be one of that number, and after that he could not be satisfied to hold slaves, believing it to be wrong. And after that he proposed to me and my brother buying our times, to pay him sixty pounds gold and silver, or two thousand dollars continental money, which we complied with in the year 17—.

We left our master's house, and I may truly say it was like leaving our father's house; for he was a kind, affectionate, and tender-hearted master, and told us to make his house our home when we were out of a place or sick. While living with him we had family prayer in the kitchen, to which he frequently would come out himself at time of prayer, and my mistress with him. At length he invited us from the kitchen to the parlour to hold family prayer, which we attended to. We had our stated times to hold our prayer meetings and give exhortations at in the neighbourhood.

I had it often impressed upon my mind that I should one day enjoy my freedom; for slavery is a bitter pill, notwithstanding we had a good master. But when we would think that our day's work was never done, we often thought that after our master's death we were liable to be sold to the highest bidder, as he was much in debt; and thus my troubles were increased, and I was often brought to weep between the porch and the altar. But I have had reason to bless my dear Lord that a door was opened unexpectedly for me to buy my time, and enjoy my liberty. When I left my master's house I knew not what to do, not being used to hard work, what business I should follow to pay my master and get my living. I went to cutting of cord wood. The first day my hands were so blistered and sore, that it was with difficulty I could open or shut them. I kneeled down upon my knees and prayed that the Lord would open some way for me to get my living. In a few days my hands recovered, and became accustomed to cutting of wood and other hardships; so I soon became able to cut my cord and a half and two cords a day. After I was done cutting, I was employed in a brick-yard by one Robert Register, at fifty dollars a month, continental money. After I was done with the brick-yard I went to days' work, but did not forget to serve my dear Lord. I used oftimes to pray sitting, standing, or lying; and while my hands were employed to earn my bread, my heart was devoted to my dear Redeemer. Sometimes I would awake from my sleep preaching and praying. I was after this employed in driving of wagon in time of the continental war, in drawing salt from Rehobar, Sussex county, in Delaware. I had my regular stops and preaching places on the road. I enjoyed many happy seasons in meditation and prayer while in this employment.

After peace was proclaimed I then travelled extensively, striving to preach the Gospel. My lot was cast in Wilmington. Shortly after I was taken sick with the fall fever and then the pleurisy. September the 3d, 1783, I left my native place. After leaving Wilmington, I went into New-Jersey, and there travelled and strove to preach the Gospel until the spring of 1784. I then became acquainted with Benjamin Abbot, that great and good apostle. He was one of the greatest men that ever I was acquainted with. He seldom preached but what there were souls added to his labour. He was a man of as great faith as any that ever I saw. The Lord was with him, and blessed his labours abundantly. He was as a friend and father to me. I was sorry when I had to leave West Jersey, knowing I had to leave a father. I was employed in cutting of wood for Captain Cruenkleton, although I preached the Gospel at nights and on Sundays. My dear Lord was with me, and blessed my labours—glory to God—and gave me souls for my hire. I then visited East Jersey, and laboured for my dear Lord, and became acquainted with Joseph Budd, and made my home with him, near the new mills—a family, I trust, who loved and served the Lord. I laboured some time there; but being much afflicted in body with the inflammatory rheumatism, was not so successful as in some other places. I went from there to Jonathan Bunn's, near Bennington, East Jersey. There I laboured in that neighbourhood for some time. I found him and his family kind and affectionate, and he and his dear wife were a father and mother of Israel. In the year 1784 I left East Jersey, and laboured in Pennsylvania. I walked until my feet became so sore and blistered the first day, that I scarcely could bear them to the ground. I found the people very humane and kind in Pennsylvania. I having but little money, I stopped at Cæsar Water's, at Radnor township, twelve miles from Philadelphia. I found him and his wife very kind and affectionate to me. In the evening they asked me if I would come and take tea with them; but after sitting awhile, my feet became so sore and painful that I could scarcely be able to put them to the floor. I told them that I would accept of their kind invitation, but my feet pained me so that I could not come to the table. They brought the table to me. Never was I more kindly received by strangers that I had never before seen, than by them. She bathed my feet with warm water and bran; the next morning my feet were better and free from pain. They asked me if I would preach for them. I preached for them the next evening. We had a glorious meeting. They invited me to stay till Sabbath day, and preach for them. I agreed to do so, and preached on Sabbath day to a large congregation of different persuasions, and my dear Lord was with me, and I believe there were many souls cut to the heart, and were added to the ministry. They insisted on me to stay longer with them. I stayed and laboured in Radnor several weeks. Many souls were awakened, and cried aloud to the Lord to have mercy upon them. I was frequently called upon by many inquiring what they should do to be saved. I appointed them to prayer and supplication at the throne of grace, and to make use of all manner of prayer, and pointed them to the invitation of our Lord and Saviour Jesus Christ, who has said, "Come unto me, all ye that are weary and heavy laden, and I will give you rest." Glory be to God! and now I know he was a God at hand and left not afar off. I preached my farewell sermon, and left these dear people. It was a time of visitation from above. many were the slain of the Lord. Seldom did I ever experience such a time of mourning and lamentation among a people. There were but few coloured people in the neighbourhood—the most of my congregation was white. Some said, this man must be a man of God; I never heard such preaching before. We spent a greater part of the night in singing and prayer with the mourners. I expected I should have had to walk, as I had done before; but Mr. Davis had a creature that he made a present to me; but I intended to pay him for his horse if ever I got able. My dear Lord was kind and gracious to me. Some years after I got into business, and thought myself able to pay for the horse. The horse was too light and small for me to travel on far. I traded it away with George Huftman for a blind horse, but larger. I found my friend Huftman very kind and affectionate to me, and his family also. I preached several times at Huftman's meeting house to a large and numerous congregation.

I proceeded on to Lancaster, Pennsylvania. I found the people in general dead to religion, and scarcely a form of godliness. I went on to Little York and put up at George Tess, a saddler, and I believed him to be a man that loved and served the Lord. I had comfortable meetings with the Germans. I left Little York and proceeded on to the State of Maryland, and stopped at Mr. Benjamin Grover's; and I believed him to be a man that loved and served the Lord. I had many happy seasons with my dear friends. His wife was a very pious woman; but their dear children were strangers to vital religion. I preached in the neighbourhood for some time, and travelled Hartford circuit with Mr. Porters, who travelled that circuit. I found him very useful to me. I also travelled with Jonathan Forest and Leari Coal.

December, 1784, General Conference sat in Baltimore, the first General Conference ever held in America. The English preachers just arrived from Europe, Rev. Dr. Coke, Richard Watcoat, and Thomas Vasses. This was the beginning of the Episcopal Church amongst the Methodists. Many of the ministers were set apart in holy orders at this Conference, and were said to be entitled to the gown; and I have thought religion has been declining in the church ever since. There was a pamphlet published by some person which stated that when the Methodists were no people, then they were a people; and now they have become a people, they were no people, which had often serious weight upon my mind.

In 1785 the Rev. Richard Watcoat was appointed on Baltimore circuit. He was, I believe, a man of God. I found great strength in travelling with him—a father in Israel. In his advice he was fatherly and friendly. He was of a mild and serene disposition. My lot was cast in Baltimore, in a small meeting-house called Methodist Alley. I stopped at Richard Mould's, and was sent to my lodgings, and lodged at Mr. McCannon's. I had some happy meetings in Baltimore. I was introduced to Richard Russell, who was very kind and affectionate to me, and attended several meetings. Rev. Bishop Asberry sent for me to meet him at Henry Gaff's. I did so. He told me he wished me to travel with him. He told me that in the slave countries, Carolina and other places, I must not intermix with the slaves, and I would frequently have to sleep in his carriage, and he would allow me my victuals and clothes. I told him I would not travel with him on these conditions. He asked me my reason. I told him if I was taken sick, who was to support me? and that I thought people ought to lay up something while they were able, to support themselves in time of sickness or old age. He said that was as much as he got, his victuals and clothes. I told him he would be taken care of, let his afflictions be as they were, or let him be taken sick where he would, he would be taken care of; but I doubted whether it would be the case with myself. He smiled, and told me he would give me from then until he returned from the eastward to make up my mind, which would be about three months. But I made up my mind that I would not accept of his proposals. Shortly after I left Hartford Circuit, and came to Pennsylvania, on Lancaster Circuit. I travelled several months on Lancaster Circuit with the Rev. Peter Morratte and Irie Ellis. They were very kind and affectionate to me in building me up; for I had many trials to pass through, and I received nothing from the Methodist connexion. My usual method was, when I would get bare of clothes, to stop travelling and go to work, so that no man could say I was chargeable to the connexion. My hands administered to my necessities. The autumn of 1785 I returned again to Radnor. I stopped at George Giger's, a man of God, and went to work. His family were all kind and affectionate to me. I killed seven beefs, and supplied the neighbours with meat; got myself pretty well clad through my own industry—thank God—and preached occasionally. The elder in charge in Philadelphia frequently sent for me to come to the city. February, 1786, I came to Philadelphia. Preaching was given out for me at five o'clock in the morning at St. George's Church. I strove to preach as well as I could, but it was a great cross to me; but the Lord was with me. We had a good time, and several souls were awakened, and were earnestly seeking redemption in the blood of Christ. I thought I would stop in Philadelphia a week or two. I preached at different places in the city. My labour was much blessed. I soon saw a large field open in seeking and instructing my African brethren, who had been a long forgotten people and few of them attended public worship. I preached in the commons, in Southwark, Northern Liberties, and wherever I could find an opening. I frequently preached twice a day, at 5 o'clock in the morning and in the evening, and it was not uncommon for me to preach from four to five times a day. I established prayer meetings; I raised a society in 1786 of forty-two members. I saw the necessity of erecting a place of worship for the coloured people. I proposed it to the most respectable people of colour in this city; but here I met with opposition. I had but three coloured brethren that united with me in erecting a place of worship—the Rev. Absalom Jones, William White, and Dorus Ginnings. These united with me as soon as it became public and known by the elder who was stationed in the city. The Rev. C—B—opposed the plan, and would not submit to any argument we could raise; but he was shortly removed from the charge. The Rev Mr. W—took the charge, and the Rev L—G—. Mr. W—was much opposed to an African church, and used very degrading and insulting language to us, to try and prevent us from going on. We all belonging to St. George's church—Rev. Absalom Jones, William White and Dorus Ginnings. We felt ourselves much cramped; but my dear Lord was with us, and we believed, if it was his will, the work would go on, and that we would be able to succeed in building the house of the Lord. We established prayer meetings and meetings of exhortation, and the Lord blessed our endeavours, and many souls were awakened; but the elder soon forbid us holding any such meetings; but we viewed the forlorn state of our coloured brethren, and that they were destitute of a place of worship. They were considered as a nuisance.

A number of us usually attended St. George's Church in Fourth street; and when the coloured people began to get numerous in attending the church, they moved us from the seats we usually sat on, and placed us around the wall, and on Sabbath morning we went to church and the sexton stood at the door, and told us to go in the gallery. He told us to go, and we would see where to sit. We expected to take the seats over the ones we formerly occupied below, not knowing any better. We took those seats. Meeting had begun, and they were nearly done singing, and just as we got to the seats, the elder said, "let us pray." We had not been long upon our knees before I heard considerable scuffling and low talking. I raised my head up and saw one of the trustees, H—M—, having hold of the Rev. Absalom Jones, pulling him up off of his knees, and saying, "You must get up—you must not kneel here." Mr. Jones replied, "wait until prayer is over." Mr. H—M—said "no, you must get up now, or I will call for aid and I force you away." Mr. Jones said, "wait until prayer is over, and I will get up and trouble you no more." With that he beckoned to one of the other trustees, Mr. L—S—to come to his assistance. He came, and went to William White to pull him up. By this time prayer was over, and we all went out of the church in a body, and they were no more plagued with us in the church. This raised a great excitement and inquiry among the citizens, in so much that I believe they were ashamed of their conduct. But my dear Lord was with us, and we were filled with fresh vigour to get a house erected to worship God in. Seeing our forlorn and distressed situation, many of the hearts of our citizens were moved to urge us forward; notwithstanding we had subscribed largely towards finishing St. George's Church, in building the gallery and laying new floors, and just as the house was made comfortable, we were turned out from enjoying the comforts of worshiping therein. We then hired a store room, and held worship by ourselves. Here we were pursued with threats of being disowned, and read publicly out of meeting if we did continue worship in the place we had hired; but we believed the Lord would be our friend. We got subscription papers out to raise money to build the house of the Lord. By this time we had waited on Dr. Rush and Mr. Robert Ralston, and told them of our distressing situation. We considered it a blessing that the Lord had put it into our hearts to wait upon those gentlemen. They pitied our situation, and subscribed largely towards the church, and were very friendly towards us, and advised us how to go on. We appointed Mr. Ralston our treasurer. Dr. Rush did much for us in public by his influence. I hope the name of Dr. Benjamin Rush and Mr. Robert Ralston will never be forgotten among us. They were the two first gentlemen who espoused the cause of the oppressed, and aided us in building the house of the Lord for the poor Africans to worship in. Here was the beginning and rise of the first African church in America. But the elder of the Methodist church still pursued us. Mr. J—M—called upon us and told us if we did not erase our names from the subscription paper, and give up the paper, we would be publicly turned out of meeting. We asked him if we had violated any rules of discipline by so doing. He replied, "I have the charge given to me by the Conference, and unless you submit I will read you publicly out of meeting." We told him we were willing to abide by the discipline of the Methodist church; "and if you will show us where we have violated any law of discipline of the Methodist church, we will submit; and if there is no rule violated in the discipline, we will proceed on." He replied, "we will read you all out." We told him if he turned us out contrary to rule of discipline, we should seek further redress. We told him we were dragged off of our knees in St. George's church, and treated worse than heathens; and we were determined to seek out for ourselves, the Lord being our helper. He told us we were not Methodists, and left us. Finding we would go on in raising money to build the church, he called upon us again, and wished to see us all together. We met him. He told us that he wished us well, and that he was a friend to us, and used many arguments to convince us that we were wrong in building a church. We told him we had no place of worship; and we did not mean to go to St. George's church any more, as we were so scandalously treated in the presence of all the congregation present; "and if you deny us your name, you cannot seal up the scriptures from us, and deny us a name in heaven. We believe heaven is free for all who worship in spirit and truth." And he said, "so you are determined to go on." We told him—"yes, God being our helper." He then replied, "we will disown you all from the Methodist connexion." We believed if we put our trust in the Lord, he would stand by us. This was a trial that I never had to pass through before. I was confident that the great head of the church would support us. My dear Lord was with us. We went out with our subscription paper, and met with great success. We had no reason to complain of the liberality of the citizens. The first day the Rev. Absalom Jones and myself went out we collected three hundred and sixty dollars. This was the greatest day's collection that we met with. We appointed a committee to look out for a lot—the Rev. Absalom Jones, William Gray, William Wilcher, and myself. We pitched upon a lot at the corner of Lombard and Sixth streets. They authorized me to go and agree for it. I did accordingly. The lot belonged to Mr. Mark Wilcox. We entered into articles of agreement for the lot. Afterwards the committee found a lot in Fifth street, in a more commodious part of the city, which we bought; and the first lot they threw upon my hands, and wished me to give it up. I told them they had authorized me to agree for the lot, and they were all well satisfied with the agreement I had made, and I thought it was hard that they should throw it upon my hands. I told them I would sooner keep it myself than to forfeit the agreement I had made. And so I did.

We bore much persecution from many of the Methodist connexion; but we have reason to be thankful to Almighty God, who was our deliverer. The day was appointed to go and dig the cellar. I arose early in the morning and addressed the throne of grace, praying that the Lord would bless our endeavours. Having by this time two or three teams of my own—as I was the first proposer of the African church, I put the first spade in the ground to dig a cellar for the same. This was the first African church or meeting house that was erected in the United States of America. We intended it for the African preaching house or church; but finding that the elder stationed in this city was such an opposer to our proceedings of erecting a place of worship; though the principal part of the directors of this church belonged to the Methodist connexion, the elder stationed here would neither preach for us, nor have any thing to do with us. We then held an election, to know what religious denomination we should unite with. At the election it was determined—there were two in favour of the Methodist, the Rev. Absalom Jones and myself, and a large majority in favour of the Church of England. The majority carried. Notwithstanding we had been so violently persecuted by the elder, we were in favour of being attached to the Methodist connexion; for I was confident that there was no religious sect or denomination would suit the capacity of the coloured people as well as the Methodist; for the plain and simple gospel suits best for any people, for the unlearned can understand, and the learned are sure to understand; and the reason that the Methodist is so successful in the awakening and conversion of the coloured people, the plain doctrine and having a good discipline. But in many cases the preachers would act to please their own fancy, without discipline, till some of them became such tyrants, and more especially to the coloured people. They would turn them out of society, giving them no trial, for the smallest offence, perhaps only hearsay. They would frequently, in meeting the class, impeach some of the members of whom they had heard an ill report, and turn them out, saying, "I have heard thus and thus of you, and you are no more a member of society"—without witnesses on either side. This has been frequently done, notwithstanding in the first rise and progress in Delaware State, and elsewhere, the coloured people were their greatest support; for there were but few of us free; but the slaves would toil in their little patches many a night until midnight to raise their little truck and sell to get something to support them more than what their masters gave them, but we used often to divide our little support among the white preachers of the Gospel. This was once a quarter. It was in the time of the old revolutionary war between Great Britain and the United States. The Methodists were the first people that brought glad tidings to the coloured people. I feel thankful that ever I heard a Methodist preach. We are beholden to the Methodists, under God, for the light of the Gospel we enjoy; for all other denominations preached so high-flown that we were not able to comprehend their doctrine. Sure am I that reading sermons will never prove so beneficial to the coloured people as spiritual or extempore preaching. I am well convinced that the Methodist has proved beneficial to thousands and ten times thousands. It is to be awfully feared that the simplicity of the Gospel that was among them fifty years ago, and that they conform more to the world and the fashions thereof, they would fare very little better than the people of the world. The discipline is altered considerably from what it was. We would ask for the good old way, and desire to walk therein.

In 1793 a committee was appointed from the African Church to solicit me to be their minister, for there was no colored preacher in Philadelphia but myself. I told them I could not accept of their offer, as I was a Methodist. I was indebted to the Methodists, under God, for what little religion I had; being convinced that they were the people of God, I informed them that I could not be any thing else but a Methodist, as I was born and awakened under them, and I could go no further with them, for I was a Methodist, and would leave you in peace and love. I would do nothing to retard them in building a church as it was an extensive building, neither would I go out with a subscription paper until they were done going out with their subscription. I bought an old frame that had been formerly occupied as a blacksmith shop from Mr. Sims, and hauled it on the lot in Sixth near Lobard street, that had formerly been taken for the church of England. I employed carpenters to repair the old frame, and fit it for a place of worship. In July, 1794, Bishop Asbury being in town I solicited him to open the church[2] for us which he accepted. The Rev. John Dickins sung and prayed, and Bishop Asbury preached. The house was called bethel agreeable to the prayer that was made. Mr. Dickins prayed that it might be a bethel[3] to the gathering in of thousands of souls. My dear Lord was with us, so that there was many hearty Amen's echoed through the house. This house of worship has been favored with the awakening of many souls, and I trust they are in the kingdom both white and colored. Our warfare and troubles now began afresh. Mr. C. proposed that we should make over the church to the conference. This we objected to, he asserted that we could not be Methodists unless we did, we told him he might deny us their name, but they could not deny us a seat in Heaven. Finding that he could not prevail with us so to do, he observed that we had better be incorporated, then we could get any legacies that were left for us, if not, we could not. We agreed to be incorporated, he offered to draw the incorporation himself, that it would save us the trouble of paying for to get it drawn. We cheerfully submitted to his proposed plan. He drew the incorporation, but incorporated our church under the Conference, our property was then all consigned to the Conference for the present Bishops, Elders, and Ministers, &c., that belonged to the white Conference, and our property was gone. Being ignorant of incorporations we cheerfully agreed thereto, we labored about ten years under this incorporation, until J—S—was appointed to take the charge in Philadelphia, he soon waked us up by demanding the keys and books of the church, and forbid us holding any meetings except orders from him, these propositions we told him we could not agree to. He observed he was elder appointed to the charge, and unless we submitted to him, he would read us all out of meeting, we told him the house was our's, we had bought it, and paid for it. He said he would let us know it was not our's, it belonged to the Conference, we took council on it; council informed us we had been taken in, according to the incorporation, it belonged to the white connexion. We asked him if it could'nt be altered, he told us it two thirds of the society agreed to have it altered, it could be altered. He gave me a transcript to lay before them, I called the society together and laid it before them. My dear Lord was with us. It was unanimously agree to by both male and female, we had another incorporation drawn that took the church from Conference, and got it passed before the elder knew any thing about it. This raised a considerable rumpus, for the elder contended that it would not be good unless he had signed it. The elder with the Trustees of St. George's called us together, and said we must pay six hundred dollars a year for their services, or they could not serve us. We told them we were not able so to do. The Trustees of St. George's insisted that we should, or should not be supplied by their preachers, at last they made a move that they would take four hundred, we told them that our house was considerable in debt, and we poor people, and we could not agree to pay four hundred, but we agreed to give them two hundred. It was moved by one of the Trustees of St. George's that the money should be paid into their treasury, we refused paying it into their treasury, but we would pay it to the preacher that served, they made a move that the preacher should not receive the money from us. The bethel Trustees made a move that their funds should be shut and they would pay none, this caused a considerable contention, at length they withdrew their motion, the elder supplied us with preaching five times in a year for two hundred dollars. Finding that they supplied us so seldom, the Trustees of Bethel church passed a resolution that they would pay but one hundred dollars a year, as the elder only preached five times in a year for us, they called for the money, we paid him twenty-five dollars a quarter, but he being dissatisfied, returned the money back again, and would not have it unless we paid him fifty dollars. The Trustees concluded it was enough for five sermons, and said they would pay no more, the elder of St. George's was determined to preach for us no more, unless we gave him two hundred dollars, and we were left alone for upwards of one year.

Mr. S—R—being appointed to the charge of Philadelphia, declared unless we would repeal the Supplement neither he nor any white preacher travelling or local, should preach any more for us; so we were left to ourselves, at length the preachers and stewards belonging to the Academy, proposed serving us on the same terms that we had offered to the St. George's preachers, and they preached for us better than a twelve month; and then demanded $150 per year; this not being complied with, they declined preaching for us, and we were once more left to ourselves, as an edict was passed by the elder that if any local preacher should serve us, he should be expelled from the connexion. John Emory, then elder of the Academy, published a circular letter in which we were disowned by the Methodists. A house was also hired and fitted up for worship not far from Bethel, and an invitation given to all who desired to be Methodists to resort thither. But being disappointed in this plan, Robert R. Roberts, the resident elder, came to Bethel, insisted on preaching to us, and taking the spiritual charge of the congregation, for we were Methodists. He was told he should come on some terms with the Trustees: his answer was that, "He did not come to consult with Richard Allen or other trustees, but to inform the congregation that on next Sunday afternoon, he would come and take the spiritual charge." We told him he could not preach for us under existing circumstances. "However, at the appointed time he came, but having taken previous advice we had our preacher in the pulpit when he came, and the house was so fixed that he could not get but more than half way to the pulpit. Finding himself disappointed he appealed to those who came with him as witnesses that "That man (meaning the preacher) had taken his appointment." Several respectable white citizens who knew the colored people had been ill used were present, and told us not to fear for they would see us righted, and not suffer Roberts to preach in a forcible manner, after which Roberts went away.

The next elder stationed in Philadelphia was Robert Birch, who following the example of his predecessor, came and published a meeting for himself. But the method just mentioned was adopted, and he had to go away disappointed. In consequence of this he applied to the Supreme Court for a writ of Mandamus, to know why the pulpit was denied him. Being elder, this brought on a law suit, which ended in our favor. Thus by the Providence of God we were delivered from a long, distressing and expensive suit which could not be resumed, being determined by the Supreme Court. For this mercy we desire to be unfeignedly thankful.

About this time our colored friends in Baltimore were treated in a similar manner by the white preachers and Trustees, and many of them drove away; who were disposed to seek a place of worship, rather than go to law.

Many of the colored people in other places were in a situation nearly like those of Philadelphia and Baltimore, which induced us in April 1816 to call a general meeting, by way of Conference.

Delegates from Baltimore and other places which met those of Philadelphia, and taking into consideration their grievances, and in order to secure the privileges, promote union and harmony among themselves, it was resolved, "That the people of Philadelphia, Baltimore, &c. &c., should become one body, under the name of the African Methodist Episcopal Church." We deemed it expedient to have a form of discipline, whereby we may guide our people in the fear of God, in the unity of the Spirit, and in the bonds of peace, and preserve us from that spiritual despotism which we have so recently experienced—remembering that we are not to lord it over God's heritage, as greedy dogs that can never have enough. But with long suffering, and bowels of compassion to bear each other's burthens, and so fulfil the Law of Christ, praying that our mutual striving together for the promulgation of the Gospel may be crowned with abundant success.

> The God of Bethel heard her cries, He let his power be seen; He stop'd the proud oppressors frown,
> And proved himself a King.
> Thou sav'd them in the trying hour, Ministers and councils joined And all stood ready to retain
> That helpless church of thine.
> Bethel surrounded by her foes, But not yet in despair, Christ heard her supplicating cries;
> The God of Bethel heard.

Notes

1. Richard Allen, *The Life, Experience, and Gospel Labours of the Rt. Rev. Richard Allen*, (Philadelphia: Martin & Boden, Printers, 1833), pp. 3–21, retrieved from UNC's Documenting the American South, http://docsouth.unc.edu/neh/allen/allen.html.
2. This church will at present accommodate between 3 and 4000 persons.
3. See Gen. chap. 28.

Sojourner Truth

Named Isabella at birth, Sojourner Truth (1797–1883) dropped her given name after a spiritual revelation that led her to take the name that she deemed divinely inspired. Truth's parents were slaves to a Dutch-speaking family in upstate New York, and Truth grew up speaking Low Dutch. It is thus important to consider the layers of translation, transcription, and coding in the words of Truth's text. The version of Truth's narrative that we read then comes to us after numerous points of intervention. Truth's first language is Dutch, in contrast to her transcriber's native English tongue. Truth does not read or write, so she speaks her narrative to a transcriber, Olive Gilbert, a White female abolitionist. Gilbert's voice and viewpoint oftentimes stand out as the articulated perspective, even though the work is credited as Truth's story. Without question, Gilbert is a pervasively intrusive voice; however, Truth's voice, especially her articulation of a spiritual ethos, is not altogether silent or mere emulation of White Christian discourse. Truth's conversion account is told in the guise of the Puritan conversion narrative; however, as Gilbert notes, Truth's conversational relationship with God and her requests that seem more like demands are not conventional. Gilbert does not connect Truth's religious ethos to any tradition; however, Truth's calls to or conversations with God are like the appeals of her mother that she recalls from childhood. Like her mother, Truth finds God in the heavens and in the wilderness, and reminiscent of African religious traditions in which individuals invoke their personal deities, she invokes God for his intercession in her daily life. Truth assumes a familiarity with God that in Calvinist discourse borders on sacrilege.

Her Brothers and Sisters

Sojourner Truth[1]

Isabella's father was very tall and straight, when young, which gave him the name of 'Bomefree'—low Dutch for tree—at least, this is Sojourner's pronunciation of it—and by this name he usually went. The most familiar appellation of her mother was 'Mau-mau Bett.' She was the mother of some ten or twelve children; though Sojourner is far from knowing the exact number of her brothers and sisters; she being the youngest, save one, and all older than herself having been sold before her remembrance. She was privileged to behold six of them while she remained a slave.

Of the two that immediately preceded her in age, a boy of five years, and a girl of three, who were sold when she was an infant, she heard much; and she wishes that all who would fain believe that slave parents have not natural affection for their offspring could have listened as *she* did, while Bomefree and Mau-mau Bett,—their dark cellar lighted by a blazing pine-knot,— would sit for hours, recalling and recounting every endearing, as well as harrowing circumstance that taxed memory could supply, from the histories of those dear departed ones, of whom they had been robbed, and for whom their hearts still bled. Among the rest, they would relate how the little boy, on the last morning he was with them, arose with the birds, kindled a fire, calling for his Mau-mau to 'come, for all was now ready for her'—little dreaming of the dreadful separation which was so near at hand, but of which his parents had an uncertain, but all the more cruel foreboding. There was snow on the ground, at the time of which we are speaking; and a large old-fashioned sleigh was seen to drive up to the door of the late Col. Ardinburgh. This event was noticed with childish pleasure by the unsuspicious boy; but when he was taken and put into the sleigh, and saw his little sister actually shut and locked into the sleigh box, his eyes were at once opened to their intentions; and, like a frightened deer he sprang from the sleigh, and running into the house, concealed himself under a bed. But this availed him little. He was re-conveyed to the sleigh, and separated for ever from those whom God had constituted his natural guardians and protectors, and who should have found him, in return, a stay and a staff to them in their declining years. But I make no comments on facts like these, knowing that the heart of every slave parent will make its own comments, involuntarily and correctly, as soon as each heart shall make the case its own. Those who are not parents will draw their conclusions from the promptings of humanity and philanthropy:—these, enlightened by reason and revelation, are also unerring.

Her Religious Instruction

Isabella and Peter, her youngest brother, remained, with their parents, the legal property of Charles Ardinburgh till his decease, which took place when Isabella was near nine years old.

After this event, she was often surprised to find her mother in tears; and when, in her simplicity, she inquired, 'Mau-mau, what makes you cry?' she would answer, 'Oh, my child, I am thinking of your brothers and sisters that have been sold away from me.' And she would proceed to detail many circumstances respecting them. But Isabella long since concluded that it was the impending fate of her only remaining children, which her mother but too well understood, even then, that called up those memories from the past, and made them crucify her heart afresh.

In the evening, when her mother's work was done, she would sit down under the sparkling vault of heaven, and calling her children to her, would talk to them of the only Being that could effectually aid or protect them. Her teachings were delivered in Low Dutch, her only language, and, translated into English, ran nearly as follows:

'My children, there is a God, who hears and sees you.' A *God*, mau-mau! Where does he live?' asked the children. 'He lives in the sky,' she replied; 'and when you are beaten, or cruelly treated, or fall into any trouble, you must ask help of him, and he will always hear and help you.' She taught them to kneel and say the Lord's prayer. She entreated them to refrain from lying and stealing, and to strive to obey their masters.

At times, a groan would escape her, and she would break out in the language of the Psalmist— 'Oh Lord, how long?' 'Oh Lord, how long?' And in reply to Isabella's question—'What ails you, mau-mau?' her only answer was, 'Oh, a good deal ails me'—'Enough ails me.' Then again, she would point them to the stars, and say, in her peculiar language, 'Those are the same stars, and that is the same moon, that look down upon your brothers and sisters, and which they see as they look up to them, though they are ever so far away from us, and each other.'

Thus, in her humble way, did she endeavor to show them their Heavenly Father, as the only being who could protect them in their perilous condition; at the same time, she would strengthen and brighten the chain of family affection, which she trusted extended itself sufficiently to connect the widely scattered members of her precious flock. These instructions of the mother were treasured up and held sacred by Isabella, as our future narrative will show.

Illegal Sale of Her Son

A little previous to Isabel's leaving her old master, he had sold her child, a boy of five years, to a Dr. Gedney, who took him with him as far as New York city, on his way to England; but finding the boy too small for his service, he sent him back to his brother, Solomon Gedney. This man disposed of him to his sister's husband, a wealthy planter, by the name of Fowler, who took him to his own home in Alabama.

This illegal and fraudulent transaction had been perpetrated some months before Isabella knew of it, as she was now living at Mr. Van Wagener's. The law expressly prohibited the sale of any slave out of the State,—and all minors were to be free at twenty-one years of age; and Mr. Dumont had sold Peter with the express understanding, that he was soon to return to the State of New York, and be emancipated at the specified time.

When Isabel heard that her son had been sold South, she immediately started on foot and alone, to find the man who had thus dared, in the face of all law, human and divine, to sell her child out of the State; and if possible, to bring him to account for the deed.

Arriving at New Paltz, she went directly to her former mistress, Dumont, complaining bitterly of the removal of her son. Her mistress heard her through, and then replied—'Ugh! a *fine* fuss to make about a little *nigger*! Why, have n't you as many of 'em left as you can see to and take care of? A pity 'tis, the niggers are not all in Guinea!! Making such a halloo-balloo about the neighborhood; and all for a paltry nigger!!!' Isabella heard her through, and after a moment's hesitation, answered, in tones of deep determination—'*I'll have my child again.*' 'Have *your child* again!' repeated her mistress—her tones big with contempt, and scorning the absurd idea of her getting him. 'How can you get him? And what have you to support him with, if you could? Have you any money?' 'No,' answered Bell, 'I have no money, but God has enough, or what's better! And I'll have my child again.' These words were pronounced in the most slow, solemn and determined measure and manner. And in speaking of it, she says, 'Oh, my God! I know'd I'd have him agin. I was sure God would help me to get him. Why, I felt so *tall within*—I felt as if the *power of a nation* was with me!'

The impressions made by Isabella on her auditors, when moved by lofty or deep feeling, can never be transmitted to paper, (to use the words of another,) till by some Daguerrian art, we are enabled to transfer the look, the gesture, the tones of voice, in connection with the quaint, yet fit expressions used, and the spirit-stirring animation that, at such a time, pervades all she says.

After leaving her mistress, she called on Mrs. Gedney, mother of him who had sold her boy; who, after listening to her lamentations, her grief being mingled with indignation at the sale of her son, and her declaration that she would have him again—said, 'Dear me! What a disturbance to make about your child! What, is *your* child better than *my* child? My child is gone out there, and yours is gone to live with her, to have enough of everything, and to be treated like a gentleman!' And here she laughed at Isabel's absurd fears, as she would represent them to be. 'Yes,' said Isabel, '*your* child has gone there, but she is *married* and my boy has gone as a *slave*, and he is too little to go so far from his mother. Oh, I must have my child.' And here the continued laugh of Mrs. G. seemed to Isabel, in this time of anguish and distress, almost demoniacal. And well it was for Mrs. Gedney, that, at that time, she could not even dream of the awful fate awaiting her own beloved daughter, at the hands of him whom she had chosen as worthy the wealth of her love and confidence, and in whose society her young heart had calculated on a happiness, purer and more elevated than was ever conferred by a kingly crown. But, alas! she was doomed to disappointment, as we shall relate by and by. At this point, Isabella earnestly begged of God that he would show to those about her that He was her helper; and she adds, in narrating, 'And He *did*; or, if He did not show them, he did me.'

Isabella's Religious Experience

We will now turn from the outward and temporal to the inward and spiritual life of our subject. It is ever both interesting and instructive to trace the exercises of a human mind, through the trials and mysteries of life; and especially a naturally powerful mind, left as hers was almost entirely to its own workings, and the chance influences it met on its way; and especially to note its reception of that divine 'light, that lighteth every man that cometh into the world.'

We see, as knowledge dawns upon it, truth and error strangely commingled; here, a bright spot illuminated by truth—and there, one darkened and distorted by error; and the state of such a soul may be compared to a landscape at early dawn, where the sun is seen superbly gilding some objects, and causing others to send forth their lengthened, distorted, and sometimes hideous shadows.

Her mother, as we have already said, talked to her of God. From these conversations, her incipient mind drew the conclusion, that God was 'a great man;' greatly superior to other men in power; and being located 'high in the sky,' could see all that transpired on the earth. She believed he not only saw, but noted down all her actions in a great book, even as her master kept a record of whatever he wished not to forget. But she had no idea that God knew a thought of hers till she had uttered it aloud.

As we have before mentioned, she had ever been mindful of her mother's injunctions, spreading out in detail all her troubles before God, imploring and firmly trusting him to send her deliverance from them. Whilst yet a child, she listened to a story of a wounded soldier, left alone in the trail of a flying army, helpless and starving, who hardened the very ground about him with kneeling in his supplications to God for relief, until it arrived. From this narrative, she was deeply impressed with the idea, that if *she* also were to present her petitions under the open canopy of heaven, speaking very loud, she should the more readily be heard; consequently, she sought a fitting spot for this, her rural sanctuary. The place she selected, in which to offer up her daily orisons, was a small island in a small stream, covered with large willow shrubbery, beneath which the sheep had made their pleasant winding paths; and sheltering themselves from the scorching rays of a noon-tide sun, luxuriated in the cool shadows of the graceful willows, as they listened to the tiny falls of the silver waters. It was a lonely spot, and chosen by her for its beauty, its retirement, and because she thought that there, in the noise of those waters, she could speak louder to God, without being overheard by any who might pass that way. When she had made choice of her sanctum, at a point of the island where the stream met, after having been separated, she improved it by pulling away the branches of the shrubs from the centre, and weaving them together for a wall on the outside, forming a circular arched alcove, made entirely of the graceful willow. To this place she resorted daily, and in pressing times much more frequently.

At this time, her prayers, or, more appropriately, 'talks with God,' were perfectly original and unique, and would be well worth preserving, were it possible to give the tones and manner with the words; but no adequate idea of them can be written while the tones and manner remain inexpressible.

She would sometimes repeat, 'Our Father in heaven,' in her Low Dutch, as taught her by her mother, after that, all was from the suggestions of her own rude mind. She related to God, in minute detail, all her troubles and sufferings, inquiring, as she proceeded, 'Do you think that's right, God?' and closed by begging to be delivered from the evil, whatever it might be.

She talked to God as familiarly as if he had been a creature like herself; and a thousand times more so, than if she had been in the presence of some earthly potentate. She demanded, with little expenditure of reverence or fear, a supply of all her more pressing wants, and at times her demands approached very near to commands. She felt as if God was under obligation to her, much more than she was to him. He seemed to her benighted vision in some manner bound to do her bidding.

Her heart recoils now, with very dread, when she recalls these shocking, almost blasphemous conversations with the great Jehovah. And well for herself did she deem it, that, unlike earthly potentates, his infinite character combined the tender father with the omniscient and omnipotent Creator of the universe.

She at first commenced promising God, that if he would help her out of all her difficulties, she would pay him by being very good; and this goodness she intended as a remuneration to God. She could think of no benefit that was to accrue to herself or her fellow-creatures, from her leading a life of purity and generous self-sacrifice for the good of others; as far as any but God was concerned, she saw nothing in it but heart-trying penance, sustained by the sternest exertion; and this she soon found much more easily promised than performed.

Days wore away—new trials came—God's aid was invoked, and the same promises repeated; and every successive night found her part of the contract unfulfilled. She now began to excuse herself, by telling God she could not be good in her present circumstances; but if he would give her a new place, and a good master and mistress, she could and would be good; and she expressly stipulated, that she would be good *one* day to show God how good she would be *all* of the time, when he should surround her with the right influences, and she should be delivered from the temptations that then so sorely beset her. But, alas! when night came, and she became conscious that she had yielded to all her temptations, and entirely failed of keeping her word with God, having prayed and promised one hour, and fallen into the sins of anger and profanity the next, the mortifying reflection weighed on her mind, and blunted her enjoyment. Still, she did not lay it deeply to heart, but continued to repeat her demands for aid, and her promises of pay, with full purpose of heart, at each particular time, that *that* day she would not fail to keep her plighted word.

Thus perished the inward spark, like a flame just igniting, when one waits to see whether it will burn on or die out, till the long desired change came, and she found herself in a new place, with a good mistress, and one who never instigated an otherwise kind master to be unkind to her; in short, a place where she had literally nothing to complain of, and where, for a time, she was more happy than she could well express. 'Oh, every thing there was *so* pleasant, and kind, and good, and all so comfortable; enough of every thing; indeed, it was beautiful!' she exclaimed.

Here, at Mr. Van Wagener's,—as the reader will readily perceive she must have been,—she was so happy and satisfied, that God was entirely forgotten. Why should her thoughts turn to Him, who was only known to her as a help in trouble? She had no trouble now; her every prayer had been answered in every minute particular. She had been delivered from her persecutors and temptations, her youngest child had been given her, and the others she knew she had no means of sustaining if she had them with her, and was content to leave them behind. Their father, who was much older than Isabel, and who preferred serving his time out in slavery, to the trouble and dangers of the course she pursued, remained with and could keep an eye on them—though it is comparatively little that they can do for each other while they remain in slavery; and this little the slave, like persons in every other situation of life, is not always disposed to perform. There *are* slaves, who, copying the selfishness of their superiors in power, in their conduct towards their fellows who may be thrown upon their mercy, by infirmity or illness, allow them to suffer for want of that kindness and care which it is fully in their power to render them.

The slaves in this country have ever been allowed to celebrate the principal, if not some of the lesser festivals observed by the Catholics and Church of England; many of them not being required to do the least service for several days, and at Christmas they have almost universally an entire week to themselves, except, perhaps, the attending to a few duties, which are absolutely required for the comfort of the families they belong to. If much service is desired, they are hired to do it, and paid for it as if they were free. The more sober portion of them spend these holidays in earning a little money. Most of them visit and attend parties and balls, and not a few of them spend it in the lowest dissipation. This respite from toil is granted them by all religionists, of whatever persuasion, and probably originated from the fact that many of the first slaveholders were members of the Church of England.

Frederick Douglass, who has devoted his great heart and noble talents entirely to the furtherance of the cause of his down-trodden race, has said—'From what I know of the effect of their holidays upon the slave, I believe them to be among the most effective means, in the hands of the slaveholder, in keeping down the spirit of insurrection. Were the slaveholders at once to abandon this practice, I have not the slightest doubt it would lead to an immediate insurrection among the slaves. These holidays serve as conductors, or safety-valves, to carry off the rebellious spirit of enslaved humanity. But for these, the slave would be forced up to the wildest desperation; and woe betide the slaveholder, the day he ventures to remove or hinder the operation of those conductors! I warn him that, in such an event, a spirit will go forth in their midst, more to be dreaded than the most appalling earthquake.'

When Isabella had been at Mr. Van Wagener's a few months, she saw in prospect one of the festivals approaching. She knows it by none but the Dutch name, Pingster, as she calls it—but I think it must have been Whitsuntide, in English. She says she 'looked back into Egypt,' and everything looked 'so pleasant there,' as she saw retrospectively all her former companions enjoying their freedom for at least a little space, as well as their wonted convivialities, and in her heart she longed to be with them. With this picture before her mind's eye, she contrasted the quiet, peaceful life she was living with the excellent people of Wahkendall, and it seemed so dull and void of incident, that the very contrast served but to heighten her desire to return, that, at least, she might enjoy with them, once more, the coming festivities. These feelings had occupied a secret corner of her breast for some time, when, one morning, she told Mrs. Van Wagener that her old master Dumont would come that day, and that she should go home with him on his return. They expressed some surprise, and asked her where she obtained her information. She replied, that no one had told her, but she felt that he would come.

It seemed to have been one of those 'events that cast their shadows before;' for, before night, Mr. Dumont made his appearance. She informed him of her intention to accompany him home. He answered, with a smile, 'I shall not take you back again; you ran away from me.' Thinking his manner contradicted his words, she did not feel repulsed, but made herself and child ready; and when her former master had seated himself in the open dearborn, she walked towards it, intending to place herself and child in the rear, and go with him. But, ere she reached the vehicle, she says that God revealed himself to her, with all the suddenness of a flash of lightning, showing her, 'in the twinkling of an eye, that he was *all over*'—that he pervaded the universe—'and that there was no place where God was not.' She became instantly conscious of her great sin in forgetting her almighty Friend and 'ever-present help in time of trouble.' All her unfulfilled promises arose before her, like a vexed sea whose waves run mountains high; and her soul, which seemed but one mass of lies, shrunk back aghast from the 'awful look' of Him whom she had formerly talked to, as if he had been a being like herself; and she would now fain have hid herself in the bowels of the earth, to have escaped his dread presence. But she plainly saw there was no place, not even in hell, where he was not: and where could she flee? Another such 'a look,' as she expressed it, and she felt that she must be extinguished forever, even as one, with the breath of his mouth, 'blows out a lamp,' so that no spark remains.

A dire dread of annihilation now seized her, and she waited to see if, by 'another look,' she was to be stricken from existence,—swallowed up, even as the fire licketh up the oil with which it comes in contact.

When at last the second look came not, and her attention was once more called to outward things, she observed her master had left, and exclaiming aloud, 'Oh, God, I did not know you were so big,' walked into the house, and made an effort to resume her work. But the workings of the inward man were too absorbing to admit of much attention to her avocations. She desired to talk to God, but her vileness utterly forbade it, and she was not able to prefer a petition. 'What!' said she, 'shall I lie again to God? I have told him nothing but lies; and shall I speak again, and tell another lie to God?' She could not; and now she began to wish for some one to speak to God for her. Then a space seemed opening between her and God, and she felt that if some one, who was worthy in the sight of heaven, would but plead *for* her in their own name, and not let God know it came from *her*, who was so unworthy, God might grant it. At length a friend appeared to stand between herself and an insulted Deity; and she felt as sensibly refreshed as when, on a hot day, an umbrella had been interposed between her scorching head and a burning sun. But who was this friend? became the next inquiry. Was it Deencia, who had so often befriended her? She looked at her with her new power of sight—and, lo! she, too, seemed all 'bruises and putrifying sores,' like herself. No, it was some one very different from Deencia.

'Who *are* you?' she exclaimed, as the vision brightened into a form distinct, beaming with the beauty of holiness, and radiant with love. She then said, audibly addressing the mysterious visitant—'I *know* you, and I *don't* know you.' Meaning, 'You seem perfectly familiar; I feel that you not only love me, but that you always *have* loved me—yet I know you not—I cannot call you by name.' When she said, 'I know you,' the subject of the vision remained distinct and quiet. When she said, 'I don't know you,' it moved restlessly about, like agitated waters. So while she repeated, without intermission, 'I know you, I know you,' that the vision might remain—'Who are you?' was the cry of her heart, and her whole soul was in one deep prayer that this heavenly personage might be revealed to her, and remain with her. At length, after bending both soul and body with the intensity of this desire, till breath and strength seemed failing, and she could maintain her position no longer, an answer came to her, saying distinctly, 'It is Jesus.' 'Yes,' she responded, 'it is *Jesus*.'

Previous to these exercises of mind, she heard Jesus mentioned in reading or speaking, but had received from what she heard no impression that he was any other than an eminent man, like a Washington or a Lafayette. Now he appeared to her delighted mental vision as so mild, so good, and so every way lovely, and he loved her so much! And, how strange that he had always loved her, and she had never known it! And how great a blessing he conferred, in that he should stand between her and God! And God was no longer a terror and a dread to her.

She stopped not to argue the point, even in her own mind, whether he had reconciled her to God, or God to herself, (though she thinks the former now,) being but too happy that God was no longer to her as a consuming fire, and Jesus was 'altogether lovely.' Her heart was now full of joy and gladness, as it had been of terror, and at one time of despair. In the light of her great happiness, the world was clad in new beauty, the very air sparkled as with diamonds, and was redolent of heaven. She contemplated the unapproachable barriers that existed between herself and the great of this world, as the world calls greatness, and made surprising comparisons between them, and the union existing between herself and Jesus,—Jesus, the transcendently lovely as well as great and powerful; for so he appeared to her, though he seemed but human; and she watched for his bodily appearance, feeling that she should know him, if she saw him; and when he came, she should go and dwell with him, as with a dear friend.

It was not given her to see that he loved any other; and she thought if others came to know and love him, as she did, she should be thrust aside and forgotten, being herself but a poor ignorant slave, with little to recommend her to his notice. And when she heard him spoken of, she said mentally—'What! others know Jesus! I thought no one knew Jesus but me!' and she felt a sort of jealousy, lest she should be robbed of her newly found treasure.

She conceived, one day, as she listened to reading, that she heard an intimation that Jesus was married, and hastily inquired if Jesus had a wife. 'What!' said the reader, '*God* have a wife?' 'Is Jesus *God*?' inquired Isabella. 'Yes, to be sure he is,' was the answer returned. From this time, her conceptions of Jesus became more elevated and spiritual; and she sometimes spoke of him as God, in accordance with the teaching she had received.

But when she was simply told, that the Christian world was much divided on the subject of Christ's nature—some believing him to be coequal with the Father—to be God in and of himself, 'very God, of very God;'—some, that he is the 'well-beloved,' 'only begotten Son of God;'—and others, that he is, or was, rather, but a mere man—she said, 'Of that I only know as I saw. I did not see him to be God; else, how could he stand between me and God? I saw him as a friend, standing between me and God, through whom, love flowed as from a fountain.' Now, so far from expressing her views of Christ's character and office in accordance with any system of theology extant, she says she believes Jesus is the same spirit that was in our first parents, Adam and Eve, in the beginning, when they came from the hand of their Creator. When they sinned through disobedience, this pure spirit forsook them, and fled to heaven; that there it remained, until it returned again in the person of Jesus; and that, previous to a personal union with him, man is but a brute, possessing only the spirit of an animal.

She avers that, in her darkest hours, she had no fear of any worse hell than the one she then carried in her bosom; though it had ever been pictured to her in its deepest colors, and threatened her as a reward for all her misdemeanors. Her vileness and God's holiness and all-pervading presence, which filled immensity, and threatened her with instant annihilation, composed the burden of her vision of terror. Her faith in prayer is equal to her faith in the love of Jesus. Her language is, 'Let others say what they will of the efficacy of prayer, I believe in it, and I shall pray. Thank God! Yes, I *shall always pray,*' she exclaims, putting her hands together with the greatest enthusiasm.

For some time subsequent to the happy change we have spoken of, Isabella's prayers partook largely of their former character; and while, in deep affliction, she labored for the recovery of her son, she prayed with constancy and fervor; and the following may be taken as a specimen:— 'Oh, God, you know how much I am distressed, for I have told you again and again. Now, God, help me get my son. If you were in trouble, as I am, and I could help you, as you can me, think I would n't do it? Yes, God, you *know* I would do it.' 'Oh, God, you know I have no money, but you can make the people do for me, and you must make the people do for me. I will never give you peace till you do, God.' 'Oh, God, make the people hear me—don't let them turn me off, without hearing and helping me.' And she has not a particle of doubt, that God heard her, and especially disposed the hearts of thoughtless clerks, eminent lawyers, and grave judges and others—between whom and herself there seemed to her almost an infinite remove—to listen to her suit with patient and respectful attention, backing it up with all needed aid. The sense of her nothingness, in the eyes of those with whom she contended for her rights, sometimes fell on her like a heavy weight, which nothing but her unwavering confidence in an arm which she believed to be stronger than all others combined could have raised from her sinking spirit. 'Oh! how little I did feel,' she repeated, with a powerful emphasis. 'Neither would you wonder, if you could have seen me, in my ignorance and destitution, trotting about the streets, meanly clad, bare-headed, and bare-footed! Oh, God only could have made such people hear me; and he did it in answer to my prayers.' And this perfect trust, based on the rock of Deity, was a soul-protecting fortress, which, raising her above the battlements of fear, and shielding her from the machinations of the enemy, impelled her onward in the struggle, till the foe was vanquished, and the victory gained.

We have now seen Isabella, her youngest daughter, and her only son, in possession of, at least, their nominal freedom. It has been said that the freedom of the most free of the colored people of this country is but nominal; but stinted and limited as it is, at best, it is an *immense* remove from chattel slavery. This fact is disputed, I know; but I have no confidence in the honesty of such questionings. If they are made in sincerity, I honor not the judgment that thus decides.

Her husband, quite advanced in age, and infirm of health, was emancipated, with the balance of the adult slaves of the State, according to law, the following summer, July 4, 1828.

For a few years after this event, he was able to earn a scanty living, and when he failed to do that, he was dependent on the 'world's cold charity,' and died in a poor-house. Isabella had herself and two children to provide for; her wages were trifling, for at that time the wages of females were at a small advance from nothing; and she doubtless had to learn the first elements of economy—for what slaves, that were never allowed to make any stipulations or calculations for themselves, ever possessed an adequate idea of the true value of time, or, in fact, of any material thing in the universe? To such, 'prudent using' is meanness—and 'saving' is a word to be sneered at. Of course, it was not in her power to make to herself a home, around whose sacred hearth-stone she could collect her family, as they gradually emerged from their prison-house of bondage; a home, where she could cultivate their affection, administer to their wants, and instil into the opening minds of her children those principles of virtue, and that love of purity, truth and benevolence, which must ever form the foundation of a life of usefulness and happiness. No—all this was far beyond her power or means, in more senses than one; and it should be taken into the account, whenever a comparison is instituted between the progress made by her children in virtue and goodness, and the progress of those who have been nurtured in the genial warmth of a sunny home, where good influences cluster, and bad ones are carefully excluded—where 'line upon line, and precept upon precept,' are daily brought to their quotidian tasks—and where, in short, every appliance is brought in requisition, that self-denying parents *can* bring to bear on one of the dearest objects of a parent's life, the promotion of the welfare of their children. But God forbid that this suggestion should be wrested from its original intent, and made to shield any one from merited rebuke! Isabella's children are now of an age to know good from evil, and may easily inform themselves on any point where they may yet be in doubt; and if they now suffer themselves to be drawn by temptation into the paths of the destrover, or forget what is due to the mother who has done and suffered so much for them, and who, now that she is descending into the vale of years, and feels her health and strength declining, will turn her expecting eyes to them for aid and comfort, just as instinctively as the child turns its confiding eye to its fond parent, when it seeks for succor or for sympathy—(for it is now their turn to do the work, and bear the burdens of life, as all must bear them in turn, as the wheel of life rolls on)—if, I say, they forget this, their duty and their happiness, and pursue an opposite course of sin and folly, they must lose the respect of the wise and good, and find, when too late, that 'the way of the transgressor is hard.'

Note

1. Sojourner Truth, "Her Brothers and Sisters," "Her Religious Instruction," "Illegal Sale of Her Son," and "Isabella's Religious Experience," in *Narrative of Sojourner Truth* (Mineola, NY: Dover, 1997 [1850]), pp. 2–4; 21–26; 31–40.

Joseph S. Cotter, Jr.

A poet and writer himself, Joseph Cotter was also the son of a poet and activist, the senior Joseph Cotter. Unlike his father, however, the junior Joseph Cotter lived a short life (1895–1919). At the dawn of the Harlem Renaissance, Cotter, a promising poet, would succumb to tuberculosis. Joseph Cotter's eleven-stanza poem presages the question posed by Langston Hughes nearly three decades later in his *Montage of a Dream Deferred*: in the opening line to the poem "Harlem," the speaker asks, "What happens to a dream deferred?" Cotter and Hughes represent a vision bordering on despair but hoping still for a future of fruitful possibilities. Like Hughes, Cotter rests his pondering in the dream, which signals a connection to God or the spiritual. In African American folk culture, dreams are often employed as the medium to divine revelation. Cotter's poem expresses a desire for life and hope that is born out of speech. Only the children in this poem have a voice: from adolescence onward there is the silence. The speaker prays for words: without words there is no life. This connection between utterance and life is integral to African and African American cosmology.

A Prayer

Joseph S. Cotter Jr.[1]

As I lie in bed,
Flat on my back;
There passes across my ceiling
An endless panorama of things—
Quick steps of gay-voiced children,   5
Adolescence in its wondering silences,
Maid and man on moonlit summer's eve,
Women in the holy glow of Motherhood,
Old men gazing silently thru the twilight
Into the beyond.   10
O God, give me words to make my dream-children live.

Note

1. Joseph S. Cotter Jr., "A Prayer," in *The Book of American Negro Poetry*, ed. James Weldon Johnson (New York: Harcourt, Brace, 1922), p. 151.

Marcus Garvey

In this Christmas Eve speech before a Black New York audience, Jamaican native Marcus Garvey illustrates the pervasiveness of the sermonic tradition in religious and secular Black oratory. In this case, Garvey recounts the story of Christ—particularly the suffering and castigation he endured, even in his innocence. His proclamation of Jesus as "the first reformer" validates Garvey's own role as modern-day reformer in a society like that of Jesus that would villify him. Garvey offers a jeremiad cry to the powerful of his era, warning that God's justice and judgment will be realized, and the powerful and wicked will fall. Although Garvey is widely known as one of the leading twentieth-century voices of Black nationalism and one of the fathers of Pan-Africanism, this speech reflects a philosophy of race uplift that is steeped not in a discourse of racial superiority but rather in a Christian discourse of a universal Christ and universal redemption. Garvey ends this speech with his theology of Spirit and flesh—one that makes a paradoxical claim if seen through Western Christianity, but one that echoes numerous West African spiritual cosmologies of the spirit and carnal worlds—that sees the flesh not as vile or in competition with the spirit but rather as a form given to man to use at his discretion. The result is a rhetoric of racial uplift that is rooted in self-determination and self-responsibility.

Philosophy and Opinions of Marcus Garvey

Marcus Garvey[1]

Christ the Greatest Reformer

Speech Delivered at Liberty Hall, New York, U.S.A., December 24, 1922.

When man had fallen in sin from his spiritual kinship to his Creator and disgust reigned even in heaven among the angels and the Holy One, who brought out of chaos the great universe, there sprang up divine sympathy, divine love—a sympathy and love within the Trinity caused the Son of God to vouchsafe Himself as the Redeemer of mankind, as the Redeemer of the world. He betook to Himself, with the authority of His Father, the duty, the work, the labor, the sacrifice, to bring man nearer to his Creator, to bring man back to his God.

The angels on that first Christmas morn notified the world that the Christ was to be born. He did not of Himself come down in His spiritual image from the heaven on high, but for the purpose of drawing Himself nearer man He took on the desh and was born of a virgin woman, and in that stable at Bethlehem; the whole world, through the message of the angels, was told of the great happening and men journeyed from far and near to see the Christ. To some, His birth was a disappointment, because He was born lowly; He was born amid poor conditions and circumstances; He was not born of the reigning household; He was born only of a carpenter, an humble laborer, and therefore to many His birth was a disappointment. The prophets foretold the birth of Christ; the prophets foretold the birth of the Redeemer, and men were looking for Him everywhere. The race to which he was to be born expected a redeemer in pomp and glory, and when He came in a manger they were disappointed; they were disgusted and they denied Him as the Christ. They said He was not the Christ; He was not the Promised One; He was not the Son of God; He was an imposter; but others who had faith believed that He was the Christ. And the lowly babe that was born to us in the sinful world 1922 years ago grew up amidst the surroundings of prejudice, amidst the surroundings of disgust and dissatisfaction to take on His work, to perform His labor as the Christ, as the redeemer of man, as the redeemer of the world.

Christ As a Living Example to Man

The man who took on flesh, physical as ours, moved among us even as we go about our daily business and occupation today. They could not believe that He was the Son of God, but in Him there was that which no man knew, which no man had; in Him was a spotless soul, was a spotless character never yet known to the world beyond the Christ in all God's creation. There never came into the world a character like Jesus, pure, spotless, immaculate, divine like unto God, as God would have each of us to be. When God created man and breathed into his nostrils the breath of life, when God gave to man a living soul, God expected that man would live the spiritual life of the Christ, and when man sinned, when man fell from grace, God became disgusted, God became dissatisfied. If we could see the sufferings of Christ, if we could see the patience of Christ, if we could see the very crucifixion of Christ, then we would see the creature, the being spiritual that God would have us be; and knowing ourselves as we do, we could well realize how far we are from God. For man to see his God, for man to face His judgment and become one of the elect of the High Divine, of the Holy One, is for man to live the life of the Christ—the spotless life, the holy life, the life without sin, and that is a journey that every one in the Christian world is called upon to make. If we cannot make it, we cannot expect to see our God. Man has fallen so low, man has fallen so far from his high estate, as created and given him by God, that even now man does not know himself except in the physical; but the physical does not make the man complete. Man is part physical as well as part spiritual; the physical life we live here to our satisfaction, the spiritual life we give to God when He calls us. And how many of us in the world today, if called for the spiritual life, will give that life as spotless as Jesus by His example taught? When we look at the world today we think of sin, we think of injustice, of iniquity, a world where man because of his strength, because of his advantage abuses the rights of his brother. When we look upon the oceans of injustice that are placed in the path of the weak, how much must we not realize the far distance that we are from God and the far distance that we are from the man Christ, who tried to teach us the life by which we should see salvation, the life that He came to redeem.

His Doctrine Rejected by the Classes

Christ brought a mission to the world. It was that of love to all mankind; that which taught man to love his brother, to be charitable, and when He taught that doctrine after He had assumed the form of manhood, what did the world do to Him? The world derided Him; the world scoffed at Him; they called Him all kinds of names. He was an imposter; He was a disturber of the public peace; He was not fit to be among good society; He was an outcast; He was a traitor to the king. That is what they said of Jesus when He went about teaching and preaching to men the way of salvation, pointing them to the light by which they would see their Heavenly Father. And even though He was the Son of God, even though He had power from on high, even though He worked miracles to prove that He was not only an ordinary man, they did not believe Him and they did not heed Him. The very people among whom He was born, the very people whom probably He loved most were the people who cried out for the destruction and the death of this man, and even though He was the Christ, the Son of God, He could not save Himself from the dissatisfied rebels of His day and of His time. He went about Jerusalem, He went about the holy places, teaching the multitude; He appealed to the masses of the people to save them from their sins, and when the masses attempted to hear Him, when the masses indicated that they would follow Him, the classes who always rule said that He was a disturber of the peace. "We cannot allow this man to travel at large, disturbing the peace of the community. This man threatens the power of the state, therefore we must imprison Him. We must place Him out of the way so that He will not teach these people this new doctrine, the doctrine of love, the doctrine of human brotherhood and the doctrine of equality."

The Character of Man

Christ was the first great reformer. Christ did not go exclusively to the classes. He devoted His life to all; the classes rejected Him because He was not born of high birth, of high parentage, because He was not born in their immediate circle, He was not born of the physical blood royal, therefore they could not follow such a man—"His doctrine is unsound, and He is receiving the plaudits of the people; He is getting the sympathy of the crowd; can we allow it?" And the answer was no. And even the Son of God—not man only, but the Son of God—was sought by the classes who have always held down the masses, because of His teaching for the spiritual glory (if not the physical) of the people whom He loved.

And so while we commemorate the birth of the Christ today, we must bear in mind the sufferings He underwent, the agony He underwent for the purpose of carrying out completely His mission,—the mission that brought Him down from heaven to earth. Christ came to save a sinful world; the world rejected him, and even at the last hour, after He had preached for years to the people; after He had aroused the suspicion and the curiosity of the masses of His time, when He was about to leave the world, He had not even twelve men who were honest enough to profess the faith; He had not made twelve faithful converts, and He was the Son of God. That proves to you the state of man's mind; that proves to you the character of man, and man has not changed much since Christ was here. If he has changed he has done so for the worse. And that brings me to the thought whether if Christ should come back to the world today in what way would He be received? If Christ were to return to the world today, born in the same lowly state, born of the same humble parentage, and attempted to preach the same redemption, He would be imprisoned, He would be executed, He would be crucified in this twentieth century even as He was crucified nineteen hundred years ago on the Mount of Calvary. Man has not changed much.

Christianity a Moving Force

But there is one lesson we can learn from the teachings of Christ. Even though man in the ages may be hard in heart and hard in soul, that which is righteous, that which is spiritually just, even though the physical man dies, the righteous cause is bound to live. Because the preaching of Jesus, the teaching of Jesus was not something physical; if it was something physical it would have died. The teaching of Jesus, the preaching of Jesus, was something spiritual, and where there is righteousness of spirit there is length of life. Jesus the man was not respected, Jesus the man was not adored, Jesus the man was not even loved by His own people, and for that they crucified Him; but the spiritual doctrines of Jesus were righteous; the doctrines of Jesus were just, and even though He died nearly nineteen hundred years ago, what has happened? After the lapse of nineteen hundred years His religion is the greatest moving force in the world today, morally and spiritually. It shows you, therefore, the power of spiritual force; it shows you, therefore, the power of a righteous cause.

Jesus, who was the first great reformer, taught us the way; after Him followed the other great reformers who shared the same fate. Born, perhaps, in the same lowly station of life, feeling with the masses of people who suffered like them, they have gone out, whether it be Luther or Saint Augustine or some other great reformer, but they have all gone out and they preached their doctrine, to suffer in their time for the doctrine to rise again on the wings of time and to flourish as the green bay tree.

Man's Kinship With His Creator

Christmas symbolizes something other than the amusement that it affords today. Christmas brings us to the realization of the fact that hundreds of years ago, when man was practically lost in his spiritual kinship with his Creator and the world probably was to be wiped away, the Son of God Himself came down from His throne on high for the purpose of saving you and saving me. We rejected Him in the past; our attitude now suggests no better consideration for Him if He should return, but with that patience, but with that love, but with that mercy, with that charity that caused Him to look down, not in revenge, but in the belief, in the hope, that some time man will change his ways—man will get to realize his true kinship with his Creator and be what his God expected him to be.

But before we reach this point we need a better understanding of self, as individuals, and may I not appeal to the strong and mighty races and nations of the world for a better and a closer consideration and understanding of the teachings of the man Christ, who went about this world in His effort to redeem fallen man? May I not say to the strong, may I not say to the powerful, that until you change your ways there will be no salvation, there will be no redemption, there will be no seeing God face to face? God is just, God is love, God is no respecter of persons; God does not uphold advantage and abuse to His own people; God created mankind to the same rights and privileges and the same opportunities, and before man can see his God, man will have to measure up in that love, in that brotherhood that He desired us to realize and know as taught to us by His Son Jesus.

Let us realize that we are our brother's keeper; let us realize that we are of one blood, created of one nation to worship God the common Father. It does not, therefore, suggest a proper understanding of our God or a proper knowledge of ourselves when in our strength we attempt to abuse and oppress the weak—as is done to Negroes today.

The Selfishness of Mankind

The statesmen of the world cry out for peace. They are meeting in many conferences with the hope that they will have peace; but I wonder if they understand the meaning of peace. There can be no peace until that peace reflects the spirit of the message of the angels of nineteen centuries ago. The real peace actuated by love, love as the Christ came to the world to give us; love for the high and mighty, love for the meek and lowly, love for all, is the only peace that will reign, is the only peace that will draw man nearer to his God.

Man is so selfish that he does not seem to realize that there is anyone else in the world but himself. The statesmen who lead America seem to believe that there is no one else in the world but the people who make up America, the statesmen who lead the British Empire (even though they cry for peace and desire peace) seem to believe that no one else lives in the world but men within the British Empire.

Up to now we have not yet got the message of the angels; up to now they have not yet fully interpreted the spirit of Christ. Christ came into the world not to save one set of humanity, otherwise He would not have been the Christ. Christ came into the world to save mankind; therefore, His love must be for all; His love could not be sectional; His love could not be partial; His love was general and universal. Therefore, before we can have peace on earth, before we can welcome the spirit of the high God; before we can get a true understanding of the spirit of the Christ, who came to us born in the lowly stable at Bethlehem, we must get to realize the brotherhood that exists, realize it in truth; realize it in fact, and practise it whether we be white, black or some other hue.

God Not Interested in the Physical Activities of Man

Realizing that Christ came to save all mankind from the fallen state, to restore man to his spiritual kinship with his God, let us practise a spirit of love, a spirit of charity, a spirit of mercy toward mankind; because in so doing we will be bringing God's kingdom down to earth. Let us live that true life, that perfect life in ourselves as spiritual beings, not forgetting that we are physical also; man must not fail to understand his dual personality.

In being charitable and sympathetic like the Christ would have us to be does not mean to say that we must ignore our physical needs. Christ was not so much interested in the physical responsibility of man; neither is God interested in the physical activities of man. That may be something strange to say at this hour when you have heard so much about religion. Christ cared so little for the physical that He offered Himself up and was satisfied to go on the cross and let the physical die. God the Father is interested in the spiritual of man, but man's physical body is for his own protection; is for his own purpose. Whatsoever you want to do with the physical God does not interfere, and I trust at this time when we are going to contemplate Christ that we will get a better understanding of Him and get a better understanding of the religion that He taught, because some of us seem to have some peculiar ideas about the religion of Jesus. Some of us seem to believe that Christ and God the Father are responsible for all our ills—physical ills. They have nothing to do with our physical ills. I repeat, God is not and Jesus is not interested in the bodies of men. If you want to care for your body, that is the privilege and prerogative given to you by God. If you want to destroy it, that is the same privilege and prerogative He has given. If you want to commit suicide, that is your business. If you want to live, that is your business. God has given you the power; He has made you a free agent as far as the physical in life goes. All that God is interested in is the spiritual; that you cannot kill, because the moment you destroy the physical body God lays claim to the spiritual with which you are endowed. The spiritual is never yours. The spiritual is always God's, but the physical is your own property. If you want to break your physical life up, that is all your business. God does not interfere and that should be the Negro's interpretation in this twentieth century of Christ's religion. It is no use to blame God and Christ for the things that happen to us in the physical; they are not responsible; they have absolutely nothing to do with it. If one man enjoys life and another does not, God has absolutely nothing to do with the difference between the two individuals. That is to say, if one man lives in a palace across the street and enjoys life and the other fellow lives in the gutter, God has nothing to do with the difference between them. It is purely a physical regulation left to man himself.

Make your interpretation of Christianity scientific—what it ought to be, and blame not God, blame not the white man for physical conditions for which we ourselves are responsible.

Note

1. Marcus Garvey, "Christ the Greatest Reformer," in *Philosophy and Opinions of Marcus Garvey*, Vol. II—Pt. 1., ed. Amy Jacques Garvey (New York: Atheneum, 1968 [1925]), pp. 27–33.

James Baldwin

Baldwin writes this open epistle in support of former U.S. ambassador to the United Nations Andrew Young. Young took controversial actions concerning the establishment of a Palestinian state under the administration of President Jimmy Carter. Invoking his religious upbringing and experiences with racism, Baldwin calls upon the born-again Christian to remember the core of his faith and convictions—particularly as an injustice is being acted against another person or group. He reminds his audience what it means to be born again, a lesson he holds dear though he is far removed from his life in ministry. Arguing that much of the Western world has betrayed the teachings of Christ through their national politics, Baldwin continues to employ the rhetoric of Christian religiosity to undermine and criticize the actions of Western powers against Jewish populations throughout history. He ultimately praises Ambassador Young for being among the few "born-again" to make a choice that supports his principles in faith rather than politics.

Open Letter to the Born Again

James Baldwin[1]

I met Martin Luther King Jr. before I met Andrew Young. I know that Andy and I met only because of Martin. Andy was, in my mind, and not because he ever so described himself, Martin's "right-hand man." He was present—absolutely present. He saw what was happening. He took upon himself his responsibility for knowing what he knew, and for seeing what he saw. I have heard Andy attempt to describe himself only once: when he was trying to clarify something about me, to someone else. So, I learned, one particular evening, what his Christian ministry meant to him. Let me spell that out a little.

The text comes from the New Testament, Matthew 25:40: *Inasmuch as ye have done it unto one of the least of these my brethren, ye have done it unto me.*

I am in the strenuous and far from dull position of having news to deliver to the Western world—for example: *black* is not a synonym for *slave*. Do not, I counsel you, attempt to defend yourselves against this stunning, unwieldy and undesired message. You will hear it again: indeed, this is the only message the Western world is likely to be hearing from here on out.

I put it in this somewhat astringent fashion because it is necessary, and because I speak, now, as the grandson of a slave, a direct descendant of a born-again Christian. *My conversion,* as Countee Cullen puts it, *came high-priced/I belong to Jesus Christ.* I am also speaking as an ex-minister of the Gospel, and therefore, as one of the born again. I was instructed to feed the hungry, clothe the naked and visit those in prison. I am far indeed from my youth, and from my father's house, but I have not forgotten these instructions, and I pray upon my soul that I never will. The people who call themselves "born again" today have simply become members of the richest, most exclusive private club in the world, a club that the man from Galilee could not possibly hope—or wish—to enter.

Inasmuch as ye have done it unto the least of these my brethren, ye have done it unto me. That is a hard saying. It is hard to live with that. It is a merciless description of our responsibility for one another. It is that hard light under which one makes the moral choice. That the Western world has forgotten that such a thing as the moral choice exists, my history, my flesh, and my soul bear witness. So, if I may say so, does the predicament into which the world's most celebrated born-again Christian has managed to hurl Mr. Andrew Young.

Let us not belabor the obvious truth that what the Western world calls an "energy" crisis ineptly disguises what happens when you can no longer control markets, are chained to your colonies (instead of vice versa), are running out of slaves (and can't trust those you think you still have), can't, upon rigorously sober reflection, really send the Marines, or the Royal Navy, anywhere, or risk a global war, have no allies—only business partners, or "satellites"—and have broken every promise you ever made, anywhere, to anyone. I know what I am talking about: my grandfather never got the promised "forty acres, and a mule," the Indians who survived *that* holocaust are either on reservations or dying in the streets, and not a single treaty between the United States and the Indian was ever honored. That is quite a record.

Jews and Palestinians know of broken promises. From the time of the Balfour Declaration (during World War I) Palestine was under five British mandates, and England promised the land back and forth to the Arabs or the Jews, depending on which horse seemed to be in the lead. The Zionists—as distinguished from the people known as Jews—using, as someone put it, the "available political machinery," i.e., colonialism, e.g., the British Empire—promised the British that, if the territory were given to them, the British Empire would be safe forever.

But absolutely no one cared about the Jews, and it is worth observing that non-Jewish Zionists are very frequently anti-Semitic. The white Americans responsible for sending black slaves to Liberia (where they are still slaving for the Firestone Rubber Plantation) did not do this to set them free. They despised them, and they wanted to get rid of them. Lincoln's intention was not to "free" the slaves but to "destabilize" the Confederate Government by giving their slaves reason to "defect." The Emancipation Proclamation freed, precisely, those slaves who were not under the authority of the President of what could not yet be insured as a Union.

It has always astounded me that no one appears to be able to make the connection between Franco's Spain, for example, and the Spanish Inquisition; the role of the Christian church or—to be brutally precise, the Catholic Church—in the history of Europe, and the fate of the Jews; and the role of the Jews in Christendom and the discovery of America. For the discovery of America coincided with the Inquisition, and the expulsion of the Jews from Spain. Does no one see the connection between *The Merchant of Venice* and *The Pawnbroker*? In both of these works, as though no time had passed, the Jew is portrayed as doing the Christian's usurious dirty work. The first white man I ever saw was the Jewish manager who arrived to collect the rent, and he collected the rent because he did not own the building. I never, in fact, saw any of the people who owned any of the buildings in which we scrubbed and uffered for so long, until I was a grown man and famous. None of them were Jews.

And I was not stupid: the grocer and the druggist were Jews, for example, and they were very very nice to me, and to us. The cops were white. The city was white. The threat was white, and God was white, Not for even a single split second in my life did the despicable, utterly cowardly accusation that "the Jews killed Christ" reverberate. I knew a murderer when I saw one, and the people who were trying to kill me were not Jews.

But the state of Israel was not created for the salvation of the Jews; it was created for the salvation of the Western interests. This is what is becoming clear (I must say that it was always clear to me). The Palestinians have been paying for the British colonial policy of "divide and rule" and for Europe's guilty Christian conscience for more than thirty years.

Finally: there is absolutely—repeat: *absolutely*—no hope of establishing peace in what Europe so arrogantly calls the Middle East (how in the world would Europe know? having so dismally failed to find a passage to India) without dealing with the Palestinians. The collapse of the Shah of Iran not only revealed the depth of the pious Carter's concern for "human rights," it also revealed who supplied oil to Israel, and to whom Israel supplied arms. It happened to be, to spell it out, white South Africa.

Well. The Jew, in America, is a white man. He has to be, since I am a black man, and, as he supposes, his only protection against the fate which drove him to America. But he is still doing the Christian's dirty work, and black men know it.

My friend, Mr. Andrew Young, out of tremendous love and courage, and with a silent, irreproachable, indescribable nobility, has attempted to ward off a holocaust, and I proclaim him a hero, betrayed by cowards.

Note

1. James Baldwin, "Open Letter to the Born Again," *The Nation*, September 29, 1979, retrieved from www.thenation.com/article/159718/open-letter-born-again#

Cornelia Walker Bailey

Cornelia Walker Bailey, lifelong resident and elder of one the last undeveloped Sea Islands along the Gullah Geechee Cultural Heritage Corridor, shares her memoir of growing up in historic Hogg Hammock community on Sapelo Island. She testifies about the convergence of Islam, Christianity, and West African spiritual traditions that have been maintained on the isolated island. She speaks eloquently about the practice of faith among generations of Sapelo residents, emphasizing how Sea Island religion has always been and remains syncretic. Drawing upon the traditions of her Muslim ancestor, Bilali Muhammed, Bailey uses her gift of storytelling to convey the rich spiritual history bequeathed to Sapelo Island by its enslaved population.

God, Dr. Buzzard, and the Bolito Man: A Saltwater Geechee Talks About Life on Sapelo Island

Cornelia Walker Bailey with Christena Bledsoe[1]

God Resides in the East

When I'd go to say my nightly prayer, I'd better not, I repeat, I'd better not let Mama catch me with my head turned to the West. I was up for a good fussing at if she did.

"What do you think you're doing? Get off your knees," Mama would say. "Do you know where you're lookin' at? You're lookin' at the West. Do you know who sits in the West? You better turn your butt around this way."

I mean, "Whew." I'd better find that East direction quick.

Mama and Papa and all the old people always said, "God resides in the East and the devil resides in the West." They firmly believed that.

The first thing I learned when it came to directions, was East and West. Forget the South and the North. I knew at an early age that the sun rose in the East, so it was easy to pinpoint, and I knew the West, because the sun sets there and the darkness begins. So I knew my directions and who I was supposed to be praying to and who I was supposed to be avoiding. It was God resides in the East. Pray to God, not the devil.

We had Muslim and Christian beliefs blended in our religious rituals and praying to the East was the most important Muslim one. Bilali was Muslim and he believed in his faith. It's said that during the War of 1812, when Thomas Spalding gave Bilali firearms so the slaves could fend off any British that came, he asked Bilali if the slaves could be trusted. Bilali answered, "I can only account for my people. I cannot account for the Christian dogs that you have."

Even if that isn't a true story, Bilali wouldn't have had much regard for them. He prayed to the Islamic God and he would have believed he had the true faith. There were Christians here, though, and while Bilali was already Muslim when he got here, we don't know how the people who were Christian got their beliefs.

On some plantations there were churches, and slaveholders would have their slaves sit up in the balcony and pray because they thought it had a "civilizing" effect on them. There's no record of a church on Sapelo in slavery days, though. The Spaldings went to church over to Darien on the mainland. So did some of the Africans get introduced to Christianity by the British before they got here? Did traveling ministers come to Sapelo, as they did some places? All I know is that Grandma said that people had to sneak out into the woods at night to pray. But were they Muslims or Christians? Or did they follow African religions? Most people probably had held to African ways. Grandma didn't say.

When freedom came, Bilali's children and grandchildren formed the First African Baptist Church. Some of them would have been Muslim still and some likely were Christians by then, and they wanted to go to church together. So they patched things up, and they used Muslim traditions in a Christian church. There must have been some resistance, though, because there were about five hundred people over here after slavery and eight people were baptized the first year. The next year a few more were baptized. So there weren't any mass baptisms. It was a gradual thing but eventually everyone joined. You prayed to the East, and the congregation faced the East. You were buried in the cemetery with your foot stone to the East. Your feet were pointed to the East, and your head was looking that way, so when Judgment Day came and you rose up, you'd be standing looking toward the East when Gabriel blew his horn.

Everybody went to church on Communion Sunday. We call it First Sunday, the first Sunday of the month. Whether you went to church in between times or not, you went then. Only a couple of the ministers we had were born and raised on Sapelo. The others came from as far away as Savannah and they would ride the company boat over for First Sunday.

We'd walk up to the Bluff and there'd be people coming by truck, by horse and wagon, or by foot, and everybody was wearing their Sunday best. The men always had suits on and the women had on dresses, but those dresses weren't sleeveless. You couldn't come to church with bare arms. Never. That's right. You had to have your shoulders and upper part of your arms covered. It was disrespectful not to, and the women also had to have their heads covered by a hat at all times.

The First African Baptist Church was a big whitewashed church that had a steeple and a bell, *the* bell. In fact that was the bell that rang when I died. The church also had a tin roof that was shiny when the church was built, but when it started to rust it was painted a dull copper-looking red.

The church had pretty lavender stained glass windows with veins of white running through them like somebody took a stick and swirled white paint in the glass.

Surrounding the church were trees with benches where people would sit before and after church and talk, gossip and catch up with any news.

We'd walk into the church together and then we'd separate, and that was another Muslim tradition. The men didn't sit with the women. Papa would join the men on the left side of the church and Mama would join the women on the right. There was a third row of benches too, a short row in the middle that was mostly for young adults and children. Asberry and I were big enough to sit there now and we had asked Mama, "Can we sit in the middle row? Can we sit in the middle row?"

The deacons and the choir would be up front, with the deacons on the left and the choir on the right, and there was an arch above the pulpit and a small hand-lettered sign that said First African Baptist Church, Organized May 2, 1866. The preacher sat in the pulpit in a high-backed chair that was simple, but it looked so regal. All the cloths on tables and the pulpit and the carpet were a wine-colored red, a holy red for the blood of Jesus.

First Sunday would start with Sunday school and when it was over, the men would go outside for a breather, but the ladies very seldom left their seats, and a few minutes later, church would begin. Two deacons would get up and begin the service and one would tell you to open your hymn book to a certain song and he'd read the first stanza, and then you'd sing it behind him. As soon as that last note was out of the congregation's mouth, then the deacon picked it up and read the next stanza, and then the congregation would sing it right behind him, and so forth. And that's called raising the hymn.

The second deacon gets down on his knees and leads the congregation in a prayer then, and there would be a song, an uplifting song like, "We Are Climbing Jacob's Ladder." That song would bring the spirit into the church, so things would start out lively and the whole service would be lively. Then, after the Lord's Prayer, and that was usually sung, it was time for the minister.

When the minister would start to preach, you were ready. We had a minister that sometimes would start off mild. He'd start teaching the text he wanted to get into, and all of a sudden, he'd start the preaching, and the tempo started going up, up, up, and the ladies started tapping their feet and the men started saying "Amen" and stomping their feet, and hands started to clap, and heads started to nod, and it would keep getting to a higher pitch. And then the minister would cut off, *bam*, and there were still some little old ladies in the back screaming, "Hallelujah! Hallelujah!"

The pianist would strike up a chord and then the music would start and the congregation and the choir would fall in line with each other like they'd been practicing for weeks, and everybody would be singing, say, "Amazing Grace." Everybody was in the same mood, they knew exactly where to come in without anybody leading the song and the whole church was rocking then. The whole church was moving. Even the building seemed like it was swinging gently with you.

The collections were taken up and prayed over by a deacon, and then the head deacon would get up and he'd talk about the text that the minister talked about. He'd say what a nice service it was, and why y'all should pay attention to what the preacher said. And sometimes, he'd go on and on. Finally the snow white cloth over the communion tray was lifted and communion was served and there were more songs and more prayers.

The kids would be getting fidgety, and grownups sleepy, and we never would have gotten out of there if it wasn't for Miss Clara. Miss Clara Hillery. She would listen for awhile and then when they'd go on too long, she'd start up. "Shut up, shut up, shut up, people wanta go home. All that long-time talk. *Sit down, sit down, sit down.* People wanta go home."

We kids couldn't say "yeah" but we were hoping they'd hear her, and her voice would go all the way up to the front. Most of the time they'd cut it off a little short because once she started, Miss Clara wasn't gonna stop. She'd say it again and again. "*Shut up, shut up, my Lord, my Lord, shut up. Shut up, now.*"

Miss Clara's son, Mr. Jimmy, was a deacon, and he'd be up front and that was his mama back there doing that, but if it bothered him, he didn't show it. He had his own thing. He had a series of musical grunts. You'd watch him and if he disapproved of what the preacher or one of the deacons was saying, he'd shake that head and go, "*Uh-uh, uh-uh, uh-uh-uh-uh.*" Then if he approved, he'd go, "*Uhm-uhmm, Uhm-uhm, um-um-um-um.*" So he and his mama were quite a combination.

One morning after my twelfth birthday, Mama told me that it was time for me to go join the church. Twelve was an important age to us. When you turned twelve, you were no longer a child. You were supposed to be responsible for your own sins and actions, and the old people would start referring to you as a sinner if you didn't get baptized then.

I couldn't just stand up and profess myself. There was a whole ritual to joining the church. Depending on your teacher, that ritual took you two or three months, and a long period where you study with a teacher may have been another Muslim tradition. You *had* to have a teacher to guide you and you would pick one of the elders of the church to be your teacher.

I picked Mr. James Spaulding, who was a deacon from Raccoon Bluff, but he was living in Hog Hammock by then, right down the road from us. He was a tall, light-skinned guy with gray hair. He was nice-looking, all the Spauldings were—and he was from a family over here who had taken the Spalding name after the Civil War, but spelled their name with a *u* in it usually—and he was nice to children. You had no fear of Mr. James Spaulding.

I went to Mr. James Spaulding's house and the first thing he said was "Alright, there ain't gonna be no more playing with your friends no more."

"Yes, sir."

"You must be good, because good dreams don't come to children who misbehave, and I want you to read, every day you come, a Bible verse for me."

So you started the process of cleansing yourself. You'd study and you'd pray, and everything led up to your having a special, spiritual dream that meant you were ready to become a member of the church. You had to prepare yourself to receive that dream.

For the first two or three weeks, you'd go to your teacher every day, and he watched you carefully. He wanted to make sure you understood what you were learning. I'd get a Bible verse from Mama or find one myself, and I'd read it to him, and then he'd explain it to me. Like, Genesis, Chapter One, Verse One. "In the beginning, God created the heavens and the earth." Mr. James Spaulding would say, "What the Bible means is that this was the beginning of time. God created the heavens and the earth and everything. The earth belongs to God, not man. We were created later to take care of the earth, and to obey him."

After awhile he told me, "Do exactly as I tell you, now. You must do exactly as I say. You have to find your own place now, a secret place, and when you go seeking, that's your own special place. Nobody must know about it but you. You go by yourself out there to pray and talk to God."

I picked a pine tree off in the woods, and I made it my tree. It was the tallest tree around and it was in an East direction, to the East of the house. Nobody went there but me. I'd go to the tree three times a day, like Mr. James Spaulding told me. Morning, noon, and at night.

When your teacher decided you were ready, you had to get out of bed at midnight and go out to your private place to pray. If I wasn't awake, Mama or Papa would wake me up when midnight came. "Okay, baby, time for you to go outside and go seeking. You go ahead out, I'll be right here when you come back." So I'd go out in the dark into the wilderness and go seeking.

I was never afraid of the dark, it was just that I had to stay by myself, and I got used to that after awhile. Papa would say, "Girl, there ain't nuttin' to be frightened of. Just go out there, nuttin' will bother you. I'll be right here when you come back." So you'd figure that God would take care of you and you weren't going to step on a snake or something. You had to believe that.

I'd go out to my pine tree and kneel down and pray for an hour, or if I didn't feel like kneeling anymore, I'd sit there with my back to the tree. I'd hear frogs and cicadas chirping and a hoot owl hooting sometimes and out in the dark by myself, the sounds were louder than they've been before, but I did not abandon my purpose. You were not supposed to let anything take you away from your purpose. If a mosquito bit me, I'd brush it off and ignore it. I went outside at midnight every night for almost a month, and then I'd go back home, and clean my feet off before bed.

I had to recite my dreams to Mr. James Spaulding too. When I first started, my dreams would be things like, say you and I were playing down the road and I'd throw a stick at a cat. Mr. James Spaulding would listen and say, "You doin' everything I tell you?"

Gradually, my dreams started changing and finally, one night I dreamed about angels. There were angels flying around in my dream, and there was one angel who wore a yellow robe. The rest wore white robes and I could understand that because we believed white's for purity, see, so they were in white, all except for that one angel in a yellow robe. I told my dream to Mr. James Spaulding and he said, "You're ready to go before them now," and I became a candidate for baptism.

I had to repeat that dream before all of the deacons, hoping I did it right and they'd give that final nod of the head that everything is okay. I repeated it as best I could and they all nodded their heads. It wasn't traditional at all, having an angel in a yellow robe, but they all nodded their heads. I never knew what it meant, but that yellow robe was pretty, and it was happy-looking. Maybe that's why I dreamed it or maybe it was just that I was a little different from most kids. Some people elsewhere believe that the color yellow can be for inspiration or quickness of mind, but I'd never heard that then. But I passed.

I was baptized in June, on the Saturday before First Sunday, which is how we always did it at that time, and the sun was warm and the water was cool but not cold. Mama made a white robe for me out of a sheet and a white head rag tied in the middle of my forehead. Mama used a white string and tied the robe around my ankles so it wouldn't fly up when I got in the water.

That day there were five of us for baptism and we marched down to Blackbeard Creek singing "Shall We Gather at the River," with the elders following us, and half the congregation was standing up on the landing watching because baptism was a big occasion. Mama and Papa were there watching and Asberry was there and Grandpa had come down to the landing too. Grandma hadn't because her arthritis was bad, but we were to her house before the baptism. The deaconess and the deacons were watching and my playmates were watching, and I'd get condemned or blessed by the elders and teased by Asberry and my friends if I didn't do right. Your friends came just so they can tease you at school on Monday.

A lot of kids were scared when they went in the water to get baptized. You didn't know how to swim, usually, and your parents had been telling you, "Stay out of that water, stay out of that water, y'all drown, messing around in that water." Then they'd tell you it was time to join the church and get baptized and all of a sudden they were saying, "Go in the water, go in the water." And it was like, "Oh, my God, I'm gonna drown."

Some kids came out of the water screaming at the top of their lungs and the ladies on the bank would be saying, "They're acting like someone gonna kill them in that water. No one's gonna kill them." And one girl panicked and knocked down the minister and the deacon one time.

I was last in line in my baptism group. I made it my business to be last in the line. I wanted to see how the other kids did, so if they made a mistake, I'd know how to behave differently.

The other kids did okay and my time came. A deacon came and got me and led me down into the water. The minister was standing in the water and he read something from his Bible and then he recited the Twenty-third Psalm, with the part that you shall not fear evil because the Lord is with you. And then he was ready to dunk me.

The deacon got on one side of me and the minister was on the other and I was facing the East. One held my head and one shoulder and the other held the other shoulder and held my nose shut and they both at the same moment tilted my head back in the water and when I came out of the water, my eyes were facing East.

So it was, "I baptize you in the name of the Father," and they dunked me in the water. I'd had my head in the water before, when I was playing, unlike some kids, but this was different. Someone was *holding* me under this time and I wasn't so sure whether to trust them.

They brought me back up kinda quick. "The Son." I was down in the water again, and this time the dunk was a little longer. "And the Holy Ghost." They held me down a little bit then. It was faith-testing time. They were testing my faith, and I knew that's when everybody was judging me. From the way I behaved, they'd say what kind of Christian I was gonna be. If I fought and sputtered, the ladies would say, "You see how she act when she came out of that water? You watch, she will be a little devil the rest of her life. Mark my words."

If I was frightened, it was just a little bit. I didn't let anybody know about it. The deacons said I was ready, so I had to be ready. I was saying to myself, "I don't care if it kills me, I'm coming out of this water with a smile on my face." And I did. All they could say about me was, "That Cornelia was ready to be baptized, alright."

The deacon led me out of the water and up to the shore and the ladies of the church dried me off with a big towel. Papa said, "I'm proud of you. You did good." Mama said that too, and then everybody dispersed and went home to get ready for the morrow.

Sunday was the big day. I wore a two-tone white dress, an organdy dress with flowers on it that Mama ordered from National Bella Hess. I had white pumps to match my dress and I had a white slip too, and that strap kept slipping off my right shoulder. I was supposed to be looking dignified and not pulling my strap up, but it'd slip off my shoulder and I couldn't stand it. I kept pulling that thing up and hoping no one saw.

The elders led the five of us who had been baptized up before the pulpit and one by one they shook our hands and the minister told us to pick an elder to guide you the rest of your life. It didn't have to be the same one who had been your teacher, but I picked Mr. James Spaulding again. Then we were led back to our seats and for that day only, we were on the first row up front with the adults.

At communion time, for the first time, those bread and wine trays did not pass me by. The deacons came down the aisle with a tray of bread, regular white bread, broken up in pieces; then they brought the wine. It was in glasses, tiny, little glasses that didn't hold much more than a thimble did, and it was sweet. After you were baptized into the church, from then on you would be able to have communion unless you were in trouble with the church. They'd refuse communion to someone who had not obeyed an order of the church. A deacon would keep an empty glass on the tray then, and when he stopped before you, he'd pick up that glass and turn it upside down, so everyone would know you had refused a direct order of the church, and that told you right there you'd better do what the church said.

At the end of the service, it was fellowship time. The congregation always marched up front and shook hands with the minister, the church officers and the deacons. Then everybody would shake hands with each other, and church was over then. This day the five of us had the honored position up front along with the ministers and other church staff. Everybody filed by and shook our hands first and congratulated us. It was the moment I had been waiting for. I was now a bona fide member of First A.B. Church. I sure was.

Note

1. Cornelia Walker Bailey, "God Resides in the East," in *God, Dr. Buzzard, and the Bolito Man: A Saltwater Geechee Talks About Life on Sapelo Island, Georgia* (New York: Anchor Books, 2000), pp. 157–168.

Akasha Gloria Hull

This essay follows the trajectory of Black women's shift from espousing conventional religious ideologies to seeking forms of spiritual wisdom that move outside of the Judeo-Christian influence. Focusing on the explosion of Black female creative expression in visual art and literary forms in the late seventies and early eighties, Hull argues that Black women have been at the center of a third revolution that has recovered and harnessed the power of ancient and African spiritual systems. Capturing dialogue and intimate conversation with Toni Cade Bambara, Luisah Teish, and Julie Dash, Hull's essay acts as both scholarship and memoir as she documents her participation in the spiritual transition of a generation of Black women artists.

The Third Revolution: A New Spirituality Arises

Akasha Gloria Hull[1]

Viewed from an inner, spiritual perspective, the late 1970s through the 1980s was a time of burgeoning transformation for humankind. On the external front, however, social and political conditions were dreadful. During the years that Ronald Reagan was president (1980–1988) domestic programs such as Medicare, federally funded student loans, summer youth employment, federally funded daycare, and welfare were drastically cut; taxes were minimally reduced for the poor and radically slashed for corporations and the wealthy; the federal government slackened its oversight of the banking industry, the natural gas industry, environmental protection, and voting and civil rights; military spending rose and the national debt soared; regressive communist scare tactics were employed to justify armed U.S. intervention in Nicaragua, El Salvador, and Grenada; the Ku Klux Klan began calling upon "white anger" as a response to busing and affirmative action. It was the period of the Savings and Loan crisis, the Iran-Contra affair, ketchup as a school lunch vegetable, and Reagan's own vilification of black mothers on Aid to Families with Dependent Children (AFDC) as "welfare queens." Seen from the outside, the picture was rather bleak.

Spiritual vision, however, mandates seeing from within as well as without, and from this viewpoint another scene emerges to balance all that was disheartening. In personal relations, science, work, education, religion, and medicine, people were evolving entirely new ways of being and seeing that sought to foster not just ameliorative measures but foundational change. Though they were discipline-and content-specific, these ways entailed leaps from accepted old material paradigms into expansive and spiritually based possibilities. Thus were born the multiplicity of discoveries, activities, and attitudes that were popularly and collectively tagged "New Age"—ranging from research in quantum physics that sought to prove mysterious, interpenetrating energies of the universe, to the employment by ordinary individuals of visualization for enhanced health, wealth, and success. On the surface, this New Age activity looked like a movement without much specific racial or gender content (since the "norm" of whiteness goes unremarked) and black women, in particular, were not very visible in it. But this was far from the reality.

Around 1980 an outburst of spirituality concomitantly erupted among African American women, just when the civil rights movement and the early ferment of the feminist movement were subsiding. This upsurge of spirituality continued from the wave of these two political movements and rippled forward as an extension of them. At the time, many concerned individuals were wondering what had happened to the energy needed to propel social change. We can now see that this transformative energy was moving to encompass spirituality in a deeper, explicit way, as preparation for grappling with social issues on a more profound level.

Black women embraced practices associated with the New Age, such as crystal work, Eastern religions, and metaphysics, and laid them alongside more traditional, culturally derived religious and spiritual foundations. The results could be seen in dramatic changes of lifestyle and life direction for many, and—even more visibly—in the remarkable outpouring of creative writing by authors such as Toni Morrison, Toni Cade Bambara, and Alice Walker, authors whose writing captured unprecedented public attention because of its blend of racial-feminist-political realism and spiritual-supernatural awareness. What African American women were creating added political dimension to the generally apolitical spiritual movement and contributed immensely to a higher collective spiritual consciousness.

Clearing Out, Moving (With)In

In my case, the shift toward spirituality around 1980 involved a physical move from one place to another. After seven years of teaching literature as my first real job at the University of Delaware and carving out a specialization in African American writing, I decided to spend the 1979–1980 year on sabbatical leave in the exciting city of Washington, D.C. (as compared to Newark, Delaware, college town), conducting scholarly research and having a good time. I had participated in the black power movement as a young graduate student, wife, and mother wholly supportive of the cause in academic and personal ways but not directly active. As a black feminist, I had been more central—generating theory and articles and working as a member of the Combahee River Collective Retreat Group, an association of fifteen to twenty African American women committed to consciousness-raising and organizing.

After I moved to Washington, D.C., the territory my own consciousness covered vastly expanded. At once, I connected with Konda, a dreadlocked sister from the west coast who was managing up-and-coming women's musical groups and fashioning for herself an alternative, black-culture-based style of living. I vividly remember walking down Columbia Road with her on a mid-August afternoon. It was hot and muggy, as Washington, D.C., can be, but I was internally fanned and exhilarated by the sounds, the energy, the international medley of dark, familiar faces.

When we stepped inside a store for something cool to drink, she bought a small bottle of apple juice. I came out with a grape "Icee," one of those sugar-water, artificial-color confections in a plastic sleeve with absolutely no redeeming nutritional value. As I happily slurped it up, Konda turned smiling and serious to me and said—out of the clear blue nowhere, "If you stop eating sugar and junk like that and stuff from cans, I bet you your skin will clear up." The right force of what she said and how she said it somehow kept me from being either shocked or offended. Thus, easy and simple as that, I began a train of changes leading to the eventual clearing up of much more than my acned skin, which had continued its distressing eruptions long past the years when first one dermatologist and then another had promised me it would smooth.

I did, indeed, "go off" sugar, processed foods, meat, and caffeine, the latter being difficult enough to teach me the little that I know about substance addiction and withdrawal. I gave up even the respectability of my short Afro and began growing dreadlocks—in those days when they were not socially acceptable, not available "bottled" in hip beauty shops, not twisted into instant glamour by limber-fingered technicians who "do" locks. I traveled to the black Caribbean. All these were external indications of deep internal change that pushed me to ask with increasing urgency to be shown my true work in this world. What was I put here for? What was I *supposed* to do? What was the way, the calling, the cause that would make me feel, as Aretha Franklin put it, "justified"? This questioning arose, I see now, from a profound urge toward spiritual identity and meaning.

My religious life and my spiritual self were not subjects I had been thinking about. The childhood years I spent walking up the Norma Street hill to attend the Zion Baptist Church in Shreveport, Louisiana, had fizzled into coerced appearances as a young adult at the mandatory

Sunday chapel of my undergraduate alma mater, Southern University, and had finally petered out altogether amidst the alien atmosphere of northern, white, academic institutions, where any possible "down-home" black churches or black people had to be painstakingly sought beyond hallowed, ivy walls. In the process of wresting from this unfamiliar system its sheepskins of validation, I shed a way of being spiritual in the world that I had always inhabited. However, both the former habitation and the shedding had taken place without considered thought or conscious choice. In 1979 my most overtly spiritual practices included saying grace at communal meals and holding hands with other women in feminist full moon circles. Maybe I prayed during desperate hours, maybe currents of language-less, thought-less faith coursed through me—but, for all intents and purposes, I had no active, deeply accessed spiritual life.

I began avidly reading popularly focused metaphysical books and articles. Many of these were current New Age titles, and quite a few were feminist-oriented. What comes most readily to mind are Jane Roberts's *The Education of Oversoul Seven;* Gary Zukav's *The Dancing Wu Li Masters;* an early twentieth-century "prosperity" author whose name I cannot remember; Migene G. Whippler's *Santeria;* Diane Mariechild's *Mother Wit;* Ann Farraday and Jungian-Senoi texts about dreams; and pamphlets and articles that turned me on to mind-body-spirit truisms and material about auras, Kirlian photography, the Tarot, astrology, Zen thinking, supernatural phenomena, the "secret life of plants," crystals, and synchronicity.

Because I was at the core a spiritually receptive, even hungry, individual, the avenues to transpersonal meaning and interconnection represented by all this reading strongly appealed to my intellect and emotions. The multiple, overlapping realities of Roberts's fable about a time-and-space-hopping supersoul intuitively struck me as accurate, and yes, it made sense that real need coupled with focused attention would make money appear, and that, in general, the universe was a wondrously mysterious but ordered and purposeful organism that could be read and entered into through any number of systems and means.

Except for Whippler's work on the African-Catholic syncretism that is Santeria, none of us would think to call any of this material "black." In fact, all of the authors are white, and the material itself is apparently raceless, that is, devoid of racial reference or implications. And it is raceless—in that the energy that is the universe, that takes form in us and in everything that exists cannot itself be regarded as raced (or sexed, or gendered, or, for that matter, anything else that happens when it reaches the dense physical plane of everyday life). And, yes, this New Age material is raceless in that every kind of people dreams, suffers, and rejoices under the same progression of planets and stars, and each and every person benefits from maintaining a peaceful and present mind. Yet, it is significant that in Washington, D.C., in 1980, a group of diverse black women including myself were passing around among ourselves Jane Roberts's *Oversoul Seven,* and that our friend Crystal was invoking some sorely needed, concrete prosperity to pay the rent and buy food for her child. This adds race—as it should be—to the picture of the emerging New Age. Spiritual wisdom and timeless principles, when run through African American women, tend to emerge with a different slant.

Toni Cade Bambara's novel *The Salt Eaters* provides the perfect means to illustrate this point. An altogether unprecedented and original act of creativity, this book is simultaneously New Age, female, *and* black. Published in 1980, the novel brought blazingly into focus the momentous happenings taking place in the consciousness of black women. *The Salt Eaters* tells the story of Velma Henry, an incredibly committed political activist in her forties who has attempted suicide and is undergoing a laying-on-of-hands healing by "the good woman" Ransom as a roomful of people look on. Velma has marched until her feet and womb bled for civil rights. She has struggled with other progressive sisters in her community to make "showboating" male leaders less sexist and more truly responsive to the people's needs. She has traveled with a troupe of Third World feminists staging educational dramas. She has put her life on the line for a healthy environment and a pacifist world. Finally, though, overtaken by negativity and despair, she slashes her wrists and sticks her head in the gas of her kitchen oven. During the difficult healing, readers experience Velma spinning through muggy memories and multiple lifetimes.

The Salt Eaters firmly contextualizes Velma within her family and community, but Toni's familiarity with both science and the supernatural takes her story into worlds every bit as vast and mind-boggling as Jane Roberts's metaphysical fable. Here, in this book, in 1980, was all the spirituality I was learning—and then some—made into a literary work that was impeccable in its daunting breadth of knowledge, difficult but dazzling style, and unimpeachable racial and feminist politics. The healing of Velma through the laying-on-of-hands is, in itself, not new or particularly startling. Nor is the circle of hard-praying church people or even, perhaps, the healer's down-to-earth spirit guide. Though these might not be staples of black spirituality, neither would they be considered unusual ingredients.

What is different in this book is the profound and wholly respectful attention accorded to these more traditional racial aspects, as well as to astrology, past lives and reincarnation, Tarot cards, the metaphysical extensions of quantum physics, chakras and energy, Sufi tales, psychic telepathy, numerology, ancient black Egyptian wisdom traditions, Eastern philosophies of cosmic connectedness, and so forth—in short, an array of alternative knowledge systems founded on the belief that this visible "phenomenal" world is the external reflection of an underlying "noumenal" reality that can—and indeed, should—be tapped for the full and optimum functioning of life in material form. In other words, The Salt Eaters validated largely unknown or discredited (by black people and whites), non-rational ways of knowing—and promoted the idea that we will function more effectively if we use the unseen energy that surrounds us.

Even more radical in the novel is the fact that all of these spiritual modalities are rooted in African and African American traditions and characters, and are geared toward the elimination of racism and other forms of social injustice and abuse. The thrust of Toni's work has always been the healing of the (black) "nation"—in this case symbolized by the repair of Velma's fractured self and psyche. Only when that internal and external work has been accomplished is health possible on larger scales. Ultimately, not only will Velma be made whole, but so too must her community, nation, the world, and the universe. As Toni outlines it, spiritual wisdom is first and foremost a force for transforming social and political ills—and those ills wear the very specific faces of racism, poverty, gender inequality, rampant capitalism, ignorance, and so forth. This is what I mean when I say that spirituality run through black women comes out with a different slant. Unlike the other New Age reading I was doing, this novel addressed issues that defined my identity-reality and lay close to my heart.

Thrilled, challenged, and totally impressed (and also slightly overwhelmed) by both the politics and the spirituality of The Salt Eaters, I became determined to write about this book, a desire inspired by my need to respond to it and the urge to help others understand the work. While I felt my experience and vocabulary would enable me to discuss its politics, I was not as proficient in the wide-ranging spiritual-metaphysical ideas and practices so casually incorporated throughout the text. I knew enough to scratch the surface, enough to identify the critical places at which to dig. But the novel's holistic spiritual command forced me to consult even more ancient and esoteric documents, pushing me into such areas as cosmic symbolism, grimoires, medieval magical texts, and the writing of Mme. Blavatsky, the famous theosophist and author of The Secret Doctrine.

Because it was within the context of late twentieth-century New Age culture that I discovered the spiritual truths underlying The Salt Eaters, that context was my immediate point of reference. Not so for Toni. She has always said that everything necessary for African American well-being exists within the black community—and this includes spiritual knowledge of any sort. Even the most esoteric learning she finds stored in the aunts and uncles, grandmothers and fathers who live in the neighborhood.

Years later as I spoke with Toni about this most challenging of her literary creations, I questioned her about where she, as the narrator, and the characters learned their spiritual knowledge—in particular, the genius Campbell (who I believe is Toni's alter ego or psychic double), a character in *The Salt Eaters* who can synthesize in one breathy sweep "voodoo, thermodynamics, I Ching, astrology, numerology, alchemy, metaphysics, everybody's ancient myths." What, I wanted to know, would she counsel an uninitiated person to do who desired to become as wise?

In response, she rattled out a string of resources and individuals including workshops with the black actress Barbara O., who played Yellow Mary in Julie Dash's film *Daughters of the Dust;* a black female university dean who can levitate; black "healing and light" temples, homeopathic clinics, and bookstores "in your neighborhood"; Luisah Teish's *Jambalaya;* three weeks of study in New Orleans with a practitioner "in the business" or the voodoo festival in Galveston or Alabama during the summer solstice; Odunde ceremonies in Philadelphia and New York City for our African ancestors; all the other "stuff" that goes on at the periphery of community observances such as Juneteenth or the Garvey Day parade. Incredulous, I said these would not enable anybody to know all that Campbell knows and that he had to have been reading New Age physics. Toni disagreed. She argued that Campbell "might have had an uncle who talks that talk," who might "lay out" the wisdom on top of his nephew's high school physics. Even though a lot of what was in the book came to *her* through reading, she was adamantly clear that "reading ain't going to get it."

This conversation left me feeling outside the kind of black community that Toni insisted existed. The closest thing I had to Campbell's uncle was a half-brother old enough to be my father, who mumbled drunken crypticisms about his Scottish Rite (mind you, not black Prince Hall) Masonic affiliation when I asked him relevant questions. And, although I stood with other displaced African sisters and brothers on the piers and prayed and tossed my offerings in the water, my presence at Odunde had not led me into any esoteric depths. Clearly, for Toni, growing up in Harlem in the late 1930s and 1940s had been an unparalleled, rich, Afrocentric cradling—especially given who she was and given her mother's revolutionary black nationalist politics—that would forever enable her to access the "black" at the heart of things.

I wondered if that world and others similar to it still flourished. I knew they did not for me or for many other African Americans of my generation and upbringing. I also acknowledged that reading alone did not "do it," but knew that for many of us it functioned as a huge resource. I wondered whether Toni was romanticizing. I never asked her this question outright. I knew she may have been doing in life what she does in her fiction, that is, sometimes painting black larger than life so that we will become visible in all our glory to ourselves and to the blind, negating white world. But she simply enlarges and highlights, never lies—so her basic premises still had to be taken as factual truths.

If I did not know exactly where to go with these matters years later, I certainly did not have the insight to even divine the issues in this way in 1980. Then, I held on to my copies of Idries Shah's tales of the mullah Nasrudin, pored through dictionaries of occult symbolism, read all the poorly printed pamphlets about healing the body that slumped on the back-aisle racks in dedicated health food stores, as well as Viktoras Kulvinskas's 1975 planetary healers manual, *Survival into the Twenty-first Century* (which my copy tells me I acquired in Washington, D.C., in 1979).

An indispensable resource in this enterprise was my then-partner Martha T. Zingo, who freely shared her rich occult library and her own extensive learning. Eternally my friend, this white, Italian-Irish-American working-class woman has always kept me spiritually and politically honest, never letting me forget that, even as I tended toward constructing seamlessly interlocked black-on-black narratives, she and other white women—some teachers, some important friends and lovers—have helped, like Toni's "muse" Khufu, to "pick the rocks up" out of my own and other black women's paths. With assistance from sources both here (acknowledged) and beyond (mostly unrecognized), I completed *The Salt Eaters* essay in an affirmed and solitary glow in 1981, sitting on the living room floor of our Northwest apartment. It is clear to me now that my heady foray into understanding Toni's work became the originating point for this present book. What I felt then was a strange, unnameable sense of having tapped into something bigger than myself that, through my expression, I had somehow helped to further.

Black Women Changing

Many other black women tell different yet similar stories of shifts and breakthroughs occurring around 1980. Michele Gibbs, a writer-artist-activist, recollects:

> Interesting—the period that you started noticing this shift in our [black women's] expression—because 1980 was a very pivotal year for me specifically. It marked the end objectively and also subjectively of long years of commitment to a certain way of inducing change, which is to say as a traditional community organizer with a very materially based approach to reaching people. And also in connection with that, I had finally concluded that not only was that particular method lacking, but that the context that I was living in was not very healthy for me, that context being the United States. That was the year I moved to Grenada.

From the day Michele set foot on the island, one extraordinary experience after another bore out her initial feeling that "this is the place I always dreamed I was from." Her father had died on March 13, 1961, the date of the Grenadian revolution. She traveled to the country to participate in Maurice Bishop's New Jewel socialist movement, not thinking of any other specific connections she might have to the place. From meeting a cab driver, however, who recognized her as a Gibbs because she "looked like all the rest of them around here," Michele discovered a family she had not known existed from the second leg of the triangular slave trade.

Events such as this, Michele says, "opened up a new way of seeing and being that I had buried within myself for many years, because as children, of course, we're open to all these things." Her father, a black American, and her mother, a white Jewish American, were both avowed and active Marxists. Growing up as the daughter of an interracial communist couple in Chicago during the early 1950s, she had lived in the few places that would rent to the family—in storefronts where "the only other people as bad off were gypsies, who very often lived next door." Although they were communists, her parents were "very clear that the best lesson they could teach me was not which line to follow, but how to think for myself." Adhering to their lead, she tried to expose herself to everything. Her family did not attend church, but she pursued her inner "mystical direction" through reading Lao-tse (whom she discovered by sneaking into the adult section of the library) and through her attraction to the beauty of the gypsies and their palm reading. Yet that "strain" of "intuition" got buried the same way that her artwork did when she turned fourteen. That was the year her father died, after having just left the Communist Party for its "final-racist-straw" failure to recognize the Algerian situation as a war of national liberation. As Michele recalls,

> I felt at that moment responsible for taking up where he had left off, and so I put down my paintbrush and picked up my picket sign, and I put down my piano and picked up the guitar, and devoted myself to social activism and being "socially responsible."

That path—which coincided with the 1960s "rising tide of everything positive and new and renewing that we could imagine then"—continued until her decision in 1980 to radically alter her life. Everybody in Detroit, where she had worked and organized, accused her of "deserting the ship," to which she replied: "Not necessarily. It's a ship that's about to sink anyway, and I'm going to get off of it. Remember J. J. Jones's injunction that 'It's not the size of the ship that makes the wave; it's the motion of the ocean.'" When she and her husband moved to Grenada, she vaguely imagined the possibility of combining picket sign and paintbrush, guitar and piano, rather than having to give up one in preference for the other.

This binary opposition is, of course, the way that politics and spirituality have been conceptualized; they have been viewed as diametric extremes, locked in conflict one with the other. Michele admits that she fell prey to this straitjacketing way of thinking because, in her words, "that was the reality I inherited." It is also the legacy that unravels Velma in *The Salt Eaters*. She breaks down as a result of being solely political and relentlessly logical, and gets well when she comes into conscious possession of her spiritual being. This political-versus-spiritual problem is, in fact, what motivated Toni to write the novel:

> There is a split between the spiritual, psychic, and political forces in my community . . . . It is a wasteful and dangerous split. The novel grew out of my attempt to fuse the seemingly separate frames of reference of the camps; it grew out of an interest in identifying bridges; it grew out of a compulsion to understand how the energies of this period will manifest themselves in the next decade.

For Michele, the combination of "spiritual consciousness in the people" combined with the "environment of social transformation" in Grenada in 1980 boded well for deconstructing this classic schizophrenia on both personal and community levels:

> Almost every encounter with somebody was a "significant encounter" where you are talking on many levels at once. You'd say, or somebody would say something like, "Nothing is known," and someone else would say, "Everything is known, it's just a question of who knows it." And so the environment itself pressed me to break through some frontiers that I might not have had courage to pursue on my own.

This "incredibly intense" melding of the spiritual and political was shattered by Grenada's internal coup and the United States' 1983 invasion of the island. Devastated and "forced back on spiritual resources," Michele fled to Lesbos, another warm, pretty island, and a place "which had a both mythical and real history as a power place for women":

> It was someplace where I knew the energy would be totally different, spiritual in its own way, but would give me the emotional space I needed to become centered again. And that took about two and a half years. It took me a year and a half just to stop being more in Grenada than where I actually physically was. I mean, like every night you close your eyes and you're back there again, you're really back there. You're not only back there the way it was, but you're back there in the present with what was happening. And, you close your eyes, you're on the bus on the same road, and you see what the U.S. presence has put in the place of what you remember. And you're there, you're just there.

This out-of-body existence was, to say the least, very hard on her, but after the two and a half years of healing on Lesbos, Michele re-emerged, ready to engage again with the Caribbean and the world.

Coming from quite different directions, Namonyah Soipan, a somewhat younger psychotherapist and global traveler, arrived at 1980 when she similarly experienced a marked solidification of gradually emergent changes. Namonyah had spent the first years of her life as an extremely sensitive young girl living in New Jersey. After having a traumatic childhood near-death experience, she became obsessed with the idea of death and fervently embraced a fire-and-brimstone fundamentalist Christianity. She adamantly maintained her faith despite confusion about how to love a god that she was supposed to fear, and was also puzzled about why the coming of the Holy Ghost—taught to be a blessing—triggered a scene filled with "punishment, screaming, shouting, people getting hurt and moving out of the way." After she became not just a baptized but a *saved* Christian at sixteen, she began "to preach and go into churches and proselytize to kids at school," still feeling afraid but thinking that, now that she was saved and doing some missionary work, her "back was covered" and she need not worry about God's wrath or retribution. The disturbing emotional dissonance within her became a cacophony when she was told that she could no longer dance (this was prohibited by many fundamentalist churches)—or even ski:

> Now this is when I began to understand the difference between being a spiritual being and being a religious being, because skiing was a spiritual experience for me. So I said to them, "Wait a minute." When I'm up on that mountain, I mean thousands of feet because I was a serious skier—I wanted to be in the Olympics, but my parents would not support that because they didn't want me to be a ski bum, so I was into slalom racing—so I would be up at the very top, up to the clouds, and when I was up there I'm talking about being enraptured. When I was skiing I was so tuned in to everything. This is before I even got into spiritual. I would tell people that it was better than an orgasm. Skiing for me was that divine, that brilliant, that magnificent, that I couldn't compare it to anything, but it was spiritual. I wasn't using that word at the time, I just knew that it was incredible and I felt close to God. When they told me that I had to stop skiing, that's when I said, "Wait a minute, something's wrong here." Because when I'm up on that mountain, I'm praying. I do prayers up there to help me down safely and never take anything for granted, but not only to help me get down the slope safely but to thank God for all this beauty. So skiing to me was not just recreational. They tried to take that away from me and that's when I started questioning and realizing these are man's rules. Religion is about following the rules, but it's about following man-made rules, and I said, "I got to get out of this, because I'm not stopping skiing."

Whereupon, Namonyah let go of the fundamentalist church but not its teaching. She continued attending the family Baptist church and went off to Boston University the next year—still proselytizing, still talking about Jesus Christ and cajoling her Japanese roommate to accompany her to services. Her aunt's warning that philosophy would challenge her religious beliefs proved true, especially after she transferred to Antioch College in 1977 where, in that more experiential setting, she came into contact with transcendental meditation, parapsychology, and a friend whom she considered a sinner who exposed her to Tarot readings. Finally, in 1980, back in New York City, she met Konda (the same unique woman I had encountered the year before), who helped her open up to the intense spirituality that had simmered inside her. Konda introduced her to yoga and to setting up an altar and, as Namonyah describes it,

> That's my first conscious glimpse at spirituality—even though I had glimpsed it years ago at fifteen when I was up on those mountains. So when Konda is talking to me now I have a frame of reference—the mountains. And, yes, it's making sense. "God is in myself." All right, I know this. This is very familiar to me. I said to her, "It's skiing." So all this is clicking.

Now, Namonyah's spiritual growth could accelerate because she realized that this spirituality is what had protected her from losing herself completely as she had journeyed through her religious trip. Thus, she discovered for herself one of the key understandings buttressing this incoming New Age—the distinction between religion and spirituality, that religion can be spiritual though not automatically, and that spirituality is a more inclusive consciousness that allows for exploration of many, even heterodox, avenues to the divine. Understanding the idea of God immanent made her aware, at an operative and active level, of her innate spiritual essence, that sense of self she had always been tapping into that was far greater than any dogma.

From that point of understanding God as immanent within herself, Namonyah rapidly opened up to diverse, broad possibilities, such as practicing Tibetan Buddhism and meditation, chanting, taking yoga, smoking marijuana, going to live in Jamaica, and just "opening up, opening up, opening up," devouring the African history that had been denied her, and studying Egyptology and learning about the ancient Egyptian kingdom of Kemet. Returning in 1982 from her first trip to Africa, where she lived with the Masai in Kenya and looked up the Falasha, the original black Hebrews, in Ethiopia, Namonyah found she had left light years behind her the person she had been at the beginning of 1980.

Masani Alexis DeVeaux is a writer and teacher who drew on these identities, as well as her religious background, to define black women's spirituality. Because of her own evolution, she understood as readily as Michele did what I was talking about when I asked about the year 1980. She began speaking about her own personal experience, but quickly catapulted to a larger perspective. Born into a Baptist family, she had religion in her life because she was "extraordinarily close" to her grandmother, whom she liked to watch wield her power as a member of the church's senior usher board. Even though she attended services because otherwise "Grammy" would withhold her allowance, she genuinely enjoyed the singing, children's programs where she recited poetry, and "the whole atmosphere."

It wasn't until she was in her early twenties that Masani Alexis rebelled, deeming church "too confining." At that point, in the early 1970s, she took off in other, less traditional directions. Eventually, she learned transcendental meditation, began studying with the Rosicrucians after responding to one of their magazine advertisements, extrapolated the Rosicrucian's emphasis on Egypt into Afro-ology, deeply explored the Yoruba religion—even wearing waist beads—but without ever wanting to become a priestess. She found and still finds it difficult to "join somebody else's thing," although she can draw from it, and she definitely cannot affiliate with anything "that's going to be anti-gay or anti-woman." Coming to the early 1980s, she incorporated tai chi, yoga, and "right eating," reaching a comfortable place that she now calls "the last major transformation of my spirituality," a convergence of different parts that has left her centered and no longer searching or, as she says, flitting around.

Masani Alexis is certain that the growth that she and her immediate milieu experienced was a breakthrough of global proportions. She expresses this certainty explicitly and enthusiastically:

> I think the thing about that period in the '80s in Brooklyn is that in our singular community—little small community that we were—we were beginning to really express black women's consciousness in a way that it had not been expressed . . . . When we come to the '80s, that consciousness was no longer in disguise . . . . And at the time that we threw the covers off, we were free to do and really become. Once that happened, everybody got big, every black woman got big. Every black woman was able to tap into every other black woman and was able to tap into every black woman in history and to a channeling. This is what we did . . . . Even people who were not conscious did—even if they tapped into one person, even if they tapped into some black actress, even if they tapped into a black woman's magazine . . . . Not to mention those of us who were consciously tapping. We were *really* blowed up, you know. But we had all that going—Alice Walker, Toni Cade Bambara, Toni Morrison, all of them, all of us, all of that. All of that was stimulating consciousness,

so there was no way we could not get big . . . . That consciousness could not be confined to the borders of North America. So then traveling connected us to that global consciousness; having a sense of the cultural experience of other women connected us to that global consciousness. Once we knew ourselves, we had to know the planet.

What I understand Masani Alexis to be saying here is that, around 1980, African American women began to have an enlarged sense of ourselves and the world. Ignited first by the movements of the 1960s and '70s that instilled racial and female pride, this sense of being "big," of "bigness," or psychic and social expansion, was further fed as we accessed our spiritual dimensions. She also implies that spiritual consciousness is a limitless force capable of crossing geographic and cultural barriers. No wonder, then, that travel beyond the United States figures so prominently in our stories, the physical action of travel being symbolic of large supra-physical change. As spiritual consciousness heightened on a planetary scale, African American women responded and contributed to that consciousness—a dynamic visible in the work and influence of the writers Masani mentions. This heightening of spiritual energy is, of course, also unmistakable in the way our life histories and patterns so sharply changed. Masani Alexis, Namonyah, Michele, and I had all adhered to certain systems of belief—whether the Baptist religion or, in Michele's case, a communist idealism that functioned as religion—which we grew to find inadequate, inconsequential, or confining. For all of us, 1980 was a turning point.

It was the year we each independently began exploring radically different spiritual teachings and paths, avenues that were less traditional for African American women and that brought us in confluence with the rapidly accreting New Age—even as we instinctively played out the realities of race and gender that defined us and gave shape and meaning to our lives. We read the usual New Age books and journals, sat before altars and meditated, rejected solely materialistic modes of existence, embraced yoga and tai chi and Buddhism—all common coin of the burgeoning New Age realm. However, we simultaneously applied our new learning to black subject matter, found spiritual transcendence in black revolutionary struggle, and sought metaphysical origins in Africa. Our consciousness as African American women worked on the new material and energies even as they worked on us, and the results were both customary and unique.

Finally, Masani Alexis's remark about connection to the "cultural experience of other women" is an important reminder that remarkable changes were also occurring among white women and other women of color. My favorite example of these collective and collaborative changes is the 1981 anthology edited by Cherríe Moraga and Gloria Anzaldúa, *This Bridge Called My Back: Writings by Radical Women of Color*. Conceived in response to racism in the white women's movement, its goal was to reflect an uncompromised definition of feminism by women of color who were committed to radical revolution. The book discusses varied subjects including: the experience of growing up as dark children; racism in the women's movement; theory that accounts for the actual, concrete realities of those who live in female bodies of color; culture, class, and homophobia; the third world woman writer; and sacred vision.

Notably, Toni Cade Bambara contributed a foreword to *This Bridge Called My Back* that speaks to the political and spiritual promise inherent in the kind of life-affirming work that the anthology represents. It began:

> How I cherish this collection of cables, esoesses, conjurations and fusile missiles. Its motive force. Its gathering-us-in-ness. Its midwifery of mutually wise understandings. Its promise of autonomy and community. And its pledge of an abundant life for us all. On time. That is to say—overdue, given the times.
>
> ("Arrogance rising, moon in oppression, sun in destruction"—Cameron)

From her position as an observant black woman, Toni concluded by looking forward to "the blueprints we will draw up of the new order we will make manifest."

Cosmic Consciousness Shifts

Change is definitely what this late 1970s–early 1980s period was all about. 1980 seems to have acted as a hinge, a moment on which the collective consciousness swung into a higher vibration, shifting toward more expanded planes of awareness and moving through available portals that initiated new modes of thought and behavior. Much occurred of historical, scientific, and artistic note, having begun years earlier with that marvelous, now near-fabulous, elongated decade that we in the United States call "the sixties." What was set in motion then took form and transformed, gathering substance and momentum until, by the early 1980s, the changes had assumed a definite enough shape that many attuned individuals began to register and name them. Marilyn Ferguson's 1980 study, *The Aquarian Conspiracy*, comes immediately to my mind.

In this "New Age watershed classic," as the book is described on its jacket, Ferguson gives both the details and broad trends of what the subtitle calls *Personal and Social Transformation in Our Time*. In the early 1970s, Ferguson conducted research about the brain and consciousness and encountered startling scientific and lay data regarding "accelerated learning, expanded awareness, the power of internal imagery for healing and problem solving, and the capacity to recover buried memories." All of her subsequent work further suggested that the social activism of the 1960s and the consciousness revolution of the 1970s "seemed to be moving toward an historic synthesis: social transformation resulting from personal transformation—change from the inside out." The characteristics and subtlety of this movement made her think of a conspiracy—in the sense of priest-scientist Pierre Teilhard de Chardin's "conspiracy of love" and in the root meaning of the word *conspiracy*, "to breathe together." In order to further "make clear the benevolent nature of this joining," Ferguson linked "conspiracy" with Aquarius, the zodiacal sign of the water bearer, "symbolizing flow and the quenching of an ancient thirst." She was also "drawn to" the cultural dream "that after a dark, violent age, the Piscean, we are entering a millennium of [Aquarian] love and light."

In one important chapter, Ferguson recounts how neuroscientist Karl Pribram and Einstein protégé David Bohm's discoveries led to the revolutionary theory that says "our brains mathematically construct 'hard' reality by interpreting frequencies from a dimension transcending time and space." This makes the brain a hologram—an organic, holistic, complete, self-perpetuating system where any piece contains the entire whole—interpreting a likewise holographic universe. Thus, each person participates in reality and affects what he or she observes. This theory, as Ferguson states, "establishes the supernatural as part of nature," since the dimension transcending time and space (the so-called supernatural) is translated into what we generally take to be natural, concrete reality.

> In this framework, psychic phenomena are only by-products of the simultaneous-everywhere matrix [this is the hologram]. Individual brains are bits of the greater hologram. They have access under certain circumstances to all the information in the total cybernetic system. Synchronicity—the web of coincidence that seems to have some higher purpose or connectedness—also fits in with the holographic model. Such meaningful coincidences derive from the purposeful, patterned, organizing nature of the matrix. Psychokinesis, mind affecting matter, may be a natural result of interaction at the primary level. The holographic model resolves one long-standing riddle of psi [psychic phenomena]: the inability of instrumentation to track the apparent energy transfer in telepathy, healing, clairvoyance. If these events occur in a dimension transcending time and space, there is no need for energy to travel from here to there. As one researcher put it, "There isn't any *there*."

Or, there isn't any "out there." Leading up to this last quarter century, such breakthrough understandings in all fields of human endeavor were expanding consciousness by bridging the apparent duality between mind and matter, science and spirit. New innovative learning techniques assigned value to inner experience, imagery, dreams, and feelings; impeccably designed medical studies proved that patients who were prayed for—even by strangers—recovered faster than those who were not.

Ferguson's *The Aquarian Conspiracy* certainly captures powerfully and persuasively the "great shift of values" that was occurring throughout the world. But nowhere in her 450 pages does she discuss race or say anything at all about black women. In her seventh chapter on "Right Power," she purports to look at "experiments in social transformation," analyzing the transformative effects that "the protest and counterculture of the 1960s" had on both their participants and society at large. There is commentary here about Jerry Rubin and the Chicago Eight, the Communist party in southern California, New Left thinkers, VISTA and the Peace Corps, and the Students for a Democratic Society. But not a word about the civil rights or black power movements. And her section in this chapter on "The Power of Women" is color blind.

Ferguson's work in this book is heavily based on questionnaire data she received from 185 respondents, whom she describes as "a powerful network of leading-edge thinkers, businesspeople, scientists, and politicians who are working to create a different kind of society based on a vastly enlarged concept of human potential." The book's appendix summarizes information about these respondents, revealing where they live, their marital status, their gender, their political self-labeling, the spiritual disciplines and growth modalities instrumental for them, body therapies they have experienced, their positions on the validity of psychic phenomena, and so forth. But here, again, the reader learns nothing about their race. In this, Ferguson further evidences an insensitivity to race and an omission of race as a vitally necessary consideration—both of which have helped to give the "New Age" a bad name—further compounded, in some cases, by the careless appropriation of spiritual lore from traditions of color. Ferguson's premise is that, after the political and social agitation of the 1960s and 1970s, change was now beginning to occur, as she put it, more from the "inside out" than the outside in. Who could better illustrate this point than individuals such as the African American women discussed in this chapter, whose superbly articulated understanding of their lives encoded this paradigmatic shift?

As a black female reader I had to enter into the wealth of this very important and informative book accepting the (unstated) idea that the "personal and social transformation" it charted was something spiritual that transcended race, and therefore, expectations for representation of the embodied self and specific material issues had to be either consciously set aside or unconsciously blanked out of active awareness. Still, there were those of us who read this New Age material and subscribed to the exciting facts it presented—because we recognized their spiritual truth intuitively and within the changed parameters of our own lives. However, we clearly had to look elsewhere for images and information that mirrored who we were on every other level. Consider the following example.

In 1981, Toni Morrison appeared on the March 30 cover of *Newsweek* magazine. The bold caption read, "Black Magic," a clever but insensitive phrase that fed into racial stereotypes associating African-derived people with *black* magic, and subtly insinuating that anything so powerful as what Toni Morrison was doing (that had white people and the white establishment paying homage to her) must have been achieved via means beyond her own natural capability. Despite all this, the phrase accurately identified the very aspect of Morrison's and other black women's writing that was causing their work to fire the minds and hearts and imaginations of an unprecedented number of readers. Morrison and her sister writers were also "Aquarian conspirators"—attuned to the rays of cosmic change sweeping over us, and, beyond that, they were translating those energies into forms that revolutionized the people who touched them, causing "personal and social transformation in our time." In the same way as the respondents in Ferguson's book, these black women writers were moving beyond outmoded Piscean ways and into the future, breaking paradigms of the old rationality and spinning new spiritual models. And they were doing this in a way that helped make the transition accessible and acceptable to large numbers of people.

In the article, Morrison talks about her family experience—about her family telling ghost stories, her grandmother using a dream book to play the numbers, and her father having some-times trickster-like communications with her after his death. She concludes, "We were intimate with the supernatural." Thus, it is not surprising that the world of her novels is filled with what the *Newsweek* editor Jean Strouse termed "signs, visitations, ways of knowing that reached beyond the five senses." Morrison's 1977 novel, *Song of Solomon*, offered up the character of a self-birthed root worker named Pilate who had no navel, roaming and protective ancestral ghosts, flying Africans imitated in their liberating "riding of the air" by their contemporary descendants, a woman named Circe who is as old as time—all set within a realistic here-and-now where the ravages of racism had yet to be battled on both internal and external fronts. Most of the outer weight of *Song of Solomon* is carried by the ostensible hero, Milkman, who embarks upon a journey through which he finds his true kin, roots, name, and self—and thus gains the knowledge and heart that will enable him to be a black man who can love and benefit his race. Pilate, his aunt, creates her starkly original existence outside societal norms, living in a shack with her daughter and granddaughter and selling homemade wine when they need cash money. She is the novel's living ancestral figure who conveys spiritual wisdom.

Tar Baby, Morrison's work published in 1981, raised to uncommon heights the handling of nature and the natural environment. Her deft insight allows her to explore what it means to carry life-consciousness in non-human mineral and vegetable form in a striking manner—through ocean, fog, and trees—as she taps the psychic pain of two black people, a dark skinned, roots-culture man and a high-yellow woman of privilege, trying to love each other.

On the one hand, in Morrison's novels, we are presented with the hard realities of what it means to be raced black, and raced and gendered black female in a predominantly white—predominantly white male—world. On the other, she validates everything that the New Age Aquarian theorists are positing about the naturalness of so-called supernatural phenomena and about our ability as spiritual human beings to function within these spaces. Her validation harks back to traditions of blackness that remind us that the New Age wisdom itself is not really new—only our enlarged capacity to accept, explain, appreciate, and benefit from it is fresh. Consequently, her unambiguous and unabashed handling of these subjects wraps us in enough traditional familiarity and inspires enough belief and courage to foster our incorporation of more daring but similar truths. The depiction of Pilate using the force of her intention to protect her unborn nephew is akin to and helps create the New Age climate where we powerfully enact our daily "affirmations" and think the "positive" thoughts that create our world.

Looking back at myself and other African American women I knew, and at the transforma-tions Ferguson documents in *The Aquarian Conspiracy*, I can see now that, around 1980, many people's lives were humming—at higher frequencies—with a brand new music and that massive identity shifts were taking place. This phenomenon was definitely about something "spiritual," a word the black women I associated with started using to denote all the unseen avenues to power that enabled us to withstand the pernicious racism-sexism-classism-heterosexism of our daily existences. The benefit we derived from taking our religious-spiritual impulses to higher levels was the strength we garnered to walk this tainted Earth. We were part of a spiritual quickening that was sweeping the planet, an inspired imperative to pierce through the received, the material, and the limited obvious into the realm of invisible and divinely potentiating energies that give rise to the physical world—a motivation no more true for the physicists' probing construction of a holographic universe than for Morrison's fictional world—a world of ghosts that heal, Africans who fly, trees that talk, and women who make magic—or the spirit guides, mud mothers in a mirror, and revolution-talking drums of Toni Cade Bambara's *The Salt Eaters*.

Note

1. Akasha Gloria Hull, "The Third Revolution: A New Spirituality Arises," in *Soul Talk: The New Spirituality of African American Women* (Rochester, VT: Inner Traditions, 2001), pp. 22–53.

Iyanla Vanzant

Iyanla Vanzant, trained in both Christian and African-centered spiritual cosmologies, has established notoriety as a spiritualist, healer, and self-help guru. Taken from her collection of prayers, *Every Day I Pray*, Vanzant's "A Mother's Prayer for Her Unborn Child" gives credence to the belief in an invisible, spirit world in which our children reside prior to physically laboring them into the world. Indeed, she privileges an African-centered connection to the divine while brilliantly crafting her language to articulate the sacred pact between a hierarchy of creative beings who, together, will be responsible for the physical, mental, and spiritual well-being of the unborn. The humility of the prayer reveals the delicate balance of that relationship, an affirmation of the belief that motherhood is a divine trust that cannot and should not be taken for granted. Vanzant's prayer offers a model for shaping one's words into a rhetoric that encourages the renewal of our spiritual purpose.

A Mother's Prayer for Her Unborn Child

Iyanla Vanzant[1]

Blessed and Merciful God,
Thank you for the gift of life.
Thank you for the life of the child growing inside me.
Thank you for your love that is shaping and forming this child's life into divine perfection.
Thank you for shaping this child's mind.
Thank you for shaping this child's bones.
Thank you for shaping this child's destiny and for writing it upon his or her heart.
Thank you for filling this child's entire being with your loving light.
Thank you for knowing and calling this child's name even as it is being formed.
Thank you for showing me how to love this child even before it is born.
Thank you for giving me a healthy appetite for those foods that are life giving and life sustaining while this child is growing inside me.
Thank you for giving me peaceful rest while this child is growing inside me.
Thank you for keeping me from harm and danger while this child is growing inside me.
Thank you for peace of mind while this child is growing inside me.
Right now I give to you all of my concerns for the health, strength and well-being for the precious life growing inside my body.
Right now I call forth your grace, mercy and the loving light of your presence to fill my being and sustain the life growing inside me.
Prepare me for this birth. Prepare my mind. Prepare my body.
Bless me and this child that its birth will happen easily and effortlessly, under the grace of your peace.
I give your angels charge of this child.
I give you charge over my entire being.
I give you thanksgiving and praise for this blessed life growing inside me.
May this prayer be lifted, heard and accepted into the highest realms of all that is good.
For this I am so grateful.
And So It Is!

Note

1. Iyanla Vanzant, "A Mother's Prayer for Her Unborn Child," in *Every Day I Pray: Prayers for Awakening to the Grace of Inner Communion* (New York: Simon & Schuster, 2001), pp. 74–77.

Joseph E. Lowery

The Reverend Dr. Joseph E. Lowery, one of the eldest living civil rights icons, gave a colorful benediction at the first inauguration of the 44th president of the United States, Barack Hussein Obama, on January 22, 2009, in front of a record crowd gathered at the National Mall. Marking a profound and powerful moment in the hallmark of African American history and culture, Lowery performed a verbal feat by showcasing the Black sermon tradition—inclusive of signifyin', rhyming, code-switching, using vernacular speech, and call-and-response—all in a single call to prayer. His prayer exemplifies the spiritual and musical traditions from which Black expressive culture is born, and it invokes a double-voiced discourse in which he addresses two separate audiences at once. Lowery's opening words brought the oratorical style of Black folks to the Capitol and succeeded in taking the nation to church.

Transcript of Rev. Lowery's Inaugural Benediction

Joseph E. Lowery[1]

Rev. Joseph Lowery, who co-founded the Southern Christian Leadership Conference with Martin Luther King Jr., delivered the benediction at the inaugural ceremony. Below is a transcription of his address, provided by CQ Transcriptwire:

LOWERY: God of our weary years, god of our silent tears, thou, who has brought us thus far along the way, thou, who has by thy might led us into the light, keep us forever in the path we pray, lest our feet stray from the places, our god, where we met thee, lest our hearts, drunk with the wine of the world, we forget thee.

Shadowed beneath thy hand, may we forever stand true to thee, oh God, and true to our native land.

We truly give thanks for the glorious experience we've shared this day.

We pay now, oh Lord, for your blessing upon thy servant Barack Obama, the 44th president of these United States, his family and his administration.

He has come to this high office at a low moment in the national, and indeed the global, fiscal climate. But because we know you got the whole world in your hands, we pray for not only our nation, but for the community of nations.

Our faith does not shrink though pressed by the flood of mortal ills.

For we know that, Lord, you are able and you're willing to work through faithful leadership to restore stability, mend our brokenness, heal our wounds, and deliver us from the exploitation of the poor, of the least of these, and from favoritism toward the rich, the elite of these.

We thank you for the empowering of thy servant, our 44th president, to inspire our nation to believe that yes we can work together to achieve a more perfect union.

And while we have sown the seeds of greed—the wind of greed and corruption, and even as we reap the whirlwind of social and economic disruption, we seek forgiveness and we come in a spirit of unity and solidarity to commit our support to our president by our willingness to make sacrifices, to respect your creation, to turn to each other and not on each other.

And now, Lord, in the complex arena of human relations, help us to make choices on the side of love, not hate; on the side of inclusion, not exclusion; tolerance, not intolerance.

And as we leave this mountain top, help us to hold on to the spirit of fellowship and the oneness of our family. Let us take that power back to our homes, our workplaces, our churches, our temples, our mosques, or wherever we seek your will.

Bless President Barack, First Lady Michelle. Look over our little angelic Sasha and Malia.

We go now to walk together as children, pledging that we won't get weary in the difficult days ahead. We know you will not leave us alone.

With your hands of power and your heart of love, help us then, now, Lord, to work for that day when nations shall not lift up sword against nation, when tanks will be beaten into tractors, when every man and every woman shall sit under his or her own vine and fig tree and none shall be afraid, when justice will roll down like waters and righteousness as a mighty stream.

Lord, in the memory of all the saints who from their labors rest, and in the joy of a new beginning, we ask you to help us work for that day when black will not be asked to get in back, when brown can stick around . . .

(LAUGHTER)

. . . when yellow will be mellow . . .

(LAUGHTER)

LOWERY: . . . when the red man can get ahead, man; and when white will embrace what is right. That all those who do justice and love mercy say Amen.

AUDIENCE: Amen.

LOWERY: Say Amen.

AUDIENCE: Amen.

LOWERY: And Amen.

AUDIENCE: Amen.

(APPLAUSE)

Note

1. Joseph E. Lowery, "Benediction at the Inauguration of President Barack Hussein Obama," Washington, DC, January 22, 2009.

⊂━━━━⊃∘∞∘⊂━━━━⊃

Section 3: Further Reading

Cooper, Anna Julia. "The Gain from a Belief." In *A Voice from the South*. New York: Oxford University Press, 1988. (pp. 286–304). (Original work published 1892).

Crummell, Alexander. "God and the Nation," and "The Fitness of the Gospel." In *The Future of Africa*. New York: Charles Scribner, 1862.

Delany, Martin. *Principia of Ethnology: The Origin of Races and Color*. Philadelphia: Harper & Brothers, 1879. (pp. 9–27 pp. 37–52, pp. 56–71).

Douglass, Frederick. "Appendix." In *Narrative of the Life of Frederick Douglass*. New York: Penguin Press, 1986. (Originally published in 1845).

Dunbar, Paul Lawrence. "An Antebellum Sermon." In *African-American Poetry of the Nineteenth-Century*. Ed. Joan R. Sherman. Chicago: Univ. of Illinois Press, 1992. (Originally published in 1895). (pp. 399–401).

Farrakhan, Louis. *The Divine Value of the Woman*. Chicago: Mosque Maryam. September 16, 2011.

Hall, Prince. *A Charge Delivered to the Brethren of the African Lodge. On the 25th of June, 1792*. Boston: Bible and Heart, 1792.

hooks, bell. "Walking in the Spirit." *Sisters of the Yam: Black Women and Self-Recovery*. Cambridge, MA: South End Press, 1993. (pp. 183–190).

Hopkins, Pauline. "From of One Blood, Chapter XI." In *The Magazine Novels of Pauline Hopkins*. New York: Oxford University Press, 1988. (pp. 520–521). (Originally published in 1903).

Hopkins, Pauline. *A Primer of Facts Pertaining to the Early Greatness of the African Race and the Possibility of Restoration by Its Descendants—with Epilogue*. Cambridge, MA: PE Hopkins & Co., 1905.

Hughes, Langston. "Goodbye Christ." *The Negro Worker*. 1932.

Hughes, Langston. "Ma Lord." In *The Dream Keeper and Other Poems*. New York: Knopf, 1996. (pp. 48–49). (Originally published in 1927).

Hughes, Langston. "A New Song." In *A New Song: A Collection of Poems*. International Workers Order, 1938.

Hughes, Langston. "Salvation." In *The Big Sea*. New York: Hill & Wang, 1940. (pp. 18–21).

Hurston, Zora Neale. *Jonah's Gourd Vine*. New York: Harper Perennial, 1990. (pp. 174–181). (Originally published in 1934).

Hurston, Zora Neale. "Uncle Monday." In *The Complete Stories*. New York: Harper Perennial, 1995. (pp. 106–116). (Originally published in 1935).

James, Marlon. *The Book of Night Women*. New York: Riverhead Books, 2009. (pp. 49–52).

Johnson, James Weldon. "The Creation." In *Norton Anthology of African American Literature*, 2nd edition. Eds. Henry Louis Gates, Jr. and Nellie McKay, New York: W.W. Norton & Co., 2004. (pp. 800–802) (Originally published in 1920).

Johnson, James Weldon. "Go Down Death." In *American Negro Poetry: An Anthology*, Revised edition. Ed. Arna Bontemps, New York: Noonday Press, 1974. (Originally published in 1908).

King, Martin L. "Eulogy for the Martyred Children." September 18, 1963.

King, Martin L. "I See the Promised Land." April 3, 1968, Memphis, TN.

Lee, Jarena. "Religious Experience and Journal of Jarena Lee (1849)." In *Spiritual Narratives*. New York: Oxford University Press, 1988. (pp. 3–13, 15–30).

Morrison, Toni. *Beloved*. New York: Vintage International, 2004. (pp. 102–105). (Originally published in 1987).

Nelson, Alice Dunbar. "In Unconsciousness," "Unknown Life of Jesus Christ." In *Violets and Other Tales*, in *The Works of Alice Dunbar Nelson*. New York: Oxford University Press, 1988. (pp. 36–43, 110–122). (Originally published in 1895).

Obama, Barack. *Dreams from My Father*. New York: Three Rivers Press, 2004. (pp. 291–295).

Reed, Ishmael. *Mumbo Jumbo*. New York: Simon & Schuster, 1972. (pp. 161–191).

Reed, Ishmael. "Neo-Hoodoo Manifesto." In *Norton Anthology of African American Literature*, 2nd edition. Eds. Henry Louis Gates, Jr. and Nellie McKay, New York: NY: W.W. Norton and Co., 2004. (pp. 2062–2066). (Originally published in 1972).

Reed, Ishmael. "Shrovetide in Old New Orleans." In *Shrovetide in Old New Orleans*. New York: Atheneum, 1989. (pp. 9–33).

Said, Nicholas. "Autobiography of Nicholas Said." (1873). (pp. 7–12, pp. 36–40, pp. 78–80). Retrieved from http://docsouth.unc.edu/neh/said/said.html

Seme, Isaka. "The Regeneration of Africa." In *Africa and America* (1891). Springfield, MA: Wiley & Co., 1865.

Stewart, Maria W. "An Address Delivered at the African Masonic Hall Boston February 27, 1833." In *Maria Stewart: America's First Black Political Writer*. Bloomington: Indiana University Press, 1987. (pp. 56–64).

Teish, Luisah. "Ancestor Reverence." In *Jambalaya: The Natural Woman's Book of Personal Charms and Practical Rituals*. New York: Harper Collins, 1988. (pp. 67–75).

Vanzant, Iyanla. "Introduction," "A Prayer for Divine Correction," "A Blessing for the Body," and "Prayer of Surrender." In *Every Day I Pray: Prayers for Awakening to the Grace of Inner Communion*. New York: Simon & Schuster, 2001. (pp. 15–24, 56–59, 63–64, 144–146).

Walker, Alice. *The Color Purple*. Orlando: Harvest Books, 2003, 1982. (pp. 192–197).

Walker, Margaret. "Molly Means." In *For My People*. New Haven, CT: Yale University Press, 1942. (pp. 33–34).

Wheatley, Phillis. "Thoughts on the Works of Providence," "An Hymn to the Morning," "An Hymn to the Evening," "Isaiah LXIII. 1–8," "On Recollection," "On Imagination," "A Funeral Poem on the Death of C.E., an Infant of twelve Months," "Atheism," "An Address to the Deist," and "An Elegy on Leaving."

Whitfield, James. "Prayer of the Oppressed." In *America and Other Poems*. James S. Leavitt, 1853.

X, Malcolm. "God's Judgment on White America." 1963.

Section 3: Discussion Questions

1. What can be discerned about African American rhetorical strategies and styles when considering the reading selections in which politics and religion cross paths?

2. Identify and discuss how the practice of Islam has influenced the oratory of African Americans in the United States. How does it shift and shape the language, themes, or political views of those who practice it? Be sure to point to specific textual passages to support your position.

3. In what way is Africa—as a spiritual concept, a geographical location, and/or as an ancestral home—used as a rhetorical tool in this section? Explore the various ways Africa is centered in African American discourse to convey meaning through both explicit and implicit methods.

4. In many of the reading selections, the writer makes use of vernacular speech expressions as well as more spiritually specific language. Is there is a sharp rhetorical distinction between the sacred and the secular? If so, delineate which selections make such a distinction and which do not. For those that do blend the sacred and the secular, discuss how vernacular forms of expression function to achieve the rhetorical aim of the text.

5. Consider how the texts in this section reveal the import of class in the diversity of spiritual ethoi that emerged among Africans during and in the aftermath of the Middle Passage.

6. What do these texts reveal about how folk spirituality and Western Christianity merge and diverge in the making of African American Christianity?

7. Consider Gloria Akasha Hull's essay "The Third Revolution: A New Spirituality Arises" and her argument toward a shift in the way African American women embrace and practice spirituality in the latter part of the twentieth century. Discuss and create a trajectory of African American women's spiritual and religious thinking that leads up to this "third revolution" as evidenced by other selections by African American women in the text.

4

LANGUAGE, LITERACY, AND EDUCATION

Edited and with an introduction by Valerie Kinloch and Donja Thomas

***

Introduction

The intellectual, linguistic, and cultural traditions of African American people are, undoubtedly, grounded in a rich history, particularly in the United States and throughout the diaspora. Such traditions, forever impacted by enslavement and targeted, systematic forms of violence, oppression, and injustice, on the one hand, and marked by fights for civil, political, and educational rights, on the other hand, have always reflected the fortitude of Black people to define and centralize their experiences in the presence of mainstream (White) spaces that have looked upon such experiences as marginal, at best. One should not assume that the experiences of African American people, to include their knowledges, subjectivities, epistemologies, and their rhetorical, cultural, linguistic, and intellectual traditions, are confined to, or hidden within, historically segregated Black spaces (e.g., Black churches, homes, communities, cultural institutions). These traditions are represented by a variety of mores, including rituals, spiritual practices, and forms of orality, aurality, and storytelling, as well as by music, literature, art, and civil and sociopolitical protests. In fact, these very same traditions have always served mainstream spaces and discourse practices well. Nevertheless, African Americans and their intellectual, linguistic, and cultural traditions have not received the deserved attention within those so-called dominant spaces and practices.

Hence, the selections included in this section on "Language, Literacy, and Education" speak to some of the intellectual, linguistic, and cultural traditions of African Americans, traditions, according to Manning Marable (2000), that highlight "the critical thought and perspectives of intellectuals of African descent and scholars of black America and Africa and the black diaspora" (p. 17). Insofar as the Black intellectual tradition is concerned, it is Marable who asserts that this tradition has three characterizing factors: "First, the black intellectual tradition has always been descriptive, that is, presenting reality of black life and experiences from the point of view of black people themselves" (p. 17). Furthermore, "the black intellectual tradition has, secondly, been corrective. It has attempted to challenge and to critique the racism and stereotypes that have been ever present in the mainstream discourse of white academic institutions" (p. 17). And finally, Marable asserts that "the black intellectual tradition has been prescriptive. Black scholars who have theorized from the black experience have often proposed practical steps for empowerment of black people" (p. 18).

From being descriptive, to corrective, to prescriptive, the Black intellectual tradition unapologetically emphasizes the various worldviews, rationalities, and epistemes that have always been, and continue to be, fundamental to Black life and culture. In this way, then, one cannot situate African American rhetorics, generally, and African American forms of language, literacy, and education, specifically, within a discourse that is exclusive to examinations of otherness and difference. Such situated-ness both de-theorizes African American rhetorics and its intellectual, cultural, and linguistic traditions and positions it against, and as inferior to, "dominant" ways of theorizing, of thinking, and of being (see Gilyard, 2011; Marable, 2000; Nunley, 2011; Richardson & Jackson, 2007; Smitherman, 2000).

Instead, one must recognize how African American rhetorics and its intellectual, cultural, and linguistic traditions are so deeply intertwined into an ontology of what it means to be Black, to struggle for freedom, to gain and sustain a strong Black consciousness, to honor Black cultural ways, and to continuously strive for equality and equity in unwelcoming, pervasively racist, dominant spaces. From David Walker, Anna Julia Cooper, and Frederick Douglass; Booker T. Washington, Carter G. Woodson, William Edward Burghardt Du Bois, and Marcus Garvey; James Baldwin, June Jordan, and Zora Neale Hurston; Geneva Smitherman, Theresa Perry, Claude Steele, and Asa G. Hilliard; to Henry Louis Gates, Keith Gilyard, and Arlette Willis, among many others, the rhetorics and traditions of African American people are theorized and conceptualized in sophisticatedly complex, artistically rich, and intellectually powerful ways. The aforementioned writers, all included in this section (whether in print here, in further readings, or on the companion website), write about the intellectual, linguistic, and cultural traditions of African American people in ways that place needed attention on their language, literacy, and education. To do this, the authors, in one way or another, emphasize how rhetorical kairos, facilitated by context, time, audience, and ensuing contingencies, can continue to motivate groups of Black people to actively respond to (and resist) various forms of civic, social, political, and educational oppressions.

Specifically, the authors of the included excerpts utilize rhetorical tactics, or devices, of ethos, logos, and pathos in remarkable ways that reveal their positions on African American language, literacy, and education. They use logic, reasoning, and evidence to both make and share their arguments for the social and educative upliftment of African American people. Simultaneously, their writings embody discourses of care, humor, and compassion as the writings, collectively, arouse the emotions of their audience and point to varied ways by which to initiate discourse, promote critical dialogue, and, one would hope, effect change through collective action. In this way, a focus on African American rhetoric, with particular attention to language, literacy, and education, is not singularly about eloquence and wit, tone, and form. It is also about related exemplum, syllogism, philosophy, history, experience, worldviews, and knowledge. In other words, African American language, literacy, and education, specifically, parallel a focus on philosophy and epistemology, given that "rhetoric itself is a serious philosophical subject that involves not only the transmission, but also the generation, of knowledge," and such transmission and generation are made possible when one "coupl[es] rhetoric to epistemology" (Leff, qtd. in Berlin, 1987, p. 165). The works included in this section all take up this focus on the intersections of, and the promises afforded by, rhetoric, philosophy, and epistemology, and knowledge generation and knowledge transmission, in the language, literacy, and education of African American people.

So, what do the included works, collectively, say about language, literacy, and education for Black people? In what ways do the works point to philosophical and epistemological understandings of Black people's civil, political, and educational rights? How might the works motivate us to seriously consider issues related to knowledge production (who gets to, and does not get to, produce and disseminate knowledge about Black people, and why?) and the utility of certain kinds of knowledge over other kinds of knowledge? How can knowledge of "the social welfare of black people" impact Black people's language, literacy, and education, and how can it serve as "an oppositional critique of the existing power arrangements and relations that are responsible for the systemic exploitation of black people" (Marable, 2000, p. 21)?

More specifically, in what ways might attention to colonization, enslavement, and brutality, as described in David Walker's (1829) "Article II: Our Wretchedness in Consequence of Ignorance," revolutionize current calls for freedom, pride, and systemic change for Black people in the United States? How can an explicit focus on Black people's language, literacy, and education take into consideration arguments posited by W.E.B. Du Bois (1903) in "The Talented Tenth," and Booker T. Washington (1901) in "Struggle for an Education"? What can we learn about Black people and language by studying June Jordan's (1988) essay "Nobody Mean More to Me Than You and the Future Life of Willie Jordan"? What can be extrapolated from Arlette Willis's (1995) article "Reading the World of School Literacy: Contextualizing the Experience of a Young African American Male," in relation to how some Black people struggle to see, value, and recognize the multiplicities of self against the gaze of whiteness, particularly as they acquire school-sanctioned forms of traditional literacy?

These questions and many others speak to the power of language, literacy, and education for African American people, especially as they have fought, and continue to fight, against systemic forms of oppression. Undoubtedly, African American rhetorics, philosophies, and epistemologies are rooted in the intellectual, linguistic, and cultural traditions of African and African American people in ways that call forth descriptive, corrective, and/or prescriptive responses. Additionally, these rhetorics, philosophies, and epistemologies point to the rich presence of historical and contemporary writings on African American language, literacy, and education.

Works Cited

Du Bois, W.E.B. *The Talented Tenth*. New York, NY: James Pott, 1903.

Gilyard, Keith. *True to the Language Game: African American Discourse, Cultural Politics, and Pedagogy*. London: Routledge, 2011.

Jordan, June. "Nobody Mean More to Me Than You and the Future Life of Willie Jordan." *Harvard Educational Review*, 58.3 (1988): 363–375.

Marable, Manning. "Black Studies and the Racial Mountain." *Souls*, 2.3 (2000): 17–36.

Nunley, Vorris L. *Keepin' it Hushed: The Barbershop and African American Hush Harbor Rhetoric*. Detroit: Wayne State University, 2011.

Richardson, Elaine and Ronald Jackson. *African American Rhetoric(s): Interdisciplinary Perspectives*. Carbondale: Southern Illinois University Press, 2007.

Smitherman, Geneva. *Talkin That Talk: Language, Culture, and Education in African America*. London: Routledge, 2000.

Walker, David. *David Walker's Appeal, in Four Articles, Together With a Preamble, to the Coloured Citizens of the World, but in Particular, and Very Expressly, to Those of the United States of America*. Boston: Black Classic Press, 1829.

Washington, Booker T. *Up From Slavery*. New York: Doubleday, 1901.

Willis, Arlette. "Reading the World of School Literacy: Contextualizing the Experience of a Young African American Male." *Harvard Educational Review*, 65.1 (1995): 30–50.

David Walker

The self-educated historian, abolitionist, orator, and author David Walker is still known as one of the most revolutionary and militant voices among the early African American protest writers. Born to a slave father and free Black mother, Walker was very aware of the degradations and injustices of slavery. In September 1829, he published his *Appeal* with the intentions of reaching his primary audience of enslaved men and women in the South. To the slaves, his words were empowering and instilled a sense of pride and hope. To the slave owners, his words were dangerous and compelled White people to ban its distribution. Nevertheless, Walker's *Appeal* speaks to the history and horrific nature of American chattel slavery. He challenges the institution of chattel slavery by exposing its animalistic and inhumane characteristics and by highlighting the spiritual repercussions he believes will come to those who endorse and support such a "wretched" institution. Walker appeals to the minds and spirits of those who experience oppression, and he encourages them to stay strong, to contend for their lawful rights, and to fight for their freedom. Walker's *Appeal*, with its rhetorical sophistication, remains one of the most powerful and radical anti-slavery documents.

Article II. Our Wretchedness in Consequence of Ignorance

David Walker[1]

Ignorance, my brethren, is a mist, low down into the very dark and almost impenetrable abyss in which, our fathers for many centuries have been plunged. The Christians, and enlightened of Europe, and some of Asia, seeing the ignorance and consequent degradation of our fathers, instead of trying to enlighten them, by teaching them that religion and light with which God had blessed them, they have plunged them into wretchedness ten thousand times more intolerable, than if they had left them entirely to the Lord, and to add to their miseries, deep down into which they have plunged them tell them, that they are an *inferior* and *distinct race* of beings, which they will be glad enough to recall and swallow by and by. Fortune and misfortune, two inseparable companions, lay rolled up in the wheel of events, which have from the creation of the world, and will continue to take place among men until God shall dash worlds together.

When we take a retrospective view of the arts and sciences—the wise legislators—the Pyramids, and other magnificent buildings—the turning of the channel of the river Nile, by the sons of Africa or of Ham, among whom learning originated, and was carried thence into Greece, where it was improved upon and refined. Thence among the Romans, and all over the then enlightened parts of the world, and it has been enlightening the dark and benighted minds of men from then, down to this day. I say, when I view retrospectively, the renown of that once mighty people, the children of our great progenitor I am indeed cheered. Yea further, when I view that mighty son of Africa, HANNIBAL, one of the greatest generals of antiquity, who defeated and cut off so many thousands of the white Romans or murderers, and who carried his victorious arms, to the very gate of Rome, and I give it as my candid opinion, that had Carthage been well united and had given him good support, he would have carried that cruel and barbarous city by storm. But they were dis-united, as the coloured people are now, in the United States of America, the reason our natural enemies are enabled to keep their feet on our throats.

Beloved brethren—here let me tell you, and believe it, that the Lord our God, as true as he sits on his throne in heaven, and as true as our Saviour died to redeem the world, will give you a Hannibal, and when the Lord shall have raised him up, and given him to you for your possession, O my suffering brethren! remember the divisions and consequent sufferings of *Carthage* and of *Hayti*. Read the history particularly of Hayti, and see how they were butchered by the whites, and do you take warning.[2] The person whom God shall give you, give him your support and let him go his length, and behold in him the salvation of your God. God will indeed, deliver you through him from your deplorable and wretched condition under the Christians of America. I charge you this day before my God to lay no obstacle in his way, but let him go.

The whites want slaves, and want us for their slaves, but some of them will curse the day they ever saw us. As true as the sun ever shone in its meridian splendor, my colour will root some of them out of the very face of the earth. They shall have enough of making slaves of, and butchering, and murdering us in the manner which they have. No doubt some may say that I write with a bad spirit, and that I being a black, wish these things to occur. Whether I write with a bad or a good spirit, I say if these things do not occur in their proper time, it is because the world in which we live does not exist, and we are deceived with regard to its existence.—It is immaterial however to me, who believe, or who refuse—though I should like to see the whites repent peradventure God may have mercy on them, some however, have gone so far that their cup must be filled . . . .

Ignorance and treachery one against the other—a grovelling servile and abject submission to the lash of tyrants, we see plainly, my brethren, are not the natural elements of the blacks, as the Americans try to make us believe; but these are misfortunes which God has suffered our fathers to be enveloped in for many ages, no doubt in consequence of their disobedience to their Maker, and which do, indeed, reign at this time among us, almost to the destruction of all other principles: for I must truly say, that ignorance, the mother of treachery and deceit, gnaws into our very vitals.

Ignorance, as it now exists among us, produces a state of things, Oh my Lord! too horrible to present to the world. Any man who is curious to see the full force of ignorance developed among the coloured people of the United States of America, has only to go into the southern and western states of this confederacy, where, if he is not a tyrant, but has the feelings of a human being, who can feel for a fellow creature, he may see enough to make his very heart bleed! He may see there, a son take his mother, who bore almost the pains of death to give him birth, and by the command of a tyrant, strip her as naked as she came into the world, and apply the cowhide to her, until she falls a victim to death in the road! He may see a husband take his dear wife, not unfrequently in a pregnant state, and perhaps far advanced, and beat her for an unmerciful wretch, until his infant falls a lifeless lump at her feet! Can the Americans escape God Almighty? If they do, can he be to us a God of Justice? God is just, and I know it—for he has convinced me to my satisfaction—I cannot doubt him. My observer may see fathers beating their sons, mothers their daughters, and children their parents, all to pacify the passions of unrelenting tyrants. He may also, see them telling news and lies, making mischief one upon another. These are some of the productions of ignorance, which he will see practised among my dear brethren, who are held in unjust slavery and wretchedness, by avaricious and unmerciful tyrants, to whom, and their hellish deeds, I would suffer my life to be taken before I would submit. And when my curious observer comes to take notice of those who are said to be free, (which assertion I deny) and who are making some frivolous pretentions to common sense, he will see that branch of ignorance among the slaves assuming a more cunning and deceitful course of procedure.—He may see some of my brethren in league with tyrants, selling their own brethren into *hell upon earth*, not dissimilar to the exhibitions in Africa, but in a more secret, servile and abject manner. Oh Heaven! I am full! ! ! I can hardly move my pen! ! ! ! and as I expect some will try to put me to death, to strike terror into others, and to obliterate from their minds the notion of freedom, so as to keep my brethren the more secure in wretchedness, where they will be permitted to stay but a short time (whether tyrants believe it or not)—I shall give the world a development of facts, which are already witnessed in the courts of heaven. My observer may see some of those ignorant and treacherous creatures (coloured people) sneaking about in the large cities, endeavouring to find out all strange coloured people, where they work and where they reside, asking them questions, and trying to ascertain whether they are runaways or not, telling them, at the same time, that they always have been, are, and always will be, friends to their brethren; and, perhaps that they themselves are absconders, and a thousand such treacherous lies to get the better information of the more ignorant! ! ! There have been and are at this day in Boston, New-York, Philadelphia, and Baltimore, coloured men, who are in league with tyrants, and who receive a great portion of their daily bread, of the moneys which they acquire from the blood and tears of their more miserable brethren, whom they scandalously delivered into the hands of our *natural enemies! ! ! ! ! !*

To show the force of degraded ignorance and deceit among us some farther, I will give here an extract from a paragraph, which may be found in the Columbian Centinel of this city, for September 9, 1829, on the first page of which, the curious may find an article, headed

"AFFRAY AND MURDER." "*Portsmouth, (Ohio) Aug. 22*, 1829.

"A most shocking outrage was committed in Kentucky, about eight miles from this place, on 14th inst. A negro driver, by the name of Gordon, who had purchased in Maryland about sixty negroes, was taking them, assisted by an associate named Allen, and the wagoner who conveyed the baggage, to the Mississippi. The men were hand-cuffed and chained together, in the usual manner for driving those poor wretches, while the women and children were suffered to proceed without incumbrance. It appears that, by means of a file the negroes, unobserved, had succeeded in separating the iron which bound their hands, in such a way as to be able to throw them off at any moment. About 8 o'clock in the morning, while proceeding on the state road leading from Greenup to Vanceburg, two of them dropped their shackles and commenced a fight, when the wagoner (Petit) rushed in with his whip to compel them to desist. At this moment, every negro was found to be perfectly at liberty; and one of them seizing a club, gave Petit a violent blow on the head, and laid him dead at his feet; and Allen, who came to his assistance, met a similar fate, from the contents of a pistol fired by another of the gang. Gordon was then attacked, seized and held by one of the negroes, whilst another fired twice at him with a pistol, the ball of which each time grazed his head, but not proving effectual, he was beaten with clubs, and left for dead. They then commenced pillaging the wagon, and with an axe split open the trunk of Gordon, and rifled it of the money, about $2,400. Sixteen of the negroes then took to the woods; Gordon, in the mean time, not being materially injured, was enabled, by the assistance of one of the women, to mount his horse and flee; pursued, however, by one of the gang on another horse, with a drawn pistol; fortunately he escaped with his life barely, arriving at a plantation, as the negro came in sight; who then turned about and retreated.

"The neighbourhood was immediately rallied, and a hot pursuit given—which, we understand, has resulted in the capture of the whole gang and the recovery of the greatest part of the money. Seven of the negro men and one woman, it is said were engaged in the murders, and will be brought to trial at the next court in Greenupsburg."

Here my brethren, I want you to notice particularly in the above article, *the ignorant* and *deceitful actions* of this coloured woman. I beg you to view it candidly, as for ETERNITY! ! ! ! Here a *notorious wretch*, with two other confederates had SIXTY of them in a gang, driving them like *brutes*—the men all in chains and hand-cuffs, and by the help of God they got their chains and hand-cuffs thrown off, and caught two of the wretches and put them to death, and beat the other until they thought he was dead, and left him for dead; however, he deceived them, and rising from the ground, this *servile woman* helped him upon his horse, and he made his escape. Brethren, what do you think of this? Was it the natural *fine feelings* of this woman, to save such a wretch alive? I know that the blacks, take them half enlightened and ignorant, are more humane and merciful than the most enlightened and refined European that can be found in all the earth. Let no one say that I assert this because I am prejudiced on the side of my colour, and against the whites or Europeans. For what I write, I do it candidly, for my God and the good of both parties: Natural observations have taught me these things; there is a solemn awe in the hearts of the blacks, as it respects *murdering* men:[3] whereas the whites (though they are great cowards) where they have the advantage, or think that there are any prospects of getting it, they murder all before them, in order to subject men to wretchedness and degradation under them. This is the natural result of pride and avarice. But I declare, the actions of this black woman are really insupport-able. For my own part, I cannot think it was any thing but servile deceit, combined with the most gross ignorance: for we must remember that *humanity, kindness* and the *fear of the Lord*, does not consist in protecting *devils*. Here is a set of wretches, who had SIXTY of them in a gang, driving them around the country like *brutes*, to dig up gold and silver for them, (which they will get enough of yet.) Should the lives of such creatures be spared? Are God and Mammon in league? What has the Lord to do with a gang of desperate wretches, who go *smeaking about the country like robbers*—light upon his people wherever they can get a chance, binding them with chains and hand-cuffs, beat and murder them as they would *rattle-snakes?* Are they not the Lord's enemies? Ought they not to be destroyed? Any person who will save such wretches from destruction, is fighting against the Lord, and will receive his just recompense. The black men acted like *blockheads.* Why did they not make sure of the wretch? He would have made sure of them, if he could. It is just the way with black men—eight white men can frighten fifty of them; whereas, if you can only get courage into the blacks, I do declare it, that one good black man can put to death six white men; and I give it as a fact, let twelve black men get well armed for battle, and they will kill and put to flight fifty whites.—The reason is, the blacks, once you get them started, they glory in death. The whites have had us under them for more than three centuries, murdering, and treating us like brutes; and, as Mr. Jefferson wisely said, they have never *found us out*—they do not know, indeed, that there is an unconquerable disposition in the breasts of the blacks, which, when it is fully awakened and put in motion, will be subdued, only with the destruction of the animal existence. Get the blacks started, and if you do not have a gang of tigers and lions to deal with, I am a deceiver of the blacks and of the whites . . . . The actions of this deceitful and ignorant coloured woman, in saving the life of a desperate wretch, whose ava-ricious and cruel object was to drive her, and her companions in miseries, through the country like cattle, to make his fortune on their carcasses, are but too much like that of thousands of our brethren in these states: if any thing is whispered by one, which has any allusion to the meliora-tion of their dreadful condition, they run and tell tyrants, that they may be enabled to keep them the longer in wretchedness and miseries. Oh! coloured people of these United States, I ask you, in the name of that God who made us, have we, in consequence of oppression, nearly lost the spirit of man, and, in no very trifling degree, adopted that of brutes? Do you answer, no?—I ask you, then, what set of men can you point me to, in all the world, who are so abjectly employed by their oppressors, as we are by our *natural enemies?* How can, Oh! how can those enemies but say that we and our children are not of the HUMAN FAMILY, but were made by our Creator to be an inheritance to them and theirs for ever? How can the slaveholders but say that they can bribe the best coloured person in the country, to sell his brethren for a trifling sum of money, and take that atrocity to confirm them in their avaricious opinion, that we were made to be slaves to them and their children? How could Mr. Jefferson but say,[4]"I advance it therefore as a suspicion only, that the blacks, whether originally a distinct race, or made distinct by time and circumstances, are *inferior* to the whites in their endowments both of body and mind?"—"It," says he, "is not against experience to suppose, that different species of the same genius, or variet-ies of the same species, may possess different qualifications." [Here, my brethren, listen to him.]

"Will not a lover of natural history, then, one who views the gradations in all the races of *animals* with the eye of philosophy, excuse an effort to keep those in the department of MAN as *distinct* as nature has formed them?"—I hope you will try to find out the meaning of this verse—its widest sense and all its bearings: whether you do or not, remember the whites do. This very verse, brethren, having emanated from Mr. Jefferson, a much greater philosopher the world never afforded, has in truth injured us more, and has been as great a barrier to our emancipation as any thing that has ever been advanced against us. I hope you will not let it pass unnoticed. He goes on further, and says: "This *unfortunate* difference of colour, and *perhaps* of *faculty*, is a powerful obstacle to the emancipation of these people. Many of their advocates, while they wish to vindicate the liberty of human nature are anxious also to preserve its *dignity* and *beauty*. Some of these, embarrassed by the question, 'What further is to be done with them?' join themselves in opposition with those who are actuated by sordid avarice only." Now I ask you candidly, my suffering brethren in time, who are candidates for the eternal worlds, how could Mr. Jefferson but have given the world these remarks respecting us, when we are so submissive to them, and so much servile deceit prevail among ourselves—when we so *meanly* submit to their murderous lashes, to which neither the Indians nor any other people under Heaven would submit? No they would die to a man, before they would suffer such things from men who are no better than themselves, and *perhaps not so good*. Yes, how can our friends but be embarrassed, as Mr. Jefferson says, by the question, "What further is to be done with these people?" For while they are working for our emancipation, we are, by our treachery, wickedness and deceit, working against ourselves and our children—helping ours, and the enemies of God, to keep us and our dear little children in their infernal chains of slavery! ! ! Indeed, our friends cannot but relapse and join themselves "with those who are actuated by *sordid avarice* only! ! ! !" For my own part, I am glad Mr. Jefferson has advanced his positions for your sake; for you will either have to contradict or confirm him by your own actions, and not by what our friends have said or done for us; for those things are other men's labours, and do not satisfy the Americans, who are waiting for us to prove to them ourselves, that we are MEN, before they will be willing to admit the fact; for I pledge you my sacred word of honour, that Mr. Jefferson's remarks respecting us, have sunk deep into the hearts of millions of the whites, and never will be removed this side of eternity.— For how can they, when we are confirming him every day, by our *groveling submissions* and *treachery?* I aver, that when I look over these United States of America, and the world, and see the ignorant deceptions and consequent wretchedness of my brethren, I am brought oftimes solemnly to a stand, and in the midst of my reflections I exclaim to my God, "Lord didst thou make us to be slaves to our brethren, the whites?" But when I reflect that God is just, and that millions of my wretched brethren would meet death with glory—yea, more, would plunge into the very mouths of cannons and be torn into particles as minute as the atoms which compose the elements of the earth, in preference to a mean submission to the lash of tyrants, I am with streaming eyes, compelled to shrink back into nothingness before my Maker, and exclaim again, they will be done, O Lord God Almighty.

Men of colour, who are also of sense, for you particularly is my APPEAL designed. Our more ignorant brethren are not able to penetrate its value. I call upon you therefore to cast your eyes upon the wretchedness of your brethren, and to do your utmost to enlighten them—*go to work and enlighten your brethren!*—Let the Lord see you doing what you can to rescue them and yourselves from degradation. Do any of you say that you and your family are free and happy, and what have you to do with the wretched slaves and other people? So can I say, for I enjoy as much freedom as any of you, if I am not quite as well off as the best of you. Look into our freedom and happiness, and see of what kind they are composed! ! They are of the very lowest kind—they are the very *dreg!*—they are the most servile and abject kind, that ever a people was in possession of! If any of you wish to know how FREE you are, let one of you start and go through the southern and western States of this country, and unless you travel as a slave to a white man (a servant is a *slave* to the man whom he serves) or have your free papers, (which if you are not careful they will get from you) if they do not take you up and put you in jail, and if you cannot give good evidence of your freedom, sell you into eternal slavery, I am not a living man: or any man of colour, immaterial who he is, or where he came from, if he is not *the fourth from the negro race!!* (as we are called) the white Christians of America will serve him the same they will sink him into wretchedness and degradation for ever while he lives. And yet some of you have the hardihood to say that you are free and happy! May God have mercy on your freedom and happiness!! I met a coloured man in the street a short time since, with a string of boots on his shoulders; we fell into conversation, and in course of which, I said to him, what a miserable set of people we are! He asked, why?—Said I, we are so subjected under the whites, that we cannot obtain the comforts of life, but by cleaning their boots and shoes, old clothes, waiting on them, shaving them &c. Said he, (with the boots on his shoulders) "I am completely happy!!! I never want to live any better or happier than when I can get a plenty of boots and shoes to clean!!!" Oh! how can those who are actuated by avarice only, but think, that our Creator made us to be an inheritance to them for ever, when they see that our greatest glory is centered in such mean and low objects? Understand me, brethren, I do not mean to speak against the occupations by which we acquire enough and sometimes scarcely that, to render ourselves and families comfortable through life. I am subjected to the same inconvenience, as you all.—My objections are, to our *glorying* and being *happy* in such low employments; for if we are men, we ought to be thankful to the Lord for the past, and for the future, Be looking forward with thankful hearts to higher attainments than *wielding the razor* and *cleaning boots and shoes*. The man whose aspirations are not *above*, and even *below* these, is indeed, ignorant and wretched enough . . . .

There is a great work for you to do, as trifling as some of you may think of it. You have to prove to the Americans and the world, that we are MEN, and not *brutes*, as we have been represented, and by millions treated. Remember, to let the aim of your labours among your brethren, and particularly the youths, be the dissemination of education and religion.[5] It is lamentable, that many of our children go to school, from four until they are eight or ten, and sometimes fifteen years of age, and leave school knowing but little more about the grammar of their language than a horse does about handling a musket—and not a few of them are really so ignorant, that they are unable to answer a person correctly, general questions in geography, and to hear them read, would only be to disgust a man who has a taste for reading, which, to do well, as trifling as it may appear to some, (to the ignorant in particular) is a great part of learning. Some few of them, may make out to scribble tolerably well, over a half sheet of paper, which I believe has hitherto been a powerful obstacle in our way, to keep us from acquiring knowledge. An ignorant father, who knows no more than what nature has taught him, together with what little he acquires by the senses of hearing and seeing, finding his son able to write a neat hand, sets it down for granted that he has as good learning as any body; the young, ignorant gump, hearing his father or mother, who perhaps may be ten times more ignorant, in point of literature, than himself, extolling his learning, struts about, in the full assurance, that his attainments in literature are sufficient to take him through the world, when, in fact, he has scarcely any learning at all!!!!

I promiscuously fell in conversation once, with an elderly coloured man on the topics of education, and of the great prevalency of ignorance among us: Said he, "I know that our people are very ignorant but my son has a good education: I spent a great deal of money on his education: he can write as well as any white man, and I assure you that no one can fool him," &c. Said I, what else can your son do, besides writing a good hand? Can he post a set of books in a mercantile manner? Can he write a neat piece of composition in prose or in verse? To these interrogations he answered in the negative. Said I, did your son learn, while he was at school, the width and depth of English Grammar? To which he also replied in the negative, telling me his son did not learn those things. Your son, said I, then, has hardly any learning at all—he is almost as ignorant, and more so, than many of those who never went to school one day in all their lives. My friend got a little put out, and so walking off, said that his son could write as well as any white man. Most of the coloured people, when they speak of the education of one among us who can write a neat hand, and, who perhaps knows nothing but to scribble and puff pretty fair on a small scrap of paper, immaterial whether his words are grammatical, or spelt correctly, or not; if it only looks beautiful, they say he has as good an education as any white man—he can write as well as any white man, &c. The poor, ignorant creature, hearing, this, he is ashamed, forever after, to let any person see him humbling himself to another for knowledge but going about trying to deceive those who are more ignorant than himself, he at last falls an ignorant victim to death in wretchedness. I pray that the Lord may undeceive my ignorant brethren, and permit them to throw away pretensions, and seek after the substance of learning. I would crawl on my hands and knees through mud and mire, to the feet of a learned man, where I would sit and humbly supplicate him to instil into me, that which neither devils nor tyrants could remove, only with my life—for coloured people to acquire learning in this country, makes tyrants quake and tremble on their sandy foundation. Why, what is the matter? Why, they know that their infernal deeds of cruelty will be known to the world. Do you suppose one man of good sense and learning would submit himself, his father, mother, wife and children, to be slaves to a wretched man like himself, who, instead of compensating him for his labours, chains, handcuffs and beats him and family almost to death, leaving life enough in them, however, to work for, and call him master? No! no! he would cut his devilish throat from ear to ear, and well do slave-holders know it. The bare name of educating the coloured people, scares our cruel oppressors almost to death. But if they do not have enough to be frightened for yet, it will be, because they can always keep us ignorant, and because God approbates their cruelties, with which they have been for centuries murdering us. The whites shall have enough of the blacks, yet, as sure as God sits on his throne in Heaven.

Some of our brethren are so very full of learning, that you cannot mention any thing to them which they do not know better than yourself! !—nothing is strange to them! !—they knew every thing years ago!—if any thing should be mentioned in company where they are, immaterial how important it is respecting us or the world, if they had not divulged it; they make light of it, and affect to have known it long before it was mentioned and try to make all in the room, or wherever you may be, believe that your conversation is nothing! !—not worth hearing! All this is the result of ignorance and ill-breeding; for a man of good-breeding, sense and penetration, if he had heard a subject told twenty times over, and should happen to be in company where one should commence telling it again, he would wait with patience on its narrator, and see if he would tell it as it was told in his presence before—paying the most strict attention to what is said, to see if any more light will be thrown on the subject: for all men are not gifted alike in telling, or even hearing the most simple narration. These ignorant, vicious, and wretched men, contribute almost as much injury to our body as tyrants themselves, by doing so much for the promotion of ignorance amongst us; for they, making such pretensions to knowledge, such of our youth as are seeking after knowledge, and can get access to them, take them as criterions to go by, who will lead them into a channel, where, unless the Lord blesses them with the privilege of seeing their folly, they will be irretrievably lost forever, while in time! ! !

I must close this article by relating the very heart-rending fact, that I have examined school-boys and young men of colour in different parts of the country, in the most simple parts of Murray's English Grammar, and not more than one in thirty was able to give a correct answer to my interrogations. If any one contradicts me, let him step out of his door into the streets of Boston, New-York, Philadelphia, or Baltimore, (no use to mention any other, for the Christians are too charitable further south or west!)—I say, let him who disputes me, step out of his door into the streets of either of those four cities, and promiscuously collect one hundred school-boys, or young men of colour, *who have been to school,* and who are considered by the coloured people to have received an excellent education, because, perhaps, some of them can write a good hand, but who, notwithstanding their neat writing, may be almost as ignorant, in comparison, as a horse.—And, I say it, he will hardly find (in this enlightened day, and in the midst of this *charitable* people) five in one hundred, who, are able to correct the false grammar of their language.—The cause of this almost universal ignorance among us, I appeal to our schoolmasters to declare. Here is a fact, which I this very minute take from the mouth of a young coloured man, who has been to school in this state (Massachusetts) nearly nine years, and who knows grammar this day, *nearly* as well as he did the day he first entered the school-house, under a white master. This young man says: "My master would never allow me to study grammar." I asked him, why? "The school committee," said he, "forbid the coloured children learning grammar—they would not allow any but the white children to study grammar." It is a notorious fact, that the major part of the white Americans, have, ever since we have been among them, tried to keep us ignorant, and make us believe that God made us and our children to be slaves to them and theirs. *Oh! my God, have mercy on Christian Americans! ! !*

Notes

1. David Walker, "Preamble" and "Article II, Our Wretchedness in Consequence of Ignorance," in *Walker's Appeal in Four Articles* (Boston: D. Walker, 1829), pp. 22–39.
2. Slave rebellion in Haiti, 1789–1803, led by Toussaint L'Ouverture.
3. Which is the reason the whites take the advantage of us. [footnote in original]
4. See his *Notes on Virginia,* page 213. [footnote in original; all references to Jefferson in this article are to Query XIV in *Notes on Virginia*]
5. Never mind what the ignorant ones among us may say, many of whom when you speak to them for their good, and try to enlighten their minds, laugh at you, and perhaps tell you plump to your face, that they want no instruction from you or any other Niger, and all such aggravating language. Now if you are a man of understanding and sound sense, I conjure you in the name of the Lord, and of all that is good, to impute their actions to ignorance, and wink at their follies, and do your very best to get around them some way or other, for remember they are your brethren; and I declare to you that it is for your interests to teach and enlighten them. [footnote in original]

Frederick Douglass

The slave narrative reached its height in 1845 when Frederick Douglass published his *Narrative of the Life of Frederick Douglass, An American Slave, Written by Himself.* Douglass's narrative spoke to his personal and political mission to uproot the evil institution of slavery for African American people. A prominent abolitionist, author, editor, and orator, Douglass was born a slave, and after his escape from the institution of slavery during his later years, he went on to become a world-renowned anti-slavery activist. In Chapter 10 of his narrative, Douglass describes the cruel conditions and the mental and physical abuse he endured from his slave master and the hired field hand, Mr. Covey. Such abuse, as Douglass writes about, solidified his decision to escape slavery and seek freedom. His story is told in such a way that captures the readers' attention through its heartfelt truths and humanizing dialogue. As Douglass himself endured and overcame the trials he faced, he provides his audience with hope that they, too, can overcome their own struggles and the struggles imposed upon them by others. Douglass's narrative continues to provide personal revelation for Black America. It remains one of the greatest literary contributions to American culture.

Chapter X

Frederick Douglass[1]

I LEFT MASTER THOMAS's house, and went to live with Mr. Covey, on the 1st of January, 1833.[2] I was now, for the first time in my life, a field hand. In my new employment, I found myself even more awkward than a country boy appeared to be in a large city. I had been at my new home but one week before Mr. Covey gave me a very severe whipping, cutting my back, causing the blood to run, and raising ridges on my flesh as large as my little finger. The details of this affair are as follows: Mr. Covey sent me, very early in the morning of one of our coldest days in the month of January, to the woods, to get a load of wood. He gave me a team of unbroken oxen. He told me which was the in-hand ox, and which the off-hand one.[3] He then tied the end of a large rope around the horns of the in-hand ox, and gave me the other end of it, and told me, if the oxen started to run, that I must hold on upon the rope. I had never driven oxen before, and of course I was very awkward. I, however, succeeded in getting to the edge of the woods with little difficulty; but I had got a very few rods into the woods, when the oxen took fright, and started full tilt, carrying the cart against trees, and over stumps, in the most frightful manner. I expected every moment that my brains would be dashed out against the trees. After running thus for a considerable distance, they finally upset the cart, dashing it with great force against a tree, and threw themselves into a dense thicket. How I escaped death, I do not know. There I was, entirely alone, in a thick wood, in a place new to me. My cart was upset and shattered, my oxen were entangled among the young trees, and there was none to help me. After a long spell of effort, I succeeded in getting my cart righted, my oxen disentangled, and again yoked to the cart. I now proceeded with my team to the place where I had, the day before, been chopping wood, and loaded my cart pretty heavily, thinking in this way to tame my oxen. I then proceeded on my way home. I had now consumed one half of the day. I got out of the woods safely, and now felt out of danger. I stopped my oxen to open the woods gate; and just as I did so, before I could get hold of my ox-rope, the oxen again started, rushed through the gate, catching it between the wheel and the body of the cart, tearing it to pieces, and coming within a few inches of crushing me against the gate-post. Thus twice, in one short day, I escaped death by the merest chance. On my return, I told Mr. Covey what had happened, and how it happened. He ordered me to return to the woods again immediately. I did so, and he followed on after me. Just as I got into the woods, he came up and told me to stop my cart, and that he would teach me how to trifle away my time, and break gates. He then went to a large gum-tree, and with his axe cut three large switches, and, after trimming them up neatly with his pocket-knife, he ordered me to take off my clothes. I made him no answer, but stood with my clothes on. He repeated his order. I still made him no answer, nor did I move to strip myself. Upon this he rushed at me with the fierceness of a tiger, tore off my clothes, and lashed me till he had worn out his switches, cutting me so savagely as to leave the marks visible for a long time after. This whipping was the first of a number just like it, and for similar offences.

I lived with Mr. Covey one year. During the first six months, of that year, scarce a week passed without his whipping me. I was seldom free from a sore back. My awkwardness was almost always his excuse for whipping me. We were worked fully up to the point of endurance. Long before day we were up, our horses fed, and by the first approach of day we were off to the field with our hoes and ploughing teams. Mr. Covey gave us enough to eat, but scarce time to eat it. We were often less than five minutes taking our meals. We were often in the field from the first approach of day till its last lingering ray had left us; and at saving-fodder time,[4] midnight often caught us in the field binding blades.

Covey would be out with us. The way he used to stand it, was this. He would spend the most of his afternoons in bed. He would then come out fresh in the evening, ready to urge us on with his words, example, and frequently with the whip. Mr. Covey was one of the few slaveholders who could and did work with his hands. He was a hardworking man. He knew by himself just what a man or a boy could do. There was no deceiving him. His work went on in his absence almost as well as in his presence; and he had the faculty of making us feel that he was ever present with us. This he did by surprising us. He seldom approached the spot where we were at work openly, if he could do it secretly. He always aimed at taking us by surprise. Such was his cunning, that we used to call him, among ourselves, "the snake."[5] When we were at work in the cornfield, he would sometimes crawl on his hands and knees to avoid detection, and all at once he would rise nearly in our midst, and scream out, "Ha, ha! Come, come! Dash on, dash on!" This being his mode of attack, it was never safe to stop a single minute. His comings were like a thief in the night. He appeared to us as being ever at hand. He was under every tree, behind every stump, in every bush, and at every window, on the plantation. He would sometimes mount his horse, as if bound to St. Michael's, a distance of seven miles, and in half an hour afterwards you would see him coiled up in the corner of the wood-fence, watching every motion of the slaves. He would, for this purpose, leave his horse tied up in the woods. Again, he would sometimes walk up to us, and give us orders as though he was upon the point of starting on a long journey, turn his back upon us, and make as though he was going to the house to get ready; and, before he would get half way thither, he would turn short and crawl into a fence-corner, or behind some tree, and there watch us till the going down of the sun.

Mr. Covey's *forte* consisted in his power to deceive. His life was devoted to planning and perpetrating the grossest deceptions. Every thing he possessed in the shape of learning or religion, he made conform to his disposition to deceive. He seemed to think himself equal to deceiving the Almighty. He would make a short prayer in the morning, and a long prayer at night; and, strange as it may seem, few men would at times appear more devotional than he. The exercises of his family devotions were always commenced with singing; and, as he was a very poor singer himself, the duty of raising the hymn generally came upon me. He would read his hymn, and nod at me to commence. I would at times do so; at others, I would not.[6] My non-compliance would almost always produce much confusion. To show himself independent of me, he would start and stagger through with his hymn in the most discordant manner. In this state of mind, he prayed with more than ordinary spirit. Poor man! such was his disposition, and success at deceiving, I do verily believe that he sometimes deceived himself into the solemn belief, that he was a sincere worshipper of the most high God; and this, too, at a time when he may be said to have been guilty of compelling his woman slave to commit the sin of adultery. The facts in the case are these: Mr. Covey was a poor man; he was just commencing in life; he was only able to buy one slave; and, shocking as is the fact, he bought her, as he said, for a *breeder*. This woman was named Caroline. Mr. Covey bought her from Mr. Thomas Lowe, about six miles from St. Michael's. She was a large, able-bodied woman, about twenty years old. She had already given birth to one child, which proved her to be just what he wanted. After buying her, he hired a married man of Mr. Samuel Harrison, to live with him one year; and him he used to fasten up with her every night! The result was, that, at the end of the year, the miserable woman gave birth to twins. At this result Mr. Covey seemed to be highly pleased, both with the man and the wretched woman. Such was his joy, and that of his wife, that nothing they could do for Caroline during her confinement was too good, or too hard, to be done. The children were regarded as being quite an addition to his wealth.

If at any one time of my life more than another, I was made to drink the bitterest dregs of slavery, that time was during the first six months of my stay with Mr. Covey. We were worked in all weathers. It was never too hot or too cold; it could never rain, blow, hail, or snow, too hard for us to work in the field. Work, work, work, was scarcely more the order of the day than of the night. The longest days were too short for him, and the shortest nights too long for him. I was somewhat unmanageable when I first went there, but a few months of this discipline tamed me. Mr. Covey succeeded in breaking me. I was broken in body, soul, and spirit. My natural elasticity was crushed, my intellect languished, the disposition to read departed, the cheerful spark that lingered about my eye died; the dark night of slavery closed in upon me; and behold a man transformed into a brute!

Sunday was my only leisure time. I spent this in a sort of beastlike stupor, between sleep and wake, under some large tree. At times I would rise up, a flash of energetic freedom would dart through, my soul, accompanied with a faint beam of hope, that flickered for a moment, and then vanished. I sank down again, mourning over my wretched condition. I was sometimes prompted to take my life, and that of Covey, but was prevented by a combination of hope and fear. My sufferings on this plantation seem now like a dream rather than a stern reality.

Our house stood within a few rods of the Chesapeake Bay, whose broad bosom was ever white with sails from every quarter of the habitable globe. Those beautiful vessels, robed in purest white, so delightful to the eye of freemen, were to me so many shrouded ghosts, to terrify and torment me with thoughts of my wretched condition. I have often, in the deep stillness of a summer's Sabbath, stood all alone upon the lofty banks of that noble bay, and traced, with saddened heart and tearful eye, the countless number of sails moving off to the mighty ocean. The sight of these always affected me powerfully. My thoughts would compel utterance; and there, with no audience but the Almighty, I would pour out my soul's complaint, in my rude way, with an apostrophe to the moving multitude of ships:

"You are loosed from your moorings,[7] and are free; I am fast in my chains, and am a slave! You move merrily before the gentle gale, and I sadly before the bloody whip! You are freedom's swift-winged angels, that fly round the world; I am confined in bands of iron! O that I were free! O, that I were on one of your gallant decks, and under your protecting wing! Alas! betwixt me and you, the turbid waters roll. Go on, go on. O that I could also go! Could I but swim! If I could fly! O, why was I born a man, of whom to make a brute! The glad ship is gone; she hides in the dim distance. I am left in the hottest hell of unending slavery. O God, save me! God, deliver me! Let me be free! Is there any God? Why am I a slave? I will run away. I will not stand it. Get caught, or get clear, I'll try it. I had as well die with ague[8] as the fever. I have only one life to lose. I had as well be killed running as die standing. Only think of it; one hundred miles straight north, and I am free! Try it? Yes!

God helping me, I will. It cannot be that I shall live and die a slave. I will take to the water. This very bay shall bear me into freedom. The steamboats steered in a north-east course from North Point. I will do the same; and when I get to the head of the bay, I will turn my canoe adrift, and walk straight through Delaware into Pennsylvania. When I get there, I shall not be required to have a pass; I can travel without being disturbed. Let but the first opportunity offer, and, come what will, I am off. Meanwhile, I will try to bear up under the yoke. I am not the only slave in the world. Why should I fret? I can bear as much as any of them. Besides, I am but a boy, and all boys are bound to some one. It may be that my misery in slavery will only increase my happiness when I get free. There is a better day coming."

Thus I used to think, and thus I used to speak to myself; goaded almost to madness at one moment, and at the next reconciling myself to my wretched lot.

I have already intimated that my condition was much worse, during the first six months of my stay at Mr. Covey's, than in the last six. The circumstances leading to the change in Mr. Covey's course toward me form an epoch in my humble history. You have seen how a man was made a slave; you shall see how a slave was made a man. On one of the hottest days of the month of August, 1833, Bill Smith, William Hughes, a slave named Eli, and myself, were engaged in fanning wheat.[9] Hughes was clearing the fanned wheat from before the fan, Eli was turning, Smith was feeding, and I was carrying wheat to the fan. The work was simple, requiring strength rather than intellect; yet, to one entirely unused to such work, it came very hard. About three o'clock of that day, I broke down; my strength failed me; I was seized with a violent aching of the head, attended with extreme dizziness; I trembled in every limb. Finding what was coming, I nerved myself up, feeling it would never do to stop work. I stood as long as I could stagger to the hopper with grain. When I could stand no longer, I fell, and felt as if held down by an immense weight. The fan of course stopped; every one had his own work to do; and no one could do the work of the other, and have his own go on at the same time.

Mr. Covey was at the house, about one hundred yards from the treading-yard where we were fanning. On hearing the fan stop, he left immediately, and came to the spot where we were. He hastily inquired what the matter was. Bill answered that I was sick, and there was no one to bring wheat to the fan. I had by this time crawled away under the side of the post and rail-fence by which the yard was enclosed, hoping to find relief by getting out of the sun. He then asked where I was. He was told by one of the hands. He came to the spot, and, after looking at me awhile, asked me what was the matter. I told him as well as I could, for I scarce had strength to speak. He then gave me a savage kick in the side, and told me to get up. I tried to do so, but fell back in the attempt. He gave me another kick, and again told me to rise. I again tried, and succeeded in gaining my feet; but, stooping to get the tub with which I was feeding the fan, I again staggered and fell. While down in this situation, Mr. Covey took up the hickory slat[10] with which Hughes had been striking off the half-bushel measure, and with it gave me a heavy blow upon the head, making a large wound, and the blood ran freely; and with this again told me to get up. I made no effort to comply, having now made up my mind to let him do his worst. In a short time after receiving this blow, my head grew better. Mr. Covey had now left me to my fate. At this moment I resolved, for the first time, to go to my master, enter a complaint, and ask his protection. In order to [do] this, I must that afternoon walk seven miles; and this, under the circumstances, was truly a severe undertaking. I was exceedingly feeble; made so as much by the kicks and blows which I received, as by the severe fit of sickness to which I had been subjected. I, however, watched my chance, while Covey was looking in an opposite direction, and started for St. Michael's. I succeeded in getting a considerable distance on my way to the woods, when Covey discovered me, and called after me to come back, threatening what he would do if I did not come. I disregarded both his calls and his threats, and made my way to the woods as fast as my feeble state would allow; and thinking I might be overhauled[11] by him if I kept the road, I walked through the woods, keeping far enough from the road to avoid detection, and near enough to prevent losing my way. I had not gone far before my little strength again failed me. I could go no farther. I fell down, and lay for a considerable time. The blood was yet oozing from the wound on my head. For a time I thought I should bleed to death; and think now that I should have done so, but that the blood so matted my hair as to stop the wound. After lying there about three quarters of an hour, I nerved myself up again, and started on my way, through bogs and briers, barefooted and bareheaded, tearing my feet sometimes at nearly every step; and after a journey of about seven miles, occupying some five hours to perform it, I arrived at master's store. I then presented an appearance enough to affect any but a heart of iron. From the crown of my head to my feet, I was covered with blood. My hair was all clotted with dust and blood; my shirt was stiff with blood. My legs and feet were torn in sundry places with briers and thorns, and were also covered with blood. I suppose I looked like a man who had escaped a den of wild beasts, and barely escaped them. In this state I appeared before my master, humbly entreating him to interpose his authority for my protection. I told him all the circumstances as well as I could, and it seemed, as I spoke, at times to affect him. He would then walk the floor, and seek to justify Covey by saying he expected I deserved it. He asked me what I wanted. I told him, to let me get a new home; that as sure as I lived with Mr. Covey again, I should live with but to die with him; that Covey would surely kill me; he was in a fair way for it. Master Thomas ridiculed the idea that there was any danger of Mr. Covey's killing me, and said that he knew Mr. Covey; that he was a good man, and that he could not think of taking me from him; that, should he do so, he would lose the whole year's wages; that I belonged to Mr. Covey for one year, and that I must go back to him, come what might; and that I must not trouble him with any more stories, or that he would himself *get hold of me*. After threatening me thus, he gave me a very large dose of salts, telling me that I might remain in St. Michael's that night, (it being quite late,) but that I must be off back to Mr. Covey's early in the morning; and that if I did not, he would *get hold of me*, which meant that he would whip me. I remained all night, and, according to his orders, I started off to Covey's in the morning, (Saturday morning,) wearied in body and broken in spirit. I got no supper that night, or breakfast that morning. I reached Covey's about nine o'clock; and just as I was getting over the fence that divided Mrs. Kemp's fields from ours, out ran Covey with his cowskin, to give me another whipping. Before he could reach me, I succeeded in getting to the cornfield; and as the corn was very high, it afforded me the means of hiding. He seemed very angry, and searched for me a long time. My behavior was altogether unaccountable. He finally gave up the chase, thinking, I suppose, that I must come home for something to eat; he would give himself no further trouble in looking for me. I spent that day mostly in the woods, having the alternative before me,—to go home and be whipped to death, or stay in the woods and be starved to death. That night, I fell in with Sandy Jenkins,[12] a slave with whom I was somewhat acquainted. Sandy had a free wife[13] who lived about four miles from Mr. Covey's; and it being Saturday, he was on his way to see her. I told him my circumstances, and he very kindly invited me to go home with him. I went home with him, and talked this whole matter over, and got his advice as to what course it was best for me to pursue. I found Sandy an old adviser.32 He told me, with great solemnity, I must go back to Covey; but that before I went, I must go with him into another part of the woods, where there was a certain *root*, which, if I would take some of it with me, carrying it *always on my right side*, would render it impossible for Mr. Covey, or any other white man, to whip me. He said he had carried it for years; and since he had done so, he had never received a blow, and never expected to while he carried it. I at first rejected the idea, that the simple carrying of a root in my pocket would have any such effect as he had said, and was not disposed to take it; but Sandy impressed the necessity with much earnestness, telling me it could do no harm, if it did no good. To please him, I at length took the root, and, according to his direction, carried it upon my right side. This was Sunday morning. I immediately started for home; and upon entering the yard gate, out came Mr. Covey on his way to meeting. He spoke to me very kindly, bade me drive the pigs from a lot near by, and passed on towards the church. Now, this singular conduct of Mr. Covey really made me begin to think that there was something in the *root* which Sandy had given me; and had it been on any other day than Sunday, I could have attributed the conduct to no other cause than the influence of that root; and as it was, I was half inclined to think the *root* to be something more than I at first had taken it to be. All went well till Monday morning. On this morning, the virtue of the *root* was fully tested. Long before daylight, I was called to go and rub, curry, and feed, the horses. I obeyed, and was glad to obey. But whilst thus engaged, whilst in the act of throwing down some blades from the loft, Mr. Covey entered the stable with a long rope; and just as I was half out of the loft, he caught hold of my legs, and was about tying me. As soon as I found what he was up to, I gave a sudden spring, and as I did so, he holding to my legs, I was brought sprawling on the stable floor. Mr. Covey seemed now to think he had me, and could do what he pleased; but at this moment—from whence came the spirit I don't know—I resolved to fight; and, suiting my action to the resolution, I seized Covey hard by the throat; and as I did so, I rose. He held on to me, and I to him. My resistance was so entirely unexpected, that Covey seemed taken all aback. He trembled like a leaf. This gave me assurance, and I held him uneasy, causing the blood to run where I touched him with the ends of my fingers. Mr. Covey soon called out to Hughes for help. Hughes came, and, while Covey held me, attempted to tie my right hand. While he was in the act of doing so, I watched my chance, and gave him a heavy kick close under the ribs. This kick fairly sickened Hughes, so that he left me in the hands of Mr. Covey. This kick had the effect of not only weakening Hughes, but Covey also. When he saw Hughes bending over with pain, his courage quailed. He asked me if I meant to persist in my resistance. I told him I did, come what might; that he had used me like a brute for six months, and that I was determined to be used so no longer. With that, he strove to drag me to a stick that was lying just out of the stable door. He meant to knock me down. But just as he was leaning over to get the stick, I seized him with both hands by his collar, and brought him by a sudden snatch to the ground. By this time, Bill came. Covey called upon him for assistance. Bill wanted to know what he could do. Covey said, "Take hold of him, take hold of him!" Bill said his master hired him out to work, and not to help to whip me; so he left Covey and myself to fight our own battle out. We were at it for nearly two hours. Covey at length let me go, puffing and blowing at a great rate, saying that if I had not resisted, he would not have whipped me at all. I considered him as getting entirely the worst end of the bargain; for he had drawn no blood from me, but I had from him. The whole six months afterwards, that I spent with Mr. Covey, he never laid the weight of his finger upon me in anger. He would occasionally say, he didn't want to get hold of me again. "No," thought I, "you need not; for you will come off worse than you did before."

This battle with Mr. Covey was the turning-point in my career as a slave. It rekindled the few expiring embers of freedom, and revived within me a sense of my own manhood. It recalled the departed self-confidence, and inspired me again with a determination to be free. The gratification afforded by the triumph was a full compensation for whatever else might follow, even death itself. He only can understand the deep satisfaction which I experienced, who has himself repelled by force the bloody arm of slavery. I felt as I never felt before. It was a glorious resurrection, from the tomb of slavery, to the heaven of freedom. My long-crushed spirit rose, cowardice departed, bold defiance took its place; and I now resolved that, however long I might remain a slave in form, the day had passed forever when I could be a slave in fact. I did not hesitate to let it be known of me, that the white man who expected to succeed in whipping, must also succeed in killing me.

From this time I was never again what might be called fairly whipped,[14] though I remained a slave four years afterwards. I had several fights, but was never whipped.

It was for a long time a matter of surprise to me why Mr. Covey did not immediately have me taken by the constable to the whipping-post, and there regularly whipped for the crime of raising my hand against a white man in defence of myself. And the only explanation I can now think of does not entirely satisfy me; but such as it is, I will give it. Mr. Covey enjoyed the most unbounded reputation for being a first-rate overseer and negro-breaker. It was of considerable importance to him. That reputation was at stake; and had he sent me—a boy about sixteen years old—to the public whipping-post, his reputation would have been lost; so, to save his reputation, he suffered me to go unpunished.

My term of actual service to Mr. Edward Covey ended on Christmas day, 1833. The days between Christmas and New Year's day are allowed as holidays; and, accordingly, we were not required to perform any labor, more than to feed and take care of the stock. This time we regarded as our own, by the grace of our masters; and we therefore used or abused it nearly as we pleased. Those of us who had families at a distance, were generally allowed to spend the whole six days in their society. This time, however, was spent in various ways. The staid, sober, thinking, and industrious ones of our number would employ themselves in making cornbrooms,[15] mats, horse-collars, and baskets; and another class of us would spend the time in hunting opossums, hares, and coons. But by far the larger part engaged in such sports and merriments as playing ball, wrestling, running footraces, fiddling, dancing, and drinking whisky; and this latter mode of spending the time was by far the most agreeable to the feelings of our masters. A slave who would work during the holidays was considered by our masters as scarcely deserving them. He was regarded as one who rejected the favor of his master. It was deemed a disgrace not to get drunk at Christmas; and he was regarded as lazy indeed, who had not provided himself with the necessary means, during the year, to get whisky enough to last him through Christmas.

From what I know of the effect of these holidays upon the slave, I believe them to be among the most effective means in the hands of the slaveholder in keeping down the spirit of insurrection. Were the slaveholders at once to abandon this practice, I have not the slightest doubt it would lead to an immediate insurrection among the slaves. These holidays serve as conductors, or safety-valves, to carry off the rebellious spirit of enslaved humanity. But for these, the slave would be forced up to the wildest desperation; and woe betide the slave-holder, the day he ventures to remove or hinder the operation of those conductors! I warn him that, in such an event, a spirit will go forth in their midst, more to be dreaded than the most appalling earthquake.

The holidays are part and parcel of the gross fraud, wrong, and inhumanity of slavery. They are professedly a custom established by the benevolence of the slaveholders; but I undertake to say, it is the result of selfishness, and one of the grossest frauds committed upon the downtrodden slave. They do not give the slaves this time because they would not like to have their work during its continuance, but because they know it would be unsafe to deprive them of it. This will be seen by the fact, that the slaveholders like to have their slaves spend those days just in such a manner as to make them as glad of their ending as of their beginning. Their object seems to be, to disgust their slaves with freedom, by plunging them into the lowest depths of dissipation. For instance, the slaveholders not only like to see the slave drink of his own accord, but will adopt various plans to make him drunk. One plan is, to make bets on their slaves, as to who can drink the most whisky without getting drunk; and in this way they succeed in getting whole multitudes to drink to excess. Thus, when the slave asks for virtuous freedom, the cunning slaveholder, knowing his ignorance, cheats him with a dose of vicious dissipation, artfully labelled with the name of liberty. The most of us used to drink it down, and the result was just what might be supposed: Many of us were led to think that there was little to choose between liberty and slavery. We felt, and very properly too, that we had almost as well be slaves to man as to rum. So, when the holidays ended, we staggered up from the filth of our wallowing, took a long breath, and marched to the field,—feeling, upon the whole, rather glad to go, from what our master had deceived us into a belief was freedom, back to the arms of slavery.

I have said that this mode of treatment is a part of the whole system of fraud and inhumanity of slavery. It is so. The mode here adopted to disgust the slave with freedom, by allowing him to see only the abuse of it, is carried out in other things. For instance, a slave loves molasses; he steals some. His master, in many cases, goes off to town, and buys a large quantity; he returns, takes his whip, and commands the slave to eat the molasses, until the poor fellow is made sick at the very mention of it. The same mode is sometimes adopted to make the slaves refrain from asking for more food than their regular allowance. A slave runs through his allowance, and applies for more. His master is enraged at him; but, not willing to send him off without food, gives him more than is necessary, and compels him to eat it within a given time. Then, if he complains that he cannot eat it, he is said to be satisfied neither full nor fasting, and is whipped for being hard to please! I have an abundance of such illustrations of the same principle, drawn from my own observation, but think the cases I have cited sufficient. The practice is a very common one.

On the first of January, 1834, I left Mr. Covey, and went to live with Mr. William Freeland, who lived about three miles from St. Michael's. I soon found Mr. Freeland a very different man from Mr. Covey. Though not rich, he was what would be called an educated southern gentleman. Mr. Covey, as I have shown, was a well-trained negro-breaker and slave-driver. The former (slaveholder though he was) seemed to possess some regard for honor, some reverence for justice, and some respect for humanity. The latter seemed totally insensible to all such sentiments. Mr. Freeland had many of the faults peculiar to slaveholders, such as being very passionate and fretful; but I must do him the justice to say, that he was exceedingly free from those degrading vices to which Mr. Covey was constantly addicted. The one was open and frank, and we always knew where to find him. The other was a most artful deceiver, and could be understood only by such as were skillful enough to detect his cunningly-devised frauds. Another advantage I gained in my new master was, he made no pretensions to, or profession of, religion; and this, in my opinion, was truly a great advantage. I assert most unhesitatingly, that the religion of the south is a mere covering for the most horrid crimes,—a justifier of the most appalling barbarity,—a sanctifier of the most hateful frauds,—and a dark shelter under which the darkest, foulest, grossest, and most infernal deeds of slaveholders find the strongest protection. Were I to be again reduced to the chains of slavery, next to that enslavement, I should regard being the slave of a religious master the greatest calamity that could befall me. For of all slaveholders with whom I have ever met, religious slaveholders are the worst. I have ever found them the meanest and basest, the most cruel and cowardly, of all others. It was my unhappy lot not only to belong to a religious slaveholder, but to live in a community of such religionists. Very near Mr. Freeland lived the Rev. Daniel Weeden, and in the same neighborhood lived the Rev. Rigby Hopkins. These were members and ministers in the Reformed Methodist Church. Mr. Weeden owned, among others, a woman slave, whose name I have forgotten. This woman's back, for weeks, was kept literally raw, made so by the lash of this merciless, *religious* wretch. He used to hire hands. His maxim was, Behave well or behave ill, it is the duty of a master occasionally to whip a slave, to remind him of his master's authority. Such was his theory, and such his practice.

Mr. Hopkins was even worse than Mr. Weeden. His chief boast was his ability to manage slaves. The peculiar feature of his government was that of whipping slaves in advance of deserving it. He always managed to have one or more of his slaves to whip every Monday morning. He did this to alarm their fears, and strike terror into those who escaped. His plan was to whip for the smallest offences, to prevent the commission of large ones. Mr. Hopkins could always find some excuse for whipping a slave. It would astonish one, unaccustomed to a slaveholding life, to see with what wonderful ease a slaveholder can find things, of which to make occasion to whip a slave. A mere look, word, or motion,—a mistake, accident, or want of power,—are all matters for which a slave may be whipped at any time. Does a slave look dissatisfied? It is said, he has the devil in him, and it must be whipped out. Does he speak loudly when spoken to by his master? Then he is getting high-minded, and should be taken down a button-hole lower. Does he forget to pull off his hat at the approach of a white person? Then he is wanting in reverence, and should be whipped for it. Does he ever venture to vindicate his conduct, when censured for it? Then he is guilty of impudence,—one of the greatest crimes of which a slave can be guilty. Does he ever venture to suggest a different mode of doing things from that pointed out by his master? He is indeed presumptuous, and getting above himself; and nothing less than a flogging will do for him. Does he, while ploughing, break a plough,—or, while hoeing, break a hoe? It is owing to his carelessness, and for it a slave must always be whipped. Mr. Hopkins could always find something of this sort to justify the use of the lash, and he seldom failed to embrace such opportunities. There was not a man in the whole county, with whom the slaves who had the getting their own home, would not prefer to live, rather than with this Rev. Mr. Hopkins. And yet there was not a man any where round, who made higher professions of religion, or was more active in revivals,—more attentive to the class, love-feast, prayer and preaching meetings, or more devotional in his family,—that prayed earlier, later, louder, and longer,—than this same reverend slave-driver, Rigby Hopkins.

But to return to Mr. Freeland, and to my experience while in his employment. He, like Mr. Covey, gave us enough to eat; but, unlike Mr. Covey, he also gave us sufficient time to take our meals. He worked us hard, but always between sunrise and sunset. He required a good deal of work to be done, but gave us good tools with which to work. His farm was large, but he employed hands enough to work it, and with ease, compared with many of his neighbors. My treatment, while in his employment, was heavenly, compared with what I experienced at the hands of Mr. Edward Covey.

Mr. Freeland was himself the owner of but two slaves. Their names were Henry Harris and John Harris. The rest of his hands he hired. These consisted of myself, Sandy Jenkins,[16] and Handy Caldwell. Henry and John were quite intelligent, and in a very little while after I went there, I succeeded in creating in them a strong desire to learn how to read. This desire soon sprang up in the others also. They very soon mustered up some old spelling-books, and nothing would do but that I must keep a Sabbath school. I agreed to do so, and accordingly devoted my Sundays to teaching these my loved fellowslaves how to read. Neither of them knew his letters when I went there. Some of the slaves of the neighboring farms found what was going on, and also availed themselves of this little opportunity to learn to read. It was understood, among all who came, that there must be as little display about it as possible. It was necessary to keep our religious masters at St. Michael's unacquainted with the fact, that, instead of spending the Sabbath in wrestling, boxing, and drinking whisky, we were trying to learn how to read the will of God; for they had much rather see us engaged in those degrading sports, than to see us behaving like intellectual, moral, and accountable beings. My blood boils as I think of the bloody manner in which Messrs. Wright Fairbanks and Garrison West, both class-leaders, in connection with many others, rushed in upon us with sticks and stones, and broke up our virtuous little Sabbath school, at St. Michael's—all calling themselves Christians! humble followers of the Lord Jesus Christ! But I am again digressing.

I held my Sabbath school at the house of a free colored man, whose name I deem it imprudent to mention; for should it be known, it might embarrass him greatly, though the crime of holding the school was committed ten years ago. I had at one time over forty scholars, and those of the right sort, ardently desiring to learn. They were of all ages, though mostly men and women. I look back to those Sundays with an amount of pleasure not to be expressed. They were great days to my soul. The work of instructing my dear fellow-slaves was the sweetest engagement with which I was ever blessed. We loved each other, and to leave them at the close of the Sabbath was a severe cross indeed. When I think that these precious souls are today shut up in the prison-house of slavery, my feelings overcome me, and I am almost ready to ask, "Does a righteous God govern the universe? and for what does he hold the thunders in his right hand, if not to smite the oppressor, and deliver the spoiled out of the hand of the spoiler?" These dear souls came not to Sabbath school because it was popular to do so, nor did I teach them because it was reputable to be thus engaged. Every moment they spent in that school, they were liable to be taken up, and given thirty-nine lashes. They came because they wished to learn. Their minds had been starved by their cruel masters. They had been shut up in mental darkness. I taught them, because it was the delight of my soul to be doing something that looked like bettering the condition of my race. I kept up my school nearly the whole year I lived with Mr. Freeland; and, beside my Sabbath school, I devoted three evenings in the week, during the winter, to teaching the slaves at home. And I have the happiness to know, that several of those who came to Sabbath school learned how to read; and that one, at least, is now free through my agency.

The year passed off smoothly. It seemed only about half as long as the year which preceded it. I went through it without receiving a single blow. I will give Mr. Freeland the credit of being the best master I ever had, *till I became my own master.* For the ease with which I passed the year, I was, however, somewhat indebted to the society of my fellow-slaves. They were noble souls; they not only possessed loving hearts, but brave ones. We were linked and interlinked with each other. I loved them with a love stronger than any thing I have experienced since. It is sometimes said that we slaves do not love and confide in each other. In answer to this assertion, I can say, I never loved any or confided in any people more than my fellow-slaves, and especially those with whom I lived at Mr. Freeland's. I believe we would have died for each other. We never undertook to do any thing, of any importance, without a mutual consultation. We never moved separately. We were one; and as much so by our tempers and dispositions, as by the mutual hardships to which we were necessarily subjected by our condition as slaves.

At the close of the year 1834, Mr. Freeland again hired me of my master, for the year 1835. But, by this time, I began to want to live *upon free land* as well as *with Freeland;* and I was no longer content, therefore, to live with him or any other slaveholder. I began, with the commencement of the year, to prepare myself for a final struggle, which should decide my fate one way or the other. My tendency was upward. I was fast approaching manhood, and year after year had passed, and I was still a slave. These thoughts roused me—I must do something. I therefore resolved that 1835 should not pass without witnessing an attempt, on my part, to secure my liberty. But I was not willing to cherish this determination alone. My fellow-slaves were dear to me. I was anxious to have them participate with me in this, my life-giving determination. I therefore, though with great prudence, commenced early to ascertain their views and feelings in regard to their condition, and to imbue their minds with thoughts of freedom. I bent myself to devising ways and means for our escape, and meanwhile strove, on all fitting occasions, to impress them with the gross fraud and inhumanity of slavery. I went first to Henry, next to John, then to the others. I found, in them all, warm hearts and noble spirits. They were ready to hear, and ready to act when a feasible plan should be proposed. This was what I wanted. I talked to them of our want of manhood, if we submitted to our enslavement without at least one noble effort to be free. We met often, and consulted frequently, and told our hopes and fears, recounted the difficulties, real and imagined, which we should be called on to meet. At times we were almost disposed to give up, and try to content ourselves with our wretched lot; at others, we were firm and unbending in our determination to go. Whenever we suggested any plan, there was shrinking—the odds were fearful. Our path was beset with the greatest obstacles; and if we succeeded in gaining the end of it, our right to be free was yet questionable—we were yet liable to be returned to bondage. We could see no spot, this side of the ocean, where we could be free. We knew nothing about Canada. Our knowledge of the north did not extend farther than New York; and to go there, and be forever harassed with the frightful liability of being returned to slavery—with the certainty of being treated tenfold worse than before—the thought was truly a horrible one, and one which it was not easy to overcome. The case sometimes stood thus: At every gate through which we were to pass, we saw a watchman—at every ferry a guard—on every bridge a sentinel—and in every wood a patrol. We were hemmed in upon every side. Here were the difficulties, real or imagined—the good to be sought, and the evil to be shunned. On the one hand, there stood slavery, a stern reality, glaring frightfully upon us,—its robes already crimsoned with the blood of millions, and even now feasting itself greedily upon our own flesh. On the other hand, away back in the dim distance, under the flickering light of the north star, behind some craggy hill or snowcovered mountain, stood a doubtful freedom—half frozen—beckoning us to come and share its hospitality. This in itself was sometimes enough to stagger us; but when we permitted ourselves to survey the road, we were frequently appalled. Upon either side we saw grim death, assuming the most horrid shapes. Now it was starvation, causing us to eat our own flesh;—now we were contending with the waves, and were drowned;—now we were overtaken, and torn to pieces by the fangs of the terrible bloodhound. We were stung by scorpions, chased by wild beasts, bitten by snakes, and finally, after having nearly reached the desired spot,—after swimming rivers, encountering wild beasts, sleeping in the woods, suffering hunger and nakedness,—we were overtaken by our pursuers, and, in our resistance, we were shot dead upon the spot! I say, this picture sometimes appalled us, and made us

> rather bear those ills we had,
> Than fly to others, that we knew not of.[17]

In coming to a fixed determination to run away, we did more than Patrick Henry, when he resolved upon liberty or death. With us it was a doubtful liberty at most, and almost certain death if we failed. For my part, I should prefer death to hopeless bondage.

Sandy, one of our number, gave up the notion, but still encouraged us. Our company then consisted of Henry Harris, John Harris, Henry Bailey, Charles Roberts, and myself. Henry Bailey was my uncle, and belonged to my master. Charles married my aunt: he belonged to my master's father-in-law, Mr. William Hamilton.

The plan we finally concluded upon was, to get a large canoe belonging to Mr. Hamilton, and upon the Saturday night previous to Easter holidays, paddle directly up the Chesapeake Bay. On our arrival at the head of the bay, a distance of seventy or eighty miles from where we lived, it was our purpose to turn our canoe adrift, and follow the guidance of the north star till we got beyond the limits of Maryland. Our reason for taking the water route was, that we were less liable to be suspected as runaways; we hoped to be regarded as fishermen; whereas, if we should take the land route, we should be subjected to interruptions of almost every kind. Any one having a white face, and being so disposed, could stop us, and subject us to examination.

The week before our intended start, I wrote several protections, one for each of us. As well as I can remember, they were in the following words, to wit:—

> This is to certify that I, the undersigned, have given the bearer, my servant, full liberty to go to Baltimore, and spend the Easter holidays. Written with mine own hand, &c., 1835.
> William Hamilton, Near St. Michael's, in Talbot county, Maryland.

We were not going to Baltimore; but, in going up the bay, we went toward Baltimore, and these protections were only intended to protect us while on the bay.

As the time drew near for our departure, our anxiety became more and more intense. It was truly a matter of life and death with us. The strength of our determination was about to be fully tested. At this time, I was very active in explaining every difficulty, removing every doubt, dispelling every fear, and inspiring all with the firmness indispensable to success in our undertaking; assuring them that half was gained the instant we made the move; we had talked long enough; we were now ready to move; if not now, we never should be; and if we did not intend to move now, we had as well fold our arms, sit down, and acknowledge ourselves fit only to be slaves. This, none of us were prepared to acknowledge. Every man stood firm; and at our last meeting, we pledged ourselves afresh, in the most solemn manner, that, at the time appointed, we would certainly start in pursuit of freedom. This was in the middle of the week, at the end of which we were to be off. We went, as usual, to our several fields of labor, but with bosoms highly agitated with thoughts of our truly hazardous undertaking. We tried to conceal our feelings as much as possible; and I think we succeeded very well.

After a painful waiting, the Saturday morning, whose night was to witness our departure, came. I hailed it with joy, bring what of sadness it might. Friday night was a sleepless one for me. I probably felt more anxious than the rest, because I was, by common consent, at the head of the whole affair. The responsibility of success or failure lay heavily upon me. The glory of the one, and the confusion of the other, were alike mine. The first two hours of that morning were such as I never experienced before, and hope never to again. Early in the morning, we went, as usual, to the field. We were spreading manure; and all at once, while thus engaged, I was overwhelmed with an indescribable feeling, in the fulness of which I turned to Sandy, who was near by, and said, "We are betrayed!" "Well," said he, "that thought has this moment struck me." We said no more. I was never more certain of any thing.

The horn was blown as usual, and we went up from the field to the house for breakfast. I went for the form, more than for want of any thing to eat that morning. Just as I got to the house, in looking out at the lane gate, I saw four white men, with two colored men. The white men were on horseback, and the colored ones were walking behind, as if tied. I watched them a few moments till they got up to our lane gate. Here they halted, and tied the colored men to the gate-post. I was not yet certain as to what the matter was. In a few moments, in rode Mr. Hamilton, with a speed betokening great excitement. He came to the door, and inquired if Master William was in. He was told he was at the barn. Mr. Hamilton, without dismounting, rode up to the barn with extraordinary speed. In a few moments, he and Mr. Freeland returned to the house. By this time, the three constables rode up, and in great haste dismounted, tied their horses, and met Master William and Mr. Hamilton returning from the barn; and after talking awhile, they all walked up to the kitchen door. There was no one in the kitchen but myself and John. Henry and Sandy were up at the barn. Mr. Freeland put his head in at the door, and called me by name, saying, there were some gentlemen at the door who wished to see me. I stepped to the door, and inquired what they wanted. They at once seized me, and, without giving me any satisfaction, tied me—lashing my hands closely together. I insisted upon knowing what the matter was. They at length said, that they had learned I had been in a "scrape," and that I was to be examined before my master; and if their information proved false, I should not be hurt.

In a few moments, they succeeded in tying John. They then turned to Henry, who had by this time returned, and commanded him to cross his hands. "I won't!" said Henry, in a firm tone, indicating his readiness to meet the consequences of his refusal. "Won't you?" said Tom Graham, the constable. "No, I won't!" said Henry, in a still stronger tone. With this, two of the constables pulled out their shining pistols, and swore, by their Creator, that they would make him cross his hands or kill him. Each cocked his pistol, and, with fingers on the trigger, walked up to Henry, saying, at the same time, if he did not cross his hands, they would blow his damned heart out. "Shoot me, shoot me!" said Henry; "you can't kill me but once. Shoot, shoot,—and be damned!

I won't be tied!" This he said in a tone of loud defiance; and at the same time, with a motion as quick as lightning, he with one single stroke dashed the pistols from the hand of each constable. As he did this, all hands fell upon him, and, after beating him some time, they finally overpowered him, and got him tied.

During the scuffle, I managed, I know not how, to get my pass out, and, without being discovered, put it into the fire. We were all now tied; and just as we were to leave for Easton jail, Betsy Freeland, mother of William Freeland, came to the door with her hands full of biscuits, and divided them between Henry and John. She then delivered herself of a speech, to the following effect:—addressing herself to me, she said, *"You devil! You yellow devil!* it was you that put it into the heads of Henry and John to run away. But for you, you longlegged mulatto devil! Henry nor John would never have thought of such a thing." I made no reply, and was immediately hurried off towards St. Michael's. Just a moment previous to the scuffle with Henry, Mr. Hamilton suggested the propriety of making a search for the protections which he had understood Frederick had written for himself and the rest. But, just at the moment he was about carrying his proposal into effect, his aid was needed in helping to tie Henry; and the excitement attending the scuffle caused them either to forget, or to deem it unsafe, under the circumstances, to search. So we were not yet convicted of the intention to run away.

When we got about half way to St. Michael's, while the constables having us in charge were looking ahead, Henry inquired of me what he should do with his pass. I told him to eat it with his biscuit, and own nothing; and we passed the word around, *"Own nothing;"* and *"Own nothing! said we all.* Our confidence in each other was unshaken. We were resolved to succeed or fail together, after the calamity had befallen us as much as before. We were now prepared for any thing. We were to be dragged that morning fifteen miles behind horses, and then to be placed in the Easton jail. When we reached St. Michael's, we underwent a sort of examination. We all denied that we ever intended to run away. We did this more to bring out the evidence against us, than from any hope of getting clear of being sold; for, as I have said, we were ready for that. The fact was, we cared but little where we went, so we went together. Our greatest concern was about separation. We dreaded that more than any thing this side of death. We found the evidence against us to be the testimony of one person; our master would not tell who it was; but we came to a unanimous decision among ourselves as to who their informant was. We were sent off to the jail at Easton. When we got there, we were delivered up to the sheriff, Mr. Joseph Graham, and by him placed in jail. Henry, John, and myself, were placed in one room together—Charles, and Henry Bailey, in another. Their object in separating us was to hinder concert.

We had been in jail scarcely twenty minutes, when a swarm of slave traders, and agents for slave traders, flocked into jail to look at us, and to ascertain if we were for sale. Such a set of beings I never saw before! I felt myself surrounded by so many fiends from perdition. A band of pirates never looked more like their father, the devil. They laughed and grinned over us, saying, "Ah, my boys! we have got you, haven't we?" And after taunting us in various ways, they one by one went into an examination of us, with intent to ascertain our value. They would impudently ask us if we would not like to have them for our masters. We would make them no answer, and leave them to find out as best they could. Then they would curse and swear at us, telling us that they could take the devil out of us in a very little while, if we were only in their hands.

While in jail, we found ourselves in much more comfortable quarters than we expected when we went there. We did not get much to eat, nor that which was very good; but we had a good clean room, from the windows of which we could see what was going on in the street, which was very much better than though we had been placed in one of the dark, damp cells. Upon the whole, we got along very well, so far as the jail and its keeper were concerned. Immediately after the holidays were over, contrary to all our expectations, Mr. Hamilton and Mr. Freeland came up to Easton, and took Charles, the two Henrys, and John, out of jail, and carried them home, leaving me alone. I regarded this separation as a final one. It caused me more pain than any thing else in the whole transaction. I was ready for any thing rather than separation. I supposed that they had consulted together, and had decided that, as I was the whole cause of the intention of the others to run away, it was hard to make the innocent suffer with the guilty; and that they had, therefore, concluded to take the others home, and sell me, as a warning to the others that remained. It is due to the noble Henry to say, he seemed almost as reluctant at leaving the prison as at leaving home to come to the prison. But we knew we should, in all probability, be separated, if we were sold; and since he was in their hands, he concluded to go peaceably home.

I was now left to my fate. I was all alone, and within the walls of a stone prison. But a few days before, and I was full of hope. I expected to have been safe in a land of freedom; but now I was covered with gloom, sunk down to the utmost despair. I thought the possibility of freedom was gone. I was kept in this way about one week, at the end of which, Captain Auld, my master, to my surprise and utter astonishment, came up, and took me out, with the intention of sending me, with a gentleman of his acquaintance, into Alabama. But, from some cause or other, he did not send me to Alabama, but concluded to send me back to Baltimore, to live again with his brother Hugh, and to learn a trade.

Thus, after an absence of three years and one month, I was once more permitted to return to my old home at Baltimore. My master sent me away, because there existed against me a very great prejudice in the community, and he feared I might be killed.

In a few weeks after I went to Baltimore, Master Hugh hired me to Mr. William Gardner, an extensive ship-builder, on Fell's Point. I was put there to learn how to calk. It, however, proved a very unfavorable place for the accomplishment of this object. Mr. Gardner was engaged that spring in building two large man-of-war brigs, professedly for the Mexican government. The vessels were to be launched in the July of that year, and in failure thereof, Mr. Gardner was to lose a considerable sum; so that when I entered, all was hurry. There was no time to learn any thing. Every man had to do that which he knew how to do. In entering the ship-yard, my orders from Mr. Gardner were, to do whatever the carpenters commanded me to do. This was placing me at the beck and call of about seventy-five men. I was to regard all these as masters. Their word was to be my law. My situation was a most trying one. At times I needed a dozen pair of hands. I was called a dozen ways in the space of a single minute. Three or four voices would strike my ear at the same moment. It was—"Fred., come help me to cant this timber[18] here."— "Fred., come carry this timber yonder."—"Fred., bring that roller here."—"Fred., go get a fresh can of water."—"Fred., come help saw off the end of this timber."—"Fred., go quick, and get the crowbar."—"Fred., hold on the end of this fall."—"Fred., go to the blacksmith's shop, and get a new punch."—"Hurra, Fred.! run and bring me a cold chisel."—"I say, Fred., bear a hand, and get up a fire as quick as lightning under that steam-box."—"Halloo, nigger! come, turn this grindstone."—"Come, come! move, move! and *bowse*[19] this timber forward."—"I say, darky, blast your eyes, why don't you heat up some pitch?"—"Halloo! halloo! halloo!" (Three voices at the same time.) "Come here!—Go there!—Hold on where you are! Damn you, if you move, I'll knock your brains out!"

This was my school for eight months; and I might have remained there longer, but for a most horrid fight I had with four of the white apprentices, in which my left eye was nearly knocked out, and I was horribly mangled in other respects. The facts in the case were these: Until a very little while after I went there, white and black ship-carpenters worked side by side, and no one seemed to see any impropriety in it. All hands seemed to be very well satisfied. Many of the black carpenters were free men. Things seemed to be going on very well. All at once, the white carpenters knocked off, and said they would not work with free colored workmen. Their reason for this, as alleged, was, that if free colored carpenters were encouraged, they would soon take the trade into their own hands, and poor white men would be thrown out of employment. They therefore felt called upon at once to put a stop to it. And, taking advantage of Mr. Gardner's necessities, they broke off, swearing they would work no longer, unless he would discharge his black carpenters. Now, though this did not extend to me in form, it did reach me in fact. My fellow-apprentices very soon began to feel it degrading to them to work with me. They began to put on airs, and talk about the "niggers" taking the country, saying we all ought to be killed; and, being encouraged by the journeymen, they commenced making my condition as hard as they could, by hectoring me around, and sometimes striking me. I, of course, kept the vow I made after the fight with Mr. Covey, and struck back again, regardless of consequences; and while I kept them from combining, I succeeded very well; for I could whip the whole of them, taking them separately. They, however, at length combined, and came upon me, armed with sticks, stones, and heavy handspikes. One came in front with a half brick. There was one at each side of me, and one behind me. While I was attending to those in front, and on either side, the one behind ran up with the handspike, and struck me a heavy blow upon the head. It stunned me. I fell, and with this they all ran upon me, and fell to beating me with their fists. I let them lay on for a while, gathering strength. In an instant, I gave a sudden surge, and rose to my hands and knees. Just as I did that, one of their number gave me, with his heavy boot, a powerful kick in the left eye. My eyeball seemed to have burst. When they saw my eye closed, and badly swollen, they left me. With this I seized the handspike, and for a time pursued them. But here the carpenters interfered, and I thought I might as well give it up. It was impossible to stand my hand against so many. All this took place in sight of not less than fifty white ship-carpenters, and not one interposed a friendly word; but some cried, "Kill the damned nigger! Kill him! kill him! He struck a white person." I found my only chance for life was in flight. I succeeded in getting away without an additional blow, and barely so; for to strike a white man is death by Lynch law,—and that was the law in Mr. Gardner's ship-yard; nor is there much of any other out of Mr. Gardner's ship-yard.

I went directly home, and told the story of my wrongs to Master Hugh; and I am happy to say of him, irreligious as he was, his conduct was heavenly, compared with that of his brother Thomas under similar circumstances. He listened attentively to my narration of the circumstances leading to the savage outrage, and gave many proofs of his strong indignation at it. The heart of my once overkind mistress was again melted into pity. My puffed-out eye and blood-covered face moved her to tears. She took a chair by me, washed the blood from my face, and, with a mother's tenderness, bound up my head, covering the wounded eye with a lean piece of fresh beef. It was almost compensation for my suffering to witness, once more, a manifestation of kindness from this, my once affectionate old mistress. Master Hugh was very much enraged. He gave expression to his feelings by pouring out curses upon the heads of those who did the deed. As soon as I got a little the better of my bruises, he took me with him to Esquire Watson's, on Bond Street, to see what could be done about the matter. Mr. Watson inquired who saw the assault committed. Master Hugh told him it was done in Mr. Gardner's ship-yard, at midday, where there were a large company of men at work. "As to that," he said, "the deed was done, and there was no question as to who did it." His answer was, he could do nothing in the case, unless some white man would come forward and testify. He could issue no warrant on my word. If I had been killed in the presence of a thousand colored people, their testimony combined would have been insufficient to have arrested one of the murderers. Master Hugh, for once, was compelled to say this state of things was too bad. Of course, it was impossible to get any white man to volunteer his testimony in my behalf, and against the white young men. Even those who may have sympathized with me were not prepared to do this. It required a degree of courage unknown to them to do so; for just at that time, the slightest manifestation of humanity toward a colored person was denounced as abolitionism, and that name subjected its bearer to frightful liabilities. The watchwords of the bloody-minded in that region, and in those days, were, "Damn the abolitionists!" and "Damn the niggers!" There was nothing done, and probably nothing would have been done if I had been killed. Such was, and such remains, the state of things in the Christian city of Baltimore.

Master Hugh, finding he could get no redress, refused to let me go back again to Mr. Gardner. He kept me himself, and his wife dressed my wound till I was again restored to health. He then took me into the ship-yard of which he was foreman, in the employment of Mr. Walter Price. There I was immediately set to calking, and very soon learned the art of using my mallet and irons.[20] In the course of one year from the time I left Mr. Gardner's, I was able to command the highest wages given to the most experienced calkers. I was now of some importance to my master. I was bringing him from six to seven dollars per week. I sometimes brought him nine dollars per week: my wages were a dollar and a half a day. After learning how to calk, I sought my own employment, made my own contracts, and collected the money which I earned. My pathway became much more smooth than before; my condition was now much more comfortable. When I could get no calking to do, I did nothing. During these leisure times, those old notions about freedom would steal over me again. When in Mr. Gardner's employment, I was kept in such a perpetual whirl of excitement, I could think of nothing, scarcely, but my life; and in thinking of my life, I almost forgot my liberty. I have observed this in my experience of slavery,—that whenever my condition was improved, instead of its increasing my contentment, it only increased my desire to be free, and set me to thinking of plans to gain my freedom. I have found that, to make a contented slave, it is necessary to make a thoughtless one. It is necessary to darken his moral and mental vision, and, as far as possible, to annihilate the power of reason. He must be able to detect no inconsistencies in slavery; he must be made to feel that slavery is right; and he can be brought to that only when he ceases to be a man.

I was now getting, as I have said, one dollar and fifty cents per day. I contracted for it; I earned it; it was paid to me; it was rightfully my own; yet, upon each returning Saturday night, I was compelled to deliver every cent of that money to Master Hugh. And why? Not because he earned it,—not because he had any hand in earning it,—not because I owed it to him,—nor because he possessed the slightest shadow of a right to it; but solely because he had the power to compel me to give it up. The right of the grim-visaged pirate upon the high seas is exactly the same.

Notes

1. Frederick Douglass, "Chapter X," in *Narrative of the Life of Frederick Douglass, an American Slave, Written by Himself* (London: H.G. Collins, 1851), pp. 51–85.
2. Actually it was January 1834, when Douglass was sixteen years old.
3. In a pair of oxen hitched to a wagon, the "in-hand" ox is on the left and the "off-hand" ox is on the right.
4. The harvesting of the crops.
5. In the context of Covey's ruthless trickery and treachery, this nickname gives the story a mythical, evil twist.
6. "How can we sing the Lord's song in a foreign land?" (see the Bible, Psalm 137:4, New American Standard version).
7. Released from confining anchors and chains.
8. Fever (as with malaria) characterized by periods of chills and sweating that come and go.
9. Using a machine to separate the wheat from the worthless husk, called chaff.
10. Wooden board.
11. Overtaken.
12. Property of William Groome, a merchant in Easton, Maryland; Jenkins was hired out to Mrs. Covey's father, Mr. Caulk.
13. That is, she was not legally a slave; further, she owned her own cabin.
14. Openly whipped, without interruption or protest.
15. Brooms made from the long stems of corn plants.

16. Author's note: This is the same man who gave me the roots to prevent my being whipped by Mr. Covey. He was "a clever soul." We used frequently to talk about the fight with Covey, and as often as we did so, he would claim my success as the result of the roots which he gave me. This superstition is very common among the more ignorant slaves. A slave seldom dies but that his death is attributed to trickery.
17. A near-quotation from Shakespeare's *Hamlet* (act 3, scene 1).
18. Toss or turn over a piece of timber.
19. Pull, haul.
20. Tools of the blacksmith.

Booker T. Washington

Booker T. Washington, African American educator, civil rights activist, and author, catapulted to a position of Black national leader toward the end of the nineteenth century, primarily because of his philosophy of self-reliance and racial solidarity. Washington, who himself was born a slave, understood far too well the misery of slavery; thus, he was an advocate for empowerment through education. As founder of the Tuskegee Normal and Industrial Institute, a Black-operated educational institution, Washington promoted and defended a philosophy of African American education and socioeconomic progress. One of his greatest literary masterpieces, titled *Up From Slavery*, tells his life story in a way that connects with and inspires its readers to think proactively about, and to constructively work to change, the racial problems that exist in America. In the third chapter of *Up From Slavery*, entitled "Struggle for an Education," Washington reveals how his pursuit of an education was his saving grace from a life of poverty. He expresses the importance of many life-changing lessons he encountered throughout his journey from West Virginia to Virginia, where he attended Hampton Institute. He learns the importance of a great work ethic, valuable life experiences, and more importantly, the value of an education. Washington's message prioritizes the necessity of self-help within the African American community and speaks to the greatness of African Americans, who, according to Washington, should be given an opportunity to obtain an education.

The Struggle for an Education

Booker T. Washington[1]

ONE day, while at work in the coal-mine, I happened to overhear two miners talking about a great school for coloured people somewhere in Virginia. This was the first time that I had ever heard anything about any kind of school or college that was more pretentious than the little coloured school in our town.

In the darkness of the mine I noiselessly crept as close as I could to the two men who were talking. I heard one tell the other that not only was the school established for the members of my race, but that opportunities were provided by which poor but worthy students could work out all or a part of the cost of board, and at the same time be taught some trade or industry.

As they went on describing the school, it seemed to me that it must be the greatest place on earth, and not even Heaven presented more attractions for me at that time than did the Hampton Normal and Agricultural Institute in Virginia, about which these men were talking. I resolved at once to go to that school, although I had no idea where it was, or how many miles away, or how I was going to reach it; I remembered only that I was on fire constantly with one ambition, and that was to go to Hampton. This thought was with me day and night.

After hearing of the Hampton Institute, I continued to work for a few months longer in the coalmine. While at work there, I heard of a vacant position in the household of General Lewis Ruffner, the owner of the salt-furnace and coal-mine. Mrs. Viola Ruffner, the wife of General Ruffner, was a "Yankee" woman from Vermont. Mrs. Ruffner had a reputation all through the vicinity for being very strict with her servants, and especially with the boys who tried to serve her. Few of them had remained with her more than two or three weeks. They all left with the same excuse: she was too strict. I decided, however, that I would rather try Mrs. Ruffner's house than remain in the coal-mine, and so my mother applied to her for the vacant position. I was hired at a salary of $5 per month.

I had heard so much about Mrs. Ruffner's severity that I was almost afraid to see her, and trembled when I went into her presence. I had not lived with her many weeks, however, before I began to understand her. I soon began to learn that, first of all, she wanted everything kept clean about her, that she wanted things done promptly and systematically, and that at the bottom of everything she wanted absolute honesty and frankness. Nothing must be sloven or slipshod; every door, every fence, must be kept in repair.

I cannot now recall how long I lived with Mrs. Ruffner before going to Hampton, but I think it must have been a year and a half. At any rate, I here repeat what I have said more than once before, that the lessons that I learned in the home of Mrs. Ruffner were as valuable to me as any education I have ever gotten anywhere since. Even to this day I never see bits of paper scattered around a house or in the street that I do not want to pick them up at once. I never see a filthy yard that I do not want to clean it, a paling off of a fence that I do not want to put it on, an unpainted or unwhitewashed house that I do not want to paint or whitewash it, or a button off one's clothes, or a grease-spot on them or on a floor, that I do not want to call attention to it.

From fearing Mrs. Ruffner I soon learned to look upon her as one of my best friends. When she found that she could trust me she did so implicitly. During the one or two winters that I was with her she gave me an opportunity to go to school for an hour in the day during a portion of the winter months, but most of my studying was done at night, sometimes alone, sometimes under some one whom I could hire to teach me. Mrs. Ruffner always encouraged and sympathized with me in all my efforts to get an education. It was while living with her that I began to get together my first library. I secured a dry-goods box, knocked out one side of it, put some shelves in it, and began putting into it every kind of book that I could get my hands upon, and called it my "library."

Notwithstanding my success at Mrs. Ruffner's I did not give up the idea of going to the Hampton Institute. In the fall of 1872 I determined to make an effort to get there, although, as I have stated, I had no definite idea of the direction in which Hampton was, or of what it would cost to go there. I do not think that any one thoroughly sympathized with me in my ambition to go to Hampton unless it was my mother, and she was troubled with a grave fear that I was starting out on a "wild-goose chase." At any rate, I got only a half-hearted consent from her that I might start. The small amount of money that I had earned had been consumed by my stepfather and the remainder of the family, with the exception of a very few dollars, and so I had very little with which to buy clothes and pay my travelling expenses. My brother John helped me all that he could, but of course that was not a great deal, for his work was in the coal-mine, where he did not earn much, and most of what he did earn went in the direction of paying the household expenses.

Perhaps the thing that touched and pleased me most in connection with my starting for Hampton was the interest that many of the older coloured people took in the matter. They had spent the best days of their lives in slavery, and hardly expected to live to see the time when they would see a member of their race leave home to attend a boarding-school. Some of these older people would give me a nickel, others a quarter, or a handkerchief.

Finally the great day came, and I started for Hampton. I had only a small, cheap satchel that contained what few articles of clothing I could get. My mother at the time was rather weak and broken in health. I hardly expected to see her again, and thus our parting was all the more sad. She, however, was very brave through it all. At that time there were no through trains connecting that part of West Virginia with eastern Virginia. Trains ran only a portion of the way, and the remainder of the distance was travelled by stage-coaches.

The distance from Malden to Hampton is about five hundred miles. I had not been away from home many hours before it began to grow painfully evident that I did not have enough money to pay my fare to Hampton. One experience I shall long remember. I had been travelling over the mountains most of the afternoon in an old-fashioned stage-coach, when, late in the evening, the coach stopped for the night at a common, unpainted house called a hotel. All the other passengers except myself were whites. In my ignorance I supposed that the little hotel existed for the purpose of accommodating the passengers who travelled on the stage-coach. The difference that the colour of one's skin would make I had not thought anything about. After all the other passengers had been shown rooms and were getting ready for supper, I shyly presented myself before the man at the desk. It is true I had practically no money in my pocket with which to pay for bed or food, but I had hoped in some way to beg my way into the good graces of the landlord, for at that season in the mountains of Virginia the weather was cold, and I wanted to get indoors for the night. Without asking as to whether I had any money, the man at the desk firmly refused to even consider the matter of providing me with food or lodging. This was my first experience in finding out what the colour of my skin meant. In some way I managed to keep warm by walking about, and so got through the night. My whole soul was so bent upon reaching Hampton that I did not have time to cherish any bitterness toward the hotel-keeper.

By walking, begging rides both in wagons and in the cars, in some way, after a number of days, I reached the city of Richmond, Virginia, about eighty-two miles from Hampton. When I reached there, tired, hungry, and dirty, it was late in the night. I had never been in a large city, and this rather added to my misery. When I reached Richmond, I was completely out of money. I had not a single acquaintance in the place, and, being unused to city ways, I did not know where to go. I applied at several places for lodging, but they all wanted money, and that was what I did not have. Knowing nothing else better to do, I walked the streets. In doing this I passed by many foodstands where fried chicken and half-moon apple pies were piled high and made to present a most tempting appearance. At that time it seemed to me that I would have promised all that I expected to possess in the future to have gotten hold of one of those chicken legs or one of those pies. But I could not get either of these, nor anything else to eat.

I must have walked the streets till after midnight. At last I became so exhausted that I could walk no longer. I was tired, I was hungry, I was everything but discouraged. Just about the time when I reached extreme physical exhaustion, I came upon a portion of a street where the board sidewalk was considerably elevated. I waited for a few minutes, till I was sure that no passers-by could see me, and then crept under the sidewalk and lay for the night upon the ground, with my satchel of clothing for a pillow. Nearly all night I could hear the tramp of feet over my head. The next morning I found myself somewhat refreshed, but I was extremely hungry, because it had been a long time since I had had sufficient food. As soon as it became light enough for me to see my surroundings I noticed that I was near a large ship, and that this ship seemed to be unloading a cargo of pig iron. I went at once to the vessel and asked the captain to permit me to help unload the vessel in order to get money for food. The captain, a white man, who seemed to be kind-hearted, consented. I worked long enough to earn money for my breakfast, and it seems to me, as I remember it now, to have been about the best breakfast that I have ever eaten.

My work pleased the captain so well that he told me if I desired I could continue working for a small amount per day. This I was very glad to do. I continued working on this vessel for a number of days. After buying food with the small wages I received there was not much left to add to the amount I must get to pay my way to Hampton. In order to economize in every way possible, so as to be sure to reach Hampton in a reasonable time, I continued to sleep under the same sidewalk that gave me shelter the first night I was in Richmond. Many years after that the coloured citizens of Richmond very kindly tendered me a reception at which there must have been two thousand people present. This reception was held not far from the spot where I slept the first night I spent in that city, and I must confess that my mind was more upon the sidewalk that first gave me shelter than upon the reception, agreeable and cordial as it was.

When I had saved what I considered enough money with which to reach Hampton, I thanked the captain of the vessel for his kindness, and started again. Without any unusual occurrence I reached Hampton, with a surplus of exactly fifty cents with which to begin my education. To me it had been a long, eventful journey; but the first sight of the large, three-story, brick school building seemed to have rewarded me for all that I had undergone in order to reach the place. If the people who gave the money to provide that building could appreciate the influence the sight of it had upon me, as well as upon thousands of other youths, they would feel all the more encouraged to make such gifts. It seemed to me to be the largest and most beautiful building I had ever seen. The sight of it seemed to give me new life. I felt that a new kind of existence had now begun—that life would now have a new meaning. I felt that I had reached the promised land, and I resolved to let no obstacle prevent me from putting forth the highest effort to fit myself to accomplish the most good in the world.

As soon as possible after reaching the grounds of the Hampton Institute, I presented myself before the head teacher for assignment to a class. Having been so long without proper food, a bath, and change of clothing, I did not, of course, make a very favourable impression upon her, and I could see at once that there were doubts in her mind about the wisdom of admitting me as a student. I felt that I could hardly blame her if she got the idea that I was a worthless loafer or tramp. For some time she did not refuse to admit me, neither did she decide in my favour, and I continued to linger about her, and to impress her in all the ways I could with my worthiness. In the meantime I saw her admitting other students, and that added greatly to my discomfort, for I felt, deep down in my heart, that I could do as well as they, if I could only get a chance to show what was in me.

After some hours had passed, the head teacher said to me: "The adjoining recitation-room needs sweeping. Take the broom and sweep it."

It occurred to me at once that here was my chance. Never did I receive an order with more delight. I knew that I could sweep, for Mrs. Ruffner had thoroughly taught me how to do that when I lived with her.

I swept the recitation-room three times. Then I got a dusting-cloth and I dusted it four times. All the woodwork around the walls, every bench, table, and desk, I went over four times with my dusting-cloth. Besides, every piece of furniture had been moved and every closet and corner in the room had been thoroughly cleaned. I had the feeling that in a large measure my future depended upon the impression I made upon the teacher in the cleaning of that room. When I was through, I reported to the head teacher. She was a "Yankee" woman who knew just where to look for dirt. She went into the room and inspected the floor and closets; then she took her handkerchief and rubbed it on the woodwork about the walls, and over the table and benches. When she was unable to find one bit of dirt on the floor, or a particle of dust on any of the furniture, she quietly remarked, "I guess you will do to enter this institution."

I was one of the happiest souls on earth. The sweeping of that room was my college examination, and never did any youth pass an examination for entrance into Harvard or Yale that gave him more genuine satisfaction. I have passed several examinations since then, but I have always felt that this was the best one I ever passed.

I have spoken of my own experience in entering the Hampton Institute. Perhaps few, if any, had anything like the same experience that I had, but about that same period there were hundreds who found their way to Hampton and other institutions after experiencing something of the same difficulties that I went through. The young men and women were determined to secure an education at any cost.

The sweeping of the recitation-room in the manner that I did it seems to have paved the way for me to get through Hampton. Miss Mary F. Mackie, the head teacher, offered me a position as janitor. This, of course, I gladly accepted, because it was a place where I could work out nearly all the cost of my board. The work has hard and taxing, but I stuck to it. I had a large number of rooms to care for, and had to work late into the night, while at the same time I had to rise by four o'clock in the morning, in order to build the fires and have a little time in which to prepare my lessons. In all my career at Hampton, and ever since I have been out in the world, Miss Mary

F. Mackie, the head teacher to whom I have referred, proved one of my strongest and most helpful friends. Her advice and encouragement were always helpful and strengthening to me in the darkest hour.

I have spoken of the impression that was made upon me by the buildings and general appearance of the Hampton Institute, but I have not spoken of that which made the greatest and most lasting impression upon me, and that was a great man—the noblest, rarest human being that it has ever been my privilege to meet. I refer to the late General Samuel C. Armstrong.

It has been my fortune to meet personally many of what are called great characters, both in Europe and America, but I do not hesitate to say that I never met any man who, in my estimation, was the equal of General Armstrong. Fresh from the degrading influences of the slave plantation and the coal-mines, it was a rare privilege for me to be permitted to come into direct contact with such a character as General Armstrong. I shall always remember that the first time I went into his presence he made the impression upon me of being a perfect man; I was made to feel that there was something about him that was superhuman. It was my privilege to know the General personally from the time I entered Hampton till he died, and the more I saw of him the greater he grew in my estimation. One might have removed from Hampton all the buildings, class-rooms, teachers, and industries, and given the men and women there the opportunity of coming into daily contact with General Armstrong, and that alone would have been a liberal education. The older I grow, the more I am convinced that there is no education which one can get from books and costly apparatus that is equal to that which can be gotten from contact with great men and women. Instead of studying books so constantly, how I wish that our schools and colleges might learn to study men and things!

General Armstrong spent two of the last six months of his life in my home at Tuskegee. At that time he was paralyzed to the extent that he had lost control of his body and voice in a very large degree. Notwithstanding his affliction, he worked almost constantly night and day for the cause to which he had given his life. I never saw a man who so completely lost sight of himself. I do not believe he ever had a selfish thought. He was just as happy in trying to assist some other institution in the South a he was when working for Hampton. Although he fought the Southern white man in the Civil War, I never heard him utter a bitter word against him afterward. On the other hand, he was constantly seeking to find ways by which he could be of service to the Southern whites.

It would be difficult to describe the hold that he had upon the students at Hampton, or the faith they had in him. In fact, he was worshipped by his students. It never occurred to me that General Armstrong could fail in anything that he undertook. There is almost no request that he could have made that would not have been complied with. When he was a guest at my home in Alabama, and was so badly paralyzed that he had to be wheeled about in an invalid's chair, I recall that one of the General's former students had occasion to push his chair up a long, steep hill that taxed his strength to the utmost. When the top of the hill was reached, the former pupil, with a glow of happiness on his face, exclaimed, "I am so glad that I have been permitted to do something that was real hard for the General before he dies!" While I was a student at Hampton, the dormitories became so crowded that it was impossible to find room for all who wanted to be admitted. In order to help remedy the difficulty, the General conceived the plan of putting up tents to be used as rooms. As soon as it became known that General Armstrong would be pleased if some of the older students would live in the tents during the winter, nearly every student in school volunteered to go.

I was one of the volunteers. The winter that we spent in those tents was an intensely cold one, and we suffered severely—how much I am sure General Armstrong never knew, because we made no complaints. It was enough for us to know that we were pleasing General Armstrong, and that we were making it possible for an additional number of students to secure an education. More than once, during a cold night, when a stiff gale would be blowing, our tent was lifted bodily, and we would find ourselves in the open air. The General would usually pay a visit to the tents early in the morning, and his earnest, cheerful, encouraging voice would dispel any feeling of despondency.

I have spoken of my admiration for General Armstrong, and yet he was but a type of that Christlike body of men and women who went into the Negro schools at the close of the war by the hundreds to assist in lifting up my race. The history of the world fails to show a higher, purer, and more unselfish class of men and women than those who found their way into those Negro schools.

Life at Hampton was a constant revelation to me; was constantly taking me into a new world. The matter of having meals at regular hours, of eating on a tablecloth, using a napkin, the use of the bathtub and of the tooth-brush, as well as the use of sheets upon the bed, were all new to me.

I sometimes feel that almost the most valuable lesson I got at the Hampton Institute was in the use and value of the bath. I learned there for the first time some of its value, not only in keeping the body healthy, but in inspiring self-respect and promoting virtue. In all my travels in the South and elsewhere since leaving Hampton I have always in some way sought my daily bath. To get it sometimes when I have been the guest of my own people in a single-roomed cabin has not always been easy to do, except by slipping away to some stream in the woods. I have always tried to teach my people that some provision for bathing should be a part of every house.

For some time, while a student at Hampton, I possessed but a single pair of socks, but when I had worn these till they became soiled, I would wash them at night and hang them by the fire to dry, so that I might wear them again the next morning.

The charge for my board at Hampton was ten dollars per month. I was expected to pay a part of this in cash and to work out the remainder. To meet this cash payment, as I have stated, I had just fifty cents when I reached the institution. Aside from a very few dollars that my brother John was able to send me once in a while, I had no money with which to pay my board. I was determined from the first to make my work as janitor so valuable that my services would be indispensable. This I succeeded in doing to such an extent that I was soon informed that I would be allowed the full cost of my board in return for my work. The cost of tuition was seventy dollars a year. This, of course, was wholly beyond my ability to provide. If I had been compelled to pay the seventy dollars for tuition, in addition to providing for my board, I would have been compelled to leave the Hampton school. General Armstrong, however, very kindly got Mr. S. Griffitts Morgan, of New Bedford, Mass., to defray the cost of my tuition during the whole time that I was at Hampton. After I finished the course at Hampton and had entered upon my lifework at Tuskegee, I had the pleasure of visiting Mr. Morgan several times.

After having been for a while at Hampton, I found myself in difficulty because I did not have books and clothing. Usually, however, I got around the trouble about books by borrowing from those who were more fortunate than myself. As to clothes, when I reached Hampton I had practically nothing. Everything that I possessed was in a small hand satchel. My anxiety about clothing was increased because of the fact that General Armstrong made a personal inspection of the young men in ranks, to see that their clothes were clean. Shoes had to be polished, there must be no buttons off the clothing, and no grease-spots. To wear one suit of clothes continually, while at work and in the schoolroom, and at the same time keep it clean, was rather a hard problem for me to solve. In some way I managed to get on till the teachers learned that I was in earnest and meant to succeed, and then some of them were kind enough to see that I was partly supplied with second-hand clothing that had been sent in barrels from the North. These barrels proved a blessing to hundreds of poor but deserving students. Without them I question whether I should ever have gotten through Hampton.

When I first went to Hampton I do not recall that I had ever slept in a bed that had two sheets on it. In those days there were not many buildings there, and room was very precious. There were seven other boys in the same room with me; most of them, however, students who had been there for some time. The sheets were quite a puzzle to me. The first night I slept under both of them, and the second night I slept on top of both of them; but by watching the other boys I learned my lesson in this, and have been trying to follow it ever since and to teach it to others.

I was among the youngest of the students who were in Hampton at that time. Most of the students were men and women—some as old as forty years of age. As I now recall the scene of my first year, I do not believe that one often has the opportunity of coming into contact with three or four hundred men and women who were so tremendously in earnest as these men and women were. Every hour was occupied in study or work. Nearly all had had enough actual contact with the world to teach them the need of education. Many of the older ones were, of course, too old to master the text-books very thoroughly, and it was often sad to watch their struggles; but they made up in earnestness much of what they lacked in books. Many of them were as poor as I was, and, besides having to wrestle with their books, they had to struggle with a poverty which prevented their having the necessities of life. Many of them had aged parents who were dependent upon them, and some of them were men who had wives whose support in some way they had to provide for.

The great and prevailing idea that seemed to take possession of every one was to prepare himself to lift up the people at his home. No one seemed to think of himself. And the officers and teachers, what a rare set of human beings they were! They worked for the students night and day, in season and out of season. They seemed happy only when they were helping the students in some manner. Whenever it is written—and I hope it will be—the part that the Yankee teachers played in the education of the Negroes immediately after the war will make one of the most thrilling parts of the history of this country. The time is not far distant when the whole South will appreciate this service in a way that it has not yet been able to do.

Note

1. Booker T. Washington, "The Struggle for an Education," in *Up From Slavery: An Autobiography* (New York: Doubleday, 1901), pp. 42–62.

W.E.B. Du Bois

W.E.B. Du Bois is known as one of the most influential Black scholars, Black authors, Black leaders, and defender of freedoms for Black America. Known as a "renaissance man" of scholarly dedication, Du Bois was a man of great intellect and purpose. A prolific writer and Black studies devotee, Du Bois used his studies and works to argue against and critique the cruel inequalities and bigotry that exist in America and beyond. In his work *The Negro Problem*, Du Bois emphasizes the importance of higher education for African Americans. In the chapter of this work entitled "The Talented Tenth," Du Bois reveals social truths that he believes supports his argument that the Negro race as a whole will be saved by its exceptional men. In contrast to Booker T. Washington's belief of privileging industrial education as a way to create African American economic advancement, Du Bois believes that

> work alone will not do it unless inspired by the right ideals and guided by intelligence. Education must not simply teach work—it must teach Life. The Talented Tenth of the Negro race must be made the leaders of thought and missionaries of culture among their people.
>
> (55)

Du Bois dedicated his life to the study and redemption of the Black man, and in this contribution and many others, he inspired entire generations to invest in racial pride and to commit to an intellectual and social mission of higher education and social justice.

The Talented Tenth

W.E.B. Du Bois[1]

A strong plea for the higher education of the Negro, which those who are interested in the future of the freedmen cannot afford to ignore. W.E.B. DuBois produces ample evidence to prove conclusively the truth of his statement that "to attempt to establish any sort of a system of common and industrial school training, without *first* providing for the higher training of the very best teachers, is simply throwing your money to the winds."

The Negro race, like all races, is going to be saved by its exceptional men. The problem of education, then, among Negroes must first of all deal with the Talented Tenth; it is the problem of developing the Best of this race that they may guide the Mass away from the contamination and death of the Worst, in their own and other races. Now the training of men is a difficult and intricate task. Its technique is a matter for educational experts, but its object is for the vision of seers. If we make money the object of man-training, we shall develop money-makers but not necessarily men; if we make technical skill the object of education, we may possess artisans but not, in nature, men. Men we shall have only as we make manhood the object of the work of the schools—intelligence, broad sympathy, knowledge of the world that was and is, and of the relation of men to it—this is the curriculum of that Higher Education which must underlie true life. On this foundation we may build bread winning, skill of hand and quickness of brain, with never a fear lest the child and man mistake the means of living for the object of life.

If this be true—and who can deny it—three tasks lay before me; first to show from the past that the Talented Tenth as they have risen among American Negroes have been worthy of leadership; secondly, to show how these men may be educated and developed; and thirdly, to show their relation to the Negro problem.

You misjudge us because you do not know us. From the very first it has been the educated and intelligent of the Negro people that have led and elevated the mass, and the sole obstacles that nullified and retarded their efforts were slavery and race prejudice; for what is slavery but the legalized survival of the unfit and the nullification of the work of natural internal leadership?

Negro leadership, therefore, sought from the first to rid the race of this awful incubus that it might make way for natural selection and the survival of the fittest. In colonial days came Phillis Wheatley and Paul Cuffe striving against the bars of prejudice; and Benjamin Banneker, the almanac maker, voiced their longings when he said to Thomas Jefferson,

"I freely and cheerfully acknowledge that I am of the African race, and in colour which is natural to them, of the deepest dye; and it is under a sense of the most pro found gratitude to the Supreme Ruler of the Universe, that I now confess to you that I am not under that state of tyrannical thraldom and inhuman captivity to which too many of my brethren are doomed, but that I have abundantly tasted of the fruition of those blessings which proceed from that free and unequalled liberty with which you are favored, and which I hope you will willingly allow, you have mercifully received from the immediate hand of that Being from whom proceedeth every good and perfect gift.

"Suffer me to recall to your mind that time, in which the arms of the British crown were exerted with every powerful effort, in order to reduce you to a state of servitude; look back, I entreat you, on the variety of dangers to which you were exposed; reflect on that period in which every human aid appeared unavailable, and in which even hope and fortitude wore the aspect of inability to the conflict, and you cannot but be led to a serious and grateful sense of your miraculous and providential preservation, you cannot but acknowledge, that the present freedom and tranquility which you enjoy, you have mercifully received, and that a peculiar blessing of heaven.

"This, sir, was a time when you clearly saw into the injustice of a state of Slavery, and in which you had just apprehensions of the horrors of its condition. It was then that your abhorrence thereof was so excited, that you publicly held forth this true and invaluable doctrine, which is worthy to be recorded and remembered in all succeeding ages: 'We hold these truths to be self evident, that all men are created equal; that they are endowed with certain inalienable rights, and that among these are life, liberty and the pursuit of happiness.'"

Then came Dr. James Derham, who could tell even the learned Dr. Rush something of medicine, and Lemuel Haynes, to whom Middlebury College gave an honorary A.M. in 1804. These and others we may call the Revolutionary group of distinguished Negroes—they were persons of marked ability, leaders of a Talented Tenth, standing conspicuously among the best of their time. They strove by word and deed to save the color line from becoming the line between the bond and free, but all they could do was nullified by Eli Whitney and the Curse of Gold. So they passed into forgetfulness.

But their spirit did not wholly die; here and there in the early part of the century came other exceptional men. Some were natural sons of unnatural fathers and were given often a liberal training and thus a race of educated mulattoes sprang up to plead for black men's rights. There was Ira Aldridge, whom all Europe loved to honor; there was that Voice crying in the Wilderness, David Walker, and saying:

"I declare it does appear to me as though some nations think God is asleep, or that he made the Africans for nothing else but to dig their mines and work their farms, or they cannot believe history, sacred or profane. I ask every man who has a heart, and is blessed with the privilege of believing—Is not God a God of justice to all his creatures? Do you say he is? Then if he gives peace and tranquility to tyrants and permits them to keep our fathers, our mothers, ourselves and our children in eternal ignorance and wretchedness to support them and their families, would he be to us a God of Justice? I ask, O, ye Christians, who hold us and our children in the most abject ignorance and degradation that ever a people were afflicted with since the world began—I say if God gives you peace and tranquility, and suffers you thus to go on afflicting us, and our children, who have never given you the least provocation—would He be to us a God of Justice? If you will allow that we are men, who feel for each other, does not the blood of our fathers and of us, their children, cry aloud to the Lord of Sabaoth against you for the cruelties and murders with which you have and do continue to afflict us?"

This was the wild voice that first aroused Southern legislators in 1829 to the terrors of abolitionism.

In 1831 there met that first Negro convention in Philadelphia, at which the world gaped curiously but which bravely attacked the problems of race and slavery, crying out against persecution and declaring that "Laws as cruel in themselves as they were unconstitutional and unjust, have in many places been enacted against our poor, unfriended and unoffending brethren (without a shadow of provocation on our part), at whose bare recital the very savage draws himself up for fear of contagion—looks noble and prides himself because he bears not the name of Christian." Side by side this free Negro movement, and the movement for abolition, strove until they merged into one strong stream. Too little notice has been taken of the work which the Talented Tenth among Negroes took in the great abolition crusade. From the very day that a Philadelphia colored man became the first subscriber to Garrison's "Liberator," to the day when Negro soldiers made the Emancipation Proclamation possible, black leaders worked shoulder to shoulder with white men in a movement, the success of which would have been impossible without them. There was Purvis and Remond, Pennington and Highland Garnett, Sojourner Truth and Alexander Crummel, and above all, Frederick Douglass—what would the abolition movement have been without them? They stood as living examples of the possibilities of the Negro race, their own hard experiences and well wrought culture said silently more than all the drawn periods of orators—they were the men who made American slavery impossible. As Maria Weston Chapman once said, from the school of anti-slavery agitation "a throng of authors, editors, lawyers, orators and accomplished gentlemen of color have taken their degree! It has equally implanted hopes and aspirations, noble thoughts, and sublime purposes, in the hearts of both races. It has prepared the white man for the freedom of the black man, and it has made the black man scorn the thought of enslavement, as does a white man, as far as its influence has extended. Strengthen that noble influence! Before its organization, the country only saw here and there in slavery some faithful Cudjoe or Dinah, whose strong natures blossomed even in bondage, like a fine plant beneath a heavy stone. Now, under the elevating and cherishing influence of the American Anti-slavery Society, the colored race, like the white, furnishes Corinthian capitals for the noblest temples."

Where were these black abolitionists trained? Some, like Frederick Douglass, were self-trained, but yet trained liberally; others, like Alexander Crummell and McCune Smith, graduated from famous foreign universities. Most of them rose up through the colored schools of New York and Philadelphia and Boston, taught by college-bred men like Russworm, of Dartmouth, and college-bred white men like Neau and Benezet.

After emancipation came a new group of educated and gifted leaders: Langston, Bruce and Elliot, Greener, Williams and Payne. Through political organization, historical and polemic writing and moral regeneration, these men strove to uplift their people. It is the fashion of to-day to sneer at them and to say that with freedom Negro leadership should have begun at the plow and not in the Senate—a foolish and mischievous lie; two hundred and fifty years that black serf toiled at the plow and yet that toiling was in vain till the Senate passed the war amendments; and two hundred and fifty years more the half-free serf of to-day may toil at his plow, but unless he have political rights and righteously guarded civic status, he will still remain the poverty-stricken and ignorant plaything of rascals, that he now is. This all sane men know even if they dare not say it.

And so we come to the present—a day of cowardice and vacillation, of strident wide-voiced wrong and faint hearted compromise; of double-faced dallying with Truth and Right. Who are to-day guiding the work of the Negro people? The "exceptions" of course. And yet so sure as this

Talented Tenth is pointed out, the blind worshippers of the Average cry out in alarm: "These are exceptions, look here at death, disease and crime—these are the happy rule." Of course they are the rule, because a silly nation made them the rule: Because for three long centuries this people lynched Negroes who dared to be brave, raped black women who dared to be virtuous, crushed dark-hued youth who dared to be ambitious, and encouraged and made to flourish servility and lewdness and apathy. But not even this was able to crush all manhood and chastity and aspiration from black folk. A saving remnant continually survives and persists, continually aspires, continually shows itself in thrift and ability and character. Exceptional it is to be sure, but this is its chiefest promise; it shows the capability of Negro blood, the promise of black men. Do Americans ever stop to reflect that there are in this land a million men of Negro blood, well-educated, owners of homes, against the honor of whose womanhood no breath was ever raised, whose men occupy positions of trust and usefulness, and who, judged by any standard, have reached the full measure of the best type of modern European culture? Is it fair, is it decent, is it Christian to ignore these facts of the Negro problem, to belittle such aspiration, to nullify such leadership and seek to crush these people back into the mass out of which by toil and travail, they and their fathers have raised themselves?

Can the masses of the Negro people be in any possible way more quickly raised than by the effort and example of this aristocracy of talent and character? Was there ever a nation on God's fair earth civilized from the bottom upward? Never; it is, ever was and ever will be from the top downward that culture filters. The Talented Tenth rises and pulls all that are worth the saving up to their vantage ground. This is the history of human progress; and the two historic mistakes which have hindered that progress were the thinking first that no more could ever rise save the few already risen; or second, that it would better the unrisen to pull the risen down.

How then shall the leaders of a struggling people be trained and the hands of the risen few strengthened? There can be but one answer: The best and most capable of their youth must be schooled in the colleges and universities of the land. We will not quarrel as to just what the university of the Negro should teach or how it should teach it—I willingly admit that each soul and each race-soul needs its own peculiar curriculum. But this is true: A university is a human invention for the transmission of knowledge and culture from generation to generation, through the training of quick minds and pure hearts, and for this work no other human invention will suffice, not even trade and industrial schools.

All men cannot go to college but some men must; every isolated group or nation must have its yeast, must have for the talented few centers of training where men are not so mystified and befuddled by the hard and necessary toil of earning a living, as to have no aims higher than their bellies, and no God greater than Gold. This is true training, and thus in the beginning were the favored sons of the freedmen trained. Out of the colleges of the North came, after the blood of war, Ware, Cravath, Chase, Andrews, Bumstead and Spence to build the foundations of knowledge and civilization in the black South. Where ought they to have begun to build? At the bottom, of course, quibbles the mole with his eyes in the earth. Aye! truly at the bottom, at the very bottom; at the bottom of knowledge, down in the very depths of knowledge there where the roots of justice strike into the lowest soil of Truth. And so they did begin; they founded colleges, and up from the colleges shot normal schools, and out from the normal schools went teachers, and around the normal teachers clustered other teachers to teach the public schools; the college trained in Greek and Latin and mathematics, 2,000 men; and these men trained full 50,000 others in morals and manners, and they in turn taught thrift and the alphabet to nine millions of men, who to-day hold $300,000,000 of property. It was a miracle—the most wonderful peace-battle of the 19th century, and yet to-day men smile at it, and in fine superiority tell us that it was all a strange mistake; that a proper way to found a system of education is first to gather the children and buy them spelling books and hoes; afterward men may look about for teachers, if haply they may find them; or again they would teach men Work, but as for Life—why, what has Work to do with Life, they ask vacantly.

Was the work of these college founders successful; did it stand the test of time? Did the college graduates, with all their fine theories of life, really live? Are they useful men helping to civilize and elevate their less fortunate fellows? Let us see. Omitting all institutions which have not actually graduated students from a college course, there are to-day in the United States thirty-four institutions giving something above high school training to Negroes and designed especially for this race.

Three of these were established in border States before the War; thirteen were planted by the Freedmen's Bureau in the years 1864–1869; nine were established between 1870 and 1880 by various church bodies; five were established after 1881 by Negro churches, and four are state institutions supported by United States' agricultural funds. In most cases the college departments are small adjuncts to high and common school work. As a matter of fact six institutions—Atlanta, Fisk, Howard, Shaw, Wilberforce and Leland, are the important Negro colleges so far as actual work and number of students are concerned. In all these institutions, seven hundred and fifty Negro college students are enrolled. In grade the best of these colleges are about a year behind the smaller New England colleges and a typical curriculum is that of Atlanta University. Here students from the grammar grades, after a three years' high school course, take a college course of 136 weeks. One-fourth of this time is given to Latin and Greek; one-fifth, to English and modern languages; one-sixth, to history and social science; one-seventh, to natural science; one-eighth to mathematics, and one-eighth to philosophy and pedagogy.

In addition to these students in the South, Negroes have attended Northern colleges for many years. As early as 1826 one was graduated from Bowdoin College, and from that time till to-day nearly every year has seen elsewhere, other such graduates. They have, of course, met much color prejudice. Fifty years ago very few colleges would admit them at all. Even to-day no Negro has ever been admitted to Princeton, and at some other leading institutions they are rather endured than encouraged. Oberlin was the great pioneer in the work of blotting out the color line in colleges, and has more Negro graduates by far than any other Northern college.

The total number of Negro college graduates up to 1899, (several of the graduates of that year not being reported), was as follows:

Table 4.1

	Negro colleges	White colleges
Before '76	137	75
'75–80	143	22
'80–85	250	31
'85–90	413	43
'90–95	465	66
'96–99	475	88
Class unknown	57	64
Total	1,914	390

Of these graduates 2,079 were men and 252 were women; 50 per cent. of Northern-born college men come South to work among the masses of their people, at a sacrifice which few people realize; nearly 90 per cent. of the Southern-born graduates instead of seeking that personal freedom and broader intellectual atmosphere which their training has led them, in some degree, to conceive, stay and labor and wait in the midst of their black neighbors and relatives.

The most interesting question, and in many respects the crucial question, to be asked concerning college-bred Negroes, is: Do they earn a living? It has been intimated more than once that the higher training of Negroes has resulted in sending into the world of work, men who could find nothing to do suitable to their talents. Now and then there comes a rumor of a colored college man working at menial service, etc. Fortunately, returns as to occupations of college-bred Negroes, gathered by the Atlanta conference, are quite full—nearly sixty per cent. of the total number of graduates.

This enables us to reach fairly certain conclusions as to the occupations of all college-bred Negroes. Of 1,312 persons reported, there were:

> Over half are teachers, a sixth are preachers, another sixth are students and professional men; over 6 per cent. are farmers, artisans and merchants, and 4 per cent. are in government service. In detail the occupations are as follows:

Table 4.2

Occupations of college-bred men		
Teachers:		
Presidents and Deans,	19	
Teacher of Music,	7	
Professors, Principals and Teachers,	675	Total 701
Clergymen:		
Bishop,	1	
Chaplains U.S. Army,	2	
Missionaries,	9	
Presiding Elders,	12	
Preachers,	197	Total 221
Physicians,		
Doctors of Medicine,	76	
Druggists,	4	
Dentists,	3	Total 83
Students,	74	
Lawyers,	62	
Civil Service:		
U.S. Minister Plenipotentiary,	1	
U.S. Consul,	1	
U.S. Deputy Collector,	1	
U.S. Gauger,	1	
U.S. Postmasters,	2	
U.S. Clerks,	44	
State Civil Service,	2	
City Civil Service,	1	Total 53
Business Men:		
Merchants, etc.,	30	
Managers,	13	
Real Estate Dealers,	4	Total 47
Farmers,	26	
Clerks and Secretaries:		
Secretary of National Societies,	7	
Clerks, etc.,	15	Total 22
Artisans,	9	
Editors,	9	
Miscellaneous,	5	

These figures illustrate vividly the function of the college-bred Negro. He is, as he ought to be, the group leader, the man who sets the ideals of the community where he lives, directs its thoughts and heads its social movements. It need hardly be argued that the Negro people need social leadership more than most groups; that they have no traditions to fall back upon, no long established customs, no strong family ties, no well defined social classes. All these things must be slowly and painfully evolved. The preacher was, even before the war, the group leader of the Negroes, and the church their greatest social institution. Naturally this preacher was ignorant and often immoral, and the problem of replacing the older type by better educated men has been a difficult one. Both by direct work and by direct influence on other preachers, and on congregations, the college-bred preacher has an opportunity for reformatory work and moral inspiration, the value of which cannot be overestimated.

It has, however, been in the furnishing of teachers that the Negro college has found its peculiar function. Few persons realize how vast a work, how mighty a revolution has been thus accomplished. To furnish five millions and more of ignorant people with teachers of their own race and blood, in one generation, was not only a very difficult undertaking, but a very important one, in that, it placed before the eyes of almost every Negro child an attainable ideal. It brought the masses of the blacks in contact with modern civilization, made black men the leaders of their communities and trainers of the new generation. In this work college-bred Negroes were first teachers, and then teachers of teachers. And here it is that the broad culture of college work has been of peculiar value. Knowledge of life and its wider meaning, has been the point of the Negro's deepest ignorance, and the sending out of teachers whose training has not been simply for bread winning, but also for human culture, has been of inestimable value in the training of these men.

In earlier years the two occupations of preacher and teacher were practically the only ones open to the black college graduate. Of later years a larger diversity of life among his people, has opened new avenues of employment. Nor have these college men been paupers and spendthrifts; 557 college-bred Negroes owned in 1899, $1,342,862.50 worth of real estate, (assessed value) or $2,411 per family. The real value of the total accumulations of the whole group is perhaps about $10,000,000, or $5,000 a piece. Pitiful, is it not, beside the fortunes of oil kings and steel trusts, but after all is the fortune of the millionaire the only stamp of true and successful living? Alas! it is, with many, and there's the rub.

The problem of training the Negro is to-day immensely complicated by the fact that the whole question of the efficiency and appropriateness of our present systems of education, for any kind of child, is a matter of active debate, in which final settlement seems still afar off. Consequently it often happens that persons arguing for or against certain systems of education for Negroes, have these controversies in mind and miss the real question at issue. The main question, so far as the Southern Negro is concerned, is: What under the present circumstance, must a system of education do in order to raise the Negro as quickly as possible in the scale of civilization? The answer to this question seems to me clear: It must strengthen the Negro's character, increase his knowledge and teach him to earn a living. Now it goes without saying, that it is hard to do all these things simultaneously or suddenly, and that at the same time it will not do to give all the attention to one and neglect the others; we could give black boys trades, but that alone will not civilize a race of ex-slaves; we might simply increase their knowledge of the world, but this would not necessarily make them wish to use this knowledge honestly; we might seek to strengthen character and purpose, but to what end if this people have nothing to eat or to wear? A system of education is not one thing, nor does it have a single definite object, nor is it a mere matter of schools. Education is that whole system of human training within and without the school house walls, which molds and develops men. If then we start out to train an ignorant and unskilled people with a heritage of bad habits, our system of training must set before itself two great aims—the one dealing with knowledge and character, the other part seeking to give the child the technical knowledge necessary for him to earn a living under the present circumstances. These objects are accomplished in part by the opening of the common schools on the one, and of the industrial schools on the other. But only in part, for there must also be trained those who are to teach these schools—men and women of knowledge and culture and technical skill who understand modern civilization, and have the training and aptitude to impart it to the children under them. There must be teachers, and teachers of teachers, and to attempt to establish any sort of a system of common and industrial school training, without *first* (and I say *first* advisedly) without *first* providing for the higher training of the very best teachers, is simply throwing your money to the winds. School houses do not teach themselves—piles of brick and mortar and machinery do not send out *men*. It is the trained, living human soul, cultivated and strengthened by long study and thought, that breathes the real breath of life into boys and girls and makes them human, whether they be black or white, Greek, Russian or American. Nothing, in these latter days, has so dampened the faith of thinking Negroes in recent educational movements, as the fact that such movements have been accompanied by ridicule and denouncement and decrying of those very institutions of higher training which made the Negro public school possible, and make Negro industrial schools thinkable. It was Fisk, Atlanta, Howard and Straight, those colleges born of the faith and sacrifice of the abolitionists, that placed in the black schools of the South the 30,000 teachers and more, which some, who depreciate the work of these higher schools, are using to teach their own new experiments. If Hampton, Tuskegee and the hundred other industrial schools prove in the future to be as successful as they deserve to be, then their success in training black artisans for the South, will be due primarily to the white colleges of the North and the black colleges of the South, which trained the teachers who to-day conduct these institutions. There was a time when the American people believed pretty devoutly that a log of wood with a boy at one end and Mark Hopkins at the other, represented the highest ideal of human training. But in these eager days it would seem that we have changed all that and think it necessary to add a couple of saw-mills and a hammer to this outfit, and, at a pinch, to dispense with the services of Mark Hopkins.

I would not deny, or for a moment seem to deny, the paramount necessity of teaching the Negro to work, and to work steadily and skillfully; or seem to depreciate in the slightest degree the important part industrial schools must play in the accomplishment of these ends, but I *do* say, and insist upon it, that it is industrialism drunk with its vision of success, to imagine that its own work can be accomplished without providing for the training of broadly cultured men and women to teach its own teachers, and to teach the teachers of the public schools.

But I have already said that human education is not simply a matter of schools; it is much more a matter of family and group life—the training of one's home, of one's daily companions, of one's social class. Now the black boy of the South moves in a black world—a world with its own leaders, its own thoughts, its own ideals. In this world he gets by far the larger part of his life training, and through the eyes of this dark world he peers into the veiled world beyond. Who guides and determines the education which he receives in his world? His teachers here are the group-leaders of the Negro people—the physicians and clergymen, the trained fathers and mothers, the influential and forceful men about him of all kinds; here it is, if at all, that the culture of the surrounding world trickles through and is handed on by the graduates of the higher schools. Can such culture training of group leaders be neglected? Can we afford to ignore it? Do you think that if the leaders of thought among Negroes are not trained and educated thinkers, that they will have no leaders? On the contrary a hundred half-trained demagogues will still hold the places they so largely occupy now, and hundreds of vociferous busy-bodies will multiply. You have no choice; either you must help furnish this race from within its own ranks with thoughtful men of trained leadership, or you must suffer the evil consequences of a headless misguided rabble.

I am an earnest advocate of manual training and trade teaching for black boys, and for white boys, too. I believe that next to the founding of Negro colleges the most valuable addition to Negro education since the war, has been industrial training for black boys. Nevertheless, I insist that the object of all true education is not to make men carpenters, it is to make carpenters men; there are two means of making the carpenter a man, each equally important: the first is to give the group and community in which he works, liberally trained teachers and leaders to teach him and his family what life means; the second is to give him sufficient intelligence and technical skill to make him an efficient workman; the first object demands the Negro college and college-bred men—not a quantity of such colleges, but a few of excellent quality; not too many college-bred men, but enough to leaven the lump, to inspire the masses, to raise the Talented Tenth to leadership; the second object demands a good system of common schools, well-taught, conveniently located and properly equipped.

The Sixth Atlanta Conference truly said in 1901:

"We call the attention of the Nation to the fact that less than one million of the three million Negro children of school age, are at present regularly attending school, and these attend a session which lasts only a few months.

"We are to-day deliberately rearing millions of our citizens in ignorance, and at the same time limiting the rights of citizenship by educational qualifications. This is unjust. Half the black youth of the land have no opportunities open to them for learning to read, write and cipher. In the discussion as to the proper training of Negro children after they leave the public schools, we have forgotten that they are not yet decently provided with public schools.

"Propositions are beginning to be made in the South to reduce the already meagre school facilities of Negroes. We congratulate the South on resisting, as much as it has, this pressure, and on the many millions it has spent on Negro education. But it is only fair to point out that Negro taxes and the Negroes' share of the income from indirect taxes and endowments have fully repaid this expenditure, so that the Negro public school system has not in all probability cost the white taxpayers a single cent since the war.

"This is not fair. Negro schools should be a public burden, since they are a public benefit. The Negro has a right to demand good common school training at the hands of the States and the Nation since by their fault he is not in position to pay for this himself."

What is the chief need for the building up of the Negro public school in the South? The Negro race in the South needs teachers to-day above all else. This is the concurrent testimony of all who know the situation. For the supply of this great demand two things are needed—institutions of higher education and money for school houses and salaries. It is usually assumed that a hundred or more institutions for Negro training are to-day turning out so many teachers and college-bred men that the race is threatened with an over-supply. This is sheer nonsense. There are to-day less than 3,000 living Negro college graduates in the United States, and less than 1,000 Negroes in college. Moreover, in the 164 schools for Negroes, 95 per cent. of their students are doing elementary and secondary work, work which should be done in the public schools. Over half the remaining 2,157 students are taking high school studies. The mass of so-called "normal" schools for the Negro, are simply doing elementary common school work, or, at most, high school work, with a little instruction in methods. The Negro colleges and the post-graduate courses at other institutions are the only agencies for the broader and more careful training of teachers. The work of these institutions is hampered for lack of funds. It is getting increasingly difficult to get funds for training teachers in the best modern methods, and yet all over the South, from State Superintendents, county officials, city boards and school principals comes the wail, "We need TEACHERS!" and teachers must be trained. As the fairest minded of all white Southerners, Atticus G. Haygood, once said: "The defects of colored teachers are so great as to create an urgent necessity for training better ones. Their excellencies and their successes are sufficient to justify the best hopes of success in the effort, and to vindicate the judgment of those who make large investments of money and service, to give to colored students opportunity for thoroughly preparing themselves for the work of teaching children of their people."

The truth of this has been strikingly shown in the marked improvement of white teachers in the South. Twenty years ago the rank and file of white public school teachers were not as good as the Negro teachers. But they, by scholarships and good salaries, have been encouraged to thorough normal and collegiate preparation, while the Negro teachers have been discouraged by starvation wages and the idea that any training will do for a black teacher. If carpenters are needed it is well and good to train men as carpenters. But to train men as carpenters, and then set them to teaching is wasteful and criminal; and to train men as teachers and then refuse them living wages, unless they become carpenters, is rank nonsense.

The United States Commissioner of Education says in his report for 1900: "For comparison between the white and colored enrollment in secondary and higher education, I have added together the enrollment in high schools and secondary schools, with the attendance on colleges and universities, not being sure of the actual grade of work done in the colleges and universities. The work done in the secondary schools is reported in such detail in this office, that there can be no doubt of its grade."

He then makes the following comparisons of persons in every million enrolled in secondary and higher education:

Table 4.3

	Whole country	Negroes
1880	4,362	1,289
1900	10,743	2,061

And he concludes: "While the number in colored high schools and colleges had increased somewhat faster than the population, it had not kept pace with the average of the whole country, for it had fallen from 30 per cent. to 24 per cent. of the average quota. Of all colored pupils, one (1) in one hundred was engaged in secondary and higher work, and that ratio has continued substantially for the past twenty years. If the ratio of colored population in secondary and higher education is to be equal to the average for the whole country, it must be increased to five times its present average." And if this be true of the secondary and higher education, it is safe to say that the Negro has not one-tenth his quota in college studies. How baseless, therefore, is the charge of too much training! We need Negro teachers for the Negro common schools, and we need first-class normal schools and colleges to train them. This is the work of higher Negro education and it must be done.

Further than this, after being provided with group leaders of civilization, and a foundation of intelligence in the public schools, the carpenter, in order to be a man, needs technical skill. This calls for trade schools. Now trade schools are not nearly such simple things as people once thought. The original idea was that the "Industrial" school was to furnish education, practically free, to those willing to work for it; it was to "do" things—i.e.: become a center of productive industry, it was to be partially, if not wholly, self-supporting, and it was to teach trades. Admirable as were some of the ideas underlying this scheme, the whole thing simply would not work in practice; it was found that if you were to use time and material to teach trades thoroughly, you could not at the same time keep the industries on a commercial basis and make them pay. Many schools started out to do this on a large scale and went into virtual bankruptcy. Moreover, it was found also that it was possible to teach a boy a trade mechanically, without giving him the full educative benefit of the process, and, vice versa, that there was a distinctive educative value in teaching a boy to use his hands and eyes in carrying out certain physical processes, even though he did not actually learn a trade. It has happened, therefore, in the last decade, that a noticeable change has come over the industrial schools. In the first place the idea of commercially remunerative industry in a school is being pushed rapidly to the back-ground. There are still schools with shops and farms that bring an income, and schools that use student labor partially for the erection of their buildings and the furnishing of equipment. It is coming to be seen, however, in the education of the Negro, as clearly as it has been seen in the education of the youths the world over, that it is the *boy* and not the material product, that is the true object of education. Consequently the object of the industrial school came to be the thorough training of boys regardless of the cost of the training, so long as it was thoroughly well done.

Even at this point, however, the difficulties were not surmounted. In the first place modern industry has taken great strides since the war, and the teaching of trades is no longer a simple matter. Machinery and long processes of work have greatly changed the work of the carpenter, the ironworker and the shoemaker. A really efficient workman must be to-day an intelligent man who has had good technical training in addition to thorough common school, and perhaps even higher training. To meet this situation the industrial schools began a further development; they established distinct Trade Schools for the thorough training of better class artisans, and at the same time they sought to preserve for the purposes of general education, such of the simpler processes of elementary trade learning as were best suited therefor. In this differentiation of the Trade School and manual training, the best of the industrial schools simply followed the plain trend of the present educational epoch. A prominent educator tells us that, in Sweden, "In the beginning the economic conception was generally adopted, and everywhere manual training was looked upon as a means of preparing the children of the common people to earn their living. But gradually it came to be recognized that manual training has a more elevated purpose, and one, indeed, more useful in the deeper meaning of the term. It came to be considered as an educative process for the complete moral, physical and intellectual development of the child."

Thus, again, in the manning of trade schools and manual training schools we are thrown back upon the higher training as its source and chief support. There was a time when any aged and wornout carpenter could teach in a trade school. But not so to-day. Indeed the demand for college-bred men by a school like Tuskegee, ought to make Mr. Booker T. Washington the firmest friend of higher training. Here he has as helpers the son of a Negro senator, trained in Greek and the humanities, and graduated at Harvard; the son of a Negro congressman and lawyer, trained in Latin and mathematics, and graduated at Oberlin; he has as his wife, a woman who read Virgil and Homer in the same class room with me; he has as college chaplain, a classical graduate of Atlanta University; as teacher of science, a graduate of Fisk; as teacher of history, a graduate of Smith,—indeed some thirty of his chief teachers are college graduates, and instead of studying French grammars in the midst of weeds, or buying pianos for dirty cabins, they are at Mr. Washington's right hand helping him in a noble work. And yet one of the effects of Mr. Washington's propaganda has been to throw doubt upon the expediency of such training for Negroes, as these persons have had.

Men of America, the problem is plain before you. Here is a race transplanted through the criminal foolishness of your fathers. Whether you like it or not the millions are here, and here they will remain. If you do not lift them up, they will pull you down. Education and work are the levers to uplift a people. Work alone will not do it unless inspired by the right ideals and guided by intelligence. Education must not simply teach work—it must teach Life. The Talented Tenth of the Negro race must be made leaders of thought and missionaries of culture among their people. No others can do this work and Negro colleges must train men for it. The Negro race, like all other races, is going to be saved by its exceptional men.

Note

1. W.E.B. Du Bois, "The Talented Tenth," in *The Negro Problem* (New York: James Pott, 1903), pp. 33–75.

Zora Neale Hurston

Zora Neale Hurston, considered one of the preeminent writers of twentieth-century African American literature, was an anthropologist, folklorist, essayist, playwright, and novelist. In her essay "How It Feels to Be Colored Me," Hurston embraces her identity in ways that demonstrate her pride in her heritage and that promote racial consciousness for African American people. Hurston directly and unapologetically confronts racism by speaking to the advantages of her blackness as opposed to the disadvantages commonly expressed by, and in, mainstream society. Hurston describes her experience of growing up in an all-Black town in the South and how this loving community informs her identity. She does not feel as if Black means blemish; to the contrary, she equates strength and the will to survive with her Black historical, cultural, and intellectual traditions. Hurston proclaims that even in the face of discrimination, Black people should be proud of their heritage and never forget their potential, intelligence, and purpose. Hurston reminds us all of the richness that exists in racial heritage.

How It Feels to Be Colored Me

Zora Neale Hurston[1]

1. I am colored but I offer nothing in the way of extenuating circumstances except the fact that I am the only Negro in the United States whose grandfather on the mother's side was *not* an Indian chief.

2. I remember the very day that I became colored. Up to my thirteenth year I lived in the little Negro town of Eatonville, Florida. It is exclusively a colored town. The only white people I knew passed through the town going to or coming from Orlando. The native whites rode dusty horses, the Northern tourists chugged down the sandy village road in automobiles. The town knew the Southerners and never stopped cane chewing when they passed. But the Northerners were something else again. They were peered at cautiously from behind curtains by the timid. The more venturesome would come out on the porch to watch them go past and got just as much pleasure out of the tourists as the tourists got out of the village.

3. The front porch might seem a daring place for the rest of the town, but it was a gallery seat for me. My favorite place was atop the gatepost. Proscenium box for a born first-nighter. Not only did I enjoy the show, but I didn't mind the actors knowing that I liked it. I usually spoke to them in passing. I'd wave at them and when they returned my salute, I would say something like this: "Howdy-do-well-I-thank-you-where-you-goin'?" Usually automobile or the horse paused at this, and after a queer exchange of compliments, I would probably "go a piece of the way" with them, as we say in farthest Florida. If one of my family happened to come to the front in time to see me, of course negotiations would be rudely broken off. But even so, it is clear that I was the first "welcome-to-our-state" Floridian, and I hope the Miami Chamber of Commerce will please take notice.

4. During this period, white people differed from colored to me only in that they rode through town and never lived there. They liked to hear me "speak pieces" and sing and wanted to see me dance the parse-me-la, and gave me generously of their small silver for doing these things, which seemed strange to me for I wanted to do them so much that I needed bribing to stop, only they didn't know it. The colored people gave no dimes. They deplored any joyful tendencies in me, but I was their Zora nevertheless. I belonged to them, to the nearby hotels, to the county—everybody's Zora.

5. But changes came in the family when I was thirteen, and I was sent to school in Jacksonville. I left Eatonville, the town of the oleanders, a Zora. When I disembarked from the river-boat at Jacksonville, she was no more. It seemed that I had suffered a sea change. I was not Zora

of Orange County any more, I was now a little colored girl. I found it out in certain ways. In my heart as well as in the mirror, I became a fast brown—warranted not to rub nor run.

6. But I am not tragically colored. There is no great sorrow dammed up in my soul, nor lurking behind my eyes. I do not mind at all. I do not belong to the sobbing school of Negrohood who hold that nature somehow has given them a lowdown dirty deal and whose feelings are all but about it. Even in the helter-skelter skirmish that is my life, I have seen that the world is to the strong regardless of a little pigmentation more of less. No, I do not weep at the world—I am too busy sharpening my oyster knife.

7. Someone is always at my elbow reminding me that I am the granddaughter of slaves. It fails to register depression with me. Slavery is sixty years in the past. The operation was successful and the patient is doing well, thank you. The terrible struggle that made me an American out of a potential slave said "On the line!" The Reconstruction said "Get set!" and the generation before said "Go!" I am off to a flying start and I must not halt in the stretch to look behind and weep. Slavery is the price I paid for civilization, and the choice was not with me. It is a bully adventure and worth all that I have paid through my ancestors for it. No one on earth ever had a greater chance for glory. The world to be won and nothing to be lost. It is thrilling to think—to know that for any act of mine, I shall get twice as much praise or twice as much blame. It is quite exciting to hold the center of the national stage, with the spectators not knowing whether to laugh or to weep.

8. The position of my white neighbor is much more difficult. No brown specter pulls up a chair beside me when I sit down to eat. No dark ghost thrusts its leg against mine in bed. The game of keeping what one has is never so exciting as the game of getting.

9. I do not always feel colored. Even now I often achieve the unconscious Zora of Eatonville before the Hegira. I feel most colored when I am thrown against a sharp white background.

10. For instance at Barnard. "Beside the waters of the Hudson" I feel my race. Among the thousand white persons, I am a dark rock surged upon, and overswept, but through it all, I remain myself. When covered by the waters, I am; and the ebb but reveals me again.

11. Sometimes it is the other way around. A white person is set down in our midst, but the contrast is just as sharp for me. For instance, when I sit in the drafty basement that is The New World Cabaret with a white person, my color comes. We enter chatting about any little nothing that we have in common and are seated by the jazz waiters. In the abrupt way that jazz orchestras have, this one plunges into a number. It loses no time in circumlocutions, but gets right down to business. It constricts the thorax and splits the heart with its tempo and narcotic harmonies. This orchestra grows rambunctious, rears on its hind legs and attacks the tonal veil with primitive fury, rending it, clawing it until it breaks through to the jungle beyond. I follow those heathen—follow them exultingly. I dance wildly inside myself; I yell within, I whoop; I shake my assegai above my head, I hurl it true to the mark yeeeeooww! I am in the jungle and living in the jungle way. My face is painted red and yellow and my body is painted blue. My pulse is throbbing like a war drum. I want to slaughter something—give pain, give death to what, I do not know. But the piece ends. The men of the orchestra wipe their lips and rest their fingers. I creep back slowly to the veneer we call civilization with the last tone and find the white friend sitting motionless in his seat, smoking calmly.

12. "Good music they have here," he remarks, drumming the table with his fingertips.

13. Music. The great blobs of purple and red emotion have not touched him. He has only heard what I felt. He is far away and I see him but dimly across the ocean and the continent that have fallen between us. He is so pale with his whiteness then and I am so colored.

14. At certain times I have no race, I am me. When I set my hat at a certain angle and saunter down Seventh Avenue, Harlem City, feeling as snooty as the lions in front of the Forty-Second Street Library, for instance. So far as my feelings are concerned, Peggy Hopkins Joyce

on the Boule Mich with her gorgeous raiment, stately carriage, knees knocking together in a most aristocratic manner, has nothing on me. The cosmic Zora emerges. I belong to no race nor time. I am the eternal feminine with its string of beads.

15. I have no separate feeling about being an American citizen and colored. I am merely a fragment of the Great Soul that surges within the boundaries. My country, right or wrong.

16. Sometimes, I feel discriminated against, but it does not make me angry. It merely astonishes me. How can any deny themselves the pleasure of my company? It's beyond me.

17. But in the main, I feel like a brown bag of miscellany propped against a wall. Against a wall in company with other bags, white, red and yellow. Pour out the contents, and there is discovered a jumble of small things priceless and worthless. A first-water diamond, an empty spool, bits of broken glass, lengths of string, a key to a door long since crumbled away, a rusty knife-blade, old shoes saved for a road that never was and never will be, a nail bent under the weight of things too heavy for any nail, a dried flower or two still a little fragrant. In your hand is the brown bag. On the ground before you is the jumble it held—so much like the jumble in the bags, could they be emptied, that all might be dumped in a single heap and the bags refilled without altering the content of any greatly. A bit of colored glass more or less would not matter. Perhaps that is how the Great Stuffer of Bags filled them in the first place—who knows? (May 11, 1928)

Note

1. Zora Neale Hurston, "How It Feels to Be Colored Me" in *World Tomorrow* (New York: Fellowship Press, 1928), pp. 215–216.

June Jordan

Born July 9, 1936, to Jamaican immigrant parents in the Harlem community in New York City, New York, June Millicent Jordan is an award-winning poet, essayist, novelist, librettist, educator, and activist who, in 1991, founded the Poetry for the People program at the University of California, Berkeley. She is author of over twenty-five books and a recipient of a Rockefeller Fellowship, Yaddo Fellowship, and, among numerous other awards, a National Endowment for the Arts Fellowship. Jordan's writings examine identity, civil rights, democracy, love, and language. For example, in "Nobody Mean More to Me Than You and the Future Life of Willie Jordan," she highlights explicit connections among language, identity, and power to argue for the import of Black English as a valuable system of communication. In the essay's opening, Jordan describes her undergraduate students' reactions to the Black English spoken by Celie, a character in Alice Walker's novel *The Color Purple*. Confronting their initial discomfort with seeing Black English in print helped Jordan's students to gain both an appreciation of their own oral use of the language and an awareness of the power of the language to ignite change within their communities. A focus on the cultural significance and linguistic richness of Black English led Jordan and her students to eventually devise rules, qualities, and guidelines for the language. Simultaneously, they wrote letters in Black English to newspapers and news stations in support of a classmate whose unarmed brother was killed by police officers. This essay not only validates Black English as a linguistic system but also situates it as a communal language of action.

Nobody Mean More to Me Than You[1] and the Future Life of Willie Jordan

June Jordan[2]

June Jordan (b. 1936) is professor of African American studies at the University of California, Berkeley. She is the author of novels, short stories, poetry, children's fiction, and biography. Her essays can be found in collections such as On Call *(1986),* Moving Toward Home: Political Essays *(1989) and* Technical Difficulties: African American Notes on the State of the Union *(1992). Jordan's most recent work is a musical,* I Was Looking at the Ceiling and Then I Saw the Sky: Earthquake-Romance *(1995), for which John Adams wrote the music. The essay "Nobody Mean More to Me than You and the Future Life of Willie Jordan" is found in* On Call. *She has also published stories and poems in numerous national magazines.*

Jordan thinks of writing, and especially of poetry, as a way toward empowerment. "Why should power and language coalesce in poetry? Because poetry is the medium for telling the truth, and because a poem is antithetical to lieslevasions and superficiality, anyone who becomes a practicing poet has an excellent chance of becoming somebody real, somebody known, self-defined and attuned to and listening and hungering for kindred real voices utterly/articulately different from his or her own voice."

Black English is not exactly a linguistic buffalo; as children, most of the thirty-five million Afro-Americans living here depend on this language for our discovery of the world. But then we approach our maturity inside a larger social body that will not support our efforts to become anything other than the clones of those who are neither our mothers nor our fathers. We begin to grow up in a house where every true mirror shows us the face of somebody who does not belong there, whose walk and whose talk will never look or sound "right," because that house was meant to shelter a family that is alien and hostile to us. As we learn our way around this environment, either we hide our original word habits, or we completely surrender our own voice, hoping to please those who will never respect anyone different from themselves: Black English is not exactly a linguistic buffalo, but we should understand its status as an endangered species, as a perishing, irreplaceable system of community intelligence, or we should expect its extinction, and, along with that, the extinguishing of much that constitutes our own proud, and singular identity.

What we casually call "English," less and less defers to England and its "gentlemen." "English" is no longer a specific matter of geography or an element of class privilege; more than thirty-three countries use this tool as a means of "intranational communication."[3] Countries as disparate as Zimbabwe and Malaysia, or Israel and Uganda, use it as their non-native currency of convenience. Obviously, this tool, this "English," cannot function inside thirty-three discrete societies on the basis of rules and values absolutely determined somewhere else, in a thirty-fourth other country, for example.

In addition to that staggering congeries of non-native users of English, there are five countries, or 333,746,000 people, for whom this thing called "English" serves as a native tongue.[4] Approximately ten percent of these native speakers of "English" are Afro-American citizens of the U.S.A. I cite these numbers and varieties of human beings dependent on "English" in order, quickly, to suggest how strange and how tenuous is any concept of "Standard English." Obviously, numerous forms of English now operate inside a natural, an uncontrollable, continuum of development. I would suppose "the standard" for English in Malaysia is not the same as "the standard" in Zimbabwe. I know that standard forms of English for Black people in this country do not copy that of whites. And, in fact, the structural differences between these two kinds of English have intensified, becoming more Black, or less white, despite the expected homogenizing effects of television[5] and other mass media.

Nonetheless, white standards of English persist, supreme and unquestioned, in these United States. Despite our multilingual population, and despite the deepening Black and white cleavage within that conglomerate, white standards control our official and popular judgments of verbal proficiency and correct, or incorrect, language skills, including speech. In contrast to India, where at least fourteen languages co-exist as legitimate Indian languages, in contrast to Nicaragua, where all citizens are legally entitled to formal school instruction in their regional or tribal languages, compulsory education in America compels accommodation to exclusively white forms of "English." White English, in America, is "Standard English."

This story begins two years ago. I was teaching a new course, "In Search of the Invisible Black Woman," and my rather large class seemed evenly divided between young Black women and men. Five or six white students also sat in attendance. With unexpected speed and enthusiasm we had moved through historical narratives of the 19th century to literature by and about Black women, in the 20th. I had assigned the first forty pages of Alice Walker's *The Color Purple*, and I came, eagerly, to class that morning:

"So!" I exclaimed, aloud. "What did you think? How did you like it?"

The students studied their hands, or the floor. There was no response. The tense, resistant feeling in the room fairly astounded me.

At last, one student, a young woman still not meeting my eyes, muttered something in my direction:

"What did you say?" I prompted her.
"Why she have them talk so funny. It don't sound right."
"You mean the language?"
Another student lifted his head: "It don't look right, neither. I couldn't hardly read it."

At this, several students dumped on the book. Just about unanimously, their criticisms targeted the language. I listened to what they wanted to say and silently marveled at the similarities between their casual speech patterns and Alice Walker's written version of Black English.

But I decided against pointing to these identical traits of syntax; I wanted not to make them self-conscious about their own spoken language—not while they clearly felt it was "wrong." Instead I decided to swallow my astonishment. Here was a negative Black reaction to a prize winning accomplishment of Black literature that white readers across the country had selected as a best seller. Black rejection was aimed at the one irreducibly Black element of Walker's work: the language—Celie's Black English. I wrote the opening lines of *The Color Purple* on the blackboard and asked the students to help me translate these sentences into Standard English:

You better not never tell nobody but God. It'd kill your mammy.
    Dear God,
    I am fourteen years old. I have always been a good girl. Maybe you can give me a sign letting me know what is happening to me.
    Last spring after Little Lucious come I heard them fussing. He was pulling on her arm. She say it too soon, Fonso. I aint well. Finally he leave her alone. A week go by, he pulling on her arm again. She say, Naw, I ain't gonna. Can't you see I'm already half dead, an all of the children.[6]

Our process of translation exploded with hilarity and even hysterical, shocked laughter: The Black writer, Alice Walker, knew what she was doing! If rudimentary criteria for good fiction includes the manipulation of language so that the syntax and diction of sentences will tell you the identity of speakers, the probable age and sex and class of speakers, and even the locale— urban/rural/southern/western—then Walker had written, perfectly. This is the translation into Standard English that our class produced:

Absolutely, one should never confide in anybody besides God. Your secrets could prove devastating to your mother.
    Dear God,
    I am fourteen years old, I have always been good. But now, could you help me to understand what is happening to me?
    Last spring, after my little brother, Lucious, was born, I heard my parents fighting. My father kept pulling at my mother's arm. But she told him, "It's too soon for sex, Alfonso. I am still not feeling well." Finally, my father left her alone. A week went by, and then he began bothering my mother, again: Pulling her arm. She told him, "No, I won't! Can't you see I'm already exhausted from all of these children?"

(Our favorite line was "It's too soon for sex, Alphonso.")

Once we could stop laughing, once we could stop our exponentially wild improvisations on the theme of Translated Black English, the students pushed me to explain their own negative first reactions to their spoken language on the printed page. I thought it was probably akin to the shock of seeing yourself in a photograph for the first time. Most of the students had never before seen a written facsimile of the way they talk. None of the students had ever learned how to read and write their own verbal system of communication: Black English. Alternatively, this fact began to baffle or else bemuse and then infuriate my students. Why not? Was it too late? Could they learn how to do it, now? And, ultimately, the final test question, the one testing my sincerity: Could I teach them? Because I had never taught anyone Black English and, as far as I knew, no one, anywhere in the United States, had ever offered such a course, the best I could say was "I'll try."

He looked like a wrestler.

He sat dead center in the packed room and, every time our eyes met, he quickly nodded his head as though anxious to reassure, and encourage, me.

Short, with strikingly broad shoulders and long arms, he spoke with a surprisingly high, soft voice that matched the soft bright movement of his eyes. His name was Willie Jordan. He would have seemed even more unlikely in the context of Contemporary Women's Poetry, except that ten or twelve other Black men were taking the course, as well. Still, Willie was conspicuous. His extreme fitness, the muscular density of his presence underscored the riveted, gentle attention that he gave to anything anyone said. Generally, he did not join the loud and rowdy dialogue flying back and forth, but there could be no doubt about his interest in our discussions. And, when he stood to present an argument he'd prepared, overnight, that nervous smile of his vanished and an irregular stammering replaced it, as he spoke with visceral sincerity, word by word.

That was how I met Willie Jordan. It was in between "In Search of the Invisible Black Woman" and "The Art of Black English." I was waiting for Departmental approval and I supposed that Willie might be, so to speak, killing time until he, too, could study Black English. But Willie really did want to explore Contemporary Women's poetry and, to that end, volunteered for extra research and never missed a class.

Towards the end of that semester, Willie approached me for an independent study project on South Africa. It would commence the next semester. I thought Willie's writing needed the kind of improvement only intense practice will yield. I knew his intelligence was outstanding. But he'd wholeheartedly opted for "Standard English" at a rather late age, and the results were stilted and frequently polysyllabic, simply for the sake of having more syllables. Willie's unnatural formality of language seemed to me consistent with the formality of his research into South African apartheid. As he projected his studies, he would have little time, indeed, for newspapers. Instead, more than 90 percent of his research would mean saturation in strictly historical, if not archival, material. I was certainly interested. It would be tricky to guide him into a more confident and spontaneous relationship both with language and apartheid. It was going to be wonderful to see what happened when he could catch up with himself, entirely, and talk back to the world.

September, 1984: Breezy fall weather and much excitement! My class, "The Art of Black English," was full to the limit of the fire laws. And, in Independent Study, Willie Jordan showed up, weekly, fifteen minutes early for each of our sessions. I was pretty happy to be teaching, altogether!

I remember an early class when a young brother, replete with his ever present pork-pie hat, raised his hand and then told us that most of what he'd heard was "all right" except it was "too clean." "The brothers on the street," he continued, "they mix it up more. Like 'fuck' and 'motherfuck.' Or like 'shit.'" He waited, I waited. Then all of us laughed a good while, and we got into a brawl about "correct" and "realistic" Black English that led to Rule 1.

Rule 1: *Black English is about a whole lot more than mothafuckin.*

As a criterion, we decided, "realistic" could take you anywhere you want to go. Artful places. Angry places. Eloquent and sweetalkin places. Polemical places. Church. And the local Bar & Grill. We were checking out a language, not a mood or a scene or one guy's forgettable mouthing off.

It was hard. For most of the students, learning Black English required a fallback to patterns and rhythms of speech that many of their parents had beaten out of them. I mean *beaten*. And, in a majority of cases, correct Black English could be achieved only by striving for *incorrect*

Standard English, something they were still pushing at, quite uncertainly. This state of affairs led to Rule 2.

Rule 2: *If it's wrong in Standard English it's probably right in Black English, or, at least, you're hot.*

It was hard. Roommates and family members ridiculed their studies, or remained incredulous, "You *studying* that shit? At school?" But we were beginning to feel the companionship of pioneers. And we decided that we needed another rule that would establish each one of us as equally important to our success. This was Rule 3.

Rule 3: *If it don't sound like something that come out somebody mouth then it don't sound right. If it don't sound right then it ain't hardly right. Period.*

This rule produced two weeks of compositions in which the students agonizingly tried to spell the sound of the Black English sentence they wanted to convey. But Black English is, preeminently, an oral/spoken means of communication. *And spelling don't talk.* So we needed Rule 4.

Rule 4: *Forget about the spelling. Let the syntax carry you.*

Once we arrived at Rule 4 we started to fly because syntax, the structure of an idea, leads you to the world view of the speaker and reveals her values. The syntax of a sentence equals the structure of your consciousness. If we insisted that the language of Black English adheres to a distinctive Black syntax, then we were postulating a profound difference between white and Black people, *per se*. Was it a difference to prize or to obliterate?

There are three qualities of Black English—the presence of life, voice, and clarity—that testify to a distinctive Black value system that we became excited about and self-consciously tried to maintain.

1. Black English has been produced by a pre-technocratic, if not anti-technological, culture. More, our culture has been constantly threatened by annihilation or, at least, the swallowed blurring of assimilation. Therefore, our language is a system constructed by people constantly needing to insist that we exist, that we are present. Our language devolves from a culture that abhors all abstraction, or anything tending to obscure or delete the fact of the human being who is here and now/the truth of the person who is speaking or listening. Consequently, *there is no passive voice construction possible in Black English.* For example, you cannot say, "Black English is being eliminated." You must say, instead, "White people eliminating Black English." The assumption of the presence of life governs all of Black English. Therefore, overwhelmingly, *all action takes place in the language of the present indicative.* And every sentence assumes the living and active participation of at least two human beings, the speaker and the listener.
2. A primary consequence of the person-centered values of Black English is the delivery of voice. If you speak or write Black English, your ideas will necessarily possess that otherwise elusive attribute, *voice*.
3. One main benefit following from the person-centered values of Black English is that of *clarity*. If your idea, your sentence, assumes the presence of at least two living and active people, you will make it understandable because the motivation behind every sentence is the wish to say something real to somebody real.

As the weeks piled up, translation from Standard English into Black English or vice versa occupied a hefty part of our course work.

Standard English (hereafter S.E.): "In considering the idea of studying Black English those questioned suggested—"

(What's the subject? Where's the person? Is anybody alive in there, in that idea?)

Black English (hereafter B.E.): "I been asking people what you think about somebody studying Black English and they answer me like this."

But there were interesting limits. You cannot "translate" instances of Standard English preoccupied with abstraction or with nothing/nobody evidently alive, into Black English. That would warp the language into uses antithetical to the guiding perspective of its community of users. Rather you must first change those Standard English sentences, themselves, into ideas consistent with the person-centered assumptions of Black English.

Guidelines for Black English

1. Minimal number of words for every idea: This is the source for the aphoristic and/or poetic force of the language; eliminate every possible word.
2. Clarity: If the sentence is not clear it's not Black English.
3. Eliminate use of the verb *to be* whenever possible. This leads to the deployment of more descriptive and, therefore, more precise verbs.
4. Use *be* or *been* only when you want to describe a chronic, ongoing state of things.
   He *be* at the office, by 9. (He is always at the office by 9.)
   He *been* with her since forever.
5. Zero copula: Always eliminate the verb *to be* whenever it would combine with another verb in Standard English.
   S.E.: She is going out with him.
   B.E.: She going out with him.
6. Eliminate *do* as in:
   S.E.: What do you think? What do you want?
   B.E.: What you think? What you want?

Rules number 3, 4, 5, and 6 provide for the use of the minimal number of verbs per idea and, therefore, greater accuracy in the choice of verb.

7. In general, if you wish to say something really positive, try to formulate the idea using emphatic negative structure.
   S.E.: He's fabulous.
   B.E.: He bad.
8. Use double or triple negatives for dramatic emphasis.
   S.E.: Tina Turner sings out of this world.
   B.E.: Ain nobody sing like Tina.
9. Never use the-*ed* suffix to indicate the past tense of a verb.
   S.E.: She closed the door.
   B.E.: She close the door. Or, she have close the door.
10. Regardless of intentional verb time, only use the third person singular, present indicative, for use of the verb *to have*, as an auxiliary.

S.E.: He had his wallet then he lost it.
B.E.: He have him wallet then he lose it.
S.E.: He had seen that movie.
B.E.: We seen that movie. Or, we have see that movie.

11. Observe a minimal inflection of verbs. Particularly, never change from the first person singular forms to the third person singular.
    S.E.: Present Tense Forms: He goes to the store.
    B.E.: He go to the store.
    S.E.: Past Tense Forms: He went to the store.
    B.E.: He go to the store. Or, he gone to the store. Or, he been to the store.

12. The possessive case scarcely ever appears in Black English. Never use an apostrophe ('s) construction. If you wander into a possessive case component of an idea, then keep logically consistent: *ours, his, theirs, mines.* But, most likely, if you bump into such a component, you have wandered outside the underlying world-view of Black English.
    S.E.: He will take their car tomorrow.
    B.E.: He taking they car tomorrow.

13. Plurality: Logical consistency, continued: If the modifier indicates plurality then the noun remains in the singular case.
    S.E.: He ate twelve doughnuts.
    B.E.: He eat twelve doughnut.
    S.E.: She has many books.
    B.E.: She have many book.

14. Listen for, or invent, special Black English forms of the past tense, such as: "He losted it. That what she felted." If they are clear and readily understood, then use them.

15. Do not hesitate to play with words, sometimes inventing them: e.g. "astropotomous" means huge like a hippo plus astronomical and, therefore, signifies real big.

16. In Black English, unless you keenly want to underscore the past tense nature of an action, stay in the present tense and rely on the overall context of your ideas for the conveyance of time and sequence.

17. Never use the suffix-*ly* form of an adverb in Black English.
    S.E.: The rain came down rather quickly.
    B.E.: The rain come down pretty quick.

18. Never use the indefinite article *an* in Black English.
    S.E.: He wanted to ride an elephant.
    B.E.: He want to ride him a elephant.

19. Invariant syntax: in correct Black English it is possible to formulate an imperative, an interrogative, and a simple declarative idea with the same syntax:
    B.E.: You going to the store?

You going to the store.
You going to the store!
Where was Willie Jordan? We'd reached the mid-term of the semester. Students had formulated Black English guidelines, by consensus, and they were now writing with remarkable beauty, purpose, and enjoyment:
I ain hardly speakin for everybody but myself so understan that.—Kim Parks
Samples from student writings:

Janie have a great big ole hole inside her. Tea Cake the only thing that fit that hole . . .

That pear tree beautiful to Janie, especial when bees fiddlin with the blossomin pear there growing large and lovely. But personal speakin, the love she get from staring at that tree ain the love what starin back at her in them relationship. (Monica Morris)

Love is a big theme in, *They Eye Was Watching God*. Love show people new corners inside theyself. It pull out good stuff and stuff back bad stuff . . . Joe worship the doing uh his own hand and need other people to worship him too. But he ain't think about Janie that she a person and ought to live like anybody common do. Queen life not for Janie. (Monica Morris)

In both life and writin, Black womens have varietous experience of love that be cold like a iceberg or fiery like a inferno. Passion got for the other partner involve, man or woman, seem as shallow, ankle-deep water or the most profoundest abyss. (Constance Evans)

Family love another bond that ain't never break under no pressure. (Constance Evans)

You know it really cold/When the friend you/Always get out the fire/Act like they don't know you/When you in the heat. (Constance Evans)

Big classroom discussion bout love at this time. I never take no class where us have any long arguin for and against for two or three day. New to me and great. I find the class time talkin a million time more interestin than detail bout the book. (Kathy Esseks)

As these examples suggest, Black English no longer limited the students, in any way. In fact, one of them, Philip Garfield, would shortly "translate" a pivotal scene from Ibsen's *Doll House*, as his final term paper.

> NORA: I didn't gived no shit. I thinked you a asshole back then, too, you make it so hard for me save mines husband life.
> KROGSTAD: Girl, it clear you ain't any idea what you done. You done exact what once done, and I losed my reputation over it.
> NORA: You asks me believe you once act brave save you wife life?
> KROGSTAD: Law care less why you done it.
> NORA: Law must suck.
> KROGSTAD: Suck or no, if I wants, judge screw you wid dis paper.
> NORA: No way, man.
>
> (Philip Garfield)

But where was Willie? Compulsively punctual, and always thoroughly prepared with neatly typed compositions, he had disappeared. He failed to show up for our regularly scheduled conference, and I received neither a note nor a phone call of explanation. A whole week went by. I wondered if Willie had finally been captured by the extremely current happenings in South Africa: passage of a new constitution that did not enfranchise the Black majority, and militant Black South African reaction to that affront. I wondered if he'd been hurt, somewhere. I wondered if the serious workload of weekly readings and writings had overwhelmed him and changed his mind about independent study. Where was Willie Jordan?

One week after the first conference that Willie missed, he called: "Hello, Professor Jordan? This is Willie. I'm sorry I wasn't there last week. But something has come up and I'm pretty upset. I'm sorry but I really can't deal right now."

I asked Willie to drop by my office and just let me see that he was okay. He agreed to do that. When I saw him I knew something hideous had happened. Something had hurt him and scared him to the marrow. He was all agitated and stammering and terse and incoherent. At last, his sadly jumbled account let me surmise, as follows: Brooklyn police had murdered his unarmed, twenty-five-year-old brother, Reggie Jordan. Neither Willie nor his elderly parents knew what to do about it. Nobody from the press was interested. His folks had no money. Police ran his family around and around, to no point. And Reggie was really dead. And Willie wanted to fight, but he felt helpless.

With Willie's permission I began to try to secure legal counsel for the Jordan family. Unfortunately Black victims of police violence are truly numerous while the resources available to prosecute their killers are truly scarce. A friend of mine at the Center for Constitutional Rights estimated that just the preparatory costs for bringing the cops into court normally approaches $180,000. Unless the execution of Reggie Jordan became a major community cause for organizing, and protest, his murder would simply become a statistical item.

Again, with Willie's permission, I contacted every newspaper and media person I could think of. But the William Bastone feature article in *The Village Voice* was the only result from that canvassing.

Again, with Willie's permission, I presented the case to my class in Black English. We had talked about the politics of language. We had talked about love and sex and child abuse and men and women. But the murder of Reggie Jordan broke like a hurricane across the room.

There are few "issues" as endemic to Black life as police violence. Most of the students knew and respected and liked Jordan. Many of them came from the very neighborhood where the murder had occurred. All of the students had known somebody close to them who had been killed by police, or had known frightening moments of gratuitous confrontation with the cops. They wanted to do everything at once to avenge death. Number One: They decided to compose personal statements of condolence to Willie Jordan and his family written in Black English. Number Two: They decided to compose individual messages to the police, in Black English. These should be prefaced by an explanatory paragraph composed by the entire group. Number Three: These individual messages, with their lead paragraph, should be sent to *Newsday*.

The morning after we agreed on these objectives, one of the young women students appeared with an unidentified visitor, who sat through the class, smiling in a peculiar, comfortable way.

Now we had to make more tactical decisions. Because we wanted the messages published, and because we thought it imperative that our outrage be known by the police, the tactical question was this: Should the opening, group paragraph be written in Black English or Standard English?

I have seldom been privy to a discussion with so much heart at the dead heat of it. I will never forget the eloquence, the sudden haltings of speech, the fierce struggle against tears, the furious throwaway, and useless explosions that this question elicited.

That one question contained several others, each of them extraordinarily painful to even contemplate. How best to serve the memory of Reggie Jordan? Should we use the language of the killers—Standard English—in order to make our ideas acceptable to those controlling the killers? But wouldn't what we had to say be rejected, summarily, if we said it in our own language, the language of the victim, Reggie Jordan? But if we sought to express ourselves by abandoning our language wouldn't that mean our suicide on top of Reggie's murder? But if we expressed ourselves in our own language wouldn't that be suicidal to the wish to communicate with those who, evidently, did not give a damn about us/Reggie/police violence in the Black community?

At the end of one of the longest, most difficult hours of my own life, the students voted, unanimously, to preface their individual messages with a paragraph composed in the language of Reggie Jordan. "*At least we don't give up nothing else. At least we stick to the truth: Be who we been. And stay all the way with Reggie.*"

It was heartbreaking to proceed, from that point. Everyone in the room realized that our decision in favor of Black English had doomed our writings, even as the distinctive reality of our Black lives always has doomed our efforts to "be who we been" in this country.

I went to the blackboard and took down this paragraph, dictated by the class:

...YOU COPS!
    WE THE BROTHER AND SISTER OF WILLIE JORDAN, A FELLOW STONY BROOK STUDENT WHO THE BROTHER OF THE DEAD REGGIE JORDAN, REGGIE, LIKE MANY BROTHER AND SISTER, HE A VICTIM OF BRUTAL RACIST POLICE, OCTOBER 25, 1984. US APPALL, FED UP, BECAUSE THAT ANOTHER SENSELESS DEATH WHAT OCCUR IN OUR COMMUNITY. THIS WHAT WE FEEL, THIS, FROM OUR HEART, FOR WE AIN'T STAYIN' SILENT NO MORE.

With the completion of this introduction, nobody said anything. I asked for comments. At this invitation, the unidentified visitor, a young Black man, ceaselessly smiling, raised his hand. He was, it so happens, a rookie cop. He had just joined the force in September and, he said he thought he should clarify a few things. So he came forward and sprawled easily into a posture of barroom, or fireside, nostalgia:

"See," Officer Charles enlightened us, "most times when you out on the street and something come down you do one of two things. Over-react or under-react. Now, if you under-react then you can get yourself kilt. And if you over-react then maybe you kill somebody. Fortunately it's about nine times out of ten and you will over-react. So the brother got kilt. And I'm sorry about that, believe me. But what you have to understand is what kilt him: Over-reaction. That's all. Now you talk about Black people and white police but see, now, I'm a cop myself. And (big smile) I'm Black. And just a couple months ago I was on the other side. But see it's the same for me. You a cop, you the ultimate authority: the Ultimate Authority. And you on the street, most of the time you can only do one of two things: over-react or under-react. That's all it is with the brother. Over-reaction. Didn't have nothing to do with race."

That morning Officer Charles had the good fortune to escape without being boiled alive. But barely. And I remember the pride of his smile when I read about the fate of Black policemen and other collaborators, in South Africa. I remember him, and I remember the shock and palpable feeling of shame that filled the room. It was as though that foolish, and deadly, young man had just relieved himself of his foolish, and deadly, explanation, face to face with the grief of Reggie Jordan's father and Reggie Jordan's mother. Class ended quietly. I copied the paragraph from the blackboard, collected the individual messages and left to type them up.

Newsday rejected the piece.

The Village Voice could not find room in their "Letters" section to print the individual messages from the students to the police.

None of the TV news reporters picked up the story.

Nobody raised $180,000 to prosecute the murder of Reggie Jordan.

Reggie Jordan is really dead.

I asked Willie Jordan to write an essay pulling together everything important to him from that semester. He was still deeply beside himself with frustration and amazement and loss. This is what he wrote, unedited, and in its entirety:

Throughout the course of this semester I have been researching the effects of oppression and exploitation along racial lines in South Africa and its neighboring countries. I have become aware of South African police brutalization of native Africans beyond the extent of the law, even though the laws themselves are catalyst affliction upon Black men, women, and children. Many Africans die each year as a result of the deliberate use of police force to protect the white power structure.

Social control agents in South Africa, such as policemen, are also used to force compliance among citizens through both overt and covert tactics. It is not uncommon to find bold-faced coercion and cold-blooded killings of Blacks by South African police for undetermined and/or inadequate reasons. Perhaps the truth is that the only reasons for this heinous treatment of Blacks rests in racial differences. We should also understand that what is conveyed through the media is not always accurate and may sometimes be construed as the tip of the iceberg at best.

I recently received a painful reminder that racism, poverty, and the abuse of power are global problems which are by no means unique to South Africa. On October 25, 1984, at approximately 3:00 P.M. my brother, Mr. Reginald Jordan, was shot and killed by two New York City policemen from the 75th precinct in the East New York section of Brooklyn. His life ended at the age of twenty-five. Even up to this current point in time the Police Department has failed to provide my family, which consists of five brothers, eight sisters, and two parents, with a plausible reason for Reggie's death. Out of the many stories that were given to my family by the Police Department, not one of them seems to hold water. In fact, I honestly believe that the Police Department's assessment of my brother's murder is nothing short of ABSOLUTE BULLSHIT, and thus far no evidence had been produced to alter perception of the situation.

Furthermore, I believe that one of three cases may have occurred in this incident. First, Reggie's death may have been the desired outcome of the police officer's action, in which case the killing was premeditated. Or, it was a case of mistaken identity, which clarifies the fact that the two officers who killed my brother and their commanding parties are all grossly incompetent. Or, both of the above cases are correct, i.e., Reggie's murderers intended to kill him and the Police Department behaved insubordinately.

Part of the argument of the officers who shot Reggie was that he had attacked one of them and took his gun. This was their major claim. They also said that only one of them had actually shot Reggie. The facts, however, speak for themselves. According to the Death Certificate and autopsy report, Reggie was shot eight times from point-blank range. The Doctor who performed the autopsy told me himself that two bullets entered the side of my brother's head, four bullets were sprayed into his back, and two bullets struck him in the back of his legs. It is obvious that unnecessary force was used by the police and that it is extremely difficult to shoot someone in his back when he is attacking or approaching you.

After experiencing a situation like this and researching South Africa I believe that to a large degree, justice may only exist as rhetoric. I find it difficult to talk of true justice when the oppression of my people both at home and abroad attests to the fact that inequality and injustice are serious problems whereby Blacks and Third World people are perpetually short-changed by society. Something has to be done about the way in which this world is set up. Although it is a difficult task, we do have the power to make a change.

—Willie J. Jordan, Jr. EGL 487, Section 58, November 14, 1984

It is my privilege to dedicate this book to the future life of Willie J. Jordan, Jr. August 8, 1985

Notes

1. Black English aphorism crafted by Monica Morris, a junior at S.U.N.Y. at Stony Brook, October, 1984.—JORDAN'S NOTE.

2. June Jordan, "Nobody Mean More to Me Than You and The Future Life of Willie Jordan," *Harvard Educational Review* 58.3 (1988): 363–375. Also published in June Jordan, *Moving Toward Home: Political Essays* (London: Virago, 1989), pp. 175–189.

3. *English Is Spreading, but What Is English?* A presentation by Professor S. N. Sridahr, Dept. Of Linguistics, S.U.N.Y. at Stony Brook, April 9, 1985; Dean's Conversation among the Disciplines.—JORDAN'S NOTE.

4. Ibid.—JORDAN'S NOTE.

5. *New York Times*, March 15, 1985, Section One, p. 14: Report on study by Linguistics at the University of Pennsylvania.—JORDAN'S NOTE.

6. Alice Walker, *The Color Purple*, p. 11, Harcourt Brace, N.Y.—JORDAN'S NOTE.

Keith Gilyard

Utilizing a sophisticated combination of autobiographical narrative writing, academic prose, and document analysis, distinguished professor of English and eminent scholar in African American Studies at Pennsylvania State University, former chair of the Conference on College Composition and Communication, and past president of the National Council of Teachers of English Keith Gilyard examines issues in language and literacy education for African Americans. In the closing chapter of his book, Gilyard reflects on his high school years by recalling his difficulties with existing "between institutions"—high school and the streets. As he reflects on his earlier experiences, he describes how public education attempts to erase people's cultural identities, and exclude one's mother tongue, instead of necessarily working to recognize and sustain linguistic and cultural pluralism. A specific way that schools work to erase one's cultural identity is by marking languages and linguistic systems other than "Standard English" as subordinate, inferior, and languages of failure. Gilyard notes that Black peoples' affirmation of Black English, or African American language, signifies a level of resistance to dominant-identified ways of talking and being. Hence, the success of public education for students and teachers, specifically, and for us all, generally, heavily depends on a redefinition of success to account for diverse cultural and linguistic practices that include Black English.

Conclusion

Keith Gilyard[1]

With a rap or two of the magistrate's gavel punctuating my junior high school experience, I reached new sociolinguistic heights. I had successfully wielded language as an instrument of power in the often-intimidating world of the legal system. This tactical success gave me greater confidence than ever my ability to manage impression in novel situations, using language as the primary device, and it also served as dramatic notice of a truth I was well aware of by then: inadequate language skills would not be my downfall. By the close of eighth grade, with my reading level at a solid 12.2 according to my performance on the Metropolitan Achievement Exam and with a healthy 86 percentile ranking on the Iowa Test of Educational Development, I had moved far beyond any barrier constructed solely with Standard English. A major purpose of this book has been to describe this movement, yet this book is not simply about positive accomplishments. Contrary to what some might have anticipated, mastery of the standard dialect did not in and of itself lead to outstanding formal academic progress and, as the narrative indicates, I foundered badly.

My average in academic subjects dropped from 84 at the end of seventh grade to 79 at the close of eighth grade to 70 at the close of ninth grade. As indicated, I made a comeback upon entering Stuyvesant High, finishing the tenth grade with a 90.2 average for the spring semester. In the process of doing so I scored the previously reported 100 on the Regents Examination in Geometry, received a grade of 94 in English, and earned a 91 in Spanish II (after failing Spanish I with a 55 just one year earlier).

Then the heroin usage began and the grades plummeted once again. I averaged 78 for the latter half of my junior year and 61.7 the last half of my senior year, this last feat highlighted by the 40 in English and 56 general absences. I was torn between institutions, between value systems. At times the tug of school was greater, therefore the 90.2 average. On other occasions the streets were a more powerful lure, thus the heroin and the 40 in English and a brief visit to the Adolescent Remand Shelter (I couldn't talk my way out of that one.) I saw no middle ground or, more accurately, no total ground on which anomalies like me could gather. I tried to be a hip schoolboy, but it was impossible to achieve that persona. In the group I most loved, to be fully hip meant to repudiate a school system in which African-American consciousness was undervalued or ignored; in which, in spite of the many nightmares around us, I was urged to keep my mind on the Dream, to play the fortunate token, to keep my head straight down in my books and "make it." And I pumped more and more dope into my arms. It was a nearly fatal response, but an almost inevitable one.

Several recent and popular books can be used to shed further light on my predicament. In fact, *Hunger of Memory* by Richard Rodriguez (1983) helped motivate me to produce this present work. Rodriguez, a Mexican-American, reveals the storm of torment he has weathered in order to assimilate into the culture of mainstream America. He has chased the middle-class dream and caught it, but the psychic costs have been enormous, as he himself well knows. He has suffered alienation to the point of feeling apart from his own family, has virtually given up his native tongue, has zealously pursued the ideals of his upper-middle-class companions, has endured the caustic rebuttals of opponents who dislike his anti-affirmative action and anti-bilingual education views, and he has felt that all the pain has been worth it. Whether it has indeed been worth it is something only Rodriguez can decide, in fact, must decide, but he is mistaken to advocate an educational policy under which his type of pain is to be justified rather than prevented. Early on in his book he writes, "I remember what was so grievously lost to define what was necessarily gained" (p. 6); I immediately scribbled a question in the margin: But was it necessarily lost? The answer, however, is not easily arrived at. Of course it (his culture) was necessarily lost inasmuch as he chose to give it up. What one does is necessary in one's own eyes. But in a larger sense, we are asking if such cultural loss is a desirable aim of public education, and this question has only one answer: No! More specifically, getting back to the issue of language, the eradication of one tongue is not prerequisite to the learning of a second. Rodriguez participated in such self-annihilation for *as long as he did* because he thought it benefited him personally. It would be tragic, however, to translate his own appraisal of his pain into pedagogy.

Rodrigues asserts that: "Radical educationalists meanwhile complain that ghetto schools 'oppress' students by trying to mold them, stifling native characteristics. The truer critique would be just the reverse: not that schools change ghetto students too much, but while they may promote the occasional scholarship student, they change most students barely at all" (p. 68). If one has ever watched the gleam in the eyes of kindergarteners fade to smoldering anger before they even reach adolescence, if the children Kohl or Kozol or Levy or Fader or Collins has taught are at all real characters, then one knows all too much about some of the damaging changes that the public school system has wrought.

Rodriguez just ignores reality. His thinking is characterized by the failure to stretch his own arguments out to logical conclusions, by the passing off of his own transactional choices as outer-determined inevitabilities, again, by pushing his pain as policy instead of using it to question policy. One would expect him to fumble a discussion of Black English and, predictably, he delivers:

> I remember the black political activists who have argued in favor of using black English in schools. (Their argument varies only slightly from that made by foreign-language bilingualists.) I have heard "radical" linguists make the point that black English is a complex and intricate version of English. And I do not doubt it. But neither do I think that black English should be a language of public instruction. What makes black English inappropriate in classrooms is not something *in* the language. It is rather what lower-class speakers make of it. Just as Spanish would have been a dangerous language for me to have used at the start of my education, so black English would be a dangerous language to use in the schooling of teenagers for whom it reinforces feelings of public separateness.
>
> (pp. 33–34)

Rodriguez has surely hit upon a dilemma, one not to be taken lightly. But I think the most potentially dangerous thing concerning public education is to allow it to remain pretty much as it has been. Important works concerning language instruction, several of which I have cited thus far, contain quite clear warnings against suppressing students' language. Such action helps create failing students, provides an inadequate support system for scholarship students, and may promote within the latter group negative self-concepts. Rodriguez is aware of these dangers, particularly those involving scholarship students. After all, he was a victim himself. However, he doesn't see that part of the solution to the problem lies in using the children's own languages in school. He insists on cultural suicide, a conclusion totally unappealing to me, one I rejected as an adolescent.

John Edgar Wideman's book, *Brothers and Keepers* (1984), provides related insights. Wideman, whose career has been even more distinguished than that of Rodriguez, has lived through a similar process of cultural self-denial. Part of what makes his book more refreshing to me, though, is that he is still trying to come to grips with his personal history; he doesn't ask anyone to emulate him. Much of this critical self-examination is motivated by the guilt he feels over the fact that his brother is doing a life sentence for murder; nevertheless, his self-exploration is quite honest and revealing.

A question that keeps nagging Wideman is this: How could he and his brother, both from the same background, undergo such vastly different experiences? But actually the answer is not all that complicated. They had different visions. John, a child of the fifties, strongly identified with mainstream America and, like Rodriguez, he was willing to commit cultural suicide to gain membership. He writes:

> To get ahead, to make something of myself, college had seemed a logical, necessary step; my exile, my flight from home began with good grades, with good English, with setting myself apart long before I'd earned a scholarship and a train ticket over the mountains to Philadelphia. With that willed alienation behind me, between us, guilt was predictable. One measure of my success was the distance I'd put between us. Coming home was a kind of bragging, like the suntans people bring back from Hawaii in the middle of winter. It's sure fucked up around here, ain't it? But look at me, I got away. I got mine. I didn't want to be caught looking back. I needed home to reassure myself of how far I'd come. If I ever doubted how good I had it away at school in that world of books, exams, pretty, rich white girls, a roommate from Long Island who unpacked more pairs of brand-new jockey shorts and T-shirts than they had in Kaufmann's department store, if I ever had any hesitations or reconsiderations about the path I'd chosen, youall were back home in the ghetto to remind me how lucky I was.
>
> (p. 27)

I had no desire, as John did, to alienate myself from my community.

Robby Wideman, a child of the sixties, ten years John's junior, only fourteen months older than I, did not, as I did not, share his brother's aspirations. His adolescent perspective could be summed up as follows:

> In the real world, the world left for me, it was unacceptable to be "good," it was square to be smart in school, it was cool to be cold to your woman and the people that loved you. The things we liked we called "bad." "Man, that was a bad girl." The world of the angry black kid growing up in the sixties was a world in which to be in was to be out—out of touch with the square world and all of its rules on what's right and wrong. The thing was to make your own rules, do your own thing, but make sure it's contrary to what society says or is.
>
> (p. 58)

Robby's reasoning was the type of reasoning that often made sense to me. It was more than coincidence, therefore, that in the summer of 1968 we both took that hard fall down into the world of heroin addiction. Robby just didn't make it back in time to avoid prison.

No one paid more for the type of cultural conflict being discussed here than Edmund Perry. He lost his life. A teenager from Harlem, Perry finished four years at Phillips Exeter, one of the most prestigious prep schools in the country, only to be killed less than two weeks after graduation, allegedly during the act of mugging an undercover police officer. A cop's bullet canceled Edmund's full scholarship to Stanford University. Edmund's brother, Jonah, a student at Cornell University, was tried as an accomplice but was subsequently acquitted. During the furor surrounding the case, when the Perry boys were symbols of general Black rage directed at the police department or useful icons for self-serving types, one thing became increasingly clear. Not many people, especially Blacks, allowed for the complexity of Edmund or Jonah. Reporter Robert Sam Anson (1987) illustrates this point well in *Best Intentions*. The argument that scholarship students couldn't be involved in street crime is a shallow conception. I happen to think the Perrys were guilty. I was saddened by the event but not surprised at all. The very day Edmund Perry died I took my oral examinations at New York University. As the last step in earning a doctorate in English Education, I was called upon to discuss much of the information contained in the book now before you.

It is significant to note that many of the students Anson interviewed at Exeter said that Edmund was too hung up on "Blackness," said that they had grown tired of hearing it. Easy enough for them to say, it wasn't their immediate problem. Many educators, however, must continue to listen. Edmund Perry wasn't the last person to suffer a kind of enforced educational schizophrenia, and the world is a more complex place than a Michael Jackson video in which the Harlem-boy-at-prep-school dilemma is resolved with a series of sublime dance steps capped by a sermon. As part of the present movement for educational reform, along with the call for increased salaries, professionalization, greater teacher input in shaping curriculum, mandatory preschool, less powerful bureaucracies, and so on, there must be an insistence that educators understand and indicate by their actions the importance of cultural and linguistic pluralism in educational settings. Why fight for better salaries for teachers so they can do a higher paid job of alienating and attempting to eradicate?

That teachers break the confines of monoculturalism is more crucial than ever before. It has been suggested in some circles, given the history of Black-White classroom confrontations, that the solution is an increase in the number of African-American teachers. If such candidates were not into cultural self-denial (a phenomenon too widespread), it seems a reasonable remedy and, indeed, there is no question that the recruitment of minority teachers should be a priority. Nonetheless, current data show that the percentage of African-American public school teachers is decreasing and probably will continue to do so. Whitaker (1989) reports that because of low pay, undesirable work conditions, and overall frustration with school systems, African-Americans are shunning careers in education. It is predicted, he reveals, that by the turn of the century 40 percent of the students in public schools will be Black while less than 5 percent of the teachers will be so.

Aside from this specific concern, demographics indicate that schools all over the nation are becoming more and more ethnically diverse. Raspberry (1988) reports that ethnic diversity is potentially upsetting to the "civic paradise" of Minneapolis-St. Paul: "For the first time, whites are on the way to becoming a minority in Twin Cities public schools. The new immigrants include Filipinos, Vietnamese, Hmong from Laos and an influx of blacks quite different from the upwardly mobile managers, technicians and educators the area is used to dealing with" (p. 3B).

As this whole educational enterprise proceeds inexorably but unsteadily toward the twenty-first century, language educators in particular must prepare themselves to function productively in multicultural classrooms. Terry Dean (1989) has suggested specific techniques that may be useful. Having worked with students from over thirty ethnic groups, he assigns writing topics about culture itself, about language itself, to ensure that student-centered discussions of difference, collision, and assimilation, are central to the course of study. Dean understands that "how students handle the cultural transitions that occur in the acquisition of academic discourse affects how successfully they acquire that discourse" (p. 23). Add a multi-cultural literature to the mix and you have a good start toward a model language arts classroom.

Over the years, roughly 85 percent of Dean's students have expressed the belief that they do not have to give up their home and cultural values to succeed in school. This has been the attitude of thousands of African-Americans all along. What has been commonly referred to by educators as "failure" to learn Standard English is more accurately termed an act of resistance: Black students affirming, through Black English, their sense of self in the face of a school system and society that deny the same. It is not at all shocking to me, as it was to many, that a more recent study by Labov (see Stevens 1985) demonstrates that the language of many Blacks is diverging more and more from Standard English. With continued lack of equal opportunity in many areas, with increased racial polarization, only those who underestimate the significance of language as a symbol of protest or group solidarity could expect otherwise.

It can be said that the cultural conflict that has confronted African-Americans in schools "got me later," as it did Robby Wideman and Edmund Perry. However, it finished off many students "sooner," caused them to shrink away from formal education before they could gain or, more importantly, even appreciate the enormous power to be had through encounters with a wide variety of books, of articles, of conversations, and, by way of writing, through encounters with their innermost selves. These students were helped to fail before they could fully develop the sociolinguistic ability necessary to educate themselves.

. . . and mostly they lead marginal lives of regret and self-blame and eventually they preach to their children about, uh hunh, the virtues of the school system . . . .

I have tried to show in this book that language instruction and school education in general can only be a widespread success, in the humanitarian sense of the word, when teachers stop assuming that students are inferior and/or have nothing to contribute to the educative process other than to sit and absorb. I don't know all that must be done, however, to break the cycle of failure. But to successfully challenge current practices that justify eradicationist attempts aimed against African-American identity and the language variety in which that identity is most clearly realized is a worthwhile place to begin.

Note

1. Keith Gilyard, "Chapter 9: Conclusion," in *Voices of the Self: A Study of Language Competence* (Detroit: Wayne State University Press, 1991), pp. 159–165.

Arlette Ingram Willis

Professor of curriculum and instruction at the University of Illinois, Urbana-Champaign, Arlette Willis's research examines the applicability of critical pedagogy, multicultural literature, and a critical history of literacy in preservice teacher education programs. Her teaching and research are framed by a critically conscious approach to language and literacy studies, and her essay "Reading the World of School Literacy" exemplifies this approach. In her essay, she describes the literacy encounters and schooling experiences of her then nine-year-old son, Jake, who struggles to see himself and have himself seen by others, including teachers, in light of his multiplicities: as an African American, a male, and a literacy learner. In highlighting Jake's struggles, Willis critiques cultural accommodation in order to posit a definition of school literacy that includes multiple understandings of culture, language, and literacy, given the diversity of students living and attending schools in the United States. In so doing, she insists that students, particularly culturally and linguistically diverse students, not be devalued or ignored in school-sponsored literacy teaching and learning. Instead, they should be seen as "valid sources of literacy acquisition" (p. 34) whose identities, lived conditions, and knowledge are central to expanded meanings of literacy. She concludes her essay by offering specific recommendations of this expanded, more inclusive view of literacy for teacher education programs that work with preservice and in-service teachers, and for the types of literacy curricula that are utilized in schools.

Reading the World of School Literacy: Contextualizing the Experience of a Young African American Male

Arlette Ingram Willis[1]

Let me share a conversation that I had with my nine-year-old son, and the context in which it occurred:

It's a cold, frosty winter morning, and everyone has left for work or school except my youngest son Jake and me. I am busy applying last-minute touches to my makeup and encouraging Jake, in the next room, to "step it up." I wonder why he is dragging around; school starts in ten minutes and we haven't yet left the house. Jake knows the routine; I wonder if something is troubling him. So, I peek around the corner and find him looking forlorn—you know, a scowl on his face, a look of growing despair and sadness. I forget about the clock and attend to him.

"Jake, what's wrong? Why are you so unhappy?" I ask.

"We have the Young Authors [writing] Contest today, and I don't have anything to write about."

"Sure you do. There are lots of things you can write about," I encourage him. [I believe people write best about those subjects they know and care about.) *"Why don't you write about baseball or soccer?"*

"No," he replies. "A kid at our school wrote about cancer last year, and the story went all the way to the next state [regionals]."

"Well," I answer, "maybe you should write about something funny—like when you go to the barbershop. You and your brothers are always talking about your trips there."[2]

"Oh no, Mom, they wouldn't understand. When I just get my haircut, they always ask me, 'Why do you have that line in your hair?' 'It's not a line, it's a part,' I try to tell them. I can't write about the barbershop. They won't understand."

"Well," I say, trying to clarify what I really mean, "I don't mean write about getting a haircut. I mean writing about all the funny people that come in and the things that happen while you are at the barbershop. You and your brothers always come home tellin' a funny story and laugh about it for the rest of the week. That's what I mean by writing about the barbershop."

"No, Mom. They won't understand," he insists.

"What do you mean, 'they won't understand?' Who is this 'they'?" I ask.

"The people in my class," he replies, somewhat frustrated.

Jake continues, "You should read this story that M. wrote. It is a mystery story and it's really good. I can't beat that story. I'll bring you a copy of it if I can. I know it will win." (Sadder now that he has had time to consider his competition, Jake turns and walks toward his room.)

Wanting him to participate in the contest, I ask, "How do you know M.'s story is good?"

"She read it in class. Everybody said it's really good," he responds.

"Well, I still think you should try. You are a really good writer. Look at all the 'good stuff' you wrote in Mrs. S.'s room. You could rewrite some of it and turn it in."

Finally he answers, "I'll think about it," and we go off to school.

As I remember the conversation, Jake's tone of voice hinted at both frustration and defensiveness. I interpreted his use of phrases like "they always ask" and "I try to tell them" to mean that since he gets his hair cut every two weeks, it gets pretty tiresome answering the same questions from his classmates so frequently.[3] Furthermore, I interpreted his intonation to mean that he has had to stand his ground with other children who either do not agree with his definition of a "part," or who try to define its meaning for him.

I believe that Jake cannot bring this aspect of his life and culture into the classroom because he doesn't feel that it will be understood by his classmates and teacher. When Jake says "They won't understand," I interpret his words to mean that if his classmates cannot understand the simplest action in getting a haircut—the barber taking less than ten seconds to place a part in his hair—how can he expect them to understand the context and culture that surround the entire event. Also, I see Jake's reluctance to share something as commonplace in his home and community life as a haircut as a way of distancing this portion of his life from the life he leads at school. It seems that he has come to understand that as an African American he must constantly make a mediating effort to help others understand events that appear to be commonplace on the surface, but are in fact culturally defined.

Several interwoven incidents have helped me to understand the conversation with Jake. I will briefly describe them to provide the context for my understanding of the subtle, yet ever-present and unquestioned role of cultural accommodation that occurs in the school literacy experiences of children from diverse backgrounds. I have been teaching courses in multicultural literature at my university for several years. After my fall 1993 course, I reflected, using journal writing, on my growing experience teaching multicultural literature courses.[4] Teaching these courses has led me to a more informed understanding of how, in the practice of school literacy, there are many culturally defined moments of conflict that call daily for cultural understanding, knowledge, and sensitivity from teachers. These "moments" also challenge non-mainstream students to choose between cultural assimilation and accommodation, or resistance. My journal entries centered on my readings, research, and, most importantly, my daily conversations about school life with my three sons, who range in age from nine to seventeen. In my classes, I have often shared my sons' school experiences and my reactions to them in an effort to help my students understand how teachers' daily subtle and seemingly inconsequential decisions can affect the learning of the children they teach.

A striking example of a teacher's unintentional disregard for the cultural history, understanding, experiences, and voice of a student occurred when my oldest son struggled to meet the requirements of a national essay contest entitled, "What it means to be an American." One of the contest's restrictions was that students should not mention the concept of race. My son thought this was an unfair and impossible task to complete, since his African American identity is synonymous with his being American. Yet, his efforts to articulate the difficulty of the task to his English teacher were frustrated by her response that, although she was empathic, she did not have the authority to change the rules. I intervened and spoke with the teacher at length about my son's values, beliefs, and his unwillingness to compromise himself in order to compete in an essay contest in which he had little or no interest other than a grade.

My second son also had a similar experience involving unintentional cultural insensitivity. He is a member of the school band, which was having its fall concert. While attending, I noticed that all the music the band played was composed by Europeans or European Americans. I spoke with one of the band directors, and asked rhetorically if there were any songs that the band members could perform that were composed by people of color. She responded that she had never considered the choices she made as nonrepresentative of all the students who had to learn them, while I could see little else than the absence of cultural diversity. I was pleased when the winter concert included some Hanukkah tunes. It was a start.

Reflections

Though my conversation with Jake is now months old, it has continued to haunt me. I have been deeply concerned about a noticeable shift in my son's attitude toward writing. Jake's early writing experiences in kindergarten and first grade revealed that he found writing to be a natural outlet for self-expression. He often wrote for pleasure and has kept all of his drafts. Jake learned the process approach to writing in first grade and treasures his portfolio, which he had originally developed in that class. I have found him in his room revisiting a piece he had written earlier. However, this past year I have noticed a change in his level of production. Jake no longer writes detailed accounts. Instead, he spends a great deal of time thinking about what to write and how to say it. While I believe these are laudatory traits of a good writer, his teachers often accuse him of being underproductive.

Reflecting on our conversation, I sense that Jake believes (understands?) that his perceived audience will neither value nor understand the cultural images and nuances he wishes to share in his writing. Jake is a child wrestling with an internal conflict that is framed by the sociohistorical and sociocultural inequities of U.S. society. He is trying to come to grips with how he can express himself in a manner that is true to his "real self," and yet please his teacher and audience of readers who are, in effect, evaluating his culture, thinking, language, and reality.

Jake's perception of an unaccepting audience is not unique. Several researchers have expressed similar concerns about the narrowly defined culture of acceptable school literacy and the growing literateness of culturally and linguistically diverse children (Delpit, 1986, 1991, 1993; Gutierrez, 1992; Heath, 1983; Labov, 1972; Ovando & Collier, 1985; Reyes & Molner, 1991; Sawyer & Rodriguez, 1992).[5] Why is it clearer to children than to adults that there are systematic, institutional inequalities in the decisions teachers make about the "appropriate" methods and materials used to enhance their students' literacy development?

Like millions of culturally and linguistically diverse people, Jake understands the unstated reality of schooling in U.S. society: It is built upon a narrow understanding of school knowledge and literacy, which are defined and defended as what one needs to know and how one needs to know it in order to be successful in school and society. As Barrera (1992) explains:

> The school culture can be seen to reflect the dominant class and, so too, the cultures of literacy and literature embedded within the school culture. For this reason, the teaching of literacy and literature are considered to be neither acultural nor neutral, but cultural and political.

(p. 236)

The real question is, why do we as educators continue this "sin of omission"—that is, allowing the cultural knowledge of culturally and linguistically diverse children to be ignored, devalued, and unnurtured as valid sources of literacy acquisition? Excerpts from the writings of five noted African Americans help to illustrate my point.

The Past Revisited

The problem of defining one's literary self is not a new one. As noted scholar W. E. B. Du Bois argued in 1903:

> After the Egyptian and Indian, the Greek and Roman, the Teuton and Mongolian, the Negro is a sort of seventh son, born with a veil, and gifted with second-sight in this American world,—a world which yields him no true self-consciousness, but only lets him see himself through the revelation of the other world. It is a peculiar sensation this double-consciousness, this sense of always looking at one's self through the eyes of others . . . . One ever feels his twoness, an American, a Negro; two souls, two thoughts, two unreconciled strivings; two warring ideals in one dark body, whose dogged strength alone keeps it from being torn asunder. The history of the American Negro is the history of this strife,—this longing to attain self conscious manhood, to merge his double self into a better and truer self.
>
> (1903/1965, pp. 214–215)

Similarly, historian Carter G. Woodson (1933/1990) stated:

> In this effort to imitate, however, those "educated people" are sincere. They hope to make the Negro conform quickly to the standard of the whites and thus remove the pretext for the barriers between the races. They do not realize, however, that if the Negroes do successfully imitate the whites, nothing new has thereby been accomplished. You simply have a larger number of persons doing what others have been doing. The unusual gifts of the race have not thereby been developed.
>
> (p. 4)

Poet Langston Hughes (1951) expressed a similar notion:

> I guess being colored doesn't make me not like
> the same things other folks like who are other races.
> So will my page be colored that I write?
> Being me, it will not be white.
> But it will be
> a part of you, instructor.
> You are white—
> yet a part of me, as I am a part of you.
> That's American.
> Sometimes perhaps you don't want to be a part of me.
> Nor do I often want to be a part of you.
> But we are, that's true!
> As I learn from you,
> I guess you learn from me—
> although you're older—and white—
> and somewhat more free.
>
> (pp. 39–40)

Novelist Ralph Ellison (1952) writes:

> I am invisible, understand, simply because people refuse to see me. Like the bodiless heads you see sometimes in circus sideshows, it is as though I have been surrounded by mirrors of hard, distorting glass. When they approach me they see only my surroundings, themselves, or figments of their imagination—indeed, everything and anything except me.
>
> (p. 3)

And, finally, Toni Morrison (1992) refers to the phenomenon of double consciousness as "writing for a white audience" (p. xii). She asks:

> What happens to the writerly imagination of a black author who is at some level *always* conscious of representing one's own race to, or in spite of, a race of readers that understands itself to be "universal" or race-free? In other words, how are "literary whiteness" and "literary blackness" made, and what is the consequence of these constructions?
>
> (p. xii)

Like other culturally and linguistically diverse people before him (including myself and every other person of color with whom I have shared this incident), Jake has encountered the struggle of literary personhood.

Questions and concerns flood my mind: Where, I wonder, has he gotten the idea of a "White" audience—that is, the sense that his classmates and others who read his writing will not appreciate what he has to share? When did his concept of a "White" audience arise? My questions persist: How long has Jake known, intuitively perhaps, that his school literacy experiences have been tempered through a mainstream lens? Will Jake continue to resist "writing for a white audience?" When do culturally and linguistically diverse children learn that they must choose between selfhood and accommodation?[6] When do they learn that "the best way, then, to succeed—that is, to receive rewards, recognition . . . is to learn and reproduce the ways of the dominant group?" (Scheurich, 1992, p. 7). Must there be only one acceptable culture reflected in current school literacy programs? What thoughts, words, and language is Jake replacing with those of the dominant culture in order to please his audience? Will he ever be able to recapture his true literate self after years of accommodation?

As a third grader, Jake is writing, but not for pleasure. Whereas once he wrote as a way of expressing himself or as a hobby, now he does not. He only writes to complete assignments. Much of the "joy" he experienced in writing for pleasure seems to have waned. I recently read some of his writings and noted that he concentrated on topics that do not reflect African American culture. For example, his most recent entries are about his spoon collection, running track, rocks, and football—pretty generic stuff.

My fears are like those of all parents who believe they have prepared their child, having done all that they have read and know a parent should do, yet see their child struggling with a history, a tradition, that is much larger than they can battle.[7] What can I do to help my son and children like him enjoy the freedom of writing and reading? How can I help them value the culturally relevant events in their lives? How can school literacy programs begin to acknowledge, respect, and encourage the diverse cultural knowledge and experiences that children bring to school?

In this article, I am speaking as a teacher educator and parent. This article is an attempt to begin conversations with my colleagues that will address cultural complexities so often ignored in literacy research and practice. For too long, the only perspective published was European Americans' understanding of literacy events. Over the past few years, other cultural perspectives have been published and, more recently, a few have questioned the connection between the theoretical notions of literacy and the historical, and daily, reality of institutionalized inequalities.

As a scholar, I can begin conversations with my colleagues about reexamining theories of literacy to include the role of culture and linguistic diversity. Moreover, teachers and teacher educators like myself can then extend these conversations to reinterpret literacy development, school literacy programs, and teacher education methods and materials to include the experiences of nonmainstream cultures. Finally, I can further extend these conversations into rethinking how we teach and practice school literacy.

Broadening the Scope

Several contemporary positions on literacy serve to enlighten our understanding of how literacy is defined in the field and how it is defined in practice. In this section, I will offer a brief look at several definitions. First, Cook-Gumperz (1986) describes two competing definitions of school literacy that are useful in framing this discussion. She states that "inherent in our contemporary attitude to literacy and schooling is a confusion between a prescriptive view of literacy, as a statement about the values and uses of knowledge, and a descriptive view of literacy, as cognitive abilities which are promoted and assessed through schooling" (p. 14). Second, a more expansive definition of how literacy is conceptualized is offered by Freire and Macedo (1987). They suggest that "literacy becomes a meaningful construct to the degree that it is viewed as a set of practices that functions to either empower or disempower people. In the larger sense, literacy is analyzed according to whether it serves a set of cultural practices that promotes democratic and emancipatory change" (p. 141). Further, they clarify their position on literacy by noting that "for the notion of literacy to become meaningful it has to be situated within a theory of cultural production and viewed as an integral part of the way in which people produce, transform, and reproduce meaning" (p. 142). Third, more general discussions of literacy define literacy as functional, cultural, or critical. Each of these concepts also refers to very different ways of thinking about literacy. *Functional literacy* refers to mastery of the skills needed to read and write as measured by standardized forms of assessment. This view of literacy is similar to Cook-Gumperz's (1986) notion of a descriptive view of literacy. The functional view promotes literacy as a cognitive set of skills that are universal, culturally neutral, and equally accessible through schooling, and is based on a positivistic ideology of learning. Further, this view is heavily dependent on the use of standardized testing measures as a proving ground for literacy acquisition. Most basal reading series and programmed reading approaches embrace the functional/descriptive view of literacy.

Cultural literacy is a term that is most often associated with E. D. Hirsch's 1987 book, *Cultural Literacy: What Every American Needs to Know*. Hirsch defines cultural literacy as "the network of information that all competent readers possess. It is the background information, stored in their minds, that enables them to take up a newspaper and read it with an adequate level of comprehension, getting the point, grasping the implications, relating what they read to the unstated context which alone gives meaning to what they read" (p. 2). Cook-Gumperz (1986) has labeled this form of literacy "prescriptive." In effect, this form of cultural literacy validates language forms, experiences, literature, and histories of some and marginalizes or ignores the language forms, experiences, literature, and histories of others. In the United States, the prescriptive view can be seen in the use of standard English, Eurocentric ways of knowing and learning, a Eurocentric literary canon, and a conventional unproblematic rendering of U.S. history. This form of the cultural/prescriptive view marginalizes the pluralistic composition of U.S. society by devaluing the language, contributions, and histories of some groups. Traditional or conventional approaches to school-based literacy take this form. McLaren (1987) argues that there is a second form of cultural literacy. He writes that this form of cultural literacy "advocates using the language standards and cultural information students bring into the classroom as legitimate and important constituents of learning" (p. 214). Cultural literacy, thus described, suggests that the language and experiences of each student who enters the classroom should be respected and nurtured. This form of cultural literacy recognizes that there are differences in language forms, experiences, literature, and histories of students that will affect literacy learning. Social constructivist theories fall into this prescriptive/cultural literacy category. These approaches to literacy emphasize the active engagement of learners in making meaning from print, the social context of literacy learning, and the importance of recognizing individual and cultural differences.

Critical literacy refers to the ideologies that underlie the relationship between power and knowledge in society. The work of Brazilian educator Paulo Freire has been influential to U.S. efforts to adopt a critical literacy position. Freire, among others, suggests that literacy is more than the construction of meaning from print: Literacy must also include the ability to understand oneself and one's relationship to the world. Giroux's (1987) discussion is worth quoting here at length:

> As Paulo Freire and others have pointed out, schools are not merely instructional sites designed to transmit knowledge; they are also cultural sites. As sites, they generate and embody support for particular forms of culture as is evident in the school's support for specific ways of speaking, the legitimating of distinct forms of knowledge, the privileging of certain histories and patterns of authority, and the confirmation of particular ways of experiencing and seeing the world. Schools often give the appearance of transmitting a common culture, but they, in fact, more often than not, legitimate what can be called a dominant culture.
>
> (p. 176)

Giroux goes on to state:

> At issue here is understanding that student experience has to be understood as part of an interlocking web of power relations in which some groups of students are often privileged over others. But if we are to view this insight in an important way, we must understand that it is imperative for teachers to critically examine the cultural backgrounds and social formations out of which their students produce the categories they use to give meaning to the world. For teachers are not merely dealing with students who have individual interests, they are dealing primarily with individuals whose stories, memories, narratives, and readings of the world are inextricably related to wider social and cultural formations and categories. This issue here is not merely one of relevance but one of power.
>
> (p. 177)

Similarly, Apple (1992) has argued for nearly a decade that "it is naive to think of the school curriculum as neutral knowledge . . . . Rather, what counts as legitimate knowledge is the result of complex power relations and struggles among identifiable class, race, gender, and religious groups" (p. 4). Critical literacy draws attention to the historical, political, cultural, and social dimensions of literacy. Most importantly, this form of literacy focuses on power relations in society and how knowledge and power are interrelated. Educationalists, practitioners in particular, have not yet fully grasped this position on literacy. The other forms of literacy, functional/descriptive and cultural/prescriptive, do not include, among other things, the notion of power relations in literacy instruction.

Philosophically, social constructivist notions (a form of prescriptive/cultural literacy) may be seen as comparable to those espoused by critical literacy. From the schema theorists of the early 1980s to the social constructivist theories of the 1990s, literacy development is understood to be a "meaning making process"—that is, socially mediated (Meek, 1982). Drawing primarily on the work of Halliday (1975), Vygotsky (1978), and Goodman (1989), a number of literacy researchers have stressed the universality of language learning. For example, Goodman's (1989) discussion of the philosophical stance of whole language is that:

> At the same time that whole language sees common strengths and universals in human learning, it expects and recognizes differences among learners in culture, value systems, experience, needs, interests and language. Some of these differences are personal, reflecting the ethnic, cultural, and belief systems of the social groups pupils represent. Thus teachers in whole-language programs value differences among learners as they come to school and differences in objectives and outcomes as students progress through school.
>
> (p. 209)

However, I argue that the role of culture in the social constructivist theories is not as well defined as it needs to be in a pluralistic or multicultural society. While it is fair to say that unidimensional views of culture would not be supported by social constructivists, it is also fair to say that the multilayered complexity of culture, especially the cultures of historically oppressed groups, is not explicitly addressed by them either. By way of example, I will examine the prescriptive/cultural literacy foundation of whole language. Goodman (1986) argues that "language begins as means of communication between members of the group. Through it, however, each developing child acquires the life view, the cultural perspective, the ways of meaning particular to its own culture" (p. 11). But this definition fails to acknowledge that in addition to acquiring culturally "neutral" knowledge, some children must also acquire a Eurocentric cultural perspective to be successful in school. It is not sufficient to suggest that the language and culture of every student is welcomed, supported, and nurtured in school without explicitly addressing the power relations in institutions, social practice, and literature that advantage some and hinder others (Delpit, 1988; Reyes, 1992). School-based literacy, in its varying forms, fails to acknowledge explicitly the richness of the cultural ways of knowing, forms of language other than standard English, and the interwoven relationship among power, language, and literacy that silences kids like Jake.[8] To fail to attend to the plurality and diversity within the United States—and to fail to take seriously the historic past and the social and political contexts that have sustained it—is to dismiss the cultural ways of knowing, language, experiences, and voices of children from diverse linguistic and cultural backgrounds. This is not to imply that programs based on such theories need to be scrapped. It does mean that social constructivist theories need to be reworked to include the complexities of culture that are currently absent. It will also mean that teacher education will need to: 1) make explicit the relationship among culture, language, literacy and power; and 2) train teachers to use cultural information to support and nurture the literacy development of all the students who enter their classrooms.

When taken at face value, social constructivist theory would lead one to assume that new holistic approaches to literacy are culturally validating for all students. An examination of Jake's home and school contexts for his developing understanding of literacy illustrates that this is not always true. That is, we need to understand where he acquired language and his understanding of culture, as well as his history of literacy instruction, to understand how he is "reading the world" of school literacy and how his experiences with a variety of school literacy forms, including holistic approaches, have not addressed his cultural ways of knowing, experiences, language, and voice.

Literacy Contexts

HOME CONTEXT

Literacy acquisition does not evolve in one context or through one type of event; rather, it is a complex endeavor that is mediated through culture. Jake's home literacy environment began with our preparations for him as a new baby. He was brought into a loving two-parent home in which two older brothers were awaiting his arrival. Jake also entered a print-and language-rich environment. He was read to when only a few months old, and continues to share reading (and now writing) with family members. Like the homes of many other middle-class children, Jake's is filled with language, and a range of standard and vernacular languages is used. Our talk centers around family issues, but also includes conversations about world events, neighborhood and school concerns, and personal interests. There are stories, prayers, niceties (manners), verbal games, family jokes, homework assignments, daily Bible reading and discussion, as well as family vacations and excursions to museums, zoos, concerts, and ball parks. Daily routines include reading and responding to mail, making schedules, appointments, grocery and chore lists, and taking telephone messages, all of which include opportunities for shared conversations. There is also a family library that consists of adult fiction, nonfiction, and reference materials. Conversations flow constantly and with ease as we enjoy sharing with each other.

Prior to Jake's entering school, we enjoyed music, games, songs, fingerplay, writing notes on unlined paper with lots of different writing tools, long nature walks, as well as trips to the store, library, barbershop, and church.[9] All these activities were accompanied by lots of talk to expand understanding and draw connections. In addition, Jake and his brothers all have their own bedroom library in which they keep their favorite books, collected since early childhood. Jake's written communications include telephone messages, calendar events, schedules, notes, recipes, invitations, thankyou notes, game brackets (Sega or Nintendo), and occasionally letters and poems.

Jake has a special interest in his collections of stickers, stamps, coins, puzzles, board games, maps, newspaper clippings, and baseball, football, and basketball cards. He also enjoys reading his bedtime story books, magazines (especially *Sports Illustrated for Kids*), and the newspaper (his favorite parts are the sports page, the comics, and the weather map).

What makes Jake's understanding of language and literacy so culturally different from his school's, although both are apparently based on middle-class standards, is that his home literacy events have been culturally defined and are mediated through his cultural understanding. Jake's world is African American; that is, his growing understanding of who and what he is has consciously and unconsciously been mediated through an African American perspective. We select our artwork, magazines, novels, television programs, music, videos, and movies to reflect interests in African American life and society.

SCHOOL CONTEXT

Like most parents, I inquired about the kindergarten's literacy program before enrolling Jake in school.[10] I wanted to have some idea of how his teachers viewed literacy development and how they planned to conduct literacy instruction. My primary question was, "What approach to literacy will you use?" Jake's private, full-day kindergarten was founded by three Jewish women, two of whom taught the kindergarten class, while the third served as school administrator. The teachers informed me that they had taught for many years and were aware of the modern trends. They had therefore designed a program that included what they considered to be the strong points of several programs. Jake's classmates included twelve European Americans (eight were Jewish) and two African American children. His teachers tried to provide all the children with what they thought the children would need to know in order to be success-ful readers and writers in grade one. As a result, the classroom was colorful and full of print. Labels were placed on cubbyholes, activity centers, children's table chairs, and charts.[11] The reading material was an eclectic mix of basals, trade books, and a small library of children's classics.

In first grade, Jake attended a public elementary school. This classroom was a mixed-age group (grades one and two) of twenty-three children, including seventeen European Americans, four African Americans, and two Asian Americans. His teacher described her literacy program as literature-based, and she stressed reading and writing. This teacher read to the children, who also read individually or in small groups. The reading materials included recipients of the Caldecott award and other award-winning books, stories, and poems by children's favorite authors, classics of children's literature, and writing "published" by the students. The children especially liked to read folk tales. As they gained reading and writing skills, the children coauthored, published, and shared their own work. Students were also encouraged to read and write for pleasure. In all these works, I recall that very few were written about or authored by people of color, except for a few on the Caldecott list.

Jake attended a different elementary school for second grade. I eagerly met his new teacher and asked my standard question about literacy. She informed me that she used the basal approach, which she believed ensured that all the "skills" needed to be a successful reader would be covered. The particular basal series she used included "universal" themes and contained illustrations of various racial/ethnic groups but made little reference to the culture of the people. There were several "ethnic" stories, but I consider their authorship suspect, at best.[12] The series also included isolated skill development, vocabulary regulated text, several thematically organized stories, informational selections, and limited writing opportunities. This class of twenty-eight children included twenty European Americans, five African Americans, and three Asian Americans.

Not wishing Jake to repeat this basal approach in grade three, I spoke with other mothers in the neighborhood, soliciting information about the "good" third-grade teachers. After much prayer, I informed the principal of my choice. Now in third grade, Jake is experiencing what his teacher refers to as a whole language approach to literacy, which includes lots of reading and writing for meaning, working in cooperative groups, process writing, and having sustained time for reading and writing. Writing is a daily activity, and Thursday mornings are designated as Writing Workshop mornings with parent volunteers who assist students in a variety of ways, from brainstorming topics to editing their writing. The teacher allows time for individual and small group readings of trade books on a daily basis. Since my conversation with Jake, I have learned his teacher had selected the books she planned to use during the school year, ahead of time, and the children were allowed only to choose which of these books to read. All of the books were written by European American authors. Even the folk tales from other countries were rewritten by European Americans. Very few books by or about U.S. minorities have been read to students by the teacher, student teachers, or in the reading groups.

I cannot account for the moment-by-moment decisions Jake's teachers have had to make each day. However, I can review the philosophies behind the programs they use. Theoretically, each literacy program purports to be culturally neutral and not mediated by any dominant view of language, when, in fact, a Eurocentric, mainstream cultural view dominates. Darder (1991) argues that it is important to understand the historicity of knowledge:

> The dominant school culture functions not only to support the interests and values of the dominant society, but also to marginalize and invalidate knowledge forms and experiences that are significant to subordinate and oppressed groups. This function is best

illustrated in the ways that curriculum often blatantly ignores the histories of women, people of color, and the working class.

(p. 79)

Having held a conference with each of Jake's teachers and observed each class setting on several occasions, I can say without hesitation that each teacher believed that she was doing her best to meet the needs of each child in her classroom. That is, she was trying to foster a growing sense of literacy competence in each child. Yet, I don't believe that any of Jake's teachers were aware that they were also narrowly defining the cultural lens through which all children in the classroom were expected to understand literacy.

Thus, in four short years Jake has experienced a wide range of philosophies, approaches, and instruction in literacy, and, at the same time, a narrow ethnocentric view of school literacy. All of his teachers have meant to encourage his growth and development as a literate person. Why, then, have they failed to acknowledge an important part of who he is and what he *culturally* brings to the school literacy program? Reyes (1992) argues that teachers often fail to make adjustments in their approaches to literacy for culturally and linguistically diverse learners because

the majority of [teachers] are members of the dominant culture, implementing programs designed primarily for mainstream students. Teachers implementing these programs tend to treat students of color as exceptions to the norm, as students who should be assimilated into the dominant group, rather than accommodated according to their own needs.

(p. 437)

Some theorists, researchers, and teachers may suggest the counterargument; that is, that elements of the mainstream culture are apparent in all "parallel cultures" and that it is easiest to teach to the mainstream (Hamilton, 1989).[13] I would argue that to ignore, consciously or not, the culture and language that each child brings to the literacy table is to miseducate him or her. As the research by Au (1993), Morrow (1992), and Reyes and Laliberty (1992), among others, has shown, when cultural and linguistic adjustments are made to school literacy programs, all children benefit.

You may wonder if I have tried to inform Jake's teachers of the narrowness of the literacy lens through which they seem to be defining literacy development and instruction. I admit that I have failed miserably to take a strong stand. Rather than confront them about the lack of culturally responsive literacy instruction, I have expressed my concerns for Jake's personal literacy growth. For example, I have shared multicultural book lists with Jake's teachers and offered to serve as a resource. I have honestly wanted to inform Jake's teachers of two things: one, the need to be more sensitive in their approach to the language and cultural experiences that children bring to the classroom; and two, the need to incorporate more books written by people of color to legitimize the contributions of all literate people. Yet I have also believed that expressing my thoughts might jeopardize Jake's educational future with some kind of backlash.

A Status Report

While literacy theorists, researchers, and practitioners continue to suggest that school literacy is culturally neutral, Jake's literacy experiences offer an intimate and compelling argument that, as currently practiced, school literacy has been and still is narrowly defined in terms of culture. Only the packaging is new.

Descriptions of my conversation with Jake have met with lots of head nodding and similar stories from many of my non-White students. Delpit (1988) has shared similar insights into what she correctly describes as the "silenced dialogue." The commonsense response among some people of color to school literacy (and schooling in general) has been to take a "way things are" attitude. Many people of color understand that there are inequalities in the educational system; however, we also understand that little can be done without massive school reform. So, to be educated in our current system requires accepting that "this is the way things are. If you want to advance you must learn to play the game." That is, institutionalized racism is something we all know, but see as an unavoidable part of education in U.S. society.

In sharing my analysis with my graduate students, several European Americans have questioned why I refer to Jake's school literacy experiences as being narrowly defined and inquired what is so "acultural" about his literacy education. They ask, "Aren't literature-based and whole language programs built upon notions of constructivist theory that embrace notions of culture?" Of course, my students' understanding is correct: Current holistic school literacy programs support constructivist theory. I guess that's what is so frightening.

While the rhetoric of school literacy programs suggests that culture is part of the theoretical framework, "culture" has been narrowly defined to mean middle-class European American culture. The tacit assumption is, then, that all children are being well served by the new literacy programs that are built on the "natural" language acquisition of middle-class European American children. However, natural language acquisition is mediated through the particular culture in which the child lives. The reality, then, as shared in this article, is that theoreticians, researchers, teacher educators, practitioners, and publishers of literacy approaches and programs are frequently unaware of their assumptions.

Some may truly believe that they are delivering on their promise to build on the culture and language of the child, but what they have been unable, or unwilling, to acknowledge is that school literacy, as it exists, is not universal or reflective of the language and culture of many children. They claim that current school literacy programs and practices are acultural. These programs, however, clearly put some children at a disadvantage, while giving an advantage to others. It is clear, even to a nine-year-old, that school literacy is narrowly defined.

Discussion

In order to meet the needs of our U.S. society, which is rapidly becoming more culturally diverse, our literacy programs should offer more than sensitivity training, human relations, or attitudinal shifts to issues of culture and linguistic diversity. Programs are needed that will also help teachers transform their thinking about the role of language and culture in literacy development. It is simply not enough to inform teachers of what they do not know. Teachers need to question "cultural bumps," or mismatches in expectations of performance in literacy development (Garcia, 1994, personal communication). As Barnitz (1994) states, "Teachers must recognize difference as manifestations of cultural discourse which can be expanded rather than interrupted or suppressed" (p. 587).

What I see is an institutionalized racism that is grounded in the theories used to discuss literacy and to inform and educate teachers and teacher educators. I believe that we need to enhance preservice teacher curricula and education. The current method of dispersing concepts of diversity, inclusivity, or multiculturalism across several courses, hoping students will synthesize these issues into a workable whole, has been ineffective. Preservice teachers also need intensive education in understanding the dynamic role that culture plays in language and literacy development and in defining school literacy.

In a preservice teacher education course I teach, I use literature authored by domestic minority men and women as a starting point for preservice teachers to begin to reflect on their cultural assumptions about how they "read the word and the world" (Freire, 1985). The method has been effective in helping many students face their own, heretofore unvoiced, assumptions of their own culture and the cultures of other groups.

Most of my students are in their early twenties and have never really concerned themselves with issues of race. Even the students who are members of U.S. minority groups prefer not to discuss race, ethnicity, or culture openly. At the opening of class, for example, many of my students think that their cultural understanding will not affect the students they teach. They believe that their most important concern should be the subject matter and how to transmit effectively a love for their subject to their students. Some of my students also have difficulty understanding the notion of institutionalized racism in U.S. public education. It is at this point in the course that I begin to share the daily occurrences in the lives of my children. Further, some of my European American students see themselves only as "American" and do not wish to deal with their heritage. They want to minimize any tie to Europe and only concentrate on their "Americanness." Some students believe that most U.S. minority group members are poor people, and that most poor people (from all racial groups, but especially those seen most frequently in the media—African Americans and Latinos) really don't care about their children's education. Some also think that children from minority groups don't care about their own education. Most of my students have not even considered how to prepare to teach in multicultural or multilingual classrooms. They tend to live under the false assumption that they can get jobs in homogeneous, suburban school districts.

As in most preservice teacher education courses nationwide, my students are predominantly European American women. However, in each of my classes, I have had at least one U.S. minority group member. The presence of members from these groups has helped give voice to the concerns of their various communities. My courses are elective, which I believe is important, because it means that the students in my class are interested in issues of diversity. In the best of all worlds, all students would be so inclined, but they are not.

One of the first things I do to help my students become aware of their own cultural understandings is to have them write an autobiographical essay. The essay requires them to trace their ancestry over four or five generations, and to explain their families' use of language, food traditions, and other interesting cultural habits. The essays are shared first in small groups and then with the whole class. In this way, students can readily understand that everyone is a product of their culture, knowingly or not. I too share my cultural and ethnic background. As a person of African, Native, and European American descent, yet who looks only African American, I use my background and life as a springboard for discussions of students' cultural diversity and the limited conception of "culture" in most schools. Since this is a semester-long course, we have the time to engage in many activities, such as community and faculty presentations, videos, and readings by U.S. minority members. However, I believe that some of the most productive work occurs in the small group discussions my students have with each other as they respond to literature written by U.S. minority group members. For example, recently we read a number of novels written by Asian Americans. Many of my students had not heard of the internment of Japanese Americans during World War II.

After my students and I have reflected upon the cultural assumptions from which we perceive our world (and those worlds that might differ from our own), we begin to address teachers' roles and how their cultural assumptions affect the decisions they make, their interactions with students, and their selection of teaching materials. I then give the students opportunities to use their growing understanding of cultural knowledge in lessons they design and teach. My students are all required to teach two literacy lessons during the semester. Many of them choose activities that require participants to work together in cooperative learning groups. Four examples come to mind. One student asked each of us to recall an event using the Native

American concept of a "skin story"—drawing on animal pelts—to create pictograph symbols to relate that event. Another student separated class members by attributes they could not control (gender, hair color, size of feet). The "minority" group members (men in this case) were seated in the front of the classroom and were the only students the leader of the exercise asked to respond to her questions. In a third example, a student distributed a series of photographs to small groups and had each group classify the people in the photos, rating them on attributes such as who appeared most intelligent, most successful, and nicest. Finally, a student asked us to read current newspaper articles about war-torn countries and write a diary entry or letter to a government official from the perspective of someone in the country. Through such exercises and activities, my students have learned that culture is a complex issue, one that cannot be taken lightly. They learn to think and act reflectively and become predisposed to considering issues of race, class, gender, age, and sexual preference. Moreover, they understand that their decisions must be based on more than theory; they must also consider the interrelationship of power and knowledge.

I also design in-class lessons around students' responses to the authentic texts they have read. Throughout their field experiences, I have been impressed by the culturally responsive approach to literacy and literature that many of my students have taken with them into the field. For example, one of my students invited recent Asian immigrants to her eighth-grade class to be interviewed by her students. She believed that the face-to-face interactions her students had during the interviews allowed them to understand better the hardships endured by the new U.S. citizens. Another student taught *Huckleberry Finn*. She began the lesson by sharing the historical context in which the novel was written, a model I insist each student use in my class. When confronted by an African American student about the use of the word "nigger" in the novel, she was able to facilitate a group discussion on the use of derogatory terms. She believed that membership in my class enabled her to deal openly with the student and the offensive term. Her experience demonstrates that it is possible to create multicultural learning communities within classrooms that are based on critical literacy theory that validates and legitimizes all learners.

Conclusion

In this chapter, I have argued that for school literacy to begin to move beyond its "neutral" conception of culture, educators at all levels must acknowledge the role and importance of more than one culture in defining school literacy. Educators have not effectively built upon the culture and language of every child, and have set arbitrary standards of acceptance and defined them as normative. I have also argued for the reconceptualization and program development of school literacy, not to dismantle, but to strengthen, literacy frameworks. We can and must do a better job of inviting all students to the literacy table and including them in conversations on school literacy.

I had initial misgivings about sharing my conversation with Jake, as I feared that my thinking would be misinterpreted. My fears lay with the "predictable inability (West, 1993) of some European Americans to consider honestly the shortcomings of programs they espouse as universal. In addition, I was concerned that my colleagues would view the conversation as one isolated event, ignoring the fact that there are countless instances of narrow cultural constructions of literacy in the daily lives of culturally and linguistically diverse children. I was also reluctant to give such an intimate look into my private world. Therefore, I hope that sharing the incident opens conversations about reconceptualizing and reforming school literacy. When I wonder if I've done the right thing, I recall Jake saying to his older brothers, "I want to share a picture of my real self."

Notes

1. Arlette Ingram Willis, "Reading the World of School Literacy: Contextualizing the Experience of a Young African American Male," *Harvard Educational Review* 65.1 (1995): 30–50.
2. Going to the barbershop and getting a haircut is a bimonthly occurrence for many African American males. A number of Jake's classmates differed in their definition of what constituted a "part"; however, the other African American children in his class have a similar cultural understanding of the term.
3. As a Writing Workshop parent volunteer in his class, I know that Jake's class consists of ten European American boys, nine European American girls, four African American boys, two African American girls, and one Asian American girl. The class is taught by a European American woman with over twenty years of experience. Also, during this school year, there have been three student teachers (all European American women) and several other parent volunteers (also European American women).
4. In the fall of 1993 I taught a pilot course, which included multicultural education, reading methods for grades six-twelve, and literature for grades six-twelve with special emphasis on multicultural literature.
5. To me, "growing literateness" means an understanding of how language, reading, and writing fit into the communication patterns of home and school life. It can also mean the development of literate behaviors, the adoption of literate attitudes, and the confidence that allows one to define oneself as a reader and a writer.
6. Selfhood, as used in this article, means the awareness of oneself as a person, in particular as a person who belongs to a specific culturally and linguistically distinct group.
7. Cose's (1993) book, *The Rage of a Privileged Class*, gives examples of the frustration experienced by other middle-class African Americans who believed that by doing everything according to plan they would reap just rewards. For example, Cose quotes Darwin Davis, senior vice president of Equitable Life Assurance Society: "They [young Black managers] have an even worse problem [than I did] because they've got M.B.A.'s from Harvard. They did all the things that you're supposed to do . . . and things are supposed to happen" (p. 76).

   By *history*, I mean how the inequalities that exist in schools reflect a much greater history of institutionalized inequalities. By *tradition*, I mean teachers' tendency to teach how they were taught. Whether history or tradition is the overriding factor in this instance, I am not sure.
8. Silencing, as used by Michelle Fine (1987), "constitutes a process of institutionalized policies and practices which obscure the very social, economic and therefore experiential conditions of students' daily lives, and which expel from written, oral, and nonverbal expression substantive and critical 'talk' about these conditions . . . . Silencing constitutes the process by which contradictory evidence, ideologies, and experiences find themselves buried, camouflaged, and discredited" (p. 157).
9. *Fingerplay* is a term often used to describe actions made with the fingers as children sing a song. For example, the motions used with the song "The Itsy Bitsy Spider" are fingerplay.
10. During my years as a classroom teacher, many parents asked what type of reading program I planned to use. While most parents do not use the term *literacy programs* or inquire about writing programs per se, they do inquire about reading. I have also found that parents are interested in the methods used to teach spelling and vocabulary.
11. Activity centers are areas set aside for special activities. For example, the science center, math center, etc., all have activities specifically designed for children interested in learning more about a selected topic.
12. Many stories contained in basals, like the one Jake used in second grade, are written by teams of authors seeking to control vocabulary or teach specific skills. Basal stories are often abridged or edited versions of original works, and in some instances, such as folk tales, legends, and fairy tales, are translations or a retelling of the original.
13. Recently, Hamilton (1989) used the term *parallel cultures* to refer to the historical experiences of domestic minorities in the United States. *Parallel* conveys a sense of coexistence with the more dominant European American culture so loosely referred to as American culture. The term *domestic minorities* is used to refer to minority groups that have a long history in this country (African Americans, Asian Americans, etc.) but whose forefathers and foremothers lived elsewhere—except in the case of Native Americans.

References

Apple, M. (1992). The text and cultural politics. *Educational Researcher*, *21*(7), 4–11, 19.

Au, K. (1993). *Literacy instruction in multicultural settings*. Fort Worth, TX: Harcourt Brace Jovanovich.

Barnitz, J. (1994). Discourse diversity: Principles for authentic talk and literacy instruction. *Journal of Reading, 37,* 586–591.

Barrera, R. (1992). The cultural gap in literature-based literacy instruction. *Education and Urban Society, 24,* 227–243.

Cook-Gumperz, J. (Ed). (1986). *The social construction of literacy.* Cambridge, Eng.: Cambridge University Press.

Cose, E. (1993). *The rage of a privileged class.* New York: Harper Collins.

Darder, A. (1991). *Culture and power in the classroom: A critical foundation for bicultural education.* New York: Bergin & Garvey.

Delpit, L. (1986). Skills and other dilemmas of a progressive Black educator. *Harvard Educational Review, 56,* 379–385.

Delpit, L. (1988). The silenced dialogue: Power and pedagogy in educating other people's children. *Harvard Educational Review, 58,* 280–298.

Delpit, L. (1991). A conversation with Lisa Delpit. *Language Arts, 68,* 541–547.

Delpit, L. (1993). The politics of teaching literate discourse. In T. Perry & J. Fraser (Eds.), *Freedom's plow: Teaching in the multicultural classroom* (pp. 285–295). New York: Routledge.

Du Bois, W. E. B. (1965). *The souls of Black folks.* New York: Bantam. (Original work published in 1903)

Ellison, R. (1952). *Invisible man.* New York: Random House.

Fine, M. (1987). Silencing in public schools. *Language Arts, 64,* 157–174.

Freire, P. (1985). Reading the world and the word: An interview with Paulo Freire. *Language Arts, 62,* 15–21.

Freire, P., & Macedo, D. (1987). *Literacy: Reading the world and the word.* South Hadley, MA: Bergin & Garvey.

Giroux, H. (1987). Critical literacy and student experience: Donald Graves' approach to literacy. *Language Arts, 64,* 175–181.

Goodman, K. (1986). *What's whole in whole language?* Portsmouth, NH: Heinemann.

Goodman, K. (1989). Whole-language research: Foundations and development. *Elementary School Journal, 90,* 207–221.

Gutierrez, K. (1992). A comparison of instructional contexts in writing process classrooms with Latino children. *Education and Urban Society, 24,* 244–262.

Halliday, M. (1975). *Learn how to mean.* London: Edward Arnold.

Hamilton, V. (1989). Acceptance speech, Boston Globe-Horn Book Award, 1988. *Horn Book, 65*(2), 183.

Heath, S. (1983). *Ways with words: Language, life and work in the communities and classrooms.* Cambridge, Eng.: Cambridge University Press.

Hirsch, E. (1987). *Cultural literacy: What every American needs to know.* Boston: Houghton Mifflin.

Hughes, L. (1951). Theme for English B. In L. Hughes, *Montage of a dream deferred* (pp. 39–40). New York: Henry Holt.

Labov, W. (1972). The logic of nonstandard English. In R. D. Abrahams & R. C. Troike (Eds.), *Language and cultural diversity in American education* (pp. 225–261). Englewood Cliffs, NJ: Prentice Hall.

McLaren, P. (1988). Culture or canon? Critical pedagogy and the politics of literacy. *Harvard Educational Review, 58,* 213–234.

Meek, M. (1982). *Learning to read.* Portsmouth, NH: Heinemann.

Morrison, T. (1992). *Playing in the dark: Whiteness and the literary imagination.* Cambridge, MA: Harvard University Press.

Morrow, L. (1992). The impact of a literature-based program on literacy achievement, use of literature, and attitudes of children from minority backgrounds. *Reading Research Quarterly, 27,* 251–275.

Ovando, C., & Collier, V. (1985). *Bilingual and ESL classrooms: Teaching in multicultural contexts.* New York: McGraw-Hill.

Reyes, M. de la Luz. (1992). Challenging venerable assumptions: Literacy instruction for linguistically different students. *Harvard Educational Review, 62,* 427–446.

Reyes, M. de la Luz, & Laliberty, E. (1992). A teacher's "Pied Piper" effect on young authors. *Education and Urban Society, 24,* 263–278.

Reyes, M. de la Luz, & Molner, L. (1991). Instructional strategies for second-language learners in content areas. *Journal of Reading, 35,* 96–103.

Sawyer, D., & Rodriguez, C. (1992). How native Canadians view literacy: A summary of findings. *Journal of Reading, 36*, 284–293.

Scheurich, J. (1992). Toward a White discourse on White racism. *Educational Researcher, 22*(8), 5–10.

Vygotsky, L. (1978). *Mind in society*. Cambridge, MA: Harvard University Press.

West, C. (1993). *Race matters*. Boston: Beacon Press.

Woodson, C. (1990). *The mis-education of the Negro*. Nashville, TN: Winston-Derek. (Original work published 1933)

Theresa Perry

Theresa Perry, professor of education and African studies at Simmons College and director of the Simmons College/Beacon Press "Race, Education, and Democracy" lecture and book series, writes the book's first chapter, titled "Up From the Parched Earth: Towards a Theory of African-American Achievement," in three parts. Part 1 is the excerpt included here, "Freedom for Literacy and Literacy for Freedom." Parts 2 and 3, respectively, are "Competing Theories of Group Achievement" and "Achieving in Post-Civil Rights America: The Outline of a Theory." In "Freedom for Literacy and Literacy for Freedom," Perry includes the narratives of eight African Americans as a way to discuss a philosophy of schooling for African American people. Relying on the slave and contemporary narratives of the likes of Frederick Douglass, Harriet Jacobs, Malcolm X, Joycelyn Elders, Haki Madhubuti, Maya Angelou, Gwendolyn Parker, Septima Clark, and Ben Carson allows Perry to demonstrate how African Americans have always sought to acquire an education and pursue academic excellence, even in the face of insurmountable odds. Perry advocated a philosophy of education that is grounded in African American oral and written forms, and that is experienced in community contexts and in institutionalized schools. The excerpt included here highlights the guiding belief in literacy for freedom and freedom for literacy by emphasizing leadership, collective action, and racial uplift.

Freedom for Literacy and Literacy for Freedom: The African-American Philosophy of Education

Theresa Perry[1]

The questions that are at the heart of the dilemma of schooling for African Americans, and perhaps for any group for whom there is not a predictable or rational relationship between effort and reward in the social, education, or economic spheres, are these: Why should one make an effort to excel in school if one cannot predict when and under what circumstances learning will be valued, seen, acknowledged? Why should one focus on learning in school if that learning doesn't, in reality or in one's imaginary community, have the capacity to affect, inform, or alter one's self-perception or one's status as a member of an oppressed group?

African Americans have historically given rich and elaborated answers to these questions. In *The Education of Blacks in the South, 1860–1935*, James Anderson unearths the answers that African Americans themselves provided—answers that were forged out of African Americans' early encounters with literacy and their struggles over time to acquire literacy and education in America. For African Americans, from slavery to the modern Civil Rights movement, the answers were these: You pursued learning because this is how you asserted yourself as a free person, how you claimed your humanity. You pursued learning so you could work for the racial uplift, for the liberation of your people. You pursued education so you could prepare yourself to lead your people.

Not coincidentally, this is the same message about literacy and education that literary scholars Henry Louis Gates and Robert Stepto have found encoded in the African-American narrative tradition, an impulse that Stepto summarizes as "freedom for literacy and literacy for freedom." I will argue that what Anderson and other historians have found in the historical record and what Gates and Stepto have seen in the African-American literary tradition are evidence for an indigenous African-American philosophy of education. I will further argue that this philosophy of education was powerfully implicated in motivating African Americans across generations to vigorously pursue education.

There is a tendency to see philosophy as an activity of specialized people, elites, who are usually ensconced in universities, far from the day-to-day activities of ordinary people. I am arguing that out of African Americans' collective experience with learning and education, and all that that implied, they developed a philosophy of education that was passed on in oral and written narratives. Moreover, narratives were not only the vehicles for passing on this philosophy, but they also had a discursive function. They were central to the identity formation of African Americans as intellectually capable people.

I want to help readers get a sense of the content and power of the African-American philosophy of schooling by doing a close reading of seven African-American narratives. My goal is to make palpable the feelings, the meanings, and the significance African Americans have attached to schooling and learning, to make visible their indigenous philosophy of education. These narratives—some literature and some not—allow us to see how this philosophy of education found expression in the real lives of people, or at least in their memory. The two slave narratives and the five contemporary narratives that I have chosen to discuss are representative of the experiences of African Americans during slavery and in the twentieth century. But I could have just as easily chosen other narratives, as there are dozens of narratives in which one can find the same messages, from Booker T. Washington's *Up from Slavery* to Vernon Jordan's recently published *Vernon Can Read*.

My primary argument is that this indigenous and operative philosophy of learning and schooling was capable of developing and sustaining the desire for learning in a people for whom educational accomplishment was not necessarily linked to comparable rewards, in the school communities created by African Americans. I will end part 1 of this essay by reflecting on how this discussion might inform contemporary conversations about African-American school achievement and what the historic African-American philosophy of education can contribute toward the development of a contemporary theory of African-American school achievement.

Slave Narratives and an African-American Philosophy of Learning

Law and custom made it a crime for enslaved men and women to learn or teach others to read and write. And yet slave narratives uniformly recount the intensity of the slaves' and ex-slaves' desire for literacy, the barriers they encountered in becoming literate, and what they were willing to endure in order to become literate. Even the threat of beating, amputation, or death did not quell the slaves' desire for literacy. According to the testimony of one slave, "The first time you was caught trying to read or write you was whipped with a cow hide the next time with a cat-o-nine and the third time they cut the first joint offen your forefinger" (Cornelius 1991, 66).

There are the stories of slaves who were hanged when they were discovered reading, and of patrollers who went around breaking up Sunday meetings where slaves were being taught to read, beating all of the adults who were present. Slaves cajoled white children into teaching them, trading marbles and candy for reading lessons. They paid large sums of money to poor white people for reading lessons and were always on the lookout for time with the blue black speller (a school dictionary), or for an occasion to learn from their masters and mistresses without their knowing.

For the slaves, literacy was more than a symbol of freedom; it *was* freedom. It affirmed their humanity, their personhood. To be able to read and write was an intrinsic good, as well as a mighty weapon in the slave's struggle for freedom. Literate slaves filed legal petitions, protesting and challenging their enslavement; they forged passes for themselves and others, thus allowing escape from the horrors of slavother literate slaves led rebellions and wrote pamphlets and tracts denouncing and exposing the slave system. They read the Bible, interpreting its message in a way that supported resistance and rebellions.

While learning to read was an individual achievement, it was fundamentally a communal act. For the slaves, literacy affirmed not only their individual freedom but also the freedom of their people. Becoming literate obliged one to teach others. Learning and teaching were two sides of the same coin, part of the same moment. Literacy was not something you kept for yourself; it was to be passed on to others, to the community. Literacy was something to share.

Maya Angelou

The graduation scene described in Maya Angelou's autobiographical narrative *I Know Why the Caged Bird Sings* asks and answers the question, Why literacy? This sequence embodies the dilemma of achievement for African Americans living in the segregated South, a people whose school and community were organized to affirm their humanity, their racial, cultural, and national identities, and to buffer them from ideologies, policies, and practices that would devalue and denigrate them.

The entire school community took on an air of celebration as Maya and her classmates prepared for graduation. All its members were involved in the preparations—building sets and preparing speeches, dramatic readings, and songs. The graduation was a celebration not only for the graduates and the families of the children attending the school, but for the entire community. While each student's achievements were noted with great fanfare, the graduation itself, and the graduation of each student, was a communal event, an accomplishment for the African-American community of Stamps, Arkansas.

Against the backdrop of this excitement and celebratory atmosphere, the inequalities represented in the physical conditions of the Black county school and the white county school loomed large. Maya reflects on the difference:

> Unlike the white high school, Lafayette County Training School distinguished itself by having neither lawn nor hedges, nor tennis court, nor climbing ivy. Its two buildings (main classrooms, the grade school, and home economics) were set on a dirt hill with no fence to limit either its boundaries, or those of the bordering farms. There was a large expanse to the left of the school, which was used alternately as a baseball diamond or basketball court. Rusty hoops on the swaying poles represented the permanent recreational equipment, although bats and balls could be borrowed from the P. E. teachers, if the borrower was qualified, and if the diamond wasn't occupied.
>
> (Angelou 1969, 151)

Despite these inequalities, Maya and her classmates were committed to academic achievement. They diligently studied Black poets and Black history, and they were also steeped in the so-called classics, given an education usually reserved for those considered "first-class citizens" by the larger society. However, only a small number of the students graduating from the high school would attend college, and many of them would attend a college with an ostensibly vocational curriculum, suggesting that they were being prepared to reproduce their social position in the larger society. The dilemma of achievement for African Americans is concretized in the very nature of separate and unequal education.

Graduation day was one of particular excitement for Maya's family and friends. Maya's grandmother had bought her a watch as a graduation present. Her brother Bailey had given her a bound leather copy of the works of Edgar Allen Poe. Maya's grandmother owned a store, and nearly every one of her customers had given Maya a gift: "a nickel, maybe a dime, with the instruction 'keep on moving to higher ground' or some other encouragement." Maya's grandmother posted a sign on her store announcing the importance of the day. It read, "Closed—graduation."

The graduation began with the traditional opening sequence for ceremonies in the Black community: the singing of the national anthem, the Pledge of Allegiance, and the singing of the

Black National Anthem. This ceremony was interrupted after the Pledge of Allegiance by two white men, representatives from the county. The graduates and other members of the audience were motioned by the principal to be seated.

One of the white men made his way to the podium, allegedly to bring greetings and congratulations to the graduates. With these greetings, he let those in attendance know, in no uncertain terms, that contrary to what they might imagine, they were not being educated for first-class citizenship, for freedom. Maya recalls the white man's message to the graduates, to their families and to the Stamps community:

> He told us of the wonderful changes we children in Stamps had in store. The Central School (naturally, the white school was "central") had already been granted improvements that would be used in the fall. A wellknown artist was coming from Little Rock to teach art to them. They were going to have the newest microscopes and chemistry equipment for their laboratory . . . .
>
> He said that he had pointed out to people at a very high level that one of the first-line halfback tacklers at Arkansas Agricultural and Mechanical College had graduated from Lafayette County Training School . . . .
>
> He went on to praise us. He went on to say how he had bragged "one of the best basketball players sank his first ball right here at Lafayette County Training School." . . .
>
> The white kids were going to have a chance to be the Galileos and Madame Curies and Edisons and Gauguins, and our boys (the girls weren't even in on it) would try to be Jessie Owenses and Joe Lewises.
>
> (151–52)

Maya's words revealed the absurdity of this graduation event. The existential dilemma about the meaning of academic achievement for African Americans was "thrown in the faces" of the graduates and their community. The magic evaporated, the spirit of celebration and excitement dissipated. Those in attendance came face-to-face with their history as a despised and degraded people, with their identity as a racially and historically oppressed people:

> Graduation, the hush-hush magic time of thrills and gifts and congratulations and diplomas, was finished for me before my name was called. The accomplishment was nothing. The meticulous maps drawn in three colors of ink, learning and spelling decasyllabic words, memorizing the whole of "The Rape of Lucrece"—it was for nothing. Donleavy [the white speaker] had exposed us . . . .
>
> We were maids and farmers, handymen and washerwomen, and anything higher that we aspired to was farcical and presumptuous.
>
> (152)

Maya writes that the ugliness that followed these remarks was palpable, that it refused to leave, even after the white men who had "hand-delivered" it left as abruptly as they had entered. Neither the singing of "Onward Christian Soldiers" nor the recitation of the poem "Invictus" cleared the air. Maya allows us access to her thoughts as the valedictorian began his speech, to her struggles with the absurdity of her community's commitment to academic achievement, to literacy:

> There was shuffling and rustling around me, then Henry Reed was giving his valedictory address, "To Be or Not to Be." Hadn't he heard the white folks? We couldn't *be*, so the question was a waste of time. Henry's voice came out clear and strong. I feared to look at

him. Hadn't he got the message? There was no "nobler in the mind" for Negroes, because the world didn't think we had minds, and they let us know it. "Outrageous fortune?" Now, that was a joke. When the ceremony was over, I had to tell him to read some things, if I still cared.

(152)

As soon as Henry Reed had completed his speech, he turned to face the graduates on stage, leading them and the entire community in singing the Black National Anthem, which had been omitted because of the visit of the white folks from downtown.

> Lift every voice and sing
> Till earth and heaven ring
> Ring with harmonies of liberty
> Stony the road we rode
> Bitter the chastening rod
> Felt in the days when hope, unborn, had died
> Yet with a steady beat
> Have not our weary feet
> Come to the place for which our fathers sighed?
> (Angelou 1969, 155)

The singing of the Black National Anthem by the entire community, and the historic meaning of this ritual, reminded the community of the answer to the question, Why literacy? The unbowed display of an individual, followed by the collective gesture together turned the community back to a focus on education as an act of freedom, as an act of resistance, as a political and communal act.

After singing the Black National Anthem, Maya recalls that the community was "on top again . . . . The depths had been icy and dark, but now bright sun spoke to our souls. I was no longer simply a member of the proud graduating class of 1940; I was a proud member of the wonderful, beautiful Negro race" (156). This graduation sequence reflects the institutionalization of the African-American philosophy of schooling, freedom for literacy and literacy for freedom, and its capacity to develop and sustain the desire to achieve in a historically oppressed group.

Reflections on the Narratives

What lessons emerge from our reading of the narratives? How can these lessons inform the contemporary conversation about African-American school achievement?

Academic achievement, doing well in school, and pursuing learning, in all of these narratives, is always accomplished in the face of considerable constraints, whether the impoverished condition of the school, the absence of a local high school, laws that made it a crime to teach slaves to read and write, or a teacher's or school's ideology of African-American intellectual inferiority. These constraints were tied to the social identity and the political location of African Americans *as* African Americans.

The pursuit of education as described in the narratives is not casual. It is seen and presented as intense, persistent, and supported and fueled by an explicit and continually articulated belief system. This explicit, and continually articulated belief system functions as a counternarrative, one that stands in opposition to the dominant society's notions about the intellectual capacity of African Americans, the role of learning in their lives, the meaning and purpose of school, and the power of their intellect.

The authors use metaphors to capture the embeddedness and the all-embracing nature of their or their community's beliefs about education. These beliefs were ground up and served as grits, communicated with the regularity of a mother's prayers, like a drumbeat, a mission.

Many of the narratives place in the foreground the set of behaviors, the routines and practices, that express in the real world the individuals' and their families' commitment to learning—from Douglass, who took his spelling book with him so that whenever he had time he could practice his reading; to Malcolm, who read whenever he had time, even late at night; to Carson, who at his mother's insistence read every night.

The narratives we have cited have a discursive function and as such are powerfully implicated in the identity formation of African Americans as learners and intellectual beings. Not only are stories passed down from generation to generation about the meaning of literacy and the meaning of the denial of literacy, but these narratives show African Americans who they can become. As Dorothy Holland and others maintain, "Identities are the stories we tell ourselves and the world about who we are, and our attempt to act in accordance with these stories." For Elders, it was the story of Edith Folb, the first woman and the first Black person to graduate from the University of Arkansas Medical School, told at Philander-Smith College's weekly chapel service, that allowed her to see herself as a doctor. It was the story of Douglass's and other slaves' pursuit of literacy "in danger and darkness," passed on orally to Elders and almost certainly read by her in written narrative text, that motivated her to be committed to learning. It was the narrative of Richard Wright that figured centrally in Haki's redefinition of himself as a literate person. And it was the stories of her family and what they were willing to do with their education that framed the identity and possibilities for Gwendolyn Parker.

The philosophy of achievement that emerges from these narratives is predicated on, is responsive to, and exists in a dialectical relationship with the specific challenges African Americans faced in their pursuit of education and literacy. It is a philosophy that is predicated on and takes seriously the sociopolitical location of African Americans. For Africans in America, literacy laws were enacted to keep them as a people from voting, from exercising their citizenship rights. African-American teachers were paid less than white teachers, less was spent on African-American schools, and so on. There was a systematic denial and limiting of educational opportunity for African Americans precisely because they were African Americans. The philosophy of education that developed was informed by the particular ways in which literacy and education were implicated in the oppression of African Americans. It informed the role that education and schooling would assume in resistance and the struggle for freedom from the time of slavery to the Civil Rights era.

But what do all of these observations have to do with the current conversation about African-American school achievement? For what groups of African Americans, for what generations, is this philosophy of education still compelling? Among contemporary African-American youth, could this philosophy of education have the power to make academic achievement coincident with being African American? How would it be manifested, ritualized, represented in the post—Civil Rights era? Can it still play a role in the identity formation of African-American children? Could it play a central role in motivating contemporary African Americans to pursue education vigorously? If it is true that the media plays a central role in the construction of racial and gender identities, can a counternarrative about African Americans as intellectuals have sufficient power to contest the negative narratives about African Americans that are expressed in the media and encoded in the ideologies and practices of schools? What would it take for this historic philosophy of education to be systematically and intentionally passed on in families, community-based organizations, and schools? Under what conditions could it be passed on in a multiracial, multicultural school community?

And finally, how can this philosophy of achievement enter into dialogue with and be used to critique the explanatory models and their variations that have been used and continue to be used to discuss school performance of African Americans and other children of color? How would it be used in the development of a theory of achievement for African Americans at the beginning of the twentieth century?

Notes

1. Theresa Perry, "Freedom for Literacy and Literacy for Freedom: The African-American Philosophy of Education," in *Young, Gifted, and Black: Promoting High Achievement Among African American Students*, ed. C. Steele and A. G. Hilliard (New York: Beacon Press, 2004), pp. 11–51.

Section 4: Further Reading

Alim, H. Samy and John Baugh, eds. *Talkin Black Talk*. New York: Teachers College Press, 2007.

Baldwin, James. "If Black English Isn't a Language, Then Tell Me, What Is?" *New York Times* (29 July 1979).

Ball, Arnetha F. "Empowering Pedagogies that Enhance the Learning of Multicultural Students." *Teachers College Record*, 102 (2000): 1006–1034.

Delpit, Lisa. *Other People's Children: Cultural Conflict in the Classroom*. New York: New Press, 1995.

Haddix, Marcelle. "Black Boys Can Write: Challenging Dominant Framings of African American Adolescent Males in Literacy Research." *Journal of Adolescent & Adult Literacy*, 53.4 (2010): 341–343.

Hale, Janice E. *Unbank the Fire: Visions for the Education of African American Children*. Baltimore: The John Hopkins University Press, 1994.

Hill, Marc Lamont. *Beats, Rhymes, and Classroom Life: Hip-Hop Pedagogy and the Politics of Identity*. New York: Teachers College Press, 2009.

hooks, bell. *Teaching to Transgress: Education as the Practice of Freedom*. New York: Routledge, 1994.

King, Joyce E. "Diaspora Literacy and Consciousness in the Struggle against Miseducation in the Black Community." *The Journal of Negro Education*, 61.3 (1992): 317–340.

Kinloch, Valerie. *Harlem on Our Minds: Place, Race, and the Literacies of Urban Youth*. New York: Teachers College Press, 2009.

Kirkland, David. "We Real Cool: Examining Black Males and Literacy." *Reading Research Quarterly*, 44.3 (2009): 278–297.

Kynard, Carmen. "'I Want to Be African': In Search of a Black Radical Tradition/African-American-Vernacularized Paradigm for 'Students' Right to Their Own Language,' Critical Literacy, and 'Class Politics.'" *College English*, 69 (2007): 360–390.

Ladson-Billings, Gloria. *The Dream Keepers: Successful Teachers of African America Children*, 2nd edition. San Francisco: Jossey-Bass, 2009.

Lanehart, Sonja. *Sista, speak! Black Women Kinfolk Talk about Language and Literacy*. Austin: University of Texas Press, 2002.

Lee, Carol D. *Culture, Literacy, and Learning: Taking Bloom in the Midst of the Whirlwind*. New York: Teachers College Press, 2007.

Mahiri, Jahiri. *Shooting for Excellence. African American and Youth Culture in New Century Schools*. Urbana, IL: National Council for the Teachers of English, 1998.

Morrell, Ernest. "Critical Literacy and Urban Youth: Pedagogies of Access, Dissent, and Liberation." In *Your Average Nigga: Performing Race, Literacy, and Masculinity*. Detroit: Wayne State University, 2007.

Morrison, Toni. *Playing in the Dark: Whiteness and the Literary Imagination*. New York: Vintage, 1993.

Richardson, Elaine. *African American Literacies*. London: Routledge, 2003.

Winn, Maisha T. "Betwixt and Between: Literacy, Liminality, and the Celling of Black Girls." *Race, Ethnicity, and Education*, 13.4 (2010): 425–447.
Woodson, Carter Goodwin. (1933). "Education Under Outside Control." In *The Miseducation of the Negro*. Trenton, NJ: Africa World Press (*Excerpt*—"Vocational Guidance," pp. 26–37).

Section 4: Discussion Questions

1. What are some of the traditions of African American rhetorical practice that are presented in the selected works included in this section? In terms of rhetorical practices, what can be learned about, and gleaned from, a focus on African American language, literacy, and education?
2. What cultural, intellectual, and rhetorical features make the selected texts distinctively African or African American?
3. What roles, purposes, and function do community and community-building play in African and/or African American forms of education?
4. In what ways does language, as a communicative form, influence the rhetorical practices of African and African American writers?
5. What does it mean to see the world through an African American rhetorical perspective? How might this way of seeing serve as commentary on understandings of African and African American language, literacy, and education?
6. What can be learned about identity, community, communal action, deliberation, and discourse from the selected texts? How might these identified lessons be used to theorize a rhetoric of community?
7. What can be learned about the social, political, and educational complexities of Black life in White America from the writings of African American authors? How might these complexities contribute to a robust understanding of African American communicative practice as a communal and expressive form?

5

BLACK PRESENCE: AFRICAN AMERICAN POLITICAL RHETORIC

Edited and with an introduction by
Michelle Bachelor Robinson and Khirsten L. Echols
with Vorris L. Nunley

———◦◦◦◦◦———

An Introduction

Since the first Black slave slipped off to the hush harbor in the woods to preach the Bible-within-the-Bible to other Black folks outside the gaze of Whites; since Martin Delaney boldly argued that the Black race is the origin of humanity; since Malcolm X and Martin Luther King Jr. advocated for differing methodologies to achieve race equality, and ultimately when President Barack Obama, then presidential candidate, spoke about race in Philadelphia, African American rhetoric has always been political.

African American politics can be productively understood as a particular iteration of "micropolitics," a politics of the ordinary,[1] yet appropriated here to politicize Black habits, dispositions, feelings, bodies, emotions, and thinking. These embodied practices and responses were and are potential sites of emancipation, domination, and resistance—below, with, and through formal democratic institutions and procedures. This section is designed to capture the rhetoric employed by these practitioners to advance these rhetorical purposes in a range of political spheres.

However, in order to begin an exploration of African American rhetoric in the political sphere, one must understand the prevalence of the concept of *nommo* (see Smith's and Gilyard's essays in Unit 1), particularly in this section, as most of these pieces were composed, delivered, or performed for the purpose of mobilization to affect change, and so the power of the word at the most basic level is critical to shaping an exploration of African American political rhetoric.

African American rhetorics are anchored in the African concept of *nommo*. Yet, they circulate with an American, contemporary slant: the power of black affectivities mediated through and between African American bodies, speech, sounds, structures of feelings, and images. All resonating through and producing material and embodied effects upon the onto-epistemological (what it is *to be*), improvisational, macro- and micropolitics of African American lifeworlds.[2]

In short, African American rhetoric is about *presence*: Black presence—African American presences and affects in all their multiple, soulful, sassy, belligerent, poetic, noisy, complicit, resistant, queered, make-it-plain complicated, sacred, secular manifestations. More than existing in a particular place and time, Black presence is both being present and *being taken into account*. Black presence resists erasure and invisibility. Sometimes, embodying visibility and legibility through showin' up and showin' out. African American rhetoric proclaims that, paraphrasing Audre Lorde, we might as well groan, moan, sing, and shout; speak, move, floss, and swagger; because our silence will not save us; our attempts at decorous visibility and respectability will not hide us. African American rhetoric then is not a choice; it is a necessity, and this necessity makes it political. And so we focus on the vocal in this section. Many pieces have been orally delivered (though they may appear in print text here); some were written when Blacks occupied a smaller share of a public platform; and still others were composed to vast, wide, and diverse audiences. Because this section houses texts from a variety of historical and contemporary movements and events (e.g., abolitionists, women's rights, civil rights, Black Lives Matter), there is the ability to capture and represent the rhetoric in its original form, and so we have included a rich media section complete with links to video or audio representation of the rhetor's delivery when available, and textual representations when video and audio are unavailable.

The included African American performances and cultural products evoke the micropolitically mediated rhetorical situations and the African American subjects/folks responding to those situations. Micropolitically mediated as the reception of Black and Black diasporic bodies and culture are, they are rarely if ever deemed neutral or innocent in their gendered, classed, caste, and queered performance; in their intellectual and cultural content; and in their various modes and platforms of delivery—primarily speeches, but also essays, animation, music, and even stand-up comedy. Our method, informed by the micropolitics of African American life, while allowing the inclusion of canonical texts, such as Sojourner Truth's "Ain't I a Woman" and Martin Luther King Jr.'s "Letter From Birmingham Jail," also clears space for African American texts and cultural productions heretofore excluded, such as Ella Baker's "More Than a Hamburger," or Richard Pryor's "Niggas vs. The Police," exclusions due to archival myopia and conservatism, the politics of publishing, and masculinist notions of charisma and power that de-privilege the rhetorical performances of Black women. The inclusion of textual representations in the media list affords us the special opportunity of offering a diverse selection of political texts for this section. We include speeches and texts from formal and informal, official and unofficial, Black and mainstream occasions and sites; from rhetors who most Black folks embrace (President Obama) and others at whom they jeer (Clarence Thomas); and from Black bodies occupying and claiming various subject positions. This gesture is not a facile attempt at inclusion; rather, it is to more accurately and efficaciously map out the increasing heterogeneity of African American rhetorical terrain—conceptual and lived terrain that more fully reflects the protean micropolitics of African American experience.

And so this section on political rhetoric includes (whether in print here, in further readings, or on the companion website) pre-emancipation rhetoric of Benjamin Banneker, Frederick Douglass, and Sojourner Truth; the well-anthologized, yet essential, juxtaposed arguments of Booker T. Washington and W.E.B. Du Bois; the powerful voices of advocacy of Victoria Earle Matthews and Ida B. Wells at the turn of the century; but also well-known debates like Martin Luther King and Malcolm X and Anita Hill and Clarence Thomas. We round out the print text with important contemporary political voices on issues from self-actualization, the prison industrial complex, and hip-hop to language diversity and how to move forward making sure to look back with Louis Farrakhan, Angela Davis, David Banner, Audre Lorde, and Zadie Smith. Finally, no reader on African American rhetoric would be complete without the voice of our first African American president, Barack Obama, represented in both print text and the media section.

The media list in this section is rich, diverse, and inclusive with the many voices that space did not allow us to represent in print and includes the rhetoric of traditional African American political figures, like Mary Church Terrell, Mary McCleod Bethune, A. Philip Randolph, Adam Clayton Powell, Paul Robeson, Ella Baker, John Lewis, Stokely Carmichael, James Baldwin, Thurgood Marshall, Shirley Chisolm, Muhammad Ali, Huey Newton, Lani Guinier, Diahann Carroll, Bill Cosby, Harold Ford, and Condelezza Rice. The list also includes texts on important political issues in more artistic representations, like Paul Lawrence Dunbar, Richard Pryor,

Grandmaster Flash, Public Enemy, Sista Souljah, *The Boondocks*, Young Jeezy featuring Nas, and Saul Williams. Finally, the media list is a place where we provide additional texts to explore rhetors that do appear in print, like Frederick Douglass, Martin Luther King Jr., Malcolm X, Audre Lorde, and President Barack Obama. Because African American rhetoric is so necessarily political, this section (if used to the extent for which it was designed) offers a comprehensive and dense exploration of African American political rhetoric.

African American political rhetoric then is about possessing the presence to deliver the word, the power, and black affectivity of that delivery, and the intensities, power, and impact that power has on the audience, both inside and outside the culture. This section was designed to provide primary texts, both in print and media forms, for students to experience a diverse exploration of political rhetoric. The guiding questions will help to frame how these texts are thematically connected, and the guiding questions for the overall text will help students place the political rhetoric in this section in the larger conversation of African American rhetoric at large.

Notes

1. Micropolitics is a concept explored in *A Thousand Plateaus: Capitalism and Schizophrenia*, by Gilles Deleuze and Felix Guattari.
2. Lifeworlds is a term employed by Michael Hanchard in his book *Party/Politics: Culture, Community, and Agency in Black Political Thought*.

Benjamin Banneker

Benjamin Banneker (1731–1806) devoted much of his life to understanding astronomy by keeping an active log of his solar and lunar eclipse projects and computed ephemerides. On August 19, 1791, Banneker forwarded his calculations accompanied with a letter that engaged the conversation of race and rights of African Americans in the United States to Thomas Jefferson, then secretary of state. Banneker, aware of his rights and abilities, acknowledges the decision to initiate this conversation by choosing "a liberty which seemed to me scarcely allowable," because of "the almost general prejudice and prepossession which is so prevalent in the world against those of my complexion." He develops the conversation by citing Jefferson's own words from the Declaration of Independence in order to challenge Jefferson and his contemporaries on their treatment of African Americans. After Jefferson's acknowledgment of Banneker's letter, he forwarded it to the Marquis de Condorcet, the secretary of the Academie des Sciences in Paris. Later, the exchanges between Banneker and Jefferson were published as a separate pamphlet. They received wide publicity when Banneker published an ephemeris in Baltimore titled *Benjamin Banneker's Pennsylvania, Delaware, Maryland and Virginia Almanack and Ephemeris, for the Year of Our Lord, 1792; Being Bissextile, or Leap Year, and the Sixteenth Year of American Independence*. Banneker's almanacs were published every year from 1792 until 1797.

A Letter to Thomas Jefferson

Benjamin Banneker[1]

SIR,

I AM fully sensible of the greatness of that freedom, which I take with you on the present occasion; a liberty which seemed to me scarcely allowable, when I reflected on that distinguished and dignified station in which you stand, and the almost general prejudice and prepossession, which is so prevalent in the world against those of my complexion.

I suppose it is a truth too well attested to you, to need a proof here, that we are a race of beings, who have long labored under the abuse and censure of the world; that we have long been looked upon with an eye of contempt; and that we have long been considered rather as brutish than human, and scarcely capable of mental endowments.

Sir, I hope I may safely admit, in consequence of that report which hath reached me, that you are a man far less inflexible in sentiments of this nature, than many others; that you are measurably friendly, and well disposed towards us; and that you are willing and ready to lend your aid and assistance to our relief, from those many distresses, and numerous calamities, to which we are reduced. Now Sir, if this is founded in truth, I apprehend you will embrace every opportunity, to eradicate that train of absurd and false ideas and opinions, which so generally prevails with respect to us; and that your sentiments are concurrent with mine, which are, that one universal Father hath given being to us all; and that he hath not only made us all of one flesh, but that he hath also, without partiality, afforded us all the same sensations and endowed us all with the same faculties; and that however variable we may be in society or religion, however diversified in situation or color, we are all of the same family, and stand in the same relation to him.

Sir, if these are sentiments of which you are fully persuaded, I hope you cannot but acknowledge, that it is the indispensible duty of those, who maintain for themselves the rights of human nature, and who possess the obligations of Christianity, to extend their power and influence to the relief of every part of the human race, from whatever burden or oppression they may unjustly labor under; and this, I apprehend, a full conviction of the truth and obligation of these principles should lead all to. Sir, I have long been convinced, that if your love for yourselves, and for those inestimable laws, which preserved to you the rights of human nature, was founded on sincerity, you could not but be solicitous, that every individual, of whatever rank or distinction, might with you equally enjoy the blessings thereof; neither could you rest satisfied short of the most active effusion of your exertions, in order to their promotion from any state of degradation, to which the unjustifiable cruelty and barbarism of men may have reduced them.

Sir, I freely and cheerfully acknowledge, that I am of the African race, and in that color which is natural to them of the deepest dye; and it is under a sense of the most profound gratitude to the Supreme Ruler of the Universe, that I now confess to you, that I am not under that state of tyrannical thraldom, and inhuman captivity, to which too many of my brethren are doomed, but that I have abundantly tasted of the fruition of those blessings, which proceed from that free and unequalled liberty with which you are favored; and which, I hope, you will willingly allow you have mercifully received, from the immediate hand of that Being, from whom proceedeth every good and perfect Gift.

Sir, suffer me to recal to your mind that time, in which the arms and tyranny of the British crown were exerted, with every powerful effort, in order to reduce you to a state of servitude: look back, I entreat you, on the variety of dangers to which you were exposed; reflect on that time, in which every human aid appeared unavailable, and in which even hope and fortitude wore the aspect of inability to the conflict, and you cannot but be led to a serious and grateful sense of your miraculous and providential preservation; you cannot but acknowledge, that the present freedom and tranquility which you enjoy you have mercifully received, and that it is the peculiar blessing of Heaven.

This, Sir, was a time when you cleary saw into the injustice of a state of slavery, and in which you had just apprehensions of the horrors of its condition. It was now that your abhorïence thereof was so excited, that you publicly held forth this true and invaluable doctrine, which is worthy to be recorded and remembered in all succeeding ages: "We hold these truths to be self-evident, that all men are created equal; that they are endowed by their Creator with certain unalienable rights, and that among these are, life, liberty, and the pursuit of happiness." Here was a time, in which your tender feelings for yourselves had engaged you thus to declare, you were then impressed with proper ideas of the great violation of liberty, and the free possession of those blessings, to which you were entitled by nature; but, Sir, how pitiable is it to reflect, that although you were so fully convinced of the benevolence of the Father of Mankind, and of his equal and impartial distribution of these rights and privileges, which he hath conferred upon them, that you should at the same time counteract his mercies, in detaining by fraud and violence so numerous a part of my brethren, under groaning captivity and cruel oppression, that you should at the same time be found guilty of that most criminal act, which you professedly detested in others, with respect to yourselves.

I suppose that your knowledge of the situation of my brethren, is too extensive to need a recital here; neither shall I presume to prescribe methods by which they may be relieved, otherwise than by recommending to you and all others, to wean yourselves from those narrow prejudices which you have imbibed with respect to them, and as Job proposed to his friends, "put your soul in their souls' stead;" thus shall your hearts be enlarged with kindness and benevolence towards them; and thus shall you need neither the direction of myself or others, in what manner to proceed herein. And now, Sir, although my sympathy and affection for my brethren hath caused my enlargement thus far, I ardently hope, that your candor and generosity will plead with you in my behalf, when I make known to you, that it was not originally my design; but having taken up my pen in order to direct to you, as a present, a copy of an Almanac, which I have calculated for the succeeding year, I was unexpectedly and unavoidably led thereto.

This calculation is the production of my arduous study, in this my advanced stage of life; for having long had unbounded desires to become acquainted with the secrets of nature, I have had to gratify my curiosity herein, through my own assiduous application to Astronomical Study, in which I need not recount to you the many difficulties and disadvantages, which I have had to encounter.

And although I had almost declined to make my calculation for the ensuing year, in consequence of that time which I had allotted therefor, being taken up at the Federal Territory, by the request of Mr. Andrew Ellicott, yet finding myself under several engagements to Printers of this state, to whom I had communicated my design, on my return to my place of residence, I industriously applied myself thereto, which I hope I have accomplished with correctness and accuracy; a copy of which I have taken the liberty to direct to you, and which I humbly request you will favorably receive; and although you may have the opportunity of perusing it after its publication, yet I choose to send it to you in manuscript previous thereto, that thereby you might not only have an earlier inspection, but that you might also view it in my own hand writing.

And now, Sir, I shall conclude, and subscribe myself, with the most profound respect, Your most obedient humble servant,

BENJAMIN BANNEKER.
University of Virginia

Note

1. Benjamin Banneker, "A Letter to Thomas Jefferson," Maryland, Baltimore County, August 19, 1791, http://digital.library.temple.edu/cdm/ref/collection/p16002coll5/id/237.

Frederick Douglass

Frederick Douglass's (1818–1895) escape from slavery prompted pursuits of freedom and abolition. Douglass's long life afforded him the opportunity to compose three autobiographies over the course of his life: *Narrative of the Life of Frederick Douglass, an American slave* (1845), *My Bondage and My Freedom* (1855), and *Life and Times of Frederick Douglass* (1881). His writing as well as his speeches worked to advance the notion that slaves were indeed intellectually capable, which served to advance the larger abolition argument as well. Many of Douglass's arguments centered on topics related to equality, both racial and gender equality. On September 24, 1847, Frederick Douglass delivered his speech "Love of God, Love of Man, Love of Country" in Syracuse, New York. During the speech, Douglass appropriated the religious explanation used by many slaveholders to justify the ills of slavery and made a counterargument that questioned the morality of those men. He brought attention not only to moral distinctions but also to those of intellect and citizenship. Douglass assessed his role as an American citizen and asserted, "If I had a country I should be a patriot." He emphasized the intellectual and moral capacity that African Americans embodied as representative of their right to be accepted as equal citizens.

"Love of God, Love of Man, Love of Country" or "If I Had a Country, I Should Be a Patriot"

Frederick Douglass[1]

I like radical measures, whether adopted by Abolitionists or slaveholders. I do not know but I like them better when adopted by the latter. Hence I look with pleasure upon the movements of Mr. Calhoun and his party. I rejoice at any movement in the slave States with reference to this system of Slavery. Any movement there will attract attention to the system—a system, as Junius once said to Lord Granby, "which can only pass without condemnation as it passes without observation." I am anxious to have it seen of all men: hence I am delighted to see any effort to prop up the system on the part of the slaveholders. It serves to bring up the subject before the people; and hasten the day of deliverance. It is meant otherwise.

I am sorry that it is so. Yet the wrath of man may be made to praise God. He will confound the wisdom of the crafty, and bring to naught the counsels of the ungodly. The slaveholders are now marshalling their hosts for the propagation and extension of the institution—Abolitionists, on the other hand, are marshalling their forces not only against its propagation and extension, but against its very existence. Two large classes of the community, hitherto unassociated with the Abolitionists, have come up so far towards the right as to become opposed to the farther extension of the crime. I am glad to hear it. I like to gaze upon these two contending armies, for I believe it will hasten the dissolution of the present unholy Union, which has been justly stigmatized as "a covenant with death, an agreement with hell." I welcome the bolt, either from the North or the South, which shall shatter this Union; for under this Union lie the prostrate forms of three millions with whom I am identified. In consideration of their wrongs, of their sufferings, of their groans, I welcome the bolt, either from the celestial or from the infernal regions, which shall sever this Union in twain. Slaveholders are promoting it—Abolitionists are doing so. Let it come, and when it does, our land will rise up from an incubus; her brightness shall reflect against the sky, and shall become the beacon light of liberty in the Western world. She shall then, indeed, become "the land of the free and the home of the brave." For sixteen years, Wm. Lloyd Garrison and a noble army of the friends of emancipation have been labouring in season and out of season, amid smiles and frowns, sunshine and clouds, striving to establish the conviction through this land, that to hold and traffic in human flesh is a sin against God. They have been somewhat successful; but they have been in no wise so successful as they might have been, had the men and women at the North rallied around them as they had a right to hope from their profession. They have had to contend not only with skillful politicians, with a deeply preju-diced and pro-slavery community, but with eminent Divines, Doctors of Divinity, and Bishops. Instead of encouraging them as friends, they have acted as enemies. For many days did Garrison go the rounds of the city of Boston to ask of the ministers the poor privilege of entering their chapels and lifting up his voice for the dumb. But their doors were bolted, their gates barred, and their pulpits hermetically sealed. It was not till an infidel hall was thrown open, that the voice of dumb millions could be heard in Boston.

I take it that all who have heard at all on this subject, are well convinced that the stronghold of Slavery is in the pulpit. Say what we may of politicians and political parties, the power that holds the keys of the dungeon in which the bondman is confined, is the pulpit. It is that power which is dropping, dropping, constantly dropping on the ear of this people, creating and mould-ing the moral sentiment of the land. This they have sufficiently under their control that they can change it from the spirit of hatred to that of love to mankind. That they do it not, is evident from the results of their teaching. The men who wield the blood-clotted cow-skin come from our Sabbath Schools in the Southern States. Who act as slave-drivers? The men who go forth from our own congregations here. Why, if the Gospel were truly preached among us, a man would as soon think of going into downright piracy as to offer himself as a slave-driver. In Farmington, two sons of members of the Society of Friends are cooly proposing to go the South and engage in the honourable office of slave-driving for a thousand dollars a year. People at the North talk cooly of uncles, cousins, and brothers who are slaveholders, and of their coming to visit them. If the Gospel were truly preached here, you would as soon talk of having an uncle or brother a brothel keeper as a slaveholder; for I hold that every slaveholder, no matter how pure he may be, is a keeper of a house of ill-fame. Every kitchen is a brothel, from that of Dr. Fuller's to that of James K. Polk's (Applause). I presume I am addressing a virtuous audience—I presume I speak to virtuous females—and I ask you to consider this one feature of Slavery. Think of a million of females absolutely delivered up into the hands of tyrants, to do what they will with them-to dispose of their persons in any way they see fit. And so entirely are they at the disposal of their masters, that if they raise their hands against them, they may be put to death for daring to resist their infernal aggression.

We have been trying to make this thing appear sinful. We have not been able to do so yet. It is not admitted, and I hardly know how to argue against it. I confess that the time for argument seems almost gone by. What do the people want? Affirmation upon affirmation,—denunciation upon denunciation,—rebuke upon rebuke?

We have men in this land now advocating evangelical flogging. I hold in my hand a sermon recently published by Rev. Bishop Meade, of Virginia. Before I read that part in favour of evan-gelical flogging, let me read a few extracts from another part, relating to the duties of the slave. The sermon, by the way, was published with a view of its being read by Christian masters to their slaves. White black birds! (Laughter.)

(*Mr. Douglass here assumed a most grotesque look, and with a canting tone of voice, read as* follows.) "Having thus shown you the chief duties you owe to your great Master in Heaven, I now come to lay before you the duties you owe to your masters and mistresses on earth. And for this you have one general rule that you ought always to carry in your minds, and that is, to do all services for them, as if you did it for God himself. Poor creatures! you little consider when you are idle, and neglectful of your master's business; when you steal, waste, and hurt any of their substance; when you are saucy and impudent; when you are telling them lies and deceiving them; or when you prove stubborn and sullen, and will not do the work you are set about, with-out stripes and vexation; you do not consider, I say, that what faults you are guilty of towards your masters and mistresses, are faults done against God himself, who hath set your masters and mistresses over you in his own stead, and expects that you will do for them just as you would do for him. And pray, do not think that I want to deceive you, when I tell you that your masters and mistresses are God's overseers; and that if you are faulty towards them, God himself will punish you severely for it."

This is some of the Southern religion. Do you not think you would "grow in grace and in the knowledge of the truth." (Applause.) I come now to evangelical flogging. There is nothing said about flogging—that word is not used. It is called correction; and that word as it is understood at the North, is some sort of medicine. (Laughter.) Slavery has always sought to hide itself under different names. The mass of the people call it "our peculiar institution." There is no harm in that. Others call it (they are the more pious sort), "our Patriarchal institution." (Laughter.) Politicians have called it "our social system"; and people in social life have called it "our domestic institution." Abbot Lawrence has recently discovered a new name for it—he calls it "unenlightened labour." (Laughter.) The Methodists in their last General Conference, have invented a new name—"the impediment." (Laughter.) To give you some idea of evangelical flogging, under the name of correction, there are laws of this description,—"any white man killing a slave shall be punished as though he shall have killed a white person, unless such a slave die under moderate correction." It commences with a plain proposition.

"Now when correction is given you, you either deserve it, or you do not deserve it." (Laughter.)

That is very plain, almost as safe as that of a certain orator:—"Ladies and Gentlemen, it is my opinion, my deliberate opinion, after a long consideration of the whole matter, that as a general thing, all other things being equal, there are fewer persons to be found in towns sparsely populated, than in larger towns more thickly settled." (Laughter.)

The Bishop goes on to say—"Whether you really deserve it or not," (one would think that would make a difference), "it is your duty, and Almighty God requires that you bear it patiently. You may perhaps think that this is a hard doctrine," (and it admits of little doubt), "but if you consider it right you must needs think otherwise of it." (It is clear as mud. I suppose he is now going to reason them into the propriety of being flogged evangelically.) "Suppose you deserve correction; you cannot but see that it is just and right you should meet with it. Suppose you do not, or at least so much or so severe; you perhaps have escaped a great many more, and are at last paid for all. Suppose you are quite innocent; is it not possible you may have done some other bad thing which was never discovered, and Almighty God would not let you escape without punishment one time or another? Ought you not in such cases to give glory to Him?" (Glory!) (Much laughter.)

I am glad you have got to the point that you can laugh at the religion of such fellows as this Doctor. There is nothing that will facilitate our cause more than getting the people to laugh at that religion which brings its influence to support traffic in human flesh. It has deceived us so long that it has overawed us.

For a long time when I was a slave, I was led to think from hearing such passages as "servants obey, &c." that if I dared to escape, the wrath of God would follow me. All are willing to acknowledge my right to be free; but after this acknowledgement, the good man goes to the Bible and says "after all I see some difficulty about this thing. You know, after the deluge, there was Shem, Ham, and Japhet; and you know that Ham was black and had a curse put upon him; and I know not but it would be an attempt to thwart the purposes of Jehovah if these men were set at liberty." It is this kind of religion I wish to have you laugh at—it breaks the charm there is about it. If I could have the men at this meeting who hold such sentiments and could hold up the mirror to let them see themselves as others see them, we should soon make head against this pro-slavery religion.

I dwell mostly upon the religious aspect, because I believe it is the religious people who are to be relied on in this Anti-Slavery movement. Do not misunderstand my railing—do not class me with those who despise religion—do not identify me with the infidel. I love the religion of Christianity—which cometh from above—which is pure, peaceable, gentle, easy to be entreated, full of good fruits, and without hypocrisy. I love that religion which sends its votaries to bind up the wounds of those who have fallen among thieves. By all the love I bear to such a Christianity as this, I hate that of the Priest and Levite, that with long-faced Phariseeism goes up to Jerusalem and worships, and leaves the bruised and wounded to die. I despise that religion that can carry Bibles to the heathen on the other side of the globe and withhold them from [the] heathen on this side—which can talk about human rights yonder and traffic in human flesh here. I love that which makes its votaries do to others as they would that others should do to them. I hope to see a revival of it—thank God it is revived. I see revivals of it in the absence of the other sort of revivals. I believe it to be confessed now, that there has not been a sensible man converted after the old sort of way, in the last five years. Le Roy Sunderland, the mesmerizer, has explained all this away, so that Knapp and others who have converted men after that sort have failed.

There is another religion. It is that which takes off fetters instead of binding them on—that breaks every yoke—that lifts up the bowed down. The Anti-Slavery platform is based on this kind of religion. It spreads its table to the lame, the halt, and the blind. It goes down after a long neglected race. It passes, link by link till it finds the lowest link in humanity's chain—humanity's most degraded form in the most abject condition. It reaches down its arm and tells them to stand up. This is Anti-Slavery—this is Christianity. It is reviving gloriously among the various denominations. It is threatening to supercede those old forms of religion having all of the love of God and none of man in it. (Applause.) I now leave this aspect of the subject and proceed to inquire into that which probably must be the inquiry of every honest mind present. I trust I do not misjudge the character of my audience when I say they are anxious to know in what way they're contributing to uphold Slavery.

The question may be answered in various ways. I leave the outworks of political parties and social arrangements, and come at once to the Constitution, to which I believe all present are devotedly attached I will not say all, for I believe I know some, who, however they may be disposed to admire some of the beautiful truths set forth in that instrument, recognize its pro-slavery features, and are ready to form a republic in which there shall be neither tyrant nor slave. The Constitution I hold to be radically and essentially slave-holding, in that it gives the physical and numerical power of the nation to keep the slave in his chains, by promising that that power shall in any emergency be brought to bear upon the slave, to crush him in obedience to his master. The language of the Constitution is you shall be a slave or die. We know it is such, and knowing it we are not disposed to have part nor lot with that Constitution. For my part I had rather that my right hand should wither by my side than cast a ballot under the Constitution of the United States.

Then, again, in the clause concerning fugitives—in this you are implicated. Your whole country is one vast hunting ground from Texas to Maine. Ours is a glorious land; and from across the Atlantic we welcome those who are stricken by the storms of despotism. Yet the damning facts remain, there is not a rood of earth under the stars and the eagle of your flag, where a man of my complexion can stand free. There is no mountain so high, no plain so extensive, no spot so sacred, that it can secure to me the right of liberty. Wherever waves the star-spangled banner there the bondman may be arrested and hurried back to the jaws of Slavery. This is your "land of the free," your "home of the brave." From Lexington, from Ticonderoga, from Bunker Hill, where rises that grand shaft with its capstone in the clouds, asks, in the name of the first blood that spurted in behalf of freedom, to protect the slave from the infernal clutches of his master. That petition would be denied, and he bid go back to the tyrant.

I never knew what freedom was till I got beyond the limits of the American eagle. When I first rested my head on a British Island I felt that the eagle might scream, but from its talons and beak

I was free, at least for a time. No slave-holder can clutch me on British soil. There I could gaze the tyrant in the face and with the indignation of a tyrant in my look, wither him before me. But republican, Christian America will aid the tyrant in catching his victim.

I know this kind of talk is not agreeable to what are called patriots. Indeed, some have called me a traitor. That profanely religious Journal "The Olive Branch," edited by the Rev. Mr. Norris, recommended that I be hung as a traitor. Two things are necessary to make a traitor. One is, he shall have a country. (Laughter and applause.) I believe if I had a country, I should be a patriot. I think I have all the feelings necessary—all the moral material, to say nothing about the intellectual. I do not know that I ever felt the emotion, but sometimes thought I had a glimpse of it. When I have been delighted with the little brook that passes by the cottage in which I was born,—with the woods and the fertile fields, I felt a sort of glow which I suspect resembles a little what they call patriotism. I can look with some admiration on your wide lakes, your fertile fields, your enterprise, your industry, your many lovely institutions. I can read with pleasure your Constitution to establish justice, and secure the blessings of liberty to posterity. Those are precious sayings to my mind. But when I remember that the blood of four sisters and one brother, is making fat the soil of Maryland and Virginia,—when I remember that an aged grandmother who has reared twelve children for the Southern market, and these one after another as they arrived at the most interesting age, were torn from her bosom,—when I remember that when she became too much racked for toil, she was turned out by a professed Christian master to grope her way in the darkness of old age, literally to die with none to help her, and the institutions of this country sanctioning and sanctifying this crime, I have no words of eulogy, I have no patriotism. How can I love a country where the blood of my own blood, the flesh of my own flesh, is now toiling under the lash?—America's soil reddened by the stain from woman's shrinking flesh.

No, I make no pretension to patriotism. So long as my voice can be heard on this or the other side of the Atlantic, I will hold up America to the lightning scorn of moral indignation. In doing this, I shall feel myself discharging the duty of a true patriot; for he is a lover of his country who rebukes and does not excuse its sins. It is righteousness that exalteth a nation while sin is a reproach to any people. But to the idea of what you at the North have to do with Slavery. You furnish the bulwark of protection, and promise to put the slaves in bondage. As the American Anti-Slavery Society says, "if you will goon branding, scourging, sundering family ties, trampling in the dust your down trodden victims, you must do it at your own peril." But if you say, "we of the North will render you no assistance: if you still continue to trample on the slave, you must take the consequences," I tell you the matter will soon be settled.

I have been taunted frequently with the want of valour: so has my race, because we have not risen upon our masters. It is adding insult to injury to say this. You belong to 17,000,000, with arms, with means of locomotion, with telegraphs. We are kept in ignorance three millions to seventeen. You taunt us with not being able to rescue ourselves from your clutch. Shame on you! Stand aside—give us fair play—leave us with the tyrants, and then if we do not take care of ourselves, you may taunt us. I do not mean by this to advocate war and bloodshed. I am not a man of war. The time was when I was. I was then a slave: I had dreams, horrid dreams of freedom through a sea of blood. But when I heard of the Anti-Slavery movement, light broke in upon my dark mind. Bloody visions fled away, and I saw the star of liberty peering above the horizon. Hope then took the place of desperation, and I was led to repose in the arms of Slavery. I said, I would suffer rather than do any act of violence—rather than that the glorious day of liberty might be postponed.

Since the light of God's truth beamed upon my mind, I have become a friend of that religion which teaches us to pray for our enemies—which, instead of shooting balls into their hearts, loves them. I would not hurt a hair of a slaveholder's head. I will tell you what else I would not do. I would not stand around the slave with my bayonet pointed at his breast, in order to keep him in the power of the slaveholder.

I am aware that there are many who think the slaves are very well off, and that they are very well treated, as if it were possible that such a thing could be. A man happy in chains! Even the eagle loves liberty.

> Go, let a cage, with grates of gold,
> And pearly roof, the eagle hold;
> Let dainty viands be his fare,
> And give the captive tenderest care;
> But say, in luxury's limits pent,
> Find you the king of birds content?
> No, oft he'll sound the startling shriek,
> And dash the grates with angry beak.
> Precarious freedom's far more dear,
> Than all the prison's pampring cheer!
> He longs to see his eyrie's seat,
> Some cliff on ocean's lonely shore,
> Whose old bare top the tempests beat,
> And round whose base the billows roar,
> When tossed by gales, they yawn like graves,—
> He longs for joy to skim those waves;
> Or rise through tempest-shrouded air,
> And thick and dark, with wild winds swelling,
> To brave the lightning's lurid glare,
> And talk with thunders in their dwelling.

As with the eagle, so with man. No amount of attention or finery, no dainty dishes can be a substitute for liberty. Slaveholders know this, and knowing it, they exclaim,—"The South are surrounded by a dangerous population, degraded, stupid savages, and if they could but entertain the idea that immediate, unconditional death would not be their portion, they would rise at once and enact the St. Domingo tragedy. But they are held in subordination by the consciousness that the whole nation would rise and crush them." Thus they live in constant dread from day to day.

Friends, Slavery must be abolished, and that can only be done by enforcing the great principles of justice. Vainly you talk about voting it down. When you have cast your millions of ballots, you have not reached the evil. It has fastened its root deep into the heart of the nation, and nothing but God's truth and love can cleanse the land. We must change the moral sentiment. Hence we ask you to support the Anti-Slavery Society. It is not an organization to build up political parties, or churches, nor to pull them down, but to stamp the image of Anti-Slavery truth upon the community. Here we may all do something.

In the world's broad field of battle,
In the bivouac of life,
Be not like dumb driven cattle—
Be a hero in the strife.

Note

1. Frederick Douglass, "Love of God, Love of Man, Love of Country" or "If I Had a Country, I Should Be a Patriot," Syracuse, New York, September 24, 1847.

Martin R. Delaney

Martin R. Delany (1812–1885) was well accomplished during his lifetime, as he was one of the first three Blacks to be admitted to Harvard Medical School. He worked with Fredrick Douglass to publish the *North Star*, and he was the first African American field officer in the United States Army during the Civil War. Due in part to his publication of *The Condition, Elevation, Emigration, and Destiny of Colored People of the United States, Politically Considered* (1852), which challenged mainstream notions of abolitionism and encouraged emigration to Central America, Delany became known to many as the first proponent of Black nationalism. He continued his Black nationalist thoughts and writings in many of his texts, including *Principia of Ethnology: The Origins of Race and Color, with an Archaeological Compendium of Ethiopian and Egyptian Civilization* (1880), which seeks to respond to the Duke of Argyll's ethnological inquiry (*Primeval Man*) about the origin of man. In his response, Delany composes a scientific and sociological treatment of the origins of race and color using biblical allusions that reveal Black as the original, dominant race.

Preface

Martin R. Delaney[1]

In presenting to the scientific and serious inquirer such a work as this, I may venture the opinion that, for the first time, public attention has been called to facts essential to a satisfactory solution of the all-important question in social science, so befittingly put forth by the Duke of Argyll, in his ethnological inquiry, Primeval Man: "That question is not the rise of kingdoms, but the Origin of Races * * * When and how did they begin? * * * And in this feature of color it is remarkable that we have every possible variety of tint from the fairest to the blackest races, so that the one extreme passes into the other by small and insensible gradations." This then is the great mystery which this little treatise purposes to solve, as well as to show the first steps in the progress of civilization, the origin and institution of letters and literature. On the delicate subject of the integrity of the races, let it also be understood that we purpose, so far as the pure races are concerned, to have once and forever settled that they are indestructible, as proven in this treatise. That, as in the substance and science of chemistry, the two extremes, saccharine and acid—the most intense sweetness and the most intense sourness—are produced by the same material and essential properties, so is it in the substance and science of animal chemistry in the human family, in relation to color or complexion of the skin; that the two extremes of color, from the most negative white—"including every possible variety of tint"—up to the blackest, are all produced by the same material and essential properties of color. This much I have deemed it proper as a preface to add, to prepare the mind of the reader for an inquiry which, I may venture to say, he will not regret having made, and which may induce others of higher attainments to prosecute the subject to different conclusions. If in this I have been successful, in aiding to find the key to the discovery of the all-important subject of variety of complexions, or Origin of Races and Color, however little that aid, I shall have reached the zenith of my desire.

M. R. D.

Charleston, May 6th. 1878.

The Origin of Races

We have shown the "method" of the Creator, in effecting his design for man to "scatter abroad upon the face of the whole earth;" to "multiply and replenish it." But we have not yet seen, how the division was brought about by the confusion of tongues, so as to settle and harmonize the people, instead of distracting and discouraging them. What mark of distinction could there have been given to the multitudes of this "one people" previous to separation, to enable them to recognize any individual of a separate division, without speaking? It must be seen, that such an act of All-wise interposition was essential to enable each individual of any one of the now three grand divisions of the new tongues, when seen, to identify the other without speaking; otherwise, there would have been produced a "confusion worse confounded."

"And one of the questions on which testimony bears, is a question of paramount importance in determining the antiquity of the human family," says the Duke of Argyll. "That question is not the rise of kingdoms, but the origin of races. The varieties of man are a great mystery. The physical differences which these varieties involve may be indeed, and often are, much exaggerated. Yet these differences are distinct, and we are naturally impelled to ask When and How did they begin? The question When stands before the question How. The fundamental problem to be solved is this: can such a variety have descended from a single stock? And if they can, then must not a vast, indefinite lapse of time have been occupied in the gradual development of divergent types?" This "mystery" we shall hope to solve by the aid of the light of science, and assistance of Divine authority, enabling us to discover the secrets of the laws of nature.

"And the Lord said, Behold the people is one, and they have all one language;" "let us go down, and there confound their language." Behold the people are one; that is they are all of one stock, descended from the same parentage, all still living, consequently they consider themselves all one family. To separate this family was the paramount object, and to sever their interest in each other was necessary to this separation.

The sons of Noah were three in number: Shem, Ham and Japheth. That these three sons were the active heads of the people as directors and patriarchal leaders, there is no doubt.

There is to us another fact of as little doubt; that is, that these three sons of Noah all differed in complexion, and proportionate numbers of the people—their dependants in and about the city and around about the Tower—also differed as did the three sons in complexion. And these different complexions in the people, at that early period, when races were unknown, would have no more been noticed as a mark of distinction, than the variation in the color of the hair of those that are white, mark them among themselves as distinct peoples.

That Shem was of the same complexion as Noah, his father and mother—the Adamic complexion—there is no doubt in our mind. And that Ham the second son was swarthy in complexion, we have as little doubt. Indeed, we believe it is generally conceded by scholars, though disputed by some, that the word Ham means "dark," "swarthy," "sable." And it has always been conceded, and never, as we know of, seriously disputed, that Japheth was white.

Of one thing we are morally certain, that after the confusion of tongues, each one of these three sons of Noah, turned and went in different directions with their followers. These followers were just so many and no more, than those who spoke one and the same language. And there can be no reasonable doubt, in our mind, that these people were all of the same complexion with each of the sons of Noah whom they followed. On leaving the ark, they were one family, relatives, continuing together as "one people," all morally and socially blind and ignorant of any difference of characteristics personal, or interests general, as much so as a family of children with themselves toward the family, till years of maturity bring about a change. Hence, when the confusion took place, their eyes became open to their difference in complexion with each other, as a division, each preferring those of their kind with whom they went, thus permanently uniting their destiny.

Shem settled in Asia, peopling the country around and about the centre from where they scattered. Ham went to the south-west, and Japheth to the north-west. And it will not be disputed, that from then to the present day, the people in those regions where those three sons are said to have located—the three grand divisions of the Eastern Hemisphere: Asia, Africa and

Europe—are, with the exceptions to be hereafter accounted for, of the distinct complexions of those attributed to Shem, Ham and Japheth—yellow,[2] black and white. And this confusion of tongues, and scattering abroad in the earth, were the beginning and origin of races.

"But the great question," says the Duke of Argyll, "is not the rise of kingdoms, but the origin of races. When and How did they begin?" This we propose to show, in the next chapter, by an indisputable explanation of the origin of color by transmission of the parents.

How Color Originates

"CAN such varieties," inquires the Duke, "have descended from a single stock?" And why not? His Grace has truly said in another place quoted, "It is not in itself inconsistent with the Theistic argument, or with belief in the ultimate agency and directing power of a Creative mind. This is clear, since we never think of any difficulty in reconciling that belief with our knowledge of the ordinary laws of animal and vegetable reproduction."

Is it reasonable to suppose that there were necessarily original parents for all the varieties in every species of animals and vegetables? Must there have necessarily been a black and white cock, and a black and white hen, of all the varieties of fowls of every species; a black and white male and a black and white female of all the cattle stock of every variety of the same species; a black and white male, and a black and white female, of all animals, canine and feline, of each variety of the same species? Were there necessarily separate creations for each of the same species of different colors among all these animals, beasts and fowls? Certainly not; and no hypothesis can make it affirmatively tenable. And just here, whence comes a black lamb, born of white stock, a circumstance happening frequently on almost every sheep farm, where every ram is white, and not the possibility of a black ram communicating with them? This certainly is a theme worthy of the attention of the leading minds in social science.

One remarkable fact of a law in procreation, which seems inexplicable, is the sexes always differ in color; the male invariably—with occasional exceptions—being white, and the female, dark or gray. We refer to the goose and gander. Why this should be so we know as little, and probably less, than we do why there should be races of man, differing in complexion, all from the same parent stock.

The Duke has wisely said, "Creation has had a method!" and again: "The same language might be applied, without the alteration of a word, to the origin of species, if it were indeed true, that new kinds, as well as new individuals, were created by being born." Shem, Ham and Japheth, the three sons of Noah, we believe to have been, and history so records them, yellow, black and white; and here hangs that mystery of the unity and brotherhood of man, that persons of three distinct complexions could possibly be born of the same father and mother of one race and color. And that which seems to be enveloped in inexplicable concealment, is indeed to our mind, a comprehensible law of God's all-wise providence.

Let us take a peep into the laws of nature, and for a little, follow them as our guide. Our present familiarity with the spectroscope, gives us a knowledge of the properties of the sun, as transmitted through the rays, reflecting all the colors of the prism or rainbow. Solid matter of mineral substances, we know to be among these properties.

Whatever has color then, whether animal, vegetable or mineral, receives these colors directly from the sun; that is, the essential properties that form or compose them. This is by a physiological process, called elaboration and selection, whether in animal, vegetable or mineral chemistry, or the natural functions of these systems, unaided by art. Of all the systems, general and particular, the human presents the most beautiful and comprehensive illustration of God's wonderful providence in the works of creation, But says his Grace of Argyll: "What of that vast continent of Africa; when and how did that negro race begin, which is both one of the most ancient and one of the most strongly marked among the varieties of man?" This is the cloud we design to dispel, and reveal the hidden secrets of a thousand ages.

The human body is covered by a structure composed of three distinct parts: the *cuticle* or external surface; the *rete mucosum*, middle or intermediate structure; and the *cutis vera* or true skin, underlying the other two, covering the whole surface of the fleshy parts or muscular system, called the hide in slaughtered animals.

The rete mucosum is a colorless jelly-like substance, composed of infinitesimal cells like a sponge or honey-comb. The cuticle or external surface is an extremely thin structure, colorless, and as perfectly clear and transparent as crystal glass. The upper surface of the cutis vera or true skin—that part in contact with the rete mucosum—is perfectly white. White is simply negative, having no color at all.

It will at once be observed, that the cuticle or external surface being transparent, the rete mucosum next below it being also colorless, and the surface of the cutis vera underlying all being white, that all human beings by nature are first white, at some period of existence, whether born white or not.

The cells of the rete mucosum are filled with limpid fluid, and whatever the complexion of an individual or race, the coloring matter is deposited in the cells of the rete mucosum, mixed with the limpid fluid. This is deposited there by the process of elaboration and selection in animal chemistry, a function simply of physiology.

This coloring matter in the Caucasian or white race is *rouge* as we shall term it, the essential properties which give redness to the rose. When a white person blushes, red matter rushes into the cells of the rete mucosum, then recedes, leaving them as before, colorless, and the complexion white. When a white person has rosy cheeks or "ruby lips," there is a fixed deposit of rouge in those parts; but where they are pale and "colorless," there is an absence of rouge or coloring matter in the rete mucosum. In the Mongolian or yellow race of Asia, the coloring matter is the same—rouge—modified by peculiar elaboration, and uniformly infused into the rete mucosum, giving the yellow tinge—one of the known properties of the sun's rays—to the complexion.

And in the African or black race of Africa, the coloring matter is *the same* as that in the other two races, being rouge concentrated, which makes a pigment—the *pigmentum nigrum* of physiology—or a black matter. Thus the color of the blackest African is produced by *identically the same* essential coloring matter that gives the "rosy cheeks and ruby lips" to the fairest and most delicately beautiful white lady.

For illustration, to prove that concentrated rouge or concrete redness is black, take blood caught in a vessel, let it cool and dry up by evaporation of the liquid part; when condensed in a solid mass it becomes perfectly black, more so than the blackest human being ever seen. Look again at the fruits, black-berries, black-cherries, poke-berries and the like. From greenness, discoloration goes on till approaching a whiteness, when a faint redness ensues, gradually increasing to a deep red, which merges into blackness, the intense color of red.

Take now this clot of dried blood, and these fruits, macerate them in water and you have not a black, but assuredly a red solution. Compare these deep red fruits called black with the color of the blackest person in complexion, and there will be the most remarkable contrast between the fruit and the skin.

May it not be seen by this, in the language of the Duke, that "new kinds as well as new individuals can be born"? Cannot God's wonderful and inscrutable providence be seen in this simple but comprehensibly beautiful law of procreation? It certainly can.

Here we see that the first son of Noah, Shem, was born with a high degree of a certain complexion or color; the second son, Ham, with a higher degree or intensity of the same color, making a different complexion; and the third son Japheth, with the least of the same color, which gives an entirely different complexion from either. The three brothers were all of the *same color*—rouge—which being possessed in different degrees simply, gave them different complexions.

Was there any miracle in this; any departure from the regular order of the laws of nature, necessary to the production in these three sons of a different complexion by the same father and mother of one complexion? Certainly not, as it is common to see parents of one complexion, and hair and eyes of one color, produce children with hair and eyes of various colors. Then the same laws in physiology, which produced the former of the variations also produced the other; but for His all-wise purposes—doubtless the production of fixed races of man—the effect was placed upon the skin instead of the eyes and hair.

For the convenience of classification, these complexions may be termed *positive, medium*, and *negative*. Ham was positive, Shem medium, and Japheth negative. And here it may be remarked as a curious fact, that in the order of these degrees of complexion which indicated the ardor and temperament of races they represented, so was the progress of civilization propagated and carried forward by them. But is it still in doubt, that the color of the African is homogeneous with that of the Mongolian and Caucasian races, or that either is identified with that of the other? In this, too, we summon the incontestable laws of nature. In this we have reference simply to the three original races—Mongolian, African and Caucasian, or yellow, black and white.

Physiology classifies the admixture of the races by a cross between the white and black, as a mulatto; between the mulatto and white, a quadroon; between the quadroon and white, a quintroon; between the quintroon and white, a sextaroon; between the sextaroon and white, a septaroon; between the septaroon and white, an octoroon. The same numerical classifications are given a like number of crosses between the offspring of the black and mulatto, with a prefix of the adjective "black"; as a black quadroon, and so on to octoroon. A cross between the American Indian and a white, is called a Mustee or Mustezo; and a cross between the Indian and black, is called a Sambo or Zambo; and the complexional distinction is precisely the same, either white or black, as that of the offspring between the mulatto and a white or black. Here the beauty and wisdom of that Divine law, creating man with a medium complexion, from whence all others originated, is apparent, the Indian being of the Adamic or original complexion.

Now, what is here to be observed as an exact and, with little variation, almost never failing result, in this law of procreation between the African and Caucasian, or white and black races is, that these crosses go on with a nicety of reducing and blending the complexion, till it attains its original standard to either pure white or pure black, on the side by which the cross is continued from the first. By this it is seen that each race is equally *reproducing, absorbing*, and *enduring*, neither of which can be extinguished or destroyed—all admixtures running out into either of the original races, upon the side which preponderates.

This is an important truth, worthy the attention and serious consideration of the social scientist, philosopher, and statesman. That two races as distinct as the black and white, may dwell together in their purity, is marvellously true, because whatever of crosses may take place, they will run out into purity on one side or the other, by intermarriage on either side continued[3] And how wonderfully typical of the first original man, is this crossing of the races; the offspring of the white and black being yellow, precisely the complexion of Adam, the first man!

Shem, Ham and Japheth, the sons of Noah and wife, who were Adamites and of one complexion, were themselves of three different complexions, as a means in the providence of God's economy, to the accomplishment of his ends in the progress of civilization.

"And the Lord said, Behold the people is one." They were one in descent, one in family, one in interest, one in design, and one in purpose; having one language, they had no other thought than remaining together. And so doubtless would have continued as one, had not some sufficient cause transpired, to completely break up their interests, and compel them to a forced separation. "So the Lord scattered them abroad from thence, upon the face of all the earth;" and this separation of these three brothers was the *origin of races*. Each of these brothers headed and led his people with a language, and in all reasonable probability, a complexion similar to his own, each settling the then known three parts of the earth—Asia, Africa and Europe.

And God's design in the creation of the races was accomplished, because it fixed in the people a desire to be separated by reason of race affinity. To "replenish and multiply," or the peopling of the earth, was a principal command by God, given to man; and by this was carried out one of the intentions of the Divine will in creation.

Can his Grace, the Duke of Argyll, now see "when and how did that negro race begin"?

Notes

1. Martin R. Delaney, *Principia of Ethnology: The Origin of Races and Color* (Philadelphia: Harper & Brother, 1880).
2. Yellow—called *brown* in South Carolina and the West Indies.
3. Hon. Henry Clay, the great statesman, years ago, when the humanitarian discussions concerning the two races in America were attracting public attention, in an able letter suggested a prohibition to the importation of the black race, and a continual cross, when they would become extinct. The distinguished statesman had by observation, evidently become acquainted with the fact, that the black race could be absorbed by the white, without probably understanding at all that this was a mutual and unalterable law of procreation between the two races, applying equally to both white and black.

Victoria Earle Matthews

Victoria Earle Matthews (1861–1907) was an activist-writer whose work was connected to the equality of rights and freedoms experienced by Americans, specifically women and African Americans. As a response to John W. Jacks's 1895 open letter addressing African American women and their "moral" state in the United States, Matthews delivered her speech "The Awakening of the Afro-American Woman" before an audience at The Christian Endeavor Convention in San Francisco, California, on July 11, 1897. Her argument offered an alternative view of Black womanhood, one that painted a picture of piety, strength, fortitude, and industriousness, one that credits Black women in the South with making something post-slavery from the nothingness that slavery left. Matthews also shed light on the lack of value and recognition assigned to Black women. She uses Jacks's claims, specifically those of Christianity, as a site for understanding universal issues, with specific attention to the needs of the African American woman.

The Awakening of the Afro-American Woman (1897)

Victoria Earle Matthews[1]

The awakening to life of any of the forces of nature is the most mysterious as it is the sublimest of spectacles. Through all nature there runs a thread of life. We watch with equal interest and awe the transformation of the rosebud into the flower and the babe into manhood. The philosopher has well said that the element of life runs through all nature and links the destinies of earth with the destinies of the stars. This is a beautiful and ennobling thought; while it binds to earth it yet lifts us to heaven. It gives us strength in adversity, when the storms beat and the thunders peal forth their diapason and confusion reigns supreme everywhere; it tempers our joys with soberness when prosperity hedges us about as the dews of the morning hedge about with gladness the modest violet shyly concealed by the wayside. Life is the most mysterious as it is the most revealed force in nature. Death does not compare with it in these qualities, for there can be no death without life. It is from this point of view that we must regard the tremendous awakening of the Afro-American womanhood, during the past three decades from the double night of ages of slavery in which it was locked in intellectual and moral eclipse. It has been the awakening of a race from the nightmare of 250 years of self-effacement and debasement. It is not within the power of any one who has stood outside of Afro-American life to adequately estimate the extent of the effacement and debasement, and, therefore, of the gracious awakening which has quickened into life the slumbering forces and filled with hope and gladness the souls of millions of the womanhood of our land. To the God of love and tenderness and pity and justice we ascribe the fullness of our thanks and prayers for the transformation from the death of slavery to the life of freedom. All the more are we grateful to the moral and Christian forces of the world, the Christian statesmen and soldiers and scholars who were the divine instruments who made it possible for this womanhood to stand in this august presence to-day, this vast army laboring for the upbuilding of the Master's kingdom among men; for it is true as Longfellow said:

> Were half the power that fills the world with terror,
> Were half the wealth bestowed on camps and courts,
> Given to redeem the human mind from error,
> There were no need of arsenals and forts.

The auction block of brutality has been changed into the forum of reason, the slave mart has been replaced by the schoolroom and the church.

As I stand here to-day clothed in the garments of Christian womanhood, the horrible days of slavery, out of which I came, seem as a dream that is told, some horror incredible. Indeed, could they have been, and are not? They were; they are not; this is the sum and substance, the shame and the glory of the tale that I would tell, of the message that I would bring.

In the vast economy of nature, cycles of time are of small moment, years are as hours, and seconds bear but small relation to the problem, yet they are as the drops of rain that fall to earth and lodge in the fastnesses of the mountain from which our rivers are formed that feed the vast expanse of ocean. So in the history of a race lifting itself out of its original condition of helplessness, time is as necessary an element as is opportunity, in the assisting forces of humankind.

When we remember that the God who created all things is no respecter [*sic*] of persons, that the black child is beloved of Him as the white child, we can more easily fix the responsibility that rests upon the Christian womanhood of the country to join with us in elevating the head, the heart and the soul of Afro-American womanhood. As the great Frederick Douglass once said, in order to measure the heights to which we have risen we must first measure the depths to which we were dragged. It is from this point of observation that we must regard the awakening of the Afro-American womanhood of the land. And what is this awakening? What is its distinguishing characteristics? It would seem superfluous to ask or to answer questions so obvious, but the lamentable truth is, that the womanhood of the United States, of the world, knows almost absolutely nothing of the hope and aspirations, of the joys and the sorrows, of the wrongs, and of the needs of the black women of this country, who came up out of the effacement and debasement of American slavery into the dazzling sunlight of freedom. My friends, call to mind the sensations of the prisoner of Chillon, as he walked out of the dungeon where the flower of his life had been spent, into the open air, and you will be able to appreciate in some sense our feelings in 1865,

When the war drums throbbed no longer,
And the battle flags were furled.

What a past was ours! There was no attribute of womanhood which had not been sullied—aye, which had not been despoiled in the crucible of slavery. Virtue, modesty, the joys of maternity, even hope of mortality, all those were the heritage of this womanhood when the voice of Lincoln and the sword of Grant, as the expression of the Christian opinion of the land, bade them stand forth, without let or hindrance, as arbiters of their own persons and wills. They had no past to which they could appeal for anything. It had destroyed, more than in the men, all that a woman holds sacred, all that ennobles womanhood. She had but the future.

From such small beginnings she was compelled to construct a home. She who had been an outcast, the caprice of brutal power and passion, who had been educated to believe that morality was an echo, and womanly modesty a name; she who had seen father and brother and child torn from her and hurried away into everlasting separation—this creature was born to life in an hour and expected to create a home.

Home, sweet home;
Be it ever so humble,
There's no place like home.

My friends, more, home is the noblest, the most sacred spot in a Christian nation. It is the foundation upon which nationality rests, the pride of the citizen and the glory of the Republic. This woman was expected to build a home for 4,500,000 people, of whom she was the decisive unit. No Spartan mother ever had a larger task imposed upon her shoulders; no Spartan mother ever acquitted herself more heroically than this Afro-American woman has done. She has done it almost without any assistance from her white sister; who, in too large a sense, has left her to work out her own destiny in fear and trembling. The color of the skin has been an almost insurmountable barrier between them, despite the beautiful lines of the gentle Cowper, that—

Skin may differ,
But affection
Dwells in black and white the same.

I am not unmindful, however, of the Northern women who went into the South after the war as the missionary goes into the dark places of the world, and helped the Afro-American women to lay the foundation of her home broad and deep in the Christian virtues. For years they did this in the schoolroom and their labors naturally had their reflex in the home life of their pupils.

Broadly speaking, my main statement holds, however, that these women, starting empty handed, were left to make Christian homes where a Christian citizenship should be nurtured. The marvel is not that they have succeeded, not that they are succeeding, but that they did not fail, *utterly fail*. I believe the God who brought them out of the Valley of the Shadow, who snatched them from the hand of the white rapist, the base slave master whose unacknowledged children are to be found in every hamlet of the Republic, guided these women, and guides them in the supreme work of building their Christian homes. The horrors of the past were forgotten in the joyous labor that presented itself. Even the ineffaceable wrongs of the past, while not forgotten, were forgiven in the spirit of the Master, who even forgave those who took His life.

If there had been no other awakening than this, if this woman who had stood upon the auction block possessed of no rights that a white man was bound to respect, and none which he did respect, if there had been no other awakening of the Afro-American woman than this, that she made a home for her race, an abiding place for husband, and son, and daughter, it would be glory enough to embalm her memory in song and story. As it is, it will be her sufficient monument through all time that out of nothing she created something, and that something the dearest, the sweetest, the strongest institution in Christian government.

But she has done more than this. The creation of a home is the central feature of her awakening, but around this are many other features which show her strong title to the countenance and respect of the sisterhood of the world. She has meekly taken her place by her husband, in the humble occupations of life as a bread winner, and by her labors and sacrifices has helped to rear and educate 50,000 young women, who are active instructors in the Christian churches of the land. In the building up of the Master's kingdom she has been and she is an active and a positive influence; indeed, in this field she has proven, as her white sister has proven, the truth of Napoleon Bonaparte's sententious but axiomatic truth, that "The hand that rocks the cradle rules the world." It is not too much to say that the 7,000,000 Afro-American church memberships would fall to pieces as a rope of sand if the active sympathy and support of the Afro-American women were withdrawn. It is demonstrable that these women are the arch of the Afro-American temple. But these women who came out of slavery have done more than this. They have not only made Christian homes for their families, and educated 50,000 Sunday-school workers, but they have given to the State 25,000 educated school teachers, who are to-day the hope and inspiration of the whole race. The black women who came out of slavery in the past thirty years, have accomplished these tremendous results as farm-laborers and house servants, and they deserve the admiration of mankind for the glorious work that they have accomplished. In the past few years the educated daughters of these ex-slave women have aroused themselves to the necessity of systematic organization for their own protection, and for strengthening their race where they find it is weak, and to this end they have in the several States 243 regularly organized and officered clubs in the Afro-American Women's National Association; there are besides hundreds of social clubs and temperance organizations working in their own way for a strong Christian womanhood. Indeed, the impulse of aspiration after the strong and the good in our civilization is manifest on all hands in our womanhood. It is all so grounded in Christian morality that we may safely conclude that it is built upon a rock and cannot be shaken by the fury of the storms.

The awakening of the Afro-American woman is one of the most promising facts in our national life. That she deserves the active sympathy and co-operation of all the female forces of the Republic, I think I have sufficiently shown. We need them. We have always needed them. We need them in the work of religion, of education, of temperance, of morality, of industrialism; and above all we need their assistance in combatting the public opinion and laws that degrade our womanhood because it is black and not white; for of a truth, and as a universal law, an injury to one woman is an injury to all women. As long as the affections are controlled by legislation in defiance of Christian law, making infamous the union of black and white, we shall have unions without the sanction of the law, and children without legal parentage, to the degradation of black womanhood and the disgrace of white manhood. As one woman, as an Afro-American woman, I stand in this great Christian presence to-day and plead that the marriage and divorce laws be made uniform throughout the Republic, and that they shall not control, but legalize, the union of mutual affections. Until this shall have been done, Afro-American womanhood will have known no full and absolute awakening. As the laws now stand, they are the greatest demoralizing forces with which our womanhood has to contend. They serve as the protection of the white man, but they leave us defenceless, indeed. I ask the Christian womanhood of this great organized Army of Christ, to lend us their active co-operation in coercing the lawmakers of the land in throwing around our womanhood the equal protection of the State to which it is entitled. A slave regulation should not be allowed to prevail in a free government. A barbarous injustice should not receive the sanction of a Christian nation. The stronger forces of society should scorn to crush to the earth one of the weakest forces.

Next to these degrading marriage and divorce laws which prevail in two [sic] many States of the Republic, the full awakening of the Afro-American woman to her rightful position in society, are the separate car regulations which prevail in most of the States of the South. They were conceived in injustice; they are executed with extraordinary cowardice. Their entire operation tends to degrade Afro-American womanhood. None who are familiar with their operation will dispute this statement of facts. From this exalted forum, and in the name of the large army of Afro-American women, I appeal to the Christian sentiment which dominates this organization, to assist us in righting the wrongs growing out of these regulations, to the end that our womanhood may be sustained in its dignity and protected in its weakness, and the heavenly Father, who hath declared, "righteousness exalteth a nation, but sin is a reproach to any people," will give His benediction to the laws made just.

I am moved here further to invoke your patience and sympathy in the efforts of our awakening womanhood to care for the aged and infirm, for the orphan and outcast; for the reformation of the penal institutions of the Southern States, for the separation of male and female convicts, and above all for the establishment of juvenile reformatories [in] those States for both races, to the end that the shame of it may be removed that children of tender age should be herded with hardened criminals from whose life all of moral sensibility has vanished forever.

I feel moved to speak here in this wise for a whole race of women whose rise or fall, whose happiness or sorrow, whose degradation or exaltation are the concern of Christian men and women everywhere. I feel moved to say in conclusion that in all Christian and temperance work, in all that lifts humanity from its fallen condition to a more perfect resemblance of Him in whose image it was made, in all that goes to make our common humanity stronger and better and more beautiful; the Afro-American women of the Republic will "do their duty as God shall give them light to do it."

Note

1. Victoria Earle Matthews, "The Awakening of the Afro-American Woman," The Christian Endeavor Convention, San Francisco, July 11, 1897. Published with the permission of the Yale Collection of American Literature, Beinecke Rare Book and Manuscript Library, Yale University.

Ida B. Wells

Ida B. Wells (1862–1931) was dedicated to addressing problems related to anti-lynching, suffrage, and women's rights and used journalism and public speaking as her primary platforms. On June 1, 1909, Ida B. Wells delivered her speech "Mob Murder in a Christian Nation" during the National Negro Conference in New York. Without any hesitation, Wells plainly states,

> The lynching record for a quarter of a century merits the thoughtful study of the American people. It presents three salient facts: First, lynching is a colorline murder. Second, crimes against women is the excuse, not the cause. Third, it is a national crime and requires a national remedy.[1]

Wells's urgency and call-to-action approach to handling matters of lynching and women's rights are revealed throughout the speech. She questions the religious stance of the nation when she asks, "Why is mob murder permitted by a Christian nation?" Similar questions of action and reaction are found throughout the speech, working to advance her primary rhetorical purpose of revealing the ills of lynching to the public.

Mob Murder in a Christian Nation

Ida B. Wells[2]

The lynching record for a quarter of a century merits the thoughtful study of the American people. It presents three salient facts: First, lynching is a colorline murder. Second, crimes against women is the excuse, not the cause. Third, it is a national crime and requires a national remedy.

Proof that lynching follows the color line is to be found in the statistics which have been kept for the past twenty-five years. During the few years preceding this period and while frontier law existed, the executions showed a majority of white victims. Later, however, as law courts and authorized judiciary extended into the far West, lynch law rapidly abated, and its white victims became few and far between.

Just as the lynch law regime came to a close in the West, a new mob movement started in the South. This was wholly political, its purpose being to suppress the colored vote by intimidation and murder. Thousands of assassins, banded together under the name of Ku Klux Klans, "Midnight Raiders," etc., spread a reign of terror by beating, shooting and killing colored people by the thousands. In a few years, the purpose was accomplished and the black vote was suppressed. But mob murder continued.

From 1882, when 52 were lynched, down to the present, lynching has been along the color line. Statistics show that 3,284 men, women and children have been put to death in this quarter of a century....

During the last ten years, from 1899 to 1908 inclusive, the number lynched was 959. Of this number, 102 were white, while the colored victims numbered 857. No other nation, civilized or savage, burns its criminals; only under that Stars and Stripes is the human holocaust possible. Twenty-eight human beings burned at the stake, one of them a woman and two of them children, is the awful indictment against American civilization—the gruesome tribute which the nation pays to the color line.

Why is mob murder permitted by a Christian nation? What is the cause of this awful slaughter? This question is answered almost daily: always the same shameless falsehood that "Negroes are lynched to protect womanhood." Standing before a Chautauqua assemblage, John Temple

Graves, at once champion of lynching and apologist for lynchers, said, "The mob stands today as the most potential bulwark between the women of the South and such a carnival of crime as would infuriate the world and precipitate the annihilation of the Negro race." This is the never-varying answer of lynchers and their apologists. All know that it is untrue. The cowardly lyncher revels in murder, then seeks to shield himself from public execration by claiming devotion to woman. But truth is mighty and the lynching record discloses the hypocrisy of the lyncher as well as his crime.

The Springfield, Illinois, mob rioted for two days, the militia of the entire state was called out, two men were lynched, hundreds of people driven from their homes, all because a white woman said a Negro assaulted her. A mad mob went to the jail, tried to lynch the victim of her charge, and, not being able to find him, proceeded to pillage and burn the town and to lynch two innocent men. Later, after the police had found that the woman's charge was false, she published a retraction, the indictment was dismissed, and the intended victim discharged. But the lynched victims were dead, hundreds were homeless, and Illinois was disgraced.

As a final and complete refutation of the charge that lynching is occasioned by crimes against women, a partial record of lynchings is cited; 285 persons were lynched for causes as follows: unknown cause, 92; no cause, 10; race prejudice, 49; miscegenation, 7; informing, 12; making threats, 11; keeping saloon, 3; practicing fraud, 5; practicing voodooism, 2; bad reputation, 8; unpopularity, 3; mistaken identity, 5; using improper language, 3; violation of contract, 1; writing insulting letter, 2; eloping, 2; poisoning horse, 1; poisoning well, 2; by white capes, 9; vigilantes, 14; Indians, 1; moonshining, 1; refusing evidence, 2; political causes, 5; disputing, 1; disobeying quarantine regulations, 2; slapping a child, 1; turning state's evidence, 3; protecting a Negro, 1; to prevent giving evidence, 1; knowledge of larceny, 1; writing letter to white woman, 1; asking white woman to marry, 1; jilting girl, 1; having smallpox, 1; concealing criminal, 2; threatening political exposure, 1; self-defense, 6; cruelty, 1; insulting language to woman, 5; quarreling with white man, 2; colonizing Negroes, 1; throwing stones, 1; quarreling, 1; gambling, 1.

Is there a remedy, or will the nation confess that it cannot protect its protectors at home as well as abroad? Various remedies have been suggested to abolish the lynching infamy, but year after year, the butchery of men, women, and children continues in spite of plea and protest. Education is suggested as a preventive, but it is as grave a crime to murder an ignorant man as it is a scholar. True, few educated men have been lynched, but the hue and cry once started stops at no bounds, as was clearly shown by the lynchings in Atlanta, and in Springfield, Illinois.

Agitation, though helpful, will not alone stop the crime. Year after year statistics are published, meetings are held, resolutions are adopted. And yet lynchings go on . . . .

The only certain remedy is an appeal to law. Lawbreakers must be made to know that human life is sacred and that every citizen of this country is first a citizen of the United States and secondly a citizen of the state in which he belongs. This nation must assert itself and protect its federal citizenship at home as well as abroad. The strong men of the government must reach across state lines whenever unbridled lawlessness defies state laws, and must give to the individual under the Stars and Stripes the same measure of protection it gives to him when he travels in foreign lands. Federal protection of American citizenship is the remedy for lynching . . . .

In a multitude of counsel there is wisdom. Upon the grave question presented by the slaughter of innocent men, women, and children there should be an honest, courageous conference of patriotic, law-abiding citizens anxious to punish crime promptly, impartially, and by due process of law, also to make life, liberty, and property secure against mob rule.

Time was when lynching appeared to be sectional, but now it is national—a blight upon our nation, mocking our laws and disgracing our Christianity. "With malice toward none but with charity for all," let us undertake the work of making the "law of the land" effective and supreme upon every foot of American soil—a shield to the innocent; and to the guilty, punishment swift and sure.

Notes

1. Robert Torricelli and Andrew Carrole, eds., *In Our Own Words: Extraordinary Speeches of the American Century* (New York: Pocket Books, 1999), p. 23.
2. Ida B. Wells, "Mob Murder in a Christian Nation," NAACP Speech Against Lynching, Baltimore, February 12, 1909.

Bayard Rustin

Bayard Rustin's (1912–1987) civil and gay rights activism was presented through several social and political agencies and movements. His work spanned a half-century in the trenches of human rights advocacy. His early years were spent working with the Fellowship of Reconciliation, but ultimately he became one of the masterminds behind the civil disobedience element of the civil rights movement, a consultant to Martin Luther King Jr. in the Montgomery Bus Boycott, and the chief organizer for the 1963 March on Washington. The fact that Rustin lived as an openly gay man in the 1940s, 1950s, and 1960s was a stumbling block to his full recognition in the movement, but in his later years, LGBTQ rights became the passion for his work. In the 1980s, Rustin worked as a monitor for Freedom House, an NGO that conducts research to encourage human rights, and testified in support of New York State's Gay Rights Bill. Rustin was dedicated to engaging conversations connected to both Black rights and gay rights, both collectively and respectively, as he worked with the Southern Christian Leadership Conference and Dr. Martin Luther King Jr. during the civil rights movement. In 2013, Rustin was awarded the Presidential Medal of Freedom for his service to these communities during his life.

"The Time Is Now" (1963)[1]

Bayard Rustin

Rustin produced this promotional pamphlet for the March on Washington.

Wednesday, August 28, 1963
America faces a crisis . . .
Millions of citizens are unemployed . . .
Millions are denied freedom . . .

The twin evils of discrimination and economic deprivation plague the nation. They rob all people, Negro and white, of dignity, self-respect and freedom. They impose a special burden upon the Negro who is denied the right to vote, refused access to public accommodations, forced to accept inferior education and relegated to sub-standard ghetto housing.

One hundred years after the Emancipation Proclamation, the American Negro still bears the brunt of economic exploitation, the indignity of second-class citizenship, and ignominy of slave wages.

The rate of Negro unemployment is almost three times higher than that of white workers, breeding misery, frustration and degradation in every community—North and South.

Discrimination in education and in apprenticeship training renders Negroes, Puerto Ricans and other minorities helpless in our mechanized, industrial society. Shunted to relief, to charity, or to living by their wits, the jobless are driven to despair, to crime, to hatred and to violence.

Yet, despite this crisis . . .

Southern Democrats and reactionary Republicans in Congress are still working to defeat any effective civil rights legislation. They fight against the rights of all workers and minority groups. They are the sworn enemies of freedom and justice. They proclaim states rights in order to destroy human rights.

The Southern Democrats came to power by disenfranchising the Negro people. They know that as long as black workers are voteless, exploited, depressed and underpaid the fight of white workers for decent wages and working conditions will fail. They know that semi-slavery for one means semi-slavery for all.

We oppose these forces. We appeal for unity to destroy this century-long hoax.

WE CALL UPON ALL AMERICANS,
REGARDLESS OF RACE OR CREED,
TO JOIN
THE MARCH ON WASHINGTON

for freedom

- To demand that Congress pass a civil rights bill that will restore the constitutional rights now denied the Negro people.
- To assure neither watering down, nor compromise, nor filibuster against civil rights legislation by either political party.
- To offer a great witness to the basic moral principle of human equality and brotherhood . . . .

March on Washington for Jobs and Freedom
170 West 130th Street, New York 27, N.Y.
FI 8–1900
A. Philip Randolph, Director
Bayard Rustin, Deputy Director

* * *

"Statement by Bayard Rustin" (August 14, 1963)[2]

On the eve of the March on Washington, Rustin responded to charges by Senator Strom Thurmond that he had been a draft dodger and a Communist.

I wish to comment on two charges leveled against me by Senator Strom Thurmond.

The first charge is that I was a draft-dodger during World War II. This is demonstrably false. As a Quaker, I refused to participate in World War II on grounds of conscientious objection. I notified my draft board accordingly. When I was sentenced to 28 months, the judge was sufficiently impressed with the sincerity of my pacifist convictions to allow me three weeks, without bail, to complete my work for the Congress of Racial Equality (CORE) before serving my sentence.

My activities in the pacifist and Quaker organizations are well known. My adherence to nonviolence in the civil rights movement is an outgrowth of the philosophical pacifism I came to accept in the course of those activities. One may quarrel with the conscientious objector, but it is neither fair nor accurate to call him a draft-dodger. I did not dodge the draft. I openly and vigorously opposed it. Twenty eight months imprisonment was the price I willingly paid for my convictions.

Senator Thurmond charges me with Communism. I am not now and never have been a member of the Communist Party. More than twenty years ago, while a student at the City College of New York, I was a member of the Young Communist League. In 1938 when I joined the YCL, I thought it was genuinely interested in peace and in racial justice. Those were the years of the Hitler-Stalin pact, when pacifists could feel relatively comfortable in the YCL. In 1941 when Hitler attacked the Soviet Union, the YCL line changed overnight. The fight for peace and for civil rights was declared subordinate to the defense of the Soviet Union. The League instructed me to stop agitating for integration of the Armed Forces on the grounds that this impaired the war effort.

I have never been willing to subordinate the just demands of my people to the foreign or domestic policy of any nation. I did not then, and I do not now, consider acquiescence in injustice the road to any kind of true democracy. Accordingly, I left the YCL in 1941.

Even before that year, my Quaker beliefs had conflicted with the basic aims and practices of the YCL. Those beliefs, strengthened over the years, remain incompatible with Communism....

I am not the first of my race to have been falsely attacked by spokesmen of the Confederacy. But even from them a minimal affection for the facts should be expected. Senator Thurmond's remarks were a disgrace to the United States Senate and a measure of the desperation of the segregationist cause.

With regard to Senator Thurmond's attack on my morality, I have no comment. By religious training and fundamental philosophy, I am disinclined to put myself in the position of having to defend my own moral character. Questions in this area should properly be directed to those who have entrusted me with my present responsibilities.

* * *

Pledge by March on Washington Participants (August 28, 1963)[3]

Text of pledge read by Rustin at conclusion of March on Washington and agreed to by the audience, promising to continue to work for its goals.

PLEDGE

Standing before the Lincoln Memorial on the 28th of August, in the Centennial Year of Emancipation, I affirm my complete personal commitment to the struggle for Jobs and Freedom for all Americans.

To fulfill that commitment, I pledge that I will not relax until victory is won.

I pledge that I will join and support all actions undertaken in good faith in accord with the time-honored democratic tradition of non-violent protest, of peaceful assembly and petition, and of redress through the courts and the legislative process.

I pledge to carry the message of the March to my friends and neighbors back home and to arouse them to an equal commitment and an equal effort. I will march and I will write letters. I will demonstrate and I will vote. I will work to make sure that my voice and those of my brothers ring clear and determined from every corner of our land.

I pledge my heart and my mind and my body, unequivocally and without regard to personal sacrifice, to the achievement of social peace through social justice.

* * *

A Black Presidential Candidacy?[4]

[1983]

RECENT WEEKS HAVE SEEN THE EMERGENCE of a spirited discussion about a possible black candidate in the Democratic Presidential race. Clearly, no black or civil rights leader would have reason to quarrel with the entry of a qualified black politician into the Presidential sweepstakes. After all, wouldn't the entry of a popular black candidate raise certain issues of vital concern to the black agenda? Would not a black Presidential candidate serve to galvanize black involvement in the electoral process? Wouldn't a black candidacy increase the number of black delegates to the Democratic Party Convention?

At first glance, the answer to all these questions might appear to be yes. Yet a closer examination of the issue provides a more complicated and less clear-cut picture.

Clearly, a black Presidential candidate would be in a position to raise issues of concern to black Americans. Yet a candidate who entered the Democratic primaries on the basis of a black candidacy and black agenda would deal a substantial setback to black community interests. The issues of greatest concern to black Americans, after all, are not exclusively black issues. The issues of jobs, unemployment, plant closings, education, crime, and poverty are part of the national agenda; they are problems which concern all Americans and must be posed in the broadest possible manner if we are to elect a candidate sensitive to the needs of blacks and all working people. A candidate who runs for President on a black platform, therefore, runs the risk of making such issues appear linked to more narrow special interests.

Clearly, a black Presidential candidacy would galvanize increased black voter interest. Yet the evidence of the 1982 elections is that blacks—who for the first time voted in higher proportions than whites—can also be motivated to vote in greater numbers purely on the basis of political issues and economic interests.

A black Presidential candidacy might increase the number of black Democratic Convention delegates; but not by any significant number. Blacks clearly will be included in substantial numbers within the delegations pledged to the candidates (Mondale, Glenn, Hart, Cranston, Hollings, and Askew). Moreover, because of a shift of delegate strength to the Southern states, where the black vote is more highly concentrated, the number of black delegates to the convention is likely to be augmented.

Thus each of the major advantages of a black Presidential candidacy may not be so substantial as it first appeared. Moreover, there are serious drawbacks to a black Presidential entry:

- Such a candidacy would take away votes from the candidates who, in the absence of a black candidate, are most attractive to the black electorate.
- A black candidacy would mean that the likely nominee won the nomination with less black support and therefore might be less responsive to black interests.
- Blacks who voted for a black candidate would almost certainly be voting for someone who will not be the likely nominee.
- A black candidacy would clearly be perceived by many nonblacks as the candidacy of a special interest and could hurt the Democratic Party by making it appear beholden to special racial, ethnic, or other group interests,
- Because many black political leaders are likely to back other candidates, a black candidacy would add to the division of the black leadership and to the splintering of the black vote.
- A black candidacy might have the effect of heightening racial tensions and weakening the coalition of blacks, labor, and liberals, which is essential to Democratic electoral success.

No one can deny the right of a qualified black or white candidate to enter into the Democratic Presidential campaign. However, any black who might choose to make the run for President should only do so on the basis of a candidacy which appeals to the entire electorate and not only to the black community. An exclusively "black candidacy" not only would end in political failure and split the black electorate, it would do harm to the strategy of coalition politics and to the interests of the black community.

Thus, it is not at all surprising that many prominent black leaders, including the leadership of the NAACP, has expressed serious doubts about the advisability of a black Presidential candidacy in 1984.

The New "Niggers" Are Gays[5]

[1986]

TODAY, BLACKS ARE NO LONGER THE LITMUS PAPER or the barometer of social change. Blacks are in every segment of society and there are laws that help to protect them from racial discrimination. The new "niggers" are gays. No person who hopes to get politically elected, even in the deep South, not even Governor Wallace, would dare to stand in the schoolhouse door to keep blacks out. Nobody would dare openly and publicly to argue that blacks should not have the right to use public accommodations. Nobody would dare to say any number of things about blacks that they are perfectly prepared to say about gay people. It is in this sense that gay people are the new barometer for social change.

Indeed, if you want to know whether today people believe in democracy, if you want to know whether they are true democrats, if you want to know whether they are human rights activists, the question to ask is, "What about gay people?" Because that is now the litmus paper by which this democracy is to be judged. The barometer for social change is measured by selecting the group which is most mistreated. To determine where society is with respect to change, one does not ask, "What do you think about the education of children?" Nor does one ask, "Do you believe the aged should have Social Security?" The question of social change should be framed with the most vulnerable group in mind: gay people.

Therefore, I would like to be very hard with the gay community, not for the sake of being hard, but to make clear that, because we stand in the center of progress toward democracy, we have a terrifying responsibility to the whole society.

There are four aspects to this responsibility. First, the gay community cannot work for justice for itself alone. Unless the community fights for *all*, it is fighting for nobody, least of all for itself. Second, gay people should not practice prejudice. It is inconsistent for gay people to be antisemitic or racist. These gay people do not understand human rights.

Third, gay people should look not only at what people are doing to us but also what we are doing to each other. Fourth, gay people should recognize that we cannot fight for the rights of gays unless we are ready to fight for a new mood in the United States, unless we are ready to fight for a radicalization of this society. You will not feed people *à la* the philosophy of the Reagan administration. Imagine a society that takes lunches from school children. Do you really think it's possible for gays to get civil rights in that kind of society? Do you really think that a society that deprives students of food will confer rights to gay people? And what about people my age who don't have my vigor at seventy-five, who are not provided with adequate Social Security? These economic concerns must go hand-in-hand and, to a degree, precede the possibility of dealing with the most grievous problem—which is sexual prejudice.

Edited from a speech delivered to the Philadelphia chapter of Black and White Men Together, March 1, 1986.

Notes

1. Bayard Rustin, "The Time Is Now," Washington: Promotional pamphlet for the March on Washington, 1963, print.
2. Bayard Rustin, "Statement by Bayard Rustin," delivered on the eve of the March on Washington in responses to accusations from Senator Strom Thurmond, August 14, 1963.
3. Bayard Rustin, "Pledge by March on Washington Participants," read by Rustin at the close of the march, August 28, 1963. Published in Jerald Podair, *Bayard Rustin: American Dreamer* (Blue Ridge Summit, PA: Rowman & Littlefield, 2008).
4. Bayard Rustin, "A Black Presidential Candidacy?," 1983.
5. Bayard Rustin "Niggers Are the New Gays," speech delivered to the Philadelphia Chapter of Black and White Men Together, March 1, 1986. Published in Devon Carbado and Donald Weise, eds., *Time on Two Crosses: The Collected Writings of Bayard Rustin* (San Francisco: Cleis Press, 2003).

Clarence Thomas

Clarence Thomas (1948–) serves as an associate justice of the Supreme Court of the United States. He is the second African American to hold this position, succeeding Thurgood Marshall. Prior to serving in this role, Thomas served as assistant secretary for civil rights at the U. S. Department of Education and as the chairman of the Equal Employment Opportunity Commission. During his 1991 confirmation hearings for the Supreme Court justice appointment, Thomas was met with allegations of sexual harassment after an FBI interview with former employee Anita Hill was uncovered. In this response to the allegations and statement from Hill, Thomas used provocative rhetoric about Blacks, equality, and achievement to react. Despite these allegations and conversations that followed, the United States Senate ultimately confirmed Thomas by a vote of 52–48.

Statement to the Judiciary Committee

Judge Clarence Thomas[1]

SENATOR BIDEN: The committee will please come to order. Judge, tough day and tough night for you, I know. Let me ask, do you have anything you'd like to say before we begin? And I understand that your preference is—which is totally and completely understandable—that we go one hour tonight, 30 minutes on each side. Is—Am I correct in that?

JUDGE THOMAS: That's right.

SENATOR BIDEN: Do you have anything you'd like to say?

JUDGE THOMAS: Senator, I would like to start by saying unequivocally, uncategorically, that I deny each and every single allegation against me today that suggested in any way that I had conversations of a sexual nature or about pornographic material with Anita Hill, that I ever attempted to date her, that I ever had any personal sexual interest in her, or that I in any way ever harassed her.

A second, and I think more important point. I think that this today is a travesty. I think that it is disgusting. I think that this hearing should never occur in America. This is a case in which this sleaze, this dirt, was searched for by staffers of members of this committee, was then leaked to the media, and this committee and this body validated it and displayed it at prime time over our entire nation. How would any member on this committee, any person in this room, or any person in this country, would like sleaze said about him or her in this fashion? Or this dirt dredged up and this gossip and these lies displayed in this manner? How would any person like it?

The Supreme Court is not worth it. No job is worth it. I am not here for that. I am here for my name, my family, my life, and my integrity. I think something is dreadfully wrong with this country when any person, any person in this free country would be subjected to this.

This is not a closed room. There was an FBI investigation. This is not an opportunity to talk about difficult matters privately or in a closed environment. This is a circus. It's a national disgrace.

And from my standpoint as a black American, as far as I'm concerned, it is a high-tech lynching for uppity blacks who in any way deign to think for themselves, to do for themselves, to have different ideas, and it is a message that unless you kowtow to an old order, this is what will happen to you. You will be lynched, destroyed, caricatured by a committee of the U.S. Senate, rather than hung from a tree.

Note

1. Clarence Thomas, "High-Tech Lynching," response to Senate Judiciary Committee for the Nomination of Clarence Thomas to the U.S. Supreme Court, October 11, 1991.

Angela Y. Davis

Angela Davis was born in Birmingham, Alabama, on January 26, 1944. Her roles within the Communist Party, the Black Panther Party, and throughout the civil rights movement shaped her positions as an activist, scholar, and author. Davis elaborated upon the idea of the prison industrial complex as she made legible the structural similarities and intersections of military production and public punishment. Davis delivered "The Prison Industrial Complex" in 1997. The speech was later released as an audio CD and then expanded to a book-length representation with the same title. Her article "Masked Racism: Reflections on the Prison Industrial Complex," published in the Fall 1998 issue of *ColorLines*, also addressed this issue. Davis was devoted to unmasking and revealing the atrocities of the American penal system as she included a chapter about the prison industrial complex in her 2003 book entitled *Are Prisons Obsolete?* With America leading at 25 percent of the world's prison population, Davis's critical assessment of the structure, pitfalls, and widespread effect of the penal system serves as a rhetorical powerhouse in conversations about intersectionality and punishment politics.

Masked Racism: Reflections on the Prison Industrial Complex

Angela Y. Davis[1]

Imprisonment has become the response of first resort to far too many of the social problems that burden people who are ensconced in poverty. These problems often are veiled by being conveniently grouped together under the category "crime" and by the automatic attribution of criminal behavior to people of color. Homelessness, unemployment, drug addiction, mental illness, and illiteracy are only a few of the problems that disappear from public view when the human beings contending with them are relegated to cages.

Prisons thus perform a feat of magic. Or rather the people who continually vote in new prison bonds and tacitly assent to a proliferating network of prisons and jails have been tricked into believing in the magic of imprisonment. But prisons do not disappear problems, they disappear human beings. And the practice of disappearing vast numbers of people from poor, immigrant, and racially marginalized communities has literally become big business.

The seeming effortlessness of magic always conceals an enormous amount of behind-the-scenes work. When prisons disappear human beings in order to convey the illusion of solving social problems, penal infrastructures must be created to accommodate a rapidly swelling population of caged people. Goods and services must be provided to keep imprisoned populations alive. Sometimes these populations must be kept busy and at other times—particularly in repressive super-maximum prisons and in INS detention centers—they must be deprived of virtually all meaningful activity. Vast numbers of handcuffed and shackled people are moved across state borders as they are transferred from one state or federal prison to another.

All this work, which used to be the primary province of government, is now also performed by private corporations, whose links to government in the field of what is euphemistically called "corrections" resonate dangerously with the military industrial complex. The dividends that accrue from investment in the punishment industry, like those that accrue from investment in weapons production, only amount to social destruction. Taking into account the structural similarities and profitability of business-government linkages in the realms of military production and public punishment, the expanding penal system can now be characterized as a "prison industrial complex."

The Color of Imprisonment

Almost two million people are currently locked up in the immense network of U.S. prisons and jails. More than 70 percent of the imprisoned population are people of color. It is rarely acknowledged that the fastest growing group of prisoners are black women and that Native American prisoners are the largest group per capita. Approximately five million people—including those on probation and parole—are directly under the surveillance of the criminal justice system.

Three decades ago, the imprisoned population was approximately one-eighth its current size. While women still constitute a relatively small percentage of people behind bars, today the number of incarcerated women in California alone is almost twice what the nationwide women's prison population was in 1970. According to Elliott Currie, "[t]he prison has become a looming presence in our society to an extent unparalleled in our history—or that of any other industrial democracy. Short of major wars, mass incarceration has been the most thoroughly implemented government social program of our time."

To deliver up bodies destined for profitable punishment, the political economy of prisons relies on racialized assumptions of criminality—such as images of black welfare mothers reproducing criminal children—and on racist practices in arrest, conviction, and sentencing patterns. Colored bodies constitute the main human raw material in this vast experiment to disappear the major social problems of our time. Once the aura of magic is stripped away from the imprisonment solution, what is revealed is racism, class bias, and the parasitic seduction of capitalist profit. The prison industrial system materially and morally impoverishes its inhabitants and devours the social wealth needed to address the very problems that have led to spiraling numbers of prisoners.

As prisons take up more and more space on the social landscape, other government programs that have previously sought to respond to social needs—such as Temporary Assistance to Needy Families—are being squeezed out of existence. The deterioration of public education, including prioritizing discipline and security over learning in public schools located in poor communities, is directly related to the prison "solution."

Profiting From Prisoners

As prisons proliferate in U.S. society, private capital has become enmeshed in the punishment industry. And precisely because of their profit potential, prisons are becoming increasingly important to the U.S. economy. If the notion of punishment as a source of potentially stupendous profits is disturbing by itself, then the strategic dependence on racist structures and ideologies to render mass punishment palatable and profitable is even more troubling.

Prison privatization is the most obvious instance of capital's current movement toward the prison industry. While government-run prisons are often in gross violation of international human rights standards, private prisons are even less accountable. In March of this year, the Corrections Corporation of America (CCA), the largest U.S. private prison company, claimed 54,944 beds in 68 facilities under contract or development in the U.S., Puerto Rico, the United Kingdom, and Australia. Following the global trend of subjecting more women to public punishment, CCA recently opened a women's prison outside Melbourne. The company recently identified California as its "new frontier."

Wackenhut Corrections Corporation (WCC), the second largest U.S. prison company, claimed contracts and awards to manage 46 facilities in North America, U.K., and Australia. It boasts a total of 30,424 beds as well as contracts for prisoner health care services, transportation, and security.

Currently, the stocks of both CCA and WCC are doing extremely well. Between 1996 and 1997, CCA's revenues increased by 58 percent, from $293 million to $462 million. Its net profit grew from $30.9 million to $53.9 million. WCC raised its revenues from $138 million in 1996 to

$210 million in 1997. Unlike public correctional facilities, the vast profits of these private facilities rely on the employment of non-union labor.

The Prison Industrial Complex

But private prison companies are only the most visible component of the increasing corporatization of punishment. Government contracts to build prisons have bolstered the construction industry. The architectural community has identified prison design as a major new niche. Technology developed for the military by companies like Westinghouse is being marketed for use in law enforcement and punishment.

Moreover, corporations that appear to be far removed from the business of punishment are intimately involved in the expansion of the prison industrial complex. Prison construction bonds are one of the many sources of profitable investment for leading financiers such as Merrill Lynch. MCI charges prisoners and their families outrageous prices for the precious telephone calls which are often the only contact prisoners have with the free world.

Many corporations whose products we consume on a daily basis have learned that prison labor power can be as profitable as third world labor power exploited by U.S.-based global corporations. Both relegate formerly unionized workers to joblessness and many even wind up in prison. Some of the companies that use prison labor are IBM, Motorola, Compaq, Texas Instruments, Honeywell, Microsoft, and Boeing. But it is not only the hi-tech industries that reap the profits of prison labor. Nordstrom department stores sell jeans that are marketed as "Prison Blues," as well as t-shirts and jackets made in Oregon prisons. The advertising slogan for these clothes is "made on the inside to be worn on the outside." Maryland prisoners inspect glass bottles and jars used by Revlon and Pierre Cardin, and schools throughout the world buy graduation caps and gowns made by South Carolina prisoners.

"For private business," write Eve Goldberg and Linda Evans (a political prisoner inside the Federal Correctional Institution at Dublin, California) "prison labor is like a pot of gold. No strikes. No union organizing. No health benefits, unemployment insurance, or workers' compensation to pay. No language barriers, as in foreign countries. New leviathan prisons are being built on thousands of eerie acres of factories inside the walls. Prisoners do data entry for Chevron, make telephone reservations for TWA, raise hogs, shovel manure, make circuit boards, limousines, waterbeds, and lingerie for Victoria's Secret—all at a fraction of the cost of 'free labor.'"

Devouring the Social Wealth

Although prison labor—which ultimately is compensated at a rate far below the minimum wage—is hugely profitable for the private companies that use it, the penal system as a whole does not produce wealth. It devours the social wealth that could be used to subsidize housing for the homeless, to ameliorate public education for poor and racially marginalized communities, to open free drug rehabilitation programs for people who wish to kick their habits, to create a national health care system, to expand programs to combat HIV, to eradicate domestic abuse—and, in the process, to create well-paying jobs for the unemployed.

Since 1984 more than twenty new prisons have opened in California, while only one new campus was added to the California State University system and none to the University of California system. In 1996–97, higher education received only 8.7 percent of the State's General Fund while corrections received 9.6 percent. Now that affirmative action has been declared illegal in California, it is obvious that education is increasingly reserved for certain people, while prisons are reserved for others. Five times as many black men are presently in prison as in four-year colleges and universities. This new segregation has dangerous implications for the entire country.

By segregating people labeled as criminals, prison simultaneously fortifies and conceals the structural racism of the U.S. economy. Claims of low unemployment rates—even in black communities—make sense only if one assumes that the vast numbers of people in prison have really disappeared and thus have no legitimate claims to jobs. The numbers of black and Latino men currently incarcerated amount to two percent of the male labor force. According to criminologist David Downes, "[t]reating incarceration as a type of hidden unemployment may raise the jobless rate for men by about one-third, to 8 percent. The effect on the black labor force is greater still, raising the [black] male unemployment rate from 11 percent to 19 percent."

Hidden Agenda

Mass incarceration is not a solution to unemployment, nor is it a solution to the vast array of social problems that are hidden away in a rapidly growing network of prisons and jails. However, the great majority of people have been tricked into believing in the efficacy of imprisonment, even though the historical record clearly demonstrates that prisons do not work. Racism has undermined our ability to create a popular critical discourse to contest the ideological trickery that posits imprisonment as key to public safety. The focus of state policy is rapidly shifting from social welfare to social control.

Black, Latino, Native American, and many Asian youth are portrayed as the purveyors of violence, traffickers of drugs, and as envious of commodities that they have no right to possess. Young black and Latina women are represented as sexually promiscuous and as indiscriminately propagating babies and poverty. Criminality and deviance are racialized. Surveillance is thus focused on communities of color, immigrants, the unemployed, the undereducated, the homeless, and in general on those who have a diminishing claim to social resources. Their claim to social resources continues to diminish in large part because law enforcement and penal measures increasingly devour these resources. The prison industrial complex has thus created a vicious cycle of punishment which only further impoverishes those whose impoverishment is supposedly "solved" by imprisonment.

Therefore, as the emphasis of government policy shifts from social welfare to crime control, racism sinks more deeply into the economic and ideological structures of U.S. society. Meanwhile, conservative crusaders against affirmative action and bilingual education proclaim the end of racism, while their opponents suggest that racism's remnants can be dispelled through dialogue and conversation. But conversations about "race relations" will hardly dismantle a prison industrial complex that thrives on and nourishes the racism hidden within the deep structures of our society.

The emergence of a U.S. prison industrial complex within a context of cascading conservatism marks a new historical moment, whose dangers are unprecedented. But so are its opportunities. Considering the impressive number of grassroots projects that continue to resist the expansion of the punishment industry, it ought to be possible to bring these efforts together to create radical and nationally visible movements that can legitimize anti-capitalist critiques of the prison industrial complex. It ought to be possible to build movements in defense of prisoners' human rights and movements that persuasively argue that what we need is not new prisons, but new health care, housing, education, drug programs, jobs, and education. To safeguard a democratic future, it is possible and necessary to weave together the many and increasing strands of resistance to the prison industrial complex into a powerful movement for social transformation.

Note

1. Angela Y. Davis, "Masked Racism: Reflections on the Prison Industrial Complex," *Colorlines: News for Action*, September 10, 1998.

David Banner

David Banner (1974–), an artist, producer, and label executive, was born in Jackson, Mississippi. On April 4, 2007, talk radio host Don Imus made harsh remarks about the Rutgers women's basketball team, describing them as "rough girls" and "nappy-headed hos" on his nationally syndicated radio show. As a result, conversations within the radio, political, hip-hop, and African American, to name a few, communities were sparked. After Imus was fired and hired by another radio station, several members of the hip-hop community came before Congress to address the lyrics of the industry on September 25, 2007.[1] Banner was one of the participants before Congress; during his statement, he made the claim that features of hip-hop found problematic are part of a larger American ethos and pathology. The video from which this statement was transcribed illustrates how Banner's black affectivity and speech contributed to ongoing conversations concerning hip-hop music, Black representation, and American life.

Address to Congress Over Hip-Hop Lyrics

David Banner[2]

Good afternoon Mr. Chairman, Mr. Stern, and members of the Committee. My name is David Banner. I am an artist for Universal Recordings, a producer, and label executive. Thank you for inviting my testimony. This dialogue was sparked by the insulting comments made by Don Imus concerning the Rutgers women's basketball team. Imus lost his job, but later secured a million dollar contract with another station. While he appears to have been rewarded, the hip-hop industry is left under public scrutiny. As this dialogue played out in the media, the voices of the people who create hip-hop and rap music were silenced. We were not invited to participate on any panels, nor given the opportunity to publicly refute any of the accusations hurled at us. While Congress lacks the power to censor, it is of the utmost importance that the people whose livelihood is at stake be made a vital part of this process.

I am from Jackson, Mississippi. Jackson is one of the most violent cities in the United States. Much like Washington, D.C., Jackson stayed in the murder capital run. When I was growing up, it always ranked as one of the top ten cities for the highest number of murders per capital. Being located right below Chicago, a lot of kids got in trouble up there and were sent to Jackson by their grandparents, who were from Jackson.

The by product of this migration was violence. I was blessed to have a very strong man for a father, and a very, very strong woman for a mother.

Honestly, rap music is what kept me out of trouble.

Statistics will never show the positive side of rap because statistics don't reflect what you do, if you don't commit a murder or a crime. When I would feel angry and would think about getting revenge, I would listen to Tupac.

His anger in a song was a replacement for my anger. I lived vicariously through his music.

Rap music is the voice of the underbelly of America.

In most cases, America wants to hide the negative that it does to its people. Hip-hop is the voice, and how dare America not give us the opportunity to be heard.

I am one of the few artists who went to college. I still see my friends who, as college graduates, are unable to get a job. The truth is that what we do sells. Often artists try to do different types of music and their music doesn't sell. In America, the media only lifts up negativity.

People consider me a philanthropist. I give away close to a quarter of my yearly earnings to send children from impoverished neighborhoods to different cities and to Disneyland. This gives them another vision. Rap music has changed my life, and the lives of those around me. It has given us the opportunity to eat. I remember sending eighty-eight kids from the inner city on a trip. I went to the local newspaper and TV station, only to be told that the trip wasn't newsworthy. But if I had shot somebody, it would have been all over the news. I threw the largest urban relief concert in history. That never made the front cover of a magazine. But as soon as I say something negative, rise up against my own, or become sharp at the mouth (no pun intended), I am perceived as being disrespectful to Black leaders. That negativity overshadows all of the positive things that I've done as a rap artist.

Some might argue that the content of our music serves as poison to the minds of our generation. If by some stroke of the pen, hip-hop was silenced, the issues would still be present in our communities. Drugs, violence, and the criminal element were around long before hip-hop existed. Our consumers come from various socioeconomic backgrounds and cultures. While many are underprivileged, a large percentage are educated professionals. The responsibility for their choices does not rest on the shoulders of hip-hop.

Still others raise concerns about the youth having access to our music. Much like the ratings utilized by the Motion Picture Association of America, our music is given ratings which are displayed on the packaging.

These serve to inform the public of possible adult content. As such, the probability of shocking the unsuspecting consumers sensibilities is virtually impossible. If the consumer is disinterested or offended by the content of our music, one could simply not purchase our CDs. The music that is played on the radio must comply with FCC guidelines. Again, this provides a safeguard. Ultimately, the burden of monitoring the music that minors listen to rests with their parents.

Some argue that the verbiage used in our music is derogatory. During slavery, those in authority used the word "nigger" as a means to degrade and emasculate. There was no push for censorship of the word back then. The abuse that accompanied the label "nigger" forced us to internalize it. This made the situation easier to digest. Our generation has since assumed ownership of the word. Now that we are capitalizing off the use of the word, why is it so important that it be censored? The intent and spirit of the word "nigga" in rap music does not even remotely carry the same meaning nor historical intent.

Attempting to censor the use of a word that merely depicts deep camaraderie is outrageous. People should focus less on the offensive words in our music, and more on the messages that are being conveyed.

The same respect is often not extended to hip-hop artists as to those in other arenas. Steven King and Steven Spielberg are renowned for their horrific creations. These movies are embraced as art. Why then is our content not merely deemed horror music?

Mark Twain's literary classic, *Huckleberry Finn*, is still required reading in classrooms across the United States of America. The word "nigger" appears in the book approximately 215 times. While some may find this offensive, the book was not banned by all school districts because of its artistic value. The same consideration should be extended to hip-hop music.

As consumers, we generally gravitate to and have a higher tolerance for things that we can relate to. As such, it is not surprising that the spirit of hip-hop is not easily understood. In the 1971 case of Cohen vs. California, Justice Harlan noted that one man's vulgarity is another man's lyric. The content and verbiage illustrated in our music may be viewed as derogatory or unnecessary, but it is a protected means of artistic expression. In 2005 Al Sharpton, who is a proponent of censorship, stated on CNN that rappers have the right to talk about the violence they come from; if they're going to rap about it and sing about it, they have the First Amendment right. Much like imagery supplied via television, literature, and by other genres of music, we merely provide a product that appeals to our patrons.

Our troops are currently at war under the guise of liberating other countries. While here in America, our rights are being threatened daily. This is illustrated by homeland security, extensive phone tapping and ill-placed attempts at censorship. If we are not careful, we will find ourselves getting closer to a dictatorship.

Traditionally multi-billion dollar industries have thrived on the premise of violence, sexuality, and derogatory content. This capitalistic trend was not created nor introduced by hip-hop. It's been here.

It's the American way.

I can admit that there are some problems in hip-hop.

But it is only a reflection of what is taking place in our society. Hip-hop is sick because America is sick.

Thank you.

Notes

1. https://www.c-span.org/video/?c4487738/david-banner
2. David Banner, "Address to Congress Over Hip-Hop Lyrics," Washington, DC, September 27, 2007.

Audre Lorde

Audre Lorde (1934–1992), poet, essayist, and—regardless of whether she claimed the designations—rhetorician and theorist, memoirist, Black woman, feminist/womanist, lesbian, educator, daughter of Grenadian immigrants, activist, and warrior. Audre Lorde is included in this collection because of her sobering, fecund, and emancipatory investment in the power of the word. And in the power of language. She explicitly addresses a distinction between rhetoric and poetry in the poem "Power." More than what words and language mean, Audre Lorde tapped into what words and language *do* (*nommo*), what they allow, their effects—the realm of rhetoric—and, after being diagnosed with cancer, in "The Transformation of Silence Into Language and Action," into what the suppression and silencing of Black affectivity and bodily intensities, Black structures of feelings and emotions do to the souls and life of everyone, but particularly to Black women. And where are those places of redemption? Possibility? Transformation? In "Poetry Is Not a Luxury," in the rhetoric informing that essay, Audre Lorde offers insight that intersects with "The Transformation of Silence Into Language and Action":

> As we learn to bear the intimacy of scrutiny and to flourish within it, as we learn to use the products of that scrutiny for power within our living, those fears which rule our lives and form our silences begin to lose their control over us. For each of us as women, there is a dark place within, where hidden and growing our true spirit rises, "beautiful/and tough as chestnut/stanchions against (y)our nightmare of weakness/" and of impotence. These places of possibility within ourselves are dark because they are ancient and hidden; they have survived and grown strong through that darkness. Within these deep places, each one of us holds an incredible reserve of creativity and power, of unexamined and unrecorded emotion and feeling. The woman's place of power within each of us is neither white nor surface; it is dark, it is ancient, and it is deep.[1]

The Transformation of Silence Into Language and Action (Excerpt)

Audre Lorde[2]

I have come to believe over and over again that what is most important to me must be spoken, made verbal and shared, even at the risk of having it bruised or misunderstood. That the speaking profits me, beyond any other effect.

I was forced to look upon myself and my living with a harsh and urgent clarity that has left me still shaken but much stronger. Some of what I experienced during that time has helped elucidate for me much of what I feel concerning the transformation of silence into language and action.

In becoming forcibly and essentially aware of my mortality, and of what I wished and wanted for my life, however short it might be, priorities and omissions became strongly etched in a merciless light, and what I most regretted were my silences. Of what had I ever been afraid? To question or to speak as I believed could have meant pain, or death. But we all hurt in so many different ways, all the time, and pain will either change or end. Death, on the other hand, is the final silence. And that might be coming quickly now, without regard for whether I had ever spoken what needed to be said, or had only betrayed myself into small silences, while I planned someday to speak, or waited for someone else's words.

I was going to die, if not sooner then later, whether or not I had ever spoken myself. My silences had not protected me. Your silence will not protect you.

What are the words you do not yet have? What do you need to say? What are the tyrannies you swallow day by day and attempt to make your own, until you will sicken and die of them, still in silence? Perhaps for some of you here today, I am the face of one of your fears. Because I am a woman, because I am Black, because I am lesbian, because I am myself—a Black woman warrior poet doing my work—come to ask you, are you doing yours?

And of course I am afraid, because the transformation of silence into language and action is an act of self-revelation, and that always seems fraught with danger. But my daughter, when I told her of our topic and my difficulty with it, said, "Tell them about how you're never really a whole person if you remain silent, because there's always that one little piece inside you that wants to be spoken out, and if you keep ignoring it, it gets madder and madder and hotter and hotter, and if you don't speak it out one day it will just up and punch you in the mouth from the inside."

In the cause of silence, each of us draws the face of her own fear—fear of contempt, of censure, of some judgment, or recognition, of challenge, of annihilation. But most of all, I think, we fear the visibility without which we cannot truly live.

And that visibility which makes us most vulnerable is that which also is the source of our greatest strength. Because the machine will try to grind you into dust anyway, whether or not we speak. We can sit in our corners mute forever while our sisters and our selves are wasted, while our children are distorted and destroyed, while our earth is poisoned; we can sit in our safe corners mute as bottles, and we will still be no less afraid.

Each of us is here now because in one way or another we share a commitment to language and to the power of language, and to the reclaiming of that language which has been made to work against us. In the transformation of silence into language and action, it is vitally necessary for each one of us to establish or examine her function in that transformation and to recognize her role as vital within that transformation.

For those of us who write, it is necessary to scrutinize not only the truth of what we speak, but the truth of that language by which we speak it. For others, it is to share and spread also those words that are meaningful to us. But primarily for us all, it is necessary to teach by living and speaking those truths which we believe and know beyond understanding. Because in this way alone can we survive, by taking part in a process of life that is creative and continuing, that is growth.

And it is never without fear—of visibility, of the harsh light of scrutiny and perhaps judgment, of pain, of death. But we have lived through all of those already, in silence, except death. And I remind myself all the time now that if I were to have been born mute, or had maintained an oath of silence my whole life long for safety, I would still have suffered, and I would still die. It is very good for establishing perspective.

We can learn to work and speak when we are afraid in the same way we have learned to work and speak when we are tired. For we have been socialized to respect fear more than our own needs for language and definition, and while we wait in silence for that final luxury of fearlessness, the weight of that silence will choke us.

The fact that we are here and that I speak these words is an attempt to break that silence and bridge some of those differences between us, for it is not difference which immobilizes us, but silence. And there are so many silences to be broken.

Notes

1. Audre Lorde, *Sister Outsider: Essays and Speeches* (New York: Crossing Press Feminist Series, 2007), pp. 36–37. Kindle edition.
2. Originally delivered at the Modern Language Association's "Lesbian and Literature Panel," Chicago, Illinois, December 28, 1977. First published in *Sinister Wisdom* 6 (1978) and *The Cancer Journals* (San Francisco: Spinsters, Ink), 1980.

Zadie Smith

Zadie Smith (1975–) was born in London, England, to her Jamaican mother and British father. The English writer has authored several fiction and nonfiction pieces and edited volumes. In 2009, Smith published her piece "Speaking in Tongues." In the piece, she travels through many places while exploring the way that speaking influences the journey and the reception of the traveler. "Speaking in Tongues" navigates the birth of speech and the mouth, and considers the ways that its speech changes as it is delivered and affects the speaker and the listeners. Smith's retelling of her own speech narrative speaks to larger conversations of class distinctions based on speech communities. She argues, "not all lettered people need to be of the same class, nor speak identically." The essay has been connected to President Barack Obama's speech journey and the changes that were observed from candidacy to office.

Speaking in Tongues

Zadie Smith[1]

The following is based on a lecture given at the New York Public Library in December 2008.

1

Hello. This voice I speak with these days, this English voice with its rounded vowels and consonants in more or less the right place—this is not the voice of my childhood. I picked it up in college, along with the unabridged *Clarissa* and a taste for port. Maybe this fact is only what it seems to be—a case of bald social climbing—but at the time I genuinely thought *this* was the voice of lettered people, and that if I didn't have the voice of lettered people I would never truly be lettered. A braver person, perhaps, would have stood firm, teaching her peers a useful lesson by example: not all lettered people need be of the same class, nor speak identically. I went the other way. Partly out of cowardice and a constitutional eagerness to please, but also because I didn't quite see it as a straight swap, of this voice for that.

My own childhood had been the story of this and that combined, of the synthesis of disparate things. It never occurred to me that I was leaving the London district of Willesden for Cambridge. I thought I was *adding* Cambridge to Willesden, this new way of talking to that old way. Adding a new kind of knowledge to a different kind I already had. And for a while, that's how it was: at home, during the holidays, I spoke with my old voice, and in the old voice seemed to feel and speak things that I couldn't express in college, and vice versa. I felt a sort of wonder at the flexibility of the thing. Like being alive twice.

But flexibility is something that requires work if it is to be maintained. Recently my double voice has deserted me for a single one, reflecting the smaller world into which my work has led me. Willesden was a big, colorful, working-class sea; Cambridge was a smaller, posher pond, and almost univocal; the literary world is a puddle. This voice I picked up along the way is no longer an exotic garment I put on like a college gown whenever I choose—now it is my only voice, whether I want it or not. I regret it; I should have kept both voices alive in my mouth. They were both a part of me. But how the culture warns against it! As George Bernard Shaw delicately put it in his preface to the play *Pygmalion*, "many thousands of [British] men and women . . . have sloughed off their native dialects and acquired a new tongue."

Few, though, will admit to it. Voice adaptation is still the original British sin. Monitoring and exposing such citizens is a national pastime, as popular as sex scandals and libel cases. If you lean toward the Atlantic with your high-rising terminals you're a sell-out; if you pronounce borrowed European words in their original style—even if you try something as innocent as *parmigiano* for "parmesan"—you're a fraud. If you go (metaphorically speaking) down the British class scale, you've gone from Cockney to "mockney," and can expect a public tar and feathering; to go the other way is to perform an unforgivable act of class betrayal. Voices are meant to be unchanging and singular. There's no quicker way to insult an ex-pat Scotsman in London than to tell him he's lost his accent. We feel that our voices are who we are, and that to have more than one, or to use different versions of a voice for different occasions, represents, at best, a Janus-faced duplicity, and at worst, the loss of our very souls.

Whoever changes their voice takes on, in Britain, a queerly tragic dimension. They have betrayed that puzzling dictum "To thine own self be true," so often quoted approvingly as if it represented the wisdom of Shakespeare rather than the hot air of Polonius. "*What's to become of me? What's to become of me?*" wails Eliza Doolittle, realizing her middling dilemma. With a voice too posh for the flower girls and yet too redolent of the gutter for the ladies in Mrs. Higgins's drawing room.

But Eliza—patron saint of the tragically double-voiced—is worthy of closer inspection. The first thing to note is that both Eliza and *Pygmalion* are entirely didactic, as Shaw meant them to be. "I delight," he wrote,

> in throwing [*Pygmalion*] at the heads of the wiseacres who repeat the parrot cry that art should never be didactic. It goes to prove my contention that art should never be anything else.

He was determined to tell the unambiguous tale of a girl who changes her voice and loses her self. And so she arrives like this:

> Don't you be so saucy. You ain't heard what I come for yet. Did you tell him I come in a taxi? . . . Oh, we are proud! He ain't above giving lessons, not him: I heard him say so. Well, I ain't come here to ask for any compliment; and if my moneys not good enough I can go elsewhere . . . . Now you know, don't you? I'm come to have lessons, I am. And to pay for em too: make no mistake . . . . I want to be a lady in a flower shop stead of selling at the corner of Tottenham Court Road. But they wont take me unless I can talk more genteel.

And she leaves like this:

> I can't. I could have done it once; but now I can't go back to it. Last night, when I was wandering about, a girl spoke to me; and I tried to get back into the old way with her; but it was no use. You told me, you know, that when a child is brought to a foreign country, it picks up the language in a few weeks, and forgets its own. Well, I am a child in your country. I have forgotten my own language, and can speak nothing but yours.

By the end of his experiment, Professor Higgins has made his Eliza an awkward, in-between thing, neither flower girl nor lady, with one voice lost and another gained, at the steep price of everything she was, and everything she knows. Almost as afterthought, he sends Eliza's father, Alfred Doolittle, to his doom, too, securing a three-thousand-a-year living for the man on the condition that Doolittle lecture for the Wannafeller Moral Reform World League up to six times a year. This burden brings the philosophical dustman into the close, unwanted embrace of what he disdainfully calls "middle class morality." By the time the curtain goes down, both Doolittles find themselves stuck in the middle, which is, to Shaw, a comi-tragic place to be, with the emphasis on the tragic. What are they fit for? What will become of them?

How persistent this horror of the middling spot is, this dread of the interim place! It extends through the specter of the tragic mulatto, to the plight of the transsexual, to our present anxiety—disguised as genteel concern—for the contemporary immigrant, tragically split, we are sure, between worlds, ideas, cultures, voices—whatever will become of them? Something's got to give—one voice must be sacrificed for the other. What is double must be made singular.

But this, the apparent didactic moral of Eliza's story, is undercut by the fact of the play itself, which is an orchestra of many voices, simultaneously and perfectly rendered, with no shade of color or tone sacrificed. Higgins's Harley Street high-handedness is the equal of Mrs. Pierce's lower-middle-class gentility, Pickering's kindhearted aristocratic imprecision every bit as convincing as Arthur Doolittle's Nietzschean Cockney-by-way-of-Wales. Shaw had a wonderful ear, able to reproduce almost as many quirks of the English language as Shakespeare's. Shaw was in possession of a gift he wouldn't, or couldn't, give Eliza: he spoke in tongues.

It gives me a strange sensation to turn from Shaw's melancholy Pygmalion story to another, infinitely more hopeful version, written by the new president of the United States of America. Of course, his ear isn't half bad either. In *Dreams from My Father*, the new president displays an enviable facility for dialogue, and puts it to good use, animating a cast every bit as various as the one James Baldwin—an obvious influence—conjured for his own many-voiced novel *Another Country*. Obama can do young Jewish male, black old lady from the South Side, white woman from Kansas, Kenyan elders, white Harvard nerds, black Columbia nerds, activist women, churchmen, security guards, bank tellers, and even a British man called Mr. Wilkerson, who on a starry night on safari says credibly British things like: "I believe that's the Milky Way." This new president doesn't just speak *for* his people. He can *speak* them. It is a disorienting talent in a president; we're so unused to it. I have to pinch myself to remember who wrote the following well-observed scene, seemingly plucked from a comic novel:

> "Man, I'm not going to any more of these bullshit Punahou parties."
> "Yeah, that's what you said the last time . . . ."
> "I mean it this time . . . . These girls are A-1, USDA-certified racists. All of 'em. White girls. Asian girls—shoot, these Asians worse than the whites. Think we got a disease or something."
> "Maybe they're looking at that big butt of yours. Man, I thought you were in training."
> "Get your hands out of my fries. You ain't my bitch, nigger . . . buy your own damn fries. Now what was I talking about?"
> "Just 'cause a girl don't go out with you doesn't make her a racist."

This is the voice of Obama at seventeen, as remembered by Obama. He's still recognizably Obama; he already seeks to unpack and complicate apparently obvious things ("Just 'cause a girl don't go out with you doesn't make her a racist"); he's already gently cynical about the impassioned dogma of other people ("Yeah, that's what you said the last time"). And he has a sense of humor ("Maybe they're looking at that big butt of yours"). Only the voice is different: he has made almost as large a leap as Eliza Doolittle. The conclusions Obama draws from his own Pygmalion experience, however, are subtler than Shaw's. The tale he tells is not the old tragedy of gaining a new, false voice at the expense of a true one. The tale he tells is all about addition. His is the story of a genuinely many-voiced man. If it has a moral it is that each man must be true to his selves, plural.

For Obama, having more than one voice in your ear is not a burden, or not solely a burden—it is also a gift. And the gift is of an interesting kind, not well served by that dull publishing-house title *Dreams from My Father: A Story of Race and Inheritance* with its suggestion of a simple linear inheritance, of paternal dreams and aspirations passed down to a son, and fulfilled.

Dreams from My Father would have been a fine title for John McCain's book *Faith of My Fathers*, which concerns exactly this kind of linear masculine inheritance, in his case from soldier to soldier. For Obama's book, though, it's wrong, lopsided. He corrects its misperception early on, in the first chapter, while discussing the failure of his parents' relationship, characterized by their only son as the end of a dream. "Even as that spell was broken," he writes, "and the worlds that they thought they'd left behind reclaimed each of them, I *occupied the place* where their dreams had been."

To *occupy* a dream, to exist in a dreamed space (conjured by both father and mother), is surely a quite different thing from simply *inheriting* a dream. It's more interesting. What did Pauline Kael call Cary Grant? "*The Man from Dream City.*" When Bristolian Archibald Leach became suave Cary Grant, the transformation happened in his voice, which he subjected to a strange, indefinable manipulation, resulting in that heavenly sui generis accent, neither west country nor posh, American nor English. It came from nowhere, *he* came from nowhere. Grant seemed the product of a collective dream, dreamed up by moviegoers in hard times, as it sometimes feels voters have dreamed up Obama in hard times. Both men have a strange reflective quality, typical of the self-created man—we see in them whatever we want to see. "*Everyone wants to be Cary Grant,*" said Cary Grant. "*Even I want to be Cary Grant.*" It's not hard to imagine Obama having that same thought, backstage at Grant Park, hearing his own name chanted by the hopeful multitude. *Everyone wants to be Barack Obama. Even I want to be Barack Obama.*

2

But I haven't described Dream City. I'll try to. It is a place of many voices, where the unified singular self is an illusion. Naturally, Obama was born there. So was I. When your personal multiplicity is printed on your face, in an almost too obviously thematic manner, in your DNA, in your hair and in the neither this nor that beige of your skin—well, anyone can see you come from Dream City. In Dream City everything is doubled, everything is various. You have no choice but to cross borders and speak in tongues. That's how you get from your mother to your father, from talking to one set of folks who think you're not black enough to another who figure you insufficiently white. It's the kind of town where the wise man says "I" cautiously, because "I" feels like too straight and singular a phoneme to represent the true multiplicity of his experience. Instead, citizens of Dream City prefer to use the collective pronoun "we."

Throughout his campaign Obama was careful always to say we. He was noticeably wary of "I." By speaking so, he wasn't simply avoiding a singularity he didn't feel, he was also drawing us in with him. He had the audacity to suggest that, even if you can't see it stamped on their faces, most people come from Dream City, too. Most of us have complicated back stories, messy histories, multiple narratives.

It was a high-wire strategy, for Obama, this invocation of our collective human messiness. His enemies latched on to its imprecision, emphasizing the exotic, un-American nature of Dream City, this ill-defined place where you could be from Hawaii and Kenya, Kansas and Indonesia all at the same time, where you could jive talk like a street hustler and orate like a senator. What kind of a crazy place is that? But they underestimated how many people come from Dream City, how many Americans, in their daily lives, conjure contrasting voices and seek a synthesis between disparate things. Turns out, Dream City wasn't so strange to them.

Or did they never actually see it? We now know that Obama spoke of *Main Street* in Iowa and of *sweet potato pie* in Northwest Philly, and it could be argued that he succeeded because he so rarely misspoke, carefully tailoring his intonations to suit the sensibility of his listeners. Sometimes he did this within one speech, within one line: "We worship an *awesome* God in the blue states, and we don't like federal agents poking around our libraries in the red states."

Awesome God comes to you straight from the pews of a Georgia church; *poking around* feels more at home at a kitchen table in South Bend, Indiana. The balance was perfect, cunningly counterpoised and never accidental. It's only now that it's over that we see him let his guard down a little, on *60 Minutes*, say, dropping in that culturally, casually black construction "Hey, I'm not stupid, *man*, that's why I'm president," something it's hard to imagine him doing even three weeks earlier. To a certain kind of mind, it must have looked like the mask had slipped for a moment.

Which brings us to the single-voiced Obamanation crowd. They rage on in the blogs and on the radio, waiting obsessively for the mask to slip. They have a great fear of what they see as Obama's doubling ways. "He says one thing but he means another"—this is the essence of the fear campaign. He says he's a capitalist, but he'll spread your wealth. He says he's a Christian, but really he's going to empower the Muslims. And so on and so forth. These are fears that have their roots in an anxiety about voice. *Who is he?* people kept asking. *I mean, who is this guy, really?* He says *sweet potato pie* in Philly and *Main Street* in Iowa! When he talks to us, he sure *sounds* like us—but behind our backs he says we're clinging to our religion, to our guns. And when Jesse Jackson heard that Obama had lectured a black church congregation about the epidemic of absent black fathers, he experienced this, too, as a tonal betrayal; Obama was "talking down to black people." In both cases, there was the sense of a double-dealer, of someone who tailors his speech to fit the audience, who is not *of* the people (because he is able to look at them objectively) but always above them.

The Jackson gaffe, with its Oedipal violence ("I want to cut his nuts out"), is especially poignant because it goes to the heart of a generational conflict in the black community, concerning what we will say in public and what we say in private. For it has been a point of honor, among the civil rights generation, that any criticism or negative analysis of our community, expressed, as they often are by white politicians, without context, without real empathy or understanding, should not be repeated by a black politician when the white community is listening, even if (*especially* if) the criticism happens to be true (more than half of all black American children live in single-parent households). Our business is our business. Keep it in the family; don't wash your dirty linen in public; stay unified. (Of course, with his overheard gaffe, Jackson unwittingly broke his own rule.)

Until Obama, black politicians had always adhered to these unwritten rules. In this way, they defended themselves against those two bogeymen of black political life: the Uncle Tom and the House Nigger. The black politician who played up to, or even simply echoed, white fears, desires, and hopes for the black community was in danger of earning these epithets—even Martin Luther King was not free from such suspicions. Then came Obama, and the new world he had supposedly ushered in, the postracial world, in which what mattered most was not blind racial allegiance but factual truth. It was felt that Jesse Jackson was sadly out of step with this new postracial world: even his own son felt moved to publicly repudiate his "ugly rhetoric." But Jackson's anger was not incomprehensible nor his distrust unreasonable. Jackson lived through a bitter struggle, and bitter struggles deform their participants in subtle, complicated ways. The idea that one should speak one's cultural allegiance first and the truth second (and that this is a sign of authenticity) is precisely such a deformation.

Right up to the wire, Obama made many black men and women of Jackson's generation suspicious. How can the man who passes between culturally black and white voices with such flexibility, with such ease, be an honest man? How *will* the man from Dream City keep it real? Why won't he speak with a clear and unified voice? These were genuine questions for people born in real cities at a time when those cities were implacably divided, when the black movement had to yell with a clear and unified voice, or risk not being heard at all. And then he won. Watching Jesse Jackson in tears in Grant Park, pressed up against the varicolored American public, it seemed like he, at least, had received the answer he needed: only a many-voiced man could have spoken to that many people.

A clear and unified voice. In that context, this business of being biracial, of being half black and half white, is awkward. In his memoir, Obama takes care to ridicule a certain black girl called Joyce—a composite figure from his college days who happens also to be part Italian and part French and part Native American and is inordinately fond of mentioning these facts, and who likes to say:

> I'm not black . . . I'm *multiracial* . . . . Why should I have to choose between them? . . . It's not white people who are making me choose . . . . No—it's *black people* who always have to make everything racial. *They're* the ones making me choose. *They're* the ones who are telling me I can't be who I am . . . .

He has her voice down pat and so condemns her out of her own mouth. For she's the third bogeyman of black life, the tragic mulatto, who secretly wishes she "passed," always keen to let you know about her white heritage. It's the fear of being mistaken for Joyce that has always ensured that I ignore the box marked "biracial" and tick the box marked "black" on any questionnaire I fill out, and call myself unequivocally a black writer and roll my eyes at anyone who insists that Obama is not the first black president but the first biracial one. But I also know in my heart that it's an equivocation; I know that Obama has a double consciousness, is black and, at the same time, white, as I am, unless we are suggesting that one side of a person's genetics and cultural heritage cancels out or trumps the other.

But to mention the double is to suggest shame at the singular. Joyce insists on her varied heritage because she fears and is ashamed of the singular black. I suppose it's possible that subconsciously I am also a tragic mulatto, torn between pride and shame. In my conscious life, though, I cannot honestly say I feel proud to be white and ashamed to be black or proud to be black and ashamed to be white. I find it impossible to experience either pride or shame over accidents of genetics in which I had no active part. I understand how those words got into the racial discourse, but I can't sign up to them. I'm not proud to be female either. I am not even proud to be human—I only love to be so. As I love to be female and I love to be black, and I love that I had a white father.

It's telling that Joyce is one of the few voices in *Dreams from My Father* that is truly left out in the cold, outside of the expansive sympathy of Obama's narrative. She is an entirely didactic being, a demon Obama has to raise up, if only for a page, so everyone can watch him slay her. I know the feeling. When I was in college I felt I'd rather run away with the Black Panthers than be associated with the Joyces I occasionally met. It's the Joyces of this world who "talk down to black folks." And so to avoid being Joyce, or being seen to be Joyce, you unify, you speak with one voice.

And the concept of a unified black voice is a potent one. It has filtered down, these past forty years, into the black community at all levels, settling itself in that impossible injunction "keep it real," the original intention of which was unification. We were going to unify the concept of Blackness in order to strengthen it. Instead we confined and restricted it. To me, the instruction "keep it real" is a sort of prison cell, two feet by five. The fact is, it's too narrow. I just can't live comfortably in there. "*Keep it real*" replaced the blessed and solid genetic fact of Blackness with a flimsy imperative. It made Blackness a quality each individual black person was constantly in danger of losing. And almost anything could trigger the loss of one's Blackness: attending certain universities, an impressive variety of jobs, a fondness for opera, a white girlfriend, an interest in golf. And of course, any change in the voice. There was a popular school of thought that maintained the voice was at the very heart of the thing; fail to keep it real there and you'd never see your Blackness again.

How absurd that all seems now. And not because we live in a postracial world—we don't—but because the reality of race has diversified. Black reality has diversified. It's black people who talk like me, and black people who talk like L'il Wayne. It's black conservatives and black liberals, black sportsmen and black lawyers, black computer technicians and black ballet dancers and black truck drivers and black presidents. We're all black, and we all love to be black, and we all sing from our own hymn sheet. We're all surely black people, but we may be finally approaching a point of human history where you can't talk up or down to us anymore, but only *to* us. *He's talking down to white people*—how curious it sounds the other way round! In order to say such a thing one would have to think collectively of white people, as a people of one mind who speak with one voice—a thought experiment in which we have no practice. But it's worth trying. It's only when you play the record backward that you hear the secret message.

3

For reasons that are obscure to me, those qualities we cherish in our artists we condemn in our politicians. In our artists we look for the many-colored voice, the multiple sensibility. The apogee of this is, of course, Shakespeare: even more than for his wordplay we cherish him for his lack of allegiance. *Our* Shakespeare sees always both sides of a thing, he is black and white, male and female—he is everyman. The giant lacunae in his biography are merely a convenience; if any new facts of religious or political affiliation were ever to arise we would dismiss them in our hearts anyway. Was he, for example, a man of Rome or not? He has appeared, to generations of readers, not of one religion but of both, in truth, beyond both. Born into the middle of Britain's fierce Catholic—Protestant culture war, how could the bloody absurdity of those years not impress upon him a strong sense of cultural contingency?

It was a war of ideas that began for Will—as it began for Barack—in the dreams of his father. For we know that John Shakespeare, a civic officer in Protestant times, oversaw the repainting of medieval frescoes and the destruction of the rood loft and altar in Stratford's own fine Guild Chapel, but we also know that in the rafters of the Shakespeare home John hid a secret Catholic "Spiritual Testament," a signed profession of allegiance to the old faith. A strange experience, to watch one's own father thus divided, professing one thing in public while practicing another in private. John Shakespeare was a kind of equivocator: it's what you do when you're in a corner, when you can't be a Catholic and a loyal Englishman at the same time. When you can't be both black and white. Sometimes in a country ripped apart by dogma, those who wish to keep their heads—in both senses—must learn to split themselves in two.

And this we *still* know, here, at a four-hundred-year distance. No one can hope to be president of these United States without professing a committed and straightforward belief in two things: the existence of God and the principle of American exceptionalism. But how many of them equivocated, and who, in their shoes, would not equivocate, too?

Fortunately, Shakespeare was an artist and so had an outlet his father didn't have—the many-voiced theater. Shakespeare's art, the very medium of it, allowed him to do what civic officers and politicians can't seem to: speak simultaneous truths. (Is it not, for example, experientially true that one can both believe and *not* believe in God?) In his plays he is woman, man, black, white, believer, heretic, Catholic, Protestant, Jew, Muslim. He grew up in an atmosphere of equivocation, but he lived in freedom. And he offers us freedom: to pin him down to a single identity would be an obvious diminishment, both for Shakespeare and for us. Generations of critics have insisted on this irreducible multiplicity, though they have each expressed it different ways, through the glass of their times. Here is Keats's famous attempt, in 1817, to give this quality a name:

> At once it struck me, what quality went to form a Man of Achievement especially in Literature and which Shakespeare possessed so enormously—I mean *Negative Capability*, that

is when man is capable of being in uncertainties, Mysteries, doubts, without any irritable reaching after fact and reason.

And here is Stephen Greenblatt doing the same, in 2004:

There are many forms of heroism in Shakespeare, but ideological heroism—the fierce, self-immolating embrace of an idea or institution—is not one of them.

For Keats, Shakespeare's many voices are quasi-mystical as suited the Romantic thrust of Keats's age. For Greenblatt, Shakespeare's negative capability is sociopolitical at root. Will had seen too many wild-eyed martyrs, too many executed terrorists, too many wars on the Catholic terror. He had watched men rage absurdly at rood screens and write treatises in praise of tables. He had seen men disemboweled while still alive, their entrails burned before their eyes, and all for the preference of a Latin Mass over a common prayer or vice versa. He understood what fierce, singular certainty creates and what it destroys. In response, he made himself a diffuse, uncertain thing, a mass of contradictory, irresolvable voices that speak truth plurally. Through the glass of 2009, "negative capability" looks like the perfect antidote to "ideological heroism."

From our politicians, though, we still look for ideological heroism, despite everything. We consider pragmatists to be weak. We call men of balance naive fools. In England, we once had an insulting name for such people: trimmers. In the mid-1600s, a trimmer was any politician who attempted to straddle the reviled middle ground between Cavalier and Roundhead, Parliament and the Crown; to call a man a trimmer was to accuse him of being insufficiently committed to an ideology. But in telling us of these times, the nineteenth-century English historian Thomas Macaulay draws our attention to Halifax, great statesman of the Privy Council, set up to mediate between Parliament and Crown as London burned. Halifax proudly called himself a trimmer, assuming it, Macaulay explains, as

a title of honour, and vindicat[ing], with great vivacity, the dignity of the appellation. Everything good, he said, trims between extremes. The temperate zone trims between the climate in which men are roasted and the climate in which they are frozen. The English Church trims between the Anabaptist madness and the Papist lethargy. The English constitution trims between the Turkish despotism and Polish anarchy. Virtue is nothing but a just temper between propensities any one of which, if indulged to excess, becomes vice.

Which all sounds eminently reasonable and Aristotelian. And Macaulay's description of Halifax's character is equally attractive:

His intellect was fertile, subtle, and capacious. His polished, luminous, and animated eloquence . . . was the delight of the House of Lords . . . . His political tracts well deserve to be studied for their literary merit.

In fact, Halifax is familiar—he sounds like the man from Dream City. This makes Macaulay's caveat the more striking:

Yet he was less successful in politics than many who enjoyed smaller advantages. Indeed, those intellectual *peculiarities which make his writings valuable* frequently impeded him in the contests of active life. For he always saw passing events, not in the point of view in which they commonly appear to one who bears a part in them, but in the point of view in which, after the lapse of many years, they appear to the philosophic historian.

To me, this is a doleful conclusion. It is exactly men with such intellectual peculiarities that I have always hoped to see in politics. But maybe Macaulay is correct: maybe the Halifaxes of this world make, in the end, better writers than politicians. A lot rests on how this president turns out—but that's a debate for the future. Here I want instead to hazard a little theory, concerning the evolution of a certain type of voice, typified by Halifax, by Shakespeare, and very possibly the President. For the voice of what Macaulay called "the philosophic historian" is, to my mind, a valuable and particular one, and I think someone should make a proper study of it. It's a voice that develops in a man over time; my little theory sketches four developmental stages.

The first stage in the evolution is contingent and cannot be contrived. In this first stage, the voice, by no fault of its own, finds itself trapped between two poles, two competing belief systems. And so this first stage necessitates the second: the voice learns to be flexible between these two fixed points, even to the point of equivocation. Then the third stage: this native flexibility leads to a sense of being able to "see a thing from both sides." And then the final stage, which I think of as the mark of a certain kind of genius: the voice relinquishes ownership of itself, develops a creative sense of disassociation in which the claims that are particular to it seem no stronger than anyone else's. There it is, my little theory—I'd rather call it a story. It is a story about a wonderful voice, occasionally used by citizens, rarely by men of power. Amidst the din of the 2008 culture wars it proved especially hard to hear.

In this lecture I have been seeking to tentatively suggest that the voice that speaks with such freedom, thus unburdened by dogma and personal bias, thus flooded with empathy, might make a good president. It's only now that I realize that in all this utilitarianism I've left joyfulness out of the account, and thus neglected a key constituency of my own people, the poets! Being many-voiced may be a complicated gift for a president, but in poets it is a pure delight in need of neither defense nor explanation. Plato banished them from his uptight and annoying republic so long ago that they have lost all their anxiety. They are fancy-free.

"I am a Hittite in love with a horse," writes Frank O'Hara.

> I don't know what blood's
> in me I feel like an African prince I am a girl walking downstairs
> in a red pleated dress with heels I am a champion taking a fall
> I am a jockey with a sprained ass-hole I am the light mist
> in which a face appears
> and it is another face of blonde I am a baboon eating a banana
> I am a dictator looking at his wife I am a doctor eating a child
> and the child's mother smiling I am a Chinaman climbing a mountain
> I am a child smelling his father's underwear I am an Indian
> sleeping on a scalp
> and my pony is stamping in
> the birches,
> and I've just caught sight of the
> Niña, the Pinta and the Santa
> Maria
> What land is this, so free?

Frank O'Hara's republic is of the imagination, of course. It is the only land of perfect freedom. Presidents, as a breed, tend to dismiss this land, thinking it has nothing to teach them. If this new president turns out to be different, then writers will count their blessings, but with or without a president on board, writers should always count their blessings. A line of O'Hara's reminds us of this. It's carved on his gravestone. It reads: "Grace to be born and live as variously as possible."

But to live variously cannot simply be a gift, endowed by an accident of birth; it has to be a continual effort, continually renewed. I felt this with force the night of the election. I was at a lovely New York party, full of lovely people, almost all of whom were white, liberal, highly educated, and celebrating with one happy voice as the states turned blue. Just as they called Iowa my phone rang and a strident German voice said: "Zadie! Come to Harlem! It's vild here. I'm in za middle of a crazy Reggae bar—it's so vonderful! Vy not come now!"

I mention he was German only so we don't run away with the idea that flexibility comes only to the beige, or gay, or otherwise marginalized. Flexibility is a choice, always open to all of us. (He was a writer, however. Make of that what you will.)

But wait: all the way uptown? A crazy reggae bar? For a minute I hesitated, because I was at a lovely party having a lovely time. Or was that it? There was something else. In truth I thought: but I'll be ludicrous, in my silly dress, with this silly posh English voice, in a crowded bar of black New Yorkers celebrating. It's amazing how many of our cross-cultural and cross-class encounters are limited not by hate or pride or shame, but by another equally insidious, less-discussed, emotion: embarrassment. A few minutes later, I was in a taxi and heading uptown with my Northern Irish husband and our half-Indian, half-English friend, but that initial hesitation was ominous; the first step on a typical British journey. A hesitation in the face of difference, which leads to caution before difference and ends in fear of it. Before long, the only voice you recognize, the only life you can empathize with, is your own. You will think that a novelist's screwy leap of logic. Well, it's my novelist credo and I believe it. I believe that flexibility of voice leads to a flexibility in all things. My audacious hope in Obama is based, I'm afraid, on precisely such flimsy premises.

It's my audacious hope that a man born and raised between opposing dogmas, between cultures, between voices, could not help but be aware of the extreme contingency of culture. I further audaciously hope that such a man will not mistake the happy accident of his own cultural sensibilities for a set of natural laws, suitable for general application. I even hope that he will find himself in agreement with George Bernard Shaw when he declared, "Patriotism is, fundamentally, a conviction that a particular country is the best in the world because you were born in it." But that may be an audacious hope too far. We'll see if Obama's lifelong vocal flexibility will enable him to say proudly with one voice "I love my country" while saying with another voice "It is a country, like other countries." I hope so. He seems just the man to demonstrate that between those two voices there exists no contradiction and no equivocation but rather a proper and decent human harmony.

Note

1. Zadie Smith, "Speaking in Tongues," *The New York Review of Books*, February 26, 2009.

President Barack Obama

Barack Hussein Obama II (1961–) was born in Honolulu, Hawaii, to his American mother, Stanley Ann Dunham, and Kenyan father, Barack Obama Sr. Obama graduated from Columbia University in 1983. Upon graduating, he served as a community organizer in Chicago, Illinois, before attending Harvard Law School, where he served as the first Black president of the Harvard Law Review. After earning his JD in 1991, Obama worked as a civil rights attorney while teaching constitutional law at University of Chicago Law School. From 1997 to 2004, he served three successful terms representing the 13th District in the Illinois Senate. During his 2004 campaign, Senator Obama received national attention when he delivered the keynote address at the Democratic National Convention. Three years later, he began a presidential campaign that would result in his election as the forty-fourth president of the United States of America, the first African American to hold this position. Nine months after his election, President Obama was named the 2009 Nobel Peace Prize laureate. In 2012, he was reelected. During his terms, President Obama signed countless pieces of legislation and policies that speak directly to, but are not limited to, economic stimulus, domestic initiatives, foreign policies, and inclusiveness of civil rights.

His terms were also marked by his eloquently powerful speeches. In March 2015, President Obama delivered an address during the fiftieth anniversary of "Bloody Sunday," commemorating the marches to Montgomery in 1965. Using the tragic events of Selma as his backdrop, President Obama argued that the Selma marchers helped to change American democracy. President Obama's speech in Selma, Alabama, commemorated an important moment in American history—one that rhetorically constructed a vision for American history that charged all American citizens to take steps toward a more hopeful future. This speech and other speeches from then-Senator Obama and President Obama can be found printed in this reader and in the supporting digital files.

Address on the 50th Anniversary of the Selma, Alabama March

Barack Obama[1]

Delivered 7 March 2015, Edmund Pettus Bridge, Selma, Alabama

It is a rare honor in this life to follow one of your heroes. And John Lewis is one of my heroes.

Now, I have to imagine that when a younger John Lewis woke up that morning 50 years ago and made his way to Brown Chapel, heroics were not on his mind. A day like this was not on his mind. Young folks with bedrolls and backpacks were milling about. Veterans of the movement trained newcomers in the tactics of non-violence—the right way to protect yourself when attacked. A doctor described what tear gas does to the body, while marchers scribbled down instructions for contacting their loved ones. The air was thick with doubt, anticipation and fear. And they comforted themselves with the final verse of the final hymn they sung:

> *No matter what may be the test, God will take care of you;*
> *lean, weary one, upon His breast, God will take care of you.*[2]

And then, his knapsack stocked with an apple, a toothbrush, and a book on government—all you need for a night behind bars—John Lewis led them out of the church on a mission to change America.

President and Mrs. Bush, Governor Bentley, Mayor Evans, Sewell, Reverend Strong, members of Congress, elected officials, foot soldiers, friends, fellow Americans:

As John noted, there are places and moments in America where this nation's destiny has been decided. Many are sites of war—Concord and Lexington, Appomattox, Gettysburg. Others are sites that symbolize the daring of America's character—Independence Hall and Seneca Falls, Kitty Hawk and Cape Canaveral.

Selma is such a place. In one afternoon 50 years ago, so much of our turbulent history—the stain of slavery and anguish of civil war; the yoke of segregation and tyranny of Jim Crow; the death of four little girls in Birmingham; and the dream of a Baptist preacher—all that history met on this bridge.[3]

It was not a clash of armies, but a clash of wills; a contest to determine the true meaning of America. And because of men and women like John Lewis, Joseph Lowery, Hosea Williams, Amelia Boynton, Diane Nash, Ralph Abernathy, C.T. Vivian, Andrew Young, Fred Shuttlesworth, Dr. Martin Luther King, Jr., and so many others, the idea of a just America and a fair America, an inclusive America, and a generous America—that idea ultimately triumphed.

As is true across the landscape of American history, we cannot examine this moment in isolation. The march on Selma was part of a broader campaign that spanned generations; the leaders that day part of a long line of heroes.

We gather here to celebrate them. We gather here to honor the courage of ordinary Americans willing to endure billy clubs and the chastening rod; tear gas and the trampling hoof; men and women who despite the gush of blood and splintered bone would stay true to their North Star and keep marching towards justice.

They did as Scripture instructed: "Rejoice in hope, be patient in tribulation, be constant in prayer." And in the days to come, they went back again and again. When the trumpet call sounded for more to join, the people came—black and white, young and old, Christian and Jew, waving the American flag and singing the same anthems full of faith and hope. A white newsman, Bill Plante, who covered the marches then and who is with us here today, quipped that the growing number of white people lowered the quality of the singing. To those who marched, though, those old gospel songs must have never sounded so sweet.

In time, their chorus would well up and reach President Johnson. And he would send them protection, and speak to the nation, echoing their call for America and the world to hear: "We shall overcome." What enormous faith these men and women had. Faith in God, but also faith in America.

The Americans who crossed this bridge, they were not physically imposing. But they gave courage to millions. They held no elected office. But they led a nation. They marched as Americans who had endured hundreds of years of brutal violence, countless daily indignities—but they didn't seek special treatment, just the equal treatment promised to them almost a century before.

What they did here will reverberate through the ages. Not because the change they won was preordained; not because their victory was complete; but because they proved that nonviolent change is possible, that love and hope can conquer hate.

As we commemorate their achievement, we are well-served to remember that at the time of the marches, many in power condemned rather than praised them. Back then, they were called Communists, or half-breeds, or outside agitators, sexual and moral degenerates, and worse—they were called everything but the name their parents gave them. Their faith was questioned; their lives were threatened; their patriotism challenged.

And yet, what could be more American than what happened in this place? What could more profoundly vindicate the idea of America than plain and humble people—unsung, the downtrodden, the dreamers not of high station, not born to wealth or privilege, not of one religious tradition but many, coming together to shape their country's course?

What greater expression of faith in the American experiment than this, what greater form of patriotism is there than the belief that America is not yet finished, that we are strong enough to be self-critical, that each successive generation can look upon our imperfections and decide that it is in our power to remake this nation to more closely align with our highest ideals?

That's why Selma is not some outlier in the American experience. That's why it's not a museum or a static monument to behold from a distance. It is instead the manifestation of a creed written into our founding documents: "We the People . . . in order to form a more perfect union." "We hold these truths to be self-evident, that all men are created equal."

These are not just words. They're a living thing, a call to action, a roadmap for citizenship and an insistence in the capacity of free men and women to shape our own destiny. For founders like Franklin and Jefferson, for leaders like Lincoln and FDR, the success of our experiment in self-government rested on engaging all of our citizens in this work. And that's what we celebrate here in Selma. That's what this movement was all about, one leg in our long journey toward freedom.

The American instinct that led these young men and women to pick up the torch and cross this bridge, that's the same instinct that moved patriots to choose revolution over tyranny. It's the same instinct that drew immigrants from across oceans and the Rio Grande; the same instinct that led women to reach for the ballot, workers to organize against an unjust status quo; the same instinct that led us to plant a flag at Iwo Jima and on the surface of the Moon. It's the idea held by generations of citizens who believed that America is a constant work in progress; who believed that loving this country requires more than singing its praises or avoiding uncomfortable truths. It requires the occasional disruption, the willingness to speak out for what is right, to shake up the status quo. That's America.

That's what makes us unique. That's what cements our reputation as a beacon of opportunity. Young people behind the Iron Curtain would see Selma and eventually tear down that wall. Young people in Soweto would hear Bobby Kennedy talk about ripples of hope and eventually banish the scourge of apartheid. Young people in Burma went to prison rather than submit to military rule. They saw what John Lewis had done. From the streets of Tunis to the Maidan in Ukraine, this generation of young people can draw strength from this place, where the powerless could change the world's greatest power and push their leaders to expand the boundaries of freedom.

They saw that idea made real right here in Selma, Alabama. They saw that idea manifest itself here in America.

Because of campaigns like this, a Voting Rights Act was passed. Political and economic and social barriers came down. And the change these men and women wrought is visible here today in the presence of African Americans who run boardrooms, who sit on the bench, who serve in elected office from small towns to big cities; from the Congressional Black Caucus all the way to the Oval Office.

Because of what they did, the doors of opportunity swung open not just for black folks, but for every American. Women marched through those doors. Latinos marched through those doors. Asian Americans, gay Americans, Americans with disabilities—they all came through those doors. Their endeavors gave the entire South the chance to rise again, not by reasserting the past, but by transcending the past.

What a glorious thing, Dr. King might say. And what a solemn debt we owe. Which leads us to ask, just how might we repay that debt?

First and foremost, we have to recognize that one day's commemoration, no matter how special, is not enough. If Selma taught us anything, it's that our work is never done. The American experiment in self-government gives work and purpose to each generation.

Selma teaches us, as well, that action requires that we shed our cynicism. For when it comes to the pursuit of justice, we can afford neither complacency nor despair.

Just this week, I was asked whether I thought the Department of Justice's Ferguson report shows that, with respect to race, little has changed in this country. And I understood the question; the report's narrative was sadly familiar. It evoked the kind of abuse and disregard for citizens that spawned the Civil Rights Movement.

But I rejected the notion that nothing's changed. What happened in Ferguson may not be unique, but it's no longer endemic. It's no longer sanctioned by law or by custom. And before the Civil Rights Movement, it most surely was.

We do a disservice to the cause of justice by intimating that bias and discrimination are immutable, that racial division is inherent to America. If you think nothing's changed in the past 50 years, ask somebody who lived through the Selma or Chicago or Los Angeles of the 1950s. Ask the female CEO who once might have been assigned to the secretarial pool if nothing's changed. Ask your gay friend if it's easier to be out and proud in America now than it was thirty years ago. To deny this progress, this hard-won progress—our progress—would be to rob us of our own agency, our own capacity, our responsibility to do what we can to make America better.

Of course, a more common mistake is to suggest that Ferguson is an isolated incident; that racism is banished; that the work that drew men and women to Selma is now complete, and that whatever racial tensions remain are a consequence of those seeking to play the "race card" for their own purposes. We don't need the Ferguson report to know that's not true. We just need to open our eyes, and our ears, and our hearts to know that this nation's racial history still casts its long shadow upon us.

We know the march is not yet over. We know the race is not yet won. We know that reaching that blessed destination where we are judged, all of us, by the content of our character requires admitting as much, facing up to the truth. "We are capable of bearing a great burden," James Baldwin once wrote, "once we discover that the burden is reality and arrive where reality is."

There's nothing America can't handle if we actually look squarely at the problem. And this is work for all Americans, not just some. Not just whites. Not just blacks. If we want to honor the courage of those who marched that day, then all of us are called to possess their moral imagination. All of us will need to feel as they did the fierce urgency of now. All of us need to recognize as they did that change depends on our actions, on our attitudes, the things we teach our children. And if we make such an effort, no matter how hard it may sometimes seem, laws can be passed, and consciences can be stirred, and consensus can be built.

With such an effort, we can make sure our criminal justice system serves all and not just some. Together, we can raise the level of mutual trust that policing is built on—the idea that police officers are members of the community they risk their lives to protect, and citizens in Ferguson and New York and Cleveland, they just want the same thing young people here marched for 50 years ago—the protection of the law. Together, we can address unfair sentencing and overcrowded prisons, and the stunted circumstances that rob too many boys of the chance to become men, and rob the nation of too many men who could be good dads, and good workers, and good neighbors.

With effort, we can roll back poverty and the roadblocks to opportunity. Americans don't accept a free ride for anybody, nor do we believe in equality of outcomes. But we do expect equal opportunity. And if we really mean it, if we're not just giving lip service to it, but if we really mean it and are willing to sacrifice for it, then, yes, we can make sure every child gets an education suitable to this new century, one that expands imaginations and lifts sights and gives those children the skills they need. We can make sure every person willing to work has the dignity of a job, and a fair wage, and a real voice, and sturdier rungs on that ladder into the middle class.

And with effort, we can protect the foundation stone of our democracy for which so many marched across this bridge—and that is the right to vote. Right now, in 2015, 50 years after

Selma, there are laws across this country designed to make it harder for people to vote. As we speak, more of such laws are being proposed. Meanwhile, the Voting Rights Act, the culmination of so much blood, so much sweat and tears, the product of so much sacrifice in the face of wanton violence, the Voting Rights Act stands weakened, its future subject to political rancor.

How can that be? The Voting Rights Act was one of the crowning achievements of our democracy, the result of Republican and Democratic efforts. President Reagan signed its renewal when he was in office. President George W. Bush signed its renewal when he was in office. One hundred members of Congress have come here today to honor people who were willing to die for the right to protect it. If we want to honor this day, let that hundred go back to Washington and gather four hundred more, and together, pledge to make it their mission to restore that law this year. That's how we honor those on this bridge.

Of course, our democracy is not the task of Congress alone, or the courts alone, or even the President alone. If every new voter-suppression law was struck down today, we would still have, here in America, one of the lowest voting rates among free peoples. Fifty years ago, registering to vote here in Selma and much of the South meant guessing the number of jellybeans in a jar, the number of bubbles on a bar of soap. It meant risking your dignity, and sometimes, your life.

What's our excuse today for not voting? How do we so casually discard the right for which so many fought? How do we so fully give away our power, our voice, in shaping America's future? Why are we pointing to somebody else when we could take the time just to go to the polling places? We give away our power.

Fellow marchers, so much has changed in 50 years. We have endured war and we've fashioned peace. We've seen technological wonders that touch every aspect of our lives. We take for granted conveniences that our parents could have scarcely imagined. But what has not changed is the imperative of citizenship; that willingness of a 26-year-old deacon, or a Unitarian minister, or a young mother of five to decide they loved this country so much that they'd risk everything to realize its promise.

That's what it means to love America. That's what it means to believe in America. That's what it means when we say America is exceptional.

For we were born of change. We broke the old aristocracies, declaring ourselves entitled not by bloodline, but endowed by our Creator with certain inalienable rights. We secure our rights and responsibilities through a system of self-government, of and by and for the people. That's why we argue and fight with so much passion and conviction—because we know our efforts matter. We know America is what we make of it.

Look at our history:

We are Lewis and Clark and Sacajawea, pioneers who braved the unfamiliar, followed by a stampede of farmers and miners, and entrepreneurs and hucksters. That's our spirit. That's who we are.

We are Sojourner Truth and Fannie Lou Hamer, women who could do as much as any man and then some. And we're Susan B. Anthony, who shook the system until the law reflected that truth. That is our character.

We're the immigrants who stowed away on ships to reach these shores, the huddled masses yearning to breathe free—Holocaust survivors, Soviet defectors, the Lost Boys of Sudan. We're the hopeful strivers who cross the Rio Grande because we want our kids to know a better life. That's how we came to be.

We're the slaves who built the White House and the economy of the South. We're the ranch hands and cowboys who opened up the West, and countless laborers who laid rail, and raised skyscrapers, and organized for workers' rights.

We're the fresh-faced GIs who fought to liberate a continent. And we're the Tuskegee Airmen, and the Navajo code-talkers, and the Japanese Americans who fought for this country even as their own liberty had been denied.

We're the firefighters who rushed into those buildings on 9/11, the volunteers who signed up to fight in Afghanistan and Iraq. We're the gay Americans whose blood ran in the streets of San Francisco and New York, just as blood ran down this bridge.

We are storytellers, writers, poets, artists who abhor unfairness, and despise hypocrisy, and give voice to the voiceless, and tell truths that need to be told.

We're the inventors of gospel and jazz and blues, bluegrass and country, and hip-hop and rock and roll, and our very own sound with all the sweet sorrow and reckless joy of freedom.

We are Jackie Robinson, enduring scorn and spiked cleats and pitches coming straight to his head, and stealing home in the World Series anyway.

We are the people Langston Hughes wrote of who "build our temples for tomorrow, strong as we know how." We are the people Emerson wrote of, "who for truth and honor's sake stand fast and suffer long;" who are "never tired, so long as we can see far enough."

That's what America is. Not stock photos or airbrushed history, or feeble attempts to define some of us as more American than others. We respect the past, but we don't pine for the past. We don't fear the future; we grab for it. America is not some fragile thing. We are large, in the words of Whitman, containing multitudes. We are boisterous and diverse and full of energy, perpetually young in spirit. That's why someone like John Lewis at the ripe old age of 25 could lead a mighty march.

And that's what the young people here today and listening all across the country must take away from this day. You are America. Unconstrained by habit and convention. Unencumbered by what is, because you're ready to seize what ought to be.

For everywhere in this country, there are first steps to be taken, there's new ground to cover, there are more bridges to be crossed. And it is you, the young and fearless at heart, the most diverse and educated generation in our history, who the nation is waiting to follow.

Because Selma shows us that America is not the project of any one person. Because the single-most powerful word in our democracy is the word "We." "We The People." "We Shall Overcome." "Yes We Can." That word is owned by no one. It belongs to everyone. Oh, what a glorious task we are given, to continually try to improve this great nation of ours.

Fifty years from Bloody Sunday, our march is not yet finished, but we're getting closer. Two hundred and thirty-nine years after this nation's founding our union is not yet perfect, but we are getting closer. Our job's easier because somebody already got us through that first mile. Somebody already got us over that bridge. When it feels the road is too hard, when the torch we've been passed feels too heavy, we will remember these early travelers, and draw strength from their example, and hold firmly the words of the prophet Isaiah:

Those who hope in the Lord will renew their strength. They will soar on wings like eagles. They will run and not grow weary. They will walk and not be faint.[4]

We honor those who walked so we could run. We must run so our children soar. And we will not grow weary. For we believe in the power of an awesome God, and we believe in this country's sacred promise.

May He bless those warriors of justice no longer with us, and bless the United States of America.

Thank you, everybody.

Notes

1. President Barack Obama, "Fiftieth Anniversary of Bloody Sunday," Edmond Pettus Bridge, Selma, Alabama, March 7, 2015. AUTHENTICITY CERTIFIED: Text version transcribed directly from audio.
2. From a hymn entitled "God Will Take Care of You" with lyrics by Civilla D. Martin and music by W. Stillman Martin. It is the third entry in the 1906 hymnal *Songs of Redemption and Praise* compiled by

John A. Davis and John Ralston Clements. Sheet music for this hymn has been digitized by and publicly preserved at Internet Archive.

3. Edmund Pettus Bridge, Wikipedia entry: "The Edmund Pettus Bridge is a bridge that carries U.S. Route 80 across the Alabama River in Selma, Alabama. Built in 1940, it is named for Edmund Winston Pettus, a former Confederate brigadier general, Democratic Party U.S. Senator from Alabama and Grand Dragon of the Alabama Ku Klux Klan . . . The Edmund Pettus Bridge was the site of the conflict of Bloody Sunday on March 7, 1965, when armed policemen attacked peaceful civil rights demonstrators who were attempting to march to the Alabama state capital of Montgomery. The bridge was declared a National Historic Landmark on March 11, 2013." (Truncated from original; retrieved and posted 12 March 2015)

4. Isaiah: 40:31

Section 5: Further Reading

King, Martin L. "Letter from Birmingham Jail." In *Why We Can't Wait*. Ed. Martin Luther King, Jr. New York: Signet Classics, 1963. (pp. 77–100).

X, Malcolm. "The Ballot or the Bullet." Detroit, Michigan. (12 April 1964).

Section 5: Discussion Questions

1. In the introduction to the African American Political Rhetoric section, the section editors assert that African American political rhetoric is about Black presence. Explore the concept of presence as you engage and analyze the rhetoric that appears in both the print text and media list of this section.

2. The section editors also assert that African American rhetoric is necessarily political. Discuss the connotation of this assertion using the variety of artifacts that appear in this section.

3. The artifacts in the political rhetoric section, as in other sections, are composed of texts from a variety of genres. What about the nature of political rhetoric allows for such a variety of representations in text?

4. Using the concept of nommo as defined in the Smith and Gilyard pieces in the first section, offer a discussion of nommo in the artifacts that appear in this section.

5. When considering the variety of artifacts included in the print and media sections, how would you thematically characterize African American political rhetoric? Is there a recurring sentiment? If so, what social, political, economic, and legislative phenomena have contributed to this sentiment?

PART III
DISCOURSES ON BLACK BODIES

INTRODUCTION: GENDERS AND SEXUALITIES

Vershawn Ashanti Young

━━━━◦∞◦━━━━

As the sociologist Patricia Hill Collins writes in *Black Sexual Politics: African Americans, Gender, and the New Racism* (2004), "Failing to address questions of gender and sexuality will compromise antiracist African American politics in the post—civil rights era" (9). Collins's observation might be modified to express the intention of this unit by saying that failing to address questions of gender and sexuality compromises any examination of African American rhetoric. Questions of gender and sexuality are important to raise and answer in African American rhetoric over the longue durée—that is, from the beginning of the Americas to today. Indeed past failures on the part of African Americans in particular and Americans in general to confront gender and sexuality in relation to racial progress has compromised social and economic equality for all. The three sections that constitute this unit then all pivot on the understood articulation among gender, race, and sexuality.

The first section, "Race Women and Black Feminisms," edited by Joy James, focuses on the rhetoric of Black women's lives, their womanhood, and Black feminisms. Many of the readings assert intersectionality as a Black feminist frame for understanding the world. And as such, intersectionality brings the topic of class into the fold of the triumvirate of gender, race, and sexuality advanced in this unit. The second slate of readings, "Motions of Manhood," edited by Vershawn Ashanti Young, presents the varied discourses concerning racialized masculinity and the self-representations of Black manhood by Black men in a patriarchal America. In the third section, "The Quare of Queer," editor Jeffrey McCune provides a sampling from the steadily growing terrain of Black queer rhetorics. He draws mostly from theoretical sources but also presents popular perspectives. As Black queer rhetoric has found a strong constellation of voices among scholars of color, the theoretical disposition of this last section in the unit is appropriate and necessary. Taken together, these sections present the articulation of gender, race, and sexuality as a key to reading African American rhetoric writ large.

As an important touchstone for understanding African American discourse and culture, it might help before engaging the readings to understand the indivisible rhetorical link among gender, race, and sexuality. Understanding this articulation means queering, or rather "quaring," as one scholar of Black queer rhetoric terms it, what appears to be obvious about this articulation. So here's the quare: in American culture, gender and sexuality are often conflated due to our society's abiding commitment to compulsory heterosexuality, which can perhaps be defined simply as the expectation and pressure for everyone to be heterosexual. In a patriarchal society, such as America, women are consistently treated as second-class citizens, rendering femininity a less desired gender performance, while manhood and masculinity are given undo

315

primacy. Thus heterosexuality for any man in such a culture is judged on the basis of two essential requirements: the enactment of an idealized masculinity and intercourse with a woman. In this environment, women are seen and often used as conduits for displays of manhood and the exhibition of a man's masculinity. When one element is out of sync—that is, when a man is not performing the right masculinity and not known to be sexually involved with women—he is negatively deemed queer, and not queer as in different or offering a non-normative alternative, but queer as in gay, an aberration of heterosexuality.

However, unlike proclamations of sexuality ("I am straight" or "I am gay"), sex acts are for the most part private practices, prohibited in public; so then gender performances must serve a dual role. A man may then attempt to use his bodily expression of masculinity to promote or disrupt expectations of his sexuality, while others assess his performance and speculate about what he does in bed and with whom he does it. In regard to race, this is as true for the White man in America as it is for the Black. However, what is not true for the White man but is certainly true for the Black is that, on the basis of race, the question of homosexuality is always present for Black men, regardless of whether they are actually gay or straight. This gender circumstance is due to the prevailing discourse on racial performance that creates restrictions on Black men's ability to behave in all the ways White men can in public, in school, in the boardroom, or in the White House, thus effectively limiting their performances of an idealized American masculinity. As sociologist Roderick A. Ferguson (2004) puts it, "African American culture has historically been deemed contrary to the norms of heterosexuality and patriarchy" on the basis of race. Black men thus must always respond to considerations of their racial difference—"the sign of nonheteronormativity presumed to be fundamental to African American culture" (20, 21). That is to say, assigning nonheteronormative behavior to Black men historically exists as a way to disenfranchise them from the opportunities reserved for White men in America and thus from perceptions of "true" manhood, and from "true" heterosexuality. A major consequence of this disenfranchisement is that it itself produces and perpetuates this nonheteronormativity, which one might better understand in this context as homonormativity.

This circumstance can be easily observed in the discourse surrounding the first president of African American descent, Barack Obama. As the most visible and discussed Black man so far in the twenty-first century, he is perceived as enacting a nontraditional American masculinity and routinely negatively profiled as gay or homosexual (see "Straight Black Queer" in the section "Motions of Manhood"). What may be surprising, however, is the rhetorical contradiction: while Obama is often praised for not being the typical, domineering man and also for not being the stereotypical Black man, he is ultimately criticized for not being either. While Obama's ascent to the office of U.S. president is a first for the Black man, the rhetorical contradiction about Black men's manhood is not new. It is in fact historical and longstanding, and certainly is explicitly revealed in many of the readings in the section "Motions of Manhood." However, one might ask, what does all this talk about how White patriarchy affects Black manhood have to do with the other rhetorics in this section, the discourses about Black women and Black quare lives? The answer is "quite a bit." Because as Black men have tried to fight against the denial of their manhood in America, they have sometimes advertently, other inadvertently, worked against or stifled the gender progress of Black women and the rights of Black queer people, particularly Black queer men. In order to not appear queer themselves or not be relegated to the second-class status of women, Black men have sometimes engaged in a detrimental disassociating rhetoric of self-separation from the concerns of Black women and Black gays in order to identify more closely with the White patriarchal order of White manhood in America.

So while one should be cautious about reading the rhetorical legacies of Black women and quare people through the lenses of White or Black manhood and heteronormativity, and should also avoid short-circuiting the voices of women and quares by turning them into self-serving patriarchal projects, it is nonetheless a fact that the rhetorics of Black women, Black men, and Black quares variously speak to, for, and against each other in a constellation of debates and discourses related to the antiracist politics pointed out at the outset by Collins. It is this constellation of discourses that the readings that follow in all three sections take up.

Works Cited

Collins, Patricia Hill. *Black Sexual Politics: African Americans, Gender, and the New Racism*. New York: Routledge, 2004.

Ferguson, Roderick A. *Aberrations in Black: Toward a Queer of Color Critique*. Minneapolis: University of Minnesota Press, 2004.

6

RACE WOMEN AND BLACK FEMINISMS

Edited and with an introduction by Joy James

———◦◦◦◦———

Acknowledgments: (1) *Gratitude* to Black women's intergenerational labors in crafting impassioned dialogues for freedom. (2) *Thanks* to the editors, and Vershawn A. Young (Dr. Vay, if I may) for patient diligence in getting me to produce. (3) *Appreciation* for scholar-student researcher Ahmad Greene-Hayes's insights and skillful contributions.

Black Feminisms and Resilience

Circulating in the national public arena, and beyond, is a centuries-old conversation initiated by Black women. This "conversation"—established in oration, sketches, photographs, memoirs, speeches, interviews, novels, pamphlets, essays, and texts—sets and resets normative "freedoms" for a democracy unsettled by its history, its present moment, and its future as accurate reflections of its romantic idealism. Black feminist rhetoric presents an aesthetic, a philosophy, and political ambitions extending beyond Black families and Black communities. This foundational discourse predates the "founding fathers," and is in dialogue with an imperial democracy. Whoever pursues life, liberty, and happiness within the American landscape does so through the rhetoric of race and gender, the language of laws, the structures of economic and political enfranchisement or disenfranchisement, the disciplining and fetishizing of sexualities, and the violations and violence reserved for "minorities." This national, often international, rhetoric is influenced by the experiences and analyses of race women and Black feminisms. The resilience and longevity of these narratives constitute the "American experience."

"Race women" are Black or African American female advocates for human equality and the freedom of African Americans to fully participate in political and economic life. Usually, race women are understood as working to benefit "the race," racially fashioned African Americans in a society and state structured under White supremacy, patriarchy, and capitalism. In 1892, the year that Negro Club women published Ida B. Wells's pamphlet on lynching, *Southern Horrors*, her contemporary Anna Julia Cooper stated to a gathering of Black clergymen that only Black women could assert "when and where I enter, in the quiet, undisputed dignity of my womanhood, without violence . . . or special patronage, then and there the whole . . . race enters with me" (31). Yet it has proven, over the last century since Cooper spoke, that not just one "race" has entered with the rising valuation (and mutating denigration) of Black female life.

Given the ideological diversity among Black women, evidenced in their rhetoric, Black feminisms or womanisms exist in plurality. Overlapping or diverging, both expressive formations have shaped language about sexuality, gender, race, power, captivity, and freedom, one that uplifts, or scorns, and thereby (de)stabilizes national democratic speech. Everyone enters in some way or fashion into greater value with the appearance of advocacy in the words of race women and Black feminisms. Consider that in the eighteenth century, the rhetoric of Black girls was not heard by the enslaved, master races, and presidents: a seven-year-old Senegambian captive-turned-child slave, renamed Philiss Wheatley (1753–1784?), authors *Poems on Various Subjects, Religious and Moral* (1773), which is noted by George Washington; an older sexualized child, named Sally Hemings, has her slave speech erased by caretakers of Thomas Jefferson's legacy, yet in Black feminist fiction (e.g., that of Barbara Chase-Riboud) and scholarship, Sally Hemings's (un)spoken thoughts haunt through centuries.

As spirit and embodied praxis, Black women's lives and words touch and infiltrate Americana thought: its notions of the family, sexuality, motherhood, manhood; its perceptions and practices of poverty, fetish, and predation; its anxiety of resistance and rebellion emanating from its most feared and despised configuration: the Black politicized body. Race women and (proto)feminists as political agents have always "talked back" to democracy based on Black exclusion; the legal proximity of sexuality to violence; state/corporate ownership of wombs; and the exploitation of productivity and reproductivity intersecting the Black female form. Through slavery, convict prison lease system, Jim Crow segregation, caste and color divisions among Blacks, world wars and imperialism, movements for labor, civil rights, women's rights, and human rights—for centuries, women of African descent talked out shared struggles and accomplishments. This volume leans into their conversations and debates.

Race women's rhetoric reflects a "neuroplasticity"—in the science of brain development, this is the ability of the brain to rematerialize with cognitive potential despite trauma—that restores itself for complex mandates concerning efficacy and power. Moving beyond the fight or flight reflexivity of primal survival, race women's speech exhibits astute forms of executive functioning. In the two centuries covered in this collection—from Maria Stewart's 1832 public addresses against slavery to Nikky Finney's 2013 acceptance of a literary award for poetry—punitive slave and neoslave codes prohibited Black rhetoric and literacy. Yet, seeking freedom with the word, Black feminisms burned sometimes fiery and sometimes frozen codes with discourse by women advocating for themselves, their families, others, a nation, a world.

We can assert that race women's and Black feminist rhetoric have functioned as shelter not just for well-adjusted citizens, or citizens-in-waiting, but also for maroons, those pushed or propelled to democracy's borders. Black women have not presented their forced alienation as solely a flight into conceptual wilderness. In this collection, their words as movements constitute a continual return that travels beyond confrontations with repressive speech and policies, animus against Black females, rage against freedom, and violence structured within Black female life.

Over centuries, race women and Black feminisms have articulated a Black matrix as a paradigm for language and vision: a spectacle and spectrum through which to view and comprehend transitions toward freedom, and intimacy beyond violence. The ability to speak and write a life beyond violation, to project a whole and peaceful existence despite one's vulnerable position, constitutes the resilient productivity of race women and Black feminisms that forged a treasure of transformative rhetoric hidden in plain sight.

Work cited

Cooper, Anna Julia. *A Voice From the South*. Xenia, Ohio: The Alden Printing House, 1892, 31. http://docsouth.unc.edu/church/cooper/cooper.html

Maria W. Stewart

In her second lecture, "Why Sit Ye Here and Die?" (delivered September 21, 1832, to the England Anti-Slavery Society in Boston, MA), Maria W. Stewart (1803–1879), the first woman to lecture in public in the United States, critiques the subjugation of both free and enslaved Black women. Propertied Black Bostonians found her to be too radical and too embarrassing in her departures from (Victorian) norms of civility and propriety. Her activism in opposition to racist rage—which led to the deaths of both her husband and their abolitionist comrade, David Walker—was deemed insufficiently "feminine."

Eventually silenced by free-Black Bostonians, Stewart later served in the Civil War.

Why Sit Ye Here and Die?

Maria W. Stewart[1]

Why sit ye here and die? If we say we will go to a foreign land, the famine and the pestilence are there, and there we shall die. If we sit here, we shall die. Come let us plead our cause before the whites: if they save us alive, we shall live—and if they kill us, we shall but die.

Methinks I heard a spiritual interrogation—'Who shall go forward, and take off the reproach that is cast upon the people of color? Shall it be a woman?' And my heart made this reply—'If it is thy will, be it even so, Lord Jesus!'

I have heard much respecting the horrors of slavery; but may Heaven forbid that the generality of my color throughout these United States should experience any more of its horrors than to be a servant of servants, or hewers of wood and drawers of water! Tell us no more of southern slavery; for with few exceptions, although I may be very erroneous in my opinion, yet I consider our condition but little better than that. Yet, after all, methinks there are no chains so galling as the chains of ignorance—no fetters so binding as those that bind the soul, and exclude it from the vast field of useful and scientific knowledge. O, had I received the advantages of early education, my ideas would, ere now, have expanded far and wide; but, alas! I possess nothing but moral capability—no teachings but the teachings of the Holy spirit.

I have asked several individuals of my sex, who transact business for themselves, if providing our girls were to give them the most satisfactory references, they would not be willing to grant them an equal opportunity with others? Their reply has been—for their own part, they had no objection; but as it was not the custom, were they to take them into their employ, they would be in danger of losing the public patronage.

And such is the powerful force of prejudice. Let our girls possess what amiable qualities of soul they may; let their characters be fair and spotless as innocence itself; let their natural taste and ingenuity be what they may; it is impossible for scarce an individual of them to rise above the condition of servants. Ah! why is this cruel and unfeeling distinction? Is it merely because God has made our complexion to vary? If it be, O shame to soft, relenting humanity! "Tell it not in Gath! publish it not in the streets of Askelon!" Yet, after all, methinks were the American free people of color to turn their attention more assiduously to moral worth and intellectual improvement, this would be the result: prejudice would gradually diminish, and the whites would be compelled to say, unloose those fetters!

Though black their skins as shades of night, Their hearts are pure, their souls are white.

Few white persons of either sex, who are calculated for any thing else, are willing to spend their lives and bury their talents in performing mean, servile labor. And such is the horrible idea that I entertain respecting a life of servitude, that if I conceived of there being no possibility of my rising above the condition of a servant, I would gladly hail death as a welcome messenger. O, horrible idea, indeed! to possess noble souls aspiring after high and honorable acquirements, yet confined by the chains of ignorance and poverty to lives of continual drudgery and toil. Neither do I know of any who have enriched themselves by spending their lives as house-domestics, washing windows, shaking carpets, brushing boots, or tending upon gentlemen's tables. I can but die for expressing my sentiments; and I am as willing to die by the sword as the pestilence; for I and a true born American; your blood flows in my veins, and your spirit fires my breast.

I observed a piece in the Liberator a few months since, stating that the colonizationists had published a work respecting us, asserting that we were lazy and idle. I confute them on that point. Take us generally as a people, we are neither lazy nor idle; and considering how little we have to excite or stimulate us, I am almost astonished that there are so many industrious and ambitious ones to be found; although I acknowledge, with extreme sorrow, that there are some who never were and never will be serviceable to society. And have you not a similar class among yourselves?

Again. It was asserted that we were "a ragged set, crying for liberty." I reply to it, the whites have so long and so loudly proclaimed the theme of equal rights and privileges, that our souls have caught the flame also, ragged as we are. As far as our merit deserves, we feel a common desire to rise above the condition of servants and drudges. I have learnt, by bitter experience, that continual hard labor deadens the energies of the soul, and benumbs the faculties of the mind; the ideas become confined, the mind barren, and, like the scorching sands of Arabia, produces nothing; or, like the uncultivated soil, brings forth thorns and thistles.

Again, continual hard labor irritates our tempers and sours our dispositions; the whole system becomes worn out with toil and failure; nature herself becomes almost exhausted, and we care but little whether we live or die. It is true, that the free people of color throughout these United States are neither bought nor sold, nor under the lash of the cruel driver; many obtain a comfortable support; but few, if any, have an opportunity of becoming rich and independent; and the employments we most pursue are as unprofitable to us as the spider's web or the floating bubbles that vanish into air. As servants, we are respected; but let us presume to aspire any higher, our employer regards us no longer. And where it not that the King eternal has declared that Ethiopia shall stretch forth her hands unto God, I should indeed despair.

I do not consider it derogatory, my friends, for persons to live out to service. There are many whose inclination leads them to aspire no higher; and I would highly commend the performance of almost any thing for an honest livelihood; but where constitutional strength is wanting, labor of this kind, in its mildest form, is painful. And doubtless many are the prayers that have ascended to Heaven from Africa's daughters for strength to perform their work. Oh, many are the tears that have been shed for the want of that strength! Most of our color have dragged out a miserable existence of servitude from the cradle to the grave. And what literary acquirements can be made, or useful knowledge derived, from either maps, books or charm, by those who continually drudge from Monday morning until Sunday noon? O, ye fairer sisters, whose hands are never soiled, whose nerves and muscles are never strained, go learn by experience! Had we had the opportunity that you have had, to improve our moral and mental faculties, what would have hindered our intellects from being as bright, and our manners from being as dignified as yours? Had it been our lot to have been nursed in the lap of affluence and ease, and to have basked beneath the smiles and sunshine of fortune, should we not have naturally supposed that we were never made to toil? And why are not our forms as delicate, and our constitutions as slender, as yours? Is not the workmanship as curious and complete? Have pity upon us, have pity upon us, O ye who have hearts to feel for other's woes; for the hand of God has touched us. Owing to the disadvantages under which we labor, there are many flowers among us that are . . . born to bloom unseen, And waste their fragrance on the desert air.

My beloved brethren, as Christ has died in vain for those who will not accept of offered mercy, so will it be vain for the advocates of freedom to spend their breath in our behalf, unless with united hearts and souls you make some mighty efforts to raise your sons, and daughters from the horrible state of servitude and degradation in which they are placed. It is upon you that woman depends; she can do but little besides using her influence; and it is for her sake and yours that I have come forward and made myself a hissing and a reproach among the people; for I am also one of the wretched and miserable daughters of the descendants of fallen Africa. Do you ask, why are you wretched and miserable? I reply, look at many of the most worthy and interesting of us doomed to spend our lives in gentlemen's kitchens. Look at our young men, smart, active and energetic, with souls filled with ambitious fire; if they look forward, alas! what are their prospects? They can be nothing but the humblest laborers, on account of their dark complexions; hence many of them lose their ambition, and become worthless. Look at our middle-aged men, clad in their rusty plaids and coats; in winter, every cent they earn goes to buy their wood and pay their rents; their poor wives also toil beyond their strength, to help support their families. Look at our aged sires, whose heads are whitened with the front of seventy winters, with their old wood-saws on their backs. Alas, what keeps us so? Prejudice, ignorance and poverty. But ah! Methinks our oppression is soon to come to an end; yes, before the Majesty of heaven, our groans and cries have reached the ears of the Lord of Sabaoth [James 5:4]. As the prayers and tears of Christians will avail the finally impenitent nothing; neither will the prayers and tears of the friends of humanity avail us any thing, unless we possess a spirit of virtuous emulation within our breasts. Did the pilgrims, when they first landed on these shores, quietly compose themselves, and say, "the Britons have all the money and all the power, and we must continue their servants forever?" Did they sluggishly sigh and say, "our lot is hard, the Indians own the soil, and we cannot cultivate it?" No; they first made powerful efforts to raise themselves and then God raised up those illustrious patriots WASHINGTON and LAFAYETTE, to assist and defend them. And, my brethren, have you made a powerful effort? Have you prayed the Legislature for mercy's sake to grant you all the rights and privileges of free citizens, that your daughters may raise to that degree of respectability which true merit deserves, and your sons above the servile situations which most of them fill?

Note

1. Maria Stewart, "Why Sit Ye Here and Die?," in *Lift Every Voice: African American Voices: Oratory*, eds. Philip Sheldon Foner and Robert J. Branham (Tuscaloosa: University of Alabama Press, 1998 [1832]), pp. 125–130, www.blackpast.org/1832-maria-w-stewart-why-sit-ye-here-and-die <accessed 25 April 2014>

Linda Brent

Harriet Ann Jacobs's (writing as Linda Brent) (1813–1897) "V. The Trials of Girlhood" is taken from her memoir *Incidents in the Life of a Slave Girl*, which offers a poignant look at childhood and rape under racial captivity. The rapist is a White enslaver, the prototypical physical domestic rapist of a Black female child from an era in which White males lived in the homes made by Black women and girls. Rather than an unlettered overseer, the embodiment of the uncouth White also constructed as the enemy of propertied, cultured Whites, Brent's predator is a doctor, a physician who has attained and represents the respectability and accomplishments of a "great White nation." Her narrative of girlhood terrifies because of its intimacy with elite domination and violation, elites who form the governing bodies of recognized civility and law. Contemporary cinema such as *12 Years a Slave*, about nineteenth-century (interracial) rape, and *Precious*, about twentieth-century intraracial rape and maternal and paternal incest, "shock" and entertain moral and cultural imaginations. Popular culture that features Black female sexuality as prey can be framed by Linda Brent's writing. Her autobiographical narrative embodies female vulnerability and resistance. Her cloistered existence in her grandmother's attic for years maps a geography of domesticity and fugitive rebellion. The "incidents" of life are shaped by childhood terrors made predictable by the routine, violent occurrences of trauma amplified by denials and silences yet nonetheless met with resilience.

The Trials of Girlhood

Linda Brent[1]

During the first years of my service in Dr. Flint's family, I was accustomed to share some indulgences with the children of my mistress. Though this seemed to me no more than right, I was grateful for it, and tried to merit the kindness by the faithful discharge of my duties. But I now entered on my fifteenth year—a sad epoch in the life of a slave girl. My master began to whisper foul words in my ear. Young as I was, I could not remain ignorant of their import. I tried to treat them with indifference or contempt. The master's age, my extreme youth, and the fear that his conduct would be reported to my grandmother, made him bear this treatment for many months. He was a crafty man, and resorted to many means to accomplish his purposes. Sometimes he had stormy, terrific ways, that made his victims tremble; sometimes he assumed a gentleness that he thought must surely subdue. Of the two, I preferred his stormy moods, although they left me trembling. He tried his utmost to corrupt the pure principles my grandmother had instilled. He peopled my young mind with unclean images, such as only a vile monster could think of. I turned from him with disgust and hatred. But he was my master. I was compelled to live under the same roof with him—where I saw a man forty years my senior daily violating the most sacred commandments of nature. He told me I was his property; that I must be subject to his will in all things. My soul revolted against the mean tyranny. But where could I turn for protection? No matter whether the slave girl be as black as ebony or as fair as her mistress. In either case, there is no shadow of law to protect her from insult, from violence, or even from death; all these are inflicted by fiends who bear the shape of men. The mistress, who ought to protect the helpless victim, has no other feelings towards her but those of jealousy and rage. The degradation, the wrongs, the vices, that grow out of slavery, are more than I can describe. They are greater than you would willingly believe. Surely, if you credited one half the truths that are told you concerning the helpless millions suffering in this cruel bondage, you at the north would not help to tighten the yoke. You surely would refuse to do for the master, on your own soil, the mean and cruel work which trained bloodhounds and the lowest class of whites do for him at the south.

Every where the years bring to all enough of sin and sorrow; but in slavery the very dawn of life is darkened by these shadows. Even the little child, who is accustomed to wait on her mistress and her children, will learn, before she is twelve years old, why it is that her mistress hates such and such a one among the slaves. Perhaps the child's own mother is among those hated ones. She listens to violent outbreaks of jealous passion, and cannot help understanding what is the cause. She will become prematurely knowing in evil things. Soon she will learn to tremble when she hears her master's footfall. She will be compelled to realize that she is no longer a child. If God has bestowed beauty upon her, it will prove her greatest curse. That which commands admiration in the white woman only hastens the degradation of the female slave. I know that some are too much brutalized by slavery to feel the humiliation of their position; but many slaves feel it most acutely, and shrink from the memory of it. I cannot tell how much I suffered in the presence of these wrongs, nor how I am still pained by the retrospect. My master met me at every turn, reminding me that I belonged to him, and swearing by heaven and earth that he would compel me to submit to him. If I went out for a breath of fresh air, after a day of unwearied toil, his footsteps dogged me. If I knelt by my mother's grave, his dark shadow fell on me even there. The light heart which nature had given me became heavy with sad forebodings. The other slaves in my master's house noticed the change. Many of them pitied me; but none dared to ask the cause. They had no need to inquire. They knew too well the guilty practices under that roof, and they were aware that to speak of them was an offence that never went unpunished.

I longed for some one to confide in. I would have given the world to have laid my head on my grandmother's faithful bosom, and told her all my troubles. But Dr. Flint swore he would kill me, if I was not as silent as the grave. Then, although my grandmother was all in all to me, I feared her as well as loved her. I had been accustomed to look up to her with a respect bordering upon awe. I was very young, and felt shamefaced about telling her such impure things, especially as I knew her to be very strict on such subjects. Moreover, she was a woman of a high spirit. She was usually very quiet in her demeanor; but if her indignation was once roused, it was not very easily quelled. I had been told that she once chased a white gentleman with a loaded pistol, because he insulted one of her daughters. I dreaded the consequences of a violent outbreak; and both pride and fear kept me silent. But though I did not confide in my grandmother, and even evaded her vigilant watchfulness and inquiry, her presence in the neighborhood was some protection to me. Though she had been a slave, Dr. Flint was afraid of her. He dreaded her scorching rebukes. Moreover, she was known and patronized by many people; and he did not wish to have his villany made public. It was lucky for me that I did not live on a distant plantation, but in a town not so large that the inhabitants were ignorant of each other's affairs. Bad as are the laws and customs in a slaveholding community, the doctor, as a professional man, deemed it prudent to keep up some outward show of decency.

O, what days and nights of fear and sorrow that man caused me! Reader, it is not to awaken sympathy for myself that I am telling you truthfully what I suffered in slavery. I do it to kindle a flame of compassion in yours hearts for my sisters who are still in bondage, suffering as I once suffered.

I once saw two beautiful children playing together. One was a fair white child; the other was her slave, and also her sister. When I saw them embracing each other, and heard their joyous laughter, I turned sadly away from the lovely sight. I foresaw the inevitable blight that would fall on the little slave's heart. I knew how soon her laughter would be changed to sighs. The fair child grew up to be a still fairer woman. From childhood to womanhood her pathway was blooming with flowers, and overarched by a sunny sky. Scarcely one day of her life had been clouded when the sun rose on her happy bridal morning.

How had those years dealt with her slave sister, the little playmate of her childhood? She, also, was very beautiful; but the flowers and sunshine of love were not for her. She drank the cup of sin, and shame, and misery, whereof her persecuted race are compelled to drink.

In view of these things, why are ye silent, ye free men and women of the north? Why do your tongues falter in maintenance of the right? Would that I had more ability! But my heart is so full, and my pen is so weak! There are noble men, and women who plead for us, striving to help those who cannot help themselves. God bless them! God give them strength and courage to go on! God bless those, every where, who are laboring to advance the cause of humanity!

Note

1. Linda Brent, "The Trials of Girlhood," in *Incidents in the Life of a Slave Girl.* (New York: Harcourt Brace, 1973 [1861]), pp. 26–29, retrieved from http://xroads.virginia.edu/~hyper/jacobs/hjch5.htm

Ida B. Wells

In the post-slavery and post-reconstruction eras, Ida B. Wells's (1862–1931) *Southern Horrors: Lynch Law in All Its Phases* (excerpts) provided an incendiary critique. This is from a pamphlet funded by the Negro Women's Club, which launched Wells's national speaking tours against slavery; it is the antithesis of the silenced voice. All of the women here are combatants as opposed to pugilists. The latter are those in the ring seeking a particular prize or attempting to avoid a specific punishment. The women seem already designated as casualties of war before the bell is even rung. Maria Stewart is a free Bostonian Black but loses her husband and her close colleague David Walker to the long reach of the punitive White hand stretching from the South or North. Brent is the slave whose proximity to whiteness flows through her veins and her rapist's blood and will lead her to a claustrophobic existence in an attic; Wells, another teenage girl without parental protection, would transform her vulnerability in the postbellum era into that of an armed militant whose weapons—her pen, intellect, activism, and pistol in purse—would alter the political and economic landscape of first Memphis, and then increasingly the South, the United States, and globally, as she framed and formed anti-lynching campaigns that shaped the rise and trajectory of the NAACP even as it refused to credit her for her labor and sacrifice. Wells's daughter, Althea Duster, would posthumously edit and publish her mother's autobiography, *Crusade for Justice*, with the University of Chicago Press.

Southern Horrors

Ida B. Wells[1]

Preface

The greater part of what is contained in these pages was published in the *New York Age* June 25, 1892, in explanation of the editorial which the Memphis whites considered sufficiently infamous to justify the destruction of my paper, the *Free Speech*.

Since the appearance of that statement, requests have come from all parts of the country that "Exiled" (the name under which it then appeared) be issued in pamphlet form. Some donations were made, but not enough for that purpose. The noble effort of the ladies of New York and Brooklyn Oct. 5 have enabled me to comply with this request and give the world a true, unvarnished account of the causes of lynch law in the South.

This statement is not a shield for the despoiler of virtue, nor altogether a defense for the poor blind Afro-American Sampsons who suffer themselves to be betrayed by white Delilahs. It is a contribution to truth, an array of facts, the perusal of which it is hoped will stimulate this great American Republic to demand that justice be done though the heavens fall.

It is with no pleasure I have dipped my hands in the corruption here exposed. Somebody must show that the Afro-American race is more sinned against than sinning, and it seems to have fallen upon me to do so. The awful death-roll that Judge Lynch is calling every week is appalling, not only because of the lives it takes, the rank cruelty and outrage to the victims, but because of the prejudice it fosters and the stain it places against the good name of a weak race.

The Afro-American is not a bestial race. If this work can contribute in any way toward proving this, and at the same time arouse the conscience of the American people to a demand for justice to every citizen, and punishment by law for the lawless, I shall feel I have done my race a service. Other considerations are of minor importance.

To the Afro-American women of New York and Brooklyn, whose race love, earnest zeal and unselfish effort at Lyric Hall, in the City of New York, on the night of October 5, 1892—made possible its publication, this pamphlet is gratefully dedicated by the author.

The Offense

Wednesday evening May 24, 1892, the city of Memphis was filled with excitement. Editorials in the daily papers of that date caused a meeting to be held in the Cotton Exchange Building; a committee was sent for the editors of the *Free Speech* an Afro-American journal published in that city, and the only reason the open threats of lynching that were made were not carried out was because they could not be found. The cause of all this commotion was the following editorial published in the *Free Speech* May 21, 1892, the Saturday previous.

Eight negroes lynched since last issue of the *Free Speech* one at Little Rock, Ark., last Saturday morning where the citizens broke(?) into the penitentiary and got their man; three near Anniston, Ala., one near New Orleans; and three at Clarksville, Ga., the last three for killing a white man, and five on the same old racket—the new alarm about raping white women. The same programme of hanging, then shooting bullets into the lifeless bodies was carried out to the letter.

Nobody in this section of the country believes the old thread-bare lie that Negro men rape white women. If Southern white men are not careful, they will overreach themselves and public sentiment will have a reaction; a conclusion will then be reached which will be very damaging to the moral reputation of their women.

The *Daily Commercial* of Wednesday following, May 25, contained the following leader:

Those negroes who are attempting to make the lynching of individuals of their race a means for arousing the worst passions of their kind are playing with a dangerous sentiment. The negroes may as well understand that there is no mercy for the negro rapist and little patience with his defenders. A negro organ printed in this city, in a recent issue publishes the following atrocious paragraph: "Nobody in this section of the country believes the old thread-bare lie that negro men rape white women. If Southern white men are not careful they will overreach themselves, and public sentiment will have a reaction; and a conclusion will be reached which will be very damaging to the moral reputation of their women."

The fact that a black scoundrel is allowed to live and utter such loathsome and repulsive calumnies is a volume of evidence as to the wonderful patience of Southern whites. But we have had enough of it.

There are some things that the Southern white man will not tolerate, and the obscene intimations of the foregoing have brought the writer to the very outermost limit of public patience. We hope we have said enough.

The *Evening Scimitar* of same date, copied the *Commercial*'s editorial with these words of comment:

Patience under such circumstances is not a virtue. If the negroes themselves do not apply the remedy without delay it will be the duty of those whom he has attacked to tie the wretch who utters these calumnies to a stake at the intersection of Main and Madison Sts., brand him in the forehead with a hot iron and perform upon him a surgical operation with a pair of tailor's shears.

Acting upon this advice, the leading citizens met in the Cotton Exchange Building the same evening, and threats of lynching were freely indulged, not by the lawless element upon which the deviltry of the South is usually saddled—but by the leading business men, in their leading business centre. Mr. Fleming, the business manager and owning a half interest the *Free Speech*, had to leave town to escape the mob, and was afterwards ordered not to return; letters and telegrams sent me in New York where I was spending my vacation advised me that bodily harm awaited my return. Creditors took possession of the office and sold the outfit, and the *Free Speech* was as if it had never been.

The editorial in question was prompted by the many inhuman and fiendish lynchings of Afro-Americans which have recently taken place and was meant as a warning. Eight lynched in one week and five of them charged with rape! The thinking public will not easily believe freedom and education more brutalizing than slavery, and the world knows that the crime of rape was unknown during four years of civil war, when the white women of the South were at the mercy of the race which is all at once charged with being a bestial one.

Since my business has been destroyed and I am an exile from home because of that editorial, the issue has been forced, and as the writer of it I feel that the race and the public generally should have a statement of the facts as they exist. They will serve at the same time as a defense for the Afro-Americans Sampsons who suffer themselves to be betrayed by white Delilahs.

The whites of Montgomery, Ala., knew J.C. Duke sounded the keynote of the situation—which they would gladly hide from the world, when he said in his paper, the *Herald*, five years ago: "Why is it that white women attract negro men now more than in former days? There was a time when such a thing was unheard of. There is a secret to this thing, and we greatly suspect it is the growing appreciation of white Juliets for colored Romeos." Mr. Duke, like the *Free Speech* proprietors, was forced to leave the city for reflecting on the "honah" of white women and his paper suppressed; but the truth remains that Afro-American men do not always rape (?) white women without their consent.

Mr. Duke, before leaving Montgomery, signed a card disclaiming any intention of slandering Southern white women. The editor of the *Free Speech* has no disclaimer to enter, but asserts instead that there are many white women in the South who would marry colored men if such an act would not place them at once beyond the pale of society and within the clutches of the law. The miscegnation laws of the South only operate against the legitimate union of the races; they leave the white man free to seduce all the colored girls he can, but it is death to the colored man who yields to the force and advances of a similar attraction in white women. White men lynch the offending Afro-American, not because he is a despoiler of virtue, but because he succumbs to the smiles of white women.

The Black and White of It

The *Cleveland Gazette* of January 16, 1892, publishes a case in point. Mrs. J.S. Underwood, the wife of a minister of Elyria, Ohio, accused an Afro-American of rape. She told her husband that during his absence in 1888, stumping the State for the Prohibition Party, the man came to the kitchen door, forced his way in the house and insulted her. She tried to drive him out with a heavy poker, but he overpowered and chloroformed her, and when she revived her clothing was torn and she was in a horrible condition. She did not know the man but could identify him. She pointed out William Offett, a married man, who was arrested and, being in Ohio, was granted a trial.

The prisoner vehemently denied the charge of rape, but confessed he went to Mrs. Underwood's residence at her invitation and was criminally intimate with her at her request. This availed him nothing against the sworn testimony of a ministers wife, a lady of the highest respectability. He was found guilty, and entered the penitentiary, December 14, 1888, for fifteen years. Some time afterwards the woman's remorse led her to confess to her husband that the man was innocent.

These are her words:

I met Offett at the Post Office. It was raining. He was polite to me, and as I had several bundles in my arms he offered to carry them home for me, which he did. He had a strange fascination for me, and I invited him to call on me. He called, bringing chestnuts and candy for the children. By this means we got them to leave us alone in the room. Then I sat on his lap. He made a proposal to me and I readily consented. Why I did so, I do not know, but that I did is true. He visited me several times after that and each time I was indiscreet. I did not care after the first time. In fact I could not have resisted, and had no desire to resist.

When asked by her husband why she told him she had been outraged, she said: "I had several reasons for telling you. One was the neighbors saw the fellows here, another was, I was afraid I had contracted a loathsome disease, and still another was that I feared I might give birth to a Negro baby. I hoped to save my reputation by telling you a deliberate lie." Her husband horrified by the confession had Offett, who had already served four years, released and secured a divorce.

There are thousands of such cases throughout the South, with the difference that the Southern white men in insatiate fury wreak their vengeance without intervention of law upon the Afro-Americans who consort with their women. A few instances to substantiate the assertion that some white women love the company of the Afro-American will not be out of place. Most of these cases were reported by the daily papers of the South.

In the winter of 1885–86 the wife of a practicing physician in Memphis, in good social standing whose name has escaped me, left home, husband and children, and ran away with her black coachman. She was with him a month before her husband found and brought her home. The coachman could not be found. The doctor moved his family away from Memphis, and is living in another city under an assumed name.

In the same city last year a white girl in the dusk of evening screamed at the approach of some parties that a Negro had assaulted her on the street. He was captured, tried by a white judge and jury, that acquitted him of the charge. It is needless to add if there had been a scrap of evidence on which to convict him of so grave a charge he would have been convicted.

Sarah Clark of Memphis loved a black man and lived openly with him. When she was indicted last spring for miscegenation, she swore in court that she was *not* a white woman. This she did to escape the penitentiary and continued her illicit relation undisturbed. That she is of the lower class of whites, does not disturb the fact that she is a white woman. "The leading citizens" of Memphis are defending the "honor" of *all* white women, *demi-monde* included.

Since the manager of the *Free Speech* has been run away from Memphis by the guardians of the honor of Southern white women, a young girl living on Poplar St., who was discovered in intimate relations with a handsome mulatto young colored man, Will Morgan by name, stole her father's money to send the young fellow away from that father's wrath. She has since joined him in Chicago.

The *Memphis Ledger* for June 8 has the following:

If Lillie Bailey, a rather pretty white girl seventeen years of age, who is now at the City Hospital, would be somewhat less reserved about her disgrace there would be some very nauseating details in the story of her life. She is the mother of a little coon. The truth might reveal fearful depravity or it might reveal the evidence of a rank outrage. She will not divulge the name of the man who has left such black evidence of her disgrace, and, in fact, says it is a matter in which there can be no interest to the outside world. She came to Memphis nearly three months ago and was taken in at the Woman's Refuge in the southern part of the city. She remained there until a few weeks ago, when the child was born. The ladies in charge of the Refuge were horrified. The girl was at once sent to the City

Hospital, where she has been since May 30. She is a country girl. She came to Memphis from her fathers farm, a short distance from Hernando, Miss. Just when she left there she would not say. In fact she says she came to Memphis from Arkansas, and says her home is in that State. She is rather good looking, has blue eyes, a low forehead and dark red hair. The ladies at the Woman's Refuge do not know anything about the girl further than what they learned when she was an inmate of the institution; and she would not tell much. When the child was born an attempt was made to get the girl to reveal the name of the Negro who had disgraced her, she obstinately refused and it was impossible to elicit any information from her on the subject.

Note the wording. "The truth might reveal fearful depravity or rank outrage." If it had been a white child or Lillie Bailey had told a pitiful story of Negro outrage, it would have been a case of woman's weakness or assault and she could have remained at the Woman's Refuge. But a Negro child and to withhold its father's name and thus prevent the killing of another Negro "rapist." A case of "fearful depravity."

The very week the "leading citizens" of Memphis were making a spectacle of themselves in defense of all white women of every kind, an Afro-American, M. Stricklin, was found in a white woman's room in that city. Although she made no outcry of rape, he was jailed and would have been lynched, but the woman stated she bought curtains of him (he was a furniture dealer) and his business in her room that night was to put them up. A white woman's word was taken as absolutely in this case as when the cry of rape is made, and he was freed.

What is true of Memphis is true of the entire South. The daily papers last year reported a farmer's wife in Alabama had given birth to a Negro child. When the Negro farm hand who was plowing in the field heard it he took the mule from the plow and fled. The dispatches also told of a woman in South Carolina who gave birth to a Negro child and charged three men with being its father, *every one of whom has since disappeared*. In Tuscumbia, Ala., the colored boy who was lynched there last year for assaulting a white girl told her before his accusers that he had met her there in the woods often before.

Frank Weems of Chattanooga who was not lynched in May only because the prominent citizens became his body guard until the doors of the penitentiary closed on him, had letters in his pocket from the white woman in the case, making the appointment with him. Edward Coy who was burned alive in Texarkana, January 1, 1892, died protesting his innocence. Investigation since as given by the Bystander in the *Chicago Inter Ocean*, October 1, proves:

1. The woman who was paraded as a victim of violence was of bad character; her husband was a drunkard and a gambler.
2. She was publicly reported and generally known to have been criminally intimate with Coy for more than a year previous.
3. She was compelled by threats, if not by violence, to make the charge against the victim.
4. When she came to apply the match Coy asked her if she would burn him after they had "been sweethearting" so long.
5. A large majority of the "superior" white men prominent in the affair are the reputed fathers of mulatto children.

These are not pleasant facts, but they are illustrative of the vital phase of the so-called race question, which should properly be designated an earnest inquiry as to the best methods by which religion, science, law and political power may be employed to excuse injustice, barbarity and crime done to a people because of race and color. There can be no possible belief that these people were inspired by any consuming zeal to vindicate God's law against miscegnationists of the most practical sort. The woman was a willing partner in the victim's guilt, and being of the "superior" race must naturally have been more guilty.

In Natchez, Miss., Mrs. Marshall, one of the *creme de la creme* of the city, created a tremendous sensation several years ago. She has a black coachman who was married, and had been in her employ several years. During this time she gave birth to a child whose color was remarked, but traced to some brunette ancestor, and one of the fashionable dames of the city was its godmother. Mrs. Marshall's social position was unquestioned, and wealth showered every dainty on this child which was idolized with its brothers and sisters by its white papa. In course of time another child appeared on the scene, but it was unmistakably dark. All were alarmed, and "rush of blood, strangulation" were the conjectures, but the doctor, when asked the cause, grimly told them it was a Negro child. There was a family conclave, the coachman heard of it and leaving his own family went West, and has never returned. As soon as Mrs. Marshall was able to travel she was sent away in deep disgrace. Her husband died within the year of a broken heart.

Ebenzer Fowler, the wealthiest colored man in Issaquena County, Miss., was shot down on the street in Mayersville, January 30, 1885, just before dark by an armed body of white men who filled his body with bullets. They charged him with writing a note to a white woman of the place, which they intercepted and which proved there was an intimacy existing between them.

Hundreds of such cases might be cited, but enough have been given to prove the assertion that there are white women in the South who love the Afro-American's company even as there are white men notorious for their preference for Afro-American women.

There is hardly a town in the South which has not an instance of the kind which is well known, and hence the assertion is reiterated that "nobody in the South believes the old thread bare lie that negro men rape white women." Hence there is a growing demand among Afro-Americans that the guilt or innocence of parties accused of rape be fully established. They know the men of the section of the country who refuse this are not so desirous of punishing rapists as they pretend. The utterances of the leading white men show that with them it is not the crime but the *class*. Bishop Fitzgerald has become apologist for lynchers of the rapists of *white* women only. Governor Tillman, of South Carolina, in the month of June, standing under the tree in Barnwell, S.C., on which eight Afro-Americans were hung last year, declared that he would lead a mob to lynch a *negro* who raped a *white* woman. So say the pulpits, officials and newspapers of the South. But when the victim is a colored woman it is different.

Last winter in Baltimore, Md., three white ruffians assaulted a Miss Camphor, a young Afro-American girl, while out walking with a young man of her own race. They held her escort and outraged the girl. It was a deed dastardly enough to arouse Southern blood, which gives its horror of rape as excuse for lawlessness, but she was an Afro-American. The case went to the courts, an Afro-American lawyer defended the men and they were acquitted.

In Nashville, Tenn., there is a white man, Pat Hanifan, who outraged a little Afro-American girl, and, from the physical injuries received, she has been ruined for life. He was jailed for six months, discharged, and is now a detective in that city. In the same city, last May, a white man outraged an Afro-American girl in a drug store. He was arrested, and released on bail at the trial. It was rumored that five hundred Afro-Americans had organized to lynch him. Two hundred and fifty white citizens armed themselves with Winchesters and guarded him. A cannon was placed in front of his home, and the Buchanan Rifles (State Militia) ordered to the scene for his protection. The Afro-American mob did not materialize. Only two weeks before Eph. Grizzard, who had only been *charged* with rape upon a white woman, had been taken from the jail, with Governor Buchanan and the police and militia standing by, dragged through the streets in broad daylight, knives plunged into him at every step, and with every fiendish cruelty a frenzied mob could devise, he was at last swung out on the bridge with hands cut to pieces as he tried to climb up the stanchions. A naked, bloody example of the blood-thirstiness of the nineteenth-century civilization of the Athens of the South! No cannon or military was called out in his defense. He dared to visit a white woman.

At the very moment these civilized whites were announcing their determination "to protect their wives and daughters," by murdering Grizzard, a white man was in the same jail for raping eight-year-old Maggie Reese, an Afro-American girl. He was not harmed. The "honor" of grown women who were glad enough to be supported by the Grizzard boys and Ed Coy, as long as the liaison was not known, needed protection; they were white. The outrage upon helpless childhood needed no avenging in this case; she was black.

A white man in Guthrie, Oklahoma Territory, two months ago inflicted such injuries upon another Afro-American child that she died. He was not punished, but an attempt was made in the same town in the month of June to lynch an Afro-American who visited a white woman.

In Memphis, Tenn., in the month of June, Ellerton L. Dorr, who is the husband of Russell Hancock's widow, was arrested for attempted rape on Mattie Cole, a neighbors cook; he was only prevented from accomplishing his purpose, by the appearance of Mattie's employer. Dorr's friends say he was drunk and not responsible for his actions. The grand jury refused to indict him and he was discharged.

Note

1. Excerpt from Ida B. Wells, *Southern Horrors: Lynch Law in All Its Phases* (1892), www.gutenberg.org/files/14975/14975-h/14975-h.htm <accessed 25 April 2014>

Mary Church Terrell

Mary Church Terrell (1863–1954) would urge a unity that allowed for an independent politics. "In Union There Is Strength" (1897) had the foresight to advocate for universal kindergartens (for Blacks), a mandate established by 2014 Mayor Bill DeBlasio (and his African American wife and "co-mayor," Charlene) and "universal preK." Over a century earlier, Mary Church Terrell, the daughter of the wealthy Memphis businessman Robert Terrell, an Oberlin graduate who would later work with presidents and leaders, such as Booker T. Washington, was president of the National Association of Colored Women's Clubs with founding members including Harriet Tubman and Ida B. Wells. The National Association of Colored Women addressed domestic life and elevated the importance of the lives of children. Denouncing severe and physical punishment of Black children, Church Terrell's address asserts,

> More than any other race at present in this country, we should strive to implant feelings of self respect and pride in our children, whose spirits are crushed and whose hearts saddened enough by indignities from which as victims of unreasonable cruel prejudice it is impossible to shield them.[1]

Note

1. See Jean Robbins, "Black Club Women's Purposes for Establishing Kindergartens in the Progressive Era, 1896–1906," (PhD diss., Loyola University Chicago, 2011), Paper 99, http://ecommons.luc.edu/luc_diss/99

In Union There Is Strength

Mary Church Terrell[1]

In Union there is strength is a truism that has been acted upon by Jew and Gentile, by Greek and Barbarian, by all classes and conditions alike from the creation of the universe to the present day. It did not take long for men to learn that by combining their strength, a greater amount of work could be accomplished with less effort in a shorter time. Upon this principle of union, governments have been founded and states built. Our own republic teaches the same lesson. Force a single one of the states of the United States to stand alone, and it becomes insignificant, feeble, and a prey to the rapacity of every petty power seeking to enlarge its territory and increase its wealth. But form a republic of United States, and it becomes one of the great nations of the earth, strong in its might. Acting upon this principle of concentration and union have the colored women of the United States banded themselves together to fulfill a mission to which they fell peculiarly adapted and especially called. We have become National, because from the Atlantic to the Pacific, from Maine to the Gulf, we wish to set in motion influences that shall stop the ravages made by practices that sap our strength and preclude the possibility of advancement which under other circumstances could easily be made.

We call ourselves an Association to signify that we have joined hands one with the other to work together in a common cause. We proclaim to the world that the women of our race have become partners in the great firm of progress and reform. We denominate ourselves colored, not because we are narrow, and wish to lay special emphasis on the color of the skin, for which no one is responsible, which of itself is no proof of an individual's virtue nor of his vice, which neither is a stamp, neither of one's intelligence nor of ignorance, but we refer to the fact that this is an association of colored women, because our peculiar status in this country at the present time seems to demand that we stand by ourselves in the special work for which we have organized. For this reason it was thought best to invite the attention of the world to the fact that colored women feel their responsibility as a unit, and together have clasped hands to assume it. Special stress has been laid upon the fact that our association is composed of women, not because we wish to deny rights and privileges to out brothers in imitation of the example they have set for us so many years, but because the work which we hope to accomplish can be done better, by the mothers, wives, daughters, and sisters of our race than by the fathers, husbands, brothers, and sons. The crying need of our organization of colored women is questioned by no one conversant with our peculiar trials and perplexities, and acquainted with the almost insurmountable obstacles in our path to those attainments and acquisitions to which it is the right and privilege of every member of every race to aspire. It is not because we are discouraged at the progress made by our people that we have uttered the cry of alarm which has called together this band of earnest women assembled here tonight.

In the unprecedented advancement made by the Negro since his emancipation, we take great pride and extract therefore both courage and hope. From a condition of dense ignorance. But thirty years ago, we have advanced so far in the realm of knowledge and letters as to have produced scholars and authors of repute. Though penniless as a race a short while ago, we have among us today a few men of wealth and multitudes who own their homes and make comfortable livings. We therefore challenge any other race to present a record more creditable and show a progress more wonderful than that made by the ex slaves of the United States and that too in the face of prejudice, proscription, and persecution against which no other people has ever had to contend in the history of the world. And yet while rejoicing in our steady march, onward and upward, to the best and highest things of life, we are nevertheless painfully mindful of our weaknesses and defects [in] which we know the Negro is no worse than other races equally poor, equally ignorant, and equally oppressed, we would nevertheless see him lay aside the sins that do so easily beset him, and come forth clothed in all these attributes of mind and grace of character that claims the real man. To accomplish this end through the simplest, swiftest, surest methods, the colored women have organized themselves into this Association, whose power for good, let us hope, will be as enduring as it is unlimited.

Believing that it is only through the home that a people can become really good and truly great, the N.A.C.W shall enter that sacred domain to inculcate right principles of living and correct false views of life. Homes, more homes, purer homes, better homes, is the text upon which our sermons to the masses must be preached. So long s the majority of people call that place home in which the air is foul, the manners bad, and the morals worse, just so long is this so called home a menace to health, a breeder of vice, and the abode of crime. Not alone upon the inmates of these hovels are the awful consequences of their filth and immorality visited, but upon the heads of those who sit calmly by and make no effort to stem the tide of disease and vice will vengeance as surely fall.

The colored youth is vicious we are told, and statistics showing the multitudes of our boys and girls who fill the penitentiaries and crowd the jails appall and discourage us. Side by side with these facts and figures of crime, I would have presented and pictured the miserable hovels from which these youthful criminals come. Crowded into alleys, many of them the haunts of vice, few if any of them in a proper sanitary condition, most of them fatal to mental and moral growth, and destructive of healthful physical development as well, thousands of our children have a wretched heritage indeed. It is, therefore, into the home, sisters of the Association, that we must go, filled with all the zeal and charity which such a mission demands.

To the children of the race we owe, as women, a debt which can never be paid, until Herculean efforts are made to rescue them from evil and shame for which they are in no way responsible. Listen to the cry of the children, my sisters. Upon you they depend for the light of knowledge, and the blessing of a good example. As an organization of women, surely nothing can be nearer our hearts than the children, many of whose lives so sad and dark we might brighten and bless. It is kindergartens we need. Free kindergartens in every city and hamlet of this broad land we must have, if the children are to receive from us what it is our duty to give. The more unfavorable the environments of children, the more necessary is it that steps be taken to counteract the hateful influences upon innocent victims. How imperative is it then that we inculcate correct principles, and set good examples for our own youth whose little feet will have so many thorny paths of prejudice, temptations, and injustice to tread. Make a visit to the settlements of colored people who in many cities are relegated to the most noisome sections permitted by the municipal government, and behold the miles of inhumanity that infest them. Here are our little ones, the future representatives of the race, fairly drinking in the permissible example of their elders, coming in contact with nothing but ignorance and vice, till at the age of six evil habits are formed that no amount of civilizing and Christianizing can ever completely break. As long as the evil nature alone is encouraged to develop, while the higher, nobler qualities in little ones are dwarfed and deadened by the very atmosphere which they breathe, the negligent, pitiless public is responsible for the results and is partner of their crimes.

Let the women of the National Association see to it that the little strays of the alleys come in contact with intelligence and virtue, at least a few times a week, that the noble aspirations with which they are born may not be entirely throttled by the evil influences which these poor little ones are powerless to escape. The establishment of free kindergartens! You exclaim Where is the money coming from? How can we do it? This charity you advocate though beautiful in theory is nevertheless impossible of attainment. Let the women of the race once be thoroughly aroused to their duty to the children, let them be consumed with desire to save them from lives of degradation and shame, and the establishment of free kindergartens for the poor will become a living, breathing, saving reality at no distant day. What movement looking toward the reformation and regeneration of mankind was ever proposed that did not instantly assume formidable portions to the fainthearted. But how soon obstacles that have once appeared insuperable dwindle into nothingness, after the shoulder is put to the wheel and united effort determines to remove them! In every organization of the Association let committees be appointed whose special mission it will be to do for the little strays of the alleys what is not done by their mothers, who in many instances fall far short of their duty, not because they are vicious and depraved, but because they are ignorant and poor.

Through mother meetings which have been in the past year and will be in the future a special feature of the Association, much useful informatics in everything pertaining to the home will be disseminated. Object lessons in the best way to sweep, to dust, to cook and to wash should be given by women who have made a special study of the art and science of housekeep. How to clothe children neatly, how to make, and especially how to mend garments, how to manage their households economically, what food is the most nutritious and best for the money, how to ventilate as thoroughly as possible the dingy stuffy quarters which the majority are forced to inhabit . . . all these are subjects on which the women of the masses need more knowledge. Let us teach mothers of families how to save wisely. Let us have heart to heart talks with our women that we may strike at the root of evil. If the women of the dominant race with all the centuries of education. refinement, and culture back of them, with all their wealth of opportunity ever present with them, if these women felt a responsibility to call a Mother's Congress that they might be ever enlightened as to the best methods of rearing children and conducting their homes, how much more do the women of our race from whom the shackles of slavery have just fallen need information on the same subjects? Let us have Mother Congresses in every community in which our women can be counseled. The necessity of increasing the self respect of our children is important. Let the reckless, ill advised, and oftentimes brutal methods of punishing children be everywhere condemned Let us teach our mothers that by punishing children inhumanely, they destroy their pride, crush their spirit and convert them into hardened culprits whom it will be impossible later on to reach or touch in anyway at all.

More than any other race at present in this country, we should strive to implant feelings of self respect and pride in our children, whose spirits are crushed and whose hearts saddened enough by indignities from which as victims of unreasonable cruel prejudice it is impossible to shield them. Let it be the duty of every friend of the race to teach children who are humiliated on learning that they are descendants of slaves that the majority of races on the earth have at some time in their history been subjects to another. This knowledge of humiliation will be important when we are victims of racism. Let us not only preach, but practice race unity, race pride, reverence and sect for those capable of leading and advising us. Let the youth of the race impressed about the dignity of labor and inspired with a desire to work. Let us do nothing to handicap children in the desperate struggle for existence in which their unfortunate condition in this country forces them to engage. Let us purify the atmosphere of our homes till it becomes so sweet that those who dwell in them carry on a great work of reform. That we have no money to help the needy and poor, I reply, that having hearts, generous natures, willing feet, and helpful hands can without the token of a single penny work miracles in the name of humanity and right.

Money we need, money we must have to accomplish much which we ape to effect. But it is not by powerful armies and the outlays of vast fortunes that the greatest revolutions are wrought and the most enduring reforms inaugurated. It is by the silent, though powerful force of individual influences thrown on the side of right, it is by arduous persistence and effort keep those with whom we come in daily contact, to enlighten the heathen our door, to create wholesome public sentiment in the communities in hick we live, that the heaviest blows are struck for virtue and right. Let us not only preach, but practice race unity, race pride, reverence, and respect for those capable of leading and advising us. Let the youth of the race Be impressed about the dignity of labor and inspired with a desire to work. Let us do nothing to handicap children in the desperate struggle for existence in which their unfortunate condition in this country forces them to engage. Let us purify the atmosphere of our homes till it become so sweet it those who dwell in them will have a heritage more precious than silver or gold.

Note

1. Mary Church Terrell, "In Union There is Strength," in *African American Perspectives: Selections from the Daniel P. Murray Collection, Library of Congress* (1897), retrieved from http://lcweb2.loc.gov/ammem/aap/

Claudia Jones

In 1949, Communist and Caribbean feminist Claudia Jones (1915–1964) wrote her most well-known and circulated essay, "An End to the Neglect of the Problems of the Negro Woman" (see Section 9 in this book, by Aaron Kamugisha and Yanique Hume). This essay would become a groundbreaking treatise of the National Women's Commission of the Communist Party of the United States of America based in New York City. "We Seek Full Equality for Women" was published in the same year and ushered in an intersectional focus for talking about Black women's oppression. Noted Caribbean scholar and feminist Carole Boyce-Davies describes "We Seek Full Equality for Women" as best capturing Claudia Jones's Black left feminism / Black socialist feminism / Black Marxist feminism. Jones situates Black women's place within Marxist-Leninist theories of modes of production. She begins with the history of the suffragists and moves right away into describing how communists were also working to advance women's rights. She outlines what a Marxist-Leninist feminism looks like and then describes how the Communist Party USA could lead the way to a progressive women's movement. She challenges any communist position that places class above race and gender, offering one of the most famous lines that has organized Black feminists for years to come: the

> triply-oppressed status of [Black] women is a barometer of the status of all women, and that the fight for the full, economic, political and social equality of the [Black] woman is in the vital self-interest of white workers, in the vital interest of the fight to realize equality for all women.

The overlap of Black feminist activism crosses decades and ideologies: the National Committee to Free the Ingram Family (which successfully lobbied to change the death sentence to life in prison) was headed by Mary Church Terrell, who helped to found the National Association of Colored Women. Terrell would not have embraced Jones's communism and critique of U.S. democracy; yet both women could champion Black women in the direct crosshairs of White supremacist violence and poverty.

We Seek Full Equality for Women

Introduction by Carole Boyce-Davies: We (Still) Seek Full Equality!

As we commemorate Claudia Jones's 100th birthday this year, it is fitting to reposition one of her most influential essays, "We Seek Full Equality for Women" (1949). Given current and ongoing discourses about lingering inequality for several subordinated groups in the United States and Europe, the mantra of "still seeking full equality" resonates in chants like "Black Lives Matter" and in the activism of LGBTQ groups. And indeed women are still seeking full equality in all fields and spheres of life.

Journalist, editor, intellectual-activist, communist theorist, community leader and human rights advocate Claudia Vera Cumberbatch Jones (1915–1964) was born February 21, 1915 in Trinidad and Tobago. After years of membership beginning as a teenager, she became the only black woman on the central committee of the Communist Party USA and Secretary of the Women's commission in 1947. In that role, she organized women's groups across the United States and wrote a Women's Rights column titled "Half the World" for *The Daily Worker*. A speech titled "International Women's Day and the Struggle for Peace" delivered on International Women's Day in 1950 was cited as the "overt act" which led to her arrest, trial, conviction, and imprisonment for being a communist in the United States. In December 1955, she was deported to England because she was still then a Commonwealth "subject." There, she became the founder of the first black newspaper in London, the *West Indian Gazette and Afro-Asian Caribbean News (WIG)* in 1958 and developed a praxis that bridged the United States and United Kingdom, informed by the world politics of decolonization. She organized a parallel March on Washington in 1963 and met world leaders like Martin Luther King, Jr., Mao Tse-Tung, Norman Manley, Cheddi Jagan, and Jomo Kenyatta of Kenya.

For Claudia Jones, communism provided a theoretical explanation for the treatment of oppressed black and working class men and women. Claudia Jones is credited with putting consistently on the platform of the Communist Party the triple oppression of black women based on their race, class, and gender and for popularizing the triple rights call on behalf of workers, women, and black people in the United States throughout the 1940s and up to the mid-1950s.[1]

"We Seek Full Equality for Women" (1949) was published in the same year as her most well-known and circulated essay "An End to the Neglect of the Problems of Negro Women" (1949). I have described this essay as best capturing Claudia Jones's art of black left feminism. In it she identifies the black woman's place in the Marxist-Leninist theorization of the mode of production. While it begins with the idea of taking up the history of struggle of the Suffragists, she hastens to describe how communists were proposing to advance women's rights. She summarizes the basics of Marxist-Leninist feminism, outlining the work that was taking place in applying this theory. She describes the organization of state branche of the Women's Commission and describes the Communist Party USA as leading the way to developing a progressive women's movement. The essay explains the causes of the inequality of women under capitalism and indicates that winning equality was determined by the extent to which the particular "problems, needs and aspirations of women—as women" were addressed. Perhaps the most famous line in the essay, one often cited by Angela Davis, is that the "triply-oppressed status of [Black] women is a barometer of the status of all women, and that the fight for the full, economic, political and social equality of the [Black] woman is in the vital self-interest of white workers, in the vital interest of the fight to realize equality for all women."

In 2015, a good 65 years after this essay was written, inequality remains. "We Seek Full Equality for Women" should therefore be read again, and included as part of the common library of thought on this subject.

—*Carole Boyce Davies (@Ca_Rule)*

"We Seek Full Equality for Women" (1949)

Taking up the struggle of the Suffragists, the Communists have set new tasks, new objectives in the fight for a new status for women. The special value of Foster's contribution:

> The leading role of the Communist Party in the struggle to emancipate women from male oppression is one of the proud contributions which our Party of Marxism-Leninism, the Communist Party, U.S.A., celebrates on its thirtieth anniversary.

Marxism-Leninism exposes the core of the woman question and shows that the position of women in society is not always and everywhere the same, but derives from woman's relation to the mode of production.

Under capitalism, the inequality of women stems from exploitation of the working class by the capitalist class. But the exploitation of women cuts across class lines and affects all women. Marxism-Leninism views the woman question as a special question which derives from the economic dependence of women upon men. This economic dependence as Engels wrote over 100 years ago, carries with it the sexual exploitation of women, the placing of woman in the modern bourgeois family, as the "proletariat" of the man, who assumes the role of "bourgeoisie."

Hence, Marxist-Leninists fight to free woman of household drudgery, they fight to win equality for women in all spheres; they recognize that one cannot adequately deal with the woman question or win women for progressive participation unless one takes up the special problems, needs and aspirations of women—as women.

It is this basic principle that has governed the theory and practice of the Communist Party for the last three decades.

As a result, our Party has chalked up a proud record of struggle for the rights of women.

American literature has been enhanced by the works of Marxists who investigated the status of women in the U.S. in the '30s. Its record is symbolized in the lives of such outstanding women Communists as Ella Reeve Bloor and Anita Whitney and others who are associated with the fight for women's suffrage, for the rights of the Negro people, for working class emancipation.

Our Party and its leadership helped stimulate the organization of women in the trade unions and helped activize the wives of workers in the great labor organizing drives; built housewives' councils to fight against the high cost of living; taught women through the boycott and other militant actions how to fight for the needs of the family; helped to train and mold women Communist leaders on all levels, working class women inspired by the convictions and ideals of their class—the working class.

A pioneer in the fight for the organization of working class women, our Party was the first to demonstrate to white women and to the working class that the triply-oppressed status of Negro women is a barometer of the status of all women, and that the fight for the full, economic, political and social equality of the Negro woman is in the vital self-interest of white workers, in the vital interest of the fight to realize equality for all women.

But it remained for the contribution of William Z. Foster, National Chairman of our Party, to sharpen the thinking of the American Communist Party on the woman question. Comrade Foster projected in a deeper way the basic necessity for the working class and its vanguard Party to fight the obstacles to women's equality, evidenced in many anti-woman prejudices, in the prevalent ideology of male superiority fostered by the monopolists imbibed by the working class men.

The essence of Foster's contribution is that it is necessary to win the masses of American women for the over-all struggle against imperialist war and fascism by paying special attention to their problems and by developing special struggles for their economic, political, and social needs. Basing himself upon the Marxist-Leninist tenet that the inequality of women is inherently connected with the exploitation of the working class, Foster called on the Party and the working class to master the Marxist-Leninist theory of the woman question, to improve our practical work on this question, and to correct former errors, errors of commission and omission with regard to this fundamental question.

Foster's special contribution lies in his unique exposé of the mask placed on the status of women in every sphere in the U.S. by American imperialism. Comrade Foster exposed the bourgeois lie that women in the U.S. have achieved full equality and that no further rights remain to be won. He shows that the ideological prop used by reactionary propagandists to perpetuate false ideas of women's 'inferiority' is to base their anti-social arguments as regards women on all kinds of pseudo-scientific assumptions, particularly the field of biology.

Any underestimation of the need for a persistent ideological struggle against all manifestations of masculine superiority must therefore be rooted out. If biology is falsely utilized by the bourgeois ideologists to perpetuate their false notions about women, Communists and progressives must fare boldly into the biological sciences and enhance our ideological struggle against bourgeois ideas and practices of male superiority.

In order to meet the tasks projected for a deeper understanding and mastery of the Marxist-Leninist approach to the woman question a special Party Commission on Theoretical Aspects of Work among Women was established.

Reflecting the great hunger for theory on the woman question on the part of Communists and progressives was the one day Conference on Marxism and the Women Question held under the auspices of the Jefferson School of Social Science held in June of this year. Nearly 600 women and men attended. Indicative, too, of how the Party is meeting its tasks in this sphere are the numerous cadre schools which have been held to facilitate the training of women for mass work among women and the training of Communist men on the woman question.

Some 10 Party women's commissions now exist, which, under the leadership and guidance of the Party district organizations, give attention to work among women in the Party and in the mass organizations. It is necessary to utilize the 30th anniversary of our Party to strengthen our mass and Party work and to turn the face of the entire Party toward this question.

This is necessary, first, because without mobilization of the masses of women, particularly working class and Negro women, the fight for peace against a third world war will not be successful. American women and their organizations have given indications in varied ways, that they oppose the Atlantic Pact, and are fearful of the implications of the arms pact.

This understanding is necessary, secondly, because of the growing reactionary offensive against the civil rights of the American people, the outstanding examples of which is the indictment and trial of the 12 leaders of our Party before a jury having a majority of women.

Finally, this understanding is necessary because without rooting ourselves among the masses of women, without building the progressive organizations of women, such as the Congress of American Women, Women's Division of the Progressive Party, the Negro women's organizations, etc., and without organizing special struggles for the demands of women, we cannot with the women against the reactionary influences of the Roman Catholic hierarchy, and the bourgeois ideologists.

By successfully mastering our theory of the woman question, organizing masses of American women, and focusing attention primarily on the problems and needs of working class women, our Party can help usher in a new status for American women.

To achieve that end, we must win the women to an over-active fight against imperialist war and fascism. For, in the words of the great Dimitroff, in his famous report, "The United Front Against Fascism":

> While fascism exacts most from youth it enslaves women with particular ruthlessness and cynicism, playing on the most painful feelings of the mother, the housewife, the single working woman, uncertain of the morrow. Fascism, posing as a benefactor, throws the starving family a few beggarly scraps, trying in this way to stifle the bitterness aroused particularly among the toiling women, by the unprecedented slavery which fascism brings them.

We must spare no pains to see that the women workers and toilers fight shoulder to shoulder with their class brothers in the ranks of the united working class front and the anti-fascist people's front.

In the spirit of the anti-fascist hero of Leipzig, let us rededicate ourselves to the fight for the complete equality of women.

Note

1. For further discussion, see Carole Boyce Davies, *Left of Karl Marx: The Political Life of Black Communist Claudia Jones* (Durham, NC: Duke University Press, 2008).

Ella Baker

During the Depression, while organizing in New York City for workers' rights, Ella Baker (1903–1986) coauthored with Marvel Cooke a critique of the Bronx "slave markets" where Black women endured domestic work or service work, often sexualized as commodities, because jobs were largely barred to them. This critique of economic exploitation and capitalist structures shaped by racism would shape Miss Baker's role in the formation of the Student Non-Violent Coordinating Committee (SNCC). SNCC became one of the most dynamic and instrumental organizations for social change during the southern civil rights movement of the 1960s. In 1960, while serving as the first de facto director of the Southern Christian Leadership Council (SCLC), having been recruited through In Friendship, an organization formed by Bayard Rustin, Ella Baker, and Stanley Levison, Baker found herself with political differences from the more conservative black male clergy, such as Rev. Martin Luther King Jr., who led the SCLC. The younger African American reverends had difficulties dealing with the more mature, politically sophisticated, and radical Baker. When Ella Baker wrote the brief article "Bigger Than a Hamburger" (1960), in essence counseling young activists not to be coopted by more established civil rights organizations that lacked their dynamism, she essentially set the stage for her departure from the SCLC. Baker explicitly and implicitly linked the freedom struggle for Blacks to economic self-determination. She raises a pointed query: "What is the point of desegregation in order to participate in consumer society without the wealth to purchase?" Central to Baker's analysis was that students not append themselves to older, more "status quo" leadership but maintain their autonomy in order to channel their militancy into structural change. The conference that led to the formation of the SNCC, which would become the most influential and radical of the civil rights organizations, was held at Ella Baker's alma mater, Shaw University, in 1960.

"Bigger Than a Hamburger" (1960)

Ella Baker[1]

Raleigh, NC-The Student Leadership Conference made it crystal clear that current sit-ins and other demonstrations are concerned with something much bigger that a hamburger or even a giant-sized COKE.

Whatever may be the difference in approach to their goal, the Negro and white students, North and South, are seeking to rid America of the scourge of racial segregation and discrimination—not only at lunch counters, but in every aspect of life. In reports, casual conversations, discussion groups, and speeches, the sense and the spirit of the following statement that appeared in the initial newsletter of the students at Barber-Scotia College, Concord, NC were echoed time and again:

"We want the world to know that we no longer accept the inferior position of second-class citizenship. We are willing to go to jail, be ridiculed, spat upon and even suffer physical violence to obtain First Class Citizenship. By and large, this feeling that they have a destined date with freedom, was not limited to a drive for personal freedom, or even freedom for the Negro in the South. Repeatedly it was emphasized that the moment was concerned with the moral implications of racial discrimination for the "whole world" and the "Human Race." This universality of approach was linked with a perspective and recognition that "it is important to keep the movement democratic and to avoid struggles for personal leadership."

It was further evident that desire for supportive cooperation from adult leaders and the adult community was also tempered by apprehension that adults might try to "capture" the student

Figure 6.1 Ella Baker Giving a Speech

movement. The students showed willingness to be met on the basis of equality, but were intolerant of anything that smacked of manipulation or domination. This inclination toward group-centered leadership, rather than toward a leader centered group pattern of organization, was refreshing indeed to those of the older group who bear the scars of battle, the frustrations and disillusionment that come when the prophetic leader out to have heavy feet of clay. However hopeful might be the signs in the direction of group-centeredness, the fact that many schools and communities, especially in the South, have not provided adequate experience for young Negroes to assume initiative and think and act independently accentuated the need for guarding the student movement against well-meaning, but nevertheless unhealthy, over-protectiveness. Here is an opportunity for adults and youth to work together and provide genuine leadership—the development of the individual to his highest potential for the benefit of the group. Many adults and youth characterized the Raleigh meeting as the greatest or most significant conference of our period. Whether it lives up to this high evaluation or not will, in large measure, be determined by the extent to which there is more effective training in and understanding of non-violent principles and practices, in group dynamics, and in the re-direction into creative channels of the normal frustrations and hostilities that result from second-class citizenship.

Note

1. Ella Baker, "Bigger than a Hamburger" (1960), retrieved from http://hutchinscenter.fas.harvard.edu/sites/all/files/Bigger%20than%20a%20Hamburger%20-%20Ella%20Baker.pdf

Fannie Lou Hamer

Fannie Lou Hamer (1917–1977), known for her civil rights activism, came to national and international prominence during the 1964 Mississippi Freedom Summer. In her leadership with the Student Nonviolent Coordinating Committee (SNCC), she worked with SNCC cofounder Ella Baker. Hamer struggled endlessly and courageously to ensure that African Americans were politically active, registered voters, informed of policies and laws that would usher them out of Jim Crow and into American citizenry. As vice-chair for the Mississippi Freedom Democratic Party (MFDP), she attended the 1964 Democratic National Convention in Atlantic City, New Jersey, where her televised testimony, which included references to the racial-sexual violence that sought to punish and end her activism, transformed consciences throughout the nation. Although her class and educational backgrounds were very different from that of Baker and other middle-class movement leaders, her autobiographical and political narratives as a dark-skinned laborer with little formal education, as well as her rendition of "negro spirituals," such as "This Little Light of Mine," transformed politics and gospel into mobilization for freedom battles. The daughter of Mississippi sharecroppers, Hamer brought the fields into organizing and organizing into the fields. She was fired from her only trained labor, banned from her home, and became a nomadic activist for Black freedom, meeting with leaders such as Malcolm X and traveling to Africa. Brutalized by beatings that she also understood and represented as sexual assault, Hamer's 1964 testimony at the 1964 Democratic National Convention, in which the SNCC and the MFDP sought to unseat or be seated with the all-White segregationist Mississippi delegation, led civil rights leaders, such as Martin Luther King Jr. and Hubert Humphrey (Johnson's vice-presidential running mate), to co-opt or silence radical agents of change. President Lyndon Johnson, who was seeking reelection, attempted to deflect from her testimony with an impromptu press conference. Nonetheless, Fannie Lou Hamer's testimony was broadcast in full during the night on all the major networks. It remains, with her activism, one of the most searing and endearing indictments of the U.S. electoral system and representative democracy. Later advocates, such as Lani Guinier, would build on the legacy of the MFDP.

Testimony Before the Credentials Committee, Democratic National Convention, Atlantic City, New Jersey, August 22, 1964

Fannie Lou Hamer[1]

Mr. Chairman, and to the Credentials Committee, my name is Mrs. Fannie Lou Hamer, and I live at 626 East Lafayette Street, Ruleville, Mississippi, Sunflower County, the home of Senator James O. Eastland, and Senator Stennis.

It was the 31st of August in 1962 that eighteen of us traveled twenty-six miles to the county courthouse in Indianola to try to register to become first-class citizens.

We was met in Indianola by policemen, Highway Patrolmen, and they only allowed two of us in to take the literacy test at the time. After we had taken this test and started back to Ruleville, we was held up by the City Police and the State Highway Patrolmen and carried back to Indianola where the bus driver was charged that day with driving a bus the wrong color.

After we paid the fine among us, we continued on to Ruleville, and Reverend Jeff Sunny carried me four miles in the rural area where I had worked as a timekeeper and sharecropper for eighteen years. I was met there by my children, who told me that the plantation owner was angry because I had gone down to try to register.

After they told me, my husband came, and said the plantation owner was raising Cain because I had tried to register. Before he quit talking the plantation owner came and said, "Fannie Lou, do you know—did Pap tell you what I said?"

And I said, "Yes, sir."

He said, "Well I mean that." He said, "If you don't go down and withdraw your registration, you will have to leave." Said, "Then if you go down and withdraw," said, "you still might have to go because we are not ready for that in Mississippi."

And I addressed him and told him and said, "I didn't try to register for you. I tried to register for myself."

I had to leave that same night.

On the 10th of September 1962, sixteen bullets was fired into the home of Mr. and Mrs. Robert Tucker for me. That same night two girls were shot in Ruleville, Mississippi. Also Mr. Joe McDonald's house was shot in.

And June the 9th, 1963, I had attended a voter registration workshop; was returning back to Mississippi. Ten of us was traveling by the Continental Trailway bus. When we got to Winona, Mississippi, which is Montgomery County, four of the people got off to use the washroom, and two of the people—to use the restaurant—two of the people wanted to use the washroom.

The four people that had gone in to use the restaurant was ordered out. During this time I was on the bus. But when I looked through the window and saw they had rushed out I got off of the bus to see what had happened. And one of the ladies said, "It was a State Highway Patrolman and a Chief of Police ordered us out."

I got back on the bus and one of the persons had used the washroom got back on the bus, too.

As soon as I was seated on the bus, I saw when they began to get the five people in a highway patrolman's car. I stepped off of the bus to see what was happening and somebody screamed from the car that the five workers was in and said, "Get that one there." When I went to get in the car, when the man told me I was under arrest, he kicked me.

I was carried to the county jail and put in the booking room. They left some of the people in the booking room and began to place us in cells. I was placed in a cell with a young woman called Miss Ivesta Simpson. After I was placed in the cell I began to hear sounds of licks and screams, I could hear the sounds of licks and horrible screams. And I could hear somebody say, "Can you say, 'yes, sir,' nigger? Can you say 'yes, sir'?"

Figure 6.2 Fannie Lou Hamer

And they would say other horrible names.

She would say, "Yes, I can say 'yes, sir.'"

"So, well, say it."

She said, "I don't know you well enough."

They beat her, I don't know how long. And after a while she began to pray, and asked God to have mercy on those people.

And it wasn't too long before three white men came to my cell. One of these men was a State Highway Patrolman and he asked me where I was from. I told him Ruleville and he said, "We are going to check this."

They left my cell and it wasn't too long before they came back. He said, "You are from Ruleville all right," and he used a curse word. And he said, "We are going to make you wish you was dead."

I was carried out of that cell into another cell where they had two Negro prisoners. The State Highway Patrolmen ordered the first Negro to take the blackjack.

The first Negro prisoner ordered me, by orders from the State Highway Petrolman, for me to lay down on a bunk bed on my face.

I laid on my face and the first Negro began to beat. I was beat by the first Negro until he was exhausted. I was holding my hands behind me at that time on my left side, because I suffered from polio when I was six years old.

After the first Negro had beat until he was exhausted, the State Highway Patrolman ordered the second Negro to take the blackjack.

The second Negro began to beat and I began to work my feet, and the State Highway Patrolman ordered the first Negro who had beat me to sit on my feet—to keep me from working my feet. I began to scream and one white man got up and began to beat me in my head and tell me to hush.

One white man—my dress had worked up high—he walked over and pulled my dress—I pulled my dress down and he pulled my dress back up.

I was in jail when Medgar Evers was murdered.

All of this is on account of we want to register, to become first-class citizens. And if the Freedom Democratic Party is not seated now, I question America. Is this America, the land of the free and the home of the brave, where we have to sleep with our telephones off the hooks because our lives be threatened daily, because we want to live as decent human beings, in America?

Thank you.

Note

1. Fannie Lou Hamer, *Mississippi Freedom Democratic Party speaks before the Credentials Committee of the Democratic National Convention in Atlantic City*, August 22, 1964, retrieved from http://american radioworks.publicradio.org/features/sayitplain/flhamer.html

Shirley Anita St. Hill Chisholm

Four years after the MFDP challenge led by Ella Baker and Fannie Lou Hamer for representation at the highest levels, Shirley Chisholm (1924–2005) became the first African American woman to be elected to the U.S. House of Representatives. She served in the House representing New York's 12th congressional district from 1969 to 1983.

In January 1972, she became the first Black presidential candidate from a major party, a fact underplayed in Barack Obama's 2008 and 2012 historic campaigns, and she was the first woman to run for the Democratic party's presidential nomination, a forerunner to Hillary Clinton's 2008 campaign against Obama. Born in Brooklyn but partly raised in Barbados, Representative Chisholm faithfully served her largely working-class Black and Puerto Rican district in Brooklyn, New York, adopting a politics that resonated with her times and her constituency. A staunch feminist, she also publicly supported the Black Panther Party's right to protest racist repression. Chisholm benefitted from the 1960s civil rights movement, a movement in which Hamer as a political outsider, seeking the right to vote for Black women and men, would set the stage for political insiders within the Congressional Black Caucus (all-male until Chisholm's entry). Like Black women before her, Chisholm galvanized energy and sparked the consciences of Americans who sought a greater democracy. After the waning of the southern civil rights movement, the martyrdoms of Martin Luther King Jr. and Robert Kennedy, with the law-and-order rhetoric of Richard Nixon, the North became the battleground for the articulation of rights. Congresswoman Chisholm's advocacy for the Equal Rights Amendment (ERA; 1972), like the anti-lynching laws sought by Ida B. Wells and Mary Church Terrell, was never legitimized in Congress. Nonetheless, she managed to seamlessly combine both gender and race as dual tensions in a razor wire stretched by bigots. Chisholm admonishes Congress for its opposition to the ERA: "If the argument [that the ERA will not end sex discrimination] were used against a civil rights bill, the prejudice that lies behind it would be embarrassing."[1] Middle-/upper-class White women organized the movement for the ERA. Chisholm faithfully and fairly worked for its passage; yet two years later she would be profoundly disappointed by the mainstream feminist movement's failure to support her presidential bid, a failure that included the betrayal also of the Congressional Black Caucus (CBC). Both the CBC and the leaders of second-wave feminism backed George McGovern and lobbied for Chisholm to abandon her "divisive" campaign. Despite this, the platform created in *Ms.* magazine allowed for other Black women several years later a national forum for analyses evocative of the ERA and Chisholm's legacy.

Note

1. Shirley Chisholm, "For the Equal Rights Amendment," speech (1970), www.americanrhetoric.com/speeches/shirleychisholmequalrights.htm <accessed 25 April 2014>

For the Equal Rights Amendment (10 August 1970), Washington D.C., Congress

Shirley Anita St. Hill Chisholm[1]

Mr. Speaker, House Joint Resolution 264, before us today, which provides for equality under the law for both men and women, represents one of the most clear-cut opportunities we are likely to have to declare our faith in the principles that shaped our Constitution. It provides a legal basis for attack on the most subtle, most pervasive, and most institutionalized form of prejudice that exists. Discrimination against women, solely on the basis of their sex, is so widespread that is seems to many persons normal, natural and right.

Legal expression of prejudice on the grounds of religious or political belief has become a minor problem in our society. Prejudice on the basis of race is, at least, under systematic attack. Their is reason for optimism that it will start to die with the present, older generation. It is time we act to assure full equality of opportunity to those citizens who, although in a majority, suffer the restrictions that are commonly imposed on minorities, to women.

The argument that this amendment will not solve the problem of sex discrimination is not relevant. If the argument were used against a civil rights bill, as it has been used in the past, the prejudice that lies behind it would be embarrassing. Of course laws will not eliminate prejudice from the hearts of human beings. But that is no reason to allow prejudice to continue to be enshrined in our laws—to perpetuate injustice through inaction.

The amendment is necessary to clarify countless ambiguities and inconsistencies in our legal system. For instance, the Constitution guarantees due process of law, in the 5th and 14th amendments. But the applicability of due process of sex distinctions is not clear. Women are excluded from some State colleges and universities. In some States, restrictions are placed on a married woman who engages in an independent business. Women may not be chosen for some juries. Women even receive heavier criminal penalties than men who commit the same crime. What would the legal effects of the equal rights amendment really be? The equal rights amendment would govern only the relationship between the State and its citizens—not relationships between private citizens. The amendment would be largely self-executing, that is, and Federal or State laws in conflict would be ineffective one year after date of ratification without further action by the Congress or State legislatures.

Opponents of the amendment claim its ratification would throw the law into a state of confusion and would result in much litigation to establish its meaning. This objection overlooks the influence of legislative history in determining intent and the recent activities of many groups preparing for legislative changes in this direction.

State labor laws applying only to women, such as those limiting hours of work and weights to be lifted would become inoperative unless the legislature amended them to apply to men. As of early 1970 most States would have some laws that would be affected. However, changes are being made so rapidly as a result of title VII of the Civil Rights Act of 1964, it is likely that by the time the equal rights amendment would become effective; no confliction State laws would remain.

In any event, there has for years been great controversy as to the usefulness to women of these State labor laws. There has never been any doubt that they worked a hardship on women who need or want to work overtime and on women who need or want better paying jobs, and there has been no persuasive evidence as to how many women benefit from the archaic policy of the laws. After the Delaware hours law was repealed in 1966, there were no complaints from women to any of the State agencies that might have been approached.

Jury service laws not making women equally liable for jury service would have been revised. The selective service law would have to include women, but women would not be required to serve in the Armed Forces where they are not fitted any more than men are required to serve. Military service, while a great responsibility, is not without benefits, particularly for young men with limited education or training.

Since October 1966, 246,000 young men who did not meet the normal mental or physical requirements have been given opportunities for training and correcting physical problems. This opportunity is not open to their sisters. Only girls who have completed high school and meet high standards on the educational test can volunteer. Ratification of the amendment would not permit application of higher standards to women.

Survivorship benefits would be available to husbands of female workers on the same basis as to wives of male workers. The Social Security Act and the civil service and military service retirement acts are in conflict. Public schools and universities could not be limited to one sex and could not apply different admission standards to men and women. Laws requiring longer prison sentences for women than men would be invalid, and equal opportunities for rehabilitation and vocational training would have to be provided in public correctional institutions. Different ages of majority based on sex would have to be harmonized. Federal, State, and other governmental bodies would be obligated to follow nondiscriminatory practices in all aspects of employment, including public school teachers and State university and college faculties.

What would be the economic effects of the equal rights amendment? Direct economic effects would be minor. If any labor laws applying only to women still remained, their amendment or repeal would provide opportunity for women in better-paying jobs in manufacturing. More opportunities in public vocational and graduate schools for women would also tend to open up opportunities in better jobs for women.

Indirect effects could be much greater. The focusing of public attention on the gross legal, economic, and social discrimination against women by hearings and debates in the Federal and State legislatures would result in changes in attitude of parents, educators, and employers that would bring about substantial economic changes in the long run.

Sex prejudice cuts both ways. Men are oppressed by the requirements of the Selective Service Act, by enforced legal guardianship of minors, and by alimony laws. Each sex, I believe, should be liable when necessary to serve and defend this country. Each has a responsibility for the support of children.

There are objections raised to wiping out laws protecting women workers. No one would condone exploitation. But what does sex have to do with it. Working conditions and hours that are harmful to women are harmful to men; wages that are unfair for women are unfair for men. Laws setting employment limitations on the basis of sex are irrational, and the proof of this is their inconsistency from State to State. The physical characteristics of men and women are not fixed, but cover two wide spans that have a great deal of overlap. It is obvious, I think, that a robust woman could be more fit for physical labor than a weak man. The choice of occupation would be determined by individual capabilities, and the rewards for equal works should be equal.

This is what it comes down to: artificial distinctions between persons must be wiped out of the law. Legal discrimination between the sexes is, in almost every instance, founded on outmoded views of society and the pre-scientific beliefs about psychology and physiology. It is time to sweep away these relics of the past and set further generations free of them.

Federal agencies and institutions responsible for the enforcement of equal opportunity laws need the authority of a Constitutional amendment. The 1964 Civil Rights Act and the 1963 Equal Pay Act are not enough; they are limited in their coverage—for instance, one excludes teachers, and the other leaves out administrative and professional women. The Equal Employment Opportunity Commission has not proven to be an adequate device, with its power limited to investigation, conciliation, and recommendation to the Justice Department. In its cases involving sexual discrimination, it has failed in more than one-half. The Justice Department has been even less effective. It has intervened in only one case involving discrimination on the basis of sex, and this was on a procedural point. In a second case, in which both sexual and racial discrimination were alleged, the racial bias charge was given far greater weight.

Evidence of discrimination on the basis of sex should hardly have to be cited here. It is in the Labor Department's employment and salary figures for anyone who is still in doubt. Its elimination will involve so many changes in our State and Federal laws that, without the authority and impetus of this proposed amendment, it will perhaps take another 194 years. We cannot be parties to continuing a delay. The time is clearly now to put this House on record for the fullest expression of that equality of opportunity which our founding fathers professed. They professed it, but they did not assure it to their daughters, as they tried to do for their sons.

The Constitution they wrote was designed to protect the rights of white, male citizens. As there were no black Founding Fathers, there were no founding mothers—a great pity, on both counts. It is not too late to complete the work they left undone. Today, here, we should start to do so.

In closing I would like to make one point. Social and psychological effects will be initially more important than legal or economic results. As Leo Kanowitz has pointed out:

> Rules of law that treat of the sexes per se inevitably produce far-reaching effects upon social, psychological and economic aspects of male-female relations beyond the limited confines of legislative chambers and courtrooms. As long as organized legal systems, at once the most respected and most feared of social institutions, continue to differentiate sharply, in treatment or in words, between men and women on the basis of irrelevant and artificially created distinctions, the likelihood of men and women coming to regard one another primarily as fellow human beings and only secondarily as representatives of another sex will continue to be remote. When men and women are prevented from recognizing one another's essential humanity by sexual prejudices, nourished by legal as well as social institutions, society as a whole remains less than it could otherwise become.

Note

1. Shirley Chisholm, "For the Equal Rights Amendment," speech (1970), www.americanrhetoric.com/speeches/shirleychisholmequalrights.htm <accessed 25 April 2014>

Johnnie Tillmon

The convergence of not just race, class, and gender but also blackness, poverty, and motherhood is prominently featured in Johnnie Tillmon's (1926–1995) "Welfare Is a Woman's Issue," published by *Ms.* magazine in 1972. Tillmon introduces her article in succinct sentences, descriptors identifying herself as what would be vilified a decade later in Ronald Reagan's stereotypical "welfare queen." Tillmon also describes welfare as a "traffic accident" that afflicts mostly women, especially women such as she. *Ms.* subscribers and readers understood that the ERA (which Shirley Chisholm championed in the House of Representatives) was a "woman's issue"; hence it was never necessary for *Ms.* to title any article to identify it as such. But with the national denigration of the beneficiaries of AFDC (Aid to Families with Dependent Children, a support system put into effect during the Nixon Administration and dismantled during the Clinton administration) as Black—although White women were in fact the majority of the recipients of aid—socially inferior, and "lazy," the mother of six needed to position welfare as an issue relevant to *Ms.*'s whiter, more affluent readership. Tillmon brilliantly frames welfare or public assistance within the political paradigm of mainstream feminism's "feminine mystique": the women's movement is about a bad marriage in which the man with money holds dictatorial power over dependent women and children in the household. *Ms.* magazine would follow Tillmon's essay three years later with one by Angela Y. Davis writing on the plight of another, impoverished Black woman whose life or death resided in the hands of the state.

"Welfare Is a Women's Issue" (1972)

Johnnie Tillmon[1]

I'm a woman. I'm a black woman. I'm a poor woman. I'm a fat woman. I'm a middle-aged woman. And I'm on welfare.

In this country, if you're any one of those things you count less as a human being. If you're all those things, you don't count at all. Except as a statistic.

I am 45 years old. I have raised six children. There are millions of statistics like me. Some on welfare. Some not. And some, really poor, who don't even know they're entitled to welfare. Not all of them are black. Not at all. In fact, the majority—about two-thirds—of all the poor families in the country are white.

Welfare's like a traffic accident. It can happen to anybody, but especially it happens to women.

And that's why welfare is a women's issue. For a lot of middle-class women in this country, Women's Liberation is a matter of concern. For women on welfare it's a matter of survival.

Survival. That's why we had to go on welfare. And that's why we can't get off welfare now. Not us women. Not until we do something about liberating poor women in this country.

Because up until now we've been raised to expect to work, all our lives, for nothing. Because we are the worst educated, the least-skilled, and the lowest-paid people there are. Because we have to be almost totally responsible for our children. Because we are regarded by everybody as dependents. That's why we are on welfare. And that's why we stay on it.

Welfare is the most prejudiced institution in this country, even more than marriage, which it tries to imitate. Let me explain that a little.

Ninety-nine percent of welfare families are headed by women. There is no man around. In half the states there can't be men around because A.F.D.C. (Aid to Families With Dependent Children) says if there is an "able-bodied" man around, then you can't be on welfare. If the kids are going to eat, and the man can't get a job, then he's got to go.

Welfare is like a super-sexist marriage. You trade in a man for the man. But you can't divorce him if he treats you bad. He can divorce you, of course, cut you off anytime he wants. But in that case, he keeps the kids, not you. The man runs everything. In ordinary marriage, sex is supposed to be for your husband. On A.F.D.C., you're not supposed to have any sex at all. You give up control of your own body. It's a condition of aid. You may even have to agree to get your tubes tied so you can never have more children just to avoid being cut off welfare.

The man, the welfare system, controls your money. He tells you what to buy, what not to buy, where to buy it, and how much things cost. If things—rent, for instance—really cost more than he says they do, it's just too bad for you. He's always right.

That's why Governor [Ronald] Reagan can get away with slandering welfare recipients, calling them "lazy parasites," "pigs at the trough," and such. We've been trained to believe that the only reason people are on welfare is because there's something wrong with their character. If people have "motivation," if people only want to work, they can, and they will be able to support themselves and their kids in decency.

The truth is a job doesn't necessarily mean an adequate income. There are some ten million jobs that now pay less than the minimum wage, and if you're a woman, you've got the best chance of getting one. Why would a 45-year-old woman work all day in a laundry ironing shirts at 90-some cents an hour? Because she knows there's some place lower she could be. She could be on welfare. Society needs women on welfare as "examples" to let every woman, factory workers and housewife workers alike, know what will happen if she lets up, if she's laid off, if she tries to go it alone without a man. So these ladies stay on their feet or on their knees all their lives instead of asking why they're only getting 90-some cents an hour, instead of daring to fight and complain.

Maybe we poor welfare women will really liberate women in this country. We've already started on our own welfare plan. Along with other welfare recipients, we have organized so we can have some voice. Our group is called the National Welfare Rights Organization (N.W.R.O.). We put together our own welfare plan, called Guaranteed Adequate Income (G.A.I.), which would eliminate sexism from welfare. There would be no "categories"—men, women, children, single, married, kids, no kids—just poor people who need aid. You'd get paid according to need and family size only and that would be upped as the cost of living goes up.

As far as I'm concerned, the ladies of N.W.R.O. are the front-line troops of women's freedom. Both because we have so few illusions and because our issues are so important to all women—the right to a living wage for women's work, the right to life itself.

Note

1. Johnnie Tillmon, "Welfare Is a Woman's Issue," *Ms. Magazine*, 1972, www.msmagazine.com/spring2002/tillmon.asp <accessed April 2014>

Combahee River Collective

Named after a military foray organized by Harriet Tubman, sparked by a series of murders against Black teen girls who were alleged sex workers and whose corpses were dumped in trash cans, with little investigative responses from police or outrage from communities, the Combahee River Collective was codified in 1977. It offers a genealogy and road map for Black feminism, identifying radical tendencies in revolutionary Black nationalism, critiquing elitism and classism among Black women (including those whose works had been promoted by *Ms.* magazine), and articulating the creative and political contributions of radical Black lesbians. Dubious about coalitions, the Combahee River Collective posits real possibilities (manifested over the decades since its publication) in its closing assertion: "As Black feminists and Lesbians we know that we have a very definite revolutionary task to perform and we are ready for the lifetime of work and struggle before us."[1]

Note

1. Combahee River Collective (April 1977), http://circuitous.org/scraps/combahee.html <accessed 25 April 2014>

The Combahee River Collective Statement (April 1977)

Combahee River Collective[1]

We are a collective of Black feminists who have been meeting together since 1974. During that time we have been involved in the process of defining and clarifying our politics, while at the same time doing political work within our own group and in coalition with other progressive organizations and movements. The most general statement of our politics at the present time would be that we are actively committed to struggling against racial, sexual, heterosexual, and class oppression, and see as our particular task the development of integrated analysis and practice based upon the fact that the major systems of oppression are interlocking. The synthesis of these oppressions creates the conditions of our lives. As Black women we see Black feminism as the logical political movement to combat the manifold and simultaneous oppressions that all women of color face.

We will discuss four major topics in the paper that follows: (1) the genesis of contemporary Black feminism; (2) what we believe, i.e., the specific province of our politics; (3) the problems in organizing Black feminists, including a brief herstory of our collective; and (4) Black feminist issues and practice.

1. The Genesis of Contemporary Black Feminism

Before looking at the recent development of Black feminism we would like to affirm that we find our origins in the historical reality of Afro-American women's continuous life-and-death struggle for survival and liberation. Black women's extremely negative relationship to the American political system (a system of white male rule) has always been determined by our membership in two oppressed racial and sexual castes. As Angela Davis points out in "Reflections on the Black Woman's Role in the Community of Slaves," Black women have always embodied, if only in their physical manifestation, an adversary stance to white male rule and have actively resisted its inroads upon them and their communities in both dramatic and subtle ways. There have always been Black women activists—some known, like Sojourner Truth, Harriet Tubman, Frances E. W. Harper, Ida B. Wells Barnett, and Mary Church Terrell, and thousands upon thousands unknown—who have had a shared awareness of how their sexual identity combined with their racial identity to make their whole life situation and the focus of their political struggles unique. Contemporary Black feminism is the outgrowth of countless generations of personal sacrifice, militancy, and work by our mothers and sisters.

A Black feminist presence has evolved most obviously in connection with the second wave of the American women's movement beginning in the late 1960s. Black, other Third World, and working women have been involved in the feminist movement from its start, but both outside reactionary forces and racism and elitism within the movement itself have served to obscure our participation. In 1973, Black feminists, primarily located in New York, felt the necessity of forming a separate Black feminist group. This became the National Black Feminist Organization (NBFO).

Black feminist politics also have an obvious connection to movements for Black liberation, particularly those of the 1960s and 1970s. Many of us were active in those movements (Civil Rights, Black nationalism, the Black Panthers), and all of our lives Were greatly affected and changed by their ideologies, their goals, and the tactics used to achieve their goals. It was our experience and disillusionment within these liberation movements, as well as experience on the periphery of the white male left, that led to the need to develop a politics that was anti-racist, unlike those of white women, and anti-sexist, unlike those of Black and white men.

There is also undeniably a personal genesis for Black Feminism, that is, the political realization that comes from the seemingly personal experiences of individual Black women's lives. Black feminists and many more Black women who do not define themselves as feminists have all experienced sexual oppression as a constant factor in our day-to-day existence. As children we realized that we were different from boys and that we were treated differently. For example, we were told in the same breath to be quiet both for the sake of being "ladylike" and to make us less objectionable in the eyes of white people. As we grew older we became aware of the threat of physical and sexual abuse by men. However, we had no way of conceptualizing what was so apparent to us, what we knew was really happening.

Black feminists often talk about their feelings of craziness before becoming conscious of the concepts of sexual politics, patriarchal rule, and most importantly, feminism, the political analysis and practice that we women use to struggle against our oppression. The fact that racial politics and indeed racism are pervasive factors in our lives did not allow us, and still does not allow most Black women, to look more deeply into our own experiences and, from that sharing and growing consciousness, to build a politics that will change our lives and inevitably end our oppression. Our development must also be tied to the contemporary economic and political position of Black people. The post World War II generation of Black youth was the first to be able to minimally partake of certain educational and employment options, previously closed completely to Black people. Although our economic position is still at the very bottom of the American capitalistic economy, a handful of us have been able to gain certain tools as a result of tokenism in education and employment which potentially enable us to more effectively fight our oppression.

A combined anti-racist and anti-sexist position drew us together initially, and as we developed politically we addressed ourselves to heterosexism and economic oppression under capitalism.

2. What We Believe

Above all else, Our politics initially sprang from the shared belief that Black women are inherently valuable, that our liberation is a necessity not as an adjunct to somebody else's may because of our need as human persons for autonomy. This may seem so obvious as to sound simplistic, but it is apparent that no other ostensibly progressive movement has ever considered our specific oppression as a priority or worked seriously for the ending of that oppression. Merely naming the pejorative stereotypes attributed to Black women (e.g. mammy, matriarch, Sapphire, whore, bulldagger), let alone cataloguing the cruel, often murderous, treatment we receive, Indicates how little value has been placed upon our lives during four centuries of bondage in the Western hemisphere. We realize that the only people who care enough about us to work consistently for our liberation are us. Our politics evolve from a healthy love for ourselves, our sisters and our community which allows us to continue our struggle and work.

This focusing upon our own oppression is embodied in the concept of identity politics. We believe that the most profound and potentially most radical politics come directly out of our own identity, as opposed to working to end somebody else's oppression. In the case of Black women this is a particularly repugnant, dangerous, threatening, and therefore revolutionary concept because it is obvious from looking at all the political movements that have preceded us that anyone is more worthy of liberation than ourselves. We reject pedestals, queenhood, and walking ten paces behind. To be recognized as human, levelly human, is enough.

We believe that sexual politics under patriarchy is as pervasive in Black women's lives as are the politics of class and race. We also often find it difficult to separate race from class from sex oppression because in our lives they are most often experienced simultaneously. We know that there is such a thing as racial-sexual oppression which is neither solely racial nor solely sexual, e.g., the history of rape of Black women by white men as a weapon of political repression.

Although we are feminists and Lesbians, we feel solidarity with progressive Black men and do not advocate the fractionalization that white women who are separatists demand. Our situation as Black people necessitates that we have solidarity around the fact of race, which white women of course do not need to have with white men, unless it is their negative solidarity as racial oppressors. We struggle together with Black men against racism, while we also struggle with Black men about sexism.

We realize that the liberation of all oppressed peoples necessitates the destruction of the political-economic systems of capitalism and imperialism as well as patriarchy. We are socialists because we believe that work must be organized for the collective benefit of those who do the work and create the products, and not for the profit of the bosses. Material resources must be equally distributed among those who create these resources. We are not convinced, however, that a socialist revolution that is not also a feminist and anti-racist revolution will guarantee our liberation. We have arrived at the necessity for developing an understanding of class relationships that takes into account the specific class position of Black women who are generally marginal in the labor force, while at this particular time some of us are temporarily viewed as doubly desirable tokens at white-collar and professional levels. We need to articulate the real class situation of persons who are not merely raceless, sexless workers, but for whom racial and sexual oppression are significant determinants in their working/economic lives. Although we are in essential agreement with Marx's theory as it applied to the very specific economic relationships he analyzed, we know that his analysis must be extended further in order for us to understand our specific economic situation as Black women.

A political contribution which we feel we have already made is the expansion of the feminist principle that the personal is political. In our consciousness-raising sessions, for example, we have in many ways gone beyond white women's revelations because we are dealing with the implications of race and class as well as sex. Even our Black women's style of talking/testifying in Black language about what we have experienced has a resonance that is both cultural and political. We have spent a great deal of energy delving into the cultural and experiential nature of our oppression out of necessity because none of these matters has ever been looked at before. No one before has ever examined the multilayered texture of Black women's lives. An example of this kind of revelation/conceptualization occurred at a meeting as we discussed the ways in which our early intellectual interests had been attacked by our peers, particularly Black males. We discovered that all of us, because we were "smart" had also been considered "ugly," i.e., "smart-ugly." "Smart-ugly" crystallized the way in which most of us had been forced to develop our intellects at great cost to our "social" lives. The sanctions In the Black and white communities against Black women thinkers is comparatively much higher than for white women, particularly ones from the educated middle and upper classes.

As we have already stated, we reject the stance of Lesbian separatism because it is not a viable political analysis or strategy for us. It leaves out far too much and far too many people, particularly Black men, women, and children. We have a great deal of criticism and loathing for what men have been socialized to be in this society: what they support, how they act, and how they oppress. But we do not have the misguided notion that it is their maleness, per se—i.e., their biological maleness—that makes them what they are. As Black women we find any type of biological determinism a particularly dangerous and reactionary basis upon which to build a politic. We must also question whether Lesbian separatism is an adequate and progressive political analysis and strategy, even for those who practice it, since it so completely denies any but the sexual sources of women's oppression, negating the facts of class and race.

3. Problems in Organizing Black Feminists

During our years together as a Black feminist collective we have experienced success and defeat, joy and pain, victory and failure. We have found that it is very difficult to organize around Black feminist issues, difficult even to announce in certain contexts that we are Black feminists. We have tried to think about the reasons for our difficulties, particularly since the white women's movement continues to be strong and to grow in many directions. In this section we will discuss some of the general reasons for the organizing problems we face and also talk specifically about the stages in organizing our own collective.

The major source of difficulty in our political work is that we are not just trying to fight oppression on one front or even two, but instead to address a whole range of oppressions. We do not have racial, sexual, heterosexual, or class privilege to rely upon, nor do we have even the minimal access to resources and power that groups who possess anyone of these types of privilege have.

The psychological toll of being a Black woman and the difficulties this presents in reaching political consciousness and doing political work can never be underestimated. There is a very low value placed upon Black women's psyches in this society, which is both racist and sexist. As an early group member once said, "We are all damaged people merely by virtue of being Black women." We are dispossessed psychologically and on every other level, and yet we feel the necessity to struggle to change the condition of all Black women. In "A Black Feminist's Search for Sisterhood," Michele Wallace arrives at this conclusion:

> We exists as women who are Black who are feminists, each stranded for the moment, working independently because there is not yet an environment in this society remotely congenial to our struggle—because, being on the bottom, we would have to do what no one else has done: we would have to fight the world.

Wallace is pessimistic but realistic in her assessment of Black feminists' position, particularly in her allusion to the nearly classic isolation most of us face. We might use our position at the bottom, however, to make a clear leap into revolutionary action. If Black women were free, it would mean that everyone else would have to be free since our freedom would necessitate the destruction of all the systems of oppression.

Feminism is, nevertheless, very threatening to the majority of Black people because it calls into question some of the most basic assumptions about our existence, i.e., that sex should be a determinant of power relationships. Here is the way male and female roles were defined in a Black nationalist pamphlet from the early 1970s:

> We understand that it is and has been traditional that the man is the head of the house. He is the leader of the house/nation because his knowledge of the world is broader, his awareness is greater, his understanding is fuller and his application of this information is wiser . . . After all, it is only reasonable that the man be the head of the house because he is able to defend and protect the development of his home . . . Women cannot do the same things as men—they are made by nature to function differently. Equality of men and women is something that cannot happen even in the abstract world. Men are not equal to other men, i.e. ability, experience or even understanding. The value of men and women can be seen as in the value of gold and silver—they are not equal but both have great value. We must realize that men and women are a complement to each other because there is no house/family without a man and his wife. Both are essential to the development of any life.

The material conditions of most Black women would hardly lead them to upset both economic and sexual arrangements that seem to represent some stability in their lives.

Many Black women have a good understanding of both sexism and racism, but because of the everyday constrictions of their lives, cannot risk struggling against them both.

The reaction of Black men to feminism has been notoriously negative. They are, of course, even more threatened than Black women by the possibility that Black feminists might organize around our own needs. They realize that they might not only lose valuable and hardworking allies in their struggles but that they might also be forced to change their habitually sexist ways of interacting with and oppressing Black women. Accusations that Black feminism divides the Black struggle are powerful deterrents to the growth of an autonomous Black women's movement.

Still, hundreds of women have been active at different times during the three-year existence of our group. And every Black woman who came, came out of a strongly-felt need for some level of possibility that did not previously exist in her life.

When we first started meeting early in 1974 after the NBFO first eastern regional conference, we did not have a strategy for organizing, or even a focus. We just wanted to see what we had. After a period of months of not meeting, we began to meet again late in the year and started doing an intense variety of consciousness-raising. The overwhelming feeling that we had is that after years and years we had finally found each other. Although we were not doing political work as a group, individuals continued their involvement in Lesbian politics, sterilization abuse and abortion rights work, Third World Women's International Women's Day activities, and support activity for the trials of Dr. Kenneth Edelin, Joan Little, and Inéz García. During our first summer when membership had dropped off considerably, those of us remaining devoted serious discussion to the possibility of opening a refuge for battered women in a Black community. (There was no refuge in Boston at that time.) We also decided around that time to become an independent collective since we had serious disagreements with NBFO's bourgeois-feminist stance and their lack of a clear political focus.

We also were contacted at that time by socialist feminists, with whom we had worked on abortion rights activities, who wanted to encourage us to attend the National Socialist Feminist Conference in Yellow Springs. One of our members did attend and despite the narrowness of the ideology that was promoted at that particular conference, we became more aware of the need for us to understand our own economic situation and to make our own economic analysis.

In the fall, when some members returned, we experienced several months of comparative inactivity and internal disagreements which were first conceptualized as a Lesbian-straight split but which were also the result of class and political differences. During the summer those of us who were still meeting had determined the need to do political work and to move beyond consciousness-raising and serving exclusively as an emotional support group. At the beginning of 1976, when some of the women who had not wanted to do political work and who also had voiced disagreements stopped attending of their own accord, we again looked for a focus. We decided at that time, with the addition of new members, to become a study group. We had always shared our reading with each other, and some of us had written papers on Black feminism for group discussion a few months before this decision was made. We began functioning as a study group and also began discussing the possibility of starting a Black feminist publication. We had a retreat in the late spring which provided a time for both political discussion and working out interpersonal issues. Currently we are planning to gather together a collection of Black feminist writing. We feel that it is absolutely essential to demonstrate the reality of our politics to other Black women and believe that we can do this through writing and distributing our work. The fact that individual Black feminists are living in isolation all over the country, that our own numbers are small, and that we have some skills in writing, printing, and publishing makes us want to carry out these kinds of projects as a means of organizing Black feminists as we continue to do political work in coalition with other groups.

4. Black Feminist Issues and Projects

During our time together we have identified and worked on many issues of particular relevance to Black women. The inclusiveness of our politics makes us concerned with any situation that impinges upon the lives of women, Third World and working people. We are of course particularly committed to working on those struggles in which race, sex, and class are simultaneous factors in oppression. We might, for example, become involved in workplace organizing at a factory that employs Third World women or picket a hospital that is cutting back on already inadequate heath care to a Third World community, or set up a rape crisis center in a Black neighborhood. Organizing around welfare and daycare concerns might also be a focus. The work to be done and the countless issues that this work represents merely reflect the pervasiveness of our oppression.

Issues and projects that collective members have actually worked on are sterilization abuse, abortion rights, battered women, rape and health care. We have also done many workshops and educationals on Black feminism on college campuses, at women's conferences, and most recently for high school women.

One issue that is of major concern to us and that we have begun to publicly address is racism in the white women's movement. As Black feminists we are made constantly and painfully aware of how little effort white women have made to understand and combat their racism, which requires among other things that they have a more than superficial comprehension of race, color, and Black history and culture. Eliminating racism in the white women's movement is by definition work for white women to do, but we will continue to speak to and demand accountability on this issue.

In the practice of our politics we do not believe that the end always justifies the means. Many reactionary and destructive acts have been done in the name of achieving "correct" political goals. As feminists we do not want to mess over people in the name of politics. We believe in collective process and a nonhierarchical distribution of power within our own group and in our vision of a revolutionary society. We are committed to a continual examination of our politics as they develop through criticism and self-criticism as an essential aspect of our practice. In her introduction to *Sisterhood is Powerful* Robin Morgan writes:

> I haven't the faintest notion what possible revolutionary role white heterosexual men could fulfill, since they are the very embodiment of reactionary-vested-interest-power.

As Black feminists and Lesbians we know that we have a very definite revolutionary task to perform and we are ready for the lifetime of work and struggle before us.

Note

1. Combahee River Collective, April 1977, http://circuitous.org/scraps/combahee.html <accessed 25 April 2014>

bell hooks

Issues of intimacy, love, and power are themes expounded on in the work of bell hooks (1952–), formerly known as Gloria Jean Watkins, who shaped feminism in 1981 with her text *Ain't I Woman?: Black Women and Feminism*, written while she was an undergraduate student at Stanford University. In the January 1999 issue of the Buddhist journal *Shambala Sun*, hooks revisits her work in the article "Ain't She Still a Woman?," where she examines the resurgence of patriarchal narratives as the uplift of the Black family. (The emphasis on strengthening the social and economic power of Black males was prevalent in the Obama administration, and some Black feminists have argued for programs supporting Black girls and women.) hooks notes that it is easier for "mainstream society to support the idea of benevolent black male domination in family life than to support the cultural revolutions that would ensure an end to race, gender and class exploitation." Including Black males on some level of a system structured on capitalism, imperialism, White supremacy, and patriarchy becomes then the "solution" to the disenfranchisement and vulnerability of Black families, particularly Black women and children.

"Ain't She Still a Woman?"

bell hooks[1]

Increasingly, patriarchy is offered as the solution to the crisis black people face. Black women face a culture where practically everyone wants us to stay in our place.

Progressive non-black folks, many of them white, often do not challenge black male support of patriarchy even though they would oppose sexism in other groups of men. In diverse black communities, and particularly in poor communities, feminism is regarded with suspicion and contempt. Most folks continue to articulate a vision of racial uplift that prioritizes the needs of males and valorizes conventional notions of gender roles. As a consequence black males and females who critique sexism and seek to eradicate patriarchy in black life receive little support.

Despite all the flaws and proven failures of patriarchal logic, many black people continue to grasp hold of the model of a benevolent patriarchy healing our wounds. Increasingly, patriarchy is offered as the solution to the collective crisis that black people face in their private and public lives.

Despite feminist critiques of patriarchal narratives of race that suggest black men suffer the most vicious assaults of white supremacy and racism because they are not empowered to be "real" men (i.e. patriarchal providers and protectors), most black people, along with the rest of the culture, continue to believe that a solid patriarchal family will heal the wounds inflicted by race and class. Frankly, many people cling to this myth because it is easier for mainstream society to support the idea of benevolent black male domination in family life than to support the cultural revolutions that would ensure an end to race, gender and class exploitation.

Many black people understand that the patriarchal two-parent black family often fares better than matriarchal single-parent households headed by women. Consequently it is not surprising that at moments of grave crisis, attempting to create a cultural climate that will promote and sustain patriarchal black families seems a more realistic strategy for solving the problems.

Of course, that appears more realistic only if one does not bring a hardcore class analysis to the crisis. For example: many conservative black males have spoken about the necessity of black men assuming economic responsibility for families, and have denounced welfare. Yet they do not address in any way where jobs will come from so that these would-be protectors and providers will be able to take care of the material well-being of their families.

Black females and males committed to feminist thinking cannot state often enough that patriarchy will not heal our wounds. On a basic level we can begin to change our everyday lives in a positive, fundamental way by embracing gender equality and with it a vision of mutual partnership that includes the sharing of resources, both material and spiritual. While it is crucial that black children learn early in life to assume responsibility for their well-being—that they learn discipline and diligence—these valuable lessons need not be connected to coercive authoritarian regimes of obedience.

While feminism has fundamentally altered the nature of white culture, the way white folks in families live both in the workplace and home, black female involvement in feminist thinking has not had enough meaningful impact on black families. The work of progressive black woman thinkers to encourage everyone in this society to think in terms of race, gender, and class has not radically altered the racist and sexist stereotypes that suggest black women succeed at the expense of black men.

Note

1. bell hooks, "Ain't She Still a Woman?," *Shambala Sun*, January 1999, www.hartford-hwp.com/archives/45a/186.html

Darnell Moore

A younger generation of Black feminists with a critique of political economies is embodied in Imani Perry, whose critique of neoliberalism, and Black feminism's economic and ideological embrace of power, has led her to note in a 2012 interview that "Black feminist thought is not simply an interest group advocating for powerful Black women, it is about seeing the world with a vision of liberation." What constitutes "liberation" is increasingly determined by class divisions among Black women and Black feminists. Increasingly the categories of "race women" or "Black feminists" are fractured and defined by ideological differences and varied if not antagonistic relations to economic and political power structures. Hence the rhetoric and vision of Black feminism become part of the political landscape of factions.

Conversation With Professor Imani Perry

Darnell Moore[1]

DM: You recently offered a compelling critique via social media in which you noted: "Black feminism used to be inherently radical, critical of classism, sexism, racism, heterosexism, and structures of domination, exploitation and imperialism everywhere. But now we have our own versions of NOW feminism, derivative 2nd wave feminism, and tone-deaf elitist middle class feminism." Can you say more about these contemporary Black feminisms that you've named and why it might be important to remember the political and intellectual frameworks out of which Black feminisms emerged?

IP: Neoliberalism has infected every area of thought, even those we think of as inherently progressive. Feminism that is about "choice" (read consumption) rather than an analysis of power, and comes through the mechanisms, and reflects the priorities, of large corporations has very limited potential to actually say much of anything about the deep structure of inequality. I think it is important to remember early Black feminisms because those women had a deep analysis of inequality, one that began with, but extended far beyond their existences as Black women to address all forms of oppression at home and abroad. Those feminists did not celebrate the powerful, but rather advocated for the least of these. And their intellectual work was never simply about the fact of someone being born in a Brown skinned xx body, but rather about the interpretive power of beginning one's thought from the experience of being Black and a girl or woman. I am worried when I read the title "Black feminism" applied to championing women like Susan Rice. I think a traditional and sophisticated Black feminist analysis does understand that she was targeted as a function of her race and gender; and yet, it also takes a critical posture towards her ideology which lies contrary to global principles of justice. Black feminist thought is not simply an interest group advocating for powerful Black women, it is about seeing the world with a vision of liberation. At least it should be.

DM: If a shift has taken place, do you think it is possible to conceive Black feminisms that reach back—to recuperate and bring into the present—a tradition of intersectional analyses and radical praxis—and push forward—to rethink and extend analyses and political work in areas under-theorized and not yet explored?

IP: I am currently writing about gender, and I am absolutely trying to do that. I think many other scholars are as well: Sara Ahmed and Sharon Holland immediately come to mind. Moreover, a lot of the women of the generation before me (I'm 40 years old) are still thinking and writing, such as Patricia Hill Collins and Bonnie Thornton Dill. The issue is: how do we get young feminists to turn to the books and to the grassroots, as much as they turn to celebrity feminists and the non-profit industrial complex, for their intellectual and political development? There is nothing more macho than corporate power and empire, feminists ought to be immediately skeptical of both even as we have to engage with them if we live in the United States. I'm worried that not enough self-proclaimed feminists have that skepticism. Black queer studies is probably the most robust area right now, in that it is a field that remains explicitly political and deeply analytical, yet connected to the lives of ordinary people: I'm thinking of scholars like E. Patrick Johnson or Rinaldo Walcott, here. All that to say, I think exposing students to sophisticated ideas and modes of analysis will provide them with the tools to push us further. Young people will be at the vanguard of a revitalized intellectual movement for gender justice.

DM: How do these questions figure into your present and/or future intellectual/political projects?

IP: As I said, I'm writing a book about gender. It is heavily theoretical, rooted in philosophy, jurisprudence and the literature of Black women of the renaissance of the 70s-90s. I'm pushing in a different direction than intersectionality. If we read the Combahee River Collective Statement, we see something that isn't so specific or sited at the crossroads, but expansive and frankly both Marxist and infused with the sensibilities of liberation movements across the globe. I'm pushing in the direction they, and others, set forth.

DM: And speaking of your work, you've mentioned that your recent book, *More Beautiful and More Terrible: The Embrace and Transcendence of Racial Inequality in the United States*, "called [you], rather than one [you] looked for." How so?

IP: I think part of being an intellectual is both being an active and constant reader of books and articles and also reading one's environment. So when I say the book called me, I mean that I didn't plan to write it but, rather, it took shape through my reading and thinking and living. The same thing with my current book projects. In academia, we are often told to have a fixed research agenda from the beginning of one's career. I have never subscribed to that approach. I write consistently, but I write where my passion lies, and that is an ever-changing and growing thing. Living as an intellectual is prayerful. You immerse yourself in ideas; you live and love the life of the mind; and at opportune times you find insight thrust upon you. It is a blessing.

DM: Lastly, who would you name as your Black feminist sheroes, those whose lives and work invigorate your own? And why?

IP: This is an extremely hard question. There are so many, so this is just a handful of them: all women I've known. Certainly, the women in my family, helmed by my late grandmother Neida Mae Garner Perry, are all models of organic feminism. The sense of personal power that I learned from them has enabled every aspiration. And, as a girl, I met Ella Baker several times. She was elderly by then, and I took her to the park. Knowing who she was, I learned early on that a woman who developed a politic around ways of thinking that are traditionally conceived of as female—collaboration, participation, inclusion, process, humility—could initiate an organization that would change the world. That had a huge impact on me. Mary Helen Washington's landmark and beautiful, *Black Eyed Susans*, was the first Black feminist anthology I ever read—I read it when I was in middle school—and she went to my church so doing this kind of work was "real" for me. When I was a young scholar, she praised me for maintaining a class analysis in my scholarship. That attention meant the world to me. Beverly Smith, one of the authors of the Combahee River Collective Statement, and other women of that community were often in my living room for gatherings when I was young, and the conversations they had influenced me. Kate Rushin encouraged me to read Black feminist writers specifically when I was a teenager. I listened. I also began to read her poetry as an adult. It is so human and so Black and so womanly.

In college, I interned at South End Press and, as a result, spent a significant amount of time with bell hooks. Her way of both naming injustice and the thought that produces it, but also remaining hopeful, was inspiring. And she did away with any thought that feminism had to be staid. And then, in my senior year of college, I read Patricia Hill Collins *Black Feminist Thought*, and I remember calling my mom and saying "THIS is what I want to do when I grow up!" It turns out she knew Pat from Black Catholic activist days. Years later, I got to know Pat myself, and I continue to be amazed by the complex maps she creates of how gender and race and class operate. Lani Guinier inspired me to go to law school and inspires me still with her ability to be critical of the site of her own privilege as a scholar who is at a very powerful institution. I try very hard to replicate that critical posture. My play-sister, Farah Jasmine Griffin, models what it means to prioritize Black women as creative and intellectual subjects, to challenge their place in dominant epistemologies, and open up new epistemological frameworks that center Black women writers and musicians. She teaches us how much we matter. And, Toni Morrison is everything. She announces to the world that the very best, the most profound, the most beautiful and the deepest cutting words emerge from the embodied lives of Black women. What better license to write could there be?

Note

1. Excerpt from Darnell Moore, "Black Feminist Intellectual: A Conversation with Professor Imani Perry," December 20, 2012, http://thefeministwire.com/2012/12/imaniperry/ <accessed April 25 2014>

Omi Osun Joni L. Jones

Joni Omi Jones, professor of performance studies and African and African diaspora studies at the University of Texas, Austin, writes of "allies" as essential; as a Black lesbian performance artist she observes how "truth telling is dangerous business because of vulnerability which is also a necessary strength." Truth telling, according to Jones, "leaves one exposed" yet also free. Jones has contributed numerous artistic projects and writings internationally, focused on Black feminism, and Black lesbian theories and praxes. The following keynote address was presented at Muhlenberg College, Allentown, Pennsylvania, on February 7, 2013.

"The Role of Allies in 2013"

Omi Osun Joni L. Jones[1]

Good afternoon Muhlenberg Community! It is so good to be here. I did undergraduate work at a small liberal arts college where I received the best education of my life. Being here makes me nostalgic in the best possible way.

I'd like to thank the department chair, Jim Peck, for inviting me to talk with you today. Jim and Jessica Bien made excellent travel arrangements and accommodations. It is no small feat to do this smoothly and professionally—while tending to countless other responsibilities. Thank you so much for your hard work.

I have entitled my talk "The Role of Allies in 2013." I applaud your community for taking freedom so seriously, for integrating the role of allies into your curriculum and into the general spirit of your campus.

I'd like you to fully visualize the concept of an ally. Some of us use the term often, but what do we really mean by it? In order to explore this, I'd like you to work with a partner. Turn to someone you don't know. Together, create a one-sentence definition of an ally. You have one-minute!

Now, make that sentence into a physical shape that you can both do from your seats. Practice it! Be ready to share it!

I'd like to divide the group into four quadrants. When I point to your quadrant, offer your shape. Quadrant 1. Quadrant 3. Quadrant 2. Quadrant 4. Don't forget your shape. You will share it again soon.

I take this opportunity to speak with you very seriously. The times require that I use every moment of public presentation to speak the truth as I know it. That is my job as an artist, a scholar, a teacher, a committed human being seeking to make a world of peace and justice for everyone.

This truth telling is dangerous business. It leaves one vulnerable—but our vulnerability is our strength. It leaves one exposed—but exposure allows the wind to whip through all those dank and musty spaces of terror, and blow away isolation and fear. Truth telling leaves us free—and that is, after all, the point.

This truth telling is especially dangerous for a Black queer woman, for me. My very safety is at stake when I speak the truth, the truth of my life, and the truth of the world as I experience it. My truths challenge the very foundation of the systems around me, systems that variously support and denigrate me, systems that both applaud and slap me.

So, as I walk, I look for mirrors, for allies who are also committed to everyone's freedom, allies willing to risk their own safety in order to ensure mine.

Allies must understand that oppressions are multiplicative—race, gender, sexuality, class, nation, ability, religion, age must *all* be considered as we work for social justice. This list is not exhaustive—oppressions and privilege lurk in many places.

As I consider the seriousness of the moment, I am reminded of the courage and power of actress Beah Richards who was invited to speak before the Chicago Peace Congress in 1951. You may know Beah Richards as Sidney Poitier's mother in "Guess Who's Coming to Dinner." She was also the passionate preacher in the groves in the film "Beloved," and the subject of a biographical documentary by Lisa Gay Hamilton. As scholar Margaret Wilkerson describes Richards' 1951 presentation, the women—all of them white—who invited Richards to speak, wanted her to address racial diversity. Instead of performing the role of the grateful colored guest, instead of predictably offering out a poem by Georgia Douglas Johnson or Paul Laurence Dunbar—Beah Richards confronted the issue of racial diversity head on in a piece she wrote especially for the occasion entitled "A Black Woman Speaks." In this poetic direct address to her all-white largely female audience, she said—

"They said, the white supremacists said,
that you were better than me
that your fair brow should never know the sweat of slavery.
They lied.
White womanhood too is enslaved.
The difference is degree.

And what wrongs you, murders me.
And eventually marks your grave
So we share a mutual death at the hand of tyranny.

He, the white supremacist, fixed your minds with poisonous thought—
'white skin is supreme.'
Set your minds on my slavery
the better to endure your own.

Cuddled down in your pink slavery
and thought somehow my wasted blood
confirmed your superiority.

Because your necklace was of gold
You did not notice that it throttled speech."[2]

That was Beah Richards in 1951, who sought to join in solidarity with white women even as she acknowledged the ways in which the lives of Black women and white women were sharply divided.

Some 28 years later, poet activist Audre Lorde was similarly invited to speak at a conference—the Second Sex Conference in New York City. Like Richards, Audre Lorde spoke of the challenge and necessity of building allies. She stated—

"As women, we have been taught either to ignore our differences, or to view them as causes for separation and suspicion rather than as forces for change. Without community there is no liberation, only the most vulnerable and temporary armistice between an individual and her oppression. But community must not mean a shedding of our differences, nor the pathetic pretense that these differences do not exist.

Those of us who stand outside the circle of this society's definition of acceptable women; those of us who have been forged in the crucibles of difference—those of us who are poor, who are lesbians, who are Black, who are older—know that survival is not an academic skill. It is learning how to stand alone, unpopular and sometimes reviled, and how to make common cause with those others identified as outside the structures in order to define and seek a world in which we can all flourish. It is learning how to take our differences and make them strengths. For the master's tools will never dismantle the master's house. They may allow us temporarily to beat him at his own game, but they will never enable us to bring about genuine change. And this fact is only threatening to those women who still define the master's house as their only source of support.

In a world of possibility for us all, our personal visions help lay the groundwork for political action. The failure of academic feminists to recognize difference as a crucial strength is a failure to reach beyond the first patriarchal lesson. In our world, divide and conquer must become define and empower."[3]

So, in the spirit of Richards who exposed the trap of "pink slavery" in order to forge allies, and Lorde who told us that we must not replicate the very structures that divide us, I offer some reflections on what it means to be an ally to queer people, to women, to poor people, and to people of color. Rules for allies may be for our own use as we acknowledge our points of privilege, or for passing along to others.

Rule #1

Allies know that it is not sufficient to be liberal. The liberal position allows those with optimal privileges to pretend that everything is "basically OK." Believing that things are "OK" means a deep mistrust of the truths that people of color, women, queer people and poor people bring to light. The liberal position says that those of us with legitimate observations about injustice are really exaggerating, paranoid, and unwilling to see how we are creating the problem we expose. In this way, the liberal position is actually a walk backwards. It creates suspicion among the very people who might be allies. The politically liberal position blinds us to what is hiding in plain sight. The liberal position supports the status quo, which means that racism, sexism, homophobia, the perils of nationhood, and a commitment to class structures that support social hierarchies will persist—unless we move toward a *radical* rather than *liberal* position.

This first rule reminds me of the powerful ideas of feminist activist/scholar Joy James who makes a critical distinction between a soldier and a warrior.[4] The soldier works for the state—and therefore supports all that that implies. The warrior works for freedom. Allies must be willing to be warriors, and risk the support of institutions in our joint move toward deep liberation.

In thinking about Rule #1, "The Liberal Position is Not Sufficient," I am reminded of Rev. Dr. Martin Luther King, Jr.'s "Letter from a Birmingham Jail" which he penned in 1963 after being jailed as a result of working with the Alabama Christian Movement for Human Rights against discrimination and oppression.

From his jail cell King addressed this point directly when he wrote—

"Shallow understanding from people of good will is more frustrating than absolute misunderstanding from people of ill will."[5]

Rule #2

Be Loud and Crazy so women, people of color, queer people, poor people won't have to be! Speak up! Say it! Name it! If you are male, YOU be the one to tell your boss that the women's salaries in your workplace must be brought in line with those of the men. If you are white, YOU be the one to advocate for the qualified person of color to be hired rather than the qualified white applicant. Change doesn't happen if you don't make change. If you are Christian, YOU be the one to be sure that Muslims in your community have safe accessible places on campus for their obligatory daily prayers. Being Loud and Crazy does not mean being reckless; *strategizing* is always important (as we will see in the next rule). Speaking up *does* mean being willing to relinquish some piece of privilege in order to create justice. Allies step up. They do the work that has left others depleted and weary.

Rule #3

Do not tell anyone in any oppressed group to be patient. Doing so is a sign of your own privilege and your unconscious, though absolute, disregard for the person with whom you are speaking. You may remember, it was a number of white ministers in Atlanta who advised King to be patient in reacting to U.S. racism. This call for patience prompted King to write—

> "We know through painful experience that freedom is never voluntarily given by the oppressor; it must be demanded by the oppressed. Frankly, I have yet to engage in a direct action campaign that was 'well timed' in the view of those who have not suffered unduly from the disease of segregation. For years now I have heard the word 'Wait!' It rings in the ear of every Negro with piercing familiarity. This 'Wait' has almost always meant 'Never.' We must come to see . . . that 'justice too long delayed is justice denied.'"[6]

Patience is not a political strategy. It is a diversionary tactic. It is a patronizing recommendation made only by those who do not believe that oppression is killing us all.

Planning while *appearing* to wait, *is* a strategy. Allies, plan with us.

Rule #4

Recognize the new racism, the new sexism, the old homophobia. It is institutional and structural. Learn to walk in a room and count the people of color—and know what you know. The absence of people of color in any space cannot be accounted for by chance or accident. Learn to see how many women are in charge. The absence of powerful women in any space cannot be accounted for by chance or accident. Learn to see and feel those spaces that are unsafe for queer people. The absence of queer people in any space cannot be accounted for by chance or accident. Allies know that racism, sexism, and homophobia are real, and NEVER tell people, "You could be wrong, you know." Such a statement presumes that you have greater insights into oppression than those with *lived experience* inside of multiple oppressions. Recognizing the new racism, the new sexism, the old homophobia means listening, means acknowledging that these oppressions have not been honestly talked about enough.

King wrote of being "humiliated day in and day out by nagging signs reading 'white' and 'colored.'"[7] We must look for the new signs. What are the signs of racism and sexism? What do they look like in 2013? Women doing work comparable to men still make less than their male counterparts. Black people around the world are still disproportionately incarcerated and impoverished. What are the other signs of racism and sexism today? Having a Black president does not absolve the nation of its racist history or present. We must learn to name what we know to be true. And the public conversation around sexuality is so new, that homophobia still lives in the socially unchallenged gay jokes, the insistence on blue for baby boys and pink for baby girls, and the refusal for school districts to allow same-gender partners at the prom.

Playwright and novelist Pearl Cleage demands that theatre be her "hollering place"—a space where Black women can tell their stories. In her "hollering place," everyone is welcome IF they are willing to truly listen to Black women and feel with the density of our lives.[8] Feeling with the person to whom you are speaking, means NOT offering an objection to the gashes of racism or sexism or homophobia that they have shared with you—even if holding onto your objection leaves your tongue bloody! In 48 hours, after contemplation and reflection, after those experiences have had a chance to marinate in you, you just might feel *inside* rather than *outside* of that person's experience. Allies know how to spot oppression and to support others as they reveal their wounds.

Rule #5

When called out about your racism, sexism or homophobia, don't cower in embarrassment, don't cry, and don't silently think "they're crazy," and vow never to interact with them again. We are all plagued by racism, sexism, homophobia, classism. Be grateful that someone took the time to expose yours—remember, exposure allows the wind to whip away isolation and fear. Exposure is a step toward freedom. Allies welcome an opportunity to see how their choices, ideas, words may be erasing people around them. It's not about your intent—that you did not intend to be sexist when you consulted with men rather than with women even though the women were in charge—it is about the effect, the damaging effect your choice had on others, the reinforcement of patriarchy that your choice made.

Allies want to know when they have contributed to the very oppressions they oppose. Men of color must be vigilant about re-routing their commitment to patriarchy. Allies know they are not above reproach.

Rule #6

Allies actively support alternative possibilities. It is these alternative possibilities that make us strong. It is diversity of thinking, believing, behaving that makes our lives, our work richer.

Because allies believe "the master's tools will never dismantle the master's house," allies consider the transgressive power in alternative possibilities, a power that works to undo patriarchy, white supremacy, the insatiability of capitalism, and the hegemony of heterosexism. Supporting alternative possibilities is the only way we can all dream ourselves into the world in which we want to live.

Rule #7

Allies work for themselves, not for others. Allies do not dole out charity, but work to create the world they want to live in. This is not about what Latinos and Latinas need or what poor folks need, it's about what the most privileged in society need in order to live as equal citizens in the human community.

Rev. Dr. Martin Luther King wisely noted, "We are caught in an inescapable network of mutuality, tied in a single garment of destiny. Whatever affects one directly, affects all indirectly."[9]

If people of color are truly the brothers and sisters to white people, it means that white people will have to reimagine themselves. So, white people are working for their *own* freedom, not merely the freedom of others. So, the middle class is working for their *own* freedom, not for the freedom of the poor. So, straight people are working for their *own* erotic and sexual and gender freedom, not for the freedom of queer folk. As long as there is oppression, it means that those with race and gender privilege maintain a false idea of themselves as superior, as smarter, as more worthy—so dismantling oppression means that white people are working to free themselves from these falsehoods as much as they are working with people of color to remove social and institutional impediments.

The late poet and activist raulrsalinas (AKA Raul R. Salinas) spoke to a group of artists and reminded them that they cannot do any work for other people.[10] Doing so is pretentious; it silently relies on the activist actually occupying a superior position to those supposedly in need. To fully adopt Raul's radical position, we must courageously explore our motives for engaging in social justice work. What may appear to be generosity can more accurately be ways of bolstering our own importance. Let us do our work because we know that humanity is intertwined. Someone else's oppression is our own, diminishes our own soul.

Rule #8

White people must take responsibility for white people. Straight people must take responsibility for straight people. The most privileged in society should make the most privileged accountable. While this group responsibility is generally understood and expected among people of color—when a Black child commits a crime, members of Black communities come together to address the issue—this is not generally true among white people. If a white person commits a crime, I do not believe white citizens gather to discuss this as evidence of a problem in the white community, in the white family structure, in white values. Instead, this is considered a general problem of society. What might happen if white people were held accountable—made to feel and be responsible—for the violence and ignorance in white communities?

Just as Black and Brown people have gone into neighborhoods mangled by gang fear, and bravely encouraged dangerous conversations that have led to peace—white folks might sit down with the KKK, with the Tea Party members, with all the white people who believe that people of color are less than them, with all the white people who would never admit to such things but whose very philosophies are predicated on the rejection of all things Black Brown Yellow Red not to mention Rainbow. Liberal white people might do more for the cause of freedom by educating their own than by "helping" people of color.

Christians must take care of other Christians, pull their coats, tell them to embody Jesus's love (not merely tolerance), show them how to love their own sexual selves and to respect the sexual selves of others. Christians must come to see how their dominance in numbers silences Muslims, Buddhists, Agnostics, Atheists—and such silencing breeds hostility and hierarchies of spirituality, not love.

This list of Rules for Allies requires that each of us know when we can be allies; those of us who are women, those of us who are queer, those of us who are people of color, those of us who are middle class must examine those times when our own privileges insist that *we* abide by these very rules. For me, my class privilege, my able-bodiedness and nationality are markers that require me to practice being an ally. This means that the Rules for Allies can be used by everyone in this room.

The habitual performance of these rules means that more and more of us have the space to fully be ourselves because we will speak our truth with the assurance of support.

Now, I'd like you to explore these rules amongst yourselves. With your partner, join another duo. Discuss which of the eight rules you find the most challenging. Be specific. The rules are: 1) Liberal is not Sufficient, 2) Be Loud and Crazy, 3) Patience is not a Political Strategy, 4) Recognize the New Racism, the New Sexism, the Old Homophobia, 5) Welcome Opportunities to Examine Your Racism, Sexism, Homophobia, 6) Support Alternative Possibilities, 7) Work for Your Own Freedom, 8) Take Responsibility for 'Your People.'

You have about 5 minutes for this discussion.

Theatrical jazz composer Sharon Bridgforth often writes of freedom. Her piece *delta dandi* ends with the character Gurl assuming the role of king as both a declaration of personal freedom and a call for community. Freedom and community are vital components in ally making. *delta dandi* seems a fitting way for me to conclude.

> "this is where it all comes together.
> this is where we meet. the shift is now.
> the Change has come. it is time.
> i move from the crossroads
> stand where all the rivers meet.
>
> life flows through me.
> i wait for you.
> come to me.
>
> ask your question child."[11]

Ask questions of each other to better support each other, to make the communities in which we want to live, to be the allies we need to be.

> Quadrant 2—ally pose!
> Quadrant 1—ally pose!
> Quadrant 3—ally pose!
> Quadrant 4—ally pose!

As you move through the rest of the week, join with others as allies in order to ensure our mutual freedom.

Practice these physical poses throughout the week. Let them be your markers of being an ally. Thank you for sharing your vulnerability and hopes with me.

Notes

1. Joni Omi Jones, "The Role of Allies in 2013," Keynote, Muhlenberg College, Pennsylvania, February 7, 2013.
2. Richards, Beah. "A Black Woman Speaks," in *9 Plays by Black Women*, ed. Margaret Wilkerson. NY: Penguin Books, 1986.
3. Lorde, Audre. "The Master's Tools Will Never Dismantle the Master's House," in *Sister Outsider: Essays and Speeches*. Trumansburg, NY: Crossing Press, 1984.
4. James, Joy. *Shadowboxing: Representations of Black Feminist Politics*. NY: St. Martin's Press, 1999.
5. King, Martin Luther. "Letter from a Birmingham Jail," in *The Atlantic Monthly*, Vol. 212, No. 2.
6. Ibid.
7. Ibid.
8. Cleage, Pearl. "Hollering Place," in *The Dramatists Guild Quarterly*. NY: The Dramatists Guild, Summer 1994.
9. King, Op. Cit.
10. Salinas, Raul R. "Work of the Spirit," in *Experiments in a Jazz Aesthetic: Art, Activism, Academia and the Austin Project*, eds. Jones, Omi Osun Joni L., Sharon Bridgforth and Lisa L. Moore. Austin, TX: University of Texas Press, 2010.
11. Bridgforth, Sharon. *delta dandi*, in *Solo, Black, Woman*, eds. Johnson, E. Patrick and Ramon Rivera-Servera. Evanston, IL: Northwestern University Press, 2013.

Nikky Finney

Nikky Finney (born Lynn Carol Finney on August 26, 1957) grew up in a civil rights activist–attorney family. The Guy Davenport Endowed Professor of English at the University of Kentucky, *Wings Made of Gauze* (1985) was her first book of poems. *Rice* (1995) received a PEN American Open Book Award, and *Heartwood* (1998) is unique for its focus on literacy.

In 1999, Finney held the Goode Chair in the Humanities at Berea College. *The World Is Round* (2003) followed her return to the University of Kentucky. She was the Grace Hazard Conkling Writer-in-Residence at Smith College, 2007–2009. *The Ringing Ear: Black Poets Lean South* (2007) was followed by *Head Off & Split* (2011), which won the National Book Award for Poetry. Her acceptance speech, published in this volume, was considered extraordinary. A founding member of the Affrilachian Poets in Lexington, Kentucky, she was entered into the Hall of Fame for Writers of African Descent in Chicago, Illinois.

National Book Awards Acceptance Speech, November 16, 2011, New York

Nikky Finney[1]

One: We begin with history. The Slave Codes of SC, 1739:

> *a fine of one hundred dollars and six months in prison will be imposed for anyone found teaching a slave to read, or write, and death is the penalty for circulating any incendiary literature.*

The ones who longed to read and write, but were forbidden, who lost hands and feet, were killed, by laws written by men who believed they owned other men. Their words devoted to quelling freedom and insurgency, imagination, all hope; what about the possibility of one day making a poem? The king's mouth and the queen's tongue arranged, perfectly, on the most beautiful paper, sealed with wax and palmetto tree sap, determined to control what can never be controlled: the will of the human heart to speak its own mind.

Tonight, these forbidden ones move all around the room as they please. They sit at whatever table they want. They wear camel-colored field hats and tomato-red kerchiefs. They are bold in their Sunday-go-to meeting best. Their cotton croker-sack shirts are black washpot clean and irreverently not tucked in. Some have even come in white Victorian collars and bustiers. Some have just climbed out of the cold wet Atlantic, just to be here. We shiver together.

If my name is ever called out, I promised my girl-poet self, so too would I call out theirs.

Two:

Parneshia Jones (Acquisitions Editor), Marianne Jankowski (Art Director), and Northwestern University Press, this moment has everything to do with how seriously, how gorgeously, you do what you do.

A.J. Verdelle, editor-partner in this language life, you taught me that repetition is holy, Courage is a daughter's name, and two is stronger than one.

Papa, chief opponent of the death penalty in South Carolina for 50 years, 57 years married to the same Newberry girl, when I was a girl you bought every encyclopedia, dictionary, and Black history tome, that ever knocked on our Oakland Avenue door.

Mama, dear mama, Newberry girl, 57 years married to the same Smithfield boy, you made Christmas, Thanksgiving, and birthdays out of foil, lace, cardboard, and paper maché, insisting beauty into our deeply segregated southern days.

Adrienne Rich, Yusef Komunyakaa, Carl Philips, and Bruce Smith, simply to be in your Finalist Company is to brightly burn.

National Book Foundation and 2011 National Book Award judges for poetry, there were special, and subversive, high school English teachers who would read and announce the highly anticipated annual report, from the National Book Foundation; the names of the winners stowed way down deep in some the only life I ever wanted, that of a poet.

Dr. Gloria Wade Gayles, great and best teacher, you asked me on a Friday, 4 o'clock, 1977, I was 19 and sitting on a Talladega College wall dreaming about the only life I ever wanted, that of a poet. "Miss Finney," you said, "do you really have time to sit there, have you finished reading every book in the library?"

Dr. Katie Cannon, what I heard you say once still haunts every poem I make, "Black People were the only people in the United States ever explicitly forbidden to become literate."

I am now, officially, speechless.

Note

1. Nikky Finney, Acceptance Speech 2011 National Book Award in Poetry, New York, November 16, 2011, http://nikkyfinney.net/yxLS9.So.79.pdf <accessed 25 April 2014>, www.youtube.com/watch?v=Y2q15iiL79g <accessed April 25 2014>

Section 6: Further Reading

Barrier Williams, Fannie. "Opportunities and Responsibilities of Colored Women." (1895), pp. 146–161. Web. Retrieved 25 April 2014. http://docsouth.unc.edu/church/haley/haley.html#p.146

Bonner, Marita. "On Being Young—a Woman—and Colored." *The Crisis* (1925).

Butler, Octavia E. NPR Essay: "UN Racism Conference." (2001). Web. Retrieved 25 April 2014. www.npr.org/programs/specials/racism/010830.octaviabutleressay.html.

Cooper, Anna Julia. *A Voice from the South.* Xenia, OH: The Aldine Printing House, 1892. Web. Retrieved 25 April 2014. http://docsouth.unc.edu/church/cooper/cooper.html

Davis, Angela. "Joan Little: The Dialectics of Rape." *Ms. Magazine* (1975). Web. Retrieved 25 April 2014. www.msmagazine.com/spring2002/davis.asp

Guinier, Lani. "Race and Reality in a Front-Porch Encounter." *The Chronicle of Higher Education* (30 July 2009). Web. Retrieved 25 April 2014. http://chronicle.com/article/RaceReality-in-a/47509/

Guy-Sheftall, Beverly. "Response from a 'Second Waver' to Kimberly Springer's 'Third Wave Black Feminism?'" *Signs*, 27.4 (Summer 2002): 1091–1094.

Harris, Cheryl. "Whiteness as Property." In *Critical Race Theory: The Key Writings that Formed the Movement.* Eds. K. Chrenshaw et al., New York: The New Press, 1995. (pp. 276–291); reprint, "Whiteness as Property," *Harvard Law Review*, 106.8 (June 1993): 1757–1773.

Hill Collins, Patricia. "Black Nationalism and African American Ethnicity: Afrocentrism as Religion." In *From Black Power to Hip Hop: Racism, Nationalism, and Feminism.* Philadelphia: Temple University Press, 2006. (pp. 75–94).

Jackson, Esther. "Interview with Esther Jackson." *Abafazi*, 9.1 (Fall/Winter 1998).

Jaffrey, Zia. "The Salon Interview—Toni Morrison." (2 February 1998). Web. Retrieved 25 April 2014. https://www.salon.com/1998/02/02/cov_si_02int/

Johnson Reagon, Bernice. "Freedom Songs: My African American Singing and Fighting Mothers." In *If You Don't Go, Don't Hinder Me.* Lincoln: University of Nebraska Press, 2001. (pp. 100–142).

Murray, Pauli. "The Negro Woman in the Quest for Equality." Speech (14 November 1963), reprinted from *The Acorn* (June 1964).

Queen Mother Moore Speech, "People's Communication Network" (1973) (See: Chris Hill, "Dialogue across Decades: BLW and People's Communication Network—Exercises in Remembering and Forgetting." *Journal of Film and Video*, 16.1–2: 17–29).

Shadd Cary, Mary Ann. "Hints to the Colored People of the North." (1849) As discussed in Rhodes, Jane. *Mary Ann Shadd Cary: The Black Press and Protest in the Nineteenth Century*. Bloomington: Indiana University Press, 1999.

Shakur, Assata. "To My People." 4 July 1973. Web. Retrieved 25 April 2014. www.thetalkingdrum.com/tmp.html

Smith, Barbara and Beverly Smith. "The Kitchen Table: A Sister-to-Sister Dialogue." In *This Bridge Called My Back: Writings by Radical Women of Color*, 1st edition. Eds. Cherrie Moraga and Gloria Anzaldua, Kitchen Table/Women of Color Press, 1981. Web. Retrieved 28 April 2014. http://queertheories.files.wordpress.com/2012/01/smith-and-smith-across-the-kitchen-table.pdf

Spillers, Hortense. "Mama's Baby, Papa's Maybe." *Diacritics*, 17.2 (1987): 64–81. Web. Retrieved 25 April 2014. http://web.calstatela.edu/faculty/jgarret/texts/spillers.pdf

Truth, Sojourner. "It Is Often Darkest Just before Dawn." Excerpt from *The Narrative of Sojourner Truth* (1850). Ed. Olive Gilbert. Web. Retrieved 25 April 2014. http://digital.library.upenn.edu/women/truth/1850/1850-17.html

Williams, Delores. "Social-Role Surrogacy: Naming Black Women's Oppression." In *Sisters in the Wilderness*. Ed. D. Williams. New York: Orbis Books, 1993.

Section 6: Discussion Questions

1. What devices have race women and Black feminists used against being "silenced" to resist the depiction of their speech as marginal, divisive, or incendiary?

2. Map the development of Black feminist rhetoric from the nineteenth through twenty-first centuries to counter censorship and shaming; to what degree has this body of rhetoric employed spirituality or idealism to overcome marginalization?

3. How does Black feminist rhetoric implicitly and explicitly position capitalism, socialism, and communism in its critiques of sexism/homophobia and racism/White supremacy?

4. What definitional norms have been established in and by Black feminist rhetoric to critique White racism, racial supremacy, and colorism, and have they been utilized or appropriated in the political rhetoric of other groups/movements?

5. How are the erotic and the sexual displayed or cloistered in Black feminist rhetoric and writing; what strategies are used to address fetishism?

6. Cite Black feminist rhetoric's insights concerning multilayered, pervasive violence and violation in state/structural, social, and intimate/personal arenas; how do these insights treat analytical and emotional intelligence?

7. Tracing the arc of Black feminist and race women rhetoric, where do intergenerational perspectives converge and diverge; are ideological diversity and elitism coherent and fixed formations through the decades/centuries?

7

MOTIONS OF MANHOOD

Edited and with an introduction by Vershawn Ashanti Young

———◦○◦○◦———

Tell us what it is to be a woman so that we may know what it is to be a man.
—from Toni Morrison's Nobel Lecture for
the Nobel Prize in Literature in 1993

In the quest for African American rights in America, the question of Black manhood has been quite salient and persistent for Black men. There is a reason for this, and some history too. For too long, the word "man" served (and in some circles, still serves) as an official linguistic stand-in for humankind. (Think here too of the current colloquial use of "you guys" to refer both to men and women.) In this discursive sense, in our patriarchal culture, men have presumptuously, perhaps even arrogantly, chosen the male gender to represent the whole of humankind. Women are implicitly understood as being a part of "mankind," but without an explicit naming that represents their gender. Rhetorically speaking, then, the word man, without the forthright inclusion of the female gender, subjugates women and in everyday language shifts them into a second-class position by sheer terminology.

Now, imagine Black men trying to argue the foregoing point, say, in 1791, when they themselves were not even considered to be fully human; and to the extent that they were considered human, they were legally designated as only three-fifths of a man, while White men were whole, a full five-fifths. On what grounds could Black men have cultivated an argument to the founding fathers and further to the White men of the legislatures that "man" was a limiting term that excluded women? Could it have been that what Black men wanted was themselves to be viewed and treated simply as men; and like White men, to come to represent humankind, including women? It would seem from the vantage point of the twenty-first century that the primary angle for an argument for the equality between Black men and White men would be about race, since they all shared the same gender. However, the racial equality argument has also been unsuccessful in this regard. How so?

Even after the enslavement period, Black men were still not considered to be men. As Marlon Ross explains in his critical assessment of Black manhood in works of literature, during legal segregation Black men encountered "an impossible paradox"—that while the logic of racial difference that began during slavery "insists on black men's natural deficiency as men," during the Jim Crow period, that logic of gender deficiency came also to include the impossible "demands that [Black men] adhere and aspire to the social codes established for the conduct of men" (2004, 2). In other words, there was a requirement for Black men born into Jim Crow to be men on the basis of gender, yet there was a continued denial of male privilege because of their race. And while it is true that legislation later came to render discrimination against color and heritage illegal, there was an entrenchment of the attachment of unjust stigmas and the codification of signifiers of blackness put upon Black male bodies. Therefore, while for both Black and White men the primary task is performing acceptable manhood, for Black men, the problem was and remains how to perform that manhood without ceasing to be Black.

Of course, under Jim Crow Black men had no choice. The racial infrastructure required that they abandon or truncate their performance of manhood publically so as not to threaten that structure. However, one might think that things would be different some sixty or seventy years post–Jim Crow. But not really so. Black men born into desegregation still face an impossible paradox of gender performance: if White men set the standard for mainstream masculinity, then Black men can try to downplay culturally Black characteristics in order to be read as sufficiently male (in a White paradigm); but this puts them at risk of being read as insufficiently Black, even though it is required by Whites. At the same time, within their own culture, more often than not, if Black men do not embrace expressions of blackness, especially those that define Black masculinity, they risk being read as both insufficiently male and insufficiently Black. As a result, readers of rhetorics of manhood must account for the historical and political circumstances and dilemmas when assessing proclamations and enactments of manhood that may seem to be hypermasculine or exaggerated displays of manliness. One way to think of this is as a Black male response to the threat of losing their manhood in a society that prefers to recognize, privilege, and honor only White manhood and White masculinity. This helps us to understand, though certainly not condone, why some Black men prefer to live in sexual closets and why others disparage Black quare men, since Black males' inability to meet the racial norms of White manhood unavoidably attaches tropes of homosexuality to Black masculine performance.

These questions and lines of reasoning are not presented to excuse any misrecognition or exclusion of women or quares at any point in history, regardless of whether that was the custom at the time. To the contrary, the real argument here is that it ought never to have been a custom to disrespect women or gays, but to the large extent that it was/is the custom helps us to understand why among some of the readings on Black manhood, we find a solidarity rhetoric, calling for Black men and women to stand together, such as in the reading on the Million Man March. But the question often is, whose gender agenda is privileged? We also find readings where Black men and women are presented as being sometimes at odds, such as in the excerpt from Wallace's *Black Macho*. The best way to approach these kinds of readings is to find and understand at least two kinds of underlying politics and ideologies that divide Black men, quares, and women: those that exert White patriarchal and linguistic pressure on the race, say, like using man to represent humankind, and those that circulate among Blacks themselves, as a race by, say, accepting the use of man to represent humankind.

All this is to say that no consideration of the rhetoric of manhood can be understood without reflecting on and considering the rhetorics of and from Black women and quares. As the epigraph from Toni Morrison begs, "Tell us what it is to be a woman so that we may know what it is to be a man" (1993). This is a must. So, while it might be that in some of the readings that follow a consideration of women and the lives of quare people is not explicitly discussed, the task of the reader is always to bring the voices of women and quares back into memory and conversation, particularly as we develop and debate viewpoints and perspectives about what it means to be a Black man.

Works Cited

Morrison, Toni. Nobel Lecture. Dec. 7, 1993. Web. Retrieved Dec. 2, 2017. www.nobelprize.org/nobel_prizes/literature/laureates/1993/morrison-lecture.html

Ross, M.B. *Manning the Race: Reforming Black Men in the Jim Crow Era*. New York: NYU Press, 2004.

The Memorial of Thomas Cole Bricklayer, P. B. Mathews, and Mathew Webb Butchers on behalf of themselves & others Free-Men of Colour. To the Honorable David Ramsay Esquire President and to the rest of the Honorable New Members of the Senate of the State of South Carolina.

As noted in the introduction to this section, the rhetoric of African American manhood has always involved an underlying question and a quest. The question is not, what is a Black man? But it is instead, how can a Black man ever be viewed as a legitimate "man" in a society that consistently designs and supports rules and institutions that seek to curtail his rights and privileges as a full citizen, and endeavors to prevent him from acting in all the ways that a White man can? The consequent mission that ensues from this question turns out to be either a futile effort to prove that Black men are the very thing that all should recognize they already are—men; or the impractical effort to convince others that Black men accept a gender status that renders them as "not quite men," men who readily accede to laws and circumstances that attempt to render them as being endowed with a lesser manhood than Whites. This first entry illustrates this historical dilemma and reveals how at least one group of Black men chose to respond to it.

In the following letter that a group of free Black men from South Carolina sent to the General Assembly of the State of South Carolina in 1791, the men are writing to request removal of clauses in laws that prevent them—just because they are Black—from participating in legal and economic transactions. The men are writing in a climate that determined that a Black man is equal to only three-fifths of a White man. This is likely one of the reasons they write that they "do not presume to hope that they shall be put upon an equal footing with free white citizens of the state" ("A Memorial" 1791). This may be considered an example of the rhetorical strategy of racial accommodation, a rhetoric that indicates acceptance of the racist views of Black men while attempting to gain political privileges. This rhetoric is not unusual among Black rhetors. It was also used, for instance, in an earlier writing in 1787 by the enslaved poet Jupiter Hammon in his "Address to the Negroes in the State of New-York," wherein he urges "his brethren" to accommodate to their lives as slaves. Such early rhetoric anticipates the core of Booker T. Washington's famous "Atlanta Compromise" speech of 1895, where he preaches accommodation to the circumstances of segregation. And elements of accommodationist rhetoric can be seen in President Barack Obama's criticism of Black fathers in his Father's Day speech of 2008.

While reading this opening entry, think of the many possible reasons why this reading was selected to begin a consideration of the rhetoric of Black manhood. Consider how the dilemma presented here and the rhetorics of Black manhood develop over the course of the readings and in American rhetorics of manhood and masculinity in general.

A Memorial to the South Carolina Senate

Thomas Cole and Mathew Webb[1]

To the Honorable David Ramsay Esquire President and to the rest of the Honorable New Members of the Senate of the State of South Carolina The Memorial of Thomas Cole Bricklayer P. B. Mathews and Mathew Webb Butchers on behalf of themselves & others Free-Men of Colour. Humbly Sheweth

That in the Enumeration of Free Citizens by the Constitution of the United States for the purpose of Representation of the Southern States in Congress Your Memorialists have been considered under that description as part of the Citizens of this State. Although by the Fourteenth and Twenty-Ninth clauses in an Act of Assembly made in the Year 1740 and intitled an Act for the better Ordering and Governing Negroes and other Slaves in this Province commonly called The Negro Act now in force Your Memorialists are deprived of the Rights and Privileges of Citizens by not having it in their power to give Testimony on Oath in prosecutions on behalf of the State from which cause many Culprits have escaped the punishment due to their atrocious Crimes, nor can they give their Testimony in recovering Debts due to them, or in establishing Agreements made by them within the meaning of the Statutes of Frauds and Perjuries in force in this State except in cases where Persons of Colour are concerned, whereby they are subject to great Losses and repeated Injuries without any means of redress.

That by the said clauses in the said Act, they are debarred of the Rights of Free Citizens by being subject to a Trial without the benefit of a jury and subject to Prosecution by Testimony of Slaves without Oath by which they are placed on the same footing.

Your Memorialists shew that they have at all times since the Independence of the United States contributed and do now contribute to the support of the Government by cheerfully paying their Taxes proportionable to their Property with others who have been during such period, and now are in full enjoyment of the Rights and Immunities of Citizens Inhabitants of a Free Independent State.

That as your Memorialists have been and are considered as Free-Citizens of this State they hope to be treated as such, they are ready and willing to take and subscribe to such Oath of Allegiance to the States as shall be prescribed by this Honorable House, and are also willing to take upon them any duty for the preservation of the Peace in the City or any other occasion if called on.

Your Memorialists do not presume to hope that they shall be put on an equal footing with the Free white citizens of the State in general they only humbly solicit such indulgence as the Wisdom and Humanity of this Honorable House shall dictate in their favor by repealing the clauses the act aforementioned, and substituting such a clause as will efectually Redress the grievances which your Memorialists humbly submit in this their Memorial but under such restrictions as to your Honorable House shall seem proper.

May it therefore please your Honors to take your Memorialists case into tender consideration, and make such Acts or insert such clauses for the purpose of relieving your Memorialists from the unremitted grievance they now Labour under as in your Wisdom shall seem meet.

And as in duty bound your Memorialists will ever pray

Note

1. South Carolina Department of Archives and History, "The Memorial of Thomas Cole Bricklayer, P. B. Mathews, and Mathew Webb Butchers on behalf of themselves & others Free-Men of Colour. To the Honorable David Ramsay Esquire President and to the rest of the Honorable New Members of the Senate of the State of South Carolina," *Records of the General Assembly, Petitions*, 1791, No. 181, www.pbs.org/wgbh/aia/part2/2h70t.html

Harriet A. Jacobs

Harriet Jacobs's autobiography, *Incidents in the Life of a Slave Girl*, is one of the most well known and widely read narratives by an ex-enslaved person. It is excerpted some three times in this reader. It is also often studied and noted for its detailed depiction of the experience of the female who is enslaved. However, in this excerpt, which comes from the fourth chapter of the novel, Jacobs mainly depicts experience of her uncle Benjamin but also highlights the character of her brother William, both of whom she describes as striving to be men in their struggles to gain their freedom. On the night that Benjamin tells Jacobs that he intends to escape, she reports, "I implored him not to go, but he paid no heed to my words. He said he was no longer a boy, and every day made his yoke more galling." The chapter ends with a statement that expresses how slavery contradicts and goes against manhood for all, men as well as women. After learning that Benjamin's escape was a success, and after learning that her grandmother has successfully purchased the freedom of Jacobs's uncle, Philip, they all share in the sentiment that closes the chapter: "He that is willing to be a slave, let him be a slave."

Jacobs's depiction of Benjamin is reminiscent, although certainly different from, Frederick Douglass's well-known self-depiction of an enslaved male first wresting his manhood from the psychological and emotional clutches of slavery by physically overpowering his master, and later seizing his physical freedom by escaping into freedom. Benjamin's narrative should be read within the constellation of enslaved male experiences that Jacobs provides. For instance, Jacobs also describes the desires of her brother William to be free, although he arguably occupies a better position than other slaves since he works in the house. Jacobs also examines in implicit details the sexual exploitation of male slaves by their male master, when describing the experience of Luke, who is chained, unclothed, to his master's bedpost (see McCune's entries in the queer section). In the excerpt that follows, however, Jacobs focuses on the fierce determination of an enslaved man to cultivate manhood, a feeling of mind, spirit, and heart that is greatly diminished by physical bondage.

Incidents in the Life of a Slave Girl Written by Herself

Harriet A. Jacobs[1]

One afternoon I sat at my sewing, feeling unusual depression of spirits. My mistress had been accusing me of an offence, of which I assured her I was perfectly innocent; but I saw, by the contemptuous curl of her lip, that she believed I was telling a lie.

I wondered for what wise purpose God was leading me through such thorny paths, and whether still darker days were in store for me. As I sat musing thus, the door opened softly, and William came in. "Well, brother," said I, "what is the matter this time?"

"O Linda, Ben and his master have had a dreadful time!" said he.

My first thought was that Benjamin was killed. "Don't be frightened, Linda," said William; "I will tell you all about it."

It appeared that Benjamin's master had sent for him, and he did not immediately obey the summons. When he did, his master was angry, and began to whip him. He resisted. Master and slave fought, and finally the master was thrown. Benjamin had cause to tremble; for he had thrown to the ground his master—one of the richest men in town. I anxiously awaited the result.

That night I stole to my grandmother's house, and Benjamin also stole thither from his master's. My grandmother had gone to spend a day or two with an old friend living in the country.

"I have come," said Benjamin, "to tell you good by. I am going away."

I inquired where.

"To the north," he replied.

I looked at him to see whether he was in earnest. I saw it all in his firm, set mouth. I implored him not to go, but he paid no heed to my words. He said he was no longer a boy, and every day made his yoke more galling. He had raised his hand against his master, and was to be publicly whipped for the offence. I reminded him of the poverty and hardships he must encounter among strangers. I told him he might be caught and brought back; and that was terrible to think of.

He grew vexed, and asked if poverty and hardships with freedom, were not preferable to our treatment in slavery. "Linda," he continued, "we are dogs here; foot-balls, cattle, every thing that's mean. No, I will not stay. Let them bring me back. We don't die but once."

He was right; but it was hard to give him up. "Go," said I, "and break your mother's heart."

I repented of my words ere they were out.

"Linda," said he, speaking as I had not heard him speak that evening, "how *could* you say that? Poor mother! be kind to her, Linda; and you, too, cousin Fanny."

Cousin Fanny was a friend who had lived some years with us.

Farewells were exchanged, and the bright, kind boy, endeared to us by so many acts of love, vanished from our sight.

It is not necessary to state how he made his escape. Suffice it to say, he was on his way to New York when a violent storm overtook the vessel. The captain said he must put into the nearest port. This alarmed Benjamin, who was aware that he would be advertised in every port near his own town. His embarrassment was noticed by the captain. To port they went. There the advertisement met the captain's eye. Benjamin so exactly answered its description, that the captain laid hold on him, and bound him in chains. The storm passed, and they proceeded to New York. Before reaching that port Benjamin managed to get off his chains and throw them overboard. He escaped from the vessel, but was pursued, captured, and carried back to his master.

When my grandmother returned home and found her youngest child had fled, great was her sorrow; but, with characteristic piety, she said, "God's will be done." Each morning, she inquired if any news had been heard from her boy. Yes, news *was* heard. The master was rejoicing over a letter, announcing the capture of his human chattel.

That day seems but as yesterday, so well do I remember it. I saw him led through the streets in chains, to jail. His face was ghastly pale, yet full of determination. He had begged one of the sailors to go to his mother's house and ask her not to meet him. He said the sight of her distress would take from him all self-control. She yearned to see him, and she went; but she screened herself in the crowd, that it might be as her child had said.

We were not allowed to visit him; but we had known the jailer for years, and he was a kind-hearted man. At midnight he opened the jail door for my grandmother and myself to enter, in disguise. When we entered the cell not a sound broke the stillness. "Benjamin, Benjamin!" whispered my grandmother. No answer. "Benjamin!" she again faltered. There was a jingle of chains. The moon had just risen, and cast an uncertain light through the bars of the window. We knelt down and took Benjamin's cold hands in ours. We did not speak. Sobs were heard, and Benjamin's lips were unsealed; for his mother was weeping on his neck. How vividly does memory bring back that sad night! Mother and son talked together. He asked her pardon for the suffering he had caused her. She said she had nothing to forgive; she could not blame his desire for freedom. He told her that when he was captured, he broke away, and was about casting himself into the river, when thoughts of *her* came over him, and he desisted. She asked if he did not also think of God. I fancied I saw his face grow fierce in the moonlight. He answered, "No, I did not think of him. When a man is hunted like a wild beast he forgets there is a God, a heaven. He forgets every thing in his struggle to get beyond the reach of the bloodhounds."

"Don't talk so, Benjamin," said she. "Put your trust in God. Be humble, my child, and your master will forgive you."

"Forgive me for *what*, mother? For not letting him treat me like a dog? No! I will never humble myself to him. I have worked for him for nothing all my life, and I am repaid with stripes and imprisonment. Here I will stay till I die, or till he sells me."

The poor mother shuddered at his words. I think he felt it; for when he next spoke, his voice was calmer. "Don't fret about me, mother. I ain't worth it," said he. "I wish I had some of your goodness. You bear every thing patiently, just as though you thought it was all right. I wish I could."

She told him she had not always been so; once, she was like him; but when sore troubles came upon her, and she had no arm to lean upon, she learned to call on God, and he lightened her burdens. She besought him to do likewise.

We overstaid our time, and were obliged to hurry from the jail.

Benjamin had been imprisoned three weeks, when my grandmother went to intercede for him with his master. He was immovable. He said Benjamin should serve as an example to the rest of his slaves; he should be kept in jail till he was subdued, or be sold if he got but one dollar for him. However, he afterwards relented in some degree. The chains were taken off, and we were allowed to visit him.

As his food was of the coarsest kind, we carried him as often as possible a warm supper, accompanied with some little luxury for the jailer.

Three months elapsed, and there was no prospect of release or of a purchaser. One day he was heard to sing and laugh. This piece of indecorum was told to his master, and the overseer was ordered to re-chain him. He was now confined in an apartment with other prisoners, who were covered with filthy rags. Benjamin was chained near them, and was soon covered with vermin. He worked at his chains till he succeeded in getting out of them. He passed them through the bars of the window, with a request that they should be taken to his master, and he should be informed that he was covered with vermin.

This audacity was punished with heavier chains, and prohibition of our visits.

My grandmother continued to send him fresh changes of clothes. The old ones were burned up. The last night we saw him in jail his mother still begged him to send for his master, and beg his pardon. Neither persuasion nor argument could turn him from his purpose. He calmly answered, "I am waiting his time."

Those chains were mournful to hear.

Another three months passed, and Benjamin left his prison walls. We that loved him waited to bid him a long and last farewell. A slave trader had bought him. You remember, I told you what price he brought when ten years of age. Now he was more than twenty years old, and sold for three hundred dollars. The master had been blind to his own interest. Long confinement had made his face too pale, his form too thin; moreover, the trader had heard something of his character, and it did not strike him as suitable for a slave. He said he would give any price if the handsome lad was a girl. We thanked God that he was not.

Could you have seen that mother clinging to her child, when they fastened the irons upon his wrists; could you have heard her heartrending groans, and seen her bloodshot eyes wander wildly from face to face, vainly pleading for mercy; could you have witnessed that scene as I saw it, you would exclaim, *Slavery is damnable!*

Benjamin, her youngest, her pet, was forever gone! She could not realize it. She had had an interview with the trader for the purpose of ascertaining if Benjamin could be purchased. She was told it was impossible, as he had given bonds not to sell him till he was out of the state. He promised that he would not sell him till he reached New Orleans.

With a strong arm and unvaried trust, my grandmother began her work of love. Benjamin must be free. If she succeeded, she knew they would still be separated; but the sacrifice was not too great. Day and night she labored. The trader's price would treble that he gave; but she was not discouraged.

She employed a lawyer to write to a gentleman, whom she knew, in New Orleans. She begged him to interest himself for Benjamin, and he willingly favored her request. When he saw Benjamin, and stated his business, he thanked him; but said he preferred to wait a while before making the trader an offer. He knew he had tried to obtain a high price for him, and had invariably failed. This encouraged him to make another effort for freedom. So one morning, long before day, Benjamin was missing. He was riding over the blue billows, bound for Baltimore.

For once his white face did him a kindly service. They had no suspicion that it belonged to a slave; otherwise, the law would have been followed out to the letter, and the *thing* rendered back to slavery. The brightest skies are often overshadowed by the darkest clouds. Benjamin was taken sick, and compelled to remain in Baltimore three weeks. His strength was slow in returning; and his desire to continue his journey seemed to retard his recovery. How could he get strength without air and exercise? He resolved to venture on a short walk. A by-street was selected, where he thought himself secure of not being met by any one that knew him; but a voice called out, "Halloo, Ben, my boy! what are you doing *here?*"

His first impulse was to run; but his legs trembled so that he could not stir. He turned to confront his antagonist, and behold, there stood his old master's next door neighbor! He thought it was all over with him now; but it proved otherwise. That man was a miracle. He possessed a goodly number of slaves, and yet was not quite deaf to that mystic clock, whose ticking is rarely heard in the slaveholder's breast.

"Ben, you are sick," said he. "Why, you look like a ghost. I guess I gave you something of a start. Never mind, Ben, I am not going to touch you. You had a pretty tough time of it, and you may go on your way rejoicing for all me. But I would advise you to get out of this place plaguy quick, for there are several gentlemen here from our town." He described the nearest and safest route to New York, and added, "I shall be glad to tell your mother I have seen you. Good by, Ben."

Benjamin turned away, filled with gratitude, and surprised that the town he hated contained such a gem—a gem worthy of a purer setting.

This gentleman was a Northerner by birth, and had married a southern lady. On his return, he told my grandmother that he had seen her son, and of the service he had rendered him.

Benjamin reached New York safely, and concluded to stop there until he had gained strength enough to proceed further. It happened that my grandmother's only remaining son had sailed for the same city on business for his mistress. Through God's providence, the brothers met. You may be sure it was a happy meeting. "O Phil," exclaimed Benjamin, "I am here at last." Then he told him how near he came to dying, almost in sight of free land, and how he prayed that he might live to get one breath of free air. He said life was worth something now, and it would be hard to die. In the old jail he had not valued it; once, he was tempted to destroy it; but something, he did not know what, had prevented him; perhaps it was fear. He had heard those who profess to be religious declare there was no heaven for self-murderers; and as his life had been pretty hot here, he did not desire a continuation of the same in another world. "If I die now," he exclaimed, "thank God, I shall die a freeman!"

He begged my uncle Phillip not to return south; but stay and work with him, till they earned enough to buy those at home. His brother told him it would kill their mother if he deserted her in her trouble. She had pledged her house, and with difficulty had raised money to buy him. Would he be bought?

"No, never!" he replied. "Do you suppose, Phil, when I have got so far out of their clutches, I will give them one red cent? No! And do you suppose I would turn mother out of her home in her old age? That I would let her pay all those hard-earned dollars for me, and never to see me? For you know she will stay south as long as her other children are slaves. What a good mother! Tell her to buy *you*, Phil. You have been a comfort to her, and I have been a trouble. And Linda, poor Linda; what'll become of her? Phil, you don't know what a life they lead her. She has told me something about it, and I wish old Flint was dead, or a better man. When I was in jail, he asked her if she didn't want *him* to ask my master to forgive me, and take me home again. She told him, No; that I didn't want to go back. He got mad, and said we were all alike. I never despised my own master half as much as I do that man. There is many a worse slaveholder than my master; but for all that I would not be his slave."

While Benjamin was sick, he had parted with nearly all his clothes to pay necessary expenses. But he did not part with a little pin I fastened in his bosom when we parted. It was the most valuable thing I owned, and I thought none more worthy to wear it. He had it still.

His brother furnished him with clothes, and gave him what money he had.

They parted with moistened eyes; and as Benjamin turned away, he said, "Phil, I part with all my kindred." And so it proved. We never heard from him again.

Uncle Phillip came home; and the first words he uttered when he entered the house were, "Mother, Ben is free! I have seen him in New York." She stood looking at him with a bewildered air. "Mother, don't you believe it?" he said, laying his hand softly upon her shoulder. She raised her hands, and exclaimed, "God be praised! Let us thank him." She dropped on her knees, and poured forth her heart in prayer. Then Phillip must sit down and repeat to her every word Benjamin had said. He told her all; only he forbore to mention how sick and pale her darling looked. Why should he distress her when she could do him no good?

The brave old woman still toiled on, hoping to rescue some of her other children. After a while she succeeded in buying Phillip. She paid eight hundred dollars, and came home with the precious document that secured his freedom. The happy mother and son sat together by the old hearthstone that night, telling how proud they were of each other, and how they would prove to the world that they could take care of themselves, as they had long taken care of others. We all concluded by saying, "He that is *willing* to be a slave, let him be a slave."

Note

1. Harriet A. Jacobs, "The Slave Who Dared to Feel Like a Man," in *Incidents in the Life of a Slave Girl* (New York, NY: Oxford University Press, 1988 [1861]).

William Wells Brown

Williams Wells Brown, a formerly enslaved man who escaped to freedom as a young adult, is known for a pair of rhetorical firsts, among other notable works. He is considered to be the first African American to publish a novel and a play. His novel, *Clotel, or, The President's Daughter: a Narrative of Slave Life in the United States*, was published in London in 1853 and is the fictional account of two daughters of Thomas Jefferson by his long-time mistress and slave concubine, Sally Hemmings. With this novel, Brown sought to challenge the contradictory and deleterious views that Jefferson propounded about Black humanity, slavery, and abolition. Brown read his play, *The Escape; or, A Leap for Freedom* (1858), aloud at abolitionist meetings. His oral reading was an early form of performance-rhetoric that dramatized the escape of those enslaved. By read-ing his play aloud at abolitionist meetings, Brown placed performance-rhetoric on par with the lecture, the typical form of abolitionist public address. The selection ahead is from one of Brown's lesser-known but nonetheless important works, a historical compilation of notable Blacks titled *The Black Man: His Antecedents, His Genius, and His Achievements* (1863). While the book is a series of profiles of well-known Black people, both men and women, such as Phillis Wheatley, Benjamin Banneker, Frederick Douglas, and Frances Ellen Watkins Harper, Brown sought to rep-resent the lives and voices of all sorts of brave Blacks, even including a write-up on Nat Turner, an enslaved man who was considered a prophet. Turner led a rebellion that led to the deaths of many Whites, and, as a result, Turner was not only killed but also vilified and considered notorious in the rhetoric of Whites slaveholders and legislators. The selection that follows is a refashioning of Brown's own personal narrative into a short story that could speak for and represent lesser-known others. The story is titled "A Man Without a Name," which indicates Brown's interest in present-ing a perspective about Black manhood that highlights the everyday bravery and moral disposition of Black men.

A Man Without a Name

William Wells Brown[1]

It was in the month of December, 1852, while Colonel Rice and family were seated around a bright wood fire, whose blaze lighted up the large dining room in their old mansion, situ-ated ten miles from Dayton, in the State of Ohio, that they heard a knock at the door, which was answered by the familiar "Come in" that always greets the stranger in the Western States. Squire Loomis walked in and took a seat on one of the three rocking-chairs, which had been made vacant by the young folks, who rose to give place to their highly influential and wealthy neighbor. It was a beautiful night; the sky was clear, the wind had hushed its deep moanings, the most brilliant of the starry throng stood out in bold relief, despite the superior light of the moon. "I see some one standing at the gate," said Mrs. Rice, as she left the window and came nearer the fire. "I'll go out and see who it is," exclaimed George, as he quitted his chair and started for the door. The latter soon returned and whispered to his father, and both left the room, evincing that something unusual was at hand. Not many minutes elapsed, however, before the father and son entered, accompanied by a young man, whose complexion showed plainly that other than Anglo-Saxon blood coursed through his veins. The whole company rose, and the stranger was invited to draw near to the fire. Question after question was now pressed upon the new-comer by the colonel and the squire, but without eliciting satisfactory replies.

"You need not be afraid, my friend," said the host, as he looked intently in the colored man's face, "to tell where you are from and to what place you are going. If you are a fugitive, as I sus-pect, give us your story, and we will protect and defend you to the last."

Taking courage from these kind remarks, the mulatto said, "I was born, sir, in the State of Kentucky, and raised in Missouri. My master was my father; my mother was his slave. That, sir, accounts for the fairness of my complexion. As soon as I was old enough to labor I was taken into my master's dwelling as a servant, to attend upon the family. My mistress, aware of my near relationship to her husband, felt humiliated, and often in her anger would punish me severely for no cause whatever. My near approach to the Anglo-Saxon aroused the jealousy and hatred of the overseer, and he flogged me, as he said, to make me know my place. My fellow-slaves hated me because I was whiter than themselves. Thus my complexion was construed into a crime, and I was made to curse my father for the Anglo-Saxon blood that courses through my veins.

"My master raised slaves to supply the southern market, and every year some of my companions were sold to the slave-traders and taken farther south. Husbands were separated from their wives, and children torn from the arms of their agonizing mothers. These outrages were committed by the man whom nature compelled me to look upon as my father. My mother and brothers were sold and taken away from me; still I bore all, and made no attempt to escape, for I yet had near me an only sister, whom I dearly loved. At last, the negro driver attempted to rob my sister of her virtue. She appealed to me for protection. Her innocence, beauty, and tears were enough to stir the stoutest heart. My own, filled with grief and indignation, swelled within me as though it would burst or leap from my bosom. My tears refused to flow: the fever in my brain dried them up. I could stand it no longer. I seized the wretch by the throat, and hurled him to the ground; and with this strong arm I paid him for old and new. The next day I was tried by a jury of slaveholders for the crime of having within me the heart of a man, and protecting my sister from the licentious embrace of a libertine. And—would you believe it, sir?—that jury of enlightened Americans,—yes, sir, Christian Americans,—after *grave* deliberation, decided that I had broken the laws, and sentenced me to receive five hundred lashes upon my bare back. But, sir, I escaped from them the night before I was to have been flogged.

"Afraid of being arrested and taken back, I remained the following day hid away in a secluded spot on the banks of the Mississippi River, protected from the gaze of man by the large trees and thick cane-brakes that sheltered me. I waited for the coming of another night. All was silence around me, save the sweet chant of the feathered songsters in the forest, or the musical ripple of the eddying waters at my feet. I watched the majestic bluffs as they gradually faded away, through the gray twilight, from the face of day into the darker shades of night. I then turned to the rising moon as it peered above, ascending the deep blue ether, high in the heavens, casting its mellow rays over the surrounding landscape, and gilding the smooth surface of the noble river with its silvery hue. I viewed with interest the stars as they appeared, one after another, in the firmament. It was then and there that I studied nature in its lonely grandeur, and saw in it the goodness of God, and felt that He who created so much beauty, and permitted the fowls of the air and the beasts of the field to roam at large and be free, never intended that man should be the slave of his fellow-man. I resolved that I would be a bondman no longer; and, taking for my guide the *north star*, I started for Canada, the negro's land of liberty. For many weeks I travelled by night, and lay by during came to live with him, and as I was a house servant, and the young master and I would, at times, get confused in the same name, orders were given for me to change mine. From that moment, I resolved that, as slavery had robbed me of my liberty and my name, I would not attempt to have another till I was free. So, sir, for once you have a man standing before you without a name."

Note

1. William Wells Brown, "A Man Without a Name," in *The Black Man: His Antecedents, His Genius, and His Achievements* (New York, NY: Arno Press, 1969 [1863]).

W.E.B. Du Bois

William Edward Burghardt Du Bois (pronounce du' boyz), known as "W.E.B." Du Bois, was a writer, sociologist, and civil rights activist. He is best known for being the first African American to receive a PhD from Harvard in 1895 and also for his searing assessment of African American history, rhetoric, and culture in his *Souls of Black Folks* (1903). The selection that follows is the oration that Du Bois was elected to give at his undergraduate graduation from Harvard in 1890. This speech reveals Du Bois's early acquiescence to ideas that held that Black men could be tutored into full manhood by the help of White men. He chose to use Jefferson Davis, a champion of slavery and the first and only president of the Confederate States of America, as a representative of the Teutonic Strong Man that would assist the submissive Black man to develop in society. Considering his audience, one might wonder if he was being so acquiescent to racist ideas of Black manhood in order not to offend those who tacitly held such views but did not want to acknowledge them. Whatever the case, it must be noted that Du Bois roundly rejected this view of Black manhood in the *Souls of Black Folk*, wherein he criticizes the accommodationist rhetoric of Booker T. Washington. He goes on in the book to more strongly reject the necessity of Black men being submissive to White men by developing a radical, even angry, educated Black man in the character of John Jones, who decides that death is better than tacit submission to a racist order. The short story that profiles John Jones is called "On the Coming of John" and is listed in further readings. But it is recommended that this story be considered along with this oration for a understanding of the dimensions, or what the title of this section calls "motions," of the rhetoric of manhood, and how such motions can develop and change over time by the same rhetor.

Jefferson Davis as a Representative of Civilization

W.E.B. Du Bois[1]

Jefferson Davis was a typical Teutonic hero; the history of civilization during the last millenium has been the development of the idea of the Strong Man of which he was the embodiment. The Anglo-Saxon loves a soldier—Jefferson Davis was a soldier. There was not a phase in that familiarly strange life that would not have graced a medieaval romance: from the fiery and impetuous young lieutenant who stole as his bride the daughter of a ruler-elect of the land, to the cool and ambitious politician in the Senate ball. So boldly and surely did that cadaverous figure with the thin nervous lips and flashing eye, write the first line of the new page of American history, that the historian of the future must ever see back of the war of Secession, the strong arm of one imperious man, who defied desease trampled on precedent, would not be defeated, and never surrendered. A soldier and a lover, a statesman and a ruler; passionate, ambitious and indomitable; bold reckless guardian of a peoples' All—judged by the whole standard of Teutonic civilization, there is something noble in the figure of Jefferson Davis; and judged by every canon of human justice, there is something fundamentally incomplete about that standard.

I wish to consider not the man, but the type of civilization which his life represented: its foundation is the idea of the strong man—Individualism coupled with the rule of might—and it is this idea that has made the logic of even modern history the cool logic of the Club. It made a naturally brave and generous man Jefferson Davis—now advancing civilization by murdering Indians, now hero of a national disgrace called by courtesy, the Mexican War and finally, as the crowning absurdity, the peculiar champion of a people fighting to be free in order that another people should not be free. Whenever this idea has for a moment escaped from the individual realm, it has found an even more secure foothold in the policy and philosophy of the State. The Strong Man and his mighty Right Arm has become the Strong Nation with its armies. Under whatever guise, however a Jefferson Davis may appear as man, as race, or as nation, his life can only logically mean this: the advance of a part of the world at the expence of the whole: the overweening sense of the and the consequent forgetting of the Thou. It has thus happened, that advance in civilization has always been handicapped by shortsighted national selfishness. The vital principle of division of labor has not only stiffled in industry, but also in civilization; so as to render it well nigh impossible for a new race to introduce a new idea into the world except by means of the cudgel. To say that a nation is in the way of civilization is a contradiction in terms, and a system of human culture whose principle is the rise of one race on the ruins of another is a farce and a lie. Yet this is the type of civilization which Jefferson Davis represented: it represents a field for stalwart manhood and heroic character, and at the same time for moral obtuseness and refined brutality. These striking contradictions of character always arise when a people seemingly become convinced that the object of the world is not civilization, but Teutonic civilization. Such a type is not wholly evil or fruitless: the world has needed and will need its Jefferson Davises; but such a type is incomplete and never can serve its best purpose untill checked by its complementary ideas. Whence shall these come?

To the most casual observer, it must have occurred that the Rod of Empire has in these days, turned towards the South. In every Southern country, however, destined to play a future part in the world—in Southern North America, South America, Australia, and Africa a new nation has a more or less firm foothold. This circumstance has, however, attracted but incidental notice, hitherto; for wherever the Negro people have touched civilization their rise has been singularly unromantic and unscientific. Through the glamor of history, the rise of a nation has ever been typified by the Strong Man crushing out an effete civilization. That brutality buried aught else beside Rome when it decended goldened haired and drunk from the blue north has scarcely entered human imagination. Not as the muscular warrior came the Negro, but as the cringing slave. The Teutonic met civilization and crushed it—the Negro met civilization and was crushed by it. The one was the hero the world has ever worshipped, who gained unthought of triumphs and made unthought of mistakes; the other was the personification of dogged patience bending to the inevitable, and waiting. In the history of this people, we seek in vain the elements of Teutonic deification of Self, and Roman brute force, but we do find an idea of submission apart from cowardice, laziness or stupidity, such as the world never saw before. This is the race which by its very presence must play a part in the world of tomorrow; and this is the race whose rise, I contend, has practically illustrated an idea which is at once the check and complement of the Teutonic Strong Man. It is the doctrine of the Submissive Man—given to the world by strange coincidence, by the race of whose rights, Jefferson Davis had not heard.

What then is the change made in the conception of civilization, by adding to the idea of the Strong Man, that of the Submissive Man? It is this: the submission of the strength of the Strong to the advance of all—not in mere aimless sacrifice, but recognizing the fact that, "To no one type of mind is it given to discern the totality of Truth," that civilization cannot afford to lose the contribution of the very least of nations for its full developement: that not only the assertion of the I, but also to the submission to the Thou is the highest Individualism.

The Teuton stands today as the champion of the idea of Personal Assertion: the Negro as the peculiar embodiment of the idea of Personal Submission: either, alone, tends to an abnormal developement—towards Despotism on the one hand which the world has just cause to fear, and yet covertly admires, or towards slavery on the other which the world despises and which, yet is not wholly despicable. No matter how great and striking the Teutonic type of impetuous manhood may be, it must receive the cool purposeful "Ich Dien" of the African for its round and full developement. In the rise of Negro people and development of this idea, you whose nation was founded on the loftiest ideals, and who many times forgot those ideals with a strange forgetfulness, have more than a sentimental duty. You owe a debt to humanity for this Ethiopia of the Out-stretched Arm, who has made her beauty, patience, and her grandeur, law.

Note

1. W.E.B. Du Bois, "Jefferson Davis as a Representative of Civilization," in *Commencement Parts* (Cambridge, MA, 1890).

Charles W. Chesnutt

"The Doll," written by novelist and story writer Charles Chesnutt (1858–1932), was submitted to *The Atlantic Monthly* in 1904. However, it was rejected, likely for being too racially provocative, and would not be published until 1912, by W.E.B. Du Bois, editor of *The Crisis*, the official journal of the NAACP. Because of the interval between the writing and publication of the story, many fail to see the rhetorical response to manhood that Chesnutt offers to Du Bois's widely read fictional profile of John Jones in "On the Coming of John," the penultimate chapter in Du Bois's *The Souls of Black Folk* (1903). Du Bois presents John Jones as the educated Black youth who becomes radicalized after becoming aware of and experiencing unrelenting racial prejudice. "The Doll" also presents the dilemma of a brother whose sister is apparently assaulted by a White man. What's more, when the father of the brother and sister confronts the assailant's family, the father is killed. When the man who killed his father comes years later to the shop where the protagonist, Tom Taylor, is now barber and owner, and chides him about the history, Chesnutt chooses to present an alternative performance of Black manhood other than the radical self-justice of Du Bois's John. Tom Taylor shows restraint, caution, and perhaps forgiveness as qualities of Black manhood, qualities that Chesnutt seems to suggest are possible antidotes to even the most virulent and violent race prejudice.

The Doll

Charles W. Chesnutt[1]

When Tom Taylor, proprietor of the Wyandot Hotel barber shop, was leaving home, after his noonday luncheon, to return to his work, his daughter, a sprightly, diminutive brown maid, with very bright black eyes and very curly, black hair, thrust into his coat pocket a little jointed doll somewhat the worse for wear.

"Now, don't forget, papa," she said, in her shrill childish treble, "what's to be done to her. Her arms won't work, and her legs won't work, and she can't hold her head up. Be sure and have her mended this afternoon, and bring her home when you come to supper; for she's afraid of the dark, and always sleeps with me. I'll meet you at the corner at half-past six—and don't forget, whatever you do."

"No, Daisy, I'll not forget," he replied, as he lifted her to the level of his lips and kissed her.

Upon reaching the shop he removed the doll from his pocket and hung it on one of the gilded spikes projecting above the wire netting surrounding the cashier's desk, where it would catch his eye. Some time during the afternoon he would send it to a toy shop around the corner for repairs. But the day was a busy one, and when the afternoon was well advanced he had not yet attended to it.

Colonel Forsyth had come up from the South to attend a conference of Democratic leaders to consider presidential candidates and platforms. He had put up at the Wyandot Hotel, but had been mainly in the hands of Judge Beeman, chairman of the local Jackson club, who was charged with the duty of seeing that the colonel was made comfortable and given the freedom of the city. It was after a committee meeting, and about 4 in the afternoon, that the two together entered the lobby of the Wyandot. They were discussing the platforms to be put forward by the two great parties in the approaching campaign.

"I reckon, judge," the colonel was saying, "that the Republican party will make a mistake if it injects the Negro question into its platform. The question is primarily a local one, and if the North will only be considerate about the matter, and let us alone, we can settle it to our entire satisfaction. The Negro's place is defined by nature, and in the South he knows it and gives us no trouble."

"The Northern Negroes are different," returned the judge.

"They are just the same," rejoined the colonel. "It is you who are different. You pamper them and they take liberties with you. But they are all from the South, and when they meet a Southerner they act accordingly. They are born to serve and to submit. If they had been worthy of equality they would never have endured slavery. They have no proper self-respect; they will neither resent an insult, nor defend a right, nor avenge a wrong."

"Well, now, colonel, aren't you rather hard on them? Consider their past."

"Hard? Why, no, bless your heart! I've got nothing against the nigger. I like him—in his place. But what I say is the truth. Are you in a hurry?"

"Not at all."

"Then come downstairs to the barber shop and I'll prove what I say."

The shop was the handsomest barber shop in the city. It was in the basement, and the paneled ceiling glowed with electric lights. The floor was of white tile, the walls lined with large mirrors. Behind ten chairs, of the latest and most comfortable design, stood as many colored barbers, in immaculate white jackets, each at work upon a white patron. An air of discipline and good order pervaded the establishment. There was no loud talking by patrons, no unseemly garrulity on the part of the barbers. It was very obviously a well-conducted barber shop, frequented by gentlemen who could afford to pay liberally for superior service. As the judge and the colonel entered a customer vacated the chair served by the proprietor.

"Next gentleman," said the barber.

The colonel removed his collar and took his seat in the vacant chair, remarking, as he ran his hand over his neck, "I want a close shave, barber."

"Yes, sir; a close shave."

The barber was apparently about forty, with a brown complexion, cleancut features and curly hair. Committed by circumstances to a career of personal service, he had lifted it by intelligence, tact and industry to the dignity of a successful business. The judge, a regular patron of the shop, knew him well and had often, while in his chair, conversed with him concerning his race—a fruitful theme, much on the public tongue.

"As I was saying," said the colonel, while the barber adjusted a towel about his neck, "the Negro question is a perfectly simple one."

The judge thought it hardly good taste in the colonel to continue in his former strain. Northern men might speak slightingly of the Negro, but seldom in his presence. He tried a little diversion.

"The tariff," he observed, "is a difficult problem."

"Much more complicated, suh, than the Negro problem, which is perfectly simple. Let the white man once impress the Negro with his superiority; let the Negro see that there is no escape from the inevitable, and that ends it. The best thing about the Negro is that, with all his limitations, he can recognize a finality. It is the secret of his persistence among us. He has acquired the faculty of evolution, suh—by the law of the survival of the fittest. Long ago, when a young man, I killed a nigger to teach him his place. One who learns a lesson of that sort certainly never offends again, nor fathers any others of his breed."

The barber, having lathered the colonel's face, was stropping his razor with long, steady strokes. Every word uttered by the colonel was perfectly audible to him, but his impassive countenance betrayed no interest. The colonel seemed as unconscious of the barber's presence as the barber of the colonel's utterance. Surely, thought the judge, if such freedom of speech were the rule in the South the colonel's contention must be correct, and the Negroes thoroughly cowed. To a Northern man the situation was hardly comfortable.

"The iron and sugar interests of the South," persisted the judge, "will resist any reduction of the tariff."

The colonel was not to be swerved from the subject, nor from his purpose, whatever it might be.

"Quite likely they will; and we must argue with them, for they are white men and amenable to reason. The nigger, on the other hand, is the creature of instinct; you cannot argue with him; you must order him, and if he resists shoot him, as I did.

"Don't forget, barber," said the colonel, "that I want a close shave."

"No, sir," responded the barber, who, having sharpened his razor, now began to pass it, with firm and even hand, over the colonel's cheek.

"It must have been," said the judge, "an aggravated case, to justify so extreme a step."

"Extreme, suh? I beg yo' pardon, suh, but I can't say I had regarded my conduct in that light. But it was an extreme case so far as the nigger was concerned. I am not boasting about my course; it was simply a disagreeable necessity. I am naturally a kind-hearted man, and don't like to kill even a fly. It was after the war, suh, and just as the reconstruction period was drawing to a close. My mother employed a Negro girl, the child of a former servant of hers, to wait upon her."

The barber was studying the colonel's face as the razor passed over his cheek. The colonel's eyes were closed, or he might have observed the sudden gleam of interest that broke through the barber's mask of self-effacement, like a flash of lightning from a clouded sky. Involuntarily the razor remained poised in midair, but, in less time than it takes to say it, was moving again, swiftly and smoothly, over the colonel's face. To shave a talking man required a high degree of skill, but they were both adepts, each in his own trade—the barber at shaving, the colonel at talking.

"The girl was guilty of some misconduct, and my mother reprimanded her and sent her home. She complained to her father, and he came to see my mother about it. He was insolent, offensive and threatening. I came into the room and ordered him to leave it. Instead of obeying, he turned on me in a rage, suh, and threatened me. I drew my revolver and shot him. The result was unfortunate; but he and his people learned a lesson. We had no further trouble with bumptious niggers in our town."

"And did you have no trouble in the matter?" asked the judge.

"None, suh, to speak of. There were proceedings, but they were the merest formality. Upon my statement, confirmed by that of my mother, I was discharged by the examining magistrate, and the case was never even reported to the grand jury. It was a clear case of self-defense."

The barber had heard the same story, with some details ignored or forgotten by the colonel. It was the barber's father who had died at the colonel's hand, and for many long years the son had dreamed of this meeting.

He remembered the story in this wise: His father had been a slave. Freed by the Civil War, he had entered upon the new life with the zeal and enthusiasm of his people at the dawn of liberty, which seem, in the light of later discouragements, so pathetic in the retrospect. The chattel aspired to own property; the slave, forbidden learning, to educate his children. He had worked early and late, had saved his money with a thrift equal to that of a German immigrant, and had sent his children regularly to school.

The girl—the barber remembered her very well—had been fair of feature, soft of speech and gentle of manner, a pearl among pebbles. One day her father's old mistress had met him on the street and, after a kindly inquiry about his family, had asked if she might hire his daughter during the summer, when there was no school. Her own married daughter would be visiting her, with a young child, and they wanted some neat and careful girl to nurse the infant.

"Why, yas ma'am," the barber's father had replied. "I reckon it might be a good thing fer Alice. I wants her ter be a teacher; but she kin l'arn things from you, ma'am, that no teacher kin teach her. She kin l'arn manners, ma'am, an' white folks' ways, and nowhere better than in yo' house."

So Alice had gone to the home of her father's former mistress to learn white folks' ways. The lady had been kind and gracious. But there are ways and ways among all people.

When she had been three weeks in her new employment her mistress's son—a younger brother of the colonel—came home from college. Some weeks later Alice went home to her father. Who was most at fault the barber never knew. A few hours afterward the father called upon the lady. There was a stormy interview. Things were said to which the ears of white ladies were unaccustomed from the lips of black men. The elder son had entered the room and interfered. The barber's father had turned to him and exclaimed angrily:

"Go 'way from here, boy, and don't talk ter me, or I'm liable ter harm you."

The young man stood his ground. The Negro advanced menacingly toward him. The young man drew his ready weapon and fatally wounded the Negro—he lived only long enough, after being taken home, to gasp out the facts to his wife and children.

The rest of the story had been much as the colonel had related it. As the barber recalled it, however, the lady had not been called to testify, but was ill at the time of the hearing, presumably from the nervous shock.

That she had secretly offered to help the family the barber knew, and that her help had been rejected with cold hostility. He knew that the murderer went unpunished, and that in later years he had gone into politics, and became the leader and mouthpiece of his party. All the world knew that he had ridden into power on his hostility to Negro rights.

The barber had been a mere boy at the time of his father's death, but not too young to appreciate the calamity that had befallen the household. The family was broken up. The sordid details of its misfortunes would not be interesting. Poverty, disease and death had followed them, until he alone was left. Many years had passed. The brown boy who had wept beside his father's bier, and who had never forgotten nor forgiven, was now the grave-faced, keen-eyed, deft-handed barber, who held a deadly weapon at the throat of his father's slayer.

How often he had longed for this hour! In his dreams he had killed this man a hundred times, in a dozen ways. Once, when a young man, he had gone to meet him, with the definite purpose of taking his life, but chance had kept them apart. He had imagined situations where they might come face to face; he would see the white man struggling in the water; he would have only to stretch forth his hand to save him; but he would tell him of his hatred and let him drown. He would see him in a burning house, from which he might rescue him; and he would call him murderer and let him burn! He would see him in the dock for murder of a white man, and only his testimony could save him, and he would let him suffer the fate that he doubly deserved! He saw a vision of his father's form, only an hour before thrilling with hope and energy, now stiff and cold in death; while under his keen razor lay the neck of his enemy, the enemy, too, of his race, sworn to degrade them, to teach them, if need be, with the torch and with the gun, that their place was at the white man's feet, his heel upon their neck; who held them in such contempt that he could speak as he had spoken in the presence of one of them. One stroke of the keen blade, a deflection of half an inch in its course, and a murder would be avenged, an enemy destroyed!

For the next sixty seconds the barber heard every beat of his own pulse, and the colonel, in serene unconsciousness, was nearer death than he had ever been in the course of a long and eventful life. He was only a militia colonel, and had never been under fire, but his turbulent political career had been passed in a community where life was lightly valued, where hot words were often followed by rash deeds, and murder was tolerated as a means of private vengeance and political advancement. He went on talking, but neither the judge nor the barber listened, each being absorbed in his own thoughts.

To the judge, who lived in a community where Negroes voted, the colonel's frankness was a curious revelation. His language was choice, though delivered with the Southern intonation, his tone easy and conversational, and, in addressing the barber directly, his manner had been courteous enough. The judge was interested, too, in watching the barber, who, it was evident, was repressing some powerful emotion. It seemed very probable to the judge that the barber might resent this cool recital of murder and outrage. He did not know what might be true of the Negroes in the South, but he had been judge of a police court in one period of his upward career, and he had found colored people prone to sudden rages, when under the influence of strong emotion, handy with edged tools, and apt to cut thick and deep, nor always careful about the color of the cuticle. The barber's feelings were plainly stirred, and the judge, a student of human nature, was curious to see if he would be moved to utterance. It would have been no novelty—patrons of the shop often discussed race questions with the barber. It was evident that the colonel was trying an experiment to demonstrate his contention in the lobby above. But the judge could not know the barber's intimate relation to the story, nor did it occur to him that the barber might conceive any deadly purpose because of a purely impersonal grievance. The barber's hand did not even tremble.

In the barber's mind, however, the whirlwind of emotions had passed lightly over the general and settled upon the particular injury. So strong, for the moment, was the homicidal impulse that it would have prevailed already had not the noisy opening of the door to admit a patron diverted the barber's attention and set in motion a current of ideas which fought for the colonel's life. The barber's glance toward the door, from force of habit, took in the whole shop. It was a handsome shop, and had been to the barber a matter of more than merely personal pride. Prominent among a struggling people, as yet scarcely beyond the threshold of citizenship, he had long been looked upon, and had become accustomed to regard himself, as a representative man, by whose failure or success his race would be tested. Should he slay this man now beneath his hand, this beautiful shop would be lost to his people. Years before the whole trade had been theirs. One by one the colored master barbers, trained in the slovenly old ways, had been forced to the wall by white competition, until his shop was one of the few good ones remaining in the hands of men of his race. Many an envious eye had been cast upon it. The lease had only a year to run. Strong pressure, he knew, had been exerted by a white rival to secure the reversion. The barber had the hotel proprietor's promise of a renewal; but he knew full well that should he lose the shop no colored man would succeed him; a center of industry, a medium of friendly contact with white men, would be lost to his people—many a good turn had the barber been able to do for them while he had the ear—literally had the ear—of some influential citizen, or held some aspirant for public office by the throat. Of the ten barbers in the shop all but one were married, with families dependent upon them for support. One was sending a son to college; another was buying a home. The unmarried one was in his spare hours studying a profession, with the hope of returning to practice it among his people in a Southern State. Their fates were all, in a measure, dependent upon the proprietor of the shop. Should he yield to the impulse which was swaying him their livelihood would be placed in jeopardy. For what white man, while the memory of this tragic event should last, would trust his throat again beneath a Negro's razor?

Such, however, was the strength of the impulse against which the barber was struggling that these considerations seemed likely not to prevail. Indeed, they had presented themselves to the barber's mind in a vague, remote, detached manner, while the dominant idea was present and compelling, clutching at his heart, drawing his arm, guiding his fingers. It was by their mass rather than by their clearness that these restraining forces held the barber's arm so long in check—it was society against self, civilization against the primitive instinct, typifying, more fully than the barber could realize, the great social problem involved in the future of his race.

He had now gone once over the colonel's face, subjecting that gentleman to less discomfort than he had for a long time endured while undergoing a similar operation. Already he had retouched one cheek and had turned the colonel's head to finish the other. A few strokes more and the colonel could be released with a close shave—how close he would never know!—or, one stroke, properly directed, and he would never stand erect again! Only the day before the barber had read, in the newspapers, the account of a ghastly lynching in a Southern State, where, to avenge a single provoked murder, eight Negroes had bit the dust and a woman had been burned at the stake for no other crime than that she was her husband's wife. One stroke and there would be one less of those who thus wantonly played with human life!

The uplifted hand had begun the deadly downward movement—when one of the barbers dropped a shaving cup, which was smashed to pieces on the marble floor. Fate surely fought for the colonel—or was it for the barber? Involuntarily the latter stayed his hand—instinctively his glance went toward the scene of the accident. It was returning to the upraised steel, and its uncompleted task, when it was arrested by Daisy's doll, hanging upon the gilded spike where he had left it.

If the razor went to its goal he would not be able to fulfil his promise to Daisy! She would wait for him at the corner, and wait in vain! If he killed the colonel he himself could hardly escape, for he was black and not white, and this was North and not South, and personal vengeance was not accepted by the courts as a justification for murder. Whether he died or not, he would be lost to Daisy. His wife was dead, and there would be no one to take care of Daisy. His own father had died in defense of his daughter; he must live to protect his own. If there was a righteous God, who divided the evil from the good, the colonel would some time get his just deserts. Vengeance was God's; it must be left to Him to repay!

The jointed doll had saved the colonel's life. Whether society had conquered self or not may be an open question, but it had stayed the barber's hand until love could triumph over hate!

The barber laid aside the razor, sponged off the colonel's face, brought him, with a movement of the chair, to a sitting posture, brushed his hair, pulled away the cloths from around his neck, handed him a pasteboard check for the amount of his bill, and stood rigidly by his chair. The colonel adjusted his collar, threw down a coin equal to double the amount of his bill and, without waiting for the change, turned with the judge to leave the shop. They had scarcely reached the door leading into the hotel lobby when the barber, overwrought by the long strain, collapsed heavily into the nearest chair.

"Well, judge," said the colonel, as they entered the lobby, "that was a good shave. What a sin it would be to spoil such a barber by making him a postmaster! I didn't say anything to him, for it don't do to praise a nigger much—it's likely to give him the big head—but I never had," he went on, running his hand appreciatively over his cheek, "I never had a better shave in my life. And I proved my theory. The barber is the son of the nigger I shot."

The judge was not sure that the colonel had proved his theory, and was less so after he had talked, a week later, with the barber. And, although the colonel remained at the Wyandot for several days, he did not get shaved again in the hotel barber shop.

Note

1. Charles W. Chesnutt, "The Doll," *The Crisis* 6 (April 3, 1912).

Nella Larsen

As the scholar M. L. Bahktin observes, there are many discourses present in any novel, and Nella Larsen's most famous novel, *Passing* (1929), is no exception. While the primary thrust of the text is a psychological examination of the two female protagonists, Irene Redfield and Clare Kendry, who pass as White, the novel presents sustained treatments of gender. In the excerpt here, Black masculinity and manhood are observed by Irene Redfield as she describes and assesses the features and disposition of her Black husband, Brian Redfield. This description comes after we are introduced to John Bellew, Clare Kendry's White racist husband, who does not know he is married to a Black woman. When Irene meets Bellew, she describes him as

> a tallish person, broadly made. His age she guessed to be some-where between thirty-five and forty. His hair was dark brown and waving, and he had a soft mouth, somewhat womanish, set in an unhealthy-looking dough-coloured face . . . But there was, Irene decided, nothing unusual about him, unless it was an Impression of latent physical power.
>
> (28)

Her description of her own husband is strikingly different. Larsen's descriptions of the two men are apparent efforts in the novel to render racism as non-manly and Black men as strong for having to endure it.

Passing

Nella Larsen[1]

"Not another damned thing!" Irene declared aloud as she drew a fragile stocking over a pale beige-coloured foot.

"Aha! Swearing again, are you, madam? Caught you in the act that time."

Brian Redfield had come into the room in that noiseless way which, in spite, of the years of their life together, still had the power to disconcert her. He stood looking down on her with that amused smile of his, which was just the faintest bit supercilious and yet was somehow very becoming to him.

Hastily Irene pulled on the other stocking and slipped her feet into the slippers beside her chair.

"And what brought on this particular outburst of profanity? That is, if an indulgent but perturbed husband may inquire. The mother of sons too! The times, alas, the times!"

"I've had this letter," Irene told him. "And I'm sure that anybody'll admit it's enough to make a saint swear. The nerve of her!"

She passed the letter to him, and in the act made a little mental frown. For, with a nicety of perception, she saw that she was doing it instead of answering his question with words, so that he might be occupied while she hurried through her dressing. For she was late again, and Brian, she well knew, detested that. Why, oh why, couldn't she ever manage to be on time? Brian had been up for ages, had made some calls for all she knew, besides having taken the boys downtown to school. And she wasn't dressed yet; had only begun. Damn Clare! This morning it was her fault.

Brian sat down and bent his head over the letter, puckering his brows slightly in his effort to make out Clare's scrawl.

Irene, who had risen and was standing before the mirror, ran a comb through her black hair, then tossed her head with a light characteristic gesture, in order to disarrange a little the set locks. She touched a powder-puff to her warm olive skin, and then put on her frock with a motion so hasty that it was with some difficulty properly adjusted. At last she was ready, though she didn't immediately say so, but stood, instead, looking with a sort of curious detachment at her husband across the room.

Brian, she was thinking, was extremely good-looking. Not, of course, pretty or effeminate; the slight irregularity of his nose saved him from the prettiness, and the rather marked heaviness of his chin saved him from the effeminacy. But he was, in a pleasant masculine way, rather handsome. And yet, wouldn't he, perhaps, have been merely ordinarily good-looking but for the richness, the beauty of his skin, which was of an exquisitely fine texture and deep copper colour.

He looked up and said: "Clare? That must be the girl you told me about meeting the last time you were out home. The one you went to tea with?"

Irene's answer to that was an inclination of the head.

"I'm ready," she said.

They were going downstairs, Brian deftly, unnecessarily, piloting her round the two short curved steps, just before the centre landing.

"You're not," he asked, "going to see her?"

His words, however, were in reality not a question, but, as Irene was aware, an admonition.

Her front teeth just touched. She spoke through them, and her tones held a thin sarcasm. "Brian, darling, I'm really not such an idiot that I don't realize that if a man calls me a nigger, it's his fault the first time, but mine if he has the opportunity to do it again."

They went into the dining-room. He drew back her chair and she sat down behind the fat-bellied German coffee-pot, which sent out its morning fragrance, mingled with the smell of crisp toast and savoury bacon, in the distance. With his long, nervous fingers he picked up the morning paper from his own chair and sat down.

Zulena, a small mahogany-coloured creature, brought in the grapefruit.

They took up their spoons.

Out of the silence Brian spoke. Blandly. "My dear, you misunderstand me entirely. I simply meant that I hope you're not going to let her pester you. She will, you know, if you give her half a chance and she's anything at all like your description of her. Anyway, they always do. Besides," he corrected, "the man, her husband, didn't call you a nigger. There's a difference, you know."

"No, certainly he didn't. Not actually. He couldn't, not very well, since he didn't know. But he would have. It amounts to the same thing. And I'm sure it was just as unpleasant."

"U-mm, I don't know. But it seems to me," he pointed out, "that you, my dear, had all the advantage. You knew what his opinion of you was, while he—Well, 'twas ever thus. We know, always have. They don't. Not quite. It has, you will admit, its humorous side, and, sometimes, its conveniences."

She poured the coffee.

"I can't see it. I'm going to write Clare. Today, if I can find a minute. It's a thing we might as well settle definitely, and immediately. Curious, isn't it, that knowing, as she does, his unqualified attitude, she still—"

Brian interrupted: "It's always that way. Never known it to fail. Remember Albert Hammond, how he used to be for ever haunting Seventh Avenue, and Lenox Avenue, and the dancing-places, until some 'shine' took a shot at him for casting an eye towards his 'sheba?'[3] They always come back. I've seen it happen time and time again."

"But why?" Irene wanted to know. "Why?"

"If I knew that, I'd know what race is."

"But wouldn't you think that having got the thing, or things, they were after, and at such risk, they'd be satisfied? Or afraid?"

"Yes," Brian agreed, "you certainly would think so. But, the fact remains, they aren't. Not satisfied, I mean. I think they're scared enough most of the time, when they give way to the urge and slip back. Not scared enough to stop them, though. Why, the good God only knows."

Irene leaned forward, speaking, she was aware, with a vehemence absolutely unnecessary, but which she could not control.

"Well, Clare can just count me out. I've no intention of being the link between her and her poorer darker brethren. After that scene in Chicago too! To calmly expect me—" She stopped short, suddenly too wrathful for words.

"Quite right. The only sensible thing to do. Let her miss you. It's an unhealthy business, the whole affair. Always is."

Irene nodded. "More coffee," she offered.

"Thanks, no." He took up his paper again, spreading it open with a little rattling noise.

Zulena came in bringing more toast. Brian took a slice and bit into it with that audible crunching sound that Irene disliked so intensely and turned back to his paper.

She said: "It's funny about 'passing.' We disapprove of it and at the same time condone it. It excites our contempt and yet we rather admire it. We shy away from it with an odd kind of revulsion, but we protect it."

"Instinct of the race to survive and expand."

"Rot! Everything can't be explained by some general biological phrase."

"Absolutely everything can. Look at the so-called whites, who've left bastards all over the known earth. Same thing in them. Instinct of the race to survive and expand."

With that Irene didn't at all agree, but many arguments in the past had taught her the futility of attempting to combat Brian on ground where he was more nearly at home than she. Ignoring his unqualified assertion, she slid away from the subject entirely.

"I wonder," she asked, "if you'll have time to run me down to the printing-office. It's on a Hundred and Sixteenth Street. I've got to see about some handbills and some more tickets for the dance."

"Yes, of course. How's it going? Everything all set?"

"Ye-es. I guess so. The boxes are all sold and nearly all the first batch of tickets. And we expect to take in almost as much again at the door. Then, there's all that cake to sell. It's a terrible lot of work, though."

"I'll bet it is. Uplifting the brother's no easy job. I'm as busy as a cat with fleas, myself." And over his face there came a shadow. "Lord! how I hate sick people, and their stupid, meddling families, and smelly, dirty rooms, and climbing filthy steps in dark hallways."

"Surely," Irene began, fighting back the fear and irritation that she felt, "surely—"

Her husband silenced her, saying sharply: "Let's not talk about it, please." And immediately, in his usual, slightly mocking tone he asked: "Are you ready to go now? I haven't a great deal of time to wait."

He got up. She followed him out into the hall without replying. He picked up his soft brown hat from the small table and stood a moment whirling it round on his long tea-coloured fingers.

Irene, watching him, was thinking: "It isn't fair, it isn't fair." After all these years to still blame her like this. Hadn't his success proved that she'd been right in insisting that he stick to his profession right there in New York? Couldn't he see, even now, that it *had* been best? Not for her, oh no, not for her—she had never really considered herself—but for him and the boys. Was she never to be free of it, that fear which crouched, always, deep down within her, stealing away the sense of security, the feeling of permanence, from the life which she had so admirably arranged for them all, and desired so ardently to have remain as it was? That strange, and to her fantastic, notion of Brian's of going off to Brazil[4] which, though unmentioned, yet lived within him; how it frightened her, and—yes, angered her!

"Well?" he asked lightly.

"I'll just get my things. One minute," she promised and turned upstairs.

Her voice had been even and her step was firm, but in her there was no slackening of the agitation, of the alarms, which Brian's expression of discontent had raised. He had never spoken of his desire since that long-ago time of storm and strain, of hateful and nearly disastrous quarrelling, when she had so firmly opposed him, so sensibly pointed out its utter impossibility and its probable consequences to her and the boys, and had even hinted at a dissolution of their marriage in the event of his persistence in his idea. No, there had been, in all the years that they had lived together since then, no other talk of it, no more than there had been any other quarrelling or any other threats. But because, so she insisted, the bond of flesh and spirit between them was so strong, she knew, had always known, that his dissatisfaction had continued, as had his dislike and disgust for his profession and his country.

A feeling of uneasiness stole upon her at the inconceivable suspicion that she might have been wrong in her estimate of her husband's character. But she squirmed away from it. Impossible! She couldn't have been wrong. Everything proved that she had been right. More than right, if such a thing could be. And all, she assured herself, because she understood him so well, because she had, actually, a special talent for understanding him. It was, as she saw it, the one thing that had been the basis of the success which she had made of a marriage that had threatened to fail. She knew him as well as he knew himself, or better.

Then why worry? The thing, this discontent which had exploded into words, would surely die, flicker out, at last. True, she had in the past often been tempted to believe that it had died, only to become conscious, in some instinctive, subtle way, that she had been merely deceiving herself for a while and that it still lived. But it *would* die. Of that she was certain. She had only to direct and guide her man, to keep him going in the right direction.

Note

1. Nella Larsen, *Passing* (New York, NY: Alfred A. Knopf, 1929).

Lorraine Hansberry

Lorraine Hansberry's well-known play, *A Raisin in the Sun*, profiles the Lee family, which has three strong women, the mother, wife, and sister of the play's protagonist, Walter Lee. That Walter is placed as the central character in a plot that moves as he interacts with the three women he lives with makes the play an assessment of the close interpersonal relations within Black families and how those relationships impact a person's display of womanhood or manhood. In the play's final scene, excerpted here, the matriarch observes that her son, Walter, has "just come into his manhood," when he demonstrates a version of manhood he had not yet reached. The play then offers the growth of Walter into a man of certain qualities, who is unselfish and who challenges racial prejudice, as a model for others to emulate in the Black community.

A Raisin in the Sun, Act III

Lorraine Hansberry[1]

RUTH: Who was that?

BENEATHA: Your husband.

RUTH: Where did he go?

BENEATHA: Who knows—maybe he has an appointment at U.S. Steel.

RUTH *(anxiously, with frightened eyes)*: You didn't say nothing bad to him, did you?

BENEATHA: Bad? Say anything bad to him? No—I told him he was a sweet boy and full of dreams and everything is strictly peachy keen, as the ofay kids say!

MAMA *enters from her bedroom. She is lost, vague, trying to catch hold, to make some sense of her former command of the world, but it still eludes her. A sense of waste overwhelms her gait; a measure of apology rides on her shoulders. She goes to her plant, which has remained on the table, looks at it, picks it up and takes it to the window sill and sits it outside, and she stands and looks at it a long moment. Then she closes the window, straightens her body with effort and turns around to her children.*

MAMA: Well—ain't it a mess in here, though? *(a false cheerfulness, a beginning of something)* I guess we all better stop moping around and get some work done. All this unpacking and everything we got to do. (RUTH *raises her head slowly in response to the sense of the line; and* BENEATHA *in similar manner turns very slowly to look at her mother.*) One of you all better call the moving people and tell 'em not to come.

RUTH: Tell 'em not to come?

MAMA: Of course, baby. Ain't no need in 'em coming all the way here and having to go back. They charges for that too. *(She sits down, fingers to her brow, thinking.)* Lord, ever since I was a little girl, I always remembers people saying, "Lena—Lena Eggleston, you aims too high all the time. You needs to slow down and see life a little more like it is. Just slow down some." That's what they always used to say down home—"Lord, that Lena Eggleston is a high-minded thing. She'll get her due one day!"

RUTH: No, Lena . . .

MAMA: Me and Big Walter just didn't never learn right.

RUTH: Lena, no! We gotta go. Bennie—tell her . . . *(She rises and crosses to* BENEATHA *with her arms outstretched.* BENEATHA *doesn't respond.)* Tell her we can still move . . . the notes ain't but a hundred and twenty-five a month. We got four grown people in this house—we can work . . .

MAMA(*to herself*): Just aimed too high all the time—

RUTH (*turning and going to* MAMA *fast—the words pouring out with urgency and desperation*): Lena—I'll work . . . I'll work twenty hours a day in all the kitchens in Chicago . . . I'll strap my baby on my back if I have to and scrub all the floors in America and wash all the sheets in America if I have to—but we got to MOVE! We got to get OUT OF HERE!!

MAMA *reaches out absently and pats* RUTH'*s hand.*

MAMA: No—I sees things differently now. Been thinking 'bout some of the things we could do to fix this place up some. I seen a second-hand bureau over on Maxwell Street just the other day that could fit right there. (*She points to where the new furniture might go.* RUTH *wanders away from her.*) Would need some new handles on it and then a little varnish and it look like something brand-new. And—we can put up them new curtains in the kitchen . . . Why this place be looking fine. Cheer us all up so that we forget trouble ever come . . . (*to* RUTH) And you could get some nice screens to put up in your room round the baby's bassinet . . . (*She looks at both of them, pleadingly.*) Sometimes you just got to know when to give up some things . . . and hold on to what you got . . .

WALTER *enters from the outside, looking spent and leaning against the door, his coat hanging from him.*

MAMA: Where you been, son?

WALTER (*breathing hard*): Made a call.

MAMA: To who, son?

WALTER: To The Man. (*He heads for his room.*)

MAMA: What man, baby?

WALTER (*stops in the door*): The Man, Mama. Don't you know who The Man is?

RUTH: Walter Lee?

WALTER: *The Man.* Like the guys in the streets say—The Man. Captain Boss—Mistuh Charley . . . Old Cap'n Please Mr. Bossman . . .

BENEATHA (*suddenly*): Lindner!

WALTER: That's right! That's good. I told him to come right over.

BENEATHA (*fiercely, understanding*): For what? What do you want to see him for!

WALTER (*looking at his sister*): We going to do business with him.

MAMA: What you talking 'bout, son?

WALTER: Talking 'bout life, Mama. You all always telling me to see life like it is. Well—I laid in there on my back today . . . and I figured it out. Life just like it is. Who gets and who don't get. (*He sits down with his coat on and laughs.*) Mama, you know it's all divided up. Life is. Sure enough. Between the takers and the "tooken." (*He laughs.*) I've figured it out finally. (*He looks around at them.*) Yeah. Some of us always getting "tooken." (*He laughs.*) People like Willy Harris, they don't never get "tooken." And you know why the rest of us do? 'Cause we all mixed up. Mixed up bad. We get to looking 'round for the right and the wrong; and we worry about it and cry about it and stay up nights trying to figure out 'bout the wrong and the right of things all the time . . . And all the time, man, them takers is out there operating, just taking and taking. Willy Harris? Shoot—Willy Harris don't even count. He don't even count in the big scheme of things. But I'll say one thing for old Willy Harris . . . he's taught me something. He's taught me to keep my eye on what counts in this world. Yeah—(*shouting out a little.*) Thanks, Willy!

RUTH: What did you call that man for, Walter Lee?

WALTER: Called him to tell him to come on over to the show. Gonna put on a show for the man. Just what he wants to see. You see, Mama, the man came here today and he told us that them people out there where you want us to move—well they so upset they willing to pay us *not* to move! (*He laughs again.*) And—and oh, Mama—you would of been proud of the way me and Ruth and Bennie acted. We told him to get out . . . Lord have mercy! We told the man to get out! Oh, we was some proud folks this afternoon, yeah. (*He lights a cigarette.*) We were still full of that old-time stuff . . .

RUTH (*coming toward him slowly*): You talking 'bout taking them people's money to keep us from moving in that house?

WALTER: I ain't just talking 'bout it, baby—I'm telling you that's what's going to happen!

BENEATHA: Oh, God! Where is the bottom! Where is the real honest-to-God bottom so he can't go any farther!

WALTER: See—that's the old stuff. You and that boy that was here today. You all want everybody to carry a flag and a spear and sing some marching songs, huh? You wanna spend your life looking into things and trying to find the right and the wrong part, huh? Yeah. You know what's going to happen to that boy someday—he'll find himself sitting in a dungeon, locked in forever—and the takers will have the key! Forget it, baby! There ain't no causes—there ain't nothing but taking in this world, and he who takes most is smartest—and it don't make a damn bit of difference *how*.

MAMA: You making something inside me cry, son. Some awful pain inside me.

WALTER: Don't cry, Mama. Understand. That white man is going to walk in that door able to write checks for more money than we ever had. It's important to him and I'm going to help him . . . I'm going to put on the show, Mama.

MAMA: Son—I come from five generations of people who was slaves and sharecroppers—but ain't nobody in my family never let nobody pay 'em no money that was a way of telling us we wasn't fit to walk the earth. We ain't never been that poor. (*raising her eyes and looking at him*) We ain't never been that—dead inside.

BENEATHA: Well—we are dead now. All the talk about dreams and sunlight that goes on in this house. It's all dead now.

WALTER: What's the matter with you all! I didn't make this world! It was give to me this way! Hell, yes, I want me some yachts someday! Yes, I want to hang some real pearls 'round my wife's neck. Ain't she supposed to wear no pearls? Somebody tell me—tell me, who decides which women is suppose to wear pearls in this world. I tell you I am a *man*—and I think my wife should wear some pearls in this world!

This last line hangs a good while and WALTER *begins to move about the room. The word "Man" has penetrated his consciousness; he mumbles it to himself repeatedly between strange agitated pauses as he moves about.*

MAMA: Baby, how you going to feel on the inside?

WALTER: Fine! . . . Going to feel fine . . . a man . . .

MAMA: You won't have nothing left then, Walter Lee.

WALTER (*coming to her*): I'm going to feel fine, Mama. I'm going to look that son-of-a-bitch in the eyes and say—(*He falters.*)—and say, "All right, Mr. Lindner—(*He falters even more.*)—that's *your* neighborhood out there! You got the right to keep it like you want! You got the right to have it like you want! Just write the check and—the house is yours." And—and I am going to say—(*His voice almost breaks.*) "And you—you people just put the money in my hand and you won't have to live next to this bunch of stinking niggers! . . ." (*He straightens up and moves away from his mother, walking around the room.*) And maybe—maybe I'll just get down on my black knees . . . (*He does so;* RUTH *and* BENNIE *and* MAMA *watch him in frozen horror.*) "Captain, Mistuh, Bossman—(*groveling and grinning and wringing his hands in profoundly anguished imitation of the slow-witted movie stereotype.*) A-hee-hee-hee! Oh, yassuh boss! Yasssssuh! Great white!—(*Voice breaking, he forces himself to go on.*)—Father, just gi' ussen de money, fo' God's sake, and we's—we's ain't gwine come out deh and dirty up yo' white folks neighborhood . . . " (*He breaks down completely.*) And I'll feel fine! Fine! FINE! (*He gets up and goes into the bedroom.*)

BENEATHA: That is not a man. That is nothing but a toothless rat.

MAMA: Yes—death done come in this here house. (*She is nodding, slowly, reflectively.*) Done come walking in my house on the lips of my children. You what supposed to be my beginning again. You—what supposed to be my harvest. (*to* BENEATHA) You—you mourning your brother?

BENEATHA: He's no brother of mine.

MAMA: What you say?

BENEATHA: I said that that individual in that room is no brother of mine.

MAMA: That's what I thought you said. You feeling like you better than he is today? (BENEATHA *does not answer.*) Yes? What you tell him a minute ago? That he wasn't a man? Yes? You give him up for me? You done wrote his epitaph too—like the rest of the world? Well, who give you the privilege?

BENEATHA: Be on my side for once! You saw what he just did, Mama! You saw him—down on his knees. Wasn't it you who taught me to despise any man who would do that? Do what he's going to do?

MAMA: Yes—I taught you that. Me and your daddy. But I thought I taught you something else too . . . I thought I taught you to love him.

BENEATHA: Love him? There is nothing left to love.

MAMA: There is *always* something left to love. And if you ain't learned that, you ain't learned nothing. (*Looking at her.*) Have you cried for that boy today? I don't mean for yourself and for the family 'cause we lost the money. I mean for him: what he been through and what it done to him. Child, when do you think is the time to love somebody the most? When they done good and made things easy for everybody? Well, then, you ain't through learning—because that ain't the time at all. It's when he's at his lowest and can't believe in hisself 'cause the world done whipped him so! When you starts measuring somebody, measure him right, child, measure him right. Make sure you done taken into account what hills and valleys he come through before he got to wherever he is.

TRAVIS *bursts into the room at the end of the speech, leaving the door open.*

TRAVIS: Grandmama—the moving men are downstairs! The truck just pulled up.

MAMA (*turning and looking at him*): Are they, baby? They downstairs?

She sighs and sits. LINDNER *appears in the doorway. He peers in and knocks lightly, to gain attention, and comes in. All turn to look at him.*

LINDNER (*hat and briefcase in hand*): Uh—hello . . .

RUTH *crosses mechanically to the bedroom door and opens it and lets it swing open freely and slowly as the lights come up on* WALTER *within, still in his coat, sitting at the far corner of the room. He looks up and out though the room to* LINDNER.

RUTH: He's here. (*A long minute passes and* WALTER *slowly gets up.*)

LINDNER (*coming to the table with efficiency, putting his briefcase on the table and starting to unfold papers and unscrew fountain pens*): Well, I certainly was glad to hear from you people. (WAL-TER *has begun the trek out of the room, slowly and awkwardly, rather like a small boy, passing the back of his sleeve across his mouth from time to time.*) Life can really be so much simpler than people let it be most of the time. Well—with whom do I negotiate? You, Mrs. Younger, or your son here? (MAMA *sits with her hands folded on her lap and her eyes closed as* WALTER *advances.* TRAVIS *goes closer to* LINDNER *and looks at the papers curiously.*) Just some official papers, sonny.

RUTH: Travis, you go downstairs—

MAMA (*opening her eyes and looking into* WALTER's): No. Travis, you stay right here. And you make him understand what you doing, Walter Lee. You teach him good. Like Willy Harris taught you. You show where our five generations done come to. (WALTER *looks from her to the boy, who grins at him innocently.*) Go ahead, son—(*She folds her hands and closes her eyes.*) Go ahead.

WALTER (*at last crosses to* LINDNER, *who is reviewing the contract*): Well, Mr. Lindner. (BENEATHA *turns away.*) We called you—(*There is a profound, simple groping quality in his speech.*)—because, well, me and my family (*He looks around and shifts from one foot to the other.*) Well—we are very plain people . . .

LINDNER: Yes—

WALTER: I mean—I have worked as a chauffeur most of my life—and my wife here, she does domestic work in people's kitchens. So does my mother. I mean—we are plain people . . .

LINDNER: Yes, Mr. Younger—

WALTER (*really like a small boy, looking down at his shoes and then up at the man*): And—uh—well, my father, well, he was a laborer most of his life . . .

LINDNER (*absolutely confused*): Uh, yes—yes, I understand. (*He turns back to the contract.*)

WALTER (*a beat, staring at him*): And my father—(*with sudden intensity*) My father almost *beat a man to death* once because this man called him a bad name or something, you know what I mean?

LINDNER (*looking up, frozen*): No, no, I'm afraid I don't—

WALTER (*A beat. The tension hangs; then* WALTER *steps back from it.*): Yeah. Well—what I mean is that we come from people who had a lot of *pride.* I mean—we are very proud people. And that's my sister over there and she's going to be a doctor—and we are very proud—

LINDNER: Well—I am sure that is very nice, but—

WALTER: What I am telling you is that we called you over here to tell you that we are very proud and that this—(*signaling to* TRAVIS) Travis, come here. (TRAVIS *crosses and* WALTER *draws him before him facing the man.*) This is my son, and he makes the sixth generation our family in this country. And we have all thought about your offer—

LINDNER: Well, good . . . good—

WALTER: And we have decided to move into our house because my father—my father—he earned it for us brick by brick. (MAMA *has her eyes closed and is rocking back and forth as though she were in church, with her head nodding the Amen yes.*) We don't want to make no trouble for nobody or fight no causes, and we will try to be good neighbors. And that's *all* we got to say about that. (*He looks the man absolutely in the eyes.*) We don't want your money. (*He turns and walks away.*)

LINDNER: (*looking around at all of them*): I take it then—that you have decided to occupy . . .

BENEATHA: That's what the man said.

LINDNER (*to* MAMA *in her reverie*): Then I would like to appeal to you, Mrs. Younger. You are older and wiser and understand things better I am sure . . .

MAMA: I am afraid you don't understand. My son said we was going to move and there ain't nothing left for me to say. *(briskly)* You know how these young folks is nowadays, mister. Can't do a thing with 'em! *(As he opens his mouth, she rises.)* Goodbye.

LINDNER *(folding up his materials)*: Well—if you are that final about it . . . there is nothing left for me to say. *(He finishes, almost ignored by the family, who are concentrating on WALTER LEE. At the door LINDNER halts and looks around.)* I sure hope you people know what you're getting into. *(He shakes his head and exits.)*

RUTH *(looking around and coming to life)*: Well, for God's sake—if the moving men are here— LET'S GET THE HELL OUT OF HERE!

MAMA *(into action)*: Ain't it the truth! Look at all this here mess. Ruth, put Travis' good jacket on him . . . Walter Lee, fix your tie and tuck your shirt in, you look like somebody's hoodlum! Lord have mercy, where is my plant? *(She flies to get it amid the general bustling of the family, who are deliberately trying to ignore the nobility of the past moment.)* You all start on down . . . Travis child, don't go empty-handed . . . Ruth, where did I put that box with my skillets in it? I want to be in charge of it myself . . . I'm going to make us the biggest dinner we ever ate tonight . . . Beneatha, what's the matter with them stockings? Pull them things up, girl . . .

The family starts to file out as two moving men appear and begin to carry out the heavier pieces of furniture, bumping into the family as they move about.

BENEATHA: Mama, Asagai asked me to marry him today and go to Africa—

MAMA *(in the middle of her getting-ready activity)*: He did? You ain't old enough to marry nobody—*(seeing the moving men lifting one of her chairs precariously)* Darling, that ain't no bale of cotton, please handle it so we can sit in it again! I had that chair twenty-five years . . .

The movers sigh with exasperation and go on with their work.

BENEATHA *(girlishly and unreasonably trying to pursue the conversation)*: To go to Africa, Mama— be a doctor in Africa . . .

MAMA *(distracted)*: Yes, baby—

WALTER: *Africa!* What he want you to go to Africa for?

BENEATHA: To practice there . . .

WALTER: Girl, if you don't get all them silly ideas out your head! You better marry yourself a man with some loot . . .

BENEATHA *(angrily, precisely as in the first scene of the play)*: What have you got to do with who I marry!

WALTER: Plenty. Now I think George Murchison—

BENEATHA: *George Murchison!* I wouldn't marry him if he was Adam and I was Eve!

WALTER *and* BENEATHA *go out yelling at each other vigorously and the anger is loud and real till their voices diminish.* RUTH *stands at the door and turns to* MAMA *and smiles knowingly.*

MAMA *(fixing her hat at last)*: Yeah—they something all right, my children . . .

RUTH: Yeah—they're something. Let's go, Lena.

MAMA *(stalling, starting to look around at the house)*: Yes—I'm coming. Ruth—

RUTH: Yes?

MAMA *(quietly, woman to woman)*: He finally come into his manhood today, didn't he? Kind of like a rainbow after the rain . . .

RUTH (*biting her lip lest her own pride explode in front of* MAMA): Yes, Lena.

WALTER'*s voice calls for them raucously.*

WALTER (*off stage*): Y'all come on! These people charges by the hour, you know!
MAMA (*waving* RUTH *out vaguely*): All right, honey—go on down. I be down directly.

RUTH *hesitates, then exits.* MAMA *stands, at last alone in the living room, her plant on the table before her as the lights start to come down. She looks around at all the walls and ceilings and suddenly, despite herself, while the children call below, a great heaving thing rises in her and she puts her fist to her mouth to stifle it, takes a final desperate look, pulls her coat about her, pats her hat and goes out. The lights dim down. The door opens and she comes back in, grabs her plant, and goes out for the last time.*

Note

1. Lorraine Hansberry, *A Raisin in the Sun* (New York, NY: Random House, 1959), Act III, pp. 127–142.

Toni Morrison

Toni Morrison's novel *Sula* (1973) is called a feminist novel for a reason. It details the experience of several Black women over the course of several generations. It also centers on the relation of these women to one another, especially the relations of the protagonist Sula and her best friend, Nel. However, it is Morrison herself who famously said in her acceptance speech for the Nobel Prize in literature, "Tell us what it is to be a woman so that we may know what it is to be a man." Thus much can be gained by analyzing the discourses about manhood and masculinity in the Morrison novels. In this excerpt from *Sula*, the protagonist discusses her take on Black manhood as perceived in a racist society.

Sula

Toni Morrison[1]

Just at that moment the children ran in announcing the entrance of their father. Jude opened the back door and walked into the kitchen. He was still a very good-looking man, and the only difference Sula could see was the thin pencil mustache under his nose, and a part in his hair.

"Hey, Jude. What you know good?"

"White man running it—nothing good."

Sula laughed while Nel, high-tuned to his moods, ignored her husband's smile saying, "Bad day, honey?"

"Same old stuff," he replied and told them a brief tale of some personal insult done him by a customer and his boss—a whiney tale that peaked somewhere between anger and a lapping desire for comfort. He ended it with the observation that a Negro man had a hard row to hoe in this world. He expected his story to dovetail into milkwarm commiseration, but before Nel could excrete it, Sula said she didn't know about that—it looked like a pretty good life to her.

"Say what?" Jude's temper flared just a bit as he looked at this friend of his wife's, this slight woman, not exactly plain, but not fine either, with a copperhead over her eye. As far as he could tell, she looked like a woman roaming the country trying to find some man to burden down with a lot of lip and a lot of mouths.

Sula was smiling. "I mean, I don't know what the fuss is about. I mean, everything in the world loves you. White men love you. They spend so much time worrying about your penis they forget their own. The only thing they want to do is cut off a nigger's privates. And if that ain't love and respect I don't know what is. And white women? They chase you all to every corner of the earth, feel for you under every bed. I knew a white woman wouldn't leave the house after 6 o'clock for fear one of you would snatch her. Now ain't that love? They think rape soon's they see you, and if they don't get the rape they looking for, they scream it anyway just so the search won't be in vain. Colored women worry themselves into bad health just trying to hang on to your cuffs. Even little children—white and black, boys and girls—spend all their childhood eating their hearts out 'cause they think you don't love them. And if that ain't enough, you love yourselves. Nothing in this world loves a black man more than another black man. You hear of solitary white men, but niggers? Can't stay away from one another a whole day. So. It looks to me like you the envy of the world."

Jude and Nel were laughing, he saying, "Well, if that's the only way they got to show it—cut off my balls and throw me in jail—I'd just as soon they left me alone." But thinking that Sula had an odd way of looking at things and that her wide smile took some of the sting from that rattlesnake over her eye. A funny woman, he thought, not that bad-looking. But he could see why she wasn't married; she stirred a man's mind maybe, but not his body.

Note

1. Toni Morrison, *Sula* (New York, NY: Penguin Books, 1973).

Michele Wallace

Michele Wallace makes a direct link between literature and rhetoric when she writes that "Richard Wright's *Native Son* was the starting point of the black writer's lover affair with Black Macho" (55). Wallace is offering a critique of a certain hypersexualized and patriarchal rhetoric of manhood that became prevalent during the Black arts and Black power movements of the 1960s and 1970s, (known together as the Black movement). The strong assertion of Black masculinity that accompanied it was often rendered in sexual language as a counterresponse to the ongoing legacy of White supremacy. As has been presented in previous readings in this book, under American systems of overt oppression, under slavery and Jim Crow, White power and dominance were exacted not only in laws and social relations but also in acts of sexual violence against—that is, in the rape and lynching of—Black men and women. Thus, in the following selection, Wallace asserts that sex and sexuality came to stand in for that dominance. In turn in art, cultural discourse, and people's lives, Black macho was used as the signature image of Black power and resistance to racial and sexual subjugation.

Black Macho and the Myth of the Super Woman

Michele Wallace[1]

Richard Wright's *Native Son* was the starting point of the black writer's love affair with Black Macho. Bigger Thomas, the product of a black Chicago ghetto, is employed as chauffeur by an upper-middle-class white family. His first night on the job he drives the daughter of his employer and her socialist boyfriend to a political meeting. They try to befriend Bigger, drink with him, go with him to a black restaurant. Later Bigger takes the drunken young woman home, barely escapes raping her, murders her accidentally, and burns her in the furnace in the basement. Lest we should doubt his viciousness, he then rapes his own black girl friend and throws her out of a window. Bigger, Wright would have us believe, had gained an identity and realized himself as a man for the first time in his life through these acts of violence.

Bigger Thomas was nothing more than the American white males's fantasy/nightmare/myth of the black man thinly disguised, expanded upon (albeit brilliantly), endowed with the detail of social reality and thrust back in the white man's face in a form recognizable enough to connect with the old terror.

In inventing such a protagonist, Wright seemed much more concerned with making a lasting impression on whites than he was with self-revelation or self-exploration. The black man could only come to life in the act of punishing the white man or, in other words, the black man could only come to life by losing his humanity. It would be some years before this view would become common currency; later writers, such as Norman Mailer, turned back to *Native Son* for confirmation.

Finally, Baldwin was right about *Native Son*.

> Recording his days of anger he has also nevertheless recorded, as no Negro before him had ever done, that fantasy Americans hold in their minds when they speak of the Negro: that fantastic and fearful image which we have lived with since the first slave fell beneath the lash. This is the significance of *Native Son* and also, unhappily, its overwhelming limitation.
>
> (James Baldwin, "Many Thousands Gone," *Notes of a Native Son*.)

> Bigger's tragedy is not that he is cold or black or hungry, not even that he is American, black; but that he has accepted a theology that denies him life, that he admits the possibility of

his being sub-human and feels constrained, therefore, to battle for his humanity according to those brutal criteria bequeathed him at his birth.

(Baldwin, "Everybody's Protest Novel," Notes of a Native Son.)

I began reading James Baldwin when I was about twelve and he remains one of the black writers whom I respect most, not because I agree with everything he has to say or even the way he says it, but because he has paid more attention to black women, to the actual mechanics of the black male/female relationship and to the myths that have been working on it, than any other black male writer (except Thomas Wideman and, perhaps, John A. Williams). At least in his earlier essays and novels, Baldwin did, in fact, explore "the disquieting complexities of ourselves." In that sense, reading him is still an education.

Baldwin seemed wiser than Wright because he maintained a sense of the double reality of being black: the white man's vision of the black man and the man the black man had to be for himself. Baldwin had in mind a more humane manhood, a manhood that would take into account the expensive lesson the black man had learned from oppression, a manhood that would perhaps turn even America's corrupting influence into something beneficial.

Negroes are Americans and their destiny is the country's destiny. They have no other experience besides their experience on this continent and it is an experience which cannot be rejected, which yet remains to be embraced. If, as I believe, no American Negro exists who does not have his private Bigger Thomas living in the skull, then what most significantly fails to be illuminated here is the paradoxical adjustment which is perpetually made, the Negro being compelled to accept the fact that this dark and dangerous and unloved stranger is part of himself forever. Only this recognition sets him in any wise free and it is this, this necessary ability to contain and even, in the most honorable sense of the word, to *exploit* the "nigger," which lends to Negro life its high element of the ironic and which causes the most well-meaning of their American critics to make such exhilarating errors when attempting to understand them. To present Bigger as a warning is simply to reinforce the American guilt and fear concerning him, it is most forcefully to limit him to that previously mentioned social arena in which he has no human validity, it is simply to condemn him to death.

(Baldwin, "Many Thousands Gone," Notes of a Native Son.)

Baldwin had no way of knowing in 1951, when he said, "it is quite beyond the limit of possibility that Negroes in America will ever achieve the means of wreaking vengeance upon the state . . . also . . . it cannot be said that they have any desire to do so," that there would indeed be those who would want to and who would try to before long.

Ralph Ellison, like Baldwin, expressed a horror of the white man's nightmare, and the realization of the inevitable lack of humanity it afforded the black man. The white man's own nightmare could not be used to conquer him. But then Ellison was more obsessed than Baldwin with the way blacks were seen, or rather not seen, by whites; with the extent to which they only existed, even for one another, if whites recognized that existence. And although I fully realize what an important literary accomplishment *Invisible Man* was, I am often tempted to wonder if that concern with white perception did not help to make it such a huge success. Ellison's hero takes the coward's way out. He retreats because he cannot deal with a world in which his existence as an individual is never allowed but must be taken—a dilemma that seems almost naïve. Ellison tells us little about how blacks relate to one another, except to the extent that whites intrude upon that intercourse. It's not surprising that he has never successfully completed another novel. There was no place for his hero to go, no reason for him to come up from underground.

Baldwin, in contrast, plunges headlong into the intricacies of the black relationship. He does not propose a solution outright, but he is clearly working out of a specific set of values, and the values are those of patriarchy. It strikes me as very appropriate that he and Martin Luther King should have been close friends. Both seemed to believe in the notion of man as God on earth in the Christian sense. This notion of man, while unacceptable to me from a feminist perspective, as well as on religious and philosophical grounds, presumed some emotional and material responsibility towards black women and children. The ideal man was distinguished by both power *and* compassion, for he would be held accountable to God for his actions towards his charges. He thus had a moral responsibility for the destiny of the entire race.

Baldwin is an emphatically moralistic writer. He has never been able to adequately justify the actions sometimes taken by black men regarding women and children. His continual struggle in print with his father testifies to that. He tells us that his father was frightened because he was unable to support the family he had created, that he was beaten down, driven mad by this society. Yet Baldwin remains unable to completely excuse his father's acts of insensitivity and cruelty toward his mother, his siblings, and himself. Throughout his earlier work there is evidence of his interior struggle over the question of whether the black man had been more right or wrong in his exploitation of the black woman; that is, in using her as a target for his anger. A tenet of patriarchal morality is the conviction that men must rule because they are more often right about what's best for everybody.

That very uncertainty was why Amiri Baraka and Eldridge Cleaver singled Baldwin out for such vicious attacks. In his novels *Go Tell It on the Mountain* and *Another Country*, Baldwin told the black woman's story with far too much empathy to ever be accepted into the ranks of the militant black male intellectuals in the Black Power days.

> Now I talked to many Southern liberals who were doing their best to bring integration about in the South, but met scarcely a single Southerner who did not weep for the passing of the old order . . . . But the old black men I looked at down there—those same black men that the Southern liberal had loved . . . they were not weeping. Men do not like to be protected, it emasculates them . . . . It is not a pretty thing to be a father and be ultimately dependent on the power and kindness of some other man for the well-being of your house.
>
> But what this evasion of the Negro's humanity has done to the nation is not so well known. The really striking thing, for me, in the South was this dreadful paradox, that the black men were stronger than the white. I do not know how they did it, but it certainly has something to do with that as yet unwritten history of the Negro woman . . .
>
> (James Baldwin, "Nobody Knows My Name: A Letter From The South,"
> *Nobody Knows My Name*, New York: Dial, 1961.)

Like Martin Luther King, Baldwin was an anachronism come the sixties; but unlike King he was not conveniently murdered, so they had to dispose of him some other way. Ironically, Baldwin's love affair with the tragic details of the black man's life, and his romanticization of them, laid the groundwork for the deification of the genitals that would later characterize the prose of the Black Movement. That is, to a degree, Baldwin, too, admired what was characterized as the brutal masculinity of the black man, also saw it as an affirmation of his existence. The biggest difference between Baldwin and the others really was that Baldwin saw in the black man as much potential for a sense of responsibility as any tendency toward brutal sexuality.

Because he is in partial agreement with Mailer, Baldwin's criticism of "The White Negro" is oddly evasive. He does not come right out and accuse Mailer of making a racist argument.

"Man," said a Negro musician to me once, talking about Norman, "the only trouble with that cat is that he's white." This does not mean exactly what it says—or, rather, it *does* mean exactly what it says, and not what it might be taken to mean—and it is a very shrewd observation. What my friend meant was that to become a Negro man, let alone a Negro artist, one had to make oneself up as one went along. This had to be done in the not-at-all-metaphorical teeth of the world's determination to destroy you. The world had prepared no place for you, and if the world had its way, no place would ever exist. Now, this is true for everyone, but, in the case of a Negro, this truth is absolutely naked: if he deludes himself about it, he will die . . . .

(Baldwin, "The Black Boy Looks at the White Boy," *Nobody Knows My Name.*)

Baldwin is patting Mailer on the head and sending him back to play with the little kids. He is saying, anybody who isn't black shouldn't dare to presume to understand why black men do the things they do.

The language is ambiguous not only because it is Baldwin's style to be so but also because he wants to make Mailer aware that black men and white men move, and must move, in different directions and toward different ends. But there is, as well, an implicit affirmation of the right of the black man to assert himself sexually, the right of the black man to be a sexual outlaw if he finds it necessary to his survival. "To become a Negro man . . . one had to make oneself up as one went along . . . ." Nor does Baldwin deny outright that black men are psychopaths or that theirs is what Mailer calls a "morality of the bottom." Rather he asks, "Why malign the sorely menaced sexuality of Negroes in order to justify the white man's sexual panic?"

Then things changed. The rhetoric of Black Power became loud and not a little idiotic. Baldwin was repeatedly attacked. He was singled out to represent everything younger blacks didn't like about the solutions and evasiveness of their parents. Cleaver, who had his own peculiar love-hate relationship with Baldwin, accused him of waging "a war . . . against black masculinity." LeRoi Jones accused him of doing "the Martyr's Shuffle in cocktail time."

In 1967, Baldwin returned to America from his long self-imposed exile in France to take his punishment, to say what other black writers wanted him to say, perhaps because he, too, desperately wanted to believe in the quixotic virility of the black man.

If Beale Street Could Talk was published in 1974. It was a novel about a young black ghetto girl. She falls in love with and becomes pregnant by a young black boy who is falsely accused of rape and imprisoned. The boy's father is an impotent drunkard. Nevertheless, he is portrayed as noble, even kindhearted, driven to drink and despair by his domineering, malicious, frigid, churchgoing wife. The girl's parents and sister, who are very poor, are curiously overjoyed to hear of the girl's pregnancy and are thoroughly supportive of the unmarried couple. All of the characters positively gush the dogma of the Black Movement, except the boy's mother, who is the perfect caricature of the man-eating black woman. Earlier, in 1972, Baldwin had said:

Every black man walking in this country pays a tremendous price for walking: for men are not women, and a man's balance depends on the weight he carries between his legs. All men, however they may face or fail to face it, however they may handle, or be handled by it, know something about each other, which is simply that a man without balls is not a man . . . .

(James Baldwin, *No Name in the Street*, New York: Dial, 1972.)

And so, by whatever means, Baldwin had finally seen the light, arrived at the theoretical premise that made the Black Movement a vehicle for Black Macho: Black males who stressed a traditionally patriarchal responsibility to their women and children, to their communities—to black people—were to be considered almost sisified. The black man's sexuality and the physical fact of his penis were the major evidence of his manhood and the purpose of it.

LeRoi Jones was the Black Movement's leading intellectual convert, having deserted success in the white world for the uncertainty of the Black Revolution. He had lived in Greenwich Village. His friends were Gregory Corso, Allen Ginsberg, Frank O'Hara, Larry Rivers. His wife was white. His poetry was individualistic, well-crafted, and lauded by the critics. Those who knew him then described him as gentle, "the nicest man you ever met."

Then one day—it seemed to happen all of a sudden according to his white friends—he was among the angriest of black voices. His new hatred of whites led him to leave his white wife and his two half-white children to marry a black woman and start a nationalist organization called New Ark in Newark, New Jersey. Now Imamu Amiri Baraka, his poetry—and he was the father of the entire 1960s black poetry movement—advocated violence, the death of all whites, the moral and physical superiority of the black man, Black Macho.

But before he severed all ties with the white world, he remained with one foot in and one foot out for a period of a few years during which he wrote an essay called "American Sexual Reference: Black Male" (1965). According to Jones the struggle of black against white was the purity of primitivism against the corruption of technology, the noble savage against the pervert bureaucrats, the super macho against the fags.

> Most American white men are trained to be fags . . . they devote their energies to the non-physical, the nonrealistic . . . even their wars move to the stage where whole populations can be destroyed by *pushing a button* . . . the purer white, the more estranged from, say, actual physical work . . . can you, for a second, imagine the average middle class white man able to do somebody harm? Alone? Without the technology that at this moment still has him rule the world? Do you understand the softness of the white man, the weakness . . . .
> (Jones, "American Sexual Reference: Black Male," *Home*.)

Whites labeled him racist, but there turned out to be no cause for worry. In time Jones would prove himself neither a politician nor a general. He was first and last a writer. As a writer, even in his essay, he was most concerned with compelling images. What did it matter whether they were real or imagined? He would frequently pass up the moderate when there was an extreme within reach. Black Macho was the stuff of which stirring, gut-spilling prose was made and Jones seized the opportunity.

> . . . the black man and the white woman were not supposed to have any connections, even in anybody's wildest fantasies. This was (is?) the great taboo of the society. This taboo did a number of things. For one, it created for such a possible blackman-white-woman union an aura of mystery and wild sensuality that could provoke either principal to investigate, if either were intrepid or curious enough.
>
> The reason the white woman was supposed to be intrigued by the black man was because he was basic and elemental emotionally (which is true for the nonbrainwashed black, simply because there is no reason he should not be; the black man is more "natural" than the white simply because he has fewer *things* between him and reality, fewer wrappers, fewer artificial rules), therefore "wilder," harder, and almost insatiable in his lovemaking.
> (Jones, "American Sexual Reference: Black Male," *Home*.)

He admonishes black men for being taken in by the trap of pursuing white women—which is not to say that black men should spurn white pussy but that they should seize it rather than grovel for it. Whereas Mailer's rallying cry to the primitives seemed half tongue-in-cheek, Jones's seemed deadly serious.

> The most heinous crime against white society would be . . . the rape, the taking forcibly of one of whitie's treasures . . . the average ofay thinks of the black man as potentially raping every white lady in sight, which is true, in the sense that the black man should want to rob the white man of everything he has . . . for most whites the guilt of the robbery is the guilt of the rape. That is, they know in their deepest hearts that they *should* be robbed, and the white woman understands that only in the rape sequence is she likely to get cleanly, viciously popped . . . . The black man, then, because he can enter into the sex act with less guilt as to its results, is freer. Because of the robbery/rape syndrome, the black man will *take* the white woman in a way that does not support the myth of The Lady.
>
> (Jones, "American Sexual Reference: Black Male," *Home*.)

Jones had transformed Mailer's "sexual outlaw" into the role model for the black revolutionary— "the black man as robber/rapist (take it further, it is murderer . . .)". A compelling fictional character, he is a fascist in real life. Black men, with the help of Jones and others like him, would take the prototype of man as warrior, as conqueror blind to the rights of all but himself, as rapist and psychopath turned soldier, and use it as the English settler had used a similar form of macho to place the American continent at his feet.

That Jones wrote with such fanaticism and hatred does not surprise me. First, Jones as an individual had to negate his former love affair with whites. Second, throughout the so-called calm period of his earlier poetry there repeatedly emerges the voice of a man who has a tremendous amount of anger bottled up inside of him. In *Dutchman*, which was written in 1964, Clay, a young black man, says to Lula, a white woman who's been hassling him for being stiff, uptight, middle class:

> . . . If I'm a middle class fake white man . . . let me be. And let me be in the way I want. I'll rip your lousy breasts off! Let me be who I feel like being. Uncle Tom. Thomas. Whoever . . . . You don't know anything except what's there for you to see. An act. Lies. Device. Not the pure heart, the pumping black heart. You don't ever know that. And I sit here, in this buttoned-up suit, to keep myself from cutting all your throats. I mean wantonly . . . . All the hip white boys scream for Bird. And Bird saying, "Up your ass, feeble-minded ofay! Up your ass." And they sit there talking about the tortured genius of Charlie Parker. Bird would've played not a note of music if he just walked up to East Sixty-seventh Street and killed the first ten white people he saw. Not a note! And I'm the great would-be poet. Yes. That's right! Poet. Some kind of bastard literature . . . all it needs is a simple knife thrust. Just let me bleed you, you loud whore, and one poem vanished a whole people of neurotics, struggling to keep from being sane. And the only thing that would cure the neurosis would be your murder . . . all it needs is that simple act. Murder. Just murder! Would make us all sane. Ahhh. Shit. But who needs it. I'd rather be a fool. Insane. Safe with my words, and no deaths, and clean, hard thoughts, urging me to new conquests . . . .
>
> (Le Roi Jones, *Dutchman and the Slave*, New York: William Morrow, 1964.)

A recurring theme in his work is this one of masks, of "Cold air blown through narrow blind eyes. Flesh,/white hot metal. Glows as the day with its sun./It is a human love, I live inside. A bony skeleton/you recognize as words or simple feeling./But it has no feeling. As the metal, is hot, it is not/given to love./It burns the thing/inside it. And that thing/screams." (LeRoi Jones, "An Agony As Now," *The Dead Lecturer*, New York: Grove Press, 1964.)

No, I cannot consider Jones's verbal violence a surprise. To some degree it was predictable that he would crack under the pressure of the kind of extreme role playing he was doing. And it was also predictable that a man like that, a black man whose father was a postal employee and whose mother was a social worker, who was born in Newark and who wrote a book called *The Systems of Dante's Hell* (New York: Grove Press, 1965.) which according to a writer in the *Village Voice*, "sent critics scurrying off to examine his sources in Homer's *Odyssey*, Dante's *Inferno*, Tennyson's 'The Lotus-Eaters,' and Joyce's *Ulysses*," would ultimately swing so violently in the other direction. But that he was taken so seriously seems to me a sad comment on the Black Movement. Just how long had it been since a race of black conquerors had marched into town, looted the churches of the enemy, smashed their gods, and raped their women!

Cleaver, Jones's ideological other half, was an even more effective voice for Black Macho. A former rapist, he described himself as a student of Norman Mailer's "The White Negro." Their definitions of a revolutionary were similar. His raping was not a crime against women but a political act. The white man's culture rendered the white impotent, but the black man a super stud. Yet Cleaver was perhaps closer to the truth than Jones. He understood that, sexually, black women and white women were victims of America's history and that the white man was a victim of his own Frankenstein monster.

Cleaver did a lot to politicize sexuality in the Black Movement. One of his most dubious contributions was the idea that black homosexuality was synonymous with reactionary Uncle Tomism. This is particularly clear in his attack on Baldwin. He describes Baldwin's criticism of Mailer's "The White Negro" as "schoolmarmish" and then turns, none too subtly, to an examination of the black male homosexual.

> . . . it seems that many Negro homosexuals, acquiescing in this racial death-wish, are outraged and frustrated because in their sickness they are unable to have a baby by a white man. The cross they have to bear is that, already bending over and touching their toes for the white man, the fruit of their miscegenation is not the little half-white offspring of their dreams but an increase in the unwinding of their nerves—though they redouble their efforts and intake of the white man's sperm . . . .
>
> The white man has deprived him of his masculinity, castrated him in the center of his burning skull, and when he submits to this change and takes the white man for his lover as well as Big Daddy, he focuses on "whiteness" all the love in his pent up soul and turns the razor edge of hatred against "blackness"—upon himself, what he is, and all those who look like him, remind him of himself. He may even hate the darkness of night . . . .
>
> (Cleaver, "Notes on a Native Son," *Soul on Ice*.)

Soul on Ice was a book that appealed to the senses. Cleaver was violent and advocated violence. Cleaver was macho and the sixties were years in which macho heroism was highly exalted and taken seriously by many people of all sorts of political and intellectual persuasions (whites did not scorn Jones's macho but his racism, assuming it is possible to separate the two). People yearned for the smell of blood on a page and Cleaver provided it.

If one is to take Cleaver at his word, the black homosexual is counterrevolutionary (1) because he's being fucked and (2) because he's being fucked by a white man. By so doing he reduces himself to the status of our black grandmothers who, as everyone knows, were fucked by white men all the time.

However, it would follow that if *a black man were doing the fucking* and the one being fucked were a white man, the black male homosexual would be just as good a revolutionary as a black heterosexual male, if not a better one. Black Macho would have to lead to this conclusion. If whom you fuck indicates your power, then obviously the greatest power would be gained by fucking a white man first, a black man second, a white woman third and a black woman not at all. The most important rule is that *nobody* fucks you.

Finally, if homosexuals are put down, even though they're males, because they get fucked, where does that leave women in terms of revolution? Black Macho allowed for only the most primitive notion of women—women as possessions, women as the spoils of war, leaving black women with no resale value. As a possession, the black woman was a symbol of defeat, and therefore of little use to the revolution except as the performer of drudgery (not unlike her role in slavery).

The white man had offered white women privilege and prestige as accompaniments to his power. Black women were offered no such deal, just the same old hard labor, a new silence, and more loneliness. The patriarchal black macho of Malcolm X might have proven functional— black women might have suffered their oppression for years in comparative bliss—but black men were blinded by their resentment of black women, their envy of white men, and their irresistible urge to bring white women down a peg. With patriarchal macho it would have taken black men years to avenge themselves. With the narcissistic macho of the Black Movement, the results were immediate.

And when the black man went as far as the adoration of his own genitals could carry him, his revolution stopped. A big Afro, a rifle, and a penis in good working order were not enough to lick the white man's world after all.

Note

1. Michele Wallace, *Black Macho and the Myth of the Super Woman* (New York, NY: The Dial Press, 1979).

Ossie Davis

In his eulogy for Malcolm X, actor Ossie Davis proclaims that "Malcolm was our manhood. Our living black manhood."[1] This was considered a controversial statement, given that many considered Malcolm to be a violent, reverse racist, without ever having so much, as Davis says in the eulogy, as talked to or listened to him. Davis felt compelled to offer a response to those who questioned why he would eulogize Malcolm X. And his reasons for it are revealing. He says in part that he always wanted to speak out on racial matters but felt constrained by how Whites would view him. He found the death of Malcolm X to be an opportunity to come into his voice. Davis thus links voice, or the ability to speak out against injustice, as a practice of manhood.

On Malcolm X

Ossie Davis[2]

Mr. Davis wrote the following in response to a magazine editor's question: Why did you eulogize Malcolm X?

You are not the only person curious to know why I would eulogize a man like Malcolm X. Many who know and respect me have written letters. Of these letters I am proudest of those from a sixth-grade class of young white boys and girls who asked me to explain. I appreciate your giving me this chance to do so.

You may anticipate my defense somewhat by considering the following fact: no Negro has yet asked me that question. (My pastor in Grace Baptist Church where I teach Sunday school preached a sermon about Malcolm in which he called him a "giant in a sick world.") Every one of the many letters I got from my own people lauded Malcolm as a man, and commended me for having spoken at his funeral.

At the same time—and this is important—most of them took special pains to disagree with much or all of what Malcolm said and what he stood for. That is, with one singing exception, they all, every last, black, glory-hugging one of them, knew that Malcolm—whatever else he was or was not—*Malcolm was a man!*

White folks do not need anybody to remind them that they are men. We do! This was his one incontrovertible benefit to his people.

Protocol and common sense require that Negroes stand back and let the white man speak up for us, defend us, and lead us from behind the scene in our fight. This is the essence of Negro politics. But Malcolm said to hell with that! Get up off your knees and fight your own battles. That's the way to win back your self-respect. That's the way to make the white man respect you. And if he won't let you live like a man, he certainly can't keep you from dying like one!

Malcolm, as you can see, was refreshing excitement; he scared hell out of the rest of us, bred as we are to caution, to hypocrisy in the presence of white folks, to the smile that never fades. Malcolm knew that every white man in America profits directly or indirectly from his position vis-à-vis Negroes, profits from racism even though he does not practice it or believe in it.

He also knew that every Negro who did not challenge on the spot every instance of racism, overt or covert, committed against him and his people, who chose instead to swallow his spit and go on smiling, was an Uncle Tom and a traitor, without balls or guts, or any other commonly accepted aspects of manhood!

Now, we knew all these things as well as Malcolm did, but we also knew what happened to people who stick their necks out and say them. And if all the lies we tell ourselves by way of extenuation were put into print, it would constitute one of the great chapters in the history of man's justifiable cowardice in the face of other men.

But Malcolm kept snatching our lies away. He kept shouting the painful truth we whites and blacks did not want to hear from all the housetops. And he wouldn't stop for love nor money.

You can imagine what a howling, shocking nuisance this man was to both Negroes and whites. Once Malcolm fastened on you, you could not escape. He was one of the most fascinating and charming men I have ever met, and never hesitated to take his attractiveness and beat you to death with it. Yet his irritation, though painful to us, was most salutary. He would make you angry as hell, but he would also make you proud. It was impossible to remain defensive and apologetic about being a Negro in his presence. He wouldn't let you. And you always left his presence with the sneaky suspicion that maybe, after all, you *were* a man!

But in explaining Malcolm, let me take care not to explain him away. He had been a criminal, an addict, a pimp, and a prisoner; a racist, and a hater, he had really believed the white man was a devil. But all this had changed. Two days before his death, in commenting to Gordon Parks about his past life he said: "That was a mad scene. The sickness and madness of those days! I'm glad to be free of them."

And Malcolm was free. No one who knew him before and after his trip to Mecca could doubt that he had completely abandoned racism, separatism, and hatred. But he had not abandoned his shock-effect statements, his bristling agitation for immediate freedom in this country not only for blacks, but for everybody.

And most of all, in the area of race relations, he still delighted in twisting the white man's tail, and in making Uncle Toms, compromisers, and accommodationists—I deliberately include myself—thoroughly ashamed of the urbane and smiling hypocrisy we practice merely to exist in a world whose values we both envy and despise.

But even had Malcolm not changed, he would still have been a relevant figure on the American scene, standing in relation as he does, to the "responsible" civil rights leaders, just about where John Brown stood in relation to the "responsible" abolitionist in the fight against slavery. Almost all disagreed with Brown's mad and fanatical tactics which led him foolishly to attack a Federal arsenal at Harpers Ferry, to lose two sons there, and later to be hanged for treason.

Yet, today the world, and especially the Negro people, proclaim Brown not a traitor, but a hero and a martyr in a noble cause. So in future, I will not be surprised if men come to see that Malcolm X was, within his own limitations, and in his own inimitable style, also a martyr in that cause.

But there is much controversy still about this most controversial American, and I am content to wait for history to make the final decision.

But in personal judgment, there is no appeal from instinct. I knew the man personally, and however much I disagreed with him, I never doubted that Malcolm X, even when he was wrong, was always that rarest thing in the world among us Negroes: a true man.

And if, to protect my relations with the many good white folks who make it possible for me to earn a fairly good living in the entertainment industry, I was too chicken, too cautious, to admit that fact when he was alive, I thought at least that now, when all the white folks are safe from him at last, I could be honest with myself enough to lift my hat for one final salute to that brave, black, ironic gallantry, which was his style and hallmark, that shocking *zing* of fire-and-be-damned-to-you, so absolutely absent in every other Negro man I know, which brought him, too soon, to his death.

Notes

1. Ossie Davis, "Eulogy for Malcolm X," in *For Malcolm: Poems on the Life and the Death of Malcolm X*, eds. Dudley Randall and Margaret G. Burroughs (Detroit, MI: Broadside Press, 1969), pp. 121–122.
2. Ossie Davis, "On Malcolm X," in Alex Haley, *The Autobiography of Malcolm X* (New York, NY: Ballantine Books, 1992).

Barack Obama

As the first African American president of the U.S. (2008–2016), Barack Obama is often presented as a role model for other African American men. As such, it is important to assess his writing about growing into manhood, which he offers in his autobiography *Dreams from my Father*. In this book, and in the selection here from it, Obama details what it means to be a Black man of biracial decent who is raised by his White grandparents. In addition to what Obama reveals in the book about manhood and masculinity, it is important to keep in mind the varied and contradictory responses that the American public have to him and his performance of Black manhood. Just as much as he is praised for his achievements as a Black man, he is vilified by his opponents for his cool, even temperament and erudite style of communication. Obama's own self-reflections reveal the discourses that influenced his concept of what it means to be a man.

Dreams From My Father, Chapter Four

Barack Obama[1]

Man, I'm not going to any more of these bullshit Punahou parties."

"Yeah, that's what you said the last time."

Ray and I sat down at a table and unwrapped our hamburgers. He was two years older than me, a senior who, as a result of his father's army transfer, had arrived from Los Angeles the previous year. Despite the difference in age, we'd fallen into an easy friendship, due in no small part to the fact that together we made up almost half of Punahou's black high school population. I enjoyed his company; he had a warmth and brash humor that made up for his constant references to a former L.A. life—the retinue of women who supposedly still called him long-distance every night, his past football exploits, the celebrities he knew. Most of the things he told me I tended to discount, but not everything; it was true, for example, that he was one of the fastest sprinters in the islands, Olympic caliber some said, this despite an improbably large stomach that quivered under his sweat-soaked jersey whenever he ran and left coaches and opposing teams shaking their heads in disbelief. Through Ray I would find out about the black parties that were happening at the university or out on the army bases, counting on him to ease my passage through unfamiliar terrain. In return, I gave him a sounding board for his frustrations.

"I mean it this time," he was saying to me now. "These girls are A-1, USDA-certified racists. All of 'em. White girls. Asian girls—shoot, these Asians worse than the whites. Think we got a disease or something."

"Maybe they're looking at that big butt of yours. Man, I thought you were in training."

"Get your hands out of my fries. You ain't my bitch, nigger . . . buy your own damn fries. Now what was I talking about?"

"Just 'cause a girl don't go out with you doesn't make her racist."

"Don't be thick, all right? I'm not just talking about one time. Look, I ask Monica out, she says no. I say okay . . . your shit's not so hot anyway." Ray stopped to check my reaction, then smiled. "All right, maybe I don't actually say all that. I just tell her okay, Monica, you know, we still tight. Next thing I know, she's hooked up with Steve 'No Neck' Yamaguchi, the two of 'em all holding hands and shit, like a couple of lovebirds. So fine—I figure there're more fish in the sea. I go ask Pamela out. She tells me she ain't going to the dance. I say cool. Get to the dance, guess who's standing there, got her arms around Rick Cook. '*Hi, Ray*,' she says, like she don't know what's going down. Rick Cook! Now you know that guy ain't shit. Sorry-assed motherfucker got nothing on me, right? Nothing."

He stuffed a handful of fries into his mouth. "It ain't just me, by the way. I don't see you doing any better in the booty department."

Because I'm shy, I thought to myself; but I would never admit that to him. Ray pressed the advantage.

"So what happens when we go out to a party with some sisters, huh? What happens? I tell you what happens. Blam! They on us like there's no tomorrow. High school chicks, university chicks—it don't matter. They acting sweet, all smiles. 'Sure you can have my number, baby.' Bet."

"Well . . ."

"Well what? Listen, why don't you get more playing time on the basketball team, huh? At least two guys ahead of you ain't nothing, and you know it, and they know it. I seen you tear 'em up on the playground, no contest. Why wasn't I starting on the football squad this season, no matter how many passes the other guy dropped? Tell me we wouldn't be treated different if we was white. Or Japanese. Or Hawaiian. Or fucking Eskimo."

"That's not what I'm saying."

"So what are you saying?"

"All right, here's what I'm saying. I'm saying, yeah, it's harder to get dates because there aren't any black girls around here. But that don't make the girls that are here all racist. Maybe they just want somebody that looks like their daddy, or their brother, or whatever, and we ain't it. I'm saying yeah, I might not get the breaks on the team that some guys get, but they play like white boys do, and that's the style the coach likes to play, and they're winning the way they play. I don't play that way.

"As for your greasy-mouthed self," I added, reaching for the last of his fries, "I'm saying the coaches may not like you 'cause you're a smart-assed black man, but it might help if you stopped eating all them fries you eat, making you look six months pregnant. That's what I'm saying."

"Man, I don't know why you making excuses for these folks." Ray got up and crumpled his trash into a tight ball. "Let's get out of here. Your shit's getting way too complicated for me."

Ray was right; things had gotten complicated. It had been five years since my father's visit, and on the surface, at least, it had been a placid time marked by the usual rites and rituals that America expects from its children—marginal report cards and calls to the principal's office, part-time jobs at the burger chain, acne and driving tests and turbulent desire. I'd made my share of friends at school, gone on the occasional awkward date; and if I sometimes puzzled over the mysterious realignments of status that took place among my classmates, as some rose and others fell depending on the whims of their bodies or the make of their cars, I took comfort in the knowledge that my own position had steadily improved. Rarely did I meet kids whose families had less than mine and might remind me of good fortune.

My mother did her best to remind me. She had separated from Lolo and returned to Hawaii to pursue a master's degree in anthropology shortly after my own arrival. For three years I lived with her and Maya in a small apartment a block away from Punahou, my mother's student grants supporting the three of us. Sometimes, when I brought friends home after school, my mother would overhear them remark about the lack of food in the fridge or the less-than-perfect housekeeping, and she would pull me aside and let me know that she was a single mother going to school again and raising two kids, so that baking cookies wasn't exactly at the top of her priority list, and while she appreciated the fine education I was receiving at Punahou, she wasn't planning on putting up with any snotty attitudes from me or anyone else, was that understood?

It was understood. Despite my frequent—and sometimes sullen—claims of independence, the two of us remained close, and I did my best to help her out where I could, shopping for groceries, doing the laundry, looking after the knowing, dark-eyed child that my sister had become. But when my mother was ready to return to Indonesia to do her field work, and suggested that I go back with her and Maya to attend the international school there, I immediately said no. I doubted what Indonesia now had to offer and wearied of being new all over again. More than that, I'd arrived at an unspoken pact with my grandparents: I could live with them and they'd leave me alone so long as I kept my trouble out of sight. The arrangement suited my purpose, a purpose that I could barely articulate to myself, much less to them. Away from my mother, away from my grandparents, I was engaged in a fitful interior struggle. I was trying to raise myself to be a black man in America, and beyond the given of my appearance, no one around me seemed to know exactly what that meant.

My father's letters provided few clues. They would arrive sporadically, on a single blue page with gummed-down flaps that obscured any writing at the margins. He would report that everyone was fine, commend me on my progress in school, and insist that my mother, Maya, and I were all welcome to take our rightful place beside him whenever we so desired. From time to time he would include advice, usually in the form of aphorisms I didn't quite understand ("Like water finding its level, you will arrive at a career that suits you"). I would respond promptly on a wide-ruled page, and his letters would find their way into the closet, next to my mother's pictures of him.

Gramps had a number of black male friends, mostly poker and bridge partners, and before I got old enough not to care about hurting his feelings, I would let him drag me along to some of their games. They were old, neatly dressed men with hoarse voices and clothes that smelled of cigars, the kind of men for whom everything has its place and who figure they've seen enough not to have to waste a lot of time talking about it. Whenever they saw me they would give me a jovial slap on the back and ask how my mother was doing; but once it was time to play, they wouldn't say another word except to complain to their partner about a bid.

There was one exception, a poet named Frank who lived in a dilapidated house in a rundown section of Waikiki. He had enjoyed some modest notoriety once, was a contemporary of Richard Wright and Langston Hughes during his years in Chicago—Gramps once showed me some of his work anthologized in a book of black poetry. But by the time I met Frank he must have been pushing eighty, with a big, dewlapped face and an ill-kempt gray Afro that made him look like an old, shaggy-maned lion. He would read us his poetry whenever we stopped by his house, sharing whiskey with Gramps out of an emptied jelly jar. As the night wore on, the two of them would solicit my help in composing dirty limericks. Eventually, the conversation would turn to laments about women.

"They'll drive you to drink, boy," Frank would tell me soberly. "And if you let 'em, they'll drive you into your grave."

I was intrigued by old Frank, with his books and whiskey breath and the hint of hard-earned knowledge behind the hooded eyes. The visits to his house always left me feeling vaguely uncomfortable, though, as if I were witnessing some complicated, unspoken transaction between the two men, a transaction I couldn't fully understand. The same thing I felt whenever Gramps took me downtown to one of his favorite bars, in Honolulu's red-light district.

"Don't tell your grandmother," he would say with a wink, and we'd walk past hard-faced, softbodied streetwalkers into a small, dark bar with a jukebox and a couple of pool tables. Nobody seemed to mind that Gramps was the only white man in the place, or that I was the only eleven-or twelve-year-old. Some of the men leaning across the bar would wave at us, and the bartender, a big, light-skinned woman with bare, fleshy arms, would bring a Scotch for Gramps and a Coke for me. If nobody else was playing at the tables, Gramps would spot me a few balls and teach me the game, but usually I would sit at the bar, my legs dangling from the high stool, blowing bubbles into my drink and looking at the pornographic art on the walls—the phosphorescent women on animal skins, the Disney characters in compromising positions. If he was around, a man named Rodney with a wide-brimmed hat would stop by to say hello.

"How's school coming, captain?"

"All right."

"You getting them *A*'s, ain't you?"

"Some."

"That's good. Sally, buy my man here another Coke," Rodney would say, peeling a twenty off a thick stack he had pulled from his pocket before he fell back into the shadows.

I can still remember the excitement I felt during those evening trips, the enticement of darkness and the click of the cue ball, and the jukebox flashing its red and green lights, and the weary laughter that ran around the room. Yet even then, as young as I was, I had already begun to sense that most of the people in the bar weren't there out of choice, that what my grandfather sought there was the company of people who could help him forget his own troubles, people who he believed would not judge him. Maybe the bar really did help him forget, but I knew with the unerring instincts of a child that he was wrong about not being judged. Our presence there felt forced, and by the time I had reached junior high school I had learned to beg off from Gramps's invitations, knowing that whatever it was I was after, whatever it was that I needed, would have to come from some other source.

TV, movies, the radio; those were the places to start. Pop culture was color-coded, after all, an arcade of images from which you could cop a walk, a talk, a step, a style. I couldn't croon like Marvin Gaye, but I could learn to dance all the *Soul Train* steps. I couldn't pack a gun like Shaft or Superfly, but I could sure enough curse like Richard Pryor.

And I could play basketball, with a consuming passion that would always exceed my limited talent. My father's Christmas gift had come at a time when the University of Hawaii basketball team had slipped into the national rankings on the strength of an all-black starting five that the school had shipped in from the mainland. That same spring, Gramps had taken me to one of their games, and I had watched the players in warm-ups, still boys themselves but to me poised and confident warriors, chuckling to each other about some inside joke, glancing over the heads of fawning fans to wink at the girls on the sidelines, casually flipping layups or tossing high-arcing jumpers until the whistle blew and the centers jumped and the players joined in furious battle.

I decided to become part of that world, and began going down to a playground near my grandparents' apartment after school. From her bedroom window, ten stories up, Toot would watch me on the court until well after dark as I threw the ball with two hands at first, then developed an awkward jump shot, a crossover dribble, absorbed in the same solitary moves hour after hour. By the time I reached high school, I was playing on Punahou's teams, and could take my game to the university courts, where a handful of black men, mostly gym rats and has-beens, would teach me an attitude that didn't just have to do with the sport. That respect came from what you did and not who your daddy was. That you could talk stuff to rattle an opponent, but that you should shut the hell up if you couldn't back it up. That you didn't let anyone sneak up behind you to see emotions—like hurt or fear—you didn't want them to see.

And something else, too, something nobody talked about: a way of being together when the game was tight and the sweat broke and the best players stopped worrying about their points and the worst players got swept up in the moment and the score only mattered because that's how you sustained the trance. In the middle of which you might make a move or a pass that surprised even you, so that even the guy guarding you had to smile, as if to say, "Damn . . ."

My wife will roll her eyes right about now. She grew up with a basketball star for a brother, and when she wants to wind either of us up she will insist that she'd rather see her son play the cello. She's right, of course; I was living out a caricature of black male adolescence, itself a caricature of swaggering American manhood. Yet at a time when boys aren't supposed to want to follow their fathers' tired footsteps, when the imperatives of harvest or work in the factory aren't supposed to dictate identity, so that how to live is bought off the rack or found in magazines, the principal difference between me and most of the man-boys around me—the surfers, the football players, the would-be rock-and-roll guitarists—resided in the limited number of options at my disposal. Each of us chose a costume, armor against uncertainty. At least on the basketball court I could find a community of sorts, with an inner life all its own. It was there that I would make my closest white friends, on turf where blackness couldn't be a disadvantage. And it was there that I would meet Ray and the other blacks close to my age who had begun to trickle into the islands, teenagers whose confusion and anger would help shape my own.

"That's just how white folks will do you," one of them might say when we were alone. Everybody would chuckle and shake their heads, and my mind would run down a ledger of slights: the first boy, in seventh grade, who called me a coon; his tears of surprise—"Why'dya do that?"—when I gave him a bloody nose. The tennis pro who told me during a tournament that I shouldn't touch the schedule of matches pinned up to the bulletin board because my color might rub off; his thin-lipped, red-faced smile—"Can't you take a joke?"—when I threatened to report him. The older woman in my grandparents' apartment building who became agitated when I got on the elevator behind her and ran out to tell the manager that I was following her; her refusal to apologize when she was told that I lived in the building. Our assistant basketball coach, a young, wiry man from New York with a nice jumper, who, after a pick-up game with some talkative black men, had muttered within earshot of me and three of my teammates that we shouldn't have lost to a bunch of niggers; and who, when I told him—with a fury that surprised even me—to shut up, had calmly explained the apparently obvious fact that "there are black people, and there are niggers. Those guys were niggers."

That's just how white folks will do you. It wasn't merely the cruelty involved; I was learning that black people could be mean and then some. It was a particular brand of arrogance, an obtuseness in otherwise sane people that brought forth our bitter laughter. It was as if whites didn't know they were being cruel in the first place. Or at least thought you deserving of their scorn.

White Folks

The term itself was uncomfortable in my mouth at first; I felt like a non-native speaker tripping over a difficult phrase. Sometimes I would find myself talking to Ray about *white folks* this or *white folks* that, and I would suddenly remember my mother's smile, and the words that I spoke would seem awkward and false. Or I would be helping Gramps dry the dishes after dinner and Toot would come in to say she was going to sleep, and those same words—*white folks*—would flash in my head like a bright neon sign, and I would suddenly grow quiet, as if I had secrets to keep.

Later, when I was alone, I would try to untangle these difficult thoughts. It was obvious that certain whites could be exempted from the general category of our distrust: Ray was always telling me how cool my grandparents were. The term *white* was simply a shorthand for him, I decided, a tag for what my mother would call a bigot. And although I recognized the risks in his terminology—how easy it was to fall into the same sloppy thinking that my basketball coach had displayed ("There are white folks, and then there are ignorant motherfuckers like you," I had finally told the coach before walking off the court that day)—Ray assured me that we would never talk about whites as whites in front of whites without knowing exactly what we were doing. Without knowing that there might be a price to pay.

But was that right? Was there still a price to pay? That was the complicated part, the thing that Ray and I never could seem to agree on. There were times when I would listen to him tell some blond girl he'd just met about life on L.A.'s mean streets, or hear him explain the scars of racism to some eager young teacher, and I could swear that just beneath the sober expression Ray was winking at me, letting me in on the score. Our rage at the white world needed no object, he seemed to be telling me, no independent confirmation; it could be switched on and off at our pleasure. Sometimes, after one of his performances, I would question his judgment, if not his sincerity. We weren't living in the Jim Crow South, I would remind him. We weren't consigned to some heatless housing project in Harlem or the Bronx. We were in goddamned Hawaii. We said what we pleased, ate where we pleased; we sat at the front of the proverbial bus. None of our white friends, guys like Jeff or Scott from the basketball team, treated us any differently than they treated each other. They loved us, and we loved them back. Shit, seemed like half of 'em wanted to be black themselves—or at least Doctor J.

Well, that's true, Ray would admit.

Maybe we could afford to give the bad-assed nigger pose a rest. Save it for when we really needed it.

And Ray would shake his head. A pose, huh? Speak for your own self.

And I would know that Ray had flashed his trump card, one that, to his credit, he rarely played. I was different, after all, potentially suspect; I had no idea who my own self was. Unwilling to risk exposure, I would quickly retreat to safer ground.

Perhaps if we had been living in New York or L.A., I would have been quicker to pick up the rules of the high-stake game we were playing. As it was, I learned to slip back and forth between my black and white worlds, understanding that each possessed its own language and customs and structures of meaning, convinced that with a bit of translation on my part the two worlds would eventually cohere. Still, the feeling that something wasn't quite right stayed with me, a warning that sounded whenever a white girl mentioned in the middle of conversation how much she liked Stevie Wonder; or when a woman in the supermarket asked me if I played basketball; or when the school principal told me I was cool. I did like Stevie Wonder, I did love basketball, and I tried my best to be cool at all times. So why did such comments always set me on edge? There was a trick there somewhere, although what the trick was, who was doing the tricking, and who was being tricked, eluded my conscious grasp.

One day in early spring Ray and I met up after class and began walking in the direction of the stone bench that circled a big banyan tree on Punahou's campus. It was called the Senior Bench, but it served mainly as a gathering place for the high school's popular crowd, the jocks and cheerleaders and partygoing set, with their jesters, attendants, and ladies-in-waiting jostling for position up and down the circular steps. One of the seniors, a stout defensive tackle named Kurt, was there, and he shouted loudly as soon as he saw us.

"Hey, Ray! Mah main man! Wha's happenin'!"

Ray went up and slapped Kurt's outstretched palm. But when Kurt repeated the gesture to me, I waved him off.

"What's his problem?" I overheard Kurt say to Ray as I walked away. A few minutes later, Ray caught up with me and asked me what was wrong.

"Man, those folks are just making fun of us," I said.

"What're you talking about?"

"All that 'Yo baby, give me five' bullshit."

"So who's mister sensitive all of a sudden? Kurt don't mean nothing by it."

"If that's what you think, then hey—"

Ray's face suddenly glistened with anger. "Look," he said, "I'm just getting along, all right? Just like I see you getting along, talking your game with the teachers when you need them to do you a favor. All that stuff about 'Yes, Miss Snooty Bitch, I just find this novel so engaging, if I can just have one more day for that paper, I'll kiss your white ass.' It's their world, all right? They own it, and we in it. So just get the fuck outta my face."

By the following day, the heat of our argument had dissipated, and Ray suggested that I invite our friends Jeff and Scott to a party Ray was throwing out at his house that weekend. I hesitated for a moment—we had never brought white friends along to a black party—but Ray insisted, and I couldn't find a good reason to object. Neither could Jeff or Scott; they both agreed to come so long as I was willing to drive. And so that Saturday night, after one of our games, the three of us piled into Gramps's old Ford Granada and rattled our way out to Schofield Barracks, maybe thirty miles out of town.

When we arrived the party was well on its way, and we steered ourselves toward the refreshments. The presence of Jeff and Scott seemed to make no waves; Ray introduced them around the room, they made some small talk, they took a couple of the girls out on the dance floor. But I could see right away that the scene had taken my white friends by surprise. They kept smiling a lot. They huddled together in a corner. They nodded self-consciously to the beat of the music and said "Excuse me" every few minutes. After maybe an hour, they asked me if I'd be willing to take them home.

"What's the matter?" Ray shouted over the music when I went to let him know we were leaving. "Things just starting to heat up."

"They're not into it, I guess."

Our eyes met, and for a long stretch we just stood there, the noise and laughter pulsing around us. There were no traces of satisfaction in Ray's eyes, no hints of disappointment; just a steady gaze, as unblinking as a snake's. Finally he put out his hand, and I grabbed hold of it, our eyes still fixed on each other. "Later, then," he said, his hand slipping free from mine, and I watched him walk away through the crowd, asking about the girl he'd been talking to just a few minutes before.

Outside the air had turned cool. The street was absolutely empty, quiet except for the fading tremor of Ray's stereo, the blue lights flickering in the windows of bungalows that ran up and down the tidy lane, the shadows of trees stretching across a baseball field. In the car, Jeff put an arm on my shoulder, looking at once contrite and relieved. "You know, man," he said, "that really taught me something. I mean, I can see how it must be tough for you and Ray sometimes, at school parties . . . being the only black guys and all."

I snorted. "Yeah. Right." A part of me wanted to punch him right there. We started down the road toward town, and in the silence, my mind began to rework Ray's words that day with Kurt, all the discussions we had had before that, the events of that night. And by the time I had dropped my friends off, I had begun to see a new map of the world, one that was frightening in its simplicity, suffocating in its implications. We were always playing on the white man's court, Ray had told me, by the white man's rules. If the principal, or the coach, or a teacher, or Kurt, wanted to spit in your face, he could, because he had power and you didn't. If he decided not to, if he treated you like a man or came to your defense, it was because he knew that the words you spoke, the clothes you wore, the books you read, your ambitions and desires, were already his. Whatever he decided to do, it was his decision to make, not yours, and because of that fundamental power he held over you, because it preceded and would outlast his individual motives and inclinations, any distinction between good and bad whites held negligible meaning. In fact, you couldn't even be sure that everything you had assumed to be an expression of your black, unfettered self—the humor, the song, the behind-the-back pass—had been freely chosen by you. At best, these things were a refuge; at worst, a trap. Following this maddening logic, the only thing you could choose as your own was withdrawal into a smaller and smaller coil of rage, until being black meant only the knowledge of your own powerlessness, of your own defeat. And the final irony: Should you refuse this defeat and lash out at your captors, they would have a name for that, too, a name that could cage you just as good. Paranoid. Militant. Violent. Nigger.

Over the next few months, I looked to corroborate this nightmare vision. I gathered up books from the library—Baldwin, Ellison, Hughes, Wright, DuBois. At night I would close the door to my room, telling my grandparents I had homework to do, and there I would sit and wrestle with words, locked in suddenly desperate argument, trying to reconcile the world as I'd found it with the terms of my birth. But there was no escape to be had. In every page of every book, in Bigger Thomas and invisible men, I kept finding the same anguish, the same doubt; a self-contempt that neither irony nor intellect seemed able to deflect. Even DuBois's learning and Baldwin's love and Langston's humor eventually succumbed to its corrosive force, each man finally forced to doubt art's redemptive power, each man finally forced to withdraw, one to Africa, one to Europe, one deeper into the bowels of Harlem, but all of them in the same weary flight, all of them exhausted, bitter men, the devil at their heels.

Only Malcolm X's autobiography seemed to offer something different. His repeated acts of self-creation spoke to me; the blunt poetry of his words, his unadorned insistence on respect, promised a new and uncompromising order, martial in its discipline, forged through sheer force of will. All the other stuff, the talk of blue-eyed devils and apocalypse, was incidental to that program, I decided, religious baggage that Malcolm himself seemed to have safely abandoned toward the end of his life. And yet, even as I imagined myself following Malcolm's call, one line in the book stayed me. He spoke of a wish he'd once had, the wish that the white blood that ran through him, there by an act of violence, might somehow be expunged. I knew that, for Malcolm, that wish would never be incidental. I knew as well that traveling down the road to self-respect my own white blood would never recede into mere abstraction. I was left to wonder what else I would be severing if and when I left my mother and my grandparents at some uncharted border.

And, too: If Malcolm's discovery toward the end of his life, that some whites might live beside him as brothers in Islam, seemed to offer some hope of eventual reconciliation, that hope appeared in a distant future, in a far-off land. In the meantime, I looked to see where the people would come from who were willing to work toward this future and populate this new world. After a basketball game at the university gym one day, Ray and I happened to strike up a conversation with a tall, gaunt man named Malik who played with us now and again. Malik mentioned that he was a follower of the Nation of Islam but that since Malcolm had died and he had moved to Hawaii he no longer went to mosque or political meetings, although he still sought comfort in solitary prayer. One of the guys sitting nearby must have overheard us, for he leaned over with a sagacious expression on his face.

"You all talking about Malcolm, huh? Malcolm tells it like it is, no doubt about it."

"Yeah," another guy said. "But I tell you what—you won't see me moving to no African jungle anytime soon. Or some goddamned desert somewhere, sitting on a carpet with a bunch of Arabs. No sir. And you won't see me stop eating no ribs."

"Gotta have them ribs."

"And pussy, too. Don't Malcolm talk about no pussy? Now you know that ain't gonna work."

I noticed Ray laughing and looked at him sternly. "What are you laughing at?" I said to him. "You've never read Malcolm. You don't even know what he says."

Ray grabbed the basketball out of my hand and headed for the opposite rim. "I don't need no books to tell me how to be black," he shouted over his head. I started to answer, then turned to Malik, expecting some words of support. But the Muslim said nothing, his bony face set in a faraway smile.

I decided to keep my own counsel after that, learning to disguise my feverish mood. A few weeks later, though, I awoke to the sound of an argument in the kitchen—my grandmother's voice barely audible, followed by my grandfather's deep growl. I opened my door to see Toot entering their bedroom to get dressed for work. I asked her what was wrong.

"Nothing. Your grandfather just doesn't want to drive me to work this morning, that's all."

When I entered the kitchen, Gramps was muttering under his breath. He poured himself a cup of coffee as I told him that I would be willing to give Toot a ride to work if he was tired. It was a bold offer, for I didn't like to wake up early. He scowled at my suggestion.

"That's not the point. She just wants me to feel bad."

"I'm sure that's not it, Gramps."

"Of course it is." He sipped from his coffee. "She's been catching the bus ever since she started at the bank. She said it was more convenient. And now, just because she gets pestered a little, she wants to change everything."

Toot's diminutive figure hovered in the hall, peering at us from behind her bifocals.

"That's not true, Stanley."

I took her into the other room and asked her what had happened.

"A man asked me for money yesterday. While I was waiting for the bus."

"That's all?"

Her lips pursed with irritation. "He was very aggressive, Barry. Very aggressive. I gave him a dollar and he kept asking. If the bus hadn't come, I think he might have hit me over the head."

I returned to the kitchen. Gramps was rinsing his cup, his back turned to me. "Listen," I said, "why don't you just let me give her a ride. She seems pretty upset."

"By a panhandler?"

"Yeah, I know—but it's probably a little scary for her, seeing some big man block her way. It's really no big deal."

He turned around and I saw now that he was shaking. "It *is* a big deal. It's a big deal to me. She's been bothered by men before. You know why she's so scared this time? I'll tell you why. Before you came in, she told me the fella was *black*." He whispered the word. "That's the real reason why she's bothered. And I just don't think that's right."

The words were like a fist in my stomach, and I wobbled to regain my composure. In my steadiest voice, I told him that such an attitude bothered me, too, but assured him that Toot's fears would pass and that we should give her a ride in the meantime. Gramps slumped into a chair in the living room and said he was sorry he had told me. Before my eyes, he grew small and old and very sad. I put my hand on his shoulder and told him that it was all right, I understood.

We remained like that for several minutes, in painful silence. Finally he insisted that he drive Toot after all, and struggled up from his seat to get dressed. After they left, I sat on the edge of my bed and thought about my grandparents. They had sacrificed again and again for me. They had poured all their lingering hopes into my success. Never had they given me reason to doubt their love; I doubted if they ever would. And yet I knew that men who might easily have been my brothers could still inspire their rawest fears.

That night, I drove into Waikiki, past the bright-lit hotels and down toward the Ala-Wai Canal. It took me a while to recognize the house, with its wobbly porch and low-pitched roof. Inside, the light was on, and I could see Frank sitting in his overstuffed chair, a book of poetry in his lap, his reading glasses slipping down his nose. I sat in the car, watching him for a time, then finally got out and tapped on the door. The old man barely looked up as he rose to undo the latch. It had been three years since I'd seen him.

"Want a drink?" he asked me. I nodded and watched him pull down a bottle of whiskey and two plastic cups from the kitchen cupboard. He looked the same, his mustache a little whiter, dangling like dead ivy over his heavy upper lip, his cut-off jeans with a few more holes and tied at the waist with a length of rope.

"How's your grandpa?"

"He's all right."

"So what are you doing here?"

I wasn't sure. I told Frank some of what had happened. He nodded and poured us each a shot. "Funny cat, your grandfather," he said. "You know we grew up maybe fifty miles apart?"

I shook my head.

"We sure did. Both of us lived near Wichita. We didn't know each other, of course. I was long gone by the time he was old enough to remember anything. I might have seen some of his people, though. Might've passed 'em on the street. If I did, I would've had to step off the side-walk to give 'em room. Your grandpa ever tell you about things like that?"

I threw the whiskey down my throat, shaking my head again.

"Naw," Frank said, "I don't suppose he would have. Stan doesn't like to talk about that part of Kansas much. Makes him uncomfortable. He told me once about a black girl they hired to look after your mother. A preacher's daughter, I think it was. Told me how she became a regular part of the family. That's how he remembers it, you understand—this girl coming in to look after somebody else's children, her mother coming to do somebody else's laundry. A regular part of the family."

I reached for the bottle, this time pouring my own. Frank wasn't watching me; his eyes were closed now, his head leaning against the back of his chair, his big wrinkled face like a carving of stone. "You can't blame Stan for what he is," Frank said quietly. "He's basically a good man. But he doesn't *know* me. Any more than he knew that girl that looked after your mother. He *can't* know me, not the way I know him. Maybe some of these Hawaiians can, or the Indians on the reservation. They've seen their fathers humiliated. Their mothers desecrated. But your grandfather will never know what that feels like. That's why he can come over here and drink my whiskey and fall asleep in that chair you're sitting in right now. Sleep like a baby. See, that's something I can never do in his house. *Never.* Doesn't matter how tired I get, I still have to watch myself. I have to be vigilant, for my own survival."

Frank opened his eyes. "What I'm trying to tell you is, your grandma's right to be scared. She's at least as right as Stanley is. She understands that black people have a reason to hate. That's just how it is. For your sake, I wish it were otherwise. But it's not. So you might as well get used to it."

Frank closed his eyes again. His breathing slowed until he seemed to be asleep. I thought about waking him, then decided against it and walked back to the car. The earth shook under my feet, ready to crack open at any moment. I stopped, trying to steady myself, and knew for the first time that I was utterly alone.

Note

1. Barack Obama, *Dreams From My Father: A Story of Race and Inheritance* (New York, NY: Three Rivers Press, 1995).

Michael Awkward

Michael Awkward is an academic who studies and writes about Black feminisms. Feminism becomes the framework through which he studies himself in his scholarly autobiography, *Scenes of Instruction* (1999). The whole book is structured around a series of significant academic events in Awkward's life. In the selection that follows, Awkward ruminates on the feats of manhood that he had to endure and overcome as he came of age and came into an understanding of himself as a man in the face of competing discourses and perceptions about what a real man should be and not be. The experiences that Awkward discusses reveals that manhood is not a single, agreed-upon construct, but is a constant negotiation of ideas and practices that begin early in life and continue well into adulthood.

Scenes of Instruction, Section II: Are You Man Enough?

Michael Awkward[1]

The graduation exercises culminated with the announcement of the winners of the outstanding female and male awards. When Mr. G. mentioned these prizes at the beginning of the proceedings, before the academic and vocational subject awards had been given out, the idea of them seemed utterly ridiculous to me. Most of the teachers didn't know most of the students, had had no contact with the great majority of them, and hence couldn't reliably assess our relative outstandingness. Also, "outstanding" in this context was so vague a term that it was virtually meaningless. What criteria did they use to determine outstandingness? Grades? Standardized test scores? Potential for future success? The one criterion I remember Mr. G. mentioning was "contributions to the school," but given Bartlett's manifest lack of organized opportunities for service, extracurricular and otherwise, it was unclear to me what we could have contributed, and to whom.

Because of my ceremonial bounty to that point, my relative success at standardized test taking, and my having been awarded a scholarship to a prestigious prep school, I sat nervously through the last minutes of the ceremony, convinced I'd be chosen. I knew I didn't deserve such recognition—in truth, I hadn't contributed much of anything to the school that I was aware of—but I wanted it, and I suspected that few in the auditorium would have been surprised if my name was called. I sat, shaking like a leaf on a tree, as Nadine, one of the North Philly yearbook girls, the head editor, in fact, tall and pretty and charismatic, walked up to receive the prize for outstanding female. As she strutted back to her seat, grinning from ear to ear, some of my friends—none of whom had known anything at all about the award before the graduation began—patted me on the back and punched me lightly on the arm, sure that I'd be called next.

Mr. G. called Steve instead. Steve was a chubby, jovial, brownnosing North Philly boy who, like Nadine, was from a section other than the star academic group. His behavior often seemed an affront to the norms of masculinity against which all of the males in my class were measured. Although we didn't tease our two budding gay classmates about their soft, high voices, loose-hipped walks, and obvious lack of interest in being anything more than friends with the girls in our class, boys had spent their entire junior high school careers referring to Steve as a "faggot." That obviously derisive characterization had very little to do with his projecting any stereotypically gay traits but was motivated by his atypicality. He eschewed sports, tough talk, girl ogling, fistfights—rituals through which we periodically tested and measured our masculinity—and instead settled on the role of good boy to teachers, for whom he ran all sorts of errands and proved exceedingly trustworthy.

For a number of teachers and a few of his female classmates, who enjoyed having their needs attended to so energetically and efficiently, his cloying, kiss-ass, choirboy, eraser-cleaning routine did not, in fact, represent the personification of all that black boys could not and should not be—as it did for the rest of us. He did not lack personal toughness and integrity, and when he was insulted by some of the boys who had known him before he came to Bartlett, he could defend himself verbally quite well. But even those defensive moments, during which he would set his jaw, gaze sincerely at his would-be assailant, and assert his right to act in any way he felt comfortable, demonstrated his difference, as he never gave any indication that he wanted to smack the shit out of someone for fucking with him too much. At such moments—in fact, at nearly every moment I witnessed his behavior—he acted on the belief that sincerity, honesty, and integrity would work for and change others' minds about him.

That he hadn't excelled academically in any appreciable way—he hadn't been even a runner-up for any of the academic awards—didn't matter to the teachers. That he hadn't won the respect of the majority of his classmates didn't matter, either. What mattered, to the teachers and perhaps to others of the assembled masses who beheld his triumph, was that he represented a safe, pliable version of black boyhood in an institutional and social context dominated by masculine unruliness.

As I watched Steve receive the congratulations of the principal, I felt a level of resentment well out of proportion with my desire for, or belief that I was indeed deserving of, that award. My academic awards began to seem merely a tease, a concession, a begrudging recognition that even in a context where it was supposed to be prized, supported, and encouraged, the only personal quality I possessed significant quantities of that the society insisted it valued—school smarts—was ultimately of no real significance.

This moment represented the culmination of a yearlong process of learning that to be deemed truly outstanding, to win the respect of my teachers, the patience, understanding, and affection of girls, and the favor—or at least the noncontempt—of my mother, I had to be different than I was. Mine was solely a quantitative accomplishment, a victory by the numbers. Qualitatively speaking, the skills and personal characteristics I'd displayed or possessed were only marginally important. Overwhelming evidence of my academic abilities didn't persuade a sufficient number of teachers to vote in my favor. My deep, sincere, tongue-tied affection for Alannah wasn't enough to compensate for my fear and romantic inexperience. And the fact that I obviously wasn't my father didn't convince my mother during her drunken episodes that females could expect to be treated in any less abusive a manner by me than he'd treated her.

After the ceremony, I ended my futile search for Alannah when I saw my mother approaching me with a big, closemouthed grin on her face. When she reached me, she touched my arm lightly and said, "My, my, aren't you something?" I smiled weakly back at her, not sure what to say, and knowing full well how much she frowned on displays of excessive self-satisfaction, vanity, or ingratitude. I wanted to avoid at all costs complaining about not being chosen as the outstanding boy.

"I guess so, huh?" I replied, as I offered her the awards, which I'd rolled neatly together and secured with the thick rubber band, and patted her hand. "Mommy, could you take these home for me? I wanna go to the movies with one of my friends."

"Sure, Michael Cycle, but be home at a reasonable hour, okay? Don't make me worry about you."

"All right, Mommy. I promise."

"I'm proud of you, you know. Four awards! Aren't you something? I thought you might even win that final award. But you can't be too greedy, right?"

"Yeah, you're right. Thanks. See you."

I'd wanted my mother to hug me, kiss me on the cheek, and tell me that she understood how overwhelmed I was by the success of which she was so proud. To tell me that she thought that my resentment—at being passed over for the chubby little brownnoser, being ignored by Alannah, and having been forced to be my mother's own whipping boy—was perfectly justified.

Instead, she turned to leave the auditorium. After she'd moved ten steps away from me, she turned back in my direction, held up the certificates, and smiled at me. I had no idea how to read her gesture.

Bird and I went to see *Shaft in Africa*, one of the sequels to the original black private dick flick starring Richard Roundtree. In this ridiculous installment (which I was viewing with the advantage of not having seen the original), Shaft traveled to some unspecified or unremembered location on the dark continent to rescue the natives who were being sold into slavery by a slimy European who rode around in a stretch limousine during most of the movie with his nymphomaniacal blonde concubine. A horribly inconsistent American condemnation of the African practice of clitorectomy, the film also featured Yvette McGee as the beguiling daughter of an urbanized tribal chief who, unbeknownst to her father, was no longer a virgin. Having firsthand knowledge of what she'd be missing if she submitted to this mutilation, McGee's character schemed to avoid coming under the knife. Like the blonde nympho, this princess quickly became an object of desire for the suave love man and former Afro Sheen model, who—despite the fact that nearly every bad guy in the movie had studied glossy photographs of him and could therefore distinguish his well-groomed do from the home cuts of the black actors with whom he shared screen time—made an effort to learn to appear culturally African so that he could liberate his brothers from slavery's late-twentieth-century manifestation.

I could barely focus on the silly, illogical story and spent much of my energy trying to elicit Bird's hushed, high-pitched laughter by asking him repeatedly, in my best ghetto nigger voice, "Ain't they got they own private dicks in Africa?" But I loved the familiar strangeness in the movie theater, the popcorn-soda-Raisinets-jujubes-musty-humanity-and-reefer smell, the rustling sounds, the hearty laughs and surprised sighs, the clear, large-screen picture, even the sticky, uncomfortable chair on which I sat and was sure would stain my silk-and-wool pants. I was excited by the love scene between the leads, set in a raised crop storage hut that appeared to be a cross between Tarzan's living quarters and a Manhattan loft. And I liked seeing how the movie's music, highlighted by the hit song "Are You Man Enough," fit and didn't fit into the flow of the narrative.

The lyrics of the song were rendered in raspy sweetness by The Four Tops' Levi Stubbs and asked questions with which all the boys I knew—myself included—were actively wrestling.

Are you man enough
Big and bad enough
Are you gonna let 'em shoot you down

How big and bad did one have to be to get the girl? To walk the street unmolested? To limit or eliminate altogether the constant sense of fear that haunted my waking hours and my dreams? Were there spaces and places I could occupy where hardness, badness, and toughness didn't define manhood, where they were only possibilities among a host of equally attractive ways of being male? I wished I could ask Bird, or Ricky, or someone who wouldn't laugh or ridicule me, wouldn't call me a little faggot, wouldn't question my manhood, and would understand, even if he or she didn't know the answers.

As we walked out of the theater and into the humid night air, I shook Bird's hand, embraced him in a back-slapping hug, and told him I'd speak with him soon. "And if you see Alannah," I joked, "tell her I love her, okay?" He smiled, shook his head in feigned exasperation, and headed toward Broad Street to catch the El to North Philly.

One evening that summer, exhausted from having played basketball for several hours in terribly uncomfortable heat and humidity, I decided that rather than walk the extra distance to the relative safety of the well-lit elevators in the back of the building, I'd use the more convenient front-lobby elevators that faced the playground. These elevators' primary function had become to provide maintenance workers with the means of transporting refrigerators, stoves, and other bulky appliances and materials. When I pushed the cold button, one of the elevators' doors opened immediately, and as I stepped toward it, I saw David and Joe, boys who were two years older than I. David, who was known throughout the neighborhood as a crazy motherfucker, and Joe, who was too fundamentally nice to appear so, greeted me. I figured that their appearance at the precise moment I pushed the elevator button was sheer coincidence, that they were leaving one of their apartments to go outside. Their sinister smiles worried me a bit, as did the darkened cabin and the fact that, rather than exit the elevator, they casually leaned against its metal walls, beckoning me to enter.

Tired and thirsty, I stepped from the streetlight-lit lobby into the nearly pitch-black elevator, offering the conventional neighborhood greeting, "What's up," as the door closed and sight of any sort became impossible. "One of y'all got a match or something?" I asked, as their silence gave way to childish snickering, and my wariness turned into real fear. I remembered an earlier elevator incident when David had pulled a knife on Joe and me and ordered us to touch his dick or he'd "fuck you up real bad." In the face of that threat, I had been consumed by a variety of cop-show images: of screaming as the knife pierced my flesh; of my blood mixing with the urine on the floor of the elevator; of David standing over me, smiling menacingly as he kicked my lifeless corpse. I'd reached my shaking right hand into his pants, touched the coarse border of his pubic hair, and removed my hand quickly, as though I'd touched a flame, which seemed to satisfy him. I remembered the look of hurt and deep betrayal on Joe's face. Suddenly I became terrified of what they'd do to me, in the dark, deserted elevator that wouldn't stop before it reached the nineteenth floor.

Hands grabbed my arms, which I struggled to free. A hand covered my mouth, stifling momentarily my efforts to reason with them or to scream or to speak menacingly. Hands and arms and pelvises pushed me to the floor, which I hit with a soft splash, coating my sweat-drenched T-shirt with what I imagined was days-old urine. Fists and knees and elbows and feet slammed against my arms, my stomach, my legs, and my back as I covered my face and tried to collect my thoughts. Why were they doing this? What had I done to them? How much would it hurt? Did it hurt? When would it end?

"What the fuck you doing?"

"Shut the fuck up, nigger!"

"Why y'all doing this? Stop it!"

"What I say? Shut the fuck up!"

When I didn't experience the intense pain I expected to feel from long, uninterrupted seconds of beating, I realized that they were pulling their punches. They weren't really trying to hurt me at all but had merely involved me in a prank, a joke, a game of victim and victimizer. That realization didn't help me to endure any better the seconds before the elevator door opened. But in that moment of clarity, all of the fighting, the posturing, the wolfing and dangerous signifying, the gang warring, seemed similarly staged efforts to manifest a sense of power that the participants were aware all along was, at most, transitory, if not wholly illusory.

Giggling like six year olds or actors playing the roles of insane asylum patients, they kicked me gently in the ass as I rolled off the elevator when it opened on the brightly lit nineteenth floor. I fumbled for my key, opened the door of the deserted apartment, and ran to the bathroom, desperately throwing off my sweat-and-urine-soaked clothing. Sitting in the cold bathtub, I ran the water as hot as I could stand, and as the tub filled and covered my sore body, aching more from hours of basketball than from the mock attack, I started to cry uncontrollably. For what felt like a half hour, I sobbed, my torso rocking involuntarily from a combination of pain, anger, and deep frustration; and I repeated over and over again, "I got to get the fuck outta here. I got to get the fuck outta here."

The day before I was scheduled to leave for Governor Dummer Academy in some place called Byfield, Massachusetts, I went to a drugstore in the Italian Market to purchase discount toiletries. I walked quickly past the pungent smells of the fruit and vegetable stands that covered much of the sidewalk of the Market, leaving shoppers very little room to manueuver their carts, wagons, and screaming children. I watched for sneaky 13th Streeters who liked catching unsuspecting boys from my neighborhood in this neutral commercial turf and robbing them or beating them up. And I avoided being seen by the proprietors of Al's Clothing Store, where I'd worked two consecutive summers with my brother and, later, after school.

As I moved past the fruit stands that dominated the Ninth and Washington Avenue corner and toward the area of the Market where meats, fish, eggs, clothes, shoes, and other items were sold, I felt that someone was following me. Suspecting I was being stalked by someone from 13th Street, I quickened my pace, but when I glanced around, I saw no one looking in my direction except a middle-aged black man dressed in khaki work clothes, who smiled broadly at me. Walking toward me as I slowed my pace a half block from the drugstore, he spoke of the weather or the crowd or some other inane subject. I barely responded. But because I was relieved that he didn't want to stab me, I started to converse with him until, after thirty seconds or so, he asked me to meet him somewhere in 7th Street territory later that evening when he got off of work. Initially, I wanted to ask why, but I quickly realized his unstated intention and sped up again until I turned toward the door of the drugstore. He blocked my path and asked if I was going to meet him. I told him I was going to be busy, that I was leaving town to go off to school, but I knew he wouldn't let me go unless I gave him something to hope for.

"You understand what I'm talking about, don't you?"

Trembling, I shook my head and ran into the store.

To make sure he wasn't waiting for me when I left the drugstore, I spent a full hour choosing deodorant, toothpaste, lotion, and a toothbrush. I walked slowly around the store under the watchful eye of the white female cashier, who seemed convinced that I was prepared to hide a large bottle of mouthwash in my underwear.

I wondered whether I looked gay, or at least potentially interested in altering my clearly conceived sense of my sexuality because of a few words from an old, smelly construction worker. Wasn't I walking tough enough? Hadn't all the work I'd done to remove that feminine switch from my walk been successful? I thought of Carol's question about my sexual orientation and wondered whether others besides my older sister and this man suspected that I wasn't who I believed myself to be.

I spent my last night in Philly before I headed to prep school at home, afraid that the man I'd met would be roaming the streets, looking for me. As I packed my trunks, watched from the porch as my friends and acquaintances played basketball, and leafed through my junior high school yearbook, I wondered whether the sort of aggressiveness that the man displayed was a significant part of what it meant to be a man. This sort of manly assertiveness would have allowed me to inform Alannah confidently that I thought she was really cute, and that I wanted to be her man. Was that the sort of behavior she'd expected of me as we played out our gendered roles of male initiator and female receptor of male interest?

Masculinity, it seemed, in addition to resulting in or helping to produce calculated violence, meant projecting a self-confidence, a fearlessness, that compelled you to go out and get what you wanted. My tentativeness, my dreamy passivity, were unmanly and unlikely to get me anything except hurt, physically and/or emotionally. Perhaps the construction worker sensed that I hadn't sufficiently embraced manhood, that I was overcome with fear of the sort that inhibits bold self-presentation and strenuous resistance to others' acts of assertiveness. If manly behavior included propositioning young boys or strange girls of one's peer group, threatening your friends and acquaintances with knives, beating boys up on pissy elevators, gang warring, and whistling and moaning at attractive women like the construction workers I'd pass as I silently and lustfully watched the objects of our desire walk in Center City, what kind of man was I? What type of man would I become?

I was stuck inside on the porch on a beautiful summer night when the stars made a rare appearance in the typically sooty air. On my last day as a permanent resident of the Southwark Projects, I listened to the thumping of basketballs and the loud squeals of children's playing in the pool, hummed along with the love songs that Debby was sharing with her boyfriend in the living room, and wondered if Alannah was thinking of me, too.

Note

1. Michael Awkward, "Section II: Are You Man Enough?," in *Scenes of Instruction* (Durham, NC: Duke University Press, 1999).

Daniel Black

Daniel Black's third novel, *Perfect Peace*, is about a mother who conceals the true gender of her seventh son from the family and the public and raises him as a girl. The novel is an intriguing investigation of society's commitment to the correlations between biological sex designations, gender performances, and sexuality. In this scene, Perfect's mother reveals to her and her family that she is really a male and should learn the ways of manhood in order to be accepted in the world. The emotional trauma on Perfect, who must henceforward be called Paul, is a powerful testament to the psychological and emotional impact that discourses of manhood have on all men.

Perfect Peace

Daniel Black[1]

"What's the matter with Momma?" Mister asked Authorly the day after Perfect's party. They were gathered for the Sunday meal. "Why ain't she eatin'?"

"I don't know," Authorly said with a drumstick in each hand. He'd noted her strangeness in church, the way she looked out the window as though in another time and place, and decided he'd ask her about it later. But now he sensed she wanted to be left alone.

Sitting on the couch with her forehead buried into both palms, Emma Jean knew there was no turning back. She wasn't afraid for herself. Her entire life had been a struggle. It was Perfect she was worried about. Was she as strong as she'd need to be? Could she withstand the frowns and verbal abuse sure to come? She was only a little girl, Emma Jean told herself. But she had to do it. It was the only way to give Perfect a life, some hope that would sustain her, regardless of what happened to Emma Jean. It was what she knew had to be done.

She'd seen Eva Mae wink at Perfect during church and that's when she decided she couldn't wait any longer. There was something that girl knew and Emma Jean feared she'd tell it. Maybe Eva Mae didn't know everything—she couldn't have known *everything*—but she knew something. And if it was what Emma Jean feared, and if Eva Mae told, her whole family would be ruined and nobody would ever trust her again. No, she had to act today. It couldn't wait.

Dreading the moment like Sisyphus must have dreaded another rolling of the stone, Emma Jean rose and said, "Perfect, honey, come with me." She slung a bag over her shoulder and walked out the front door without ever turning back.

The boys gathered at the screen and watched Perfect walk behind Emma Jean until both vanished down the road. Emma Jean turned and led Perfect into the forest. She hadn't had the time to grab Olivia, and she would soon regret having left her behind. Perfect thought that maybe they were headed to the Jordan for some reason.

"Sit on that stump there," Emma Jean said, and pointed.

"Okay, Momma."

Emma Jean couldn't face her. All she could think about was what she was prepared to do and whether Perfect could handle it. She paced several seconds with her eyes closed, then said, "Listen, sweetie. Momma's got somethin' to tell you, and I need you to hear me. This ain't gon' be easy, but it's gon' be okay. At least afterwhile."

Perfect smiled. "Is this about my birthday party yesterday? I know it was ruined, but it's okay. We can always have another one if you want to."

"No, honey, this ain't got nothin' to do with that." Emma Jean chewed her thumbnail and continued, "This got to do with you. Just you."

"What about me, Momma?"

Emma Jean looked heavenward and asked for strength. "You just gotta hear what I'm 'bout to say and believe I wouldn't never do nothin' to hurt you. I swear I wouldn't."

"I know." Perfect nodded.

"And I'm doin' this for your own good. You understand that, don't you?"

"Yes, ma'am." Perfect had no idea what Emma Jean was talking about.

"This ain't gon' be easy, sweetie," she repeated, "but it's the only way."

"Okay."

Emma Jean knelt. "Years ago, I did . . . um . . . something I shouldn't have done."

Perfect frowned. "What?"

"And I need to fix it now. So no one hurts you in the future."

Perfect's blank stare made Emma Jean's purging difficult. "See, honey . . . um . . . when you was born I wanted a little girl so bad I woulda done anything to get one."

"Then you got one!"

"Um . . . yes . . . well . . . sorta."

"Whatcha mean?"

Emma Jean huffed and shook her head. "I mean that . . . um . . . I wanted a girl so bad that I . . . um . . ."

"What, Momma? You can tell me anything."

" . . . that I . . . um . . . made you into one." She glanced into Perfect's eyes and saw nothing but confusion. Then she reached for her small, soft hands and clutched them harder than she had intended.

"I know this don't make no sense, baby, but you gotta know. Before somebody else tell you."

Perfect's brow furrowed. "Tell me what?"

Emma Jean blurted, "That you ain't no girl!"

"What do you mean, Momma? Of course I'm a girl. I got long hair and everything."

Emma Jean stood. "Listen, Perfect. You been thinkin' you a girl yo' whole life. I understand that, because that's how I raised you, but you wunnit born that way."

"Huh?" Perfect began to tear up. "I don't understand, Momma."

Emma Jean struggled to remain composed. "I know you don't, baby, but just listen to what I'm telling you."

"I ain't no girl?" Perfect whimpered.

"No. Not really. I mean, no. When you was born I decided to raise you as a girl 'cause I wanted one so bad, but—"

"Then what am I?" Perfect cried.

"You're a boy. That's what you are." Emma Jean covered her mouth at the horror of it all.

"No I'm not! I'm a girl. Just like you."

"Honey, listen," Emma Jean tried to explain. "I know you're confused and don't none of this make much sense to you right now, but you gotta believe me. You was meant to be a boy."

"But I don't wanna be no boy!"

"It don't make no difference what you want!" Emma Jean screeched. "You was born a boy. I *made* you a girl, but that ain't what you was suppose to be."

"How you know, Momma? Huh? How you know?"

Emma Jean began unbuttoning her dress.

"I like bein' a girl and havin' pretty things and stuff. You even said yourself that I was a girl and that I was gon' grow up and marry a handsome man and—"

"I know what I said, Perfect," Emma Jean said as she lifted her dress over her head. "But I was wrong. I shouldn't o' said those things to you. You ain't no girl."

"Yes I am, Momma!" Perfect was inconsolable.

"No, you ain't!"

Perfect nodded and sobbed.

Emma Jean pointed to her panties and said, "This is what girls have!"

Perfect gawked. Where was the lump?

"Only boys have what you have. I'm sorry, honey. I'm really, really sorry."

She hadn't meant to be crude, but she couldn't think of another way to convince Perfect of the truth.

"Now. I know this ain't easy, but we can survive it," Emma Jean said, pulling her dress back over her head. "If I hadn't told you, somebody else would've, and then you'd been real upset with me, and you probably wouldn't ever trust me again. This way, you heard the truth from me. I know I was wrong, but this is the best I can do now. Trust me. I'm lovin' you more right now than I ever have before."

Perfect hadn't said a word since beholding Emma Jean's nakedness. Where was her *thing*? She thought desperately. It couldn't be true, could it? Was she really supposed to be a *boy*?

"So from now on, you gon' be a boy. A handsome little black boy. It'll be strange at first, but you'll get used to it, and this'll all be over afterwhile."

"But, Momma, I—"

"Shut up! I done told you the truth and ain't no more to say about it. I'm sorry for what I did, and this is the only way I know to fix it." Her tone softened. "I know this hurts, Perfect, but if somebody else told you, you wouldn't ever forgive me. You might be mad at me now, but you'll thank me one day for telling you the truth."

"But I cain't be no boy!"

"Yes, you can. And you will. We gon' start with this." She extracted a battered pair of overalls from the bag. "Here. Put 'em on."

Perfect sat transfixed.

"I said, put 'em on!"

She received the overalls with tremulous hands. Emma Jean lifted Perfect's dress and manipulated it over her head. "Put these on first."

Perfect wept as she removed her panties and slid on a brand-new pair of boy's underwear. They felt thick and heavy, and Perfect didn't like them, but she was too perplexed to argue. She needed Olivia now. Someone who understood her. Someone who could verify that, in fact, she was a girl and had always been.

"Now. Step into these." Emma Jean held open the overalls as Perfect obeyed. "Good. You're gonna be fine." Emma Jean buckled the straps.

Perfect stared at her mother as though she had never seen her. Was this some sort of joke? Why was Emma Jean doing this? Perfect couldn't be a boy for real. Not really. Could she?

"Now. One more thing."

Emma Jean motioned for Perfect to sit, and, like a robotic zombie, she complied. Her tears continued to flow, but the sobbing had ceased. She gazed straight ahead as though out of touch with reality. The straps of the overalls drooped over her thin shoulders, and she still wasn't sure why Emma Jean was doing this to her.

After rummaging through the bag, Emma Jean removed a pair of scissors and stood behind the paralyzed child. "This hurts me more than it does you. Believe me. I wish there was another way, but there ain't. If I didn't do this now, you'd hate me later, and I couldn't live with that. This way, we'll go through everything together." She removed the ribbons from Perfect's hair and began to clip it away in clusters. Stray pieces fell slowly, quietly across her shoulders and onto her lap, and all Perfect could do was weep. She couldn't imagine what she'd look like without hair, but she had a feeling others wouldn't call her pretty anymore. "You gon' always be my baby," Emma Jean assured her. "Don't make no difference if you a girl or boy." She cut the hair as short as she could manage with a pair of scissors, then tried her best to shape it. "There. That'll do for now." She stepped from behind Perfect and inspected her work. "You real handsome." She collected the clumps of hair and put them in the bag. Perfect never moved.

Emma Jean then pulled her to her feet. "All right. This is a new beginning. You a boy now. It ain't got to be hard 'less you make it hard. It'll feel a little awkward at first, but, like I said, you'll get used to it. Now wipe your face and let's go."

Emma Jean was speaking jibberish for all Perfect knew. She felt like unwanted lint, picked and, tossed to the wind without a care. What would her brothers say? Wouldn't they ask where their sister had gone?

Every few steps, Perfect stumbled or bumped into trees as Emma Jean dragged her home. Years later, she would try to recall exactly how the transition had occurred, only to find a blank space in her memory where details should have been. All she remembered was crying and begging her mother to stop—had she actually said it or did she just think it?—but Emma Jean was determined to accomplish the mission at hand. She had decided that Perfect's life as a girl was over, so, without warning or preamble, she ended it—just like that. That's what she remembered. And her life was never the same again.

Emma Jean had practiced what she would say to Gus and the boys, but when she stepped through the door, her mind went blank. Authorly was the first to notice, and his "Oh shit!" captured everyone's attention.

Gus turned, prepared to slap Authorly in the mouth, but froze when he saw his distorted daughter.

"Everyone," Emma Jean announced slowly, "ain't no easy way to say this, so I'm just gon' say it." She positioned Perfect in front of her and rested her hands on Perfect's shoulders.

Mister's mouth fell open. His brothers stared and waited. Gus glanced from Perfect to Emma Jean, unable to imagine why someone had done this to his baby girl. He stood slowly.

Gus's facial contortions ruined Emma Jean's resolve. She had planned to tell the truth, and then to ask the men for forgiveness. Simple as that. It would be awkward, she knew, but she could endure it. She hadn't planned for Gus to rise and gape at her like one prepared to destroy her if her explanation wasn't sufficient.

"When Perfect was born," Emma Jean muttered, "I wanted a girl. Gus, you remember. I always wanted girls, but I didn't have none. You boys was fine, but I needed a girl. Someone I could dress up and make feel pretty. You know what I mean?" She tried to smile, but no one smiled in return. "So I did . . . something I shouldn't've done." Her voice broke. Perfect had been crying the entire time. "I lied. I told y'all the child was a girl, but it wasn't." She dropped her head. "It was a boy."

Now Bartimaeus understood.

Gus inched forward in slow motion, studying Emma Jean's face.

"I needed a girl!" she proclaimed. "Cain't you understand that? Every mother wants a girl. It's a woman's dream."

"What?" Gus whispered in fury. "You did what?" He was approaching like a starving lioness before the kill.

"Gus, listen. Please. I know this don't make much sense to you right now, but you gotta try to understand where I was then."

"I ain't understandin' nothin' you sayin', woman!" he screamed. Authorly stood beside him.

"I'm sorry," Emma Jean whined. "I didn't mean for it to happen like this. It just got out of hand."

Gus lifted Perfect's bowed head and, for the first time, saw his own reflection, although he still didn't believe what Emma Jean was saying.

"You lyin', Emma Jean. My baby girl ain't no boy."

Authorly touched his father's shoulder, but Gus jerked away violently.

"Do you think I'd lie about something like this, man?"

Gus looked at Perfect and said, "You my little girl. You gon' always be my little girl, and ain't nothin' gon' change that."

"Stop, Gus! Listen to what I'm sayin'! I lied to you, I lied to everybody when this child was born 'cause I needed a girl. I knew it couldn't last forever, but I—"

Gus slapped Emma Jean so hard the boys gasped and held their breaths. Authorly stepped toward him, but the look in Gus's eyes made the boy halt.

"I don't know what you done done," he whispered vehemently, "but this ain't no boy." His pointed finger trembled.

Emma Jean sobbed and nodded. "Yes, it is, Gus. Yes it is. I'm sorry. I didn't know it would do this to you. I never knew you even wanted a girl."

"I wanted a girl when I got one!" he shouted. "Now I don't know why you cut her hair off and I don't know why she got on them clothes—"

" 'Cause he's a boy, Gus," Emma Jean sniffled. "He's a boy."

Gus's eyes watered and his mouth quivered. "If what you sayin' is true, you prove it to me right now."

"I'm tellin' you—"

"Don't *tell* me nothin'! I said prove it!"

"But the only way you gon' know for sure—"

Suddenly he turned to Perfect. "Take them clothes off."

"Oh no, honey. Don't do this. Not now. Don't embarrass him in front o' his brothers. He ain't ready for nothin' like that."

"I said, take them damn clothes off!"

Emma Jean reached to assist, but Gus wouldn't allow it.

"Not you!" He pushed her hands away. "You," he said to Perfect. "You do it yo'self."

Perfect submitted, dropping his overalls to the floor. Only his underwear remained. Gus thought he saw a bulge, but was still unsatisfied.

"Take 'em off," he demanded.

"Please, Gus, don't do this! Not in front of the boys! Take him in the room or outside, but don't—"

"Shut the hell up, Emma Jean!"

Perfect's sobbing returned as he lowered his underwear to his ankles.

When Gus saw the miniature penis, he screamed, "No! Oh God, no!" and crumpled to his knees. Authorly embraced him.

The brothers looked on in disbelief.

"I'm sorry! I'm so, so sorry!" Emma Jean repeated. "If I could do it all over again, I'd do it different." She knelt beside Gus. "Baby, I know you upset, but please try to understand."

Gus lunged at her before Authorly could restrain him. He smacked Emma Jean's face three or four times, then pinned her neck to the floor with his thick, rough hands. "What did you do this for! You ain't got no right to do nobody like this! What the hell is wrong with you!" Emma Jean couldn't breathe. "You didn't have to do this!" He might have strangled her to death had Authorly not jumped on Gus's back and, with Woody's assistance, wrestled Gus's hands away from her throat.

Emma Jean squirmed upon the floor in breathless agony. Perfect had closed his eyes once he removed his underwear, and never knew that it was Mister who had replaced them.

Gus sat panting in the middle of the living room floor. Emma Jean's heavy gasping meant nothing to him. A boy? Perfect was a boy? All these years he had been kissing a boy? He thought of Perfect in his lap and shook his head. Gus had absolutely no way to comprehend what, now, he couldn't deny—he had seen the penis himself. How had Emma Jean done it? How had she lied to him—and everyone else—without detection? Why didn't he suspect something? He had never been clever, he admitted, but shouldn't a father know instinctively about his own kids? Shouldn't he at least have *sensed* that something was different?

Mister escorted Perfect to the sofa and wiped his face with a ball of tissue. His quivering elicited Mister's sympathy and caused him to whisper, "Just be still. It's gonna be okay. Don't say nothin' right now. Just be quiet."

Perfect nodded. His uneven, partially straight, stubby hair made him look as though he had been in a brawl and lost badly. Wedged between Mister and Sol, who kept looking at him sympathetically, Perfect watched Emma Jean crawl into the bedroom and kick the door closed behind her. As the rains of '48 began, Gus exited clumsily, tripping over the upturned edge of the battered living room rug, but never made it to the Jordan. Too angry and confused to purge, he simply escaped to the barn and shouted every curse word he knew instead of murdering the mother of his children. With no one to guide him, Bartimaeus skipped the cleansing, too, and wept openly, right in the middle of the living room, about all the ways he could have protected his family. Especially Gus. He didn't deserve this. He was a good daddy, Bartimaeus thought, who worked hard and treated people kindly. And now Gus was devastated, all because Bartimaeus was too afraid to act.

An hour later, Authorly gathered the brothers together in the living room. He sat in the chair opposite the sofa and, with the coffin/coffee table between them, said, "Woody, Sol, Mister, James Earl, Bartimaeus . . . we got ourselves another brother. I ain't sho how this happened, but we all know it's true. Can't nobody deny that. We done seen it for ourselves. Ain't nothin' nobody can do about it now but accept it and keep on livin'."

Perfect never lifted his head. He knew he wasn't beautiful anymore. His brothers' energies convinced him that, now, he was ordinary, simple, common just like them. It was strange to Perfect how his world was shifting without his consent. He didn't feel safe like he once did in his brothers' presence. Sitting on the sofa shivering, with his head practically touching his knees, he felt his previous life ooze away as his brothers ushered him into a more harsh, less sympathetic reality. And they did this without uttering a word. Perfect sensed that if he cried now, Authorly's normally protective gaze would be replaced with something more corrective, so Perfect trembled and covered his mouth. What he really wanted was to run and hide in Emma Jean's bosom, but somehow he knew that wasn't an option. Who would touch and hold him now? Usually when he cried, someone embraced him and reassured his heart, but now all hands avoided him. That's how he knew he was different. Or no longer different. His pain was insignificant to his brothers and, for the first time in his life, he was responsible for his own healing.

Sol dragged his heavy heart to the edge of the porch and sang sweetly, "Sometimes I feel like a motherless chiiiiild, sometimes I feel like a motherless chiiiiiild, sometimes I feel like a motherless child, a looooong way from hooooome, a loooooong way from home," while Perfect sat transfixed in a sea of sorrow.

Chapter 15

Moments later, Authorly knocked on Emma Jean's bedroom door. "Momma?" he whispered, then entered uninvited.

Emma Jean was curled in a fetal position upon the floor. She had tried to lift herself to the bed, but simply didn't have the strength. Gus had caught her off guard. She didn't know he had it in him to fight, but now she knew. He would've killed her, she was certain, had Authorly and Woody not intervened. Now she couldn't help but wonder what Gus might do when the rains ended.

"You all right, Momma?"

Her groan revealed that at least she was alive. Authorly lifted her as though carrying a new bride across a threshold and laid her gently upon the bed. He saw where Gus's fingernails had scratched her neck, and he knew that, for a while, she'd be terrified of him. *Good,* Authorly thought. *She deserves everything she gets.*

Emma Jean cleared her throat and massaged her neck. "Thank you, son. I'm all right."

Authorly walked to the window and noticed Mister talking to Perfect in the yard. "What's wrong with you, Momma? Why would you do something like this?"

Emma Jean sighed. "I don't know, son. It made sense then, I guess. I'm not sayin' it was right, but it made so much more sense then than it does now."

"You lied to everybody, Momma." Authorly turned from the window. "And you made Perfect think he was somethin' he ain't."

"I know what I did, and I'm gon' have to live with it the rest o' my life. But I meant well."

Note

1. Daniel Black, *Perfect Peace* (New York, NY: St. Martin's Press, 2010).

Vershawn Ashanti Young

It is perhaps not very well known that the first president of African American descent, Barack Obama, has been routinely profiled as a closeted homosexual throughout his campaign and tenure as president. The suspicion arises because of his performance of manhood. This selection examines why a slew of White-run media outlets consistently and unfavorably queer Obama, amplifying his nonnormative masculine traits and then, on that basis, assigning him a deceitful, nonheteronormative sexuality. The fact that Obama, as the highest-achieving Black man in the world, is relentlessly categorized as homosexual also helps explain why so many other Black men are wary of the rhetoric that school is a path for success for them and resist the discourse that standards for professional success are just as applicable to them as they are to White men.

Straight Black Queer: Obama, Code-Switching, and the Gender Anxiety of African American Men

Vershawn Ashanti Young[1]

Globe Magazine featured a "world exclusive," not even a year into Barack Obama's first term as president of the United States, charging him with homosexual infidelity and his wife, Michelle, with coordinating a cover-up ("Obama Gay Cover-Up!"). The magazine followed up two months later, asserting that Obama's lover resided in the White House and was none other than his personal aide, Reggie Love ("Obama's Gay Lover").[2] *Globe*, of course, is a dime-store rag whose mission is to sensationalize. I refer to it here because it is perhaps the most relentless among a slew of white-run media outlets that consistently and unfavorably queer Obama, amplifying his nonnormative masculine traits and then, on that basis, assigning him a deceitful, nonheteronormative sexuality.

Globe's profiling of Obama is connected to the gender anxiety that African American men more broadly experience in regard to educational and professional success. Signithia Fordham reports in her ethnographic study of African American high school students, for instance, that "male students at Capital [High] are fearful of the pursuit of academic excellence [because] they fear being labeled gay" (*Blacked Out* 279). The fact that Obama, as the highest-achieving black man in the world, is relentlessly categorized as homosexual supports their concern. But despite this evidence, the gender anxiety of African American men is often overlooked or dismissed because their culture is assumed to privilege anti-intellectualism as a marker of authentic masculinity, to equate being smart with having less gender privilege—that is, with being gay. And so it is believed that a pathological masculine conformity causes African American men to resist academic success.

Two editorialists of the *Washington Post* debated this very topic. When Kathleen Parker, a white straight woman, criticized Obama for "acting too much like a woman" ("Obama"), her colleague Jonathan Capehart, an African American gay man, told her that "black men are held to a different standard than whites. They are practiced in keeping their emotions under wraps. They can't 'go off,' as some have urged Obama to do" (qtd. in Parker, "Following Up"). Capehart writes, "African American men are taught at very young ages (or learn the hard way) to keep our emotions in check" ("Rage"). As an African American male, I agree with Capehart, which is why I argue against the gendered and racialized instruction of African American males, particularly the pedagogical method of code-switching employed in schools.

Code-switching, as reductively deployed in educational contexts, is a sociolinguistic method of teaching African Americans to adopt a double set of behaviors, Englishes, and rhetorical styles, one for blacks and another for whites. This effort is often conceived during instruction as learning different languages for different contexts. In this light, code-switching becomes an institutionalized form of language instruction that perpetuates a sense of the educational inferiority of African American English and the professional and social inferiority of African American people. I argue that code-switching contributes to the subordinated gender status of African American men and leads to the negative, antimasculine queering of them, whether they are straight or gay. Ironically, this antimasculine queering partly accounts, as Capehart suggests, both for the success of a few black men, such as Obama, Capehart, and even myself, and for the widespread underachievement of African American males who resist such queering, as Fordham's research subjects illustrate.

The most prevalent argument for teaching African Americans to switch codes used to be based on employability and job security. But as the linguist James Sledd bluntly put it in 1973, the proponents of code-switching "themselves do not claim to have produced substantial numbers of psychologically undamaged doublespeakers, whose mastery of Whitey's talk has won them jobs which would have been otherwise denied them" (193). Even current proponents of code-switching admit that African American English speakers occupy a wide range of professional jobs, many in the public sector. So the conversation has turned from the loss of financial possibilities to what it has always really been about—the hope that code-switching will protect African Americans from the deleterious consequences of racism. For example, Patricia Edwards, past president of the International Reading Association, and her team of literacy experts write, "Most teachers of African American Children . . . believe . . . that their students' life chances will be further hampered if they do not learn Standard English. *In the stratified society in which we live*, they are absolutely right" (Edwards, McMillon, and Turner 73; emphasis added).

Fear of racism leads some African Americans to accept code-switching; but others reject it, as Donald McCrary does:

> Hold up. I know what you gonna say. Talkin' that black English is okay at home and with your friends, but don't be speakin' that foolishness in school or at the j-o-b. And don't be tellin' no students they can speak that mess either. You want people (read: white) to think they ignorant? Right. Right. I hear you. I hear you. But let's be real. America loves itself some black English. Half the announcers on ESPN speak it, and I'm talking about the white dudes, too. Americans know more black English than they like to admit . . . . [So] students should be allowed to combine standard English with other languages when they speak and write in the academy.
>
> (73–74)

McCrary's writing reflects and advocates what I call code-meshing, which simply means blending, merging, meshing dialects. Code-meshing offers a resolution to the emotional, psychological, and linguistic dilemmas that code-switching—separating Englishes according to setting—presents for many African Americans. It also has the potential to encourage more African American men to stay in school. Houston Baker's code-meshing, for instance, had an encouraging educational effect on Michael Awkward. Awkward recalls that during a call recruiting him to attend graduate school at the University of Pennsylvania, Baker's speech "slipped effortlessly between King's English and hood dialect, between authoritative assertion and sizzling slang" (154). Awkward admits that "as his voice assumed, abandoned, and took up again a range of discursive styles, I questioned the efficacy of my having spent seven years unlearning modes of speech that virtually all the people with whom I grew up employed as a rule . . . . When I got off the phone, I smiled at my mother and told her that I planned to accept Penn's offer" (155).

However, some may get it twisted, thinking that the only purpose for discussing code-meshing is to exemplify the kind of blended speech or writing that African American English speakers might produce and to explain the egalitarian reasons why they should be allowed to do it. But as Judith Bradford and Crispin Sartwell eloquently put it, "How to speak is one problem; how to listen is another." In their work on white privilege and on how racial and gender expectations limit the ability of the marginalized to speak, they find that too little attention has been paid "to the problem of *how to learn to hear* people's voices" (201). So the work of code-meshing also involves asking others to learn to hear and read diverse voices.

Capehart and Parker's dialogue illustrates both an attempt to encourage a deeper hearing of others' voices and the practiced failure to do so. In her column "Obama: Our First Female President," Parker writes that while she is not "calling Obama a girlie president," she is concerned that "he may be suffering a rhetorical-testosterone deficit when it comes to dealing with crises, with which," she says, invoking a sexual metaphor, "he has been richly endowed."[3] She then compares him to his predecessor: "it shouldn't surprise anyone that Obama's rhetoric would simmer next to George W. Bush's boil. But passivity in a leader is not a reassuring posture." She ends the article predicting Obama's fate: "Obama may prove to be our first male president who pays a political price for acting too much like a woman."

Capehart both phoned Parker and wrote a response, trying to school her on some of the gender and racial reasons for Obama's public style. What he wrote is worth quoting at length:

> Let me ask you a question. When was the last time you saw your black male colleague, especially if you're in a white-collar profession, show anger or rage in public? My hunch is never. There's a reason for that. African American men are taught at very young ages (or learn the hard way) to keep our emotions in check, to not lose our cool, lest we be perceived as dangerous or menacing or give someone a reason to doubt our ability to handle our jobs. Think of the emotional corset women in leadership positions are expected to maintain to ensure they never cry in public or show TOO much compassion for fear of raising the same doubt and seeming weak.

Although there are African American males, including myself, who have shown some degree of anger in public—in, say, department meetings at predominantly white institutions—Capehart is right. We, and certainly I, have not done so without consequence. The one or two other African American faculty members keep a respectful distance from you in public, especially around white colleagues, or they may even feel a sense of pressure to compensate for your behavior by being overconciliatory. Whether white colleagues appear stunned or sympathic, as Capehart writes, they "doubt our ability to handle our jobs." For instance, although I am an advanced associate professor, I am regularly passed over for leadership appointments, monitored when guests visit, and ignored in meetings. This is in contrast to my white male colleagues, who show even more passion and anger than I do, but who constitute the administrative echelon of the department. One of them even has the reputation for being snarky, yet that demeanor is forgiven, envied even.

Capehart's comparison of African American men to women in "white-collar professions" reveals, as my own experience does, that African American men, like all women, are subject to subordination and scrutiny by white males. But in our still patriarchal and prejudiced society, (white) women are regarded as unequal to white men on the basis of gender, while African American men share this gendered circumstance on the basis of race.[4] This is a point that E. Franklin Frazier made some time ago (*Black Bourgeoisie* [1957]) and that Marlon Ross made more recently (*Manning the Race* [2004]). Commenting on middle-class African American men, Frazier writes that they "are not allowed to play the 'masculine role' as defined by American culture" and therefore they "resemble women who use their 'personalities' to compensate for their inferior status in relation to [white] men" (220, 221). These personalities, Frazier explains, are the gender identities that they "have tended to cultivate," such as code-switching, in the presence of whites to gain influence and position (220).

Thus, code-switching is not limited to the grammatical features of African American English but includes racialized behavior that African American men are taught culturally and, I argue, officially throughout their education. Thus, code-switching is also gendered and thereby sexualized, which may explain why *Globe* and other media outlets view Obama's gender performance as representative of the emasculated homosexual. Think of it this way: in American culture, gender and sexuality are often conflated by our society's abiding commitment to compulsory heterosexuality, the expectation that everyone is heterosexual. And heterosexuality for men is judged on the basis of two essential requirements: the performance of ideal masculinity, which includes the ability to freely express justified anger and rage and to act protectively on behalf of others, particularly women and children, and the engagement in intercourse with women. When one of these is absent, the man is deemed queer.

However, since sexual intercourse remains for the most part a private practice, gender performance serves dual roles: it must also represent what and whom a man does in bed. This is as true for the white man as it is for the African American. However, unlike white men, African American men are relegated to an inferior status in educational, professional, and social relations. That is, their performances of masculinity are limited, since they cannot behave in ways white men can in public, in the boardroom, in Congress, or in the White House. Thus, African American men who make it in the mainstream are already queered because they must limit their performance of gender to be there in the first place. This may help explain why Fordham's male subjects showed little interest in education—because they understood that mainstream, middle-class success requires a racial and gender subordination that they were unwilling to negotiate. So when Parker says that Obama's rhetoric "simmer[s] next to Bush's boil," she is unwittingly commenting on Obama's probable acceptance of code-switching behavior and outing her queering of it.

Yet perhaps most surprising to some is that the queer performance of gender that African American men are required to give in order to achieve mainstream success is the same behavior that later breeds *Globe*'s sexual suspicion and Parker's harsh criticism. For instance, Parker didn't always view Obama as unsatisfyingly womanly. In an earlier column, "Obama's Unmacho Diplomacy," she defends the president against analysts who "focused on whether he was manly enough" during his "first European tour." She writes, "Obama seems to have his [testosterone] under control. He doesn't strut, swagger, or flex." Comparing him with his predecessor, she says, "If George W. Bush was a cowboy, Obama is a hug." Obama's leadership style, which is defined by "listening," "partnership," and "humility," "is of course," she explains, "pure porn for women." And even though she cautions that "women don't rule the world" and that we still "have to worry whether Obama will be viewed as weak and the U.S., therefore, vulnerable," she concludes that "a man who listens may be perceived as weak by those who prefer to talk big. But playground wisdom holds that showoffs are usually overcompensating, and the strongest one has nothing to prove. [Obama's] saber is understood."

Now, how could Obama's rhetorical style turn from a scintillating pleasure ("pure porn") into a national sin? Parker answers this question herself. After Capehart's response, she published "Following Up on 'The First Female President.'" "The two most common complaints I heard," she reports, were "one, a black man cannot show anger in public lest he be considered an Angry Black Man. And two, to suggest that a black man has any feminine characteristics, even when framed as an 'evolutionary achievement,' is to emasculate and reduce him to a figure from Jim Crow days." She responds, "Do I think people are too sensitive? Yes. Do I think I may have overstepped the line? No." She then explains why she's absolved: being white, she asserts, "allows me both the luxury of seeing people without the lens of race, but also (sometimes) to fail to imagine how people of other backgrounds might interpret my words."

Parker's turn in opinion of Obama's rhetorical style illustrates something pernicious about the burden of code-switching—that it operates in only one direction. African Americans are required to shape-shift, to change their language styles and behaviors, but whites are not required to do anything except assess the acceptability of African Americans' linguistic performance. African American men are caught in a double bind: they are required to become one stereotype, docile and unmasculine, in order to escape another, dangerous and menacing. If Obama behaved in a more traditionally masculine way, another columnist would be writing about him as the dangerous black man. Thus, code-switching creates in African Americans a hyperawareness about race and gender. It also contributes to the unjustified conceit of those who believe that it is a privilege of whiteness to ignore race, which as Parker confesses leads to her inability to hear diverse voices or anticipate others' perceptions regarding her own.

For although Parker is an intellectual, a writer, her racial naïveté makes her deaf to the easily accessible historical perceptions of African American men, perceptions she perpetuates. Her profile of Obama as too rhetorical and not action-oriented, for example, echoes sentiments uttered in 1921, yes, during Jim Crow, by the sociologist Robert E. Park. Like Parker in "Obama's Unmacho Diplomacy," Park intended his comments effeminizing African American men to be complimentary. "The Negro is, by natural disposition," Park explains, "neither an intellectual nor an idealist, like the Jew; nor a brooding introspective, like the East Indian; nor a pioneer and frontiersman, like the Anglo-Saxon. He is primarily an artist, loving life for its own sake. His *metier* is expression rather than action. He is, so to speak, the lady among the races" (Park and Burgess 136).

While Park received some disapproval from African Americans of his time, perhaps the most famous critique came in 1964, when Ralph Ellison wrote, "I had undergone, not too many months before taking the path which led to writing, the humiliation of being taught in a class in sociology at the Negro college (from Park and Burgess, the leading textbook in the field) that Negroes represented the 'lady of the races.' . . . I had no intention of being bound by any such humiliating definition . . . " (xx). Ellison's refusal as a writer to be hemmed in by any such racial stereotype, whether promoted with good intentions or not, anticipates my critique of code-switching, which, despite good intentions, likewise results in rhetorical, emotional, and gender confinement.

However, there is hope. And the hope I point to is, oddly, couched in Parker's concluding criticism of Obama:

> Obama elected to employ a certain type of rhetoric in the Oval Office that put him in line with feminine rhetorical traditions and at odds with historical precedent and the expectations for his gender. Such a choice ultimately may prove to be a crucial step forward toward a better world. But the backlash against his rhetoric suggests we're not there yet . . . .
>
> ("Following Up")

So how do we get to the "better world" in which Obama's demonstration of "feminine rhetorical traditions," his atypical masculine style, first is not a requirement for academically successful black men and second does not provoke a backlash? We will not get there by requiring the assimilation of women into masculine rhetorical styles or of African Americans into white rhetorical patterns. Nor will we get there by restricting women's and African Americans' expression of humanity, of emotions, or by meting out consequences when they do express themselves freely, consequences from which the dominant group is often relieved. However, when folks from the streets, from the hoods, from the diverse cultures that constitute America and the world bring their unique voices and expressions and personalities into schools, businesses, and the Oval Office, and when we accept them, unconditionally, without assimilationist restrictions that stem from racial and gendered prejudices, then we may be on our way toward that better world.

Notes

1. Vershawn A. Young, "Straight Black Queer: Obama, Code-Switching, and the Gender Anxiety of African American Men," *PMLA* 129.3 (May 2014).
2. *Globe*'s articles appeared years before Obama's unequivocal defense of same-sex marriage, support that led *Newsweek* to dub him "the first gay president" on the cover of its 21 May 2012 issue.
3. In "The First Woman President?" printed in *Newsweek* during the 2008 primary campaign, the Harvard professor Martin Linsky writes that Obama "displays qualities and values that women bring to organizational life." His opponent, "Hillary Clinton, on the other hand, is taking a more traditional (and male?) authoritarian approach." Though Linsky says both Barack Obama and Hillary Clinton bend the traditional conventions of their genders and even, for good measure, refers once to the presumptive Republican nominee, John McCain, as "androgynous," one can't help noticing the distinction in the way he assesses the Democratic candidates. Whereas the parenthetical "(and male?)" leaves uncertain the masculinity of Clinton's assertive performance, Linsky is unequivocal in his other characterization. "This campaign will always be remembered," he writes, "for the emergence of the first serious woman candidate for president: Barack Obama."
4. Fordham discusses how code-switching and the racial dilemma of educational and professional success affect African American women ("Beyond Capital High").

Works Cited

Awkward, Michael. *Scenes of Instruction: A Memoir*. Durham: Duke UP, 1999. Print.

Bradford, Judith, and Crispin Sartwell. "Voiced Bodies/Embodied Voices." *Race/Sex: Their Sameness, Difference, and Interplay*. Ed. Naomi Zack. New York: Routledge, 1997. 191–203. Print.

Capehart, Jonathan. "Rage: Why Obama Won't and Can't Give You What You Want." *The Washington Post*. Washington Post, 8 June 2010. Web. 19 Apr. 2014.

Edwards, Patricia A., Gwendolyn Thompson McMillon, and Jennifer D. Turner. *Change Is Gonna Come: Transforming Literacy Education for African American Students*. New York: Teachers Coll. P—Intl. Reading Assn., 2010. Print.

Ellison, Ralph. Introduction. *Shadow and Act*. New York: Random, 1964. xi—xxiii. Print.

Fordham, Signithia. "Beyond Capital High: On Dual Citizenship and the Strange Career of 'Acting White.'" *Anthropology and Education Quarterly* 39.3 (2008): 227–46. Print.

———. *Blacked Out: Dilemmas of Race, Identity, and Success at Capital High*. Chicago: U of Chicago P, 1996. Print.

Frazier, E. Franklin. *Black Bourgeoisie*. 1957. New York: Free, 1997. Print.

Linsky, Martin. "The First Woman President? Obama's Campaign Bends Gender Conventions." *Newsweek*. Newsweek, 26 Feb. 2008. Web. 19 Apr. 2014.

McCrary, Donald. "Represent, Representin', Representation: The Efficacy of Hybrid Texts in the Writing Classroom." *Journal of Basic Writing* 24.2 (2005): 72–91. Print.

"Obama Gay Cover-Up!" *Globe*. American Media, 8 June 2009. Web. 19 Apr. 2014.

"Obama's Gay Lover Works in White House." *Globe*. American Media, 3 Aug. 2009. Web. 19 Apr. 2014.

Park, Robert Ezra, and Ernest Watson Burgess. *Introduction to the Science of Sociology*. Chicago: U of Chicago P, 1921. Print.

Parker, Kathleen. "Following Up on 'The First Female President.'" *The Washington Post*. Washington Post, 4 July 2010. Web. 19 Apr. 2014.

————. "Obama: Our First Female President." *The Washington Post*. Washington Post, 30 June 2010. Web. 19 Apr. 2014.

————. "Obama's Unmacho Diplomacy." *The Washington Post*. Washington Post, 8 Apr. 2009. Web. 19 Apr. 2014.

Ross, Marlon Bryan. *Manning the Race: Reforming Black Men in the Jim Crow Era*. New York: New York UP, 2004. Print.

Sledd, James. "Doublespeak: Dialectology in the Service of Big Brother." *Black Language Reader*. Ed. Robert H. Bentley and Samuel D. Crawford. Glenview: Foresman, 1973. 191–98. Print.

Charles M. Blow

It has long been believed that African American families are plagued by either absent fathers or fathers who are not involved in their children's lives or both. The following editorial by Charles M. Blow, who writes for the *New York Times*, says that these are persistent myths that paint an unnecessary and bleak portrait of African American men and fathers. In fact, the opinion seeks to present both sociological and statistical data that show that, among fathers of different ethnic and racial backgrounds, African American fathers exceed expectations in terms of involvement in their children's lives. This opinion seeks to intervene into the negative discourse that is pervasive about African American fathers with factual information that challenges and corrects the negative perceptions of African American men and fathers.

Black Dads Are Doing Best of All

Charles M. Blow[1]

JUNE 8, 2015

One of the most persistent statistical bludgeons of people who want to blame black people for any injustice or inequity they encounter is this: According to data from the Centers for Disease Control and Prevention (C.D.C.), in 2013 in nearly 72 percent of births to non-Hispanic black women, the mothers were unmarried.

It has always seemed to me that embedded in the "If only black men would marry the women they have babies with . . . " rhetoric was a more insidious suggestion: that there is something fundamental, and intrinsic about black men that is flawed, that black fathers are pathologically prone to desertion of their offspring and therefore largely responsible for black community "dysfunction."

There is an astounding amount of mythology loaded into this stereotype, one that echoes a history of efforts to rob black masculinity of honor and fidelity.

Josh Levs points this out in his new book, "All In," in a chapter titled "How Black Dads Are Doing Best of All (But There's Still a Crisis)." One fact that Levs quickly establishes is that most black fathers in America live with their children: "There are about 2.5 million black fathers living with their children and about 1.7 million living apart from them."

Fathers' Involvement

Involvement of fathers with activities of their children under age 5.

"So then," you may ask, "how is it that 72 percent of black children are born to single mothers? How can both be true?"

Good question.

Here are two things to consider: First, there are a growing number of people who live together but don't marry. Those mothers are still single, even though the child's father may be in the home. And, as The Washington Post reported last year:

"The share of unmarried couples who opted to have 'shotgun cohabitations'—moving in together after a pregnancy—surpassed 'shotgun marriages' for the first time during the last decade, according to a forthcoming paper from the National Center for Health Statistics, part of the Centers for Disease Control and Prevention."

Furthermore, a 2013 C.D.C. report found that black and Hispanic women are far more likely to experience a pregnancy during the first year of cohabitation than white and Asian women.

Table 7.1

Fathers Living With Children	Hisp.	White	Black
		(Percentages)	
Fed or ate meals with children daily	63.9	73.9	78.2
Bathed, diapered or dressed children daily	45.0	60	70.4
Played with children daily	74.1	82.7	82.2
Read to children daily	21.9	30.2	34.9

Fathers Not Living With Children	Hisp.	White	Black
Fed or ate meals with children daily	8.6	*	12.6
Bathed, diapered or dressed children daily	7.3	6.6	12.7
Played with children daily	10.0	6.6	16.5
Read to children daily	*	3.2	7.8

Note: Many differences between white, black or Hispanic fathers were not significant due to margins or error. Fathers who live with some children and live apart from others were asked separately about each set of children and their different answers were counted in the two different categories.

* Figure does not meet standards of reliability or precision.

Source: Los Angeles Times, National Center for Health Statistics.

Second, some of these men have children by more than one woman, but they can only live in one home at a time. This phenomenon means that a father can live with some but not all of his children. Levs calls these men "serial impregnators," but I think something more than promiscuity and irresponsibility are at play here.

> "An important but unreported indicator of Ferguson's dilemma is that half of young African-American men are missing from the community. According to the U.S. Census Bureau, while there are 1,182 African-American women between the ages of 25 and 34 living in Ferguson, there are only 577 African-American men in this age group. In other words there are more than two young black women for each young black man in Ferguson."

In April, The New York Times extended this line of reporting, pointing out that nationally, there are 1.5 million missing black men. As the paper put it: "Incarceration and early deaths are the overwhelming drivers of the gap. Of the 1.5 million missing black men from 25 to 54— which demographers call the prime-age years—higher imprisonment rates account for almost 600,000. Almost one in 12 black men in this age group are behind bars, compared with one in 60 nonblack men in the age group, one in 200 black women and one in 500 nonblack women." For context, there are about eight million African-American men in that age group overall.

Mass incarceration has disproportionately ensnared young black men, sucking hundreds of thousands of marriage-age men out of the community.

Another thing to consider is something that The Atlantic's Ta-Nehisi Coates pointed out in 2013: "The drop in the birthrate for unmarried black women is mirrored by an even steeper drop among married black women. Indeed, whereas at one point married black women were having more kids than married white women, they are now having less." This means that births to unmarried black women are disproportionately represented in the statistics.

Now to the mythology of the black male dereliction as dads: While it is true that black parents are less likely to marry before a child is born, it is not true that black fathers suffer a pathology of neglect. In fact, a C.D.C. report issued in December 2013 found that black fathers were the most involved with their children daily, on a number of measures, of any other group of fathers—and in many cases, that was among fathers who didn't live with their children, as well as those who did.

There is no doubt that the 72 percent statistic is real and may even be worrisome, but it represents more than choice. It exists in a social context, one at odds with the corrosive mythology about black fathers.

Note

1. Charles Blow, "Black Dads Are Doing Best of All," *New York Times*, June 8, 2015, A21.

Section 7: Further Reading

Brooks, Gwendolyn. "Malcolm X." In *The Mecca*. New York: Harper & Row, 1968. (p. 39).

Cleaver, Eldridge. *Soul on Ice*. New York: Dell Publishing, 1968. (pp. 106–111).

Cullen, Countee. "Tableau." In *Norton Anthology of African American Literature*. Eds. Henry L. Gates Jr. and Nellie Y. McKay. New York: Norton, 2004. (p. 1341).

Davis, Ossie. "Eulogy for Malcolm X." Funeral of Malcolm X. Harlem, NY. 27 February 1965. Speech.

Douglass, Frederick. *Narrative of the Life of Frederick Douglass*. London, Hampshire: H. G. Collins, 1851. (pp. 55–89). (Originally published in 1845).

Ellison, Ralph. "Chapter 1." In *Invisible Man*. New York: Random House, 1952. (pp. 13–26).

Johnson, Helene. "Sonnet to a Negro in Harlem." In *Norton Anthology of African American Literature*. Eds. Henry L. Gates Jr. and Nellie Y. McKay. New York: Norton, 2004. (p. 1352).

Mance, Ginger. "No Space between Our Men." In *Million Man March/Day of Absence: A Commemorative Anthology*. Chicago, IL; Los Angeles: Third World Press; University of Sankore Press, 1996. (pp. 122–124).

McKay, Claude. "If We Must Die." In *The Liberator*, July 2, 1919.

McKay, Claude. "To the White Fiend." In *Norton Anthology of African American Literature*. Eds. Henry L. Gates Jr. and Nellie Y. McKay. New York: Norton, 2004. (p. 1007).

Wilson, August. *Fences*, Act I. New York: Samuel French, Inc., 1986.

Wright, Eric L. *Boyz-n-the-hood. N.W.A. and the Posse*. Los Angeles, 1987. Music CD.

Wright, Richard. "How 'Bigger'g Was Born." In *Native Son*. New York: Harper & Brothers, 1969. (pp. vii–xxxiv). (Originally published in 1940).

Section 7: Discussion Questions

1. What is the relationship among race, gender, sex, and sexuality in the discourses of manhood? How do each of these intertwine in African American rhetoric?
2. What similar themes, situations, and arguments about manhood do you recognize among the works produced during the enslavement period (and other earlier periods) and now?
3. Describe how the selections depict an evolving relationship among school, education, and manhood. How has the relationship among school, education, and manhood changed over time? Identify how different works portray this relationship during different periods.
4. How have Blacks tried to reveal their manhood to Whites? How have Blacks tried to reveal their manhood to other Blacks? What are the differences and similarities in the appeals that are made to each racial group? What accounts for any differences and similarities?
5. Explain how female rhetors, such as Larsen, Morrison, Brent, Hansberry, or Wallace, represent and/or portray manhood. Compare these women's representations of manhood to representations of manhood by men.

8

THE QUARE OF QUEER

Edited and with an introduction by Jeffrey McCune

—————◦◦◦◦◦—————

To understand queer rhetoric is to understand what is produced at the site of queer practice. Whether it be the creation of space, the production of peculiar knowledge, or the distillation of particular experiences, we can witness how queer rhetoric is produced and recorded. This section of this anthology attempts to gather how Black queer subjects narrate how they do queer differently. Alexander and Rhodes (2012) remind us,

> Queer practice in this regard is robustly rhetorical in that it sees discourse as densely persuasive—a set of textual, visual, and auditory tools through which bodies and psyches are shaped and cast in particular identity formations and through which such bodies and psyches might potentially be recast and reformed.
>
> (1)

Indeed, the intent of this section is to bring to the fore these textual, visual, and auditory tools—illuminating the cultural-political verve that is stored within. Though the musical-audio component of blackness and queerness could not be utilized here, the voices collected incorporate and anticipate the sonic, as much as they provide a window into some other ways of knowing Black experience, Black expression, and of course Black knowledges.

Through these collected works and their specific focus on Black experience, largely outside of the White queer archive, these collected works represent the myriad of ways that Black public address have employed nonnormative cultural forms/genre and engaged nonnormative sexualities. Together, this body of texts persuades us that there was much queer about blackness before queerness was in vogue," prior to its elevation as White academic articulations of the nonnormative way of being in the world. This collection—of diverse texts and ideas—attempts to unveil the multiple ways that Black subjects use multiple genres, forms of expression, and archives to articulate race, gender, and sexuality on their own terms. Whether it is literary work that prioritizes the marginal voice, scholarly work that asks new questions, or a letter to speak one's truth on one's own terms, the work persuades the reader that materiality of blackness does alter worldview and how the world responds to the "doing of difference."

In E. Patrick's Johnson's field-shifting essay "Quare Studies, or [Almost] Everything I Know About Queer Studies I Learned From My Grandmother," he uses the rhetoric of his grandmother to anchor his quare orientation, one that he understands to capture "a way to critique stable notions of identity and, at the same time, to locate racialized and class knowledges" (p. 3). For me, this essay is as much about Johnson's coming into his own comfort in his skin as it is

449

about the ways in which the established language used to discuss, perform, and distill sexual desire was insufficient for Black life. In the offering here, I also suggest that the performances, texts, and artifacts classically included to chronicle Black gay and lesbian culture are largely insufficient as well. Rather, many kinds of texts, literatures, and performances tell the story of the "quare within the queer." What does that mean? It is more than just locating Black queer experiences among a homogenous White gay movement. Instead, I might suggest that to read quarely, or to quare the texts, we arrive at an orientation that understands the importance of Black nonnormative gender and sexual manifestations not only to the larger queer movement but also to Black studies project more generally. In essence, this body of material represents a quaring of sorts—the incorporation of Black gay voice and nonnormative presence in the larger schema of African American rhetoric and performance. In my quaring I have decided to "recruit texts"—selecting works that in different ways capture multiple experiences of the quare within the queer. Here, the "quare within the queer" is a move to recognize that blackness is always already a queer in the White marketplace of desire. My queer here is not indexing a particularly sexual experience, or some larger LGBT movement, but rather a gesture toward a discrete sexual or social presence that has always edged up and against the Black heteronormative struggle for mobility and respectability. Thus, my quare is not necessarily a contemporary revelation but an emergence from texts across time that signify the tardiness of queer theorists and queer inclusionists to read and account for the "the quare of the queer."

Works Cited

Alexander, Jonathan and Jackie Rhodes. "Queer Rhetoric and the Pleasures of the Archive." *Enculturation* (6 January 2012).

Johnson, E. Patrick. "'Quare' Studies, or (Almost) Everything I Know about Queer Studies I Learned from My Grandmother." *Text and Performance Quarterly*, 21.1 (2001).

Olaudah Equiano

Historically, this narrative has been touted as a cosmopolitan slave narrative, which explores the dual worlds that some slaves live between slavery and free. Olaudah Equiano's travels were largely financed by White men, with whom he shares intimate space and narrates exceptionally intimate moments. This narrative introduces male-male intimacies, in ways that quare the historical account of the slave-free experience. In addition, this narrative has been met with great scrutiny and faced with a set of questions around truth, accuracy of birthplace, and authenticity of the life story. The text is doubly quare as it not only disorients the reader from an assertion of the slave text as pure nonfiction but also unveils the erotic workings of White-Black post-slavery contexts. Regardless of truth(s), this text serves to introduce a particular brand of historical ex-slave narrative that explores the quare-world making and the rhetoric of intimacy—thereby complicating the relationship of its reader to all that is chronicled in this telling of Olaudah Equiano's life.

The Interesting Narrative of the Life of Olaudah Equiano, or Gustavus Vassa, the African

Olaudah Equiano[1]

I now saw myself deprived of all chance of returning to my native country, or even the least glimpse of hope of gaining the shore which I now considered as friendly; and I even wished for my former slavery in preference to my present situation, which was filled with horrors of every kind, still heightened by my ignorance of what I was to undergo. I was not long suffered to indulge my grief; I was soon put down hinder the decks, and there I received such a salutation in my nostrils as I had never experienced in my life: so that, with the loathsomeness of the stench and crying together, I became so sick and low that I was not able to eat, nor had I the least desire to taste anything. I now wished for the last friend, death, to relieve me; but soon, to my grief, two of the white men offered me eatables; and on my refusing to eat, one of them held me fast by the hands, and laid me across I think the windlass and tied my feet, while the other flogged me severely. I had never experienced anything of this kind before; and although, not being used to the water, I naturally feared that element the first time I saw it, yet nevertheless, could I have got over the nettings, I would have jumped over the side, but I could not; and, besides, the crew used to watch us very closely who were not chained down to the decks, lest we should leap into the water: and I have seen some of these poor African prisoners most severely cut for attempting to do so, and hourly whipped for not eating. This indeed was often the case with myself. In a little time after, amongst the poor chained men, I found some of my own nation, which in a small degree gave ease to my mind. I inquired of these what was to be done with us; they gave me to understand we were to be carried to these white people's country to work for them.

I then was a little revived, and thought, if it were no worse than working, my situation was not so desperate: but still I feared I should be put to death, the white people looked and acted, as I thought, in so savage a manner; for I had never seen among any people such instances of brutal cruelty; and this not only shewn towards us blacks, but also to some of the whites themselves. One white man in particular I saw, when we were permitted to be on deck, flogged so unmercifully with a large rope near the foremast that he died in consequence of it; and they tossed him over the side as they would have done a brute. This made me fear these people the more.

On the 21st of April we renewed our efforts to land the men, while all the men of war were stationed along the shore to cover it, and fired at the French batteries and breastworks from early in the morning till about four o'clock in the evening, when our soldiers effected a safe landing.

They immediately attacked the French; and, after a sharp encounter, forced them from the batteries. Before the enemy retreated they blew up several of them, lest they should fall into our hands. Our men now proceeded to besiege the citadel, and my master was ordered on shore to superintend the landing of all the materials necessary for carrying on the siege; in which service I mostly attended him. While I was there I went about to different parts of the island; and one day, particularly, my curiosity almost cost me my life. I wanted very much to see the mode of charging the mortars and letting off the shells and for that purpose I went to an English battery that was but a very few yards from the walls of the citadel. There, indeed, I had an opportunity of completely gratifying myself in seeing the whole operation, and that not without running a very great risk, both from the English shells that burst while I was there, but likewise from those of the French. One of the largest of their shells bursted within nine or ten yards of me: there was a single rock close by, about the size of a butt; and I got instant shelter under it in time to avoid the fury of the shell. Where it burst the earth was torn in such a manner that two or three butts might easily have gone into the hole it made, and it threw great quantities of stones and dirt to a considerable distance. Three shot[s] were also fired at me and another boy who was along with me, one of them in particular seemed

   "Wing'd with red lightning and impetuous rage;"
for with a most dreadful sound it hissed close by me, and struck a rock at a little distance, which it shattered to pieces. When I saw what perilous circumstances I was in, I attempted to return the nearest way I could find, and thereby I got between the English and the French sentinels. An English sergeant, who commanded the outposts, seeing me, and surprised how I came there (which was by stealth along the seashore), reprimanded me very severely for it, and instantly took the sentinel off his post into custody, for his negligence in suffering me to pass the lines. While I was in this situation I observed at a little distance a French horse, belonging to some islanders, which I thought I would now mount, for the greater expedition of getting off. Accordingly I took some cord which I had about me, and making a kind of bridle of it, I put it round the horse's head, and the tame beast very quietly suffered me to tie him thus and mount him. As soon as I was on the horse's back I began to kick and beat him, and try every means to make him go quick, but all to very little purpose. I could not drive him out of a slow pace. While I was creeping along, still within reach of the enemy's shot, I met with a servant well mounted on an English horse. I immediately stopped; and, crying, told him my case; and begged of him to help me, and this he effectually did; for, having a fine large whip, he began to lash my horse with it so severely, that he set off full speed with me towards the sea, while I was quite unable to hold, or manage him. In this manner I went along till I came to a craggy precipice. I now could not stop my horse; and my mind was filled with apprehensions of my deplorable fate should he go down the precipice, which he appeared fully disposed to do: I therefore thought I had better throw myself off him at once, which I did immediately with a great deal of dexterity, and fortunately escaped unhurt. As soon as I found myself at liberty I made the best of my way for the ship, determined I would not be so foolhardy again in a hurry.

Note

1. Olaudah Equiano, *The Interesting Narrative of the Life of Olaudah Equiano*, ed., Henry Louis Gates (New York: Penguin Books, 1987 [1814]), pp. 73–75; pp. 163–165.

Harriet Jacobs

In this passage Jacobs presents another side of the slave narrative. In essence, she records a moment of quare pain (slave subjection to violent erotic gaze) and queer pleasure (White slave master's violent gaze). Jacobs narrates an act of violence upon a fellow slave named Luke, which speaks to the erotic life of racism (Holland) and the sexual formations produced in the slave arrangements. This particular narrative introduces the idea of the "slave watching the slave," which can be understood as a cross-viewing practice that is as much cautionary as it is erotic. Specifically, *how* Jacobs narrates this moment provides evidence of quare disgust—rooted in queerness as an act of White racist violence against men and their manhood.

The Fugitive Slave Law

Harriet Jacobs[1]

My brother, being disappointed in his project, concluded to go to California; and it was agreed that Benjamin should go with him. Ellen liked her school, and was a great favorite there. They did not know her history, and she did not tell it, because she had no desire to make capital out of their sympathy. But when it was accidentally discovered that her mother was a fugitive slave, every method was used to increase her advantages and diminish her expenses.[1]

I was alone again. It was necessary for me to be earning money, and I preferred that it should be among those who knew me. On my return from Rochester, I called at the house of Mr. Bruce, to see Mary, the darling little babe that had thawed my heart, when it was freezing into a cheerless distrust of all my fellow-beings. She was growing a tall girl now, but I loved her always. Mr. Bruce had married again, and it was proposed that I should become nurse to a new infant.[2] I had but one hesitation, and that was my feeling of insecurity in New York, now greatly increased by the passage of the Fugitive Slave Law. However, I resolved to try the experiment. I was again fortunate in my employer. The new Mrs. Bruce was an American, brought up under aristocratic influences, and still living in the midst of them; but if she had any prejudice against color, I was never made aware of it; and as for the system of slavery, she had a most hearty dislike of it. No sophistry of Southerners could blind her to its enormity. She was a person of excellent principles and a noble heart. To me, from that hour to the present, she has been a true and sympathizing friend. Blessings be with her and hers!

About the time that I reentered the Bruce family, an event occurred of disastrous import to the colored people. The slave Hamlin, the first fugitive that came under the new law, was given up by the bloodhounds of the north to the bloodhounds of the south. It was the beginning of a reign of terror to the colored population. The great city rushed on in its whirl of excitement, taking no note of the "short and simple annals of the poor."[3] But while fashionables were listening to the thrilling voice of Jenny Lind in Metropolitan Hall,[4] the thrilling voices of poor hunted colored people went up, in an agony of supplication, to the Lord, from Zion's church.[5] Many families, who had lived in the city for twenty years, fled from it now.[6] Many a poor washerwoman, who, by hard labor, had made herself a comfortable home, was obliged to sacrifice her furniture, bid a hurried farewell to friends, and seek her fortune among strangers in Canada. Many a wife discovered a secret she had never known before—that her husband was a fugitive, and must leave her to insure his own safety. Worse still, many a husband discovered that his wife had fled from slavery years ago, and as "the child follows the condition of its mother," the children of his love were liable to be seized and carried into slavery. Every where, in those humble homes, there was consternation and anguish. But what cared the legislators of the "dominant race" for the blood they were crushing out of trampled hearts?

When my brother William spent his last evening with me, before he went to California, we talked nearly all the time of the distress brought on our oppressed people by the passage of this iniquitous law; and never had I seen him manifest such bitterness of spirit, such stern hostility to our oppressors. He was himself free from the operation of the law; for he did not run from any Slaveholding State, being brought into the Free States by his master. But I was subject to it; and so were hundreds of intelligent and industrious people all around us. I seldom ventured into the streets; and when it was necessary to do an errand for Mrs. Bruce, or any of the family, I went as much as possible through back streets and by-ways.[7] What a disgrace to a city calling itself free, that inhabitants, guiltless of offence, and seeking to perform their duties conscientiously, should be condemned to live in such incessant fear, and have nowhere to turn for protection! This state of things, of course, gave rise to many impromptu vigilance committees. Every colored person, and every friend of their persecuted race, kept their eyes wide open. Every evening I examined the newspapers carefully, to see what Southerners had put up at the hotels. I did this for my own sake, thinking my young mistress and her husband might be among the list; I wished also to give information to others, if necessary; for if many were "running to and fro," I resolved that "knowledge should be increased."[8]

This brings up one of my Southern reminiscences, which I will here briefly relate. I was somewhat acquainted with a slave named Luke, who belonged to a wealthy man in our vicinity. His master died, leaving a son and daughter heirs to his large fortune. In the division of the slaves, Luke was included in the son's portion. This young man became a prey to the vices growing out of the "patriarchal institution," and when he went to the north, to complete his education, he carried his vices with him. He was brought home, deprived of the use of his limbs, by excessive dissipation. Luke was appointed to wait upon his bed-ridden master, whose despotic habits were greatly increased by exasperation at his own helplessness. He kept a cowhide beside him, and, for the most trivial occurrence, he would order his attendant to bare his back, and kneel beside the couch, while he whipped him till his strength was exhausted. Some days he was not allowed to wear any thing but his shirt, in order to be in readiness to be flogged. A day seldom passed without his receiving more or less blows. If the slightest resistance was offered, the town constable was sent for to execute the punishment, and Luke learned from experience how much more the constable's strong arm was to be dreaded than the comparatively feeble one of his master. The arm of his tyrant grew weaker, and was finally palsied; and then the constable's services were in constant requisition. The fact that he was entirely dependent on Luke's care, and was obliged to be tended like an infant, instead of inspiring any gratitude or compassion towards his poor slave, seemed only to increase his irritability and cruelty. As he lay there on his bed, a mere degraded wreck of manhood, he took into his head the strangest freaks of despotism; and if Luke hesitated to submit to his orders, the constable was immediately sent for. Some of these freaks were of a nature too filthy to be repeated. When I fled from the house of bondage, I left poor Luke still chained to the bedside of this cruel and disgusting wretch.

One day, when I had been requested to do an errand for Mrs. Bruce, I was hurrying through back streets, as usual, when I saw a young man approaching, whose face was familiar to me. As he came nearer, I recognized Luke. I always rejoiced to see or hear of any one who had escaped from the black pit; but, remembering this poor fellow's extreme hardships, I was peculiarly glad to see him on Northern soil, though I no longer called it *free* soil. I well remembered what a desolate feeling it was to be alone among strangers, and I went up to him and greeted him cordially. At first, he did not know me; but when I mentioned my name, he remembered all about me. I told him of the Fugitive Slave Law, and asked him if he did not know that New York was a city of kidnappers.

He replied, "De risk ain't so bad for me, as 'tis fur you. 'Cause I runned away from de speculator, and you runned away from de massa. Dem speculators vont spen dar money to come here fur a runaway, if dey ain't sartin sure to put dar hans right on him. An I tell you I's tuk good car 'bout dat. I had too hard times down dar, to let 'em ketch dis nigger."

He then told me of the advice he had received, and the plans he had laid. I asked if he had money enough to take him to Canada. " 'Pend upon it, I hab," he replied. "I tuk car fur dat. I'd bin workin all my days fur dem cussed whites, an got no pay but kicks and cuffs. So I tought dis nigger had a right to money nuff to bring him to de Free States. Massa Henry he lib till ebery body vish him dead; an ven he did die, I knowed de debbil would hab him, an vouldn't vant him to bring his money 'long too. So I tuk some of his bills, and put 'em in de pocket of his ole trousers. An ven he was buried, dis nigger ask fur dem ole trousers, an dey gub 'em to me." With a low, chuckling laugh, he added, "You see I didn't *steal* it; dey *gub* it to me. I tell you, I had mighty hard time to keep de speculator from findin it; but he didn't git it."

This is a fair specimen of how the moral sense is educated by slavery. When a man has his wages stolen from him, year after year, and the laws sanction and enforce the theft, how can he be expected to have more regard to honesty than has the man who robs him? I have become somewhat enlightened, but I confess that I agree with poor, ignorant, much-abused Luke, in thinking he had a *right* to that money, as a portion of his unpaid wages. He went to Canada forthwith, and I have not since heard from him.

All that winter I lived in a state of anxiety. When I took the children out to breathe the air, I closely observed the countenances of all I met. I dreaded the approach of summer, when snakes and slaveholders make their appearance. I was, in fact, a slave in New York, as subject to slave laws as I had been in a Slave State. Strange incongruity in a State called free!

Spring returned, and I received warning from the south that Dr. Flint knew of my return to my old place, and was making preparations to have me caught. I learned afterwards that my dress, and that of Mrs. Bruce's children, had been described to him by some of the Northern tools, which slaveholders employ for their base purposes, and then indulge in sneers at their cupidity and mean servility.

I immediately informed Mrs. Bruce of my danger, and she took prompt measures for my safety. My place as nurse could not be supplied immediately, and this generous, sympathizing lady proposed that I should carry her baby away.[9] It was a comfort to me to have the child with me; for the heart is reluctant to be torn away from every object it loves. But how few mothers would have consented to have one of their own babes become a fugitive, for the sake of a poor, hunted nurse, on whom the legislators of the country had let loose the bloodhounds! When I spoke of the sacrifice she was making, in depriving herself of her dear baby, she replied, "It is better for you to have baby with you, Linda; for if they get on your track, they will be obliged to bring the child to me; and then, if there is a possibility of saving you, you shall be saved."

This lady had a very wealthy relative, a benevolent gentleman in many respects, but aristocratic and pro-slavery. He remonstrated with her for harboring a fugitive slave; told her she was violating the laws of her country; and asked her if she was aware of the penalty. She replied, "I am very well aware of it. It is imprisonment and one thousand dollars fine. Shame on my country that it *is* so! I am ready to incur the penalty. I will go to the state's prison, rather than have any poor victim torn from *my* house, to be carried back to slavery."

The noble heart! The brave heart! The tears are in my eyes while I write of her. May the God of the helpless reward her for her sympathy with my persecuted people!

I was sent into New England, where I was sheltered by the wife of a senator, whom I shall always hold in grateful remembrance.[10] This honorable gentleman would not have voted for the Fugitive Slave Law, as did the senator in "Uncle Tom's Cabin;" on the contrary, he was strongly opposed to it; but he was enough under its influence to be afraid of having me remain in his house many hours. So I was sent into the country, where I remained a month with the baby. When it was supposed that Dr. Flint's emissaries had lost track of me, and given up the pursuit for the present, I returned to New York.

Note

1. Harriet Jacobs (Jean Yellin), *Incidents in the Life of a Slave Girl: Written by Herself* (Cambridge, MA: Harvard University Press, 1987 [1861]), pp. 191–193.

E. Franklin Frazier

In this problematic framing of the Black middle-class "negro" as "prevented from playing the masculine role," Frazier exposes the queer position of some men. In this chapter, he unveils the working of masculine scripts in Black middle-class life as used to police and surveil Black male doings. In this interpretation of Black life, Frazier sets forth a narrative that essentially speaks to how Black middle-class status queers Black men, producing a set of quare arrangements that endanger his masculine ideals. Through this largely essentialist and overdetermining rhetoric, Frazier uncovers his own ideological bias, while also uncovering the ways in which interpretations of Black life can short-circuit the legitimacy of nonnormative gender and sexuality. To do this, Frazier also utilizes women to be the litmus tests for the functionality of nontraditional sexuality, as well as middle-class labor demands. In his engagement with Black female experience, he paints a picture of quare performances by women within relationships where class mobility, according to Frazier, recalibrates the whole family structure.

Black Bourgeoisie

E. Franklin Frazier[1]

There is much frustration among the black bourgeoisie despite their privileged position within the segregated Negro world. Their "wealth" and "social" position can not erase the fact that they are generally segregated and rejected by the white world. Their incomes and occupations may enable them to escape the cruder manifestations of racial prejudice, but they can not insulate themselves against the more subtle forms of racial discrimination. These discriminations cause frustrations in Negro men because they are not allowed to play the "masculine role" as defined by American culture. They can not assert themselves or exercise power as white men do. When they protest against racial discrimination there is always the threat that they will be punished by the white world. In spite of the movement toward the wider integration of the Negro into the general stream of American life, middle-class Negroes are still threatened with the loss of positions and earning power if they insist upon their rights.[4] After the Supreme Court of the United States ruled that segregation in public education was illegal, Negro teachers in some parts of the South were dismissed because they would not sign statements supporting racial segregation in education.

As one of the results of not being able to play the "masculine role," middle-class Negro males have tended to cultivate their "personalities"[5] which enable them to exercise considerable influence among whites and achieve distinction in the Negro world. Among Negroes they have been noted for their glamour.[6] In this respect they resemble women who use their "personalities" to compensate for their inferior status in relation to men. This fact would seem to support the observation of an American sociologist that the Negro was "the lady among the races," if he had restricted his observation to middle-class males among American Negroes.[7]

In the South the middle-class Negro male is not only prevented from playing a masculine role, but generally he must let Negro women assume leadership in any show of militancy. This reacts upon his status in the home where the tradition of female dominance, which is widely established among Negroes, has tended to assign a subordinate role to the male. In fact, in middle-class families, especially if the husband has risen in social status through his own efforts and married a member of an "old" family or a "society" woman, the husband is likely to play a pitiful role. The greatest compliment that can be paid such a husband is that he "worships his wife," which means that he is her slave and supports all her extravagances and vanities. But, of course, many husbands in such positions escape from their frustrations by having extra-marital sex relations. Yet the conservative and conventional middle-class husband presents a pathetic picture. He often sits at home alone, impotent physically and socially, and complains that his wife has gone crazy about poker and "society" and constantly demands money for gambling and expenditures which he can not afford. Sometimes he enjoys the sympathy of a son or daughter who has not become a "socialite." Such children often say that they had a happy family life until "mamma took to poker."

Preoccupation with poker on the part of the middle-class woman is often an attempt to escape from a frustrated life. Her frustration may be bound up with her unsatisfactory sexual life. She may be married to a "glamorous" male who neglects her for other women. For among the black bourgeoisie, the glamour of the male is often associated with his sexual activities. The frustration of many Negro women has a sexual origin.[8] Even those who have sought an escape from frustration in sexual promiscuity may, because of satiety or deep psychological reasons, become obsessed with poker in order to escape from their frustrations. One "society" woman, in justification of her obsession with poker remarked that it had taken the place of her former preoccupation with sex. Another said that to win at poker was similar to a sexual orgasm.

The frustration of the majority of the women among the black bourgeoisie is probably due to the idle or ineffectual lives which they lead. Those who do not work devote their time to the frivolities of Negro "society." When they devote their time to "charity" or worth-while causes, it is generally a form of play or striving for "social" recognition. They are constantly forming clubs which ostensibly have a serious purpose, but in reality are formed in order to consolidate their position in "society" or to provide additional occasions for playing poker. The idle, over-fed women among the black bourgeoisie are generally, to use their language, "dripping with diamonds." They are forever dieting and reducing only to put on more weight (which is usually the result of the food that they consume at their club meetings). Even the women among the black bourgeoisie who work exhibit the same frustrations. Generally, they have no real interest in their work and only engage in it in order to be able to provide the conspicuous consumption demanded by "society." As we have indicated, the women as well as the men among the black bourgeoisie read very little and have no interest in music, art or the theater. They are constantly restless and do not know how to relax. They are generally dull people and only become animated when "social" matters are discussed, especially poker games. They are afraid to be alone and constantly seek to be surrounded by their friends, who enable them to escape from their boredom.

The frustrated lives of the black bourgeoisie are reflected in the attitudes of parents towards their children. Middle-class Negro families as a whole have few children, while among the families that constitute Negro "society" there are many childless couples.[9] One finds today, as an American observed over forty years ago, that "where the children are few, they are usually spoiled" in middle-class Negro families.[10] There is often not only a deep devotion to their one or two children, but a subservience to them. It is not uncommon for the only son to be called and treated as the "boss" in the family. Parents cater to the transient wishes of their children and often rationalize their behavior towards them on the grounds that children should not be "inhibited." They spend large sums of money on their children for toys and especially for clothes. They provide their children with automobiles when they go to college. All of this is done in order that the children may maintain the status of the parents and be eligible to enter the "social" set in Negro colleges. When they send their children to northern "white" colleges they often spend more time in preparing them for what they imagine will be their "social" life than in preparing them for the academic requirements of these institutions.

In their fierce devotion to their children, which generally results in spoiling them, middle-class Negro parents are seemingly striving at times to establish a human relationship that will compensate for their own frustrations in the realm of human relationships. Devotion to their children often becomes the one human tie that is sincere and free from the competition and artificiality of the make-believe world in which they live. Sometimes they may project upon their children their own frustrated professional ambitions. But usually, even when they send their children to northern "white" universities as a part of their "social" striving within the Negro community, they seem to hope that their children will have an acceptance in the white world which has been denied them.

Note

1. E. Franklin Frazier, *Black Bourgeoisie* (New York: Simon & Schuster, 1957), pp. 220–224.

Eldridge Cleaver

Written from prison, prominent Black Panther leader Eldridge Cleaver writes a collection of essays that espouse his political views on the state of blackness and Black political action. In this particular essay, Cleaver uses James Baldwin as a syndecdoche for Black peril at the hands of whiteness. Here, he establishes Baldwin as the antithesis of Black manhood, the homosexual Black who embraces a "racial death-wish." Queerly, Cleaver separated Baldwin's work from his sexuality and praises his contribution to Black rhetorical and political tradition. This excerpt serves as an example of how rhetoric meant to critique queerness can be ridden with its own set of quare voices—exposing a discourse that arises out of the scene of heightened truculence and masculine braggadocio. Indeed, Cleaver engages in a performance of the essential "Black man" by discounting Baldwin's position in the schema of Black manhood and connecting him to the "White homosexual." This indictment on sexuality, while it has often been talked about as an allegory for White racism, situates all nonnormative sexuality as a product of whiteness, or quintessentially anti-Black.

Soul on Ice

Eldridge Cleaver[1]

In the autobiographical notes of *Notes of a Native Son*, Baldwin is frank to confess that, in growing into his version of manhood in Harlem, he discovered that, since his African heritage had been wiped out and was not accessible to him, he would appropriate the white man's heritage and make it his own. This terrible reality, central to the psychic stance of all American Negroes, revealed to Baldwin that he hated and feared white people. Then he says: "This did not mean that I loved black people; on the contrary, I despised them, possibly because they failed to produce Rembrandt." The psychic distance between love and hate could be the mechanical difference between a smile and a sneer, or it could be the journey of a nervous impulse from the depths of one's brain to the tip of one's toe. But this impulse in its path through North American nerves may, if it is honest, find the passage disputed: may find the leap from the fiber of hate to that of love too taxing on its meager store of energy—and so the long trip back may never be completed, may end in a reconnaissance, a compromise, and then a lie.

Self-hatred takes many forms; sometimes it can be detected by no one, not by the keenest observer, not by the self-hater himself, not by his most intimate friends. Ethnic self-hate is even more difficult to detect. But in American Negroes, this ethnic self-hatred often takes the bizarre form of a racial death-wish, with many and elusive manifestations. Ironically, it provides much of the impetus behind the motivations of integration. And the attempt to suppress or deny such drives in one's psyche leads many American Negroes to become ostentatious separationists, Black Muslims, and back-to-Africa advocates. It is no wonder that Elijah Muhammad could conceive of the process of controlling evolution whereby the white race was brought into being. According to Elijah, about 6300 years ago all the people of the earth were Original Blacks. Secluded on the island of Patmos, a mad black scientist by the name of Yacub set up the machinery for grafting whites out of blacks through the operation of a birth-control system. The population on this island of Patmos was 59,999 and whenever a couple on this island wanted to get married they were only allowed to do so if there was a difference in their color, so that by mating black with those in the population of a brownish color and brown with brown—but never black with black—all traces of the black were eventually eliminated; the process was repeated until all the brown was eliminated, leaving only men of the red race; the red was bleached out, leaving only yellow; then the yellow was bleached out, and only white was left. Thus Yacub, who was long since dead, because this whole process took hundreds of years, had finally succeeded in creating the white devil with the blue eyes of death

This myth of the creation of the white race, called "Yacub's History," is an inversion of the racial death-wish of American Negroes. Yacub's plan is still being followed by many Negroes today. Quite simply, many Negroes believe, as the principle of assimilation into white America implies, that the race problem in America cannot be settled until all traces of the black race are eliminated. Toward this end, many Negroes loathe the very idea of two very dark Negroes mating. The children, they say, will come out ugly. What they mean is that the children are sure to be black, and this is not desirable. From the widespread use of cosmetics to bleach the black out of one's skin and other concoctions to take Africa out of one's hair, to the extreme, resorted to by more Negroes than one might wish to believe, of undergoing nose-thinning and lip-clipping operations, the racial death-wish of American Negroes—Yacub's goal—takes its terrible toll. What has been happening for the past four hundred years is that the white man, through his access to black women, has been pumping his blood and genes into the blacks, has been diluting the blood and genes of the blacks—i.e., has been fulfilling Yacub's plan and accelerating the Negroes' racial death-wish.

The case of James Baldwin aside for a moment, it seems that many Negro homosexuals, acquiescing in this racial death-wish, are outraged and frustrated because in their sickness they are unable to have a baby by a white man. The cross they have to bear is that, already bending over and touching their toes for the white man, the fruit of their miscegenation is not the little half-white offspring of their dreams but an increase in the unwinding of their nerves—though they redouble their efforts and intake of the white man's sperm.

In this land of dichotomies and disunited opposites, those truly concerned with the resurrection of black Americans have had eternally to deal with black intellectuals who have become their own opposites, taking on all of the behavior patterns of their enemy, vices and virtues, in an effort to aspire to alien standards in all respects. The gulf between an audacious, bootlicking Uncle Tom and an intellectual buckdancer is filled only with sophistication and style. On second thought, Uncle Tom comes off much cleaner here because usually he is just trying to survive, choosing to pretend to be something other than his true self in order to please the white man and thus receive favors. Whereas the intellectual sycophant does not pretend to be other than he actually is, but hates what he is and seeks to redefine himself in the image of his white idols. He becomes a white man in a black body. A self-willed, automated slave, he becomes the white man's most valuable tool in oppressing other blacks.

The black homosexual, when his twist has a racial nexus, is an extreme embodiment of this contradiction. The white man has deprived him of his masculinity, castrated him in the center of his burning skull, and when he submits to this change and takes the white man for his lover as well as Big Daddy, he focuses on "whiteness" all the love in his pent up soul and turns the razor edge of hatred against "blackness"—upon himself, what he is, and all those who look like him, remind him of himself. He may even hate the darkness of night.

The racial death-wish is manifested as the driving force in James Baldwin. His hatred for blacks, even as he pleads what he conceives as their cause, makes him the apotheosis of the dilemma in the ethos of the black bourgeoisie who have completely rejected their African heritage, consider the loss irrevocable, and refuse to look again in that direction. This is the root of Baldwin's violent repudiation of Mailer's *The White Negro*.

To understand what is at stake here, and to understand it in terms of the life of this nation, is to know the central fact that the relationship between black and white in America is a power equation, a power struggle, and that this power struggle is not only manifested in the aggregate (civil rights, black nationalism, etc.) but also in the interpersonal relationships, actions, and reactions between blacks and whites where taken into account. When those "two lean cats,"

Baldwin and Mailer, met in a French living room, it was precisely this power equation that was at work.

It is fascinating to read (in *Nobody Knows My Name*) in what terms this power equation was manifested in Baldwin's immediate reaction to that meeting: "And here we were, suddenly, circling around each other. We liked each other at once, but each was frightened that the other would pull rank. He could have pulled rank on me because he was more famous and *had more money* and also *because he was white;* but I could have pulled rank on him precisely because I was black and knew more about that periphery he so helplessly maligns in *The White Negro* than he could ever hope to know." [Italics added.]

Pulling rank, it would seem, is a very dangerous business, especially when the troops have mutinied and the basis of one's authority, or rank, is devoid of that interdictive power and has become suspect. One would think that for Baldwin, of all people, these hues of black and white were no longer armed with the power to intimidate—and if one thought this, one would be exceedingly wrong: for behind the structure of the thought of Baldwin's quoted above, there lurks the imp of Baldwin's unwinding, of his tension between love and hate—love of the white and hate of the black. And when we dig into this tension we will find that when those "two lean cats" crossed tracks in that French living room, one was a Pussy Cat, the other a Tiger. Baldwin's purr was transmitted magnificently in *The Fire Next Time*. But his work is the fruit of a tree with a poison root. Such succulent fruit, such a painful tree, what a malignant root!

It is ironic, but fascinating for what it reveals about the ferment in the North American soul in our time, that Norman Mailer, the white boy, and James Baldwin, the black boy, encountered each other in the eye of a social storm, traveling in opposite directions; the white boy, with knowledge of white Negroes, was traveling toward a confrontation with the black, with Africa; while the black boy, with a white mind, was on his way to Europe. Baldwin's nose, like the North-seeking needle on a compass, is forever pointed toward his adopted fatherland, Europe, his by intellectual osmosis and in Africa's stead. What he says of Aimé Césaire, one of the greatest black writers of the twentieth century, and intending it as an ironic rebuke, that "he had penetrated into the heart of the great wilderness which was Europe and stolen the sacred fire . . . which . . . was . . . the assurance of his power," seems only too clearly to speak more about Peter than it does about Paul. What Baldwin seems to forget is that Césaire explains that fire, whether sacred or profane, burns. In Baldwin's case, though the fire could not burn the black off his face, it certainly did burn it out of his heart.

I am not interested in denying anything to Baldwin. I, like the entire nation, owe a great debt to him. But throughout the range of his work, from *Go Tell It on the Mountain*, through *Notes of a Native Son, Nobody Knows My Name, Another Country*, to *The Fire Next Time*, all of which I treasure, there is a decisive quirk in Baldwin's vision which corresponds to his relationship to black people and to masculinity. It was this same quirk, in my opinion, that compelled Baldwin to slander Rufus Scott in *Another Country*, venerate André Gide, repudiate *The White Negro*, and drive the blade of Brutus into the corpse of Richard Wright. As Baldwin has said in *Nobody Knows My Name*, "I think that I know something about the American masculinity which most men of my generation do not know because they have not been menaced by it in the way I have been." O.K., Sugar, but isn't it true that Rufus Scott, the weak, craven-hearted ghost of *Another Country*, bears the same relation to Bigger Thomas of *Native Son*, the black rebel of the ghetto and a man, as you yourself bore to the fallen giant, Richard Wright, a rebel and a man?

Somewhere in one of his books, Richard Wright describes an encounter between a ghost and several young Negroes. The young Negroes rejected the homosexual, and this was Wright alluding to a classic, if cruel, example of a ubiquitous phenomenon in the black ghettos of America: the practice by Negro youths of going "punk-hunting." This practice of seeking out homosexuals on the prowl, rolling them, beating them up, seemingly just to satisfy some savage impulse to inflict pain on the specific target selected, the "social outcast," seems to me to be not unrelated, in terms of the psychological mechanisms involved, to the ritualistic lynchings and castrations inflicted on Southern blacks by Southern whites. This was, as I recall, one of Wright's few comments on the subject of homosexuality.

I think it can safely be said that the men in Wright's books, albeit shackled with a form of impotence, were strongly heterosexual. Their heterosexuality was implied rather than laboriously stated or emphasized; it was taken for granted, as well all take men until something occurs to make us know otherwise. And Bigger Thomas, Wright's greatest creation, was a man in violent, though inept, rebellion against the stifling, murderous, totalitarian white world. There was no trace in Bigger of a Martin Luther King-type self-effacing love for his oppressors. For example, Bigger would have been completely baffled, as most Negroes are today, at Baldwin's advice to his nephew (*The Fire Next Time*), concerning white people: "You must accept them *and accept them with love.* For these innocent people have no other hope." [Italics added.]

Rufus Scott, a pathetic wretch who indulged in the white man's pastime of committing suicide, who let a white bisexual homosexual fuck him in his ass, and who took a Southern Jezebel for his woman, with all that these tortured relationships imply, was the epitome of a black eunuch who has completely submitted to the white man. Yes, Rufus was a psychological freedom rider, turning the ultimate cheek, murmuring like a ghost, "*You took the best so why not take the rest,*" which has absolutely nothing to do with the way Negroes have managed to survive here in the hells of North America! This all becomes very clear from what we learn of Erich, the archghost of *Another Country*, of the depths of his alienation from his body and the source of his need: "And it had taken him almost until this very moment, on the eve of his departure, to begin to recognize that part of Rufus' great power over him had to do with the past which Erich had buried in some deep, dark place; was connected with himself, in Alabama, *when I wasn't nothing but a child;* with the cold white people and the warm black people, warm at least for him . . . ."

So, too, who cannot wonder at the source of such audacious madness as moved Baldwin to make this startling remark about Richard Wright, in his ignoble essay "Alas, Poor Richard": "In my own relations with him, I was always exasperated by his notions of society, politics, and history, for they seemed to me utterly fanciful. I never believed that he had any real sense of how a society is put together."

Richard Wright is dead and Baldwin is alive and with us. Baldwin says that Richard Wright held notions that were utterly fanciful, and Baldwin is an honorable man.

Note

1. Eldridge Cleaver, from "Notes on a Native Son," in *Soul on Ice* (New York: Random House, 1968), pp. 101–107.

Huey P. Newton

Contrary to Cleaver, Black Panther cofounder Huey P. Newton turns his Black radical and political energies in the direction of coalitional and anti-oppression politics. In this excerpt, he performs a quare alliance with the women's movement and the larger LGBT movement. In this letter, he attempts to speak to Black leaders and the constituents of the LGBT and women's organizations. Here, Newton actually posits that women, and particularly gays and lesbians, can be revolutionary—contributing members to the larger cause of Black liberation. This letter is a rhetorical device deployed to encourage Black revolutionary embrace of women and LGBT in the larger Black power movement while also offering support for their independent efforts toward equality.

On the Women's and Gay Liberation Movements

Huey P. Newton[1]

SUPREME COMMANDER
Black Panther Party

During the past few years, strong movements have developed among women and homosexuals seeking their liberation. There has been some uncertainty about how to relate to these movements.

Whatever your personal opinion and your insecurities about homosexuality and the various liberation movements among homosexuals and women (and I speak of the homosexuals and women as oppressed groups) we should try to unite with them in a revolutionary fashion.

I say "whatever your insecurities are" because, as we very well know, sometimes our first instinct is to want to hit a homosexual in the mouth and to want a woman to be quiet. We want to hit the homosexual in the mouth as soon as we see him because we're afraid we might be homosexual and want to hit the woman or shut her up because she might castrate us or take the nuts that we may not have to start with.

We must gain security in ourselves and therefore have respect and feelings for all oppressed people. We must not use the racist-type attitudes like the white racists use against people because they are black and poor. Many times the poorest white person is the most racist because he's afraid that he might lose something or discover something that he doesn't have. You're some kind of threat to him. This kind of psychology is in operation when we view oppressed people and we're angry with them because of their particular kind of behavior or their particular kind of deviation from the established norm.

Remember we haven't established a revolutionary value system; we're only in the process of establishing it. I don't remember us ever constituting any value that said that a revolutionary must say offensive things toward homosexuals or that a revolutionary would make sure that women do not speak out about their own particular kind of oppression.

Matter of fact, it's just the opposite, we say that we recognize the woman's right to be free. We haven't said much about the homosexual at all and we must relate to the homosexual movement because it is a real movement. And I know through reading and through my life experience, my observation, that homosexuals are not given freedom and liberty by anyone in this society. Maybe they might be the most oppressed people in the society.

What made them homosexuals? Perhaps it's a whole phenomena that I don't understand entirely. Some people say that it's the decadence of capitalism—I don't know whether this is the case, I rather doubt it. But whatever the case is, we know that homosexuality is a fact that exists and we must understand it in its purest form; that is, a person should have the freedom to use his body whatever way he wants to.

That's not endorsing things in homosexuality that we wouldn't view as revolutionary. But there is nothing to say that a homosexual can not also be a revolutionary. And maybe I'm now injecting some of my prejudice by saying "even a homosexual can be a revolutionary." Quite the contrary, maybe a homosexual could be the most revolutionary.

When we have revolutionary conferences, rallies and demonstrations, there should be full participation of the Gay Liberation Movement and the Women's Liberation Movement. We understand there are factions within the Women's Liberation Movement. Some groups might be more revolutionary than others. We shouldn't use the actions of a few to say that they're all reactionary or counterrevolutionary because they're not.

We should deal with factions just as we deal with any other group or party that claims to be revolutionary. We should try to judge somehow whether they're operating sincerely in a revolutionary fashion from a really oppressed situation (and we'll grant that if they're women they're probably oppressed.) If they do things that are unrevolutionary or counterrevolutionary, then criticize that action. If we feel that the group in spirit means to be revolutionary in practice but they make mistakes in interpretation of the revolutionary philosophy or they don't understand the dialectics of the social forces in operation, we should criticize that and not criticize them because they are women trying to be free. And the same is true for homosexuals.

We should never say a whole movement is dishonest when in fact they are trying to be honest; they're just making honest mistakes. Friends are allowed to make mistakes. The enemy is not allowed to make mistakes because his whole existence is a mistake and we suffer from it. But the Women's Liberation Front and Gay Liberation Front are our friends, they are our potential allies and we need as many allies as possible.

We should be willing to discuss the insecurities that many people have about homosexuality. When I say, "insecurities" I mean the fear that there is some kind of threat to our manhood. I can understand this fear. Because of the long conditioning process that builds insecurity in the American male, homosexuality might produce certain hangups in us. I have hangups myself about male homosexuality where on the other hand I have no hangups about female homosexuality and that's a phonomena in itself. I think it's probably because that's a threat to me maybe, and the females are no threat. It's just another erotic sexual thing.

We should be careful about using terms which might turn our friends off. The terms "faggot" and "punk" should be deleted from our vocabulary and especially we should not attach names normally designed for homosexuals to men who are enemies of the people such as Nixon or Mitchell. Homosexuals are not enemies of the people.

We should try to form a working coalition with the Gay Liberation and Women's Liberation groups. We must always handle social forces in an appropriate manner and this is really a significant part of the population—both women and the growing number of homosexuals that we have to deal with.

Note

1. Huey P. Newton, "On the Women's and Gay Liberation Movements," in *Traps: African American Men on Gender and Sexuality*, eds. Rudolph P. Byrd and Beverly Guy Sheftall (Indianapolis: Indiana University Press, 1970), pp. 281–283.

Assotto Saint

Assotto Saint's manifesto for radical writing provides a critical ethos for writing during the onset of AIDS in the Black gay community and in today's contemporary production of knowledge through writing. This piece, rather than writing against a dominant White (gay) community, speaks through a centering of the Black gay experience in the age of AIDS. This is significant, as Saint draws from his experiences both within the community and as a writer for the community, giving us a sense of a longer rhetorical tradition to which he is an heir. For Saint, the quare is a push past the queer limits, where Black life is far too important to be concerned with dominant standards and traditions.

Why I Write

Assotto Saint[1]

As a poet and playwright, whose themes are mainly inspired by the gay black community, I am often told that I will always have a "limited" readership and audience. This implies that my writings perhaps will never enjoy broad commercial success. As though such success should be the primary gauge of an artist's works. Although I do want my writings to be published, staged, bought, read, discussed, and remembered, the perennial question that challenges me is not will my audience always be limited, but rather am I limiting myself?

When I started to write thirteen years ago, I felt a need to present the gay black experience, as I, an "openly" gay black man, lived it. And as others, meaning a non-gay and non-black readership and audience, seldom had the chance to acquaint themselves with it, except for the writings of Richard Bruce Nugent, Langston Hughes, and Samuel Delany. Their works always left me in a high spirit, deepening my appreciation of the past, but needing much more, especially in the field of nonfiction.

Right from the start, my writings, especially my plays (*Risin' to the Love We Need*, *Black Fag*, and *New Love Song*), became what I call a necessary theater. I was cognizant of the wants and needs of our emerging community; my writings needed to serve its visibility and empowerment. Most revolutions—be they political, social, spiritual, or economic—are usually complemented by one in literature. The Civil Rights Movement counted on numerous literary voices, from Maya Angelou to Bobby Seale, to fuel outrage and inspire justice, while Simone de Beauvoir, Betty Friedan, and Gloria Steinem led the feminist cause.

Along with a few other writers, most notably the members of the Blackheart Collective (whose founder, Issac Jackson, was a ground-breaker in openly gay black publishing by putting out four issues of *The Blackheart Collective Journal*), and the late Philip Blackwell (writer of numerous plays, such as *Two Heads*, *A Lover's Play*, *City Men*, which was successfully produced), I not only committed myself toward an affirmation of the gay black community, but also toward the liberation of an audience from its own misconceptions of gay black life.

Occasionally I have been asked if I seriously expect non-gay blacks to identify with my writings. This infuriates me. It reminds me of the degree of my dehumanization, the extent of my oppression, and ultimately my invalidation as a gay black man.

Why should I not hope that any audience could identify with all these abstract yet very tangible things, which characterize my humanity. After all, I have had to identify with countless non-gay black characters. My pursuit of happiness is not unlike that of most human beings who, enthralled by the sensation of being alive, hunger for financial stability, thirst for spiritual fulfillment, and crave for love and respect through "family" and community.

As gay black poets and playwrights, we are persons of the roads still looking for the other side of the rainbow. The best answer to the question of who we are resides in our experiences; from whence our strongest writings are derived. Old myths explode as new ones of our own molding take their place, in turn recreating us.

While we map our this new wilderness of our experiences, we must also bear witness. Like archaeologists, we have to file those reports in the form of our finely crafted poems and plays, which we must then make available to the world. It is our duty to share the writings with others, not just file them away in our computers or in our desk drawers. Our writings should very much be a public process that reflects private passions.

Yes, this telling of us will bring the pain of rejection. Too often, as gay black men, our lives have been so painful that we do not last beyond the pain. We can take all sorts of mental pills for the hurt, but painful feelings are destroyed once we start to pinpoint them, analyze them, and write about them. Dodging these emotions or being frightened by them gets us nowhere. Any learning process involves fear. We overcome fear when it ceases to hamper our ability to tell the truth, something writers have to vigilantly, even violently, guard.

We must fight our numerous detractors, who will try to block our visions as well as the world's visions of us. Nor can we cover our own eyes from the glaring sunlight and pretend that it is night.

When we sacrifice our authenticity as gay black writers "to pass" in order to secure a book contract from a major publishing house (nowadays, most of the large companies are actively seeking out gay authors), when we sell out our dreams, thereby causing our art to mask our true feelings, when we inhabit a world of lies, which turn us into frauds in our own language and ideas, we resign ourselves to the status quo of this unsettling world we live in.

We must become whistle-blowers. We must become muthafuckhas with messages and a mission. We must become powerful enough to stand tall and not fall, thrive and not just survive. A tremendous amount of common sense, arrogance, and defiance will get us through.

American is a capitalist society. Let us save, beg, and borrow money to keep building our autonomous publications and other cultural institutions. Let us make sure that these institutions outlast us and do not become self-serving. Let us live beyond the here and now by nurturing each other and supporting one another's works.

Although we should not let the "white" gay and the "straight" black literary publications and theater institutions off the hook for tokenizing, not publishing our writings, or not producing our plays, we cannot make grievances the primary focus of our writings or of our lives. So much of gay and black art depicts its heroes as victims, in a realm of reverie or on the roads to calvary, constantly at the mercy of others. Puzzling over our predicaments and commitments, we can be skeptical, but never comfortable in the cynical blame game.

Nor can we take the high road behind our writings and evade our social responsibility as human beings to dirty our hands and feet when we need to publicly pick and kick shit out of our way. This especially applies to the handful of us who have proudly and productively assumed either the "gay black writer" or "black gay writer" label and benefited from our tokenization and overpresentation. The promise of a new world order lives not just in our words, but in our actions.

We should not just try to internalize our oppression through our writings, but externalize it by fighting bigotry tooth and nail, no matter what form it takes. Whether it's in confronting AIDS, apartheid, dictatorships, homophobia, racism, sexism, anti-Semitism, and silence that's foisted upon us or that we force upon ourselves. Our destiny must always be confronted with our conscience.

In this current health crisis, many of us gay black writers are dying much sooner than we anticipated. The numbers are already overwhelming. Thirteen contributors to the anthology *The Road Before Us: 100 Gay Black Poets*, which I edited and published in November 1991, have so far died. Among these dead are such notables as Melvin Dixon, David Frechette, Roy

Gonsalves, Craig G. Harris, and Donald Woods. Over half of the contributors to the same volume are people with AIDS (PWAs), such as myself, or have tested HIV-positive. The same ratio applies to previous gay black anthologies such as *In the Life* (Alyson Publications, 1986), edited by Joseph Beam, who died of AIDS in 1988, and *Brother to Brother* (Alyson Publications, 1991), edited by Essex Hemphill, who is open about his seropositive status. Five of the fifteen editors of the first volume of *Other Countries: Black Gay Voices*, which was published in 1988, have since died of AIDS. *Sojourner: Black Gay Voices in the Age of AIDS*, recently published by the Other Countries collective, lists in the bio section almost one half of its contributors as dead or living with/dying of AIDS. Its chief editor, B. Michael Hunter, is seropositive, as is Rodney Dildy, the editor and publisher of *The Pyramid Periodical*, one of our three gay black literary journals. The HIV's death toll in our community keeps beating its drum with no abatement in sight.

We must strive before it is too late to realize this creative wish: that the writings of our experiences serve as testaments to those who passed along this way, testimonies to our times, and legacies to future generations. These works should offer our readers and audience inspiration, consolation, and hope in the advent of a new millennium. Our words indeed do triumph over silence, despair, and death.

As our strength is constantly being tested, the only time to play it safe is inside our coffins. Even then, when we are disfigured by the horrors of HIV, we should morally and legally leave instructions for our life-partners, families, and friends not to close the damn caskets, not to hide or deny the real cause of our deaths, not to falsely rewrite our history in our obituaries. So what if people are uncomfortable!

I don't ever want to show anyone my physical and psychological wounds and scars without telling them what caused me to hurt, what it will take to heal me, and what collectively and responsibly should be done to prevent similar injuries from ever happening again—to me or to others.

In these dire times, I'd much rather engage myself reading works that are didactic and political instead of precious and arty stuff, where there's a lack of passion, integrity of feelings, sense of commitment beyond the self; but this constant romanticization of inertia, unfulfilling sex, along with the usual indulgence in alcohol and substance abuse because mother/father were not loving enough. Tired shit!

To the original question: Am I limiting myself? I answer emphatically, "No." Through poetry and playwriting I go to the limits of my being to forever discover the essence of rebirth within. I explore the world and how it closes in on itself with its prejudices. My poems and plays are weapons and blessings that I use to liberate myself, to validate our realities as gay black men, and to elucidate the human struggle. What better place to celebrate this movement than on the page and on the stage.

—Assotto Saint

Note

1. Assotto Saint, "Why I Write," in *Spells of a Voodoo Doll* (Michigan: Masquerade Books, 1996), pp. 3–17.

Dwight McBride

Dwight McBride's essay takes seriously the role of racial essentialism in the cultural framing of Black gay experience. In essence, he proposes that the lack of accounting for quare life has to do with the limited, essentializing understanding of Black life. As an early articulation of "quare studies," in this excerpt he speaks back to scholars who defend Black homophobia, in order to position the marginal experience of Black life. This essay suggests that to forget Black quare life is to forget the totality of the Black community. Indeed, McBride challenges Black scholars and the Black community—using bell hooks as a case study—to never simply reduce Black homophobia to a response strictly as a product of Black oppression. Instead, he suggests that we better interrogate the myriad of ways our anti-racist discourse, in its default to the impact of oppression, may encourage a rationale for homophobia and leave Black LGBT without voice or opportunities to challenge discursive and physical violences related to gender and sexuality.

Can the Queen Speak?: Racial Essentialism, Sexuality and the Problem of Authority[1]

*Dwight A. McBride**

The gay people we knew then did not live in separate subcultures, not in the small, segregated black community where work was difficult to find, where many of us were poor . . . Sheer economic necessity and fierce white racism, as well as the joy of being there with black folks known and loved, compelled many gay blacks to live close to home and family. That meant, however, that gay people created a way to live out sexual preferences within the boundaries of circumstances that were rarely ideal no matter how affirming. In some cases, this meant a closeted sexual life. In other families, an individual could be openly expressive, quite out.

> . . . Unfortunately, there are very few oral histories and autobiographies which explore the lives of black gay people in diverse black communities. This is a research project that must be carried out if we are to fully understand the complex experience of being black and gay in this white-supremacist, patriarchal, capitalist society. Often we hear more from black gay people who have chosen to live in predominately white communities, whose choices may have been affected by undue harassment in black communities. We hear hardly anything from black gay people who live contentedly in black communities.
>
> bell hooks, *Talking Back*

> I speak for the thousands, perhaps hundreds of thousands of men who live and die in the shadows of secrets, unable to speak of the love that helps them endure and contribute to the race. Their ordinary kisses of sweet spit and loyalty are scrubbed away by the propaganda makers of the race, the "talented Tenth" . . .
>
> The Black homosexual is hard pressed to gain audience among his heterosexual brothers; even if he is more talented, he is inhibited by his silence or his admissions. This is what the race has depended on in being able to erase homosexuality from our recorded history. The "chosen" history. But the sacred constructions of silence are futile exercises in denial. We will not go away with our issues of sexuality. We are coming home.
>
> It is not enough to tell us that one was a brilliant poet, scientist, educator, or rebel. Whom did he love? It makes a difference. I can't become a whole man simply on what is fed to me: watered-down versions of Black life in America. I need the ass-splitting truth to be told, so I will have something pure to emulate, a reason to remain loyal.
>
> Essex Hemphill, *Ceremonies*

The fundamental question driving this essay is who speaks for "the race," and on what authority? In partial answer to this query, elsewhere[2] I have argued that African American intellectuals participate, even if out of political necessity, in forms of racial essentialism to authorize and legitimate their positions in speaking for or representing "the race." This essay is in some ways the culmination of a tripartite discussion of that argument. Of course, the arguments made here and in those earlier essays need not be limited solely to the field of African American intellectuals. Indeed, the discursive practices described in these essays are more widely disseminated. Nevertheless, because I am quite familiar with African American intellectualism and am actively invested in addressing that body of discourse, it makes sense that I locate my analysis of racial essentialism in the context of a broader discussion of how we have come to understand what "black" is.

My essay moves from an examination of African American intellectuals' efforts to problematize racial subjectivity through black anti-racist discourse to a critique of their representation, or lack thereof, of gays and lesbians in that process. I will further have occasion to observe the political process that legitimates and qualifies certain racial subjects to speak for (represent) "the race," and excludes others from that very possibility. I use three exemplary reading sites to formulate this analysis. First, I examine bell hooks's essay, "Homophobia in Black Communities." I then move to an exchange, of sorts, between essays by the controversial black psychiatrist Frances Cress Welsing and the late black gay poet, essayist and activist Essex Hemphill, "The Politics Behind Black Male Passivity, Effeminization, Bisexuality and Homosexuality" and "If Freud Had Been a Neurotic Colored Woman: Reading Dr. Frances Cress Welsing," respectively. Finally, I consider two moments from the documentary on the life and art of James Baldwin entitled *James Baldwin: The Price of the Ticket*.

In her now oft-cited intervention into the 2 Live Crew controversy of a few years ago, "Beyond Racism and Misogyny: Black Feminism and 2 Live Crew," Kimberlé Williams Crenshaw asserts that the danger in the misogyny of the group's lyrics cannot simply be read as an elaborate form of cultural signifying as Henry Louis Gates, Jr. argues in his defense of 2 Live Crew. On the contrary, Crenshaw maintains that such language is

> no mere braggadocio. Those of us who are concerned about the high rates of gender violence in our communities must be troubled by the possible connections between such images and violence against women. Children and teenagers are listening to this music, and I am concerned that the range of acceptable behavior is being broadened by the constant propagation of antiwoman imagery. I'm concerned, too, about young Black women who together with men are learning that their value lies between their legs. Unlike that of men, however, women's sexual value is portrayed as a depletable commodity: By expending it, girls become whores and boys become men.
>
> (30)

My concerns are similar in kind to those of Crenshaw. Having come of age in a small rural black community where any open expression of gay or lesbian sexuality was met with derision at best and violence at worst; having been socialized in a black Baptist church which preached the damnation of "homosexuals"; having been trained in an African American Studies curriculum which provided no serious or sustained discussion of the specificity of African American lesbian and gay folk; and still feeling—even at the moment of this present writing—the overwhelming weight and frustration of having to speak in a race discourse that seems to have grown all too comfortable with the routine practice of speaking about a "black community" as a discursive unit wholly separate from black lesbians and gay men (evidenced by the way we always speak in terms of the relationship of black gays and lesbians to the black community or to how we speak of the homophobia of the black community, etc.); all of this has led me to the conclusion that as a community of scholars who are serious about political change, healing black people, and speaking truth to black people, we must begin the important process of undertaking a truly more inclusive vision of "black community" and of race discourse. As far as I am concerned, any treatment of African American politics and culture, and any theorizing of the future of Black America, indeed, any black religious practice or critique of black religion that does not take seriously the lives, contributions and presence of black gays and lesbians (just as we take seriously the lives of black women, the black poor, black men, the black middle-class, etc.) or any critique that does no more than to render token lip-service to black gay and lesbian experience is a critique that not only denies the complexity of who we are as a representationally "whole people," but denies the very "ass-splitting truth" which Essex Hemphill referred to so eloquently and so very appropriately in *Ceremonies*.

I mean this critique quite specifically. Too often, African American cultural critique finds itself positing an essential black community that serves as a point of departure for commentary. In other cases, it assumes a kind of monolith in general when it calls upon the term "black community" at all. Insofar as the position of such a construct might be deemed essential to the critical project, it is not that gesture to which I object. Rather, it is the narrowness of the vision for what is constitutive of that community that is most problematic. If we accept the fact that the term "community," regardless of the modifier which precedes it, is always a term in danger of presuming too much, I favor making sure that our use of the term accounts for as much of what it presumes as possible.

At present, the phrase "the black community" functions as a shifter or floating signifier. That is, it is a term whose meaning shifts in accordance with the context in which it is articulated. But at the same time the phrase is also most often deployed in a manner which presumes a cultural specificity which works as much on a politics of exclusion as it does on a politics of inclusion. There are many visions and versions of the black community that get posited in scholarly discourse, popular cultural forms and in political discourse. Rarely do any of these visions include lesbians and gay men, except perhaps as an afterthought. I want to see a black anti-racist discourse that does not need to maintain such exclusions in order to be efficacious.

Insofar as there is a need to articulate a black anti-racist discourse to address and to respond to the real and present dangers and vicissitudes of racism, essential to that discourse is the use of the rhetoric of community. Perhaps in the long term it would be best to explode all of the categories having to do with the very notion of "black community" and all of the inclusions and exclusions that come along with it. That is a project the advent of which I will be among the first to applaud. However, in the political meantime, my aim here is to take seriously the state of racial discourse, especially black anti-racist discourse and the accompanying construct of "the black community," on the very irksome terms in which I have inherited it.

As I think again on the example of the exchange between Crenshaw and Gates over the misogyny charges against 2 Live Crew, it also occurs to me that similar charges of homophobia or heterosexism could be waged against any number of rap or hip-hop artists, though this is a critique that seems to have been given very little attention.[3] If similar charges could be made, could not, then, similar defenses of heterosexism be mounted as well? The argument would go something like this: What appears to be open homophobia on the part of black rap and hip-hop artists is really engaged in a complicated form of cultural signifying that needs to be read not as homophobia, but in the context of a history of derisive assaults on black manhood. This being the case, what we really witness when we see and hear these artists participate in what appears to be homophobia is an act involved in the project of the reclamation of black manhood that does not really mean the literal violence that it performs. This is, in fact, similar to the logic used by bell hooks in her essay, "Homophobia in Black Communities," when she speaks of the contradiction that is openly expressed homophobia among blacks:

Black communities may be perceived as more homophobic than other communities because there is a tendency for individuals in black communities to verbally express in an outspoken way antigay sentiments. I talked with a straight black male in a California community who acknowledged that though he has often made jokes poking fun at gays or expressing contempt, as a means of bonding in group settings, in his private life he was a central support person for a gay sister. Such contradictory behavior seems pervasive in black communities. It speaks to ambivalence about sexuality in general, about sex as a subject of conversation, and to ambivalent feelings and attitudes toward homosexuality. Various structures of emotional and economic dependence create gaps between attitudes and actions. Yet a distinction must be made between black people overtly expressing prejudice toward homosexuals and homophobic white people who never make homophobic comments but who have the power to actively exploit and oppress gay people in areas of housing, employment, etc.

(122)

Hooks's rhetoric here is at once to be commended for its critique of the claims by many that blacks are more homophobic than other racial or ethnic groups, and to be critiqued as an apology for black homophobia. For hooks to offer as rationale for black homophobia, as in her anecdote of the "straight black male in a California community," the fact that "bonding" (since it is unspecified, we can assume both male and racial bonding here) is the reason he participates in homophobic "play," is both revealing and inexcusable. This is precisely the kind of play that, following again the logic of Crenshaw, we cannot abide given the real threats that still exist in the form of discrimination and violence to gays and lesbians. While hooks may want to relegate systemic discrimination against gays and lesbians to the domain of hegemonic whites, anti-gay violence takes many forms—emotional, representational and physical—and is not a practice exclusive to those of any particular race. Furthermore, it seems disingenuous and naive to suggest that what we say about gays and lesbians and the cultural representations of gays and lesbians do not, at least in part, legitimate—if not engender—discrimination and violence against gays and lesbians.

The rhetorical strategy which she employs here is a very old one, indeed, wherein blacks are blameless because "powerless." The logic implied by such thinking is that because whites constitute a hegemonic racial block in American society which oppresses blacks and other people of color, blacks can never be held wholly accountable for their own socio-political transgressions. Since this is sensitive and volatile territory upon which I am treading, let me take some extra care to make sure that I am properly understood. I do not mean to suggest that there is not a grain of truth in the reality of the racial claims made by hooks and sustained by a history of black protest. However, it is only a grain. And the grain is, after all, but a minute particle on the vast shores of discursive truth. For me, any understanding of black oppression that makes it possible, and worse permissible, to endorse at any level sexism, elitism or heterosexism is a vision of black culture that is finally not politically consummate with liberation. We can no more excuse black homophobia than black sexism. One is as politically and, dare I say, morally suspect as the other. This is a particularly surprising move on the part of hooks when we consider that in so many other contexts her work on gender is so unrelenting and hard-hitting.[4] So much is this the case that it is almost unimaginable that hooks would allow for a space in which tolerance for black sexism would ever be tenable. This makes me all the more suspect of her willingness not just to tolerate but to apologize for black homophobia.

There is still one aspect of hooks's argument that I want to address here, which is her creation of a dichotomy between black gays and lesbians who live in black communities and those who live in predominately white communities. It is raised most clearly in the epigraph with which I began this essay. She laments that "often we hear more from black gay people who have chosen to live in predominately white communities, whose choices may have been affected by undue harassment in black communities. We hear hardly anything from black gay people who live contentedly in black communities" (122). This claim about the removal of black gays and lesbians from the "authentic" black community is quite bizarre for any number of reasons. Is it to say that those who remain in black communities are not "unduly harassed"? Or is it that they can take it? And is undue harassment the only factor in moves by black gays and lesbians to other communities? Still the statement is problematic even beyond these more obvious curiosities in that it plays on the kind of authenticity politics that are under critique here. Hooks faults many black middle-class gays and lesbians, and I dare say many of her colleagues in the academy, who live in "white communities" in a way that suggests that they are unable to give us the "real" story of black gays and lesbians. What of those experiences of "undue harassment" that she posits as potentially responsible for their exodus from the black community? Are those narratives, taking place as they do in hooks's "authentic" black community, not an important part of the story of black gay and lesbian experience, or are those gays and lesbians unqualified because of the geographical locations from which they speak? It appears that the standard hooks ultimately establishes for "real" black gay commentary here is a standard that few black intellectuals could comfortably meet any more—a by-product of the class structure in which we live. In most cases the more upwardly mobile one becomes, the whiter the circles in which one inevitably finds oneself circulating—one of the more unfortunate realities of American society.[5]

The logic used by hooks on black homophobia is dangerous not only for the reasons I have already articulated, but because it exists on a continuum with thinkers like Frances Cress Welsing. They are not, of course, the same; but each does exist in a discursive field which makes the other possible. Therefore, hooks's implied logic of apology played out to its fullest conclusion bears a great deal of resemblance to Welsing's own heterosexist text.

Welsing's[6] sentiments are exemplary of and grow out of a black cultural nationalist response to gay and lesbian sexuality, which has most often read homosexuality as "counter-revolutionary."[7] She begins first by dismissing the entirety of the psychoanalytic community which takes its lead from Freud. Freud is dismissed immediately by Welsing because he was unable to deliver his own people from the devastation of Nazi Germany. This "racial" ineffectualness for Welsing renders moot anything that Freud (or any of his devotees) might have to say on the subject of sexuality. The logic is this: since the most important political element for black culture is that of survival and Freud didn't know how to do that for his people, nothing that Freud or his devotees could tell us about homosexuality should be applied to black people. The idea of holding Freud responsible for not preventing the Holocaust is not only laughable, but it denies the specific history giving rise to that event. Furthermore, if we use this logic of victim blaming in the case of the Jews and Freud, would it not also follow that we would have to make the same critique of slavery? Are black Africans and the tribal leaders of West Africa, then, not also responsible for not preventing the enslavement of blacks? It is precisely this sort of specious logic that makes a very articulate Welsing difficult and frustrating when one tries to take her seriously.

But take her seriously we must. Welsing continues to speak and to command quite a following among black cultural nationalists.[8] We have to be concerned, then, about the degree to which Welsing's heterosexist authentication of blackness contributes to the marginalization of black gays and lesbians. For Welsing, black Africa is the site of an "originary" or "authentic" blackness. At the beginning of her essay, Welsing makes the following statement:

> Black male passivity, effeminization, bisexuality and homosexuality are being encountered increasingly by Black psychiatrists working with Black patient populations. These issues are being presented by family members, personnel working in schools and other social institutions or by Black men themselves. Many in the Black population are reaching the conclusion that such issues have become a problem of epidemic proportion amongst

Black people in the U.S., although it was an almost non-existent behavioral phenomenon amongst indigenous Blacks in Africa.

(81)

From the beginning, Welsing describes homosexuality in a language associated with disease. It is a "problem of epidemic proportion" which seems to be spreading among black people. This rehearses a rhetorical gesture I mentioned earlier by speaking of the black community as an entity wholly separate from homosexuals who infect its sacrosanct authenticity. Of course, it goes without saying that Welsing's claim that homosexuality "was an almost non-existent behavioral phenomenon amongst indigenous Blacks in Africa" is not only unsupported by anthropological study,[9] but it also suggests the biological or genetic link, to use her language, which non-indigenous blacks have to indigenous black Africans. Welsing more than adopts an Afrocentric worldview in this essay by positing Africa as the seat of all real, unsullied, originary blackness. In this way she casts her lot with much of black cultural nationalist discourse, which is heavily invested in Afrocentrism. For further evidence of this, we need look no further than Welsing's own definition of "Black mental health":

> The practice of those unit patterns of behavior (i.e., logic, thought, speech, action and emotional response) in all areas of people activity: economics, education, entertainment, labor, law, politics, religion, sex and war—which are simultaneously self-and group-supporting under the social and political conditions of worldwide white supremacy domination (racism). In brief, this means Black behavioral practice which resists self-and group-negation and destruction.
>
> (82)

Here, as elsewhere, Welsing prides herself on being outside of the conceptual mainstream of any currently held psychiatric definitions of mental illness. She labels those the "'European' psycho-analytic theories of Sigmund Freud" (82). She seems here to want to be recognized for taking a bold, brazen position as solidly outside any "mainstream" logic. This is because all such logic is necessarily bad because it is mainstream, which is to say, white. One, then, gets the sense that homosexuality too is a by-product of white supremacy. And further, that if there were no white supremacy, homosexuality would not at best exist or at worst be somehow okay if it did. The overriding logic of her argument is the connection between white supremacy and homosexuality. The former is produced by the latter as a way to control black people. Hence, it follows that the only way to be really black is to resist homosexuality.

From this point on, Welsing's essay spirals into an ever deepening chasm from which it never manages to return. For example, she argues that it is "male muscle mass" which oppresses a people. Since white men understand this fact and the related fact of their genetic weakness in relation to the majority of the world's women (women of color), they are invested in the effeminization and homosexualization of black men (83–84). She also states that the white women's liberation movement—white women's response to the white male's need to be superior at least over them—has further served to weaken the white male's sense of power, "helping to push him to a *weakened* and *homosexual* stance" (my emphasis—the two are synonymous for Welsing). Feminism, then, according to Welsing, leads to further "white male/female alienation, pushing white males further into the homosexual position and . . . white females in that direction also" (85–86). Finally, she suggests that it is black manhood that is the primary target of racism, since black men, of course, are the genetically superior beings who cannot only reproduce with black women, but who can also reproduce with white women. And since the off-spring of such unions, according to Welsing's logic, are always black (the exact opposite of the result of such sexual pairings for white men and black women), black manhood is the primary target of a white supremacist system. Welsing's words are significant enough here that I quote her at some length:

> . . . Racism (white supremacy) is the dominant social system in today's world. Its fundamental dynamic is predicated upon the genetic recessive deficiency state of albinism, which is responsible for skin whiteness and thus the so-called "white race." This genetic recessive trait is dominated by the genetic capacity to produce any of the various degrees of skin melanation—whether black, brown, red or yellow. In other words, it can be annihilated as a phenotypic condition. Control of this potential for genetic domination and annihilation throughout the world is absolutely essential if the condition of skin whiteness is to survive. "White" survival is predicated upon aggressiveness and muscle mass in the form of technology directed against the "non-white" melanated men on the planet Earth who constitute the numerical majority. Therefore, white survival and white power are dependent upon the various methodologies, tactics and strategies developed to control all "non-white" men, as well as bring them into cooperative submission. This is especially important in the case of Black men because they have the greatest capacity to produce melanin and, in turn, the greatest genetic potential for the annihilation of skin albinism or skin whiteness.
>
> (83)

This passage demonstrates, to my mind, the critical hazards of privileging the category of race in any discussion of black people. When we give "race," with its retinue of historical and discursive investments, primacy over other signifiers of difference, the result is a network of critical blindnesses which prevent us from perceiving the ways in which the conventions of race discourse get naturalized and normativized. These conventions often include, especially in cases involving— though not exclusive to—black cultural nationalism, the denigration of homosexuality and the accompanying peripheralization of women. Underlying much of race discourse, then, is always the implication that all "real" black subjects are male and heterosexual. Therefore, in partial response to the query with which I began this essay, only these such subjects are best qualified to speak for or to represent the race.

Unfortunately, Welsing does not stop there. She continues her discussion of black manhood to a point where what she means by the appellation far-and-above exceeds her mere genetic definition. Though she never clearly defines what she intends by black manhood, we can construct a pretty clear idea from the ways that she uses the term in her argument. "The dearth of black males in the homes, schools and neighborhoods," Welsing proclaims,

> leaves Black male children no alternative models. Blindly they seek out one another as models, and in their blindness end up in trouble—in juvenile homes or prisons. But fate and the dynamics of racism again play a vicious trick because the young males only become more alienated from their manhood and more feminized in such settings.
>
> (89)

It is clear from this statement that black manhood is set in opposition to femininity, and is something that is retarded by the influence of women, especially in female-headed households. She describes the effect of effeminizing influences on black men as the achievement of racist programming. This achievement is, in part, possible because of the clothing industry as well, according to Welsing: "The white run clothing industry is all too pleased to provide the costumes of feminine disguise for Black male escape. However, they never would provide uniforms or combat gear if customers were willing to pay $1000 per outfit" (89). She also faults television as "an important programmer of behavior in this social system" which "plays a further major role in alienating Black males (especially children) from Black manhood" (89). The examples she cites are Flip Wilson's persona Geraldine and Jimmy Walker's character, J.J., on the 1970s television series, *Good Times*. "These weekly insults," she maintains, "to Black manhood that we have been programmed to believe are entertainment and not direct racist warfare, further reinforce, perhaps in the unconscious thinking of Black people, a loss of respect for Black manhood while carrying that loss to even deeper levels" (90). Most telling, perhaps, is that the clinical method she endorses for "disorders" of "passivity, effeminization, bisexuality, homosexuality" is to have the patients "relax and envision themselves approaching and opposing, in actual combat, the collective of white males and females (without apology or giving up in the crunch)" (91–92). Again, there is an essence to what black manhood is that never receives full articulation except implicitly. But what is implied could be described as monstrous, combative, and even primitive. There is certainly no room for a nurturing view of manhood here. To be a man is to be strong. And strength, in Welsing's logic, is the opposite of weakness, which can only signify at best as effeminacy or passivity and at worst as bisexuality or homosexuality. Still another of the vexatious implication of this logic is that in a world devoid of racism or white supremacy, there would be no black male homosexuality. The result is that black male homosexuality is reducible to being a by-product of racist programming. Once again, this is the function of an argument which privileges race discourse over other forms of difference in its analysis of black oppression.

Let me turn my attention for a moment to Essex Hemphill's response to Welsing's troublesome essay. Hemphill's rhetoric demonstrates how even in a very astute and well-wrought "reading" of Welsing—and it is fair to say that Hemphill "reads" her in both the critical and the more campy sense of the word—the move is never made to critique the structure (and by "structure" here I mean the implied rules governing the use of) and function of race discourse itself. It is clear to me, as I have tried to demonstrate, that this is precisely what is missing from hooks's logic which undergirds her discussion of homophobia in black communities as well. Hemphill's response to Welsing is thoughtful, engaging and identifies the faulty premises upon which Welsing bases her arguments. Still, Hemphill's own essay and rhetoric falls prey to the conventions of race discourse in two very important ways. First, in order to combat Welsing's homophobia/heterosexism, Hemphill himself feels the pressure to legitimize and authorize himself as a speaker on race matters by telling his own authenticating anecdote of black/gay experience at the beginning of his essay:[10]

> In 1974, the year that Dr. Frances Cress Welsing wrote "The Politics Behind Black Male Passivity, Effeminization, Bisexuality, and Homosexuality," I entered my final year of senior high school.
>
> By that time, I had arrived at a very clear understanding of how dangerous it was to be a homosexual in my Black neighborhood and in society . . . Facing this then-limited perception of homosexual life, I could only wonder, where did I fit in? . . .
>
> Conversely, I was perfecting my heterosexual disguise; I was practicing the necessary use of masks for survival; I was calculating the distance between the first day of class and graduation, the distance between graduation from high school and departure for college—and ultimately, the arrival of my freedom from home, community, and my immediate peers . . .
>
> During the course of the next sixteen years I would articulate and politicize my sexuality. I would discover that homo sex did not constitute a whole life nor did it negate my racial identity or constitute a substantive reason to be estranged from my family and Black culture. I discovered, too, that the work ahead for me included, most importantly, being

able to integrate all of my identities into a functioning self, instead of accepting a dysfunctional existence as a consequence of my homosexual desires.

(52–53)

While Hemphill's personal anecdote demonstrates his access to the various categories of identity he claims, it is not a critique of the very idea of the categories themselves. In fact, he plays the "race/sexuality" card in a way that is similar to the way in which Welsing plays the "race" card.

And second, while his critique of Welsing is thorough and extremely insightful, it does not move to critique the methodological fault Welsing makes in her analysis—that is, the fact that much of what is wrong with Welsing's argument is a result of the privileging of "race" over other critical categories of difference. Instead, Hemphill treats Welsing's heterosexism itself as the critical disease instead of as symptomatic of a far more systemic critical illness.

One of the most noteworthy things about Hemphill's anecdotal testimony is that while it insists, and rightly so, upon the integration of what Welsing has established as the dichotomous identities of race and homosexuality, it also participates in a familiar structural convention of race-discourse in its necessity to claim the racial identification as a position from which even the black homosexual speaks. In other words, part of the rhetorical strategy enacted by Hemphill in this moment is that of claiming the category of racial authenticity for himself as part of what legitimizes and authorizes the articulation of his corrective to Welsing's homophobic race logic. The net result is the substitution of heterosexist race logic with a homo-positive or homo-inclusive race logic. Still, the common denominator of both positions is the persistence of race as the privileged category in discussions of black identity.

The first clue we get of Hemphill's failure to identify the larger systemic problem of Welsing's argument is when he compares Welsing to Shahrazad Ali:

Dr. Welsing is not as easily dismissable as Shahrazad Ali, author of the notorious book of internal strife, *The Black Man's Guide to Understanding the Black Woman* (Philadelphia: Civilized Publications, 1989) . . . By dismissing the lives of Black lesbians and gay men, Ali is clearly not advocating the necessary healing Black communities require; she is advocating further factionalization. Her virulently homophobic ideas lack credibility and are easily dismissed as incendiary.

Dr. Welsing is much more dangerous because she attempts to justify *her* homophobia and heterosexism precisely by grounding it in an acute understanding of African-American history and an analysis of the psychological effects of centuries of racist oppression and violence.

(54)

Hemphill is right in his reading of Welsing, though his reading does not go far enough: Ali is not more easily dismissable than Welsing. In fact, Ali's ideas are rooted in a history of sorts as well, a history shared by Welsing's arguments—that is, the history of race discourse itself which, in its privileging of the dominant category of analysis, has always sustained the derision or exclusion of black gays and lesbians.

Another such moment in Hemphill's essay comes when he identifies what he seems to understand as the central problem of Welsing's text. He writes:

Welsing refutes any logical understanding of sexuality. By espousing Black homophobia and heterosexism—imitations of the very oppressive forces of hegemonic white male heterosexuality she attempts to challenge—she places herself in direct collusion with the forces that continually move against Blacks, gays, lesbians, and all people of color. Thus, every time a gay man or lesbian is violently attacked, blood *is* figuratively on Dr. Welsing's hands as surely as blood is on the hands of the attackers. Her ideas reinforce the belief that gay and lesbian lives are expendable, and her views also provide a clue as to why the Black community has failed to intelligently and coherently address critical, life-threatening issues such as AIDS.

(55)

Hemphill's statement is true. Welsing's logic does imitate that of the oppressive forces of white male heterosexuality which she tries to refute. The difference is that Welsing does not view the latter category as crucial to her analysis. The problem with Welsing's argument does not end where Hemphill supposes it does. Much of race discourse, even the discourse of racial liberation, participates in a similar relationship with hegemonic anti-gay forces. This is especially the case, and some might even argue that it is inevitable, when we consider the history and development of black liberationist or anti-racist discourse with its insistence on the centrality of black masculinity (in the narrowest sense of the term) as the essential element of any form of black liberation. If racial liberationist discourse suggests at best the invisibility of homosexuality and at worst understands homosexuality as racially antagonistic, Dr. Welsing radically manifests one of the more unseemly truths of race discourse for blacks—the demonization of homosexuality.

The critical blindness demonstrated by Hemphill does not alone express the extent of what happens when a gay black man takes up the mantle of race discourse. Another example worth exploring is that of James Baldwin. In the documentary of his life done in 1989, *James Baldwin: The Price of the Ticket*, there are at least two moments to which I want to call attention. The first is a statement made by Amiri Baraka and the second is a statement made by Baldwin himself from interview footage from *The Dick Cavett Show*. I turn to these less literally textual examples to demonstrate that in our more causal or less scripted moments, our sub-conscious understanding of the realities of race discourse is laid bare even more clearly.

Baraka's regard for Baldwin is well-documented by the film. He talks about how Baldwin was "in the tradition" and how his early writings, specifically *Notes of a Native Son*, really impacted him and spoke to a whole generation. In an attempt to describe or to account for Baldwin's homosexuality, however, Baraka falters in his efforts to unite the racially significant image of Baldwin that he clings to with the homosexual Baldwin with whom he seems less comfortable. Baraka states the following:

Jimmy Baldwin was neither in the closet about his homosexuality, nor was he running around proclaiming homosexuality. I mean, he was what he was. And you either had to buy that or, you know, *mea culpa*, go somewhere else.

The poles of the rhetorical continuum which Baraka sets up here for his understanding of homosexuality are very telling and should remind us of the earlier dichotomy set up by bell hooks between homosexuals who live somewhat closeted existences in black communities and those who do not. To Baraka's mind, one can either be in the closet or "running around proclaiming homosexuality" (the image of the effete gay man or the gay activist collide here it would seem). What makes Baldwin acceptable to enter the pantheon of race men for Baraka is the fact that his sexual identity is unlocatable. It is neither here nor there, or perhaps it is everywhere at once, leaving the entire question an undecided and undecidable one. And if Baldwin is undecided about his sexual identity, the one identity to which he is firmly committed is his racial identity. The rhetorical ambiguity around his sexual identity, according to Baraka, is what makes it possible for Baldwin to be a race man who was "in the tradition."

Baldwin himself, it seems, was well aware of the dangers of, indeed, the "price of the ticket" for trying to synthesize his racial and sexual identities. He understood that his efficacy as race man was, in part at least, owing to limiting his activism to his racial politics. The frame of the documentary certainly confirms this in the way it represents Baldwin's own response to his sexuality. In one interview, he makes the following statement:

> I think the trick is to say yes to life . . . It is only we of the twentieth century who are so obsessed with the particular details of anybody's sex life. I don't think those details make a difference. And I will never be able to deny a certain power that I have had to deal with, which has dealt with me, which is called love; and love comes in very strange packages. I've loved a few men; I've loved a few women; and a few people have loved me. That's . . . I suppose that's all that's saved my life.

It may be of interest to note that while making this statement, the camera pans down to Baldwin's hands which are fidgeting with the cigarette and cigarette holder. This move on the part of the camera undercuts the veracity of Baldwin's statement here. In fact, it suggests what I think of as a fair conclusion about this statement. That is, Baldwin himself does not quite believe all of what he is saying in this moment. From the 1949 essay, "The Preservation of Innocence," that he wrote and published in *Zero*, a small Moroccan journal, Baldwin knows just how profoundly important sexuality is to discussions of race. But the desire registered here for sexuality not to make a difference is important to recognize. When we understand this statement as spoken in a prophetic mode, it imagines a world in which the details of a person's sex life can "matter" as part of a person's humanity but not have to usurp their authority or legitimacy to represent the race.

If Baldwin's statement raises the complications of speaking from a complex racial/sexual identity location, the following excerpt from his interview on *The Dick Cavett Show* illustrates this point all the more clearly:

> I don't know what most white people in this country feel, but I can only conclude what they feel from the state of their institutions. I don't know if white Christians hate Negroes or not, but I know that we have a Christian church which is white and a Christian church which is black. I know as Malcolm X once put it, "The most segregated hour in America is high noon on Sunday." That says a great deal to me about a Christian nation. It means that I can't afford to trust most white Christians and certainly cannot trust the Christian church. I don't know whether the labor unions and their bosses really hate me. That doesn't matter. But I know that I'm not in their unions. I don't know if the real estate lobby has anything against black people, but I know the real estate lobby keeps me in the ghetto. I don't know if the board of education hates black people, but I know the text books they give my children to read and the schools that we go to. Now this is the evidence! *You want me to make an act of faith risking myself, my wife, my woman, my sister, my children on some idealism which you assure me exists in America which I have never seen.*
>
> [emphasis added]

Interesting for both the rich sermonic quality and the vehement tone for which Baldwin was famous, this passage is also conspicuous for the manner in which Baldwin assumes the voice of representative race man. In the very last sentence, when Baldwin affects the position of race man, part of the performance includes the masking of his specificity, his sexuality, his difference. And in race discourse when all difference is concealed what emerges is the heterosexual black man "risking [himself], [his] wife, [his] woman and [his] children." The image of the black man as protector, progenitor and defender of the race—which sounds suspiciously similar to the image fostered by Welsing and much of black cultural nationalism—is what Baldwin assumes here. The truth of this rhetorical transformation—the hard, difficult worrisome truth—is that in order to be representative race man, one must be hetero-sexual. And what of women? They would appear, in the confines of race discourse, to be ever the passive players. They are rhetorically useful in that they lend legitimacy to the black male's responsibility for their care and protection, but they cannot speak any more than the gay or lesbian brother or sister can. If these are part of the structural demands of race discourse, the erasure of subtlety and black difference, it is time to own up to that truth. As black intellectuals and cultural workers, we have to demand, insist upon, and be about the business of helping to create new and more inclusive ways of speaking about race that do not cause even good, thorough thinkers like hooks, Hemphill and Baldwin (and there are many others), to compromise their/our own critical veracity by participating in the form of race discourse that has been hegemonic for so long. Race is, indeed, a fiction, an allegory, if you will, with an elaborate linguistic court. Knowing that, more needs to be done to reimagine race; to create new and inclusive mythologies to replace the old, weather-worn, heterosexual masculinity-centered ones; to reconstitute "the black community" as one which includes our various differences as opposed to the monolith to which we inevitably seem to return.

For far too long the field of African American/Afro-American/Black Studies has thought about race as the primary category of analysis for the work that proceeds from the field. The problem with such work has always been, and continues to be, that African Americans and African American experience are far more complicated than this. And it is time that we begin to understand what that means in the form of an everyday critical and political practice. Race is not simple. It has never been simple. It does not have the history that would make it so, no matter how much we may yearn for that degree of clarity. This is a point I have argued in a variety of venues. The point being, if I am thinking about race, I should already be thinking about gender, class and sexuality. This statement, I think, assumes the very impossibility of a hierarchy or chronology of categories of identity. The point is not just one of intersection—as we have thought of it for so long—it is one of reconstitution. That is, race is already more than just race. Or put another way, race is always already everything that it ever was, though some of its constitutive aspects may have been repressed for various nefarious purposes and/or for other strategic ones. Either way, it is never simple, never to be taken for granted. What I say is not revolutionary or revelatory. The theory, in this way, has gotten ahead of the critical practice. Almost all good race theorists these days will recognize the merit of this approach; the point is that the work we produce has not fully caught up. That explains why it is still possible today to query: what does a race theory, of which all of these categories of identity are constitutive, look like? And more importantly, how do the critiques, the work informed by such theory, look different from what we now see dominating the field? I have great hope in the future for the work of scholars like Lindon Barrett who are beginning to theorize racial blackness in relationship to the category of value with all the trappings of desire, commodification and exchange inherent in that operation. This may be just the kind of critical innovation needed to help us to reconstitute our ideas about "race" and race discourse.[11]

Of course, it is not my intention in these reflections to suggest that there are not good heterosexual "race men" and "race women" on the scene who have progressive views about sexuality and are "down" with their gay and lesbian brothers and sisters. In fact, quite the contrary. In many instances, it adds an extra dimension of cachet and progressivism to hear such heterosexual speakers be sympathetic to gays and lesbians. So long as they are not themselves gay or lesbian, it would appear on the open market to enhance their "coolness" quotient. The issue that needs more attention exists at the level at which we authenticate our authority and legitimacy to speak for the race as representational subjects. In other words, there are any number of narratives that African American intellectuals employ to qualify themselves in the terms of race discourse to speak for the race. And while one routinely witnesses the use of narratives of racial discrimination, narratives of growing up poor and black and elevating oneself through education and hard work, narratives about how connected middle-class black intellectuals are to "the black community" or "the hood," we could scarcely imagine an instance in which narrating or even claiming one's gay or lesbian identity would authenticate or legitimate oneself as a racial representative. And as we see in the case of James Baldwin, when black gays and lesbians do don the racial representational mask, they often do so at the expense of effacing (even if only temporarily) their sexual identities.

Given the current state of black anti-racist discourse, it is no wonder that even now there is only one book-length critical, literary investigation of the work of James Baldwin by Trudier Harris;[12] it is no wonder that Langston Hughes's biographer even in 1986 felt the need to defend him against the "speculation" surrounding his homosexuality; it is no wonder that even to this day we can still say with Cheryl Clark and bell hooks that there exists no sustained sociological study of black lesbians and gays; and it is no wonder that among the vanguard of so-called black public intellectuals there is the notable near absence of openly gay and lesbian voices. Lamentable though this state of affairs may be, we cannot deny that part of the responsibility for it has much to do with the limits of black anti-racist discourse: that is, what it is still considered appropriate to say about race, and the policing of who speaks for the race.

Notes

1. Dwight McBride, "Can the Queen Speak? Racial Essentialism, Sexuality and the Problem of Authority," *Callaloo*, 21.2 (Spring 1998): pp. 363–368.

* Let me thank Bob E. Myers (UCLA), Darieck Bruce Scott (Stanford) and Prof. Toni Morrison (Princeton) for listening to and responding to these ideas in their even more unfinished conversational form. I also wish to thank Professors Arthur Little (UCLA), Prof. Jonathan Holloway (UCSD), and Prof. Chris Cunningham (UCLA) for reading and responding to an earlier draft of this essay. And finally let me acknowledge the careful and instructive readings of Kara Keeling (U Pittsburgh) and of Professors Eric Clarke (U Pittsburgh) and Lindon Barrett (UCI).

2. See my two essays "Speaking the Unspeakable: On Toni Morrison, African American Intellectuals and the Uses of Essentialist Rhetoric," *Modern Fiction Studies* (Fall/Winter 1993): 755–76, and "Transdisciplinary Intellectual Practice: Cornel West and the Rhetoric of Race Transcending," *Harvard BlackLetter Law Journal* (Spring 1994): 155–68.

3. Thinkers like Kobena Mercer at the Black Nations/Queer Nations Conference in 1995 represent one among a few of the exceptions to this claim. Still, such critique of homophobia has not been a part of the more public debates about the objectionable qualities of rap and hip-hop.

4. See, for example, any number of hooks's essays in *Yearning: Race, Gender, and Cultural Politics* (Boston: South End, 1990), and *Black Looks: Race and Representation* (Boston: South End, 1992).

5. This is not to say that those of us who exist (at least professionally) in predominately white circles do not interact with the "black community." It is to suggest that our interaction is, in a sense, constructed.

6. For a fuller discussion of how homosexuality is counter-revolutionary, see Eldridge Cleaver's *Soul on Ice* (New York: McGraw-Hill, 1968). The chapters entitled "The Allegory of the Black Eunuchs" and "The Primeval Mitosis" are especially noteworthy. In order to relate this to the earlier discussion of Crenshaw and Gates's exchange over 2 Live Crew, it is interesting to note the point made by Essex Hemphill in his essay on Welsing that she has been a highly "sought-after public speaker, and in recent years, her ideas have been embraced in the reemergence of Black cultural nationalism, particularly by rap groups such as Public Enemy" (53–54).

7. Welsing herself is no exception to this rule. The last sentence of her essay reads as follows: "Black male bisexuality and homosexuality has been used by the white collective in its effort to survive genetically in a world dominated by colored people, and Black acceptance of this position does not solve the major problem of our oppression [read here the race problem] but only further retards its ultimate solution" (92).

8. Even as recently as a few weeks ago at the time of this writing, Welsing appeared on NPR speaking about her famous Cress Theory of race. The theory is based on the genetic inferiority of whites to blacks. Since whites have knowledge of this, they fear genetic annihilation. This fear, according to Welsing, has been the cause of the history of racism as we know it.

9. For some preliminary discussion of anthropological evidence of the existence of homosexual practices among certain African cultures and other peoples of color, see Pat Caplan, ed., *The Cultural Construction of Sexuality* (London and New York: Tavistock, 1987).

10. See my essay "Transdisciplinary Intellectual Practice: Cornel West and the Rhetoric of Race-Transcending" where I argue that one of the essentializing gestures in which African American intellectuals participate in order to legitimate themselves as speakers for the race is to relate racially affirming anecdotes from their own experience. Also in fairness to Hemphill, his use of the anecdotal gesture of self-authorization is somewhat different from the usual race-based model. His narrative authority derives from the simultaneity of his gay and black experience. He insists upon them both. Still the need to narrate the two side by side, indeed, to narrate his story at all is interesting to note as a response to Welsing's very problematic position.

11. See Lindon Barrett's forthcoming book *Seeing Double: Blackness and Value* (Cambridge University Press).

12. I am also aware of the work-in-progress of Maurice Wallace at Yale entitled *Hostile Witness: Baldwin as Artist and Outlaw*.

Works Cited

Baldwin, James. "Preservation of Innocence." *OUT/LOOK* 2.2 (Fall 1989): 40–45.

Caplan, Pat. "Introduction." *The Cultural Construction of Sexuality*. London: Tavistock, 1987. 1–30.

Cleaver, Eldridge. *Soul on Ice*. New York: McGraw-Hill, 1968.

Crenshaw, Kimberlé Williams. "Beyond Racism and Misogyny: Black Feminism and 2 Live Crew." *Boston Review* 16.6 (December 1991): 6, 30.

Dixon, Melvin. "This Light, This Fire, This Time: James Arthur Baldwin." *OUT/LOOK* 2.2 (Fall 1989): 38–39.

Gates, Henry Louis, Jr. "To the Editor." *Boston Review* 17.1 (February 1992): 11–12.

Harper, Philip Brian. *Are We Not Men?: Masculine Anxiety and the Problem of African-American Identity*. New York: Oxford University Press, 1996.

Hemphill, Essex. "If Freud Had Been a Neurotic Colored Woman: Reading Dr. Frances Cress Welsing." *Ceremonies: Prose and Poetry*. New York: Plume, 1992. 52–62.

hooks, bell. "Homophobia in Black Communities." *Talking Back*. Boston: South End, 1989. 120–26.

McBride, Dwight A. "Speaking the Unspeakable: On Toni Morrison, African American Intellectuals and the Uses of Essentialist Rhetoric." *Modern Fiction Studies*. 39.3&4 (Fall/Winter 1993): 755–76.

———. "Transdisciplinary Intellectual Practice: Cornel West and the Rhetoric of Race-Transcending." *Harvard BlackLetter Law Journal* 11 (Spring 1994): 155–68.

Rampersad, Arnold. *The Life of Langston Hughes, Volume I: 1902–1941*. New York: Oxford, 1986.

Rose, Tricia. *Black Noise: Rap Music and Black Culture in Contemporary America*. Middletown: Wesleyan University Press, 1994.

Ross, Marlon B. "Some Glances at the Black Fag: Race, Same-Sex Desire, and Cultural Belonging." *Canadian Review of Comparative Literature* 28.1–2 (March—June 1994): 193–219.

Spivak, Gayatri. "Can the Subaltern Speak?" *Marxism and the Interpretation of Culture*. Eds. Cary Nelson and Lawrence Grossman. Urbana and Chicago: University of Illinois Press, 1988. 271–313.

Thomas, Kendall. " 'Ain't Nothin' Like the Real Thing': Black Masculinity, Gay Sexuality, and the Jargon of Authenticity." *The House that Race Built: Black Americans, U.S. Terrain*. Ed. Wahneema Lubiano. New York: Pantheon, 1997. 116–35.

Welsing, Frances Cress. "The Politics Behind Black Male Passivity, Effeminization, Bisexuality and Homosexuality." *The Isis Papers: The Keys to the Colors*. Chicago: Third World, 1991. 81–92.

E. Patrick Johnson

E. Patrick Johnson's groundbreaking essay anchors this section of the anthology. His use of the everyday to capture how queers of color do things differently has shifted how we discuss the intersections of race, gender, class, and sexuality. Inadvertently, this essay opens up a new field of study where Black LGBT individuals and non-LGBT folks can better address the everyday needs, practices, and desires of the "margins of the margins." The "quare" as a construct becomes a shorthand opportunity not only to mark people of color's experience of sexuality but also to speak to how "feeling queer" or marginal operates differently in the life of those whose lives have always already been suspect and subjected to discursive and material violence.

"Quare" Studies, or (Almost) Everything I Know About Queer Studies I Learned From My Grandmother

E. Patrick Johnson[1]

Although queer studies has the potential to transform the way scholars theorize sexuality in conjunction with other identity formations, the paucity of attention given to race and class in queer studies represents a significant theoretical gap. Most current formulations of queer theory either ignore the categories of race and class altogether or theorize their effects in discursive rather than material terms. To suture that gap, this essay proposes "quare" studies as a vernacular rearticulation and deployment of queer theory to accommodate racialized sexual knowledge.

Keywords: queer studies, performance, performativity, race, class.

I love queer. Queer is a homosexual of either sex. It's more convenient than saying "gays" which has to be qualified, or "lesbians and gay men." It's an extremely useful polemic term because it is who we say we are, which is, "Fuck You."

—Spike Pittsberg (qtd. in C. Smith 280)

I use queer to describe my particular brand of lesbian feminism, which has much to do with the radical feminism I was involved with in the early '80s. I also use it externally to describe a political inclusivity—a new move toward a celebration of difference across sexualities, across genders, across sexual preference and across object choice. The two link.

Linda Scmple (qtd. in C. Smith 280)

I'm more inclined to use the words "black lesbian," because when I hear the word queer I think of white, gay men.

—Isling Mack-Nataf (qtd. in C. Smith 280)

I define myself as gay mostly. I will not use queer because it is not part of my vernacular—but I have nothing against its use. The same debates around naming occur in the "black community." Naming is powerful. Black people and gay people constantly renaming ourselves is a way to shift power from whites and hets respectively.

—Inge Blackman (qtd. in C. Smith 280)

Personally speaking, I do not consider myself a "queer" activist or, for that matter, a "queer" anything. This is not because I do not consider myself an activist; in fact, I hold my political work to be one of my most important contributions to all of my communities. But like other lesbian, gay, bisexual, and transgendered activists of color, I find the label "queer" fraught with unspoken assumptions which inhibit the radical political potential of this category.

—Cathy Cohen ("Punks" 451)

"Quare" Etymology (With Apologies to Alice Walker)

Quare (Kwâr), *n.* 1. meaning *queer;* also, opp. of *straight;* odd or slightly off kilter; from the African American vernacular for queer; sometimes homophobic in usage, but always denotes excess incapable of being contained within conventional categories of *being;* curiously equivalent to the Anglo-Irish (and sometimes "Black" Irish) variant of queer, as in Brendan Behan's famous play, *The Quare Fellow.*

— *adj.* 2. a lesbian, gay, bisexual, or transgendered person of color who loves other men or women, sexually or nonsexually, and appreciates black culture and community.
— *n.* 3. one who *thinks* and *feels* and *acts* (and, sometimes, "acts up"); committed to struggle against all forms of oppression—racial, sexual, gender, class, religious, etc.
— *n.* 4. one for whom sexual and gender identities always already intersect with racial subjectivity.
5. quare is to queer as "reading" is to "throwing shade."[2]

I AM going out on a limb. This is a precarious position, but the stakes are high enough to warrant risky business. The business to which I refer is reconceptualizing the still incubating discipline called queer studies. Now, what's in a name? This is an important question when, as James Baldwin proclaims in the titles of two of his works, I have "no name in the street" or, worse still, "nobody *knows* my name" (emphasis added). I used to answer to "queer," but when I was hailed by that naming, interpellated in that moment, I felt as if I was being called "out of my name." I needed something with more "soul," more "bang," something closer to "home." It is my name after all!

Then I remembered how "queer" is used in my family. My grandmother, for example, used it often when I was a child and still uses it today. When she says the word, she does so in a thick, black, southern dialect: "That sho'll is a quare chile." Her use of "queer" is almost always nuanced. Still, one might wonder, what, if anything, could a poor, black, eighty-something, southern, homophobic woman teach her educated, middle-class, thirty-something, gay grandson about queer studies? Everything. Or *almost* everything. On the one hand, my grandmother uses "quare" to denote something or someone who is odd, irregular, or slightly off kilter—definitions in keeping with traditional understandings and uses of "queer." On the other hand, she also deploys "quare" to connote something excessive—something that might philosophically translate into an excess of discursive and epistemological meanings grounded in African American cultural rituals and lived experience. Her knowing or not knowing vis-à-vis "quare" is predicated on her own "multiple and complex social, historical, and cultural positionality" (Henderson 147). It is this culture-specific positionality that I find absent from the dominant and more conventional usage of "queer," particularly in its most recent theoretical reappropriation in the academy.

I knew there was something to "quare," that its implications reached far beyond my grandmother's front porch. Little did I know, however, that its use extended across the Atlantic. Then, I found "quare" in Ireland.[3] In *Quare Joyce,* Joseph Valente writes,

[…] I have elected to use the Anglo-Irish epithet *quare* in the title as a kind of transnational/transidiomatic pun. *Quare,* meaning odd or strange, as in Brendan Behan's famous play,

The Quare Fellow, has lately been appropriated as a distinctively Irish variant of *queer*, as in the recent prose collection *Quare Fellas*, whose editor, Brian Finnegan, reinterprets Behan's own usage of the term as having "covertly alluded to his own sexuality."

(4, emphasis in original)

Valente's appropriation of the Irish epithet "quare" to "queerly" read James Joyce establishes a connection between race and ethnicity in relation to queer identity. Indeed, Valente's "quare" reading of Joyce, when conjoined with my grandmother's "quare" reading of those who are slightly off kilter, provides a strategy for reading racial and ethnic sexuality. Where the two uses of "quare" diverge is in their deployment. Valente deploys quare to devise a queer literary exegesis of Joyce. Rather than drawing on "quare" as a *literary* mode of reading/theorizing, however, I draw upon the *vernacular* roots implicit in my grandmother's use of the word to devise a strategy for theorizing racialized sexuality.

Because much of queer theory critically interrogates notions of selfhood, agency, and experience, it is often unable to accommodate the issues faced by gays and lesbians of color who come from "raced" communities. Gloria Anzaldúa explicitly addresses this limitation when she warns that "queer is used as a false unifying umbrella which all 'queers' of all races, ethnicities and classes are shored under" (250). While acknowledging that "at times we need this umbrella to solidify our ranks against outsiders," Anzaldúa nevertheless urges that "even when we seek shelter under it ["queer"], we must not forget that it homogenizes, erases our differences" (250).

"Quare," on the other hand, not only speaks across identities, it *articulates* identities as well. "Quare" offers a way to critique stable notions of identity and, at the same time, to locate racialized and class knowledges. My project is one of recapitulation and recuperation. I want to maintain the inclusivity and playful spirit of "queer" that animates much of queer theory, but I also want to jettison its homogenizing tendencies. As a disciplinary expansion, then, I wish to "quare" "queer" such that ways of knowing are viewed both as discursively mediated and as historically situated and materially conditioned. This reconceptualization foregrounds the ways in which lesbians, bisexuals, gays, and transgendered people of color come to sexual and racial knowledge. Moreover, quare studies acknowledges the different "standpoints" found among lesbian, bisexual, gay, and transgendered people of color—differences that are also conditioned by class and gender.[4]

Quare studies is a theory of and for gays and lesbians of color. Thus, I acknowledge that in my attempt to advance quare studies, I run the risk of advancing another version of identity politics. Despite this, I find it necessary to traverse this political mine field in order to illuminate the ways in which some strands of queer theory fail to incorporate racialized sexuality. The theory that I advance is a "theory in the flesh" (Moraga and Anzaldúa 23). Theories in the flesh emphasize the diversity within and among gays, bisexuals, lesbians, and transgendered people of color while simultaneously accounting for how racism and classism affect how we experience and theorize the world. Theories in the flesh also conjoin theory and practice through an embodied politics of resistance. This politics of resistance is manifest in vernacular traditions such as performance, folklore, literature, and verbal art.

This essay offers an extended meditation on and intervention in queer theory and practice. I begin by mapping out a general history of queer theory's deployment in contemporary academic discourse, focusing on the lack of discourse on race and class within the queer theoretical paradigm. Following this, I offer an analysis of one queer theorist's (mis)reading of two black gay performances. Next, I propose an intervention in queer theory by outlining the components of quare theory, a theory that incorporates race and class as categories of analysis in the study of sexuality. Quare theory is then operationalized in the following section where I offer a quare reading of Marlon Riggs' film *Black Is . . . Black Ain't*. The final section calls for a conjoining of academic and political praxis.

"Race Trouble": Queer Studies or the Study of White Queers

At a moment when queer studies has gained momentum in the academy and forged a space as a legitimate disciplinary subject, much of the scholarship produced in its name elides issues of race and class. While the epigraphs that open this essay suggest that the label "queer" sometimes speaks across (homo)sexualities, they also suggest that the term is not necessarily embraced by gays, bisexuals, lesbians, and transgendered people of color. Indeed, the statements of Mack-Nataf, Blackman, and Cohen reflect a general suspicion that the label often displaces and rarely addresses their concerns.[5]

Some queer theorists have argued that their use of "queer" is more than just a reappropriation of an offensive term. Cherry Smith, for example, maintains that the term entails a "radical questioning of social and cultural norms, notions of gender, reproductive sexuality and the family" (280). Others underscore the playfulness and inclusivity of the term, arguing that it opens up rather than fixes identities. According to Eve Sedgwick, "What it takes—all it takes—to make the description 'queer' a true one is the impulsion to use it in the first person" (9). Indeed, Sedgwick suggests, it may refer to

> pushy femmes, radical faeries, fantasists, drags, clones, leatherfolk, ladies in tuxedos, femi-nist women or feminist men, masturbators, bulldaggers, divas, Snap! queens, butch bottoms, storytellers, transsexuals, aunties, wannabes, lesbian-identified men or lesbians who sleep with men, or [. . .] people able to relish, learn from, or identify with such.
>
> (8)

For Sedgwick, then, it would appear that "queer" is a catchall term not bound to any particular identity, a notion that moves us away from binaries such as homosexual/heterosexual and gay/lesbian. Micheal Warner offers an even more politicized and polemical view:

> The preference for "queer" represents, among other things, an aggressive impulse of generalization; it rejects a minoritizing logic of toleration or simple political interest-representation in favor of a more thorough resistance to regimes of the normal. For academics, being interested in Queer theory is a way to mess up the desexualized spaces of the academy, exude some rut, reimagine the public from and for which academic intellectuals write, dress, and perform.
>
> (xxvi)

The foregoing theorists identify "queer" as a site of indeterminate possibility, a site where sexual practice does not necessarily determine one's status as queer. Indeed, Lauren Berlant and Michael Warner argue that queer is "more a matter of aspiration than it is the expression of an identity or a history" (344). Accordingly, straight-identified critic Calvin Thomas appropriates Judith Butler's notion of "critical queerness" to suggest that "just as there is more than one way to be 'critical', there may be more than one (or two or three) to be 'queer'" (83).

Some critics have applied Butler's theory of gender to identity formation more generally. Butler calls into question the notion of the "self" as distinct from discursive cultural fields. That is, like gender, there is no independent or pure "self" or agent that stands outside socially and culturally mediated discursive systems. Any move toward identification, then, is, in her view, to be hoodwinked into believing that identities are discourse free and capable of existing outside the systems those identity formations seek to critique. Even when identity is contextualized and qualified, Butler still insists that theories of identity "invariably close with an embarrassed 'etc.'" (*Gender* 143). Butler's emphasis on gender and sex as "performative" would seem to undergird a progressive, forward-facing theory of sexuality. In fact, some theorists have made the theoretical leap from the gender performative to the racial performative, thereby demonstrating the potential of her theory for understanding the ontology of race.[6]

But to riff off of the now popular phrase "gender trouble," *there is some race trouble here with queer theory*. More particularly, in its "race for theory" (Christian), queer theory has often failed to address the material realities of gays and lesbians of color. As black British activist Helen (Charles) asks, "What happens to the definition of 'queer' when you're washing up or having a wank? When you're aware of misplacement or displacement in your colour, gender, identity? Do they get subsumed [. . .] into a homogeneous category, where class and other things that make up a cultural identity are ignored?" (101–102). What, for example, are the ethical and material implications of queer theory if its project is to dismantle all notions of identity and agency? The deconstructive turn in queer theory highlights the ways in which ideology functions to oppress and to proscribe ways of knowing, but what is the utility of queer theory on the front lines, in the trenches, on the street, or anyplace where the racialized and sexualized body is beaten, starved, fired, cursed—indeed, where the body is the site of trauma?[7]

Beyond queer theory's failure to focus on materiality, it also has failed to acknowledge consistently and critically the intellectual, aesthetic, and political contributions of nonwhite and non-middle-class gays, bisexuals, lesbians, and transgendered people in the struggle against homophobia and oppression. Moreover, even when white queer theorists acknowledge these contributions, rarely do they self-consciously and overtly reflect on the ways in which their whiteness informs their critical queer position, and this is occurring at a time when naming one's positionality has become almost standard protocol in other areas of scholarship. Although there are exceptions, most often white queer theorists fail to acknowledge and address racial privilege.[8]

Because transgendered people, lesbians, gays, and bisexuals of color often ground their theorizing in a politics of identity, they frequently fall prey to accusations of "essentialism" or "anti-intellectualism." Galvanizing around identity, however, is not always an unintentional "essentialist" move. Many times, it is an intentional strategic choice.[9] Cathy Cohen, for example, suggests that "queer theorizing which calls for the elimination of fixed categories seems to ignore the ways in which some traditional social identities and communal ties can, in fact, be important to one's survival" ("Punks" 450). The "communal ties" to which Cohen refers are those which exist in communities of color across boundaries of sexuality. For example, my grandmother, who is homophobic, nonetheless must be included in the struggle against oppression in spite of her bigotry. While her homophobia must be critiqued, her feminist and race struggles over the course of her life have enabled me and others in my family to enact strategies of resistance against a number of oppressions, including homophobia. Some queer activists groups, however, have argued fervently for the disavowal of any alliance with heterosexuals, a disavowal that those of us who belong to communities of color cannot necessarily afford to make.[10] Therefore, while offering a progressive and sometimes transgressive politics of sexuality, the seams of queer theory become exposed when that theory is applied to identities around which sexuality may pivot, such as race and class.

As a counter to this myopia and in an attempt to close the gap between theory and practice, self and Other, Audre Lorde proclaims:

Without community there is no liberation, only the most vulnerable and temporary armistice between an individual and her oppression. But community must not mean a shedding of our differences, nor the pathetic pretense that these differences do not exist. [...] *I urge each one of us here to reach down into that deep place of knowledge inside herself and touch the terror and loathing of any difference that lives there. See whose face it wears. Then the personal as the political can begin to illuminate all our choices.*

(112–13, emphasis in original)

For Lorde, a theory that dissolves the communal identity—in all of its difference—around which the marginalized can politically organize is not a progressive one. Nor is it one that gays, bisexuals, transgendered people, and lesbians of color can afford to adopt, for to do so would be to foreclose possibilities of change.

"Your Blues Ain't Like Mine": The Invalidation of "Experience"

As a specific example of how some queer theorists (mis)read or minimize the work, lives, and cultural production of gays, lesbians, bisexuals and transgendered people of color and to lay the groundwork for a return to a focus on embodied performance as a critical praxis, I offer an analysis of one queer theorist's reading of two black gay performances. In *The Ethics of Marginality*, for example, queer theorist John Champagne uses black gay theorists' objections to the photographs of Robert Mapplethorpe to call attention to the trouble with deploying "experience" as evidentiary.[11] Specifically, Champagne focuses on a speech delivered by Essex Hemphill, a black gay writer and activist, at the 1990 OUTWRITE conference of gay and lesbian writers. In his speech, Hemphill critiqued Mapplethorpe's photographs of black men.[12] Champagne takes exception to Hemphill's critique, arguing that Hemphill's reading is "monolithic" and bespeaks "a largely untheorized relation between desire, representation, and the political" (59). What I wish to interrogate, however, is Champagne's reading of Hemphill's apparent "emotionality" during the speech.

In Champagne's account, Hemphill began to cry during his speech, to which there were two responses: one of sympathy/empathy and one of protest. Commenting on an overheard conversation between two whites in the audience, Champagne writes, "Although I agreed with much of the substance of this person's comments concerning race relations in the gay and lesbian community, I was suspicious of the almost masochistic pleasure released in and through this public declaration of white culpability" (58). I find it surprising that Champagne would characterize what appears to be white self-reflexivity about racial and class privilege as "masochistic" given how rare such self-reflexivity is in the academy and elsewhere. After characterizing as masochistic the two whites who sympathetically align themselves with Hemphill, Champagne aligns himself with the one person who displayed vocal disapproval by booing Hemphill's speech:

> I have to admit that I admired the bravura of the lone booer. I disagreed with Hemphill's readings of the photographs and felt that his tears were an attempt to shame the audience into refusing to interrogate the terms of his address. If, as Gayatri Spivak has suggested, we might term the politics of an explanation the means by which it secures its particular mode of being in the world, the politics of Hemphill's reading of Mapplethorpe might be described as the politics of tears, a politics that assures the validity of its produced explanation by appealing to some kind of "authentic," universal, and (thus) uninterrogated "human" emotion of experience.

(58–59)

Champagne's own "bravura" in *his* reading of Hemphill's tears illuminates the ways in which many queer theorists, in their quest to move beyond the body, ground their critique in the discursive rather than the corporeal. I suggest that the two terrains are not mutually exclusive, but rather stand in a dialogical/dialectical relationship to one another. What about the authenticity of pain, for example, that may supercede the cognitive and emerges from the heart—not *for* display but *despite* display? What is the significance of a black *man* crying in public? We must grant each other time and space not only to talk *of* the body but *through* it as well.[13] In Champagne's formulation however, bodily experience is anti-intellectual, and Hemphill's black bodily experience is manipulative. This seems to be an unself-reflexive, if not unfair, assumption to make when, for the most part, white bodies are discursively and corporeally naturalized as universal. Historically, white bodies have not been trafficked, violated, burned, and dragged behind trucks because they embody racialized identities. In Champagne's analysis, bodily whiteness goes uninterrogated.[14]

In order to posit an alternative reading of Hemphill's tears, I turn to bell hooks' insights regarding the ways in which whites often misread emotionality elicited through black cultural aesthetics. "In the context of white institutions, particularly universities," hooks writes, "that mode of address is questionable precisely because it moves people. Style is equated in such a setting with a lack of substance" (21). hooks believes that this transformation of cultural space requires an "audience [to] shift [. . .] paradigms," and, in that way, "a marginal aspect of black cultural identity [is] centralized" (22). Unlike Champagne's own diminution of the "subversive powers [and politics] of style" (127–28), hooks affirms the transgressive and transformative potential of style, citing it as "one example of counter-hegemonic cultural practice," as well as "an insertion of radical black subjectivity" (22). Despite Champagne's statements to the contrary, his reading of Hemphill constitutes himself as a "sovereign subject" within his theory of anti-subjectivity, a positionality that renders him "overseer" of black cultural practices and discourse. On the other hand, Hemphill's tears, as a performance of black style that draws upon emotionality, may be read as more than simply a willful act of manipulation to substantiate the black gay "experience" of subjugation and objectification. More complexly, it may be read as a "confrontation with difference which takes place on new ground, in that counter-hegemonic marginal space where radical black subjectivity is *seen*, not overseen by an authoritative Other claiming to know us better than we know ourselves" (hooks 22). In his reading of Hemphill, Champagne positions himself as "authoritative Other," assuming, as he does, the motivation behind Hemphill's tears.[15]

Champagne also devotes an entire chapter to *Tongues Untied*, a film by black gay film maker, Marlon Riggs. Once again critiquing what he sees as the films problematic reliance on "experience" as evidentiary, Champagne offers a queer reading of Riggs' film to call into question the filmic representation of blackness and class:

> In *Tongues Untied*, one of the consequences of failing to dis-articulate, in one's reading, the hybrid weave of discursive practices deployed by the film might be the erasure of what I would term certain discontinuities of class, race, and imperialism as they might interweave with the necessarily inadequate nominations "Black" and "gay." For example, much of the film seems to employ a set of discursive practices historically familiar to a middle-class audience, Black and non-Black alike. The film tends to privilege the (discursive) "experience" of middle-class Black gay men, and is largely articulated from that position. The film privileges poetry, and in particular, a poetry that seems to owe as much historically to Walt Whitman and William Carlos Williams as to Langston Hughes or Countee Cullen; moreover, the film's more overtly political rhetoric seems culled from organized urban struggles in the gay as well as Black communities, struggles often headed by largely middle-class people.
>
> Another moment in the film that suggests a certain middle-class position is arguably one of the central images of the film, a series of documentary style shots of what appears to be a Gay Pride Day march in Manhattan. A group of Black gay men carry a banner

that reads "Black Men Loving Black Men Is a Revolutionary Act," apparently echoing the rhetoric of early middle-class feminism. Furthermore, the men who carry this banner are arguably marked as middle-class, their bodies sculpted into the bulging, muscular style so prominent in the gay ghettos of San Francisco and New York.

(68–69)

Champagne's critique is problematic in several ways. First, it is based on the premise that *Tongues Untied* elides the issue of class in its focus on race and homosexuality. However, Champagne then goes on to demonstrate the ways in which the film speaks to a middle-class sensibility. What is missing here is an explanation as to why black middle-class status precludes one from socially and politically engaging issues of race and sexuality. Because Champagne does not provide such an explanation, the reader is left to assume that a black middle-class subject position, as Valerie Smith has suggested, "is a space of pure compromise and capitulation, from which all autonomy disappears once it encounters hegemonic power" (67). Second, in his class-based analysis, Champagne reads literary selections, material goods, and clothing aesthetics as "evidence" of the film's middle-class leanings. However, he fails to recognize that the *appearance* of belonging to a particular class does not always reflect one's actual class status. In the black community, for instance, middle-class status is often performed—what is referred to in the vernacular as acting "boojee" (bourgeois). The way a black person adorns herself or publicly displays his material possessions may not necessarily reflect his or her economic status. Put another way, one might *live* in the projects but not necessarily *appear* to.[16] Champagne however, misreads signs of class in the film in order to support his thesis that middle-class status in the film is symptomatic of deeply rooted sexual conservatism and homophobia. Incredibly, he links this conservatism not only to that of anti-porn feminists, but also to political bigots like Jesse Helms.[17]

I am perplexed as to why the film cannot privilege black, middle-class gay experience. Is *Tongues Untied* a red herring of black gay representation because it does not do the discursive work that Champagne wishes it to do? Is it *The Cosby Show* in "gay face" because it portrays black middle-class life, (and I'm not so sure that it does)? Positioning the film in such a light seems to bespeak just the kind of essentialism that Champagne so adamantly argues against. That is, he links class and epistemology to serve the purpose of his critique, yet dismisses race-based ways of knowing. Why is class privileged epistemologically while "raced" ways of knowing are dismissed? Champagne states that "to point out that Riggs' film seems to privilege the (discursive) experience of largely middle-class urban Black gay men and to employ conventions of filmmaking familiar to a middle-class audience is not, in and of itself, a criticism of the video" (69). This disclaimer notwithstanding, Champagne goes on to do a close (mis)reading of various moments and aesthetics of the film—from specific scenes to what he argues is the film's "experimental documentary" style—to substantiate his class critique.

Unlike Champagne's deployment of queer theory, the model of quare studies that I propose would not only critique the concept of "race" as historically contingent and socially and culturally constructed/performed, it would also address the material effects of race in a white supremacist society. Quare studies requires an acknowledgement by the critic of her position within an oppressive system. To fail to do so would, as Ruth Goldman argues, "[leave] the burden of dealing with difference on the people who are themselves different, while simultaneously allowing white academics to construct a discourse of silence around race and other queer perspectives" (173). One's "experience" within that system, however discursively mediated, is also materially conditioned. A critic cannot ethically and responsibly speak from a privileged place, as Champagne does, and not own up to that privilege. To do so is to maintain the force of hegemonic whiteness, which, until very recently, has gone uninterrogated.[18]

"Quaring" the Queer: Troping the Trope

Queer studies has rightfully problematized identity politics by elaborating on the processes by which agents and subjects come into being; however, there is a critical gap in queer studies between theory and practice, performance and performativity. Quare studies can narrow that gap to the extent that it pursues an epistemology rooted in the body. As a "theory in the flesh" quare necessarily engenders a kind of identity politics, one that acknowledges difference within and between particular groups. Thus, identity politics does not necessarily mean the reduction of multiple identities into a monolithic identity or narrow cultural nationalism. Rather, quare studies moves beyond simply theorizing subjectivity and agency as discursively mediated to theorizing how that mediation may propel material bodies into action. As Shane Phelan reminds us, the maintenance of a progressive identity politics asks "not whether we share a given position but whether we share a commitment to improve it, and whether we can commit to the pain of embarrassment and confrontation as we disagree" (156).

Quare studies would reinstate the subject and the identity around which the subject circulates that queer theory so easily dismisses. By refocusing our attention on the racialized bodies, experiences, and knowledges of transgendered people, lesbians, gays, and bisexuals of color, quare studies grounds the discursive process of mediated identification and subjectivity in a political praxis that speaks to the material existence of "colored" bodies. While strategically galvanized around identity, quare studies should be committed to interrogating identity claims that exclude rather than include. I am thinking here of black nationalist claims of "black authenticity" that exclude, categorically, homosexual identities. Blind allegiance to "isms" of any kind is one of the fears of queer theorists who critique identity politics. Cognizant of that risk, quare studies must not deploy a totalizing and homogeneous formulation of identity. Rather, it must foster contingent, fragile coalitions as it struggles against common oppressive forms.

A number of queer theorists have proposed potential strategies (albeit limited ones) that may be deployed in the service of dismantling oppressive systems. Most significantly, Judith Butler's formulation of performativity has had an important impact not only on gender and sexuality studies, but on queer studies as well. While I am swayed by Butler's formulation of gender performativity, I am disturbed by her theory's failure to articulate a meatier politics of resistance. For example, what are the implications of dismantling subjectivity and social will to ground zero within oppressive regimes? Does an emphasis on the discursive constitution of subjects propel us beyond a state of quietism to address the very real injustices in the world? The body, I believe, has to be theorized in ways that not only describe the ways in which it is brought into being, but what it *does* once it *is* constituted and the relationship between it and the other bodies around it. In other words, I desire a rejoinder to performativity that allows a space for subjectivity, for agency (however momentary and discursively fraught), and, ultimately, for change.

Therefore, to complement notions of performativity, quare studies also deploys theories of performance. Performance theory not only highlights the discursive effects of acts, it also points to how these acts are historically situated. Butler herself acknowledges that the conflation of "performativity to performance would be a mistake" (*Bodies* 234). Indeed, the focus on performativity alone may problematically reduce performativity and performance to one interpretative frame to theorize human experience. On the other hand, focusing on both may bring together two interpretative frames whose relationship is more dialogical and dialectical.

In her introduction to *Performance and Cultural Politics*, Elin Diamond proposes such a relationship between performance and performativity:

When being is de-essentialized, when gender and even race are understood as fictional ontologies, modes of expression without true substance, the idea of performance comes to the fore. But performance both affirms and denies this evacuation of substance. In the sense that the "I" has no interior secure ego or core identity, "I" must always enunciate itself: there is only performance of a self, not an external representation of an interior truth. But in the sense that I do my performance in public, for spectators who are interpreting and/or performing with me, there are real effects, meanings solicited or imposed that produce relations in the real. Can performance make a difference? A performance, whether it inspires love or loathing, often consolidates cultural or subcultural affiliations, and these affiliations, might be as regressive as they are progressive. The point is, as soon as performativity comes to rest on *a* performance, questions of embodiment and political effects, all become discussible.

Performance [...] is precisely the site in which concealed or dissimulated conventions might be investigated. When performativity materializes as performance in that risky and dangerous negotiation between doing (a reiteration of norms) and a thing done (discursive conventions that frame our interpretations), between somebody's body and the conventions of embodiment, we have access to cultural meanings and critique. Performativity [...] must be rooted in the materiality and historical density of performance.

(5, emphasis in original)

I quote Diamond at length here because of the implications her construals of performance and performativity have for reinstating subjectivity and agency through the performance of identity. Although fleeting and ephemeral, these performances may activate a politics of subjectivity.

The performance of self is not only a performance/construction of identity for/toward an "out there" or merely an attachment or "taking up" (Butler, *Gender* 145) of a predetermined, discursively contingent identity. It is also a performance of self for the self in a moment of self-reflexivity that has the potential to transform one's view of self in relation to the world. People have a need to exercise control over the production of their images so that they feel empowered. For the disenfranchised, the recognition, construction and maintenance of self-image and cultural identity function to sustain, even when social systems fail to do so. Granted, formations/performances of identity may simply reify oppressive systems, but they may also contest and subvert dominant meaning systems. When gays, lesbians, bisexuals, and transgendered people of color "talk back," whether using the "tools of the master" (Lorde 110) or the vernacular on the street, their voices, singularly or collectively, do not exist in some vacuous wasteland of discursivity. As symbolic anthropologist Victor Turner suggests, their performances

are not simple reflectors or expressions of culture or even of changing culture but may themselves be active *agencies* of change, representing the eye by which culture sees itself and the drawing board on which creative actors sketch out what they believe to be more apt or interesting "designs for living." [...] Performative reflexivity is a condition in which a sociocultural group, or its most perceptive members, acting representatively, turn, bend, or reflect back upon themselves, upon the relations, actions, symbols, meanings, codes, roles, statuses, social structures, ethical and legal rules, and other sociocultural components which make up their public selves.

(24, my emphasis)

Turner's theory of performative cultural reflexivity suggests a transgressive aspect of performative identity that neither dissolves identity into a fixed "I" nor presumes a monolithic "we." Rather, Turner's assertions suggest that social beings "look back" and "look forward" in a manner that wrestles with the ways in which that community exists in the world and theorizes that existence. As Cindy Patton warns, not everyone who claims an identity does so in the ways critics of essentialist identity claim they do (181).

Theories of performance, as opposed to theories of performativity, also take into account the context and historical moment of performance (Strine 7). We need to account for the temporal and spatial specificity of performance not only to frame its existence, but also to name the ways in which it signifies. Such an analysis would acknowledge the discursivity of subjects, but it would also "unfix" the discursively constituted subject as always already a pawn of power. Although many queer theorists appropriate Foucault to substantiate the imperialism of power, Foucault himself acknowledges that discourse has the potential to disrupt power:

> Discourses are not once and for all subservient to power or raised up against it, any more than silences are. We must make allowances for the complex and unstable process whereby discourse can be both an instrument and an effect of power, but also a hindrance, a stumbling-block, a point of resistance and a starting point for an opposing strategy. Discourse transmits and produces power; it reinforces it, *but also undermines and exposes it, renders it fragile and makes it possible to thwart it.*
>
> (100–101, my emphasis)

Although people of color may not have theorized our lives in Foucault's terms, we have used discourse in subversive ways because it was necessary for our survival. Failure to ground discourse in materiality is to privilege the position of those whose subjectivity and agency, outside the realm of gender and sexuality, have never been subjugated. The tendency of many lesbians, bisexuals, gays, and transgendered people of color is to unite around a racial identity at a moment when their subjectivity is already under erasure.

Elaborating more extensively on the notion of performance as a site of agency for lesbian, gay, bisexual, and transgendered people of color, Latino performance theorist José Muñoz proposes a theory of "disidentification" whereby queers of color work within and against dominant ideology to effect change:

> Disidentification is the third mode of dealing with dominant ideology, one that neither opts to assimilate within such a structure nor strictly opposes it; rather, disidentification is a strategy that works on and against dominant ideology. Instead of buckling under the pressures of dominant ideology (identification, assimilation) or attempting to break free of its inescapable sphere (counteridentification, utopianism), this "working on and against" is a strategy that tries to transform a cultural logic from within, always laboring to enact permanent structural change while at the same time valuing the importance of local and everyday struggles of resistance.
>
> (11–12)

Muñoz's concept of "disidentification" reflects the process through which people of color have always managed to survive in a white supremacist society: by "working on and against" oppressive institutional structures.

The performance strategies of African Americans who labored and struggled under human bondage exemplify this disidentificatory practice. For instance, vernacular traditions that emerged among enslaved Africans—including folktales, spirituals, and the blues—provided the foundation for social and political empowerment. These discursively mediated forms, spoken and filtered through black bodies, enabled survival. The point here is that the inheritance of hegemonic discourses does not preclude one from "disidentifying," from putting those discourses in the service of resistance. Although they had no institutional power, enslaved blacks refused to become helpless victims and instead enacted their agency by cultivating discursive weapons based on an identity as oppressed people. The result was the creation of folktales about the "bottom rail becoming the top riser" (i.e., a metaphor for the slave rising out of slavery) or spirituals that called folks to "Gather At the River" (i.e., to plan an escape).

These resistant vernacular performances did not disappear with slavery. Gays, lesbians, bisexuals, and transgendered people of color continued to enact performative agency to work on and against oppressive systems. Quare singers such as Bessie Smith and Ma Rainey, for instance, used the blues to challenge the notion of inferior black female subjectivity and covertly brought the image of the black lesbian into the American imaginary.[19] Later, through his flamboyant style and campy costumes, Little Richard not only fashioned himself as the "emancipator" and "originator" of rock-n-roll, he also offered a critique of hegemonic black and white masculinity in the music industry. Later still, the black transgendered singer Sylvester transformed disco with his high soaring falsetto voice and gospel riffs. Indeed, Sylvester's music transcended the boundary drawn between the church and the world, between the sacred and profane, creating a space for other quare singers, like Blackberri, who would come after him. Even RuPaul's drag of many flavors demonstrates the resourcefulness of quares of color to reinvent themselves in ways that transform their material conditions. Quare vernacular tools operate outside the realm of musical and theatrical performance as well. Performance practices such as vogueing, snapping, "throwing shade," and "reading" attest to the ways in which gays, lesbians, bisexuals, and transgendered people of color devise technologies of self-assertion and summon the agency to resist.[20]

Taken together, performance and quare theories alert us to the ways in which these disidentificatory performances serve material ends, and they do this work by accounting for the context in which these performances occur. The stage, for instance, is not confined solely to the theater, the dance club, or the concert hall. Streets, social services lines, picket lines, loan offices, and emergency rooms, among others, may also serve as useful staging grounds for disidentificatory performances. Theorizing the social context of performance sutures the gap between discourse and lived experience by examining how quares use performance as a strategy of survival in their day-to-day experiences. Such an analysis requires that we, like Robin Kelley, reconceptualize "play" (performance) as "work." Moreover, quare theory focuses attention on the social consequences of those performances. It is one thing to do drag on the club stage but quite another to embody a drag queen identity on the street. Bodies are sites of discursive effects, but they are sites of social ones as well.

I do not wish to suggest that quare vernacular performances do not, at times, collude with sexist, misogynist, racist, and even homophobic ideologies. Lesbian, bisexual, gay, and transgendered people of color must always realize that we cannot transgress for transgression's sake lest our work end up romanticizing and prolonging our state of struggle and that of others. In other words, while we may occasionally enjoy the pleasures of transgressive performance, we must transgress responsibly or run the risk of creating and sustaining representations of ourselves that are anti-gay, anti-woman, anti-transgender, anti-working class, and anti-black. Despite this risk, we must not retreat to the position that changes within the system are impossible. The social movements of the past century are testament that change is possible.

Ultimately, quare studies offers a more utilitarian theory of identity politics, focusing not just on performers and effects, but also on contexts and historical situatedness. It does not, as bell hooks warns, separate the "politics of difference from the politics of racism" (26). Quare studies grants space for marginalized individuals to enact "radical black subjectivity" (hooks 26) by adopting the both/and posture of "disidentification." Quare studies proposes a theory grounded in a critique of naïve essentialism and an enactment of political praxis. Such theorizing may *strategically* embrace identity politics while also acknowledging the contingency of identity, a double move that Angelia Wilson adroitly describes as "politically necessary and politically dangerous" (107).

Seeing Through Quare Eyes: Marlon Riggs' *Black Is . . . Black Ain't*

In Riggs' documentary, *Black Is . . . Black Ain't*, we find an example of quare theory operationalized. Thus, in order to demonstrate the possibilities of quare, I turn now to an analysis of this film. Completed after Riggs' death in 1994, this documentary chronicles the filmmaker's battle with AIDS and also serves as a meditation on the embattled status of black identity. *Black Is . . . Black Ain't* "quares" "queer" by suggesting that identity, although highly contested, manifests itself in the flesh and, therefore, has social and political consequences for those who live in that flesh. Further "quaring" queer, the film also allows for agency and authority by visually privileging Riggs' AIDS experience narrative. Indeed, the film's documentation of Riggs' declining health suggests an identity and a body in the process of *being* and *becoming*. Quare theory elucidates the mechanics of this both/and identity formation, and, in so doing, it challenges a static reading of identity as only performativity or only performance.

Initially, I focus on how the film engages performativity, focusing as it does on problematizing notions of essential blackness. One of the ways in which the film engages this critique is by pointing out how, at the very least, gender, class, sexuality and region all impact the construction of blackness. Indeed, the title of the film points to the ways in which race defines, as well as confines, African Americans. The recurrent trope used by Riggs to illuminate the multiplicity of blackness is gumbo, a dish that consists of whatever the cook wishes. It has, Riggs remarks, "everything you can imagine in it." This trope also underscores the multiplicity of blackness insofar as gumbo is a dish associated with New Orleans, a city confounded by its mixed race progeny and the identity politics that mixing creates. The gumbo trope is apropos because, like "blackness," gumbo is a site of possibilities. The film argues that when African Americans attempt to define what it means to be black, they delimit the possibilities of what blackness can be. But Riggs' film does more than just stir things up. In many ways it reduces the heat of the pot, allowing everything in the gumbo to mix and mesh, yet maintain its own distinct flavor. Chicken is distinct from andouille, rice from peas, bay leaves from thyme, cayenne from paprika. Thus, Riggs' film suggests that African Americans cannot begin to ask dominant culture to accept their difference as "others" until African Americans accept the differences that exist among themselves.

Class represents one significant axis of difference and divisiveness within black communities. As Martin Favor persuasively argues, "authentic" blackness is most often associated with the "folk" or working class blacks. Moreover, art forms such as the blues and folklore that are associated with the black working class are also viewed as more genuinely black. This association of the folk with black authenticity necessarily renders the black middle class as inauthentic and apolitical. In *Black Is . . . Black Ain't*, Riggs intervenes in this construction of the black middle class as "less black," by featuring a potpourri of blacks from various backgrounds. Importantly, those who might be considered a part of the "folk" questionably offer some of the most anti-black sentiments, while those black figures most celebrated in the film—Angela Davis, Barbara Smith, Michele Wallace, and Cornel West—are middle-class members of the baby boomer generation. Riggs undermines the idea that "authentic" blackness belongs to the black working class by prominently displaying interviews with Angela Davis, Michelle Wallace and Barbara Smith. While ostracized for attending integrated schools and speaking Standard English or another language altogether, these women deny that their blackness was ever compromised. The film critiques hegemonic notions of blackness based on class status by locating the founding moment of black pride and radical black activism within black middle-class communities in the '60s, thereby reminding us that "middle class" is also an ideological construct as contingently constituted as other positionalities.

Riggs also unhinges the link between hegemonic masculinity and authentic blackness. By excerpting misogynist speeches by Louis Farrakhan, a southern black preacher, and the leader of an "African" village located in South Carolina and by juxtaposing them with the personal narratives of bell hooks and Angela Davis, Riggs undermines the historical equation of "real" blackness with black masculinity. The narrative that hooks relates regarding her mother's spousal abuse is intercut with and undercuts Farrakhan's sexist and misogynist justification of Mike Tyson's sexual advances that eventually led to his being convicted for raping Desiree Washington. The narrative set forth by hooks also brackets the sexism inherent in the black preacher's and African leader's justification of the subjugation of women based on biblical and African mythology. Musically framing this montage of narratives is rap artist Queen Latifah's performance of "U-N-I-T-Y," a song that urges black women to "let black men know you ain't a bitch or a 'ho." Riggs' decision to use Queen Latifah's song to administer this critique is interesting on a number of levels. Namely, Queen Latifah's own public persona, as well as her television and motion picture roles, embody a highly masculinized femininity or, alternatively what Judith Halberstam might call "female masculinity" (1–42). Riggs uses Latifah's song and the invocation of her persona, then, to disrupt hegemonic constructions of black masculinity and to illuminate the sexism found within the black community.

While I find the film's critique of essentialized blackness persuasive, I find its critique of homophobia in the black community and its demand for a space for homosexual identity within constructions of blackness even more compelling. As a rhetorical strategy, Riggs first points to those signifiers of blackness that build community (e.g., language, music, food, and religion). Indeed, the opening of the film with the chant-like call and response of black folk preaching references a communal cultural site instantly recognizable to many African Americans. But just as the black church has been a political and social force in the struggle for the racial freedom of its constituents, it has also, to a large extent, occluded sexual freedom for many of its practitioners, namely gays and lesbians. Thus, in those opening scenes, Riggs calls attention to the double standard found within the black church by exemplifying how blackness can "build you up, or bring you down," hold you in high esteem or hold you in contempt. Riggs not only calls attention to the racism of whites; he also calls attention to homophobia in the black community and particularly in the black church. Throughout the film, however, Riggs challenges the traditional construction of the black church by featuring a black gay and lesbian church service. Given the black church's typical stance on homosexuality, some might view this avowal of Christianity as an instance of false consciousness. I argue, however, that these black gay and lesbians are employing disidentification insofar as they value the cultural rituals of the black worship service yet resist the fundamentalism of its message. In the end, the film intervenes in the construction of black homosexuality as anti-black by propagating gay Christianity as a legitimate signifier of blackness.

Riggs' film implicitly employs performativity to suggest that we dismantle hierarchies that privilege particular black positionalities at the expense of others, that we recognize that darker hue does not give us any more cultural capital or claim to blackness than does a dashiki, braids, or a southern accent. Masculinity is no more a signifier of blackness than femininity; heterosexuality is no blacker than homosexuality; and living in the projects makes you no more authentically black than owning a house in the suburbs. Indeed, Riggs suggests that we move beyond these categories that define and confine in order to realize that, depending on where you are from and where you are going, black is and black ain't.

While the film critically interrogates cleavages among blacks, it also exposes the social, political, economic and psychological effects of racism, and the role it has played in defining blackness. By adopting this dual focus, Riggs offers a perspective that is decidedly quare. He calls attention to differences among blacks and between blacks and their "others";[21] he grounds blackness in lived experience; and he calls attention to the consequences of embodied blackness. The montage of footage from the LA riots and interviews with young black men who characterize themselves as "gang bangers" bring into clear focus the material reality of black America and how the black body has historically been the site of violence and trauma.

Nowhere in the film is a black body historicized more pointedly and powerfully, however, than in the scenes where Riggs is featured walking through the forest naked or narrating from his hospital bed from which his t-cell count is constantly announced. According to Riggs, these scenes are important because he wants to make the point that not until we expose ourselves to one another will we be able to communicate effectively across our differences. Riggs' intentions notwithstanding, his naked black body serves another important function within the film. It is simultaneously in a state of being *and* becoming. I intend here to disrupt both these terms by refusing to privilege identity as either solely performance or solely performativity and by demonstrating the dialogical/dialectical relationship of these two tropes.

Paul Gilroy's theory of diaspora is useful in clarifying the difference between being and becoming. According to Gilroy, "Diaspora accentuates *becoming* rather than *being* and identity conceived diasporically, along these lines, resists reification" (24, emphasis in original). Here, Gilroy associates "being" with the transhistorical and transcendental subject and "becoming" with historical situatedness and contingency. In what follows, I supplement Gilroy's use of both terms by suggesting that "being" and "becoming" are sites of performance *and* performativity. I construe "being" as a site of infinite signification *as well as* bodily and material presence. "Being" calls the viewer's attention not only to "blackness" as discourse, but also to embodied blackness in that moment where discourse and flesh conjoin in performance. If we look beyond Riggs' intent to "expose" himself in order to encourage cross-difference communication, we find that his nakedness in the woods functions ideologically in ways that he may not wish. For example, his nakedness may conjure up the racist stereotype of the lurking, bestial, and virile black male that became popular in the 18th and 19th century American imaginary. On the other hand, his embodied blackness in the woods and in his hospital bed also indicate a diseased body that is fragile, vulnerable, and a site of trauma, a site that grounds black discursivity materially in the flesh. At the literal level, Riggs' black male body is exposed as fragile and vulnerable, but it also synecdochically stands in for a larger body of racist discourse on the black male body in motion. This trope of black bodily kinesthetics is manifest in a variety of forms (e.g., the vernacular expression "keep the nigger running," the image of the fugitive slave, and contemporary hypermasculinized images of black athletes). Racist readings of Riggs' black male body are made possible by the context in which Riggs' body appears, the woods. Within this setting, blackness becomes problematically aligned with nature, reinscribing the black body as bestial and primal. This imagery works against Riggs' intentions—namely, running naked in the woods as a way to work through the tangled and knotty web that is identity. Indeed, the images of Riggs running naked through the woods signify in multiple and troubling ways that, once let loose, cannot be contained by either Riggs' authorial intentions or the viewer's gaze. The beauty of *being*, however, is that where it crumbles under the weight of deconstruction, it reemerges in all its bodily facticity. Although Riggs' body may signify in ways that constrain his agency, his embodied blackness also enlivens a discussion of a "fleshy" nature. Whatever his body signifies, the viewer cannot escape its material presence.

Riggs' body is also a site of *becoming*. He dies before the film is completed. Riggs' body physically "fades away," but its phantom is reconstituted in our current discourse on AIDS, race, gender, class, and sexuality. Thus, Riggs' body discursively rematerializes and intervenes in hegemonic formulations of blackness, homosexuality, and the HIV-infected person. As a filmic performance, *Black Is . . . Black Ain't* resurrects Riggs' body such that when the film is screened at universities, shown to health care providers, viewed in black communities or rebroadcast on PBS, the terms and the stakes for how we think about identity and its relation to HIV/AIDS are altered. Like Toni Morrison's character Sula, Riggs dreams of water carrying him over that liminal threshold where the water "would envelop [him], carry [him], and wash [his] tired flesh always" (149). After her death, Sula promises to tell her best friend, Nel, that death did not hurt, ironically announcing her physical death alongside her spiritual rebirthing. Her rebirthing is symbolized by her assuming a fetal position and traveling "over and down the tunnels, just missing the dark walls, down, down until she met a rain scent and would know the water was near" (149). Riggs dreams of a similar journey through water. In his dream, Harriet Tubman serves as a midwife who cradles his head at the tunnel's opening and helps him make the journey. Once on the other side, Riggs, like Sula, lives on and also makes good on his promise to return through his living spirit captured in the film. The residual traces of Riggs' body become embedded in the ideological battle over identity claims and the discourse surrounding the disproportionate number of AIDS-infected people of color. His becoming, then, belies our being.

Ultimately, *Black Is . . . Black Ain't* performs what its title announces: the simultaneity of bodily presence and absence, being and becoming. Although Riggs offers his own gumbo recipe that stands in for blackness, he does so only to demonstrate that, like blackness, the recipe can be altered, expanded, reduced, watered down. At the same time, Riggs also asks that we not forget that the gumbo (blackness) is contained within a sturdy pot (the body) that has weathered abuse, that has been scorched, scoured, and scraped, a pot/body that is in the process of becoming but nonetheless *is*.

Unlike queer theory, quare theory fixes our attention on the discursive constitution of the recipe even as it celebrates the improvisational aspects of the gumbo and the materiality of the pot. While queer theory has opened up new possibilities for theorizing gender and sexuality, like a pot of gumbo cooked too quickly, it has failed to live up to its full critical potential by refusing to accommodate *all* the queer ingredients contained inside its theoretical pot. Quare theory, on the other hand, promises to reduce the spillage, allowing the various and multiple flavors to co-exist—those different flavors that make it spicy, hot, unique and sumptuously brown.

Bringin' It on "Home": Quare Studies on the Back Porch

Thus far, I have canvassed the trajectory for quare studies inside the academy, focusing necessarily on the intellectual work that needs to be done to advance specific disciplinary goals. While there is intellectual work to be done inside the academy—what one might call "academic praxis"—there is also political praxis outside the academy.[22] If social change is to occur, gays, bisexuals, transgendered people, and lesbians of color cannot afford to be armchair theorists. Some of us need to be in the streets, in the trenches, enacting the quare theories that we construct in the "safety" of the academy. While keeping in mind that political theory and political action are not necessarily mutually exclusive, quare theorists must make theory work for its constituency. Although we share with our white queer peers sexual oppression, gays, lesbians, bisexuals, and transgendered people of color also share racial oppression with other members of our community. We cannot afford to abandon them simply because they are heterosexual. Cohen writes that "although engaged in heterosexual behavior," straight African Americans "have often found themselves outside the norms and values of dominant society. This position has most often resulted in the suppression or negation or their legal, social, and physical relationships and rights" (454). Quare studies must encourage strategic coalition building around laws and policies that have the potential to affect us across racial, sexual, and class divides. Quare studies must incorporate under its rubric a praxis related to the sites of public policy, family, church,

THE QUARE OF QUEER • **499**

and community. Therefore, in the tradition of radical black feminist critic Barbara Smith ("Toward"), I offer a manifesto that aligns black quare academic theory with political praxis.

We can do more in the realm of public policy. As Cohen so cogently argues in her ground-breaking book, *The Boundaries of Blackness*, we must intervene in the failure of the conservative black leadership to respond to the HIV/AIDS epidemic ravishing African American communities. Due to the growing number of African Americans infected with and contracting HIV, quare theorists must aid in the education and prevention of the spread of HIV as well as care for those who are suffering. This means more than engaging in volunteer work and participating in fund raising. It also means using our training as academics to deconstruct the way HIV/AIDS is discussed in the academy and in the medical profession. We must continue to do the important work of physically helping our brothers and sisters who are living with HIV and AIDS through outreach services and fundraising events, but we must also use our scholarly talents to combat racist and homophobic discourse that circulates in white as well as black communities. Ron Simmons, a black gay photographer and media critic who left academia to commit his life to those suffering with AIDS by forming the organization US Helping US, remains an important role model for how we can use both our academic credentials and our political praxis in the service of social change.

The goal of quare studies is to be specific and intentional in the dissemination and praxis of quare theory, committed to communicating and translating its political potentiality. Indeed, quare theory is "bi"-directional: it theorizes from bottom to top and top to bottom (pun intended!). This dialogical/dialectical relationship between theory and practice, the lettered and unlettered, ivory tower and front porch is crucial to a joint and sustained critique of hegemonic systems of oppression.

Given the relationship between the academy and the community, quare theorists must value and speak from what hooks refers to as "homeplace." According to hooks, homeplace "[is] the one site where one [can] freely confront the issue of humanization, where one [can] resist" (42). It is from homeplace that people of color live out the contradictions of our lives. Cutting across the lines of class and gender, homeplace provides a place from which to critique oppression. I do not wish to romanticize this site by dismissing the homophobia that circulates within homeplace or the contempt that some of us (of all sexual orientations) have for "home."[23] I am suggesting, rather, that in spite of these contradictions, homeplace is that site that first gave us the "equipment for living" (Burke 293) in a racist society, particularly since we, in all of our diversity, have always been a part of this homeplace: housekeepers, lawyers, seamstresses, hair-dressers, activists, choir directors, professors, doctors, preachers, mill workers, mayors, nurses, truck drivers, delivery people, nosey neighbors, and (an embarrassed?) "etc." SNAP!.

Homeplace is also a site which quare praxis must critique. That is, we may seek refuge in homeplace as a marginally safe place to critique oppression outside its confines, but we must also deploy quare theory to address oppression within homeplace itself. One might begin, for instance, with the black church, which remains for some gays and lesbians, a sustaining site of spiritual affirmation, comfort, and artistic outlet. Quare studies cannot afford to dismiss, cavalierly, the role of the black church in quare lives. However, it must never fail to critique the black church's continual denial of gay and lesbian subjectivity. Our role within the black church is an important one. Those in the pulpit and those in the congregation should be challenged whenever they hide behind Romans and Leviticus to justify their homophobia. We must force the black church to name us and claim us if we are to obtain any liberation within our own communities.[24]

Regarding ideological and political conflicts in gay, lesbian, and transgendered communities of color, quare praxis must interrogate and negotiate the differences among our differences, including our political strategies for dealing with oppression and our politics of life choice and maintenance. Consequently, quare studies must also focus on interracial dating and the identity politics such couplings invoke. Writer Darieck Scott has courageously addressed this issue, but we need to continue to explore our own inner conflicts around our choices of sexual partners across racial lines. Additionally, quare studies should interrogate another contested area of identity politics: relations between "out" and "closeted" members of our community. Much of this work must be done not in the academy, but in our communities, in our churches, in our homes.

Unconvinced that queer studies is soon to change, I summon quare studies as an interventionist disciplinary project. Quare studies addresses the concerns and needs of gay, lesbian, bisexual, and transgendered people across issues of race, gender, class, and other subject positions. While attending to the discursive constitution of subjects, quare studies is also committed to theorizing the practice of everyday life. Because we exist in material bodies, we need a theory that speaks to that reality. Indeed, quare studies may breathe new life into our "dead" (or deadly) stratagems of survival.

Coda

Because I credit my grandmother for passing on to me the little bit of common sense I still have, I conclude this essay with a story about her use of "gaydar,"[25] a story that speaks to how black folk use "motherwit" as a "reading" strategy, as well as a way to "forget all those things they don't want to remember, and remember everything they don't want to forget" (Hurston 1).

My grandmother lives in western North Carolina. When I went to live with her to collect her oral history for my dissertation, she spent a considerable amount of time catching me up on all of the new residents who had moved into her senior citizens' community. Dressed in her customary polyester cut-off shorts and cotton makeshift blouse, loosely tied sheer scarf draped around her dyed, jet black hair, legs crossed and head cocked to the side, my grandmother described for me, one by one, each of the new residents. She detailed, among other things, their medical histories and conditions, the number of children they had, their marital status and, perhaps most importantly, whether they were "pickles" or not. She uses the term euphemistically to describe people she believes are "not quite right in the head."

There was one resident, David, about whom my grandmother had a particular interest. I soon learned that David was a seventy-four year-old white man who had to walk with the support of a walker and who had moved to my grandmother's community from across town, but that was not the most important thing about David. My grandmother revealed to me what that was one day: "Well, you know we got one of them 'homalsexuals' living down here," she said, dryly. Not quite sure I had heard her correctly but also afraid that I had, I responded, "A what?" "You know, one of them 'homalsexuals,'" she said again just as dryly. This time, however, her voice was tinged with impatience and annoyance. Curious, a bit anxious about the turn the conversation was taking (I am not "out" to my grandmother), I pursued the issue further: "Well, how do you know the man's a homosexual, Grandmama?" She paused, rubbed her leg, narrowed her eyes and responded, "Well, he gardens, bakes pies, and keeps a clean house." Like a moth to the flame, I opened the door to my own closet for her to walk in and said, "Well, I cook and keep my apartment clean." Then, after a brief pause, "But I don't like gardening. I don't like getting my hands dirty." As soon as the words "came out" of my mouth, I realized what I had done. My grandmother said nothing. She simply folded her arms and began to rock as if in church. The question she dare not ask sat behind her averted eyes: "You ain't quare are you, Pat?" Yes, Grandmama, quare indeed.

Notes

1. E. Patrick Johnson, "'Quare' Studies, or (Almost) Everything I Know About Queer Studies I Learned From My Grandmother," *Text and Performance Quarterly* 21:1 (2001): 18–20.

2. See Johnson, "SNAP! Culture" 125–128.

3. I have long known about the connection between African Americans and the Irish. As noted in the film *The Commitments*, "The Irish are the blacks of Europe." The connection is there—that is, at least until the Irish became "white." For a sustained discussion of how Irish emigrants obtained "white" racial privilege, see Ignatiev.

4. For more on "standpoint" theory, see Collins.

5. In *Bodies That Matter*, Judith Butler anticipates the contestability of "queer," noting that it excludes as much as it includes but that such a contested term may energize a new kind of political activism. She proposes that "[. . .] it may be that the critique of the term will initiate a resurgence of both feminist and anti-racist mobilization within lesbian and gay politics or open up new possibilities for coalitional alliances that do not presume that these constituencies are radically distinct from one another. The term will be revised, dispelled, rendered obsolete to the extent that it yields to the demands which resist the term precisely because of the exclusions by which it is mobilized" (228–29). To be sure, there are gay, bisexual, lesbian and transgendered people of color who embrace "queer." In my experience, however, those who embrace the term represent a small minority. At the "Black Queer Studies at the Millennium Conference" held at the University of North Carolina on April 7–9, 2000, for example, many of the conference attendees were disturbed by the organizers' choice of "queer" for the title of a conference on black sexuality. So ardent was their disapproval that it became a subject of debate during one of the panels.

6. See, for example, Hall and Gilroy, " 'Race'."

7. I thank Michelé Barale for this insight.

8. While it is true that some white queer theorists are self-reflexive about their privilege and incorporate the works and experiences of gays, bisexuals, lesbians, and transgendered people of color into their scholarship, this is not the norm. Paula Moya calls attention to how the theorizing of women of color is appropriated by postmodernist theorists: "[Judith] Butler extracts one sentence from [Cherríe] Moraga, buries it in a footnote, and then misreads it in order to justify her own inability to account for the complex interrelations that structure various forms of human identity" (133). David Bergman also offers a problematic reading of black gay fiction when he reads James Baldwin through the homophobic rhetoric of Eldridge Cleaver and theorizes that black communities are more homophobic than white ones (163–87). For other critiques of simplistic or dismissive readings of the works of gays, bisexuals, lesbians, and transgendered people of color see Ng, (Charles), and Namaste. One notable exception is Ruth Goldman's "Who is That *Queer* Queer," in which she, a white bisexual, calls other white queer theorists to task for their failure to theorize their whiteness: "[. . .] those of us who are white tend not to dwell on our race, perhaps because this would only serve to normalize us—reduce our queerness, if you will" (173).

9. For more on "strategic" essentialism, see: Case 1–12; de Lauretis; and Fuss 1–21.

10. For a sustained discussion of queer activists' disavowal of heterosexual political alliances, see Cohen, "Punks" 440–52.

11. Champagne draws from Joan Scott's "The Evidence of Experience," where she argues that "experience" is discursively constituted, mediated by and through linguistic systems and embedded in ideology. Like all discursive terrains, the ground upon which "experience" moves is turbulent and supple, quickly disrupting the foothold we think we might have on history and the "evidentiary." Scott writes, "Experience is at once always already an interpretation and is in need of interpretation. What counts as experience is neither self-evident nor straightforward; it is always contested, always therefore political. The study of experience, therefore, must call into question its originary status in historical explanation. This will happen when historians take as their project not the reproduction and transmission of knowledge said to be arrived at through experience, but the analysis of the production of that knowledge itself" (37, emphasis in original). Scott is particularly concerned here with histories that draw on "experience" as evidentiary in order to historicize difference. "By remaining within the epistemological frame of orthodox history," Scott argues, "these studies lose the possibility of examining those assumptions and practices that excluded considerations of difference in the first place" (24–25).

12. Robert Mapplethorpe's photographs of black gay men continue to be a source of controversy in the black gay community. Reactions to the photos range from outrage to ambivalence to appreciation. I believe the most complex reading of Mapplethorpe is found in Isaac Julien and Kobena Mercer's "True Confessions: A Discourse on Images of Black Male Sexuality." They write: "While we recognize the oppressive dimension of these images of black men as Other, we are also attracted: We want to look but don't always find the images we want to see. This ambivalent mixture of attraction and repulsion goes for images of black gay men in porn generally, but the inscribed or preferred meanings of

these images are not fixed; they can at times, be pried apart into alternative readings when different experiences are brought to bear on their interpretation" (170).

13. I thank Soyini Madison for raising this issue.

14. I do not mean to deny that white gay, lesbian, bisexual, and transgendered people have been emotionally, psychologically, and physically harmed. The recent murder of Matthew Shepard is a sad testament to this fact. Indeed, given how his attackers killed him, there are ways in which we may read Shepard's murder through a racial lens. What I am suggesting, however, is that racial violence (or the threat of it) is enacted upon black bodies in different ways and for different reasons than it is on white bodies.

15. Emotionality as manipulative or putatively repugnant may also be read through the lens of gender. Generally understood as a "weak" (read "feminine") gender performance, emotional display among men of any race or sexual orientation represents a threat to heteronormativity and, therefore, is often met with disapproval.

16. I do not wish to suggest that the appearance of poverty or wealth never reflects that one is actually poor or wealthy. What I am suggesting, however, is that in many African American communities, style figures more substantively than some might imagine. Accordingly, there exists a politics of taste among African Americans that is performed so as to dislodge fixed perceptions about who one is or where one is from. In many instances, for example, performing a certain middle-class style has enabled African Americans to "pass" in various and strategically savvy ways. For more on the performance of style in African American communities see B. Smith's "Home" and Beam's "Leaving." For a theoretical perspective on the politics of taste, see Bourdieu.

17. Champagne writes that, "like the white antiporn feminists whose rhetoric they sometimes share, intellectuals like Riggs and Hemphill may in fact be expressing in *Tongues Untied* a (middle-) class-inflected sense of disgust related to sexuality—obviously, not related to all sexuality, but to a particularly culturally problematic kind. It is perhaps thus not a coincidence at all that the rhetoric deployed by Hemphill in his reading of Mapplethorpe should be so similar to that of Dworkin, Stoltenberg, and even Jesse Helms" (79).

18. For examples of white critics who interrogate "whiteness," see Frankenberg, Hill, and Roediger.

19. For an analysis of Bessie Smith's explicitly lesbian blues songs, see Harrison 103–104.

20. See Riggs "Black Macho" and Johnson "SNAP!" and "Feeling."

21. Paul Gilroy's insights regarding the theoretical utility of the concept "diaspora" are similar to what I mean here insofar as he posits that diaspora "allows for a complex conception of sameness and an idea of solidarity that does not repress the differences within in order to maximize the differences between one 'essential' community and others" (" . . . to be real," 24).

22. I do not wish to suggest that the academy is not always already a politicized site. Rather, I only mean to suggest that the ways in which it is politicized are, in many instances, different from the ways in which nonacademic communities are politicized.

23. For a critique of the notion of "home" in the African American community vis-à-vis homophobia and sexism, see Clarke, Crenshaw, hooks, and Simmons.

24. For a sustained critique of homophobia in the black church, see Dyson 77–108.

25. "Gaydar" is a term some gays and lesbians use to signal their ability to determine whether or not someone is gay.

Works Cited

Anzaldúa, Gloria. "To(o) Queer the Writer: *Loca, escrita y chicana.*" *Inversions: Writing by Dykes and Lesbians.* Ed. Betsy Warland. Vancouver: Press Gang, 1991. 249–259.

Baldwin, James. *Nobody Knows My Name: More Notes of a Native Son.* New York: Vintage, 1993.

———. *No Name in the Street.* New York: Dial, 1972.

Beam, Joseph. "Making Ourselves from Scratch." *Brother to Brother: New Writings by Black Gay Men.* Ed. Essex Hemphill. Boston: Alyson, 1991. 261–262.

———. "Leaving the Shadows Behind." *In the Life.* Ed. Joseph Beam. Boston: Alyson, 1986. 13–18.

Bergman, David. *Gaiety Transfigured: Gay Self-Representation in American Literature.* Madison: U of Wisconsin P, 1991.

Berlant, Lauren, and Michael Warner. "What Does Queer Theory Teach Us about X?" *PMLA* 110 (1995): 343–349.

Black Is . . . Black Ain't. Dir. Marlon Riggs. Independent Film Series, 1995.

Bourdieu, Pierre. *Distinction: A Social Critique of the Judgement of Taste.* Trans. Richard Nice. Cambridge: Harvard UP, 1984.

Burke, Kenneth. *Philosophy of Literary Form.* Baton Rouge: Louisiana State UP, 1967.

Butler, Judith. *Bodies That Matter: On the Discursive Limits of "Sex."* New York: Routledge, 1993.

———. *Gender Trouble: Feminism and the Subversion of Identity.* New York: Routledge, 1990.

Case, Sue-Ellen. *The Domain Matrix: Performing Lesbian at the End of Print Culture.* Bloomington: Indiana UP, 1996.

Champagne, John. *The Ethics of Marginality: A New Approach to Gay Studies.* Minneapolis: U of Minnesota P, 1995.

(Charles), Helen. " 'Queer Nigger': Theorizing 'White' Activism." *Activating Theory: Lesbian, Gay, Bisexual Politics.* Eds. Joseph Bistrow and Angelia R. Wilson. London: Lawrence and Wishart, 1993. 97–117.

Christian, Barbara. "The Race for Theory." *Cultural Critique* 6 (1985): 51–63.

Clarke, Cheryl. "The Failure to Transform: Homophobia in the Black Community." *Home Girls: A Black Feminist Anthology.* Ed. Barbara Smith. New York: Kitchen Table, 1983. 197–208.

Cohen, Cathy. *The Boundaries of Blackness: AIDS and the Breakdown of Black Politics.* Chicago: U of Chicago P, 1999.

———. "Punks, Bulldaggers, and Welfare Queens: The Radical Potential of Queer Politics?" *GLQ: A Journal of Lesbian & Gay Studies* 3 (1997): 437–465.

Collins, Patricia Hill. "The Social Construction of Black Feminist Thought." *Words of Fire: An Anthology of African-American Feminist Thought.* Ed. Beverly Guy-Sheftall. New York: New Press, 1995. 338–357.

The Commitments. Dir. Alan Parker. Lauren Films, 1991.

Crenshaw Kimberlé Williams. "Mapping the Margins: Intersectionality, Identity Politics, and Violence Against Women of Color." *Stanford Law Review* 43 (1991): 1241–99.

de Lauretis, Teresa. "The Essence of the Triangle, or Taking the Risk of Essentialism Seriously: Feminist Theory in Italy, the U.S. and Britain." *differences* 1.2 (1989): 3–37.

Diamond, Elin, ed. Introduction. *Performance & Cultural Politics.* New York: Routledge, 1996. 1–9.

Dyson, Michael Eric. "The Black Church and Sex." *Race Rules: Navigating the Color Line.* Reading, MA: Addison-Wesley, 1996. 77–108.

Favor, Martin. *Authentic Blackness: The Folk in the New Negro Renaissance.* Durham: Duke UP, 1999.

Foucault, Michel. *The History of Sexuality, Vol. 1.* Trans. Robert Hurley. New York: Random House, 1980.

Frankenberg, Ruth, ed. *Displacing Whiteness: Essays in Social and Cultural Criticism.* Durham: Duke UP, 1997.

Fuss, Diana. *Essentially Speaking: Feminism, Nature & Difference.* New York: Routledge, 1989.

Gilroy, Paul. " ' . . . to be real': The Dissident Forms of Black Expressive Culture." *Let's Get It On: The Politics of Black Performance.* Ed. Catherine Ugwu. Seattle: Bay, 1995. 12–33.

———. " 'Race', Class, and Agency." *There Ain't No Black in the Union Jack: The Cultural Politics of Race and Nation.* London: Hutchinson, 1987. 15–42.

Goldman, Ruth. "Who Is That *Queer* Queer?" *Queer Studies: A Lesbian, Gay, Bisexual and Transgender Anthology.* Eds. Brett Beemyn and Mickey Eliason. New York: NYU P, 1996. 169–182.

Halberstam, Judith. *Female Masculinity.* Durham: Duke UP, 1998.

Hall, Stuart. "Subjects in History: Making Diasporic Identities." *The House That Race Built.* Ed. Wahneema Lubiano. New York: Pantheon, 1997. 289–299.

Harrison, Daphne Duval. *Black Pearls: Blues Queens of the 1920's.* New Brunswick: Rutgers UP, 1998.

Henderson, Mae. "Speaking in Tongues." *Feminist Theorize the Political.* Eds. Judith Butler and Joan W. Scott. New York: Routledge, 1992. 144–165.

Hill, Mike, ed. *Whiteness: A Critical Reader.* New York: NYU P, 1997.

hooks, bell. *Yearning.* Boston: South End, 1990.

Hurston, Zora Neale. *Their Eyes Were Watching God.* New York: Harper & Row, 1990.

Ignatiev, Noel. *How the Irish Became White.* New York: Routledge, 1995.

Johnson, E. Patrick. "Feeling the Spirit in the Dark: Expanding Notions of the Sacred in the African American Gay Community." 21 *Callaloo* (1998): 399–418.

———. "SNAP! Culture: A Different Kind of 'Reading.'" *Text and Performance Quarterly* 3 (1995): 121–142.

Julien, Isaac, and Kobena Mercer. "True Confessions: A Discourse on Images of Black Male Sexuality." *Brother to Brother: New Writings by Black Gay Men.* Ed. Essex Hemphill. Boston: Alyson, 1991. 167–173.

Kelley, Robin D.G. "Looking to Get Paid: How Some Black Youth Put Culture to Work." *Yo Mama's Disfunktional!: Fighting the Culture Wars in Urban America.* Boston: Beacon, 1997. 43–77.

Latifah, Queen. "U.N.I.T.Y." *Black Reign.* Motown. 1993.

Lorde, Audre. *Sister Outsider.* Freedom, CA: Crossing, 1984.

Moraga, Cherríe, and Gloria Anzaldúa, eds. *This Bridge Called My Back: Writings by Radical Women of Color.* New York: Kitchen Table, 1983.

Morrison, Toni. *Sula.* New York: Knopf, 1973.

Moya, Paula M.L. "Postmodernism, 'Realism', and the Politics of Identity: Cherríe Moraga and Chicano Feminism." *Feminist Genealogies, Colonial Legacies, Democratic Futures.* Eds. M. Jacqui Alexander and Chandra Talpade Mohanty. New York: Routledge, 1997. 125–50.

Muñoz, José Esteban. *Disidentifications: Queers of Color and the Performance of Politics.* Minneapolis: U of Minnesota P, 1999.

Namaste, Ki. " 'Tragic Misreadings': Queer Theory's Erasure of Transgender Identity." *Queer Studies: A Lesbian, Gay, Bisexual and Transgender Anthology.* Eds. Brett Beemyn and Mickey Eliason. New York: NYU P, 1996. 183–203.

Ng, Vivien. "Race Matters." *Lesbian and Gay Studies: A Critical Introduction.* Eds. Andy Medhurst and Sally R. Munt. London: Cassell. 215–231.

Patton, Cindy. "Performativity and Social Distinction: The End of AIDS Epidemiology." *Performativity and Performance.* Eds. Andrew Parker and Eve Kosofsky Sedgwick. New York: Routledge, 1995. 173–196.

Phelan, Shane. *Getting Specific.* Minneapolis: U of Minnesota P, 1994.

Riggs, Marlon. "Black Macho Revisited: Reflections of a SNAP! Queen." *Brother to Brother: New Writings by Black Gay Men.* Ed. Essex Hemphill. Boston: Alyson, 1991. 253–257.

Roediger, David. *Towards the Abolition of Whiteness.* London: Verso, 1994.

Scott, Darieck. "Jungle Fever?: Black Gay Identity Politics, White Dick, and the Utopian Bedroom." *GLQ: A Journal of Lesbian & Gay Studies* 3 (1994): 299–32.

Scott, Joan V. "Experience." *Feminist Theorize the Political.* Eds. Judith Butler and Joan W. Scott. New York: Routledge, 1992. 22–40.

Sedgwick, Eve Kosofsky. "Queer and Now." *Tendencies.* Durham: Duke UP, 1993. 1–20.

Simmons, Ron. "Some Thoughts on the Issues Facing Black Gay Intellectuals." *Brother to Brother: New Writings by Black Gay Men.* Ed. Essex Hemphill. Boston: Alyson, 1991. 211–228.

Smith, Barbara. "Home." *Home Girls: A Black Feminist Anthology.* Ed. Barbara Smith. New York: Kitchen Table, 1983. 64–72.

———. "Toward a Black Feminist Criticism." *All the Women Are White, All the Blacks Are Men, But Some of Us Are Brave.* Eds. Gloria T. Hull, Patricia Bell Scott, and Barbara Smith. Old Westbury, NY: Feminist Press, 1982. 157–175.

Smith, Cherry. "What Is This Thing Called Queer?" *Material Queer: A LesBiGay Cultural Studies Reader.* Ed. Donald Morton. Boulder: Westview, 1996. 277–285.

Smith, Valerie. *Not Just Race, Not Just Gender: Making Feminist Readings.* New York: Routledge, 1998.

Strine, Mary. "Articulating Performance/Performativity: Disciplinary Tasks and the Contingencies of Practice." National Speech Communication Association Conference. San Diego, CA. November 1996.

Thomas, Calvin. "Straight with a Twist: Queer Theory and the Subject of Heterosexuality." *The Gay '90's: Disciplinary and Interdisciplinary Formations in Queer Studies.* Eds. Thomas Foster, Carol Siegel, and Ellen E. Berry. New York: NYU P, 1997. 83–115.

Turner, Victor. *The Anthropology of Performance.* New York: Performing Arts Journal, 1986.

Valente, Joseph. "Joyce's (Sexual) Choices: A Historical Overview." *Quare Joyce.* Ed. Joseph Valente. Ann Arbor: U of Michigan P, 1998. 1–18.

Walker, Alice. *In Search of Mothers' Gardens: Womanist Prose.* San Diego: Harcourt Brace Jovanovich, 1983.

Warner, Michael. Introduction. *Fear of a Queer Planet: Queer Politics and Social Theory.* Ed. Michael Warner. Minneapolis: U of Minnesota P, 1993. vii—xxxi.

Wilson, Angelia R. "Somewhere Over the Rainbow: Queer Translating." *Playing With Fire: Queer Politics, Queer Theories.* Ed. Shane Phelan. New York: Routledge, 1997. 99–111.

Sharon Bridgforth

This excerpt from performance artist Sharon Bridgforth's performance novel, *Love Conjure/Blues*, illustrates the beauty of a Black queer world. The characters in the following piece are in a junk joint in the Black South. This joint is filled with lively personas who are trans, straight, queer, and more. The rhetorical impulses at work seek to establish queer lives as central to Black identity and cultural struggles.

Love Conjure/Blues

Sharon Bridgforth[1]

throw in a word when slim take a breath.
probably is all slim really want after all
somebody to listen
talk for a bit.
anyway
we all know
slim call himself running a ho house
but slim ain't running nothing or nobody.
so the place he call figure's flavors/we calls it
bettye's.
yessuh/cause slim's sister bettye be the one running
that jernt.
and what it is is the best blues inn in the country.
first off bettye know how to keep a clean room
so the stopovers always be happy/feel rested and cared
for
but more important/bettye can cook so gotdamngood
make you want to kick your own ass. i trying to watch
see if bettye been throwed some powders off in them
pots/make
the cooking so much excitement
for the tastes.
anyway
chile/musicians from states away haul they music over
to bettye's just
to be up in there get some. don't even charge bettye
to play/course na
some of them tasting more than good cooking from
bettye.
look like her favorites be extra fed. but they all of
them gets tips meals and a room/long as they willing to
work/and play hard.
and do the jernt be packed!
mens womens some that is both some that is neither/be
rolling all up and between the sounds/laying up in
them rent rooms/and dancing off all bettye's home
cooking.

anyway
it was a hot night after a hot day.
the peoples was in they finest/fresh pressed and set for
whatever bettye's was about to bring. it was rib night
the start of the weekend. folk was still eyes bright
hearts light pockets packed full of laughter/and on the
ready.
that night was a wo'mn named big bill what rose up out
of bettye's room.
big bill had on the finest suit i have seen to this day.
come in with she suit black/hat low/glasses dark/and
shoes so shining make your head hurt. big bill walk
through
the crowd part/as she make way to the piano in the
corner of the room.
big bill's long legs reach strong
one powerful in front the other/her unbuttoned jacket
open close open close
as she walk/pants pull here here
here
material ripple across she crotch which appear
packing a large and heavy surprise i glance over to
bettye/see she seeing too/smiling down where big bill
pants pull and ripple large/and not so subtle in the
crotch. bettye fanning
still sweat run all around her face.
i ain't got time be looking at bettye/look back
big bill taking she jacket off/take she hat off/slowly roll
up one crisp sleeve/then the other/loosen she tie/turn
her big broad back to the room/sit down/and ever so
slightly nodd she nappy head. at that guitar sam pull
up take a chair next to she. big bill nodd again even
more slight/and a big ole powerful sample of wo'mness
stroll center the room. sway step smile sway step smile
sway sway she went till she in place standing center
inside a moment of stillness. then suddenly/the three
of them hit a note
all at the same time/*aaaaaaawwwwwwhhhhhh*
went the sound and i declare some kind of hunger-
spirit swept through the room.
took everybody's mind in one swoop.
after that
wasn't nothing but bodies feeding the feeling till
sunday sunrise just before first service. shiiit. we still
rest-broken from all that business.
big mama sway/singing

  i gots geechee lips
  i gots geechee hips

i gots a geechee kiss
that you'll never forget
but you got to
show me that you want it
show me that you need/so
if you can't show me that you want it
go on/pack your thangs and go.

chile
what a time.
something about they sound almost stop my heart.
i knew it weren't the liquor
cause wasn't nothing in my cup but that
strong-ass coffee bettye serve/which could been
overwork my heart/but i don't think so.
see/bettye don't allow no drinking in she jernt.
not since she lost her first love lushy boudreaux to the
guzzle.
naw/lushy ain't dead
thats her yonder holding up the back of the jernt.
bettye lost lushy from she bed when she kicked that
drunk ass out one last time.
been upset about that ever since. mostly at herself/say
she got so caught up loving what lushy could have
been/she wouldn't see what lushy really was.
anyway
lushy don't drink no more/bettye don't like the smell
of the drink/reminding her of the hard times/so we all
forced stay in our right minds when we come to bettye's
well not all of us/cause you know any fool can
find a way to tilt they cup if they want to. but
bettye's no liquor rule do cut down on the free
flowingness of it
which is a relief really
because usually with the drinking come the looking and
the looking bring the knives/cause folk can't just look at
they own peoples they gots to always cast a looking at
somebody's somebody else/and the knives bring the
cussing and the cussing bring the swoll chest and the
swoll chest
always
interrupt the good time.
but the good time don't hardly get stopped at bettye's

Note

1. Sharon Bridgforth, *Love Conjure/Blues* (Washington, D.C.: RedBone Press, 2004), pp. 9–11.

David Malebranche

In this short but pointed essay, David Malebranche takes up the figure of the "down low brotha," the construction within the public imagination of a Black man who had sex with men while often having a wife/girlfriend. Looking closely at the field of public health, he dispels the prominence of this enigmatic Black man spreading AIDS in the Black community. Using the idea of "black dick as weapon of mass destruction," he uncovers the power of this "down low" narrative and offers a pointed critique of its role in crafting public mythology and dangerous data.

The Black Dick as a Weapon of Mass Destruction: George Bush, Oprah Winfrey, "Down Low," and the Politics of HIV Blame

David Malebranche, MD, MPH[1]

The most amazing feat that George Bush has pulled off in the past four years is convincing the country that his current "War on Iraq" is actually analogous to the "War on Terror," with little evidence of a connection between Iraq and Al-Qaeda. First we were looking for "weapons of mass destruction," then when we couldn't find them, it became "Operation: Iraqi Freedom"; now it's the "War on Terror," since we have supposedly succeeded in "freeing" Iraq. If you haven't taken this class already, it's called "Marketing a War 101."

The state of our country post-9/11 has been so preoccupied with fear and blame that it has been relatively easy for the Bush administration to blur distinctions between the foreign faces of the "enemy" and brainwash people to believe that we are actually "safer" now that hundreds of our troops have died in Iraq, airport security is tighter than ever, billions of dollars have been spent on improving our armed forces, and since we have captured Saddam Hussein. But are we really "safer" now than before 9/11? And can we really point the finger at one person, organization or political administration to ease our collective conscious on why thousands of Americans had to needlessly in the World Trade Center bombings? Who is to blame for these atrocities?

I thought about all these dynamics as I watched the Oprah Winfrey show last week. For those of you who missed it, Oprah did a show about "Down Low" black men, or as the current textbook definition states, "a man who lives a 'heterosexual' lifestyle (whatever that means), but has sex with men on the side." On the show, Oprah showcased the current George Bush of HIV prevention, JL King, who is currently trying to promote media hype for the May 11th release of his upcoming book "Living on the Down Low." The show was filled with misquoted HIV statistics, sensationalistic rhetoric, and showcased this man who reportedly was previously married with kids, but had sex with men on the side, but now has "courageously" come forward to expose this "secret" world of underground sex.

They interviewed other "Down Low" brothers who were HIV positive, portraying them as hedonistic predators without morals or ethics as they carelessly navigated through the sexual landscape of America, infecting any and all comers. Oprah then lamented the fact that of all current AIDS cases among women in the United States, 72% are among black women. And of course the main reason that black women were getting HIV nowadays was because of this elusive "Down Low" brutha, who has sex with men, but refuses to admit he is "gay," thereby causing him to have unprotected sex. Makes sense, right?

For those of you who answered "yes" to that last question, you probably have been caught up in all the media blame game around "Down Low" black men and HIV in the black community, similar to the way Neo believed the life messages programmed into his brain in the movie "The Matrix." So let me play Morpheus for a minute. From articles in Jet, Ebony, Essence, the New York Times and the Washington Post, to featured stories on news and popular syndicated programs such as "ER," "Law and Order: Special Victims Unit," and "Soul Food," pathologizing this mythi-cal "Down Low" black man as the "vector" of HIV transmission in the black community has become the topic du jour. Here's the template for all these media stories: "black man has same sex desires, confused over identifying as 'gay' for fear of compromising his hyper-heterosexual black manhood, maliciously chooses to have unprotected sex with men secretly while being married or with a girlfriend and having unprotected sex with her, gets HIV and transmits it to unsuspecting victimized female sexual partner, and either dies or murders gay lover in a fit of self-hatred and rage." Yes, ladies and gentleman, the current vessel of HIV transmission in this country has become the insatiable black dick—preying on unsuspecting women, men, anyone it can hunt down, and refusing to take precautions to protect against HIV. Essentially, the take home message is that these "Down Low" black men as hypersexualized beings who don't think rationally, and are so mired in a cesspool of self-hate over their primal homosexual urges that they take the entire black community down with them. According to many media outlets, this is a "good story" that sells papers.

Unfortunately, the American preoccupation with the sexualizing and demonizing of the black dick has been a staple of American culture since the days of slavery, where the 2 major masculine roles for black men were to "work" and "breed." We all know the stereotypes of the mythical Mandingo with the 12 inch dick and the insatiable appetite for screwing women (specifically white women), which inspired a 1970s movie of the same name starring Ken Norton. White slavemasters hung black male slaves out of irrational fear that they were trying to rape their wives.

Recent history has exposed our preoccupation with this image of black manhood through the real-life court TV drama biographies of OJ Simpson, Mike Tyson and Kobe Bryant. Most people in America, black or white, understand fully that when it comes to charging a black man with sexual misconduct or rape, we are guilty until proven innocent. Today, overzealous white police officers promote racial profiling and beat innocent black boys and men on a daily basis because of their fear and loathing of the so-called sexual and physical prowess of black men. Young black high school athletes in Georgia are put in jail for having consensual sex with white girls because they do it in the wrong city at the wrong time (see Marcus Dixon), and the sexuality and physicality of black male athletes are paraded around in media endorsements and professional NBA and NFL drafts like so many slaves sold for labor at the auction block. Don't get it twisted, the black dick in all its masculine and sexual glory is to be celebrated when it can be used for the entertainment and economic advancement of the white community, but con-demned when it is actually used for its anatomical purpose: having sex and procreating. Or God forbid extends its repertoire to developing a brain and critical thinking to accompany the sexual myth. Now that's really scary.

And so we come to the current "War on HIV" that is currently being fought in this country, with black men being the convenient scapegoat. Despite not having any concrete statistics on this elusive and ephemeral "Down Low" population of black men, Oprah and other media out-lets have confidently misstated that down low bruthas are the "major reason why black women are getting HIV." They parade a couple of examples of black women who got infected while hav-ing sex with a husband or male partner who had sex with men on the side, and then they create the "face" for HIV in the black community. And similar to the "deck of cards" that George Bush and his less-than-clever staff came up with to personalize (and trivialize) who we are fighting against, so has the war against black men who don't identify as "gay" been created, and a similar parade of faces like JL King and other characters are shown in every media outlet possible. You identify a group of people in the midst of tough emotional and economic times (the American people or heterosexual black women), and you give them a face or profile of someone they can blame (any Middle Eastern Muslim male or the "Down Low" brutha). He is the reason for your problems. He is the cause of your sickness. He is the one we are fighting against. And voila! Instant fear, instant outrage, instant division, instant war, instant excuses.

Unfortunately, the majority of public health and behavioral research doesn't support the theory of "Down Low" black men as the "bridge" of HIV to the general black community. In fact, reports from the Centers for Disease Control and Prevention (CDC) and other public health studies have demonstrated that black men who are either bisexual or don't disclose their homosexuality (i.e., "in the closet) report using condoms with anal sex more than black men who solely identify as "gay" or are "out of the closet." And when one closely examines the popularly quoted statistic of "one out of every three black men who have sex with men are HIV positive," it becomes clear that these studies were conducted predominantly with "gay" identified black men who were recruited at popular "gay" social spots in major metropolitan cities. Those of us who do HIV research know for a fact that we currently have no studies on so-called "Down Low" black men, just studies on black men recruited from "gay" venues who may have checked their sexuality on a survey as "bisexual" or "heterosexual." But does that necessarily make them "Down Low?" How is it that we aren't talking about men of other ethnicities who engage in the same discreet homosexual behavior? Why isn't there outrage over HIV ravaging the black "gay" community? And why have the facts of HIV transmission among black men and between black men and women been obscured in favor of sensationalistic rhetoric claiming that "Down Low" bruthas are fanning the flames of HIV in the black community? These, my friends, are the million dollar questions that no one appears willing to try to answer.

Without caring about the context of how black men are getting HIV, our society has deemed the "Down Low" brutha as the "vector of transmission" from the black homosexual community to the black straight community, similar to the way a mosquito transmits malaria to its host. The black male population that is currently being decimated by HIV/AIDS has been conveniently swept under the carpet as a side note between epidemics that previously plagued white gay men and now plague black women. It is easier for the white gay community to demonize black men who don't adopt a "gay" identity and "come out of the closet," for it allows them to avoid looking in the mirror at their own pathological behaviors of circuit parties, testosterone, ecstasy and Viagra abuse, as well as current barebacking parties that are currently refueling syphilis and HIV outbreaks in their own community. And its easier for black women to pathologize and blame "Down Low" bruthas for the current HIV epidemic among black women, for it takes them away for examining the issues of low self-esteem, substance abuse, teenage pregnancy, loneliness, pressure to get married and poor condom negotiation skills that are equally relevant explanations for the behaviors that may be fueling the HIV crisis they are facing as well. Yet we continue to eat our "freedom fries," brainlessly post American flags on our cars and say that terrorists are "jealous of our freedom" to mask our reluctance to acknowledge the role of irresponsible and arrogant United States foreign policy history in developing al Quida and feelings of anti-American sentiment that are prevalent around the world.

George Bush focuses on distorting the truth about "weapons of mass destruction" and changing colors of "terror alert" on a monthly basis to divert our attention from the fact that we are living in a country with unprecedented national debt, unemployment, crumbling educational and health institutions, and increasing divisions among our people based primarily on race, culture and class. Similarly, we seem to be preoccupied distorting the truth about and blaming "Down Low" black men for the current HIV epidemic in the black community to divert our attention from the real "down low" issues we are facing: oppression, racism, low self-esteem, trauma, sexual abuse, substance abuse, joblessness, hopelessness and despair. Sorry, people, the black dick is not an elusive "weapon of mass destruction" that public health officials can send inspectors around to uncover in covert areas. And "Down Low" bruthas (and all black men for that matter) are more than mindless black dicks. The time for irrational fear-based HIV prevention tactics is over. We need more than a few George Bush wannabees unintelligently stirring the collective pot of our fears and insecurities if we are to win this war.

Note

1. David Malebranche, "The Black Dick as a Weapon of Mass Destruction," (Unpublished Manuscript, 2005).

Mirielle Miller-Young

Mirielle Miller-Young offers the Black female pornography artist as a work agent from whom we can learn much about labor, sexual subjectivity, and processes of consumption. This essay challenges the idea that bodies in pornographic space are always repugnant or without agency but rather are sites of complex possibilities and productions. Miller-Young's attention to this nonnormative setting, as well as the nonnormative body, allows her to trace the "illicit erotic"—a formation that works against "respectable" sexual politics.

Hip-Hop Honeys and Da Hustlaz: Black Sexualities in the New Hip-Hop Pornography

Mireille Miller-Young[1]

Hip-hop pornography propels the conventions of the nearly soft-core hip-hop video to the extreme, the explicit, the hard-core. The convergence of the outlaw cultures of hip-hop and pornography offers a compelling narrative about how black sexual subjects define authority, legitimacy, legibility, and power. Hip-hop porn provides black women and men an arena for labor and accumulation as well as self-presentation, mediation, and mobility. As a space for work, survival, consumption, and identity-formation, the genre proffers an opportunity to explore the gendering of black (post)modern desires, as well as the potential to think through historical echoes of the current controversies and debates around exactly what constitutes "appropriate" black sexuality. Even as it offers a venue for acts of self-representation, pleasure, and exchange, hip-hop porn's brand of eroticism raises important questions about contemporary black gender and sexual politics. Within the space of hip-hop porn, these gender and sexual politics are produced within a sexual economy of illicit eroticism. The "illicit erotic" challenges ideas that fix the hypersexuality of the black body as always already repugnant, by using fetishized hypersexuality to strategically work with and through modern capitalism. This essay is primarily concerned with exploring how black sexual subjects engage illicit erotic economies as sites to self-fashion themselves according to the values and practices of "radical consumerism," "play-labor," and self-or counter-fetishization.

From *Hot Chocolate* (1984) to *Desperate Blackwives* (2005), during the last twenty years black sexuality has been increasingly incorporated into the production of modern hard-core pornography in the United States. The pornography business began to appropriate black culture and black bodies in the late nineteenth century in the secret trade of erotic photography and "stag" films, but the modern adult entertainment industry has used hip-hop culture as a primary tool for the development of a specialized fetish market for black sexuality in hard-core video since the 1990s. Meanwhile, the hip-hop industry has also become increasingly interested in exploiting pornographic codes and accessing the pornography industry's broad marketing of subversive sexualities to consumers at revenues of ten to fourteen billion dollars a year (O'Toole 1999; Rich 2001; Business Wire 2005; Free Speech Coalition 2006).

From the hip-hop-influenced adult video series *My Baby Got Back* to the recent celebrity-focused hip-hop porn productions, such as Snoop Dog's *Doggystyle* and *Hustlaz: Diary of a Pimp*, hip-hop and pornography have partnered to commodify black sexuality in a new genre form, employing black women's bodies as the hard currency of exchange. The result has been a lucrative synthesis that has brought fans of both media together as consumers, while lining the pockets of music and adult industry business-people. They have observed the coming together of genres, as well as the broader "pornification" of hip-hop and the mainstreaming and "diversification" of pornography, with the glee of robber barons. As one adult industry critic observed: "Hip Hop and porn are a natural marriage; from underground traditions and celebrating outlaw lifestyles, they have both become the source of eye-popping profits for savvy investors" (Weasels n.d.).

Hip-hop music videos, as advertisements for hip-hop artists or entertainers, have been the principal location for a growing pornographic sensibility that functions to market black bodies, aesthetics, and culture to a global consumer audience. These commercials-to-a-beat have been essential for the expansive financial success of corporate television media, including Viacom's MTV, VH1, and BET, "bling" lifestyle products and brands (De Beers, General Motors, Louis Vuitton Moet Hennessy—LVMH), and for quite a few rappers as well as others in the industry such as music video directors, producers, agents, designers, stylists, and film crews. Yet the tremendous wealth produced for all these "players" in the hip-hop "game" rests largely on the pornographic performance of the "video model," sometimes known as the "video ho."[2] She is the "eye candy" that sells the rapper, the products of his supposed "lifestyle," and finally, the song, with every wiggle of her body, sway of her hips, and glisten of her skin. Indeed, there is a widely shared consensus that "many hip-hop videos are very nearly soft-core porn already, and they wouldn't be the same without the everpresent [sic] background of rump-shakin', booty-quakin' honeys" (Weasels n.d.).

Hip-hop porn propels the conventions of the "nearly soft-core" hip-hop video to the extreme, the explicit, the hard-core. If porn and hip-hop are both, as the critic above stated, "underground traditions" and "outlaw cultures," the convergence of these forms offers a compelling narrative about authority, legitimacy, legibility, and power. Hip-hop porn provides black women and men an arena for labor and accumulation as well as self-presentation, mediation, and mobility. As a space for work, survival, consumption, and identity-formation, the genre proffers an opportunity to explore the gendering of black (post)modern desires, as well as the potential to think through historical echoes of the current controversies and debates around what exactly constitutes "appropriate" black sexuality. In addition, even as it offers a venue for acts of self-representation and exchange, hip-hop porn's brand of eroticism raises important questions about contemporary black gender and sexual politics.

Hip-hop femininities and masculinities are subject to market concerns of white supremacist, patriarchal, multinational, corporate capitalism and are positioned as marginal to the means of material production and institutional political power. It is thus the close attention to the race-gender-sex-class reconstitution of hip-hop identities that makes the genre form of hip-hop pornography legible. Yet what also needs to be teased out is how these hip-hop identities are defined as well by black cultural investments in authentic, ever subversive, and pleasure-giving performances, visualities, and soundscapes (Kelley 1994; Rose 1994). How do we account for the ways in which pleasure intersects with politics, identity, and power?

The convergence of hip-hop and porn illuminates the constructions and fissures of black femininity, but also black masculinity, as it engages the myths and fascinations of black sexual deviance (Crenshaw 1991; Rose 2001). Particularly revealing is the productive dependence on black women, specifically their sexualized bodies, by black men in authenticating their claims and representations of manhood. Black women's excessive and accessible heterosexuality as performed in hard-core and soft-core hip-hop acts as a signifier that undergirds the performance of black hypermasculinity (Sharpley-Whiting 2007). At the same time, black video models and sex workers mobilize their sexualities in the marketplace of desire for their own interests of access, opportunity, mobility, and fame (Hopkinson and Moore 2006). Within the space of hip-hop porn, these gender politics are produced within what I argue is a sexual economy of *illicit eroticism*.

The illicit erotic economy symbolically and strategically produces gender identities *through* the commodification and manipulation of private (sex) acts. These identities are reflective of the historical engagement by African Americans with underground, illegal, and quasi-legal economies—from gambling to prostitution and beyond—which offered marginalized ways to survive and prosper within the U.S. political economy (Harley 2002). But more than a continuation of survival skills, illicit eroticism is an attempt to refigure the racial logic of sexual respectability and normativity.

In this essay I outline how both mainstream and African American hetero-patriarchal discourses have been mediated by the hybrid medium of hip-hop porn, and pose questions as to what extent the representations and labor politics of this emergent genre expand the tradition of fetishizing black sexuality as a site of desire and disgust, expression and exploitation, subjectivity and objectification. As hip-hop porn is an emerging genre that is still in flux, its meanings and characteristics still undetermined, I offer notes toward a theory of how hip-hop and porn intersect and interact and what they mean for black sexual politics in this contemporary moment.

Considering the global dominance of hip-hop music and culture in the current moment (in 2006, hip-hop music earned $1.3 billion, 11.4% of the music market),[3] how does capital's circulations of black culture impact the currency of black masculinities and femininities? Moreover, how does hip-hop porn, in its production and reception, violate taboos in black communities about sexual disclosure that are rooted in discourses of heteronormative bourgeois respectability? This project challenges what Mattie Udora Richardson describes as "[t]he tradition of representing black people as decent and moral historical agents," as it has "meant the erasure of the broad array of black sexuality and gendered being in favor of a static heterosexual narrative" (Richardson 2003, 64).

Anxieties

There is a profound anxiety within "the black community" over the moral and political value of contemporary mainstream hip-hop cultural production.[4] This anxiety is reflective of a tendency toward viewing certain youth subcultures in the African diaspora, including hip-hop but also dancehall, soukous, kwaito, and parkour, as dangerous, immoral, even pathological. David Scott's discussion of dancehall, which, like American hip-hop, is seen by some as a "disturbing mirror of contemporary Jamaican society," is insightful. Like hip-hop, dancehall constitutes, Scott argues, "simultaneously a social site and an ensemble of cultural practices that circulate around music and dance; it is at once a venue (where the popular is constituted and performed) and a style of (sartorial and linguistic) self-fashioning" (Scott 1999, 191–92).

Moreover, according to Scott, dancehall in Jamaica is perceived to embody "debased values— values that openly embrace materialism, hedonism, and violence," instead of those of the church, the family, and other institutions that have "lost their moral authority" (Scott 1999, 192). Like dancehall in Jamaica, hip-hop in the U.S. context is a deeply contested social site for music and dance (among other cultural expressions like graffiti art). Perceived to embrace "materialism, hedonism, and violence," hip-hop proffers a space where the self is constantly refashioned and performed in ways that subvert bourgeois values or responsibility, sexual propriety, and decency. Referencing Foucault, Scott argues that this self-fashioning is a "practice of freedom," whereby "the subject deliberately acts upon the self in an effort to alter the dimensions already imposed upon it, to reconstitute the energies already shaped by existing relations of power" (Scott 1999, 213–14; see also Foucault 1986). Reading hip-hop through Scott and Foucault, one can understand the culture as a space where participants radically recuperate subjectivities that are both at odds with and shaped by hegemonic power.

What exactly are the anxieties that hip-hop and porn provoke in this contemporary moment? Is the black middle-class establishment anxious over its inability to discipline the bodies of hip-hop hustlers and ho's into a "patriarchal model of the bourgeois family as the cornerstone for [African American and] U.S. social, economic, and political progress" of which Daniel Patrick

Moynihan would be proud (Ross 1998, 603)? Are the unseen, border sexualities of the hip-hop porn world frighteningly unobservant of the dangers to black bodies, such as the pandemic of HIV/AIDS as it ravages the black population throughout the African Diaspora? Do the apparent misogyny and violence against women, represented in much of contemporary hip-hop media, subsume the possibilities for non-coercive consent and even pleasure by the women in such productions?

Not a simple story of domination or liberation, hard-core hip-hop practitioners and black pornography workers both challenge and are constituted by the racialized, gendered, and sexualized terms of representation in pornography and hip-hop, as they negotiate ways to strategically *re-present* themselves as subjects of fetishistic desire. Nonetheless, can the exploitations of fetishization and commodification be subverted through the politics of self-fashioning and *counter-fetishization* (or what I view as self-authored fetishization) by black sexual subjects? Could the hip-hop porn genre be critically conceived as a productive space of pleasure and desire attempting to transgress or problematize what Celine Parreñas Shimizu terms the "bind of representation?" "To assume that sexuality gives bad impressions of racial subjects," Parreñas Shimizu suggests, "keeps us from looking at how these images critique normative subjectivities" (Parreñas Shimizu 2005, 248). How do hip-hop porn representations critique normativity and respectability in black sexual politics, even as they perhaps comply with hegemonic codifications? Can our analyses "move beyond a one-dimensional understanding of sexual representation as always already injurious, dangerous, and damaging" while taking stock of the ways in which hip-hop has been accountable for the iconographic and material sexual abuse of black women (Parreñas Shimizu 2005, 248)?

Sexual Revolutions

Historically, the pornography industry has been both a venue for the production of sexual culture and for the mobilization of sexual labor. Pornography acts as a racialized economy of desire that is intensely policed and regulated by state and social apparatuses, but that is also widely consumed by all Americans, especially white middle-class men, as well as men of color. A powerful fascination with racial difference as sexual performance underlines how pornography acts as, Laura Kipnis points out, acts as a form of "political theater" where social and cultural ideologies of desire and taboo are staged and manipulated, as sexual norms and categories are simultaneously upheld and transgressed (Kipnis 1999, 164). Because pornography functions as a "festival of social infractions," its "allegories of transgression reveal, in the most visceral ways, not only our culture's edges, but how intricately our own identities are bound up in all of these quite unspoken, but relentless, cultural dictates" (Kipnis 1999, 167). The fascination with racial difference penetrates and organizes multiple levels of power in ways that are at once subtle and extreme, covert and overt, and thoroughly bound to a historical imaginary of black sexuality as inevitably the marker of deviance and the problematic of interracial desire (Williams 2004).

Within this context of the creation and management of racialized desire as both transgressive and policed, pornography has excelled at the production, marketing, and dissemination of categories of difference as special subgenres and fetishes in a form of "racialized political theater." Empowered by technological innovations such as video, camcorders, cable, satellite, digital broadband, CD-ROMs, DVDs, and the internet, the pornography business has exploited new media technology in the creation of a range of specialized sexual commodities that are consumed in the privacy of the home. The reorientation of pornography as consumed in male-only spaces during the early "stag" film era and public theatrical venues during the "golden era" of film pornography in the 1970s to the private consumption of the video and digital eras prompted the profound transformation of the political economy of the adult entertainment industry (Williams 1999; Slade 2000). Moreover, domestic consumption allowed the massive industrialization of racial fetishism in hard-core, including black and interracial heterosexual porn, because it vitally transformed the viewer's relationship to taboo sites of desire and fantasy. As a result of these technological developments, according to feminist film and pornography theorist Constance Penley, viewers could "find out what their own fantasies [were] and what [were] the limits of their fantasies" ("Part 5" 1999). Hence, technology enabled spectators of hard-core to explore the limits and boundaries of their desires, at precisely the point where taboo fantasies of interracial sex acts were situated in the American mass psychic imaginary.

Black performers, who have been depicted in pornographic media for over one hundred years, began to be professionalized as porn actors in the 1980s with the creation of black and interracial porn as specialized economies within hard-core. In hard-core fantasies of race, they were marginalized within the productive visual and political economies of the industry, and were featured only as actors, rather than as directors, producers, manufacturers, distributors, or retailers. Generally not employed in the mainstream and primarily white pornography genre of "features"—defined by more complicated plot schemes and higher production values—black performers were usually segregated into more marginal black and interracial video genres. Because the black and interracial genres were treated as a sideline to the industry, the producers did not mind cheapening many facets of the production—including the time for filming, crew, set design, equipment, and support and funding for the cast. Therefore the growth in available jobs for black women and men in the black and interracial fetish market was tempered by the broad racial segregation and devaluation of the videos. Hip-hop porn has allowed more opportunities for black performers in pornography to gain work opportunities, including in acting and filmmaking; nevertheless, the now popular genre sustains the segregation of the performers from the mainstream, more lucrative and dominant segment of the adult industry. Hence the representation of black and interracial sexualities and bodies continues to exist in a somewhat separate sphere than normative white sexual economies in hard-core, and as a consequence, these sexualities maintain the emblem of racial difference as a border, outlaw, and deviant economy of desire.

During the late 1980s and early 1990s pornography began to infiltrate mainstream media representations and sexual culture, and so did hip-hop. In fact, popular media's appropriation of hip-hop music inspired the adult industry to seize upon the currency of the urban black cultural movement. Video Team, one of the most successful black and interracial film production companies (now owned by Vivid), was probably the first company to capitalize on the mainstreaming of hip-hop with *In Loving Color* (1990), an interracial sex spoof based on the popular Wayans Brothers' hip-hop-influenced comedy television show *In Living Color*. Video Team followed the video's success with the all-black genre series *My Baby Got Back* (1992–2007), named after the controversial Sir Mix-a-Lot rap song *Baby Got Back* (1991). As Sir Mix-a-Lot raps, "I like big butts," the song celebrates black women's voluptuous butts as symbols of desirability and beauty, a radical revision of the historical representation of black women's butts as loci of their deviance and hypersexuality vis à vis the trope of the "Hottentot Venus." The music video provides an alternative iconography, where the round posteriors of black women dancers and enormous sculptures of brown butts are figured both as trumping normative (white) beauty standards and as sites of intense desire from black and white men alike (Hobson 2003, 95–96).

Since both pornography and hip-hop elicit complex responses of desire and disgust, pleasure and danger, and as illicit erotic economies embrace deviance, transgression, and subversion of sexual codes of decency, they have been similarly policed and regulated by the state. Nevertheless, both have been eagerly consumed in public and private contexts alike. The massive appeal of hip-hop as a subversive, urban, youth-oriented cultural form attracted pornographers interested in expanding their markets—historically focused mainly on white men—to urban men of color. Christian Mann, former president of Video Team, explained his interest in engaging hip-hop in the development of black pornography:

> I came up with a video called *My Baby Got Back*. Just a slight variation on the [original song] title. And it was going to be about butt worship! And the video went through the roof! We had a front box cover that was similar to the photograph that 2 Live Crew used for their *Nasty as They Want to Be* CD. It was really the first intersection of hip-hop marketing and pornography, I believe.
>
> (Mann 2002)

With the rise to popularity of rap music in the early 1990s, Mann, among other producers, tapped into the frenzy by marketing hip-hop-oriented porn to a growing urban black and Latino consumer base. Mann references 2 Live Crew, a rap group that garnered intense controversy when their album *As Nasty as They Want to Be* and live performances were prosecuted for obscenity in 1990. 2 Live Crew also sparked a national debate, including among black intellectuals, as to whether the music constituted unadulterated misogyny against black women, as charged by black feminists like Kimberlé Crenshaw, or the cultural signifying of black men as a vernacular tradition, as argued by black literary scholar Henry Louis Gates, Jr. (Sharpley-Whiting 2007, 61–63). That Video Team's *My Baby Got Back* video series was inspired by the likes of Sir Mix-a-Lot and 2 Live Crew with their ultra-popular and lucrative exploitations of black women's bodies, specifically their derrières, is not surprising, given the widespread popularity, controversy, and salaciousness of these rappers at the time.

White pornographers were acutely interested in how black men consumed images of black women—how they fetishized them in popular culture—so that they could expand their market beyond the standard white male consumers who generally purchased adult tapes featuring black sexuality. Christian Mann argues that the hip-hop-oriented black porn genre that he was instrumental in developing was fashioned to cater to the specific libidinal desires of black male consumers:

> I believed this interest in black women with large butts was something that was being fueled by black men's interest and was about black men wanting to see black women . . . . I didn't think it made sense to have these women with white guys . . . . All-black video is marketed to black consumers. Interracial video is more likely marketed to white men who like black women.
>
> (Mann 2002)

Mann's comment underscores how significant hip-hop's *counter-fetishization* of black women's butts is to this story. Long a symbol of deviant, repulsive, and grotesque black sexuality and black womanhood (recall the "Hottentot Venus"), black women's rear ends became newly fetishized through hip-hop music in ways that sought to recognize, reclaim, and reify their bodies as desirable, natural, and attractive. Mann also points to the ways in which black women's bodies featured in hard-core functioned to define markets for white and black male consumers. Reflecting the dominant belief in the adult business that men prefer to identify with male performers of their own race in hard-core movies, we begin to see how hip-hop became an effective tool for white pornographers to create a separate and parallel economy for "all-black" sexualities. This process occurred over time, whereas in the early 1990s, even hip-hop-influenced racialized titles like *Girlz in Da Hood 1* (1991), *Booty Ho* (1993), *Booty in the House* (1994), and *Booty By Nature* (1994) were all interracial (black–white) videos that not only included white men, but also white women. However, during the late 1990s it seems that much more segregation emerged, where such titles as *Ghetto Girlz* (1996), *Bootylicious 10: Ghetto Booty* (1996), *Girlz in Da Hood 7* (1997), and *Booty Talk 1* (1998), demarcated films where black women were the primary attraction.

During this period, commercial hip-hop came under the influence of west coast gangsta rap, with the enormous popularity of artists like N.W.A., Ice T, and Snoop Doggy Dogg. The adult entertainment industry, located just miles from the black working-class post-industrial landscape of south central Los Angeles, was influenced by the trend. Adult companies like Video Team and Heatwave exploited the gangster trend and produced a sub-genre often referred to as "ghetto porn." Ghetto porn was hip-hop-influenced hard-core that glamorized representations of the inner city, poverty, gangsta life, pimping, and whores. The tapes, like *South Central Hookers* (1997–2002), usually posed black women performers as prostitutes and constructed sets to romanticize the "hood," with bars on the windows, graffiti walls, trash-strewn concrete floors, and garbage cans arranged decoratively around a profusion of black women's butts. This ghetto fantasy signifies white production companies' attempts to authenticate black sexuality on screen for black, but also presumably white, male audiences, with seeming icons of the ghetto, including black women as street prostitutes.

The desire to maintain and legitimize the hyperaccessibility of black women's bodies to the sexual needs of men, while simultaneously iconographically devaluing those bodies, is illustrated in the cooptation of hip-hop as a space for the articulation and visualization of black sexualities. Black men in these videos are often gangsters, and white men the businessmen or pornographers who go to and then find in the ghetto experienced prostitutes or young unassuming women (portrayed by professional porn actresses) for sexual encounters. Sometimes guns are used as props, and there is conflict or violence invoked (though never actuated on the women; it's usually between men) to charge the scene and mark the fantasy as authentic and "ghetto." However, the performance of violent hip-hop masculinities and degraded femininities is marked by its mimetic, voyeuristic quality—it's a poor, even comedic, imitation by bad actors. Yet what it does is reveal the scopic desires of pornographers and consumers for "the 'ghetto' [as] a place of adventure, unbridled violence, erotic fantasy, and/or an imaginary alternative to suburban boredom" (Kelley 1994, 181).

Pimp/Stud: Performing Black Masculinity

Hip-hop is the main form of legibility for black American culture in this contemporary moment, one that has diasporic and global effects. The massive popularity of mainstream hip-hop, which celebrates an anti-establishment, outlaw aesthetic, and largely defines itself as a masculinist, commodified terrain of cultural production, has prompted porn companies to go further than merely referencing the form. They noticed the hypersexualization of hip-hop videos and the intense controversy the form has continued to garner, and as a result set their eyes on acquiring actual rappers for an emergent genre of celebrity hip-hop hard-core videos. Of course, the rappers were also looking to hard-core for an opportunity to expand their entrepreneurial interests and illicit erotic desires. Rappers like Tupac Shakur, whose 1996 soft-core music video "How Do You Want It" featured legendary porn stars Heather Hunter, Angel Kelly, Jeannie Pepper, and Nina Hartley, were willing to collaborate and cross over into the new realm of hip-hop celebrity pornification.[5] In the raunchy, largely misogynist tradition of rappers like Luke Campbell of 2 Live Crew (who once owned a black hard-core magazine called *Black Gold*, and had an interest in strip clubs of the same name in Miami), Larry Flynt's Hustler Productions collaborated with west coast rapper Snoop Doggy Dogg to make *Snoop Dogg's Doggystyle*, the highest selling hard-core video of 2001 (Salomon 2001; Edlund 2004).

"*Snoop Dogg's Doggystyle* is a prime example of how adult oriented erotic entertainment is crossing over into the mainstream," asserts Scott Schalin, former president of the (now defunct) adult internet company Interactive Gallery. Snoop's first video sold over 100,000 copies (outstanding by porn industry standards, where 4,000 copies sold is considered a success), and his second video, *Hustlaz: Diary of a Pimp* (2002), nearly matched that sales figure (Salomon 2001; Edlund 2004). Both won best-selling video awards from *Adult Video News* (AVN), the main adult industry trade publication, which suggests that the appeal was huge among white consumers as well as people of color, men and women (and is remarkable because so few "ethnic themed" videos win AVN awards). *Hustler* founder and publisher Larry Flynt revealed how pornographers identified and appreciated the outlaw nature of commercial hip-hop, which they also saw as an ideal cash cow: "The rappers have this 'don't give a damn' attitude which is great. They don't care who criticizes them for what. So it's been a pleasure working for Snoop and it's been a successful relationship for both of us" (Majors 2003).

Following the overwhelming success of the Snoop and Hustler Video collaboration, other companies like Video Team, Metro, and Heatwave jumped on the bandwagon, producing videos for Lil' Jon, Mystikal, Digital Underground, and G-Unit. Like ghetto porn productions of the all-black video genre, these celebrity-oriented videos purported to highlight raw, uneroticized sex, but with a hip-hop celebrity, hypercapitalist twist. They were situated within the fantastical lifestyle of famous rappers as they perform on the road or have raucous parties with a harem of sex workers—mostly real-life black women exotic dancers and porn stars—at multimillion-dollar estates. In fact, Snoop's *Doggystyle* was filmed at his home, lending a feel of authenticity to his claims for luxuriously authoritative player status. At the same time, his pimp/player performance is fraught with the impossibility of this fantasy; we know that this is not "real" life, at least of the everyday for these men (Shock G 2004). Yet the emphasis of these videos on the sexual bacchanal—as seen in the final orgy scene in *Hustlaz: Diary of a Pimp*, or the "Sex Olympics" scene in Digital Underground's *Sex and the Studio* (2003)—illuminates the contemporary significance of sexuality, specifically an abundant, unrestrained, and commodified sexuality, to black hypermasculinity as it is articulated through illicit eroticism.

The assumption of hip-hop performers' "celebrity lifestyles" as always already hard-core porn organizes the genre. The form is invested in the repetition of symbols and practices that reflect a kind of self-rendering by black men—specifically the rappers as co-producers of the videos—that engages hypermasculinity and illicit eroticism. Interestingly, the rappers conduct the show by playing "host" to the sexual narrative and sexual labor, but they do not perform sex acts within it. The rappers thus perform as pimps or players directing the sex workers; black male porn actors are "studs" and women (including women of color and white women, but primarily black women) are the "ho's." Therefore, the rappers in hip-hop porn objectify the bodies of black men and women in their self-representations of black masculine authority. Through their performances these men mobilize deviance as well as illicit eroticism to construct themselves through, and against, dominant discourses of black masculinity that render black men powerless in relation to white patriarchal hegemony (Gray 1995; Perry 2004).

The performance of hip-hop celebrity/pimp/player is a self-articulation that makes use of black men's outsider status and reframes it as an oppositional and autonomous masculinity that is defined by a consciously chosen hypersexuality. This complicated process of subject-formation actually participates in the historical use of the pimp, player, hustler, and badman figures as vernacular sites of identification and legibility for African American men (Kelley 1994; Perry 2004). According to Eithne Quinn, the pimp's symbolic lifestyle is very much about "impression management":

The affluent "pimp daddy" is preoccupied with the conspicuous display of material wealth . . . the commodification of women . . . by the supersexual pimp is recounted in the lewd vernacular. The dandified spectacle foregrounds the importance of impression management: naming . . . reputation . . . and recognition.

(Quinn 2000, 121–22)

Here black masculinity is invested in "conspicuous display" as a mode of sexual self-rendering and self-recognition. These rappers define their sexual agency in ways that diverge from the traditional black middle-class adherence to respectability as the only path to access, opportunity, and citizenship. Of course, this self-construction is tied to the performance of fantasy: fantasies of entrepreneurial empowerment, of sexual prowess, and of power over women and other men.

In hard-core pornography, rappers mobilize an illicit or "counter-public" site of self-definition, recognition, and desire in very public and lucrative ways (Cohen 2004). Lil' Jon, describing his *Lil' Jon and the Eastside Boyz Worldwide Sex Tour* (2004) reveals how the performance of celebrity lifestyle is tied to claims of hypersexual authenticity:

> Our shit is different because it's kind of like our lifestyle, like you are hanging out with us for the duration of the tape. You are hanging out with us, partying, wiling out, doing crazy shit, it's funny. And you got some good sex on the tape . . . . I mean sex is a part of every man's lifestyle nowadays. I'm just happy to be an entertainer. So I get more sex thrown at me than the average.

(Lil' Jon 2004)

These cultural productions reflect the ways in which we may view black masculinity as always performative, and as a mythology that is impossible for men to achieve (Johnson 2003). Rappers perform a kind of hypersexual black manhood, but cannot really "perform" as studs, because doing so means living up to an impossible "standard" (at least ten inches long) that very few men can achieve. These rappers prefer to perform the pimp or player, therefore, because performing the stud would open their performances up to critique and vulnerability.

Compulsory heterosexuality, fear of homoeroticism, and homophobia disallow desire to be gauged on their bodies (arousal of the phallus) and exposed. Hegemonic white masculinity defines black masculinities as non-normative, monstrous, dangerous, and feminized; these performances of hypermasculinity thus attempt to subvert such constructions by embracing them on one's own terms. This self-fashioning produces new spaces for desire and pleasure through counter-fetishization. Yet with regard to the notion of self-care in the Foucauldian sense, what are the implications of this for the community and for women?

While hip-hop porn rappers prefer not to perform the sexual labor on screen, black male sex workers are called upon to fill the role of stud. Proud descendants of Sweetback (the cocksman vigilante of Melvin Van Peeble's 1971 film *Sweet Sweetback's Baadasssss Song*), black men working in the pornography industry benefit from the fetishization of black masculine sexuality in popular culture, which has translated into a demand for their sexual labor in hard-core (Guerrero 1993). More successful at gaining investors and distribution contracts than black women sex workers, many of these actors have directed their own videos and video series and have started production companies, which address the desires of black male consumers and white male voyeurs of interracial genre video.[6]

The adult entertainment industry has taken on increasing significance for modern black life. As a space for labor, consumption, networking, leisure, and sociality, the strip club has also become a particularly significant site of late, and this has been reflected in hip-hop music, cultural production, and music videos (Sharpley-Whiting 2007). Nelly's controversial music video[7] for "Tipdrill" represents the fluidity of pornography, strip club, and rap video conventions. Set in a sprawling mansion and filled with more than fifty black women exotic dancers in bikinis, the video, like most rap videos that signify the benefits of heterosexist playerdom, proffers a sense of luxury, abundance, and sexual possibility that is consciously figured within a sexual marketplace. Yet this is a marketplace over which these rappers believe that they have authority. The most compelling moment in the video happens as Nelly swipes a credit card through a dancer's butt and then smiles into the camera. Is this a gesture of possession, the black woman as both currency and a device of exchange in the flow of capital and masculinity? And what does the woman in the video get out of this configuration?

Can the Ho' Speak?

Here, I would like to follow the lead of Northwestern University Professor Dwight A. McBride's work, specifically his essay titled "Can the Queen Speak?," itself an allusion to Spivak's "Can the Subaltern Speak?" My section title, "Can the Ho' Speak?" intends to explore the question of how racial essentialism "legitimates and qualifies certain racial subjects to speak for (represent) 'the race' and excludes others from that very possibility" (McBride 1998, 364). McBride's work analyzes and critiques how African American gays and lesbians are so often written out of discourses about "the black community"; they are understood as discursively separate from and outside of whatever constitutes authentic (read normative, heterosexual) blackness.

In a similar way racial essentialism defines black "ho's" (normatively lumped together, they include video models, street prostitutes, private escorts, exotic dancers, phone-sex workers, skeezers, freaks, chicken-heads, golddiggers, and others) as existing outside of black moral respectability. Black ho's are not as invisible as gays and lesbians in homophobic black intellectual discourses of "the black community"—often because of their symbolic power to represent multiple crises (black matriarchy, the black family, teen pregnancy, HIV/AIDS, welfare, the materialism of black youth culture, the limits of black feminism, etc.)—but they are similarly derided (Collins 2000). They are often constructed as between, not entirely powerless victims and blameful agents of false consciousness. For many, it's better to be a "bitch" than a "ho." Ho's are embarrassing and retrograde to the black progress narrative; they lend legitimacy to negative stereotypes about black women, and they make the "real" black community look bad.

Not only does the figure of the black whore exist as an outcast—part outlaw, part victim—she is dangerously positioned in relationship to material and discursive abuse. This point brings me to the second part of McBride's essay that I find so useful: it is critical that we take hip-hop to task for its sexism and misogyny *and* homophobia. Following Kimberlé Crenshaw's feminist intervention in critiquing the ways in which acts like 2 Live Crew do more than signify in a vernacular about black manhood, McBride agrees that sexist and homophobic cultural productions "legitimate—if not engender" gender and sexual violence in black communities (McBride 1998, 367). So by exploring the ways in which black manhood is trying to find expression through the fetishization and commodification of black women's bodies and the mobilization of self-representations of hypermasculinity, I do not intend to offer a "political apologia" or rationale for black sexism, abuse, or misogyny (Zook 1995; Carbado 1998). At the same time, I argue here and elsewhere that, although sexism and misogyny exist in much of pornography, this does not mean that it is present in the entire media form. Nor can we consider the women involved in the productions hapless victims or traitors to the race (Miller-Young 2007).

Additionally, because there is so much diversity in porn subjects and subjective spectatorship, possibilities and potentials exist within the form that I believe should exclude it from being written off as only productive of discrimination, violence, and abuse. Significantly, we do not know enough about pornography and adult entertainment—the industry has been taboo even for researchers to explore—and much of the work written by black feminist cultural critics about the images of black women in pornography has not included the voices of women, sustained analyses of women's participation as labor, or their own productions within pornographic media.[8] Because black women "whores" have been written out of discourses of "the black community" or have been focused on only as the problems of contemporary black femininity, we are missing an opportunity to understand and illuminate the choices and self-articulations young black women today are making about their sexualities.

T. Denean Sharpley-Whiting's *Pimps Up, Ho's Down: Hip Hop's Hold on Young Black Women* (2007) is a new work that productively advances the discussion of black women's sexuality in relation to hip-hop culture. In considering how second-wave feminism and the civil rights and black power movements have contributed to the ways in which young black men and women of the hip-hop generation experience sex within our consumer-oriented media culture, Sharpley-Whiting unpacks how the "twin myths"—"hypersexuality and easy accessibility"—about black women shape the terrain of their lives and render them "too hot to be bothered." She questions how the women's movement has allowed black women to pursue sexual autonomy, yet the trafficking of their sexuality within the corporate, transnational hip-hop industry functions to reproduce them as stereotypical objects "rendered fair game for rape and sexual assault" (Sharpley-Whiting 2007, 58):

> The sad irony about the notion of "choice" and "autonomy" for us black women who choose to appropriate and project the twin myths whether as rap artists, "video ho's" or Jane Does . . . is that the choice is never fully ours, and thus the sexual freedom is illusory . . . . Black women's sexuality in the marketplace of hip hop—in this instance, the supine or prostrate variety—is then devalued and heavily discounted.
>
> (Sharpley-Whiting 2007, 66)

Sharpley-Whiting's work helpfully elucidates the complexity of black women's sexual subjectivities in light of the many powerful economic, political, and social influences of hip-hop and contemporary black sexual politics. Black women's sexual choices and self-articulations within contemporary hip-hop cultural production are complicated by the multiple stigmas and abuses that devalue, commodify, appropriate, mystify, and violate black women's sexual integrity.

I agree that the ways in which black women are constructed through representation as hypersexual, accessible, and devalued contributes to their subjugation. I also believe that the fact that so many women still engage the media and culture, and find it engaging, compelling, and even instrumental to their subject-formation (or as preferred spaces of labor), means that we have to look carefully at how we as cultural critics, in naming the desires of others as illusory or somehow false, contributes to the assumption of representation, consumption, and desire as good versus bad or other binary valuations. That is to say, representation is an encounter with history and power that unleashes pain and horror as well as recognition and seduction. If we concentrate on how some representations are injurious and damaging to our sense of progress or integrity, we might miss reading the unreliability, unknowability, and ambiguity of black women's complex sexual desires, fantasies, and pleasures (Parreñas Shimizu 2007). This is not to discount in any way the structural issues of sexism and violence as they are reproduced constantly in hip-hop and pornography; it is to propose that we take seriously how and why black people are finding their own legibility in these forms, and how they self-fashion themselves through and against hypersexuality. I suggest that even though black women are stereotyped, and indeed in many ways mistreated, this does not mean that we need to call into question their power for sexual choice, autonomy, or freedom. And if we do, do we not risk denying them the very agency we seek to provide?

If we turn again to hip-hop porn and the question of how black women negotiate sexuality within the genre, we see that black women's position in relation to the powerful gendered and racialized influences of corporate media is shaped by what Sharpley-Whiting (2007) calls the "twin myths" of their hypersexuality and super-accessibility. The adult industry's interest in appropriating black urban youth culture, in its most heterosexist and masculinist forms, has had important implications for black women performers. Hip-hop porn has brought about increased work opportunities for black sex workers, but has also continued the often racially exploitative and sexist roles for black women that have been prevalent since pornography's inception. Black women's appearance in a variety of high-and low-budget films with an increasingly "ghetto culture" theme signifies their general ghettoization within the representational economy of hard-core as well as within the political economy of the adult industry as sex workers. Yet more black women than ever have gravitated to the sex industry as a site of labor and sexual expression—why?

During the 1970s there were fewer than five professional black and Latina porn actresses—including the famed Vanessa Del Rio, and the less well-known Desiree West.[9] During the 1980s there were fewer than twenty black women performers, but during the 1990s, hundreds, if not thousands, of black women chose to appear in hard-core films, as well as in erotic magazines and websites. In other sectors of the sex industry, black women, who have traditionally participated in sex work as a labor option, have increasingly sought to make livelihoods in the fields of exotic dance, street prostitution, private escorting, and phone sex. With the growing incorporation of black actresses into an increasingly profitable and mainstream adult industry, how have black women performers perceived their participation in pornography? Why have black women chosen pornography as a labor option? While these questions are too complex to fully investigate here, I think it is important to point out that the stigma of sex work has elided a conversation over the productive aspects of women's labor in the sex industries, including the pornography industry, within black feminist cultural criticism. Considering the marginalization of black women's labor in low-level service sector jobs, and the feminization of work and poverty in the late twentieth century (Woody 1992), we should begin to ask to what extent does their labor in the sexual economy represent a broader strategy of black women's attempts at survival and mobility? What are the specific motivations behind black women's choice of sex work as a labor option? How has the mainstreaming of pornography impacted young women's ambitions to be the "video ho'"?

Through my research on black women in the adult video industry, I found that these women are also seeking access, recognition, mobility, independence, and sexual pleasure as they practice an everyday politics of survival. They are aspiring actresses trying to gain access to the entertainment industry; mothers attempting to have more work flexibility and income so they can raise their children; students trying to pay rent, tuition, and fees; young women desperate to leave home and be independent; sex radicals exploring exhibitionism and polyamorous sex; budding entrepreneurs hoping to control the means of production; and much more. Coming from a variety of class and social contexts, sex workers in porn, like those in other areas of the sex industry, are sometimes casual laborers in it for the short term and sometimes professionals carefully constructing a career with an eye on the long-term, big picture. Their everyday negotiations are punctuated by moments of both defiance and complicity within the limits of the racialized sexual economy that figure as dangerous black women who engage in sexual labor and construct non-normative sexual autonomy (Hammonds 1997). Black women in hard-core engage in the illicit erotics of sexual economy. Through illicit eroticism they mobilize deviant, outlaw racialized sexuality as vehicles of consumption and labor, as well as of contestation and consent.

Though they strategically utilize non-normative sexualities deemed dangerous, they are also critical of the structural and symbolic limits to their sexual autonomy as they are articulated in hard-core, including hip-hop hard-core. Sasha Brabuster, a beautiful 44KK busty model and performer, chooses to avoid working in hip-hop-oriented pornography, preferring to appear in the BBW (Big Beautiful/Black/Busty Women) genres. Identifying hip-hop porn as problematic because of its narrow racial and gender stereotyping, Sasha told me that she mainly works in interracial BBW videos in order to protect herself from the kinds of limited representations that narrowly define black women in the hip-hop genre. "I choose movies that put me in a positive light," she says, "that will market me in all positive ways" (Brabuster 2005). Sierra, a former professional exotic dancer and porn star from Atlanta, shared Sasha's concerns about the misogyny in hip-hop, including music videos and adult videos. Sierra turned down many opportunities to work in both and shared with me why:

> It's sickening. It is sickening! That's why I won't do [music] video work. People have tried to get me to do rap videos. No, sorry, I'm not going to sit there and let you call me a bitch. I'm not having it . . . I just refuse to be called that and smile. Sorry, someone has to put their foot down. Why can't it be "See this pretty girl over here? Watch her do this" . . . Sex is a beautiful thing. It's not something you should use to degrade people with.
>
> (Sierra 2003)

While Sierra was critical of how hip-hop pornographic production abused black women by attacking them as "bitches" and the like, she also discussed its growing influence in the hard-core industry. This presented a double bind: while hip-hop encouraged the industry to produce even more films highlighting black and interracial sex—and thus provided more opportunities for black women to work in the videos—more of the roles were explicitly "ghettoizing" black women, literally and symbolically. Although she was critical of the genre, Sierra also worked in several hip-hop-themed porn videos, which reveals the primacy of the genre for black women working in hard-core.

Sinnamon Love, a savvy adult performer and illicit erotic businesswoman with more than fourteen years in the industry, exposes the complexity of this issue. She has appeared in numerous videos with hip-hop themes—*Snoop Dogg's Doggystyle* (2000), *South Central Hookers 10* (1995), *Black Jack City* (1995)—and is critical of the problematic nature of ghettoizing black women's sexuality. At the same time, she sees the production of black women's sexuality as assimilative to whiteness as also limiting. Nevertheless, she underscores that as the adult industry is being run by men for men's interests, if she is to survive and achieve success, she must commodify her sexuality in ways that maintain her own interests:

> It's almost as if companies are saying that men of color or white men, either have interest in seeing black women who either look extremely ghetto, or are assimilative to their own [white]. It's gotta be one or the other, there is no in-between. The girl has to be either in a mansion setting or she has to be "Ghetto Bitches in the Hood vol. 17." It's as if the companies think or feel that there is no middle-class market, there is no market to see just an average black girl that has a nice body, that is pretty, that also likes to have down and dirty and nasty sex. It either has to be pimps and hoes or [assimilation] . . . well, when it comes down to the girls, the guys is a different story . . . the companies really only care what the last movie was she spread her ass in. They don't, because this is a male run industry. I recognize that my power in the business comes from the core. The core being your center [*presses her two hands down towards vagina*] and if women don't realize how much power they have between their legs . . . I feel like if I have to continue to present myself in a way that they, they being the companies, and company owners, will deem [acceptable] in order to get what I want, then that's what I'm going to do, because I'm gonna get what I want.
>
> (Love 2002)

Love's testimony reveals the complicated negotiations that are part of the everyday strategies of survival and mobility for black women in adult entertainment. She illuminates how one can be both critical of the normative limits of representation as they structure the labor options and experiences of sex workers in pornography and can still choose to engage sexual expression within that space. She also argues compellingly for the need for women to understand their sexual power—which she articulates as their "core"—as they navigate an industry that does not necessarily have their best interests in mind. She is clear about her desire to mobilize her sexuality—including a pleasure in "down and dirty nasty sex"—in the marketplace of desire for her own interests of access, opportunity, mobility, and fame. While I can't explore further the complexities of these testimonies in this context, I want to situate the experiences of these women, and their illicit erotic labor, in further discussion about commodification and racial/sexual subjectivity.

The policing of women's sexual autonomy within the black community means that, despite the fact that sexual exploration is an important motivating factor for many young black women to enter the sex industries, such sexual self-fashioning remains taboo, especially because commodification is equated with objectification rather than subjectivity. Implicit critiques of these women are bound up in assumptions that it is, first, morally wrong for a woman to use her sexuality as a commodity (because it is sacred or only to be given as a "gift" in the context of love, romance, or heterosexual marriage, for example) and, second, that because of the history of racialized sexual coercion of black women by legal and economic institutions in the Americas, black women should protect their sexualities from the exploitations of the marketplace. Discussions of sexual self-commodification often ignore the ways in which even hetero-normative relationships in the context of marriage are bound up with monetary or commodity exchange (Zelizer 2005). In addition, the act of fetishizing oneself as a consumable commodity in order to gain access to other kinds of consumptions for self-care is not unique to sex work. As Luise White (1990) suggests, sex work is not a capitalist social relationship because capitalism has commodified sex, but because it has commodified *all* labor. Moreover, we often ignore that sex work is "family labor" in that as women participate in the sexual economy, they "reproduce" themselves and their families (White 1990, 2).

Self-commodification and reproductive labor enables consumption. Deborah Thomas's work on working-class Jamaican youth culture suggests the concept of "radical consumerism" as a way to understand how for some minoritarian subjects "consumption is a creative and potentially liberatory process" that works through rather than against capitalism (Thomas 2002, 43):

> However, taking "radical consumerism" seriously may reveal that the lower-class black Jamaican man driving a "Bimma" has more on his mind than individualist conspicuous consumption. Instead, he is refashioning selfhood and reshaping stereotypical assumptions about racial possibilities through—rather than outside—capitalism.
>
> (Thomas 2002, 44–45)

Thompson underscores how subjects may selectively appropriate, as well as creatively redefine, aspects of the capitalist ethos as a way to survive economic crises or as a path to social mobility. Robin D. G. Kelley's work (1997) underscores the ways in which selective appropriation of self-commodification is both strategic and creative in its engagement with capitalism. African Americans have mobilized self-commodification through the form of "play"—that is, the transformation of leisure, pleasure, and creative expression into labor. This "play-labor" is not necessarily resistant to hegemonic institutions of power, nor is it meant to be. It is one strategy by which young people, women, minoritarian subjects, the working class, and others may navigate the political economy by using their corporeal resources (Kelley 1997, 45–46).

Black women sex workers transform "labor not associated with wage work—sexual play and intercourse—into income" (Kelley 1997, 73).

Yet these women's labor may not necessarily be about getting paid cold hard cash. As Joan Morgan points out about music video models, "Very, very, very few women make any money doing music videos" (Carpenter 2006b). This leads us to wonder if there are other engagements at play as women participate in the sexual economy—be it soft-core music videos or hard-core porn videos.

The question is intricately bound to the issue of how black women should use their sexualities in the marketplace in light of the perceived misogyny and abuses of much of contemporary commercial hip-hop culture as it reproduces the historical violence against black womanhood. This issue intersects with what Darlene Clark Hine (1989) has described as black women's "culture of dissemblance," or self-imposed silences about issues of sexuality. A necessary strategy of self-protection from abuse, the "culture of dissemblance" has tended to deny sexualities that might provoke further stigmatization. As it became a dominant articulation and identification for black women in post-slavery America, it coincided with black women's attempts to define themselves as citizens deserving of equal rights, including the right to be protected from abuse.

Black women embraced what Evelyn Brooks Higginbotham (1993) has described as a "politics of respectability," or a radical form of discursive self-representation that refigured black women as strategically conforming to hegemonic manners and morals around gender and sexual propriety as an attempt to access social power and legitimacy. A weapon against racist discourse that rendered black women as sexual monsters, the politics of respectability, supported by the culture of dissemblance, actually functioned to limit notions of acceptable sexual behavior among black communities to the realm of conservative hetero-normativity. Although the porn actresses seem to agree with the prevailing black feminist criticism that hip-hop pornography can only be oppressive to black women—even when they, like Sinnamon Love, attempt to explore sexual self-fashioning within the genre precisely because it offers an alternative to white normative hard-core fantasies—what is also expressed is a pressing need for a liberatory space where the imaginary for black female sexuality transcends the dominant sexual economy in which black women continue to "give birth to white wealth" (Davis 2002). To that end, black women's continued reliance on the politics of respectability and the culture of dissemblance in the public sphere does little to advance counter-discourses on their sexual expressions and representations.

Deviance vs. Defiance: Concluding Thoughts

Questions of the policing of sexual expressions, including the illicit erotic, may be theorized through the lens of the historical disciplining of urban youth sexualities as discussed by Hazel Carby: "The dance hall and cabaret . . . are the most frequently referenced landscapes in which Black female promiscuity and sexual degeneracy were described" (Carby 1992, 750). Referencing the 1927 sociologist William Jones, Carby posits that dance halls were perceived to encourage a "quick intimacy," potentially giving rise to crime and working-class pathologies among youth, and that Jones sought to mobilize social disapproval of the black middle class in order to frame dance-hall culture as undermining the moral health and progress of the black community. Like the dance hall and cabaret of the early twentieth century, the strip club, dance club, party, music video, and porn set are all seen as spaces of the illicit erotic economy that actually threaten the moral health (and physical—as the inhabitants are seen as vectors of disease) of the black (middle-class) community. Can we defy or move beyond the stigma of the illicit erotic to explore other terrains of possibility?

This cultural work of non-conformity to normalizing and oppressive social structures must be analyzed as daily tactics of agency and autonomy, through which pleasure is a political act of reclamation in the context of social annihilation. Here, pleasure may be a way to *disidentify* with dominant regimes that police black bodies (Muñoz 2000). Cathy Cohen argues that we must queer black studies in order to understand how the most "deviant" groups (such as poor single mothers, the incarcerated, queer and transgender people of color, HIV+, and I would add sex-worker populations) seek out the "basic human goals of pleasure, desire, recognition, and respect" as they live "counternormative behaviors" (Cohen 2004, 30). Within our scholarly traditions of focusing on formal political movements and the social politics of respectability, we have elided and actually repathologized the lived experiences and political culture of the deviant, and missed out on conceptualizing the "full range of political acts of resistance." Cohen suggests:

> Through the repetition of deviant practices by multiple individuals, new identities, communities, and politics emerge where seemingly deviant, unconnected behavior can be transformed into conscious acts of resistance that serve as a basis for a mobilized politics of deviance.

(Cohen 2004, 43)

Cohen's understanding of the utility of deviance parallels Celine Parreñas Shimizu's concept of "productive perversity" as a way to redefine perverse, non-normative hypersexuality "in order to create new morphologies in representation and in history" (Parreñas Shimizu 2007, 26).

The celebration of the corporeal grotesqueries of hip-hop pornography is perhaps a useful example of mobilizing this politics of deviance, best understood through Mikhail Bakhtin's paradigm (1993) of the *carnivalesque* as an expressive politics of the public, collective, and common body. Within the carnivalesque revelry of the explicit, exposed, sensual spectacle of black sexuality, perhaps hip-hop pornography offers a new morphology or legibility of the black body as a site of counter-fetishized desire. This self-fetishization or counter-fetishization allows black sexual subjects in the public sphere to create a dialectical tension with the historical politics of respectability. This visual body remains firmly wedded to the pains and exploitations of hetero-patriarchal capital, yet is also framed within a discourse of pleasure and possibility authored by hip-hop subjectivities.

Can pleasure, particularly sexual pleasure, become an anti-racist and anti-sexist platform in the way that pain and struggle has become for black communities? Moreover, in the context of the "new racism" (Collins 2004), late capitalism, neo-liberalism, and global cultural distribution of hip-hop, are our definitions of hip-hop culture as a counter-culture still relevant? Finally, are there other possibilities for black women, including queer spectatorship, in the new hip-hop pornography?

I raise these questions in the interest of challenging ideas that fix hypersexuality of the black body as always already repugnant. Perhaps we can read these oversexed bodies in another way. The realm of sexuality embeds complex power relations in which the subaltern subject is often conquered and colonized. However, sexual practices and representations are rich with possibilities for self-actualization and empowerment. Exploring illicit erotic economies is one way we can better understand how black sexual subjects self-fashion and refigure themselves according to the values and practices of radical consumerism, play-labor, and counter-fetishization. In light of dominant markets perpetuating white supremacist, capitalist, and hetero-patriarchal narratives of black sexuality, it is imperative that we create black sexual subjectivities that move beyond respectability politics and the culture of dissemblance to recuperate a radical sexual counter-public.

Acknowledgments

I wish to thank the editors and blind readers of *Meridians* and the editors of this special issue for their patience, enthusiasm, and support of this work. I would also like to thank those who consented to be interviewed, as well as my fellow panelists and the audience at the 2006 American Studies Annual Meeting in Oakland, CA for the panel titled "Performing Diasporas: Gender and Sexual Transgressions, Transformations, and Transactions," organized by Marlon M. Bailey, and including Matt U. Richardson, Roshanak Kheshti, and Linda Carty for helping me to develop the arguments presented here. Thanks also go to Rebecca Wanzo, Xavier Livermon, Robin D. G. Kelley, Celine Parreñas Shimizu, Constance Penley, Paul Amar, Nicole Starosielski, and all the scholars cited in this piece.

Notes

1. Mirielle Miller-Young, "Hip-Hop Honeys and Da Hustlaz: Black Sexualities in the New Hip-Hop Pornography," *Meridians* 8.1 (2008): 261–292.
2. Railton and Watson argue that "the display of the sexualised body and the potential for that body to be figured as an object of desire or fantasy are crucial to the economies of both pleasure and profit in the pop music video" (Railton and Watson 2005, 52). This observation includes the conventions of hip-hop music videos. Furthermore, the authors rightly point out that "despite the problematic nature of some of the imagery, pop music videos provide one of the, still very few, mainstream cultural spaces where there are a significant number of representations of black women." (Railton and Watson 2005, 52)
3. According to the Recording Industry Association of America 2006 Consumer Profile, hip-hop/rap has fluctuated at between 9.7% and 13.8% of the overall music industry during the years 1997–2006. This figure does not include hip-hop-influenced R&B music, which has been between 9.7% and 12.8% of the music market during the same period. R&B music videos often use similar conventions as hip-hop music videos, including the fetishization of consumer products and the bodies of women of color. Rap/hip-hop has been the second or third most popular music genre behind rock, and in competition with country music.
4. Here I'm interested in complicating the often reductionist use of "the black community" that is used within popular culture as well as among black intellectuals. According to Dwight McBride (1998), the term often leaves out black lesbians and gay men, and I would argue, other sexual minorities including sex workers and transsexuals.
5. The "How Do You Want It" music video was directed by former black adult actor Ron Hightower. Two versions of the video were shot, one that included partial nudity and one that was filmed with no nudity due to censorship (Pepper 2002).
6. Whereas black men were treated as marginal and mildly threatening to masculine dominance in porn of the 1970s and 80s (performers such as Johnny Keyes, Ray Victory, Jack Baker, and Billie Dee), the popularization of black and interracial genres and the appropriation of hip-hop themes in the 90s meant increased opportunities for work. The growing demand for extreme sex acts, cheaply made reality-based (or "gonzo") productions, and interracial performances (which in porn primarily means black men with white women) also centralized the roles of black male performers like Sean Michaels, Lexington Steele, Mr. Marcus, Jake Steed, and Byron Long. These men appropriated the role of the hypersexual stud as they mobilized their sexualities for labor and pleasure, opening up representational and labor space for a new cadre of black male porn actors to follow. Taking advantage of being in demand within the adult industry—and they are, somewhat, just as or more popular than the leading white male performers like Rocco Siffredi and Evan Stone—black male sex workers in porn counter-fetishized the representation of black men as sexual beasts with gigantic genitals through their performances and creations of hardcore productions. Jake Steed's series *Little White Chicks and Big Black Monster Dicks* (1999–2003) is one example of how these men fetishize their own sexualities while recognizing and exploiting the market's demand for certain types of illicit erotic performances by black men.
7. For fascinating insight into the black feminist critique of the music video, see Carpenter 2006a.
8. Black feminist cultural critics have been very critical of pornography as a field of media and representation, arguing that it constitutes the abuse of women and is especially abusive for black women. See, for example, Gardner 1980; Collins 2000, 2004; and Walker 1980, 2000.
9. There were few black and Latina women in golden-age hard-core films of the 1970s, but according to my research there were thousands who appeared in other erotic venues such as magazines like *Players,*

Playboy, and *Eros* in the U.S., and *Femme Souillee, Inhalt, Emanuel, Whitelady, La Cousine,* and *Samy* in Europe (especially France, Germany, the Netherlands, Britain, and Spain).

Works Cited

Bakhtin, Mikhail M. 1993. *Rabelais and His World,* translated by Hélène Iswolsky. Bloomington: Indiana University Press.

Brabuster, Sasha. 2005. Personal Interview. January 20.

Business Wire. 2005. "Adult Industry Generates $12.6 Billion in 2005, AVN Estimates; State of the U.S. Adult Industry Report Highlights Diverse Products and Delivery Options." December 13.

Carbado, Devon. 1998. "Black Male Racial Victimhood." *Callaloo* 21, no. 2: 337–61.

Carby, Hazel. 1992. "Policing the Black Woman's Body in the Urban Context." *Critical Inquiry* (Summer): 738–55.

Carpenter, Faedra Chatard. 2006a. "An Interview with Moya Bailey." *Callaloo* 29, no. 3: 753–60.

———. 2006b. "An Interview with Joan Morgan." *Callaloo* 29, no. 3: 764–72.

Cohen, Cathy. 2004. "Deviance as Resistance: A New Research Agenda for the Study of Black Politics." *Du Bois Review* 1, no. 1: 27–45.

Collins, Patricia Hill. 2000. *Black Feminist Thought: Knowledge, Consciousness and the Politics of Empowerment.* 2nd ed. New York: Routledge.

———. 2004. *Black Sexual Politics: African Americans, Gender, and the New Racism.* New York: Routledge.

Crenshaw, Kimberlé Williams. 1991. "Beyond Racism and Misogyny: Black Feminism and 2 Live Crew." *Boston Review* 16, no. 6 (December): 6, 30.

Davis, Adrienne. 2002. "'Don't Let Nobody Bother Yo' Principle': The Sexual Economy of American Slavery." In *Sister Circle: Black Women and Work,* edited by Sharon Harley and the Black Women and Work Collective, 103–27. New Brunswick, NJ: Rutgers University Press.

Edlund, Martin. 2004. "Hip Hop's Crossover to the Adult Aisle." *New York Times* (March 7). http://query.nytimes.com/gst/fullpage.html?res=9C01E0DD153FF934A35750C0A9629C8B63. Accessed November 27, 2007.

Free Speech Coalition. 2006. *Adult Entertainment in America: State of the Industry Report.* www.freespeechcoalition.com/FSCViewR.asp. Accessed October 1, 2007.

Foucault, Michel. 1986. *The History of Sexuality,* vol. 3: *The Care of the Self.* New York: Random House.

Gardner, Tracy A. 1980. "Racism in Pornography and the Women's Movement." In *Take Back the Night: Women on Pornography,* edited by Laura Lederer. New York: William & Morrow.

Guerrero, Ed. 1993. *Framing Blackness: The African American Image in Film.* Philadelphia: Temple University Press.

Gray, Herman. 1995. *Watching Race: Television and the Struggle for "Blackness."* Minneapolis: University of Minnesota Press.

Hammonds, Evelyn. 1997. "Towards a Genealogy of Black Female Sexuality: The Problematic of Silence." In *Feminist Genealogies: Colonial Legacies, Democratic Futures,* edited by M. Jacqui Alexander and Chandra Talpade Mohanty, 170–81. New York: Routledge.

Harley, Sharon. 2002. "'Working for Nothing But a Living': Black Women in the Underground Economy." In *Sister Circle: Black Women and Work,* edited by Sharon Harley and the Black Women and Work Collective, 48–66. New Brunswick, NJ: Rutgers University Press.

Higginbotham, Evelyn Brooks. 1993. *Righteous Discontent: The Women's Movement in the Black Baptist Church,* 1880–1920. Cambridge, MA: Harvard University Press.

Hine, Darlene Clark. 1989. "Rape and the Inner Lives of Black Women in the Middle West: Preliminary Thoughts on the Culture of Dissemblance." *Signs* 14, no. 4: 912–20.

Hobson, Janell. 2003. "The 'Batty' Politic: Toward an Aesthetic of the Black Female Body." *Hypatia* 18, no. 4: 87–105.

Hopkinson, Natalie and Natalie Y. Moore. 2006. *Deconstructing Tyrone: A New Look at Black Masculinity in the Hip Hop Generation.* San Francisco: Cleis Press.

Johnson, E. Patrick. 2003. *Appropriating Blackness: Performance and the Politics of Authenticity.* Durham, NC: Duke University Press.

Kelley, Robin D. G. 1994. *Race Rebels: Culture, Politics, and the Black Working Class.* New York: Free Press.

———. 1997. *Yo Mama's Disfunktional: Fighting the Culture Wars in Urban America.* Boston: Beacon Press.

Kipnis, Laura. 1999. *Bound and Gagged: Pornography and the Politics of Fantasy in America.* Durham, NC: Duke University Press.

Lil' Jon. 2004. Personal Interview. January 11.

Love, Sinnamon. 2002. Personal Interview. December 5.

Majors, Frank. 2003. "The Porn-To-Rap Connection." *Adult Video News Magazine* (January 21). www.avn.com/index.cfm?objectId=ED9C0F09-1372-4B41-C4FA3458342950C1. Accessed June 1, 2004.

Mann, Christian. 2002. Personal Interview. November 27.

McBride, Dwight A. 1998. "Can the Queen Speak? Racial Essentialism, Sexuality and the Problem of Authority." *Callaloo* 21, no. 2: 363–79.

Miller-Young, Mireille. 2007. "Let Me Tell Ya 'Bout Black Chicks: Black Women in 1980s Video Pornography." In *Blackness and Sexualities*, edited by Michelle Wright and Antje Schuhmann, 143–63. Forum for European Contributions to African American Studies (FORECAAST) 16. Berlin: Lit Verlag.

Muñoz, Jose Esteban. 2000. *Disidentifications: Queers of Color and the Performance of Politics.* Minneapolis: University of Minnesota Press.

O'Toole, Laurence. 1999. *Pornocopia: Porn, Sex, Technology and Desire.* 2nd ed. London: Serpent's Tail.

Parreñas Shimizu, Celine. 2005. "The Bind of Representation: Performing and Consuming Hypersexuality in Miss Saigon." *Theater Journal* 57, no. 2: 247–65.

———. 2007. *The Hypersexuality of Race: Performing Asian/American Women on Screen and Scene.* Durham, NC: Duke University Press.

"Part 5: Sex Lives on Videotape" 1999. *Pornography: The Secret History of Civilisation.* Directed by Kate Williams, Christopher Rodley, and Dev Varma. London and Los Angeles: World of Wonder.

Pepper, Jeannie. 2002. Personal Interview. December 8.

Perry, Imani. 2004. *Prophets of the Hood: Politics and Poetics in Hip-Hop.* Durham, NC: Duke University Press.

Quinn, Eithne. 2000. " 'Who's the Mack?' The Performativity and Politics of the Pimp Figure in Gangsta Rap." *Journal of American Studies* 34, no.1: 115–36.

Railton, Diane and Paul Watson. 2005. "Naughty Girls and Red Blooded Women: Representations of Female Heterosexuality in Music Video." *Feminist Media Studies* 5, no. 1: 51–62.

Recording Industry Association of America. 2006 *Consumer Profile.* Year-End Report. www.riaa.com/keystatistics.php?content_selector=consumertrends. Accessed November 27, 2007.

Rich, Frank. 2001. "Naked Capitalists." *New York Times Magazine* (May 20): 50–56, 80–82, 92.

Richardson, Mattie Udora. 2003. "No More Secrets, No More Lies: African American History and Compulsory Heterosexuality." *Journal of Women's History* 15, no. 3: 63–76.

Rose, Tricia. 1994. *Black Noise: Rap Music and Black Culture in Contemporary America.* Middletown, CT: Wesleyan University Press.

———. 2001. "Never Trust a Big Butt and A Smile." In *Black Feminist Cultural Criticism*, edited by Jacqueline Bobo, 233–54. Malden, MA: Blackwell.

Ross, Marlon. 1998. "In Search of Black Men's Masculinities." *Feminist Studies* 24, no. 3 (Autumn): 599–626.

Salomon, Yves. 2001. "Snoop Dogg Ventures into the World of Porn." *Adult Industry News*, 26 February. www.ainews.com/Archives/Story1547.phtml. Accessed November 27, 2007.

Scott, David. 1999. *Refashioning Futures: Criticism after Postcoloniality.* Princeton: Princeton University Press.

Sharpley-Whiting, T. Denean. 2007. *Pimps Up, Ho's Down: Hip Hop's Hold on Young Black Women.* New York: New York University Press.

Shock G. 2004. Personal Interview. January 10.

Sierra. 2003. Personal Interview. April 23.

Slade, Joseph. 2000. "Erotic Motion Pictures and Videotapes." In *Pornography in America: A Reference Handbook.* Santa Barbara: ABC-CLIO.

Thomas, Deborah. 2002. "Modern Blackness: 'What We Are and What We Hope to Be.' " *Small Axe* 6, no. 2: 25–48.

Walker, Alice. 1980. "Coming Apart." In *Take Back the Night: Women on Pornography*, edited by Laura Lederer. New York: William & Morrow.

———. 2000. "Porn." In *Feminism and Pornography*, edited by Drucilla Cornell. New York: Oxford.

Weasels, P. n.d. "Porn 101: Hip Hop Porn Primer." Editorial. www.gamelink.com/news.jhtml?news_id=news_nt_primer_hip_hop_porn. Accessed November 27, 2007.

White, Luise. 1990. *The Comforts of Home: Prostitution in Colonial Nairobi*. Chicago: University of Chicago Press.

Williams, Linda. 1999. *Hard Core: Power, Pleasure, and the "Frenzy of the Visible."* 2nd ed. Berkeley: University of California Press.

———. 2004. "Skin Flicks on the Racial Border: Pornography, Exploitation and Interracial Lust." In *Porn Studies*, edited by Linda Williams, 271–308. Durham, NC: Duke University Press.

Woody, Bette. 1992. *Black Women in the Workplace: Impacts of Structural Change in the Economy*. New York: Greenwood Press.

Zelizer, Viviana A. 2005. *The Purchase of Intimacy*. Princeton: Princeton University Press.

Zook, Kristal Brent. 1995. "A Manifesto of Sorts for a Black Feminist Movement." *New York Times* (November 12): F86.

Frank Ocean

This famous singer and songwriter's letter on his blog to anonymous male interest prompted an outpouring of public discourse around Black artistry, sexuality, and politics of "coming out." Rather than taking a traditional approach in announcing "I'm Black and gay," Ocean rhetorically frames a letter that speaks directly to a male love interest. This strategy of public confession marked a shift in the rhythm and blues music culture as we knew it, as well as remixed the "coming out" genre form. Ocean quares the queer "coming out" tradition by casually remarking upon his same-sex desire, but doing so as he excelled at the cross section of hip-hop and R&B music. This letter would become viral material, being circulated worldwide, producing a global buzz around Frank Ocean and Black male sexuality. To accompany his rhetorically powerful move, his music would also oscillate between female and male interest in an unapologetic mode that produced controversy and critical public discourse around race and sexuality.

Open Letter

Frank Ocean[1]

WHOEVER YOU ARE. WHEREVER YOU ARE. . I'M STARTING TO THINK WE'RE A LOT ALIKE. HUMAN BEINGS SPINNING ON BLACKNESS. ALL WANTING TO BE SEEN, TOUCHED, HEARD, PAID ATTENTION TO. MY LOVED ONES ARE EVERYTHING TO ME HERE. IN THE LAST YEAR OR 3 I'VE SCREAMED AT MY CREATOR. SCREAMED AT CLOUDS IN THE SKY. FOR SOME EXPLANATION. MERCY MAYBE. FOR PEACE OF MIND TO RAIN LIKE MANNA SOMEHOW. 4 SUMMERS AGO, I MET SOMEBODY. I WAS 19 YEARS OLD. HE WAS TOO. WE SPENT THAT SUMMER, AND THE SUMMER AFTER, TOGETHER. EVERYDAY ALMOST. AND ON THE DAYS WE WERE TOGETHER, TIME WOULD GLIDE. MOST OF THE DAY I'D SEE HIM, AND HIS SMILE. I'D HEAR HIS CONVERSATION AND HIS SILENCE. . UNTIL IT WAS TIME TO SLEEP. SLEEP I WOULD OFTEN SHARE WITH HIM. BY THE TIME I REALIZED I WAS IN LOVE, IT WAS MALIGNANT. IT WAS HOPELESS. THERE WAS NO ESCAPING, NO NEGOTIATING WITH THE FEELING. NO CHOICE. IT WAS MY FIRST LOVE, IT CHANGED MY LIFE. BACK THEN, MY MIND WOULD WANDER TO THE WOMEN I HAD BEEN WITH, THE ONES I CARED FOR AND THOUGHT I WAS IN LOVE WITH. I REMINISCED ABOUT THE SENTIMENTAL SONGS I ENJOYED WHEN I WAS A TEENAGER. . THE ONES I PLAYED WHEN I EXPERIENCED A GIRLFRIEND FOR THE FIRST TIME. I REALIZED THEY WERE WRITTEN IN A LANGUAGE I DID NOT YET SPEAK. I REALIZED TOO MUCH, TOO QUICKLY. IMAGINE BEING THROWN FROM A PLANE. I WASN'T IN A PLANE THOUGH. I WAS IN A NISSAN MAXIMA, THE SAME CAR I PACKED UP WITH BAGS AND DROVE TO LOS ANGELES IN. I SAT THERE AND TOLD MY FRIEND HOW I FELT. I WEPT AS THE WORDS LEFT MY MOUTH. I GRIEVED FOR THEM, KNOWING I COULD NEVER TAKE THEM BACK FOR MYSELF. HE PATTED MY BACK. HE SAID KIND THINGS. HE DID HIS BEST, BUT HE WOULDN'T ADMIT THE SAME. HE HAD TO GO BACK INSIDE SOON, IT WAS LATE AND HIS GIRLFRIEND WAS WAITING FOR HIM UPSTAIRS. HE WOULDN'T TELL ME THE TRUTH ABOUT HIS FEELINGS FOR ME FOR ANOTHER 3 YEARS. I FELT LIKE I'D ONLY IMAGINED RECIPROCITY FOR YEARS. NOW IMAGINE BEING THROWN FROM A CLIFF. NO, I WASN'T ON A CLIFF. I WAS STILL IN MY CAR TELLING MYSELF IT WAS GONNA BE FINE AND TO TAKE DEEP BREATHS. I TOOK THE BREATHS AND CARRIED ON. I KEPT UP A PECULIAR FRIENDSHIP WITH HIM BECAUSE I COULDN'T IMAGINE KEEPING UP MY LIFE WITHOUT HIM. I STRUGGLED TO MASTER MYSELF AND MY EMOTIONS. I WASN'T ALWAYS SUCCESSFUL.

THE DANCE WENT ON. . I KEPT THE RHYTHM FOR SEVERAL SUMMERS AFTER. IT'S WINTER NOW. I'M TYPING THIS ON A PLANE BACK TO LOS ANGELES FROM NEW ORLEANS. I FLEW HOME FOR ANOTHER MARRED CHRISTMAS. I HAVE A WINDOW-SEAT. IT'S DECEMBER 27, 2011. BY NOW I'VE WRITTEN TWO ALBUMS. THIS BEING THE SECOND. I WROTE TO KEEP MYSELF BUSY AND SANE. I WANTED TO CREATE WORLDS THAT WERE ROSIER THAN MINE. I TRIED TO CHANNEL OVERWHELMING EMOTIONS. I'M SURPRISED AT HOW FAR ALL OF IT HAS TAKEN ME. BEFORE WRITING THIS I'D TOLD SOME PEOPLE MY STORY. I'M SURE THESE PEOPLE KEPT ME ALIVE, KEPT ME SAFE. . SINCERELY, THESE ARE THE FOLKS I WANNA THANK FROM THE FLOOR OF MY HEART. EVERYONE OF YOU KNOWS WHO YOU ARE. . GREAT HUMANS, PROBABLY ANGELS. I DON'T KNOW WHAT HAPPENS NOW, AND THAT'S ALRITE. I DON'T HAVE ANY SECRETS I NEED KEPT ANYMORE. THERE'S PROBABLY SOME SMALL SHIT STILL, BUT YOU KNOW WHAT I MEAN. I WAS NEVER ALONE, AS MUCH AS I FELT LIKE IT. . AS MUCH AS I STILL DO SOMETIMES. I NEVER WAS. I DON'T THINK I EVER COULD BE. THANKS. TO MY FIRST LOVE, I'M GRATEFUL FOR YOU. GRATEFUL THAT EVEN THOUGH IT WASN'T WHAT I HOPED FOR AND EVEN THOUGH IT WAS NEVER ENOUGH, IT WAS. SOME THINGS NEVER ARE. . AND WE WERE. I WON'T FORGET YOU. I WON'T FORGET THE SUMMER. I'LL REMEMBER WHO I WAS WHEN I MET YOU. I'LL REMEMBER WHO YOU WERE AND HOW WE'VE BOTH CHANGED AND STAYED THE SAME. I'VE NEVER HAD MORE RESPECT FOR LIFE AND LIVING THAN I HAVE RIGHT NOW. MAYBE IT TAKES A NEAR DEATH EXPERIENCE TO FEEL ALIVE. THANKS. TO MY MOTHER. YOU RAISED ME STRONG. I KNOW I'M ONLY BRAVE BECAUSE YOU WERE FIRST. . SO THANK YOU. ALL OF YOU. FOR EVERYTHING GOOD. I FEEL LIKE A FREE MAN. IF I LISTEN CLOSELY. . I CAN HEAR THE SKY FALLING TOO.

-FRANK

Note

1. Frank Ocean, "Frank Ocean's Open Letter," July 4, 2012, http://frankocean.tumblr.com/post/264737 98723

Section 8: Further Reading

Allen, Jafari. ¡Venceremos?: The Erotics of Black Self-making in Cuba. Durham, NC: Duke University Press, 2011.

Bailey, Marlon M. Butch Queens up in Pumps: Gender, Performance, and Ballroom Culture in Detroit. Ann Arbor: University of Michigan Press, 2013.

Brim, Matt. James Baldwin and the Queer Imagination. University of Michigan Press, 2014.

Eguchi, Shinsuke, and Myra N. Roberts. "Gay Rapping and Possibilities: A Quare Reading of 'Throw that Boy P*** y'." Text and Performance Quarterly (2015): 1–16.

Holland, Sharon Patricia. The Erotic Life of Racism. Durham, NC: Duke University Press, 2012.

McCune Jr, Jeffrey Q. Sexual Discretion: Black Masculinity and the Politics of Passing. Chicago, IL: University of Chicago Press, 2014.

Nash, Jennifer Christine. The Black Body in Ecstasy: Reading Race, Reading Pornography. Durham, NC: Duke University Press, 2014.

Richardson, Matt. The Queer Limit of Black Memory: Black Lesbian Literature and Irresolution. Columbus: Ohio State University Press, 2013.

Scott, Darieck. *Extravagant Abjection: Blackness, Power, and Sexuality in the African American Literary Imagination.* New York: NYU Press, 2010.

Walcott, Rinaldo. "Outside in black studies: reading from a queer place in the diaspora." *Queerly Canadian: An Introductory Reader in Sexuality Studies* (2012): 23–34.

Williams, Erica Lorraine. *Sex Tourism in Bahia: Ambiguous Entanglements.* Urbana-Champaign: University of Illinois Press, 2013.

Section 8: Discussion Questions

1. What constitutes Black quare rhetoric?
2. What is the Black quare archive and what is included inside of it? How might it differ from dominant archival structures?
3. How does Black quareness get articulated in multiple forms?
4. How does the discourse of Black homophobia also produce kernels of quareness?
5. How do performances of "deviance" complicate the Black archive generally?

PART IV
THE NEW BLACKNESS
Multiple Cultures, Multiple Modes

INTRODUCTIONS:

COURAGEOUS RHETORIC: CARIBBEAN FOUNDATIONS, NEW MEDIA, AND BLACK AESTHETICS

Vershawn Ashanti Young

EVERYDAY RHETORIC: RHETORIC EVERYDAY

Michelle Bachelor Robinson

⤙━⋙⋘━⤚

Courageous Rhetoric: Caribbean Foundations, New Media, and Black Aesthetics

Vershawn Ashanti Young

Every year, in February, we attempt to recognize and to appreciate black history. It is a worthwhile endeavor for the contributions of African Americans to this great nation are numerous and significant. Even as we fight a war against terrorism, deal with the reality of electing an African American as our President for the first time and deal with the other significant issues of the day, the need to confront our racial past, and our racial present, and to understand the history of African people in this country, endures. One cannot truly understand America without understanding the historical experience of black people in this nation. Simply put, to get to the heart of this country one must examine its racial soul.
—First Black attorney general Eric Holder, 2009, Black History
Month speech to the Justice Department employees

When Eric Holder, the first African American U.S. attorney general, gave his opening speech to his employees in the Justice Department, he shocked some Americans with this statement: "Though this nation has proudly thought of itself as an ethnic melting pot, in things racial we have always been and continue to be, in too many ways, essentially a nation of cowards." Many wondered: Who was Holder calling cowards? After all, hadn't Americans from various racial and ethnic backgrounds courageously come together to elect its first ever Black president just a few months earlier, a victory that led to Holder's own appointment? And didn't the dream of Barack Obama becoming president come more sharply into focus after he gave, while still a candidate, his engrossing and well-received speech on race relations in the U.S.? So who was Holder really talking to, and what was he talking about? Holder's speech exemplifies the continuing legacy of African American rhetoric that is (re)presented in this book. So a brief consideration of his speech and its historical context should answer questions about audience and subject matter that Holder's statement raises. Further, such a reflection will also show why Holder's words are relevant to readers of this book as a whole, particularly this part, with its four multifarious sections that present the African American rhetorics of new media, hip-hop, Caribbean discourse, and cultural aesthetics.

537

Now, consider some of the cultural context that gave rise to Holder's words: it has been a month or so since Barack Obama's first presidential inauguration. Commentators are still reporting the offense some expressed at how culturally Black the inauguration was, that the president had an activist pray for "brown to stick around" and "for that day when black will not be asked to get in back" (Armbruster 2009). Some even expressed concern that Obama had stopped by a diner owned by a Trinidadian, Ben's Chilli Bowl, that had once served Black nationalists, and that he used African American English while talking to a White waitress while there. Some were calling for Obama to manage and downplay his blackness in order to appease—that is, not scare—his White liberal constituency, who get skittish about race-talk and who believe that Black cultural expressivity might best be limited to interactions with other Blacks. Others were warning that conservatives were keenly observant of Obama's words and actions, and stockpiling evidence of reverse racism, and claiming that Obama had the interests of only Black people in mind. Consider further that the housing market was in dire straits, and many families had lost their homes and were in high debt due to subprime lending. The country was also still in recession, the unemployment rate was high, and all of these conditions affected African Americans more significantly than any other racial group—so much so that economists, sociologists, and philosophers remarked that the period was a second nadir, the lowest point of African American experience. Those familiar with African American history know that the period after slavery and the end of reconstruction is considered the first nadir—due to rampant lynching, high mortality rates and incarceration rates, and low employment and other legal and social prospects. These circumstances were also evident at the time of Holder's speech—low literacy levels and graduation rates, as well as questionable killings of Black men and women by both White laypeople and police officers.

In view of the political and social environment of the time, it is undeniable that it would take courage for any Black man, especially the head of the U.S. Justice Department, to give a speech that in essence announced that his office would focus on ending gross racial disparity and pursue racial justice. He is unequivocal on this point, saying,

> Through its work and through its example this Department of Justice, as long as I am here, must—and will—lead the nation to the "new birth of freedom" so long ago promised by our greatest President. This is our duty and our solemn obligation.
>
> (Holder 2009)

Holder's speech undoubtedly keeps with the traditions of African American rhetoric contained in this book, and thus the audience and subject of his statement are made clear when considered in this light: when Holder called America a nation of cowards when it comes to talking about race, he could not have been referring to Black people. For although some Black people would rather avoid race-talk and get uncomfortable when racial politics are discussed, far more Blacks find such conversation necessary and instructive. Holder himself did, as have scores of other Black rhetors over the centuries.

Indeed, the four parts of this book, containing as they do umpteen selections, show that Black people have consistently and courageously engaged in talk about race—certainly since the early seventeenth century. And the sections in this part make this legacy perhaps even more clear as it presents hip-hop as an important genre of Black rhetoric that emerges out of and remixes African diasporic and African American discursive practices, such as folktales, protests, raps, and rhymes, often doing so with a view toward social justice and highlighting the unabashed performance of blackness. In addition, the diasporic connection between African American Americans and other Blacks in the world, particularly in the Caribbean, reveals important efforts toward justice that link Black and Brown bodies across the globe. Further, African Americans have always taken advantage of and in fact invented and spearheaded technological and digital resources, often using these means to communicate on behalf of racial progress. To that end, technological advances have continually served the African American social justice cause. It was the television cameras in Birmingham in the 1960s that caused White America to look at Bull Connor's practices of fire hoses and attack dogs on peaceful citizens and children and feel compassion. It was the camcorders of the 1980s that gave America a front row seat to police brutality in LA. And now the handheld camera on every cell phone and the power of social media have given everyone the power to be a rhetor, to use the camera as a tool to affect change and their voices, through social media, to start a new revolution to combat the daily injustices that have plagued Black Lives and have compelled Patrisse Kahn-Cullors, Alicia Garza, and Opal Tometi to begin a movement to assert that Black Lives Matter. And it seems almost too obvious to state that in the relationship between the arts and technology, one is essential to the other. However, understanding African American arts, culture, and aesthetics, as Holder mentions in his speech, is to understand American culture, and without it, there can be no true recognition of what America means. This truly is the challenge that Holder puts forth in his speech, calling for Americans to place African American experience at the center of American history and discourse. By calling America a nation of cowards, he is referring to persistent marginalization of African American experience, even though that experience is inherently, thoroughly, and significantly American. The challenge that Holder presents, one that this part, with its four sections, echoes in its many voices and readings, is for all to understand, embrace, and pursue blackness—or as Holder put it, to examine our "racial soul."

Everyday Rhetoric: Rhetoric Everyday

Michelle Bachelor Robinson

African American rhetoric has continued to manifest in very traditional and mainstream ways with the beautifully eloquent and authentically Black words of the first African American President of the United States. At the same time, artistic productions have reached new heights in the music industry through multi-genre renditions of the old and the new. However, in our current political and social climate, where white supremacy has escalated and is taking new approaches in the way of sanctioned killings and brutalization of Black bodies, African American Rhetoric is also reinventing itself. Discursive practices once fostered by television news cameras and heavily reliant on Black print media have evolved into online and real time communication with "live" image capturing with immediate consumption and response.

In this multi-modal world, technology has provided African American rhetors with new platforms and unmediated agency. To that end, technological advances have continually served the Black social justice cause. It was the television cameras in Birmingham in the 1960s that caused White America to look at Bull Connor's practice of using fire hoses and attack dogs on peaceful citizens and children and feel compassion. It was the camcorders of the 1980s that gave America a front row seat to police brutality and the response in Los Angeles, and today smartphones, equipped with internet connections and cameras capable of still and video imaging, have essentially changed the rules of engagement. In 21st Century Black Rhetoric, everyone's a rhetor, with the power to tweet, post, chat, as well as assert, argue, shape, craft, advocate, and protest to an immediate and responsive audience. In 2016 through a Facebook live feed, the world watched Philando Castille's life expire after being shot by a police officer on a "routine" traffic stop. And through the reposting of dash-cam footage, we witnessed the unwarranted harassment of Sandra Bland that led to her death after being unlawfully incarcerated. These incidents, and many more, received worldwide attention because African American rhetors employed their available technological and rhetorical tools. This kind of agency has taken African American rhetorical engagement to a new level—fostering community, birthing movements, shaping discourse.

Works Cited

Armbruster, Ben. "Beck Outraged at Inauguration Benediction, Accuses Rev. Lowery of Calling America 'Racist.'" *Think Progress*. Jan. 21, 2009. Web. Retrieved on Dec. 2, 2017. https://thinkprogress.org/beck-outraged-at-inauguration-benediction-accuses-rev-lowery-of-calling-america-racist-951113bc7953/

Holder, Eric. "Attorney General Eric Holder at the Department of Justice African American History Month Program." US Department of Justice. 2009. Web. www. justice. gov/ag/speeches/2009/ag-speech-090218. html

9

CARIBBEAN THOUGHT AND ITS CRITIQUE OF SUBJUGATION

Edited and with an introduction by Aaron Kamugisha and Yanique Hume

The Caribbean region—historically constituted by some of the most oppressive regimes of modern history—genocide, transatlantic slavery, and indentured labor—has long been a site of remarkable rebellion against colonial rule. The forms that this resistance have taken are vast and include the creation of new African diasporic religions in the Americas, musical traditions that have had a decisive impact on twentieth-century global popular culture, dance and performance traditions that have functioned as sites of embodied memory, and oral and writing traditions that have raised pivotal questions concerning sovereignty, history, and the reclamation of identity. The last of these creative expressions—traditions of orality and anti-hegemonic inspired writing—is the focus of our presentation of Caribbean rhetoric.

We have sought to capture the best of Caribbean rhetoric—rhetoric here defined as the art of meaning making and a style of persuasion—by culling sources from the expansive intellectual tradition of the region, which dates back to the early nineteenth century. Many of the themes covered in this corpus of work and the amazing array of thinkers devoted to the resuscitation of humanity beyond barbarism emerged out of the very history of violence and depersonalization experienced in the Caribbean. Vested in the urgency of the moment to give voice to the atrocities of the past and present while articulating a future beyond domination, Caribbean thinkers honed a style of reasoning that went far beyond that of a vindicationist appeal to be counted as human. Rather than protest literature, Caribbean thought at its best has proffered anti-colonial thought to the world—a demand for a world reconstructed based on the dignity and self-determination of the masses, rather than for the benefit of the few. While cataloguing the enormity of the crimes of colonialism to economies and societies and to dignity and self-worth, this body of thought always seeks the unknown form—a community beyond coloniality, secured by freedom and justice.

Many of the Caribbean's finest rhetoricians may be immediately recognized as political figures using commonplace Western understandings of what constitutes the sphere of formal politics. Heads of state in the persons of Jean-Jacques Dessalines, Fidel Castro, and Maurice Bishop are represented in this collection (whether in print here, in further readings, or on the companion website), along with easily recognizable Caribbean political thinkers—Marcus Garvey, Pedro Campos, Jacques Roumain, Aimé Césaire, Frantz Fanon, C.L.R. James, and Walter Rodney. The reduction of human beings to the status of property by chattel slavery, the destruction and reproduction of landscapes to serve the commercial needs of a predatory European colonialism, and the racist logic that undergirds it all meant that the political in Caribbean thought occupies a terrain far greater than in the Western-colonial inspired academy. To speak of self-determination in the cultural sphere, of economic enfranchisement, or against self-alienation *is* political speech in the colonial situation, as colonialism wages war on the freedom of its subjects, which many writers in these pages recognized and paid for with their lives.

Self-determination, autonomy, and freedom are then talismanic concepts that are behind the thought of many of the Caribbean thinkers gathered in this collection. The "Declaration of Rights of the Negro Peoples of the World" from the 1920 Congress of the Universal Negro Improvement Association is one of the greatest collective manifestos produced by an organized body of people of African descent. Its demand for Black freedom beyond second-class citizenship resonates with clarity and insightful contemporary meaning a century later. In the midst of a global neoliberalism determined to reduce the globe to the logic of the market and supported by a sturdy racism determined to reverse the halting gains by Black populations since the 1960s, we find ourselves faced with the persistence of inequality and growing asymmetries of power. Decades prior to this contemporary moment, many Caribbean leaders and rhetoricians of the region spoke vehemently about the dangers of succumbing to imperial forces while living amid their preying presence. The ability of Caribbean states to chart autonomous paths rather than exist as colonial adjuncts of Europe or the victims of American hegemony is most searingly addressed by Dessalines and Bishop, leaders of Caribbean revolutions three centuries apart, and Pedro Campos's struggle for a free Puerto Rico, while the region's rich contribution to global anti-colonial thought is seen well in Aimé Césaire's classic text, *Discourse on Colonialism*.

It is in the arena of cultural sovereignty that many of the most enduring positions on Caribbean freedom have been articulated, as the legacy of the tissue of deceptions and distortions of colonialism has been particularly difficult to resolve at the level of the intimate lives of Caribbean people. One well-known response to this question came in the form of the Négritude school, co-founded by Aimé Césaire, Léon Damas, and Leopold Senghor in 1930s Paris. French colonialism's offer of equal citizenship predicated on full cultural assimilation to its subjects, though an ingenious and relatively transparent fiction, sharpened the gravity of the question of cultural alienation for Francophone Caribbean intellectuals. British colonialism's greater commitment to social apartheid meant that this tradition of critique developed later and was given a fillip by the global uprisings of the 1960s, as can be seen in the articles of George Lamming and Walter Rodney. Lamming gives a scathing critique of the philistine bourgeois tastes of the middle class that took the helm after the moment of independence. Rodney captures the essence of this argument but places it within a history of the development of Caribbean people, which culminated at the time of his first major radical intervention—1968 Jamaica—with the need for Black power. The experience of the first independent Caribbean state, Haiti, shows, as Michel-Rolph Trouillot points out, that some of imperialism's greatest work comes in how it enmeshes its subjects in an epistemological web of colonial knowledge that is tremendously difficult to undo. In "The Odd and the Ordinary," Trouillot weaves an evocative argument that critiques the narrative concerning Haiti's exceptionalism and singularity, indicating the manner through which knowledge systems shroud Haiti in a cloak of "otherness" that prohibits full theoretical and sociopolitical engagement with the country.

The grand political-aesthetic arguments made by Négritude, Black power, and class-centered critiques of the Caribbean present form but part of the aesthetic revolution that has swept the Caribbean in the last two generations, influencing historical consciousness, style, and understandings of value in the region. Rohlehr terms this a "revolution in self-perception," and in the last generation, the most seismic progressive change in the Caribbean has been an outpouring of a tremendous body of genre-defying work on (and by) Caribbean women and gender relations in the region. Claudia Jones, writing as a committed Communist in 1949, would excoriate the neglect of Black women's experiences in a blueprint of action among the left, and register her disgust at the lack of social honor and respect given to them by all members of American society. Poet and essayist Audre Lorde, represented here through her path-breaking essay "The Transformation of Silence Into Language and Action," has inspired a generation to revise and re-enchant their ideas about racism, language, and social freedom, and to recognize necessity of revolt against the world order in which we live. Edwidge Danticat's playfully ironic affirmation of self has understated importance—"we are ugly but we are here! And here to stay!" Cognizant of how others fail to recognize us, Danticat speaks our defiant stance to be counted among the world's people.

The question of aesthetics and freedom comes together most eloquently in the arena of language and orality, spaces of expression that have been pivotal sites of struggle but also ones that illuminate the creative genius of our people. The creole tongues that give voice to the history of cultural change and adaptation have always provided a space of refuge from oppression and a place of validation and connection to a past and present reality, where the tensions between memory and reclamation of identity are able to manifest. Our "wordsmiths," as they are locally dubbed in the English-speaking Caribbean, are some of the world's most recognizable voices working in mediums that run the spectrum of popular music, spoken word, and academic scholarship. From the globally acclaimed reggae artists Bob Marley and Peter Tosh to dub poets Michael Smith and Mutaburuka, we see how orality is the bedrock through which Caribbean people articulate freedom, combat the colonial stranglehold, and redress the imbalances of power. It has likewise been the source through which our musical expressions have been realized—the Caribbean expressive form most readily available and known globally. At the same time, we see in the rich traditions of orality some of our most valiant and aesthetically provocative critiques of subjugation. The latter can be seen in the work of both Kamau Brathwaite and Edouard Glissant (included in the Further Reading section), who developed theories on identity formation that moved beyond models of stasis and fixity to that of process and dynamism. Braithwaite extends his analysis of the voice and its rhythmic cadence to a study of its cultural and sociopolitical dimensions. Language is thus seen as a site for submerged identities to surface, a platform for exploring oppositional practices, play, and resistance to dominant codes of being and the means through which Africa could be reconstituted in the New World and, by extension, new creole nation-language and identities formulated. In Glissant's work on language and in particular his concept of forced, natural, and counter poetics, we are introduced to the concept of opacity and thus begin from the perspective that language use in the Caribbean was an instrument of resistance as it both revealed and concealed meanings. Secrecy and cunning are therefore central features of vernacular expressions and an essential aspect of an indigenous aesthetic of which memory and fragmentation are paramount.

Our selections here have been profoundly secular in orientation, though some of the greatest charismatic and rhetorical sources in the region one can persuasively claim come from the spiritual and sacred traditions. The difficulties of including the performance, the speech, and the sermon are relatively obvious here, especially given the question of whether the appeal extends beyond the distinctive community of adherents who are members of this movement. Yet in our selections, it is hard to miss a style of rhetoric that speaks to prophecy and vision, from Dessalines to Fidel Castro, in Garvey and Sylvia Wynter. C.L.R. James's exhortation in his introduction to *Party Politics in the West Indies* that "people of the West Indies, you do not know your own power. No one dares to tell you" (1962, 4) and Wynter's demand that we overturn the overrepresentation of Western man as the human speak to the power and potential of a region that must, and can, overturn the burdens of history. In all of the work here, a uniting theme is the desire that their notations would be a prolegomena for a Caribbean writing beyond coloniality. This work would then constitute a beginning toward an end we must anticipate and create—and would be the future of the writing and rhetoric of Caribbean thought.

Jean-Jacques Dessalines

Jean-Jacques Dessalines (1758–1806) was a Haitian Revolutionary leader of great courage who led his people to victory on the field of battle against European colonizers. He became the first ruler of independent Haiti and one of the most important world historical figures of the early nineteenth century. His speech on declaring the independence of Haiti, reproduced ahead, is perhaps the finest anti-imperialist speech made by a Caribbean head of state.

Liberty or Death: Proclamation

Jean-Jacques Dessalines[1]

JEAN JAQUES DESSALINES Governor General to the inhabitants of Hayti.

CRIMES, the most atrocious, such as were until then unheard of, and would cause nature to shudder, have been perpetrated. The measure was over-heaped. At length the hour of vengeance has arrived, and the implacable enemies of the rights of man have suffered the punishment due to their crimes.

My arm, raised over their heads, has too long delayed to strike. At that signal, which the justice of God has urged, your hands righteously armed, have brought the axe upon the ancient tree of slavery and prejudices. In vain had time, and more especially the infernal politics of Europeans, surrounded it with triple brass; you have stripped it of its armour; you have placed it upon your heart, that you may become (like your natural enemies) cruel and merciless. Like an overflowing mighty torrent that tears down all opposition, your vengeful fury has carried away every thing in its impetuous course. Thus perish all tyrants over innocence, all oppressors of mankind!

What then? Bent for many ages under an iron yoke: the sport of the passions of men, or their injustice, and of the caprices of fortune; mutilated victims of the cupidity of white Frenchmen; after having fattened with our toils these insatiate blood suckers, with a patience and resignation unexampled, we should again have seen that sacrilegious horde make an attempt upon our destruction, without any distinction of sex or age; and we, men without energy, of no virtue, of no delicate sensibility, should not we have plunged in their breast the dagger of desperation? Where is that vile Haytian, so unworthy of his regeneration, who thinks he has not accomplished the decrees of the Eternal, by exterminating these bloodthirsty tygers? If there is one, let him fly; indignant nature discards him from our bosom; let him hide his shame far from hence: the air we breath is not suited to his gross organs; it is the pure air of Liberty, august and triumphant.

Yes, we have rendered to these true cannibals war for war, crime for crime, outrage for outrage; Yes, I have saved my country; I have avenged America. The avowal I make of it in the face of earth and heaven, constitutes my pride and my glory. Of what consequence to me is the opinion which contemporary and future generations will pronounce upon my conduct? I have performed my duty; I enjoy my own approbation; for me that is sufficient. But what do I say? The preservation of my unfortunate brothers, the testimony of my own conscience, are not my only recompence: I have seen two classes of men, born to cherish, assist and succour one another—mixed, in a word, and blended together—crying for vengeance, and disputing the honor of the first blow.

Blacks and Yellows, whom the refined duplicity of Europeans has for a long time endeavored to divide; you, who are now consolidated, and make but one family; without doubt it was necessary that our perfect reconciliation should be sealed with the blood of your butchers. Similar calamities have hung over your proscribed heads: a similar ardour to strike your enemies, has signalized you: the like fate is reserved for you: and the like interests must therefore render you for ever one, indivisible, and inseparable. Maintain that precious concord, that happy harmony amongst yourselves: it is the pledge of your happiness, your salvation, and your success: it is the secret of being invincible.

Is it necessary, in order to strengthen these ties to recall to your remembrance the catalogue of atrocities committed against our species: the massacre of the entire population of this Island meditated in the silence and sangfroid of the Cabinet: the execution of that abominable project, to me unblushingly proposed and already begun by the French with the calmness and serenity of a countenance accustomed to similar crimes. Guadaloupe, pillaged and destroyed: its ruins still reeking, with the blood of the children, women and old men put to the sword, PELAGE (himself the victim of their craftiness) after having basely betrayed his country and his brothers: The brave and immortal DELGRESSE, blown into the air with the fort which he defended, rather than accept their offered chains. Magnanimous warrior! that noble death, far from enfeebling our courage, serves only to rouse within us the determination of avenging or of following thee. Shall I again recall to your memory the plots lately framed at Jeremie? The terrible explosion which was to be the result, nothwithstanding the generous pardon granted to these incorrigible beings at the expulsion of the French army? The deplorable fate of our departed brothers in Europe? And (dread harbinger of death) the frightful despotism exercised at Martinique? Unfortunate people of Martinique, could I but fly to your assistance, and break your letters! Alas! an insurmountable barrier separates us. Perhaps a spark from the same fire which inflames us, will alight into your bosoms: perhaps at the found of this commotion, suddenly awakened from your lethargy, with arms in your hands, you will reclaim your sacred and inprescriptable rights.

After the terrible example which I have just given, that sooner or later Divine Justice will unchain on earth some mighty minds, above the weakness of the vulgar, for the destruction and terror of the wicked; tremble, tyrants, usurpers, scourges of the new world! Our daggers are sharpened; your punishment is ready! Sixty thousand men, equipped, inured to war, obedient to my orders, burn to offer a new sacrifice to the names of their assassinated brothers. Let that nation come who may be mad and daring enough to attack me. Already at its approach, the irritated genius of Hayti, rising out of the bosom of the ocean appears; his menacing aspect throws the waves into commotion, excites tempests, and with his mighty hand disperses ships, or dashes them in pieces; to his formidable voice the laws of nature pay obedience; diseases, plague, famine, conflagration, poison, are his constant attendants. But why calculate on the assistance of the climate and of the elements? Have I forgot that I command a people of no common cast, brought up in adversity, whose audacious daring frowns at obstacles and increases by dangers? Let them come, then, these homicidal Cohort? I wait for them with firmness and with a steady eye. I abandon to them freely the sea-shore, and the places, where cities have existed; but woe to those who may approach too near the mountains! It were better for them that the sea received them into its profound abyss, than to be devoured by the anger of the children of Hayti.

"*War to Death to Tyrants!*" this is my motto; "*Liberty! Independence!*" this is our rallying cry.

Generals, officers, soldiers, a little unlike him who has preceded me, the ex-general Toussaint Loverture, I have been faithful to the promise which I made to you when I took up arms against tyranny, and whilst the last spark of life remains in me I shall keep my oath. *Never again shall a Colonist or an European set his foot upon this territory with the title of master or proprietor.* This resolution shall hence-forward form the fundamental basis of our constitution.

Should other chiefs, after me, by pursuing a conduct diametrically opposite to mine, dig their own graves and those of their species, you will have to accuse only the law of destiny which shall have taken me away from the happiness and welfare of my fellow-citizens. May my successors follow the path I shall have traced out for them! It is the system best adapted for consolidating their power; it is the highest homage they can render to my memory.

As it is derogatory to my character and my dignity to punish the innocent for the crimes of the guilty, a handful of whites, commendable by the religion they have always professed, and who have besides taken the oath to live with us in the woods, have experienced my clemency. I order that the sword respect them, and that they be unmolested.

I recommend anew and order to all the generals of department &c. to grant succours, encouragement, and protection, to all neutral and friendly nations who may wish to establish commercial relations in this Island.

Head Quarters at the Cape, 28th April, 1804, first year of independence.

The Governor General,

(Signed) DESSALINES.

A true Copy. The Secretary-General,

JUSTE CHANLATTE.

Note

1. Jean-Jacques Dessalines, "Liberty or Death: Proclamation," in *The Balance and Columbian Repository, Vol. III* (Hudson, NY: Harry Croswell, 1804), pp. 197–199.

Declaration of Rights of the Negro Peoples of the World (1920)

The "Declaration of Rights of the Negro Peoples of the World" is the greatest collective manifesto produced by the Garvey movement. Produced when the Universal Negro Improvement Association was at the height of its powers at its convention in New York in August 1920, it stands as a definitive document of its time of the anger felt by people of African descent at their relegation to second-class citizenship in the Americas, with clear resonances to their predicament a century later.

Declaration of Rights of the Negro Peoples of the World[1]

Drafted and adopted at Convention held in New York, 1920, over which Marcus Garvey presided as Chairman, and at which he was elected Provisional President of Africa.

(Preamble)

"Be it Resolved, That the Negro people of the world, through their chosen representatives in convention assembled in Liberty Hall, in the City of New York and United States of America, from August 1 to August 31, in the year of our Lord, one thousand nine hundred and twenty, protest against the wrongs and injustices they are suffering at the hands of their white brethren, and state what they deem their fair and just rights, as well as the treatment they propose to demand of all men in the future."

We complain:

I. "That nowhere in the world, with few exceptions, are black men accorded equal treatment with white men, although in the same situation and circumstances, but, on the contrary, are discriminated against and denied the common rights due to human beings for no other reason than their race and color."

"We are not willingly accepted as guests in the public hotels and inns of the world for no other reason than our race and color."

II. "In certain parts of the United States of America our race is denied the right of public trial accorded to other races when accused of crime, but are lynched and burned by mobs, and such brutal and inhuman treatment is even practised upon our women."

III. "That European nations have parcelled out among themselves and taken possession of nearly all of the continent of Africa, and the natives are compelled to surrender their lands to aliens and are treated in most instances like slaves."

IV. "In the southern portion of the United States of America, although citizens under the Federal Constitution, and in some states almost equal to the whites in population and are qualified land owners and taxpayers, we are, nevertheless, denied all voice in the making and administration of the laws and are taxed without representation by the state governments, and at the same time compelled to do military service in defense of the country."

V. "On the public conveyances and common carriers in the Southern portion of the United States we are jim-crowed and compelled to accept separate and inferior accommodations and made to pay the same fare charged for first-class accommodations, and our families are often humiliated and insulted by drunken white men who habitually pass through the jim-crow cars going to the smoking car."

VI. "The physicians of our race are denied the right to attend their patients while in the public hospitals of the cities and states where they reside in certain parts of the United States."

"Our children are forced to attend inferior separate schools for shorter terms than white children, and the public school funds are unequally divided between the white and colored schools."

  VII. "We are discriminated against and denied an equal chance to earn wages for the support of our families, and in many instances are refused admission into labor unions, and nearly everywhere are paid smaller wages than white men."

 VIII. "In Civil Service and departmental offices we are everywhere discriminated against and made to feel that to be a black man in Europe, America and the West Indies is equivalent to being an outcast and a leper among the races of men, no matter what the character and attainments of the black man may be."

   IX. "In the British and other West Indian Islands and colonies, Negroes are secretly and cunningly discriminated against, and denied those fuller rights in government to which white citizens are appointed, nominated and elected."

    X. "That our people in those parts are forced to work for lower wages than the average standard of white men and are kept in conditions repugnant to good civilized tastes and customs."

  XI. "That the many acts of injustice against members of our race before the courts of law in the respective islands and colonies are of such nature as to create disgust and disrespect for the white man's sense of justice."

  XII. "Against all such inhuman, unchristian and uncivilized treatment we here and now emphatically protest, and invoke the condemnation of all mankind."

"In order to encourage our race all over the world and to stimulate it to a higher and grander destiny, we demand and insist on the following Declaration of Rights:

1. "Be it known to all men that whereas, all men are created equal and entitled to the rights of life, liberty and the pursuit of happiness, and because of this we, the duly elected representatives of the Negro peoples of the world, invoking the aid of the just and Almighty God do declare all men women and children of our blood throughout the world free citizens, and do claim them as free citizens of Africa, the Motherland of all Negroes."

2. "That we believe in the supreme authority of our race in all things racial; that all things are created and given to man as a common possession; that there should be an equitable distribution and apportionment of all such things, and in consideration of the fact that as a race we are now deprived of those things that are morally and legally ours, we believe it right that all such things should be acquired and held by whatsoever means possible.

3. "That we believe the Negro, like any other race, should be governed by the ethics of civilization, and, therefore, should not be deprived of any of those rights or privileges common to other human beings."

4. "We declare that Negroes, wheresoever they form a community among themselves, should be given the right to elect their own representatives to represent them in legislatures, courts of law, or such institutions as may exercise control over that particular community."

5. "We assert that the Negro is entitled to even-handed justice before all courts of law and equity in whatever country he may be found, and when this is denied him on account of his race or color such denial is an insult to the race as a whole and should be resented by the entire body of Negroes."

6. "We declare it unfair and prejudicial to the rights of Negroes in communities where they exist in considerable numbers to be tried by a judge and jury composed entirely of an alien race, but in all such cases members of our race are entitled to representation on the jury."

7. "We believe that any law or practice that tends to deprive any African of his land or the privileges of free citizenship within his country is unjust and immoral, and no native should respect any such law or practice."

8. "We declare taxation without representation unjust and tyrannous, and there should be no obligation on the part of the Negro to obey the levy of a tax by any law-making body from which he is excluded and denied representation on account of his race and color."

9. "We believe that any law especially directed against the Negro to his detriment and singling him out because of his race or color is unfair and immoral, and should not be respected."

10. "We believe all men entitled to common human respect, and that our race should in no way tolerate any insults that may be interpreted to mean disrespect to our color."

11. "We deprecate the use of the term 'nigger' as applied to Negroes, and demand that the word 'Negro' be written with a capital 'N.' "

12. "We believe that the Negro should adopt every means to protect himself against barbarous practices inflicted upon him because of color."

13. "We believe in the freedom of Africa for the Negro people of the world, and by the principle of Europe for the Europeans and Asia for the Asiatics; we also demand Africa for the Africans at home and abroad."

14. "We believe in the inherent right of the Negro to possess himself of Africa, and that his possession of same shall not be regarded as an infringement on any claim or purchase made by any race or nation."

15. "We strongly condemn the cupidity of those nations of the world who, by open aggression or secret schemes, have seized the territories and inexhaustible natural wealth of Africa, and we place on record our most solemn determination to reclaim the treasures and possession of the vast continent of our forefathers."

16. "We believe all men should live in peace one with the other, but when races and nations provoke the ire of other races and nations by attempting to infringe upon their rights, war becomes inevitable, and the attempt in any way to free one's self or protect one's rights or heritage becomes justifiable."

17. "Whereas, the lynching, by burning, hanging or any other means, of human beings is a barbarous practice, and a shame and disgrace to civilization, we therefore declare any country guilty of such atrocities outside the pale of civilization."

18. "We protest against the atrocious crime of whipping, flogging and overworking of the native tribes of Africa and Negroes everywhere. These are methods that should be abolished, and all means should be taken to prevent a continuance of such brutal practices."

19. "We protest against the atrocious practice of shaving the heads of Africans, especially of African women or individuals of Negro blood, when placed in prison as a punishment for crime by an alien race."

20. "We protest against segregated districts, separate public conveyances, industrial discrimination, lynchings and limitations of political privileges of any Negro citizen in any part of the world on account of race, color or creed, and will exert our full influence and power against all such."

21. "We protest against any punishment inflicted upon a Negro with severity, as against lighter punishment inflicted upon another of an alien race for like offense, as an act of prejudice and injustice, and should be resented by the entire race."

22. "We protest against the system of education in any country where Negroes are denied the same privileges and advantages as other races."

23. "We declare it inhuman and unfair to boycott Negroes from industries and labor in any part of the world."

24. "We believe in the doctrine of the freedom of the press, and we therefore emphatically protest against the suppression of Negro newspapers and periodicals in

various parts of the world, and call upon Negroes everywhere to employ all available means to prevent such suppression."

25. "We further demand free speech universally for all men."
26. "We hereby protest against the publication of scandalous and inflammatory articles by an alien press tending to create racial strife and the exhibition of picture films showing the Negro as a cannibal."
27. "We believe in the self-determination of all peoples."
28. "We declare for the freedom of religious worship."
29. "With the help of Almighty God, we declare ourselves the sworn protectors of the honor and virtue of our women and children, and pledge our lives for their protection and defense everywhere, and under all circumstances from wrongs and outrages."
30. "We demand the right of unlimited and unprejudiced education for ourselves and our posterity forever."
31. "We declare that the teaching in any school by alien teachers to our boys and girls, that the alien race is superior to the Negro race, is an insult to the Negro people of the world."
32. "Where Negroes form a part of the citizenry of any country, and pass the civil service examination of such country, we declare them entitled to the same consideration as other citizens as to appointments in such civil service."
33. "We vigorously protest against the increasingly unfair and unjust treatment accorded Negro travelers on land and sea by the agents and employees of railroad and steamship companies and insist that for equal fare we receive equal privileges with travelers of other races."
34. "We declare it unjust for any country, State or nation to enact laws tending to hinder and obstruct the free immigration of Negroes on account of their race and color."
35. "That the right of the Negro to travel unmolested throughout the world be not abridged by any person or persons, and all Negroes are called upon to give aid to a fellow Negro when thus molested."
36. "We declare that all Negroes are entitled to the same right to travel over the world as other men."
37. "We hereby demand that the governments of the world recognize our leader and his representatives chosen by the race to look after the welfare of our people under such governments."
38. "We demand complete control of our social institutions without interference by any alien race or races."
39. "That the colors, Red, Black and Green, be the colors of the Negro race."
40. "Resolved, That the anthem 'Ethiopia, Thou Land of Our Fathers,' etc., shall be the anthem of the Negro race."

The Universal Ethiopian Anthem

(Poem by Burrell and Ford)

I

Ethiopia, thou land of our fathers,
Thou land where the gods loved to be,
As storm cloud at night suddenly gathers
Our armies come rushing to thee.
We must in the fight be victorious

When swords are thrust outward to gleam;
For us will the vict'ry be glorious
When led by the red, black and green.

Chorus
Advance, advance to victory,
Let Africa be free;
Advance to meet the foe
With the might
Of the red, the black and the green.

II
Ethiopia, the tyrant's falling,
Who smote thee upon thy knees,
And thy children are lustily calling
 From over the distant seas.
Jehovah, the Great One has heard us,
 Has noted our sighs and our tears,
With His spirit of Love he has stirred us
To be One through the coming years.
CHORUS—Advance, advance, etc.

III
O Jehovah, thou God of the ages
Grant unto our sons that lead
The wisdom Thou gave to Thy sages
When Israel was sore in need.
Thy voice thro' the dim past has spoken,
Ethiopia shall stretch forth her hand,
By Thee shall all fetters be broken,
And Heav'n bless our dear fatherland.
CHORUS—Advance, advance, etc.

41. "We believe that any limited liberty which deprives one of the complete rights and prerogatives of full citizenship is but a modified form of slavery."
42. "We declare it an injustice to our people and a serious impediment to the health of the race to deny to competent licensed Negro physicians the right to practise in the public hospitals of the communities in which they reside, for no other reason than their race and color."
43. "We call upon the various governments of the world to accept and acknowledge Negro representatives who shall be sent to the said governments to represent the general welfare of the Negro peoples of the world."
44. "We deplore and protest against the practice of confining juvenile prisoners in prisons with adults, and we recommend that such youthful prisoners be taught gainful trades under humane supervision."
45. "Be it further resolved, that we as a race of people declare the League of Nations null and void as far as the Negro is concerned, in that it seeks to deprive Negroes of their liberty."
46. "We demand of all men to do unto us as we would do unto them, in the name of justice; and we cheerfully accord to all men all the rights we claim herein for ourselves."

47. "We declare that no Negro shall engage himself in battle for an alien race without first obtaining the consent of the leader of the Negro people of the world, except in a matter of national self-defense."

48. "We protest against the practice of drafting Negroes and sending them to war with alien forces without proper training, and demand in all cases that Negro soldiers be given the same training as the aliens."

49. "We demand that instructions given Negro children in schools include the subject of 'Negro History,' to their benefit."

50. "We demand a free and unfettered commercial intercourse with all the Negro people of the world."

51. "We declare for the absolute freedom of the seas for all peoples."

52. "We demand that our duly accredited representatives be given proper recognition in all leagues, conferences, conventions or courts of international arbitration wherever human rights are discussed."

53. "We proclaim the 31st day of August of each year to be an international holiday to be observed by all Negroes."

54. "We want all men to know we shall maintain and contend for the freedom and equality of every man, woman and child of our race, with our lives, our fortunes and our sacred honor."

These rights we believe to be justly ours and proper for the protection of the Negro race at large, and because of this belief we, on behalf of the four hundred million Negroes of the world, do pledge herein the sacred blood of the race in defense, and we hereby subscribe our names as a guarantee of the truthfulness and faithfulness hereof in the presence of Almighty God, on the 13th day of August, in the year of our Lord one thousand nine hundred and twenty.

Marcus Garvey, James D. Brooks, James W. H. Eason, Henrietta Vinton Davis, Lionel Winston Greenidge, Adrion Fitzroy Johnson, Rudolph Ethelbert Brissaac Smith, Charles Augustus Petioni, Thomas H. N. Simon, Richard Hilton Tobitt, George Alexander McGuire, Peter Edward Baston, Reynold R. Felix, Harry Walters Kirby, Sarah Branch, Marie Barrier Houston, George L. O'Brien, F. O. Ogilvie, Arden A. Bryan, Benjamin Dyett, Marie Duchaterlier, John Phillip Hodge, Theophilus H. Saunders, Wilford H. Smith, Gabriel E. Stewart, Arnold Josiah Ford, Lee Crawford, William McCartney, Adina Clem. James, William Musgrave La Motte, John Sydney de Bourg, Arnold S. Cunning, Vernal J. Williams, Frances Wilcome Ellegor, J. Frederick Selkridge, Innis Abel Horsford, Cyril A. Crichlow, Samuel McIntyre, John Thomas Wilkins, Mary Thurston, John G. Befue, William Ware, J. A. Lewis, O. C. Kelly, Venture R. Hamilton, R. H. Hodge, Edward Alfred Taylor, Ellen Wilson, G. W. Wilson, Richard Edward Riley, Nellie Grant Whiting, G. W. Washington, Maldena Miller, Gertrude Davis, James D. Williams, Emily Christmas Kinch, D. D. Lewis, Nettie Clayton, Partheria Hills, Janie Jenkins, John C. Simons, Alphonso A. Jones, Allen Hobbs, Reynold Fitzgerald Austin, James Benjamin Yearwood, Frank O. Raines, Shedrick Williams, John Edward Ivey, Frederick Augustus Toote, Philip Hemmings, F. F. Smith, E. J. Jones, Joseph Josiah Cranston, Frederick Samuel Ricketts, Dugald Augustus Wade, E. E. Nelom, Florida Jenkins, Napoleon J. Francis, Joseph D. Gibson, J. P. Jasper, J. W. Montgomery, David Benjamin, J. Gordon, Harry E. Ford, Carrie M. Ashford, Andrew N. Willis, Lucy Sands, Louise Woodson, George D. Creese, W. A. Wallace, Thomas E. Bagley, James Young, Prince Alfred McConney, John E. Hudson, William Ines, Harry R. Watkins, C. L. Halton, J. T. Bailey, Ira Joseph Touissant Wright, T. H. Golden, Abraham Benjamin Thomas, Richard C. Noble, Walter Green, C. S. Bourne, G. F. Bennett, B. D. Levy, Mary E. Johnson, Lionel Antonio Francis, Carl Roper, E. R. Donawa, Philip Van Putten, I. Brathwaite, Jesse W. Luck, Oliver Kaye, J. W. Hudspeth, C. B. Lovell, William C. Matthews, A. Williams, Ratford E. M. Jack, H. Vinton Plummer, Randolph Phillips, A. I. Bailey, duly elected representatives of the Negro people of the world.

Sworn before me this 15th day of August, 1920.

[Legal Seal] JOHN G. BAYNE.

Notary Public, New York County.
New York County Clerk's No. 378; New York County Register's
No. 12102. Commission expires March 30, 1922.

Note

1. "Declaration of Rights of the Negro Peoples of the World," in *The Philosophy and Opinions of Marcus Garvey, or Africa for the Africans, Vol. 1&2*, ed. Amy Jacques Garvey (Dover, MA: The Majority Press, 1986), pp. 135–143.

Léon Damas

Léon Gontran Damas (1912–1978) was a poet born in Cayenne, French Guiana, who furthered his studies in Martinique and later France. While in secondary school he established a lifelong friendship with Aimé Césaire, whom he would go on to meet again while a student in Paris. Damas, along with Césaire and a young Senegalese student, Leopold Senghor, founded *L'etudiant noir*, a publication that aimed to break down the nationalistic barriers that had existed among Black students in France. Its demise in 1940 marked the first phase of the Négritude movement. Damas was the first of the three founders of Négritude to publish his own book of poems. His volume, *Pigments*, has been termed the "manifesto of the movement," influencing countless other texts on Négritude. Damas also served as contributing editor of *Présence Africaine*, as well as senior adviser and UNESCO delegate for the Society of African Culture.

Sell Out

Léon Damas[1]

Sell Out *for Aimé Césaire*

I feel ridiculous
in their shoes
their dinner jackets
their starched shirts
and detachable collars
their monocles and
their bowler hats

I feel ridiculous
my toes not made
to sweat from morning until night's relief
from this swaddling that impedes my limbs
and deprives my body of the beauty of its hidden sex

I feel ridiculous
my neck caught smokestack style
with this head that aches
but stops
each time I greet someone

I feel ridiculous
in their drawing rooms
among their manners
their bowings and scrapings
and their manifold need of monkeyshines

I feel ridiculous
with all their talk
until they serve each afternoon
a bit of tepid water and
some teacakes snuffling rum

I feel ridiculous
with theories they season
to the taste of their needs
their passions
their instincts
laid out neatly every night
like doormats

I feel ridiculous
among them
like an accomplice
like a pimp
like a murderer among them
my hands hideously red
with the blood of their
ci-vi-li-za-tion

Note

1. Léon Damas, "Sell Out," in *The Negritude Poet*, ed. Ellen Kennedy (New York, NY: Thunder's Mouth Press, 1989), pp. 50–51.

Pedro Albizu Campos

Pedro Albizu Campos (1891-1965) was Puerto Rico's greatest nationalist leader of the 20th century. An outstanding orator and committed anti-colonialist of great courage, he was incarcerated for over twenty years for his political beliefs and actions, and is for many the emblematic symbol of Puerto Rican resistance to U.S. imperialism.

Puerto Rican Nationalism

Pedro Albizu Campos

Sixty-Eight years ago, our republic was formed. On September 23, 1868, we declared our independence from Spain. Puerto Rico was rich in name and in our soil. Our Christian foundation had created a family model that was to be a vanguard of modern civilization.

Influential, independent men have made a difference in our society. Men such as musician Morel Campos; intellectuals such as Eugenio María de Hostos; and poets like Gautier Benítez were among the great men who built and founded this nation.

The founders of our republic in 1868 held that our nation and its people would be sovereign – never belonging to another nation or people. This idea is not original, but is the basis of universal civilization, of international law. It is the basis of the family of free nations.

Our mother nation, Spain, founder of North and South American civilization, recognized this basic principle of sovereignty and, in 1868, paved the way for Puerto Rico to enter the family of free nations.

The United States (after the Spanish American War), on the other hand, saw Puerto Rico not as a nation, but as island property, and therefore took Puerto Rico through military intervention, and kept it.

Military intervention is the most brutal and abusive act that can be committed against a nation and a people. We demanded then, as we do today, the retreat of United States armed forces from Puerto Rico in order to embrace the liberty we held all too briefly in 1868.

We are not as fortunate as our forebears in 1868, who struggled to attain sovereignty. They never had a complaint against Spain, for Spain had every intention of granting Puerto Rico its liberty.

We stand today, docile and defenceless, because, since 1868, our political and economic power has been systematically stripped away by the United States for its own political and economic gain.

We stand as a nation forced not only to demand our liberty, but to demand reparations for having our political and economic liberty taken away.

We stand as a nation surrounded by industry, but with little of it belonging to our people. The business development in Puerto Rico since the United States intervention should have made the island one of the most prosperous islands in the world, but that is not the case.

The United States controls our economy, our commerce. Puerto Rico must determine a price for its products that is acceptable to the United States, while the United States issues their products to Puerto Rico at a rate that is comfortable to its own manufacturers and not the Puerto Rican consumer. The result is exploitation and abuses perpetrated at will, resulting in poverty for our people and wealth for the United States.

Seventy-six per cent of the wealth is in the hands of United States corporations, and their stability is ensured by the United States military. This economic exploitation will have a long-lasting impact. Our family structure will be weakened, and the intellectual, spiritual, and moral advancement of our race will be jeopardized as we are made to be more 'North American.'

Already United States government agencies, under the guise of Christian virtue and goodwill, are simply controlling our people, destroying its culture. By imposing its own culture and language, the United States destroys our own culture and language.

What will we have when we have nothing but dependency on those who destroyed us?

This is why I am dismayed by the effort among our own people to defeat the spirit of those who struggle for our liberation. Our own people see Puerto Rican nationalism as nothing but a path of terrorism and murder; but they defeat our spirit in denouncing themselves. They defeat our spirit by ignoring the historical terrorism and murder of the United States. In the end, they help only the United States, its industry, its imperialist objectives.

It stands to reason – it stands to common sense – that we must be a free nation in order to survive as a people. The future of those not yet born depends on respecting the independence of Puerto Rico. That respect alone – the respecting of Puerto Rico's independence – is what Puerto Rican nationalism is all about.

Reference

Reprinted as Pedro Albizu Campos, "Puerto Rican Nationalism," in O. Nigel Bolland ed., *The Birth of Caribbean Civilisation: A Century of Ideas about Culture and Identity, Nation and Society* (Kingston, Jamaica: Ian Randle Press, 2004): 77-78

Originally published as Pedro Albizu Campos, "Puerto Rican Nationalism," in Robert Santiago ed., *Boricuas: Influential Puerto Rican Writings – An Anthology*. Translated by Roberto Santiago. New York: Ballantine, 1995.

Claudia Jones

Claudia Jones (1915–64) was a Trinidadian communist and Black nationalist, whose activist work in mid-century America and Britain made her an enemy of the state targeted for deportation in the former. Her work as a community organizer in Britain led to what is now known as the Notting Hill Carnival, Europe's biggest Caribbean-influenced carnival. She was a perceptive critic both of imperialism and of the intersecting dominations produced by race, class, and gender. "An End to the Neglect of the Problems of Negro Women!" is her best-known and most poignant single piece of writing and a classic of the Black radical tradition.

An End to the Neglect of the Problems of Negro Women!

Claudia Jones[1]

An outstanding feature of the present stage of the Negro liberation movement is the growth in the militant participation of Negro women in all aspects of the struggle for peace, civil rights, and economic security. Symptomatic of this new militancy is the fact that Negro women have become symbols of many present-day struggles of the Negro people. This growth of militancy among Negro women has profound meaning, both for the Negro liberation movement and for the emerging anti-fascist, anti-imperialist coalition.

To understand this militancy correctly, to deepen and extend the role of Negro women in the struggle for peace and for all interests of the working class and the Negro people, means primarily to overcome the gross neglect of the special problems of Negro women. This neglect has too long permeated the ranks of the labor movement generally, of Left-progressives, and also of the Communist Party. The most serious assessment of these shortcomings by progressives, especially by Marxist-Leninists, is vitally necessary if we are to help accelerate this development and integrate Negro women in the progressive and labor movement in our own Party.

The bourgeoisie is fearful of the militancy of the Negro woman, and for good reason. The capitalists know, far better than many progressives seem to know, that once Negro women undertake action, the militancy of the whole Negro people, and thus of the anti-imperialist coalition, is greatly enhanced.

Historically, the Negro woman has been the guardian, the protector, of the Negro family. From the days of the slave traders down to the present, the Negro woman has had the responsibility of caring for the needs of the family, of militancy shielding it from the blows of Jim Crow insults, of rearing children in an atmosphere of lynch terror, segregation, and policy brutality, and of fighting for an education for the children. The intensified oppression of the Negro people, which has been the hallmark of the postwar reactionary offensive, cannot therefore but lead to an acceleration of the militancy of the Negro woman. As mother, as Negro, and as worker, the Negro woman fights against the wiping out of the Negro family, against the Jim Crow ghetto existence which destroys the health, morale and the very life of millions of her sisters, brothers, and children.

Viewed in this light, it is not accidental that the American bourgeoisie has intensified its oppression, not only of the Negro people in general, but of Negro women in particular. Nothing so exposes the drive to fascization in the nation as the callous attitude which the bourgeoisie displays and cultivates toward Negro women. The vaunted boast of the ideologists of Big Business—that American women possess 'the greatest equality' in the world is exposed in all its hypocrisy in the Soviet Union, the New Democracies and the formerly oppressed land of China, women are attaining new heights of equality. But above all else, Wall Street's boast stops at the water's edge where Negro and working-class women are concerned. Not equality, but degradation and super-exploitation: this is the actual lot of Negro women!

Consider the hypocrisy of the Truman Administration, which boasts about 'exporting democracy throughout the world' while the state of Georgia keeps a widowed Negro mother of twelve children under lock and key. Her crime? She defended her life and dignity—aided by her two sons—from the attacks of a 'white supremacist'. Or ponder the mute silence with which the Department of Justice has greeted Mrs. Amy Mallard, widowed Negro school teacher, since her husband was lynched in Georgia because he had bought a new Cadillac and become, in the opinion of the 'white supremacists', 'too uppity'. Contrast this with the crocodile tears shed by the US delegation to the United Nations for Cardinal Mindszenty, who collaborated with the enemies of the Hungarian People's Republic and sought to hinder the forward march to fuller democracy by the formerly oppressed workers and peasants of Hungary. Only recently, President Truman spoke solicitously in a Mother's Day Proclamation about the manifestation of 'our love and reverence' for all mothers of the land. The so-called 'love and reverence' for the mothers of the land by no means includes Negro mothers who, like Rosa Lee Ingram, Amy Mallard, the wives and mothers of the Trenton Six, or the other countless victims, dare to fight back against lynch law and 'white supremacy' violence.

Economic Hardships

Very much to the contrary, Negro women—as workers, as Negroes, and as women—are the most oppressed stratum of the whole population.

In 1940, two out of every five Negro women, in contrast to two out of every eight white women, worked for a living. By virtue of their majority status among the Negro people, Negro women not only constitute the largest percentage of women heads of families, but are the main breadwinners of the Negro family. The large proportion of Negro women in the labor market is primarily a result of the low-scale earnings of Negro men. This disproportion also has its roots in the treatment and position of Negro women over the centuries.

Following the emancipation, and persisting to the present day, a large percentage of Negro women—married as well as single—were forced to work for a living. But despite the shift in employment of Negro women from rural to urban areas, Negro women are still generally confined to the lowest-paying jobs. The Women's Bureau, US Department of Labor, *Handbook of Facts for Women Workers* (1948, Bulletin 225), shows white women workers as having median earnings more than twice as high as those of non-white women, and non-white women workers (mainly Negro women) as earning less than $500 a year! In the rural South, the earnings of women are even less. In three large Northern industrial communities, the median income of white families ($1,720) is also 60 percent higher than that of Negro families ($1,095). The super-exploitation of the Negro woman worker is thus revealed not only in that she receives, as woman, less than equal pay for equal work with men, but in that the majority of Negro women get less than half the pay of white women. Little wonder, then, that in Negro communities the conditions of ghetto-living—low salaries, high rents, high prices, etc.—virtually become an iron curtain hemming in the lives of Negro children and undermining their health and spirit! Little wonder that the maternity death rate for Negro women is triple that of white women! Little wonder that one out of every ten Negro children born in the United States does not grow to manhood or womanhood!

The low scale of earnings of Negro woman is directly related to her almost complete exclusion from virtually all fields of work except the most menial and underpaid, namely, domestic service. Revealing are the following data given in the report of 1945, *Negro Women War Workers* (Women's Bureau, US Department of Labor, Bulletin 205): Of a total 7½ million Negro women, over a million are in domestic and personal service. The overwhelming bulk—about 918,000—of these women workers are employed in private families, and some 98,000 are employed as cooks, waitresses, and in like services in other than private homes. The remaining 60,000 workers in service trades are in miscellaneous personal service occupations (beauticians, boarding house and lodging-house keepers, charwomen, janitors, practical nurses, housekeepers, hostesses, and elevator operators).

The next largest number of Negro women workers are engaged in agricultural work. In 1940, about 245,000 were agricultural workers. Of them, some 128,000 were unpaid family workers.

Industrial and other workers numbered more than 96,000 of the Negro women reported. Thirty-six thousand of these women were in manufacturing, the chief groups being 11,300 in apparel and other fabricated textile products, 1,000 in tobacco manufacturers, and 5,600 in food and related products.

Clerical and kindred workers in general numbered only 13,00. There were only 8,300 Negro women workers in civil service.

The rest of the Negro women who work for a living were distributed along the following lines: teachers, 50,000; nurses and student nurses, 6,700; social and welfare workers, 1,700; dentists, pharmacists, and veterinarians, 120; physicians and surgeons, 129; actresses, 200; authors, editors and reporters, 100; lawyers and judges, 39; librarians, 400; and other categories likewise illustrating the large-scale exclusion of Negro women from the professions.

During the anti-Axis war, Negro women for the first time in history had an opportunity to utilize their skills and talents in occupations other than domestic and personal service. They became trail blazers in many fields. Since the end of the war, however, this has given way to growing unemployment, to the wholesale firing of Negro women, particularly in basic industry.

This process has been intensified with the development of the economic crisis. Today, Negro women are being forced back into domestic work in great numbers. In New York State, for example, this trend was officially confirmed recently when Edward Corsi, Commissioner of the State Labor Department, revealed that for the first time since the war, domestic help is readily obtainable. Corsi in effect admitted that Negro women are not voluntarily giving up jobs, but rather are being systematically pushed out of industry. Unemployment, which has always hit the Negro woman first and hardest, plus the high cost of living, is what compels Negro women to re-enter domestic service today. Accompanying this trend is an ideological campaign to make domestic work palatable. Daily newspaper advertisements which base their arguments on the claim that most domestic workers who apply for jobs through USES 'prefer this type of work to work in industry', are propagandizing the 'virtues' of domestic work, especially of 'sleep-in positions'.

Inherently connected with the question of job opportunities where the Negro woman is concerned, is the special oppression she faces as Negro, as woman and as worker. She is the victim of the white chauvinist stereotype as to where her place should be. In the film, radio and press, the Negro woman is not pictured in her real role as breadwinner, mother, and protector of the family, but as a traditional 'mammy' who puts the care of children and families of others above her own. This traditional stereotype of the Negro slave mother, which to this day appears in commercial advertisements, must be combatted and rejected as a device of the imperialists to perpetuate the white chauvinist ideology that Negro women are 'backward', 'inferior', and the 'natural slaves' of others.

Historical Aspects

Actually, the history of the Negro woman shows that the Negro mother under slavery held a key position and played a dominant role in her own family grouping. This was due primarily to two factors: the conditions of slavery, under which marriage, as such, was non-existent, and the Negro's social status was derived from the mother and not the father; and the fact that most of the Negro people brought to these shores by the slave traders came from West Africa where the position of women, based on active participation in property control, was relatively higher in the family than that of European women.

Early historians of the slave trade recall the testimony of travelers indicating that the love of the African mother for her child was unsurpassed in any part of the world. There are numerous stories attesting to the self-sacrificial way in which East African mothers offered themselves to the slave traders in order to save their sons and Hottentot women refused food during famines until after their children were fed.

It is impossible within the confines of this article to relate the terrible sufferings and degradation undergone by Negro mothers and Negro women generally under slavery. Subject to legalized rape by the slaveowners, confined to slave pens, forced to march for eight to fourteen hours with loads on their backs and to perform back-breaking work even during pregnancy, Negro women bore a burning hatred for slavery, and undertook a large share of the responsibility for defending and nurturing the Negro family.

The Negro mother was mistress in the slave cabin, and despite the interference of master or overseer, her wishes in regard to mating and in family matters were paramount. During and after slavery, Negro women had to support themselves and the children, necessarily playing an important role in the economic and social life of her people.

The Negro Woman Worker

The negligible participation of Negro women in progressive and trade union circles is thus all the more startling. In union after union, even in those unions where a large concentration of workers are Negro women, few Negro women are to be found as leaders or active workers. The outstanding exceptions to this are the Food and Tobacco Workers' Union and the United Office and Professional Workers' Union.

But why should these be exceptions? Negro women are among the most militant trade unionists. The sharecroppers' strike of the '30's were sparkplugged by Negro women. Subject to the terror of the landlord and white supremacist, they waged magnificent battles together with Negro men and white progressives in that struggle of great tradition led by the Communist Party. Negro women played a magnificent part in the pre-CIO days in strikes and other struggles, both as workers and as wives of workers, to win recognition of the principle of industrial unionism, in such industries as auto, packing, steel, etc. More recently, the militancy of Negro women unionists is shown in the strike of the packing-house workers, and even more so, in the tobacco workers' strike—in which such leaders as Moranda Smith and Velma Hopkins emerged as outstanding trade unionists. The struggle of the tobacco workers led by Negro women later merged with the political action of Negro and white which led to the election of the first Negro in the South (in Winston-Salem, North Carolina) since Reconstruction days.

It is incumbent on progressive unionists to realize that in the fight for equal rights for Negro workers, it is necessary to have a special approach to Negro women workers, who, far out of proportion to other women workers, are the main breadwinners in their families. The fight to retain the Negro woman in industry and to upgrade her on the job, is a major way of struggling for the basic and special interests of the Negro woman worker. Not to recognize this feature is to miss the special aspects of the effects of the growing economic crisis, which is penalizing Negro workers, particularly Negro women workers, with special severity.

The Domestic Worker

One of the crassest manifestations of trade union neglect of the problems of the Negro woman worker has been the failure, not only to fight against relegation of the Negro woman to domestic and similar menial work, but to *organize* the domestic worker. It is merely lip-service for progressive unionists to speak of organizing the un-organized without turning their eyes to the serious plight of the domestic worker, who, unprotected by union standards, is also the victim of exclusion from all social and labor legislation. Only about one in ten of all Negro women workers are to be found in states having minimum-wage laws. All of the arguments heretofore projected with regard to the real difficulties of organizing the domestic workers—such as the 'casual' nature of their employment, the difficulties of organizing day workers, the problem of organizing people who work in individual households, etc.,—must be overcome forthwith. There is a danger that Social-Democratic forces may enter this field to do their work of spreading disunity and demagogy, unless progressives act quickly.

The lot of the domestic worker is one of unbearable misery. Usually, she has no definition of tasks in the household where she works. Domestic workers may have 'thrown in', in addition to cleaning and scrubbing, such tasks as washing windows, caring for the children, laundering, cooking etc., and all at the lowest pay. The Negro domestic worker must suffer the additional indignity, in some areas, of having to seek work in virtual 'slave markets' on the streets where bids are made, as from a slave block, for the hardiest workers. Many a domestic worker, on returning to her own household, must begin housework anew to keep her own family together.

Who was not enraged when it was revealed in California, in the heinous case of Dora Jones, that a Negro woman domestic was enslaved for more than 40 years in 'civilized' America? Her 'employer' was given a minimum sentence of a few years and complained that the sentence was for 'such a long period of time'. But could Dora Jones, Negro domestic worker, be repaid for more than 40 years of her life under such conditions of exploitation and degradation? And how many cases, partaking in varying degrees of the condition of Dora Jones, are still tolerated by progressives themselves!

Only recently, in the New York State Legislature, legislative proposals were made to 'fingerprint' domestic workers. The Martinez Bill did not see the light of day, because the reactionaries were concentrating on other repressive legislative measures; but here we see clearly the imprint of the African 'pass' system of British imperialism (and of the German Reich in relation to the Jewish people!) being attempted in relation to women domestic workers.

It is incumbent on the trade unions to assist the Domestic Workers' Union in every possible way to accomplish the task of organizing the exploited domestic workers, the majority of whom are Negro women. Simultaneously, a legislative fight for the inclusion of domestic workers under the benefits of the Social Security Law is vitally urgent and necessary. Here, too, recurrent questions regarding 'administrative problems' of applying the law to domestic workers should be challenged and solutions found.

The continued relegation of Negro women to domestic work has helped to perpetuate and intensify chauvinism directed against all Negro women. Despite the fact that Negro women may be grandmothers or mothers, the use of the chauvinist term 'girl' for adult Negro women is a common expression. The very economic relationship of Negro women to white women, which perpetuates 'madam-maid' relationships, feeds chauvinist attitudes and makes it incumbent on white women progressives, and particularly Communists, to fight consciously against all manifestations of white chauvinism, open and subtle.

Chauvinism on the part of progressive white women is often expressed in their failure to have close ties of friendship with Negro women and to realize that this fight for equality of Negro women is in their own self-interest, inasmuch as the super-exploitation and oppression of Negro women tends to depress the standards of all women. Too many progressives, and even some Communists, are still guilty of exploiting Negro domestic workers, of refusing to hire them through the Domestic Workers' Union (or of refusing to help in its expansion into those areas where it does not yet exist), and generally of participating in the vilification of 'maids' when speaking to their bourgeois neighbours and their own families. Then, there is the expressed 'concern' that the exploited Negro domestic worker does not 'talk' to, or is not 'friendly' with, her employer, or the habit of assuming that the duty of the white progressive employer is to 'inform' the Negro woman of her exploitation and her oppression which she undoubtedly knows quite intimately. Persistent challenge to every chauvinist remark as concerns the Negro woman is vitally necessary, if we are to break down the understandable distress on the part of the Negro women who are repelled by the white chauvinism they often find expressed in progressive circles.

Manifestations of White Chauvinism

Some of the crassest expressions of chauvinism are to be found at social affairs, where, all to often, white men and women and Negro men participate in dancing, but Negro women are neglected, the acceptance of white ruling-class standards of 'desirability' for women (such as light skin), the failure to extend courtesy to Negro women and to integrate Negro women into organizational leadership, are other forms of chauvinism.

Another rabid aspect of the Jim Crow oppression of the Negro woman is expressed in the numerous laws which are directed against her as regards property rights, inter-marriage (originally designed to prevent white men in the South from marrying Negro women), and laws which hinder and deny the right of choice, not only to Negro women, but Negro and white men and women.

For white progressive women and men, and especially for Communists, the question of social relations with Negro men and women is above all a question of strictly adhering to social equality. This means ridding ourselves of the position which sometimes finds certain progressives and Communists fighting on the economic and political issues facing the Negro people, but 'drawing the line' when it comes to social intercourse or inter-marriage. To place the question as a 'personal' and not a political matter, when such questions arise, is to be guilty of the worst kind of Social-Democratic bourgeois-liberal thinking as regards the Negro question in American life; it is to be guilty of imbibing the poisonous white-chauvinist 'theories' of a Bilbo or a Rankin. Similarly, too, with regard to guaranteeing the 'security' of children. This security will be enhanced only through the struggle for the liberation and equality of all nations and peoples, and not by shielding children from the knowledge of this struggle. This means ridding ourselves of the bourgeois-liberal attitudes which 'permit' Negro and white children of progressives to play together at camps when young, but draw the line when the children reach teenage and establish boy-girl relationships.

The bourgeois ideologists have not failed, of course, to develop a special ideological offensive aimed at degrading Negro women, as part and parcel of the general reactionary ideological offensive against women of 'kitchen, church and children'. They cannot, however, with equanimity or credibility, speak of the Negro woman's 'place' as in the home; for Negro women are in other people's kitchens. Hence, their task has been to intensify their theories of male 'superiority' as regards the Negro woman by developing introspective attitudes which coincide with the 'new school' of 'psychological inferiority' of women. The whole intent of a host of articles, books, etc., has been to obscure the main responsibility for the oppression of Negro women by spreading the rotten bourgeois notion about a 'battle of the sexes' and 'ignoring' the fight of both Negro men and women—the whole Negro people—against their common oppressors, the white ruling class.

Chauvinist expressions also include paternalistic surprise when it is learned that Negroes are professional people. Negro professional women workers are often confronted with such remarks as 'Isn't your family proud of you?' Then, there is the reverse practice of inquiring of Negro women professionals whether 'someone in the family' would like to take a job as a domestic worker.

The responsibility for overcoming these special forms of white chauvinism rests, not with the 'subjectivity' of Negro women, as it is often put, but squarely on the shoulders of white men and white women. Negro men have a special responsibility particularly in relation to rooting out attitudes of male superiority as regards women in general. There is need to root out all 'humanitarian' and patronizing attitudes toward Negro women. In one community, a leading Negro trade unionist, the treasurer of her Party section, would be told by a white progressive woman after every social function: 'Let me have the money; something may happen to you'. In another instance, a Negro domestic worker who wanted to join the Party was told by her employer, a Communist, that she was 'too backward' and 'wasn't ready' to join the Party. In yet another community, which since the war has been populated in the proportion of sixty percent Negro to forty percent white, white progressive mothers maneuvered to get their children out of the school in this community. To the credit of the initiative of the Party section organizer, a Negro woman, a struggle was begun which forced a change in arrangements which the school principle, yielding to the mothers' and his own prejudices, had established. These arrangements involved a special class in which a few white children were isolated with 'selected Negro kids' in what was termed an 'experimental class in race relations'.

These chauvinist attitudes, particularly as expressed toward the Negro woman, are undoubtedly an important reason for the grossly insufficient participation of Negro women in progressive organizations and in our Party as members and leaders.

The American bourgeoisie, we must remember, is aware of the present and even greater potential role of the masses of Negro women, and is therefore not loathe to throw plums to Negroes who betray their people and do the bidding of imperialism.

Faced with the exposure of their callous attitude to Negro women, faced with the growing protests against unpunished lynchings and the legal lynchings 'Northern style', Wall Street is giving a few token positions to Negro women. Thus, Anna Arnold Hergeman, who played a key role in the Democratic National Negro Committee to Elect Truman, was rewarded with the appointment as Assistant Federal Security Administrator Ewing. Thus, too, Governor Dewey appointed Irene Diggs to a high post in the New York State Administration.

Another straw in the wind showing attempts to whittle down the militancy of Negro women was the State Department's invitation to a representative of the National Council of Negro Women—the only Negro organization so designated—to witness the signing of the Atlantic Pact.

Key Issues of Struggle

There are many key issues facing Negro women around which struggle can and must be waged.

But none so dramatizes the oppressed status of Negro womanhood as does the case of Rosa Lee Ingram, widowed Negro mother of fourteen children—two of them dead—who faces life imprisonment in a Georgia jail for defending herself from the indecent advances of a 'white supremacist'. The Ingram case illustrates the landless, Jim Crow oppressed status of the Negro family in America. It illumines particularly the degradation of Negro women today under American bourgeois democracy moving to fascism and war. It reflects the daily insults to which Negro women are subjected in public places, no matter what their class, status, or position. It exposes the hypocritical alibi of the lynchers of Negro manhood who have historically hidden behind the skirts of white women when they try to cover up their foul crimes with the 'chivalry' of 'protecting white womenhood'. But white women, today, no less than their sisters in the abolitionist and suffrage movements, must rise to challenge this lie and the whole system of Negro oppression.

American history is rich in examples of the cost—to the democratic rights of both women and men—of failure to wage this fight. The suffragists, during their first failings, were purposely

placed on cots next to Negro prostitutes to 'humiliate' them. They had the wisdom to understand that the intent was to make it so painful, that no women would dare to fight for her rights
if she had to face such consequences. But it was the historic shortcoming of the women's suffrage
leaders, predominantly drawn as they were from the bourgeoisie and the petty-bourgeoisie, that
they failed to link their own struggles to the struggles for the full democratic rights of the Negro
people following emancipation.

A developing consciousness on the woman question today, therefore, must not fail to recognize that the Negro question in the United States is *prior* to, and not equal to, the woman question; that only to the extent that we fight all chauvinist expressions and actions as regards the
Negro people and fight for the full equality of the Negro people, can women as a whole advance
their struggle for equal rights. For the progressive women's movement, the Negro woman, who
combines in her status the worker, the Negro, and the woman, is the vital link to this heightened
political consciousness. To the extent, further, that the cause of the Negro woman worker is promoted, she will be enabled to take her rightful place in the Negro-proletarian leadership of the
national liberation movement, and by her active participation contribute to the entire American
working class, whose historic mission is the achievement of a Socialist America—the final and
full guarantee of woman's emancipation.

The fight for Rosa Lee Ingram's freedom is a challenge to all white women and to all progressive forces, who must begin to ask themselves: How long shall we allow this dastardly crime
against all womenhood, against the Negro people, to go unchallenged? Rosa Lee Ingram's plight
and that of her sisters also carries with it a challenge to progressive cultural workers to write and
sing of the Negro woman in her full courage and dignity.

The recent establishment of the National Committee to Free the Ingram Family fulfills a need
long felt since the early movement which forced commutation to life imprisonment of Mrs.
Ingram's original sentence of execution. This National Committee, headed by Mary Church Terrell, a founder of the National Association of Colored Women, includes among its leaders such
prominent women, Negro and white, as Therese Robinson, National Grand Directoress of the
Civil Liberties Committee of the Elks, Ada B. Jackson, and Dr. Gene Weltfish.

One of the first steps of the Committee was the visit of a delegation of Negro and white citizens to this courageous, militant Negro mother imprisoned in a Georgia cell. The measure of
support was so great that the Georgia authorities allowed the delegation to see her unimpeded.
Since that time, however, in retaliation against the developing mass movement, the Georgia
officials have moved Mrs. Ingram, who is suffering from a severe heart condition, to a worse
penitentiary, at Reedsville.

Support to the work of this committee becomes a prime necessity for all progressives, particularly women. President Truman must be stripped of his pretense of 'know-nothing' about
the Ingram case. To free the Ingrams, support must be rallied for the success of the million-
signatures campaign, and for UN action on the Ingram brief soon to be filed.

The struggle for jobs for Negro women is a prime issue. The growing economic crisis, with
its mounting unemployment and wage-cuts and increasing evictions, is making its implact felt
most heavily on the Negro masses. In one Negro community after another, Negro women, the
last to be hired and the first to be fired, are the greatest sufferers from unemployment. Struggles
must be developed to win jobs for Negro women in basic industry, in the white-collar occupations, in the communities, and in private utilities.

The successful campaign of the Communist Party in New York's East Side to win jobs for
Negro women in the five-and-dime stores has led to the hiring of Negro women throughout the
city, even in predominantly white communities. This campaign has extended to New England
and must be waged elsewhere.

Close to 15 government agencies do not hire Negroes at all. This policy gives official sanction to, and at the same time further encourages, the pervasive Jim Crow policies of the capitalist exploiters. A campaign to win jobs for Negro women here would thus greatly advance the whole struggle for jobs for Negro men and women. In addition, it would have a telling effect in exposing the hypocrisy of the Truman Administration's 'Civil Rights' program.

A strong fight will also have to be made against the growing practice of the United States Employment Service to shunt Negro women, despite their qualifications for other jobs, only into domestic and personal service work.

Where consciousness of the special role of Negro women exists, successful struggle can be initiated which will win the support of white workers. A recent example was the initiative taken by white Communist garment workers in a shop employing 25 Negro women where three machines were idle. The issue of upgrading Negro women workers became a vital one. A boycott movement has been initiated and the machines stand unused as of this writing, the white workers refusing to adhere to strict seniority at the expense of Negro workers. Meanwhile, negotiations are continuing on this issue. Similarly, in a Packard UAW local in Detroit, a fight for the maintenance of women in industry and for the upgrading of 750 women, the large majority of whom where Negro, was recently won.

The Struggle for Peace

Winning the Negro women for the struggle for peace is decisive for all other struggles. Even during the anti-Axis war, Negro women had to weep for their soldier-sons, lynched while serving in a Jim Crow army. Are they, therefore, not interested in the struggle for peace?

The efforts of the bipartisan war-makers to gain the support of the women's organizations in general, have influenced many Negro women's organizations, which, at their last annual conventions, adopted foreign-policy stands favouring the Marshall Plan and Truman Doctrine. Many of these organizations have worked with groups having outspoken anti-imperialist positions.

That there is profound peace sentiment among Negro women which can be mobilized for effective action is shown, not only in the magnificent response to the meetings of Eslande Goode Robeson, but also in the position announced last year by the oldest Negro women's organization, under the leadership of Mrs. Christine C. Smith, in urging a national mobilization of American Negro women in support of the United Nations. In this connection, it will be very fruitful to bring to our country a consciousness of the magnificent struggles of women in North Africa, who, though lacking in the most elementary material needs, have organized a strong movement for peace and thus stand united against a Third World War, with 81 million women in 57 nations, in the Women's International Democratic Federation.

Our Party, based on its Marxist-Leninist principles, stands four-square on a program of full economic, political and social equality for the Negro people and of equal rights for women. Who, more than the Negro woman, the most exploited and oppressed, belongs in our Party? Negro women can and must make an enormous contribution to the daily life and work of the Party. Concretely, this means prime responsibility lies with white men and women comrades. Negro men comrades, however, must participate on this task. Negro Communist women must everywhere now take their rightful place in Party leadership on all levels.

The strong capacities, militancy and organizational talents of Negro women, can, if well utilized by our Party, be a powerful lever for bringing forward Negro workers—men and women— as the leading forces of the Negro people's liberation movement, for cementing Negro and white unity in the struggle against Wall Street imperialism, and for rooting the Party among the most exploited and oppressed sections of the working class and its allies.

In our Party clubs, we must conduct an intense discussion of the role of the Negro women, so as to equip our Party membership with clear understanding for undertaking the necessary struggles in the shops and communities. We must end the practice, in which many Negro women who join our Party, and who, in their churches, communities and fraternal groups are leaders of masses, with an invaluable mass experience to give to our Party, suddenly find themselves involved in our clubs, not as leaders, but as people who have 'to get their feet wet' organizationally. We must end this failure to create an atmosphere in our clubs in which new recruits—in this case Negro women—are confronted with the 'silent treatment' or with attempts to 'blueprint' them into a pattern. In addition to the white chauvinist implications in such approaches, these practices confuse the basic need for Marxist-Leninist understanding which our Party gives to all workers, and which enhances their political understanding, with chauvinist disdain for the organizational talents of new Negro members, or for the necessity to promote them into leadership.

To win the Negro women for full participation in the antifascist, anti-imperialist coalition, to bring her militancy and participation to even greater heights in the current and future struggles against Wall Street imperialism, progressives must acquire political consciousness as regards her special oppressed status.

It is this consciousness, accelerated by struggles, that will convince increasing thousands that only the Communist Party, as the vanguard of the working class, with its ultimate perspective of Socialism, can achieve for the Negro women—for the entire Negro people—the full equality and dignity of their stature in a Socialist society in which contributions to society are measured, not by national origin, or by color, but a society in which men and women contribute according to ability, and ultimately under Communism receive according to their needs.

Note

1. Claudia Jones, "An End to the Neglect of the Problems of Negro Women!," in *"I Think of My Mother": Notes on the Life and Times of Claudia Jones*, ed. Buzz Johnson (London: Karia Press, 1985), pp. 103–120.

Aimé Césaire

Poet, statesman, and revolutionary theorist Aimé Césaire (1915–2008) was one of the most important intellectuals of the twentieth-century Caribbean and the most influential figure in that period in Martinique, the birthplace also of Frantz Fanon and Edouard Glissant. In the 1930s in Paris, he coined the term "négritude" and founded a movement based on that name with Leopold Sédar Senghor and Léon Damas. Césaire's body of work contains some of the most thrilling and experimental poetry written in the Caribbean, plays, and revolutionary tracts. His incisive critique of colonialism, *Discourse on Colonialism* (1950), is excerpted ahead.

Discourse on Colonialism

Aimé Césaire[1]

A civilization that proves incapable of solving the problems it creates is a decadent civilization.

A civilization that chooses to close its eyes to its most crucial problems is a stricken civilization.

A civilization that uses its principles for trickery and deceit is a dying civilization.

The fact is that the so-called European civilization—"Western" civilization—as it has been shaped by two centuries of bourgeois rule, is incapable of solving the two major problems to which its existence has given rise: the problem of the proletariat and the colonial problem; that Europe is unable to justify itself either before the bar of "reason" or before the bar of "conscience"; and that, increasingly, it takes refuge in a hypocrisy which is all the more odious because it is less and less likely to deceive.

Europe is indefensible.

Apparently that is what the American strategists are whispering to each other.

That in itself is not serious.

What is serious is that "Europe" is morally, spiritually indefensible.

And today the indictment is brought against it not by the European masses alone, but on a world scale, by tens and tens of millions of men who, from the depths of slavery, set themselves up as judges.

The colonialists may kill in Indochina, torture in Madagascar, imprison in Black Africa, crack down in the West Indies. Henceforth the colonized know that they have an advantage over them. They know that their temporary "masters" are lying.

Therefore that their masters are weak.

And since I have been asked to speak about colonization and civilization, let us go straight to the principal lie that is the source of all the others.

Colonization and civilization?

In dealing with this subject, the commonest curse is to be the dupe in good faith of a collective hypocrisy that cleverly misrepresents problems, the better to legitimize the hateful solutions provided for them.

In other words, the essential thing here is to see clearly, to think clearly—that is, dangerously—and to answer clearly the innocent first question: what, fundamentally, is colonization? To agree on what it is not: neither evangelization, nor a philanthropic enterprise, nor a desire to push back the frontiers of ignorance, disease, and tyranny, nor a project undertaken for the greater glory of God, nor an attempt to extend the rule of law. To admit once and for all, without flinching at the consequences, that the decisive actors here are the adventurer and the pirate, the wholesale grocer and the ship owner, the gold digger and the merchant, appetite and force, and behind them, the baleful projected shadow of a form of civilization which, at a certain point in its history, finds itself obliged, for internal reasons, to extend to a world scale the competition of its antagonistic economies.

Pursuing my analysis, I find that hypocrisy is of recent date; that neither Cortéz discovering Mexico from the top of the great teocalli, nor Pizzaro before Cuzco (much less Marco Polo before Cambuluc), claims that he is the harbinger of a superior order; that they kill; that they plunder; that they have helmets, lances, cupidities; that the slavering apologists came later; that the chief culprit in this domain is Christian pedantry, which laid down the dishonest equations *Christianity = civilization, paganism = savagery*, from which there could not but ensue abominable colonialist and racist consequences, whose victims were to be the Indians, the Yellow peoples, and the Negroes.

That being settled, I admit that it is a good thing to place different civilizations in contact with each other; that it is an excellent thing to blend different worlds; that whatever its own particular genius may be, a civilization that withdraws into itself atrophies; that for civilizations, exchange is oxygen; that the great good fortune of Europe is to have been a crossroads, and that because it was the locus of all ideas, the receptacle of all philosophies, the meeting place of all sentiments, it was the best center for the redistribution of energy.

But then I ask the following question: has colonization really *placed civilizations in contact*? Or, if you prefer, of all the ways of *establishing contact*, was it the best?

I answer *no*.

And I say that between *colonization* and *civilization* there is an infinite distance; that out of all the colonial expeditions that have been undertaken, out of all the colonial statutes that have been drawn up, out of all the memoranda that have been dispatched by all the ministries, there could not come a single human value.

∗∗∗∗

First we must study how colonization works to *decivilize* the colonizer, to *brutalize* him in the true sense of the word, to degrade him, to awaken him to buried instincts, to covetousness, violence, race hatred, and moral relativism; and we must show that each time a head is cut off or an eye put out in Vietnam and in France they accept the fact, each time a little girl is raped and in France they accept the fact, each time a Madagascan is tortured and in France they accept the fact, civilization acquires another dead weight, a universal regression takes place, a gangrene sets in, a center of infection begins to spread; and that at the end of all these treaties that have been violated, all these lies that have been propagated, all these punitive expeditions that have been tolerated, all these prisoners who have been tied up and "interrogated," all these patriots who have been tortured, at the end of all the racial pride that has been encouraged, all the boastfulness that has been displayed, a poison has been distilled into the veins of Europe and, slowly but surely, the continent proceeds toward *savagery*.

And then one fine day the bourgeoisie is awakened by a terrific boomerang effect: the gestapos are busy, the prisons fill up, the torturers standing around the racks invent, refine, discuss.

People are surprised, they become indignant. They say: "How strange! But never mind—it's Nazism, it will pass!" And they wait, and they hope; and they hide the truth from themselves, that it is barbarism, the supreme barbarism, the crowning barbarism that sums up all the daily barbarisms; that it is Nazism, yes, but that before they were its victims, they were its accomplices; that they tolerated that Nazism before it was inflicted on them, that they absolved it, shut their eyes to it, legitimized it, because, until then, it had been applied only to non-European peoples; that they have cultivated that Nazism, that they are responsible for it, and that before engulfing the whole edifice of Western, Christian civilization in its reddened waters, it oozes, seeps, and trickles from every crack.

Yes, it would be worthwhile to study clinically, in detail, the steps taken by Hitler and Hitlerism and to reveal to the very distinguished, very humanistic, very Christian bourgeois of the twentieth century that without his being aware of it, he has a Hitler inside him, that Hitler *inhabits* him, that Hitler is his *demon*, that if he rails against him, he is being inconsistent and that, at bottom, what he cannot forgive Hitler for is not *the crime* in itself, *the crime against man*, it is not *the humiliation of man as such*, it is the crime against the white man, the humiliation of the white man, and the fact that he applied to Europe colonialist procedures which until then had been reserved exclusively for the Arabs of Algeria, the "coolies" of India, and the "niggers" of Africa.

And that is the great thing I hold against pseudo-humanism: that for too long it has diminished the rights of man, that its concept of those rights has been—and still is—narrow and fragmentary, incomplete and biased and, all things considered, sordidly racist.

I have talked a good deal about Hitler. Because he deserves it: he makes it possible to see things on a large scale and to grasp the fact that capitalist society, at its present stage, is incapable of establishing a concept of the rights of all men, just as it has proved incapable of establishing a system of individual ethics. Whether one likes it or not, at the end of the blind alley that is Europe, I mean the Europe of Adenauer, Schuman, Bidault, and a few others, there is Hitler. At the end of capitalism, which is eager to outlive its day, there is Hitler. At the end of formal humanism and philosophic renunciation, there is Hitler.

And this being so, I cannot help thinking of one of his statements: "We aspire not to equality but to domination. The country of a foreign race must become once again a country of serfs, of agricultural laborers, or industrial workers. It is not a question of eliminating the inequalities among men but of widening them and making them into a law."

That rings clear, haughty, and brutal, and plants us squarely in the middle of howling savagery. But let us come down a step.

Who is speaking? I am ashamed to say it: it is the Western *humanist*, the "idealist" philosopher. That his name is Renan is an accident. That the passage is taken from a book entitled *La Réforme intellectuelle et morale*, that it was written in France just after a war which France had represented as a war of right against might, tells us a great deal about bourgeois morals.

The regeneration of the inferior or degenerate races by the superior races is part of the providential order of things for humanity. With us, the common man is nearly always a déclassé nobleman, his heavy hand is better suited to handling the sword than the menial tool. Rather than work, he chooses to fight, that is, he returns to his first estate. *Regere imperio populos*, that is our vocation. Pour forth this all-consuming activity onto countries which, like China, are crying aloud for foreign conquest. Turn the adventurers who disturb European society into a *ver sacrum*, a horde like those of the Franks, the Lombards, or the Normans, and every man will be in his right role. Nature has made a race of workers, the Chinese race, who have wonderful manual dexterity and almost no sense of honor; govern them with justice, levying from them, in return for the blessing of such a government, an ample allowance for the conquering race, and they will be satisfied; a race of tillers of the soil, the Negro; treat him with kindness and humanity, and all will be as it should; a race of masters and soldiers, the European race. Reduce this noble race to working in the *ergastulum* like Negroes and Chinese, and they rebel. In Europe, every rebel is, more or less, a soldier who has missed his calling, a creature made for the heroic life, before whom you are setting *a task that is contrary to his race*, a poor worker, too good a soldier. But the life at which our workers rebel would make a Chinese or a fellah happy, as they are not military creatures in the least. *Let each one do what he is made for, and all will be well.*

Hitler? Rosenberg? No, Renan.

But let us come down one step further. And it is the long-winded politician. Who protests? No one, so far as I know, when M. Albert Sarraut, the former governor-general of Indochina, holding forth to the students at the Ecole Coloniale, teaches them that it would be puerile to object to the European colonial enterprises in the name of "an alleged right to possess the land one occupies, and some sort of right to remain in fierce isolation, which would leave unutilized resources to lie forever idle in the hands of incompetents."

And who is roused to indignation when a certain Rev. Barde assures us that if the goods of this world "remained divided up indefinitely, as they would be without colonization, they would answer neither the purposes of God nor the just demands of the human collectivity"?

Since, as his fellow Christian, the Rev. Muller, declares: "Humanity must not, cannot allow the incompetence, negligence, and laziness of the uncivilized peoples to leave idle indefinitely the wealth which God has confided to them, charging them to make it serve the good of all."

No one.

I mean not one established writer, not one academic, not one preacher, not one crusader for the right and for religion, not one "defender of the human person."

And yet, through the mouths of the Sarrauts and the Bardes, the Mullers and the Renans, through the mouths of all those who considered—and consider—it lawful to apply to non-European peoples "a kind of expropriation for public purposes" for the benefit of nations that were stronger and better equipped, it was already Hitler speaking!

What am I driving at? At this idea: that no one colonizes innocently, that no one colonizes with impunity either; that a nation which colonizes, that a civilization which justifies colonization—and therefore force—is already a sick civilization, a civilization which is morally diseased, which irresistibly, progressing from one consequence to another, one denial to another, calls for its Hitler, I mean its punishment.

Colonization: bridgehead in a campaign to civilize barbarism, from which there may emerge at any moment the negation of civilization, pure and simple.

Elsewhere I have cited at length a few incidents culled from the history of colonial expeditions.

Unfortunately, this did not find favor with everyone. It seems that I was pulling old skeletons out of the closet. Indeed!

Was there no point in quoting Colonel de Montagnac, one of the conquerors of Algeria: "In order to banish the thoughts that sometimes besiege me, I have some heads cut off, not the heads of artichokes but the heads of men."

Would it have been more advisable to refuse the floor to Count d'Hérisson: "It is true that we are bringing back a whole barrelful of ears collected, pair by pair, from prisoners, friendly or enemy."

Should I have denied Saint-Arnaud the right to profess his barbarous faith: "We lay waste, we burn, we plunder, we destroy the houses and the trees."

Should I have prevented Marshal Bugeaud from systematizing all that in a daring theory and invoking the precedent of famous ancestors: "We must have a great invasion of Africa, like the invasions of the Franks and the Goths."

Lastly, should I have cast back into the shadows of oblivion the memorable feat of arms of General Gérard and kept silent about the capture of Ambike, a city which, to tell the truth, had never dreamed of defending itself: "The native riflemen had orders to kill only the men, but no one restrained them; intoxicated by the smell of blood, they spared not one woman, not one child . . . . At the end of the afternoon, the heat caused a light mist to arise: it was the blood of the five thousand victims, the ghost of the city, evaporating in the setting sun."

Yes or no, are these things true? And the sadistic pleasures, the nameless delights that send voluptuous shivers and quivers through Loti's carcass when he focuses his field glasses on a good massacre of the Annamese? True or not true? And if these things are true, as no one can deny, will it be said, in order to minimize them, that these corpses don't prove anything?

For my part, if I have recalled a few details of these hideous butcheries, it is by no means because I take a morbid delight in them, but because I think that these heads of men, these collections of ears, these burned houses, these Gothic invasions, this steaming blood, these cities that evaporate at the edge of the sword, are not to be so easily disposed of. They prove that colonization, I repeat, dehumanizes even the most civilized man; that colonial activity, colonial enterprise, colonial conquest, which is based on contempt for the native and justified by that contempt, inevitably tends to change him who undertakes it; that the colonizer, who in order to ease his conscience gets into the habit of seeing the other man as *an animal*, accustoms himself to treating him like an animal, and tends objectively to transform *himself* into an animal. It is this result, this boomerang effect of colonization that I wanted to point out.

Unfair? No. There was a time when these same facts were a source of pride, and when, sure of the morrow, people did not mince words. One last quotation; it is from a certain Carl Siger, author of an *Essai sur la colonisation* (Paris, 1907):

> The new countries offer a vast field for individual, violent activities which, in the metropolitan countries, would run up against certain prejudices, against a sober and orderly conception of life, and which, in the colonies, have greater freedom to develop and, consequently, to affirm their worth. Thus to a certain extent the colonies can serve as a safety valve for modern society. Even if this were their only value, it would be immense.

Truly, there are sins for which no one has the power to make amends and which can never be fully expiated.

But let us speak about the colonized.

I see clearly what colonization has destroyed: the wonderful Indian civilizations—and neither Deterding nor Royal Dutch nor Standard Oil will ever console me for the Aztecs and the Incas.

I see clearly the civilizations, condemned to perish at a future date, into which it has introduced a principle of ruin: the South Sea Islands, Nigeria, Nyasaland. I see less clearly the contributions it has made.

Security? Culture? The rule of law? In the meantime, I look around and wherever there are colonizers and colonized face to face, I see force, brutality, cruelty, sadism, conflict, and, in a parody of education, the hasty manufacture of a few thousand subordinate functionaries, "boys," artisans, office clerks, and interpreters necessary for the smooth operation of business.

I spoke of contact.

Between colonizer and colonized there is room only for forced labor, intimidation, pressure, the police, taxation, theft, rape, compulsory crops, contempt, mistrust, arrogance, self-complacency, swinishness, brainless elites, degraded masses.

No human contact, but relations of domination and submission which turn the colonizing man into a classroom monitor, an army sergeant, a prison guard, a slave driver, and the indigenous man into an instrument of production.

My turn to state an equation: colonization = "thingification."

I hear the storm. They talk to me about progress, about "achievements," diseases cured, improved standards of living.

I am talking about societies drained of their essence, cultures trampled underfoot, institutions undermined, lands confiscated, religions smashed, magnificent artistic creations destroyed, extraordinary *possibilities* wiped out.

They throw facts at my head, statistics, mileages of roads, canals, and railroad tracks.

I am talking about thousands of men sacrificed to the Congo-Océan.[2] I am talking about those who, as I write this, are digging the harbor of Abidjan by hand. I am talking about millions of men torn from their gods, their land, their habits, their life—from life, from the dance, from wisdom.

I am talking about millions of men in whom fear has been cunningly instilled, who have been taught to have an inferiority complex, to tremble, kneel, despair, and behave like flunkeys.

They dazzle me with the tonnage of cotton or cocoa that has been exported, the acreage that has been planted with olive trees or grapevines.

I am talking about natural *economies* that have been disrupted—harmonious and viable *economies* adapted to the indigenous population—about food crops destroyed, malnutrition permanently introduced, agricultural development oriented solely toward the benefit of the metropolitan countries; about the looting of products, the looting of raw materials.

They pride themselves on abuses eliminated.

I too talk about abuses, but what I say is that on the old ones—very real—they have superimposed others—very detestable. They talk to me about local tyrants brought to reason; but I note that in general the old tyrants get on very well with the new ones, and that there has been established between them, to the detriment of the people, a circuit of mutual services and complicity.

They talk to me about civilization, I talk about proletarianization and mystification.

For my part, I make a systematic defense of the non-European civilizations.

Every day that passes, every denial of justice, every beating by the police, every demand of the workers that is drowned in blood, every scandal that is hushed up, every punitive expedition, every police van, every gendarme and every militiaman, brings home to us the value of our old societies.

They were communal societies, never societies of the many for the few.

They were societies that were not only ante-capitalist, as has been said, but also *anti-capitalist*.

They were democratic societies, always.

They were cooperative societies, fraternal societies.

I make a systematic defense of the societies destroyed by imperialism.

They were the fact, they did not pretend to be the idea; despite their faults, they were neither to be hated nor condemned. They were content to be. In them, neither the word *failure* nor the word *avatar* had any meaning. They kept hope intact.

Whereas those are the only words that can, in all honesty, be applied to the European enterprises outside Europe. My only consolation is that periods of colonization pass, that nations sleep only for a time, and that peoples remain.

This being said, it seems that in certain circles they pretend to have discovered in me an "enemy of Europe" and a prophet of the return to the pre-European past.

For my part, I search in vain for the place where I could have expressed such views; where I ever underestimated the importance of Europe in the history of human thought; where I ever preached a *return* of any kind; where I ever claimed that there could be a *return*.

The truth is that I have said something very different: to wit, that the great historical tragedy of Africa has been not so much that it was too late in making contact with the rest of the world, as the manner in which that contact was brought about; that Europe began to "propagate" at a time when it had fallen into the hands of the most unscrupulous financiers and captains of industry; that it was our misfortune to encounter that particular Europe on our path, and that Europe is responsible before the human community for the highest heap of corpses in history.

In another connection, in judging colonization, I have added that Europe has gotten on very well indeed with all the local feudal lords who agreed to serve, woven a villainous complicity with them, rendered their tyranny more effective and more efficient, and that it has actually tended to prolong artificially the survival of local pasts in their most pernicious aspects.

I have said—and this is something very different—that colonialist Europe has grafted modern abuse onto ancient injustice, hateful racism onto old inequality.

That if I am attacked on the grounds of intent, I maintain that colonialist Europe is dishonest in trying to justify its colonizing activity *a posteriori* by the obvious material progress that has been achieved in certain fields under the colonial regime—since *sudden change* is always possible, in history as elsewhere; since no one knows at what stage of material development these same countries would have been if Europe had not intervened; since the introduction of technology into Africa and Asia, their administrative reorganization, in a word, their "Europeanization," was (as is proved by the example of Japan) in no way tied to the European *occupation*; since the Europeanization of the non-European continents could have been accomplished otherwise than under the heel of Europe; since this movement of Europeanization was in progress; since it was even slowed down; since in any case it was distorted by the European takeover.

The proof is that at present it is the indigenous peoples of Africa and Asia who are demanding schools, and colonialist Europe which refuses them; that it is the African who is asking for ports and roads, and colonialist Europe which is niggardly on this score; that it is the colonized man who wants to move forward, and the colonizer who holds things back.

****

One of the values invented by the bourgeoisie in former times and launched throughout the world was *man*—and we have seen what has become of that. The other was the nation.

It is a fact: the *nation* is a bourgeois phenomenon.

Exactly; but if I turn my attention from *man* to *nations*, I note that here too there is great danger; that colonial enterprise is to the modern world what Roman imperialism was to the ancient world: the prelude to Disaster and the forerunner of Catastrophe. Come, now! The Indians massacred, the Moslem world drained of itself, the Chinese world defiled and perverted for a good century; the Negro world disqualified; mighty voices stilled forever; homes scattered to the wind; all this wreckage, all this waste, humanity reduced to a monologue, and you think all that does not have its price? The truth is that this policy *cannot but bring about the ruin of Europe itself,* and that Europe, if it is not careful, will perish from the void it has created around itself.

They thought they were only slaughtering Indians, or Hindus, or South Sea Islanders, or Africans. They have in fact overthrown, one after another, the ramparts behind which European civilization could have developed freely.

I know how fallacious historical parallels are, particularly the one I am about to draw. Nevertheless, permit me to quote a page from Edgar Quinet for the not inconsiderable element of truth which it contains and which is worth pondering.

Here it is:

People ask why barbarism emerged all at once in ancient civilization. I believe I know the answer. It is surprising that so simple a cause is not obvious to everyone. The system of ancient civilization was composed of a certain number of nationalities, of countries which, although they seemed to be enemies, or were even ignorant of each other, protected, supported, and guarded one another. When the expanding Roman Empire undertook to conquer and destroy these groups of nations, the dazzled sophists thought they saw at the end of this road humanity triumphant in Rome. They talked about the unity of the human spirit; it was only a dream. It happened that these nationalities were so many bulwarks protecting Rome itself . . . . Thus when Rome, in its alleged triumphal march toward a single civilization, had destroyed, one after the other, Carthage, Egypt, Greece, Judea, Persia, Dacia, and Cisalpine and Transalpine Gaul, it came to pass that it had itself swallowed up the dikes that protected it against the human ocean under which it was to perish. The magnanimous Caesar, by crushing the two Gauls, only paved the way for the Teutons. So many societies, so many languages extinguished, so many cities, rights, homes annihilated, created a void around Rome, and in those places which were not invaded by the barbarians, barbarism was born spontaneously. The vanquished Gauls changed into Bagaudes. Thus the violent downfall, the progressive extirpation of individual cities, caused the crumbling of ancient civilization. That social edifice was supported by the various nationalities as by so many different columns of marble or porphyry.

When, to the applause of the wise men of the time, each of these living columns had been demolished, the edifice came crashing down; and the wise men of our day are still trying to understand how such mighty ruins could have been made in a moment's time.

And now I ask: what else has bourgeois Europe done? It has undermined civilizations, destroyed countries, ruined nationalities, extirpated "the root of diversity." No more dikes, no more bulwarks. The hour of the barbarian is at hand. The modern barbarian. The American hour. Violence, excess, waste, mercantilism, bluff, conformism, stupidity, vulgarity, disorder.

In 1913, Ambassador Page wrote to Wilson:

"The future of the world belongs to us . . . . Now what are we going to do with the leadership of the world presently when it clearly falls into our hands?"

And in 1914: "What are we going to do with this England and this Empire, presently, when economic forces unmistakably put the leadership of the race in our hands?"

This Empire . . . And the others . . .

And indeed, do you not see how ostentatiously these gentlemen have just unfurled the banner of anti-colonialism?

"*Aid to the disinherited countries*," says Truman. "The time of the old colonialism has passed." That's also Truman.

Which means that American high finance considers that the time has come to raid every colony in the world. So, dear friends, here you have to be careful!

I know that some of you, disgusted with Europe, with all that hideous mess which you did not witness by choice, are turning—oh! in no great numbers—toward America and getting used to looking upon that country as a possible liberator.

"What a godsend!" you think.

"The bulldozers! The massive investments of capital! The roads! The ports!"

"But American racism!"

"So what? European racism in the colonies has inured us to it!"

And there we are, ready to run the great Yankee risk.

So, once again, be careful!

American domination—the only domination from which one never recovers. I mean from which one never recovers unscarred.

And since you are talking about factories and industries, do you not see the tremendous factory hysterically spitting out its cinders in the heart of our forests or deep in the bush, the factory for the production of lackeys; do you not see the prodigious mechanization, the mechanization of man; the gigantic rape of everything intimate, undamaged, undefiled that, despoiled as we are, our human spirit has still managed to preserve; the machine, yes, have you never seen it, the machine for crushing, for grinding, for degrading peoples?

So that the danger is immense.

So that unless, in Africa, in the South Sea Islands, in Madagascar (that is, at the gates of South Africa), in the West Indies (that is, at the gates of America), Western Europe undertakes on its own initiative a policy of *nationalities*, a new policy founded on respect for peoples and cultures—nay, more—unless Europe galvanizes the dying cultures or raises up new ones, unless it becomes the awakener of countries and civilizations (this being said without taking into account the admirable resistance of the colonial peoples primarily symbolized at present by Vietnam, but also by the Africa of the Rassemblement Démocratique Africain), Europe will have deprived itself of its last *chance* and, with its own hands, drawn up over itself the pall of mortal darkness.

Which comes down to saying that the salvation of Europe is not a matter of a revolution in methods. It is a matter of the Revolution—the one which, until such time as there is a classless society, will substitute for the narrow tyranny of a dehumanized bourgeoisie the preponderance of the only class that still has a universal mission, because it suffers in its flesh from all the wrongs of history, from all the universal wrongs: the proletariat.

Notes

1. Aimé Césaire, *Discourse on Colonialism*, trans. Joan Pinkham. (New York: Monthly Review Press, 2000), pp. 31–37; 42–46.
2. A railroad line connecting Brazzaville with the port of Pointe-Noire (Trans.).

Walter Rodney

Walter Rodney's (1942–1980) life and work have deservedly become renowned in the Caribbean and African diasporic world since his assassination at age thirty-eight, which deprived the Caribbean and the Third World of one of its leading radical intellectual voices. A Marxist Pan-Africanist of great commitment and brilliance, his *How Europe Underdeveloped Africa* (1972) is his best-known work and a classic text about African underdevelopment. In 1968, the year he spent teaching at the University of the West Indies, Mona Campus, in Jamaica before he was refused reentry by the Jamaican government, he made several speeches on Black Power, one of which is reproduced ahead.

Black Power—Its Relevance to the West Indies

Walter Rodney[1]

About a fortnight ago I had the opportunity of speaking on Black Power to an audience on this campus.[2] At that time, the consciousness among students as far as the racial question is concerned had been heightened by several incidents on the world scene—notably, the hangings in Rhodesia and the murder of Dr. Martin Luther King. Indeed, it has been heightened to such an extent that some individuals have started to organise a Black Power movement. My presence here attests to my full sympathy with their objectives.

The topic on this occasion is no longer just 'Black Power' but 'Black Power and You'. Black Power can be seen as a movement and an ideology springing from the reality of oppression of black peoples by whites within the imperialist world as a whole. Now we need to be specific in defining the West Indian scene and our own particular roles in the society. You and I have to decide whether we want to think black or to *remain* as a dirty version of white. (I shall indicate the full significance of this later.)

Recently there was a public statement in *Scope* where Black Power was referred to as 'Black supremacy'. This may have been a genuine error or a deliberate falsification. Black Power is a call to black peoples to throw off white domination and resume the handling of their own destinies. It means that blacks would enjoy power commensurate with their numbers in the world and in particular localities. Whenever an oppressed black man shouts for equality he is called a racist. This was said of Marcus Garvey in his day. Imagine that! We are so inferior that if we demand equality of opportunity and power that is outrageously racist! Black people who speak up for their rights must beware of this device of false accusations. It is intended to place you on the defensive and if possible embarrass you into silence. How can we be both oppressed and embarrassed? Is it that our major concern is not to hurt the feelings of the oppressor? Black People must now take the offensive—if it is anyone who should suffer embarrassment it is the whites. Did black people roast six million Jews? Who exterminated millions of indigenous inhabitants in the Americas and Australia? Who enslaved countless millions of Africans? The white capitalist cannibal has always fed on the world's black peoples. White capitalist imperialist society is profoundly and unmistakably racist.

The West Indies have always been a part of white capitalist society. We have been the most oppressed section because we were a slave society and the legacy of slavery still rests heavily upon the West Indian black man. I will briefly point to five highlights of our social development: (1) the development of racialism under slavery; (2) emancipation; (3) Indian indentured labour; (4) the year 1865 in Jamaica; (5) the year 1938 in the West Indies.

Slavery. As C. L. R. James, Eric Williams and other W.I. scholars have pointed out, slavery in the West Indies started as an economic phenomenon rather than a racial one. But it rapidly became racist as all white labour was withdrawn from the fields, leaving black to be identified with slave labour and white to be linked with property and domination. Out of this situation where blacks had an inferior status in practice, there grew social and scientific theories relating to the supposed inherent inferiority of the black man, who was considered as having been created to bring water and hew wood for the white man. This theory then served to rationalise white exploitation of blacks all over Africa and Asia. The West Indies and the American South share the dubious distinction of being the breeding ground for world racialism. Naturally, our own society provided the highest expressions of racialism. Even the blacks became convinced of their own inferiority, though fortunately we are capable of the most intense expressions when we recognise that we have been duped by the white men. Black Power recognises both the reality of black oppression and self-negation as well as the potential for revolt.

Emancipation. By the end of the 18th century, Britain had got most of what it wanted from black labour in the West Indies. Slavery and the slave trade had made Britain strong and now stood in the way of new developments, so it was time to abandon those systems. The Slave Trade and Slavery were thus ended; but Britain had to consider how to squeeze what little remained in the territories and *how to maintain the local whites in power*. They therefore decided to give the planters £20 million compensation and to guarantee their black labour supplies for the next six years through a system called apprenticeship. In that period, white society consolidated its position to ensure that slave relations should persist in our society. The Rastafari Brethren have always insisted that the black people were promised £20 million at emancipation. In reality, by any normal standards of justice, we black people should have got the £20 million compensation money. We were the ones who had been abused and wronged, hunted in Africa and brutalised on the plantations. In Europe, when serfdom was abolished, the serfs usually inherited the land as compensation and by right. In the West Indies, the exploiters were compensated because they could no longer exploit us in the same way as before. White property was of greater value than black humanity. It still is—white property is of greater value than black humanity in the British West Indies today, especially here in Jamaica.

Indian Indentured Labour. Britain and the white West Indians had to maintain the plantation system in order to keep white supreme. When Africans started leaving the plantations to set up as independent peasants they threatened the plantation structure and therefore Indians were imported under the indenture arrangements. That was possible because white power controlled most of the world and could move non-white peoples around as they wished. It was from British-controlled India that the indentured labour was obtained. It was the impact of British commercial, military and political policies that was destroying the life and culture of 19th century India and forcing people to flee to other parts of the world to earn bread. Look where Indians fled—to the West Indies! The West Indies is a place black people want to leave not to come to. One must therefore appreciate the pressure of white power on India which gave rise to migration to the West Indies. Indians were brought here solely in the interest of white society—at the expense of Africans already in the West Indies and often against their own best interests, for Indians perceived indentured labour to be a form of slavery and it was eventually terminated through the pressure of Indian opinion in the homeland. The West Indies has made a unique contribution to the history of suffering in the world, and Indians have provided part of that contribution since indentures were first introduced. This is another aspect of the historical situation which is still with us.

1865. In that year Britain found a way of perpetuating White Power in the West Indies after ruthlessly crushing the revolt of our black brothers led by Paul Bogle. The British Government took away the Constitution of Jamaica and placed the island under the complete control of the Colonial Office, a manoeuvre that was racially motivated. The Jamaican legislature was then largely in the hands of the local whites with a mulatto minority, but if the gradual changes continued the mulattoes would have taken control—and the blacks were next in line. Consequently, the British Government put a stop to the process of the gradual takeover of political power by blacks. When we look at the British Empire in the 19th century, we see a clear difference between white colonies and black colonies. In the white colonies like Canada and Australia the British were giving white people their freedom and self-rule. In the black colonies of the West Indies, Africa and Asia the British were busy taking away the political freedom of the inhabitants. Actually, on the constitutional level, Britain had already displayed its racialism in the West Indies in the early 19th century when it refused to give mulattoes the power of Government in Trinidad, although they were the majority of free citizens. In 1865 in Jamaica it was not the first nor the last time on which Britain made it clear that its white 'kith and kin' would be supported to hold dominion over blacks.

1938. Slavery ended in various islands of the West Indies between 1834 and 1838. Exactly 100 years later (between 1934–38) the black people in the West Indies revolted against the hypocritical freedom of the society. The British were very surprised—they had long forgotten all about the blacks in the British West Indies and they sent a Royal Commission to find out what it was all about. The report of the conditions was so shocking that the British government did not release it until after the war, because they wanted black colonials to fight the white man's battles. By the time the war ended it was clear in the West Indies and throughout Asia and Africa that some concessions would have to be made to black peoples. In general, the problem as seen by white imperialists was to give enough power to certain groups in colonial society to keep the whole society from exploding and to maintain the essentials of the imperialist structure. In the British West Indies, they had to take into account the question of military strategy because we lie under the belly of the world's imperialist giant, the U.S.A. Besides, there was the new and vital mineral bauxite, which had to be protected. The British solution was to pull out wherever possible and leave the imperial government in the hands of the U.S.A., while the local government was given to a white, brown and black petty-bourgeoisie who were culturally the creations of white capitalist society and who therefore support the white imperialist system because they gain personally and because they have been brainwashed into aiding the oppression of black people.

Black Power in the West Indies means three closely related things: (1) the break with imperialism which is historically white racist; (ii) the assumption of power by the black masses in the islands; (iii) the cultural reconstruction of the society in the image of the blacks.

I shall anticipate certain questions on who are the blacks in the West Indies since they are in fact questions which have been posed to me elsewhere. I maintain that it is the white world which has defined who are blacks—if you are not white then you are black. However, it is obvious that the West Indian situation is complicated by factors such as the variety of racial types and racial mixtures and by the process of class formation. We have, therefore, to note not simply what the white world says but also how individuals perceive each other. Nevertheless, we can talk of the mass of the West Indian population as being black—either African or Indian. There seems to have been some doubts on the last point, and some fear that Black Power is aimed against the Indian. This would be a flagrant denial of both the historical experience of the West Indies and the reality of the contemporary scene.

When the Indian was brought to the West Indies, he met the same racial contempt which whites applied to Africans. The Indian, too, was reduced to a single stereotype—the coolie or labourer. He too was a hewer of wood and a bringer of water. I spoke earlier of the revolt of the blacks in the West Indies in 1938. That revolt involved Africans in Jamaica, Africans and Indians in Trinidad and Guyana. The uprisings in Guyana were actually led by Indian sugar workers. Today, some Indians (like some Africans) have joined the white power structure in terms of economic activity and culture; but the underlying reality is that poverty resides among Africans and Indians in the West Indies and that power is denied them. Black Power in the West Indies, therefore, refers primarily to people who are recognisably African or Indian.

The Chinese, on the other hand, are a former labouring group who have now become bastions of white West Indian social structure. The Chinese of the People's Republic of China have long broken with and are fighting against white imperialism, but *our* Chinese have nothing to do with that movement. They are to be identified with Chiang-Kai-Shek and not Chairman Mao Tse-tung. They are to be put in the same bracket as the lackeys of capitalism and imperialism who are to be found in Hong Kong and Taiwan. Whatever the circumstances in which the Chinese came to the West Indies, they soon became (as a group) members of the exploiting class. They will have either to relinquish or be deprived of that function before they can be re-integrated into a West Indian society where the black man walks in dignity.

The same applies to the mulattoes, another group about whom I have been questioned. The West Indian brown man is characterised by ambiguity and ambivalence. He has in the past identified with the black masses when it suited his interests, and at the present time some browns are in the forefront of the movement towards black consciousness; but the vast majority have fallen to the bribes of white imperialism, often outdoing the whites in their hatred and oppression of blacks. Garvey wrote of the Jamaican mulattoes—'I was openly hated and persecuted by some of these coloured men of the island who did not want to be classified as Negroes but as white'. Naturally, conscious West Indian blacks like Garvey have in turn expressed their dislike for the browns, but there is nothing in the West Indian experience which suggests that browns are unacceptable when they choose to identify with blacks. The post-1938 developments in fact showed exactly the opposite. It seems to me, therefore, that it is not for the Black Power movement to determine the position of the browns, reds and so-called West Indian whites—the movement can only keep the door open and leave it to those groups to make their choice.

Black Power is not racially intolerant. It is the hope of the black man that he should have power over his own destinies. This is not incompatible with a multi-racial society where each individual counts equally. Because the moment that power is equitably distributed among several ethnic groups then the very relevance of making the distinction between groups will be lost. What we must object to is the current image of a multi-racial society living in harmony—that is a myth designed to justify the exploitation suffered by the blackest of our population, at the hands of the lighter-skinned groups. Let us look at the figures for the racial composition of the Jamaican population. Of every 100 Jamaicans,

76.8%	are visibly African
0.8%	European
1.1%	Indian
0.6%	Chinese 91% have African blood
0.1%	Syrian
14.6%	Afro-European
5.4%	other mixtures

This is a black society where Africans preponderate. Apart from the mulatto mixture all other groups are numerically insignificant and yet the society seeks to give them equal weight and indeed more weight than the Africans. If we went to Britain we could easily find non-white groups in the above proportions[3]—Africans and West Indians, Indians and Pakistanis, Turks, Arabs and other Easterners—but Britain is not called a multi-racial society. When we go to Britain we don't expect to take over all of the British real estate business, all their cinemas and most of their commerce as the European, Chinese and Syrian have done here. All we ask for there is some work and shelter, and we can't even get that. Black Power must proclaim that Jamaica is a black society—we should fly Garvey's Black Star banner and we will treat all other groups in the society on that understanding—they can have *the basic right of all individuals* but *no privileges to exploit Africans* as has been the pattern during slavery and ever since.

The present government knows that Jamaica is a black man's country. That is why Garvey has been made a national hero, for they are trying to deceive black people into thinking that the government is with them. The government of Jamaica recognises black power—it is afraid of the potential wrath of Jamaica's black and largely African population. It is that same fear which forced them to declare mourning when black men are murdered in Rhodesia, and when Martin Luther King was murdered in the U.S.A. But the black people don't need to be told that Garvey is a national hero—they know that. Nor do they need to be told to mourn when blacks are murdered by White Power, because they mourn everyday right here in Jamaica where white power keeps them ignorant, unemployed, ill-clothed and ill-fed. They will stop mourning when things change—and that means a revolution, for the first essential is to break the chains which bind us to white imperialists, and that is a very revolutionary step. Cuba is the only country in the West Indies and in this hemisphere which has broken with white power. That is why Stokely Carmichael can visit Cuba but he can't visit Trinidad or Jamaica. That is why Stokely can call Fidel 'one of the blackest men in the Americas' and that is why our leaders in contrast qualify as 'white'.

Here I'm not just playing with words—I'm extending the definition of Black Power by indicating the nature of its opposite, 'White Power', and I'm providing a practical illustration of what Black Power means in one particular West Indian community where it had already occurred. White Power is the power of whites over blacks without any participation of the blacks. White Power rules the imperialist world as a whole. In Cuba the blacks and mulattoes numbered 1,585,073 out of a population of 5,829,029 in 1953—i.e. about one quarter of the population. Like Jamaica's black people today, they were the poorest and most depressed people on the island. Lighter-skinned Cubans held local power, while real power was in the hands of the U.S. imperialists. Black Cubans fought alongside white Cuban workers and peasants because they were all oppressed. Major Juan Almeida, one of the outstanding leaders of Cuba today, was one of the original guerrillas in the Sierra Maestra, and he is black. Black Cubans today enjoy political, economic and social rights and opportunities of exactly the same kind as white Cubans. They too bear arms in the Cuban Militia as an expression of their basic rights. In other words, White Power in Cuba is ended. The majority of the white population naturally predominates numerically in most spheres of activity but they do not hold dominion over blacks without regard to the latter's interests. The blacks have achieved power commensurate with their own numbers by their heroic self-efforts during the days of slavery, in fighting against the Spanish and in fighting against imperialism. Having achieved their rights they can in fact afford to forget the category 'black' and think simply as Cuban citizens, as Socialist equals and as men. In Jamaica, where blacks are far greater in numbers and have no whites alongside them as oppressed workers and peasants, it will be the black people who alone can bear the brunt of revolutionary fighting.

Trotsky once wrote that Revolution is the carnival of the masses. When we have that carnival in the West Indies, are people like us here at the university going to join the bacchanal?

Let us have a look at our present position. Most of us who have studied at the U.W.I. are discernibly black, and yet we are undeniably part of the white imperialist system. A few are actively pro-imperialist. They have no confidence in anything that is not white—they talk nonsense about black people being lazy—the same nonsense which was said about the Jamaican black man after emancipation, although he went to Panama and performed the giant task of building the Panama Canal—the same nonsense which is said about W.I. unemployed today, and yet they proceed to England to run the whole transport system. Most of us do not go to quite the same extremes in denigrating ourselves and our black brothers, but we say nothing against the system, and that means that we are acquiescing in the exploitation of our brethren. One of the ways that the situation has persisted especially in recent times is that it has given a few individuals like you and I a vision of personal progress measured in terms of front lawn and of the latest model of a huge American car. This has recruited us into their ranks and deprived the black masses of articulate leadership. That is why at the outset I stressed that our choice was to *remain* as part of the white system or to break with it. There is no other alternative.

Black Power in the W.I. must aim at transforming the Black intelligensia into the servants of the black masses. Black Power, within the university and without must aim at overcoming white cultural imperialism. Whites have dominated us both physically and mentally. This fact is brought out in virtually any serious sociological study of the region—the brainwashing process has been so stupendous that it has convinced so many black men of their inferiority. I will simply draw a few illustrations to remind you of this fact which blacks like us at Mona prefer to forget.

The adult black in our West Indian society is fully conditioned to thinking white, because that is the training we are given from childhood. The little black girl plays with a white doll, identifying with it as she combs its flaxen hair. Asked to sketch the figure of a man or woman, the black schoolboy instinctively produces a white man or a white woman. This is not surprising, since until recently the illustrations in our text books were all figures of Europeans. The few changes which have taken place have barely scratched the surface of the problem. West Indians of every colour still aspire to European standards of dress and beauty. The language which is used by black people in describing ourselves shows how we despise our African appearance. 'Good hair' means European hair, 'good nose' means a straight nose, 'good complexion' means a light complexion. Everybody recognises how incongruous and ridiculous such terms are, but we continue to use them and to express our support of the assumption that white Europeans have the monopoly of beauty, and that black is the incarnation of ugliness. That is why Black Power advocates find it necessary to assert that BLACK IS BEAUTIFUL.

The most profound revelation of the sickness of our society on the question of race is our respect for all the white symbols of the Christian religion. God the Father is white, God the Son is white, and presumably God the Holy Ghost is white also. The disciples and saints are white, all the Cherubim, Seraphim and angels are white—except Lucifer, of course, who was black, being the embodiment of evil. When one calls upon black people to reject these things, this is not an attack on the teachings of Christ or the ideals of Christianity. What we have to ask is 'Why should Christianity come to us all wrapped up in white?' The white race constitute about 20 per cent of the world's population, and yet non-white peoples are supposed to accept that all who inhabit the heavens are white. There are 650 million Chinese, so why shouldn't God and most of the angels be Chinese? The truth is that there is absolutely no reason why different racial groups should not provide themselves with their own religious symbols. A picture of Christ could be red, white or black, depending upon the people who are involved. When Africans adopt the European concept that purity and goodness must be painted white and all that is evil and dammed is to be painted black then we are flagrantly self-insulting.

Through the manipulation of this media of education and communication, white people have produced black people who administer the system and perpetuate the white values— 'white-hearted black men', as they are called by conscious elements. This is as true of the Indians as it is true of the Africans in our West Indian society. Indeed, the basic explanation of the tragedy of African/Indian confrontation in Guyana and Trinidad is the fact that both groups are held captive by the European way of seeing things. When an African abuses an Indian he repeats all that the white men said about Indian indentured 'coolies'; and in turn the Indian has borrowed from the whites the stereotype of the 'lazy nigger' to apply to the African beside him. It is as though no black man can see another black man except by looking through a white person. It is time we started seeing through our own eyes. The road to Black Power here in the West Indies and everywhere else must begin with a revaluation of ourselves as blacks and with a redefinition of the world from our own standpoint.

Notes

1. Walter Rodney, "Black Power—Its Relevance to the West Indies," in *The Groundings With My Brothers* (London: Bogle-L'Ouverture, 1990), pp. 24–34.
2. The U.W.I. campus.
3. As the non-blacks in Jamaica. Editor's note.

Maurice Bishop

Maurice Bishop (1944–1983) was the charismatic leader of the Grenadian Revolution, a revolution that captured the world's imagination and attention in the early 1980s. The circumstances around its catastrophic demise continue to haunt the Caribbean left a generation later. In one of his most arresting speeches, Bishop demands sovereignty beyond neocolonialism for his revolution—and the people of the Caribbean.

In Nobody's Backyard

Maurice Bishop[1]

National Broadcast on RFG, 13 April 1979

Today, one month after our historic People's Revolution, there is peace, calm and quiet in our country. Indeed, there has been a tremendous drop in the crime rate since our Revolution. Foreign residents in the Levera/Bathway are feeling so comfortable and safe nowadays that they have advised the Commissioner of Police that he could close down the sub-Police Station in that area. An unusually high number of tourists for an off-season period are presently enjoying the beauty of our land and the warmth of our people, and this is so in spite of the fact that we have just had a Revolution and that a real and present threat of mercenary invasion is faced by our country. In fact, it is almost impossible to rent a vehicle or to find an empty cottage at this point.

Tourists and visitors to our country have all been greatly impressed by the discipline of our troops, and the respect that has been shown for the lives and property of local and foreign residents and visitors. From all over the island the same report have come to us that the tourists are commenting on the warmth, friendliness and discipline of our people and the People's Revolutionary Army. The same comments are being daily made by the hundreds of medical students studying in Grenada.

The annual boat race from Trinidad to Grenada took place as usual last night with a bigger than ever participation. The great sense of relief and happiness of our people are obvious to all. In fact, it is clear that there is no sense of panic here or hesitation by the tourists who daily continue to stream into Grenada.

Big Stick and Carrots

For this reason we want the people of Grenada and the Caribbean to realize that if all of a sudden tourists start panicking and leaving the country, or stop coming to our country, then they should note that this came after veiled threats by the United States Ambassador with respect to our tourist industry. The Ambassador, Mr Frank Ortiz, on his last visit to Grenada some days ago, went out of his way to emphasise the obvious importance of tourism to our country. He argued that as Grenada imported some $32 million a year in goods but exported only $13 million, we had a massive trade deficit of some $19 million, which earnings from the tourist industry could substantially lessen. His point was, and we accept that point, that tourism was and is critical to the survival of our economy. The Ambassador went on to advise us that if we continue to speak about what he called 'mercenary invasions by phantom armies' that we could lose all our tourists. He also reminded us of the experience which Jamaica had had in this regard a few years ago.

As some of you will undoubtedly recall, Jamaica at that time had gone through a period of intense destabilisation. Under this process the people of Jamaica were encouraged to lose faith and confidence in themselves, their government and their country and in the ability of their government to solve the pressing problems facing the country and meeting the expectations of their people. This was done through damaging news stories being spread in the local, regional and international media, particularly newspapers, aimed at discrediting the achievements of the Jamaican government. It was also done through violence and sabotage and by wicked and pernicious attempts at wrecking the economy through stopping the flow of tourist visitors, and hence much needed foreign exchange earnings of the country. The experience of Jamaica must therefore remind us that the economies of small, poor Third World countries which depend on tourism can be wrecked by those who have the ability and the desire to wreck them. In his official meetings with Minister of Finance Brother Bernard Coard, and then with me on Tuesday of this week, and in his unofficial discussions with a leading comrade of the People's Revolutionary Army at Pearls Airport on Wednesday, the Ambassador stressed the fact that his government will view with great displeasure the development of any relations between our country and Cuba. The Ambassador pointed out that his country was the richest, freest and most generous country in the world, but, as he put it, 'We have two sides'. We understood that to mean that the other side he was referring to was the side which stamped on freedom and democracy when the American government felt that their interests were being threatened. 'People are panicky and I will have to report that fact to my government', he advised us. However, the only evidence of panic given by the Ambassador was the incident which took place last Monday when the People's Revolutionary Army, as a result of not having been warned beforehand, shot at a plane which flew very low, more than once over Camp Butler. He calls that panic. The people of Grenada call it alertness.

At the end of our discussion on Tuesday the Ambassador handed me a typed statement of his instructions from his government, to be given to us. The relevant section of that statement reads, and I quote:

> Although my Government recognises your concerns over allegations of a possible counter-coup, it also believes that it would not be in Grenada's best interests to seek assistance from a country such as Cuba to forestall such an attack. We would view with displeasure any tendency on the part of Grenada to develop closer ties with Cuba.

We Are No One's Lackey

It is well established internationally that all independent countries have a full, free and unhampered right to conduct their own internal affairs. We do not, therefore, recognise any right of the United States of America to instruct us on who we may develop relations with and who we may not.

From day one of the Revolution we have always striven to have and develop the closest and friendliest relations with the United States, as well as Canada, Britain and all our Caribbean neighbours—English, French, Dutch and Spanish speaking, and we intend to continue to strive for these relations. But no one must misunderstand our friendliness as an excuse for rudeness and meddling in our affairs, and no one, no matter now mighty and powerful they are, will be permitted to dictate to the government and people of Grenada who we can have friendly relations with and what kind of relations we must have with other countries. We haven't gone through 28 years of fighting Gairyism, and especially the last six years of terror, to gain our freedom, only to throw it away and become a slave or lackey to *any* other country, no matter how big and powerful.

Every day we fought Gairy we put our lives on the line. On the day of the Revolution we started out with almost no arms and in so doing we again put our lives on the line.

We have demonstrated beyond any doubt that we were prepared to *die* to win our freedom. We are even more prepared to die to maintain that freedom now that we have tasted it.

We feel that people of Grenada have the right to know precisely what steps we have taken in our attempts to establish relations at various levels with the United States, and the response which we have so far received.

From the second day of our Revolution, during our first meeting with American government representatives in Grenada, we were at pains to emphasise the deplorable and ravished state in which the Gairy dictatorship had left our economy and our country. We pointed out then that massive assistance, technical and financial, would be required in order to begin the process of rebuilding the economy. The American Consul-General told us that he was not surprised to hear this, and assured us that he would encourage his government to give us the necessary assistance, particularly as he had been so impressed by the bloodless character and the self-evident humanity of our prompt assurances in the first hours of the Revolution that the safety, lives and property of American and other foreign residents were guaranteed. Indeed, he freely admitted that his American residents had all reported to him that they were happy, comfortable and felt secure. However, one month later, no such aid has arrived, It is true that the Ambassador did point out—and correctly so—that his Government generally grants aid on a multilateral basis through the Caribbean Development Bank. It is also true that he said his government would prefer to maintain that approach rather than help directly, despite his admission that red tape and bureaucracy could cause delays of up to one year in receiving such multilateral aid.

It is also true that he advised us that his Government is monitoring movements and that it is against United States law for Gairy to recruit mercenaries in the United States of America. This we appreciate.

US $5,000 Is Not the Price of Our Dignity

However, we must point out that the fact is, that in place of the massive economic aid and assistance that seemed forthcoming, the only aid the American Ambassador has been able to guarantee that he could get to Grenada in a reasonably short time would be $5,000.00 (US) for each of a few small projects.

Sisters and brothers, what can a few $5,000.00 (US) do? Our hospitals are without medicines, sheets, pillowcases and proper equipment. Our schools are falling down. Most of our rural villages are in urgent need of water, electricity, health clinics and decent housing. Half of the people in the country who are able to and would like to work are unable to find jobs. Four out of every five women are forced to stay at home or scrunt for a meagre existence. $5,000.00 cannot build a house, or a health clinic. We feel forced to ask whether the paltry sum of a few $5,000.00 is all that the wealthiest country in the world can offer to a poor but proud people who are fighting for democracy, dignity and self-respect based on real and independent economic development.

Let us contrast this with the immediate response of our Caribbean brothers. We will take two examples: Guyana and Jamaica, countries thousands of times poorer than the United States of America; countries, indeed, like ourselves, poor, over-exploited and struggling to develop. These two countries have given us technical assistance, cheaper goods, and are actively considering our request for arms and military training. This assistance has included a shipment of rice which arrived two days ago, a six-man team of economic and other experts from Guyana presently in our country, and the imminent arrival of Mr Roy Jones, Deputy Governor of the Bank of Jamaica and Professor George Eaton, a leading authority on public service structures. And notwithstanding these concrete and much appreciated acts of assistance and solidarity they have never once attempted to instruct us as to the manner in which we should conduct our own internal affairs or as to which countries we should choose to develop relations with.

The American Ambassador is taking very lightly what we genuinely believe to be a real danger facing our country. Contrary to what anyone else may think we know that the dictator Gairy is organising mercenaries to attack Grenada in order to restore him to his throne. We know the man Gairy. Nobody knows him better than we the people of Grenada and we recognise the meaning and implications of the evidence which has come before us.

We say that when Frank Mabri Jr. and Mustaphos Hammarabl, Gairy's underworld friends, write to him indicating how much and what kind of arms are available, and when Gairy says on radio broadcasts and in newspaper interviews that he will never give up and that he intends to return to Grenada as prime minister, that he can only mean that he will use force in order to achieve these ends. And because our Revolution is a popular one, supported by the vast majority of our population, and because many of our patriots are armed, force here can only mean getting another country to intervene on his behalf, or hiring mercenaries to do his dirty work for him. And this in turn could only mean the mass killing of thousands of innocent Grenadians, regardless of which political party they support. It is in these circumstances, and because we have an undoubted freedom that we called on the Americans, Canadians, British, our fellow-countries in CARICOM, like Guyana and Jamaica, Venezuela and Cuba, to assist us with arms.

And we reject *entirely* the argument of the American Ambassador that we would only be entitled to call upon the Cubans to come to our assistance *after* mercenaries have landed and commenced the attack. Quite frankly, and with the greatest respect, a more ridiculous argument can hardly be imagined. It is like asking a man to wait until his house is burning down before he leaves to buy a fire extinguisher. No, we intend if possible to provide ourselves with the fire extinguisher before the fire starts! and if the government of Cuba is willing to offer us assistance, we would be more than happy to receive it.

We Are Not in Anybody's Backyard and We Are Definitely Not For Sale

Sisters and brothers, what we led was an *independent process*. Our Revolution was definitely a popular revolution, not a *coup d'etat*, and was and is in no way a minority movement. We intend to continue along an independent and non-aligned path. We have stayed in the Commonwealth, we have stayed in the Organization of American States and in CARICOM; despite pressures we have stayed in the Eastern Caribbean Common Market and in the expanded West Indies Associated States Organization (WISA). We have applied to join the Non-Aligned Movement. We will be applying to join the International Labour Organization—the ILO.

We are a small country, we are a poor country, with a population of largely African descent, we are a part of the exploited Third World, and we definitely have a stake in seeking the creation of a New International Economic Order which would assist in ensuring economic justice for the oppressed and exploited peoples of the world, and in ensuring that the resources of the sea are used for the benefit of all the people of the world and not for a tiny minority of profiteers. Our aim, therefore, is to join all organisations and work with all countries that will help us to become more independent and more in control of our own resources. In this regard, nobody who understands present-day realities can seriously challenge our right to develop working relations with a variety of countries.

Grenada is a sovereign and independent country, although a tiny speck on the world map, and we expect all countries to strictly respect our independence, just as we will respect theirs. No country has the right to tell us what to do or how to run our country, or who to be friendly with. We certainly would not attempt to tell any other country what to do. We are not in anybody's backyard, and we are definitely not for sale. Anybody who thinks they can bully us or threaten us, clearly has no understanding idea or clue as to what material we are made of. They clearly have no idea of the tremendous struggles which our people have fought over the past seven years. Though small and poor, we are proud and determined. We would sooner give up our lives before we compromise, sell out, or betray our sovereignty, our independence, our integrity, our manhood and the right of our people to national self-determination and social progress.

LONG LIVE THE REVOLUTION!

LONG LIVE GRENADA!

Note

1. Maurice Bishop, "In Nobody's Backyard," in *In Nobody's Backyard: Maurice Bishop's Speeches, 1979– 1983: A Memorial Volume*, ed. Chris Searle (London: Zed Books, 1984), pp. 9–14.

Audre Lorde

Audre Lorde (1934–1992) was a poet, human rights activist, feminist, and lesbian born in New York City to Caribbean immigrants. Through her critical essays, novels, and prose, Lorde remained steadfast in her commitment to unmasking the notion of difference (i.e., identities that were sexually, racially, or otherwise marked as existing outside of a normative White male ideal). Decades before the reflective turn in cultural inquiry, Lorde situated herself and experiences as central to her analysis of structures of power, racism, and sexism. She further explored the dynamics of coming into one's own sense of self while simultaneously being deemed invisible by the society at large. Her scholarship represented her activism and commitment to social justice. In "The Transformation of Silence Into Language and Action," we see how Lorde expands the idea of Black women's anger and creative and linguistic power that can be harnessed to invoke change against social oppressions that impose silenced categories, experiences, and challenges.

The Transformation of Silence Into Language and Action

Audre Lorde[1]

I have come to believe over and over again that what is most important to me must be spoken, made verbal and shared, even at the risk of having it bruised or misunderstood. That the speaking profits me, beyond any other effect. I am standing here as a Black lesbian poet, and the meaning of all that waits upon the fact that I am still alive, and might not have been. Less than two months ago I was told by two doctors, one female and one male, that I would have to have breast surgery, and that there was a 60 to 80 percent chance that the tumor was malignant. Between that telling and the actual surgery, there was a three-week period of the agony of an involuntary reorganization of my entire life. The surgery was completed, and the growth was benign.

But within those three weeks, I was forced to look upon myself and my living with a harsh and urgent clarity that has left me still shaken but much stronger. This is a situation faced by many women, by some of you here today. Some of what I experienced during that time has helped elucidate for me much of what I feel concerning the transformation of silence into language and action.

In becoming forcibly and essentially aware of my mortality, and of what I wished and wanted for my life, however short it might be, priorities and omissions became strongly etched in a merciless light, and what I most regretted were my silences. Of what had I *ever* been afraid? To question or to speak as I believed could have meant pain, or death. But we all hurt in so many different ways, all the time, and pain will either change or end. Death, on the other hand, is the final silence. And that might be coming quickly, now, without regard for whether I had ever spoken what needed to be said, or had only betrayed myself into small silences, while I planned someday to speak, or waited for someone else's words. And I began to recognize a source of power within myself that comes from the knowledge that while it is most desirable not to be afraid, learning to put fear into a perspective gave me great strength.

I was going to die, if not sooner then later, whether or not I had ever spoken myself. My silences had not protected me. Your silence will not protect you. But for every real word spoken, for every attempt I had ever made to speak those truths for which I am still seeking, I had made contact with other women while we examined the words to fit a world in which we all believed, bridging our differences. And it was the concern and caring of all those women which gave me strength and enabled me to scrutinize the essentials of my living.

The women who sustained me through that period were Black and white, old and young, lesbian, bisexual, and heterosexual, and we all shared a war against the tyrannies of silence. They all gave me a strength and concern without which I could not have survived intact. Within those weeks of acute fear came the knowledge—within the war we are all waging with the forces of death, subtle and otherwise, conscious or not—I am not only a casualty, I am also a warrior.

What are the words you do not yet have? What do you need to say? What are the tyrannies you swallow day by day and attempt to make your own, until you will sicken and die of them, still in silence? Perhaps for some of you here today, I am the face of one of your fears. Because I am woman, because I am Black, because I am lesbian, because I am myself—a Black woman warrior poet doing my work—come to ask you, are you doing yours?

And of course I am afraid, because the transformation of silence into language and action is an act of self-revelation, and that always seems fraught with danger. But my daughter, when I told her of our topic and my difficulty with it, said, "Tell them about how you're never really a whole person if you remain silent, because there's always that one little piece inside you that wants to be spoken out, and if you keep ignoring it, it gets madder and madder and hotter and hotter, and if you don't speak it out one day it will just up and punch you in the mouth from the inside."

In the cause of silence, each of us draws the face of her own fear—fear of contempt, of censure, or some judgment, or recognition, of challenge, of annihilation. But most of all, I think, we fear the visibility without which we cannot truly live. Within this country where racial difference creates a constant, if unspoken, distortion of vision, Black women have on one hand always been highly visible, and so, on the other hand, have been rendered invisible through the depersonalization of racism. Even within the women's movement, we have had to fight, and still do, for that very visibility which also renders us most vulnerable, our Blackness. For to survive in the mouth of this dragon we call America, we have had to learn this first and most vital lesson—that we were never meant to survive. Not as human beings. And neither were most of you here today, Black or not. And that visibility which makes us most vulnerable is that which also is the source of our greatest strength. Because the machine will try to grind you into dust anyway, whether or not we speak. We can sit in our corners mute forever while our sisters and our selves are wasted, while our children are distorted and destroyed, while our earth is poisoned; we can sit in our safe corners mute as bottles, and we will still be no less afraid.

In my house this year we are celebrating the feast of Kwanza, the African-American festival of harvest which begins the day after Christmas and lasts for seven days. There are seven principles of Kwanza, one for each day. The first principle is Umoja, which means unity, the decision to strive for and maintain unity in self and community. The principle for yesterday, the second day, was Kujichagulia—self-determination—the decision to define ourselves, name ourselves, and speak for ourselves, instead of being defined and spoken for by others. Today is the third day of Kwanza, and the principle for today is Ujima—collective work and responsibility—the decision to build and maintain ourselves and our communities together and to recognize and solve our problems together.

Each of us is here now because in one way or another we share a commitment to language and to the power of language, and to the reclaiming of that language which has been made to work against us. In the transformation of silence into language and action, it is vitally necessary for each one of us to establish or examine her function in that transformation and to recognize her role as vital within that transformation.

For those of us who write, it is necessary to scrutinize not only the truth of what we speak, but the truth of that language by which we speak it. For others, it is to share and spread also those words that are meaningful to us. But primarily for us all, it is necessary to teach by living and speaking those truths which we believe and know beyond understanding. Because in this way alone we can survive, by taking part in a process of life that is creative and continuing, that is growth.

And it is never without fear—of visibility, of the harsh light of scrutiny and perhaps judgment, of pain, of death. But we have lived through all of those already, in silence, except death. And I remind myself all the time now that if I were to have been born mute, or had maintained an oath of silence my whole life long for safety, I would still have suffered, and I would still die. It is very good for establishing perspective.

And where the words of women are crying to be heard, we must each of us recognize our responsibility to seek those words out, to read them and share them and examine them in their pertinence to our lives. That we not hide behind the mockeries of separations that have been imposed upon us and which so often we accept as our own. For instance, "I can't possibly teach Black women's writing—their experience is so different from mine." Yet how many years have you spent teaching Plato and Shakespeare and Proust? Or another, "She's a white woman and what could she possibly have to say to me?" Or, "She's a lesbian, what would my husband say, or my chairman?" Or again, "This woman writes of her sons and I have no children." And all the other endless ways in which we rob ourselves of ourselves and each other.

We can learn to work and speak when we are afraid in the same way we have learned to work and speak when we are tired. For we have been socialized to respect fear more than our own needs for language and definition, and while we wait in silence for that final luxury of fearlessness, the weight of that silence will choke us.

The fact that we are here and that I speak these words is an attempt to break that silence and bridge some of those differences between us, for it is not difference which immobilizes us, but silence. And there are so many silences to be broken.

Note

1. Audre Lorde, "The Transformation of Silence Into Language and Action," *Women's Studies Quarterly* 25.1/2 (Spring–Summer 1997): 278–285

Gordon Rohlehr

Gordon Rohlehr, professor emeritus of West Indian literature at the University of the West Indies, St. Augustine, was born in Guyana in 1942. After completing his doctorate in England in 1967 he returned to the Caribbean and established his academic career in the fields of oral poetry, West Indian literature, Caribbean popular culture, and aesthetics. Rohlehr is one of the leading cultural critics of Caribbean expressive forms who pioneered the academic study of the sociocultural and musical art form of calypso. Through masterful intellectual history of the region from slavery to contemporary times, Rohlehr interprets the culture and politics of the postindependent Caribbean.

Articulating a Caribbean Aesthetic: The Revolution of Self-Perception

Gordon Rohlehr[1]

During the period of slavery in the Caribbean, the "selves" of master and slaves, white and black, were prescribed by the rigidities of slavery and the plantation system. These were really imposed selves, hardened by the fact that the system endured for over three centuries and was thorough in its methods, most of which were directed towards the restriction of human potential and the reduction of people to tools, objects.

The limits within which Caribbean people lived were visible in every area of life; in the economics of primitive capitalism, which shackled the fragile island economies to that of the metropole; in the class stratification which resulted from the economic system, and was reinforced by the factor of race; by the various slave codes or laws, which anticipated the psychology of the modern concentration camp by several centuries. But the limits within which Caribbean people lived were most clearly visible in the need which the dominant race, class and civilization felt, to create and perpetuate stereotypes, systems of coercion (laws), and propaganda which reinforced stereotypes (education), both during and after slavery.

There is no doubt that much was destroyed, much lost or obliterated. Many minds were shattered, most accepted and adapted to the limits which had been placed on human potential. Hence we have the role-playing Black, the jive-ass Black, the Uncle Tom stereotype, and the dozens of other well-known stereotypes which have existed since slavery and have gone through several cycles of permutation since Emancipation. Du Bois in several of his works, Ellison in *Invisible Man*, Edward Brathwaite in *Rights of Passage*, have all dealt with the phenomenon of the enduring stereotype. Frantz Fanon has given it psycho-philosophical definition in his now seminal testament *Black Skin White Masks*.

The "revolution of self-perception" really began with the inner resistance of the slaves to the self imposed on them by the plantation system and slavery. In its most fundamental form it was the refusal to be a thing, an object, a tool, mere chattel: the *negation of a process of reification*.

The positive aspect of this revolution involved *the constant affirmation of the validity of the submerged self* the self—to borrow Edward Kamau Brathwaite's phrase—in maroonage; the marooned, submerged and often subversive self. This *self-in-maroonage* was affirmed in infinite ways:

a. Rebellion and constant resistance on the plantation (suicide, malingering, rioting, the Haitian Revolution, Cannes Brulées, etc)

b. The preservation of religions with an African base, or the adaptation of these under pressure of the plantation system/structure during slavery. After Emancipation several religions existed in face of constant harassment from the Law and pressure from the Established Churches. The anthropological work on Afro-Caribbean religions is beginning to constitute an important body of literature. Off-hand, I can list a number of concerns which have emerged from the study of these religions.

(1) The continuity of West African heritages in the Caribbean. Factors instrumental in such continuity have been the isolation of some communities; the inadequacy of the education system; the fact that during the post-emancipation period communities of "liberated Africans" who had never been enslaved, were settled in various islands (Trinidad, e.g.)

(2) The notion of a continuum stretching between religions with the greatest "African" content and those with the greatest "European" content. Donald Hogg in *Jamaica Religions: A Study in Variations* advances this thesis for Jamaica. Continuum theory allows for overlapping, syncretism, conflict and consensus, and leads to a notion of religion as lived process within the framework of a total society, rather than as static, fixed structures.

(3) The syncretic blending of West African and European proletarian heritages, in religions such as Zion Revival, Pukkumina, Rastafarianism in Jamaica, the Spiritual Baptists or Shouters in Trinidad. Vodun in Haiti reveals another dimension of syncretism, including a post-Medieval Catholicism and a Dahomean cosmology in a single seamless theological system.

(4) The relationship between religion and social institutions, such as communities and political parties. The cult/sect and charismatic or authoritarian political leadership. The cult/sect as an exploitable reservoir of popular lumpen-proletarian faith and emotion.

These are some of the concerns which have emerged from the study of Afro-Caribbean religions. That these religions are capable of leading scholars to such fundamental questions is the surest testimony of their vital and vibrant existence as the ground of being for large numbers of Caribbean people. It is also the clearest evidence of the survival of the *self-in-maroonage* after so many years of hostile laws, education, economic suppression and the cultural contempt of the white, brown and black servitors of the establishment.

(c) The survival of folktales, proverbs, rhetoric, patterns of performance, and the capacity to create style, are further evidence of the continued existence of the self-in-maroonage. If the original folktale has almost disappeared, the capacity for storytelling has not. Hence the storytelling tradition is maintained in The Calypso, Paul Keens-Douglas, Abdul Malik, Brathwaite's *The Arrivants*, and a growing corpus of short stories and anecdotes, which exactly parallels what has been taking place in the Afro-American tradition.

If the original propensity for proverbs and aphorisms has been modified, a tradition of moralizing still exists, and is evident in the weighty didactic element in some reggae and a few calypsoes; the desire to instruct through art.

The revolution of self-perception, then, is process, is ongoing *self-affirmation* which, in the face of the unchanging rigidity of oppression generally means self-assertion. In asking what that revolution means today we are in fact attempting to assess the quality of our self-affirmation in all the areas of our conscious living. These include:

(a) Politics and the on-going class struggle.
(b) Literature and that constant, complex exploration of the no-longer-submerged inner self; the no-longer-marooned personality.
(c) Music—Blues, Jazz, Gospel, Calypso, Funk, Reggae—and the life-styles, both sacred and secular, which sustain the music. Hence we shall have to ask ourselves what is the meaning

of our capacity for celebration, dance, carnival on the one hand, and the trauma, agony and constant struggle which celebration masks. For our music, whether created by 'Trane, Sanders, 'Tosh, Marley, Chalkdust, Black Stalin or Bird, is connected with the phenomenon of survival. Sometimes as with "Trane, it seeks to energize and humanize a city of stone and steel. Sometimes as with Chalkdust, Valentino, Marley and 'Tosh it cries out against, attacks and erodes a stone-deaf politics which, like the old plantation system it has succeeded, still regards people as things, objects, tools.

The body of my paper will be an outline of some of the trends in West Indian literature in English, which together constitute part of the on-going revolution of self-perception. For pur-poses of convenience I have arbitrarily divided my time-period into three interlocking phases: 1920–1950, 1950–1960 and 1960 to the present.

1920–1950

The twenties was the period of Garvey, Claude McKay and the Harlem Renaissance, to whose political and literary aspects both of these outstanding Jamaicans contributed. The thirties saw C. L. R. James's *Minty Alley*, his play *Toussaint L'Ouverture* (1936). The novels of Portuguese author Alfred Mendes (*Pitch Lake, Black Fauns*) and the short stories of Seepersad Naipaul *Gurudeva and Other Tales* indicated the multi-ethnic nature of the Trinidad experience. The forties were a period of steady growth in which regional periodicals such as Frank Collymore's *Bim* and A.J. Seymour's *Kyk-Over-Al* emerged. Louise Bennett, whose creative acceptance and dramatization of the language of the Jamaican people was in itself a revolution, had begun to write her poems in the late thirties, and had by 1950 become an artist whose work was known throughout the archipelago and in Panama. One of her contributions to West Indian letters was to establish the fact that the little people had not only a voice, but a way of seeing, placing and reducing the world of their social superiors.[1]

The Calypso emerged during this period from the traditional structures of *kalinda* and *sans humanité picong*[2] to a flexible medium capable of accommodating narrative, social and politi-cal protest, scatological humour, and celebration. An entire and virtually unexplored body of oral literature exists in the Calypso. It is a literature which has intimately reflected social change, and can provide the scholar with a documentary of the changing attitudes of grass-roots Trinidad.

The literature of this period was being accompanied by serious inquiry into the roots and heritage of the people of the African diaspora. There had already been the substantial work of Edward Wilmot Blyden. In America this work was to be built upon and augmented by W. E. B. DuBois. The impulse to understand, explore and vindicate an African heritage was politicized by Garvey, whose *Philosophy and Opinions* (1923) is one of the few Afro-Caribbean publications which have survived the rigid censorship of that period.

Equally remarkable was Norman Cameron's *The Evolution of the Negro*[3] (1929). Cameron was a Guyanese student of mathematics at Cambridge, whose vocation to teach in Liberia impelled him to find out all he could about that country. This awakened in him an appetite to know more about Africa itself, particularly in the pre-European period: he read all the col-lected works of all the early travellers. He augmented these with French translations of Arab and Moorish documents. He developed a keen interest in African art and sculpture which led him to those museums in England which house artifacts stolen from Africa during the scramble. Thirty years before Basil Davidson's now famous *Old Africa Rediscovered*. Cameron had already posited the link between Egypt, the Western Sudan and Africa south of the equator. He had already refuted the then current notions that excellence in African sculpture in bronze, iron and gold was the result of European influence.

He was interested in other things besides. In Chapter 11 on the Mali Empire he showed an interest in oral traditions such as the drum and elephant horn orchestras; the praise songs and use of poetry for the recording of oral history. He felt that our poets and playwrights ought to be interested in such things and wrote poetry and didactic plays himself, in some of which he consciously sought to include an "African" presence and ethos. Forty years later in Edward Brathwaite's *Masks* (1968), there at last emerged a Caribbean poet who could give impressive shape to identifiably West African oral traditions: the drum, atumpan, mmenson, the idea of masks, as well as the history, old ceremonies, dances and aspects of Akan cosmology.

Cameron, in his introduction, anticipated the criticism that there was nothing worth studying in African history. He also anticipated the now current accusation that to be seriously concerned with the African past is to be atavistic or nostalgic. *The Evolution of the Negro* was based on the idea that the past should explored as part of one's duty to oneself. One doesn't free oneself from the trauma of history by forgetting the past. One needed, instead, to accept past struggle as the basis for a self-confidence necessary for facing the present and creating a future. Thus, besides the descriptions of the pre-European kingdoms of Africa, Cameron dealt with the effects of contact with Europeans, slave life on the plantations and the Abolition of Slavery and emergence of the Afro-Caribbean person.

If his reading suggested the destructive nature of slavery, his vision was directed towards what was or would become possible if Afro-Guyanese people were to discover their roots. Thus *The Evolution of the Negro* sought to define these roots. Cameron spent some time describing the layout of villages as well as social institutions, laws, aspects of local government in Africa. He was interested in things such as cloth designs and hair styles, things which did not reenter popular black consciousness until the 1960's.

Cameron's book, which went into two volumes (1929 & 1934), was about History as continuity, and the historian as healer, bridger of hiatuses in our knowledge and consciousness. But the conscious or unconscious aim of education in the English-speaking Caribbean was to divorce the Caribbean person from issues and concerns of central relevance to his knowledge of self and milieu. Thus Cameron's profound and scholarly work, self-published and distributed, reached only a few people, went out of print to resurface in 1970 when it was reprinted in America. Unlike many other such reprints, it hasn't appeared on the shelves of Caribbean bookstores. Garvey's vision, too, remained in the borders of our consciousness and was for years beyond the reach of our curricula.

This is essentially what we are up against, then, a *tradition of discontinuity* by which our most crucial perceptions and discoveries are relegated to the margins of consciousness. *The Black Jacobins* (1938) C.L.R. James' great study of the Haitian revolution, took twenty-two years to be republished (1962). George Padmore is still a name. Sylvester Williams remote, despite Owen Mathurin's fairly recent publication. Robert Love is virtually unknown. F.E.M. Hercules has scarcely been heard about. This is probably why an era which produced work such as Garvey's, Cameron's and the early work of Eric Williams, should have produced artists who were generally little more than excellent observers of the surface of actions and recorders of manners.

The creative sensibility of the period was largely divorced from the creative thought of the period. One of the obvious reasons for this was the fact that Caribbean people were not in control of their political destinies, or of their economies. This point had been made over and over again in the polemics of the 1930's and 1940's. It resurfaced in the various discussions about the possibility of a West Indian Federation. One of the most interesting blueprints for a federation was A.P. Maloney's *After England We* (1949) which examined the potential and the limitations of the region as a whole, and envisioned a multi-lingual federation, and the emergence of a "cosmic race". Maloney was one of a family of distinguished Trinidad scholars, resident in the United States.

1950–1960

The period of 1950–1960 saw the evolution of a substantial body of literature. Mais, Lamming, Selvon, Salkey, Carew, Hearne, Mittelholzer, Harris, Reid, Carter, Walcott, V.S Naipaul, Keane, Roach and Brathwaite all emerged in this decade. Dennis Williams and Edward Brathwaite lived in Africa during this period, as had Peter Blackman (*My Song Is For All Men*). Reid, without having actually lived there had written in *The Leopard* an imaginatively impressive novel, set in Kenya. The theme of African continuity or conversely of divorce from Africa appeared in the poetry of Roach and Walcott, while Brathwaite was writing plays for Akan school children, and had by 1962 already given shape to the first half of *Masks*. Dennis Williams *Other Leopards* (1963) explored the split sensibility of the Caribbean *omowale* and left his schizophrenic hero in a desert, almost stripped of his old self, and savouring possibilities of growth in an inscrutable future.

The writers of this decade had a better opportunity to draw on a body of emerging thought and scholarship than had those of the generation before. In anthropology alone, for example, there was the work Melville and Frances Herskovits, George Eaton Simpson, M.G. Smith, Raymond Smith, Andrew Pearse and Daniel Crowley. Afro-Caribbean folklore, religions, folkways, folktales, rhetoric and patterns of performance suddenly became "visible", and we find Edward Brathwaite in an early essay; "Sir Galahad and The Islands" (BIM, 1957) suggesting that in these discoveries lay the basis for a new and alternative aesthetic.[4] We also find him writing reviews of West Indian literature while in Ghana, suggesting, as Cameron had done earlier, that a knowledge of African oral traditions would help Afro-Caribbean writers in defining and using their own still vibrant oral traditions.[5] He was in addition, a contributor to radio programmes in Ghana, and as an education officer, part of the new thrust towards the indigenization of education there, in that early post-Independence period.

In history, the impact of Eric Williams's *Capitalism and Slavery* began to be felt on the Mona Campus of the University of the West Indies. Elsa Goveia's *A Study on the Historiography of the British West Indies* provided those who were interested with a means of locating most of the current notions about the history and potential of Caribbean peoples in their historical context. George Lamming read and was deeply influenced by the ideas of C.L.R. James.

Horizons widened during this decade. Lamming's "The Negro Writer and His World", (1956)[6] for example, moved far beyond the normal stereotyped discussion, to suggest the complex situation of the Black as diasporan, as twentieth century man, and as one who had to refashion both for himself and the benefit of the Other, that image which the Other had imposed on him, The artist is seen as rebel, as adamic refashioner of word and world, as lonely descender into private hell, and as illuminator of social and political reality. Lamming, who had read Richard Wright's *Black Boy* years before, was aware of himself as one of an international group of New World writers who were involved in a process of transforming the historic stereotypes which had been imposed on Black people, by speaking from within the self-in-maroonage. Significantly, "The Negro Writer and his World", was a conference paper read at the First International Conference of Negro Writers, held in Paris in 1956. James Baldwin also attended that conference, and provides a perceptive account of that crucial period in one of his essays.

1960 to Present

Janheinz Jahn in *Muntu* (1958) had helped lift Afro-Caribbean literature out of its solitude and to locate it—often erroneously—in a wide Pan-Africanist context which had existed before in the dreams of a handful of scholars. His main concern was the literature of the Francophone Caribbean. Gabriel Coulthard's *Race and Colour in Caribbean Literature* (1962) began for the

Anglophone Caribbean the crucial business of comparative Caribbean literature. As we have seen, this was taking place while the writers themselves were, through exile, in the process of widening their horizons and deepening dimensions.

The Pan-African context, however, was but one of the possible contexts within which the literature of the diaspora could be placed. V.S. Naipaul was an outsider to such a context. His position of outsider/insider enabled him to mock it, caricature it, critically analyze it. Never for one moment could he be fully part of it, however much of it was part of him. For "seepage" from the world of Creoledom was viewed by him as violation and chaos.[7] Naipaul, after a decade of wrestling with the problems confronting the *Asiatic* presence in a post-colonial society where the Afro-Creole presence was only just beginning to be defined and accepted as such, wrote *The Mimic Men*. In this novel he posits that the violations of history have impaired both the public and the private selves; both what I have termed *the imposed self and the self-in-maroonage*. Because of this each ethnic group is seen as festering in its separate cell; while the public forum of school, parliament or business provides them with no real possibility, no common ground for dialogue. "Mimicry" in that novel is more than simple copying of other people's stuff. It is the result of the attenuation and destruction of will through historical process, the loss of the capacity for choice and the possibility of self-hood and because of these things, the openness of the psyche's shell to every chance, opinion, fashion and style, and the replacement of willed choice by role-playing.

Derek Walcott could not be satisfactorily placed in a Pan-African context either. His stance, which he eventually defined as "mulatto"[8] was one of Janus-faced ambivalence which could at one and the same time theoretically reject and accept both Africa and Europe in the Caribbean. Lamming, indeed, notes ambivalence as one of the major aspects of the Caribbean sensibility, particularly when it faces the dilemma of affirming an 'African' presence.[9] Walcott's seminal work seems always to grow out of this ambivalence. He has called it "making creative use of schizophrenia." In practice, this has meant the display of considerable strength in the affirmation of a European presence in the Caribbean sensibility and a considerable bitterness in confronting the resurgence of an African one.[10]

Just as Naipaul is able to deny the validity of the inner self-in-maroonage, Walcott is, in "The Muse of History" able to reject all the manifestations of this inner self—the drums, music style, rhetoric, religion, symbolism, etc.—as the basis for a new aesthetic. The difference between the outsider/insider position of the "Asiatic" and the "schizophrenic" position of the "mulatto" is that the latter is generally forced to affirm whatever he denies. Hence Walcott accepts the drums, music, style rhetoric, folklore, dance and so forth as a viable basis for the construction of a New World drama, and has recently included in his poetry some of the very elements for which he has roundly abused a host of unnamed other Caribbean poets.

Wilson Harris could not be fitted into a Pan-African context. He started with the notion of the Caribbean and New World sensibility as "the latent ground of old and new personalities"—a meeting place of the crumbling old world and the unborn new one. In the unnamed, untamed, osmotic heartland of this New World—aptly symbolized by the virgin forests, black inland rivers, and extensive savannahs of Guyana—all primal cosmologies, mythologies, dreams of civilization and conquest meet, intersect, echo or parallel each other, creating tension conflict, and at the same time infinite possibility. Yet the vessels within which these cosmologies meet are an odd collection of rum guzzlers, murderers, delirious pork-nockers, money-lenders, whores, cattle-ranchers, rustlers, land-surveyors, and psychotics from the coast of "domesticity and lights," who find themselves like white America's newest Thoreau, Jim Jones, in the Guyana forest of the night. There, all these people find nothing but themselves; the self stripped of its social, ethnic or economic prop; and the result of such encounter is disintegration and the possibility of transformation through lived ordeal.

Harris's preoccupation with inner quest and cosmic issues had its base in a very particular sense and knowledge of the Guyanese political scenario. There, more than anywhere else in the English-speaking Caribbean, was the visible evidence of that plural, schismatic society, which the sociologists were trying to define in the sixties.[11] There is no doubt that the break-up of the PPP and with it the African and East Indian coalition in Guyana (1954–57) is partially responsible for the themes of Harris's first four novels *Palace of the Peacock, The Far Journey of Oudin, The Whole Armour* and *The Secret Ladder* (1961–65). In these novels—the first two in particular—history is ordeal, a legacy of bitterness and guilt. It has maimed the psyches of both colonizer and colonized, and established brutal authoritarian and materialist patterns, not only in Euro/Afro-Creole society but also within the world of the indentured East Indian peasantry and their descendants. The ghost of this legacy of guilt, materialism, brutality and psychic crippledom cannot be laid by amnesia or evasion, but by confrontation and atonement, and since the crippledom exists within the psyche and has been maintained by ex-colonial peoples long after the physical withdrawal of the colonizers, then confrontation and atonement have to occur within the psyche.

Where Naipaul's people remain paralyzed before their crippledom, and Walcott, faced with the maimed remains of history at one point advocates amnesia, Harris like the Hindus or the Buddhists, involves the psyche in terrible and agonizing Kharmic processes, in which the intolerable burden of history has to be borne and worn because it is our own burden. Time has to be imaginatively re-entered and relived until one becomes worthy of reprieve or movement beyond. The price of becoming a person in the sense that Harris understands personhood requires a *movement through history* then *movement beyond history*; a gradual peeling off of the old personality, a divestment of the props of colour, status, race, power and authority. Walcott eventually adopts a similar position in his play *Dream on Monkey Mountain* which owes much conceptually to Harris.

By the mid-sixties, then, the Pan-African paradigm had proven inadequate in the face of the multi-faceted complexity of the total Caribbean experience. It was qualified by the notion of an ethnically plural and culturally diverse archipelago; by the idea of a mulatto heritage in which European and African elements are blended; and by the notion of an emerging indigenized Caribbean tradition which was flexible, complex and had grown, or was growing out of the confrontation, competition, intersection and collapse of several peoples, life-styles and cultures over a process of time and under pressure from a rigid, authoritarian and exploitative system.

If Harris's work suggests the interior dimensions of this shift in perception, Lamming's *Of Age and Innocence* was the first serious attempt to deal with its political aspect. Coming in the wake of the collapse of multi-ethnic politics in Guyana, this novel reveals the deep sense of schism running through West Indian society, as well as the desperate or resolute hope of unity in an open and ominous future. Secrecy and communion constitute the opposite poles of this novel. True political liberation can only be based on open dialogue, shared experience and communion both within and between ethnic groups; and communion requires trust, absolute candour and honesty between the leadership and the people on the one hand, and between the different ethnic groups in a culturally diverse society.

But these qualities of openness, trust and candour have never been permitted existence in a colonial situation such as the one described earlier in this paper. Thus secrecy and mistrust permeate the relationship between Africans and Indians, the major ethnic groups in *Of Age and Innocence*, and become the catalyst for the tragic divisions which occur towards the end of the novel. If *In the Castle of My Skin* (1953) ended with a perception of the complexity of the African heritage, and an emerging vision of the spiritual and emotional oneness of the Black experience, *Of Age and Innocence* ends with the more complex vision of a multi-ethnic society in which the African heritage is only one of the many heritages competing for visibility and political presence, and Pan-Africanism a source of strength or a prop only to one segment of the population. *Of Age and Innocence* also ends with the embryonic dream of the younger generation; a dream—like Martin Luther King's—of openness, graciousness, cultural exchange in a world where there are no secrets, only a sharing of modes of living and seeing. It is the single hopeful possibility Lamming permits in a horizon of omen and smouldering catastrophe.

The intolerable wrestle between dream and reality has intensified since the mid-sixties. Far from achieving dialogue and communion among the oppressed, Caribbean societies have deepened the divisions of class and race. Central to this development was the Black Power movement in America, which forty years after Garvey reopened the questions about the self-perception, economic position, and real presence of Black people in America. These questions had to be reopened; and viewed positively, the profound reassessment of the situation of Black people in the diaspora has led to a deepening of consciousness both in America and the Caribbean. There are far more people who are aware of their history and of the continuity of struggle, survival and creativity. While the system still seeks to marginalize Black people in general, there are far more people at every level of life who are articulate, resolute and conscious. There is far more publishing being done, more to read.

But it is also true to say that in places such as Trinidad and Guyana, the situation which Lamming explored in *Of Age and Innocence* still obtains. In those two countries, the two major races view each other as competitors and thus view each assertion of racial presence by the other, as a threat to self-hood. The masses of both African and Indians remain exploitable, divided and open to manipulation by politicians who because of the deepening of ethnic consciousness, have had for the last twenty years to project themselves as charismatic, ethnic culture heroes. Elsewhere in the Caribbean, politicians have even manipulated the religions of the oppressed, drawing on the fervour of the cult for political support which at points reaches fanaticism. This is true of Jamaica and Guyana and was true of Grenada and of course Haiti.

What one is dealing with in the 1970's then, is no longer the denial of racial presence to Afro-Caribbean people, but the exploitation of awakened racial consciousness by Black political leaders. So that the deepening of consciousness which could be a strength has ironically become the basis of fresh exploitation. Attempts to transcend racial and class divisions have taken the form of (a) verbal nationalism (b) a renewal of Marxist/Leninist ideology. The struggle for both of these ideals is just beginning, and promises to be long, paradoxical and bitter. Nationalism, for example, can easily become traditional insularity, which renders the region as a whole even more vulnerable in the world. Marxism/Leninism is, so far, advocated in a rigid and doctrinaire fashion, which seems to me to ignore the multi-faceted complexity of the Caribbean situation. It isn't surprising that in both Trinidad and Guyana, the cleavages along racial lines have remained and been most pronounced even in parties which have proclaimed a universalist Marxist ideology.

Since the mid-sixties various "directions" have been evident in the literature. Edward Kamau Brathwaite's trilogy *The Arrivants* (1967–1969) has been the mature fruit of an intense and richly various enquiry into the meaning of the African presence in the Caribbean and the Americas. One of his most important contributions has been his ceaseless experimentation with form, and his ability to use models drawn from the basic folk, folk-urban and proletarian forms of Black people of the diaspora, and on the continent of Africa.[12]

What has happened in Jamaica since then has resulted in an entirely different sort of poetry, best seen in his collection *Black + Blues* (1976). There, the poetry emerges out of the bleak mood which succeeded the assassination of the Black Power and Civil Rights movement in America and its collapse in the Caribbean. It constantly asks questions about the connection between Revolution and consciousness. In "Glass", for example, the poet posits that Revolution must be based on spiritual continuity with past revolutionary effort. But Blacks have inherited a tradition of discontinuity which, as Brathwaite had already illustrated in *Rights of Passage*, forces them to alternate between creative action and role-playing, revolutionary consciousness and the minstrel dance of death. How does one, beginning as colonials have had to begin, break the circle or repression/reprisal/retribution/revolution/repression? What creative action brings the necessary release from this wheel?

Brathwaite asks these questions with respect to a society which is half-urban and half-primal, facing the full stress of modern life with very few visible resources. Under pressure this world begins to prophesy; to create song, legend, myth and dread omen out of the materials of every-day horror. Black people caught in the system, whether they jive in Harlem ("Glass"), or sharpen their ratchet knives in Kingston ("Springblade", "Starvation") become representative of all sub-jugated peoples, disoriented since the break-up of the Roman Empire and the formation of Western European civilizations. The Caribbean diaspora is placed in a long and vast historical context which has seen movement of peoples, disorientation, the extermination of millions of primal peoples in the Americas by the bearers of a superior technology of warfare, the confron-tation of the materialistic West with the kingdoms of spirit in India, Africa and meso-America; the elevation of Western materialism into skyscraper, rocket, spaceship and mushroom cloud, until today the West predicts its own destruction, sees each new invention as an omen of catas-trophe, (*Future Shock, The Greening of America, Silent Spring*) and longs for its now abolished sense of wonder, the reinstatement of its dead gods.

Brathwaite's problem becomes that of the entire New World sensibility; that of locating his ex-primordial peoples in this context of movement, disequilibrium and destruction. It is Wal-cott's problem, that of Lamming's last two novels (*Water with Berries* and *Natives of My Person*, that of Carpentier, (*The Lost Steps, Explosion in a Cathedral*), Harris and Fuentes (*Terra Nostra*). It involves a profound reassessment of the meaning of European history, which Brathwaite had already begun in some of his earlier poems, (e.g., "Heretic," "Judas of Barcelona" in *Other Exiles*).

The two sets of possibilities represented by Harris's *Palace of the Peacock* and Naipaul's *The Mimic Men* now become the poles between which our self-perception swings. On the one hand there is the possibility of rebuilding the lost kingdoms of the spirit whose ruins remain as reminders of who we were. How we are to do this becomes the basis of fresh debate. Is Tom's transformation into Ogun still possible? Can Makak really return to the green beginnings? Will Donne ever attain the palace of the peacock or Mohammed be purged by the refining fire of spirit? Naipaul's constant answer to this has been a resolute NO.

Brathwaite, with all his hopes for revolutionary transformation, has grave doubts. On the one hand the ruined city man has created roots and prophecy, and his rumble of consciousness moves like an earthquake under the frail structures of "our mindless architects." But on the other hand, the city man is a victim who sees "vistas of rot only." Each new generation is "a new gen-eration of clogged gutters," and constantly betrays its lightning flashes of intuitive vision: "the flash of dark into which I have carved no holy place." ("Caliban").

So that if *The Arrivants* moved with the faith of spiritual dialectic towards an equilibrium of negation and affirmation, void and structured form, silence and widening circle of sound, *Black + Blues*, constitutes a veritable *de profundis* of catastrophe. The landscape is more dreary the manscape more ravaged. The result in terms of form is directness and plainness of statement on the one hand, and a restless unfocussed turbulence on the other. There is a greater intellectual width and depth and a burning intensity of inner search.

Fierceness and bleakness of vision are characteristic of the 1970's. Our poets at home have become furiously driven men. Walcott, Carter, Brathwaite, McNeill, Scott, Roach or Questel all share this "driven" quality, which is a direct response to the quality of chaos which exists in the contemporary Caribbean. One has travelled a considerable distance from the simple vision of the thirties and forties. The revolution of self-perception has always been taking place;

and it continues, grows increasingly more complex and multi-faceted. It embraces now both the notion of ethnic heritages and their competition and confrontation in the contemporary post-independence Caribbean. It involves the relentless class struggle, and the survival of the structures and instruments of exploitation and repression. It hovers between the alternatives of adamic renewal or return, and existentialist sense of void. It challenges conventional notions of history and is part of a vast worldwide movement to relocate the submerged cultures of the devastated in the kingdom of human and humane achievement.

(*Paper read at the Conference on "Caribbean Expressions: African Diaspora in the Americas," sponsored by the Visual Arts Research and Resource Center Relating to the Caribbean, New York, September 18, 1979. First published in* Caribe: Report; Caribbean Expressions Festival 1, *New York, 1980 pp. 7–15*).

Note

1. Gordon Rohlehr, "Articulating a Caribbean Aesthetic: The Revolution in Self-Perception," in *My Strangled City and Other Essays* (Port-of-Spain: Longman Trinidad, 1992), pp. 1–16.

References

1 Rohlehr, G., "The Folk in Caribbean Literature," *Tapia* Vol. 2 Nos. 11 and 12 (December 17 & 24, 1973).

2 Rohlehr, G., "Forty Years of Calypso," *Tapia* Vol. 2 Nos. 1, 2 & 3 (September 1972).

3 Cameron, N., *The Evolution of the Negro*, Greenwood Press, Westport Connecticut, 1970 Originally published in 1926 & 1934, Georgetown, Guyana.

4 Rohlehr, G., "The Creative Writer and Society," *Kaie*, (Guyana) No. 11, (August 1973) pp 48–77.

5 Brathwaite, E., *Review of Voices from Ghana, Bim* 30, Jan—June 1960, pp 88–90.

6 Lamming, G., "The Negro Writer and His World," *Caribbean Quarterly* Vol. 5 No. 2 (February 1958).

7 Rohlehr, G., "Predestination, Frustration and Symbolic Darkness in Naipaul's *A House for Mr. Biswas*," *Caribbean Quarterly* Vol. X, No. 1, (1964) pp 3–11 also Rohlehr, G., "The Ironic Approach" in *Modern Black Novelists*, Prentice Hall, Englewood Cliffs, NJ 1971, pp 162–176.

8 Walcott, D., "What the Twilight Says: An Overture," Introduction to *Dream On Monkey Mountain and Other Plays* Farrar, Straus & Giroux, NY 1970 "The Muse of History" in Coombs O, ed *Is Massa Day Dead?* Doubleday Anchor, NY 1974.

9 Lamming, G., "Caribbean Literature: the Black Rock of Africa," in *African Forum*, Vol. 1, No. 4 (Spring 1966) pp. 32–52 1965.

10 Walcott, D.,—opus cit. For my comments on this aspect of Walcott's work see: Rohlehr G., "My Strangled City," *Caliban* Vol. 3, No. 1, (Fall/Winter 1976) pp 50–122.

11 Smith, M. G., *The Plural Society in the British West Indies*, California, The University of California Press, 1965.

12 For a full-length study of Brathwaite's *Arrivants*, see Rohlehr, G., *Pathfinder: Black Awakening in The Arrivants of Edward Kamau Brathwaite*, Port-of-Spain, 1981.

George Lamming

George Lamming, a Barbadian author born in June 1927, is one of the most highly regarded and perhaps best-known contemporary writers from the Caribbean. His corpus of work spans nearly sixty years and encompasses an impressive array of fiction, critical essays, and prose. Lamming stands as a stalwart of the Caribbean intellectual, literary, and cultural traditions and is a critical voice of anti-colonial thought. Lamming is best known for his novels *In the Castle of My Skin*, *The Emigrants*, *Of Age and Innocence*, *Season of Adventure*, and *Natives of My Person*, which cover such themes as migration, alienation and identity formation, processes of cultural change, and colonization. Pivotal to Lamming's work has been his exploration of the relationship between the political and the aesthetic as well as the relationship between history and identity.

The Honourable Member[1]

George Lamming[2]

I want to offer you the social portrait of a man you have often seen, and whom many of you may have some reason to admire. He was born some 40-odd years ago in an urban village with a local primary school. Later he attended two secondary schools before going on a Government scholarship to a university abroad. He qualified as a lawyer, felt a passing interest in the study of economics, but was persuaded by his godfather, a senior public figure, to return to Barbados where his chances of a political career looked very promising. He had a moderate success at the bar, before he successfully contested an election. He has served as a Minister of Government and represented his country in various international negotiations. Today he owns three houses and a chicken farm. There is also substantial rumour of investments in an auxiliary transport service locally known as the mini-bus, and shares in various tourist resorts. His known assets are estimated to be in the region of a figure, not under three quarters of a million dollars.

He occupies a large four-bedroom house in the rural suburbs with an ample view of six parishes, and a horizon of sky that disappears into the deep-water harbour. His tastes have been influenced by foreign travel. The furniture is modern Scandinavian. There is a conspicuous assortment of Moroccan rugs, exquisitely patterned in crimson and gold. These were acquired as a gift after a brief romance in southern Spain. The walls, on all sides, are disfigured by juvenile souvenirs of illuminated nights in New York, eating out along the Bay in San Francisco, racially mixed couples at play around a kidney-shaped swimming pool in Miami. There are no books anywhere. An electric trolley moves itself around with drinks. The family has two cars: one Italian, the other Japanese. But his cultural preference in magazine reading and film is irreversibly American.

He is careful in his choice of clothes. Abroad he was known to wear pink carnations in his button hole, but promptly dropped this style of decoration on his return, since flowers on a man encourage Barbadians to question his sexual tendencies. He lunches frequently in hotel restaurants on the south coast; dines about twice a week on the west coast. On Sundays he may take small parties for a buffet feast at the Atlantis hotel. Much of this eating has to do with political business.

He has two children: a girl who went to St Winifred's from a junior school called St Gabriel's and a son who, after problems at home, was placed in a minor public school in the South of England. Neither has ever seen the inside of a government elementary school. Neither has any recollection of ever travelling by bus in Barbados.

I refrain from offering you a physical description of the Honourable Member, since he is of a type who bitterly resent any reference to the skin in analysing social relationships in this island. It is a sufficient guide to add that his wife is a lady, distinguished by her hair, which we have been trained to call, 'good.' They have both retained certain travel documents which allow them indefinite residence elsewhere.

Many of his contemporaries had a privilege of schooling similar to his. They may have been less enterprising, but they have all made notable contributions in education and at the upper levels of the Civil Service. Some have been chairmen of corporations; junior functionaries in development banks of one kind or another. A few are in general medical practice. No one of his acquaintance went into business.

Let us identify him as the Honourable Member, a man who sees his achievements as the base for an expanding personal prosperity in the years ahead. If we are to understand the true history of this man, and his relations to his public duties, we cannot concentrate only on the period of those 40-odd years you have seen him around. Nor can we view him exclusively in the context of his personal life without any reference to his social formation. Such a limited perspective can only lead to fruitless and self-degrading gossip. So let us try to see that process of social evolution which has brought him to this criterion of success which he and a whole class of men like himself now embrace as the most desirable reward of their efforts in this life: social power and material wealth.

His great grandfather was born in the parish of St George in 1877, a year after the Confederation Riots. He was put out to labour as an estate hand at the age of nine. Twelve years later, an ox-cart crippled him for life. He had already had a son of four. But it would have been useless in those days to argue a case for compensation. He lingered until the age of 40, elaborating on the stories he had heard in his childhood about the great insurrection which had engaged a turbulent underclass of workers against elements of the merchant/planter class of the day. Plantation families fled their homes to seek refuge on the ships at anchor in Carlisle Bay. In St George alone, at Salters plantation, labourers had stolen or captured 12 acres of potatoes. Their adversaries said it was the work of communistic agitators. That charge, as you will see, has been the official explanation of any disruptive social action for more than a century. It is amazing that, to this day, men can still successfully make it their major appeal in what is thought to be an honest election.

The Honourable Member would be in this category.

His grandfather who was born in 1894 continued to pass on his own father's recollections of the Confederation Riots. He could never understand why Governor Hennessy should have included in his famous six points the outrageous proposal that 'the mental asylum in Barbados should open its doors to receive lunatics from other islands'. It made him adopt a conservative and unwelcoming restraint towards all foreigners who looked a little like himself. But he is very important for our understanding of his grandson, the Honourable Member, since his own work career introduces us to a remarkable category of men whose struggle for an independent form of employment influenced a development which led towards the achievement of the Honourable Member. This grandfather had distinguished himself as a cooper. He made and repaired every kind of wooden cask and tub you could imagine, and by this achievement of a technical skill, also made himself and the artisan class he represents indispensable to the technical function of the plantation. They were stubborn men, this artisan class of coopers, carpenters, masons and blacksmiths. They were men who had cultivated an immense pride in the excellent quality of the things they made. They had a simple and genuine dignity.

The Honourable Member would hardly remember him. But it was this grandfather who preached the absolute necessity of education. He perceived the school as the only possible means of rescuing his offspring from the humiliations his ancestors had endured. The book, the lesson, pen and ink: these were his images of redemption. And that's why his son, the Honourable Member's father, born in 1914, was destined to be a teacher. The elementary school became their chapel, Harrison College their cathedral, and an English university, the Kingdom of Heaven.

And behind this immense effort was an even greater sacrifice of courage and will: the women who fathered many a household, nursed man and child without a wage and have remained to this day the last surviving example of legalised slave-labour.

Those indolent critics who treat the past as though it were an amputated limb to be buried and forgotten and who complain about my insistence on restoring it do not pay serious, critical attention to the society they describe. For a large proportion of those who rule our lives today from the executive, the judiciary, and all corners of the bureaucracy are the products of that tutelage I have described, and profoundly shaped by that social experience which has made the Honourable Member who he is. And I do not have to argue with you this morning that our rulers are not only very much alive, but may be with us for some time to come. And this is the point I want this social portrait to emphasise.

If we follow, in greater detail, that honourable line of ancestry from the estate hand in the 1880s to the professional great grandson in 1981, we shall not find a single dominant landlord, a powerful merchant banker, certainly no industrial capitalist or great shipowner. But it is precisely these categories of men and their representatives whom the Honourable Member and his class have to deal with in very complex negotiations on our behalf in the political and industrial centres of the world: from Tokyo to Toronto, London, Brussels, and New York. Our Honourable Member and his class, bright, ambitious and often patriotic men, assume these challenging tasks without any historical social experience of ownership and control of the means of production in their own country: just functionaries who take care of other people's business. It makes for a certain fragility at the heart of all their protestations against unfair terms of trade, or the subtle and not so subtle bullying by capitalist powers to make us shape a foreign policy that may not be in the interests of our people. It is a grave predicament for the Honourable Member and his class; and it is made all the more dangerous when this class, putting its own self-interests above and beyond social incentives, is so eager to separate itself, by lifestyle and the hunger for status, from the working-class base from which it derived. It is important for you, on the fortieth anniversary of this great Union of yours, to recognise very clearly that such a division in the social fabric makes you, the working class, the main bastion in the people's national defence. Not the army, nor the police, nor any arm of the state power, but you whose productive labour is the foundation of the country's survival and the major factor which will always determine what are our objective needs and how these should relate to genuine social demand. There is little or nothing mercenaries can do before a united working class that is absolutely clear about what it has to defend. But if we were to follow the lifestyle of the Honourable Member, a style which now threatens to be the dominant value for all ranks of the people; we shall stumble into a way of living where we consume what we do not produce, and produce what we scarcely consume.

Barbados will cease to be a distinct and recognisable society. All it would aspire to be is an efficient service station. Then, one mercenary could be enough.

It is clear, therefore, that the responsibilities of the Trade Union movement are essentially, and inescapably, political. There are dangers you must attend to, the most serious of which is the strategy to distract your attention from the politics of your life as an organised body of labour, and a distinct class in the country's production relations: to pin you down to concerns and preoccupations which do not go beyond disputes about wages and conditions of work: to limit your capacity to intervene as a dominant force in the creation of national policy.

Karl Marx is very prophetic on this point. In a speech to a delegation of German trade unionists in 1869, he said:

Trade Unions are the schools of socialism. It is in Trade Unions that workers educate themselves and become socialists, because under their very eyes and every day the struggle with capital is taking place. Any political party, whatever its nature and without exception, can only hold the enthusiasm of the masses for a short time, momentarily; unions, on the other hand, lay hold on the masses in a more enduring way.

They alone are capable of representing a true working class party, and opposing a bulwark to the power of capital.

The fundamental basis of democracy should be the workers' control of their place of work, where every choice of programme and personnel from management to the floor, remains decisively within workers' power. That would be the most authentic arena of elections. Those who are afraid of such a development are afraid of genuine democracy.

The trade union, as a school of socialism, has a duty to encourage responsible debate about the relevance, and the function, of certain inherited models of government which evolved out of a social history that is not our own. It is not true that this particular electoral system is the only guarantee of a people's freedom, or that it is, indeed, such a guarantee from fear.

Since the independence of Barbados in 1965, both political parties have come to power. I think it is true to say that neither the Democratic Labour Party, nor the Barbados Labour Party, can be accused of repressive rule. Neither party in power has any history of political harassment of the people. Neither party has produced a leader who remotely resembles Gairy or Burnham. It would be impossible to defend a Barbadian who, any time after 1965, would claim abroad that he was a political refugee. On that score the record of both parties is excellent.

But I have observed the hardening of a social attitude which may confront the society with one of its greatest dangers: I refer to the increasing party tribalism which smothers all critical judgement about social and political issues, and makes the ordinary decent citizen afraid of being overheard.

It is as though members of the political parties see themselves as loyal warriors of two rival primitive tribes, each regarding the other's existence as a threat to his own; and where the tribe that comes to power takes possession of the total political estate, free at last to reward prizes to the most diligent of its own henchmen; and to punish, by careful exclusion, those whose tribal allegiance lies elsewhere. This party tribalism has nothing to do with politics, but leads to an exercise in petty victimisation which imposes silence on those who might otherwise contribute to shaping the critical intelligence of the nation.

It would be unjust to identify such practice exclusively with the present Administration; for I have listened, in the past, to volumes of similar complaint during the reign of the other party. In any case, it is idle at this stage to engage in distributing blame. The fact of the matter is that such an atmosphere exists; and members of this great national institution, the Barbados Workers' Union, who straddle both parties, have a political duty to deal with this example of dysfunction. I put it that way because I do not believe that such practice derives from the particular viciousness or vindictiveness of any particular Minister of Government at any time. The average professional politician is no less virtuous than the average citizen in other occupations: the businessman or the academic who conducts a faculty politics of a particularly sinister kind. But there is, I think, an important connection between the practice of punishment and reward, and a system which confers such an undemocratic range of patronage on those who hold office. This dysfunction becomes particularly acute in the tribal politics of small islands.

Sir Arthur Lewis in *The Agony of the Eight*, speaking of small islands and Government says:

Everybody depends on the Government for something, however small, so most are reluctant to offend it. The civil servants live in fear; the police avoid unpleasantness; the Trade Unions are tied to the party: the newspapers depend on Government advertisements.

A one party mentality advocating a two party arrangements, is a recipe for disaster. I have followed political movements in Jamaica very closely since the 1950s and observed during my visits over the years how this party tribalism grew; became institutionalised; and ultimately nurtured the political violence that was to afflict that country.

There is another danger you have lived with, and which has been eroding the consciousness of our people, almost without notice. It is what Professor Gordon Lewis, of the University of Puerto Rico, has referred to as 'recolonisation by religion'. Capitalist promotion of liberal democracy in developing countries goes hand in hand with the commercial sponsorship of Jesus Christ; and it has nothing to do with Jesus, who was not a man for the marketplace.

I take the view that among the most undesirable bandits probing Caribbean society are the vagrant religious evangelists. They have been able to buy their way into the approval of those who manage our radio stations. They wake us at dawn, and pursue us throughout the day, with these militant appeals to withdraw our attention from the most urgent issues that affect our lives. It is a form of collective hypnosis by radio; and no one seems to question their motives. They have an assignment to put the minds of our people to sleep, and to mobilise that psychic energy which has no outlet into other and more honourable forms of organisational activity.

The success of the People's Cathedral reflects a critical failure of the Trade Union Movement in educating the consciousness of our people out of such joyful stupor.

These are not anti-religious sentiments; for I have a deep respect for the religious sensibility in its search to give life a creative meaning. But what you ought to place at the centre of national debate is this unforgivable, commercial blasphemy against our people's capacity to believe; for it weakens their resistance to all other forms of external penetration.

My predecessor in this role drew attention to the tasks of education which confront the Union. The Labour college should be a national institution familiar as the political parties throughout the land, as the main centre of a popular intellectual culture, attracting men and women of all races and social backgrounds, and of every level of learning.

The Trade Union Movement has the financial capacity and the human resources to give birth to a popular theatre, assigning its own actors, directors, and writers to translate the day-to-day problems of the working class into a form of entertainment and instruction with which every member of the working class can immediately identify. It may perhaps win back the victims of the People's Cathedral to an arena of genuinely spiritual communion.

I don't know what are the creative consequences of Carifesta. But whatever critics of its organisation may justly say, as a cultural event, it was a most remarkable success. There was the demonstration of the Jamaicans that their country has now provided us with a formidable school of drama, the admirable professionalism of the Cubans who came and left without doing us any harm, and were even admired and embraced by those who saw them, and the vibrancy of the Surinamese at all times. This was a moment of cultural resistance in which the Barbados Workers Union might have played a central role. It must prepare itself for such a role.

The political sovereignty of a people is impossible unless it rests upon an authentic cultural base created by its working people.

Notes

1. This address, made to the 40th Annual Conference of the Barbados Workers Union on August 29, 1981, is a detailed treatment of the Caribbean middle class, particularly—but not only—those of the class who function as "Honourable Members." Parts of this description recur, explicitly or by echo, in other speeches by Lamming.
2. George Lamming, "The Honourable Member," in *The George Lamming Reader: The Aesthetics of Decolonisation*, ed. Anthony Bogues (Kingston, Jamaica: Ian Randle, 2011), pp. 101–109.

Michel-Rolph Trouillot

Michel-Rolph Trouillot (1949–2012) was an acclaimed anthropologist, historian, and writer born in Port-au-Prince, Haiti. Growing up in an inquisitively intellectual family, where history, politics, and the arts were central themes for family debates, provided a strong foundation on which Trouillot would develop his keen scholastic legacy. Vested in interrogating the structures of power that animates social life, political economy, and historiography, Trouillot's scholarship moves beyond disciplinary silos as it questions dominant paradigms of history and notions of the native in anthropological discourse. As a staunch advocate of interdisciplinarity and comparative research, Trouillot envisioned his academic work as a lifelong pursuit that expressed his passion for producing and interrogating knowledge.

The Odd and the Ordinary: Haiti, the Caribbean, and the World[1]

Michel-Rolph Trouillot[2]

How does one explain Haiti? What is Haiti? Haiti is the eldest daughter of France and Africa. It is a place of beauty, romance, mystery, kindness, humor, selfishness, betrayal, cruelty, bloodshed, hunger and poverty. It is a closed and withdrawn society whose apartness, unlike any other in the New World, rejects its European roots."

Nice passage, isn't it? Well, those of you who know my work may have guessed that I am trying to trick you. These words are not mine. They constitute the very first paragraph of *Written in Blood*, a sensationalist account of Haitian history written by Marine Colonel Robert Heinl and his wife Nancy.[3] I quote this paragraph in lieu of an introduction because it typifies a viewpoint widely shared in Haitian studies, one that I wish to challenge, namely the fiction of Haiti's exceptionalism. Heinl and Heinl start with a question: "How does one explain Haiti?" The question is then set aside for a laundry list of particulars. Then, at the end of that list, the emphasis shifts to Haiti's apartness: Haiti is unique. It is unlike any other country in the New World. And indeed, if we keep reading the next 700 pages, we soon discover that it is unlike any other country—period.

The notion of Haitian exceptionalism permeates both the academic and popular literature on Haiti under different guises and with different degrees of candidness. At first glance, this insistence on Haiti's special status seems to be a simple acknowledgment of the country's admittedly spectacular trajectory. I suggest, however, that there are hidden agendas—intellectual and political—behind this insistence, and that these agendas, rather than genuine interest in the particulars of Haitian history, underpin Haitian exceptionalism.

Haiti is unique. Haiti is different. Haiti is special. At a superficial level, these sayings could simply mean that a particular set of environmental, historical, and social features contribute in varied ways to make Haiti quite different from other places: that Haiti is not Argentina, or Canada, or Germany, or Senegal. I have absolutely no quarrel with such a statement. I can assure you that no one born in Aquín, Gonaïves, or Cité Soleil thinks of them as Buenos Aires, Frankfurt, or Dakar.

But those who insist most often on Haiti's uniqueness do not simply mean that Haiti is easily unique. For each and every society is unique, distinguishable from each and every other society. Indeed, regions within the same country can be distinguishable from other regions. Societies, countries, or regions are historical products and all historical products are unique—by definition and by necessity. And the more we know a place or a person, the more this place or this person appears unique. But we do not keep on repeating it: life is too short for that. To my knowledge, foreign or native writers who write about, say, the Dominican Republic, Paraguay, Bolivia, Thailand, Madagascar, or Gabon—to cite only a few remarkable places—do not go on repeating ad nauseam how unique these societies are. They assume this uniqueness and proceed from there. So the celebrated uniqueness of Haitian society and culture must mean more than the distinctiveness that characterizes any historical product from any other historical products.

If all historical products are unique, not all of them are distinguishable in the same way. It is quite probable that a particular configuration of circumstances will lead to a historical product of which the uniqueness is dazzling: an individual, a group of individuals, an institution, or a phenomenon that strikes us more than otherwise similar entities. In short, some historical products are more remarkable than others, at least to certain groups of observers. However unique we may all be, it makes sense to insist that Julius Caesar, Napoleon, Shaka the Zulu, Toussaint Louverture, François Duvalier, or Mikhaïl Gorbachev are unique in ways that need to be noticed. It makes sense to insist upon the fact that the Holy See is a unique religious institution. That the French Academy is a unique combination of culture and politics. That German fascism was a unique political movement. That the state of Israel is a unique geopolitical entity. That the United States, Cuba, Brazil, Liberia, Tibet, or the Philippines are quite distinguishable countries, the uniqueness of which both strikes out and needs to be emphasized in the context of their own immediate environment or even perhaps in the context of world history.

In that sense, of course, Haiti seems more unique than many other countries. The list of features that makes it special is long, starting with the history of Saint-Domingue and the Haitian Revolution: first and only successful slave revolution in modern history. First independent country of the Americas, and for a long time the only one, where freedom meant freedom for every one. First and for a long time sole black republic in world history, indeed, the first non-white modern state. The most peasant country of the Americas. Largest creole speaking population of the world. And so on. And so on. And so on.

In that sense, of course, Haiti is indeed unique. And if we want to play semantic games, it is not just unique: it is exceptional, the result of a striking convergence of historical particulars. This is the distinctiveness that accounts for Haiti's cultural resilience. This is the distinctiveness that attracts many foreigners—tourists and academics, for good or for bad. This is the distinctiveness that succors Haitian national pride—for good *and* for bad. This is the distinctiveness that Haitian tourism officials have banked on for more than twenty years with the slogan "Vive la différence!"

I have no quarrel with such a view of Haiti's particularisms, even though I may question the use some make of them. For all the reasons I have mentioned, and probably many more, Haiti is in many ways exceptional. I would insist, though, that this exceptionalism is only one way to look at Haitian reality. There are much less petulant continuities embedded in this spectacular trajectory. The majority of Haitians live quite ordinary lives. They eat what is for them—and for many others—quite ordinary food. They die quite ordinary deaths from quite ordinary accidents, quite ordinary tortures, quite ordinary diseases. Accidents so ordinary that they could be prevented. Tortures so ordinary that the international press does not even mention them. Diseases so ordinary that they are easily treated almost anywhere else. Exceptional, is it?

Certainly more exceptional than India, Java, Burma, or Ethiopia—which are of course exceptional in their own way. Listen to Blair Niles, the author of *Black Haiti*: "I am familiar with the measured posturing dances of Japan, of India, Java and Burma. I have watched the head-hunting dance of the Dyaks of Borneo. That was savage enough; primitive enough . . . But savage as it was, that too had been in a way sophisticated." For Blair Niles discovered Haiti and its dances. That, says Niles, "went further back than the hunt [of Borneo]; back to the beginning . . ." (Niles 1926: 27).

Note that Blair Niles is writing in admiration, in this passage at least. Elsewhere in the book, he heavily criticizes foreigners who denigrate the Haitian people. Further, there is ample evidence throughout the text that Niles made a more genuine effort than many other visitors, both before and after him, to understand Haiti. At any rate, no one can accuse him of disliking Haitians. Quite the opposite: he is attracted to them. But he is attracted to them the way one can be attracted to a sexual fetish or a taboo. That is, he is attracted to Haiti as deviance. What he likes in Haiti is what he finds aberrant, the reverse image of a world of normalcy. That is not unique. That is not even exceptional. That is weird.

Listen to Professor Heinz Lehman of McGill University talking to student Wade Davis of *Serpent and Rainbow* fame: "Let me relieve you of any further suspense, Mr. Davis. We understand . . . that you are attracted to unusual places. We propose to send you to the frontier of death" (Davis 1985: 15). Davis is attracted to "unusual" places. Unusual here does not mean unique, and the reference to the frontier of death as well (as the Hollywood version of the book) is there to testify to the nuance. No, unusual here means odd, strange, peculiar, freakish, queer, bizarre. Weird, indeed, don't you think?

To be sure, Davis is careful not to use these words; but that may be a reflection of the times. Even travel guides and *National Geographic* have learned not to present so-called exotic places in explicitly condescending or derogatory terminology. Further, since the nineteenth century, a Haitian tradition of sharp rebuttal has kept many foreign writers, French and North American in particular, on their guard. Thus, for instance, Davis—of all people!—tries to distance himself from "sensational films and pulp fiction" (1985: 3). The Heinls (one of whom epitomized the worst of U.S. interference in Haitian politics) dedicate their book to Haitian nationalist heroes. It has become stylish for foreign writers to denounce Haiti's bad press while contributing to it in fact.

In that context, Haitian exceptionalism tends to function at the level of the subtext in most books published outside the country in the second half of this century. While it permeates the entire work, there are very few sentences that actually articulate it, except perhaps on the back cover or in the ad copy (e.g., Davis 1985; Abbott 1988).[4] At times, however, writers—including respected academics—can be less careful, or nonchalant enough for Haitian exceptionalism to appear clearly in the text. One more quote among many: "Haiti, like eighteenth-century Sicily has always been a place apart," a place with "a penchant for the bizarre and the grotesque" (Rotberg 1971: 7,8). As the French used to put it, with debonair condescension, "Singulier petit pays."

I am, of course, bothered by this condescension. But there is more to it. The most important problem with the overemphasis on Haiti's singularity—even if not phrased in derogatory terms—is both methodological and political. My own intolerance is less toward the narrow-mindedness often implicit in such statements (which, after all say more about their authors than about Haiti) than toward the practical consequences of this narrow-mindedness. When we are being told over and over again that Haiti is unique, bizarre, unnatural, odd, queer, freakish, or grotesque, we are also being told, in varying degrees, that it is unnatural, erratic, and therefore unexplainable. We are being told that Haiti is so special that modes of investigation applicable to other societies are not relevant here.

In her remarkable book, *Haiti and the Great Powers*, Brenda Gayle Plummer criticizes the myth of Haitian exceptionalism and exposes some of its consequences. In Plummer's view, "The idea that Haiti could fit no paradigm prohibited the development of any but the most conservative policies" on the part of international powers, including the United States (Plummer 1988). One could add that the very same view continues today to influence some policy-makers in the United States, in France or in the Vatican—to cite only three states involved in Haitian affairs. Plummer is much more indulgent than I am, however, toward Haitian politicians and intellectuals, even though she admits that they share some of the blame. In my view, in both cases Haitian exceptionalism acts as a shield.

Though not the privy of non-native writers, the fiction that Haiti escapes analysis and comparison emerged out of the minds of European and North American observers, mostly white males, who wrote about Haiti in the early nineteenth century, at the time when the very existence of a "black" state that had issued from an anticolonial revolution appeared to them as an aberration. For a plethora of writers from James Franklin to Gustave d'Alaux, to Spencer St. John to Robert and Nancy Heinl, Haitian exceptionalism has been a shield that masks the negative contribution of the Western powers to the Haitian situation. Haitian exceptionalism functions as a shield to Haiti's integration into a world dominated by Christianity, capitalism, and whiteness. The more Haiti appears weird, the easier it is to forget that it represents the longest neocolonial experiment in the history of the West.

Even James Leyburn was guilty of the same sin of omission. In the third chapter of his important book, *The Haitian People*, Leyburn (1941: 32) wrote: "If ever a country had an opportunity to start absolutely fresh in choosing its own social institutions, Haiti had that opportunity in 1804 . . . The Haitians might (theoretically, at least) have invented an entire new little world of economic, political, religious, and social life. All paths were open to them." Leyburn concluded that unfortunately Dessalines's mental limitations set the Haitians on the road to disaster.

Well, that won't do. Neither theoretically nor in practice. With one stroke of the pen, Leyburn erases three centuries of direct colonial domination and a century and a half of neocolonialism. And this from an author who remains, in my view, one of the best observers, foreign or Haitian, of Haitian society and culture.

The Haitian side is no more glorious, even though at times it looks better on paper. Indeed, many Haitian intellectuals and politicians continue to repeat the same nonsense, more loudly even than their foreign counterparts. The reality is that this fiction is as convenient to the Haitian elites as it is to many foreigners, even though for different reasons.

Before the twentieth century, Haitian writers rarely if ever promoted Haitian singularity in their studies of Haitian reality. In fact, quite the opposite, especially for the early part of the nineteenth century. Indeed, Haitian intellectuals rightly saw the theories of Haitian exceptionalism that were spreading in Europe and North America as implicitly—and often explicitly—racist. In the immediate aftermath of independence, a writer such as Baron de Vastey relied on the universalist principles of the Enlightenment to herald the Haitian Revolution and reject theories associating physical appearance and national character.[5] In the late nineteenth and early twentieth centuries, writers such as Demesvar Delorme, Louis-Joseph Janvier, Anténor Firmin, Edmond Paul, down to Jean Price-Mars and Dantès Bellegarde tried in varying degrees to make sense of Haiti in an international context, and to apply some of the prevalent theories of their times to the Haitian situation. This is particularly true in the social sciences and economics. However much one may now question the economic liberalism of an Edmond Paul, the sociology of Louis-Joseph Janvier, or the ethnology of Jean Price-Mars, these authors did not think that Haiti escaped the paradigms of their times.

But even as these writers quoted famous European thinkers, political practice in Haiti fed on exceptionalism. The Haitian elites acted as if, theories aside, Haiti was exceptional and should therefore be led in an exceptional manner. Thus the politics of a Delorme or a Firmin were not that much different from the illiterate generals who supported or opposed them and may have believed in Haitian exceptionalism. Still, the public and unchallenged assumption, in all intellectual circles, that Haiti was indeed a country like any other limited the damages inflicted by the pragmatic acceptance of practices otherwise deemed unconventional.

With the 1915–1934 U.S. occupation, however, Haitian studies took a sharp turn for the worse with increasing acceptance of theories based on Haiti's apartness. The occupation had led to a reevaluation of Haitian identity among the elites, including from writers such as Jean Price-Mars. But the ideological malaise of the times also opened the door to a possible questioning of the universals inherited from the Enlightenment. Drawing from Price-Mars but rejecting his

Enlightenment heritage, the Griot school in particular—one member of which was François Duvalier—insisted on the particularities of the Haitian *mentalité*.[6]

From the 1930s on, research, political practice and legislation emphasized Haiti's singularity, and indeed helped to increase this singularity with such aberrations as the infamous anti-Communist law of 1969. Among the many reasons cited for forbidding even the belief in Communism, the law notes "the incompatibility of *imported doctrines*, notably Marxism-Leninism, with the social, political, and economic order of Haiti" (cited in Trouillot and Pascal-Trouillot 1978: 445; emphasis added). According to Duvalier, Haiti could draw its ingredients for progress only from its own culture, a culture that is, of course, unique in the almost mystical sense emphasized by the Griot doctrine.[7]

I would be the last to say that Haitian culture is not unique, or that Haiti should not use its cultural resources. The point is that before and during the Duvalier years, the particularities of Haiti were used to shield the Haitian elites. Haiti is unique; therefore it evades foreign theories, including class analysis. Indeed, it evades all analysis in the strict sense of the term. It also evades comparison. Therefore, we can rule this country in ways that seem to defy the imagination of most foreigners and quite a few Haitians. Haiti is special; thus it deserves custom-made institutions and a custom-made government. The political maneuver is obvious. So is the intellectual fallacy upon which it rests.

It seems to me that we learn much less about Haiti if we read it as an aberration that defies any explanation than if we learn to place it in a comparative framework. One of the most serious limitations of Haitian studies, in Haiti and elsewhere, comes from the propensity of Haitianists, and especially of Haitianborn scholars, to study Haiti and nothing but Haiti. The assumption is that nothing we learn from looking at another society can teach us anything about Haiti, since Haiti is so unique. To be sure, insularism is a feature of Caribbean studies. Jamaicans study Jamaica, Cubans study Cuba, and few foreigners spread their wings over linguistic boundaries within the archipelago. Yet the irony in this case is that Haiti's exceptional history provides so many features that can benefit from the observation of other societies, especially in Latin America and more particularly in the other Antilles.

In the little space remaining, I will only mention a few of the areas where Haitian studies can surely benefit from the light of neighboring cases. I rest on the shoulders of so many colleagues that I cannot mention them all. Nor can I cover all the potential areas for comparative research.

The peasantry is one such area, and an important one. I spent fifteen months doing fieldwork among the peasantry of Dominica, and I believe that I learned much more about the Haitian peasantry during those months than I did during eighteen years in Port-au-Prince. Haiti, like the Windward Islands, like Jamaica, like Puerto Rico or to a lesser extent like Trinidad and Tobago, has a substantial post-plantation peasantry. How do theories of the impact of the plantation economy or on the passage from plantation to peasantry in a context dominated by capitalism (Trouillot 1988) fit the Haitian case? To my knowledge Alex Dupuy may be the first Haitian scholar to have tackled this question head on. Haitian studies in general would benefit from a more systematic reading of Walter Rodney, George Beckford, Raymond Smith, and J.R. Mandle. Sidney Mintz's comparative essays on Caribbean peasantries (1989) would serve as an excellent starting point for such research.

There are so many questions left unanswered in Caribbean studies that have a direct impact on the way Haitianists could look at Haiti that I can only start such a list. Why are mating patterns similar to Haitian *plaçage*, or rural institutions similar to the Haitian *lakou* or the *coumbite* present elsewhere in the Caribbean? How far do these similarities go? Are they surviving or disappearing at the same rate? For the same reasons? How do these tie in with gender? Market women in Haiti are strikingly similar to market women in Jamaica—or in Ghana, for that matter. Why? How far into social roles can we carry the post-plantation paradigm, Mintz's reconstituted peasantry?

Just as there is a post-plantation peasantry, there may also be a post-plantation state. My own comparison of the post-slavery elites of Dominica and Haiti reveals striking similarities. It is no accident that one of the most important slogans of nineteenth century Haiti—"Le plus grand bien au plus grand nombre" ("the greatest good to the greatest number")—was the slogan of the mulatto elite in British-dominated Dominica, but it was the leit-motif of the darker Parti National in mulatto-dominated Haiti (Trouillot 1992). Does the post-plantation situation lead to specific forms of state power, including specific forms of state rhetoric (Trouillot 1992)?

One could tie to that issue matters well debated in Latin American studies, such as authoritarianism and the role of the military. Is there such a thing as a social authoritarianism that can effect forms of political power? The Haitian army, just like the army in Panama, just like the army in the Dominican Republic, just like—until recently—the army in Nicaragua, is the product of a U.S. invasion. What are the similarities and the differences between these institutions as they function in societies admittedly different but also in many ways similar?

Religion is another domain. To my knowledge, no one has yet systematically picked up the trail opened by Roger Bastide in his sketchy comparisons of Brazil and Haiti. There is also a trail to pick up in the work of Melville Herskovits on Africanisms—with the necessary corrections, of course, but also with a much needed rereading of Price-Mars. Now that we know more about, say, both Suriname and Brazil, how "African" does Haiti appear in a hemispheric perspective? And of course we could push the comparison all the way to Africa.

And similarly we should look at Haitian creole in the light of what we now know about creole languages as far away as Réunion. At the very least, Haitian creole studies would benefit much from greater familiarity with such works as that of Louis-Félix Prudent on Guadeloupe-Martinique, and especially the writings of Marvyn Alleyne on St. Lucian creole and other Afro-American languages. And I have still not said anything about music . . .

I have scratched the tip of the iceberg to make a more general point. Haitian studies has experienced a small but noticeable revival since the late 1970s. But there is more to do. Much more. There are threads to pick up, new connections to be made. One would hope that, when the overemphasis on Duvalierism—if not on state politics—quiets down, practicing Haitianists will seriously start reading not only Bellegarde and Price-Mars (whom I consider to be the last of an intellectual lineage) but their precursors, the classics of nineteenth-century Haitian social thought.[8] In fact, all aspects of nineteenth-century life in Haiti will benefit from serious attention, since nineteenth-century studies have been unjustly outflanked by the dual emphasis on the slave revolution of 1791 and on twentieth-century politics. I emphasize social thought simply because the writers of that era, with their faith in universals and their desire to defend Haiti in a context of open ostracism, may have given us the most potent antidote to the myth of Haitian exceptionalism: specific questions, tuned to Haitian particulars but informed by the international debates of the times.

For Haitian studies cannot proceed without making a theoretical leap. Quite simply, we need to drop the fiction, inherited from the nineteenth-century racist literature, that Haiti is unique—if by unique one means that it escapes analysis and comparison. Haiti is not that weird. It is the fiction of Haitian exceptionalism that is weird.

Notes

1. This text was first prepared as the keynote address at a conference on "Haiti in Comparative Perspective," sponsored by Columbia/The New York University Consortium on Latin American and Caribbean Studies, New York University, New York, 9 February 1990. It is reproduced here with minor modifications. I thank Susan Lowes for valuable editorial suggestions.
2. Michel-Rolph Trouillot, "The Odd and the Ordinary: Haiti, the Caribbean and the World," *Cimarrón: New Perspectives on the Caribbean* 2.3 (1990): 3–12.

3. The Heinls lived in Haiti in the 1960s, when the Colonel acted as an adviser to François Duvalier's regime. For the introductory passage, see Heinl and Heinl 1978:1.
4. Publishers and reviewers are less cautious and more candid than writers themselves. So, Warner Books presents Davis's *The Serpent and the Rainbow* as a "journey of discovery across the border between life and death, between good and evil." The back cover of the paperback edition of the same book quotes reviews from the *Wall Street Journal* and the *Washington Post*: "Exotic and far-reaching . . . just the way Indi-ana Jones would tell it . . . . Replete with bizarre details to titillate the curious . . . . " (Davis 1985).
5. At the same time, yet in a more subtle way, Haitian poets and, later, novelists, replied to the negative mythification of Haitians by the West with myth-making writings of their own, a process that continues today (e.g., Dash 1988).
6. Because members of the Griot school claimed to be followers of Jean Price-Mars, Price-Mars has passed for a proponent of Haitian exceptionalism, a charge for which I find no justification in his voluminous writings. Price-Mars (1929) certainly did not at the outset reject what he took for science, not even Justin Dévot's unsuccessful tentative effort to introduce positivism in Haiti. Rather, in a move that anticipated both Bastide and Herskovits, Price-Mars simply insisted that Haiti could not be studied as if it were an avatar of Europe with no African influence, and that Haiti's African heritage was itself amenable to scientific study. Both points are now unquestioned among anthropologists, although they may derive from them quite different conclusions. That the first point was also repeated by Duvalier as part of a new *problématique* (Denis and Duvalier 1936) does not make Price-Mars an exceptionalist. At any rate, in Price-Mars's own words, his seminal *Ainsi parla l'oncle* (1928) is "an endeavor to integrate the popular Haitian thought into the discipline of traditional ethnography" (Price-Mars 1983:7).
7. Two preceding laws on Communist activities under Presidents Estimé (February 1948) and Magloire (September 1951) make no reference to Haitian culture as such (Trouillot and Pascal-Trouillot 1978:443–44).
8. A good deal of this corpus is available. Further, publisher Henri Deschamps has recently issued the entire work—including hitherto unpublished volumes—of Thomas Madiou, Haiti's first comprehensive historian.

References

Abbott, Elizabeth. 1988. *Haiti*. New York: McGraw-Hill.

Dash, J. Michael. 1988. *Haiti and the United States: Stereotypes and the Literary Imagination*. London: Macmillan.

Davis, Wade. 1985. *The Serpent and the Rainbow*. New York: Warner Books.

Heinl, Robert Debs and N. Heinl. 1978. *Written in Blood. The Story of the Haitian People, 1492–1971*. Boston: Houghton Mifflin.

James, C.L.R. "Introduction." *Party Politics in the West Indies*. Trinidad: Vedic Enterprises, 1962.

Leyburn, James. 1941. *The Haitian People*. New Haven: Yale University Press.

Mintz, Sidney W. 1989 [1974]. *Caribbean Transformations*. New York: Columbia University Press.

Moral, Paul. 1961. *Le Paysan haitien. Etude sur la vie rurale en Haiti*. Paris: Maisonneuve Larose.

Niles, Blair. 1926. *Black Haiti: A Biography of Africa's Eldest Daughter*. New York: Grosset and Dunlap.

Plummer, Brenda Gayle. 1988. *Haiti and the Great Powers*. Baton Rouge: University of Louisiana Press.

Price-Mars, Jean. 1929. *Une étape de l'évolution haitienne*. Port-au-Prince: Imprimerie de la Presse.

———. 1983 [1928]. *So Spoke the Uncle*. Washington, D.C.: Three Continents Press.

Rotberg, Robert, with Christopher C. Clague. 1971. *Haiti: The Politics of Squalor*. Boston: Houghton Mifflin.

Trouillot, Ernst and Ertha Pascal-Trouillot. 1978. *Codes de lois usuelles*. Port-au-Prince: Editions Henri Deschamps.

Trouillot, Michel-Rolph. 1988. *Peasants and Capital: Dominica in the World Economy*. Baltimore: The Johns Hopkins University Press.

———. 1990. *Haiti: State against Nation—The Origins and Legacy of Duvalierism*. New York: Monthly Review Press.

———. 1992. "The Inconvenience of Freedom: Free People of Color and the Aftermath of Slavery in Dominica and Saint-Domingue/Haiti." In S. Drescher and F. McGlynn, eds., *The Meaning of Freedom*. Pittsburgh: University of Pittsburgh Press.

Edwidge Danticat

Edwidge Danticat is an internationally renowned writer who was born in Port-au-Prince, Haiti, in 1969 and later immigrated to the United States to join her parents and two other siblings at age twelve. Influenced and inspired by the many storytellers of her childhood, Danticat weaves history, politics, and biographical experiences, as well as the struggles and triumphs of Haitian women, throughout her literary works. Known for her deftly simple yet powerfully evocative prose, Danticat's fierce humanism shines through her engagements with the Haitian immigrant experience and broader questions of belonging, memory, forgetting, history, family, resistance, and hope. For her unwavering commitment to "create dangerously" and give voice to the countless who remain silent and shed light on the many realities that remain unseen, Danticat was awarded the 2009 MacArthur Foundation "genius award."

We Are Ugly, But We Are Here

Edwidge Danticat[1]

One of the first people murdered on our land was a queen. Her name was Anacaona and she was an Arawak Indian. She was a poet, dancer, and even a painter. She ruled over the western part of an island so lush and green that the Arawaks called it Ayiti land of high. When the Spaniards came from across the sea to look for gold, Anacaona was one of their first victims. She was raped and killed and her village pillaged in a tradition of ongoing cruelty and atrocity. Anacaona's land is now the poorest country in the Western hemisphere, a place of continuous political unrest. Thus, for some, it is easy to forget that this land was the first Black Republic, home to the first people of African descent to uproot slavery and create an independent nation in 1804.

I was born under Haiti's dictatorial Duvalier regime. When I was four, my parents left Haiti to seek a better life in the United States. I must admit that their motives were more economic that political. But as anyone who knows Haiti will tell you, economics and politics are very intrinsically related in Haiti. Who is in power determines to a great extent whether or not people will eat.

I am twenty six years old now and have spent more than half of my life in the United States. My most vivid memories of Haiti involve incidents that represent the general situation there. In Haiti, there are a lot of "blackouts," sudden power failures. At those times, you can't read or study or watch TV, so you sit around a candle and listen to stories from the elders in the house. My grandmother was an old country woman who always felt displaced in the city of Port-au-Prince where we lived and had nothing but her patched-up quilts and her stories to console her. She was the one who told me about Anacaona. I used to share a room with her. I was in the room when she died. She was over a hundred years old. She died with her eyes wide open and I was the one who closed her eyes. I still miss the countless mystical stories that she told us. However, I accepted her death very easily because in Haiti death was always around us.

As a little girl, I attended more than my share of funerals. My uncle and legal guardian was a Baptist minister and his family was expected to attend every funeral he presided over. I went to all the funerals he presided over. I went to all the funerals in the same white lace dress. Perhaps it was because I attended so many funerals that I have such a strong feeling that death is not the end, that the people we bury are going off to live somewhere else. But at the same time, they will always be hovering around to watch over us and guide us through our journeys.

When I was eight, my uncle's brother-in-law went on a long journey to cut cane in the Dominican Republic. He came back, deathly ill. I remember his wife twirling feathers inside his nostrils and rubbing black pepper on his upper lip to make him sneeze. She strongly believed that if he sneezed, he would live. At night, it was my job to watch the sky above the house for signs of falling stars. In Haitian folklore, when a star falls out of the sky, it means someone will die. A star did fall out of the sky and he did die.

I have memories of Jean Claude "Baby Doc" Duvalier and his wife, racing by in their Mercedes Benz and throwing money out of the window to the very poor children in our neighborhood. The children nearly killed each other trying to catch a coin or a glimpse of Baby Doc. One Christmas, they announced on the radio that the first lady, Baby Doc's wife, was giving away free toys at the Palace. My cousins and I went and were nearly killed in the mob of children who flooded the palace lawns.

All of this now brings many questions buzzing to my head. Where was really my place in all of this? What was my grandmother's place? What is the legacy of the daughters of Anacaona? What do we all have left to remember, the daughters of Haiti?

Watching the news reports, it is often hard to tell whether there are real living and breathing women in conflict-stricken places like Haiti. The evening news broadcasts only allow us a brief glimpse of presidential coups, rejected boat people, and sabotaged elections. The women's stories never manage to make the front page. However they do exist.

I know women who, when the soldiers came to their homes in Haiti, would tell their daughters to lie still and play dead. I once met a woman whose sister was shot in her pregnant stomach because she was wearing a t-shirt with an "anti-military image." I know a mother who was arrested and beaten for working with a pro-democracy group. Her body remains laced with scars where the soldiers put out their cigarettes on her flesh. At night, this woman still smells the ashes of the cigarette butts that were stuffed lit inside her nostrils. In the same jail cell, she watched as paramilitary "attaches" raped her fourteen-year-old daughter at gun point.

Then mother and daughter took a tiny boat to the United States, the mother had no idea that her daughter was pregnant. Nor did she know that the child had gotten the HIV virus from one of the paramilitary men who had raped her. The grandchild the offspring of the rape was named Anacaona, after the queen, because that family of women is from the same region where Anacaona was murdered. The infant Anacaona has a face which no longer shows any trace of indigenous blood; however, her story echoes back to the first flow of blood on a land that has seen much more than its share.

There is a Haitian saying which might upset the aesthetic images of most women. Nou led, Nou la, it says. We are ugly, but we are here. Like the modesty that is somewhat common in Haitian culture, this saying makes a deeper claim for poor Haitian women than maintaining beauty, be it skin deep or otherwise. For most of us, what is worth celebrating is the fact that we are here, that we against all the odds exist. To the women who might greet each other with this saying when they meet along the countryside, the very essence of life lies in survival. It is always worth reminding our sisters that we have lived yet another day to answer the roll call of an often painful and very difficult life. It is in this spirit that to this day a woman remembers to name her child Anacaona, a name which resonates both the splendor and agony of a past that haunts so many women.

When they were enslaved, our foremothers believed that when they died their spirits would return to Africa, most specifically to a peaceful land we call Guinin, where gods and goddesses live. The women who came before me were women who spoke half of one language and half another. They spoke the French and Spanish of their captors mixed in with their own African language. These women seemed to be speaking in tongue when they prayed to their old gods, the ancient African spirits. Even though they were afraid that their old deities would no longer understand them, they invented a new language our Creole patois with which to describe their new surroundings, a language from which colorful phrases blossomed to fit the desperate circumstances. When these women greeted each other, they found themselves speaking in codes.

How are we today, Sister?
-I am ugly, but I am here.

These days, many of my sisters are greeting each other away from the homelands where they first learned to speak in tongues. Many have made it to other shores, after traveling endless miles on the high seas, on rickety boats that almost took their lives. Two years ago, a mother jumped into the sea when she discovered that her baby daughter had died in her arms on a journey which they had hoped would take them to a brighter future. Mother and child, they sank to the bottom of an ocean which already holds millions of souls from the middle passage the holocaust of the slave trade that is our legacy. That woman's sacrifice moved then-deposed Haitian President Jean Bertrand Aristide to the brink of tears. However, like the rest of us, he took comfort in the past sacrifices that were made for all of us, so that we could be here.

The past is full of examples when our foremothers and forefathers showed such deep trust in the sea that they would jump off slave ships and let the waves embrace them. They too believed that the sea was the beginning and the end of all things, the road to freedom and their entrance to Guinin. These women have been part of the very construction of my being ever since I was a little girl. Women like my grandmother who had taught me the story of Anacaona, the queen.

My grandmother believed that if a life is lost, then another one springs up replanted somewhere else, the next life even stronger than the last. She believed that no one really dies as long as someone remembers, someone who will acknowledge that this person had in spite of everything been here. We are part of an endless circle, the daughters of Anacaona. We have stumbled, but have not fallen. We are ill-favored, but we still endure. Every once in a while, we must scream this as far as the wind can carry our voices: We are ugly, but we are here! And here to stay.

Note

1. Edwidge Danticat, "We Are Ugly, But We Are Here," *Caribbean Writer* 10 (1996), http://faculty.webster.edu/corbetre/haiti/literature/danticat-ugly.htm

Sylvia Wynter

Sylvia Wynter (1928-) is a Jamaican theorist, novelist, and dramatist whose published nonfiction essays are among the most impressive bodies of work of any living Caribbean theorist. In the 1960s Caribbean, Wynter wrote a number of thoughtful essays on the question of culture and self-determination, which was followed by a series of remarkable interventions on questions of aesthetics, colonialism, intellectual history, and the history and fate of our species. Only recently has attention been paid to her ever-increasing corpus of critical essays and her quest to undo the fictions of colonial thought that have presented Western bourgeois man as the human. The following is the introduction to her landmark essay "Unsettling the Coloniality of Being/ Power/Truth/Freedom: Towards the Human, After Man: Towards His Overrepresentation—An Argument."

Unsettling the Coloniality of Being/Power/Truth/Freedom: Towards the Human, After Man, Its Overrepresentation—An Argument

Sylvia Wynter[1]

Introduction

The argument proposes that the struggle of our new millennium will be one between the ongoing imperative of securing the well-being of our present ethnoclass (i.e., Western bourgeois) conception of the human, Man, which overrepresents itself as if it were the human itself, and that of securing the well-being, and therefore the full cognitive and behavioral autonomy of the human species itself/ourselves. Because of this overrepresentation, which is defined in the first part of the title as the Coloniality of Being/Power/Truth/Freedom, any attempt to unsettle the coloniality of power will call for the unsettling of this overrepresentation as the second and now purely secular form of what Aníbal Quijano identifies as the "Racism/Ethnicism complex," on whose basis the world of modernity was brought into existence from the fifteenth/sixteenth centuries onwards (Quijano 1999, 2000),[2] and of what Walter Mignolo identifies as the foundational "colonial difference" on which the world of modernity was to institute itself (Mignolo 1999, 2000).

The correlated hypothesis here is that all our present struggles with respect to race, class, gender, sexual orientation, ethnicity, struggles over the environment, global warming, severe climate change, the sharply unequal distribution of the earth resources (20 percent of the world's peoples own 80 percent of its resources, consume two-thirds of its food, and are responsible for 75 percent of its ongoing pollution, with this leading to two billion of earth's peoples living relatively affluent lives while four billion still live on the edge of hunger and immiseration, to the dynamic of overconsumption on the part of the rich techno-industrial North paralleled by that of overpopulation on the part of the dispossessed poor, still partly agrarian worlds of the South[4])—these are all differing facets of the central ethnoclass Man vs. Human struggle. Central to this struggle also is the usually excluded and invisibilized situation of the category identified by Zygmunt Bauman as the "New Poor" (Bauman 1987). That is, as a category defined at the global level by refugee/economic migrants stranded outside the gates of the rich countries, as the postcolonial variant of Fanon's category of les damnés (Fanon 1963)—with this category in the United States coming to comprise the criminalized majority Black and dark-skinned Latino inner-city males now made to man the rapidly expanding prison-industrial complex, together with their female peers—the kicked-about Welfare Moms—with both being part of the ever-expanding global, transracial category of the homeless/the jobless, the semi-jobless, the criminalized drug-offending prison population. So that if we see this category of the damnés that is internal to (and interned within) the prison system of the United States as the analog form of a global archipelago, constituted by the Third- and Fourth-World peoples of the so-called "under-developed" areas of the world—most totally of all by the peoples of the continent of Africa (now stricken with AIDS, drought, and ongoing civil wars, and whose bottommost place as the most impoverished of all the earth's continents is directly paralleled by the situation of its Black Diaspora peoples, with Haiti being produced and reproduced as the most impoverished nation of the Americas)—a systemic pattern emerges. This pattern is linked to the fact that while in the post-sixties United States, as Herbert Gans noted recently, the Black population group, of all the multiple groups comprising the post-sixties social hierarchy, has once again come to be placed at the bottommost place of that hierarchy (Gans, 1999), with all incoming new nonwhite/non-Black groups, as Gans's fellow sociologist Andrew Hacker (1992) earlier pointed out, coming to claim "normal" North American identity by the putting of visible distance between themselves and the Black population group (in effect, claiming "normal" human status by distancing themselves from the group that is still made to occupy the nadir, "nigger" rung of being human within the terms of our present ethnoclass Man's overrepresentation of its "descriptive statement" [Bateson 1969] as if it were that of the human itself), then the struggle of our times, one that has hitherto had no name, is the struggle against this overrepresentation. As a struggle whose first phase, the Argument proposes, was first put in place (if only for a brief hiatus before being coopted, reterritorialized [Godzich 1986]) by the multiple anticolonial social-protest movements and intellectual challenges of the period to which we give the name, "The Sixties."

The further proposal here is that, although the brief hiatus during which the sixties' large-scale challenge based on multiple issues, multiple local terrains of struggles (local struggles against, to use Mignolo's felicitous phrase, a "global design" [Mignolo 2000]) erupted was soon to be erased, several of the issues raised then would continue to be articulated, some in sanitized forms (those pertaining to the category defined by Bauman as "the seduced"), others in more harshly intensified forms (those pertaining to Bauman's category of the "repressed" [Bauman 1987]). Both forms of "sanitization" would, however, function in the same manner as the law-like effects of the post-sixties' vigorous discursive and institutional re-elaboration of the central overrepresentation, which enables the interests, reality, and well-being of the empirical human world to continue to be imperatively subordinated to those of the now globally hegemonic ethnoclass world of "Man." This, in the same way as in an earlier epoch and before what Howard Winant identifies as the "immense historical rupture" of the "Big Bang" processes that were to lead to a contemporary modernity defined by the "rise of the West" and the "subjugation of the rest of us" (Winant 1994)—before, therefore, the secularizing intellectual revolution of Renaissance humanism, followed by the decentralizing religious heresy of the Protestant Reformation and the rise of the modern state—the then world of laymen and laywomen, including the institution of the political state, as well as those of commerce and of economic production, had remained subordinated to that of the post-Gregorian Reform Church of Latin-Christian Europe (Le Goff 1983), and therefore to the "rules of the social order" and the theories "which gave them sanction" (See Konrad and Szelenyi guide-quote), as these rules were articulated by its theologians and implemented by its celibate clergy (See Le Goff guide-quote).

The Janus face of the emergence of Mignolo's proposed "modernity/coloniality" complementarity is sited here. As also is the answer to the why of the fact that, as Aníbal Quijano insists in his Qué tal Raza! (2000), the "idea of race" would come to be "the most efficient instrument of social domination invented in the last 500 years." In order for the world of the laity, including that of the then ascendant modern European state, to escape their subordination to the world of the Church, it had been enabled to do so only on the basis of what Michel Foucault identifies as the "invention of Man": that is, by the Renaissance humanists' epochal redescription of the human outside the terms of the then theocentric, "sinful by nature" conception/ "descriptive statement" of the human, on whose basis the hegemony of the Church/clergy over the lay world of Latin-Christian Europe had been supernaturally legitimated (Chorover 1979). While, if this redescription was effected by the lay world's invention of Man as the political subject of the state, in the transumed and reoccupied place of its earlier matrix identity Christian, the performative enactment of this new "descriptive statement" and its master code of symbolic life and death, as the first secular or "degodded" (if, at the time, still only partly so) mode of being human in the history of the species, was to be effected only on the basis of what Quijano identifies as the "coloniality of power," Mignolo as the "colonial difference," and Winant as a huge project demarcating human differences thinkable as a "racial longue durée." One of the major empirical effects of which would be "the rise of Europe" and its construction of the "world civilization" on the one hand, and, on the other, African enslavement, Latin American conquest, and Asian subjugation.

Note

1. Excerpt from Sylvia Wynter, "Unsettling the Coloniality of Being/Power/Truth/Freedom: Towards the Human, After Man: Towards His Overrepresentation—An Argument," *Centennial Review* 3.3 (2003): 260–63.

⋯◦◦◦⋯

Section 9: Further Reading

Abrahams, Roger. *The Man-of-Words in the West Indies: Performance and the Emergence of Creole Culture.* Baltimore: John Hopkins University Press, 1983.

Bolland, O. Nigel, ed. *The Birth of Caribbean Civilisation: A Century of Ideas About Culture and Identity, Nation and Society.* Kingston, Jamaica: Ian Randle Press, 2004.

Brathwaite, Edward Kamau. *Contradictory Omens: Cultural Diversity and Integration in the Caribbean.* Mona, Kingston: Savacou, 1974.

Brathwaite, Edward Kamau. *History of the Voice: The Development of Nation Language in Anglophone Caribbean Poetry.* London: New Beacon Books, 1984. (pp. 5–17).

Brown, Stewart, Mervyn Morris and Gordon Rohlehr, eds. *Voiceprint: An Anthology of Oral and Related Poetry from the Caribbean.* San Juan, Trinidad: Longman Caribbean, 1989.

Browne, Kevin Adonis. *Tropic Tendencies: Rhetoric, Popular Culture, and the Anglophone Caribbean.* Pittsburgh: University of Pittsburgh Press, 2013.

Campos, Pedro Albizu. "Puerto Rican Nationalism." In *The Birth of Caribbean Civilisation: A Century of Ideas About Culture and Identity, Nation and Society.* Ed. O. Nigel Bolland. Kingston, Jamaica: Ian Randle Press, 2004. (pp. 77–78).

Castro, Fidel. "History Will Absolve Me." In *The Cuba Reader.* Eds. Aviva Chomsky, Barry Carr and Pamela Maria Smorkaloff. London: Duke University Press, 2004. (pp. 306–14).

Glissant, Edouard. *Caribbean Discourse: Selected Essays.* Trans. Michael Dash. Charlottesville: University of Virginia Press, 1989.

Gordon, Lewis. *An Introduction to Africana Philosophy.* Cambridge and New York: Cambridge University Press, 2008.

Gregg, Veronica. *Caribbean Women: An Anthology of Non-Fiction Writing.* Notre Dame, IN: University of Notre Dame Press, 2005.

Hume, Yanique and Aaron Kamugisha, eds. *Caribbean Cultural Thought: From Plantation to Diaspora.* Kingston: Ian Randle, 2013.

Hume, Yanique and Aaron Kamugisha, eds. *Caribbean Popular Culture: Power, Politics and Performance.* Kingston: Ian Randle, 2016.

James, C. L. R. *The Black Jacobins: Toussaint L'Ouverture and the San Domingo Revolution.* London and New York: Vintage, 1963.

James, C. L. R. "The West Indian Middle Classes." In *Party Politics in the West Indies.* Trinidad: Vedic Enterprises, 1962. (pp. 130–139).

Kamugisha, Aaron. *Caribbean Political Thought: The Colonial State to Caribbean Internationalisms.* Kingston and Miami: Ian Randle, 2013.

Mathurin Mair, Lucille. "Reluctant Matriarchs." *Savacou* 13 (1977): 1–6.

Nettleford, Rex. *Inward Stretch, Outward Reach.* London: Macmillan Press, 1993.

Pollard, Velma. *Dread Talk: The Language of Rastafari.* Kingston: Canoe Press, 2000.

Rodney, Walter. *Walter Rodney Speaks: The Making of an African Intellectual.* Trenton, NJ: Africa World Press, 1990.

Warner, Keith Q. *The Trinidad Calypso: A Study of the Calypso As Oral Literature.* London: Heinemann, 1983.

Wynter, Sylvia. "Unsettling the Coloniality of Being/Power/Truth/Freedom: Towards the Human, after Man, Its Overrepresentation—An Argument." *CR: The New Centennial Review*, 3.3 (2003): 257–337.

Section 9: Discussion Questions

1. Interrogate the role that history and colonialism have played in constructing a Caribbean citizenry.
2. Why does the plantation occupy such a key place in Caribbean theorists' debates on Caribbean culture?
3. How does a study of the Haitian revolution and its aftermath allow us to understand the condition of Haiti today?
4. Is the idea of a Caribbean aesthetic essential for the articulation of a distinctive Caribbean culture?
5. Discuss the evolution and agenda of Garveyism and account for its diasporic appeal.
6. Critically evaluate the nexus between culture, agency, and resistance as espoused in the anti-colonial writings of Aimé Césaire and Frantz Fanon.
7. Why are gender and sexuality so omnipresent in discourses about Caribbean culture?
8. What are the major perspectives that emerged about Caribbean culture as a result of the twentieth-century anti-colonial movement?
9. To what extent does the legacy of colonialism influence discourses of gender in the Caribbean?
10. Discuss the impact of twentieth-century Black consciousness, as expressed in Garveyism, Black power, and négritude, on Caribbean societies.
11. What is the relationship between colonialism, language, and liberation in the thought of Kamau Brathwaite and Edouard Glissant?
12. Can we discern a tradition of resistance to neocolonialism in Caribbean thought?
13. To what extent have the dynamics of race, ethnicity, and class shaped Caribbean identities and their notions of belonging?

10

BLACK TECHNOCULTURAL EXPRESSIVITY

Edited and with an introduction by Dara N. Byrne

The concept of Black Power rests on a fundamental premise: *Before a group can enter the open society, it must first close ranks.* By this we mean that group solidarity is necessary before a group can operate effectively from a bargaining position of strength in a pluralistic society.

—Stokely Carmichael and Charles V. Hamilton

The foregoing quotation from Stokely Carmichael and Charles V. Hamilton's instructive text, *Black Power*, provides a useful—albeit unlikely—entrance into this section's conversation about digital and visual technologies. Though their work addresses the political future of the Black community in America, Carmichael and Hamilton's notion that Black liberation requires the development of a "new consciousness" and "sense of community" provides an appropriate starting point for organizing the growing range of theories, artifacts, and methodologies that can be applied to the study of African American technoculture and expressivity. To address the schematic challenge intrinsic to this broad subject, the selections here offer a contextual framework for exploring African American rhetoric of/with technology, particularly the ways in which technological engagement furthers African Americans' solidarity and their advancement toward liberation and justice.

According to Carmichael and Hamilton, affirmation of group identity—the closing of ranks—was an essential step toward the strengthening of a Black public sphere, which in turn would lead to self-determination and political modernization. In so doing, Blacks would be better positioned to question the validity of oppressive mainstream values and institutions, to consider which political structures could best redress conditions of social and economic inequality, and to widen participation in the larger decision-making process. When applied to this chapter, these notions help thread together what would otherwise seem like infinite approaches to studying or defining the nexus between technology and African American rhetoric.

Any broad-stroke review of African American engagement with communication technologies, for example, will show the myriad ways these tools have been used to close ranks and to address a range of societal challenges. Though not included in the current volume, articles by Armistead Pride and Clint Wilson (1987) and Anna Everett (2001) document the role the Black press played in voicing community opposition to Jim Crow, in chronicling anti-Black violence and lynching, and in shedding light on grassroots activism. Advocacy was part of the de facto mission of early Black editors and publishers who, in harnessing the power of the technology of their day, cultivated spaces for public dialogue and mobilized community activity around civic issues. In fact, in 1827, when Samuel Cornish and John Russwurm, the coeditors of the first Black newspaper, the *Freedom's Journal*, penned their mission statement on the front page of its inaugural issue, they stated that the very raison d'être for Black papers—as mouthpieces for the people—was to centralize Black opinions, Black issues, and grassroots organizing around the struggle for freedom and equality. This view, of being in service of the struggle, remained relatively intact to the height of the civil rights and Black power movements.

An Internet search of the *Chicago Defender's* rhetoric about Emmett Till's murder or the litigation surrounding *Brown v. Board of Education* will yield a generous sample of the newspaper's coverage during this period. After viewing the archival images online, it should come as no surprise that Thurgood Marshall recognized the role the Black press played in documenting the local and national efforts of the NAACP Legal Defense Fund as they pushed forward to the Supreme Court. Though there are debates today about the future and purpose of the Black press, research by Ronald Jacobs (2000) shows that mainstream coverage of African American issues has never surpassed 4 percent of news content. Though not included in this volume, his comparative analysis of the rhetoric surrounding the beating of Rodney King in 1991 illustrates how the Black press continues to cultivate important spaces for cultural and political discussion.

As a matter of practicality, the readings in this section are limited to African American technoculture from the mid-twentieth century to the present and mass communication technology from print to new media. The selections (whether in print here, in further readings, or on the companion website) address the history of African American engagement with technology, the role of digital and visual technologies in the communication of and among African Americans, the role of African traditions in shaping African American use of technology, the methods and theories used in the study of African American technoculture, the popularization of technology by African Americans, the effect of the Internet on African American communication and public life, and the impact of African American digital and visual technologies on pedagogy. Though by no means exhaustive, the aim here is to provide a historical sample of how African American innovations, broadly speaking, tend to reaffirm discursive traditions, renew commitments to long-standing goals of freedom and liberation, improve the ability to access a mass audience, and increase the capacity for networking in a diasporic context.

Additionally, the organizing schema of this section is not meant to suggest that *all* African American rhetoric of/with technology, by virtue of its attention to Black audiences, *must* actively engage in consciousness building or support an activist agenda. Rather, it illustrates a liminal tension in the African American experience with technology and the ongoing quest to use these tools to advance the community agenda. For example, digital technologies today might allow African Americans to actualize Marcus Garvey's early vision of diaspora-wide interconnectivity. In the 1920s, Garvey used print technology to spread his publication, *Negro World*, throughout the Americas, The Caribbean, Africa, The United Kingdom, and even into Russia. Though his readership was rather sizeable, *Negro World* was unable to overcome the substantial costs associated with cultivating community across such massive landscape at that time. Can digital technologies be used to close ranks and deepen diasporan interconnectivity? Can new media serve as a galvanizing force that furthers goals such as liberation, justice, and self-determination? If examples such as the way Keith Boykin (2006) used his blog to mobilize activism against antigay musicians is any indication, the future of African American public life online is promising.

As Everett's (2006) work shows, the Black public sphere online has been thriving since the late 1980s, with early examples such as The Drum (launched in 1988), Melanet (launched in 1989), and NetNoir (launched in 1995). These sites were especially popular because they focused on cultural politics, incorporated Black rhetorical elements in their design, and provided space for members to articulate their sense of community. The last decade or so of scholarship in this area has documented the significance of community-specific content to African American participation online. Research has also shown that African Americans tend to spend more time on Black-targeted sites and are able to recall more of the information from targeted ones than from mainstream sites. The implications for findings such as these are as relevant to consumer and political interests as they are to educational outcomes. Consider, for example, the work of Carmen Kynard (2007), who demonstrates how African American students use digital technologies, such as Blackboard, to recreate their raced community.

This chapter is deliberately lacking in a unified definition of technology or approach to the study of it. The practice of "fixing" innovation weakens the ability to apply the definition beyond current uses and understandings of that innovation. Instead, to remain relevant to future developments in technology, the selections herein provide some (tentative) parameters on how African American artists, critics, and scholars have cast Black technoculture, from past to present, and its relationship to African American expressivity. There are three organizing strands to the selections. First, research by subject scholars provides a critical frame for understanding the history of African Americans' engagement with technology and the ways it has been used to express their sense of identity and culture. Second, artifacts such as print images, radio techniques, digital art, and chatroom discussions illustrate how form meets function when traditional African American rhetorical devices sync with technological innovation. Third, debates about identity and authenticity in Black technoculture contextualize the widespread impact of African American discursive practices in popular culture.

Readers will notice a diversity of positions. Some authors, like Imamu Amiri Baraka (1971), argue that Black engagement with technology should be grounded in cultural traditions. That is, what makes for African American rhetoric of technology is not just its functional role—usage by African Americans—but also the ways the technology can be used to map rhetorical traditions and advance conversations about the common good, even if this means transforming its original purpose. Authors like Alexander Weheliye (2005) and Rayvon Fouché (2006) equip readers with an analytical lens for exploring African American sonic technology. These readings, along with Alondra Nelson's (2002) framework for Afrofuturism, will help to contextualize the diasporic and futuristic work of artists like Sun Ra and the Arkestra, Afrika Bambaatta, Parliament Funkadelic, the Fugees, and Janelle Monáe, artists whose work are all featured in this unit. Weheliye's and Fouché's essays also provide a baseline for understanding the methodological challenge of cinematographers, like Arthur Jafa (1998), who attempt to develop culturally specific filmic techniques, such as Black visual intonation.

Unlike some of the sections in this anthology that feature primary works, many of the selections that follow or are listed in further readings and on the website are critical in nature. Part of this is because of the necessity of contextualizing debates relevant to African American rhetorical traditions, African American discourse about technology, and the ways such innovations have allowed African Americans to lay claims in the larger civil society. Aside from this, capturing digital, visual technology in book form places certain limitations on the multimodal function and capabilities of current digital technologies. To address this, readers are at times asked to access specific websites or conduct a basic Internet search before reading some selections. Further, as useful as digital technology is for documenting and transmitting cultural artifacts, an argument that Abdul Alkalimat (2001) addresses in his discussion on eBlack studies, its ability to preserve is also dependent on the content provider's desire to make the material publicly accessible. On the one hand, the early work of disc jockeys like Alley Pat and Jack "The Rapper" Gibson is currently preserved on free sites, like YouTube. This gives readers the unique opportunity to view and listen to early radio broadcasts that incorporated African American rhetorical traditions. On the other hand, when digital performance artists like Damali Ayo remove their work from websites such as rent-a-negro.com, the only (free) way to critique her approach to digital art is through the scholarly interpretations of authors like Brandi Catanese (2005).

Lastly, mixing critical scholarship with cultural artifacts is necessary for challenging readers' norms and assumptions about technology as well as the ownership and privilege associated with it. Bruce Sinclair (2004), for example, problematizes "invention" as the standard measure of technological innovation and ushers in epistemological questions about African American material engagement with technology. Given that African Americans, who were often denied access to the legal system, could not file for patents, much less finance mass production of their inventions, interrogating the African American relationship with technology will always be a more substantial critical project. By challenging mainstream values about progress and agency, we engage with new paradigms for approaching and studying African American rhetoric of/ with technology.

Works Cited

Alkalimat, A. eBlack: A 21st-Century Challenge. 2001. Web. Retrieved from www.eblackstudies.org/eblack. html

Banks, A. "Fade: Notes Toward an African American Rhetoric 2.0." *Digital Griots: African American Rhetoric in a Multimedia Age.* Carbondale: Southern Illinois Press, 2011.

Byrne, D. "Public Discourse, Community Concerns, and Civic Engagement: Exploring Black Social Networking Traditions on BlackPlanet.com." *Journal of Computer Mediated Communication,* 13.1 (2007): 319.

Baraka, A. "Technology and Ethos." In *Raise Race Rays Raze: Essays Since 1965.* New York: Random House, 1971 (p. 157).

Barlow, W. "Microphones in the Riot Zone." In Voice Over: The Making of Black Radio. Philadelphia: Temple University Press, 1999.

Boykin, K. "Black Gay Bloggers Unite Against Homophobic Artists." 2006. Web. Retrieved from http://www.keithboykin.com/arch/2006/07/11/black_gay_blogg (A reprint can be found here: http://and-reallen.blogspot.ca/2006/07/black-gay-bloggers-unite-against.html)

Catanese, B. W. (2005). "How Do I Rent a Negro? Racialized Subjectivity and Digital Performance Art." *Theatre Journal,* 57.4 (2005): 699–714.

Eglash, R. and J. Bleecker. "The Race for Cyberspace: Information Technology in the Black Diaspora." *Science as Culture* 10.3 (2001): 353–374.

Everett, A. "The Black Press in the Age of Digital Reproduction: Two Exemplars." In *The Black Press: New Literary and Historical Essays.* Ed. T. Vogel. New Brunswick: Rutgers University Press, 2001.

Fouché, R. "Say It Loud, I'm Black and I'm Proud: African Americans, American artifactual Culture, and Black Vernacular Technological Creativity." *American Quarterly,* 58.3 (2006): 639–661.

Jacobs, R.N. "The Rodney King Beating." *Race, Media, and the Crisis of Civil Society: From Watts to Rodney King.* Cambridge, UK: The University of Cambridge Press, 2000.

Jafa, A. "Black Visual Intonation." In *The Jazz Cadence of American Culture.* Ed. R.G. O'Meally. New York: Columbia University Press, 1998.

Kynard, C. "'Wanted: Some Black Long Distance Writers': Blackboard Flava-Flavin and Other Afro-Digitized Experiences in the Classroom." *Computers and Composition,* 24.3 (2007): 329–345.

Nelson, A. "Future Texts." *Social Text,* 20.2 (2002): 1–15.

Pride, A.S. and C.C. Wilson. "Survival Debates and the Common Cause." In *A History of the Black Press.* Washington, DC: Howard University Press, 1987.

Sinclair, B. "Integrating the Histories of Race and Technology." In *Technology and the African American Experience: Needs and Opportunities for Study.* Boston: Massachusetts Institute of Technology Press, 2004.

Weheliye, A.G. "Sounding Diasporic Citizenship." *Phonographies: Grooves in Sonic Afro-Modernity.* Durham: Duke University Press, 2005.

Imamu Amiri Baraka

Baraka's essay, reprinted here in its entirety, is itself an exercise in rhetorical analysis. What might become of the typewriter, he asks, if users moved beyond its original function? Similarly, how might African Americans benefit from technology if its function and design were grounded in Black culture and expression? For Baraka, Black technological engagement must be rooted in cultural knowledge if it is to be used to advance new forms and strategies for self-determination. As such, a Black technological ethos is centered on African American traditions, committed to African American freedom, and completely reimagined from its original function.

Technology and Ethos

Imamu Amiri Baraka[1]

Machines (as Norbert Weiner said) are an extension of their inventor-creators. That is not simple once you think. Machines, the entire technology of the West, is just that, the technology of the West.

Nothing *has* to look or function the way it does. The West man's freedom, unscientifically got at the expense of the rest of the world's people, has allowed him to xpand his mind—spread his sensibility wherever it *cd*go, & so *shaped* the world, & its powerful artifact-engines.

Political power is *also* the power to create—not only what you will—but to be freed to go where ever you can go—(mentally physically as well). Black creation—creation powered by the Black ethos brings very special results,

Think of yourself, Black creator, freed of european restraint which first means the restraint of self determined mind development. Think what would be the results of the unfettered blood inventor-creator *with the resources of a nation behind him.* To imagine—to think—to construct—to energize!!!

How do you communicate with the great masses of Black people? How do you use the earth to feed masses of people? How do you cure illness? How do you prevent illness? What are the Black purposes of space travel?

It staggers the mind. To be free go let the mind do what it will as constructive progress force, availed of the total knowledge resource energy of a nation.

These white scientists on lifetime fellowships, or pondering problems at Princeton's Institute For Advanced Study.

So that a telephone is one culture's solution to the problem of sending words through space. It is political power that has allowed this technology to emerge, & seem the sole direction for the result desired.

A typewriter?—why shd it only make use of the tips of the fingers as contact points of flowing multi directional creativity. If I invented a word placing machine, an "expression-scriber," *if you will*, then I would have a kind of instrument into which I could step & sit or sprawl or hang & use not only my fingers to make words express feelings but elbows, feet, head, behind, and all the sounds I wanted, screams, grunts, taps, itches, I'd have magnetically recorded, at the same time, & translated into word—or perhaps even the final xpressed thought/feeling wd not be merely word or sheet, but *itself*, the xpression, three dimensional—able to be touched, or tasted or felt, or entered, or heard or carried like a speaking singing constantly communicating charm. *A typewriter is corny!!*

The so called fine artist realizes, those of us who have *freed* ourselves, that our creations need not emulate the white man's, but it is time the engineers, architects, chemists, electronics craftsmen, ie film too, radio, sound, &c., that learning western technology must not be the end of our understanding of the particular discipline we're involved in. Most of that west shaped information is like mud and sand when you're panning for gold!

The actual *beginnings* of our expression are post Western (just as they certainly are prewestern). It is only necessary that we arm ourselves with complete self knowledge the whole technology (which is after all just *expression* of who ever) will change to reflect the essence of a freed people. Freed of an oppressor, but also as Touré has reminded we must be "free from the oppressor's spirit," as well. It is this spirit as emotional construct that can manifest as expression as art or technology or any form.

But what is our spirit, what will it project? What machines will it produce? What will they achieve? What will be their morality? Check the different *morality* of the Chinese birthday celebration firecracker & the white boy's bomb. Machines have the morality of their inventors.

See everything fresh and "without form"—then make forms that will express us truthfully and totally and by this certainly free us eventually.

The new technology must be spiritually oriented because it must aspire to raise man's spirituality and expand man's consciousness. It must begin by being "humanistic" though the white boy has yet to achieve this. Witness a technology that kills both plants & animals, poisons the air & degenerates or enslaves man.

The technology itself must represent human striving. It must represent at each point the temporary perfection of the evolutional man. And be obsolete only because nothing is ever *perfect*, the only constant is change.

Amiri Baraka
Amistad 2, 1970
soulsista:shineifa

Note

1. Imamu Amiri Baraka, "Technology and Ethos," *Raise Race Rays Raze: Essays Since 1965* (New York, NY: Random House, 1971), p. 157.

Arthur Jafa

Absent from the introduction to this chapter is a discussion of the role of television and film technology in shaping and popularizing African American rhetorical traditions. While literature on the impact of Black rhetoric on this media is widely available, less well known is the discussion about how visual technology can be grounded in African American traditions. The work by cinematographer Arthur Jafa provides a fruitful response to Amiri Baraka's call "to not emulate the white man." Jafa attempts to develop a methodology for Black filmmaking. He calls this technique Black visual intonation and explains that it includes the use of camera techniques to replicate, visually, Black orality and intonation. Jafa suggests that Black film is more than Black content (characters, themes, or concerns), as Black cinema also employs visual methodologies to support the full range of African American expressivity. The author also draws the parallel to Black music to make the illustrative point that audiences understand Black sonic style, regardless of the racial identification of the artist.

Black Visual Intonation

Arthur Jafa[1]

When I was thinking about what I wanted to do at this conference, the first thing I thought about was giving my talk with my back to the audience as a sort of allusion to Miles Davis, you know, postural semantics and all. But then I had this dream, which I'm going to tell you about.

I was in Clarksdale, Mississippi, where I grew up. I was in my bedroom, the room I remember growing up in, sitting and listening to music—the kind of music my mom used to call psychological music. You know, jazz, rock, reggae, anything that was strange (to her). And I was sitting in the room with The Alien—I don't know how many of you saw the movie *The Alien*—and we were just chilling, you know, just grooving, like me and my friends did when we were growing up. And my mom pops her head in the room occasionally like she did when I was with my friends and smiles and sort of steps back out. And my father creeps in without saying anything and turns down the volume on the music. Eventually, my friend The Alien gets up and splits. And then my father comes in and says, "Who was that big-headed nigger you were in here with?"

I don't want to be a big-headed nigger, so I'm not going to do this with my back to the audience. But, I am going to use digressions like Marlon Riggs did in his talk. One thing that's been interesting for me to see so far in this conference is the anxiety around what I would call the performative. The very first night Stuart Hall stood up and gave his talk, and I felt a little bit like that guy in the Memorex commercial. I thought, damn, he's relentless. I mean, I turned to the people next to me and said it was like listening to John Coltrane—it just didn't stop. And then after that Cornel West came out and did his thing, you know, "Give me an Amen!" He doesn't say it, but you know what he wants. Then bell hooks came on, and she did her thing, and Marlon did his incredible thing. And then there was Hazel Carby. She was interesting. She was the only person who got the "oooh" effect. She got this effect when she was pointing out the relationship between certain male academics and Zora Neale Hurston.

My primary interest is in Black film. When I first got into film at Howard University, the people who were there—Haile Gerima, Alonzo Crawford, Abiyi Ford—were very much concerned with questions around Black cinema and with defining what it was. At that time, they would have probably defined Black film as something like "We're against Hollywood," which is interesting because that definition allows you to get to certain kinds of places, and it's clear. But eventually I started to ask myself, well, is that enough? It seems they had put us in this binary opposition with Hollywood that can be kind of limited. I thought we had to ask more sophisticated questions about what Black cinema was and, in fact, could be.

One of the first things I asked was, well, if this work is supposed to be Black film, why does it use what is essentially strictly classical Hollywood spatial continuity? You know, was it significant that you respected all of the 180-, 360-degree rules around spatial organization? Was that arbitrary?

They would show the work of Oscar Micheaux, whom anyone who's interested in Black cinema, or American cinema, for that matter, should be familiar with. (I find it incredible that Black filmmakers don't know Oscar Micheaux. That's kind of like being a jazzman and not knowing Louis Armstrong.) And they would always present Oscar Micheaux's work as an example of what not to do. I got this a lot: it was incompetently realized; its class and color politics were all messed up. But I felt like they never really looked deeply into his work and saw what was worth studying.

David Bordwell and Kristin Thompson did a very interesting analysis of Ozu, the master Japanese filmmaker. They demonstrated that the spatial paradigm Ozu employed wasn't a deficient control of a Hollywood spatial paradigm, but that, in fact, it was an alternative paradigm—which oftentimes ran parallel to the Hollywood one, but just as often would transgress it.[2] Donald Ritchie, who is considered an early expert on Ozu, would say, "This is a guy who's considered one of the most controlled formal filmmakers in the world, but he got sloppy at those moments." Right.

But what was interesting about Bordwell's and Thompson's analysis was that it provided an entrée into analyzing Black film. And I started to look at Micheaux's work and said, wow, this is not an accident; this is consistent over the course of his career (and I think he made more than thirty-eight feature films). It just got badder and badder and badder.

I'm going to do a little jump right here.

I had read the anti-essentialist position in that last cinema issue of *Screen*,[3] and I said, wow, I really don't agree with some of the things that the anti-essentialists are saying. I mean, I had a hard time understanding (and perhaps it was my misunderstanding) what they were trying to say. So I said, well, I must be an essentialist. And then I read what the essentialists were saying, what they were supposed to be saying, and I said, well, maybe I'm just an "anti-anti-essentialist." What I've come to now is what a friend told me when I asked how she would describe me. She called me a "materialist retentionist" (something like that).

What that means is that I have a belief in certain levels of cultural retention. People carry culture on various levels, down to the deepest level, which I would call a kind of core stability. Nam Jun Paik, the godfather of video art, has this great quote: "The culture that's going to survive in the future is the culture that you can carry around in your head." The middle passage is such a clear example of this, because you see Black American culture particularly developed around those areas we could carry around in our heads—our oratorical prowess, dance, music, those kinds of things. There are other things not so easy to carry. Architecture, for example. When we got here, we didn't have an opportunity to make many buildings. Not right off, at least. So I have this notion of core stability and how that informs what we do, of cultural sophistication and how we apply that to the task of constructing Black cinema.

I like to think about films and the kinds of things that are possible. For example, I want to do Martin Luther King's life in the style of *In the Realm of the Senses* (Nagisa Oshima's amazing hard-core feature). I want to do Malcolm X's life as a series of moments—Malcolm arriving home at two o'clock in the morning and looking in at his little girls asleep. I like the stories that Bruce Perry tells in his biography of Malcolm X—like when he says that Malcolm X was, in fact, in love with another Betty. And in his anxiety about whether Betty was actually going to accept his proposal of marriage, he asked Betty Shabazz to marry him instead. A few weeks later, he ran into the first Betty's brother, and was being congratulated by him, you know, "Congratulations on your marriage, brother Malcolm. But why didn't you ever call our sister back? She's been waiting for you. She wanted to accept the proposal." And Malcolm X broke down and started crying.[4] That's the Malcolm X I want to see. And I would like to know what kind of version of Little Richard's life Andrei Tarkovsky would do.

I think understanding culture and having a sophisticated understanding of applying culture to the construction of Black cinema means we have to understand how culture gets played out in various arenas. And we have to be able to look at these arenas to see how Black people have intervened to transform them into spaces where we can most express our desires. A classic example, of course, is basketball. Like the question that went around for a long time (before Michael Jordan made it irrelevant) about who was the best basketball player, Magic Johnson or Larry Bird. That depends on what you mean by best, obviously. If you use a rational Western evaluation of what's best, then you come up with the statistical, which means who can put the most balls in the hoop, right? And by that definition, certainly Larry Bird can be measured with the best there's ever been. Bird can put the ball in the hoop. Anybody that tells you he can't has got a serious racial anxiety thing happening. But then you have to ask yourself, if Black people enter into this game, which was invented by Dr. Hans Nasmith (and we know he certainly didn't create it with Black folks in mind), how has it been transformed? And how many levels does that play itself out on? I mean, is it just that we function as players, or have we affected other aspects of the game? And if you ask yourself these kinds of questions, then the question of who's the best basketball player becomes irrelevant. What you're going to end up with is Larry Bird coming down the floor, going up for a shot. Two points. He comes down again. Two points. Then maybe he'll shoot one of those long ones he's good for. Three points, you know. But then Michael Jordan will come down, spinning acrobatically in apparent defiance of all known laws of gravity. Ten points.

Black pleasure (not joy)—what are its parameters, what are its primal sites, how does Black popular culture or Black culture in general address Black pleasure? How does it generate Black pleasure? How do those strategies in Black music play out the rupture and repair of African-American life on the structural level? How do they play out the sense of the lost and the found? How are Black people preoccupied with polyventiality (a term of mine)? "Polyventiality" just means multiple tones, multiple rhythms, multiple perspectives, multiple meanings, multiplicity. Why do we find these particular things pleasurable? How do African retentions coalesce with the experiential sites in the New World, with new modes of cultural stability? What does Wesley Brown's "tragic magic" mean when he says, "I played in a Bar Mitzvah band. And it was a great job until I got hit by that tragic magic, and I start playing a little bit before the beat, a little bit behind the beat. I couldn't help myself. I lost the job." This whole question of addressing Black pleasure is a critical thing.

I've heard people talk about issues of representation and the content of culture. But I'm trying to figure out how to make Black films that have the power to allow the enunciative desires of people of African descent to manifest themselves. What kinds of things do we do? How can we interrogate the medium to find a way Black movement in itself could carry, for example, the weight of sheer tonality in Black song? And I'm not talking about the lyrics that Aretha Franklin sang. I'm talking about *how she sang them*. How do we make Black music or Black images vibrate in accordance with certain frequential values that exist in Black music? How can we analyze the tone, not the sequence of notes that Coltrane hit, *but the tone itself*, and synchronize Black visual movement with that? I mean, is this just a theoretical possibility, or is this actually something we can do?

I'm developing an idea that I call Black visual intonation (BVI). What it consists of is the use of irregular, nontempered (nonmetronomic) camera rates and frame replication to prompt filmic movement to function in a manner that approximates Black vocal intonation. See, the inherent power of cinematic movement is largely dependent on subtle or gross disjunctions between the rate and regularity at which a scene is recorded and the rate and regularity at which it is played back. Nonmetronomic camera rates, such as those employed by silent filmmakers, are transfixing precisely because they are irregular. The hand-cranked camera, for example, is a more appropriate instrument with which to create movement that replicates the tendency in Black music to "worry the note"—to treat notes as indeterminate, inherently unstable sonic frequencies rather than the standard Western treatment of notes as fixed phenomena. Utilizing what I term alignment patterns, which are simply a series of fixed frame replication patterns (and I have 372 at this point), the visual equivalencies of vibrato, rhythmic patterns, slurred or bent notes, and other musical effects are possible in film. You could do samba beats, reggae beats, all kinds of things. This is just a beginning for trying to talk about certain possibilities in Black cinema.

Notes

1. Excerpt from Arthur Jafa, "Black Visual Intonation," in *The Jazz Cadence of American Culture*, ed. R. G. O'Meally (New York: Columbia University Press, 1998), pp. 264–268.
2. David Bordwell and Kristin Thompson, "Space and Narrative in the Films of Ozu," *Screen* 17, no. 2 (Summer 1976), 41–73.
3. *Screen* 29, no. 4 (Fall 1988).
4. Bruce Perry, *Malcolm: The Life of a Man Who Changed Black America* (Barrytown, N.Y.: Station Hill Press, 1991). Distributed by The Talman Co.

William Barlow

Readers should visit the Alley Pat documentary on YouTube before reading the excerpt by William Barlow. Clips from the documentary provide the rare opportunity to interact with Black radio of the 1950s and 1960s, specifically how disc jockeys like Alley Pat used the technology to broadcast African American rhetoric to Black and White audiences. The link for the Alley Pat documentary can be found here: www.youtube.com/user/AlleyPatMovie/videos. With this sonic experience in mind, Barlow's essay will further contextualize Black talk radio during this era and how this technology helped to popularize African American oral traditions and create the commercial taste for multicultural listeners. Barlow also underscores the role of the disc jockey in advancing the civil rights agenda. A griot of the airwaves, the disc jockey infused news and cultural references along with entertainment. For example, WERD's Jack "The Rapper" Gibson, who was the owner of the first Black-owned radio station, is as famed for modifying radio technology as he was for broadcasting messages from Dr. Martin Luther King and the Southern Christian Leadership Conference.

Microphones in the Riot Zones

William Barlow[1]

During the mid-1960s, the struggle for racial equality achieved significant political gains, but racial tension and inner-city violence spread across the nation. Massive pressure from below finally compelled the U.S. Congress to pass the Civil Rights Act and the Voting Rights Act in 1964. But in the same year, the civil rights movement—backed Mississippi Freedom Party was denied recognition at the Democratic National Convention. It was also in 1964 that a long, hot summer of violence erupted in New York, Chicago, and Philadelphia. In each instance, spontaneous protests against "police brutality" in African American neighborhoods rapidly degenerated into a frenzy of looting and burning. A year later, in the summer of 1965, the Watts ghetto in Los Angeles exploded after an altercation between the police and black citizens, who were outraged by the white officers' treatment of a reckless-driving suspect. Over the next few days the rioting raged out of control, and order was restored only when the California National Guard moved in to occupy the riot zone. The toll of the Watts uprising was staggering: thirty-four dead, over one thousand injured, close to four thousand arrested, and property damage estimated at $40 million.

It was also in 1965 that Martin Luther King Jr. was awarded the Nobel Peace Prize. But there was no peace. Violence flared in the cities over the next two summers, with major eruptions in San Francisco (1966) and Newark, New Jersey, and Detroit (1967). Dr. King's assassination on April 4, 1968, unleashed another wave of destruction across the country. Over that tragic Easter weekend, as the nation watched the television coverage in shock and horror, rioters looted stores, fought with the police, and burned down inner-city business districts with Molotov cocktails. Smoke and flames from Washington, D.C.'s famous "Black Broadway," the U Street corridor, could be seen from the White House a few miles away.

Peacemakers in the Neighborhoods

African American disc jockeys were literally on alert during the urban race riots of the 1960s. They worked around the clock to save lives and minimize destruction in the black community. Over the airwaves, they urged restraint and caution, implored people to stay off the streets, and gave out information on the location and extent of each disturbance, as well as any reports of casualties. The DJs also stayed in touch with local police, politicians, and civil rights leaders, giving them access to the audience as part of an effort to quell the burning, looting, and killing. When not on the air, some of the black DJs even took to the streets, visiting the riot zones to urge calm or mediate confrontations between police and angry mobs of African Americans. In some instances, their presence at potential flash points in black neighborhoods helped defuse tense situations that could have led to more bloodshed. They were the peacekeepers, as well as the eyes and the ears, of their audience at a time of crisis.

During the summer of 1964, Jocko Henderson found himself on the air in two major markets where racial disturbances broke out: "I was there . . . in New York when they had the riots, and in Philadelphia when they had the riots. I was on the scene with my quiet machine tryin' to keep 'em quiet." Georgie Woods was also caught up in the Philadelphia disturbances, but not on the airwaves: "No I wasn't on the air, I was out in the streets for three days, telling people to stop rioting . . . . We finally got the riot under control, Cecil [Moore] and I teamed up together, we got the woman who was supposedly shot by police who was supposed to be pregnant—and that sparked the riots. We got her and put her in an open convertible and drove her around the neighborhood to quiet things down."

Woods was initially summoned to the scene of the riots by Howard Leary, the Philadelphia police commissioner at the time. According to Sid Booker, a friend and business associate of Woods who witnessed the outbreak of hostilities:

> George came on the scene, the police were standing there, and they were throwing things at the police . . . . The cops were getting ready to move on 'em, and George walked up from behind the police, they saw George and said—"Hey Georgie! Hey Georgie!" George said— "Come on man, let's cool this out." He walked over there and they said—"OK Georgie, OK!" The whole crowd turned around and went home. And the police, they were getting ready to crash. But they all listened to him, 'cause he had gained their respect. As soon as they saw him that was it. It was over with.

Georgie Woods never received a word of thanks from the city for his peacekeeping efforts: "So we were able to stop the riots and save the city an awful lot of money. Did they give me a commendation? No. Did they say thank you? Nope, never, but that's OK, we did our job anyway." This snub may have been connected to an event on the final day of the trouble. On that Sunday, with the lawlessness waning, Commissioner Leary ordered Woods to close down a scheduled R & B show at the Uptown Theater. According to Woods: "We had a full house with twenty-two hundred people inside and a line of five hundred people outside. The police commissioner called me and said he was gonna close me down, and I wanted to know why; there had been no trouble at the Uptown, no disturbances whatsoever around that area. I said—'No way, you want to see a riot, close me down and we're gonna take all these people in the Uptown and march straight down to the First Philadelphia Bank, and we'll show you what a riot really is!' They panicked, and the Uptown didn't close."

Georgie Woods's heroics in Philadelphia went unnoticed by the mainstream media, but the "Magnificent" Montague was not so lucky. The Los Angeles press demonized him for allegedly inciting the Watts rebellion. At the time of the 1965 uprising, the mercurial Nathanial Montague was the top-rated black disc jockey in the local market; 75 percent of the city's African American listeners regularly tuned in to his nightly show on KGFJ. Before moving to Los Angeles, the Texas-born spin doctor had perfected his unorthodox style of broadcasting in San Antonio, Chicago, New York City, and Tijuana, Mexico. By the time he was hired by KGFJ early in 1965, the Magnificent Montague was known for his honey-coated baritone voice, keen wit, and chameleon-like radio persona. When in a romantic mood, he would recite love poems to his female listeners over the soul ballads of Sam Cooke and Otis Redding. When playing the hottest dance tracks of the day, he would punctuate them with wild exhortations, such as his trademark "Burn, baby, burn." Moreover, Montague was an avid collector of books on African American history and culture, a streetwise philosopher who peppered his radio discourses with historical anecdotes and cautionary tales about the black experience in America. This innovative style made him an overnight sensation on KGFJ. One of his fans was fellow Los Angeles DJ Larry McCormick: "I have a lot of admiration for Montague. He had a dynamite style—it was a fiery style that got people excited . . . he was a pioneer in L.A., he was the earliest to pot down a record and talk over it—talk with it. He played himself with the record and people loved that. That was something nobody out here did in those days, so it was kind of daring."

The Magnificent Montague was riding a wave of popularity in August 1965 when the Watts rebellion erupted. The mobs of black rioters who took to the streets spontaneously adopted "Burn, baby, burn" as their battle cry—many of them using it interchangeably with "Burn, Whitey, burn"—while Montague, on the air, was urging them to go home. Nevertheless, the mainstream Los Angeles media blamed him for the mayhem, and the police chief and the mayor demanded that Montague be taken off the air. KGFJ's white owners, however, were reluctant to fire him outright—perhaps fearing they would spark another uprising. Instead, they reduced his airtime and barred him from saying "Burn, baby, burn" over mike. Unrepentant, Montague started to use "Have mercy, baby" or "Keep the faith, baby" as his audio signature piece. But his days on KGFJ were numbered. According to Larry McCormick: "After the Watts riots, some people in official positions accused him of instigating the riots by doing what he had always done, and the radio station, they didn't back him up . . . they cut him slowly, cut him away and eventually cut him loose."

The Magnificent Montague's fall from grace was startling and unusual. Few black DJs were scapegoated during the urban riots in the mid-1960s, if for no other reason than that they were actively involved in efforts, both on and off the air, to restore the peace. While these peacemaking efforts were unknown to most of the outside world, they were much appreciated by the black residents of the riot zones. DJs Georgie Woods and Martha Jean Steinberg were among those who repeatedly defused volatile situations. At the height of the 1967 race riot in Detroit, for example, Steinberg mediated a tense standoff between the local police and a group of Black Panthers:

> I remember that the Black Panthers were in a house and they wouldn't come out. And they [the police] had tanks all ready to blow up the house. And I'll never forget, they called me and asked me to try to talk to the leaders . . . and the white police chief. So I begged him—all his lieutenants wanted to blow up the house—they were mad. But I asked the man please don't blow that place up. I said just give us a few more minutes. We had several leaders go in and talk to those young people. They finally came out, the Black Panthers finally came out, and we did not have blood on our hands.

Helping a Nation in Mourning

It was during the bleakest hours of the civil rights struggle, just after the assassination of Martin Luther King Jr., that African American DJs rose to an enormous challenge as communicators. All over the country, black disc jockeys suspended regular programming and gathered people around the microphone to ponder and probe the unfolding American tragedy with the listeners. Throughout the Easter weekend, they continued their on-air vigils for Dr. King, as well as their appeals for calm and restraint. While it is difficult to gauge their effectiveness, most of the DJs who experienced that ordeal believed they played a decisive role in containing the destruction and bloodshed. In the words of New York City DJ Del Shields: "On the night that Dr. King was killed . . . on that night, all across the country, the black disc jockey went on the microphone and talked to the people. It was black radio that doused the incendiary flames burning all across America."

Del Shields's assertion has been confirmed by some unlikely sources on the other side of the color line. In Denver, Colorado, police chief George L. Station publicly praised KDKO, the city's premier black appeal station, for its actions in the aftermath of the King assassination: "The sound judgement and counseling that was broadcast by your staff is to be commended. I am sure that it was only by the tremendous cooperative efforts of each and every person on the air that Denver remained peaceful." In Memphis, both the police chief and the mayor paid tribute to WDIA for its role in helping the city through its most tragic ordeal in decades. And in Los Angeles, the city leaders this time around passed a resolution praising KGFJ (now without the Magnificent Montague) for having been "instrumental in keeping racial trouble from developing, and maintaining a helpful, informative approach to assist in easing tensions when any trouble did have an opportunity to blossom."

On the evening that Dr. King was murdered, African American disc jockeys on the air responded to the crisis immediately. In New York City, Del Shields was hosting *The Total Black Experience in Sound* on WLIB-FM. As he recalled: "Somebody came running down the hall and said Dr. King was shot. I said—'Get out of here!' He said—'No man, it's on the AP'—and he brought me the [Associated Press] wire. I said—'Oh my God!'—and I made the announcement." Shields also turned on WLIB-AM, which was required to go off the air at sunset, and broadcast over both stations simultaneously. When the news reached the streets, trouble broke out: "Within an hour . . . the word came back that people were rioting in Harlem." Shields played excerpts from Dr. King's recorded speeches until the rest of the staff could get to the station; they, in turn, expanded the coverage: "We put community leaders and reporters on the air to talk and relate and try and keep the people abreast of what was going on." In addition, Shields and the WLIB staff contacted other black stations around the country, to exchange news and information: "We discovered all across the country everybody was doing the same thing. Some of the disc jockeys were going into the community and talking to the people. And the people were listening in to us to find out what was going on. They weren't tuned into NBC or CBS—no way . . . . Had we not been on, telling the people—'Don't burn, baby'—and all of that, it would have been worse."

Georgie Woods again went into the streets of his community: "I was on WHAT at the time that he died and that was devastating, and again I had to take to the streets, and we were able to get a handle on it before anything got started here. I left the air immediately and went to the streets of the city and said—'Hey, cool it, chill out'—and the people listened." In Chicago, WVON DJ Purvis Spann also hit the streets, but after the rioting had erupted: "The city was burning away. West Side looked like a war zone. Buildings burning. Sirens, gunshots . . . the National Guard. Just like a war zone. I would go in and talk with folks, saying that violence was not the way." As the most listened-to black radio station in Chicago, WVON played a pivotal role in containing the riot. According to WVON's Lucky Cordell: "Our guys came into the station, everybody. All of them came in and stayed there, must have been twenty-four hours, imploring the people not to do this, and the basic theme was, this is disrespectful to Dr. King . . . . Don't do this and call yourself a follower of King."

Baltimore and Washington, D.C., were also involved in racial conflagrations during the aftermath of the King assassination. In Baltimore, the National Guard was called in to restore order. Federal troops patrolled the riot zones in the nation's capital. Maurice "Hot Rod" Hulbert was on the air in Baltimore when the trouble broke out:

They had riots all over the country, and Baltimore, we had our share too—burnings and whatnot. Gus Harris was a major in the state militia, and they told me on the air to talk to our people and quiet them. So I said something to the effect—"OK everybody, go home. Let's get off the streets. We cannot solve the problem by burning down our businesses. Let's get off the streets and do it now!" So we were trying to get everybody off the streets, because as long as they were out there, the more problems we were going to have. And problems were jumping up all over—down off Gay Street, on North Avenue, in different sections of the city . . . and the state militia came out and quelled it.

Washington, D.C's top black disc jockey in the mid-1960s was the outspoken Bob "Nighthawk" Terry, who was heard nightly on the city's leading soul station, WOL. On the night that Dr. King was killed, Terry was openly outraged—not only by the assassination but also at the "brothers on the block," whom he challenged: "Why ya burnin' down your own communities, brothers? Don't see no riotin' down at the White House and the Congress, no siree, everybody up on U Street lootin' and shootin' your own!" In addition, Nighthawk had some harsh words for white listeners who "run back to Maryland and Virginia suburbs every evening and leave the problems back here in the city." Terry's outburst is understandable, given the dire circumstances, but most black DJs refrained from voicing their anger and frustration on the air during the crisis. Instead, they urged their listeners to honor Dr. King's commitment to nonviolence. The loss of King, however, marked a critical turning point in the civil rights struggle. In particular, it fueled the rise of a militant Black Power movement, which attracted a growing number of adherents among the younger African American disc jockeys. This change becomes especially clear when one examines the fortunes of the NARA—the National Association of Radio Announcers.

The Rise and Fall of the NARA

During the civil rights era, although the cultural and political influence of black disc jockeys was rising, their economic situation hardly changed at all. For the most part, African American DJs remained ghettoized in black appeal stations, where their salaries were, at best, about half of what their white counterparts were making in the same market. Nearly all black appeal outlets were white owned and managed; African Americans rarely filled the better-paying staff positions in management and advertising. While payola was still legal, it was common knowledge in the radio business that the record companies paid white DJs a lot more to promote new releases, including R & B discs, than they paid black DJs. These conditions had existed since the inception of black appeal formats in the late 1940s, and they led to the formation of the first trade association for African American DJs in the mid-1950s.

Originally called the National Jazz, Rhythm & Blues Disc Jockey Association, the organization was founded in the basement of a Harlem cabaret, Tommy Smalls's Paradise Club, in 1955 by the "Original Thirteen." The group, which included Jack Gibson, Maurice Hulbert, Hal Jackson, Jack Walker, and Tommy Smalls, discussed their common grievances—from low salaries, to lack of employment opportunities in mainstream radio, to the uneven distribution of payola along racial lines. At a national convention in New York City a year later, with about one hundred black disc jockeys in attendance, the organization renamed itself the National Association of Radio Announcers (NARA) in order to be more inclusive of black radio broadcasters, whatever their on-air staff positions, as well as to attract financial support from the record companies and the radio station owners.

Disinclined to support a national trade organization of black DJs, most white owners of black appeal stations saw NARA as a potential threat to their power. However, the record companies that recorded African American artists recognized black DJs' pivotal role in popularizing their new releases and proved eager to bankroll NARA's annual conventions. Beginning in 1957, the record industry became the major patron of the NARA's annual gathering, giving record companies an ideal opportunity to promote their new records and artists, as well as to cultivate contacts among the black jocks. All the key labels producing black popular music set up lavish hospitality suites at the convention; they sponsored the official luncheons and dinners, provided free entertainment showcases, and even paid hotel and travel expenses for many DJs. This infusion of music industry cash and talent transformed the annual NARA convention into a weekend of around-the-clock revelry and high jinks. Gala receptions, concerts, cocktail and dinner parties, as well as nightclub and gambling excursions, were so plentiful that the delegates were hard pressed to find the time for the annual business meeting, much less any organized discussion of the grievances that brought them together in the first place. As Jack Gibson put it: "We partied until it was time to go to church."

By the 1960s, the NARA had developed a reputation in the entertainment world as a "payola-prone group of party boys." But the situation was about to change. For openers, the congressional hearings and subsequent legislation outlawing payola had a sobering effect on the organization. Like the infamous 1959 Miami Beach convention for white DJs, the NARA gatherings had become conduits for payola—which was, actually, the hidden agenda of the early gatherings. But in view of the public uproar, the NARA was forced to renounce the practice, in statement if not in deed, to protect itself from the payola fallout. At the same time, the prominence of the civil rights movement in the early 1960s politicized many African American DJs around the country, especially the younger ones, who began to demand that the NARA become actively involved in the struggle for racial equality within the radio industry.

By the 1964 convention, the NARA was developing a new sense of purpose and mission. Held in Chicago, the annual gathering was attended by more than 250 disc jockeys and record company representatives. While the record labels continued to foot the bill, they no longer set the agenda—at least, not during daylight hours. Morning and afternoon strategy sessions were now scheduled to discuss the association's new political agenda, and the record companies were asked to close down their hospitality suites during the sessions. In addition, one of the evenings was devoted to a benefit concert at the Chicago Coliseum, which was open to the public; it proved to be the NARA's first major fund-raising effort.

One of the highlights of the 1964 convention's business sessions was the report given by Charles Johnson, the young president of the association's Los Angeles chapter and chairman of a year-old legislative committee. The committee's investigation of employment practices in the radio industry had uncovered widespread racial discrimination. Of the sixty thousand people employed in radio broadcasting, fewer than six hundred were African Americans. The ownership ratio was even more lopsided: only five of the nation's fifty-five hundred commercial stations were black owned. Johnson had met with FCC and NAB officials to discuss these committee findings. Expressing "surprise" at the figures, the officials of both organizations had promised to support any NARA initiatives to close the gaps in employment and ownership. The FCC officials even suggested that the NARA bring specific incidents of discrimination to their attention, so that they could form a test case. Johnson also reported on his chapter's successful campaign to integrate KFWB, the top station in the Los Angeles market. Noting that Larry McCormick, the station's first African American DJ, had been hired earlier in the year as a result of picketing at KFWB by supporters from local NAACP and CORE chapters, Johnson argued that any station which violated the fair-employment provisions of the 1964 Civil Rights Act should be subject to such actions.

While discussion of tactics and strategies to combat job discrimination tended to dominate the work sessions at the Chicago convention, the NARA also took action on other fronts. Since 1964 was an election year, the association decided to conduct a vigorous voter registration campaign over the airwaves, in conjunction with civil rights organizations working to get out the black vote. In addition, the delegates approved a reorganization plan that set up five regional divisions with their own elected officers and volunteer staff. The intent was both to decentralize national decision making and to facilitate more activism at the grass roots.

There was also a good deal of internal criticism among the disc jockeys at the 1964 convention. In their ongoing efforts to clean up their tarnished public image, the delegates revisited the payola issue, not only reaffirming the 1960 policy prohibiting NARA members from accepting payola but also chastising those DJs who still allowed the record labels to pay their hotel and travel expenses. Del Shields, a leading spokesman for the newly emerging activist wing of the association, delivered a fiery speech at the convention that cataloged the deficiencies of his more complacent colleagues: their lack of "professionalism," their "playboy" mentality, their lack of racial pride, and their habit of "Uncle Tomming" for white employers. He also lambasted the white owners of black appeal stations, who "got into the business by default," knew nothing about "what the black man needs," and refused to "share the profits with us." Shields concluded by reminding the delegates: "You are important. I don't think you realize your worth. Look at all the record people here . . . look at all the money they're spending. They came because you are important."

After the 1964 Chicago convention, some NARA dissidents who felt the organization was not doing enough began to organize an insurgency among the rank and file. Most of the leaders of this group, such as Georgie Woods and Del Shields in Philadelphia (WDAS), Al Bell in Washington, D.C. (WUST), Ed Wright in Cleveland (WACQ), and Charles Johnson in Los Angeles (KAPP), were DJs with ties to the civil rights movement. Al Bell, for example, had been a disc jockey on KOKY in Little Rock, Arkansas, during the 1957 integration crisis at Central High School. The experience radicalized him, and for a period of time in the late 1950s, he was an organizer for the SCLC, attending training workshops led by Dr. King in Georgia and helping mobilize people for local demonstrations. The NARA dissident group's most influential adviser was Clarence Avant, a savvy entertainment industry insider who managed jazz organist Jimmy Smith and film-score composer Lalo Shiffren, Avant urged the group to come up with a new plan of action for the NARA—one that included expanding the association to include television broadcasters and establishing a professional broadcasting school for African Americans. In addition, he suggested that they field a slate of candidates in the upcoming NARA election, in order to wrest control of the organization away from the old guard.

At the 1965 NARA convention in Houston, Texas, the insurgents' slate of candidates, headed by Ed Wright and Del Shields and calling themselves the "New Breed" (a name they borrowed from a line in the James Brown hit "Papa's Got a Brand New Bag"), scored an upset victory over the incumbents. The next year, in New York City, the association officially changed its name to the National Association of Radio and Television Announcers (NARTA) and endorsed the New Breed's ambitious agenda for change. Among other things, that agenda called for increasing black ownership of broadcast outlets, formation of a black radio news service, increasing black employment in the broadcast industry (especially at the management level), and establishing a professional college of broadcasting to train African Americans for jobs in the industry.

The more-politicized thrust of the organization was evident at the historic 1967 NARTA convention in Atlanta, where delegates heard not only Dr. King praising their efforts on behalf of the civil rights cause but also SNCC firebrand H. Rap Brown. Voting overwhelmingly for two more years of New Breed leadership, delegates elected Del Shields as the executive director of the association and again supported plans to found a black college of broadcasting. Shields—now based in New York at WLIB-FM—and Clarence Avant began making the rounds of the record companies and television networks, seeking funds and broadcast equipment for the college. Shields also organized a meeting between a group of white black appeal station owners and a delegation of New Breed DJs to discuss job discrimination and to solicit financial and technical support for the school. Within a year, Shields and Avant had lined up pledges from ten record companies for $50,000 each, to be used as the down payment on a school site in northern Delaware. The formal announcement was put on the agenda for the upcoming NARTA convention.

Then the sky fell on the New Breed, wiping out four years of hard work and damaging beyond repair their leadership position within the NARTA. First came the murder of Dr. King and its bitter aftermath as the mood of the country turned ugly and racial divisions deepened. Then, in the summer of 1968, when word of the impending deal with the record labels hit the black radio grapevine, Shields and Avant's lives were threatened by anonymous callers, who had their own agenda for the record industry's "reparations." Shields was even beaten up in Harlem by thugs whom he felt were agents of the "Black Mafia." To be sure, a black criminal element had long been associated with the music industry, mainly through their control of nightclubs; hence it is certainly possible that some in their ranks sought to muscle in on NARTA's good fortune. But the rhetoric of those making the threats was laced with militant Black Power slogans, which suggests that the culprits were rogue political opportunists—or even agent provocateurs.

Whatever their source, the provocations came to a head at the 1968 NARTA convention, held in Miami, and the thugs targeted both the New Breed leadership and white record industry executives in attendance. On the first day, a bomb threat at the convention hotel and rumors of a "contract" out on Del Shields's life persuaded Shields to return to New York. White record executives, such as Atlantic's Jerry Wexler, and Phil Walden, Otis Redding's manager, were threatened with violence by roving bands of unidentified "militants" unless they paid "reparations" on the spot. New Orleans record producer Marshall Sehorn and others were actually beaten up when they refused to pay. As word got out, the record industry representatives left—taking their half-million dollars in pledges with them. As a result of all this, dissension split the ranks of the black disc jockeys who remained at the convention. Many blamed the debacle on the New Breed's attempts to radicalize the association.

The New Breed led the NARTA for another year, but with their ambitious plans for the association now in shambles, they piloted a sinking ship. With help from Georgie Woods, Del Shields persuaded Motown's Berry Gordy to donate $25,000 to the NARTA, which, in turn, announced the pledge at the 1969 convention in Washington, D.C., and honored Gordy as the organization's man of the year. But the good news was not enough to offset financial wrongdoing charges against Shields, or the delegates' rage when they learned he had spent $10,000 on security for the convention. The association elected new leadership, a Southern faction that vowed to put their financial house in order. Although Georgie Woods was elected to the executive director post two years later, much of the New Breed leadership, including Del Shields, Clarence Avant, and Al Bell, had withdrawn from the association by the 1970s. The New Breed had disintegrated. The association also floundered; the schisms between the old guard, the moderate Southern faction, and the black power advocates only widened. The record industry withdrew its financial support and no longer sent its executives to the conventions.

With the quiet death of the NARTA in the mid-1970s, African American broadcasters lost the little political clout they had in the radio industry. With no power base, they could do little to address economic and other forms of discrimination in the workplace. In the coming years, the organizational sites of struggle would shift to the realm of ownership, and black entrepreneurs would supplant the disc jockeys as the activists and power brokers in broadcast circles.

Note

1. William Barlow, "Microphones in the Riot Zone," in *Voice Over: The Making of Black Radio* (Philadelphia: Temple University Press, 1999), pp. 212–226.

Abdul Alkalimat

Eblackstudies.org is an archival site maintained by Professor Abdul Alkalimat. The content and structure of the website are the virtual representation of Alkalimat's vision of the changing context of Black studies in the twenty-first century. The website hosts debates and lectures as well as a documentary history of Black studies in America. In the essay ahead, however, Alkimat explicates what he sees as the changing context of Black studies in the information age. He describes both the challenge of information technologies and the transformative potential this will have for the field. Arguing that eBlack is the basis for the next stage of the discipline, Alkalimat advances operating principles such as cyberdemocracy through access and participation, intellectual production through archiving, analysis and use of Black discourse, and the free sharing of resources through a knowledge network.

eBlack: A 21st Century Challenge

Abdul Alkalimat[1]

> "Every generation has a mission. It can fulfill it or betray it."
> Frantz Fanon, *Wretched of the Earth*

The information revolution is a concept that sums up a complex historical process, a process of struggle. In sum, this process is over throwing our old ways. No sector of society, no community of people, is exempt. This includes Black Studies in all its manifestations: Afrocentricity, Afrology, Afro-American and African American Studies, Africana and African Studies, as well as all forms of ethnic or minority studies. This article is a call for the transformation of Black Studies, a move from ideology to information. My argument is that eBlack, the virtualization of the Black experience, is the basis for the next stage of our academic discipline.

The information revolution is manifest in a new reality called cyberspace, the world-wide-web and the Internet. We inhabit cyberspace by digitizing information about our experience including our artistic and intellectual production, and conversations via email and chat rooms. This is the evolution of survival—if we are not digital then we do not exist. The dominant reality of the world is cyberspace. This is why the challenge of the 21st century is to develop eBlack as a positive force for Africa and the African Diaspora. eBlack forces on a global level will represent the rebirth of Pan-Africanism and a new era of struggle against all enemies—from poverty, to AIDS, to anti-democratic regimes.

The impact of the information revolution can lead to a renaissance of community development, cultural creativity, and liberation politics. We need to have theoretical principles, practical projects, and a strategic plan to create eBlack Studies. In this article we will discuss three fundamental theoretical principles. Five case studies of the eBlack Studies Program at the University of Toledo will be described as practical examples, models being proposed for more general adoption. Finally, we will propose a strategic plan to unleash a new national trend of productivity under conditions of cooperation and unity.

From Ideology to Information

Black Studies began as part of the Black Liberation Movement. It originated as a Black power project in higher education. The early adopters of the fight for Black Studies advanced their cause based on community struggle. A second generation emerged in a career stream delinked from these struggles. They cultivated academic careers rooted in the struggle for tenure. Both generations were ideological: the founders fought the century old Marxist–Nationalist debate, and the second generation wages its debate on the terrain of the Post Modernist–Afrocentrist debate.

Ideology is a form of intelligence and ignorance at the same time. Ideology easily becomes a way of life: ideas are dogma, actions are morally sanctioned, and the role of institutions is to isolate and protect members against outsiders. We become ideological as an intellectual short cut to freedom, as a way of organizing and joining large numbers of people to change the world. All too often adherents of one ideology show no interest in and even refuse to study other ideological positions. We appoint ourselves victors before we fight and win the war.

While ideological struggle has persisted the information revolution has undercut the material conditions for ideological ignorance. The information revolution has increased our capacity to produce, store, distribute, and consume all texts—written, oral, and visual. The move from ideology (Black Studies) to information (eBlack Studies) is when we chose to know about not just which texts we believe, but all the texts including ones we don't believe. The information revolution requires global consciousness. This means knowing about or wanting to know about and having access to all ideas.

This move to eBlack, from ideology to information, is consistent with the profound changes taking place in other related contexts. Library schools are schools of information science, newspapers are online sources of information, and massive efforts are underway to digitize the major library collections of the world. This is the future.

Three Theoretical Principles of eBlack Studies

eBlack Studies relies on at least three theoretical concepts: cyber democracy, collective intelligence, and information freedom. These general principles will guide the necessary discussion and debate to win faculty and students to create eBlack.

> **Principle One**: *Cyberdemocracy. eBlack depends upon everyone having access and becoming active users of cyber technology.*

The current explosion of information technology is class based. The new concept being used to describe the growth of information rich and poor is the "digital divide." This is a critical problem. Hoffman and Novak report the following recent data (1999). In 1997, on a percentage basis, Blacks were 75% as likely to use the web than whites, but by 1998 they were only 60% as likely. On the other hand the rate of increase in these same figures indicate that from 1997 to 1998 whites increased by 62.5% and Blacks by 75.8%. Blacks are not on the web as much as whites, but it looks like they are trying to be.

The Commerce Department (1999) makes a further clarification: "Nevertheless, the news is not all bleak. For Americans with incomes of $75,000 and higher, the divide between whites and Blacks has actually narrowed considerably in the last year."

Table 10.1 Comparison of Recent Black–White Web Use

Date	White		Black	
	%	*#Millions*	*%*	*#Millions*
Spring 1997	22.4	35.2	16.6	3.9
Fall 1997	30.0	48.4	17.0	4.0
Spring 1998	35.8	60.4	21.9	5.2

The principle of cyberdemocracy is being promoted in society by a variety of forces, especially ecommerce. It is very likely that computer access will become similar to telephone access (whites 95.0%, Blacks 85.4%). This is suggested by free email, free Internet access through institutions like the library and school, and community computing centers. In higher education cyberdemocracy is mandated to promote fundamental skill for the 21st century, a standard of literacy. Access is fast coming to every campus on a 24/7 basis.

> **Principle Two**: *Collective Intelligence. eBlack depends upon all intellectual production being collected, analyzed, and utilized.*

An elite runs Black Studies, usually in a very undemocratic manner. Small handfuls of people tend to dominate the activities of each ideological network. This means we see the same names in texts, anthologies, journals, academic programs, professional organizations, invitational conferences as well as annual meetings, and as editors of reprints. This is a vertical structure, a hierarchy. It protects the ideology by sustaining an authoritative source, and creates a more manageable market through name recognition.

There continues to be a remarkable expansion of cyberspace (Moore's Law = every 18 months memory of a microchip doubles, and the price is cut in half). Every text of a particular type can be included in a digital library and utilized in the aggregate, e.g., all African American Novels, all slave narratives, all the documented words of leaders like Malcolm X and Martin Luther King. This includes the written word, and also spoken and visual material as well. Everything that encodes meaning can be aggregated into a data set. This will redefine the role of scholarship. There are many examples of data sets that have never been systematically studied before: e.g., graduate level theses and dissertations at HBCU's, records of every ship involved in the slave trade, every speech given by a Black elected official during the Reconstruction, and every novel written by an African American.

> **Principle Three**: *Information Freedom. eBlack depends upon intellectual production being freely available to everyone.*

Knowledge for sale has governed the logic of the academic marketplace. The hard copy commercial publishers of books and journals, as well as the popular press, especially the New York Times, have been the gatekeepers of legitimacy and the main mechanisms for knowledge distribution. eCommerce has helped to equalize this distribution through Amazon.com and BarnesandNobles.com, but the major centers of culture and the major academic institutions will continue to dominate. Class is the best way to predict book purchases. In sum, information flows through conduits owned and controlled by big money.

On the other hand, great traditions of information freedom have been crucial for the Black Freedom struggle. The most important one is the free public library. Anyone can go and read any book for free. Literacy for Black people has required information freedom more than any thing else.

Now, information freedom is taking off in cyberspace. It is possible to go the web and get any census data you need for free. The National Institute of Health has announced its intention to make all health related scientific research available for free. H-Net has set up over 100 listservs and websites in all disciplines of the Humanities and Social Sciences that offer free subscriptions. Information from the radio and television is free. We need to give our system a makeover based on information freedom.

These three theoretical principles are revolutionary. All ideological tendencies and schools of thought in Black Studies can embrace these principles as the basis for eBlack. We can use them to guide us through the next decade of transformation toward a unified discipline based in cyberspace.

The Toledo Model: Five Practical Projects

For the last three years we have been working to build an eBlack studies program at the University of Toledo. The importance of this is that we are similar to most places. We have had only modest resources in a working class based urban public university. This work is an experiment in eBlack Studies. Other institutions with similarly modest resources are also experimenting in eBlack Studies. More experiments will advance this next stage.

LISTSERV: H-AFRO-AM WWW.H-NET.MSU.EDU

H-Afro-Am is edited at the University of Toledo. It is part of H-Net based at Michigan State University. H-Afro-Am was launched in 1998 as a vehicle for professional discourse in Afro-American Studies. There are over 1,000 subscribers from 25 countries. The list is free and open to everyone. It is a moderated list averaging up to 10 messages a day. Faculty, students, and others use H-Afro-Am to make announcements to the field, share information about curriculum development and research, and discuss theoretical and practical issues of relevance to the Black experience. People of all ideological positions are involved, and everyone shares information.

Our goal is to have every faculty and graduate student in the field in communication via this and other related listservs. This is a necessary complement to face-to-face gatherings and more expensive forms of telecommunications such as voice and fax phone.

DISTANCE LEARNING: THE UG/UT PROJECT HTTP://WEBCT.UTOLEDO.EDU

The World Bank created the Virtual African University to send courses from the USA into Africa. At the University of Toledo we have set up a partnership with the University of Ghana to send courses from Africa to the world. We invited Dr. G. K. Nukunya, Professor of Sociology and former University of Ghana Pro Vice Chancellor, to be a visiting professor for academic year 1999–2000. He taught two courses on our campus during the fall and is currently teaching the same courses for the spring via the Internet from Ghana. We are using the WebCT software to teach "Introduction to the African Experience" and "Foundations of Culture in the African Diaspora."

Table 10.2 eBlack as a Practical Project: The Toledo Experience

	Black studies	*eBlack studies*	*The Toledo Experience*
Professional discourse	Conference (face to face discussions)	Listserv discussions	H-Afro-Am
Curriculum development	Classroom based campus courses	Distance learning	Joint project with University of Ghana
Research productivity	Hard copy publications	Research web sites	*Malcolm X: A Research Site*
Public policy	Consulting and internships	Advocacy web sites and petitions	1998 Black Radical Congress
Community service	Volunteering in an actual community	Building a virtual community	Toledo Black Church web project

Distance learning is a threat to teachers if it is used to downsize faculty and seize ownership of course materials. However, it can be used to fight racism, empower Black faculty, level the academic playing field, build partnerships with community institutions, globalize education, and reverse the brain drain out of Africa.

This UG/UT project is the first project to use cyberspace in this manner. We intend to expand this to a global Pan-African Studies Program via the Internet. Geography, language, ideology, or institution will never again limit us.

WEB RESEARCH SITE: MALCOLM X WWW.BROTHERMALCOLM.NET

Scholarship in the age of information is a public exercise. The history of Black Studies, as with all academic fields, has been linked to specific institutions that have been able to house information in archives, often under conditions of limited access. Major examples include public library collections (e.g., the Schomberg in New York or the Harsh Collection in Chicago), University archives (e.g., Fisk, Howard, University of Mass., or Yale), and special research institutions (e.g., Martin Luther King Center, and the Smithsonian). Archival material usually requires the support of major funding and acceptance into one of these institutions. W.E.B. DuBois, Booker T. Washington, Frederick Douglass, Marcus Garvey, and Martin Luther King all have major university based archives and even digitized projects. There is no such project for Malcolm X, nor any Black woman.

The University of Toledo has been engaged in a program of research, production, and advocacy about the life and legacy of Malcolm X since the 1960's. There are hundreds of people all over the world as colleagues in these activities. We decided to develop a web site to share information and establish an empirical baseline for studies of Malcolm X. This web site, based on the principles of eBlack, is now the authoritative source about Malcolm X other than his published writings. It's only a click away for anyone online anywhere at anytime.

Our goal is to standardize the research site type of web page as a peer reviewed formal intellectual product of eBlack Studies. Specifically, we hope to use the Malcolm X site as a model to build a major archive of Black intellectual history, especially the radical Black tradition. This must include all ideological tendencies and be built on the principles of eBlack.

BLACK LIBERATION MOVEMENT: BRC, 1998 HTTP://208.234.16.110/INDEX2.HTML

The 1990's included a major international conference on Malcolm X (1990), an unprecedented uprising in South Central LA and over 40 other cities (1992), and the Million Man March (1996). Black radicals had not had a coordinated major national movement since the African Liberation Support Committee of the 1970's. Reformism replaced radicalism by the electoral campaigns of the 1980's and the resurgence of Black middle class mainstream leadership. We began a process to reverse this.

What began as a couple of conversations expanded to a group that then organized thousands of activists into a process to reinvigorate Black radicalism. The main vehicle for this was a web-based source of information. Many radicals were not convinced that cyberspace was the major tool for national coordination, but the BRC web site stands as a triumph of the technology. The BRC was the first organization of any kind that created the cyber organizer as an elected position. A cyber organizer includes the duties of a webmaster, managing the web site, but also building the movement based on the principles of eBlack.

The BRC cyber activity included a listserv discussion and debate. This activity demonstrated that rather than promoting factionalism and a hardening of ideological lines, participants found an open exchange over the most controversial and polemical issues to be refreshing. It gathered a webliography of contemporary Black radicalism, posted official BRC documents, and posted a report (including sound and photos) of the national congress attended by over 2,000 people. The cyber action of the BRC continues under the able leadership of the Internet pioneer Art McGee.

The BRC cyber organizers turned ideology into information and built a movement of people who otherwise would not have spent the time of day with each other. We discovered that cyber-activism made the gulf between advocacy and archiving disappear. Our 1998 experience is a model for future national campaigns of Black radical activists. Our goal is to reorganize the organizational tactics of Black radicalism around the principles of eBlack.

COMMUNITY SERVICE: BLACK CHURCH PROJECT WWW.BLACKTOLEDO.NET/RELIGION

The Black church anchors the lives of Black people and serves as a foundation for the community. The church is total theater, and includes music, lectures, ritual, pageantry, and the largest mass following of any institution. The rhetorical and organizational skills of the Black ministry are unrivaled. The Black church has been the basis for all major protest movements. When the Black church makes a commitment to recreating itself in a digital format the entire Black community will soon be online.

The University of Toledo recruited Rev. Al Reed, a local Toledo minister, to prepare a course on the Black Church. This was part of an ongoing strategy to utilize local talent to diversify our program as we had done in politics, jazz and theatre. The course met every Saturday morning and focused on rereading the Black church through the lens of Black liberation theology. As a requirement for the course each student selected a church to gathered material for a web site. The University of Toledo has established a service called MetroNet that local nonprofit organizations can use to host web pages for free. In addition, we are part of a local community-computing program, the Murchison Center and the Community Math Academy, (www.murchisoncenter.org). We are establishing a weekly workshop in which church members can learn web development software and keep their church web site updated on a regular basis.

Our goal is to get every church online via a common portal, all faiths, as a virtual ecumenical environment for Black liberation theology. Our vision is a virtual Black community. Creating this virtual world in cyberspace is a step toward recreating the actual world we live in.

Strategy for eBlackStudies

So, where do we go from here? What is a strategy to use the three basic principles, and implement the transition from Black Studies to eBlack Studies? We need a new course, a new concentration, and a new conception of mapping our existence in cyberspace.

Our academic programs need a new course: Introduction to eBlack or Information Technology and the Black Experience. This course should provide basic cyber skills to access and search the Internet, knowledge of web-based information on the Black experience, and basic skills to produce web sites. Students will grow to love this course to keep them up to date and more viable in the job market.

We need to build on this course and create a new major by linking our curriculum to information science, either through Library Science, Business, Education, Computer Science, or Engineering. This should lead to cyber organizing becoming a concentration in eBlack Studies, and route our students to exciting careers and able to make practical contributions to digitizing the experience of their family and community. We need a national plan of research collaboration, state by state, to build portals for all digital formats of the Black experience, all Black content web sites state by state. This is a vital service waiting to be done by Black Studies Programs.

The state parameters give us a rational matrix to coordinate such a comprehensive webliography project. We can use federal work-study money to hire students to carry out this activity. Further we can partner with local chapters of the Black Data Processing Associates, the Society of Black Engineers, the Community Technology Centers network, BRC cyber organizers and other local information technologists such as librarians.

This is not the time to be a slave to the past. We live in a revolutionary age that will likely go far beyond our current imagination. We need a fundamentally new approach to the 21st century. This eBlack Studies proposal begins the discussion of new theory, new practice and new strategy. Please join in this process. When we do what is necessary in cyberspace the actual material transformation of the world will surely follow.

The time for eBlack is now.

Note

1. Abdul Alkalimat, *eBlack: A 21st Century Challenge* (2001), www.eblackstudies.org/eblack.html

Selected Webliography

Campus Web Sites

1. Africana Studies, University of Pittsburgh <www.pitt.edu/~bjgrier/links.htm>
2. African and African Diaspora Studies, Tulane University <www.tulane.edu/~adst/links.htm>
3. Center for Afro-American and African Studies, University of Michigan (Ann Arbor) <www.umich.edu/~iinet/caas/links/index.html>
4. Africana Studies Research Center, Cornel University, <www.library.cornell.edu/africana/index.html>
5. Center for the Study of Race, Politics and Culture, University of Chicago, <http://social-sciences.uchicago.edu/ucrpc/>

Digital Divide Sites

1. Donna Hoffman and Thomas Novak, "The Evolution of the Digital Divide: Examining the Relationship of Race to Internet Access and Usage Over Time,"
2. Commerce Department <http://digitaldivide.gov/>
3. Benton Foundation <www.benton.org/Library>
4. Art McGee, Class Culture and Cyberspace <www.igc.org/amcgee/e-race.html>
5. Abdul Alkalimat, The Technological Revolution and Prospects for Black Liberation in the 21st Century <www.cyrev.net/Issues/Issue4/TechnologicalRevolutionAndProspectsfor-BlackLiberation.htm>

Information Revolution Sites

1. The Community Connector, School of Information, University of Michigan <www.si.umich.edu/Community>
2. Information Technology in Africa <www.sas.upenn.edu/AfricanStudies/AboutAfrican/wwtech.html>
3. cyRev: A Journal of Cybernetic Revolution, Sustainable Socialism and Radical Democracy

4. Media Lab, MIT
5. `H-Net: Humanities and Social Sciences Online

Selected Bibliography

1. Abdul Alkalimat, Doug Gills, and Kate Williams, *Job-Tech: The Technological Revolution and Its Impact on Society* (Chicago: 21st Century Books, 1995)
2. Jim Davis, et. al., *Cutting Edge: Technology, Information Capitalism and Social Revolution* (London: Verso, 1997)
3. Bosah Ebo, ed., *Cyberghetto or Cybertopia: Race, Class, and Gender on the Internet* (Westport, Conn.: Praeger, 1998)
4. Timothy Jenkins and Khafra K Om-Ra-Seti, *Black Futurists in the Information Age* (San Francisco: KMT, 1997)
5. Eric Lee, *The Labour Movement and the Internet* (London: Pluto Press, 1997)
6. Pierre Levy, *Collective intelligence: Mankind's Emerging World in Cyberspace* (New York: Plenum Press, 1997)
7. Steven Miller, *Civilizing Cyberspace: Policy, Power, and the Information Superhighway* (Reading, Mass.: Addison-Wesley, 1996)
8. Michael Perelman, *Class Warfare in the Information Age* (New York: St. Martins Press, 1998)
9. Douglas Schuler, *New Community Networks: Wired for Change* (Reading, Mass.: Addison-Wesley, 1996)
10. Nick Dyer-Witheford, *Cyber-Marx: Cycles and circuits of Struggle in High Technology Capitalism* (Urbana: University of Illinois Press, 2000)

Ron Eglash and Julian Bleecker

Eglash and Bleecker discuss the rich layers of invention and identity in the Black diaspora. Their essay illustrates how appropriation of technology can lead to resistance, or what they term a "cyberliberation." The authors make use of Barbara Christian's essay "The Race for Theory" to draw attention to the parallel need to locate communities of Black cybernetics rather than a cybernetics of Black communities. To do this, the authors begin by historicizing African innovations in technology. They also show how the appropriation of Western information technologies, when fused with African practices, serves as cultural capital, or a syncretism between culture and technology.

The Race for Cyberspace: Information Technology in the Black Diaspora

Ron Eglash and Julian Bleecker[1]

Analog Representation in Indigenous African Knowledge Systems

While binary coding is widely used in African divination systems, there is also an extraordinary precolonial utilization of analog representation. Unlike digital representation, which is based on physically arbitrary signals, analog representation is created when variation in the physical structure of the signal is proportionate to variation in the information structure it represents. In a digital medium, like a CD-ROM, music is encoded as a series of binary digits, strings of ones and zeros represented by long bumps and short bumps in the aluminum layer of the plastic disk. But in an analog medium, like a record player (phonograph), the waveforms we see in the vinyl grooves are proportionate to (that is, tiny models of) the waveforms we hear in the air. Analog systems are not necessarily "old-fashioned" however, since contemporary cybernetics includes neural net computation, nonlinear phase space analysis, and other sophisticated, cutting-edge technologies that are forms of analog representation.

Indigenous African analog representation forms are closely related to two pervasive cultural traditions: music and animism. Animism is a religion in which the life force that sustains living beings can be transferred to other systems (organic, inorganic, or mixtures of the two), often by sacrifice. Bamana divination priests have diagrammed this force as a spiral waveform, marked by their binary code and emanating from the sacrificed life.

A vodun priest in Benin provided a similar interpretation for the helix in the royal memorial staff of King Ghezo (1818–1858). He told a story in which Ghezo defeated a buffalo by grabbing his horns with his hands, and explained that the royal staff showed this *puissance* (power or energy) flowing between his hands. Blier (1995) notes that such representations are closely related to images of the umbilical cord, as a symbol of the life force. As in the case of the Bamana waveform, this energy in vodun is closely associated with communication (cf. Ellipsis 1997 p. 23). The power of the ancestors to solve particular problems, for example, can be released if they are dancing the appropriate dance, so the use of particular drum patterns in vodun rituals is actually a communication system with the dead.

Visualization of these waveforms can be quite sophisticated, as shown on a textile from the Ijebu Yoruba which they describe as the pattern of movement made by the drummembrane when it is struck (Aronson 1992:56). In European mathematical physics these are know as Chladni patterns, and they have been an important source for the development of theories of waves and vibrations (Waller 1961).

Concepts of phase relations are also evident in African textiles. Robert Farris-Thompson (1983:207) describes such patterns as a visualization of "the famed off-beat phrasing of melodic accents in African music," noting that indigenous terminology used to describe these strip cloth weavings makes explicit use of musical analogies. Jola musicians in the Casamance region of Senegal also report striking indigenous terminology, distinguishing between oscillation ("owowogene," which applies to both instrument strings and the way that palm trees sway in the wind), resonance ("ebissa," in which a plucked string can cause a nearby string tuned in harmony to vibrate), and pitch.

The pitch terms are inversely linked to owowogene, such that high frequency ("chob") is said to have short owowogene, and low frequency ("xi") has long owowogene; an indigenous counterpart of the western equation $\omega = 1/\lambda$ (frequency is the inverse of wavelength).

Movement is also closely linked to the indigenous understanding of these analog waveforms, as most vividly portrayed in dance, where resonance, hysterisis, feedback, and phase relations are used to provide visual analogs for social dynamics (Chernoff 1979, Kozel 1997). Such traditions are quite old in Africa; even ancient Egyptian images often show movement as an oscillatory waveform in time.

Mathematics Across the Middle Passage: Africanisms in
American Information Technology

In the 1940s a debate raged between Melville Herskovits, who had documented the cultural retention of African traditions in the Americas, and E. Franklin Frazier, who argued that slavery had caused American blacks to be "stripped of their social heritage." Phillips (1990), reviewing this debate and its contemporary legacy, suggests a synthesis, noting that in addition to Africanisms among blacks, there are African cultural influences among white Americans, non-African cultural legacies of slavery among black Americans, and various syncretic mixtures of all three. Phillips' interest in de-racializing cultural heritage is particularly appropriate to the history of information technology, where such mixtures can thrive, recombine, and mutate in ways unpredicted by static social codes.

Christian (1972:23) notes that this double helix is "reminiscent of a piece of sculpture out of African ancestor worship," and indeed the geographic areas that Christian notes as origins for most slaves brought for iron work—from present day Benin to Angola—do have helical sculptures; usually in reference to the umbilical cord as a symbol of life (e.g. Swiderski 1970 fig 12).

What would such cultural and technological syncretism mean to the enslaved blacksmith who created this? Under such circumstances survival itself is an act of resistance, and this is true not only for physical survival but cultural and technological as well. Taking a line from poet Audre Lourde, "never meant to survive" became the title for Aimee Sand's interview with Evelynn Hammonds, a description of Hammond's experience as a black physics graduate student at MIT. In his aptly titled essay, "Tools of the Spirit," Alton Pollard (1996:1–2) reflects on Africanisms in American slavery as a survival strategy:

> It is of course a given that the demeaned and oppressed will develop strategies of subversion, resistance, even armed combat against those who persecute them. But always, beyond the immediate goals of liberation, they also strive to create other images—cultural signposts, hope-filled intimations of a more just and humane world.

Africanisms in American culture include many of the indigenous African technologies, such as waveform representations in textiles, numeric and symbolic doubling, scaling geometries in hairstyles, and animist concepts of spiritual energy embedded in artifice (contrary to the western stereotype that animism is "nature worship"). If we examine the work of African-American scientists such as Benjamin Banneker, George Washington Carver, and Ernest Everett Just, we can often see possibilities for African cultural survivals in their technological work (Eglash 1995, 1997b). Ernest Everett Just (1883–1941), for example, is often cited in social studies of science because his social critique of the "master-slave" model for nucleus-cytoplasm interactions motivated his discovery of cytoplasm dynamics (e.g. Hess 1994). But these descriptions often overlook the possibility of African influence. Just grew up on James Island, South Carolina, where the black population still spoke Gullah (a mixture of English and West African languages), and had retained a wide variety of African customs and traditions (Manning 1983:15). Just's work was not just a critique of nucleus versus cytoplasm, but also digital versus analog: information transmitted by the genetic code versus information transmitted by the propagation of biochemical waves through the cell. In his technical writing Just used an analogy to music to describe how such analog waveforms could carry information. In his private communication to anthropologists (including Melville Herskovits, who came to Howard University at Just's invitation), Just remarked that music offered the best case for African cultural retentions in American blacks. There was a strong resemblance between the information waves in Just's scientific models and those he heard echoing across the middle passage.

Information Technologies and African American Identity in the Modern Era

Just's work did not remain isolated; G. Ross Henderson brought his framework to the scientific community that would later become General Systems Theory. This is part of a longer history in which more subtle influences from black culture were also at work, informing, contesting, and appropriating mainstream technologies. Historian Rayvon Fouché, for example, has described the ways in which black inventors used both social and technical strategies to get around Jim Crow restrictions from patent rights. Fouché notes that Granville Woods (1856–1910), inventor of the Synchronous Multiplex Railway Telegraph, developed expertise in patent interference claims to counter corporate attempts to use his race to cheat on contracts. Technology often served as a sign of white privilege, and it is no surprise that black fiction often played with new visions of technology. In 1938 African American journalist George Schuyler published *Black Empire*, a science fiction in which a black revolt of "intellectuals, scientists, and engineers" includes a black biologist named "Ransom Just." Even black literature not typically considered science fiction, such as Ellison's *Invisible Man* or Bambara's *Salt Eaters*, often have strong technological themes.

Science fiction is also credited by some black scientists as playing a pivotal role in their dedication to technological careers. Derek Harris, the president of the first black-owned computer company, recalled that the *Mission Impossible* character "Barney Collier," an African American electronics wizard, was a major influence in his childhood fascination with technology. There is, of course, a big difference between black science fiction, and black characters in science fiction written by white authors. Samuel Delany makes this point in an interview where he rejects the figures of the "Rastas" in Gibson's *Neuromancer* as providing an oppositional political stance (Dery 1994:194–197). And it is worth keeping in mind how those fictional roles are filled. During the 1960s, for example, we saw black technological characters restricted to the roles of "communications officer" (read secretary?)—as in the case of Greg Morris' Barney Collier, Ivan Dixon's "Sgt. Ivan Kinchloe" in *Hogan's Heros*, and Nichelle Nichols' "Lieutenant Uhura" in *Star Trek*. But when Nichols announced that she was planning to leave the show at the end of the first season, she was confronted by none other than Dr. Martin Luther King Jr., who told her "you cannot leave . . . you have opened a door that must not be allowed to close." Decades later, the first African-American woman in space, Dr. Mae Jemison, credited Nichols with her early aspirations towards space.

While the intertwinings between black popular culture, science, and science fiction are an important part of this story (and typically disregarded by the "minorities in science education" efforts), the success of African Americans in information technology is hardly a matter of easy dreaming. Best known is probably John P. Moon, a silicon valley engineer who dedicated years of work to studying memory storage systems, culminating in what is still the most popular transportable storage medium in existance today, the 3.5 floppy disk. At the other end of the high-tech/lowtech spectrum, black appropriations of information technology by members of economically disadvantaged communities have often utilized a bricollage of cast-off hardware, as described in this 1995 message from a DJ at KPOO radio in San Francisco to the listserv for the National Urban League:

> The folks working with the Save Mumia Committee utilized CDs, ISDN lines, the internet, laser printers and faxes to quickly spread information about Mumia's case that would have cost tens of thousands of dollars if done using traditional means of organizing (printers, newspaper ads, phone trees). . . . [W]e have found that the biggest thing keeping technology from marginalized communities are the myths that the technology is expensive and hard to use. It's not in the best interest of the computer industry, trying to make a buck off of everyone having the biggest and fastest computer, 600×600 dpi laser printer and . . . T-3 links. [We need] to let people know that they can successfully get on line free with an XT, 2400 baud modem and a inexpensive dot matrix printer. This is what I'm using right now and my whole setup cost less than $75, and it's not hard to find people willing to give away XTs or 286s. The San Francisco Public library offers free, text only internet dial-in access and the San Francisco Bay Guardian has free e-mail service. However you won't hear about this in the computer press . . . . The key is getting the word out and making low cost online communications as accessible in the hood as Old English and St. Ides.

Postmodernity and the Afrofuturists

If television in the late modern era turned technologically adept African Americans into the black secretary, the postmodern equivalent would have to be the black cyborg. This includes LeVar Burton's "Lt. Geordi LaForge" from *Star Trek: the next generation*, Philip Akin's "Norton Drak" from *War of the Worlds*, and Carl Lumbly's "Dr. Miles Hawkins" from M.A.N.T.I.S. Like the double edged status of "communications officer," there are both advantages and disadvantages to this position. On the negative side, one might cynically read this as a diversity two-for-one (you get both a disabled character and a black character in one blow). More ominously, one wonders if the figure of a technologically empowered African American man (there are apparently no female black cyborgs) was considered too threatening for an American audience, and thus the disability was required to keep him in check. Certainly such muted disguises or balances for non-white race abound in postmodern simulations (cf. Bleecker 1995).

On the other hand, one could not ask for a position more imbricated with technology than that of the cyborg. M.A.N.T.I.S. (Mechanically Augmented Neuro Transmitter Interception System), for example, is loosely based on a black comic book hero, *Hardware*, which was written and drawn by African American artists at Milestone Media (Dery 1994). Here a disabled black scientist seeks revenge on the corporate forces which cheated him (and eventually left him a paraplegic) by creating an alter-ego powered by a cybernetic exo-skeleton. Although gutted of much of its original political message, the television version did manage to occasionally convey themes connecting racial identity, disability, and resistance through technological metaphors.

Music critic and writer Mark Dery (1994) coined the term "Afrofuturist" to describe the self-conscious appropriation of technological themes in black popular culture, particularly that of rap and other hip-hop representations. The term has been used as an organizing principle by Alondra Nelson and Paul Miller in creating a listserv dedicated to "explor[ing] futurist themes in black cultural production and the ways in which technological innovation is changing the face of black art and culture." Nelson is a graduate student at NYU, and manager for a cybercafe in a mixed working class/middle class neighborhood in Brooklyn. Paul Miller is a senior editor at *Artbyte* magazine, and performs as D.J. Spooky, master of "illambiant" digital sound collage (most recently featured in the soundtrack for the film "Slam"). These dual roles in Nelson and Miller's own lives reflects the potent mixture of cultural analysis and cultural production promised by the Afrofuturist perspective.

Members of Nelson and Miller's listserv have suggested a wide spectrum of afrofuturist forerunners and fellow travellers: analog musicians Lee "Scratch" Perry (Ska), George Clinton (funk) and Sun Ra (jazz), science fiction writers Samuel R. Delany, Octavia Butler, Charles Sanders, and Nalo Hopkinson, cultural critics Greg Tate, Mark Sinker, Kodwo Eshun, and Mark Dery, digital musicians Singe, Tricky, and Dr Octagon, visual artists Fatima Truggard, Keith Piper, and Hype Williams, and performance artists Rammelzee and Carlinhos Brown. Conspicuously absent from this mix are the engineers and scientists. For example, Philip Emeagwali, a Nigerian-American who received the 1989 Gordon Bell Prize (based on an application of the CM-2 massively-parallel computer for oil-reservoir modeling) takes a strongly historical approach, drawing on sources as diverse as the African origin of the Fibonacci sequence and the 1938 Risenkampf partial differential equations. If there is a downside to the Afrofuturist movement, it is the tendency to dwell too much in the imaginary spaces created by fiction and music, rather than work at fusing these domains with functional science and technology.

Miller points to Bob Powell, "African american physicist, philosopher, and architect who studied in west africa and who worked with NASA and [at 80 years] still has really interesting ideas on physics, music, and African and African American art" as one of the exceptions to this elision. Writing in *Black Noise*, Tricia Rose suggests a promising area for historical study in positing that many of the early innovations in computer graphics, such as morphing, were based on early hip-hop visual arts such as graffiti and breakdancing. Also promising are the small clusters of black scientists engineers in particular domains. In opto-electronics, for example, we find Earl D. Shaw (physicist, co-inventor of spin-flip laser), William R. Northover (chemical innovations for laser fiber optics), Thomas C. Cannon (mechanical innovations for fiber optic cables). One wonders if this is due to the "founder effect" (similar to immigrant neighborhoods in cultural geography); if so it speaks well for the Afrofuturist thesis that culture and technology can have collaborative results. More recently black computer engineers have become leading entrepreneurs; these include Clarity CEO Howard Smith, Vice Presidents Kenneth Coleman and Marc Hannah of Silicon Graphics, Myra Peterson, President of Omniverse Digital Solutions, and Dr. Glen Toney of Applied Materials.

The Politics of Information Technology: Black Web Networks

The celebration of the "cyborg" identity in recent pop culture representations, such as "Robocop," is an important warning to those who would see the Afrofuturists' contribution as purely one of "transgressing boundaries" or "bricollage." We now live in an era in which cyborg bricollage is no longer a shocking transgression, but rather a technique for computer programming and postindustrial labor management. Nor should we rely on the mimetic theory that "role models" of black achievement will counter problems in "self-esteem." What is significant for the Afrofuturist movement—artists and inventors alike—is the ability to reveal the relations of social power in the construction of technoscience. It is the ways in which this syncretism can politicize information technology that make Afrofuturism a powerful technocultural syncretism.

Perhaps the best case for such collaboration between African American cultural politics and information technology is the emergence of black web networks. The oldest of these is The Drum; launched in 1988 as an informal group of computer users it was a pioneer of Afrocentric on-line services. Another pioneer is Melanet, started 1989 by William and Rodney Jordan. Averaging 40,000 hits per month, it maintains a focus on black culture and spirituality. Net Noir, the largest commercial success, was started in 1995 by David Ellington and Malcom CasSelle. Averaging 120,000 hits per month, it includes web channels under the categories of Culture, Entertainment, News, Business and Politics, and Shopping. The separation of culture and entertainment categories is unusual for web organization, and reflects Net Noir's responsibility to black cultural issues; meanwhile the fusion of Business and Politics in to a single category reflects their emphasis on entrepreneurship as a means to black liberation. The City of New Elam network was started 1994 by Rey Harris and Stafford Battle. Averaging 2,000 hits per month, they have focused on introducing black-owned small business to the web. Perhaps the strongest commercial potential can be found in SOHH ("Support On-line Hip-Hop"): started in 1995 with Felicia Palmer and Steve Samuel as "cybermics," they are currently negotiating with Intel, CNET and Mediadome for on-line sales of music that could mount into the millions.

Conclusion

We began Barbara Christian's framework, which shifted the focus of literary analysis from theories of Black womens' writing to Black women writers' theories. Our technological translation of this calls for a change of strategy would shift the focus of political analysis from the attempts to devise a cybernetics of Black communities, to searching instead for the communities of Black cybernetics. Such histories of Black contribution and collaboration to information technologies are, we maintain, masked by the narrative of cyberliberation, the trucage of a culture-free technoscience. In examining this history of Black cybernetics we find that the invention of technology and cultural identity are deeply intertwined.

Bleecker (1995) described the ways in which the absence of race in the virtual game SimCity allows for "raceless" urban riots; one can see that the simulation parameters of heat, crime and unemployment are all related to the propensity for urban riots, but race itself does not exist as a simulation variable. But writing race back into SimCity—putting race back into our social accounts of information technology in general—means not just adding a pessimistic realism. We can seek sources of more positive confluence between the cultural capital of personal identity and the political economy of information technology in ways that offer reconfiguration and resistance.

Note

1. Ron Eglash and Julian Bleecker, "The Race for Cyberspace: Information Technology in the Black Diaspora," *Science as Culture* 10.3 (2001): 353–374.

References

Ansu-Kyeremeh, Kwasi. *Perspectives on Indigenous Communication in Africa*. NY: University Press of America 1998.

Aronson, Lisa. "Ijebu Yoruba Aso Olona: a contextual and historical overview." *African Arts*, vol XXV #3, pp. 52–57, July 1992.

Badaway, Alexandre. "Figurations egyptiennes a schema ondulatoire." *Chronique d'Egypte* 34(68) July 1959.

Bleecker, Julian. "Urban Crisis: past, present and virtual." Socialist Review 24, 189–221, 1995.

Blier, Susan Preston. *African Vodoun*. Chicago: Univ. of Chicago Press, 1995

Chernoff, John. *African Rhythm and African Sensibility*, U. Chic. Press, 1979.

Christian, Barbara. "The Race for Theory." *Contemporary postcolonial theory: a reader*. edited by Padmini Mongia. London; New York: Arnold; New York 1996.

Christian, Marcus. *Negro Ironworkers in Louisiana, 1718–1900*. Gretna: Pelican Publishing 1972.

Dery, Mark. "Black to the Future." in *Flame Wars: the discourse of cyberculture*. Durham" Duke University Press 1994.

Eglash, R. *African Fractals: modern computing and indigenous design*. New Brunswick: Rutgers University Press 1999.

Eglash, R. "Bamana sand divination: recursion in ethnomathematics." *American Anthropologist*, v99 n1, p. 112–122, March 1997a.

Eglash, R. "The African heritage of Benjamin Banneker." *Social Studies of Science*, v27 pp. 307–15, April 1997b.

Eglash, R. "African influences in cybernetics." in *The Cyborg Handbook*, Chris Gray (ed), NY: Routledge 1995.

Ellipsis Arts. *Angels in the Mirror: vodou music of Hati*. New York: Ellipsis Arts 1997.

Gates, H.L. *The Signifying Monkey*. Oxford: Oxford Univ Press 1988.

Gilroy, P. *The Black Atlantic*. Cambridge: Harvard U Press 1993.

Graves, Ralph A. "Lousianna, land of perpetual romance." *National Geographic Magazine*, LVII, pp. 443, 450 April 1930.

David Hess, *Science and Technology in a Multicultural World* (Columbia Univ. Press 1994).

Kozel, Susan. "Material Mapping: Review of Digital Dancing 1997." The Dance & Technology Zone (D&TZ), http://art.net/~dtz/kozel2.html, Dec 1997.

Manning, Kenneth R. *Black Apollo of science: the life of Ernest Everett Just*. New York: Oxford University Press, 1983.

Pollard, Alton B. "Tools of the Spirit." *African Impact on the Material Culture of the Americas*. Winston-Salem State University Conference proceedings, May 30—June 2, 1996.

Skinner, S. *Terrestrial Astrology*. London: Routledge & Kegan Paul 1980.

Swiderski, S. "Le symbolism du poteau central au Gabon." *Anthropologische Gesellschaft in Wien*, pp. 299–315, 1970.

Thompson, Robert Farris. *Flash of the spirit: African and Afro-American art and philosophy*. New York: Random House, 1983.

Trautmann, R. "La divination a la Cote des Esclaves et a Madagascar. Le Vodou—le Fa—le Sikidy," *Memoires de l'Institut Francais d'Afrique Noire*, no. 1, Larose, Paris, 1939.

Waller, Mary. *Chladni Figures: a study in symmetry*. London: Bell 1961.

Zaslavsky, Claudia. *Africa Counts*. Boston: Prindle, Weber & Schmidt. 1973.

Alondra Nelson

One of the central voices in Afrofuturism, this essay by Nelson helps readers interpret issues like alienation, subjectivity, agency, and futuristic notions of race and identity. Nelson's essay is also an instructive foreword for readers who explore the fiction of writers like Samuel Delany, Octavia Butler, Colson Whitehead, and Nalo Hopkinson. Nelson's essay also shows how Afrofuturistic approaches, which often mix African mythology, science fiction, fantasy, and the realities of the Black experience, provide for a more critical position for engaging in discussions about race and access to technology.

Introduction to "Future Texts"

Alondra Nelson[1]

We will make our own future Text.
   —Ishmael Reed, *Mumbo Jumbo*

and on to post now
post new
   —Amiri Baraka, "Time Factor a Perfect Non-Gap"

In popular mythology, the early years of the late-1990s digital boom were characterized by the rags-to-riches stories of dot-com millionaires and the promise of a placeless, raceless, bodiless near future enabled by technological progress. As more pragmatic assessments of the industry surfaced, so too did talk of the myriad inequities that were exacerbated by the information economy—most notably, the digital divide, a phrase that has been used to describe gaps in technological access that fall along lines of race, gender, region, and ability but has mostly become a code word for the tech inequities that exist between blacks and whites. Forecasts of a utopian (to some) race-free future and pronouncements of the dystopian digital divide are the predominant discourses of blackness and technology in the public sphere. What matters is less a choice between these two narratives, which fall into conventional libertarian and conservative frameworks, and more what they have in common: namely, the assumption that race is a liability in the twenty-first century—is either negligible or evidence of negligence. In these politics of the future, supposedly novel paradigms for understanding technology smack of old racial ideologies. In each scenario, racial identity, and blackness in particular, is the anti-avatar of digital life. Blackness gets constructed as always oppositional to technologically driven chronicles of progress.

   That race (and gender) distinctions would be eliminated with technology was perhaps the founding fiction of the digital age. The raceless future paradigm, an adjunct of Marshall McLuhan's "global village" metaphor, was widely supported by (and made strange bedfellows of) pop visionaries, scholars, and corporations from Timothy Leary to Allucquère Rosanne Stone to MCI. Spurred by "revolutions" in technoscience, social and cultural theorists looked increasingly to information technology, especially the Internet and the World Wide Web, for new paradigms. We might call this cadre of analysts and boosters of technoculture, who stressed the unequivocal novelty of identity in the digital age, neocritics. Seemingly working in tandem with corporate advertisers, neocritics argued that the information age ushered in a new era of subjectivity and insisted that in the future the body wouldn't bother us any longer. There was a peculiar capitalist logic to these claims, as if writers had taken up the marketing argot of "new and improved."

   There was also much that was familiar in this rhetoric. As rapturous proclamations of the Internet's ability to connect everyone, everywhere echoed the predictions that greeted the age of the telephone, so did neocriticism's imperative to embrace the new and transform the body fall neatly in line with older narratives of technology and forgetting—most notably, the futurism movement of the turn of the twentieth century. In 1909 Filippo Tommaso Marinetti, an Italian artist, published "The Foundation and Manifesto of Futurism," in which he called for a new aesthetic that could properly represent the sensation of living in a rapidly modernizing world. Marinetti glorified the creative destruction of war, exalted the beauty of "eternal, omnipresent speed," and promised to sing of the revolutionary potential of factories, shipyards, locomotives, and airplanes. He called for the end of the old, proclaiming, "But we want no part of it, the past, we the young and strong *Futurists!*"[2] In constructing his vision of the future, Marinetti implicitly evoked a subjectivity that was decidedly male, young, and carved out in relation to the past and the "feminine."

While neocriticism's take on identity tended more toward the glorification of the self's dissolving than its hardening, it was propelled by a similar impetus to understand the technological transformations that characterized the beginning of a new era. Technoevangelist Timothy Leary proclaimed that advances in technology augured the end of burdensome social identities. Out with those old categories from the social movements of the 1960s, in with the new. Leary predicted that "in the future, the methods of information technology, molecular engineering, biotechnology, nanotechnology (atom stacking), and quantum-digital programming could make the human form a matter totally determined by individual whim, style, and seasonal choice."[3] Leary's prediction was social science fiction, a rendering of the not-now, a possible future without a certain end but loaded with assumptions. He assumed that "ever-loosening physical constraints" would free us from our cumbersome bodies and imagined that in the future identity would be driven by the consumer imperatives of whim and choice. Technology offered a future of wholly new human beings—unfettered not only from the physical body but from past human experience as well. Leary presupposed that such freedom would be widely available and universally sought after. Yet as Andrew Ross cautioned, "radical humanism" of the sort Leary advocated would, by choice or circumstance, "only free a minority of humans."[4] Bodies carry different social weights that unevenly mediate access to the freely constructed identity that Leary advocated. To be sure, his theory is an extreme example of the neocriticism that characterizes much writing about the social impact of computer technology. And yet the spirit of Leary's discourse of disembodiment, which fit an unrelentingly progressive and libertarian vision of the future, became an important inspiration for theories of identity in the digital age.

For others, technological change was the catalyst for a transformation of conceptions of the self.[5] In the influential work *The War of Desire and Technology at the Close of the Mechanical Age*, Allucquère Rosanne Stone marshaled theory, observation, and fictionalized anecdote to describe the nature of contemporary identity. According to Stone, in the "virtual age" our awareness of the fragmented self is heightened by computer-mediated communication.[6] In crafting her argument, Stone was influenced by two theories of identity and multiplicity. One held that the decentered self is the reaction of the body/subject/citizen to absolute state power; by this logic, fragmented identity is an assertion of agency under a system of complete subjugation. Stone's argument was also informed by psychological literature on multiple personality disorders (MPDs), in which "split personalities" are explained as responses to violence, trauma, and other "less overt methods of subjection." In this model, manifold selves are understood as a tactic for negotiating forms of oppression.

Despite the grave implications of these hypotheses, Stone aspired to recoup such multiplicity as a practice of pleasure and desire. But in her rush to celebrate the possibilities opened up by computer technology, Stone overlooked the fact that, as Kalí Tal has suggested, over a century's worth of "sophisticated tools for the analysis of cyberculture" already existed in African American thought.[7] These extant theories, Tal insists, provide political and theoretical precedents for articulating and understanding "multiple identities, fragmented personae and liminality"—most notably W.E.B. DuBois's concept of double consciousness. They also "contradict the notion that the absence of the (illusion of) unitary self is something new": despite the easy proliferation of selves in the digital age, the flux of identity that Stone extolled has long been the experience of African diasporic people.

DuBois's double consciousness was not simply an uncritical assertion of multiple personalities but rather a dogged analysis of both the origins and stakes of this multiplicity. What falls by the wayside in Stone's analysis—and neocriticism more generally—is an appraisal of identity that does not simply look to what is seemingly new about the self in the "virtual age" but looks backward *and* forward in seeking to provide insights about identity, one that asks what was *and* what if. While Stone gives poignant witness to the ontology of multiplicity, she is less able to show how the dialectic between defining oneself in light of ties to one's history and experience and being defined from without (be it in virtual or physical space, by stereotypes or the state) determines the shape of computer-mediated aggregate identities as much or more than the leisurely flux of personality.

Like Leary's predictions, Stone's argument begged the question of who would be able to so easily cast aside identity and, moreover, what was at stake in doing so. While Stone is careful to maintain that there is indeed a link between virtual and physical selves, she nevertheless deploys an identity politics that privileges personality performance. Yet understanding the changing terrain of identity in the virtual age requires not only attention to the technical construction of selves over a distributed network but a sense of how multiplicity works to both deflect and buttress structures of power and an understanding of how selves are differently situated both within and outside of this network.

In contrast, the shifting ecology of racialization in the virtual age has been most thoroughly explored in the scholarship of Lisa Nakamura. Nakamura's analyses of sci-fi films, technology advertisements, and identity tourism in MUDs and MOOs have offered counterpoints to the often hidden racial ideologies of the information era.[8] In a study of late-1990s ads for computer companies, Nakamura explored how the promise of a liberated world of tomorrow, free of the cumbersome weight of racial identity, is proliferated by corporations in television commercials and print advertising—most memorably in a 1997 commercial for MCI entitled "Anthem," which pronounced that there was no age, gender, or race on the Internet. Nakamura examined how several corporations deployed images of people of color, often in "exotic" locales, to sell their wares; yet these representations were merely colorful backdrops to commercial disavowals of racial difference. As Nakamura explained: "The iconography of these advertising images demonstrates that the corporate image factory *needs* images of the Other in order to depict its product: a technological utopia of difference. It is not however, a utopia *for* the Other or one that includes it in any meaningful or progressive way. Rather, it proposes an ideal world of virtual social and cultural reality based on specific methods of 'Othering.'"[9]

One such method of "othering" was the ads' use of imagery of exotic people and places, emancipated from past histories and contemporary sociopolitical context. As Nakamura observed, "ethnic difference in the world of Internet advertising is visually 'cleansed' of its divisive, problematic, tragic connotations. The ads function as corrective texts for readers deluged with images of racial conflicts and bloodshed both at home and abroad. These advertisements put the world right." The experiences of the people depicted were rendered negligible or, in Nakamura's words, "made 'not to count,' through technology."[10]

Public discourse about race and technology, led by advertisers (and aided and abetted by cybertheorists), was preoccupied with the imagined new social arrangements that might be made possible by technological advance. Advertisers relied on a shared message about race and ethnicity—the disappearance of the DuBoisian "color line"—to promote their products.

Nakamura's study elucidated how centrally race figures in contemporary narratives of technology, even in its (putative) absence. Representations of race and ethnicity created a cognitive dissonance in tech advertising; dissimilitude was slyly neutralized but never fully erased, for this alterity was necessary to the ideology of the technology being sold.

If the ads scrutinized by Nakamura can be said to reflect the high-tech, raceless promised land (and its internal inconsistencies), a recent South African ad for Land Rover illuminates the stakes of the other predominant discourse of race and technology, the digital divide. The ad, which ran in popular magazines in South Africa, depicts a Himba woman from Namibia in traditional attire. Much like an image from *National Geographic* (Nakamura makes a similar observation regarding the advertisements she discussed), the woman is shown bare-breasted. She stands alone in the desert, her only companion the latest model of the Land Rover Freelander, speedily departing. The force of the vehicle's back draft as it accelerates pulls her breasts toward it. Her "feminine primitiveness" and the slick silver veneer of the sport-utility vehicle are in sharp contrast; the Freelander rapidly heads toward the future, leaving her in the past. In this single image, we are presented with a visual metaphor for the ostensible oppositionality of race (primitive past) and technology (modern future) that is the most cutting side of the double-edged concept of the digital divide.[11]

If a sport-utility vehicle leaves people of African descent literally blowing in the wind, then the information age surely comes on like a tornado. Though meant to draw attention to true disparities, the well-meant concept of the digital divide is Janus-faced: there are indeed critical gaps in technological access and computer literacy that are comprehensible through the prisms of race, gender, socioeconomics, region, and age. Nonetheless, this paradigm is frequently reduced to race alone and thus falls all too easily in stride with preconceived ideas of black technical handicaps and "Western" technological superiority. Like the Himba woman left eating the dust of technology, the underlying assumption of much digital divide rhetoric is that people of color, and African Americans in particular, cannot keep pace with our high-tech society.

The digital divide paradigm obscures the fact that uneven access to technology is a symptom of economic inequalities that predate the Arpanet (the prototype of the Internet) and the World Wide Web.[12] Moreover, this "myth of black disingenuity with technology," to borrow a phrase from historian of science and medicine Evelynn Hammonds, does not account for the centrality of black people's labor in modernization and industrialization as well as the historical truths of black participation in technological development.[13] Examples of such participation include the contributions of inventor Garret Morgan, who invented the traffic light in 1923; the vernacular chemistry of Madame C. J. Walker, who created a multimillion-dollar black beauty business; the creation of the Lingo computer language by programmer John Henry Thompson; and pioneering music production techniques.[14]

The racialized digital divide narrative that circulates in the public sphere and the bodiless, color-blind mythotopias of cybertheory and commercial advertising have become the unacknowledged frames of reference for understanding race in the digital age. In these frameworks, the technologically enabled future is by its very nature unmoored from the past and from people of color. Neocritical narratives suggest that it is primitiveness or outmodedness, the obsolescence of something or someone else, that confirms the novel status of the virtual self, the cutting-edge product, or the high-tech society.

Post New

As Kalí Tal maintains, African diasporic history contains a wealth of theoretical paradigms that turn the reified binary between blackness and technology on its head, readily lending themselves to the task of constructing adequate frames of reference for contemporary theories of technoculture. From the early model of fractured consciousness offered by W.E.B. DuBois to the fractal patterns found in West African architecture, examples of black cultural prefigurations of our contemporary moment abound.[15]

For the purposes of this essay, Ishmael Reed's acclaimed 1972 novel *Mumbo Jumbo* offers particularly fertile ground. The novel, which took the form of a detective story, was less a who-dunit than an epistemological mystery. *Mumbo Jumbo* details one episode of an ongoing contest between the JGC's—the carriers of "jes grew," the meme of African diasporic culture—and the Atonists, supporters of the "Western civilization" mythology of world history. The novel's plot centers around competing efforts to encourage and restrain the itinerant cultural virus, "jes grew."

Reed has used the word *necromancy* to describe his project as a writer, defining it as "us[ing] the past to explain the present and to prophesize about the future."[16] Reed's understanding of a usable past runs counter to the futurism of the early twentieth century. Russian poet Kasimir Malevich described futurism as a way to pull oneself out of "the catacombs into the speed of our time. I affirm that whoever has not trod the path of Futurism as the exponent of modern life, is condemned to crawl for ever among the ancient graves and feed on the crusts of the past."[17] For Reed, on the other hand, the catacombs are not an archaic, occult place to be left behind for the clean light of modern science and technology but rather the gateway to a more complete understanding of the future. "Necromancers used to lie in the guts of the dead or in the tombs to receive visions of the future. That is prophecy. The black writer lies in the guts of old America, making readings about the future," he explained.[18] With this definition of necromancy, Reed presented a temporal orientation that seem to contradict discourses of the future predicated on either ignoring the past or rendering it as staid and stagnant. Unlike neocritics, Reed conjured "readings" of a living past, retained in the present and carried into the future.

The "jes grew" of *Mumbo Jumbo* is perhaps the best example of this. Reed borrows this phrase from civil rights activist and cultural theorist James Weldon Johnson, who used it to describe the proliferation of ragtime songs, commenting that they "jes grew" (or just grew). In the novel, "jes grew" refers to African diasporic cultures that live and evolve in the forms of gesture, music, dance, visual culture, epistemology, and language, crossing geography and generations by mov-ing from carrier to carrier and thus threatening the knowledge monopoly of the "West": " 'Jes Grew' traversed the land in search of its Text: the lost liturgy seeking its litany. Its words, chants held in bondage by the mysterious Order . . . . Jes Grew needed its words to tell its carriers what it was up to. Jes Grew was an influence which sought its text, and whenever it thought it knew the location of its words and Labanotations it headed in that direction."[19] The missing text, which originated in ancient Africa, represents the opportunity to encode African diasporic vernacular culture and create a tangible repository of black experience.

Throughout the novel, PaPa LaBas—the novel's protagonist, spiritual detective, and pro-prietor of the Mumbo Jumbo Kathedral, a HooDoo holistic health-gathering place—tracks "jes grew" as it seeks its text. Toward the novel's end, having discovered that the text has been destroyed, PaPa LaBas optimistically predicts, "We will make our own future Text. A future gen-eration of young artists will accomplish this." At first take, this statement seems to fall in line with the utopian aspirations of contemporary neocriticism. Yet LaBas is no unsophisticated booster of the new: this forecast is a vision of the future that is purposely inflected with tradi-tion. Rather than despair when he finds out that the Text has been destroyed, LaBas believes that the next generation will be successful in creating a text that can codify black culture: past, pres-ent, and future. Rather than a "Western" image of the future that is increasingly detached from the past or, equally problematic, a future-primitive perspective that fantasizes an uncomplicated return to ancient culture, LaBas foresees the distillation of African diasporic experience, rooted in the past but not weighed down by it, contiguous yet continually transformed.

The "anachronism" that is an element of much of Reed's work is used to express a unique perspective on time and tradition. This effect is achieved in his writing through what he terms "synchronizing": "putting disparate elements into the same time, making them run in the same time, together."[20] Such an approach is characteristic of how technology works in *Mumbo Jumbo*. Reed's synchronous model defies the progressive linearity of much recent technocultural criticism. As Sämi Ludwig has observed, technologies exist independently of time in the novel; though it is set in the 1920s, the story contains references to technologies that will not be readily available until years later.[21] For example, Ludwig notes that a leader of the Wall Flower Order, the military arm of the Atonists, made use of video and television to monitor the progress of "jes grew" from his headquarters. In this case, technologies from the setting's future and the author's present inhabit a story situated in the past.

Reed's synchronicity extends to the placement of obsolete technologies in the present. Though not hardware as such, a communication technique called "knockings" is used by PaPa LaBas to receive information from beyond. Ludwig likens the "knockings" to radio waves; they could also be sensory perceptions, premonitions, or communiqués from the past that live through those who, like LaBas, continue to make use of them.[22] (Importantly, Reed does not pit his protagonists against other forms of technology. LaBas also makes use of hardware like his Kathedral radio, and a multicultural gang in the novel, the Mu'tafikah, which repatriates artworks to their countries of origin, employs dictaphones in its campaign.)[23] Reed might be said to use synchronicity to reprioritize technologies. Like his critique of the dominant mythos of "Western civ," his anachronistic use of technology in *Mumbo Jumbo* begs the question of what tools are valued by whom, and to what ends. With his innovative novel as an exemplar, Ishmael Reed has supplied a paradigm for an African diasporic technoculture.

Afrofuturism

The contributions to this issue are perhaps those "future texts" hoped for by Papa LaBas in Reed's *Mumbo Jumbo*. The text and images gathered here reflect African diasporic experience and at the same time attend to the transformations that are the by-product of new media and information technology. They excavate and create original narratives of identity, technology, and the future and offer critiques of the promises of prevailing theories of technoculture. In addition, these contributions, gathered under the term *Afrofuturism*, offer takes on digital culture that do not fall into the trap of the neocritics or the futurists of one hundred years past. These works represent new directions in the study of African diaspora culture that are grounded in the histories of black communities, rather than seeking to sever all connections to them.

Many of the essays in this collection grew out of the relationships formed in an on-line community called Afrofuturism that I founded in the fall of 1998, and many of them expand, deploy, and take up the themes first discussed there. Afrofuturism can be broadly defined as "African American voices" with "other stories to tell about culture, technology and things to come."[24] The term was chosen as the best umbrella for the concerns of "the list"—as it has come to be known by its members—"sci-fi imagery, futurist themes, and technological innovation in the African diaspora."[25] The AfroFuturism listserv began as a project of the arts collective apogee with the goal of initiating dialogue that would culminate in a symposium called AfroFuturism | Forum.[26] Besides the community of thinkers, artists, and writers that has formed and been sustained through the listserv, perhaps its most meaningful function has been as an incubator of ideas.

The AfroFuturism list emerged at a time when it was difficult to find discussions of technology and African diasporic communities that went beyond the notion of the digital divide. From the beginning, it was clear that there was much theoretical territory to be explored. Early discussions included the concept of digital double consciousness; African diasporic cultural retentions in modern technoculture; digital activism and issues of access; dreams of designing technology based on African mathematical principles; the futuristic visions of black film, video, and music; the implications of the then-burgeoning MP3 revolution; and the relationship between feminism and Afrofuturism.

The contributors to this volume approach their themes from several angles: as unique analytical frameworks for interpreting black cultural production, as imagery of the near-future, as poetry. Essays by Alexander G. Weheliye and Ron Eglash consider identities of the digital age. With "'Feenin': Posthuman Voices in Contemporary Black Popular Music," Weheliye reimagines one of the most vaunted contemporary social categories, that of the posthuman. Resisting a single totalizing elaboration of posthumanity that is remarkably yet unsurprisingly similar to the Western liberal subject, Weheliye turns away from preoccupations with the ocular (in the form of the iconography of the computer screen and the spectacle of visually apparent prosthetic posthumanity) in favor of the aurality and orality of R&B music. Weheliye recoups contemporary R&B as a witness to African diasporic life that articulates human longings and at the same time reveals how these longings are mediated by technologies. The vocoder is an example of this particular conjunction of "man" and machine: "a speech-synthesizing device that renders the human voice robotic," producing an "audibly machinic black voice" that amplifies questions of race and technology. Weheliye offers a theory of digital age subjectivity centered around the encoding of black diasporic forms in terms of the new technologies that contribute to the daily realities of black life.

Ron Eglash reconfigures another hardwired persona of the digital age, that of the nerd or geek. Eglash argues that during a time when hackers with business made inroads in the halls of power, access to geek identity may perhaps smooth the path to influence and capital. In his essay "Race, Sex, and Nerds: From Black Geeks to Asian American Hipsters," Eglash traces the racial, gendered, and sexual identities that have adhered to the figure of the nerd. The typically white male nerd, Eglash argues, eked out a representational space between "primitivism," which cast people of African descent as oversexed and "closer to nature" than culture, and "orientalism," which stereotyped people of Asian descent as "undersexualized," overly abstract thinkers. Given that geek identity is carved out in opposition to other racial and gender myths, Eglash considers whether the appropriation of nerd identity can be a politically efficacious means of gaining technocultural capital.

While the benefits of black nerd identity may be debatable, African diasporic technophilia has a long history, according to Anna Everett. In her essay "The Revolution Will Be Digitized," Everett argues that the African diaspora that resulted from chattel slavery encouraged, long before the term became chic, "self-sustaining virtual communities through paralinguistic and transnational communicative systems" that sustained a "diasporic consciousness." She claims that the networked consciousness of the African diaspora of necessity prefigured the network consciousness often hailed as one of the benefits of the Internet. She maintains that this community consciousness persists "in cyberspace and the digital age." According to Everett, even as the rhetoric of the digital divide prevailed, 1995 was a "watershed moment" for black connectivity, evidence of a "black technolust" that belied the prevailing narratives about race and technology in the public sphere. Everett believes that African diasporic communities in cyberspace offer the opportunity for fostering the black public sphere and for strengthening the links of the African diaspora using information technology as a tool of activism and social cohesion.

For Kalí Tal in "That Just Kills Me," the "information revolution" provides inspiration to reconsider existing texts as counternarratives to the futurism of neocriticism. Tal reflects on black militant near-future fiction of the nineteenth and twentieth centuries. Among the generic characteristics of what she identifies as a distinct subgenre of cautionary tales are a utopian vision that is actualized through violence and the decimation of the white population, secret societies, and alternative uses of technology. In the works she discusses, the near future is a utopia in which blacks free themselves from the constraints of racism; the racist past and present are dystopic. This work begs the question of how social utopias might be variously imagined and how the past and present shape what we imagine as a positive future. Tal asserts that the writings she discusses by Sutton Griggs, George Schuyler, John A. Williams, and Chester Himes reveal a little-known history of African American futurism that both provides another lens for interpreting black literature and sets compelling precedents for the more widely known black science fiction that has emerged in the past forty years.

Novelist Nalo Hopkinson is an heir apparent to this tradition of literary speculation. She presents her own visions of the future in her critically acclaimed fiction, which is an exemplar of the living past that Ishmael Reed advocates. Hopkinson writes speculative fiction, mixing fantasy, horror, and science fiction with African mythology, spirituality, and culture. Noting that many of the metaphors of science and science fiction are derived from ancient Greek and Roman language origins, including the words *cyborg* and *telephone*, Hopkinson contemplates what words a "largely African diasporic culture might build, what stories its people might tell themselves about technology."[27] In the interview "Making the Impossible Possible," Hopkinson discusses how she writes speculative fiction that incorporates diverse African traditions. With her contributions, "Afro-Future—Dystopic Unity," "Mother Earth," and "Vertical," poet Tracie Morris offers elegiac reflections on "Western" science and technology. With this verse, Morris, a well-known performance poet and published writer, forges new directions with poetic language. She is less than sanguine about technoscience—each poem conjures the affect of loss and deception—linking it not to the promise of bright new futures but to biological abominations, genocidal campaigns, and environmental catastrophe.

The imagery of Tana Hargest and Fatimah Tuggar relies on digital-age tools to create visual speculation. Tuggar employs digital photomontage to construct a collision of time, place, and culture in a manner reminiscent of Ishmael Reed's synchronicity. Her images of northern Nigerian women in their everyday lives, using technologies both new and arcane, convey complex, often conflicting messages. Working with scale and color contrast, Tuggar hopes that the viewer will be conscious of, in the words of one reviewer, "the constructed nature of all images of Africa," in particular the continent's usual representation as an outmoded region, the opposite of what is modern and high-tech.[28] At first glance, Tuggar's cut-and-paste images seem to depict Nigerian women as victims of modern technology and Western imperialism, yet they ultimately reveal women as agents of technoculture. Placing traditional and more recent technologies on the same plane, Tuggar wants the viewer to understand them as tools that may have more in common than we think.

Tana Hargest uses computer-aided design technology to draw insights into the dilemmas of black life after the civil rights movement. Taking niche marketing to its speculative extreme, Hargest's project is a corporation, of which she is the CEO, called Bitter Nigger Inc. (BNI) that creates lifestyle products for African Americans living within the gilded cage of the color-blind aspirations of the information age. As she details in the letter to shareholders, BNI is comprised of several divisions, with one devoted to pharmaceuticals. The clever products developed by the pharmaceutical wing of BNI parody drugs like Claritin and Celebrex, the ads for which promise their own version of chemically enhanced utopia. In a manner reminiscent of George Schuyler's satirical novel *Black No More*, each BNI product identifies a "social problem" and offers a product as remedy; yet all have side effects. It isn't such a far leap from pharmacogenomics, the promise of drugs tailored for specific populations made possible by the coding of the human genome,[29] to Hargest's Tominex, a pill that helps the "buppie" consumer to "get along to go along." (The catch being that the pill is so big that in attempting to swallow the product/concept the consumer will choke.) Another product, "the Enforcer," is a behavior-correcting microchip implanted in whites that works to curb racism. The Big Brother aspect of this technology would seem to place it squarely in a dystopic world but, similar to the fiction that Kalí Tal discusses, this surveillance chip promises a utopian world in which racism is curtailed.

Notes

1. Alondra Nelson, "Future Texts," *Social Text* 20.2 (2002): 1–15.
2. Filippo Tommaso Marinetti, "The Foundation and Manifesto of Futurism," in *Art in Theory, 1900–1990: An Anthology of Changing Ideas*, ed. Charles Harrison and Paul Wood (Oxford: Blackwell, 1992), 148.
3. Timothy Leary and Eric Gullichsen, "High-Tech Paganism," in *Chaos and Cyber Culture* (Berkeley, Calif.: Ronin, 1994), 236.
4. Andrew Ross, "The New Smartness," in *Culture on the Brink: Ideologies of Technology*, ed. Gretchen Bender and Timothy Druckery (Seattle: Bay, 1994), 335. For a further critique of this type of post-humanity, see Alexander G. Weheliye's contribution to this issue, " 'Feenin': Posthuman Voices in Contemporary Black Popular Music."
5. See also Sherry Turkle, *Life on the Screen: Identity in the Age of the Internet* (New York: Simon and Schuster, 1995) and Brenda Laurel, *Computers As Theatre* (New York: Addison-Wesley, 1995).
6. Allucquère Rosanne Stone, *The War of Desire and Technology at the Close of the Mechanical Age* (Cambridge: MIT Press, 1996), 36.
7. My critique of Stone's argument draws on insights provided by Kalí Tal, who makes a similar challenge to Sherry Turkle. See Kalí Tal, "The Unbearable Whiteness of Being: African American Critical Theory and Cyberculture," www.kalital.com/Text/Writing/Whitenes.html.
8. Lisa Nakamura, " 'Where Do You Want to Go Today?': Cybernetic Tourism, the Internet, and Transnationality," in *Race in Cyberspace*, ed. Beth E. Kolko, Lisa Nakamura, and Gilbert B. Rodman (New York: Routledge, 2000), 15–26; Lisa Nakamura, "Race In/For Cyberspace: Identity Tourism and Racial Passing on the Internet," *Works and Days* (spring/fall 1995). *MUD* is an acronym for "multi-user domain" and *MOO* for "MUD, object-oriented." Both are virtual spaces or communities in which a participant choses an avatar or virtual character or assumes another identity. In her study of LambdaMOO, Nakamura observes that participants who chose a "race" as part of their identity profile were subject to accusations of introducing "politics" into the virtual space. See "Race In/For Cyberspace: Identity Tourism and Racial Passing on the Internet," www.English.iup.edu/publications/works&days/index.html.
9. Nakamura, " 'Where Do You Want to Go Today?' " 25 (emphasis in original).
10. Ibid., 21–22, 16.
11. Unfortunately, Land Rover of South Africa (now a division of the Ford Motor Company) would not grant permission for the reproduction of the advertisement referred to here. For more information about this controversial ad and to view the image, see *Adbusters*, no. 34 (March—April 2001): 38. It also appeared in "Bust in the Wind," *Harpers*, no. 1815 (August 2001): 23.
12. Alondra Nelson, "Braving the New World—AfroFuturism: Beyond the Digital Divide," in *Race and Public Policy*, ed. Makani Themba (Oakland, Calif.: Applied Research Center, 2000): 37–40.
13. Evelynn Hammonds, interview with author, 23 April 2001, Cambridge, Mass.
14. James C. Williams, *At Last, Recognition in America: A Reference Handbook of Unknown Black Inventors and Their Contribution to America* (Chicago: B.C.A., 1978), 1:27–28. For more on John Thompson, see www.lingoworks.com. See Tricia Rose, *Black Noise: Rap Music and Black Culture in Contemporary America* (Hanover, N.H.: University Press of New England, 1994), esp. chap. 3.
15. Ron Eglash, *African Fractals: Modern Computing and Indigenous Design* (New Brunswick, N.J.: Rutgers University Press, 1999).
16. Ishmael Reed, interview by Gaga [Mark S. Johnson], in *Conversations with Ishmael Reed*, ed. Bruce Dick and Amritjit Singh (Jackson: University Press of Mississippi, 1995), 51.
17. Kasimir Malevich, "From Cubism and Futurism to Suprematism: The New Realism in Painting," in Harrison and Wood, *Art in Theory*, 169.
18. John O'Brien, "Ishmael Reed," in Dick and Singh, *Conversations with Ishmael Reed*, 16.
19. Ishmael Reed, *Mumbo Jumbo* (1972; reprint, New York: Scribner, 1996), 211.
20. *Conversations with Ishmael Reed*, 53.
21. Sämi Ludwig, *Concrete Language: Intercultural Communication in Maxine Hong Kingston's "The Warrior Woman" and Ishmael Reed's "Mumbo Jumbo"* (New York: Peter Lang, 1996), 320.
22. Ludwig, *Concrete Language*, 319.

23. Ibid.
24. The term *Afro-futurism* was coined by Mark Dery in 1993 in an introductory essay that accompanied an interview with cultural critics Tricia Rose and Greg Tate and theorist and sci-fi writer Samuel Delany. See "Black to the Future: Interviews with Samuel R. Delany, Greg Tate, and Tricia Rose," in "Flame Wars: The Discourse of Cyberculture," ed. Mark Dery, *South Atlantic Quarterly* 94.4 (1993): 735–78; quotation at 738. Though this catchall term was first used by Dery in 1993, the currents that comprise it existed long before. See Kowdo Eshun, "Motion Capture (Interview)," in *More Brilliant Than the Sun: Adventures in Sonic Fiction*, 175–93 (London: Quartet, 1998). An extensive list of Afrofuturist resources has been compiled by Kalí Tal at www.afrofuturism.net.
25. This phrase is taken from my description of the listserv, which can be found at www.groups.yahoo.com/group/afrofuturism.
26. The focus of the listserv was initially on science fiction metaphors and technocultural production in the African diaspora and expanded from there into a freewheeling discussion of any and all aspects of contemporary black life. A series of moderators—including Paul D. Miller, Nalo Hopkinson, Ron Eglash, and David Goldberg—gave generously of their time and energy in periodically setting themes for the list to consider in the first year of its existence. Now three years old and still going strong, the AfroFuturism list continues to evolve: recent moderators have included Sheree Renee Thomas and Alexander Weheliye.

    Organized by Alondra Nelson, AfroFuturism | Forum, "a critical dialogue on the future of black cultural production," was held at New York University on 18 September 1999 as part of the Downtown Arts Festival. This project was made possible by assistance from the Peter Norton Family Foundation as well as the American Studies and Africana Studies programs at NYU. The panels focused on various aspects of African diasporic digital culture. Participants included Beth Coleman, Kodwo Eshun, Leah Gilliam, Jennie C. Jones, Raina Lampkins-Fielder, Kobena Mercer, Tracie Morris, Erika Dalya Muhammad, Alondra Nelson, Simon Reynolds, Tricia Rose, Franklin Sirmans, and Reggie Cortez Woolery.
27. "Filling the Sky with Islands: An Interview with Nalo Hopkinson," www.space.com/sciencefiction/books/hopkinson_intv_000110.html.
28. Amanda Carlson, "Amongst and Between Culture: The Art of Fatimah Tuggar," unpublished essay, 1999.
29. "This Heart Drug Is Designed for African Americans," *Business Week*, 26 March 2001.

Bruce Sinclair

Sinclair shows the necessity of developing new paradigms for exploring African American technology. He argues that technology is often the product of political, ideological, and economic interest, and these determine how we measure technological invention. Given that African Americans were denied access to the legal system in 1865 and could not file for patents, inventions by slaves would ordinarily be excluded from public celebration of American ingenuity. By moving beyond mainstream values, such as invention and progress, the contributions of African Americans in technical and creative areas become more evident for study. Conceiving of technology in much more broad terms also provides new insights into the role of technology and material culture by African Americans in and across American society.

Integrating the Histories of Race and Technology

Bruce Sinclair[1]

This volume brings together two subjects strongly connected but long segregated from each other. The history of race in America has been written as if technologies scarcely existed, and the history of technology as if it were utterly innocent of racial significance. Neither of these assumptions bears scrutiny. Indeed, in both cases the very opposite is true; an ancient and pervasive set of bonds links their histories. But there is little by way of an established literature that directly explores this relationship, nor a body of teaching that unites the two subjects. So we must begin the project of constructing a joint history by re-thinking our own assumptions, by borrowing useful ideas from related fields of scholarship, and by selecting examples of method and subject matter that promise fruitful lines of investigation—and in that fashion lay a groundwork. That is why this book is subtitled "Needs and Opportunities for Study." Its goal is simply to open up the topic for further exploration.

There are reasons why the past we seek to reveal has been so long denied, and racial prejudice dominates all of them. But more particularly, perceptions about inventiveness, presentations in our history about the nation-building role of technological talent, and the disciplinary boundaries between the fields of study themselves—as well as the politics that drove their own development—have all served to mask reality, and they are among the issues I want to consider in this introductory essay. A good place to start is with our oldest, most obvious attitudes. White Americans, including those as committed to Enlightenment ideals as Thomas Jefferson—even as he corresponded with Benjamin Banneker, the African-American astronomer and almanac maker—believed the black people among them were mentally inferior, and by that they didn't just mean a capacity for advanced intellectual accomplishment.[2] What good would freedom be, one Southern planter put it, to a field hand whose highest faculties were taxed "to discriminate between cotton and crop-grass, and to strike one with a hoe without hitting the other"?[3] Crude preconceptions of mental inferiority went well beyond simple tool using to include almost any aptitude for technological competence, and these notions flowered in the basic conditions of forced servitude. Owners linked the supposed endurance for hard, menial labor to brutish intelligence, and then justified enslavement on the grounds of such limited capacities. Besides that casual kind of rationalization, a substantial eighteenth-century literature invidiously compared African and other non-Western civilizations in terms of their relative backwardness in science and technology, making it easy for Europeans and Americans to take it as given that inventive talent was not to be found in any people of color.[4]

The idea that technical competence was related to race grew even more fixed with time. Even in the relatively tolerant city of Philadelphia, the Franklin Institute, established in 1824 explicitly to encourage the development of the mechanic arts, refused to allow blacks to attend lectures or classes. As Nina Lerman shows in her essay in this volume, the city's educational institutions increasingly planned occupations for its black students that required only minimal training. The great industrial expositions of the latter part of the nineteenth century made the same point graphically in the contrasts they drew between exhibits of the savagery of the dark-skinned peoples of the world and the brilliant flowering of civilized progress epitomized in Chicago's 1893 "White City."[5] But rather than simply the shell or emblem of racist thinking, defining African-Americans as technically incompetent and then—in a kind of double curse—denying them access to education, control over complex machinery, or the power of patent rights lay at the heart of the distinctions drawn between black and white people in this country. That formulation always served important political, economic, and social functions, and it is fundamentally why race and technology have for such a long time seemed different, even immiscible, categories of analysis. Racism may have colored all our history, but it whitened the national narrative.

Now, without looking very hard, we can see that this deeply ingrained and long perpetuated myth of black disingenuity has been a central element in attempts to justify slavery, as well as a whole array of racialized behaviors in the centuries after emancipation. But we are still left to wonder why scholars haven't stepped in with a more critically satisfying analysis of the relation between race and technology. The answer to that question lies at least partly in the evolution of the disciplines most concerned with those subjects.

In the United States, the history of technology emerged on a wave of post-World War II technological enthusiasm and economic ebullience. Perhaps naturally, it took on a celebratory character, emphasizing a triumphant technics, and Cold War politics reinforced that tendency. This kind of attention to great men and technological progress drove research into rather limited and exclusive channels that centered on big capital, complex technologies, and the small fragment of the population acting on that narrow stage. Inevitably, it dismissed all those who, to use Carroll Pursell's apt language, "were effectively barred by law, habit, and social expectation from the design and development stages of technical praxis."[6] It was a tale, in other words, of advantage and the successes that flowed from it.

This essentially conservative approach had its own theory. Brooke Hindle, one of the field's early spokesmen, claimed that there was a deep, interior logic to technology, crucial to the understanding of its meaning, and accessible only through rigorous study of its internal complexities.[7] That position argued the need for technical as well as historical training, and more selectively defined who and what was worth study. It took a new generation of historians to realize that technology is as much about process as about product, and that its history legitimately comprises the field as well as the factory, the home as well as the engineering site.

George Washington Williams published his *History of the Negro Race in America from 1619 to 1880* in 1882, though most people would date the origins of African-American history as a discipline to Carter Woodson's founding of the Association for the Study of Negro Life and History in 1915.[8] Still, it was not until the 1960s that African-American Studies became established in the academy, largely as a consequence of the civil rights movement and the research of a group of historians who wrote out of strong ideological conviction. The field that emerged continued a tradition of writing about race relations, implicitly if not explicitly, as a basis for political action. As it matured, however, scholars produced increasingly complex and subtle conceptual frameworks for analyzing race, including new understandings of agency—the ways in which men and women shape their own lives, even under disadvantageous circumstances.

These theoretical advances in both fields now open the way for an enriched history of technology and for new insights into the role of technology in African-American life. We have learned for a certainty that race is not a fixed, immutable concept—that definitions of who is white and who is black have changed with time, place, and circumstance. That technology is also a product of interest—political and ideological as well as economic—is also now widely accepted as an analytical point of departure. And we can begin to see that these subjects are more tightly connected than we imagined. Technology has long been an important element in the formation of racial identity in America. Whiteness and technological capability, Susan Smulyan points out, were usually seen as "natural" parts of each other, and as fundamental elements of masculinity.[9] By the end of the nineteenth century, these ideas had found widespread acceptance in such best-selling novels as *Trail of the Lonesome Pine* and *The Winning of Barbara Worth*, each subsequently made into a movie that featured a rugged, intelligent, problem-solving white engineer as the leading male character. An opposite calculus—the imputation of foolish incompetence in blacks, and thus the want of a key ingredient for independent manhood—found equally widespread acceptance. How and why these constructions were framed and how they interact thus becomes not just a good object of study, but a critical one.

There is a very reasonable argument to be made for the proposition that all discussions of race should go beyond the simple juxtaposition of black and white, and this is certainly true in the case of technology. But there is an equally persuasive logic for starting with African-Americans—because they are the classic American minority group, because they have been the focus of most American civil rights efforts, and because in their case American ideals of justice and equity are most specifically at issue.[10]

Yet, even with an enhanced appreciation of the complexities of these subjects and of their interrelatedness, we need also to be reminded that, although archival holdings and museum collections influence what historians study, people also make choices about what history gets written. Until feminist scholars created the analytical tools that revealed the women who had been there all along, historians could hardly imagine their existence.[11] Similarly, until very recently few historians have sought analytical tools that might link the study of African-Americans and technology. Just as it took new approaches to put women back into the story of America, so we now seek the means to write blacks back into the history of American technology.

To conceive such tools, we need to start not with African-Americans but with the ways in which white Americans have represented themselves. From the eighteenth century on, white Americans described themselves as an inventive people. They claimed to have a natural disposition for quick and novel solutions to the practical problems of life. That is what "Yankee ingenuity" meant—a self-attached label, applied early on.[11] And that distinct image, explicitly and repeatedly articulated over the next two centuries, was ideologically linked to the exploitation of the continent's natural resources as well as to the historic destiny white Americans imagined to be the just consequence of their political experiment. Democratic ideals would triumph by releasing the people's energies, and they would prosper by exploiting the resources that had been given them.

But that romantic vision was always framed in racial terms. European-Americans almost never considered the Africans among them, whether enslaved or enfranchised, to be capable of creative technical thought—and they translated that difference into an explicit point of contrast. Hundreds of examples illustrate that conviction, but they are all summed up in the sarcasm of a Massachusetts lawyer in a patent case when he said "I never knew a negro to invent anything but lies."[12]

And even as colonial newspaper advertisements by the hundreds described the considerable craft skills of runaways, plantation owners insisted that enslaved Africans broke or misused their tools because they could not understand how to use them, not as deliberate acts of resistance.[13]

More than that, Ron Takaki points out, technology was perceived as the means by which people of color throughout the United States—African, Native American, Hispanic, and Asian—were to be subordinated to the grander purposes of American civilization.[14] All down these long decades, white, Anglo-Saxon, Protestant Americans made technology and the capacity for its skillful management central both to the task of nation-building and to the way they represented themselves. Just as plainly, they contrasted themselves to people of color, whom they judged incapable of such things. That's what Toni Morrison means by "Africanism," an explicit kind of marginalization against which privileged status can be defined.[15]

Our history with technology, then, has always been entangled in ideas about race. But the curious consequence is that we have written that history blind to color—as if accepting all those earlier assumptions about who was inventive and who was not, as if the ways in which a people thought about and used technologies were essentially irrelevant. This limited kind of understanding is currently under attack. The work of Takaki, Robert Rydell, and Michael Adas reveals the extent to which our historic concepts of technology and of our own technological prowess have been infused by racial ideology.[16] Even *Technology and Culture*—the principal journal on the history of technology—has started publishing articles that explicitly engage the issue of race and technology. One example, reprinted here, shows how rice cultivation in South Carolina and Georgia depended on knowledge brought to those places by enslaved Africans. We already knew from Peter Wood's work that lowland South Carolina planters preferred slaves from the rice-growing regions of Africa, and we knew that those slave owners were themselves originally ignorant of the techniques and processes of rice cultivation.[17] Now we can appreciate in more explicit detail the specifics of field layout, of irrigation methods, and of the technics of rice processing (all African imports), and what we learn directly challenges the notion that blacks contributed only their labor.[18] Another recent article in *Technology and Culture* describes the relation between race, changing technology, and work assignments at Bell Telephone, and shows how the technological displacement of labor was biased by color.[19] We always thought that happened; now we have a compelling analysis of the process; So, even if slowly, we begin to see that in our country technology and race have always been tied closely together, just as we begin to sense that those connections are much more intertwined and ubiquitous than we ever realized.

How can we throw even more light on these complexities? We might start by searching out all the black inventors who have never received appropriate credit. That approach not only gives the lie to the myth of disingenuity, but also offers the comfort of familiar ground. In this country we have always celebrated our inventors. We love telling success stories, imagining them to say something important about both our past and our future. And in fact we are now beginning to see some interesting work about black inventiveness. A good place to start is Portia James's *The Real McCoy*, an extensive catalog written to accompany an exhibit she developed at the Anacostia Museum of the Smithsonian Institution. In a revised form, her essay from that book is included in this volume.[20] Another source that will prove valuable is Rayvon Fouché's *Black Inventors in the Age of Segregation*, soon to be released by the John Hopkins University Press

Invention is, however, a problematic category of analysis. The patent system has always worked worst for the poor, who have had least access to its law and processes, and that proved doubly so for black inventors. Before 1865, they were even denied the right to a patent, so that slave owners could lay claim to the intellectual as well as the physical labor of their property. After 1865 blacks more often than not lacked the economic resources to develop their ideas into patentable or marketable form, and for that reason were often forced to sell their interest in inventions prematurely. The romance of invention focuses on the flash of creative insight, to use A. P. Usher's dramatic phrase, but financial rewards more often depend on the legal manipulation of patent rights—something else not easily managed from the margins of society.[21] Finally, it is important to realize that patents describe only a fragment of human inventive activity and are only a small part of the story of people's experiences with technologies. On the other hand, if that familiar model doesn't work very well, what new paradigms do we need in order to discover the connections we seek?

In fact, all it takes to reveal a much more richly populated and therefore more authentic history is to turn the older approach on its head. If, instead of concentrating on the production of new technology, we look equally hard at the worlds of labor and of consumption, then whole new casts of characters emerge. Let's start with work. After all, it was the work of African-Americans that created the rice, tobacco, and cotton economies of the South, and thus so much of America's eighteenth- and nineteenth-century agricultural wealth. Some of that labor also took place in factories, both before and after the Civil War. Charles B. Dew originally pointed out the crucial role played by skilled slave ironworkers in Richmond's Tredegar Ironworks, one of the South's largest industrial enterprises. In a subsequent analysis of smaller furnaces and forges in the great valley of Virginia, Dew revealed both the extent to which slave artisans (who couldn't go on strike) became the preferred work force and how their skills gave them some control over their own work assignments.[22] W. E. B. Du Bois, in *The Negro Artisan*, identified black workers with "considerable mechanical ingenuity" across a broad range of craft and manufacturing occupations.[23] World War I opened up new opportunities for black people in Northern factories, breaking the agricultural "job ceiling" (to use the words of Trotter and Lewis) and making blacks important contributors to the nation's industrial economy.[24]

Thinking about labor means establishing the historical worth of the work in which most people have always been engaged, and it means exploring more creatively the relations between work, technologies, and skill. I don't at all mean to suggest that we relegate the inventive imagination of Elijah McCoy or Granville Woods to a place of lesser historic importance. But if we intend a truly inclusive history, an argument Lonnie Bunch cogently advances in an essay reprinted here, then we have to take into account all those people whose most crucial encounter with machines and technological systems takes place on the job. And surely it is the case that, in the normal, daily working of the world, skill and experience count for as much as abstract knowledge and formal training. What makes this fact important to us is that by defining technical knowledge and creativity in broad terms we immediately reveal hosts of African-Americans who had previously been excluded from the story. We find them planning the layout of South Carolina rice fields, creating pottery, fashioning the furniture now highly prized by collectors, using sewing machines, running and fixing cotton gins, molding iron in Henry Ford's assembly-line factories, and fishing in the ocean for schools of menhaden.[25]

Frederick Douglass understood the critical importance of these kinds of skills in American society, and more particularly he recognized the precise connection in our society between skill and manly status. In an 1848 letter to Harriet Beecher Stowe, he wrote: "We must become mechanics—we must build, as well as live in houses—we must make, as well as use furniture—we must construct bridges, as well as pass over them—before we can properly live, or be respected by our fellow men."[26]

Work has been an important theme of recent studies in African-American history. But in addition to the relation between labor and the creation of wealth, we also need to think about the connections between work and craft and about the affinity between craft skill and knowledge. Since the nineteenth century, engineering in this country has depended on a published literature and on advanced formal instruction that has included physics and mathematics. Craft skill depends on a different kind of knowledge, most of it unwritten and learned on the job. Apprenticeship—whether institutionalized or not—rests on emulation and repetitive practice in the interest of acquiring manual skills, and it is married to experience with the ways in which materials behave in different circumstances. Not only is this kind of knowledge complex and difficult to transfer; it gains importance when considered in the context of the history of American slavery, the formal acquisition of knowledge by slaves having been forbidden by law.

In the seventeenth century, there was little hesitancy at exploiting the technical talents of African labor. Edmund White, for instance, wrote in 1688 to Joseph Morton, twice governor of the Carolina colony: "let yr negroes be taught to be smiths, shoemakers & carpenters & bricklayers: they are capable of learning anything."[27] And learn they did. Robert Fogel estimates that by the eighteenth century 10 percent of all black women were engaged in cloth production, while upwards of half of all male slaves were employed in blacksmithing, leather-working, cooperage, and carpentry—all considered elite occupations, as were such subsequent pursuits as the management of steam engines, boilers, and other machinery.[28] Indeed, Fogel points out, plantations were industrial enterprises that employed advanced technologies and depended upon a wide variety of skills. A more complex division of labor yields more complex labor, and this fact is important as a corrective to the notion that enslaved blacks were ignorant of current technics and untouched by them.

Almost from the beginning, slavery in America was characterized by substantial technical talent and an elaborate occupational hierarchy. Moreover, planters encouraged the development of hierarchies, seeing it as a means of ensuring a tractable work force. As Fogel argues, "the critical decision made by the planters, the decision that allowed the eventual emergence of a many-sided and often quasi-autonomous slave society, was the switch from whites to slaves as the source of personnel for their various managerial and craft slots."[29] There were risks to this approach. Even as their owners encouraged legislation to prohibit the education of slaves, the teaching of craft skills often required some book learning. And knowledge combined with skill brought other contradictions. One planter ruefully observed that, analogous to the profit he made, these elite occupations rewarded their black practitioners with "an extra measure of pride."[30] So perhaps we shouldn't be surprised to learn that skilled craftsmen led most slave rebellions.

Identity through one's work has always been a fundamental part of our culture. Consider the maritime occupations, for example. Long before Frederick Douglass learned the ship caulker's trade, blacks—both free and unfree—worked at shipbuilding, as sailmakers, and as sailors.[31] On both sides of the Chesapeake, where waterways provided the dominant means of transportation, as well as the source of seafood and game, generations of African-American watermen and boat builders, down to the present, have practiced their crafts, as family histories are now beginning to reveal.[32]

Pursuing these kinds of investigations will amplify our understanding both of technology and of the diverse people engaged with it. And field is as relevant as factory; agriculture depends on a set of technologies, just as does fishing, mining, and forestry. Each also requires varied kinds of expertise in the management of its techniques, some of which, Barbara Garrity-Blake's essay provocatively suggests, can even be invisible in character.

Finally, examining the links between race and labor gives us more useful conceptual tools. Scholars have already noticed that while access to technology-related jobs has often been made a matter of color, that relationship has often changed as technologies have changed, and the assignments have also differed geographically. At one end of the range technologies displace labor, while at the other technologies create a demand for low-wage labor in high-risk conditions, some of which can include strikebreaking. Thus, new technologies constantly force the renegotiation of racialized work, and the whole history of that process remains to be written.[33]

An examination of the role of consumption similarly reveals a much more interesting picture of the relation between technology and race and promises an especially fruitful line of inquiry. Leaving aside the idea that consumers play a role in the design process, it can at least be said that outside of work, most of us encounter technologies as consumers—that is, through use. Patents, after all, have little historical importance if no one uses the thing invented, as happens more often than one might realize. Moreover, we know that people employ technologies differently. Black families in Atlanta used automobiles not only for work or personal convenience, but also to escape the humiliating experience of segregated systems of public transit—thus giving that technology a distinctly political purpose.[34] Indeed, Langdon Winner claims that technologies actually have politics embedded in their forms—an argument that might sound right to anyone familiar with the effects of technological unemployment on blacks.[35] And it works the other way, too. The furnaces and foundries at the Ford Motor Company, for example, replicated the social politics of the outside world when white workers decided that, regardless of pay scales, they would not work at such dirty jobs.[36]

Besides whatever practical ends or economic ambitions it serves, access to technology defines status and power. Electrical technicians of the late nineteenth century, in an attempt to establish their own primacy as experts in the fluid occupational demographics of that period, consistently belittled the technological competence of blacks and women.[37] People use technology that way—to maintain existing social arrangements, or to escape them. We can most clearly see how these behaviors and strategies play out in the case of novel technologies; Kathleen Franz's essay in this volume shows the rich research possibilities of this approach.

People also appropriate technologies for their own ends, which are often different than those originally intended. Women have been known to cook turkeys in dishwashers, using the drying cycle. A decade ago, young African-American musicians experimentally scratched a stylus across vinyl records to create an alternative sound that carried political and cultural meaning. Despite the subsequent commercialization of that sound, it is still a good example of people using their politics to rethink technologies.[38] And here we come back to that matter of representation. Bell hooks has focused our attention on "the politics of representation," and that issue bears with particular force for us here because it has been such a struggle for blacks to represent themselves as technically competent. Photography is an oblique but good example of the case. When black people used it, the camera became "a political instrument, a way to resist misrepresentation, as well as a means by which alternative images could be produced." The camera was crucial to the way they could picture themselves. It gave them a means to "participate fully in the production of images," regardless of class—an ability that was enormously important in a world where someone else usually controlled the ways in which African-Americans were represented. Photography became, as hooks puts it, "a powerful location for the construction of an oppositional black aesthetic."[39] This power to define reality provides a starting point from which to shape politics and culture differently. And it works two ways: cameras in black hands—just like the technology of music in black hands—allows for the creation of an alternative image, but that image also enables African-Americans to represent themselves as skillful in the management of those technologies.

Thus, the way we think about race is often shaped by the technology employed in the debate. That connection becomes clear if we look at communications media, and it tells us something important about the control of radio that "Amos 'n' Andy" was the first serial program broadcast nationally in the United States. Even though that particular show employed white actors who imitated Negro speech, in many other cases the networks depended on black artists for talent, an important reality for people of color. According to Stanley Crouch, African-Americans could "remember radio waves smacking down segregation and making the jazz and dance band broadcasts, for instance, national experiences in the most democratic sense possible."[40]

African-Americans have always been interested in new technologies. And, like most other Americans, they have believed in the regenerative powers of technology. Inevitably, they ascribed an array of possibilities to machines such as cars and airplanes—new economic opportunities, an escape from racism, the chance to claim a place for themselves in American society. But technologies that you cannot own are different. Blacks could and did buy phonograph records as a way of managing the content of that technology within their own homes. The content of radio, however, was much more difficult to control, as those "Amos 'n' Andy" broadcasts so blatantly revealed. Yet even in this case, the politics of radio technology allowed African-Americans at least one chance to manipulate programming for their own ends.

Barbara Savage tells the story in her recent book *Broadcasting Freedom*. The central character in this episode is Ambrose Calliver, Senior Specialist in Education of Negroes in the U.S.

Department of Education.[41] Long interested in radio as a medium, Calliver wanted to develop a series of programs that would showcase African-American contributions to the nation's history, culture, and intellectual life. To that end, he adroitly linked technology and politics. First, he knew that the Roosevelt administration was concerned about the extent to which blacks would support the war effort, particularly since A. Philip Randolph—using the very rhetoric employed against Hitlerism to address the problems of racism at home—was threatening a march on Washington to protest discriminatory hiring in defense jobs. Calliver also appreciated the fact that government control of frequency allocation gave him leverage with network broadcasters, and he understood that this public character of radio made it especially suitable for educational content. Calliver skillfully manipulated these factors to push NBC into broadcasting a series called "Freedom's People," starting in the fall of 1941. Using an experienced science writer, he artfully orchestrated a message that began with comfortable, non-threatening music such as "Go Down Moses" and featured celebrated artists such as Paul Robeson. Then, in a conscious and deliberate way, Calliver progressed to shows on literature, science, discovery, invention, military service, and the skills of black workers—building his argument for the intellectual abilities, the inventive talents, the courage, and the capabilities of African-Americans, past and present.

Besides serving as a nice example of the intersection of race, politics, and technology, Calliver's radio series raises interesting questions that call for further study. We might ask, for instance, how race gets represented in communications media. African-Americans were anxious to counteract the vulgarity of "Amos 'n' Andy" and the way blacks were portrayed on programs like "The Jack Benny Show," but in casting "Freedom's People" Calliver and his advisors were also concerned not to have an announcer whose voice didn't sound black enough. So, one might ask, how do race and technology reconstruct each other in radio and in other media?

We can give meaning and form to our technologies as consumers, and we can shape their applications through politics, but it is important to understand that they do not come to us as a given. They are not the result of a neutral process, and they are certainly not the consequence of some inevitable technical logic. They are the result of choices, of social processes, and consequently they embody interests, positions, and attitudes. Steven Lubar puts it as follows: "Machines and technological systems, like other forms of material culture, render cultural and social relations visible, tangible, and artifactual, objectifying and externalizing them. Our machines reflect our culture and society."[42] More than that, even, one could argue that machines and technical processes—whether simple or complex—don't just mirror us, but rather they *are* our culture and society. In other words, all these objects, techniques, and systems, as well as the ways in which they are imagined, produced, employed, consumed, and experienced, are embodiments of the ways in which we think and act.

In their own work, historians of technology have demonstrated that technologies emerge from a rich mix of choices and constraints that are social, economic, political, and technical. But for all that effort, the notion of technology as a black box—something that comes to us in an inescapable form—is still widely popular. Consider, for example, a recent feature story in the *New York Times* about an array of small electronic devices, often installed and deployed without the knowledge of the car owner, that are increasingly being used to monitor people and their automobiles. In fact, these intrusive technologies are promoted by an array of interests that include insurance companies, fast food chains, and car rental agencies. Yet in speaking of their use, a faculty member at the University of Pennsylvania's law school concluded—as if the outcome were predetermined—that "technology goes forward and people are either forced to accept the loss of privacy or lose out on the benefits."[43] That casual observation, so reminiscent of the slogan of the 1933 Chicago World's Fair, "Science Finds, Industry Applies, Man Conforms," ignores both the contingent nature of technology and the unequal power relations in these transactions. And that is where including race in our analysis brings especially useful insights. Looking at technology from the vantage point of African-American history throws the issue of power into sharp relief. Technology may be socially constructed, but the players are not all on the same footing—a truth familiar to people of color, who have also long known that both its benefits and consequences are distributed unequally.

Once we understand technology in these broader terms, we can appreciate the fact that the history of technology in America must necessarily comprise a much larger segment of the population, black and white, than we have imagined. And this understanding of the material world we have created for ourselves, while more complex than our earlier ideas about these things, ultimately yields a truer, more empowering history. But this history will not write itself. The problem of sources is real; for want of written historical records, we know little of the enslaved African potter "Dave," of South Carolina, beyond the remarkable examples of his talent now housed in museums, and not much more of Thomas Day, the celebrated African-American furniture maker.[44] But, of course—it is worth repeating—what gets remembered is not simply a matter of documents but also of choice, of deciding what we will write about. And that decision often rests on what we imagine it possible to write about. More and more, we are coming to see that there is an interesting and important history to be written about race and technology in America. Recent Ph.D. dissertations such as Linda Tucker's "Science at Hampton Normal and Agricultural Institute," Nina Lerman's on nineteenth-century industrial and vocational education in Philadelphia, Rayvon Fouché's on the African-American inventor Granville Woods, Jill Snider's "Flying to Freedom: African-American Visions of Aviation, 1910–1927," and Angela Lakwete's on the cotton gin are a few examples. But there is yet a great deal to be done. "Invisible Hands," an exhibit of black craftsmanship held at Macon, Georgia, suggested the possibilities of future work in material culture study. And anyone interested in pursuing the subject should begin with Theodore C. Landsmark's "Bibliography of African-American Material Culture," deposited at the Henry Francis du Pont Winterthur Library in Wilmington, Delaware.

Much is still to be discovered about the history of black scientific and technical educational institutions. Nina Lerman has written insightfully about race and education in nineteenth-century Philadelphia, and contributes an essay to this volume that suggests important larger themes on the subject, as well as an innovative conceptual framework. But while there were hundreds of technical colleges and institutes created to educate African-Americans, there is very little information about schools other than Tuskegee and Hampton. Amy Slaton's essay in this volume on more contemporary educational practice neatly outlines a research program that, besides providing an example of a successful grant proposal, might help us understand some of the roots of contrasting professional experiences between black and white engineers.

We also need a more complete exploration of African-American participation in the industrial exhibitions of the nineteenth and twentieth centuries—from regional fairs such as the Cotton States Expositions in Atlanta to national exhibitions such as the one held in Louisiana in 1904 and on to the great international expositions in Paris that Du Bois wrote about.[45] The Columbian Exposition in Chicago in 1893 presents especially rich materials for further examination. *The Reason Why the Colored American Is Not in the World's Columbian Exposition*, edited by Robert Rydell, is a good place to begin.[46]

At the local level, the study of African-American communities with technology in mind will reveal a wide range of technical knowledge and skills practiced by women and men, in their homes, stores, and shops. That was true of free black neighborhoods before 1865, and was certainly so in the urban centers of the later nineteenth and the twentieth century.[47]

We can see, then, that there is a great deal more to the interrelatedness of race and technology than scholars once thought, and a variety of interesting ways to come at this history. Upsetting as her story is, now that we know the dangers of overexposure to radiation, Rebecca Herzig's exploration of x-ray hair removal and skin whitening provides a provocative example of the varieties in analysis this subject offers. Furthermore, there is quite a substantial amount of rewarding material for study available both to teachers and students. The broad scope of Amy Bix's bibliographic essay reveals a surprising array of source materials and of research possibilities, and—together with the footnote references from the essays assembled here, many of which she incorporated into her essay—interested students will find all they need to make a start. Indeed, as we continue to explore the richness of this subject, the only surprise will be that we have waited so long to discover what lies at hand.

Notes

1. Excerpt from Bruce Sinclair, "Integrating the Histories of Race and Technology," in *Technology and the African American Experience: Needs and Opportunities for Study* (Boston: Massachusetts Institute of Technology Press, 2004), pp. 1–14.
2. For the details of that correspondence, see Silvio Bedini, *The Life of Benjamin Banneker* (Scribner, 1971).
3. Frederick Law Olmsted, *A Journey in the Back Country, 1853–1854* (Schocken, 1970), reprint, p. 382.
4. The best source for the ways in which racial characteristics were defined in terms of scientific and technological accomplishment is Michael Adas, *Machines as the Measure of Men: Science, Technology, and Ideologies of Western Dominance* (Cornell University Press, 1989).
5. Robert Rydell, *All the World's a Fair: Visions of Empire at American International Expositions, 1876–1916* (University of Chicago Press, 1984).
6. Carroll W. Pursell, Listening for the Silences, position paper presented at a workshop on Technology and the African-American Experience, Atlanta, February 4, 1994.
7. Brooke Hindle, *Technology in Early America: Needs and Opportunities for Study* (University of North Carolina Press, 1966).
8. See Robert L. Harris, "The Flowering of Afro-American History," *American Historical Review* 92 (1987), December: 1150–1161.
9. Susan Smulyan, The Social Construction of Race in the United States, a position paper presented at workshop on Technology and the African-American Experience, Atlanta, February 4, 1994.
10. This case is well made by Ron Takaki on p. 7 of *A Different Mirror: A History of Multicultural America* (Little, Brown, 1993).
11. For examples of how feminist scholars have changed the history of technology, see Judy Wajcman, *Feminism Confronts Technology* (Pennsylvania State University Press, 1991); Angela
12. A good example of this notion of a predisposition toward inventiveness, as well as a telling case of postwar technological enthusiasm, can be found in John A. Kouwenhoven, *Made in America: The Arts in Modern American Civilization* (Branford, 1948).
13. W. E. Burghardt Du Bois, "The American Negro at Paris," *American Monthly Review of Reviews* 22 (1900), p. 576.
14. Ira Berlin, *Many Thousands Gone: The First Two Centuries of Slavery in North America* (Harvard University Press, 1998), p. 120.
15. Ron Takaki, *Iron Cages: Race and Culture in 19th-Century America* (Oxford University Press, 1990).
16. Toni Morrison, *Playing in the Dark: Whiteness and the Literary Imagination* (Harvard University Press, 1992).
17. Adas, *Machines as the Measure of Men*; Robert Rydell, *All the World's a Fair* (University of Chicago Press, 1987).
18. "Literally hundreds of black immigrants were more familiar with the planting, hoeing, processing, and cooking of rice than were the European settlers who purchased them." (Peter H. Wood, *Black Majority: Negroes in Colonial South Carolina, From 1670 through the Stono Rebellion*, Norton, 1974, p. 61) See also Peter H. Wood, "'It Was a Negro Taught Them': A New Look at African Labor in Early South Carolina," *Journal of Asian and African Studies* 9 (1974): 160–179.
19. Judith Carney, "Landscapes of Technology Transfer: Rice Cultivation and African Continuities," *Technology and Culture* 37 (1996), January: 5–35.
20. Venus Green, "Goodbye Central: Automation and the Decline of 'Personal Service' in the Bell System," *Technology and Culture* 36 (1995), October: 912–949.
21. Pursell, *Listening for the Silences*.
22. Abbott Payson Usher, *A History of Mechanical Inventions* (McGraw-Hill, 1929). On the manipulation of patents, see also Carolyn C. Cooper, *Shaping Invention: Thomas Blanchard's Machinery and Patent Management in Nineteenth-Century America* (Columbia University Press, 1991).

23. Charles B. Dew, *Ironmaker to the Confederacy: Joseph Anderson and the Tredegar Iron Works* (Yale University Press, 1966), pp. 29–31; Dew, *Bond of Iron: Master and Slave at Buffalo Forge* (Norton, 1994), pp. 67–70.

24. W. E. Burghardt Du Bois, *The Negro Artisan* (Atlanta University Press, 1902), p. 188.

25. Joe W. Trotter and Earl Lewis, eds., *African Americans in the Industrial Age: A Documentary History, 1915–1945*.

26. John Michael Vlach has provided the best information on African-American craft workers. See, for example, his book *The Afro-American Tradition in Decorative Arts* (Cleveland Museum of Art Press 1978). Barbara Garrity-Blake's *The Fish Factory: Work and Meaning for Black and White Fishermen of the American Menhaden Industry* (University of Tennessee Press, 1994) is a fascinating study of the intersection of work, mechanism, and social relations.

27. "Proceedings of the 1853 Colored National Convention at Rochester, New York" (Frederick Douglass to Harriet Beecher Stowe, March 8, 1848), in *Minutes of the Proceedings of the National Negro Conventions, 1830–1864*, ed. H. Bell (Arno, 1969). Another useful source of information on the subject of work and skill is *A Guide to the Microfilm Edition of Slavery in Ante-Bellum Southern Industries*, ed. M. Shipper (University Publications of America, 1997).

28. Peter H. Wood, *Black Majority: Negroes in Colonial South Carolina From 1670 through the Stono Rebellion* (Norton, 1974), pp. 43-44.

29. Robert William Fogel, *Without Consent or Contract: The Rise and Fall of American Slavery* (Norton, 1989), p. 50.

30. Ibid., p. 58.31.

31. Berlin, *Many Thousands Gone*, p. 137.

32. Jeffrey Bolster, *Black Jacks: African American Seamen in the Age of Sail* (Harvard University Press, 1997).

33. Harold Anderson, "Black Men, Blue Waters: African Americans on the Chesapeake," *Maryland Marine Notes* 16 (1998), March-April: 1–3, 6–7.

34. One example of this literature is Jaqueline Jones, *American Work: Four Centuries of Black and White Labor* (Norton, 1998). For an account of the ways in which technologies create demand for low wage, high-risk jobs see Armando Solorzano and Jorge Iber, "Digging the 'Richest Hole on Earth': The Hispanic Miners of Utah, 1912–1945," *Perspectives in Mexican American Studies* 7 (2000): 1–27.

35. Blaine A. Brownell, "A Symbol of Modernity: Attitudes toward the Automobile in Southern Cities in the 1920s," *American Quarterly* 24 (1972), March, p. 35.

36. Langdon Winner, *The Whale and the Reactor: A Search for Limits in an Age of High Technology* (University of Chicago Press, 1986).

37. Joyce S. Peterson, "Black Automotive Workers in Detroit, 1910–1930," *Journal of Negro History* 64 (1978): 177–190. See also Warren Whatley, *African Americans, Technology, Work and the Reproduction of Racial Differencing*, unpublished research paper, 1994.

38. Carolyn Marvin, *When Old Technologies Were New: Thinking About Electrical Communication in the Late Nineteenth Century* (Oxford University Press, 1988).

39. Tricia Rose, *Black Noise: Rap Music and Black Culture in Contemporary America* (Wesleyan University Press, 1994).

40. bell hooks, "In Our Glory," in *Picturing Us*, ed. D. Willis (New Press, 1994), p. 49.

41. Stanley Crouch, *The All American Skin Game, or The Decoy of Race* (Vintage, 1995), p. 110.

42. Barbara Dianne Savage, *Broadcasting Freedom: Radio, War, and the Politics of Race, 1938-1948* (University of North Carolina Press, 1999).

43. Steven Lubar, *Technology and Race*, a position paper presented at workshop on Technology and the African-American Experience, Atlanta, Feruary 5, 1994.

44. *New York Times,* October 25, 2001.

45. See Vlach, *The Afro-American Tradition in Decorative Arts.*

45. See Du Bois, "The American Negro at Paris," and Philip S. Foner, "Black Participation in the Centennial of 1876," *Phylon* 39 (1978): 283–295. Nicholas Murray Butler of Columbia University also presented an exhibit of American higher education at the Paris exposition, irresistibly suggesting a comparison with Du Bois's experience there.

46. Robert Rydell, ed., *The Reason Why the Colored American Is Not in the World's Columbian Exposition* (University of Illinois Press, 1999).

47. For an example of a study of free black communities, see James O. Horton, *Free People of Color: Inside the African American Community* (Smithsonian Institution Press, 1993). See also his more recent studies *In Hope of Liberty* (Oxford University Press, 1997) and *Black Bostonians* (Holmes & Meier, 1999).

Brandi Wilkins Catanese

Exploring controversial digital art like http://trophyscarves.com will give some background on ethical questions around some iterations of Black performance art and the ways in which artists use new media to incite responses or debate from their audiences. One of the first such sites to draw this type of criticism was Damali Ayo's "How To Rent A Negro." Although the work itself is no longer active on the website rent-a-negro, Catanese's analysis of Ayo's work raises important questions about the ethics of digital performance art and the ways other artists of this genre engage in racial dialogues with "invisible" audiences. These questions can be applied to the current controversy surrounding Nate Hill's *Trophy Scarves* and other curated texts that profess to offer an artist's critique of dominant discourses about race, sexuality, or gender. As Catanese argues, in such instances, Black bodies, and ultimately Black perspectives, become subject, object, or both. For a broad discussion of how artists approach race in their art, readers can visit http://documentingblackperformanceart.tumblr.com and http://learn.walkerart.org/karawalker/Main/RepresentingRace.

"Your Own White Privilege": The Ethics of Play

Brandi Wilkins Catanese[1]

In this essay, I have suggested that ayo's digital project has both discursive and ethical dimensions (as if the two are ever divisible). However, damali ayo is not the only black artist challenging sacrosanct codes about the reverence with which we must approach racial discourse. Artists such as Adrian Piper, Carrie Mae Weems, Michael Ray Charles, Kara Walker, Tana Hargest, and Mendi+Keith Obadike have variously criticized the ways in which whiteness and blackness are deployed within artistic institutions and quotidian patterns of socialization. Michael D. Harris identifies the strategies such work often employs as inversion, recontextualization, and reappropriation, yet he asks, "Are these strategies truly effective or merely diversionary chimera?"[2] The answer may lie, in part, in the types of responses the art works accommodate.

Of the artists I mentioned above, Tana Hargest and Mendi+Keith Obadike also use digital media satirically to offer their indictments of contemporary racial practices, and, interestingly, also locate their critiques in the realm of commerce. For the Studio Museum in Harlem exhibition *Freestyle*, Hargest shared an interactive CD-ROM for Bitter Nigger, Inc., which marketed, among other things, pharmaceutical products, a concept that emerged from Hargest's "fundamental assumption that difficult concepts—especially those concerning race in America—are easier to consider if packaged as purchasable items."[3] Mendi+Keith Obadike jointly created the 2002 Internet piece *The Interaction of Coloreds*, advertising the IOC Color Check System, which would use "patented technology . . . [to offer] more precise readings of the body online" in a brilliant response to anxiety about the racial subterfuge made possible by the invisibility the Internet affords.[4] This piece followed Keith Obadike's 2001 *Blackness for Sale*, which used eBay in an effort to profit from the extreme marketability of blackness at the beginning of the twenty-first century.

One of the key features that distinguish interactive digital art from other more traditional forms of art is the way in which interactivity facilitates audiences' response to the work. While all artists, presumably, want to elicit a response from their audiences, digital interactive art requires the externalization of that response, and builds said response into the work itself. Hargest, Obadike, and ayo provide systems through which the questions their work poses may be answered.[5] How interested are you in using medical science to transform your racialized participation in American culture? Click here! What price would you place on claiming someone else's blackness for yourself? Submit your maximum bid now! Under what circumstances would you objectify a black person? Fill out the rental request form!

Rent-a-negro.com may be ayo's most famous piece in a career comprising a series of works that interrogate the processes of identity formation in contemporary culture along raced and gendered lines. She defines her work as "dialogue-driven conceptual art that engages contemporary social issues through the media of visual, virtual, written and performance art. [. . . Her] work is performative in its relentless desire to engage the audience and generate an audience reaction as an on-site companion piece."[6] Thus, by her own admission, ayo sees audience participation as a component of the work itself, and even wittily conveys this within one of her pieces. In *ontology* (2001), a found pair of Black Americana[7] salt and pepper shakers discuss ayo's work; the male shaker says, "her fundamental conceptual strategy is to implicate the spectator as complicit—not only in the society manufacturing such constructs, but in the art itself as audience is unwittingly transformed into medium."[8] This strategy seems quite clear in rent-a-negro. com, as the act of completing the rental form makes site visitors' subjectivity a part of rent-a-negro.com itself.

Audience responsiveness forms a throughline for much of ayo's oeuvre, whether these responses are as structured as the rent-a-negro.com request form or as ostensibly passive as bearing living witness to her investigations of methods through which racializing tendencies that marginalize blackness function in the present as reminders of the past. She describes her 2001 exhibition, *shift: we are not yet done*, as "an exploration of contemporary racism using everyday objects and cultural icons."[9] In addition to a critique of the Rolling Stones' song *Brown Sugar* and an exposé of Mickey Mouse's minstrel antecedents making him a "monument to racist mockery of black people," *shift* includes an on-site performance called *race tags*, in which audience members receive seemingly common adhesive identification tags on which "Hello my name is" becomes "Hello my race is . . . " Patrons are offered the classifications black, white, or other. The familiar ID tag is transformed, deployed not for the more individual naming ritual but to catalog racial membership, a playful instantiation of the pressure to see and be seen in narrow racial terms before other aspects of one's identity are considered. As *race tags* demonstrates, racial identity is not simply a private fact but also a public and social negotiation, an act of affiliation as well as an imposition. Furthermore, *race tags* underscores the imperfection of this discursive system, as demonstrated by those who become othered by the piece. In invoking the binary of black/white politics and blithely homogenizing all else as "other," ayo demonstrates the limited agency available to people within the performative discourse of race.

I mention *race tags* because its process of racial subjectification provides an interesting counterpoint to rent-a-negro.com in several ways: first, *race tags* takes place in the material world of live, person-to-person interaction, while rent-a-negro.com operates in the remote world of cyberspace, where invisibility and disembodiment mediate person-to-person interaction. The processes of sociocorporeal ratification that regulate the racial economy of *race tags* are not similarly available within rent-a-negro's e-conomy. Rather than an attendant deeming you black, white, or other after a physical inspection, your race online is seemingly produced by your behavior alone, and its intersection with the degree to which an interface allows you to register that racial identity. Additionally, *race tags* acknowledges the problematics of the simultaneously overflowing and empty signifier of the racial other. While the heterogeneity of those defined as other is elided, the label does provide an alternative to the essentialist definitions of black and white that form the center of American racial discourse (although this alternative is assigned rather than claimed). Conversely, rent-a-negro.com seems to offer its customer/consumer only one racialized subject position: whiteness.

In the homogeneity of the spectator position ayo affords rent-a-negro audiences, she knowingly replicates the assumptions that structure much of cyberspace. Although, as David Crane suggests, "cyberspace still generally connotes an 'other' world ontologically and phenomeno-logically distinct from the real one,"[10] Beth Kolko, Lisa Nakamura, and Gilbert Rodman remind us that "users bring their assumptions and discursive patterns regarding race with them when they log on, and when the medium is interactive, they receive such assumptions and patterns as well."[11] Although ayo's Web site does not offer the real-time interaction that other forms of online communication such as Multi-User Domains (MUDs) do, it does indeed invite and disseminate certain assumptions about race that we learn in the real world in order to, in her words, "reflect society back to itself in a kind of mirror."[12] The society she recreates through rent-a-negro.com is one in which "you" are always white, a default which makes common sense of the process of "subjectively objectifying"[13] herself as a black woman that ayo stages with this project. The structure of rent-a-negro.com seems to support Beth Kolko's description of how the Internet produces raced subjects: she writes, "technology interfaces carry the power to prescribe representative norms and patterns, constructing a self-replicating and exclusionary category of 'ideal' user, one that, in some very particular instances of cyberspace, is a definitively white user."[14] Rent-a-negro.com certainly falls within that category, but what does "definitively white" mean when no one can see you?

In keeping with Cameron Bailey's discussion of race in cyberspace, we must ask, what pro-duces "the special glow of virtual skin"?[15] When there are no cabs to be hailed and no jobs to be gotten, is black-identified the same as black? Once we take for granted that there are in fact a host of raced and gendered people participating in online activity, we assume that they exert complete control over the ways in which their race signifies (or does not). The acts of commu-nication that form the basis for virtual identification (as definition and as affinity) are meant to reflect our experiences in the real/material world. Yet, without the forced compatibility of what one looks like and what one says, cyberspace seems to transform identity from a negotia-tion between the signals one's physical presence gives off and the ways in which our behavior modifies these signals, into a pure representation of a freely determined, true self unfettered by external misapprehension. However, as Lisa Nakamura explains, such self-determination is not strictly coterminous with (racial) truth: she refers to the "identity tourist" as "one who engages in superficial, reversible, recreational play at otherness, a person who is satisfied with an episodic experience as a racial minority."[16] In her book *Cybertypes*, Nakamura goes on to suggest that identity tourism, rather than fostering understanding between different racial groups, reinforces misunderstanding through its reliance upon stereotypes. However, her definition focuses on those who pass down from the white summit of the racial hierarchy, rather than on other moves disembodied users might make to assume different identities. Acts of passing up for white by accepting the defaults of cyberspace's racial discourse are seen as nonthreatening because they preserve "the integrity of the national sense of self that is defined as white."[17]

Nakamura's observation offers an instructive insight into the situational malleability of race in American culture. Cyberspace takes us through the looking glass into the perverse inverse of America's racial logic. In cyberspace, all acts of passing seem to ratify the status quo one way or another: passing up for white demonstrates one's proficiency with (if not adoption of) the attitudes that preserve a white "national sense of self"; in Nakamura's characterization, passing down to a nonwhite identity seems only to happen in an effort to appropriate and/or objectify nonwhiteness in the service of some fantasy that coalesces with the very same "national sense of self." Conversely, in embodied practice, all forms of racial passing "challenge the essentialism that is often the foundation of identity politics," doing so in both qualitative and quantita-tive terms.[18] For whiteness, this foundation is shaken as much when one who was not born into whiteness performs her way into it, gaining access to the social and economic privileges that subtend an ostensibly biologically secure category, as it is when someone born into white-ness insults the category by—unfathomably—choosing to leave behind its comforts and alleged superiority. Examining these practices side by side proves that articulations of race and power remain equally and deeply invested in the biological and the behavioral understandings of racial meaning, because, as Althusser reminds us, "There is no such thing as a purely ideological apparatus."[19]

While rent-a-negro.com does exploit a whiteness that *How to Rent a Negro* later defines as pertaining to "descendents of European and some Semitic people. Confusing due to the word's association with all things good,"[20] the site does so in a way that challenges the category in an effort to force white ignorance to take responsibility for itself. Whereas whiteness as neutrality is usually attributed to its alleged vacuity as a racial category, ayo's white customer is anything but benign. Curiosity over the home page notwithstanding, each decision to click a link that ventures more deeply into the site increases the viewer's entrenchment within the white user perspective that structures ayo's relationship with site visitors. Therefore, it is not the specificity of embodiment that ayo uses to construct her "ideal white user." Instead, she exploits the disembodiedness of the Internet and makes the act of looking, along with Cameron Bailey's "imaginative act required to project into cyberspace," the determinants of racial subjectivity online. Just as Laura Mulvey argued for the male gaze as a functional apparatus that was not coterminous with male bodies watching films,[21] so does rent-a-negro.com both produce and rely upon the white gaze as the digital apparatus that helps to construct the meaning of ayo's performance project.

While this white gaze structures the ways in which ayo is knowable to her viewers through the Web site, the project also offers viewers opportunities to know themselves racially, positing blackness and alterity as cultural competencies or modes of reading rather than mere bodily facts. Although Internet art is not constrained by temporal logic in the ways that other media are, linear time does help to explain the racial awareness that rent-a-negro.com gradually fosters. In all likelihood, audiences experience the "Home" page first, which offers testimonials from satisfied customers. The primary objective of the home page is to establish the commercial credibility of the project, providing the veneer of respectability by employing the formal properties of e-commerce: testimonials intimate the services the site offers, the list of frequently asked questions (FAQs) promises to allay any concerns that viewers might have, and the credit card logos promise the integrity of any financial relationship that will ensue between the site (ayo) and the viewer.[22] Shock, offense, and/or curiosity might propel viewers to the next page, "About," on which ayo explains the rationale behind the service in greater detail and attempts to entice site viewers into becoming customers. Text written in the second person asserts a level of familiarity with the viewer, as ayo promises, "your comfort and enjoyment are valued," and reciprocates by offering a bit of biographical information about herself.[23] Taken together, the "Home" and "About" pages establish the parameters of the hoax as well as the two interactive subject positions the hoax will sustain: the renter and the rented. Some viewers will understand the joke as such, while others will have been fooled into believing the site's offer of services is real.

The remaining pages offer crucial opportunities for racial differentiation. The "Pricing" page functions as the first litmus test. After absorbing the premise of the site, visitors who recognize their own experiences in the tasks ayo offers to complete for pay are authenticated as black/identified viewers. If people have "Touch[ed Your] Hair," "Compare[d Their] Skin Tone to Yours," or asked you to "Challeng[e] Racist Family Members,"[24] you have earned the right to laugh at the Web site from the perspective of one who understands the frustrations that motivated ayo to create it.[25] You are demonstrating your awareness that "[b]lack humor most often satirizes the demeaning views of non-blacks, celebrates the unique attributes of black community life, or focuses on outwitting the oppressor."[26] You may view the site as a coping mechanism, a perverse wish-fulfillment fantasy.[27] If you do not share muscle memory with ayo of these objectifying experiences, then you are white/identified in relation to the site. However, you may recognize the tasks that ayo indicates she will no longer perform without compensation, and you may want to disavow the behaviors the site criticizes. For these viewers, the Web site becomes an instruction manual: the "Pricing" page functions as a "what not to do" list against offensive interracial contact and provides an opportunity for reflection on one's past potential racial sins. The last broad category of responses falls victim to what Richard Schechner refers to as "dark play," in which "some of the players don't know they are playing" and which "subverts order, dissolves frames, and breaks its own rules."[28] These visitors might be seduced into revealing their desire to appropriate blackness, but are denied the satisfaction of having that wish fulfilled, even at a price. White/identifiedness therefore splits into self-conscious and, for lack of a better word, duped subgroups.

The "FAQs" page is inserted between the "Pricing" and "Rent Now!" pages, and serves dual purposes: for two of the three groups identified above (black/identified and self-conscious white/identified), the FAQs alleviate curiosity and expose just how far ayo is willing to take her concept. For the duped viewer, the FAQs offer a promise of feasibility for the relationship that the site claims to sell, cultural awkwardness notwithstanding. Finally, as the interactive component of the project, the "Rent Now!" page offers a last opportunity to self-identify racially, but also ushers in an ethical crisis. Overall, rent-a-negro.com demands that its audiences assume the (perhaps fictive) role of majoritarian subject with a racially segregated life, and if visitors simply view the pages of the Web site but fail to succumb to the sales pitch, this summons is incomplete, as it fails to pull them into the realm of the externally performative. Their structured white gaze is somewhat passive, in that they accept the looking relationship that ayo has consciously built into the site but do not act on the privileges associated with their position. Yet in choosing not to become customers of the service, audiences limit the version of white or white-identified subject that they will allow themselves to become, in a strange way retaining greater agency than if they do participate in the performance. Their conscientious objection to the demands that the site makes of whiteness demonstrates the potential for transforming that identity category from one inevitably aligned with exploitation. If, instead, they complete ayo's rental request form, they are accepting a deeper level of affiliation with the whiteness that ayo wants to satirize: even without the body to substantiate the subject position, any customers can become white/identified through their willingness to commodify damali ayo.

Regardless of the racial status earned by passing through the previous four pages of the site, submitting the rental request form seems to be the sine qua non of total absorption into the white/identified space of the normative virtual self. The form threatens to level the distinctions between black/identified recognition, self-conscious white/identifiedness, and dupe status. According to ayo, "This service comes without the commitment of learning about racism, challenging your own white privilege, or being labeled 'radical.'"[29] Therefore, completing the rental form produces an implicit admission of possessing some degree of white privilege, whether or not one believes herself to have an embodied experience of this. Suddenly, the FAQ "How do I rent a Negro?"[30] becomes not a procedural but an ethical question that raises the stakes of the entire project by demanding a very personal decision by each visitor. How do I, for example, as a black woman, rent a Negro and thereby lay claim to the white privilege that the work indicts? More importantly, why would I want to engage in this dark play? In the raced and raceless interface that is the request form, how do I register my blackness, and therefore my disidentification with the easy white privilege that this site attempts to critique? Without the silent salience of my black body, how do I ironize my rental request?

While it may be difficult to understand why site visitors would want to assume the role of the dupe in order to become a customer of rent-a-negro.com, ayo's potential motive in requesting this racial charade from all of her visitors is clearer. By offering a combination of structured and relatively free responses, the site mimics the paradoxical autonomy and restrictiveness of our racial experiences and especially requires contemplating the effect of these experiences upon black people. The "successful" audience engagement with the piece seems to be the one that is willing to do as the Web site requests and "examine the impact of black people in your environment and discuss this openly in your rental agreement."[31] However imaginary the business is, the questions that it provokes are quite real. ayo herself says that "audience response becomes a live and dynamic part of the work," and viewers/customers must think carefully about the dynamic contributions that they wish to make to the meaning and cultural efficacy of rent-a-negro.com. Will their contributions be dishonest honesty ("this isn't me, but I'm giving you a glimpse of the sort of person who would want this service"), or honest dishonesty ("I know you won't really rent yourself out to me, but here's what I'd ask for if you actually would")?

Conclusion: The Ethics of In/visibility

ayo has acknowledged receiving hundreds (and by now, I'm sure, thousands) of responses that fall into three camps: those that play along, those that are angry, and those that do not understand the site is insincere and actually wish to pay ayo for her services.[32] In order to assess the significance of such cultural activity, rent-a-negro.com requires us to grapple with both the invisibility of ethics and the ethics of invisibility at the same time. What does it mean to objectify ayo when no one sees you doing so, and if no one (including ayo) can see you doing it, is it still wrong? Earlier in this essay, I drew a distinction between the externalization of response that interactive digital art affords its audiences and the internalization of response that seems more characteristic of other disembodied visual art forms. This assessment does not properly account for the rich tradition of performance art, in which artists demand embodied, externalized responses to their work. The difference between digital and embodied performance art is related to ethics: in its impersonal nature, digital performance art uses the structural means of retreat in order to achieve the ethical ends of advance. By providing an invisible opportunity to participate in racial dialogue that is less constrained by physical mobility or embodied social expertise, more people are afforded the opportunity of participating in the ethical project of expanding and augmenting racial discourse. Whereas embodied performance art often provides opportunities for the externalization of audience response, the impact of any one work is determined by the number of people it can reach at one time. Conversely, digital performance art defies many of the constraints of time and place that circumscribe material art in order to expand its reach into our social framework.

The lack of real-time, bodily accountability for our online behavior (which may include acts of hate and/or deception) suggests that there is no such thing as blackness, only black-identified-ness, in the virtual realm. As I mentioned before, *race tags* offers its audience-participants no such black-identified-ness, no chance for their behavior to supercede the racial stories their bodies tell. Conversely, the online potential for equal access to and participation in histories into which we were not biologically born distends the meaning of race to allow for imagined communities of an entirely different sort. In her Web-art-performance work, damali ayo seems both to rely upon the essentialist definitions of race that created the misapprehensions rent-a-negro.com critiques, and also to want to destroy these, in offering one mode of interaction that allows/requires participants to assume the position of white subject even if it involves an act of racial masquerade. Her setup attempts to challenge Lisa Nakamura's claim that passing toward whiteness is unthreatening. She aims to demonstrate that in contemporary society whiteness is a mode of behavior more than a particular type of body; perhaps the fact that all people have equal opportunity or responsibility to answer the question "Have you ever used black people?" is ayo's way of forcing the question of racial accountability and community into another sphere in which we do not use bodies as excuses for the oversimplification of the conversation about how racism, as a discursive and a bodily practice, exacts such a toll from all of American society. Gwendolyn DuBois Shaw's depiction of Kara Walker, another controversial young African American woman artist, seems apt here: like Walker, ayo "has been allowed to critique the dominant culture virtually unfettered by its proponents in part because she does not spare her own community in the exercise."[33] In rent-a-negro.com, the liberatory potential and benefits of re-evaluating racialized behaviors affect both blackness and whiteness.

The ethical ambiguity of cyberspace, in which anonymity is heightened, has become a very potent vehicle for fostering conversations about race. Performance artist Guillermo Gomez-Peña, whose work often invites audiences to find and/or expose their inner racist, transplanted his cultural project to the Internet with his 1995 online "Temple of Confessions," in which site visitors could "confess [their] intercultural cyber sins."[34] According to Gomez-Peña, "The total anonymity offered by the Internet, along with the invitation to discuss painful and sensitive matters of race and identity in an artificially safe environment, seems to allow for the surfacing of forbidden or forgotten zones of the psyche. In a sense, through digital technology, we enabled thousands of Internet users to involuntarily collaborate with us in the creation of a new sociocultural mythology of the Latino and the Indigenous 'Other.' "[35] The idea that Internet users are "involuntarily" contributing to a racial project that they don't understand compromises the authority with which the normative Internet user is commonly invested. Within the context of rent-a-negro.com, the duped visitors fulfill the same function, involuntarily helping ayo expose the persistence of certain counterproductive racial practices.

Overall, rent-a-negro.com sculpts and catalogs a dialogue on interracial contact that has, to borrow Lisa Blackman's language about a different interactive Web art piece, "transformative potential":

> It forces us to confront the way we draw limits around what we take so-called normality to be. It resignifies those terms, images, and languages central to our subjectification and shows how they function to maintain a particular regulatory ideal we hold up to ourselves. It shows the contingency of these terms by exploring the gaps, silences, and contradictions created through these regulatory images, i.e. the way that certain people, behaviours and experiences are simply thrust into oblivion, signifying as "other" within the cultural landscape. It produces a range of affects—not pleasure—but difficult emotions that lock into our deepest psychic and social defences.[36]

Blackman's characterization of the potential of digital interaction to change the process through which we become subjects in the real/material world as well as online has major implications for the discussion of race. Digital performance projects that call us into being in ways that are alienating can facilitate an awareness of the codes embedded in the behavioral patterns that constitute our personal set points and which we often take for granted, giving us the opportunity to redefine racial communities by adopting different patterns of behavior.

With the unique advantages that digital media offer to ayo's project, her decision to publish *How to Rent a Negro*, and thereby shift the venue through which the satire functions, is in some ways surprising. The book serves as an extension, rather than a replacement, of the Web site. It includes samples of the completed rental request forms ayo has received electronically since the performance began, and lays bare the mechanisms of participation in the rental relationship by educating both renters and rentals in the behaviors that will ensure a productive professional encounter. However, the book itself does not demand externalized response in the way that the Web site does. There are questionnaires to be completed and templates to be used for forms and certificates, but the feedback loop of the project is disrupted in print, as it does not automatically return to the artist herself.

Nevertheless, the dialogue that ayo wishes to foster is taking place, and communities of conversation regarding practices of racial objectification are taking root, even online. However, it was the publication and sale of *How to Rent a Negro*, rather than rent-a-negro.com alone, which facilitated this. Whereas rent-a-negro.com offers people the opportunity to perform race satirically, there is no online community in which visitors may respond ethically and out of character to the issues ayo raises. Of all places, the site of self-reflection and interpersonal dialogue about the ideas contained in the concept of renting a Negro is the reader reviews section of the Amazon.com Web page for ayo's book. At the time of this writing, there are only a few reader reviews listed, but they already run the gamut from white liberal epiphanies about one's own lapses into objectification, to black empathy for the practices ayo condemns in the dominant culture, to the condemnation of ayo's (alleged) pessimistic assertion that true respect and communication across racial lines are impossible. ayo offers site visitors (and now, book readers) the opportunity to participate in satirical play, while Amazon hosts the discussion board where visitors may share their ethical responses to the project. Perhaps when taken together, the cultural and capitalistic work of damali ayo and Amazon founder Jeff Bezos, respectively, do tend toward the infinite possibilities of identity by making productive use of the fragmented experience of racial meaning that postmodern life in general, and virtuality in particular, afford us.

Notes

1. Excerpt from Brandi Wilkins Catanese, "'How Do I Rent a Negro?': Racialized Subjectivity and Digital Performance Art," *Theatre Journal* 57.4 (2005): 699–714.
2. Michael D. Harris, *Colored Pictures: Race and Visual Representation* (Chapel Hill: University of North Carolina Press, 2003), 192.
3. Debra Singer, "Tana Hargest," in *Freestyle*, ed. Thelma Golden (New York: The Studio Museum in Harlem, 2001), 40.
4. Mendi+Keith Obadike, "The Interaction of Coloreds," www.blacknetart.com/HR.html. Accessed July 15, 2005.
5. Obviously, the greatest distinction is to be found between interactive digital art and other (purely) visual works of art. However, I will address the differences between digital performance art and embodied performance art later in this essay.
6. www.rent-a-negro.com/damali%20ayo%20dot%20com/pages/statement.htm. Accessed May 1, 2005.
7. "Black Americana" is a collector's euphemism for racist memorabilia. See David Pilgrim, "The Garbage Man: Why I Collect Racist Objects," www.ferris.edu/news/jimcrow/collect/. Accessed May 1, 2005.
8. www.rent-a-negro.com/damali%20ayo%20dot%20com/pages/gallery2.htm. Accessed May 1, 2005.
9. www.rent-a-negro.com/damali%20ayo%20dot%20com/pages/exhibitions.htm. Accessed May 1, 2005.
10. David Crane, "*In Medias* Race: Filmic Representation, Networked Communication, and Racial Intermediation," in Kolko et al., *Race in Cyberspace*, 87–116.
11. Kolko et al., *Race in Cyberspace*, 9.
12. www.rent-a-negro.com/damali%20ayo%20dot%20com/pages/interview.htm. Accessed May 1, 2005.
13. www.rent-a-negro.com/damali%20ayo%20dot%20com/pages/interview2001.htm. Accessed May 1, 2005.
14. Kolko, "Erasing @race," 218.
15. Bailey, "Virtual Skin," 32.
16. Lisa Nakamura, *Cybertypes: Race, Ethnicity, and Identity on the Internet* (New York: Routledge, 2002), 55.
17. Ibid., 37. At the same time, Nakamura also cites the term "black panic," coined by *New York Times* reporter Dana Canady to describe the cognitive dissonance instantiated for some of her business contacts when they met her in person, after having had only telephone contact with her previously (142).
18. Elaine K. Ginsberg, "Introduction: The Politics of Passing," in *Passing and the Fictions of Identity* (Durham: Duke University Press, 1996), 4.
19. Louis Althusser, "Ideology and Ideological State Apparatuses (Notes towards an Investigation)," in *Essays on Ideology* (London: Verso, 1984), 18.
20. damali ayo, *How to Rent a Negro* (Chicago: Lawrence Hill Books, 2005), 56.
21. Laura Mulvey, "Visual Pleasure and Narrative Cinema," *Screen* 16.3: 6–18.

22. Indeed, I taught a class in which, without prejudice, I instructed students to view the Web site. Several students began by thinking that the site had to be a joke, but were swayed by the credit card icons into believing that it was real.

23. www.rent-a-negro.com/negroabout.html. Accessed May 1 2005.

24. www.rent-a-negro.com/negropricing.html. Accessed May 1, 2005.

25. Or, conversely, to take offense, as some have, at the thought that the site trivializes the ways in which blacks continue to suffer dehumanization at the hands of the dominant culture.

26. Mel Watkins, *On the Real Side: Laughing, Lying, and Signifying—The Underground Tradition of African American Humor, from Slavery to Richard Pryor* (New York: Simon & Shuster, 1994), 29.

27. Let me be clear: the wish being fulfilled with this Web site is not to be objectified, but rather to profit from rather than simply be victimized by the economic imperatives that motivate such practices of racial objectification.

28. Schechner, *Performance Studies*, 106–7.

29. www.rent-a-negro.com/negroabout.html. Accessed May 1 2005.

30. www.rent-a-negro.com/negrofaqs.html. Accessed May 1, 2005.

31. www.rent-a-negro.com/negroabout.html. Accessed July 26, 2004. As of 15 July 2005, this is no longer the wording of the question. ayo has revised the form to make it subtly less confrontational, now asking, "Do you have previous experience with black people?" "Please describe." www.rent-a-negro.com/negrorental.html. Accessed July 15, 2005.

32. Lonnae O'Neal Parker, "Hon, Guess Who's Coming to Dinner?; Satirical rent-a-negro.com: Performance Art With a Jolt," *Washington Post* 28 May 2003: C01. Incidentally, many of these responses are published in *How to Rent a Negro*.

33. Gwendolyn DuBois Shaw, *Seeing the Unspeakable: The Art of Kara Walker* (Durham: Duke University Press, 2004), 118. It is nevertheless important to acknowledge the differing levels of entrenchment within the mainstream art world that distinguish Walker from ayo: Walker has received several marks of mainstream approval, including a MacArthur Fellowship, and is controversial in part because her fame and professional opportunities have so rapidly eclipsed those of older artists in her field. ayo, while certainly in possession of a body of provocative and engaging work, is likely only at the beginning of her professional notoriety.

34. www.echonyc.com/~confess/. Accessed May 1, 2005. The interactive component of this site is no longer functional.

35. Fifth International Conference on Cyberspace, www.fundacion.telefonica.com/at/egomez.html. Accessed May 1, 2005.

36. Lisa M. Blackman, "Culture, Technology and Subjectivity: an 'ethical' analysis," in *The Virtual Embodied: Presence/Practice/Technology*, ed. John Wood (New York: Routledge, 1998), 142.

Rayvon Fouché

While Bleecker and Eglash's lens expands the historical perspective on Black cybernetics, Fou-ché's essay provides a deeper understanding of how African Americans interact with technol-ogy to produce what he calls a "black vernacular technological creativity." Critiquing the notion that technology is value-neutral, Fouché shows how Black vernacular technological creativity reflects the Black experience in the United States—from practice to knowledge. The author also demonstrates how material participation influenced a specifically African American techno-culture, one that reflects their specific sociocultural position. In so doing, Fouché emphasizes African American technological agency.

Say It Loud, I'm Black and I'm Proud: African Americans, American Artifactual Culture, and Black Vernacular Technological Creativity

Rayvon Fouché[1]

The actual *beginnings* of our expression are post Western (just as they certainly are pre-western). It is only necessary that we arm ourselves with complete self knowledge[;] the whole technology (which is after all just *expression* of who ever) will change to reflect the essence of a freed people. Freed of an oppressor, but also as [Askia] Touré has reminded we must be "free from the oppressor's spirit," as well. It is this spirit as emotional construct that can manifest as expression as art or technology or any form.

Amiri Baraka[2]

Black Vernacular Technological Creativity

Martin Luther King Jr., in his posthumously published book *Where Do We Go from Here: Chaos or Community?*, began to critically examine the deepening divide between morality and technology. In the chapter titled "The World House," King expressed concern about the ways he saw modern science and technology and freedom revolutions shaping the emerging global community. He saw a great deal of change, but he also was unsure if we had the capac-ity to embrace each other as equal human beings, break the tradition of human exploitation, and use technology to bring communities together rather than destroy them. King wrote, "We must work passionately . . . to bridge the gulf between scientific progress and our moral progress. One of the great problems of mankind is that we suffer from a poverty of spirit which stands in glaring contrast to our scientific and technological abundance." He signaled his concern that "the richer we have become materially, the poorer we have become morally and spiritually" and cautioned that "when scientific power outruns moral power, we end up with guided missiles and misguided men."[3] King pressed for a revolution in values not only cultural but also technological. He argued that technological development did not have to be oppositional to a global moral vision. He was also troubled by what he saw as the potential for technology, if used inhumanly, to exploit individuals, communities, and societies. King was calling for "a shift from a 'thing'-oriented society to a 'person'-oriented society," and declared that "when machines and computers, profit motives and property rights are considered more important than people, the giant triplets of racism, materialism, and militarism are incapable of being conquered."[4]

Of course King's critique was situated within the context of sixties-era protest, which demanded the reassessment of the expanding military industrial complex.[5] But his critique also was situated within the context of the emerging technological medium of television. King, and the civil rights movement, effectively appropriated the power of television. Sasha Torres contends that television, as a technology of representation, powerfully displayed the civil rights protests to the larger, primarily white, American society and altered the way that white America saw and viewed African Americans.[6] The technologically mediated televisual representation of terrible events such as the attack on the Selma-to-Montgomery marchers as they crossed the Edmund Pettis Bridge changed how many people saw the movement. White audiences began to sympathize with the civilized marchers, who were being brutalized as they peacefully demonstrated for their rights. Torres shows that television can be a fertile location to ask questions about technology in relation to American race relations, politics of representation, and African American life. However, this appropriation does not specifically represent black vernacular technological creativity. Civil rights activists were not actively engaging the technology of the television to alter the way they were presented to American society. Thus, as much as television recontextualized the civil rights movement, the change in black televisual representation was quite serendipitous.

White audiences' newly found sympathy for the nonviolent civil rights protesters did not carry over to the Black Panther Party for Self Defense. The potent images of gun-toting Huey P. Newton, Bobby Seale, and a host of other Black Panther Party members redeployed the gun and precipitated an important reversal of its technological power. Guns were instruments traditionally used to control—in the loosest sense of the word—black bodies. But the Black Panther Party members inverted this power. They redeployed guns as effective and visible artifacts to create a sense of fear among many white Americans, the same fear that many African Americans had felt for generations. This appropriation by the Black Panther Party of the material and symbolic power of the gun, against those who had used it so powerfully to subjugate African Americans, enabled them to claim power African Americans infrequently access.[7]

Following in this black nationalist tradition, Amiri Baraka would level a critique of technology from a black perspective. In "Technology & Ethos," Baraka wrote that "machines (as Norbert Weiner said) are an extension of their inventor-creators. That is not simple once you think. Machines, the entire technology of the West, is just that, the technology of the West . . . . Political power is also the power to create—not only what you will—but to be freed to go where ever you can go—(mentally and physically as well). Black creation—creation powered by the Black ethos brings very special results."[8] Baraka felt that the West had long ago gone down the wrong path in attempting to technologize humanity rather than humanizing technology. In his opinion, the Western technological tradition of creating "technology that kills both plants & animals, poisons the air & degenerates or enslaves man" was misguided.[9]

Baraka was equally interested in probing what could happen and the questions that could be asked if black people had technological power and became agents of technological change:

> Think of yourself, Black creator, freed of european [sic] restraint which first means the restraint of self determined mind development. Think what would be the results of the unfettered blood inventor-creator with the resources of a nation behind him. To imagine— to think—to construct—to energize!!! How do you communicate with the great masses of Black people? How do you use the earth to feed masses of people? How do you cure illness? How do you prevent illness? What are the Black purposes of space travel?[10]

In a sense he was asking how black people could express their own creativity and design technology that would represent their social, cultural, and technological aesthetics. He would get to the heart of this question through an analysis of a typewriter.

> A typewriter?—why shd [sic] it only make use of the tips of the fingers as contact points of flowing multi directional creativity. If I invented a word placing machine, an

"expression-scriber," *if you will*, then I would have a kind of instrument into which I could step & sit or sprawl or hang & use not only my fingers to make words express feelings but elbows, feet, head, behind, and all the sounds I wanted, screams, grunts, taps, itches, I'd have magnetically recorded, at the same time, & translated into word—or perhaps even the final xpressed thought/feeling wd not be merely word or sheet, but *itself,* the xpression, three dimensional—able to be touched, or tasted or felt, or entered, or heard or carried like a speaking singing constantly communicating charm. *A typewriter is corny!!* The so called fine artist realizes, those of us who have *freed* ourselves, that our creations need not emulate the white man's, but it is time the engineers, architects, chemists, electronics craftsmen, ie film too, radio, sound, &c., that learning western technology must not be the end of our understanding of the particular discipline we're involved in. Most of that west shaped information is like mud and sand when you're panning for gold![11]

Baraka clearly stated that the typewriter—a technology designed by someone who did not see the world from a black perspective—could not fit his aesthetic sensibilities. He used the typewriter to ponder what the results of black technological creativity would look like if black people were freed from Western technological domination. But Baraka, like King, would cautiously ask, "What is our spirit, what will it project? What machines will it produce? What will they achieve?" He demanded that black technological expression be humanistic, which in his words "the white boy has yet to achieve."[12]

A more recent example of what Baraka alluded to can be seen with the creative technological reconception at Black Liberation Radio. In 1986 DeWayne Readus (soon to be known as Mbanna Kantako) began Afrikan Liberation Radio (which became known as Black Liberation Radio in 1988 and is now Human Rights Radio) in his apartment located in the John Hay Homes public housing complex in Springfield, Illinois. Readus was already well known locally for his activism regarding public housing issues.[13] The radio station began as a means for the John Hay Homes Tenants Rights Association to organize the residents and began weekly broadcasts in January 1988.[14] Initially, the station mainly aired mixes, rap, reggae, political and social commentary, and occasionally listener phone calls. The station had a total power of one watt, and, due to the segregated nature of Springfield, most of Springfield's black population could receive the broadcast. The event that changed the position of Black Liberation Radio with Springfield's black community was the broadcast of what would become known as the Gregory Court massacre.

The events began to unfold on March 19, 1989, when the emotionally unstable Douglas "Dougie" Thomas held his girlfriend, Karen Lambert, and her sister, Nicole, hostage. During the forty-two-hour standoff, Thomas's family members wanted to talk to him, convince him to let the women go, and surrender. The Springfield police apparently were minimally responsive to the family's requests and eventually entered the apartment by force after shooting two canisters of tear gas through a window. In the end, Thomas shot the two women and himself; only Nicole was not fatally injured.[15] In the following week there was a great deal of disagreement between the black residents and the police regarding the order of the events that resulted in the deaths of Dougie Thomas and Karen Lambert. It was unclear to many if Thomas had shot himself and the Lambert sisters before the tear gas or because of the tear gas. After this incident, Black Liberation Radio led the questioning of Springfield's police and began to broadcast police activity and air the resident encounters with police brutality. Soon Black Liberation Radio was harassed for its activism, as well as for broadcasting without an FCC license.[16]

Readus/Kantako said his station was a form of electronic civil disobedience. Thus, he clearly knew what he was doing. His technologically driven response was not an accidental by-product of his hobby. He understood this set of technological objects as a potent means of regaining power and a voice within an oppressive local system. More important, Black Liberation Radio rearticulated the politics of surveillance in this African American community. The station supported an "inverted 'neighborhood watch,' " and observed "the police [and city officials] as the [violent and] threatening intruder."[17] Black Liberation Radio creatively reconceived surveillance technology to surveil the surveillants. As a result of this technologically and culturally rooted inversion of power, African Americans living in the Hay Homes renegotiated their relationships with the oppressive dominant power structure. This powerful reconception of a set of technological products of surveillance was based on the needs and desires of a black community.[18]

In similar ways to the Black Panther Party and Black Liberation Radio, resistance has been a motivating factor for musicians in the reconception of technological artifacts, practices, and knowledge.[19] One example of this can be seen with DJs and the act of scratching. Scratching is the purposeful manual manipulation of an LP recording in the reverse direction of the spinning turn-table to produce a "scratching" noise. Depending on the speed, duration, and the music already inscribed on the LP record, scratching can produce a plethora of sounds. When DJs began scratching, they subverted the fundamental meaning constructed for record players as well as for that of the LP records. What is significant about this basic maneuver is that it drastically diverges from the principal meaning embedded in the technological network associated with records and record players: to listen to prerecorded sound/music. DJs were thus able to creatively reconceive the technological products associated with recorded music and the knowledge associated with their functions based on their own black/ethnic musical sensibilities.[20]

The sonic and cultural priorities that led these musicians to reconceive recording equipment began to exert a broader influence as the popularity of hip-hop music exploded in the 1980s and 1990s. Initially, existing technology was incapable of reproducing the desired sounds. Musicians such as Herbie Hancock, who embraced the tonal flexibility of synthesizers, would often have to "hack" them to produce sounds like those exhibited in his Grammy award-winning single "Rockit".[21] Others, like Eric Sadler—one of the producers of Public Enemy's incendiary hip-hop album "Fear of a Black Planet" (1990)—who desired to reproduce a gritty, dirty, and for him, more authentic sound, had to rely on a different approach. During an interview, Sadler explained why he preferred to work in a less than pristine studio. "One of the reasons I'm here in this studio is because the board is bullshit. It's old, it's disgusting, a lot of stuff doesn't work, there are fuses out . . . to get the old sound. The other room, I use for something else. All sweet and crispy clear, it's like the Star Wars room. This is the Titanic room."[22] Even though he had access to a much newer studio, he specifically wanted to use this seemingly inferior equipment because it allowed him to create a rich, rough, bass-heavy sound that emulated the "old sound" of records from the 1960s and 1970s that he valued. What he called the "sweet and crispy clear" sound produced by the newer equipment simply did not fit his aesthetic, sonic, or cultural priorities.

As hip-hop became an important part of American culture, and represented an extremely lucrative market, the music industry came to embrace the technological tweaks of early hip-hop musicians and directly supported the development of equipment designed specifically to tap into this market. DJ legend and hip-hop pioneer Grandmaster Flash was instrumental in recreating a set of new technological objects and practices that addressed black cultural needs. Moreover, Grandmaster Flash's engagement with technology, like Readus/Kantako's, was not an accident. He had a history of technological innovation. He commented that it was his "love of technology, and specifically electronic equipment, that got me into DJing over 20 years ago. I remember stepping to the packed schoolyard jam with my equipment and records in hand ready to debut my new innovation, The Quick Mix Theory. Like a mad technoscientist, I had spent months holed up in my room testing dozens of needles, sampling sounds and perfecting my newest experiment."[23] His technological rhetoric acknowledges that he understood he was re-creating technology based on his own personal aesthetics as well as using scientific methods to develop his technique.[24] A newer extension of his technologically rooted creativity can be seen in Rane Corporation's Empath mixer. Grandmaster Flash played a key role in this device's technical design, and in a 2003 interview he spoke of his often contentious, but ultimately successful, working relationship with Rane:

> The items on a mixer that you touch the most were too far away and other items that you touch weren't there. So when I made that phone call to Rane, I told them that . . . I did have a problem with some things. So when I had conversations with [Rane's director of sales] Dean Standing, all my frustrations of 25 years were coming up. They finally said, "Flash, what do you want with the mixer?" And I just flooded them with what I wanted. I met with [Rane engineer] Rick [Jeffs] and that was probably the closest thing to a fistfight that it could possibly get. With his genius, he'd say, "Flash, but it's not normally done this way." And I'd say, "But you must!" He'll say, "The mixer doesn't have enough room for that." And I'd say, "Well, you gotta squeeze it." He said, "What's going to be the output format?" And I told him XLR, quarter-inch, and RCA! He'd come back with, "Why don't we do two of the three," and I'd say no. As I gave him my wish list, he'd have to keep going back to the schematic diagram and make it work.[25]

Flash overrode the reservations of the engineers to produce one of the most innovative DJ mixers on the market today. In the end, whether it is the valorization of old equipment, the subversion of the phonograph through scratching, or the collaboration between turntablists and the music industry, the vernacular technological creative innovations of hip-hop musicians have deeply imprinted black cultural aesthetics, priorities, values, beliefs, and sensibilities on the dominant culture. I think Tricia Rose says it best when she writes:

> Rap technicians employ digital technology as instruments, revising black musical styles and priorities through the manipulation of technology. In this process of techno-black cultural syncretism, technological instruments and black cultural priorities are revised and expanded. In a simultaneous exchange rap music has made its mark on advanced technology and technology has profoundly changed the sound of black music.[26]

Within the exploration of techno-black cultural syncretism and black vernacular technological creativity lies the potential to end the silence surrounding African American technological experiences.

Conclusion

African American technological experiences need to be studied to alter the current discourse of American technology, rather than to multiculturalize our narrow understanding of technology in America. With new multicultural and multiracial approaches to understanding the nature of technology and American culture, traditional narratives can no longer produce, contain, and maintain the explanatory power they once possessed. To develop a more thoughtful analysis of African American technological experiences, we need to think differently about the questions we ask and the tools we use to answer those questions. Technological knowledge must be interrogated, because it is inextricably intertwined with relations of power that are regularly applied to regulate black existences. Stuart Hall writes, "Knowledge linked to power not only assumes the authority of 'the truth' but has the power to make itself true. All knowledge, once applied in the real world has real effects, and in that sense at least, 'becomes true.'"[27] Following from Hall, it can be said that what we know about the relations between black people and technology primarily comes from dominant subject positions that unfortunately tell us more about how African Americans are controlled and regulated than about how black people engage technology from their own locations within American culture. The existing approaches used to understand technology in American society and culture overlook racialized power and conflict when they reduce everything to various forms of negotiation. This is not to implicate or label social theories of technology as forms of epistemological imperialism in the manner in which Edward Said writes about orientalism; but Said's thoughts are insightful.[28] In writing about colonialism and imperialism, Said inveighs that "both are supported and perhaps even impelled by impressive ideological formations that include notions that certain territories and people require and beseech domination, as well as forms of knowledge affiliated with domination."[29] Just as the intellectual work of which Said writes is tainted from the very beginning, social theories of technology are besmirched by similar dominant cultural efforts that are intended to maintain domination, but are concealed within the rhetoric of flexibility and freedom.

To gain a deeper understanding of black vernacular technological creativity, it is vital to examine the experiences of African Americans from where they stand in American society and culture rather than from the dominant position reflecting back on black lives. Black vernacular technological creativity is rich in historical value and replete with rebellion, resistance, assimilation, and appropriation in forms we would often not recognize and in places we are not accustomed to looking. It is from this space that we can see how black people reclaim a level of technological agency by redeploying, reconceiving, and re-creating material artifacts in their world. By focusing on black vernacular technological creativity and engaging in uncovering the multiple layers of black communities and their interactions with technology, we can avoid making the "they are all the same" essentialization of the marginalized mistake regarding African Americans.[30]

Technology is often thought of as a value-neutral "black box" for inputs and outputs. Critical studies of technology have opened the black box, but there are many hidden compartments that still need to be explored. To access these concealed compartments, or the "blackness" in the black box, we need to reassess and expand our study of technology to examine how racially marginalized people, such as African Americans, interact with technology and how technology mediates multiple African American experiences with racism. To address African Americans and technology, we must think about the ways in which black people see race and racism—important realities of everyday black existence. This is difficult because race and racism, in relation to technology, have always been hidden in a mysterious place of "unlocation."[31] By uncovering African Americans creating technological artifacts, practices, and knowledge that have become parts of the American material and technological cultures, black people will become visible metaphorically and materially. This work will enable black people to move out of the shadows, lift the veil, remove the mask, and solidify and develop decidedly positive technological representations and existences for African Americans within American society and culture.

Notes

1. Excerpt from Rayvon Fouché, "Say It Loud, I'm Black and I'm Proud: African Americans, American Artifactual Culture, and Black Vernacular Technological Creativity," *American Quarterly* 58.3 (2006): 639–661.
2. Imamu Amiri Baraka, "Technology & Ethos," in *Raise, Race, Rays, Raze: Essays Since 1965* (New York: Random House, 1971), 157.
3. Martin Luther King Jr., *Where Do We Go from Here: Chaos or Community?* (New York: Harper & Row, 1967), 171–72.
4. Ibid., 186.
5. Howard Brick, *Age of Contradiction: American Thought and Culture in the 1960s* (Ithaca, N.Y.: Cornell University Press, 2001); Robert A. Rhoads, *Freedom's Web: Student Activism in an Age of Cultural*

Diversity (Baltimore: Johns Hopkins University Press, 1998); Theodore Roszak, *The Making of a Counter Culture: Reflections on the Technocratic Society and Its Youthful Opposition* (Garden City, N.Y.: Doubleday, 1969); Kirkpatrick Sale, *SDS* (New York: Random House, 1973).

6. Sasha Torres, *Black, White, and in Color: Television and Black Civil Rights* (Princeton, N.J.: Princeton University Press, 2003).

7. The Black Panther Party members were not the first black people to redeploy the power of the gun in the twentieth century. Black activist Robert F. Williams powerfully advocated black armed resistance in the late 1950s and early 1960s (Timothy B. Tyson, *Radio Free Dixie: Robert F. Williams and the Roots of Black Power* [Chapel Hill, N.C.: University of North Carolina Press, 1999]).

8. Baraka, "Technology & Ethos," 155.

9. Ibid., 157.

10. Ibid., 155–56.

11. Ibid., 156–57.

12. Ibid., 157.

13. Doug Pokorski, "Hay Homes Group Again Seeks Bus Service," *The State Journal-Register* (Springfield, Ill.), October 23, 1985, sec. local 10; "Readus to Head Hay Tenants Group," *The State Journal-Register* (Springfield, Ill.), February 23, 1986, sec. local 35.

14. Mary Nolan, "FCC Turns Off Hay Homes Radio Station," *The State Journal-Register* (Springfield, Ill.), April 12, 1989, sec. local 9.

15. Jay Fitzgerald, Mike Matulis, Cathy Monroe, Michael Murphy, and Jacqueline Price, "Hostage Ordeal Ends," *The State Journal-Register* (Springfield, Ill.), March 20, 1989, sec. local 1; Jay Fitzgerald, "With 2 Dead the Questions Remain," *The State Journal-Register* (Springfield, Ill.), March 21, 1989, sec. local 1.

16. Nolan, "FCC Turns Off Hay Homes Radio Station"; Ron Sakolsky and Stephen Dunifer, eds., *Seizing the Airwaves: A Free Radio Handbook* (Oakland, Calif.: AK Press, 1998), 117–20.

17. Fiske, *Media Matters*, 273.

18. In light of the racialized nature of American culture, surveillance has become a technology of whiteness. This is primarily because black people have been constructed as the "others" in American society. In part due to skin color, the "difference" of blackness (or brownness) is regularly the object and target of surveillance. That which is not normal is surveilled, and black people within American society and culture have traditionally been the abnormal against which normal is judged.

19. Trevor Pinch and Karin Bijsterveld, "Sound Studies: New Technologies and Music," *Social Studies of Science* 34 (October 2004): 635–48; Mark Katz, *Capturing Sound: How Technology Has Changed Music* (Berkeley: University of California Press, 2004); Joseph Schloss, *Making Beats: The Art of Sample-Based Hip-Hop* (Middletown, Conn.: Wesleyan University Press, 2004); Jonathan Sterne, *The Audible Past: Cultural Origins of Sound Reproduction* (Durham, N.C.: Duke University Press, 2003); Timothy D. Taylor, *Strange Sounds: Music, Technology, and Culture* (New York: Routledge, 2001); Paul Théberge, *Any Sound You Can Imagine: Making Music/Consuming Technology* (Hanover, N.H.: Wesleyan University Press, 1997).

20. David Albert Mhandi Goldberg, "The Scratch in Hip-Hop: Appropriating the Phonographic Medium," in Eglash et al., *Appropriating Technology*, 107–44.

21. Siva Vaidhyanathan, *Copyrights and Copywrongs: The Rise of Intellectual Property and How It Threatens Creativity* (New York: New York University Press, 2001), 149–51.

22. Trisha Rose, *Black Noise: Rap Music and Black Culture in Contemporary America* (Hanover, N.H.: University Press of New England, 1994), 77.

23. See www.grandmasterflash.com/ (accessed June 8, 2006).

24. Jeff Chang, *Can't Stop Won't Stop: A History of the Hip-Hop Generation* (New York: Picador, 2005), 112–13.

25. Jim Tremayne, "With a Hot New Mixer on the Market and a Revitalized Career in Motion, DJ Pioneer Grandmaster Flash Finds that Necessity Is Still the Mother of Invention," *DJ Times*, March 2003.

26. Rose, *Black Noise*, 96.

27. Stuart Hall, ed., *Representation: Cultural Representations and Signifying Practices* (Thousand Oaks, Calif.: Sage Publications, 1997), 49.

28. Edward Said, *Orientalism* (New York: Pantheon Books, 1978).

29. Edward Said, *Culture and Imperialism* (New York: Knopf, 1994), 8.

30. Cornel West, "The New Cultural Politics of Difference," in *Out There*, ed. Ferguson et al., 19–36.

31. Heidi Mirza, ed., *Black British Feminism* (New York: Routledge, 1997), 5.

Dara N. Byrne

Byrne's work investigates community life on a Black social network site, BlackPlanet, to see whether and how participants engage in public discussions, if these discussions center on issues considered to be critical to the Black community, and if so, the extent to which participants' online networks are used to foster some level of civic engagement. Findings from the rhetorical analysis show that while participants are deeply committed to community issues, none of these discussions moved beyond a discursive level of civic engagement. This selection engages important questions as to whether digital technologies can in fact be used to close ranks, to deepen diasporan interconnectivity, or to serve as a galvanizing force that furthers goals such as liberation, justice, and self-determination.

Public Discourse, Community Concerns, and Civic Engagement: Exploring Black Social Networking Traditions on BlackPlanet.com

Dara N. Byrne[1]

Methodology

In order to explore public life on BlackPlanet and the extent to which participation in this online social network site fosters civic engagement, it was necessary to generate a sizeable yet manageable pool of data. I limited my sample to community forum threaded discussions, because more members contributed to this area on a daily basis than to all of the other communal areas on the site. I used a multi-step, multi-method design that included calculating the participation rate in the discussion forums, a simplified content analysis, and a thematic analysis. This three-step procedure enabled me to identify the most popular forums, the prevalence of discussions around black community concerns, the relationship between race-specific threads and member participation, and the relationship between discussing common concerns and civic engagement. Table 1 summarizes the basic research structure, along with the methods and research questions associated with each step in the study:

Although I have been studying BlackPlanet for several years, this particular study was conducted over a six-month period, from September 2006 to February 2007. However, BlackPlanet forums are archived as far back as February 2006, and the data used are not limited to threads initiated during the time period of this study. In some instances, threads continued to receive responses even though they may have started months prior to the study period; those earlier portions of the threads were also included in the study.

Table 1 Multi-step, multi-method process designed to examine public discussions and civic engagement on BlackPlanet

Step	Methods	Research questions
I	Calculation of participation rate (Discussion forums)	RQ1: What are the most popular forums on BlackPlanet?
	Calculation of participation rate (Discussion thread title sampling)	RQ2: Is there a relationship between forum popularity and race?
II	Content analysis (Keyword search of discussion forums)	RQ3: Are participants discussing issues of common concern to the community?
III	Content analysis (Hurricane Katrina and Darfur threads) Thematic analysis	RQ4: Is there a relationship between common concern and civic engagement?

ANALYTICAL PROCEDURES

Step 1

There are 18 discussion forums on BlackPlanet: Automobiles, Campus Life, Current Events, Family & Home, Finance, Food, Health & Beauty, Heritage & Identity, Movies & TV, Men, Music, Relationships, Religion & Spirituality, Site Feedback, Sports & Fitness, Style, Technology, and Women. To assess which forums were the most popular, I compared the number of discussion threads[2] with the number of responses. Since the forums are cached as far back as February 2006, this measure could be calculated in a straightforward way. I did not calculate the rate of participation during the study, because BlackPlanet added a new forum after the study commenced, and threads are often deleted or moved by moderators due to inappropriate content. Because of the volume of threads and responses, it is unclear whether the tallies for each forum reflect only the number of posts available for one to read or whether the tallies reflect the actual number of posts submitted to the forum. Nevertheless, the calculations provided are useful in generally identifying where activity, and thus the center of public life, is likely to be.

In order to explore whether the "race specificity" of the thread topic had any impact on the popularity of certain threads or forums, I collected the thread titles from the 20 most active discussions within the most popular subcategories of the most popular and least popular forums. I examined only the most popular subcategories within these forums, because each forum has a varying number of subcategories. For example, there are five subcategories within the Heritage & Identity forum, whereas the Religion & Spirituality forum only has one subcategory. I collected the 20 most active discussion thread titles on the first and last Saturday of each month for four months (November to February; n = 1600).

Each discussion thread title was then coded as "race-specific" or "race-neutral." I defined a race-specific thread as one in which the topic is clearly focused on a particular racial group. For example, "Are we lagging behind in academic achievement?" or "Are blacks lagging behind in academic achievement?" would both be coded as race-specific, even though in the first instance racial specificity is implicit with the use of "we." I defined a race-neutral thread as one in which the topic did not explicitly or implicitly invite participants to address race. "How important has higher education been to your career?" or "How do you heal from infidelity?" would both be coded as race-neutral. In cases where a famous black figure was noted in the title, I also coded the thread in terms of whether it also explicitly or implicitly invited participants to discuss race. For example, a thread with the title "Oprah's new house" was coded as race-neutral, while "Sistas! What does Oprah Winfrey's success mean to us?" was coded as race-specific. Volume of and participation in race-specific and race-neutral threads were then calculated and compared.

Step 2

In order to assess whether participants discuss issues of common concern to the black community, I conducted a keyword search based on a list of issues extracted from noted journalist and commentator Tavis Smiley's (2006) *The Covenant with Black America*. *The Covenant with Black America* is a collection of essays on 10 issues that Smiley and key black leaders and thinkers such as Marc Morial, President and CEO of the National Urban League, and David Satcher, former U.S. Surgeon General have identified as being of central importance to the black community. The issues are: healthcare and wellbeing, education, criminal justice, police accountability, affordable neighborhoods, voting, rural development, economic prosperity, environmental justice, and the digital divide. *The Covenant with Black America* has been at the top of the *New York Times* bestseller list, a first for a non-fiction book published by a black-owned press (Wheeler, 2006). In addition, Smiley and other community leaders host "State of the Black Union" forums and have called on grassroots organizations to use their networks at the local level. Similar forums have taken place in countless cities across the country.

Using the 10 issues identified in *The Covenant with Black America* as a framework for determining issues of common concern, I developed a list of 31 keywords that were then used to search the forums. It should be noted that the keywords were generated using three to five descriptive terms found in the opening paragraph of each of the *Covenant*'s chapters; thus, this list was not exhaustive. The keyword search of all of the forums was used as a means of establishing, empirically, whether public life on BlackPlanet involved these larger community issues. The keyword search returned a list of all threads in which one or more of the keywords appeared. BlackPlanet's search engine provides results based on the appearance of a keyword in the discussion thread title or in the body of the initiating message.

Step 3

Given the large amount of data generated in steps 1 and 2, a smaller sample was extracted for the thematic analysis. The purpose of the thematic analysis was to explore the relationship between public discourse about community issues and civic engagement, specifically whether participants were pooling resources and forging alliances to address issues that were of contemporary/immediate concern. When I began this study in September 2006, the two major issues on center stage in the black community, and in the U.S. at large, were the one-year anniversary of Hurricane Katrina and the genocide in Darfur. Conversations in black and mainstream media repeatedly covered these topics; Spike Lee's HBO documentary *When the Levees Broke* (2006) had aired just days before on August 29th; organized protests about relief efforts in the Sudan were ongoing; and the United Nations Security Council recently approved a resolution to send a coalition of peacekeeping troops to further relief efforts.

Given this context, I explored forum activity around Hurricane Katrina and the genocide in Darfur and found that threads on these topics were among the most active in three of the five most popular forums. I subsequently monitored activity in all Hurricane Katrina and genocide in Darfur threads for the duration of the study. I collected all thread titles and responses, read them carefully and noted participants' views on community action, whether any encouraged taking action, if alliances were developing or had already taken place, and the extent to which participants treated the online network as a resource for bringing about some form of change.

My search for "Hurricane Katrina" (or "Louisiana" or "levee") or "Darfur" (or "genocide" or "Sudan") yielded 466 threads in total. Threads in which the only responses were advertisements or chronicled an individual experience (e.g., a Hurricane Katrina survival story) were not used. I also eliminated threads with fewer than two unique participant screen names and any in which the conversation did not address either Hurricane Katrina or Darfur, even if this appeared to be the focus in the thread title or initial description.[3] For example, the thread "Levees in New Orleans Sabotaged" initiated by whiteKKKman[4] began with "God hates lazy people, so He breached the dikes to punish the lazy people of New Orleans . . . only the people too lazy to leave would still be in New Orleans." Although there were 54 responses, making this by far the most popular of the Hurricane Katrina threads initiated in October, I eliminated it from the sample, because all subsequent responses focused on whiteKKKman's racist attitudes, rather than on anything connected to Hurricane Katrina.

After following the procedure described above, I was left with 43 topic threads. The Hurricane Katrina sample included 23 threads and 460 responses, while the Darfur sample yielded 20 threads and 280 responses. Since some participants became inactive users during the time when the sample was collected (a screen name is replaced with the generic "inactive user" when a profile has been deleted from the site), it is unclear exactly how many "inactive users" participated and what their contributions were to these discussions. Excluding the inactive users, there were 42 unique screen names in the Hurricane Katrina sample and 35 unique screen names in the genocide in Darfur sample. The length of postings varied; the longest response by a participant was 1,217 words in length, while the shortest was four words in length.

I drew on Ehrlich's (2000) definition of civic engagement as my framework for coding. Ehrlich conceives of civic engagement as:

> working to make a difference in the civic life of our communities and developing the combination of knowledge, skills, values, and motivation to make that difference. It means promoting the quality of life in a community, through both political and non-political processes.

(p. vi)

Delli Carpini's (n.d.) definition of civic engagement was also useful for developing a list of codes to explore the Hurricane Katrina and Darfur threads. Delli Carpini explains that civic engagement can include a range of actions such as:

> individual volunteerism to organizational involvement to electoral participation. It can include efforts to directly address an issue, work with others in a community to solve a problem or interact with the institutions of representative democracy. Civic Engagement encompasses a range of activities such as working in a soup kitchen, serving on a neighborhood association, writing a letter to an elected official, or voting.

(p. 1)

Among the 12 codes used for the analysis were: volunteerism, committee membership and service, electoral participation, advocacy, activism, and community involvement. Advocacy was perhaps the broadest code, because it ranged from urging forum participants to take a particular course of action to an informational thread about events or activities. For example, "let's meet next Thursday to protest for Darfur" would be considered as reflective of civic engagement. Similarly, a post that asked participants to write letters to their Congressional representatives and included a sample letter and list of official addresses would be considered as reflective of civic engagement. In all cases, I was searching for some indication that participants were moving toward some course of action to address their common concern. I applied the codes systematically to the sample to produce counts of the frequency of each code. Another CMC researcher also read and coded the sample based on the aforementioned codes for civic engagement. The results differed on our interpretation of "taking action." The other coder counted all instances where "taking action" was discussed specifically and generally. I only counted instances where participants discussed a specific strategy. To address this difference, I modified my coding to include any suggestions to "take action," whether they were specific plans or abstract discussions about what ought to be in the plan. I also noted any indications as to whether discussions about community involvement included cooperation or the combining of resources from the online social network.

Findings

The first research question asked what were the most popular forums on BlackPlanet. At the conclusion of this study, there were 45,692 discussion threads and 367,017 responses across the 18 BlackPlanet forums. The most popular forums were Relationships, Heritage & Identity, Current Events, Religion & Spirituality, and Women. As the composite image of threads and responses below shows, Relationships accounts for 55% of threads, Heritage & Identity accounts for 9% of threads, Religion and Spirituality for 6.6% of threads, Current Events accounts for 4.2% of threads, and Women accounts for 3% of threads. Relationships accounts for 66% of responses, Heritage & Identity accounts for 12.2% of responses, Religion & Spirituality accounts for 8% of responses, Current Events accounts for 4.4% of responses, and Women accounts for 2.7% of responses.

These five forums represent 77.8% of all forum threads and 93.3% of all forum responses. Thus, for any BlackPlanet member wishing to participate actively in the community at large, these five forums would likely figure prominently in their day-to-day public activities.

The second research question asked whether there is a relationship between forum popularity and race-related topics. As Table 2 shows, while race-specific threads (n = 267) only accounted for 33% of the top threads in the most popular forums, race-specific content accounted for 48% (n = 14,090) of the total responses in the sample.

In the most popular forums, each race-specific thread attracted 52.8 responses, on average, while each race-neutral thread attracted only 29.1 responses. More race-specific threads and responses occurred in the Heritage & Identity forum than in any other. On average, each thread in the Heritage & Identity forum had approximately 72.2 responses, while race-neutral threads had 43.3 responses. Even in Religion & Spirituality, where the volume of race-neutral threads and responses significantly outweighed the race-specific threads, each race-specific thread yielded 26.7 responses, while the race-neutral threads yielded about 38.3 responses per thread.

In the least popular forums, race-specific threads account for about 12% (n = 92) of all threads and about 13% of responses, as Table 3 shows.

Closer examination of the results indicates that there is a relationship between a race-specific thread and a higher response rate in the least popular threads, as well. On average, race-specific forums generated more responses per thread than race-neutral threads, even though there were 616 more race-neutral threads across the least popular forums. These results suggest that race-specific threads still draw more responses and interest, and that the absence of race-specific discussions in these forums may be related to the lower overall participation rate by the membership.

The third research question asked whether participants were discussing issues of common concern to the community. As Table 5 shows, the keywords education (n = 1,332), slavery (n = 805), racism (n = 666), AIDS (n = 654), voting (n = 633), and justice (n = 593) were found in the largest numbers of discussion threads. The 31 keywords were found in 9,258 discussion threads in total.

Table 2 A comparison of race-specific and race-neutral threads and response activity in the most popular threads

Forum title	Most popular forums					
	Race-specific discussions			Race-neutral discussions		
	Threads	Responses	Ratio	Threads	Responses	Ratio
Heritage & Identity (General)	89	6,427	72.2	70	3,031	43.3
Current Events (General)	76	5,271	69.4	84	625	7.3
Women (General)	55	1,251	22.7	102	3,321	32.6
Relationships (General)	28	634	22.6	132	2,959	22.4
Religion & Spirituality (General)	16	407	26.7	145	5,557	38.3
Totals	267	14,090	52.8	533	15,493	29.1

Table 3 A comparison of race-specific and race-neutral threads and response activity in the least popular threads

| Forum title | Least popular forums | | | | | |
| | Race specific discussions | | | Race neutral discussions | | |
	Threads	Responses	Ratio	Threads	Responses	Ratio
Style (Talk to Ford Models)	20	412	**20.6**	140	1,784	**12.7**
Automobiles (Customizing)	12	180	**15.0**	148	948	**6.4**
Food	20	88	**4.4**	140	1,604	**11.5**
Campus Life (General)	40	72	**1.8**	120	128	**1.1**
Technology (Video Games)	0	0	**NA**	160	616	**3.9**
Totals	92	752	**8.2**	708	5,080	**7.2**

Table 4 Keyword search for threaded discussions on issues of common concern

| Common concern keyword search | |
Keyword	No. of threads
Activism	33
AIDS	654
Affirmative Action	98
Barack Obama	90
Black Power	103
Boycott	6
Building Wealth	17
Civil Rights	385
Cops	336
Community Empowerment	3
Crime	841
Diabetes	80
Digital Divide	2
Education	1332
Economic Empowerment	17
Grassroots	19
Healthcare	101
Incarceration	72
Justice	593
Leadership	279
Police Brutality	47
Poverty	500
Protest	152
Prison	649
Racism	666
Reparations	115
Slavery	805
Solidarity	74
Unity	320
Voting	633
Voting Rights	236

Because of the number of these threads, it was impossible at this stage of the study to calculate the total number of responses each thread received, since this would mean sifting through all 805 thread titles from the "slavery" keyword search, for example, to see the number of responses within each thread. Thus, this keyword search only shows that participants do create forum topics around these issues; this alone does not reveal the nature of the discussions. Nonetheless, the fact that these 31 keywords identified a total of 9,258 threads indicates that community issues are a prominent feature of black public life on BlackPlanet.

The fourth research question asked whether there was a relationship between discussion on issues of contemporary/immediate concern and civic engagement. Three significant patterns emerged from these discussions: 1) participants discuss "taking action" on an ideological or theoretical level, rather than in terms of specific courses of action appropriate for immediately addressing the issue at hand; 2) when specific courses of action are proposed, the initiators are often dismissed or called "irrational;" and 3) although participants acknowledge the "power of numbers," none explores the power of the numbers or resources available within the online social network. In the remainder of this section, I explain each of these findings, providing examples to highlight their most prominent characteristics.

Only three discussions were initiated with a request for specific forms of action. These particular threads also had the lowest participation (7 unique screen names in "Boycott anyone," 6 unique screen names in "Calling Black America," and 6 unique screen names in "Darfur—What can we do to stop the genocide"). It was more common for the person creating the topic to ask participants to reflect on the issue at hand, for example, "What can we do as a people" (33 unique screen names), than to suggest organized action. Thirty-nine of the discussions threads followed this "reflection" style; there were 583 messages and 120 unique screen names in these 39 discussion threads. When organized action was suggested, more than half of the respondents (58% or 70 unique screen names) engaged with the possibilities, 30% dismissed the notion outright, and the remaining 12% did not engage at all, but rather extended pleasantries like "good idea [screen name] good idea" or "let me think on this."

The most common precursor to organized action came in the form of a question, usually, "Where do we go from here?" It was rare for participants to enter the discussion with a preset, detailed plan. The following statement by MsRead in a Hurricane Katrina thread illustrates this point (spelling, grammar, and typography are left as in the original):

MsRead
    Female, 31, Little Rock, AR
    [Cruzlan], well said once again. what do we do now? They screwed us, as they have since we got here. Things will have to start at the smallest levels and gradually grow over time. We have to invest in our families, education, health, business, and communities. I am a strong proponent in all black prosperous communities. Lets get black doctors in black towns, black mayors governing black towns, black business owners in black areas. THAT IS WHAT WE HAVE TO DO TO GROW AS A PEOPLE AND ENSURE OUR KIDS KIDS HAVE SOMETHING TO LOOK FORWARD TO!

Of the instances where specific courses of action were proposed—candlelight vigils and "civil disobedience" once a week, a six-month boycott of "Pepsi, Coke, and pork," and letters to state Senators urging them to help save Darfur—only the letters to State Senators idea was not immediately dismissed. The other two posters were labeled "irrational," "unrealistic," or their plans "made no sense." However, none of their critics presented alternative courses of action. Similarly, the poster who described the letter writing campaign and went so far as to post two sample letters was simply acknowledged with "thanks," "you're the best," and "great idea, good luck." Participation in the thread ended shortly thereafter.

Instead of exploring the letter writing option, two participants in this same thread expressed their sense of hopelessness, even though a possible course of action had already been suggested:

SuperStar
Female, 26, Washington, DC
I have read some . . . Its just really sad and I feel helpless . . . Im not in a position to really help with anything . . .
TechGurl
Female, Private [User's age was not made public], Chicago, IL
I know . . . I hate that feeling . . . .
You know that it's unfair . . . . but you can't really make a big difference . . .

Participants in the more ideological threads frequently noted that "times have changed" since the Civil Rights Movement, the community is no longer "as one," and civic organizations are no longer fulfilling their role:

Sahara
Female, Private, Houston, TX
Furthermore, I think that organizations like the NAACP need to change their name—no one has heard a peep from them on any of this since it happened. Where is the so-called 'advancement'? . . . Groups like the NAACP used to stand for something and lead the way on issues such as this—now they fall for everything and are meaningless.
We have no activism or strength in numbers anymore.

Although members critiqued longstanding associations like the NAACP, they recognized the significance of such organizations. However, no participants indicated whether they were involved in any traditional black social networks, black associations, committees, or working in any other capacity to address the issues they spoke about.

In a similar vein, participants did not express any interest in cultivating their online networks. In the extended exchange below, not one of the participants explores the possibilities of incorporating the online network into the quest for "numbers:"

BlakkPanther
Male, 32, Denver, CO
"Well we have to start somewhere. We can start by simply putting our resources together.
I don't mean just networking, but imagine this.
10,000 black men coming together, Who make at least 30,000 per year. starting businesses, franchises under one large organization and keeping their current jobs. Each individual would make a little money, but the company as a whole should be in the high millions, possibly billions. There's power in numbers.
That would be a start.
That's just a thought."
MrEbb
Male, 55, San Francisco, CA
I also believe pooling resources will be a must. But we should start with a grassroots movement.

> I think once you get passed a certain financial strata you find people are satisfied with the status quo. That's the place where you find Black Republicans! that's why I think we need to start with education. Making people aware how bad is the situation.
> MrEbb
> Male, 55, San Francisco, CA
> We don't have to "reinvent the wheel". We can use the various examples of movements and investigate their failures.
> I give Marcus Garvey's movement as an example.
> The success of that movement was the unification of a large portion of Black people.
> That unification began with education and building trust.
> CrystalSunshine
> Female, 28, Beverly Hills, CA
> That would be a great start.
> I'm down for this movement for sure.
> Let me know when it starts.

Aside from the fact that this discussion is removed from the initial question, "how can we continue to help the victims of Hurricane Katrina," it is notable that the participants do not explore their online contacts as community resources. In fact, BlakkPanther explicitly indicates that networking is not part of his vision of a solution. Similarly, when BlackVoiceinDC suggests in another thread that "we" need to show solidarity with the people in Darfur, she consistently speaks about blacks "everywhere" but never directly solicits the assistance of the participants in the discussion, nor do any of them offer to play a role. Even though JDinChiTown expresses sympathy for "the cause" and notes that reading BlackVoiceinDC's post three days earlier inspired her to attend a meeting, neither one expresses an interest in collaborating.

After closely reading all 43 threads in the sample, I found that while participants are deeply interested in the well-being of Hurricane Katrina victims and the genocide in Darfur, civic engagement is not moving beyond the discursive commitment (the initial call for action, e.g., "we must do something to help"). In the rare instances when specific courses of action are proposed, the initiators are summarily dismissed, called "irrational," or placated with polite acknowledgments. Most interestingly, the analysis reveals no instances where participants explored the possibility of working together on the issues they all recognized as being of great concern to themselves and to black people everywhere.

Discussion

While it was clear that participants are deeply committed to ongoing discussions about black community issues, these discussions did not move beyond a discursive level of civic engagement. As the findings show, much of public life on BlackPlanet centers on daily discussions of larger community concerns, yet meaningful action beyond the discussions has yet to emerge. Although the purpose of this study was not to assess the efficacy of black SNSs for collective action, it does suggest that collective action will not be the inevitable outcome of ongoing interaction in such environments, in spite of the black community's longstanding history of promoting social networking for this purpose.

Diani's (2000) study of online social movements underscores the difficulty of using computer-mediated communication technologies for this form of organizing. After investigating three types of political organizations, Diani concluded that while there was potential to build social movements out of online communities, success was highest in those networks that had pre-existing offline relationships. Interestingly, his research also shows that groups with the least radical interests benefited the most from computer-mediated communication.

Diani's (2000) research and the findings of the present study suggest that the connective power SNSs provide will not translate easily or automatically into civic engagement, without this purpose being clearly articulated. The absence of such efforts on BlackPlanet also likely reflects the persistent absence of voices of locally, nationally, or internationally known black leaders on the site. The effects of this absence can be seen by comparing BlackPlanet with the July 2006 success of a coalition of well-connected black gay bloggers, such as scholar and commentator Keith Boykin. These bloggers, when they became outraged by an HIV/AIDS fundraising concert's roster of performances by anti-gay artists, were able to turn their swell of online dialoguing into offline protest in just a few days (Byrne, in press). This is not to say that organized efforts cannot emerge on BlackPlanet without "real" (offline) faces to legitimize them. However, the absence of "known" community figures or leaders on online social networks is one of the major distinctions between traditional black social networks and these online ones.

That participants are so heavily invested in ongoing dialogues about black community issues but do not take steps to address them raises three important questions for future research on black SNS:

1)   Is the limited interest in civic engagement found in this study the result of the medium?
2)   Is the limited interest in civic engagement found in this study indicative of a decline in such activities in the community in general?
3)   Is the limited interest in civic engagement found in this study perhaps just an early stage in the transition to online social networking?

The literature includes several examples where blacks have used community websites (Everett, 2002) and blogs (Byrne, in press; Pole, 2007) to encourage civic engagement. Further work should explore whether participants on black SNSs see these spaces as being purely for entertainment or socializing purposes, without any ability to impact their real world conditions. As the example of First Fridays at the beginning of this article showed, black social networks have typically serviced members' social as well as civic interests—the two were not seen as mutually exclusive. Given this history, research should investigate further whether black online social networks represent a shift away from offline traditions.

Although limited interest in community issues is a seemingly common criticism of young people today, research that explores social network usage by blacks would be a significant contribution to the literature. Given that some research shows that African American youth are "the most politically engaged racial/ethnic group" (Ketter, Zukin, Andolina, & Jenkins, 2002), of special interest is whether young black participants in online social network sites are less inclined to become involved in the community or are just less inclined to take online discussions about the community as seriously as they would face-to-face discussions.

While there is little indication in the findings that participants currently use the connective capabilities of a site like BlackPlanet for traditional civic engagement, this does not necessarily mean that such uses are not on the horizon. Given that BlackPlanet is fairly unique, as one of the few black sites that is long running, has millions of users, and fits within the SNS genre, it is much too early to predict whether the near-complete absence of civic engagement seen in this study is a pattern that will hold. The online social networking format itself is still relatively new, and figuring out how to employ it to serve a higher social purpose may take some time, even for a community that has an extensive tradition of civically-minded social networks.

Notes

1. Excerpt from Dara N. Byrne, "Public Discourse, Community Concerns, and Civic Engagement: Exploring Black Social Networking Traditions on BlackPlanet.com," *Journal of Computer-Mediated Communication* 13.1 (2007): 319–340.
2. In this article, the term "discussion thread" is used to refer to an initiating message (topic) and all responses it receives.
3. Forum threads are usually created by site members, although in some cases, BlackPlanet staff will create threads, especially about current events. In order to create a thread, registered members click on "start a new topic" within the desired forum; a title and description of the issue, topic, or question can then be added. Once a new topic is submitted to the forum, other members can respond to it. Responses are threaded, with the most recent post appearing below the initial description. The initial description always remains at the top of the screen.
4. All screen names of BlackPlanet participants quoted in this study have been modified.

References

Appiah, O. (2003). Americans online: Differences in surfing and evaluating race-targeted websites by black and white users. *Journal of Broadcasting & Electronic Media*, **47**(4), 537–555.

Banks, A. (2005). *Race, Rhetoric, and Technology: Searching for Higher Ground*. Mahwah, NJ: Lawrence Erlbaum Associates.

boyd, d. m. (2008). Why youth (heart) social network sites: The role of networked publics in teenage social life. In D. Buckingham (Ed.), *Youth, Identity, and Digital Media* (pp. 119–142). Cambridge, MA: MIT Press.

Brady, D. (2005, September 15). Black women and the web. *Business Week*. Retrieved October 16, 2007 from www.businessweek.com/technology/content/sep2005/tc20050915_9194_tc024.htm

Burkhalter, B. (1999). Reading race online: Discovering racial identity in Usenet discussions. In M. A. Smith & P. Kollock (Eds.), *Communities in Cyberspace* (pp. 60–75). London: Routledge.

Byrne, D. N. (in press). The future of (the) 'race:' Identity, discourse and the rise of computer-mediated public spheres. In A. Everett (Ed.), *Race and Ethnicity*. Cambridge, MA: MIT Press.

Diani, M. (2000). Social movement networks virtual and real. *Information, Communication, & Society*, **3**(3), 386–401.

Davis, E. L. (1996). *Lifting As They Climb*. New York: G.K. Hall.

Delli Carpini, M. (n.d.). Definitions of civic engagement. *CampusCares*. Retrieved February 23, 2007 from www.facet.iupui.edu/events/leadership/2006%20Syllabi/ALL/Definition%20-%20Civic%20Engagement.pdf

Detlefsen, E. G. (2004). Where am I to go? Use of the Internet for consumer health information by two vulnerable communities. *Library Trends*, **53**(2), 283–300.

Edgecombe, N. T. (2004). *An Echo in the Bone: An Exploration of the Relationship Between Caribbean Cultural Identity, Intercultural Exposure, and Psychological Well-Being of Indigenous Peoples*. Ph.D. dissertation, Howard University, District of Columbia, U.S. Retrieved February 21, 2007 from ProQuest Digital Dissertations database. (Publication No. AAT 3147533.)

Eglash, R. & Bleecker, J. (2001). The race for cyberspace: Information technology in the black diaspora. *Science as Culture*, **10**(3), 353–374.

Ehrlich, T. (2000). *Civic Responsibility and Higher Education*. New York: Oryx Press.

Everett, A. (2002). The revolution will be digitized: Afrocentricity and the digital public sphere. *Social Text*, **20**(2), 125–146.

First Fridays United. (n.d.). About us. Retrieved January 12, 2006 from http://firstfridaysunited.com/about Us.php

First Fridays United. (n.d.). Events. Retrieved January 12, 2006 from http://firstfridaysunited.com/events.php

Fraser, N. (1992). Rethinking the public sphere: A contribution to the critique of actually existing democracy. In C. Calhoun (Ed.), *Habermas and the Public Sphere* (pp. 109–142). Cambridge, MA: MIT Press.

Gangemi, J. (2006, September 20). A MySpace that speaks your language. *Business Week*. Retrieved August 15, 2006 from www.businessweek.com/smallbiz/content/sep2006/sb20060920_307149.htm

Graham, L. O. (2000). *Our Kind of People: Inside America's Black Upper Class*. New York: Harper Perennial.

Habermas, J. (1989). *The Structural Transformation of the Public Sphere*. (T. Burger, Trans.). Cambridge, MA: MIT Press.

Harris, K. L. (2005) *Searching for Blackness: The Effectiveness of Search Engines in Retrieving African-American Websites*. Ph.D. dissertation, Howard University, District of Columbia, U.S. Retrieved October 19, 2007 from ProQuest Digital Dissertations database. (Publication No. AAT 3228587.)

Herd, D., & Grube, J. (1996). Black identity and drinking in the US: A national study. *Addiction*, **91**(6), 845–857.

Hutcheson, P. A., & Kimbrough, W. M. (1998). The impact of membership in Black Greek-letter organizations on black students' involvement in collegiate activities and their development of leadership skills. *The Journal of Negro Education*, **67**(2), 96–105.

Isajiw, W. (1974). Definitions of ethnicity. *Ethnicity*, **1**, 111–124.

Johnson, T. D. (2006). APHA working with black sororities to prevent diabetes. *Nation's Health*, **36**(9), 5.

Kaplan, S. J., & Alsup, R. (1995). Participatory action research: A creative response to AIDS prevention in diverse communities. *Convergence*, **28**(1), 38–57.

Kant, I. (1990). *Foundations of the Metaphysics of Morals and, What is Enlightenment*. (L. White Beck, Trans.). New York: Macmillan.

Ketter, S., Zukin, C., Andolina, M., & Jenkins, K. (2002). The civic and political health of a nation: A generational portrait. *CIRCLE and The Pew Charitable Trusts*. Retrieved May 28, 2007 from www.civicyouth.org/research/products/youth_index.htm

Kimbrough, W. M. (2003). *Black Greek 101: The Culture, Customs, and Challenges of Black Fraternities and Sororities*. Madison, NJ: Fairleigh Dickinson University Press.

Kolko, B. E. (2002). Erasing @race: Going white in the inter(face). In B. E. Kolko, L. Nakamura, & G. Rodman (Eds.), *Race in Cyberspace* (pp. 213–232). London: Routledge.

Lee, B. A., Campbell, K. E., & Miller, O. (1991). Racial difference in urban neighboring. *Sociological Forum*, **6**(3), 525–561.

Lekhi, R. (2000). The politics of African America on-line. *Democratization*, **7**(1), 76–102.

Lorence, D. P., Park, H., & Fox, S. (2006). Racial disparities in health information access: Resilience of the digital divide. *Journal of Medical Systems*, **30**(4), 241–249.

Marcia, J. E. (1989). Identity and intervention. *Journal of Adolescence*, **12**, 401–410.

McPherson, T. (2002). I'll take my stand in Dixie-Net: White guys, the South, and cyberspace. In B. E. Kolko, L. Nakamura, & G. Rodman (Eds.), *Race in Cyberspace* (pp. 117–132). London: Routledge.

McGlure, S. M. (2006). Voluntary association membership: Black Greek men on a predominantly white campus. *Journal of Higher Education*, **77**(6), 1036–1057.

Miller, E. A., West, D. M., & Wasserman, M. (2007). Health information websites: Characteristics of US users by race and ethnicity. *Journal of Telemedicine & Telecare*, **13**(6), 298–302.

Nakamura, L. (2002). *Cybertypes: Race, Ethnicity, and Identity on the Internet*. New York: Routledge.

Nuwer, H. (2001). *Wrongs of Passage: Fraternities, Sororities, Hazing, and Binge Drinking*. Bloomington: Indiana University Press.

Partridge, D. C. (1974). Adult education projects sponsored by Negro college fraternities and sororities. *The Journal of Negro Education*, **14**(3), 374–380

Pole, A. (2007). Black bloggers and the blogosphere. *The International Journal of Technology, Knowledge, and Society*, **2**(6), 9–16.

Rouse, J. A. (1984). The legacy of community organizing: Lugenia Burns Hope and the Neighborhood Union. *The Journal of Negro History*, **69**, 114–133.

Rovai, A. P., & Gallien, Jr., L. B. (2005). Learning and sense of community: A comparative analysis of African American and Caucasian online graduate students. *Journal of Negro Education*, **74**(1), 53–62.

Scott, A. F. (1990). Most invisible of all: Black women's voluntary associations. *The Journal of Southern History*, **56**(1), 3–22, 92–111.

Smiley, T. (Ed.). (2006). *The Covenant with Black America*. Chicago: Third World Press.

Uyeki, E. S. (1960). Correlates of ethnic identification. *American Journal of Sociology*, **65**, 468–474.

Wilson, J. J., Mick, R., Wei, S. J, Rustgi, A. K., Markowitz, S. D., Hampshire, M., & Metz, J. M. (2006). Clinical trial resources on the Internet must be designed to reach underrepresented minorities. *Cancer Journal*, **12**(6), 475–481.

Adam J. Banks

Alkalimat's principles for eBlack studies are a companion for Banks's reflections on how Black cultural approaches to technology can be incorporated into rhetoric and composition courses. Representing a ten-year trajectory, these two excerpts prompt readers to think more strategically about the future of knowledge networks and how interdisciplinarity impacts the teaching and learning of African American rhetoric. This excerpt from the final chapter in Banks's work outlines broad strategies for how African American rhetorical theory and practice can synchronize with the field of digital studies. Banks argues that this would mean greater opportunity for activism and democratic engagement around issues like technological access and inequality.

Fade: Notes Toward an African American Rhetoric 2.0

Adam J. Banks[1]

And we return to the very beginning, the initial invocation that launched this book project: DJing is writing, writing is DJing. Paul Miller's statement, important fort both its clarity and reciprocity in the copula and the flip—DJing is not like writing, writing is not similar to DJing, each *is* the other—calls us to consider what the DJ offers to conceptions of writing when we move beyond a few mentions of individual writing practices completely lifted from context, from tradition, from social, cultural, political, and technological networks. When the DJ is viewed as a crucial component of a griotic tradition and linked to other griots in the forms of storytellers, preachers, standup comics, and everyday people, practices like the mix, remix, and mixtape push beyond general postmodern free-floating signifiers and begin to suggest, yes, exciting writing practices, but practices linked to principles, priorities, and purposes for understanding the complexities of writing in a multimedia age.

When I was invited to be one of the visiting scholars at Ohio State University's digital media and composition seminar a couple of years ago, I was asked my take on the differences between some of the various terms used to describe the intersection of writing and digital technologies: computers and writing, new media, digital writing, multimedia writing. I wandered, somewhat clumsily, through the question at the time, attempting to avoid some of the political issues attendant in the various terms and the different visions of what writing instruction should be that were loaded in or onto them. I wish I had not been so circumspect in that moment, as watching some of these debates unfold (as departments or programs attempt to decide what they name themselves and individual scholars position their work) has demonstrated even more clearly than I might have realized then just how important academic nomenclature can be. The saturation of digital, networked technologies in our culture and in the education system means many changes for what we think of as writing, but for me the most important of those changes is not the information literacy argument, as we have always talked about information literacy as central to the education process. It is not the technological tools themselves, as every era introduces different tools, systems, and ways of knowing and thinking about technologies that demand that we shift our attitudes toward writing and communication. The most important issue in this particular convergence of digital, networked technologies and writing or composition is the fact that composing in everyday and academic contexts is far more multimedia and multimodal than it has been at other times in our history (although rhetoric and composition's history has many reminders that notions of the oral and visual have always been a part of our conceptions of writing on some level).

Beyond the changes that we have witnessed in composing practices, processes, and products over the last two decades, however, the rise and saturation of digital technologies and the narratives about their importance that have emerged and even become hegemonic lead me to believe that writing in this multimedia age must be more than multimodal, more than multimedia: it must be a digital humanities project—in other words, intellectual work connecting technologies, in all the layered senses in which we use the word, to humanistic inquiry. Acts of writing, the social networks and cultural contexts in which they occur, and the technological networks in which they take place and are disseminated still involve systems of power, still reflect the relationships between individuals and groups within those systems, and still entail questions of what it means to be and how we come to see, hear, sense, and know the world with all of those technologies, power relations, social networks, and cultural contexts.

I have attempted to argue in this book that African American oral traditions, understood particularly from the perspective of the figure of the griot, offer writers, teachers, and scholars powerful ways to link oral performance, print literacies, and digital technologies in a truly multimedia approach to writing. On the level of purpose, or exigence, black griotic traditions call for an approach to writing that is committed to the range and flexibility to "teach in the idiom of the people" and committed to writing as not just remix but as rememory, or the passionate collective memory to which Manning Marable calls scholars. These traditions also call writers to something larger and more important than mainstream notions of success, to a commitment to long-term work and struggle with the difficult questions and issues an individual, community, or society might face. In terms of principles, the digital griot demonstrates a synthesis of deep, searching (crate-digging) knowledge of the traditions and cultures of his or her community and futuristic vision; the skills, ability, and comfort level to produce in multiple modalities; the ability to employ those skills toward the purpose of building and serving communities with which he or she is aligned; an awareness of the complex and layered ethical commitments and questions facing that community; and the ability to "move the crowd," to use those traditions and technologies for the purposes of persuasion.

By moving beyond specific practices and into a broader conception of the purposes, principles, and priorities that the digital griot, seen as an important part of a broader griotic tradition, offers understandings of writing in a multimedia age, we see that the DJ and the tropes of mix, remix, and mixtape provide a place from which to begin the work of reimagining African American rhetoric as a field of study in a new century. Therefore, a second (implied) argument throughout this book has been that we must imagine an African American rhetoric 2.0, as a digital humanities project, as a thorough linking of texts, techne, and technologies in the examination of how black people have engaged in the techno-dialogic, or the mutually constitutive relationships that endure between humans and their technologies.

The beauty of the remix as trope is that in its focus on renewed vision, on re-vision, those doing the remixing never discard the original text. The antecedent remains an important part of the next text, the next movement; ancestors and elders remain clear, and even central, to the future text. This is the way I view the relationship between an African American rhetoric 2.0 that I want to see scholars and students flesh out and the definitions and articulations of African American rhetoric that we have in place today. Let me call up a few of those definitions as I make an argument for a new mix, remix, and mixtape for this field of inquiry:

> [African American rhetoric is the] study of culturally and discursively produced knowledge-forms, communication practices, and persuasive strategies rooted in freedom struggles of people of African Ancestry in America.
>
> (Richardson and Jackson xiii)

> Black discourses have been the major means by which people of African descent in the American colonies and subsequent republic have asserted their collective humanity in the face of an enduring White supremacy and have tried to persuade, cajole, and gain acceptance for ideas relative to Black survival and Black liberation.
>
> (Gilyard, "Introduction," 1)

Hush Harbor rhetoric is composed of the rhetorics and commonplaces emerging from those rhetorics, articulating distinctive social epistemologies and subjectivities of African Americans and directed toward predominantly Black audiences in formal and informal Black publics or African American centered cultural geographies.

(Nunley 221)

African American rhetoric is the set of traditions of discursive practices—verbal, visual, textual, performative, digital—used by individuals and groups of African Americans toward the ends of full participation in American society on their own terms. These traditions and practices have both public and private dimensions and embrace communicative efforts directed at African Americans and at other groups in the society: hence, directly persuasive public address and less overtly persuasive day to day performances that contribute to the creation of group identities are all viable subjects of African American rhetorical study."

(Banks 2)

Jacqueline Jones Royster, in her foreword to Elaine Richardson and Ronald Jackson's anthology *African American Rhetoric(s): Interdisciplinary Perspectives*, describes the definition Richardson and Jackson present in language that really applies to all of the articulations above:

They centralize the use of cultural frameworks in rhetorical analysis as they emphasize the importance of the practices that they are showcasing having emerged from people with a particular ancestry—African. They focus on discursive forms, which underscores the importance of verbality and rationality, rather than just orality and literacy. They acknowledge persuasion as the abiding purpose of interactive engagement within and across communities, and they make clear that the mandate that is quite compelling in these discursive forms is tied unequivocally to struggles for freedom among this group. What's more, they present this view as part of knowledge-making processes, rather than as simply expressive traditions, suggesting that there are consequences for language use in terms of the ways that we think, act, and consider ourselves in the world.

(ix)

All of these definitions work for me as continuing definitions of African American rhetoric as an area of study, even as I am pushing here for scholars to limn out this area of study as a fully developed digital humanities project moving forward. It would be rather easy to say that an African American rhetoric 2.0 means taking the definitional work of Gilyard, Royster, Richardson, and Jackson and applying it to digital means and spaces. By calling for a remixed conception of the field, however, I mean far more than scholars asking, "What are blackfolk doing online?" I also mean something richer than the American Council of Learned Societies describes in its 2006 report, *Our Cultural Commonwealth*, in its articulation of digital humanities as a project that "cultivates leadership in support of cyberinfrastructure" and "encourages digital scholarship."

A revised vision of African American rhetoric as a digital humanities project for me certainly means rich, thorough examinations of African American discourse in technologized and online spaces and developing infrastructure and digital scholarship. But for me, those goals just scratch the surface. I'm interested in what Joel Dinerstein and Alex Weheliye identify as black survival technologies and a black techno-dialogic. How have "African Americans created the nation's survival technology" (Dinerstein 22)? How have black people imagined and reimagined what it means to be in relationship with everchanging technological landscapes? Landscapes where, as Johndan Johnson-Eilola argues in his book *Datacloud*, large-scale changes are difficult to document in the ways we are used to (by charting history-making major or cataclysmic events) because the accumulation of many interconnected small changes over long periods of time leads to wholesale change we often don't recognize until we are fully enmeshed in them. I hope to see scholars and students explore the complicated ways in which micro- and macro-level technological developments in American society affect African American life and the discursive production that emerges from those moments.

The role of Hip Hop offers just one example, one metaphor, that shows how we might reimagine our work with Alondra Nelson's and Afrofuturism's synchronizing project in mind. Generation 2.0 of African American rhetoric scholars has done amazing work using Hip Hop primarily through the figure of the rapper or MC to explain black discursive practices, launched needed debates about representation, interrogated systems of power and privilege, and created space in the writing classroom for black bodies and their languages to be respected. An African American rhetoric 2.0 would continue that work and still have love for the MC but begin with the DJ and link digital technologies and practices and processes and all their attendant issues to the questions it raises and the answers it finds. African American rhetoric 2.0 should still examine issues of representation and language in the lyrics of black music, but, as Barbara Garrity-Blake does with fish chanteys in her essay "Raising Fish with a Song: Technology, Chanteys, and African Americans in the Atlantic Menhaden Industry," it would examine prison songs, work songs, and field hollers as powerful examples of techne and "invisible technology" that not only made labor, like laying railroad track and menhaden fishing, possible but fueled the larger American technological enterprise and "signified . . . expressed resistance to white authority, freedom" (114) and built community and shared the worldviews of black people in those communities. A couple more examples of the differences I mean might be illustrative here. The famous debates between Booker T. Washington and W. E. B. Du Bois about the scope and goals of education for black people was just as much about the transition from an agrarian to an industrial age as it was about "skills" versus/with "critical literacies." African American rhetoric 2.0 would continue to examine this debate but would also begin to ask how everyday discursive practices and broader attempts to move the people were rooted in the realities of how technological change affected and affects black life, individual and communal identities, discourse, and persuasive efforts. Ben Williams's masterful examination of the history of techno music in Detroit in the 1980s provides another example. In his essay "Black Secret Technology," he describes the emergence of techno music in terms of the sonic and intellectual influences on the music and also the story of how Juan Atkins and other legendary techno DJs used technologies to create a new form of music. In addition, Williams documents how techno's history was deeply rooted in, and was a direct response to, the relationships between race, technology, class, and labor that marked the United States and post-industrial Detroit.

Bold, creative, innovative uses of technologies; deep inquiry into technologies' influences on African American lives and African American influences on technologies; African American survival technologies across eras; digital scholarship; development of cyberinfrastructure for studying black texts and discourses—all of these and more are crucial to the development of African American rhetoric as a twenty-first-century discipline that thoroughly values and thoroughly weaves together spoken, oral, visual, and digital means of persuasion. By isolating the mix, remix, and mixtapes as tropes for reimagining African American rhetoric and its links to composition, I have suggested that training writers to be digital griots can help them develop skill and expertise in oral, print, and digital modes of presentation in ways that promote an ability to build from one's own cultures and traditions even as writers enter ever-changing cultural and digital spaces.

Beyond synchronizing and bringing more critical attention to the relationships between technologies, oral traditions, print, and multimedia writing, however, an even greater task for an African American rhetoric 2.0 is in synthesizing the many poles and continua that mark black rhetorical production and academic work:

- old school/new school—tradition and innovation
- Saturday night and Sunday morning: street and church, secular and sacred

- Malcolm X's focus on black communities and Martin Luther King Jr.'s aims for a broader, transformed Beloved Community
- the block and the rock—a commitment to addressing local, national, and transnational issues
- specificities in black experiences and issues and searing intersectional interrogation and critique of sexism, racism, class, and sex oppression
- radical democracy and black nationalisms
- public discourse and vernacular traditions/practices in the underground
- disciplinary and interdisciplinary concerns

By advocating synchronizing and synthesis as theoretical goals for the study of African American rhetoric, I'm in no way suggesting that the tensions in these areas can or should be "resolved" by scholarly attention to them, even though my own rhetorical move, if you will, is to search for moments and traditions of synthesis in and amid what seem to be dichotomies. Instead, I mean that we should look to examine the poles of the polemics together. Therefore, regardless of one's own inclination for, say, Malcolm over Martin or jazz over Hip Hop or religious rhetoric over the secular, I am arguing here for a conception of what it means to study African American rhetoric that demands that students in this area be exposed to the polemics and the continua in the tradition in such a way that they understand that there is no such thing as a "pure integrationist" or a "pure nationalist," as Manning Marable and Leith Mullings note, or that one cannot appreciate King without knowing X, as James Cone teaches, or that P-Funk gets sampled in gospel music just like it does in Hip Hop, and that even public rhetoric by blackfolk often still has yet other layers of meaning in the underground—just as arguments and discursive patterns that have their roots and intended audiences in the underground, whether by design or appropriation, can always find their way into public, mainstream discourse.

Beyond the argument for such an approach, however, questions remain: What does it mean to take the abilities and practices of the griot in African American culture and put them to use in digital writing and activism? What does it look like to teach students in school and out to become like Papa LaBas and to have that approach define how they view writing with technologies and in the ever-changing environment that marks writing in digital spaces? The combination of the many griotic figures in African American culture—the storytellers, the preachers, the everyday griots in their recreations of history and future, the DJs—offers us both a set of abilities and skills in addition to the framework for an outlook that allows us to see writing as serving local communities as well as the official purposes we assign writing in schools and workplaces. This framework includes an understanding of writing and technology as tools to preserve cultures even while planning future agendas; a focus on technologies as tools for reform, resistance, and renewal—as possible elements of a progressive politics of transformation; a set of ethical commitments that requires us to confront systems of oppression and exploitation in solidarity with those who have been systematically excluded from our society; the ability to produce in multiple modalities and to understand the conventions, possibilities, and constraints of various modalities; a deep and searching understanding of the traditions and cultures of one's community; and a rhetorical focus on being able to move the crowd, which requires (among other things) an ability and willingness to speak across the continua or tensions that mark a particular community at a particular time.

The specific projects shouted out through the text—digNubia, Cyber-Church, Arthur Flowers's Rootsblog, Diva Delight, and Marcyliena Morgan's Hiphop Archive—show digital griots at work, using digital writing and technologies to build and sustain community through flow, layering, and rupture. Scholars like Carmen Kynard and Elaine Richardson demonstrate uses of technologies toward liberationist pedagogies building from and through Tricia Rose's concepts of flow, layering, and rupture. As they point the way forward, Katie Cannon and James Cone, everyday griots, keep us moving forward by keeping us connected to traditions, to "surviving the blight" and engaging in creative struggle against those external constraints still on people's lives while maintaining dignity in the midst of the madness. Reimagining the work ahead, for me, means understanding that writing changed in the Bronx in 1973: completely rooted in the tradition and opening up possibilities that few, if any, saw besides the DJ. African American rhetoric in 2010 and beyond finds itself in a new era defined by amazing new possibilities and brutal realities that its study can help elucidate, in ways that few other areas can, if it proceeds committed to community, linking the truths and discursive practices found in oral traditions to rigorous analysis of the relationships between society and its technologies.

There are voices on the scholarly scene to show us what these relationships can look like, as well. Richardson's important volume *Hip Hop Literacies* provides an important spotlight for those of us wading into new literacies waters, with analysis of wide-ranging literate practices from poetry to beat-making to video gaming, and Jon Yasim makes valuable contributions for scholars looking to build pedagogical bridges between young people, Hip Hop culture, writing, and technology. Dara Byrne and Tyrone Taborn, with essays published in Anna Everett's volume *Learning Race and Ethnicity*, also begin to point the way to scholarly agendas for the future. Taborn's "Separating Race and Technology: Finding Tomorrow's IT Progress in the Past" points to the cultural dimensions at work between race and technology when youth in all strata of our society idolize Kobe Bryant but have never heard of Dr. Mark Dean, the black engineer who played crucial roles with IBM in the development of the personal computer. He reminds us again that histories, current circumstances, and future visions are all linked and challenges us to continue to work for real, meaningful technology access: "Saying that the Digital Divide is closing because minorities have greater access to computers is like saying minorities have a stake in the automobile industry because they drive cars" (39). Taborn calls us to mine the pasts of African American achievement in science and technology to destroy thoroughly the myths of black disinterest in science, technology, engineering, and math fields and introduces the concept of "cyber mentoring" to bring African American and other students of color fully into digital networks.

Byrne's essay "The Future of (the) Race: Identity, Discourse, and the Rise of Computer-Mediated Public Spheres" is an ambitious study of more than three thousand discussion threads on the early social networking sites BlackPlanet, MiGente, and Asian Avenue in order to better understand the relationships that endure between rhetorical production and racial and ethnic identities in online spaces. Her analysis helps us see that social networking sites and other digital spaces that adults might dismiss as insignificant are potentially powerful vehicles for civic engagement (32) and that regardless of our views of young people's interests or discourse, we must understand the contours of the conversation as they see it, if there is to be any potential for community-building or connecting with young people. Similarly, there is much that we can do in order to see that youth understand that "there is a fundamental relationship between collective voice and social change" (32).

Taken together, Taborn's and Byrne's articles push us to think more carefully about how rhetoric and technology might be brought together in both scholarship and collective action. We need major, detailed studies of how African Americans from many different social locations are using social networking tools like SecondLife, Facebook, Twitter, and LinkedIn, and the particular flavors and valences they bring to technology convergence. We need students and scholars following up on important developments black people have brought to e-government conversations: how should people organize to use digital tools to have better access to and influence on policy debates, budgetary processes, and dialogue with government officials? We need to extend Royster's and Shirley Wilson Logan's examinations of the lyceums that sparked nineteenth-century social movements to see if and where such spaces exist online and what kinds of rhetorical principles black people are learning in them. We need careful, thoughtful exploration of ways Juneteenth and Pullman porters and black women's organizations developed and maintained social and activist information networks in order to see what we might learn from them and apply to today's scholarship on network theory. And we need many studies detailing precisely how black students, scholars, and laypeople use technologies in the writing process—the strategies they employ, the tools they use, the assumptions they bring to writing tasks, the ways they engage with digital interfaces in order to begin conversations with human-computer interaction. We need to pay careful attention to the many episodes of digital activism in which African Americans are engaged as well as they ways they are using digital tools to participate in movements that black people are not usually associated with, like environmental justice. And maybe most of all, we need painstaking digital documentation and preservation of African American stories, sayings, oral histories, proverbs, toasts, jokes, and other oral texts across generations in order to have a fuller historical record preserved as we continue to develop new bodies of folklore.

African American rhetoric 2.0 must build a strong focus on studying and changing the relationships that endure between race, ethnicity, culture, rhetoric, and technologized spaces. The generation of scholars that has entered the academy since "Writing in the Spaces Left" has a critical opportunity to help reshape both African American rhetoric and all of composition studies by mixing, remixing, and mixtaping these intersections. Theoretically, this means an imperative to "noisily bring together competing and complementary beats without sublimating their tensions," as Weheliye reminds us (13). Ethically, it is a call to identify whom and what we are here to serve, willing to stand not only with black people but also with others who still struggle against oppression. Pedagogically, it means a firm commitment to build from the truths and tropes of black experience in writing curricula, courses, assignments, evaluation, feedback, and teacher stance and delivery—not just for black students but as a part of the education all students receive. It means building assignments that invite students not only to work across modalities but also to link those multiple modalities, individual assignments, and assignment cycles and in critical examination of the power relations and material conditions inscribed in technological tools, networks, and discourses. Practically, it means working to increase meaningful, transformative access to digital technologies for people on their own terms. It means mix, remix, mixtape. Access and transformation. Healing, celebration, self-examination, and critique. Community. Flow, layering, rupture. Innovation, vision, quality, tradition. Afrodigitized. Word.

Note

1. Adam J. Banks, "Fade: Notes Toward an African American Rhetoric 2.0.," in *Digital Griots: African American Rhetoric in a Multimedia Age* (Carbondale: Southern Illinois Press, 2011), pp. 153–168.

Section 10: Further Reading

Arnold, P. W. "Chuck D Explains How Bill Clinton Ruined Radio and Why You Have No Choice But to Re-Elect Barack Obama." *Hip Hop DX* (2012). Retrieved from www.hiphopdx.com/index/news/id.19022/title.chuck-d-explains-how-bill-clinton-ruined-radio-and-why-you-have-no-choice-but-to-re-elect-barack-obama

Atlanta Daily World. "Two Held in Connection with Chicago Lad's Death." (1 Sept. 1955): 1.

Bogle, D. "The 1980s: 'Superstars.'" In *Primetime Blues: African Americans on Network Television.* New York: Farrar Straus Giroux, 2001. Excerpt from pp. 290–303.

Bould, M. "The Ships Landed Long Ago: Afrofuturism and Black SF." *Science Fiction Studies*, 102 (2007): 177–186.

Boykin, K. "Black Gay Bloggers Unite against Homophobic Artists." (2006). Retrieved from www.keithboykin.com/arch/2006/07/11/black_gay_blogg

Boyle, E. "Vanishing Bodies: 'Race' and Technology." In *Midnight Robber* by Nalo Hopkinson. *African Identities*, 7.2 (2009): 177–191. Excerpt from pp. 180–183.

Brock, A. "Race Matters: African Americans on the Web Following Hurricane Katrina." In *Proceedings of Cultural Attitudes Towards Communication and Technology*. Eds. F. Sudweeks, H. Hrachovec, and C. Ess, 2008. (pp. 91–105). Excerpt from pp. 100–104. Retrieved from www.academia.edu/175030/Race_Matters_African_Americans_Online_Following_Hurricane_Katrina15–17

The Chicago Defender. "Demand Justice in Lynching" (10 Sept. 1955): 1.

The Chicago Defender. "Mother's Tears Greet Son Who Died a Martyr" (10 Sept. 1955): 1.

The Chicago Defender. "We'll Be Back" (17 June 1944): 10.

Contee, C. "In Defense of Black Bloggers Having a Relationship with the White House." *Jack and Jill Politics* (2010). Retrieved from www.jackandjillpolitics.com/2010/10/in-defense-of-black-bloggers-having-a-relationship-with-the-white-house/

Corbett, J. "Brothers from another Planet: The Space Madness of Lee 'Scratch' Perry, Sun Ra, and George Clinton." In *Extended Play: Sounding Off from John Cage to Dr. Funkenstein*. Durham: Duke University Press, 1994. (pp. 7–24). Excerpt from pp. 19–23.

The Crisis. "Mississippi Barbarism." (October 1955): 480.

Curry, G. E. "Viacom's BET Turns into ET." Retrieved from http://georgecurry.com/columns/index1.shtml?id=1059847337

Davis, B. "An Open Letter to Cathy Hughes." *Soul Patrol Online*. (2004). Retrieved from www.soul-patrol.com/search/index.php?cmd=view&id=20151

Eglash, R. "A Two-Way Bridge across the Digital Divide." *The Chronicle of Higher Education*, 48 (2002): 41.

Eshun, K. "Further Considerations on Afrofuturism." *CR: The New Centennial Review*, 3.2 (2003): 287–302.

EURWeb. "Black Gay Bloggers Launch Protest: Target Is Music Industry's Anti-Gay AIDS Concert." (2006). Retrieved from www.eurweb.com/story/eur27394.cfm

EURWeb. "An Open Letter to Cathy Hughes: Radio One Owner Accused of 'Setting Black America Back 40 Years.'" (2004). Retrieved from www.eurweb.com/story/eur17546.cfm

Everett, A. "The Revolution Will Be Digitized: Afrocentricity and the Digital Public Sphere." *Social Text*, 20.2 (2002): 125–146.

Hargest, T. "Bitter Nigger Inc." *Social Text*, 20.2 (2002): 115–123.

Henriques, J. "Sonic Diaspora, Vibrations, and Rhythm: Thinking through the Sounding of the Jamaican Dancehall Session." *African and Black Diaspora: An International Journal*, 1.2 (2008): 215–236. Retrieved from http://eprints.gold.ac.uk/4259/1/HenriquesSonicDiaspora**.pdf. Excerpt from pp. 8–11.

Gaiter, L. "Is the Web too Cool for Blacks?" (1997). Retrieved from www.salon.com/june97/21st/cool970605.html

Greer, O. J. "Yes We Can: (President) Barack Obama and Afrofuturism." *Anamesa: An Interdisciplinary Journal*, 7 (2009): 34–42.

Jacobs, R.N. (2000). *The Rodney King beating. Race, media, and the crisis of civil society: From Watts to Rodney King*. Cambridge, UK: The University of Cambridge Press.

James, R. "Robo-Diva R&B: Aesthetics, Politics, and Black Female Robots in Contemporary Popular Music." *Journal of Popular Music Studies*, 20.4 (2009): 402–423. Excerpt from pp. 410–418.

Jet Magazine. "Nation Horrified by Murder of Kidnapped Chicago Youth" (15 Sept. 1955): 7.

Kimberley, M. "Obama Ignores Black Unemployment." *The Black Agenda Report*. (2009). Retrieved from http://thepinehillsnews.com/wp/2009/07/30/obama-ignores-black-unemployment/

Kynard, C. (2007).'Wanted: Some black long distance writers': Blackboard flava-flavin and other Afro-digitized experiences in the classroom. *Computers and Composition 24*(3): 329-345.

Maddox Jr., A. H. From "Jim Crow Travel to Jim Crow Radio." *New York Amsterdam News* (2006). Retrieved from www.ebscohost.com

New York Amsterdam News. "50,000 Line Chicago Streets for Look at Lynch Victim" (10 Sept. 1955): 1.

New York Amsterdam News. "Mass Meet on Till Murder" (10 Sept. 1955): 14.

New York Amsterdam News. "Public Meet to Protest Miss" (24 Sept. 1955), killing: 1.

Ott, D. "Excerpt Titled Electronic Media and the Promotion of Democracy in Africa." *Power to the People: The Role of Electronic Media in Promoting Democracy in Africa*. (1998) First Monday 3. Retrieved from www.firstmonday.org/htbin/cgiwrap/bin/ojs/index.php/fm/article/view/588/509. Excerpt section entitled Electronic Media and The Promotion of Democracy in Africa.

Poussaint, A. "Why Is TV So Segregated?" *Family Education*. (2010). Retrieved from http://fun.familyeducation.com/television/african-americans/35259.html

Rambsy II, H. "The Rise of Colson Whitehead: Hi-Tech Narratives and Literary Ascent." In *New Essays on the African American Novel: From Hurston and Ellison to Morrison and Whitehead*. Eds. L. King and L. F. Selzer, 2008. (p. 221). Excerpt section entitled Upgrading the content of character.

Rice, J. "Appropriation." In *Rhetoric of Cool*. Carbondale: Southern Illinois University Press, 2007. Excerpt section entitled "Cool Cities", pp. 48–54.

Sinker, M. "Loving the Alien." *The Wire* (1992): 96. Retrieved from www.thewire.co.uk/articles/218/

Squires, C. R. "Black Talk Radio: Defining Community Needs and Identity." *Harvard International Journal of Press/Politics*, 5.2 (2000): 73–93. Excerpt from pp. 82–89.

Stites, J. "Prospectus; As Black Technology Entrepreneurs Organize, They Are Spreading the Word about the Benefits of 'Digital Freedom'." *The New York Times* (22 Feb. 1999). Retrieved from www.nytimes.com/1999/02/22/business/prospectus-black-technology-entrepreneurs-organize-they-are-spreading-word-about.html?pagewanted=all&src=pm

Tyree, T. C. M. and A. Krishnasamy. "Bringing Afrocentricity to the Funnies: An Analysis of Afrocentricity" within *The Boondocks*. *Journal of Black Studies* by Aaron McGruder. 42.1 (2011): 23–42. Excerpt from pp. 31–36.

Walton, A. "Technology versus African Americans." *The Atlantic Monthly* (1999). Retrieved from www.theatlantic.com/past/docs/issues/99jan/aftech.htm

Williams, B. "Black Secret Technology: Detroit Techno and the Information Age." In *Technicolor: Race, Technology, and Everyday Life*. Eds. A. Nelson, T.LN. Tu, & A. Headlam Hines. New York: New York University Press, 2001. Excerpt section from pp. 154–167.

Zachary, G. P. "Black Star: Ghana, Information Technology and Development in Africa." *First Monday* (2004): 9. Retrieved from http://firstmonday.org/htbin/cgiwrap/bin/ojs/index.php/fm/article/view/1126/1046. Excerpt section entitled Chapter one—To the promised land: Information technology and Ghana's "destiny."

Zuberi, N. "Is This the Future? Black Music and Technology Discourse." *Science Fiction Studies*, 34.2 (2007): 283–300. Excerpt from pp. 289–292.

Section 10: Discussion Questions

1. Based on your interpretation of technology, explain how the changing uses of technology have impacted African American rhetoric of/with technology.

2. Theorists like Arthur Jafa, Rayvon Fouché, and Alexander Weheliye explore African American engagement with differing technologies. Are there any similarities in their theoretical approaches or analyses of technology? How do their approaches differ?

3. Create an outline for a story in which Afrofuturistic principles like those articulated by Nalo Hopkinson or Alondra Nelson are used to address a contemporary racial challenge. How did you address race, culture, and identity? How did you transcend the contemporary challenge?

4. Select three African American and three mainstream news publications, whether print or online. Compare their coverage of one or two issues of concern to the African American community. Did any of the news sources frame the issue in a way that identifies African American cultural perspectives? Did any of the news sources engage in an activist agenda?

5. What role can academic institutions play in challenging the way society values African American contribution to and participation with technology? Identify three or four strategies.

6. After listening to examples of Black radio broadcasts from the 1950s and 1960s, describe how some of the disc jockeys incorporated African American oral traditions. Do you think any of those traditions persist on the radio today? How has the sonic presence of the disc jockey changed?

7. Is digital media better positioned than other mass communication technologies to help African Americans achieve long-standing goals of liberation, justice, and self-determination? Why or why not?

11

BEAT REBELS *CORRUPTING YOUTH* AGAINST BABYLON

Edited and with an introduction by Greg Thomas

———————⟫∘∘∘⟪———————

Rap in general dates all the way back to the motherland, where tribes would use call-and-response chants. In the 1930s and 1940s, you had Cab Calloway pioneering his style of jazz rhyming. In the '60s you had the love style of rapping, with Isaac Hayes, Barry White and the poetry style of rapping with the Last Poets, the Watts poets and the militant style of rapping with brothers like Malcolm X and Minister Louis Farrakhan. In the '60s you also had "The Name Game," a funny rap by Shirley Ellis, and radio DJs who would rhyme and rap before a song came on.

—Afrika Bambaataa (1993)

Introduction

Around the same time that some academic critics in North America were debating whether the history of rhetoric on a certain definition had come to an end, Lauryn Hill ("*Don't trust it/This cosmology's busted!*") of the Fugees could be seen explaining to BET audiences that this society is threatened by articulate Black people in general and articulate Black youth in particular. The potent and much dreaded figure of the "rapper" strikes fear. Ironies abounding, such young Black people have become the international image of wordsmithing, word-sorcery, and word-slinging in the present day. His or her mode of articulation does not fail to challenge Western bourgeois conceptions of articulation, however. Fluid and fluent in the extreme, hip-hop emcees wreak havoc on the still unexamined assumptions of establishment conceptions of not just who but also what counts as articulate in a society of White racist domination that fetishizes literacy to the exclusion of oral fluency—as if literacy were some White racial property despite the African origins of writing and human civilization itself. Hip-hop on the whole leaves this rhetoric dazed and confused, dumbstruck or mute, threatened and panicking in a frenzy, as a rule.

Hip-hop and rap are not one and the same, for hip-hop is composed of verbal as well as non-verbal elements, so to speak: *graffiti-writing*, *deejaying*, and *break-dancing* as well as *emceeing*. The pioneering figures of hip-hop include a "Holy Trinity" of sorts: DJ Kook Herc, Grandmaster Flash, and Afrika Bambaataa, who was hailed as the "Master of Records" and who founded the Universal Zulu Nation to promote the four basic elements of hip-hop as "hip-hop" worldwide. Making history and positivity out of negativity in a grisly neocolonial age, he and the "Mighty Zulus" would also posit a powerful "fifth element" of hip-hop: that is, *knowing* or *knowledge*, the most cosmic of hip-hop elements thought to hold them all together.

More than anyone, "Bam" grounds hip-hop in its African foundations in multiple ways. He takes an African name, after a trip to the African continent, where he locates his inspiration to launch a movement or organization, which he names after an African uprising captured on film. Out of a diverse African diaspora grounded in North America, he and his came to champion hip-hop in terms of a dual motto centered around "peace, love, unity and having fun" as well as being "warriors for the community." For him and many subsequent scholars of the hip-hop movement (e.g., R. F. Thompson, H. Osumare), hip-hop is globally *Negro-Africaine* in its origins, aesthetics, and outlook, while for many other artists and scholars (e.g., O. Sembène), further, contemporary hip-hop grounds itself back onto continental African foundations from Senegal and Azania to the "*banlieues*" of a Blackened or Afro-Arabized France.

Free of Hellenomania, hip-hop can nonetheless signify another discourse and dispersion of "civilization," indeed "out of Africa," like all "human civilization" proper. So when purportedly "other" populations assume it, now—"loving Blackness," in "revolutionary solidarity," and so forth—they might even be considered "new diasporas" of global Africa at the level of cultural bodies rather than racializing biologies of Euro-imperialism. The case of hip-hop from Palestine or Palestinians could be most interesting in this respect (e.g., S. Maira). This is argued best by one such emcee himself, 'Adi (of Wlad il 7ara): "African American history and connection to African poetic and musical traditions is a connection with another 'outside,' with Africa via Arab communities in the north of the continent. He situates Palestinians and Arabs inside this geography and connects Palestinian Hip-Hop to its diasporic forms, as part of the Black Mediterranean and Afro-Arab histories" (Maira & Shihade 2012, 22). At any rate, as a cultural-political movement, hip-hop intersects seriously with the official practice of "rhetoric" in its own political movement across ancient and modern or "trans-modern" spaces of human life, where "civilization" is often systematically confused with *colonization* again and again.

Quiet as it may be kept, "graffiti artists" tend to refer to themselves quite simply as "writers" (e.g., J. Ferrell). Deejays, beat-makers, and producers of the musical sounds of hip-hop craft *compositions* (see J. Schloss 2004). What's more, as Katrina Hazzard-Gordon (now Hazzard-Donald) maintains here, hip-hop dancers have something to *say* in their "waacking" and "breaking" and "boogaloo," not to mention their fashion and their thinking and their physics-defying body language in motion. The lyrical emceeing of hip-hop rap then appears, historically, to make all of this "extra-verbal" communication *extra* verbal in a fundamentally unmistakable manner, rocking the planet Earth to the absolute joy of some and the total, depressed, and distressed dismay of others.

KRS-One philosophizes about "Our Language" and our language use in "Nostra Lingua," a chapter from *Ruminations* (2003), slyly and graphically capping on standard English arrogance, rhetorically. *That fly ass motherfucker is dope as shit!* It is this line that encapsulates most for him the linguistic code of hip-hop, a sophisticated system of inverted meaning, cloaked irony, and exacted freedom in speech. He recognizes that, "The truth of the matter is speech and language create both reality and identity for the user. Culture reflects language and language reflects culture." "Language serves the internal communication of a group. It allows a group to share pleasure, pain, dreams, and creative intelligence." "The need for an outcast wing of society to create its own system of discourse has always been felt." When he deftly addresses the matter of hip-hop's radical and self-protective reinvention of the word "nigga," he does not hesitate to ask that reinvention's single-minded critics, "Why do we choose to rely on the master's definition? Why are we afraid to define ourselves?" (KRS-One 2003, 94–95).

One might compare or contrast this reclamation with the "Head Negro in Charge" posture of Henry Louis Gates Jr.—or his manic need to publically profess his hatred of hip-hop and proclaim his distance from the masses of Black people at large while scurrying for every possible privilege of a plantation "H.N.I.C." designation yet and still. In any case, L. H. Stallings comes through with a corrective here in "Representin' for the Bitches: Queen B(?) in Hip-Hop Culture." Her discussion of "nigga" as well as "bitch" traces the bold continuity between "bad" trickster folklore, rap lyrical personae, and much-needed Black revolutionary body language, to boot.

This style of work goes much further than simple sexual politics of affirmation of essentially unquestioned, established sexual identity categories (e.g., "gay/lesbian," "LGBT," and "queer") in the anglophone and anglophile, White- and bourgeois-dominated Western world. See in this regard Amoeblog's interview here with Juba Kalamka, "Homohop's Role Within Hip-Hop," given some of his heretical or "politically incorrect" criticism of now conventional platitudes all around. Beyond the rhetorical racialization of "sexism" and "homophobia" as well as "anti-sexism" and "anti-homopobia," then, what indigenously Black identity labels, erotic cosmologies, and sexual histories (e.g., "Zami" and "in the Life") emerge from Pan-African hip-hop internationally? What sex or body work is done musically and culturally beyond the elaboration of established colonial or neocolonial sexual categories of identity of the modern Western-European middle-class establishment, whether "heterosexual" or "homosexual" in orientation?

The hip-hop duo known as Nightjohn would themselves publish a "genius liberation handbook" in which they propose a marvelous notion: hip-hop's poetry in motion should entail an equal and fearless appreciation of mind, soul, and body—against elitism, bourgeois anti-intellectualism, and puritanism. So despite the various genteel rhetorics of gender and sexuality upheld by the establishment, some of the most stigmatized hip-hop lyricism can be embraced for its virtuoso practice of orality as a mode of intelligence, a method of communication, and a means of erotic pleasure, whether this pleasure is sexual or verbal or both in fact at once. As a result, we can hear the intense and intrinsic metaphorical connections between "orals," "head," and "genius" (e.g., G. Thomas); and we can think and feel "the word made flesh" without any missionary postures at all. Such scandalous heresies of hip-hop may assert themselves on the live stage, the mixtape circuit, *and/or* the vexed commercial outlets of television and radio (*pace* J. Ball 2011).

There are countless reasons for hip-hop music to be the menace that it is to this particular society. Pan-Africanist and profoundly humanist in its original foundation and formulation, it remains a sign of the Blackest Blackness, and the Black "corruption" of non-Black youth, everywhere it moves or finds itself trafficked. Here, like Harry Allen elsewhere, Kenyon Farrow confronts the White-supremacist and anti-Black appropriation of all that emits from Black bodies or Black people in the wake of the European enslavement of Africans; and Marc D. Perry observes how the very efforts of commercial exploitation of hip-hop inadvertently assist in the counter-production of global practices of Black self-fashioning through hip-hop from Brazil and Cuba in the Americas back to southern Africa, just for example. Among more privileged others, there has been little interest in sharing the physical or metaphysical conditions lived by the diverse African diaspora populations who would create hip-hop music in the early 1970s and recreate it day after day, decade after decade, as an originally Black music or "*musica negra*" (see W. Marshall 2009), all across Africa now as well as the African diaspora. Perhaps nothing illustrates this more than the ever-multiplying targets of what many have dubbed "Rap COINTELPRO" (e.g., C. Muhammad), the supremely Negrophobic program of persecution, policing, and prosecution paralleling the FBI's murderous "COunter-INsurgent inTELigence PROgram of an earlier epoch."

In and beyond rap, hip-hoppers should call to mind the radical Sophists of Western histories of "classical rhetoric" more than, say, Socrates, who was a ruling-class citizen of the Athenian slave state to which he liberally submits by drinking hemlock in Ancient Greece. After all, Marimba Ani wrote in *Yurugu* (1994),

the Sophists were the most effective critics of the Platonic Order from those among the 'ancestors' of the European. They apparently presented the greatest threat to his new state, as they attacked it at its epistemological base . . . We would do well to look more closely at the writings of the Sophists from an African-centered perspective.

(Ani 1994, 73)

The official field of rhetoric traditionally concerns the political and axiological as well as the epistemological. From its first element to its fifth, hip-hop does much to upset the established order of politics, the established order of values, and the established order of knowledge, hailing from deeper, Ancient African origins and incurring the wrath of many a neocolonial imperialist state. It also destabilizes the conventional intellectual opposition between rhetoric as the art of persuasion and rhetoric as the art of speaking well in addition to that between rhetoric narrowly or forensically construed and "rhetoricality" as a general atmosphere of meaning-making that permeates life as we know it. Rhetorically, then, hip-hoppers do it all—in graphic writing spraying on walls and trains; musical compositions and recompositions spinning on wax and wheels of steel, booming across the atmosphere; in cosmic cyphers of dance speaking volumes and volumes through time and space; and in hypnotic lyrical writing taking place orally both on and off Papyrus's printed page.

Afrika Bambaataa & the Mighty Zulu Nation

This selection is taken from a general oral history of hip-hop that briefly focuses on the tremendous importance of Afrika Bambaataa and the Universal Zulu Nation in the articulation and development of hip-hop as a nationwide and worldwide cultural movement. It consists of a series of firsthand accounts that pivot around "Bam," the "Master of Records," and the "Mighty Zulus," an organization whose geopolitical scope moves out from the Bronx River in New York to become as international as Marcus Garvey's Universal Negro Improvement Association. This selection highlights the mass significance of their partying and their record-playing, rhetorically, as hip-hop pioneers transform the negative context of oppression into a positive site of resistance in the global context of the African diaspora and now Planet Earth at large.

Afrika Bambaataa & the Mighty Zulu Nation[1]

AFRIKA BAMBAATAA: I grew up in the southeast Bronx. It was an area where back in the late '60s, early '70s there was "broken glass everywhere," like Melle Mel said in "The Message." But it was also an area where there was a lot of unity and a lot of social awareness going on, at a time when people of color was coming into their own, knowin' that they were Black people, hearing records like James Brown's "Say It Loud—I'm Black and I'm Proud," giving us awareness. Hearing people like Sly and the Family Stone telling you to "Stand!" "You Can Make It If You Try," "Everyday People."

Seeing all the violence that was going on with the Vietnam War and all the people in Attica and Kent State, and being aware of what was going on in the late '60s, with Woodstock and the Flower Power, the Love Power movement . . . just being a young person and seeing all this happening around me put a lot of consciousness in my mind to get up and do something; it played a strong role in trying to say, "We've got to stop this violence with the street gangs."

Basically the Bronx was looking for something new. The gang scene was starting to fade out because a lot of the women was getting tired of all the gang-banging and drugs that were coming into the community. You had the police crackdown on the gangs, and you also had religious organizations and Black leaders trying to speak to the gangs, trying to bring down gang activity. Hearing the teachings of the Nation of Islam made a lot of people get up and try to get the drugs out of their community, and seeing a lot of the struggles that was going on all around the world through television gave a lot of hope to this area to do something for itself.

What I did is I took all these elements from all these great leaders and teachers that we had at that time and said I will start a group called the Zulu Nation—from seeing a movie back in the early '60s called Zulu. Just to see these Black people fighting for what was theirs against the British, that always stuck in my mind. I said when I get of age, I will start this organization and put all these ideologies together in this group called the Zulu Nation. So what I did, with myself and a couple other of my comrades, is get out in the street, start talking to a lot of the brothers and sisters, trying to tell them how they're killing each other, that they should be warriors for their community.

And when we started this music called hip-hop, which didn't have a name at the time, it brought a lot of the elements of these different movements together. We still had little spots of violence here and there, you know, at parties and stuff, but a lot of time you had people who was coming together to kick the drug dealers out of the area—we used violence against a lot of the dope pushers and all that. We went from a negative thing to a positive thing.

* * *

AFRIKA BAMBAATAA: Before the father, Kool Herc; myself, the Godfather; and Grandmaster Flash even started DJ-ing, there was a lot of disco DJs happening, as well as a lot of radio jocks. You know, you had Jocko, we had WLIB with Eddie O-Jay, we had Gary Byrd, who was on WRL, Cousin Brucie on WABC. You had Murray the K doing his shows at the Brooklyn Fox. You had the Apollo Theater with all the MCs there . . . all these different people who was doing what we call jive-talking rap, and then as they got into the disco era, it was the disco style of rappin'. We just took the different forms that was happening, what they was doing, but then we started adding new rhymes, and Herc came in with the beats.

I started DJ-in' in 1970. Not with the two turntables and the mixers: you went and got your mother's set or your father's set, and you would come down to a recreation center, you would put up your speakers and turntable—that's the kind where you put five records on there, and then the needle would go back and the record would drop. You had one guy that was set up on this side of the room, and I was set up on another side. We had a flashlight, so if he was playing the Jackson Five, "I Want You Back," when his record was going down low, he would flash at me, and that would give me the time to put on "Stand" or "Everyday People" by Sly and the Family Stone. And that's how we started DJ-in' back and forth, before they came with the two turntables and a mixer.

In the early '70s, we was already indoors in many of the community centers in the area. One of the first DJs that came out of the Black Spades organization was a guy by the name of Kool DJ D and his brother Tyrone, and they had a MC by the name of Love Bug Starski. Then Kool Herc came out from the West Side of the Bronx, and he was doing these beat-type records, whereas on our side of the Bronx we had the disco era still going strong. But after awhile we got tired of hearing the Hustle and disco records—we wanted that funk. We was missing the James Brown, the Sly, the Mandrill, Earth Wind and Fire, so we kept that funk alive with the break-beat sound. When that break come on, the b-boys hit the floor, start doing their different dances.

We was young entrepreneurs, when we didn't even know we was entrepreneurs. We would rent out the gymnasiums for parties. A lot of times we couldn't rent certain places, so we had to get an adult to do it for us, but we were still more in control of what was happening. We'd have to get out there to make a flyer—sometimes we'd get these flyer makers that made some extraordinary flyers, and you had the other ones that made the cheap type of flyers. But the thing was getting out there and doing promotions, hitting all the high schools or the junior high schools, hitting all the different communities, walking up and down the street doing hand-to-hand contact, leaving flyers in record stores, and if you got on the bus, sticking it up on the bus signs—you'd cover over the advertising signs. It was a lot of work.

Master of Records

DJ BREAKOUT: Bambaataa used to play the wildest records in the whole entire world. He played stuff like Bugs Bunny—it's got a beat on it. Everybody was break-dancin' to that.

AFRIKA BAMBAATAA: I was looking for beats all over the place. I even had people who used to follow me in the stores, because a lot of times we had spies from other DJ groups. I had a broad taste in sound, and I was checkin' all into the rock section or the soul sections or the different African sections or the sections of the Latin records. Back then you didn't have the stores where you can listen to records or turntables where you could put the record on, so the cover had to grab me. If the words sounded funky or if it had a certain way they wrote it, I would say, "Well, this must be funky. Let me take it home." Sometimes you got some records that was a piece of . . . but then you had some that was just great—I heard the sound and I said, "Well, this is funky here." It had a nice break-beat, or the groove was kicking, or the patterns was right, so that's how I try to pick records to put on my audience.

AFRIKA ISLAM: I heard Afrika Bambaataa play at Bronx River Center, and the only thing he lacked was somebody that would be behind him, working with him, who knew the technical aspects of it in order to build a better sound system. (Afrika Islam took over that role.)

His music influenced me because he listened to the same music I listened to. Everything from rock and roll, J. Geils, "Honky Tonk Woman" by the Rolling Stones, all the way to James Brown, Funkadelic, Sly Stone, R&B, funk. And that's what I came up under, so I knew where my allegiance was, you know? My allegiance was definitely to the music and the record. The techniques, the more technical style came from Flash, and as far as sound systems, that came from Herc. That's the way it was.

AFRIKA BAMBAATAA: The Bronx River Community Center was one of the original hip-hop big spaces—hundreds of people could fit in at one time. Then we had another place called Junior High School 123, which we renamed the Funky 3. We used to always give tribute to James Brown, Sly and the Family Stone, and then later on to Uncle George Clinton of Parliament-Funkadelic for bringing us the funk. Everybody was known for certain records they brought out, and that made your audience come to see you. My audience was the most progressive of all, because they knew I was playing all types of weird records for them. I even played commercials that I taped off the television shows, from Andy Griffith to the Pink Panther, and people looked at me like I was crazy.

You could be playing records with your group, and other people is sneaking up, trying to get next to you, to see what you was doing. So I used to peel the labels off or put water on there and take the cover off so they couldn't see.

VAN SILK: An Afrika Bambaataa party was totally different from a Grandmaster Flash party, because Bam played more obscure records. I'll be honest with you: I hated going to Bam parties. Bam would be playing the break-beats and then would jump off and start playing some calypso, or playing some reggae, or playing some rock. I was like, "What is Bam doin'?" But Bambaataa's mind-set was that hip-hop was an open field of music. He'd take an Aerosmith record, "Walk This Way," and slow it, or speed it up.

AFRIKA BAMBAATAA: It might just be slammin', the people sweating, breaking, everything. And I would just stop in the middle of the thing and throw on "Sweet Georgia Brown," and then everybody'd just start doing that basketball-type dance. I would tell them, "I want you to take it back to the day when your mama and papa used to dance," and started playing a lot of the '60s records, and you would see people trying to do the Monkey, the Jerk, the Twist, and all these other type of dances. So when you came to an Afrika Bambaataa party, you had to be progressive-minded and knew that you was going to hear some weird type of stuff.

Note

1. "Afrika Bambaataa & the Mighty Zulu Nation," in *Yes, Yes, Y'all: The Experience Music Project Oral History of Hip-Hop's First Decade*, eds. Jim Fricke and Charlie Ahearn (Cambridge, MA: Da Capo Press, 2002), pp. 44–49.

Robert Farris Thompson

Perhaps the premiere art historian in North America, and a Yale professor of Black studies, Robert Farris Thompson would introduce readers of *Rolling Stone* to hip-hop aesthetics, cosmologies, and demographics in this striking article originally published in 1986. Scrupulously, he identifies the Kongo and Angolan foundations of hip-hop music and dance (e.g., break-dancing, Uprock specifically, and electric boogaloo) as it ranges from the East Coast to the West in the United States, well beyond New York City alone. He also identifies five different yet complementary streams of African diaspora populations that contribute to hip-hop culture's emergence in North America before boldly proclaiming its historical permanence without any hesitation at all.

Hip Hop 101

Robert Farris Thompson[1]

Hip hop ain't no Hula-Hoop, no matter what the trend spotters say. In 1984, of course, hip hop was hot news. Everywhere you looked, you could see hip hop in one or more of its manifestations: break and electric-boogie dancing, rap music and graffiti. Then the media moved on, leaving the impression that hip hop was a fad. Here today, gone later today. Over and out.

But traditions just don't work that way. Hip hop is still with us in all its sainted sassiness, and its impact is likely to reverberate for years and years. Rappers in concert crisscross the nation. During his last tour, Prince shared the limelight with Tony Draughon, a break dancer known as Mr. Wave. Michael Jackson's 3-D Disney project, *Captain Eo*, will feature one of the main innovators of electric boogaloo, Pop'in Pete (Timothy Solomon) of Fresno, California. And this summer, Mr. Wave, along with the New York City Breakers, will bring his inimitable body lightning to sixty American cities.

All of this is simply part of an enduring cultural evolution. And the roots go back, baby. *Way* back.

Consider Charles Dickens in 1842. He's in New York, digging the action at the Cotton Club of that era, Almack's, in a tough but vibrant Manhattan district known as Five Points. The scene, which he wrote about at length in a travel book, *American Notes*, really blows his mind. He describes the manager of Almack's, an elegant black woman in a multicolored African-style head tie. Then he zeroes in on the work of a master black dancer, of that city and of that time, performing what the landlord of the bar actually calls "a regular break-down":

> Single shuffle, double shuffle, cut and cross-cut: snapping his fingers, rolling his eyes, turning in his knees, presenting the backs of his legs in front, spinning about on his toes and heels . . . dancing with two left legs, two right legs, two wooden legs, two wire legs, two spring legs.

What does this have to do with hip hop and its roots? A lot. For example, in 1986, as part of his New York electric boogie, Tony Draughon turns in his knees, then spins around to present the backs of his legs. African American dance history is evident in other moves that Dickens witnessed. There were intimations of Kongo, an ancient and distinguished Black civilization in central Africa, in the shuffle and double shuffle (in the Kongo language, these contrasting modes of perambulation are called *ta masamba* and *ta masamba n'swalu*). And the Kongo people, apparently since the Middle Ages, have poked fun at a knock-kneed bird in a dance they call *ta minswele* and have patted their thighs and chests and snapped their fingers for extra percussion in a dance called *mbele*, which was described by a French priest in May 1698.

Back to the future. It's 1969. James Brown, Soul Brother Number One, needing no further praise or introduction, is performing onstage at Madison Square Garden. *Newsweek* is there, taking down the moves: "dazzling double shuffles, knock-kneed camel-walks and high-tailed, chicken-pecking atavisms." The imperative was clear: get loose and let loose. A cultural threshold had been reached. Moves Dickens had seen, and some he hadn't, were coming into play again. And all creative hell was breaking loose. James Brown begat soul. And soul begat George Clinton and the funk movement. And James Brown and George Clinton and others, in combination with cultural forces including jazz, salsa, and reggae (dub and the sound-system style of record playing more than the music itself), begat Afrika Bambaataa and the Zulu Nation—in short, the hip hop revolution.

Watching James Brown and listening to George Clinton from afar were young black dancers like the Solomon brothers in Fresno and Afrika Bambaataa and his followers along 174th Street in the Bronx. Out of the Bronx emerged breakdancing, turntable percussion, the beat-box sound, and rap. And out of Fresno and black Los Angeles emerged electric boogaloo, which New York renamed electric boogie. All of which takes us up to where we are today.

Of course, it's easier to savor the influence of tropical Africa in the DUN-tuh-PAH, DUN-DUN-tuh-PAH, DUN-tuh-PAH, DUN-DUN-tuh-PAH now resounding from a thousand beat boxes than to comprehend that sound as an aspect of a serious historical tradition. But in the effort to do just that, we might discover why 12.2 percent of our population, black Americans, are consistently responsible for more than 50 percent of our popular music.

Hip hop is a tale of three cities. As I've said, breakdancing and the hip hop sound emerged in the Bronx, electric-boogaloo poppin' and tickin' moves arose in Fresno and Los Angeles (Watts, Long Beach, Crenshaw Heights). Naturally, the outsider might wonder how the devastated lots of the South Bronx and the suburban sprawl of Fresno and Los Angeles could have sustained the energy and the beauty of the hip hop arts. Well, in the Bronx at least, it seems the young men and women of that much-misunderstood borough *had* to invent hip hop to regain the voice that had been denied them through media indifference or manipulation. By manipulation I mean filmmakers' exploitation of what they took to be prototypical ruins, along the southernmost edges of the South Bronx, as back-drops for the social apocalypse—witness the film *1990: The Bronx Warriors*.

Michael Ventura, in the fascinating chapter "We All Live in the South Bronx," from his *Shadow Dancing in the USA*, describes how the cameramen in the streets would seek negative local color and apparently little else: "In roughly six hours of footage—*Fort Apache, Wolfen,* and *Koyaamsqatsi*—we haven't been introduced to one soul who actually lives in the South Bronx. We haven't heard one voice speaking its own language. We've merely watched a symbol of ruin: the South Bronx [as] last act before the end of the world."

How wonderful, then, when the Bronx started to talk back. In the late spring of 1981, there was a panel at a Bronx-based conference on the folk culture of that borough with the title "This Is Not Fort Apache, This Is Our Home: Students Document Their South Bronx." Tony Draughon, who grew up on 169th Street near Yankee Stadium, maintains: "That performing-in-the-ruins stuff is all a crock. There are no abandoned buildings where I live, and breakdancing didn't start where all those broken buildings were—we danced at Bronx River, where Bambaataa and the Zulu Nation was, and Poe Park and the schoolyards and even the back of classrooms when the bell would ring." It also happens that Bambaataa grew up in a comfortable apartment in the Bronx River Project, on East 174th Street, with his mother, a nurse. The bottom line is that Bambaataa, Grandmaster Flash, DJ Kool Herc, and the other South Bronx hip hop performers transcended and transmuted violence with music and peacemaking.

Nor were the original hip hoppers confined, as some outsiders imagined, to a single, monolithic black culture. If lesson one is that a living, creative, ebullient people live in the Bronx, then lesson two in hip hop history is the appreciation that these creative people can be divided into at least five distinct African-influenced cultures:

First, English-speaking blacks from Barbados live in the Bronx. Afrika Bambaataa's mother and her two sisters were from Barbados, as was the family of that other prominent Bronx DJ, Grandmaster Flash.

Second, black Jamaicans live in the Bronx. Among them figures most famously DJ Kool Herc (Clive Campbell), originally from Kingston, who was immortalized in the 1984 film *Beat Street*.

Third, thousands of blacks from Cuba live in the Bronx. The smell of Cuban coffee and the sound of Cuban mambos enliven the streets. (As early as 1954, a blind black Cuban guitarist, Arsenio Rodríguez, had extolled in song the talents of a legendary "guy from the Bronx," or "el elemento del Bronx," according to the original Spanish lyric. In line after swinging line, Rodríguez praised him because he could dance mambo and *danzón* like a Cuban, right in the middle of the Bronx.) It was only natural for Afro-Cuban conga drums to become one of the favored percussive springboards for early breakdance improvisation. "Afro-Cuban bongos gave power to our dance," says Draughon.

Fourth, there are thousands and thousands more of *boricuas*—Puerto Ricans—and they not only augmented the Afro-Cuban impact, in the timbales of Tito Puente and the salsa of Eddie Palmieri and Willie Colón, but eventually provided an able-bodied army of knowing dancers who were to take breakdancing to its second, efflorescent phase between 1979 and 1982, after its invention in the South Bronx by black dancers, circa 1975.

Fifth and finally, there are the North American blacks, whose music was jazz and soul and funk. And the Bronx also loved rock. In the sixties and seventies, James Brown, Sly and the Family Stone, and George Clinton were the main men. Bambaataa elaborates: "I loved their *funk*—hard-hitting bass and heavy percussion. Before James Brown, funk meant the smell of sweat. But James Brown turned it into a sign of life. And George Clinton changed it into a *way* of life, with funk adverbs, the funk sign [pointer and little finger up, other digits and thumb tucked behind the palm], funky costumes, funky glasses—all that came in with him. And Sly took rock and crossed it with funk, and had 500,000 people rising to their feet at Woodstock."

In short, to live in the Bronx was to live in a multicultural happening. The Bronx blacks had the cultural depth and confidence to talk back, when challenged by the media, staying loose, creative, different. "They stayed fresh, they maintained that certain volatility that hip hop craves," recalls Michael Holman, a young black hip hop impresario, student filmmaker, and author. No fear of the end of the world, just fear of being stuck: "If you became classifiable," Holman says, "you became all the things that kept you in check."

In 1975, the lines of cultural brilliance, North American black, Afro-Cuban, et al., were beginning to crisscross. Many of these musics, however different, shared Kongo qualities of sound and motion. The wheel of creative creole interaction was turning again, as it had once in New Orleans, Havana, and Rio de Janeiro when Kongo rhythmic impulses collided with Western dance and music. One reason for the Kongo tinge in New World dancing is the sheer number of Kongo and Angolan peoples brought to our shores in the Atlantic slave trade—a miracle of cultural resistance, demographically reinforced. The historian Joseph C. Miller tells us that some 40 percent of the ten million or so Africans brought to the New World between 1500 and 1870 in the slave trade came from the ports of Kongo and neighboring Angola.

These powerful numbers, in combination with the spiritual and artistic gifts of the Kongo people, changed the course of the popular music of the world. In New Orleans, the city of jazz, the Kongo people were so numerous and their Kongo dance was so famous (in Mississippi, too) that the place where everyone hung out to hear the latest sounds and check out the newest moves, a vast dancing plaza called Congo Square, was named after them. Dena J. Epstein, an expert in the history of black folk music, has discovered a letter from New Orleans, dated 1819, that includes this telling sentence: "On sabbath evening the African slaves meet on the green . . . and rock the city with their Congo dances."

They also took creole Kongo beats and rocked Havana with rumba and Rio de Janeiro with samba. (Both *rumba* and *samba* are Kongo words for certain dance moves.) The upshot?

First, black Rio taught us how to samba, to dance to the sound of tambourines and Angolan friction drums.

Second, from Cuba came rumba and the conga line, the circling line of dancers moving one-two-three-*kick*. This style has returned to the spotlight in 1986 with the Miami Sound Machine's "Conga," the first Latin song since the sixties to become a major U.S. hit.

Third, from the Kongo dance of Congo Square, from jazz dance, and from rumba came "the Congo grind" (*tienga*), the hip-rotating sign of life that kept missionaries to Kongo muttering for centuries, that gave American Puritans cardiac arrest, that ultimately inspired Elvis Presley's famous suite of moves. Some of these motions have become part of the dance code of American people, white and black.

Fourth, wherever the Kongo people came in significant numbers, you frequently found their concept of the dance performance break: in Haiti, where *cassé* ("break") stands for the deliberate disruption of the beat of the drums, which throws the dancers into ecstasy, or in Cuba, where *rumba abierta* refers to the dropping out of melodic instrumentation and the taking over of the conga drums.

Must we know this to pass what music critic Robert Christgau calls raptitude tests? Bet. Because a fusion of break musics in the Bronx sparked the rise of hip hop. Afrika Bambaataa explains what happened in *The Beginning of Break Beat (Hip-Hop) Music:*

Break music has been around for a long time, but not until the early '70s . . . brought to popularity. Break music is that certain part of the record that you just be waiting for to come up and when that certain part comes, that percussion part with all those drums, congas, it makes you dance real wild . . . . That break is so short in the record, you get mad, because the break was not long enough for you to really get down to do your thing.

How to restore the delicious length of live music breaks in a mechanical, turntable situation? The answer was found around 1973. The Jamaican DJ Kool Herc armed himself with gigantic speakers and thundering frequency ranges and defined a world where, as one hip hopper put it, "the loudest noises were the newest." Herc took a conga drum break and extended it across two copies of the same record on two turntables. As soon as one break ended, he switched to its beginning on the second record, and the beat went on. This was the birth of Bronx-style break music.

In response, no later than 1975, young black dancers in the Bronx were improvising moves to match the new length and intensity of the music. They danced to break music, so they called themselves breakdancers. Or b-boys, for short.

In neighborhood gyms and in the parks and playgrounds, they would break to the percussion portion of a tune. I remember running full tilt into one of these scenes while driving in the Bronx in the late seventies. There was a park filled with fifty or more radios, *all playing the same thing.* It left me thrilled and reeling. This was the musical background for the earliest forms of breakdancing as seen in 1976 on the schoolyard of P.S. 110 in the Bronx by G.L.O.B.E. and Pow Wow, two prominent rappers now working with Afrika Bambaataa: "Like, it'd be two guys, both doing uprock, stand-up moves, side to side, profile, and then one of them would fall back and the other guy would catch him."

Uprock was martial posing. Uprock meant battle mime. It was danced combat, a fight with steps instead of fists. One basic sequence: hop, step, *lunge*. Or the hands were used as if they were a knife in a form of uprock known as zipping, witnessed by a historian of breakdancing, Sally Sommer. Uprock is not unlike *nsunsa*, a fast-moving Kongo battle dance—a sport, really—that's also one-on-one and also very popular with men. Can this also be the black social amusement called *soesa*, which J. G. Stedman observed in Suriname in South America and described in a book published in 1796: "[It] consists in footing opposite to each other and clapping with their hands upon their sides to keep in time."

The Bronx fall-back-and-be-caught moves recall another Kongo dance game, *lukaya lweto*, "our leaf that never falls." In this game, the child who is "it" leans back precariously and is spun around in the hands of children seated in a circle on the ground around him. They spin him roughly, quickly, but never let him fall.

Then the b-boys brought breakdancing down to the level of the ground. G.L.O.B.E. and Pow Wow elaborate:

> We got tired of just stand up and catch. We started kicking side to side and hitting the ground. Jump down, bend, crouch and take a set, all down, doing whatever moves we could, spinning top, sweep, back spin. There were guys who danced [these moves] so much they said every week they had to get a new pair of sneakers. Anyhow, you'd fall, touch your hand on the ground, improvise something, bounce right up, and freeze.

Tony Draughon participated in the creation of these early moves. He says these strokes of prowess deliberately set up a contrast between the spin and the freeze: "Imagine, man, you're *spinning*, as fast as you can, and then you *stop*, in a beautiful position, in the twinkling of an eye."

Tradition built this tone of confidence, this arsenal of instant moves and creative options. What kinds of tradition? Why, freeze and swipes and spins, of course.

Move-and-freeze sequences were legendary in the history of jazz dance. From the fifties, I remember the New York mambo picture step, in which William Pittman and Teresita Pérez, two well-known mambo dancers at the Palladium on Broadway, turned and froze, becoming momentary sculpture. I also remember the legend of a rock & rolling freeze dancer in Dallas in the fifties. It is told that he'd show up with an alarm clock concealed within his britches. He'd sweat and dance and freeze, then shake and shimmy and freeze. The ladies loved him. And then an alarm clock would go off in his pants, signaling departure time for an amorous rendezvous, and he'd disappear, mysteriously.

But there is nothing mysterious about the origins of the sweeps and swipes of early breakdancing. They clearly represent an ingenious adaptation of the pommel-horse exercises of Western gymnastics to the Africanizing "get down" level of the ground. Keep the muscle, get rid of the horse, and get on down.

The spin also recalls, in part, the virtuosic whirls of Kongo dances. In the summer of 1985, I saw a dancer spin on his right hand in the middle of a revolving, chanting circle of children in Kiluango, a hilltop village near Luozi not far from the river Congo. In other villages, I saw standing children link arms with horizontal children, spinning them close to the ground. In another town, a youngster spun on his back.

What are we to make of all this? Simply that it's no more surprising to find spin dancing in the black Bronx than it is to find "London Bridge Is Falling Down" on the playgrounds of Anglo-Saxon America. In fact, some intervening links between Kongo and the Bronx can be found:

> First, a marvelously detailed nineteenth-century Cuban engraving shows a black dancer, bare chested and with a belt of bells, spinning on his left palm in the streets of Havana on

Epiphany, the Day of the Kings. His pose is like a stop frame from a film of today's New York breaking step, the four corners.

Second, hand spins came from Angola to Brazil, where they turn up as one of the moves of *capoeira de Angola*, the black martial art of the city of Salvador, in the state of Bahia.

Third, as we learn in Lydia Parrish's classic *Slave Songs of the Georgia Sea Islands*, a ring shout in black Georgia includes a sequence in which one member "gets down on his knees and, with head touching the floor, rotates with the group as it moves around the circle."

Fourth, powerfully illustrative is a silent, very early kinescope, *Three-Man Dance*, probably from the period between 1890 and 1910. This film bears an extraordinary relation both to ancient Kongo and to the modern Bronx. While one black man plays a harmonica and another beats time with his hands, a third comes in and choreographically introduces himself with a time step. (One of the other men has just danced a rudimentary version of today's moonwalk.) Then he turns his back to the camera, and he *breaks*. Suddenly, he's dropping on the ground, touching the floor with his hand, flipping his body upside down, then resuming, in a twinkling, verticality.

Spin-pattern vocabulary, coming down the body line from Kongo culture, was very likely reinforced by other sources. Blues historian Samuel Charters saw a West African Fula dancer fling himself down on the ground, land on one hand and begin spinning wildly, and I have seen similar stunts among the Gelede dancers of Ketu, an ancient town in what is now the Republic of Benin. But however blended and recombined, the spins in the Bronx were far from fixed or static. Indeed, the special intensity of the breakdance revolution split the atom of the spins and released more creative energy than had probably ever before been seen in this particular suite of moves.

Enter the Puerto Ricans. They took breakdancing to another level in the late seventies and early eighties. They built tough, athletic structures around the original spins, mirroring an age of joggers, Adidas outfits, and Nautilus-trained bodies. For one thing, as suggested by hip hop scholar David Sternbach, they added a fast-stepping entry pattern that strongly recalled the flash and celerity of some of the steps of the Puerto Rican dance known as the *bomba*. The Puerto Ricans added new spins to the lexicon: head spins, windmills (a variation on the back spin, with flaring legs), and helicopters (one person spins two other dancers like human blades), plus a superathletic bit of virtuosity, a whirling one-arm handstand called the 1990.

By April 1981, when Sally Banes published the first article on breakdancing, the original black and subsequent Puerto Rican improvisations had fused to form the full-blown, break-dance sequence: entry (rapid-fire stepping), break (down to the hands), swipes (the ground gymnastics imparting momentum and special flair), spins (on the hands, the back, the shoulders, the head, and other body parts), finishing with a freeze and then an exit (returning the performer to verticality).

Some dancers pushed these moves to the limits of human anatomy. One dancer, for example, who dreamed that he had spun on his chin, tried it in real life and damn near broke his jaw. But the way some spins dissolved into the freeze could be truly magical. In the end there was no way of confusing the daredevil baroque of breakdancing with the straightforward spin games of ancient Kongo. For one was early and the other was late, and enormous amounts of time and creativity had intervened.

Note

1. Robert Farris Thompson, "Hip Hop 101," *Rolling Stone* #407, March 27, 1986, "On Campus" section, reprinted in William Eric Perkins, ed., *Droppin' Science: Critical Essays on Rap Music and Hip Hop Culture* (Philadelphia, PA: Temple University Press, 1996), pp. 212–218.

Houston A. Baker Jr.

The eminent Black literary critic Houston A. Baker examines a wide assortment of high-tech hip-hop textualities on the cusp of a new century here—compositions, embodiments, productions, and so forth. Suggesting we are positioned at the crossroads of still modernist pedagogies and postmodernist cultural-historical realities, he is pleased to accept hip-hop's invitation to leave anachronistic rhetorical as well as literary or aesthetic canons behind, be they represented by Shakespeare or Plato and Aristotle in the academy. In contrast, he upholds the diverse, international soundings of hip-hop as a fresh mode and object of critical analysis, urging Black studies to orchestrate a hearing for it in a dominant society that seems to be able only to give it a juridical hearing or put hip-hop on trial.

Hybridity, Rap, and Pedagogy for the 1990s: A Black Studies Sounding of Form

Houston A. Baker, Jr.[1]

Why listen—the early hip hop DJs asked—to an entire commercial disc if the disc contained only twenty (or two) seconds of worthwhile sound? Why not *work* that sound by having two copies of the same disc on separate turntables, moving the sound on the two tables in DJ-orchestrated patterns, creating thereby a worthwhile sound? The result was an indefinitely extendable, varied, reflexively signifying hip-hop sonics—indeed, a deft sounding of postmodernism.

The techniques of rap were not simply ones of selective extension and modification. They also included massive archiving. Black sound (African drums, bebop melodies, James Brown shouts, jazz improvs, Ellington riffs, blues innuendos, doo-wop croons, reggae words, calypso rhythms) were gathered into a reservoir of threads that DJs wove into intriguing tapestries of anxiety and influence. The word that comes to mind is *hybrid*.

Discotechnology was hybridized through the human hand and ear—the DJ turned wildman at the turntable. The conversion produced a rap DJ who became a postmodern ritual priest of sound rather than a passive spectator in an isolated DJ booth making robots turn. A reverse cyborgism was clearly at work in the rap conversion. The high technology of advanced sound production was reclaimed by and for human ears and the human body's innovative abilities. A hybrid sound then erupted in seemingly dead urban acoustical spaces. (By *postmodern* I intend the nonauthoritative collaging or archiving of sound and styles that bespeaks a deconstructive hybridity. Linearity and progress yield to a dizzying synchronicity.)

The Bronx, Brooklyn, Queens—called by the Reagan/Bush era black "holes" of urban blight—became concentrated masses of a new style, a hybrid sonics hip-hoppingly full of that piss, sass, and technological vinegar that tropes Langston Hughes, saying: "*I'm still here!*" This is a *blackhole* shooting hip hop quasars and bum-rushing sucker, political DJs.

What time was it? Time to get busy from the midseventies into the wildstyle popularizations of the eighties. From Parks to Priority Records, from random sampling to Run DMC. Fiercely competitive and hugely braggadocious in their energies, the quest of the emergent rap technologists was for the baddest toasts, boasts, and signifying possible. The form was male-dominant—though KRS-One and the earliest male posses will tell you the "ladies" were *always* there. Answering back, dissing the ways of menfolk and kinfolk alike who tried to ease them into the postmodern dozens. Hey, Millie Jackson had done the voiceover with musical backdrop—had talked to wrongdoing menfolk (at length) before Run or Daryl had ever even figured out that some day they might segue into each other's voices talking 'bout some "dumb girl." Indeed!

Rap technology includes *scratching*: rapidly moving the "wheels of steel" (i.e., turntables) back and forth with the disc cued, creating a deconstructed sound. There is *sampling*: taking a portion (phrase, riff, percussive vamp, etc.) of a known or unknown record (or a video game squawk, a touch-tone telephone medley, verbal tag from Malcolm X or Martin Luther King) and combining it in the overall mix. (The sample was called a *cut* in the earliest days.) *Punch phrasing:* to erupt into the sound of turntable #1 with a percussive sample from turntable #2 by def cuing.

But the most acrobatic of the technics is the verb and reverb of the human voice pushed straight out, or emulated by synthesizers, or emulating drums and falsettos, rhyming, chiming sound that is a mnemonic for black-urbanity.

The voice is individual talent holding the mic for as long as it can invoke and evoke a black tradition that is both prefabricated and in formation. "Yo, man, I hear Ellington, but you done put a new (W)rap on it!" For the rap to be defly *yours* and properly original, it has got to be *ours*—to sound like *us*.

The voice, some commentators have suggested, echoes African griots, black preachers, Apollo DJs, Birdland MCs, Muhammed Ali, black streetcorner males' signifying, oratory of the Nation of Islam, and get-down ghetto vernacular. The voice becomes the thing in which, finally, rap technology catches the consciousness of the young.

What time is it? The beginning of the decade to end a century. It is postindustrial, drum machine, synthesizer, sampling, remix, multitrack studio time. But it is also a time in which *the voice*, and *the bodies* of rap and dance beat the rap of technologically induced (reproduced) indolence, impotence, or (in)difference.

Why?

Because sales figures are a mighty index. But also—the motion of the ocean of dancers who fill vast, olympian spaces of auditoriums and stadiums transnationally when you are (*à la* Roxanne) "live on stage" is still a principal measure of rap-success. Technology can create a rap disc, but only the voice dancing to wheels of steel and producing a hip-hopping, responsive audience gives testimony to a full-filled *break*. You ain't busted a move, in other words, until the audience lets you know you're in the groove.

What time is it? It's "hardcore" and "message" and "stop the violence" and "ladies first," 1990's time. Microcomputers, drum machines, electric keyboards, synthesizers are all involved in the audio. And MTV and the grammarians of the proper Grammy Awards have had their hands forced.

Rap is a too-energetic category for the Grammies to ignore, and Fab Five Freddy and "Yo! MTV Raps" have multiple billing these days. Jesse Jackson and Quincy Jones proclaim that "Rap is here to stay." Quincy has even composed and orchestrated a cross-generational album (*Back on the Block*) on which he announces his postmodernity in the sonics of rap. Ice-T and Big Daddy Kane prop him up "on every leaning side."

But it is also time to "fight the power" as Public Enemy knows—the power of media control. In their classic rap "Don't Believe the Hype," PE indicates that prime-time media is afraid of rap's message, considering it both offensive and dangerous. In Philadelphia, one of the principal popular music stations confirms PE's assessment. For WUSL ("Power 99") proudly advertises its "no-rap workday." Secretaries fill a sixty-second ad spot with kudos for the station's erasure of rap. Hence, FCC "public" space is contoured in Philly in ways that erase the energy of rap's soundings. *Work* (defined as tedious office labor) is thus publicly constructed as incompatible with *rap*. Ethics and outputs of wage-labor are held to be incommensurate with postmodern black expressive culture. Implicit in a *no-rap workday*, of course, is an agon between industrial ("Taylorite") strategies of typing-pool (Word Processing Pool?) efficiency and a radical hybridity of sound and morals. For rap's sonics are disruptive in themselves. They become even more cacophonous when they are augmented by the black voice's anti-establishment injunctions, libido urgings, and condemnations of coercive standardization. To "get the job done" or "paid in full" in the economies of rap is scarcely to sit for eight hours cultivating carpal tunnel syndrome. Nope. To get the job done with rap style is to "get busy," innovative, and outrageous with *fresh* sounds and defly nonstandard moves. One must be undisciplined, that is to say, to be "in effect."

Eric B. and Rakim, Redman, Twin Hype, BDP, Digital Underground, EPMD, De La Soul, Q-Tip, The DOC—the names in themselves read like a Toni Morrison catalogue of nonstandard cultural denomination. And such named rap ensembles and the forms they produce are scarcely local or parochial. For rap has become an international, metropolitan hybrid. From New Delhi to Ibadan, it is busy interrupting the average workday.

Microcomputation, multitrack recording, video imaging, and the highly innovative vocalizations and choreography of black urban youth have produced a form that is fiercely intertextual, open-ended, hybrid. It has not only rendered melody virtually anomalous for any theory of "New Music," but also revised a current generation's expectations where "poetry" is concerned.

Technology's effect on student expectations and pedagogical requirements in, say, English literature classrooms is tellingly captured by recent experiences that I have had and would like to share. To prepare myself for a talk I was to give at New York's Poetry Project symposium entitled "Poetry for the Next Society" (1989) I decided to query students enrolled in a course devoted to Afro-American women writers. "What," I asked, "will be the poetry for the next society?" To a man or woman, my students responded "rap" and "MTV."

We didn't stop to dissect their claims, nor did we attempt a poetics of the popular. Instead, we tried to extrapolate from what seemed two significant forms of the present era a description of their being-in-the-world. Terms that emerged included: *public, performative, audible, theatrical, communal, intrasensory, postmodern, oral, memorable*, and *intertextual*. What this list suggests is that my students (yes, they were graduate students) believe the function of poetry belongs in our era to a telecommunal, popular space in which a global audience interacts with performative artists. A link between music and performance—specifically popular music and performance—seems determinative in their definition of the current and future function of poetry.

They are heirs to a history in which art, audience, entertainment, and instruction have assumed profoundly new meanings. The embodied catharsis of Dick Clark's bandstand or Don Cornelius's soultrain would be virtually unrecognizable—or so one thinks—to Aristotle. Thus, Elvis, Chuck Berry, and the Shirelles foreshadow and historically overdetermine The Boss, Bobby Brown, and Kool Moe Dee as, let us say, *People's Poets*.

My students' responses, however, are not nearly as natural or original as they may seem on first view. In fact, they have a familiar cast within a history of contestation and contradistinction governing the relationship between poetry and the state.

The exclusion of poets from the republic by Plato is the primary Western site of this contest. (One envisions a no-poetry workday, as it were.) In Egypt it is Thoth and the King; in Afro-America it is the Preacher and the Bluesman. It would be overly sacramental to speak of this contest as one between the letter and the spirit, and it would be too Freudian by half to speak of it as a struggle between the law and taboo. The simplest way to describe it is in terms of a tensional resonance between homogeneity and heterogeneity.

Plato argues the necessity of a homogeneous state designed to withstand the bluesiness of poets who are always intent on worrying such a line by signifying and troping irreverently on it and continually setting up conditionals. "What if this?" and "What if that?" To have a homogeneous line, Plato advocates that philosophers effectively eliminate poets. (Which is rather a forecast, I think, of the Alan Bloom cry of the heart in our own day.)

If the state is the site of what linguists call the *constative*, then poetry is an alternative space of the *conditional*. If the state keeps itself in line, as Benedict Anderson suggests (and, yes, I did eventually get to read his book) through the linear, empty space of homogeneity, then poetry worries this space or line with heterogeneous performance. If the state is a place of reading the lines correctly, then poetry is the site of audition, of embodied sounding on state wrongs such as N.W.A's " . . . Tha Police," or PE's "Black Steel in the Hour of Chaos."

Note

1. Houston A. Baker Jr., "'Hybridity, Rap, and Pedagogy': A Black Studies Sounding of Form," in *Black Studies, Rap and the Academy* (Chicago: The University of Chicago Press, 1993), pp. 88–96.

Jeff Ferrell

This selection treats the writing of graffiti artists as a writing against establishmentarian regimes of art, style, and authority. The politics of this aesthetic nonconformity in public spaces controlled by guardians of private as well as public property considerations is placed on full critical display. The criminalization of this school of writing is as literal as its transgression of the letter of the law of the land. In and out of hip-hop, the writing of graffiti is shown to recast the literary and the rhetorical under the weight of a potentially crushing political authoritarianism.

Crimes of Style: Aesthetics of Authority

Jeff Ferrell[1]

Denver graffiti has also developed out of cultural contexts which extend beyond local art worlds to encompass national media, music, and style. Many Denver writers first became aware of and interested in graffiti not only through direct exposure to the works of Z13 and other early kings, but through mediated visions of graffiti writing and graffiti subcultures elsewhere. Z13 himself first encountered contemporary graffiti when in the early 1980s he saw the graffiti film *Wild Style* (1983) on a Denver public television station. As he says, this became his "main influence," since "there weren't any artists around here doing that sort of thing." Around the same time, Fie likewise discovered hip hop graffiti when he saw another graffiti film, *Style Wars!* (1985), on television. Inspired by the film, and Z13's first Colorado Boulevard piece, Fie and a friend "tried to research, and we got any books we could find. I got *Getting Up*, and I read that and you know, from then on I was just addicted."[17] Voodoo also drew inspiration, and a sense of graffiti's dynamics, from the media:

> I'd seen a couple of movies. Different movies that had to do with spray art, graffiti. I saw this one, *King 65*, and they showed how he went out in the railyards and sprayed at night, and that movie kind of inspired me. I mean, I saw that when I was about, shit, 17 or 18. And he'd go out and spray and some of his pieces would get buffed . . . . And then I'd seen some other things about New York graffiti and how it was like a world of its own . . . . To me, I'd always been kind of in the background, kind of not really in the mainstream—put it that way. And this just seemed like the ultimate way to do what I wanted to do.

These recollections, of course, implicate not only the mass media as a primary channel of cultural and subcultural dissemination, but hip hop culture as the primary stylistic influence in the development of Denver graffiti. As shown earlier, Denver writers were not just seeing generic graffiti on television and in books; they were seeing graffiti redefined and restyled by the hip hop culture of the Bronx and New York City. These mediated encounters with hip hop graffiti were in turn cemented by direct experience. Rasta 68 began doing graffiti when he lived in New York City, continued in Seattle and Las Vegas, and ultimately brought his attitudes and expertise to Denver. Fie visited New York City for only a week in the summer of 1985, but once there "went nuts" viewing and photographing graffiti. While photographing a piece, he also met a New York graffiti writer, Shock, who painted a t-shirt and autographed the book *Subway Art* for him.[18] "Blown away" by the encounter, Fie tagged "Shock" for a time after his return to Denver.

Denver writers are well aware of hip hop's influence on the local subculture. Voodoo notes that Denver writers have for the most part been "following the codes of what New York and Chicago and all those places set down." Lamenting the relative lack of innovation in Denver, Eye Six adds that Denver graffiti "usually has words of some sort generally relating to hip hop culture. And characters which generally relate to hip hop culture—B-boys and pop characters" (in Ferrell, 1990: 10,11). He further sees graffiti—in New York and in Denver—as a component of "a whole culture. There's fashion, there's music, and then there's graffiti." Within this culture, there also exists for Eye Six a "real tie between graffiti and rap," in that both "sample" popular culture and play with the "appropriation of imagery":

> The pop culture and the cultural industrialists are throwing out so many images that it's almost, in some regards, not really necessary to invent any new images. You could just pull from one day's worth of t.v., newspaper and radio and just mash 'em all together into a style that's not like anything else—like a mass media collage. That's all that sampling is really doing; they pull phrases and sounds from mainstream radio, announcements and that kind of thing, and collage them into the music.

Eye Six puts this sense of an integrated hip hop culture into practice by not only doing graffiti, but mixing and dj'ing rap and industrial music. Mac also dubs and mixes rap and other sounds; and while other local writers may not mix, they do consistently play and listen to the music, to the point that rap constitutes an ongoing soundtrack for subcultural activities. This hip hop soundtrack flows from writers' beat boxes and headphones and into the texture of the graffiti itself. Mac, Japan and Corey originally formed the group "3XB" as much to make rap music as to write graffiti. The "3XB" crew tag thus abbreviates the phrase "3 times (the) beat," a reference to its three founders' fame as "human beat boxes"—that is, rappers adept at reproducing verbally the beat and rhythm of rap music. The "Syndicate" crew tag likewise makes reference not only to the general sense of an underground organization, but to the explicit use of "syndicate" by rap musicians like Ice-T ("Rhyme Syndicate Productions," "rollin' with the SYNDICATE my unstoppable battalion") and Donald D and the Rhyme Syndicate.

Rappers like Ice-T provide not only the context of meaning for crew tags, but the text for crew pieces. When, for example, Rasta 68 and The Kid wrote "Remember, if they don't know who you are . . . they don't know what you've done" beside an illegal piece, they took this sentiment from a lyric in Ice-T's song, "Drama":

> "What's your date of birth?" "What's your real name?"
> I stuck to my alias, I know the game.
> If they don't know who you are, then they don't know what you've done.[19]

Similarly, Phaze3—whose tag itself recalls Phase II, one of the "early pioneers" (Cooper and Chalfant, 1984: 17) of New York City graffiti—adapted a lyric from Ice-T's song "Squeeze the Trigger" (1987) in creating the text which accompanies his "CRIME" piece on Denver's second "wall of fame":

> What is crime? What is not?
> What is art? I think I forgot!!!

Hip hop sets the look and feel of Denver graffiti even more broadly than these specific examples convey. Denver writers speak, tag, and piece the language of hip hop, as they "bomb" back walls and alleys with graffiti and deride the "toyz" who lack the expertise to bomb with them. "Toyz," of course, carries hip hop culture with it doubly: in the word itself, and in its pluralization with a "z" rather than "s." This hip hop convention of "z" for "s" also shows up in tags and pieces, such as Rasta 68's "R.I.P. TOYZ" piece on the first wall of fame, or the "METALZ" piece he created for Atlas Metals Company. Moreover, local conventions of lettering and coloring derive from "wild style" and other hip hop innovations.

Note

1. Jeff Ferrell, "Crimes of Style: Aesthetics of Authority," in *Crimes of Style: Urban Graffiti and the Politics of Criminality* (Boston: Northeastern University Press, 1996), pp. 42–46.

Katrina Hazzard-Donald

This selection is an article by Katrina Hazzard-Donald, the remarkable scholar of Afro-North American and global African social dance formations. She historicizes and contextualizes hip-hop dance, which in her subtle analysis includes "waack," break-dancing, and "rap dance," across different time periods and regional spaces within the United States. What's more, she answers the question, "What does hip-hop dance *say*?" The speech of such dance is thus revealed with respect to hip-hop body language, fashion, lifestyles, personas, and the general social standpoint of socioeconomic outsiders.

"Waack and Breakin'," "Rap Dancing," and "What Hip Hop Dance Says"

Katrina Hazzard-Donald[1]

Waack and Breakin'

Hip hop dance can be characterized in three stages; waack, breakdancing, and rap dance. Waack dancing appears about 1972. Dance moves such as locking (later known on the East Coast as pop-locking), the robot, and the spank, along with splits and rapidly revolving spins combined with unexpected freezes, were part of waack's outrageous style. Here the fusion of theatrical expectation and outrageous showmanship occurs that would mark later hip hop styles known as breakdancing.

A staple in the vocabularies of waack, breaking, and, to a lesser degree, rap dance was the pop and lock, a movement technique that was part of the jerk in the late 1950s before that dance left black communities and crossed over to mainstream America in the mid- to late 1960s. (The

Figure 11.1 Chillski, a longtime Miami b-boy, leads a cypher on South Beach in 2008
(Credit: Noelle Theard)

mainstream version is almost unrecognizable to the dancers who performed the original.) The pop and lock is both a way of handling the body and a movement quality in which a jerking and freezing of movement takes place. In this particular style a segmented body part such as the foot or hand initiates a free-flowing, undulating movement that flows up the leg or arm and ends with a jerking and freezing in place. It can be done with almost any combination of body parts but is most often performed with the torso, arms, and legs. The pop-and-lock technique could also be observed in the snakehips, as that dance was performed by the Cotton Club's Earl "Snakehips" Tucker in the 1920s. Going farther back, a dance called the snakehips was popular in the Georgia Sea Islands and throughout the antebellum plantation South, and I have no reason to doubt that it resembled the version I learned in a 1950s midwestern African American community.

As with later stages of development, clothing was an essential part of hip hop style. Big apple hats (an oversized style cap popularized by the late Donny Hathaway and soon to be replaced by Kangol caps, then by baseball caps); knickers, or suspenders with baggy pants, or pants tucked into striped knee socks; open-laced combat boots (soon to be replaced by open-laced sneakers); sun visors—all were part of waack's style of dress. Through mass-media exposure, particularly on the TV dance show *Soul Train*, the dance group the Lockers and the Outrageous Waack Dancers popularized the early hip hop dancing styles, helped along by TV sitcoms such as *What's Happening*, featuring Fred "Rerun" Berry. Rerun was often allowed short solos to demonstrate the early hip hop dance and clothing style. Both the Waacks' and Lockers' dancing was full of jerks and staccato movement, with up-and-down motion providing the center from which flashy embellishments such as high kicks and sudden unexpected turns emanated.

Breakdancing, the second stage of hip hop dancing, draws on a traditional and familiar concept in African American music, dance, and verbal arts: competitive one-upmanship. In music, breaking appears in the cutting contests of Harlem rent-party musicians, or in the competitive dialogue between musician and dancer. Look for it in the verbal arts of toasting, signifying, burnin', or "cutting his mouth out," usually performed with rhyming dexterity, articulation, and style; this verbal skill is highly valued in certain contexts. The principle of competitive dialogue shows up in African American street rhyme (e.g., the Signifying Monkey, Stackolee, and Shine rhymes), in the ritual of insult known as "the dozens," in contemporary rap music, and in a sacred context in the African American sermon. It is not surprising that the competitive acrobatics involved in breakdancing were labeled *breaking* or that this traditional principle provides the form through which rappers and DJs would express themselves.

It is generally agreed that breaking as a dance style emerged around 1973 or 1974, concurrent with disco but confined to the African American youth subculture of male street associations known as crews. Breakdancing involved acrobatics that used headspins, backspins, moonwalking (a recycled version of the late 1950s, early 1960s dance the creep), waving, and the robot; it was mediated by a preparatory step known as top rockin' and pressed into competitive virtuosity. By 1976 the Zulus, a group of African American teenagers from the Bronx (the Zulu Nation formed as an alternative to the gangs in that community), had perfected the top rockin' footwork, backspins, and headspins. By 1978 many black youth had given up breaking and moved on to DJing, but the dance form would be rejuvenated among Puerto Rican youth, who took it up later than blacks and extended its longevity.

Breaking's introduction to the general public by the mass media in April 1981 surely marked the beginning of its decline as a functional apparatus for competitive challenge among rival groups or individuals. Breakdancers began rehearsing in order to be discovered and appear in movies or for competitive street exhibition rather than practicing to compete with a rival. Far more acrobatic than either preceding or subsequent hip hop dance forms, without competition, breaking loses its thrust, its raison d'être. Movement into the mainstream negated its status as countercultural by redefining it from a subcultural form to one widely accepted and imitated, a move that inadvertently linked breakers with the society that had previously excluded them. Breaking became so popular that it was featured as entertainment in the opening extravaganza of the 1984 Olympics.

Rap Dancing

The third stage of hip-hop dance, which I will label rap dance, developed as a response to the popularity and athletic requirements of breaking. Combining aspects of both breaking and waack, it is influenced and cross-fertilized by a less athletic form of popular dance, house dancing, which uses much of the traditional African American vocabulary. Further influenced by the older rhythm-and-blues dances of the 1950s and 1960s, rap dance is male oriented, even male dominated, but unlike breakdancing not exclusively male. Its movements suit male-female partnering better than those of either waack or breaking, but less well than older popular dance forms such as the lindy hop or the rhythm-and-blues dances.

Like the lindy hop, hip hop dance is often athletic, youth oriented, and competitive, but rap dancing, and hip hop dance generally, require considerably less cooperation between partners. In the era of both rhythm and blues and the lindy hop, the contingencies of African American life required and fostered a firmer cooperation and interdependence from the racial group and the extended family to an extent virtually unknown to most of today's young hip hoppers. The lindy demonstrates a celebratory exuberance foreign to the breakdancing phase of hip hop dance and largely absent from the other two phases as well. This exuberance was fed by the celebration of the individual bound by in-group solidarity, community accountability, and cooperation.

Though I would not categorize rap dance as a dance of celebration, it does appear to celebrate male solidarity, strength, and competitiveness, themes that might be expected to emerge via the social dance in an era of high black male unemployment and of scarce jobs for which men are increasingly forced to compete with women. At the same time, the lack of commitment to the traditional partnering ritual also breaks with at least one function found in earlier African American social dancing: selecting a romantic partner. Dancers who want to couple off romantically must return to the dance styles of a previous era. Hip hop shows no trace of the male-leadership themes expressed in the lindy and its 1950s and 1960s variants (the strand, off-time, jitterbug, and hand dancing), although they are still observable in the slow drag variations of what is now called slow dancing.

I was ambivalent about the hip hop phenomenon until I noticed the dancing that accompanied the rapping; it was energetic, athletic, and noticeably male dominated, using a very African movement vocabulary. It revived movements that had been out of popular use for thirty years, like splits and rapidly revolving turns (movements still employed by performers). "Splits have made a comeback," I thought. Over time I observed more of this "new" dancing and spoke with African American youth about where they got their dance steps. Many had learned them from friends, but most of the young people I spoke with in West Philadelphia also identified several dance steps with a popular hip hop artist or said that they learned the step from watching a particular performer. This indicated to me that the interplay between the popular/vernacular dance and the black commercial performer is still very strong. In observing rap dance I have seen the following traditional African American dances or dance fragments recycled and recontextualized: the black bottom, roach, Watusi, splits, boogaloo, mashed potatoes, funky butt (funky bottom, boodie green, 'da butt), chicken, four corners, worm, snakehips, and horse (old and new versions). I have also observed the use of traditional opposition or counterpoint as well as traditional characteristics such as percussive phrasing, polyrhythm, derision, mimetic play, and competition.

The rappers whose dance movements best encompass and personify the extremes in the genre of hip hop movement are Flavor Flav, of the group Public Enemy, and M.C. Hammer. Flavor Flav resembles the contemporary urban Esu-Elegba, or deity (principle) of uncertainty and unpredictability, also known as the trickster deity. M.C. Hammer's well-choreographed movements draw directly from a strong rhythm-and-blues tradition. Hammer credits James Brown, a rhythm-and-blues artist, as the most powerful influence on his dance-performance style.

Contemporary rap dances such as the pump, running man, and Roger Rabbit, as well as the dance styles from a concurrent genre, house dancing, all exhibit structural and functional continuity with previous dances. House dancing and rap dance are cross-fertilizing each other. Like most African dance styles, these exhibit angularity, asymmetry, polyrhythmic sensitivity, derision themes, segmentation and delineation of body parts, earth-centeredness, and percussive performance. To this list we can add apart dancing.

Apart dancing describes dancing in which the partners do not touch each other during the dance, yet the commitment to the partnering ritual is clear; this quality helps characterize both the traditional West African dance styles and many dance styles in African communities in the Americas. In the old rhythm-and-blues forms, apart dancing was a dominant theme, and little competition between partners emerged. Individual virtuosity often took the form of display rather than challenge as a dominant governing principle. Themes of challenge pervade both breakdancing and rap dance to a greater degree than occurs in either waack dancing or the older rhythm-and-blues dances such as the twist, the slop, or the horse. Challenge could and did emerge in these older dances, however, particularly when there was a dispute to be settled.

What Hip Hop Dance Says

The richness of gesture and motion in hip hop dance, as in numerous other forms of popular American dance styles that develop among marginalized African American, West Indian, and Puerto Rican youth, reflects the effect of social and economic marginalization on their lives.

Competitiveness in hip hop dance occurs not only against these backdrops but also with strained gender relations thrown into the mix. Since U.S. society regards young African American males as threatening, attitudes of fear and suspicion restrict their entry into the mainstream service economy as well as other areas of mainstream life. That economy thus more easily absorbs African American female workers than males; add the effects of the feminist movement on black women's attitudes toward traditional female roles, and you have raised the potential for cultural expression of rivalry and self-assertion between black men and women.

Hip hop dance permits and encourages a public (and private) male bonding that simultaneously protects the participants from and presents a challenge to the racist society that marginalized them. This dance is not necessarily observer friendly; its movements establish immediate external boundaries while enacting an aggressive self-definition. Hip hop's outwardly aggressive postures and gestures seem to contain and channel the dancer's rage.

The whole of African American dance reflects the postures and gestures that African Americans esteem. Observe today's popular dancing and note how important unpredictability is; reflected in the term "fresh" and emphasized in the new movement styles, this unpredictability has a certain logic that calls forth praise and admiration.

Hip hop dance reflects an alienation not only of young African American males from mainstream society and of African American males from females but also of one African American generation from another. Despite the many continuities and similarities to earlier dances, hip hop represents a clear demarcation between generations in ways previously unknown in African American dance culture. Because of its athletic nature, its performance in popular arenas is largely confined to those under about twenty-five years of age. This might reflect the commodity market's emphasis on youth; it certainly coincides with current marketing strategies that appeal to the "cult of youth," strategies that do not exclude African American cultural commodities. Or it might simply reflect the cultural leadership of young black men in creating African American dances.

Although hip hop dance possesses an air of defiance of authority and mainstream society that reflects a critical vision observable in earlier dances of derision, it lacks the dominant or strongly stated derision that one finds in dances such as the Pee Wee Herman or the Patty Duke of the 1970s, or even the cake-walk. True, hip hop's critical vision comes out of a marginalized youth culture with its own language, its own values and symbols, its own dance and style, yet unlike a true counterculture, hip hop does not reject the mainstream materialism of designer leisure wear, brand-name kicks, expensive cars, and (until recently) dookie gold. Perhaps this embracing or materialism by the later hip hop stylists modifies or otherwise influences the emergence of derision themes, but this connection is by no means clear-cut.

Still, as dance has done for youth in other times, hip hop dance does more than express the view of the social and economic outsider, or even of the wanna-be insider. It encompasses a highly functional system of symbols that affect individual identity development, peer-group status, and intergroup dynamics and conflict. For example, youth in New York City used the breaking form of hip hop to settle lower-level gang disputes and assert territorial dominance. A similar function for dancing was observed among gang members in Chicago in the late 1950s and early 1960s: "Dancing is even more important in Vice Lord life. Almost all Vice Lords take intense pride in their dancing ability and lose few opportunities to demonstrate it."

Malcolm X describes the importance of dancing ability in facilitating peer-group inclusion for him: "Like hundreds of thousands of country-bred Negroes who had come to the Northern black ghetto before me, and have come since, I'd also acquired all the other fashionable ghetto adornments—the zoot suits and conk that I have described, liquor, cigarettes, then reefers—all to erase my embarrassing background. But I harbored one secret humiliation: I couldn't dance."

I have understood the significance of dance in negotiating peer-group inclusion since childhood. As in many African American communities, dancing was important among the young people I knew for peer-group status and acceptance. In the mid-1950s a dance known as the slop was extremely popular. I heard my peers joyfully discussing this dance that I knew nothing about, and I felt excluded. One day I asked an older girl (about twelve or thirteen years old), Thelmari Workman, who lived downstairs from me, to demonstrate the dance for me. She teased me, taunted me, told me that I was "too little to learn the slop." She had me crying. I begged her, "Thelmari, please, please teach me how to do the slop." I knew that dance could help me to belong with my peers and garner admiration from within my community, and it could open an entire new realm of being, self-definition, and socialization.

Just as the jookers and jitterbugs of another era were given their monikers, African American working- and lower-class youth who participate in the hip hop genre, who adopt its persona as their personal presentation style, are sometimes called b-boys, b-girls, or hip hop people. Like their forerunners, they are the product of a specific sociohistoric backdrop and time-bound cultural experience. And like the *rumbista* with Cuban rumba and the *sambista* with Brazilian samba, hip hop people identify with, embrace, and live the genre completely, however short-lived it may be.

The hip hop persona emphasizes converting postures that in another context would indicate alienation and defeat into postures of self-assurance in the face of unbeatable odds. For instance, holding one's arms crossed high on the chest might be interpreted as an insecure and withdrawing posture; in hip hop dance I interpret this posture as affirming African American maleness, strength, and readiness for physical and sexual competition. It also indicates the vision of an inside observer who is simultaneously on the outside. "Laying in the cut," this observer sees something invisible to most people; his bobbing head and crossed arms reaffirm this secretly observed universal truth.

Though hip hop music and dance are today enjoyed by virtually every socioecnomic segment of American society, hip hop postures and presentation of self are born of the African-derived core culture of the street, and they are still used to negotiate a place there. Fear was among the general white public's initial reaction to the latter-day hip hop genre. I have observed young men with hip hop carriage and in hip hop attire—sneaker laces open, baseball cap, sweatsuit—listening to and carrying their beat boxes blasting rap music in the public space of the street, and I have observed whites threatened and intimidated by their presence.

Note

1. Katrina Hazzard-Donald, "Waack and Breakin'," "Rap Dancing," and "What Hip Hop Dance Says," from the "Dance in Hip Hop Culture," in *Droppin' Science: Critical Essays on Rap Music and Hip Hop Culture*, ed. William Eric Perkins (Philadelphia, PA: Temple University Press, 1996), pp. 225–231.

Kenyon Farrow

This electronic post by writer, speaker, activist, and blogger Kenyon Farrow confronts matters of race, anti-blackness, and cultural appropriation in the public consumption of hip-hop as a commodity in Anglophone North America. The specific case under consideration regards a certain assumption of the U.S. category of "Asian Americans." Despite bourgeois liberal notions of a "common culture" to be shared by all "human beings," "beyond race," he continues to ask what happens to Black culture, Black bodies, and Black people as White, non-Black, and some Black-individual entities exercise their power or privilege of playing in Blackness without paying the cost of living in Blackness or opposing White supremacism and its myriad race-and-class hierarchies.

We Real Cool?: On Hip-Hop, Asian-Americans, Black Folks, and Appropriation

Kenyon Farrow[1]

I went to an event in Philly on Friday, November 19, at the Asian Arts Initiative, an Asian American "community arts" space, entitled "Changing the Face of the Game: Asian Americans in Hip-Hop." I cannot pretend I didn't already know what I was getting myself into. The title of the event itself expresses a level of hostility to Black people—since Black people are the current face of the game, and for whatever reason, that needs to be changed. But anyhow, I went, ready to see what was gonna go down . . .

The Main Event

Oliver Wang, Asian American writer, cultural critic and graduate student at UC Berkeley (where he teaches courses on pop culture), the opening speaker and panel moderator, gave an opening talk about the historical presence of Asians in hip-hop. Mr. Wang's research into the annals of hip-hop history unearthed an emcee (who claims to have cut a record before "Rapper's Delight") from the South Bronx, whom Wang declares as the "first Asian in hip-hop." He then describes him as "half Filipino and half Black." I couldn't help but wonder how this emcee identified himself and how he physically looked, and why his Blackness was now a footnote in Wang's historical re-write. As Wang continued on, he painted hip-hop music and culture as this multi-culti "American" artform that everyone's had a hand in developing. By doing so, Wang very skillfully ignored the reality that Rap was in fact created by Black youth (and Latinos from the Caribbean—many of whom are also of African descent and certainly ghettoized as "Black" in the NYC socio-economic landscape) in the South Bronx (or in Queens, depending on whom you ask). Wang went on to say that the only reason why Asians were drawn to hip-hop was because of the music. He also said that "hip-hop is the most democratic music because it doesn't take the same skill as playing classical music."

Wang then asked a follow-up question to the panelists. Uh-oh! The panel included spoken word duo Yellow Rage, DJ Phillie Blunt, Chops of the Mountain Brothers, a Cambodian-American rapper named Jim, and his friend, the lone Black panelist who is an MC from Philly. Borrowing from the hip-hop romantic comedy Brown Sugar, Wang asked each panelist to talk about when they "first fell in love with hip-hop." All of the panelists, save the Black man, talked about hearing some rap song on the radio and falling in love, because it expressed "who they were" and "their experience." Jim admitted he grew up in the burbs and came to hip-hop out of his isolation. At least that was honest. Michelle, from Yellow Rage, anointed herself the hip-hop historian (or shall I shay griot?) for the evening. Making jokes about her age, Michelle reminded the audience to pay respect to hip-hop's roots and remember "the old school." The panel was asked another question by Wang and then he opened the floor for questions from the audience.

After squirming in my third-row seat for the duration of the talk, I had my opportunity. Quickly raising my hand, I was passed the mic. My question/statement was: In all of the talk thus far, we have conveniently skirted around the issue of race. But let's be real, when we're talking about hip-hop and hip-hop culture, we mean Black people, which you de-emphasized and de-historicized in your intro talk, Mr Wang . . . Now, we know about the history of Black popular culture being appropriated and stolen by whites, as in the case of Blues, Jazz, and Rock & Roll. And now there's hip-hop, and since we live in this multiracial state which still positions Blackness socio-economically and politically at the bottom, how does the presence of Asian Americans in hip-hop, this black cultural artform, look any different than that of white folks in Jazz, Blues, and Rock & Roll?

The jig was up. I was the rain that ended the parade (or shall I say charade?). The room quickly turned to palpable hostility and anger. Since they were already clearly pissed, I decided to throw out a follow-up question: Mr. Wang, you [said] that Asian people in hip-hop just like the music, which I find hard to believe since hip-hop also came into prominence in the day and age of music video—where image and representation are as important (if not more) than the music itself. That being the case, what is it about Black people (and especially Black masculinity in the case of hip-hop), and what they represent to others, that is so attractive to other people, including non-white people of color?

The Body Slam

Well, that did it. They were mad as hell. I mean, how dare I bring up Black people and appropriation, as if Asians can't possibly appropriate Blackness in the same manner that white folks do! It couldn't be, not while I'm in a standing-room only crowd of "conscious" Asian youth with locks and hair teased out (and often chemically treated) to look like afros! Well, that panel couldn't get that mic around fast enough! Some of the responses were too asinine to even bother with a critique. But I will tackle the main points. The first to respond was the lone Black man on the panel. Responding to my second question, he spoke in a condescending, yet gentle tone (you know, "brother to brother") about us "being a soulful people" and that's why everyone wants to get with our shit and how I should see it as a "compliment." Well, I am fine with you getting with it—on the radio or video or whatever—but does that mean you get to have it? Better yet, take it, and then use it against Black people to promote the image of us as intimidating and politically and culturally selfish? This is exactly the narrative that was used to promote Eminem and is being used now for Jin: both of them are framed as real "artists" and "lyricists" who stand dignified in the face of Black "reverse racism" and hostility (watch 8 Mile, read much of the press written about Jin's appearances on 106th & Park)—as if Nas, Bahamadia, or Andre 3000 & Big Boi aren't really artists but, as Black people are expected to do, just use "the race card" to get ahead. And to treat Blacks as "soulful people" is the same as seeing us as primitives (with some genetic code programming us to gleefully wail and shout, shake and shimmy) who make this lovely music yet are too docile to be really intelligent, ingenious and artistic.

Several of the panelists at this event went on to critique commercial rap artists for being materialistic, etc. For example, after putting his arm on his Black friend's shoulder and telling me that we need to "recognize that Blacks are on the bottom," Jim concluded by telling me that "it's about class, not race" and how he tries his hardest to be "conscientious." This is the same guy who earlier emphasized how capitalism diluted the politics of hip-hop without talking about Asian Americans' role in the capitalist structure. Instead of dealing with this very important issue, the Asian-American panelists acted as if they were "more real" than Black commercial artists. So, because they get to be "underground" (which loosely means someone without a record deal), they get to be "real" and "authentic" over Black artists who have been commercially successful. I have my own critiques of commercially successful Black hip-hop artists and their materialism, misogyny, violence and homophobia—which I have written and spoken about as well—but I was not about to give that over to some hostile non-Black people to use to make themselves more "down."

Michelle of Yellow Rage flat out screamed on me, in an effort, I guess, to "keep it real" with her duo's namesake. Starting several of her sentences with the phrase, "You need to acknowledge . . .," she went on an on about how she is sick of people (I guess Black people) saying that hip-hop is a Black thing. This Ph.D. candidate (who specializes in both Asian and African American Literature) went on to tell me that I need to "stop being so divisive" and "read my history" via the likes of cultural critics Tricia Rose and Nelson George so that I can learn and ultimately "acknowledge" that "nobody has a monopoly on culture."

And least of all Black people. As the descendants of slaves, the property of others, nothing belongs to us. Everything we do, including hip-hop and spoken word, can be done by anyone else. And yet, Yellow Rage made a name for itself by critiquing appropriation of Asian culture by non-Asians, including Black people (specifically hip-hop artists). So, to the author of *Ancestor Worship* (a phrase generally referring to Black African traditional religious practice) and member of Asians Misbehavin' (which appropriates the name from the Black musical revue of Fats Waller's music, Ain't Misbehavin') I say to you, Michelle, if Asians have certain cultural boundaries that need to be respected (e.g. Chinese/Japanese tattoos, chopsticks in the hair, etc.), then why does that not apply to Black people? Maybe this is something Michelle can ponder as she works on her dissertation called "Untying Tongues" (which appropriates the title of the late Black Gay filmmaker Marlon Rigg's work, Tongues Untied).

So I asked the first, and apparently last question of the Q&A. Not caring to see the "performance" part of the evening (though I'd have to call the panel a performance as much as the concert), I left the event, dealing with the angry glares on my way out. I thought it was over. But then a friend sent me a link to a commentary on the cultural possessiveness of Blacks over hip-hop on Oliver "aka O-Dub" Wang's site written by Mr. Wang himself (www.o-dub.com/weblog/2004/11/hes-your-chinaman-jin-jin-everywhere.html).

The Aftermath

So, in a larger blog about Jin and Asians in hip-hop, Wang writes about the Asian Arts Initiative event. Describing how I raised the question I did, Wang responds:

> "I'm constantly frustrated by these kinds of defensive attitudes around cultural ownership though I am quite aware of how they arise. The gentleman in this case was correct in noting that African American culture has suffered through a long history of being exploited to the gains of others and there is great concern that hip-hop is simply next on the list . . . Communities may think they 'own' a culture but that's not how culture works. It's not an object you can chain up. Culture doesn't care about borders—it spreads as fast and as far as the people who consume it will take it. I agree, yes, culture can also be misappropriated and exploited. But if people are really worrying about hip-hop becoming the latest example of Black culture being emptied of content and turned into a deracinated commodity, the problem doesn't lie with Asian American youth. Or Latino youth. Or even white youth really."

It's interesting—or more accurately, disturbing—that Wang uses the metaphor of culture being "chained up" in relation to African Americans. Wang, like Michelle from Yellow Rage, refuses to deal with what the legacy of being property (always owned, and never owners) means in the case of Black people and claims of ownership over culture. So, where Black people are concerned, both historically and contemporarily, it's all good. We make everything for everybody. Wang goes on assert that the "The color line here is painted in green. You want to talk about cooptation? Talk about corporations . . . " (right now W.E.B. DuBois is rolling over in his grave). So I guess, as Wang puts it, the real (and I guess only) problem is corporations who promote hip-hop and make money off of it—of which some executives are Black, Wang is eager to point out.

That's almost slick, Ollie. But not quite. People who don't want to deal with their own complicity in the reproduction of anti-Black racism are very quick to point out corporations as the culprit. Interestingly, while emphasizing corporations, Wang doesn't talk about his own relationship to them or that he makes a living writing for such corporations about a music that allegedly doesn't require much skill or that he works for a university—which is also a corporation—and gets to have some control over the production of knowledge about hip-hop. Instead of addressing this, Wang goes out of his way to point out that there are one or two Black people in some level of decision making capacity in the music industry. But why doesn't he talk about how virtually none of them actually own the labels, and fewer are in control of any means of production and distribution?

The narrative of blame the corporation, but not me (or any living breathing person), and don't talk about the bodies it oppresses in the meantime is such a mirror of the white nationalist narrative. It, to me, is the same as the white person saying, "Don't blame me for slavery. My grandparents didn't own any slaves. They came from Russia in 1902. And didn't Africans sell their own people into slavery? And didn't some Blacks own slaves?"

Well, maybe your "immigrant" ancestor did not own slaves, but they certainly benefited from a nation that valued whiteness above all else. And they got jobs in industry (that Black people clearly needed and couldn't get easy or any access to) and amass wealth in a way Black people have been prevented from doing collectively. A handful of rappers, athletes and talk-show hosts doesn't change the fact that a recent study by the Pew Hispanic Center deemed that Black families are the only racial group in the United States who saw their wealth decrease in recent years. And your grandparents didn't end up here by accident, no more than mine accidentally left the shores of Africa—"chained up." They came because the US wanted to balance a growing Black non-enslaved population with more white people. So the US took who they could get.

By the 1960's the US again decided to balance a "mad and organized-as-all-hell" Black population by relaxing immigration to bring in more non-Black people of color. So, in many cases, the non-Black presence in the US was specifically set up in relationship against Black people. Even if your family was here before the 1960s, look at the history of every contiguous state formed between the American Revolution and the Civil War. The question of slavery is at the heart of the founding of every single one. The "slave," the "nigger," and the "criminal" are historical and contemporary positions that Blackness occupies. This reality is something everyone is forced to deal with, and yet nobody wants to be one of them. So, what Asian Americans and Asian American politics (and I think "People of Color" politics as well) has yet to fully deal with is that we can't talk about capitalism and corporations in some abstract sense. If we do then we ignore how one's positionality against Blackness and Black people in a white supremacist context helps to define the issues of ownership, property and parameters and how they are racialized. Just because you aren't phenotypically white doesn't mean you can't uphold white interests politically—as Wang likes to point out in his example of the Black executive—but Black people as a whole cannot function politically in the same way that non-Black people of color can in the current global paradigm (Yes! Global. Let's talk about sub-Saharan Africa in relation to South

America, the Middle East or Asia, if you must). So, not being Black is what seems to matter more under capitalism than being white.

The Final Round

So, corporations are but one manifestation of the American project. But history and culture are also an equally important part of that project. History and culture inform narratives that form people's logic and assumptions, which root themselves in the subconscious. We could overthrow all corporations tomorrow, and if our narratives stay the same, or simply shift shape without being utterly transformed, some other new and oppressive shit (aimed at Black people!) will take its place. And take the prison's place. So, don't put all your focus on corporations, or laws, or cages, without dealing with the logic that makes us assume we need them in the first place. There's an old saying my grandmother has: "I'm not dealing with the form, I'm dealing with the essence!"

The essence is exactly this: Let's un-assume that because we're all up in hip-hop that we're all on the same page. Let's un-assume that because you might try to look like me or sound like me (or how you think I do both), that we are working towards the same goal, or that we even have the same enemy. I don't think, despite efforts to think otherwise, that this was really ever Black people's assumption.

To close, let me share a story that I think is very telling and illustrates everything I've been getting at here. I was living in New Orleans last year, and had just arrived for 2003 Satchmo Festival celebrating the life of Louie Armstrong. The event takes place in the gentrified Fabourg Marigny, and over that August weekend, cafes and restaurants fill with Brass Bands, Jazz and Blues artists. I sat outside a coffee shop one day listening to an incredible quartet with a group of Black people I had just met, while the cafe was filled with folks from all over, including whites, Japanese tourists and Asian-American college students. One Black woman said to her friend, "Girl let's go in!" The other replied, "No, I'd rather stay out here. I can't experience it the way I would if it was just us. I always feel like part of the minstrel show when they be up in it. And there ain't no place in New Orleans where they don't go now . . . " I turned to her, and gave an "Uh-huh," wanting her to know I was there to bear witness to what she'd said, and glad she'd said it. I, too, chose to stay on the outside for the very same reason. Asian Americans in hip-hop need to consider this Black woman's concern, as well as this question: If first-generation white European immigrants like Al Jolson could use minstrelsy (wearing blackface, singing black popular music and mimicking their idea of Black people) to not only ensure their status as white people, but also to distance themselves from Black people, can Asian Americans use hip-hop (the music, clothing, language and gestures, sans charcoal makeup), and everything it signifies to also assert their dominance over Black bodies, rather than their allegiance to Black liberation? People who now think that jazz is for everybody never think about what the process was to get jazz to that place, nor what that means for the people who invented it. This thought leaves me with one last—albeit very frightening—question: Will my niece and nephews be at a festival for Lauryn Hill fifty years from now, also standing on the outside looking in?

Note

1. Excerpt from Kenyon Farrow, "We Real Cool?: On Hip-Hop, Asian-Americans, Black Folks, and Appropriation," June 2, 2005, www.kenyonfarrow.com

Sunaina Maira

This selection plots and thinks through hip-hop's reach to Palestine and Palestinians transnationally, a particularly explosive connection at this point in global historical time, to be sure. At bottom, it understands hip-hop as a "poetics of displacement and protest." While hip-hop gets casually described as "multiethnic" in current global terms, this selection carefully traces Palestinian rap identifications with the experiences of racism and anti-racist resistance shared by Black, African Diasporic youth (and thereby other youth of color) in North America.

Palestinian and Palestinian American Hip Hop

Sunaina Maira[1]

An emerging generation of Arab and Palestinian American youth is using popular culture, particularly hip hop, as a medium through which to raise awareness of the Palestinian question. Hip hop emerged in the United States in the late 1970s as a subculture created by marginalized African American and Puerto Rican youth in the South Bronx who responded to urban restructuring, deindustrialization, poverty, and racism by producing a new cultural expression of their experiences of political abandonment and alienation and imaginings of the past, present, and future (Chang 2005; Rose 1994). Hip hop, which consists of rap (MCing), graffiti, deejaying, and break dancing, has been described by Tricia Rose as a hybrid cultural form that mixes Afro-Caribbean and African American musical, oral, visual, and dance practices with contemporary technologies and urban cultures to create a "counter-dominant narrative" (1994, 82) The "heavy reliance on lyricism" makes hip hop a genre that can be powerfully used for social and political commentary by layering poetry over beats (Youmans 2007, 42).

Palestinian and Palestinian/Arab American rap is a poetics of displacement and protest. In fact, some scholars such as Joseph Massad (2005) situate the political rap produced by Palestinian youth in a longer tradition of revolutionary, underground Arabic music and political songs that have supported Palestinian liberation since the 1950s and that mix nationalist poetry with hybrid Arab-Western musical instrumentation. Others, such as Will Youmans (2007, 46–47), who is himself a hip hop artist ("Iron Sheik"), acknowledge that some forms of improvised and folk poetry that are performed by Palestinians and Arabs (such as zajal, mawwal [mawwaliya], and saj') could be likened to Arabic spoken word—not to mention the percussiveness and lyricism of Arabic music—but argue that the impetus for Arab American hip hop is the mainstreaming and globalization of rap. The question of cultural influences is not an either/or one; clearly Palestinian and Palestinian American rappers are responding to both the global popularity of hip hop and to Arab musical and poetic traditions they have grown up with and are incorporating into a new cultural form. These artists acknowledge this hybridity themselves; for example, DAM, a Palestinian crew from Israel, notes that its influences are "Jamal Abdel Nasser, Naji al-Ali, Ghassan Kanafani, Fadwa Tuqan, Tupac Shakur, Toufiq Ziyyad, Malcolm X, Marcel Khalife, Fairuz, El Sheikh Imam, The Notorious BIG, George Habash, Edward Said, Nas, and KRS One."

As hip hop has crossed ethnic and class boundaries, it has become a multiethnic and globalized art form even as it has become increasingly mainstream. Many fans of political or so-called conscious rap lament that the oppositional thrust of hip hop has waned as it has become increasingly commercialized; some argue that this is part of the "politics of containment" directed at youth of color in the post-civil rights era (Chang 2005). It is apparent that, although hip hop culture may in some instances be critical or implicitly subversive of consumerism, it is always engaged with the realm of commerce and does not exist outside of U.S. or global capitalism, like all other forms of popular culture that are marketed, distributed, and consumed (Lipsitz

1994; Kelley 1997). Palestinian and Palestinian/Arab American and Palestinian hip hop is getting increased attention, but it is still, for the most part, an underground music that has not yet entered the mainstream music industry and is distributed via the Internet and Arab/Arab American stores.

Yet young Palestinian and Arab American rappers who are part of the hip hop underground are getting increasing attention, such as Iron Sheik (from Oakland but now based in Ann Arbor, Michigan), Excentrik (Oakland), the Philistines (Los Angeles), the NOMADS (also from L.A.), and the Brooklyn-based Hammer Brothers, who wrote a "Free Palestine" anthem. Numerous other Palestinian and Arab American MCs around the United States do political rap, such as Masari (San Francisco), MC Shaheed (New Orleans), Gaza Strip (New York), ASH ONE (New Jersey), and Arabic Assassin (Houston), not to mention well-known music producers such as Fredwreck (Los Angeles) and spoken word poets such as Suheir Hammad (New York), star of Def Jam Broadway (Alim 2005; Davey D 2007; Youmans 2007). In fact, Iron Sheik, who was inspired to produce and write rap in high school because of politically conscious groups such as Public Enemy and A Tribe Called Quest, suggests that the "message rap" produced by Palestinian American youth is reinvigorating the progressive potential of hip hop: "I feel ambivalent about what hip hop has become in the U.S. and I'm happy to see messages in rap again" (2008). Arab and Palestinian American hip hop artists are part of a transnational hip hop movement that includes young artists in Palestine/Israel—such as DAM and MWR in Israel; the Ramallah Underground, Checkpoint 303, and Boikutt in the West Bank; PR (Palestine Rapperz) in Gaza; and Clotaire K, Aksser, and DJ Lethal Skillz in Lebanon—as well as MCs in the larger Arab diaspora (such as I AM and MC Solaar in France, and Palestine a.k.a. Ref-UG in Sweden) who increasingly perform all over Europe and North America (Gross et al. 1996).

A new generation of Palestinian and Arab American youth have grown up identifying with the experiences of racism shared with other youth of color in the United States, and are increasingly vocal about critiquing their profiling after 9/11 and linking it to older structures of Orientalism and anti-Arab racism. Similarly, a politicized generation of Palestinian youth inside the 1948 borders of Israel (the '48 Palestinians) are critical of the painful and paradoxical condition of being "citizens without citizenship" or without the full rights of Jewish citizens in Israel (Sultany 2003). Tamer Nafar of DAM identified with the rap of African American artists such as Tupac Shakur, who commented on the poverty and racism affecting inner-city youth that Nafar, too, experienced growing up in Lid, Israel: "My reality is hip hop. I listened to the lyrics and felt they were describing me, my situation. You can exchange the word 'nigger' with 'Palestinian.' Lid is the ghetto, the biggest crime and drug center in the Middle East. When I heard Tupac sing 'It's a White Man's World,' I decided to take hip hop seriously" (in El-Sabawi 2005). The music created by these Palestinian youth—in the diaspora, the West Bank, Gaza, and Israel—demonstrates transnational and cross-ethnic linkages among Palestinians, Palestinian and Arab Americans, African Americans, Asian Americans, Native American, and Latino/a youth through popular culture.

Note

1. Sunaina Maira, "Palestinian and Palestinian American Hip Hop," *CR: The New Centennial Review* 8.2 (2008): 164–167.

Hishaam Aidi

This selection documents the explosion of hip-hop culture in the form of rap, break-dancing, and graffiti art in the sub-urban hoods of France in the wake of Afrika Bambaataa's tour of Europe of 1982 with the Double Dutch Girls and the Rock Steady Crew. The overwhelming Black and Arab African space of these "*banlieues*" has become internationally known for their political as well as musical-cultural upsurges; and the French imperial state has never failed to equate fiery riots with fiery raps in recent years, interestingly enough. The hip-hop movement documented here is now officially classified as the second largest movement in the world after hip-hop in the United States and before hip-hop in Senegal, West Africa.

B-Boys in "Les Banlieues": Hip Hop Culture in France

Hishaam Aidi[1]

According to British cultural critic, Steven Cannon, who studies hip-hop in Europe, ever since Afrika Bambaataa and the breakdancing groups Double Dutch Girls and the Rock Steady Crew toured France in 1982, b-boy culture—rap, breakdancing and graffiti art—has gained a mass following in France, making the European nation the second largest consumer and producer of hip hop after the United States. After its introduction to French teens by American performers, breakdancing ("le smurf") flourished in France and remained popular through the 1990s, while French rappers began to compile a growing and increasingly sophisticated body of work.

Now, French hip hop has emerged as the voice of France's impoverished African and Arab minorities, expressing the rage and alienation of life in "les cités" (housing projects) in an era of welfare retrenchment and rising anti-immigrant sentiment. The bulk of France's minority communities are concentrated in the "banlieues," dilapidated zones of high-rise project housing, sub-standard schooling and high unemployment that encircle French cities. Unlike in the U.S., France's ghettoes are suburban, but this has not stopped "banlieusards" ("ghetto-dwellers") from identifying with the African American experience and life in America's inner cities. Rap for many French banlieusards represents "a turn to speak" ("la prise de parole") and an opportunity to express rejectionist attitudes and "la haine" (hatred) of the French establishment. More broadly, hip hop has emerged as a cultural vehicle for France's blacks and browns (Arabs) struggling to carve a space and identity for themselves in an often inhospitable environment.

Senegalese-born rapper MC Solaar is one of French rap's most prominent pioneers. His hit "Bouge de La" ("Move From There," 1991) brought rap into the French mainstream, and found a receptive audience among African, Arab and West Indian (from the French Antilles) fans in the French banlieues. Before Solaar's ground-breaking album "Qui Sème le Vent Récolte le Tempo" ("Who Sows the Wind Reaps the Rhythm," 1991), rap was mainly played on independent stations such as Paris's Radio Nova, whose rap show led to the "discovery" of Solaar and French rap contemporaries Ministère Amer and Suprême NTM. On their famous Sunday show, Radio Nova's Dee Nasty and Lionel D opened up their microphones to aspiring "champions" from different banlieues, who would free-style over Dee Nasty's remixes. Now, French rap achieves ample airplay on Fun-Radio, Sky-Rock, and NRJ, and is no longer ghettoized on independent stations.

Despite the inter-banlieue and inter-project rivalries, throughout the French hip hop nation there is an over-arching sense of belonging to an international hip hop community. One important source of this collective identity was the Zulu Nation, founded by Bambaataa in New York in the early 1980s to promote hip hop culture and mobilize youth in a peaceful alternative to street gangs. In 1984, a branch of the Nation was established in France with its own "King" and

"Queen," its own fanzine, *The Zulus' Letter*, and block celebrations called "Zulu Parties." A number of other community fanzines have since appeared—*Down With This, From Da Underground*, and *Black News*—further solidifying a sense of collective identity among French hip hop fans.

French hip hop posses ("les bandes") have popped up around the banlieues as well, with names like Black Dragons and Black Tiger Force, and can be seen loitering on the Champs Elysees sporting the same hip hop gear worn by their American counterparts—Karl Kani boots, Tommy Hilfiger jeans, and Fubu sweatshirts. The "bandes" speak an argot that blends American hip hop slang, Arabic words (given that North Africans are France's largest ethnic minority) and French "verlan"—hipsterist word play in which syllables are reversed (for example, "noires" (blacks) become "renois," and "arabe" (Arab) becomes "beur"). French posses claim they are not gangs of delinquents, but simply trying to overcome racism and stay out of trouble by participating in hip hop festivals, dancing competitions, and graffiti art contests ("competition des taggeurs").

Rap artists of African and Arab origin voice the sentiments of France's impoverished ethnic underclass, and often try to mobilize the ghetto youth for causes such as interracial solidarity and the unity of "black, beur, blanc" (blacks, Arabs and whites), the slogan of an annual anti-racist French hip hop festival and the title of France's first rap radio show, which began in 1991 on a station in Lille. Rap artists from different banlieues tend to spurn traditional politics, affirming their loyalty to their "families" from their cités, yet calling for a multi-ethnic alliance and political movement with hip hop at its core.

Despite French hip hop's predominantly black and Arab following, this effort to use hip hop as a means of forging unity across racial lines is an increasingly central theme in French rap. Unlike their American counterparts, French rap groups are often multiracial. The Marseilles-based rap crew IAM (Imperial Asiatic Men), who use Pharaonic nicknames (Kheops, Akhenaton, Imhotep and Divin Khepren), are actually of Malian, Algerian, Spanish, and Italian origin. And while they celebrate humanity's origins in Africa, the motherland ("la terre-mere"), and condemn slavery and apartheid, IAM stress the importance of racial tolerance and unity, and on the track "Blanc et Noire" compare Louis Farrakhan to France's radically conservative messenger of hate, Jean-Marie le Pen of the National Front.

The rapper Assassin, who hails from Paris's 18th Arrondissement (district), echoes IAM's call for racial harmony: "Le drapeau de l'unité est planté dans le 18eme/Alliance d'idées, alliance de culture/le métissage est notre force, cette force de future" ("The flag of unity is planted in the 18th/Alliance of ideas, alliance of cultures/this mixing is our strength, the strength of the future.") In the same way that the multi-ethnic collection of French soccer players who won the World Cup in 1998 (popularly referred to in France as "les blacks") symbolized the emergence of a new multi-racial generation of French youth, French hip hop often expresses a pluralistic vision of racial unity and tolerance.

Despite the existence of such positive, optimistic messages in French rap, the genre's more militant perspectives tend to get more attention from the French media. Rap artists have virulently denounced police brutality and the state's apathy towards conditions in the ghetto, often in a confrontational style. Joey Starr of Suprême NTM (NTM stands for "Nique Ta More," "F—k Your Mother") observed in an interview with *Libération* magazine, "For people like me, a government of the left or the right is the same . . . voting is like pissing in a violin case . . . I fulfill my obligations as a citizen, every day, in writing my raps."

Similarly, IAM often rap about "ce putain d'état" ("this f—king state"), while on the song "Le Future Que Nous Reserve t-il?" ("What does the future hold for us?"), Assassin unleashes his lyrical, analytical skills on the European Economic Community: "La CEE organise à travers l'application de ces institutions/L'appauvrissement des pays en voie de developpement" ("The EEC condemns to poverty all developing countries"). IAM also critique European imperialism on the track "J'aurais pu croire" ("I could've believed"): "J'aurais pu croire en l'Occident/Si tout ces pays n'avaient pas eu des colonies/et lors de l'indépendance ne les avaient pas decoupées comme des tartes/aujourd'hui il y a des guerres à cause de problèmes des cartes" ("I could've believed the West/if these countries did not have colonies/if independence hadn't meant the slicing of these lands/wars rage today because of these maps"). On "Frère Faut que Tu Saches" ("Brother, you have to Know"), the group Mafia Maghrebine considers France's hidden hand in Algeria's bloody civil war: "Trop d'hypocrisie . . . . Maghreb détruit pendant que l'Europe s'enrichie" (Too much hypocrisy . . . . Maghreb [North Africa] destroyed while Europe gets rich").

French rap's incendiary lyrics have met with mainstream criticism, most notably when Suprême NTM's hit "Nique la Police" ("F—k The Police," obviously inspired by the American group NWA's song of the same name) triggered a political and legal firestorm. Performing at an anti-racism Bastille Day concert, the two rappers Kool Shen and Joey Starr encouraged the audience to shout "nique la police" in the direction of the concert security guards. Found guilty by a court of "orally abusing" the security forces, NTM was sentenced to six months in prison, fined 50,000 francs, and disbanded for six months. Leftist activists protested the decision, denouncing the punishment as evidence of a legal double standard: they noted that Jean-Marie Le Pen of the Front National has denied the Holocaust (a crime in France), while Front National-funded punk rock groups call for violence against the police and Zionists, but have not suffered similar repercussions.

Although, on appeal, NTM's ban from "professional activity" was reduced to two months, "l'affaire NTM" and further anti-state rhymes provoked a political and cultural backlash. Suprême NTM's "Qu'est-ce qu'on attend?" ("What are we waiting for?") calls for the ghetto youth "to first burn down the police state and/then send the republic to burn on the same pyre . . . . unite ourselves and incinerate this system/so why are we waiting to start this fire?"— "Just to be a few more in number," they respond on their most recent album, "Odeurs de Souffre" ("Fumes of Sulphur," 1998).

Government officials have blamed NTM's lyrics for increased street violence and attacks on the police, and government spokesman Eric Roualt has rebuked rappers for not being positive role models. "I'm not a leader, only a loudspeaker," rapped back Kool Shen. Le Pen's xenophobic National Front has denounced rap as "a dangerous art which originated in Algiers" and warned that graffiti appearing on banlieues walls is threatening French civilization. In early January, legislation was passed mandating sterilization of the 40,000 pit bulls and other "chiens d'attaque" owned by French ghetto youth; non-sterilized "attack dogs" will be rounded up by the "Brigade K-9," and their owners will be fined 10,000 francs and sentenced to six months in prison.

The popularity of hip hop is partly responsible for the infamous Toubon Law of 1994, which guards the French language against Americanisms, Arabisms, and the word play that makes up the slang of the banlieues. The law, advanced by Minister of Culture Jacques Toubon (referred to by critics as Monsieur "Allgood"), in conjunction with the 1994 Carignon Law, dictates that a minimum of 40 percent of France's musical programming must be in French and by contemporary French artists.

Ironically, state attempts to control or suppress hip hop have only seemed to aid "le mouv" (the movement). The NTM affair (and subsequent media attention to Joey Starr's assault of a flight attendant) has helped the group secure platinum sales, a multi-record deal with Epic-Sony and a contract with Adidas. While lamenting money's tendency to "rot people" ("L'argent pourrit les gens"), Joey Starr and Kool Shen have established production companies (IV My People and Boss), which have released albums by new artists like Busstaflex and Zoxea.

Note

1. Excerpt from Hishaam Aidi, "B-Boys in 'Les Banlieues': Hip Hop Culture in France," *Planète Afrique* (2000), www.planete-afrique.com/hip-hop/b_boys.htm

Cedric Muhammad

This article is the fifth installment of an expansive series on the persecution, policing, and prosecution of hip-hop figures in the United States. A local, state, and federal practice of counterin-
surgency that targets not only artists but also entourages, entrepreneurs, and activists is visible
and came to be known colloquially among critics as "Rap COINTELPRO." That nomenclature
links it to the FBI's infamous "COunter-INTELligence PROgram," directed by J. Edgar Hoover
in the U.S. settler state's effort to "neutralize" and "liquidate" the Black liberation and other
oppressed movements of the 1950s, 1960s, and 1970s.

"Rap COINTELPRO Part V . . . The NYPD Zeros in on Hip-Hop"

Cedric Muhammad[1]

For nearly a year now, we have been writing about the documented relationship between the
FBI, local law enforcement and the media in the 1960s and 1970s and comparing that relationship with its real and potential counterpart today, in reference to the Hip-Hop industry. Any
skepticism for what we have been arguing should have been swept away by Jay-Z's arrest two
weeks ago, by the NYPD street crime unit, and by this week's admission from the NYPD, that
its gang intelligence unit has been monitoring Hip-Hop artists and the nightspots that they and
their fans frequent.

Having said that we hope that no one is really so naïve as to believe the NYPD's explanation
of their activities, that they are doing what they are, to protect Hip-Hop artists. We argue to the
contrary and believe that their explained efforts to "serve and protect" the Hip Hop industry is
a cover story, or a front to really arrest Hip-Hop artists on gang, drug and racketeering charges.
This has been their aim for some time now.

To be sure, there are certainly a few who may be guilty of crimes. But a full-scale monitoring
of an entire industry, in its biggest city, is evidence of more than good police work. After all, if
drugs and gangs are what they are after, the police would be better staking out raves, heavy metal
concerts and the homes of Rock artists in search of heroin, cocaine and ecstasy drug use, as well
as ties to organized crime.

Far from an effort to save rap artists, the effort is an indication of a return to the FBI's Counter Intelligence Program—a program that was aimed at organizations like the Nation Of Islam,
the 5% Nation Of Islam, the Black Panthers, SCLC and SNCC. Interestingly, two of the biggest
files that the FBI kept during COINTELPRO were its files on the NOI and the 5 Percenters—the
two communities that arguably have had more impact on Hip-Hop than any other.

So now, an entire music industry joins that rarified air, previously the domain of activist and
progressive organizations and those concerned with political consciousness, social change and
community development. Now that we have established this fact, we hope that the Hip-Hop
community in general, and Hip-Hop artists in particular, are prepared for what awaits them
and what has already been happening to them. We hope that they are prepared for their telephone lines to be tapped; their vehicles and homes to be bugged; agents to be placed within their
organizations; their friends turned into government informants; letters and communications
attributed to them, and even their forged signatures attached to such, without their knowledge;
conflicts started between rivals and competitors; lies and half-truths about them planted in various media outlets, and yes, even violent action taken against them.

Every one of these acts, and much, much more were performed in COINTELPRO, with the
help of the FBI and local police departments. In order to get an idea of how extensive the FBI's
efforts were, and for evidence of what we have described above, one should visit the FBI's reading room, in person or online: http://foia.fbi.gov/foiaindex.htm.

You maybe surprised at some of the names the FBI has in its file index as a part of COINTEL-PRO or other surveillance programs. The list includes several celebrities (www.fbi-files.com/celebrities/index.html) who[m] the Bureau feared could move the public in ways counter to the desired direction of the status quo. Many of the most famous were White actors. The same fear exists today for Hip-hop artists who may have the most loyal fans in all of the entertainment industry.

The NYPD's program is already being described as illegal and unconstitutional. Many believe that the program represents "profiling"—a practice that is increasingly coming under fire. It will be interesting to see if civil libertarians or the liberals and progressives which dominate the industry will come to the aid of the Hip-Hop community and defend them from what, at the very least, is a massive invasion of privacy and, at the most, an act of war.

We advise that Hip-hop artists should not be surprised to find little support from the labels that employ their services. For years, several record executives have been handing over marketing plans and providing information on a variety of artists to federal law enforcement officials. And on the local level, we know of at least two record label executives who have silent alarm buttons in their offices that connect them to the NYPD, in the case of an emergency or violent altercation. Of course these record label execs have their own artists in mind as the likely perpetrators of aggression.

Which leads us to a final point. If the Hip-Hop community is going to avoid the mistakes that the targets of COINTELPRO previously made, they will have to 1) begin to question their "friendships" with record label executives, lawyers and business managers who seem to have no problem providing privileged information to law enforcement officers 2) compare notes with one another 3) discontinue their recently increased leaning toward public disputes, 4) End any activities that can be construed as illegal and 5) they must seek ways to peacefully resolve conflicts and unite.

Note

1. Cedric Muhammad, "Rap COINTELPRO Part V … The NYPD Zeros in on Hip-Hop," April 27, 2001, www.blackelectorate.com/articles.asp?ID=34

Nightjohn (Arnett Kale Powell and Adebayo Alabi Olorunto)

This selection is a chapter from Nightjohn's *The Hiphop Driven Life: A Genius Liberation Handbook* (2005). Arnette Kale ("A.K.") Powell and Adebayo Alabí Olorunto are "Nightjohn," a hip-hop duo who take their collective moniker from a novel by Gary Paulsen (and now a film by Charles Burnett) about an enslaved African who escapes the U.S. South but returns to teach literacy and help others escape to freedom as well. Both writers of books and performers of rhyme, this hip-hop Nightjohn practices a literacy of resistance, too: "Practice and Preserve Your Rights as a Genius . . . Discover Your Divine Purpose" is their motto. Their handbook includes a praxis of hip-hop "Poetry in Motion," which promotes a holistic approach to body, mind, and soul, a polemical-rhetorical approach in which each is valued and tended to equally, carefully, and passionately.

Poetry in Motion: Mind = Body = Soul

Nightjohn (Arnett Kale Powell and Adebayo Alabi Olorunto)[1]

Both of us are athletes and martial artists, so we value our physical bodies just as much as we value our mental or Spiritual attributes. There are three 120° aspects of the human spherical cipher of 360°. This infinitely Divine shape (the shape of earth, moon, sun, and stars) is a Universal representation of a person's whole Self. There is mind, body, and soul sphericity that is essential to a genius's life. All should be balanced and maintained in equivalent measure. We call this "Poetry in Motion." We're not sure of where else you may have heard this term, or what you may specifically relate to poetry in motion. For us, poetry in motion is the actualization of our thought and feeling into a physical manifestation that revolves around knowledge, wisdom, and overstanding. To manifest ourselves, we balance mind, body, and soul appropriately through sphericity.

Part of your Divine Purpose is to keep your cipher in equilibrium using the principle of sphericity. You must maintain physical, mental, and Spiritual balance. Have you ever heard of the game "rock, scissors, paper" that is played with your hands? Have you ever played that game? Well, if you recall, rock breaks scissors, paper covers rock, and scissors cut paper. When you put out your hand you are displaying a gesture that could resemble rock, paper, or scissors. It would seem that one would be better than the other, but intellectually you know that you can win against your opponent if you balance your choice of rock, paper, or scissors. You wouldn't just play rock every single time, your opponent would catch on and play paper to cover your rock. You wouldn't just play scissors every time, your opponent would catch on and play rock to break your scissors. You wouldn't play paper every time, your opponent would catch on and play scissors and cut your paper. Psychologically, you know that to win you would have to vary your plays so the odds are in your favor. Likewise, you must vary your exertion of mind, body, and soul, so the game of life's odds are in your favor.

Think of your physical body as being like the rock. If you are all muscle and no brains or soul, what do you have? A blockhead. A caveman. A gorilla pimp. Always using force to reach an objective is not wise. Only perfecting the body makes a person simplistic and controllable. The strong rule the weak, but the wise rule the strong. It also chimes in that the tougher they are the harder they fall. Bruce Lee was notorious for demonstrating that balance, rather than brawn alone, is always victorious. Muhammad Ali could "float like a butterfly and sting like a bee," and tell you about it in a freestyle rhyme before he did it! Ali and Bruce Lee are prime examples of Poetry in Motion. Those two men were not just athletes alone, they had mental and Spiritual power behind their skills, which made them unstoppable. They were living Hiphop Driven lives as Divine geniuses . . . . only they didn't know at the time.

Think of your mental capacity as being like the scissors. If all you know how to do is read, analyze things, and intellectualize what do you have? An A.I. robot. A hermit. A computer brain. Only relying on knowledge alone to reach objectives is not wise either. Only perfecting the mind makes a person too theoretical and not capable of living freely. Such a person then normally suffers from terrible bouts of paralysis by analysis. Like scissors the brain and mind can be sharpened, using decision to cut off courses of action not in alignment with a person's best interests. However, if all a person can do is plan and strategize, when does the action start! When does a person fully live. Bill Gates was a computer whiz kid, but did he just sit around in his garage forever? No. He got off his ass and hustled. He found a way to APPLY his ideas. It took Spirit and physical stamina to run around marketing his ideas to reach his objective. He had a vision, Purpose, and goals . . . though he may have achieved them in his own unique way.

Think of your Spiritual capacity as being like paper. If all you know how to do is meditate, fast, and channel energy? What do you have? A fairy. A wisp. A feather that can be easily blown adrift like a thin sheet of paper. Only relying on Spirit alone to reach objectives is not wise either. Only evolving the Spirit and inner being makes a person too abstract and incapable of living with functioning Purpose. Meditating on a mountain top for a few days is cool, but life is more than celibacy and esoteric practices. Like paper, the Spirit can mold itself into form. It can animate living beings.

Without a physical body, the Spirit might as well go to another galaxy. Without a mind, the Spirit has nowhere to direct its energy. On Earth, we have to deal with bodily functions, hunger, love, sex, human reproduction, children, mind control, police brutality, and taxes. Martin Luther King, Jr. and Malcolm X were very Spiritual men. What if Dr. King was not physically fit enough to lead a march on Washington . . . and get up enough mental power to speak to influence. It would be hard for him to declare he had a dream if he was meditating in the wilderness somewhere.

What if Brother Malcolm was not capable of disciplining himself to mentally absorb and study various forms of knowledge as diligently as he did, then jump in his car opening up temples for the Nation of Islam everywhere . . . and use his mental power to speak, influence, debate, evolve, and even travel to Africa. These brothers had the lightest Spirits, almost as light as sheets of paper or feathers for that matter; because they were serving humanity. However, they kept their bodies strong and their minds sharp to combat evil forces that wished to prevent the masses of people from getting their Divine message. In retrospect, Malcolm and Martin were living Hiphop Driven lives, and they still are through the multi-skilled, multi-cultural, multi-faith, multi-racial people all over the world who are currently establishing Hiphop as an International Kulture for peace and prosperity with their legacy.

Note

1. Nightjohn (Arnett Kale Powell and Adebayo Alabi Olorunto), "Poetry in Motion: Mind = Body = Soul," in *The Hiphop Driven Life: A Genius Liberation Handbook* (Baltimore, MD: The O.L.O.R.U.N., 2005), pp. 213–216.

Ameoblog

This selection features a probing interview conducted by Amoeblog with Juba Kalamka (aka "Pointfivefag"), a founding member of Deep Dickollective, after the DVD release of the "homohop" documentary *Pick Up the Mic* (2009). The artist, educator, and activist responds to a series of questions that centrally address "homohop's" relationship to hip-hop at large, commercialism and assimilationism.

Homohop's Role Within Hip-Hop: Juba Kalamka Interview

Ameoblog[1]

AMOEBLOG: I just realized that it is now eight years since your former group, Deep Dickollective, appeared on that *Independent Sounds Amoeba Music Compilation Vol. III.* That is a long time ago, but how much have things changed in terms of "homohop" in the time period since then—specifically in acceptance and growth of this expanding hip-hop sub-genre?

JUBA KALAMKA: There's been huge growth of the number of visibly out LGBT hip-hop artists because there's more attention on the scene over the last few years because of the documentary. There are tools available that didn't exist in 2001 as well, most notably **MySpace,** which has been really important for people to have a way to get music out for little or no cost.

As far as "acceptance" I'd say there have been some important cultural inroads made in terms of visibility and validation—self acceptance—for young queer people because hip-hop is such a reflective space for many of them, and they weren't seeing many positive [images of] themselves in mainstream media. There's much more opportunity for that to happen now because there are a lot of different ways that people are expressing themselves as "out" hip-hop artists in terms of aesthetics, subject matter, and the like.

As far as overcultural or mainstream "acceptance" of queer hip-hop artists, that hasn't changed any more than it has in mainstream community in general. Racism/white supremacy is still there. Homophobia is still there. Classism is still there. The mainstream music industry is certainly aware of the LGBT hip-hop scene, but they aren't any more accepting in a general sense. It's become a bit more tense in some instances because the "gay rapper" isn't a mythology anymore . . . there's tons of 'em.

Now, if you're asking the $64,000 question of "when will we see an out queer mainstream rap artist from the United States," I'd say that will happen when a) An established, successful straight emcee decides to come out or, b) An established, successful straight emcee is outed by the mainstream press, their own label, etc.

As much as many of those involved with the various incarnations, factions and subsets of the homohop scene are loathe to admit it, it just ain't happening there, if for no other reason than it makes absolutely no economic sense for a major label. . . . Major labels are selling to the lowest common denominator—trying to get the biggest bang for their buck, and anything that's new or different or messing with the formula is going to get shunned, especially given the economic issues the industry has had over the past ten years.

. . .

Recently, the artists who have been getting the most attention from gay and mainstream press, as well as the most bookings at pride festivals and the like, are the ones least likely to fit into hip-hop's hypermasculinist and femiphobic normatives that much of the gay hip-hop scene is heavily invested in mirroring.

Lots of sissy boys and transwomen doing fun, club-friendly party music are getting the bulk of the shine lately. For a variety of reasons, this particular set is resonating with a broad swath of fans across the net and in real time. They also work really hard at self-promotion as opposed to waiting around for straight folks—or entitled, navel-gazing "straight acting" gay emcees—to validate or authenticate them.

That's something that for better and worse I've always loved about this particular subculture. Writer Michelle Tea said to me once at a PeaceOUT event that it was what made the genre so interesting. Because it's "queered," there's been a huge opening made for people to express and expand and reexamine "hip-hop" on their own terms, and in the context of their own experiences. I'm glad to see that happening despite the intra-communal resistance to it.

. . .

AMOEBLOG: Should there even be a term "homohop"—should it be ghettoized or shouldn't it simply be a part of hip-hop in general? Thoughts?

JUBA KALAMKA: I can't say that's something I really sweat . . . or ever have. I don't know. Should there be a separate term for female emcees like "femcee?" Or ones like "gangsta?" Crunk? Trap music? Snap? Africentrist? Conscious? Whatever. In many cases the terms get created or reappropriated by people because they need something make them stand out, or to validate their cultural or social space.

"Homohop," like any other subcultural sub-genre designation, gave and still gives a listener or fan something to grab onto. The first person I heard say "homohop" was my former band-mate Tim'm West in the context of an interview in 2001 . . . and even then it was a big joke, totally tongue-in-cheek. If you called it "Fruit Rollup," people would be saying that now.

. . .

AMOEBLOG: Are there regular homohop nights in the Bay Area?

JUBA KALAMKA: There have been regular nights of queer DJs spinning major label hip hop records, but nothing really consistent in terms of a space(s) where out independent hip hop artists do live shows here . . . There really aren't many places straight ones do either. That's about bars making more money by hiring a DJ or drag shows than when they hire live musical entertainment. It's just the economic reality of running a club. At the same time, I don't know of any LGBT hip hop artists who've ever had significant enough distribution or made an imprint on college or indie radio where it would make sense for a club to do that anyway . . . if I owned a gay bar, I wouldn't hire myself, or any of the artists I know in the scene . . . that's just the nature of that particular business model. It's not designed to "break" artists.

. . .

There's a lot of blathering on different homohop centered websites around "the move-ment" that's unfortunately steeped in a lot of typical entitled attitudes about who should be paying attention, opportunity that's "owed" to them or merited and such . . . .

I've talked about this before in other places, and I've alluded to it in the paragraphs above. A lot of people in the scene missed the point of *PUTM*. I think a lot of people thought the movie (which a lot of people spent a lot of time, sweat and money on, that they didn't have to com-plete) was supposed to create this magical roadway into mainstream validation or acceptance for those who appeared in it, and others who were validated by its existence. When that didn't happen, there was a lot of grousing about what people thought should have happened, or should be happening now.

Note

1. Excerpts from "Homohop's Role Within Hip-Hop: Juba Kalamka Interview," July 7, 2009, www.amoeba. com/blog/2009/07/jamoeblog/homohop-s-role-within-hip-hop-juba-kalamka-interview.html

L. H. Stallings

This selection analyzes gender and sexual politics in the context of hip-hop culture in order to challenge sexism and homophobia in and outside of rap as well as gender and sexual conformism or conservatism in what might be called "hip-hop studies" (or "hip-hop journalism") and academia at large. L. H. Stallings underscores an oft-ignored tradition of sexual militancy within hip-hop and reconnects it with the similarly ignored traditions of trickster Black folklore. Focused on Lil' Kim here, specifically, she demonstrates that such a sexual vernacular is hardly confined to a later subgenre of hip-hop, like "homohop." Her critical text reclaims "bitch," desire, and badness through hip-hop, which proves to be more "queer," so to speak, yet in its own Black vernacular, than "queer theory."

BITCH: The Death of Wifeable Women and a Queer Intervention

L. H. Stallings[1]

Had Annie Christmas not been reared in the rural South, ruled by the levee, or committed suicide, she'd be the present-day manifestation of Black female trickster urbanity, the Queen Bitch, but as this text prefers, Queen B(?). The tone and insistence of sovereign bodies found in Black female rap performances signal an assertion not to be denied. When producers of Black female customs forgo representations of victimization and self-sacrificing women for something more human and flawed, like a Queen B(?) model, transformations seem boundless and too complicated.

One of the well-known controversies in debates about hip-hop, Black women, and language is the use of "bitch," a word that Lil' Kim and several female rappers frequently use. The word means female dog in heat, but it is spoken as a way to refer to females, males, objects, and places. Few of these debates attempt to really understand why its usage is so pervasive in female hip-hop culture, as much as they argue for its erasure in the name of love. Yet female hip-hop's ambivalence about the word is telling. Though Queen Latifah won a Grammy for her song "U.N.I.T.Y.," in which she asks a male, "Who you calling a bitch?" she has been careful to avoid policing women's use of the term to discuss themselves. Indeed, many of the actual women in hip-hop culture, comedians Monique, Adele Givens, and Sommore, as well as musicians Missy Elliott, Salt-N-Pepa, TLC, and a host of others have either used the word or have commented on the word in ways that refuse to regulate and make deviant those women who would use it or want to use it. While one cannot easily dismiss Pough's engagement with debates about the word and her valid concerns about self-respect and self-love, there should also be room to examine the word for its potential disruption of gender and sexual binaries. Female use of the word and its personification of the word in Black women's hip-hop are about total annihilation of gender hierarchies.

In "Are the Revolutionary Techniques Employed in *The Battle of Algiers* Applicable to Harlem?" Francee Covington's claim that "revolution—the overthrow of a government, form of government, or social system with another taking its place—is not an easy task" (Covington 245) suggests why it is not so easy to replace current models of gender and sexuality. Perhaps one of the reasons it is not easy is that there is simply no single way to achieve such a radical action. It takes both political and cultural movements to replace one social system for another. Take for example the way both political and cultural moves solidified the changing of the word "black." In general, the meaning and use of "black" exposes the inconsistencies of language to express self-respect and self-love. If the various dictionaries and reference tools constitute legitimate assessment of meaning, the use of "black" by many Black Americans is an appropriation of a negative term. How does a term that connotes negativity and absence on the one hand become a cultural representation of love and power? If we dismiss appropriating measures, then "Black is beautiful" is an oxymoron. But rather than accept Eurocentric definitions of "black," Black people, politically and culturally, appropriate the word and successfully replace Western meanings of "black" with their very own values. This attention to language use reveals the truth of revolutionary techniques in regard to radical Black female sexual subjectivity. If usage and nonusage of the word "bitch" is really a question of self-love and self-respect, then I also return to a question that this text has been asking all along: Why do Black females continue to use damaging words like "woman" and "lady," which are all words constructed by white Western discursive models that attempt and fail to describe and connote Black female subjectivity? Why is this appropriation of words deemed acceptable, but the appropriation of other words by some Black females deemed wrong? Aren't we all involved in reappropriation of terms and words at some level, unless we come up with new terms for Black female subjectivity and identity? The use of "bitch" by women in hip-hop appears to be another way to unname gender, impolite as it may be, and logistically is not any less valid than other means.

The use of the word acts as some Black women's trickster-troping to overthrow the passive agenda of Black womanhood with a new social system, a queer system. The appropriating gesture that occurs with women's usage of "bitch" makes it a queer word. Its usage in contemporary Black culture has evolved to be somewhat gender flexible. It can refer to a weak man or woman, as well as a strong, assertive, and vocal woman. Dependent on context and user, the word connotes positive, negative, ugliness, beauty, good, bad, and badd. It's versatile, and it has been used and appropriated by heterosexual, gay, lesbian, and trans communities. Its use in Black women's hip-hop culture have surely reflected both its problematic demeaning of women, as well as the queer possibilities for non-heteronormative Black female subjects. Yet in any hip-hop context, the word has come to be less about a female dog and more about women who do not fit proscribed notions of womanhood. The word will never be associated with wifeable women, and, depending upon what type of revolution one is really seeking, representing one's self as a Queen B(?) is not necessarily a bad and self-loathing thing. Whereas Gayl Jones's unwifeable woman becomes a healer, hip-hop's unwifeable woman is the Queen B(?).

The use of "bitch" in hip-hop is also a queer intervention meant to remark on the overabundance of rhetoric and the absence of militancy and selfishness (self-preservation) in Black feminism, womanism, and even hip-hop feminism. Unfortunately, none of these schools of thoughts has really devised a way in which radical Black female sexual subjectivity comes first. Whether it's the fear of being deemed a traitor to the Black (male) nation, the threat of being called a lesbian, or legitimate concerns over how mainstream systems dehumanize Black women, none of the aforementioned branches of thought have made it possible for Black women to desire themselves or express their object's desires in ways that are revolutionary. Hip-hop women's use of the word attempts to create a space of selfishness that has been missing from woman, womanist, and feminist.

When bitch is used as an affirmation of assertive and aggressive women, it places Black women's desires first and foremost. And the philosophy of putting "ladies first" has been a marker of Black women's hip-hop culture from its birth. Laura Jamison's "Ladies First" renders a worthy womanist histography on the legacy of women in hip-hop, and gender remains the main issue of analysis for the critic. Jamison offers a declaration from Ms. Melodie, a female member of the Boogie Down Productions crew, that brings legitimacy to her historicist piece: "It wasn't that the male started rap, the male was just the first to be put on wax. Females were always into rap, and females always had their little crews and were always known for rockin' house parties and streets, school yards the corner, the park, whatever it was" (Jamison 178). "Ladies First" provides a critical account and record of female hip-hop, but it fails to connect this tradition to remnants of other Black female popular culture.

Notably, female rappers' use of "bitch" is unavoidably retro in its nod to 1970s radical Black female subjectivity. Francee Covington said it best when she stated, "When someone says 'Freedom by any means necessary' and someone else suggests that the earnings of prostitutes be used for procuring guns—that's by any means necessary" (Covington 245). A traditional and contemporary feminist response would heave at the thought of women using their bodies in such a way, but a Queen B(?) would comprehend its objective of self-preservation in the face of enormous odds. This is not to suggest that freedom is the aim of every female rapper who uses "bitch," but the use of the word does aim to carve out a discursive niche that legitimizes Black women's "selfish" attempt to achieve one's heart's desire by any means necessary. A militant stance of self-preservation and the desire toward a better quality of life in that self-preservation marks Black women's hip-hop culture as different than any other women's empowerment movement. While some Black women choose to take up the mantle of womanhood, there are those who choose to pick up themselves. Covington's statements are phenomenal and relevant to this text's task of emphasizing that the complete and total destruction of Western categories of gender and sexuality is what should be encouraged. After all, there is a war being waged, and trickster figures play pivotal roles in social and cultural wars of the oppressed.

As a trope of trickster, bitch, or Queen Bitch, serves as a symbolic site of identity that relies on the force of desire to propel marginalized individuals to cross established boundaries to satisfy the self, in spite of what the consequence may mean for a dominant community/society. As with most post-emancipation human tricksters, the Queen B(?) seeks an appropriate expressive location for direct confrontation, as opposed to the ambiguity and guile of Tar Baby and Br'er Rabbit tales. In the past, "antebellum animal tricksters had never been beyond murder to accomplish their ends, but they had almost always murdered through trickery. Now they frequently did so in direct confrontation with their more powerful adversaries" (Levine 383). Accordingly, when social circumstances change, trickster models change. Hip-hop culture serves as the most recent Black oral form to provide the most rigorous vehicle for tricksters who would violate taboos and borders through violence and sexuality, or sexual violence. Although this has been a widely acknowledged fact, few have broached these elements in a specifically female hip-hop culture. As indicated by tales discussed in this book, a wide majority of trickster tales (African and African American) are extremely violent, and "sexual exploits abound in most trickster myths" (Hynes, 43).

However, violence has been projected as an ends to a means necessary for survival in many trickster tales. In animal tales and early slave tales, murder occurs through coincidental trickery. Yet the "crucial change marking black folklore after emancipation was the development of a group of heroes who confronted power and authority directly, without guile and tricks, and who functioned on a secular level" (Levine 386). Black female culture adapts the philosophy of the greater Black community to its own situation. In jook joints, via the Hurston-defined element of Black idiom, other elements of Black expression flourished: the absence of the concept of privacy and myths of cultural icons. In the greatest tradition of tricksterism, Zora Neale Hurston's conception about the absence of privacy evolves into the deliberated use of excessive or overt sexuality in Black female culture. It serves as a strategic rejection of conformity to any nation's limitation and binding of individual sexuality and expression of sexual desire. It provides sexual militancy in a sphere threatened by the excessive forces of colonized regimes.

As Cornel West once noted, "White fear of black sexuality is a basic ingredient of white racism . . . black sexuality is a taboo subject in America principally it is a form of black power over which whites have little control" (West 305). Arguably, West is partially correct: post-emancipated Black sexuality is a form of Black power. As seen in the narrative of Harriet Jacobs, as well as texts by other slave authors, enslaved Black people never enjoyed control over their sexuality. After the decimation of chattel slavery, it is the loss of control over Black sexuality by white America that producers of Black culture very often work to exploit and manipulate to their own advantage. This chapter is concerned with such strategies in regard to taboos of Black female sexuality and Black female urban culture. Trickster's goals of taboo breaking picks apart the Black nation's goal of normative sexuality, as well as white America's fear of Black sexuality. Since the dominant myths of Black female sexuality in Black and white America can be categorized as "Jezebel (the seductive temptress), Sapphire (the evil, manipulative bitch) or Aunt Jemima (the sexless, long-suffering nurturer)" (West 301), then modern trickeration occurs in gaps between the performances or depictions of these types by Black females.

There are culturally historic reasons, outside of hip-hop culture, as to why female rappers are drawn to and continue to use Queen B(?) performances. As opposed to the 1960s asexual strategy of crossover-happy Motown, the dominant themes of love, relationships, and explicit sexuality from the classic blues era were reborn in soul, R&B, and disco music of the 1970s. One need only heed the words and voice of Millie Jackson to appreciate how the Queen B(?) figure morphs from generation to generation: "Don't start something you can't finish, frustration ain't no fun . . . got to be an all the way, all the way, all the way loverrrr." Like true second-wave post-emancipation tricksters, Jackson, Donna Summer, and others moved away from subtle connotations onto blunt proclamations of their sexual desires. Recently, female rappers such as Da Brat, Lil' Kim, and Jackie O have claimed to be influenced by the 1970s idols. Jackson's work serves as the necessary link to understanding how female rappers and MCs unconsciously took up the Queen B(?) role for their own generation.

The remainder of this Queen B(?) chapter seeks a complex negotiation between the genres and values of various popular culture forms informed by urban vernacular. As suggested by the opening section, these are not safe spaces but tabooed open secrets of Black popular culture. Black female hip-hop artists reveal the complexities of the QueenB(?) figure and what it can offer to disturb the continuities of established sexual boundaries. The transgressive behavior negatively described as sexually promiscuous and lascivious in popular criticism offers an alternative version to the clean sanitized representations of Black sexuality offered up by the Black bourgeoisie. Sexually has ties to eroticism and the uses of the erotic, but it has also been used as currency in various cultures. What urban Black female culture manages to do is to simultaneously explicate on sexual desire as part of eros and sexuality as currency, and it exploits the instability of the terrain in which Western society tries to define and limit sexual desires. When we examine urban Black female culture, we find the liminal Queen B(?) negotiating the fine line of currency and eros, moving back and forth between Queen Bee, Queen Bulldagger, and Queen Bitch but never fully relinquishing the unfixed Queen B(?) subjectivity.

In a genre of music heavily based on Black masculinity and masculine culture and where Black women are typically relegated to the margins (as they are in U.S. society in general), female rappers rely on and manipulate the threat of female sexual desire to their advantage. As Queen B(?) figures, they have trickster-troped all over their assigned roles as asexual butches and hypersexualized femmes in hip-hop by blurring the philosophies of normative gender and desire to get rich, reconfiguring the margins of hip-hop, and offering mechanisms for exploring unpoliticized desire in Black female culture. Through an examination of the gritty lyrics and personas of selected female rappers, we will learn how Black female culture employs Queen B(?) philosophy to usurp traditional binary canons that split sexuality in terms of homosexual/heterosexual, good/evil, sacred/profane, use value/abuse value.

While Jamison documents the songs and artists of as many female endeavors as possible, cultural critic Tricia Rose, in her "Never Trust a Big Butt and a Smile," offers a more critical assessment not only of the music genre and gender, but about the critics who have attempted to analyze hip-hop culture. Piece by piece, Rose examines the output and production of female hip-hop culture and its importance in discussions of gender and sexuality. In addition, she readily connects her analysis to Angela Davis's work on blues women, "Black Women and Music: A Historical Legacy of Struggle." Perceptively, Rose's work encourages us to move beyond comparative boy/girl frameworks and issues of status and hierarchy along gender lines to complete a more sustained analysis of sexuality and Black female in hip-hop culture. Such a study reveals that verbosity about sexuality acts as a form of militancy necessary for the survival of the Queen B(?). Without sexual militancy delivered through trickster performances, Black females and their culture remain either a lesser demonstration of greater blackness (male), mimetic mirror of "the woman," or an endangered "other."

While today's hip-hoppers enjoy the verbal battles between 50 Cent and The Game, Nas and Jay-Z, Benzino and Eminem, and Tupac and Biggie, some people still remember a playing field that suggested that female MCs could be as bold and cold as their male counterparts, and the issue of sexuality (sexual desires) created this level playing field. In 1985–86, whether you were in New York, Los Angeles, or some inner city in the Midwest or the South, if you had an urban radio station to listen to you became embroiled in the soap opera appeal of a battle that pit males against females in a way that has yet to be seen ever again: U.T.F.O. versus the Roxannes versus the other Roxanne-like female rappers. In terms of bravado and exaggeration, these battles were reminiscent of the lion and the monkey, Br'er Rabbit and Tar Baby, and Sis Goose and Fox! Lyrical wit mattered more than male privilege.

As Jamison notes: "The firestorm started when an unsuspecting trio of male rappers, U.T.F.O., cut a song called 'Roxanne, Roxanne' about a stuck-up girl who had the nerve to resist their charms. Suddenly out of nowhere, a record featuring a 14-year-old with a high voice and a debilitating wit slammed U.T.F.O: She was Roxanne Shante" (Jamison 179). Roxanne Shante's response, "Roxanne's Revenge," to UTFO's rap provided a narrative that suggested that females were not simply game to be pursued by warrior males on the mic. In spouting her rap, Roxanne Shante placed herself on the offense and suggested that she had choices/options as to how to fulfill her own desires:

> You thought you was cute, yeah, you thought you was a prince
> You're walkin' down the block, holdin' your jock. But everybody
> knows that you're all on my yacht I'm just the devastatin,' always
> rockin,' always have the niggas clockin.' Everybody knows it's me,
> yeah, the R-O-X-A-N-N-E, yeah . . .

Clearly, the fourteen-year-old girl did not need someone else to champion her. Roxanne responded in a way in which she did not have to defend her sexuality because to do so would weaken her position. Instead of rapping about if she was "stuck-up" or sexually promiscuous, she chose instead to deconstruct the performance of hypermasculinity by young Black males. This tactic reveals that more powerful than male bravado is the self-control she could exercise over her sexuality. Further, Roxanne's lyrics set a precedent for use of Queen B(?) skills of rhetorical exaggeration, direct baiting, and confrontation used by Black females in hip-hop culture to dismiss and handle Black male sexism and misogyny.

In the end, this game of the dozens initiated by three young men and one little girl spawned one hundred Roxanne-related records to be released over urban airwaves, a feat that mirrors the proliferation of various trickster tales, as well as productions of numerous Bessies and Mas by the Race Records era after the initial success of Bessie Smith and Ma Rainey. Trickster culture evolved with its original blueprint still intact. In the hands of a young female MC, the hip-hop generation revises the Queen B(?) figure. While her style and demeanor may have changed, Queen B(?) trickery still protects the female's need for self-definition, independence, self-preservation, and voicing of sexual desires. It is no coincidence that the subject of these early urban battles was sexuality. Despite the negative criticism that some female rappers receive for using exaggerated sexuality, today's performers all accept that aggressively asserting control over sexuality, as exemplified via the Roxanne records, gave birth and longevity to female rap artists in hip-hop culture. The Roxanne battles showed that rap thematically concerned with sexuality makes it impossible to ignore Black females, takes away the gendered master narratives, and levels the playing field.

Rose dissects male fear about leveling the playing field in the production of male hip-hop culture, hence her title "Never Trust a Big Butt and a Smile." She includes rapper Ice Cube's comments on the power of female sexuality: "I mean the power of sex is more powerful than the motherfuckers in Saudi Arabia. A girl you want to get with can make you do damn near anything" (Rose 239). A female rapper who raps about sexuality places the male MC or rapper in a vulnerable position because she can undermine the legitimacy of just about any boast or toast that he makes, and as blues women demonstrated, concerns about propriety need not be obstacles in the way of dominating the mic. Rose rightly assesses that Ice Cube's comments reflect a male fear and "that many men are hostile towards women because the fulfillment of male heterosexual desire is significantly checked by women's capacity for sexual rejection and/or manipulation of men" (Rose 239). If that is the case, why put female sexuality in check or chains? Rose's piece, published in the early 1990s, had a much easier task of critiquing sexuality in female rap since its focus was on acts such as Salt-N-Peppa, MC Lyte, and Queen Latifah. These acts fit well into Rose's notion of traditional love and relationships as the driving force behind sexual themes in female rap music.

Yet as a diversity of women on and off the mic became front and center in hip-hop culture, certain critics seemed totally incapable of understanding the negotiation female rap artists make concerning sexuality. In briefly addressing the likes of Foxy Brown and Lil' Kim, Joan Morgan's *When Chickenheads Come Home to Roost: My Life as a Hip-Hop Feminist* negates the power that might evolve from exploiting such fear by calling women who choose to explicitly use sexual power to gain social position or economic gains "chickenheads." *When Chickenheads Come Home* accepts the presentation of overt sexuality simply as denigration, or as females being co-opted by a male system, all the while implying acceptance of social regulations of women's sexuality through notions of romantic love and marriage as systems less denigrating to women. It also misses the evidence afforded us by important historical moments like the Roxanne battles. Fortunately, Suzanne Bost's "Be Deceived If Ya Wanna Be Foolish" offers a more complicated analysis of female hip-hop culture. Focusing on Da Brat, Ursula Rucker, Dana Bryant, and Sarah Jones, Bost explodes Morgan's simplistic framework of skeeza, hoochies, whores, and freaks versus the good girls by focusing on fluidity, manipulation of the whore image, and theorizing about excessive bodies as a counter-theory to commodified contained bodies.

While some female rappers address more traditional themes of love and relationships, some consciously write lyrics or create images with the manipulation of sexual power in mind, and that is what moves them from the realm of female rapper to trickster Queen B(?) icon. The Black female rapper who performs Queen B(?) uses sexuality as a weapon because sexuality is one of the trickster's weapons of choice: "In both ritual actions and artistic depictions, the trickster sometimes carries a phallus or phallic club" (Hynes 43). In the absence of a phallus or phallic club for Queen B(?), we can substitute the presence of her deliberate decision to harness the use value of female sexuality for her own purposes and goals, rather than society's intended uses of simply wife and mother.

The harnessed female sexuality (phallic club) connotes and correlates with a theme of sexual violence seen in human trickster tales. Traditionally criticized from a non-folklore viewpoint, the elements of violence and explicit sexuality make it difficult to grasp gestures of rebelliousness of certain female rap artists in the way of trickster. Queen B(?)'s sexual militancy derives from trickster's hypersexuality. Lil' Kim is a Queen B(?) figure who, in very distinct ways, harnesses the use value of sexual desire and makes her depiction of that desire a weapon to be wielded in the struggle to maintain control over Black women's identities, lives, and images. Like Gayl Jones's fictional Harlan Eagleton, who must realize the transformative power of her Turtle Woman heritage, cultural performances by female rappers allow them a fluidity of sexuality almost impossible in other spheres of Black popular culture.

Note

1. L. H. Stallings, "BITCH: The Death of Wifeable Women and a Queer Intervention," a section of "Representin' for the Bitches: Queen B(?) in Hip-Hop Culture," in *Mutha' Is Half a Word: Intersections of Folklore, Vernacular, Myth, and Queerness in Black Female Culture* (Columbus: The Ohio State University Press, 2007), pp. 258–267.

Greg Thomas

This selection explores the rhetorical and political significance of diverse modes of oral expression audible in hip-hop lyricism. It is part of an extended case study of hip-hop's "QUEEN B@#$H" lyricism. It thus regards how orality is presented in rhyme as an instrument of knowledge or intelligence; a sign of the power of speech or communication; and, furthermore, as a means of pleasure—whether sexual or erotic and even verbal or both, despite the widespread stigmatization of certain schools of hip-hop lyricism as "mindless" and "unconscious," paradoxically enough.

Orals . . . Head . . . Genius: The Power, Knowledge, and Pleasure of *Hard Core*

Greg Thomas[1]

"[I] Chose My Life to Be *Hard Core*"—Lil' Kim

Lil' Kim certainly lives up to her provocative billing on *Hard Core*. . . . There's plenty of substance as well as style, though the Queen Bitch herself gives it to you raw and salaciously like you'd expect, yet also quite wittily and nimbly . . . . [I]t's hard to think of such a categorically dirty [*sic*] rap album that's this accomplished, and it's furthermore refreshing to hear a woman turn the tables for once, particularly so cleverly with such a venerable supporting cast.

(Jason Birchmeier, *All Music Guide to Hip-Hop* [n.d.])

Representing art and resistance, Lil' Kim would make a self on her rap premiere; and it is a self that is offered as a model of identity and politics. Her gender and sexual politics may be most apparent to the ear; after all, they are undeniably audacious. Yet, further still, these radical politics of sexuality and identity promote a new form of humanity insofar as they picture a radical new relationship between mind and body—with spirit. Or does she radically reinscribe a much older set of relations that have been suppressed, until now, in the white bourgeois West, most especially outside of art? Out of her mouth, the mind and body are lyrically united rather divided, mutual rather than hostile, organically whole rather than split, severed or separated. Later, she would sing, chant and whisper on "I'm Human" from *The Notorious K.I.M.* (2000): "'I'm human, you're human,' so they say/But inside we're all animals." This aggressive, verbal embrace of an animal biology for a humanity unafraid of its animal biology is at the heart of her brilliant Hip-Hop expression. To censor or criticize it as "obscene" is to safeguard Western bourgeois humanism, a historically racist-sexist order of language, "knowledge," pleasure and power. To embrace it is to embrace a poetics and politics that can emancipate us from the puritanism of this humanism, explosively.

And explosively is certainly how *Hard Core* begins. After its opening skit ("Intro in A-Minor"), the first official lines will scandalize puritans and light a fire in Hip-Hop. She says she used to be scared of the "dick," but "now I throw lips to tha shit/Handle it like a real bitch." Punning with extreme wit—as if her life depended on it, Lil' Kim epitomizes "uncensored speech." She embodies it in an ultra-erotic militancy that is relentless; and, sex-wise, she is all about revolution. She owns a previous fear of "the dick," at least rhetorically, on "Big Momma Thang." This "dick" might stand for sexuality in general, a sexuality that is conventionally assumed to be a male domain. It might stand for any "taboo" sex (such as anal or oral sex), if not male sexuality in particular and the power it is thought to wield. It might equally stand for the desire of a female sexuality that she is intent or "hell-bent" on reclaiming from anyone and everyone who would deny it. The idea of "throwing lip" to it is no less versatile. On the surface, it may be read or heard as a simple although mind-blowing reference to oral sex performed on a male, or men, who have seriously lost their ability to intimidate. It makes a more symbolic statement about her skills on the mic. So "throwing lip" to anything (including "dick") signifies her capacity to rhyme, to speak or "spit," and to "drop science" or knowledge in Hip-Hop. Here is in fact *Hard Core*'s massive claim to fame: Lil' Kim handles all of the above, sexuality across the board; the language of emceeing; and traditional Hip-Hop intelligence—like a "real bitch," "Queen *Bitch*" that she lyrically is.[3] When all is said and done, it's hard to believe she was ever scared.

Orality as an Instrument of Knowledge (or Intelligence)

A handling of male domination is at the center of this work on wax. This subject has always been at the center of Western humanism, white racist imperialism, or Western bourgeois domination. The Europe that historically characterizes itself as "Christian" and non-Europeans as "Heathen" characterizes its own commitment to patriarchy (a society based on male domination) as a sign of its "superior" culture or "civilization." It categorizes matriarchy (a society in which females hold power, collectively) as a "pre-historic" state of "savagery" or "barbarism," where sexuality is out of patriarchal control. There can be no separation of the issue of racism from the issue of sexism or sexuality since a sexist and sexual racism defines the white-supremacist West. It invents an evolutionary historical scheme that construes culture or "civilization" as a progressive "social" development from matrilineage or "mother right" and matriarchy to pseudo-monogamy, father-headed nuclear family, and the male power and privilege of patriarchy. This scheme of gender and sexuality similarly sees culture or "civilization" as arising out of Africa, which is at the very bottom of this system of values, on to the Mediterranean and then to Western Asia until Europe is pitched as the high point of human culture, history, or "civilization" itself. The great Cheikh Anta Diop unmasks Europe's "masculine imperialism" in *The Cultural Unity of Black Africa: The Domains of Matriarchy and of Patriarchy in Classical Antiquity* (1959), most notably, while Ifi Amadiume expands this perspective in *Re-Inventing Africa: Matriarchy, Religion and Culture* (1997), for example. A symbolic and sexual motherhood royally in check, it is in line with these Pan-African values of radical female empowerment that Lil' Kim emcees as *Hard Core*'s "Big Momma/Queen *Bitch*."

Her use of language as lyricism is nothing if not a matter of knowledge, as she seeks to school men and women or males and females on how she triumphs against all odds in the late-twentieth century context of the African diaspora. Once, she would testify in *Vibe* magazine: "Things I rap about now is things I been through. And God knows I don't want to go back to doin' what I had to do before. So I talk about it to get it away from me" (Lil' Kim in Saxon 1997, 79). She raps about it as a way of gaining control over it and its meaning. Aside from Afrika Bambaataa and the Universal Zulu Nation's declaration of "knowledge" as the all-important "fifth element" of Hip-Hop,[4] KRS-One and the Temple of Hip-Hop have named "street knowledge" as one of their nine basic elements of Hip-Hop, alternatively.[5] Knowledge is knowledge; and knowledge is where knowledge is. "Street knowledge" should not have to be qualified. Yet it is vital not to overlook the special knowledge it takes for the poor and Black to survive on the streets of white social and economic oppression—in North America and beyond. Whereas KRS-One and Afrika Bambaataa speak from the Bronx, New York, Chester Himes spoke of Harlem, similarly, as an ex-prisoner, novelist and expatriate in his poignant Blues play, *Baby Sister* (1961). Describing ghetto life conditions under which the oppressed and exploited are coerced into preying upon one another for survival, he writes in prologue:

> [I]t is perfectly reasonable and natural that these people should be hungry, the wolves and the sheep alike. If your own food—food for the soul and food for the spirit as well as food

for the stomach—had been held just out of your reach for three hundred years, or longer, you would be hungry too. And one way to keep from starving in this land of plenty when you have no food is to eat your baby sister.

(Himes 12)

Rhyming from Brooklyn, New York, Lil' Kim does not simply write stories of "baby sisters" (or "baby girls") being eaten alive by "wolves," however. She tells stories that turn the tables on these wolves and the whole system or politics of sexual domination. In her profound tricksterism, the hunter becomes the hunted; the predator, prey. The men who would make "sweet meat" of her and hers are set up to be slayed in one fashion or another instead. Many preach on endlessly about ethics and Hip-Hop without ever thinking to question gender and sexual politics in the least. But her preoccupation is with sexual and poetic justice without fail. This is her Hip-Hop, how she deploys language, sexuality and knowledge in and through and for Hip-Hop—as a brazen "pedagogy of the oppressed" and exploited, no less. The unforgettable young "bitch" from the street ("guaranteed to stay down") heard on Junior M.A.F.I.A.'s "Get Money" (*Conspiracy*, 1995) will triumphantly boast on "Spend a Little Doe" that she was "lost in the field no more." Now, she's the "shit": "Go by tha name of 'Lil' Kim, tha Queen *Bitch*.'" And, of course, this M.A.F.I.A.'s her clique.

On "Kim Gets Deeper" from *Ms. G.O.A.T.* (2007), where is she is unmistakably proud to have been "taught" by "the streets," she will lay claim to *original* knowledge of her own: "Amazin Queen *B*(ee) in tha place/My thoughts paint pictures(,) y'all just copy and trace." The interpretation of her meaning can be typically double. Her orally expressed thoughts are novel and innovative (perhaps *ab*original), while others fail to think innovatively or against the contemporary grain. Either they just unoriginally copy and trace establishment thought or they just copy and trace her creative, imaginative, anti-establishment thoughts, unoriginally. Insofar as this is the case, *Ms. G.O.A.T.*'s "Kim Gets Deeper" also seems to maintain that it is better to duplicate *her* knowledge, at least, and its subversive Hip-Hop revolutionary stance.

First, on *Hard Core*, she would establish a "street knowledge" along with her knowledge of rap or Hip-Hop or rhyming and a serious knowledge of sexual politics as they play out "in the streets," on record, "in the bedroom," etc. She makes it known that she has "know-how," or that she knows how to rap her way to the top of the world of Hip-Hop; to hustle her way out of a world full of wolves (and "haters"); and to hijack no small measure of pleasure in a puritanical and patriarchal world that hands out power and privilege according to race and class as well as gender. As she imparts her knowledge of the physical and its pleasures, she does it in a language which is oral and which rewrites the relationship between the mental and the physical, infectiously. Knowledge of all kinds is rewritten through an orality that showcases the oral as *a sign of the power of speech (or communication)* and as *a means of pleasure (sexual or erotic at large or even verbal or both)* in addition to orality as *an instrument of intelligence (or knowledge, "street" and otherwise)*: Lil' Kim's *Hard Core* poetics operate in each vein simultaneously to undo the soulless mind/body split of the white bourgeois West.

Orality as a Sign of the Power of Speech (or Communication)

The power of speech, language, or verbal expression is vocalized by Lil' Kim in countless forms. There are her signature gutturals or "grunts" and "groans," which preface and punctuate a variety of messages even as they appear to signify something beyond conventional language on their own. Linguists might refer to this speech as "extra-linguistic," meaning outside of formal language usage; they are extremely linguistic nonetheless. They express what is otherwise inexpressible within established customs of language. These utterances represent a trademark of Lil' Kim's rap: "*Unh!*" "*Wha, wha!*" and so on. They mark the potency of her words and her wordsmithing persona. Plus, they prepare (and excite) you for what else she has in store. To communicate effectively and to expand the parameters or possibilities of communication, she will constantly change up her accent, her cadence, her pitch, and her styles of enunciation, for example, both within a specific song (verse or line) and across an entire album. An emcee of many voices, she thus employs the widest range of oral and literary devices, from *alliteration, assonance,* and *consonance, metaphor, simile,* and *repetition* to *onomatopoeia,* over and above *rhyme,* no matter how much rhyming is thought to be the exclusive focus of rapping or Hip-Hop lyricism by most non-emcees. This is all done to the beat of music selected to vary and help diversify what she says and how she says it, powerfully.

Indeed, Lil' Kim may provide a most potent illustration of what French-Bulgarian critic Julia Kristeva tried to theorize in *Desire in Language: A Semiotic Approach to Literature and Art* (1980) and *Revolution in Poetic Language* (1984). Yet another approach might argue convincingly that any such gutturals, "grunts" and "groans" in a Pan-African context should be understood as a Black artist's spoken interaction with the inspirational spirit of music descended and detected in the Wolof or West African processes of *deeree* (or *di re*) and *djakharlee,* both of which call to mind the critical musical concept of "worrying the line" in many discussions of the Blues and other, twentieth-century Black, African diasporic vocal traditions.

When it comes to standard classifications, moreover, her *Hard Core* cannot be said to confine itself to just one specific language. If it is primarily in "English," per se, Lil' Kim's diction is the Blackest of "Black English," no doubt. This is what is more popularly known as "Ebonics." Plus, "No Time" will playfully dabble in French (for a censored version or radio edit: "*Ooh la, la . . . Oui, oui . . . C'est la vie*"), Spanish ("Tryna stick a nigga for his *pesos,* if you say so . . . "), and then a very prominent Afro-Jamaican "*Creole*" or *patois* ("*Pun pun nani dani punnani dani*"); "Spend a Little Doe" will echo some Spanish ("*Hasta la vista!*"); and a perhaps Tina Turner-inspired Buddhist chant ("*Nam-ryoho-renge-kho*"); "Drugs" will offer a truly stunning line of Arabic ("*Sharmoot elhasi teezi*"); and "M.A.F.I.A. Land" will articulate (or rearticulate) some Italian ("*Modano . . . Milano*") with its nimble oral choreography. There will be a lot more of this to come, throughout the length of her recording career; and her remarkable rap multilingualism expands even further when language is understood as "discourse" to include, for example, the language of Hip-Hop, broadly construed; the language of street-hustling; the language of male domination or young black female resistance to it; and her lyrical body language, that is, her discourse of sex, gender, sexuality, or eroticism. The power of speech to communicate thoughts or ideas and intentions is on full and marvelous display. Literacy is fluency in virtually every sense of the word in Lil' Kim's *Hard Core* expression.

Orality as a Means of Pleasure (Sexual or Erotic, Even Verbal)

Her agile use of many "tongues" blurs any distinction between "sex play" and "word play," particularly as the oral comes to refer to oral pleasure and the politics thereof. There is great pleasure taken in punning for the sake of punning, playing with words physically as much as mentally; and then there is her militant politicization of oral-sex relations between males and females, most of all. Outside the imagination of *Hard Core* and the tradition it will artfully establish, oral sex is supposed to be a special source of shame—at least or especially for women who are socialized to never ask for it and only reluctantly perform it on men. The act is supposed to be "degrading," if not "sinful," never satisfying or stimulating. This taboo and its sexist double-standard are attacked record after record by Lil' Kim as she rewrites scenario after scenario in order to command pleasure, reciprocity and power in every sexual exchange or interaction: "No Time" orders an unspecified male to lick her "twat" (in the uncensored version), and to lick her where its "hot" (in the censored, radio edit). In the next verse, she responds in kind but in a fashion that will have her take both control and pleasure in the performance. No longer "Daddy," the man in question is turned into a mere voyeur of her sexual mastery. He is ordered say her name ("Momma"), to signify her sexual dominance; and he complies in the background. The female hustler of "No Time" will give us a number of oral-sexual adages or sexual-political slogans in Hip-Hop, as in: "No money-money, no licky-licky/Fuck ya dicky-dicky and ya quicky!" She revels in her accentuation of these messages and their addictive play on words, relishing everything she is able to exact from the men under reference. There is literally "no shame in her game" as she reinvents or reinscribes sexuality—sexual mores—for her enjoyment and empowerment.

The stutter-stepping two-syllable rhyme scheme she uses in parts (to rhyme suggestive words like "wet," "forget," "bet" and "let," all attached to the repetitive "it" of her sexual imagination), this is often termed "a feminine rhyme" by academic studies of poetry. One-syllable rhyme schemes are termed "masculine." This would suggest that "feminine rhyming" is harder, more complex than "masculine rhyming," so to speak. It also suggests that all poetry or rhyming is always related to sex or gender, some way, somehow. At any rate, Lil' Kim's rap routinely resists the repression of that which is labeled "femininity" as she rejects the limitations of any and all gender, or the whole opposition between "masculinity" and "femininity," lyrically combining "sex play" and "word play" in a manner that the "tongue" metaphor for language actually, classically implies. The message of "No Time" regarding gender and sexuality communes well then with its sample of screams and a piano loop from a record by one of James Brown's Soul Sisters: "Message from the Soul Sisters" by Vicki Anderson (1970), who is also known as Myra Barnes (*Mother Popcorn: The Vicki Anderson Anthology*, 2005).

This is not to exclude all of the erotic pleasure Lil' Kim enjoys and expresses in "polyvocality," or her countless changes in voices, vocal styles and verbal intonation, verse after verse, song after song, sometimes mid-sentence—none of which can be adequately represented "on the page" as spoken articulations or enunciations. A verbal-physical as well as intellectual pleasure is taken in Lil' Kim's erotically charged Hip-Hop, on the regular. In a number of respects, it linguistically satisfies.

The oral commentary on oral sex continues on *Hard Core* after "No Time" on "We Don't Need It" and "Not Tonight." Each storytelling track is a "didactic" anthem, "teacherly" yet very far from prudish. Men will not dominate women in society and freely take advantage of them in sexuality (erotically or economically), if this emcee has anything to say about it. Nor will they leave her with no other option except to boycott sex, like a sex-starved puritan on the sidelines. Junior M.A.F.I.A. joins in on "We Don't Need It" to stage a dramatic conflict over "suckin' dick" and "lickin' clit," as it were. It is her stance that supplies the climax. She commands her man to do his "duty," to use his tongue to "click" her "booty," before there is any kind of sex for his pleasure: "You wanna steal tha pussy like a thief/Now twist tha lips without tha teeth." The double-entendre (or multiple meanings) should be unmistakable, as twisting lips without teeth calls her labia and cunnilingus to mind. The title of "Not Tonight" signifies sharply on the middle-class suburban housewife's cliché reply to a husband's desire for sex, which is conventionally cast as her "wifely duty." The duty is his. There will be sex, tonight; however, he won't control it. This tale refers to a time when "a dude named Jimmy" did everything for Kim, except "eat pussy" or perform oral sex. The story is then transformed into a tale about how her participation in sex is now categorically conditional ("to 'see' me, you have to eat me," in other words); and this strategy is offered as a striking, collective strategy for all women. Named after his genitalia, or "dick," since he was selfishly only into genital sex, an evidently fictional "Jimmy" is quickly forgotten by *Hard Core* as it makes its "object lesson" simple and plain. The moral of the story is this: "You ain't lickin' this, you ain't hittin' this." And there are witnesses, according to Lil' Kim, who will vouch for this sexual-political policy, just as the remix of "Not Tonight" came to relabel it "Ladies Night" with a crew of popular female rappers (namely Da Brat, Left-Eye of TLC, and Missy Elliot as well as Angie Martinez of New York's HOT-97 radio station).

Hard Core Orality: Power, Knowledge and Pleasure—All Told

The power and pleasure of *Hard Core* orality may combine most perfectly on "Drugs" where the power of the emcee's words is said to be felt most in the pleasures of the body, the flesh, physically and figuratively. The Notorious B.I.G. opens this seventh song of the album by testifying to Lil' Kim's flawlessness on the mic. She identifies herself as the source of "a different kind of high," asking or instructing her audience to "feel" her on this claim to greatness that is her literal highness as a lyrical narcotic. The "host" of "Drugs" describes herself as "dope" as well as extravagance embodied. She leaves others awestruck with both her body and her body of work. The "niggaz" in earshot are left with "cum stains," such is the excitement she brings. She likens the effect of her rap-speech to a "Dillinger" firearm thrown to a jaw. This is how she can keep "niggaz" in "awe," and why she can join Biggie in claiming her rhyming has no flaws, here or anywhere, now or ever. The "Cleopatra" of "No Time" reappears as the Black "Princess" of "Magnificence" on "Drugs" precisely because her "flow" is "phenom," or phenomenal; it hits like a "bomb." At this point, she speaks of what pleases her and "freaking" it Arabic style: "*Sharmoot elhasi teezi*" is a stock phrase that can be translated as "Lick my ass, bitch." The power of her lyrical orality enables her to command a sexual orality from the *male* "bitch" in question. There is a bilingual double-entendre here of reading or writing "backwards," as in Arabic, and of giving her pleasure "from the back," orally, back and forth—both acts being achieved with "tongue." This is "word play" and/or as "sex play," par excellence. Lyrically "electrifying," Lil' Kim's mind and mouth are pictured as a stimulant, a drug that stimulates the bodies (and "heads") of her listeners. The comparison will be a constant throughout her career. Any distinction between mind and body is disintegrated by this physical metaphor for orality's rhetorical effect, hence Biggie's testimony on the chorus of "Drugs" where he likens her to different mixes of marijuana—"La," "Ganja" and "Sensimilla". He *feels* "Big Momma/Queen Bitch" to be "The Ultimate Rush."

A royal title song, for certain, "QUEEN B@#$H" begins with her boasting about "dusting off" foes like Pledge (the furniture polish). Rap similes proliferate. Now, she is hitting them as hard as sledgehammers, continuing the mind/body connection of "Drugs." Even this last song's mid-stream dedication/shout-out had reflected her complete dedication to every aspect of the oral: "To my niggaz that trick a little/To my bitchez that suck dick a little." These "bitchez" do it while their "niggaz" lick their "middles," Lil' Kim reminds us. When she states that she receives all the "*ooh's*" and "*aah's*," onomatopoeically, along with all the jewels and cars, these sounds could be the sounds of an applauding crowd (literally because lyrically electrified); and they could be the sounds of erotic pleasure, which both her physical-sexual as well as and lyrical-textual performance would typically elicit. "QUEEN B@#$H" insists that her rhymes melt in our mouths, blending with the body once more. Her personal style is further, duly punctuated by another flamboyant, gender-flipping line in which she claims to have "buffoons" eating her "pussy" while she watches cartoons, having just compared her gun and/or sexual potency to hurricanes and typhoons. So mob thugs bow down to her. The multiple meanings of her punnings are incomparable as usual: "I got that bomb-ass cock, a good-ass shot/wit hard-core flows that keep a nigga dick rock." The "cock" in question is hers. The shot may be her sex, her sex-shooting, her gun-fire as much as her spit-fire. The powerful flow of *Hard Core* is best signified in the end by arousal, if not erection, extreme stimulation of the body via the mind and mouth behind her Hip-Hop lyricism.

This is how "Intro in A-Minor" sets up the oral-to-aural experience of *Hard Core*. It's not a concerto. It's a skit, ironically. An unidentified male is heard to exit a taxi in front of a movie theater, as if on the streets of New York's Times Square. He enters and encounters a box office worker from whom he purchases a ticket for "Lil' Kim, *Hard Core.*" Her music, "Big Momma Thang" begins to play in the background. A concession stand is approached for a small order of popcorn, a large order of butter and a lot of napkins. The customer is next heard walking into a screen room or booth filled with moaning and groaning, which is when stereotypical "porn music" begins to play as a background soundtrack. The rapper would be the star of this show. The patron or spectator unzips his pants and calls out her name, masturbating noisily as he yells. Anticipation builds. What he or we must anticipate is more action from her, his climax and perhaps hers. The acoustics of his visual pleasure at the sight of her morphs into our aural pleasure at the sound of her. Soon, this fantasy explodes in ecstasy ("*Work it, bitch!*"), an orgasm, exactly as the first song of her *Hard Core* orality explodes into the foreground, as if it were the cause and content of ecstasy itself.

"Big Momma" and "Queen *Bitch,*" Lil' Kim makes it plain that her rap "thang" is stronger than "porn" with regard to sensual power and impact, whether the senses activated are explicitly sexual or not; whether or not the gender or genitalia of reference is male or masculine, female or feminine. The effect of lyrical skill and intelligence is supposed to be *felt* in Hip-Hop—not just "reasoned" or rationalized; it is supposed to be felt *collectively* in a mind/body nexus that is full of soul as well. For this reason, "Dreams" tells us to "watch this rap bitch bust all ova ya nuts." Her orgasm and lyricism come together in one fell swoop. For *anyone* can "nut" in this, her context. "Dreams" also tells us that she "fucks" mics in the "fly" way. Provocatively, she penetrates the oral tool of the microphone, by whatever means. Lastly, "Dreams" boasts at another point that she is "on fire" and "getting head" by the Harlem Boys Choir. The spiritual orality of their singing in church is rechristened as an erotic tribute to her sacred and sexual divinity on earth, as a "mic-god/dess" supreme. The closing track of her debut solo album, "**** You" (or "Fuck You") confirms this logic in true Hip-Hop fashion. It tells us that she keeps her "pussy fresh, like Doug E." The supreme metaphor for her supreme female anatomy is a human beat-boxer and show-stopping emcee, Doug E. Fresh. The supreme metaphor for emceeing a supreme show is, conversely, her supreme female anatomy or genitalia. This "fresh" phrasing hearkens back to the wild and witty bravado of "Big Momma Thang," orally, when she asks the "cunninlinguist" what's on his mind when his tongue is inside her "pussy"—it's not marriage, or a baby carriage; it's strictly her. "Big Momma" is "Queen *Bitch*" (and vice versa) inasmuch as her sex and speech are undomesticated by marriage or motherhood under patriarchy or male domination: Lil' Kim's rap and her sex were in full political effect when she rhymed—with unquestionable passion: "[I] chose my life to be *Hard Core.*"

Hip-Hop Coda: Sexology and Musicology—or Minding Bodies With Words . . . on Wax

It may be very useful to think about this Hip-Hop obliteration of the racist-sexist mind/body split of the bourgeois West with regard to "sexology" as well as "musicology." In the anti-body or body-phobic intellectual context of European and Euro-American culture, sexologists operate as the licensed "experts" on sexual embodiment—at least for the "professionals" of "medical science." In Hip-Hop, *The Notorious K.I.M.* adopts a comparable posture on "Off the Wall," explicitly telling audiences to call her "Dr. Ruth" as she speaks the truth. A photo of popular sex therapist (and former Israeli sniper) Dr. Ruth Westheimer and Lil' Kim taken at a Grammy's party was once published by the "In the Mix" section of the tenth anniversary edition of *Vibe* magazine (September 2003, 140). Still, it is rather telling that no professional textbook on "human sexuality" seems to rival the catalogue of erotic possibilities captured by this Hip-Hop songbook. Her records form a true taxonomy of things sexual that the elite culture of sexology tries to keep under lock and key—with "bourgeois respectability" intact; and its scope is nothing short of stunning. Moreover, unlike most Western sexologists, Lil' Kim's systematic exploration of sex and it pleasures in music does not hide the sexual pleasures of its author or stigmatize any kind of sex outside white middle-class social norms or ideals. An exception to this rule would be the anti-fascist Wilhelm Reich, whose radical conception of "oral orgasms" or "orgasms of the mouth" can be radically expanded by her Hip-Hop. This is an art of the oral that is scrupulous about minding bodies . . . on wax.

While there is *sex work* all over *Hard Core*, a lush life of *sex fantasy* was laid out on "Dreams," which maps a whole field of sexual scenarios, enhancements and positions to be confronted without end. There is *sex with or enhanced by drink or drugs* (as she boasts about "all the Rhythm & Blues singers" up to Case). There is *group sex* rather than sex between two individuals or a couple (as she moves on to Troop and H-Town). There is *sex climaxed by female ejaculation* (after she runs through Babyface, Brian McKnight, Joe, and D'Angelo, when she has 112 "nuts to bust," before she celebrates with a reference to Hi-Five). There is *sex with "water sports,"* which give added meaning to *oral sex* (as she calls for "pussy-eating positions" and "Men of Vizion," after [a] "New Edition," not to mention the Harlem Boys Choir). There is *"rimming"* or *"salad-tossing," oral-anal sex* apart from *oral-vaginal sex* (as she scatologically puns on Mista and their song "Blackberry Molasses"). There is an invitation to *voyeurism* and *public sex* (as she leaves Intro and Skin Deep in the wake of her desire). There is *sex with women on top*, physically (as her climbing leaves R. Kelly jumping and whining, not "bumping and grinding"). There is *sex-role play or reversal* (as she casts Joe as her "ho" and Tony Rich as her "bitch"). There is *masturbation*, besides (as she disses Jason [Wheeler] and rhymes through Solo and After 7). And, strikingly, this is all from a single song, "Dreams (of Fuckin' an R&B Dick)," whose chorus may give the impression that it will concern *"missionary sex"* alone!

If *Hard Core*'s "Dreams" can be seen as an actual erotic guide, a musical-sexological map to the rest of her explorations of sex on record, it does not exhaust her lyrical imagination or possibilities. If there was "69-ing" and *toe-licking* before (on "Big Momma Thang" and "Drugs"), and light *sado-masochism* (on "I Need You Tonight" from Junior M.A.F.I.A.'s *Conspiracy* [1995] as well as "Call Me" with Too Short from *Booty Call: The Original Motion Picture Soundtrack* [1997]), she would later pull out a menstrual whip for an unreleased track with Rupaul entitled "Bad Girls" (*circa* 2000). She also threatens a man with *sexual mutilation* or *castration* there— again, for her sexual-political pleasure. There was *pornographic sex* or sex with the aid of adult video or visuals along with *phone sex* on "Call Me," just as her unlikely cameo on Will Smith's "Da Butta" (*Willennium*, 1999) redefines "real phone sex" as visually focused sex with live, multimedia TV cameras or camera phones. Lil' Kim documents and rails against "minute men" or *premature ejaculation* time and time again: "No Time" and "We Don't Need It" set the stage for her verse on Methods of Mayhem's "Get Naked" (*Methods of Mayhem*, 1999), a rock-rap collaboration featuring her and George Clinton (Fred Durst and Mix Master Mike). This happens to be the same song on which she screams: "Fuck a blow-job/It's a muthafuckin hobby!" Finally, the *sex with dildos* heard during "Spend a Little Doe's" spectacular stick-up is heard again in her guest verse on Usher's "Just Like Me" (*My Way*, 1997). The erotic or sexological intelligence of Lil' Kim's lyricism seems as inexhaustible as her Hip-Hop orality overall.

Such a coda would be lacking without some critical attention to *"safe(r) sex"* since, without it, neither mind nor body could be kept alive in contemporary times—to think or feel; to enjoy life or sex; or, in certain cases, to condemn sex in moralistic rants and tones. Lil' Kim's sexual consciousness could be said to climax, once, in "Rockin'" or Funkmaster Flex's *The Mix Tape, Volume 4: 60 Minutes of Funk* (2000). A rarely discussed piece of work, it raises and reinterprets the question of safety in the practice of sex or sexuality. One specific passage begins with an initial check for erection, after which Lil' Kim requires her partner to pass her inspection, before she will give him any love and affection. There is a bass line shouted out and a base line of sexual principles. A man is first instructed to meet her on a mezzanine and, second, to hop up into her limousine. Both references conjure the prospect of *public or semi-public sex*. He is told that he can "trick" or "treat," like it's Halloween, but the trick or treat must be "squeaky clean." She entices him by saying she can gargle—something (ejaculate?)—like it's Listerine, even if in the act she messes up her makeup made by Maybelline. After her alluring, verbal seduction of him, he is instructed to stick "it" in here like a *vaccine*: "Then I cud cum clean like a hygiene and a pocket full of D/dreams." On command, she is to be penetrated (vaginally or anally and, of course, orally) as we are all penetrated when vaccinated (or "getting a shot"). These images picture sexual act after sexual act with purifying puns, the most cleansing of metaphors possible. Oral sex comes in the language of "mouthwash," after inspection. Otherwise penetrative sex comes in the language of protection, or immunization, after inspection. At this point, similes stacked, Lil' Kim can herself "cum clean," again couching orgasm in the language of hygiene, redundantly, or abundantly. The pocket full of Dreams (or dreams) in the end punctuates this idea impressively. "Dreams" signify desire (ambition and aspiration) as well as sexual fantasy. In addition, it calls forth that fantastic song from *Hard Core*. But the "pocket full" also sends us to store for condoms. "Dreams" is or was a brand of condom: "Condoms from a Woman's Perspective," this is how they have been advertised. Conventional "safe sex" campaigns strike many or most as "sterile," anti-erotic, if not anti-sex. They are unsuccessful in a number of senses as a result. A kind of female "Dr. Feelgood-*cum*-oral poet," Lil' Kim crafts by contrast a *"fresh and clean" aesthetic* that eroticizes the "wildest" episodes of sex as "safe(r) sex," lyrically leaving us "disease-free," super-satisfied as well as physically and mentally alive. What better way to dismiss the mind/body split of the West than to use the mind and the mouth to discover more ways to satisfy the human body, the historically defamed body in which every human mind (and "soul") is organically lodged?

Note

1. Excerpt from Greg Thomas, "Orals . . . Head . . . Genius: The Power, Knowledge, and Pleasure of *Hard Core*," in *Hip-Hop Revolution in the Flesh: Power, Knowledge, and Pleasure in Lil' Kim's Lyricism* (New York: Palgrave Macmillan, 2009), pp. 15–26.

Halifu Osumare

This selection traces the traditional African concept of *Nommo*—the power of language or "the word"—as it is manifested in hip-hop lyricism. Emcees such as Common, Lauryn Hill, Mos Def, and KRS-One are interpreted to embody this sacred and ancestral power in rhyme. The more cosmic resources of philosophy and folklore centered around Esu-Elegbara as well as Anansi the Spider are mobilized to chart the ancestral Africanist dimensions of hip-hop's powerful practice of languaging in the present day.

The Africanist Aesthetic in Global Hip-Hop Power Moves

Halifu Osumare[1]

Dope Rhymes: *Nommo* and the Power of the Word

As I am writing this, James Brown singing "Please, Please, Please" bellows from my middle-aged white neighbor's apartment, giving audible reference to the entrenchment and the pervasiveness of black music in our lives. Gottschild would probably interpret this moment of Brown's familiar vocal improvisational nuances as the Godfather of Soul's crooning subjunctive mood—the Word as "verbal movement" (Gothschild 11) Dances done to James Brown's soul music become physical manifestations of *Nommo*, the power of the Word. In Black cultural production like James Brown's music, the interchangeable dynamics of movement and sound cojoin to form the first principle of an aesthetic that is not merely product, but indeed about *process*, always in motion, always becoming. The African concept of *Nommo* is a principle that emphasizes the changing now, the improvisatory self.

Word power is one of the first principles of the Africanist aesthetic. The power of the word, as African cosmological tenet, was first introduced to Western letters through anthropologist Marcel Griaule's 1948 *Conversations with Ogotomeli*. The text gave voice to an elder Dogon priest who revealed that particular culture's cosmological knowledge, previously withheld from Europeans for centuries. Janheinz Jahn built upon Griaule's foundation cross-culturally in his 1961 *Muntu, The New African Culture*, conflating several African and New World African American cultures under one epistemological rubric. In doing so, Jahn decoded the conception that *Nommo*'s influence extends not only to *muntu*, Bantu-speaking people's word for human, but also to things or *bintu*.

The anthropomorphic emphasis, even when interfacing with nature and inanimate objects, is central to Dogon philosophy. Ogotomeli told Griaule, "since man has power over the Word, it is he who directs the life force." Human beings, charged with cosmological duty, are equipped through *Nommo* to administer this life force and indeed to direct it. "Through the Word he receives it, shares it with other beings, and so fulfills the meaning of life." Furthermore, Ogotemeli instructed Griaule that "The *Nommo* is water and heat. The vital force that carries the Word issues from the mouth in a water vapor that is both water and Word. The vital force of the earth is water" (Griaule 1970). Thus, this ability to wield *Nommo*, viewed as a gift from God, charges humankind with the vitality of cocreation with each invocation of word power. Simultaneously, each human has an attendant responsibility to the power invoked through verbal pronunciation (orality and singing) and physical gesture (embodiment and dance).

The hip-hop slang phrase "word up," first commercialized in Cameo's 1986 funk hit "Word Up," unconsciously encompasses the concept of using this primal force called *Nommo*. In the call and response culture of hip-hop music, "word up," or just simply "word," is often used to punctuate a statement just made, as a response to one's own or someone else's calling forth of word energy through the power of voicing; while at other times the phrase is also used as a greeting to a fellow "head" or a recognized member of hip-hop subculture. It seems no coincidence that a vernacular hip-hop slang term is in actuality recognition of the ancient first principle at the root of an African cosmology.

With *Nommo* as an anthropomorphic foundation, each human has the capacity to bring forth divine power, and hip-hop culture implicitly reflects this understanding in a place and time other than that of Ogotemeli. As Gottschild articulately reflects about hip-hop's use of word power,

> [r]ap's form—the rhythmic base, together with the characteristic signifying, or making ironic, double-edged social and personal commentary through rhymed stanzas or couplets—is African. The concept of *Nommo*, the power of the word, is alive and well in hip-hop. Acknowledgment of the connection means opening the door to empowerment. The African heritage shows off its resilience and flexibility in the fact that it can be channeled in so many different ways. Music as a vehicle of power and identity is integral to understanding the Africanist aesthetic and its role in hip-hop.
>
> (Gottschild 138–39)

The power of music and dance to bolster and enhance the human spirit, as Dunham told us, has been the bedrock of the survival of African-based cultures in the Americas, and is now the inspiration for that same power, through hip-hop, to propagate throughout the world.

This relationship between expressive culture and sociohistorical dynamics is reinforced as the foundation of global hip-hop culture. The power of the word spread through rap music has indeed empowered the voices of many marginalized peoples throughout the globe. From NTM's voicing of North African Arab class issues in France to DJ Krush's authentication of the rebellious perspective of Japanese hip-hop youth, rap's word power and pumping bass beats have proliferated, empowering youth internationally.

Several African master musicians have recognized rap's cultural roots in African word power. Nigerian talking drum master and scholar Francis Awe, based in Los Angeles, offered direct verification of the transatlantic connection of rapping as an extension of a particularized African use of *Nommo* that continues even today. Awe, who also has an MFA degree in African Studies from UCLA, identifies rap's form and function as a revision of a musical tradition among his own Ekiti Yoruba in Kwara State, Nigeria:

> When I first heard rapping here, I said "Omowale [Awe's African American wife], who are those people?" And she answered, "They are what we call rappers." Then I said, "That is a Yoruba tradition. That's the way we sing. *Alamo* chanting of the Ekiti Yoruba peoples sometimes is a song, sometimes it is speech. Sometimes it is not a song and it is not a speech; it becomes a speech-song."
>
> (Personal interview, June 11, 1999)

The oral tradition among the Ekiti Yoruba, such as *alamo* rhythmic speech form, can be viewed as a part of the well-documented general category of *oriki* (praise-poetry) of the Yoruba. This poetry as *Nommo*-like invocation can take the form of praise-chant for an individual (particularly of royal status), an ancestor, a particular ancestral lineage or household, or a deity. However, the literary form has surprising resonance with rap's potential in what Clifford Geertz calls "thick description," with its convoluted allusions and connections. David Zeitlyn, in his review of Karin Barber's *I Could Speak Until Tomorrow: Oriki, Women and the Past in a Yoruba Town* (1991), analyzes *oriki* praise poems and says that they

> are distinguished by the insistence with which they are chanted (shouted or screamed) at the individual being addressed .... The performer weaves a web of allusion by combining

many disparate elements—the more skillful the performer the more radical the breaks and twists she can succeed in introducing while maintaining the thread.

(http://www.lucy.ukc.ac.uk/dz/zreviews/barber.html)

Awe elaborates on this aesthetic usage in Yoruba orality when he explains why the Ekiti Yoruba utilizes alamo rhythmic speech, rather than singing.

> So people are singing, and then they just change it and talk. It becomes more effective, because you don't need to care for tone there, *but you're still talking in rhythm* [my emphasis]. People [Ekiti Yoruba] sing and then they are overcome with emotion, and they just [start] talking, because a lot of the things they want to say, the song cannot carry that. It's like a priest worshipping. All of a sudden, they are transformed from this physical world to a metaphysical world, and then everything he is saying is not like a normal person.
>
> (Personal interview)

Awe's sentiments about the place of alamo chanting in that ethnic group's singing style has surprising resonance with statements made by Grammy-winning emcee Lauryn Hill in discussing her own neo-soul style of hip-hop that utilizes both rap word play and R&B singing:

> I knew that when I got the opportunity to do my own sound, it would be a fusion of raw hip-hop beats and the instrumentation that I grew up listening to . . . Aretha Franklin, Stevie Wonder and Marvin Gaye . . . [who were] heartfelt.
>
> (Ewey 202)

Part of Hill's perspective on popular music is that R&B singers need to learn from the intensity of rappers as wordsmiths who are not afraid to strongly contest the social ills of the nation as well as those of the black community. Contemporary rap and R&B collaborations, such as Lil' Bow Wow and Jagged Edge, Ja Rule and Ashanti, Da Brat and Destiny's Child, Mos Def and Common with Bilal, and Kanye West and John Legend, attest to this link in the Africanist oral tradition between the spoken word and melodic singing. Hill's sentiments resonate with Awe's account of the role of *alamo* chant among the Ekiti Yoruba:

> You see those rappers? They are stronger than those who just sing. You see, the singers sing with emotion. A rapper is talking, but *he* is not talking. Somebody is talking through him. And he's going to say whatever he wants to say, regardless of who is around. And a lot of people don't like that. And the same thing with those who do *alamo*; Everything strong about the people, most cannot just mention; but the *alamo* people will break through that. And sometimes it will result in fighting.
>
> (Personal interview)

Awe's latter point alludes to the competitive challenge at the basis of the Africanist aesthetic that manifests as battling in hip-hop:

> You see, here [the U.S.], the people will ask, "who did that [challenge]?" It is usually the rapper in the United States. That surprised me, and I said, it is like I'm living among the Yoruba people, but only here in the United States. It is those [kinds of] things that make me say that I need to go back to my roots, to Nigeria. And wherever I go, here, I tell all of the African Americans, "Make sure you go to Nigeria, and especially to Yorubaland."
>
> (Ibid.)

Throughout our interview, Awe insisted on the existence of direct links between African American culture and Yoruba culture, emphasizing modes of religious worship, secular dancing, and singing styles. African American orality, as exhibited in hip-hop culture, is a part of Afro-diasporic cultural practices that have direct and persisting resonances with specific African ethnic groups, such as the Yoruba, Bakongo, and Wolof.

It is equally important, however, to acknowledge hip-hop culture's foundation in twenty-first century technology. Tricia Rose reminds us that rap music, and by extension hip-hop culture, "is in part an expression of what Walter Ong has referred to as 'post-literate orality'" (Rose 1994, 86) and thereby is situated in the African aesthetic continuum at a particular historical moment of postindustrialism.

> Rap then, is not simply a linear extension of other orally based African-American traditions with beat boxes and cool European electronics added on. Rap is a complex fusion of orality and postmodern technology.
>
> (Ibid., 85)

That is, hip-hop deejays' unique use of turntables, mixers, drum machines, such as the Roland TR-808, and sampling machines such as the S900, create technical styles and sound ranges not intended by inventors of those machines. Hip-hop producers' studio techniques position these artists as new-age technological innovators. In the words of hip-hop spokesperson Harry Allen, rap artists have "humanize[d] technology and [made] it tactile" (Allen 10). Hip-hop, therefore, as in all eras of the manifestation of Black cultural production, has its own exigencies, dictated by its historical moment, that, in turn, shape its particular style and contribution to the ongoing Africanist aesthetic.

Hip-hop must be interpreted, therefore, both within the Africanist aesthetic continuum and as an articulation of the postmodern moment of intertexuality. This bifurcated view of hip-hop culture allows both for its uses of the *Nommo* word power and technological wizardry of the twenty-first century. Hip-hop's ability to bridge aeons of time and space makes this globally circulating subculture a potent and intoxicating sign of the postmodern times. Relativity Records recording artist Chicago-based Common captures some of these ancient-future cultural nuances in his "Invocation" (*One Day It'll All Make Sense*, Relativity Records, 1997):

> *Envisioning the hereafter, listenin to Steve*
> *Wonder On a Quest for Love like the Proceed drummer*
> *I strike like lightning and don't need thunder*
> *Inhale imagination and breathe wonder.*

Emcees, such as Common, invoke *Nommo* to connect the cosmological to the sociopolitical ("It's a cold world and niggaz need summer") and personal ("That's your lady, I used to run up in her and G weed from her"), and in the process make quintessential, existential hip-hop statements. The Africanist power of the word continues to transmute into new manifestations over time and space, made possible by those adept at wielding its power.

(W)Rapped in Illusion: The Emcee as Trickster

However important hip-hop's contemporary position at the beginning of the twenty-first century may be, it has always drawn from the wellspring of the Africanist aesthetic. Part of this defining aesthetic is the recuperative process of *naming*. As a manifestation of the power of the Word, naming, or better still renaming, is the empowering process so common in African American history. Ralph Ellison eloquently explained the historical basis for naming among African Americas:

> We must charge them with all our emotions, our hopes, hates, loves, aspirations. They must become our masks and our shields and the containers of all those values and traditions which we learn and/or imagine as being the meaning of our familial past.
>
> (Ellison 148)

Gottschild further politicizes the process by emphasizing renaming as the telling of one's own story. Who is foregrounded and how he/she is framed become crucial dynamics of contemporary politics of identity. Whose story is being told and by whom are always of paramount importance, and have become even more crucial in the high stakes postmodern era of the twenty-first century. As she contends, "If language is the exercise of power, and the act of naming is an act of empowerment, then what is not named, or misnamed, becomes an impotent backdrop for someone else's story" (Gottschild 5). Even as rap has often abused the naming process through myriad misogynistic and homophobic lyrics, renaming in other empowering ways in the hands of groups like Public Enemy has, along with the b-boy's power moves, graf art, and deejay mixing, continued significant counter-hegemonic and recuperative processes for marginalized hip-hop youth.

Utilizing the naming process with the power of *Nommo*, coupled with the contemporary politics of persona and spectacle in popular culture, labeling and nicknaming have become ubiquitous in hip-hop culture. Prominent hip-hop (re)names are Kool DJ Herc (Clive Campbell) Grand Master Flash (Joseph Saddler), Crazy Legs (Richard Colon), Mr. Wiggles (Steve Clemente) Flavor Flav (Rico Drayton), Queen Latifah (Dana Owens), (P) Diddy (Sean Combs), Master P (Percy Miller), Common (Derek Dudley), and the list continues. Rose positions "hip-hop's prolific self-naming" as "a form of reinvention and self-definition" in African and Afro-diasporic cultural traditions, "Rappers, DJs, graffiti artists, and breakdancers all take on hip-hop names and identities that speak to their role, personal characteristics, expertise, or 'claim to fame.' "[41] Public imaging through naming has been a part of American cultural history since minstrelsy (i.e., Coon, Sambo, Tambo, Dandy). Russell Potter notes that "Black Americans . . . have had the singular historical experience of having their blackness made into a spectacular commodity of great value, even as they themselves have been denied the profits of such commodification" (Porter 8). Today's hip-hop naming maps the current stage of this intricate representation of subjectivity in the United States as it interfaces with economics and pop culture at the beginning of the new millennium.

Hip-hop's renaming proclivity is a complex of contemporary revisioning of Africanist rhetorical strategies, diasporic historical reclaiming, and postmodern exhibitionism. In popular culture, exhibitionism or spectacle has had increasing media currency ever since the explosion of the multimedia rock concerts of the 1960s and 1970s. As did its pop culture predecessors, hip-hop culture utilizes a commodified image and spectacle that is reflective of the "cult of personality" so prevalent in today's popular culture. These new age dynamics can and do usurp hip-hop's Africanist naming process passed down over time. Guy Debord has analyzed that "[t]he spectacle is not a collection of images; rather, it is a social relationship between people that is mediated by images" (Debord 12). We saw this relationship mediated by images in the 2003 Super Bowl Halftime Show production of "Walk This Way" that included the original Aerosmith, Justin Timberlake, Mary J. Blige, Nelly, and Britney Spears. This was an attempt within a worldwide spectacle to demonstrate a consolidated American popular culture front of music artists from different historically racialized categories of music (rock, rap, R&B, and pop). This contrived imaging configured around the quintessential song touted as hip-hop's first cross-over foray into the then more mainstream rock genre, RUN-DMC/Aerosmith's "Walk This Way" (1986). In an international event like the Super Bowl, the choreographed Halftime production, with each artist having his/her image and associated music genre, was an attempt to create a coalesced sign of American popular music for the world to consume. In the process, imaging, personal persona, the racialized American music business, and hip-hop history merged into an international spectacle.

However, the central image of hip-hop itself has changed over time. The rapper has indeed replaced the deejay as axial figure. The principal trope of hip-hop has been transferred from the early days of a turntablist-deejay's beat-drenched soundscape to the intricate word play of today's rapper/emcee. As such, the hip-hop emcee is the current incarnation of an African trick-ster figure known as *ananse* among the Akan of West Africa, and transformed in the Americas into *nansi* in Jamaica and Brer Rabbit in the U.S. south. The Yoruba also have an iconic trickster, *Esu-Elegbara*, a combination trickster-crossroads deity. Literary critic Henry Louis Gates, Jr. in *Signifying Monkey: A Theory of African-American Literary Criticism* (1988) traced the Yoruba trickster deity Esu-Elegbara to both the U.S. Brer Rabbit slave folktales and the black male rhe-torical tradition of playing the dozens or the signifying monkey, revived in today's rap battles that often create multiplatinum market potential.

As trickster, Esu never quite seems as he appears; illusion is his game, and challenge to the status quo brings him fame. The status quo at one historical point might be the social system of slavery or at another juncture an individual's perception of himself or herself within the human condition. As Gates adeptly analyzes, "these variations of Esu-Elegbara speak eloquently of an unbroken arc of metaphysical presupposition and a pattern of figuration shared through time and space among certain black cultures in West Africa, South America, the Caribbean, and the United States" (Gates 6). Gates reminds us that Esu-Elegbara's other sacred role as mediator of the crossroads is made perceptible through profane vernacular. "Esu-Elegbara presides over [the] liminal crossroads, a sensory threshold barely perceptible without access to the vernacular, a word taken from the Latin *vernaculus* ('native,' taken in turn from *verna* 'slave born in his master's house')" (Ibid.).

Though all hip-hop emcees don't mediate the sacred and the secular as Esu, the skillful rap-per as trickster figure does provide access to the illusory world of representations. There is no better site for representing illusion than American popular culture. The textual strategies of Brooklyn rapper Mos Def, for example, transport the mind to sociometaphysical signs. In "New World Water" he signifies on the first George Bush's slogan "New World Order" that justified the Gulf War, while examining the relationship of the element of water, justice, and black history,

> *New World Water make the tide rise high*
> *Come inland and make your house go "Bye"*
> *Fool done upset the Old Man River*
> *Made him carry slave ships and fed him dead nigga.*

Mos Def, thereby, conjoins the political and cosmic in a few deft lines. In the wake of hurricanes Katrina and Rita in 2005, his words become even more prophetic when he clarifies that, "Now his belly full and he about to flood something; So I'm a throw a rope that ain't tied to nothing; Tell your crew use the H2 in wise amounts since; It's the New World Water; and every drop counts."

Another of Esu's personas is that of divine linguist, an even closer connection to the word-smith's ability of the "dope" rhymer. As master linguist, Esu-Elegbara translates the language of the gods to humans and vice versa and in the process becomes the master of literacy. In the diaspora, his codified literature, such as the signifying monkey tales, according to VèVè Clark, is "a hermeneutics of black criticism" (Clark 45). Signifying raps, as poetic literature, then, might also be considered within Mikhail Bakhtin's historicity of the novel as a parodic genre. "Of particular interest are those eras when the novel becomes the dominant genre. All literature is then caught up in the process of 'becoming,' and in a special kind of 'generic criticism'" (Bakhtin 5). Indeed, rap *is* the critical poetry of our era, promoting a generic criticism of the assumptions that the twentieth century harbored about the place of Africans, the American liberal republic, and indeed subjectivity itself. Thus, the hip-hop emcee as both writer and performer is the master of the vernacular language and the invoker of *Nommo* that is the legacy of the original trickster-linguist. Notwithstanding the abusive, misogynistic lyric content of the raps of some male emcees, even Esu-Elegbara's phallic, generative role of fecundity may also be situated within the boastful raps about sexual prowess and females' attraction to them. Thus, the dope rhyme of rap music, with the emcee as the translator of signs and representations, has become the global "generic criticism" mapped onto our contemporary postmodern times.

Nommo, actualized in the voice through the orality of the divine linguist, occupies a position of enormous and far-reaching power. Most of today's emcees and b-boys are only partially aware of their skills' connection to an ancient source of spiritual power or their vital link to the trickster-linguist role. However, awareness of *Nommo* or the place of the trickster in African cosmology is not a requisite of the mythology's power over individual purveyors. Artists of any musical genre reflect their finite, human understanding of the world and their place within it, while their creative genius may generate far-reaching masterpieces, often in spite of the artist as an individual.

Today's hip-hop emcees exhibit various levels of acknowledgment of hip-hop's ancestral link to the linguist's responsibility as mediator of *Nommo*. Lauryn Hill, who has sold over 12 million copies of the *Miseducation of Lauryn Hill* (Columbia/Ruff House, 1998) worldwide, demonstrates a more conscious awareness of the power of the Africanist spiritual first principle than many on "Everything is Everything":

> *I philosophy*
> *Possibly speak tongues*
> *Beat drum, Abyssinian, street Baptist*
> *Rap this in fine linen*
> *From the beginning.*

Her philosophy speaks in (many) tongues extending all the way back to the beginning of time and can be heard in the drumbeat, in a continuum from the origins of Christianity to today's street evangelists. In this context, she portrays herself as a part of a long lineage of black female representations of the Word.

> *My practice extending across the atlas*
> *I begat this*
> *Flippin' in the ghetto on a dirty mattress*
> *You can't match this rapper/actress*
> *More powerful than two Cleopatras.*

As her philosophy extends across the globe, she conflates Afrocentric allusions to East Africa and Egypt with references to the poverty of the black ghetto and she positions herself as a continuation of a line of black "royalty" ("Bomb graffiti on the tomb of Nefertiti; MCs ain't ready to take it to the Serengeti; My rhymes is heavy like the mind of Sister Betty, L. Boogie spars with stars and constellations."). In the verse, Hill, as L. Boogie (her underground hip-hop name), "spars with stars and constellations [and] then came down for a little conversation." Through her rhymes, her spiritual and profane roles merge as one.

Hill invokes an illusory figure that might appear to most as a poor ghetto dweller, but in reality, is the personification of the divine trickster power. As female, she "beget this" first principle that extends "across the atlas," while she was "flippin' in the ghetto on a dirty mattress." Through her own power as an emcee-linguist she invokes the divine Word and is able to demonstrate how "hip-hop meets scripture," and thereby she develops "a negative into a positive picture." Hill deftly represents the initiatory energy of the life force of *Nommo* descending to earth through her personas as a dialogic force. The brilliance of Hill's imagery conflates the understanding of *Nommo*, Esu-Elegbara, and postmodern radical juxtaposition in one deft stroke.

Hill's layered imagery creates a particular kind of "cipher," as it is known in hip-hop vernacular. Perry defines the cipher as "a conceptual space in which heightened consciousness exists . . . a privileged outlaw space" (Perry 107). Hill's motives are certainly to create a heightened consciousness that, in turn, provides a space for those "insiders" who want to be outside the laws of mundane time and space to gather and flourish where the ancient, present, and future coalesce. While many of her fans may not be able to truly *decipher* the depth of her imagery, they love it anyway. Cognitive awareness notwithstanding, the affective, psychophysical, and spiritual transpersonal levels at which music affects human consciousness have always ensured a strong pop music audience.

Similarly, long-term rapper KRS-One (acronym for Knowledge Reigns Supreme Over Nearly Everyone—his renaming process) has proven his staying power in the hip-hop business, and shares lyrics that directly relate to the initiatory principle of *Nommo*. After pulling himself out of homelessness in the Bronx, he became known for his "conscious" raps that he produced on his own Boogie Down Production label. Dubbed "The Teacher," KRS-One has a reputation for being both "hardcore" and didactic about the realities of violence in poor communities and the music business that so many young would-be emcees view as a way out of that poverty.

His emphasis on knowledge, as evidenced in his signature body stance—his index fingers held to each side of his head—is both esoteric and practical. On "Health, Wealth, Self" that ends his *KRS-One* (Zomba Recording/BMG, 1995) album he drops a slow, funky musical introduction that reveals his understanding of his esoteric role as emcee in relation to the divine order. In the introduction, directed to a male fan whom he met on the way to the studio to record the album, KRS-One answers the fan's question about why he uses the term "Goddess" instead of "God" as his creative source, sending the veteran rapper into a combination prose/rhyme style response: "You might know her as God/But I know her as the Goddess, the Universal Mother. The Mother of Everything you see in existence." After ironically locating his inspiration as a hardcore male rapper in a female organizing principle, he precedes in a strictly rhyming cadence to situate this gift clearly in the power of the Word:

> *Me not believe nothing else*
> *but health, wealth and knowledge of myself*
> *In the beginning was the Word*
> *The Word was made flesh.*

"Health, Wealth, Self" expresses KRS-One's ultimate "religion." Through his beliefs, he represents his understanding of the role of the emcee as an extension of the Word, the gift that comes from the "Goddess." In this case, Esu-Elegbara, the linguist who extends the gift of the *Nommo* force in language and rhyme has a feminine persona not inconsistent with many African belief systems that reflect male and female as mirror opposites of the same deity. He says, "I asked her for her gift in lyrical persistence, and she gave it to me under one condition: She said, "I'll give you the gift, but use the gift to uplift." The gift that KRS-One has received from her is not the longevity of staying in the game—but of rhyming, the grace of the Word. In Ellisonian terms, it is the mastery of the techniques and disciplines of the culture that constitute the worth of the artist. This reinforces the Thompsonian Africanist perspective, namely, that the worth of the individual artist is measured by his/her ability to tap into the

> philosophic streams of creativity and imagination, running parallel to the massive musical and choreographic modalities that connect black persons of the western hemisphere, as well as millions of European and Asian people attracted to and performing their styles, to Mother Africa.
>
> (Thompson xviii–xiv)

Lauryn Hill and KRS-One are not necessarily indicative of the majority of emcees who represent the hip-hop genre. Even if a conscious positioning of an Africanist epistemology has not always been a part of rap's content, Africanist methodologies have been. The emcee's art has implicitly utilized African oral systems of social commentary through rhyme and music. Although their branch of rap music might share some roots with the other so-called conscious rap trends inspired by the Nation of Islam and the Five Percent Nation philosophy, my purpose here in using these emcees is to illuminate the often more elusive "philosophically conscious" rap—the verbally articulated rap parallel of Thompson's "philosophical streams" that link hip-hop with African and Caribbean cultural practices and symbols like the trickster.

The Akan trickster figure, Ananse the Spider, as mentioned earlier, is one such symbol. Ananse is the weaver of tall tales. His stories are often brilliantly colored webs that even ensnare the trickster himself. His stories and his illusory persona are intricately linked to his spider web. Today's network of globally linked virtual sites, the World Wide Web, has always intrigued me as a metaphoric association with Ananse's web of stories. Suffice it to say here that the current stage of hip-hop's implications in postmodernity is a long way from its original Bronx origins. Clearly, at every turn, hip-hoppers have utilized technology to channel the power of *Nommo*. In the process, they have changed the technology's original intent, or at least, with each new technological innovation, its possibilities—the use of the sampler being one prime example. Although the Marshall McLuhan adage, "the medium is the message" has currency, rap has demonstrated how the message also *alters* the medium. Hip-hop culture that has come of age in the last two decades of the twentieth century is particularly indicative of human agency in the history of technology. Hip-hop's technology-web culture guru, Harry Allen, assessed the deejay-producer's impact on the burgeoning electronic technology in hip-hop music thus:

> Hip-hop . . . is an intrinsically electronic African-American music, the first which, from its inception, performance or creation was impossible without electronics . . . . In hip-hop, no higher praise can be given a vocalist than to cut 'n' scratch their voice. Call it a form of ancestor worship. The scratch is incantatory.
>
> (Allen 10)

Allen, then, predicts that hip-hop is not in danger of succumbing to the dehumanizing aspects of the computer age. Although I further explore the computer age as a part of hip-hop's postmodernism in chapter 4, it is important to note here that music is now being produced through the same *Nommo*-inspired factors as it was in earlier times and as it is today in sub-Saharan Africa; conscious and unconscious links continue to be invoked across time and space.

Note

1. Halifu Osumare, "Dope Rhymes: *Nommo* and the Power of the Word" and "(W)Rapped in Illusion: The Emcee as Trickster," in *The Africanist Aesthetic in Global Hip-Hop: Power Moves* (New York: Palgrave Macmillan, 2007), pp. 31–43.

Marc D. Perry

This selection regards hip-hop as a practice of the self—a political aesthetic of existence, in other words. The collective self fashioned in and through hip-hop is fashioned in the context of Global Africa, moreover, for a blackness that is both necessary and desirable for transnational Black communities of the Afro-Atlantic world. The category of youth is key here, as hip-hop movements in Brazil, Cuba, and South Africa provide clear-cut examples of this global Black self-fashioning in lyrical, musical motion.

Hip Hop as Contemporary Ontology of Blackness

Marc D. Perry[1]

As I have argued, it is precisely through the political framings of diaspora that such contestive self-racializations find their most poignant expression. Nationally transcendent modes of Black diasporic identification prove strategic in challenging local conditions of racial oppression, while at the same time remaining critically responsive to the ways global processes are increasingly reshaping such conditions. In the case of Brazil, hegemonic discourses tied to notions of "racial democracy" are increasingly unhinged as Afro-Brazilian youth use the diasporically configured Black racial contours of hip hop to construct new identities as the basis to critically interrogate the racialized social realities of their everyday. Along analogous lines in Cuba, *raperos* are using hip hop to contest longstanding ideologies of Cuban national racelessness, while

Figure 11.2a A young man in a youth prison near Caracas, Venezuela, is one of the inmates who produce an underground radio show that broadcasts from the prison in 2006

(Credit: Noelle Theard)

Figure 11.2b YONE, a graffiti artist paints a piece in an abandoned warehouse turned graffiti gallery just north of Paris in 1999

(Credit: Noelle Theard)

providing acute public critiques of the racialized workings of neoliberal transformations in a rapidly shifting Cuban social landscape. In South Africa a new generation of colored youth has attempted to position themselves amidst shifting racial paradigms of "old" and "new" where current claims to "non-racialism" run counter to the continued lived consequences of hierarchical racial privilege.

The cartography of maneuvers elucidates the social significance of hip hop not simply in terms of its international circulation and consumption but, rather, through the ways it is actively lived and politically used abroad as a site of racial mobilization and self-formation. Among these Black-identified youth, the space of diaspora—through the performative lens of hip hop—operates as a key paradigm of both identity and politics, and as such has been instrumental in enabling transnationally engaged strategies of Black self-fashioning and action in response to new, globally conditioned modes of racialization. In doing so, these young people not only marshal Black selves but ultimately realize the Afro-Atlantic itself as a lived social formation. Hip hop in this way can be seen as an active site for the global (re)mapping of Black political imaginaries via social dynamics of diaspora. Or, to return to Los Paisanos' more poetic rendering, "*¡Fundamentalmente hip hop quiere decir negro! Corto, pero penetrante.*" ["Fundamentally hip hop means black! Concise, but penetrating"].

Note

1. Marc D. Perry, "Hip-Hop as Contemporary Ontology of Blackness," from "Global Black Self-Fashioning: Hip-Hop as Diasporic Space," *Identities: Global Studies in Culture and Power* 15.6 (2008): 658–659.

Ousmane Sembène

This is a very special text from the late, great Ousmane Sembène, the reputed "Father of African Cinema" and a revolutionary Pan-Africanist legend for multiple generations. He was a great fan of hip-hop, especially rap in traditional African languages. Emcees on the continent were great fans of his as well, dubbing him "*Ousmane la Hache*" (or "Ousmane the Axe") as a kind of mic-name or rap moniker in effect. They often sampled his film soundtracks in their own Hip-Hop audio tracks in the hip-hop movement of Dakar, Senegal. Here is Sembene's rich, detailed response to a question about the political voice of hip-hop rap in continental Africa, a statement made only a couple of years before his passing on June 9, 2007.

"Hip-Hop / Rap"

Ousmane Sembène[1]

Hip-Hop! Rap! I love rap—in the national languages. What they say is found neither in the press nor in books nor in film. From the point of view of musicality and the use of instruments, they have reinvented something. Yet rap is not a new thing among us. We have a lot of names or appellations for it, one of which is the Kébétou. In the Kébétou, as soon as people get together, there is one or two who start to speak and then the others respond. But, actually, rap is the best of the musics listened to by the youth. They started calling me "le vieux jeune," "the old-young man," because I am in it—among them. They nicknamed me Ousmane-the-Axe! Also, there are the texts of my films that they sing—*Guelwaar* and all the others. Rap is a music of the future. But the people who are older than I am, politically, they don't want to listen. If you speak Wolof or Toucouleur or Bambara—*whew!*—it's the baddest of what anyone could ever say on matters of democracy and expression. I prefer rap in the national languages to French. It's a music that should enter the university as a part of the curriculum. The mixture of sounds come calling from different musics of different cultural horizons and the intonations of the respondents come from different cultural horizons as well.

Note

1. Ousmane Sembène, "Hip-Hop / Rap," quoted in Greg Thomas, *Hip-Hop Revolution in the Flesh: Power, Knowledge, and Pleasure in Lil' Kim's Lyricism* (New York: Palgrave Macmillan, 2005), pp. 106–107.

Section 11: Works Cited

Alim, H. Samy. "A New Research Agenda: Exploring the Transglobal Hip Hop Umma." In *Muslim Networks from Hajj to Hip Hop*. Eds. Miriam Cooke and Bruce B. Lawrence, 264–74. Chapel Hill: University of North Carolina Press, 2005.

Allen, Harry. "Invisible Band." *Electromag: Village Voice Consumer Electronics Special* (October 13, 1988), 10.

Bahktin, Mikhail. *The Dialogic Imagination: Four Essays*. Ed. Michael Holquist. Austin, TX: University of Austin Press, 1981.

Birchmeier, Jason. "Review of Lil' Kim's *Hard Core*." *All Music Guide*. n.d. Web. Retrieved October 15, 2008. http://www.all-music.com/cg/amg.dll?p=amg&sql=10:gxfqxqehld6e~T1

Bost, Suzanne. "Be Deceived If Ya Wanna Be Foolish: (Re)constructing Body, Genre, and Gender in Feminist Rap." *Postmodern Culture*, 12.1 (2001): 1–38. Chang, Jeff. *Can't Stop, Won't Stop: A History of the Hip-Hop Generation*. New York: St. Martin's Press, 2005.

Clarke, Vévé A. "Developing Diaspora Literacy and Marasa Consciousness." In *Comparative American Identities: Race, Sex, and Nationality in the Modern Text*. Ed. Hortense Spillers. New York: Routledge Press, 1991.

Covington, Francee. "Are the Revolutionary Techniques Employed in *The Battle of* Algiers Applicable to Harlem?" In *The Black Woman: An Anthology*. Ed. Toni Cade. New York: Signet, 1970, 244–52.

Davey, D. "Fear of an Arab Planet: Hip Hop Is Everywhere." *The Hip Hop Cosign: Breakdown FM*. November 2007. Web. Retrieved February 2, 2007. http://beta.odeo.com/episodes/18230308-Breakdown-FM-Fear-of-An-Arab-Planet-Hip-Hop-in-the-Middle-East-pt1

Debord, Guy. *Society of the Spectacle*. Detroit, MI: Red & Black, 1970.

Ellison, Ralph. *Shadow and Act*. New York: Quality Paper Back Book Club, 1994.

El-Sabawi, Taleed. "Palestinian Convict Bounces to a New Beat." *AngeLingo* 2, no. 2. 2005. Web. Retrieved February 4, 2007. http://angelingo.usc.edu/issue03/politics/a_palhiphop.php

Ewey, Melissa. "Lauryn Hill Smashes Records and Tells How Much Motherhood Changed Her Life." *Ebony* (November 1998), 202.

Gates, Henry Louis, Jr. *The Signifying Monkey: A Theory of African-American Literary Criticism*. New York: Oxford University Press, 1988.

Gottschild, Brenda Dixon. *Digging the Africanist Presence in American Performance: Dance and Other Contexts*. Westport, CT: Greenwood Press, 1996.

Griaule, Marcel. *Conversations With Ogotomeli: An Introduction to Dogon Religious Ideas*. London: Oxford University Press, 1970.

Gross, Joan, David McMurray, and Ted Swedenburg. "Arab Noise and Ramadan Nights: Rap, Rai, and Franco-Maghrebi Identities." In *Displacement, Diaspora, and Geographies of Identity*. Eds. Smadar Lavie and Ted Swedenburg, 119–55. Durham, NC: Duke University Press, 1996.

Himes, Chester. *Black on Black: Baby Sister and Selected Writings*. Garden City, NY: Doubleday, 1973.

Hynes, William. "Mapping the Characteristics of Mythic Tricksters: A Heuristic Guide." In *Mythical Trickster Figures: Contours, Contexts, and Criticisms*. Eds. William Hynes and William Doty. Tuscaloosa: University of Alabama Press, 1993, 33–45.

Iron Sheik (Will Youmans). Interview with author, January 29, 2008.

Jahn, Janheinz. *Muntu: The New African Culture*. New York: Grove Press, 1961.

Jamison, Laura. "Ladies First." In *The Vibe History of Hip Hop*. Ed. Alan Light. New York: Three Rivers Press, 1999, 177–86.

Kelley, Robin. *Yo' Mama's Disfunktional! Fighting the Culture Wars in Urban America*. Boston: Beacon Press, 1997.

Levine, Lawrence. *Black Culture and Black Consciousness: Afro-American Folk Thought From Slavery to Freedom*. New York: Oxford University Press, 1977.

Lipsitz, George. "We Know What Time It Is: Race, Class, and Youth Culture in the Nineties." In *Microphone Fiends: Youth Music, Youth Culture*, 17–28. New York: Routledge, 1994.

Maira, Sunaina, and Magid Shihade. "Hip-Hop from '48 Palestine: Youth, Music, and the Present/Absent." *Social Text*, (112) 30.3 (2012): 1–26.

Massad, Joseph. "Liberating Songs: Palestine Put to Music." In *Palestine, Israel, and the Politics of Popular Culture*. Eds. Rebecca Stein and Ted Swedenburg, 175–201. Durham, NC: Duke University Press, 2005.

Morgan, Joan. *When Chickenheads Come Home to Roost: My Life as a Hip-Hop Feminist*. New York: Simon and Schuster, 1999.

Perry, Imani. *Prophets of the Hood: Politics and Poetics of Hip-Hop*. Durham, NC: Duke University Press, 2004.

Porter, Russell. *Spectacular Vernaculars: Hip-Hop and the Politics of Postmodernism*. Albany, NY: State University of New York Press, 1995.

Rose, Tricia. *Black Noise: Rap Music and Black Culture in Contemporary America*. Hanover, NH: Wesleyan University Press of New England, 1994.

Rose, Tricia. "Never Trust a Big Butt and a Smile." In *Black Feminist Cultural Criticism*. Ed. Jacqueline Bobo. Malden, MA: Blackwell, 2001, 233–55.

Sultany, Nimer. *Citizens Without Citizenship: Israel and the Palestinian Minority 2000–2002*. Haifa, Israel: Mada-Arab Center For Applied Social Research, 2003.

Thompson, Robert Farris. *Flash of the Spirit: African and Afro-American Art and Philosophy*. New York: Vintage Books, 1984.

West, Cornel. "Black Sexuality: The Taboo Subject." In *Traps: African American Men on Gender and Sexuality*. Eds. Rudolph P. Byrd and Beverly Guy-Sheftall. Bloomington: Indiana University Press, 2001, 301–307.

Youmans, Will. "Arab American Hip-Hop." In *Etching Our Own Image: Voices From Within the Arab American Art Movement*. Eds. Anan Ameri and Holly Arida, 42–58. Newcastle, UK: Cambridge Scholars, 2007.

Section 11: Further Reading

Allen, Harry. "The Unbearable Whiteness of Emceeing: What the Eminence of Eminem Says about Race." *The Source* (February 2003), 91–92.

Ani, Marimba. *Yurugu: An African-Centered Critique of European Cultural Thought and Behavior*. Trenton, NJ: Africa World Press, 1994.

Ball, Jared A. "I Mix What I Like!: In Defense and Appreciation of the Rap Music Mixtape as 'National' and 'Dissident' Communication." *International Journal of Communication* 5 (2011): 278–97.

Brewster, Bill and Broughton, Frank. "Hip-Hop & Hip Hop 2." In *Last Night a DJ Saved My Life: The History of the Disc Jockey*. New York: Grove Press, 2000, 165–265.

Calderon, Tego. "Black Pride." February 15, 2007. Web. www.nypost.com/p/lifestyle/tempo/item_A0DRdN 2NxyDhJsGjzGqzVL;jsessionid=12D5E 06321822E5B2A3B1B42B0915697

E-PROPS. "The Myth of Reggaeton. Online at Davey D's Political Palace." 2005. Web. www.daveyd.com (http://p076.ezboard.com/fpoliticalpalacefrm57.showMessage?topicID=349.topic)

Fricke, Jim and Ahearn, Charlie. (eds.). *Yes, Yes, Y'all: The Experience Music Project Oral History of Hip-Hop's First Decade*. New York: Da Capo Press, 2002.

Giovanni, Nikki. "Shoulders Are for Emergencies Only." In *Quilting the Black-Eyed Pea: Poems and Not Quite Poems*. New York: Harper Perennial, 2011, 15.

KRS-One. Nostra Lingua." In *Ruminations*. New York: Welcome Rain, 2003, 89–95.

Marshall, Wayne. "From Musica Negra to Reggaeton Latino: Migration and the Mainstream." In *Reggaeton*. Eds. Racquel Z. Rivera and Wayne Marshall. Durham, NC: Duke University Press, 2009, 55–58.

Oa Magogodi, Kgafela. "I Mike What I Like." In *Outspoken*. Johannesburg: Laugh It Off Media, 2004, 1–3.

Perkins, William Eric (ed.). *Droppin' Science: Critical Essays on Rap Music and Hip Hop Culture*. Philadelphia: Temple University Press, 1996.

Schloss, Joseph. *Making Beats: The Art of Sample-Based Hip-Hop*. Middletown, CT: Wesleyan University Press, 2004.

Senghor, Fatou Kande (ed.). *Wala Bok: L'Histoire Orale de Hip Hop au Sénégal*. Dakar: Amalion, 2015.

Section 11: Discussion Questions

1. How is the Dogon or traditional African concept of *Nommo* at work in the lyricism of hip-hop emcees?

2. Why is it important for anti-rap establishments to represent all elements of hip-hop as devoid of meaning, or incapable of meaning-making, despite every indication to the contrary?

3. What kinds of things does hip-hop dance say, and how?

4. How can the function of the "rhetor" or the dreaded "Sophist" in academic discourse on ancient Greek rhetoric in the West be recast in terms of the "rapper" today, without Aryanism or Occidentalism framing our interpretations?

5. How does rap, graffiti art, and/or deejaying, as well as sampling in hip-hop, compel us to rethink academic studies of composition?

6. What happens to the canonical definition of who or what is "articulate" as hip-hop artists of all kinds disrupt the canonical Western bourgeois (or White middle-class) conception of "articulate," or "articulation," in various ways?

7. Why might some envision hip-hop as a new political-rhetorical discourse of Pan-Africanism and the "new humanism" once championed by classical anti-colonialists of old, such as Frantz Fanon in *The Wretched of the Earth*?

8. How is it useful to think of hip-hop as a "meta-language", if not an "anti-language" itself, given the internationalism and multilingualism of Hip-Hop as a worldwide phenomenon?

12

BLACK ARTS: BLACK ARGUMENT

Edited and with an introduction by
Michelle Bachelor Robinson

As we attempt to capture [African American Performance] through definitions, dialogues, or performative writing, we discover two important truths: that black sensibilities emerge whether there are black bodies present or not; and that while black performance may certainly become manifest without black people, we might best recognize it as a circumstance enabled by black sensibilities, black expressive practices, and black people.
—Thomas F. DeFrantz and Anita Gonzalez (Introduction to
Black Performance Theory, p. 1)

African American people have historically expressed themselves artistically, and those artistic expressions have functioned rhetorically since they chanted and danced on slave ships to signal uprisings. Artistic expressions have provided a medium through which we can express pain and suffering in the early years of chattel slavery and advocate for change during Jim Crow, but mostly artistic expression has functioned as a balm for African American people, always providing ways to shape and mode a diasporic culture in a hostile environment. This section compiles writings of African American artists who have used a variety of modes of expression to make meaning and make argument, and some of the selections have been chosen specifically because an artist articulates the rhetorical work of their art.

As early as the eighteenth century, African Americans in chattel slavery were writing poetry and novels (Hammon, Wheatley, Wilson), but equally if not more importantly, they were doing the work of author and critic. Phillis Wheatley writes a poem to Scipio Moorehead (S.M.) to offer a critique and praise of his painting. In Harriet Wilson's preface to *Our Nig* and in countless renderings of slave narratives and biographies, African Americans contextualize their lives and work for mainstream audiences. The historical work of African Americans is frequently credited as artistic achievement both past and present, but the intellectual labor of critic and activist is more carefully assigned to well-known figures, like Douglass and Du Bois. This section is opening up the conversations about Black artistic expression with a focus on the contextual work that the artistic artifacts cultivate.

We frequently look at the work of Zora Neale Hurston for her anthropological excursions collecting folklore and her artistic genius in creating characters in her fiction that each and every one of us knows back home, but we rarely consider the work she has done in helping us to theorize and collectively understand Black expression. Likewise, we frequently consider the powerful political work that W.E.B. Du Bois has contributed to both African American literature and rhetoric in kind, but here we engage his pageantry and the rhetorical work of his artistry.

More than anything, this section gives space for artists to talk about Black artistic expression in epistemological and critical ways.

When we consider the ways that rhetoric is situated in artistic expression, it is often done in subversive ways. Think of hymns Harriet Tubman sang to signal would-be runaways of her presence and purpose. Think of all of the necessary rhetorical moves that African American abolitionists make when telling the tales of woe, assuring their audiences of the humility of their station in life and the limitations of their prose. This kind of craft is a display of rhetorical savvy and discursive genius, and these kinds of coded messages continue to permeate African American artistic expression to this day.

Phillis Wheatley

Phillis Wheatley (May 8, 1753–December 5, 1784) was born in West Africa, sold into slavery at age seven, and transported to North America. There, she was purchased by the Wheatley family of Boston. They taught her to read and write and consistently supported her poetry. In 1773, Wheatley was noted as the first Black poet to publish a book. *Poems on Various Subjects, Religious and Moral*, complete with thirty-nine poems, explored Christian and racial themes. Within this volume was Wheatley's critique and praise of artist Scipio Moorhead, whose art, a portrait of Wheatley, is included in the text. (Moorhead drew the portrait of Wheatley is included in the text. "To S. M., a Young African Painter, on Seeing His Work" reflects on the artistry of creation and viewing. Wheatley presents her perspective as a fellow artist and, to some degree, a critic. She paints a vivid picture of his efforts to capture her while reflecting on the pleasure she experiences as a member of his audience. Although the Wheatley family was supportive of Wheatley's artistic pursuits, after she was emancipated, after the death of her master, they did not necessarily support her. Soon after her emancipation, she married and attempted to have children; two of her children died as infants. In 1784, her husband was imprisoned for debt. As a result, Wheatley experienced extreme poverty and illness until her death. Her surviving infant son's death quickly followed hers.

To S. M. a Young African Painter, on Seeing His Works

Phillis Wheatley[1]

TO show the lab'ring bosom's deep intent,
And thought in living characters to paint,
When first thy pencil did those beauties give,
And breathing figures learnt from thee to live,
How did those prospects give my soul delight, 5
A new creation rushing on my sight?
Still, wond'rous youth! each noble path pursue,
On deathless glories fix thine ardent view:
Still may the painter's and the poet's fire
To aid thy pencil, and thy verse conspire! 10
And may the charms of each seraphic theme
Conduct thy footsteps to immortal fame!
High to the blissful wonders of the skies
Elate thy soul, and raise thy wishful eyes.
Thrice happy, when exalted to survey 15
That splendid city, crown'd with endless day,
Whose twice six gates on radiant hinges ring:
Celestial *Salem* blooms in endless spring.

Calm and serene thy moments glide along,
And may the muse inspire each future song!   *20*
Still, with the sweets of contemplation bless'd,
May peace with balmy wings your soul invest!
But when these shades of time are chas'd away,
And darkness ends in everlasting day,
On what seraphic pinions shall we move,   *25*
And view the landscapes in the realms above?
There shall thy tongue in heav'nly murmurs flow,
And there my muse with heav'nly transport glow:
No more to tell of *Damon's* tender sighs,
Or rising radiance of *Aurora's* eyes,   *30*
For nobler themes demand a nobler strain,
And purer language on th' ethereal plain.
Cease, gentle muse! the solemn gloom of night
Now seals the fair creation from my sight.

Note

1. Phillis Wheatley, "To S. M., a Young African Painter, on Seeing His Works" (1773).

Harriet E. Wilson

Our Nig: Sketches from the Life of a Free Black is an autobiographical novel by Harriet E. Wilson (March 15, 1825–June 28, 1900). The novel, published in 1859 and rediscovered in 1982 by Henry Louis Gates Jr., is considered the first novel published by an African American woman. In the novel's preface, Wilson alludes to the authenticity of the novel by acknowledging the limitations of her narrative, based on the omission of some facts and details of her life that she felt might "provoke shame" in her anti-slavery friends as well as her "inability to minister to the refined and cultivated." She asserts concerns for criticism of these authorial decisions, fearing that her writings would appear to "palliate" slavery in the South. Nevertheless, Wilson asks for support of the novel.

Excerpt from the preface of *Our Nig*

Harriet E. Wilson[1]

Preface

In offering to the public the following pages, the writer confesses her inability to minister to the refined and cultivated, the pleasure supplied by abler pens. It is not for such these crude narrations appear. Deserted by kindred, disabled by failing health, I am forced to some experiment which shall aid me in maintaining myself and child without extinguishing this feeble life. I would not from these motives even palliate slavery at the South, by disclosures of its appurtenances North. My mistress was wholly imbued with *southern* principles. I do not pretend to divulge every transaction in my own life, which the unprejudiced would declare unfavorable in comparison with treatment of legal bondmen; I have purposely omitted what would most provoke shame in our good anti-slavery friends at home.

My humble position and frank confession of errors will, I hope, shield me from severe criticism. Indeed, defects are so apparent it requires no skilful hand to expose them.

I sincerely appeal to my colored brethren universally for patronage, hoping they will not condemn this attempt of their sister to be erudite, but rally around me a faithful band of supporters and defenders.

H. E. W.

Note

1. Excerpt from Harriet E. Wilson, "Preface," in *Our Nig* (1859).

W.E.B. Du Bois

W.E.B. Du Bois was born in Great Barrington, Massachusetts, on February 23, 1868. Although Du Bois grew up in a seemingly integrated community, he was no stranger to social differences within American culture. Du Bois was the first African American to earn a doctorate from Harvard University, and he devoted his life's work to matters of social, historical, and civil rights equality. Among his many accomplishments, Du Bois was one of the cofounders of the National Association for the Advancement of Colored People (NAACP), an organization that is well-known for its commitments to social justice and racial equality for black and brown people across the globe. As an author and editor, Du Bois became well known as the founder of the official magazine of the NAACP, *The Crisis*. After experiencing issues with the United States Passport Office, DuBois was not allowed to return to the United States after a visit to Accra, Ghana. He continued to work in Accra until his death on August 27, 1963. *The Star of Ethiopia* is an American historical pageant written by W.E.B. Du Bois in 1911. The pageant genre aimed to highlight and outline American history. Du Bois was particularly attached to the educational value that the pageant embodied. He felt the pageant could be used as an instructional tool, which educated African Americans about their history and that enlightened Whites. The pageant, complete with a prologue and five scenes (The Gift of Iron, The Dream of Egypt, The Glory of Ethiopia, The Valley of Humiliation, and The Vision Everlasting), was performed a total of four times in New York (1913), Washington, DC (1915), Philadelphia (1916), and Los Angeles (1925). Though intended to empower the education of African Americans, the pageant movement was not as successful as Du Bois imagined. In a 1916 issue of *The Crisis* magazine, Du Bois wrote, "The white public has shown little or no interest in the movement. The American Pageant Association has been silent [and] within my own race the usual petty but hurting insinuations of personal greed and selfishness" caused him a great deal of disappointment.

The National Emancipation Exposition

W.E.B. Du Bois[1]

IN NEW YORK CITY, OCTOBER 22–31, 1913

> *THE pageant of Negro history as written by W. E. B. Du Bois and produced by Charles Burroughs, Master; Daisy Tapley, Dora Cole Norman, Marie Stuart Jackson, Augustus G. Dill and 350 others, during the exhibition, and entitled "The People of Peoples and Their Gifts to Men." This pageant would later come to be titled "The Star of Ethiopia."*

Prelude

The lights of the Court of Freedom blaze. A trumpet blast is heard and four heralds, black and of gigantic stature, appear with silver trumpets and standing at the four corners of the temple of beauty cry:

"Hear ye, hear ye! Men of all the Americas, and listen to the tale of the eldest and strongest of the races of mankind, whose faces be black. Hear ye, hear ye, of the gifts of black men to this world, the Iron Gift and Gift of Faith, the Pain of Humility and the Sorrow Song of Pain, the Gift of Freedom and of Laughter, and the undying Gift of Hope. Men of the world, keep silence and hear ye this!"

Four banner bearers come forward and stand along the four walls of the temple. On their banners is written:

"The First Gift of the Negro to the world, being the Gift of Iron. This picture shall tell how, in the deep and beast-bred forests of Africa, mankind first learned the welding of iron, and thus defense against the living and the dead."

What the banners tell the heralds solemnly proclaim.
Whereat comes the

FIRST EPISODE. THE GIFT OF IRON

The lights grow dim. The roar of beasts is heard and the crash of the storm. Lightnings flash. The dark figure of an African savage hurries across the foreground, frightened and cowering and dancing. Another follows defying the lightning and is struck down; others come until the space is filled with 100 huddling, crowding savages. Some brave the storm, some pray their Gods with incantation and imploring dance. Mothers shield their children, and husbands their wives. At last, dimly enhaloed in mysterious light, the Veiled Woman appears, commanding in stature and splendid in garment, her dark face faintly visible, and in her right hand Fire, and Iron in her left. As she passes slowly round the Court the rythmic roll of tomtoms begins. Then music is heard; anvils ring at the four corners. The arts flourish, huts arise, beasts are brought in and there is joy, feasting and dancing.
A trumpet blast calls silence and the heralds proclaim

THE SECOND EPISODE, SAYING

"Hear ye, hear ye! All them that come to know the Truth, and listen to the tale of the wisest and gentlest of the races of men whose faces be black. Hear ye, hear ye, of the Second Gift of black men to this world, the Gift of Civilization in the dark and splendid valley of the Nile. Men of the world, keep silence and hear ye this." The banners of the banner bearers change and read:

"The Second Gift of the Negro to the world, being the Gift of the Nile. This picture tells how the meeting of Negro and Semite in ancient days made the civilization of Egypt the first in the world."

There comes a strain of mighty music, dim in the distance and drawing nearer. The 100 savages thronged round the whole Court rise and stand listening. Slowly there come fifty veiled figures and with them come the Sphinx, Pyramid, the Obelisk and the empty Throne of the Pharaoh drawn by oxen. As the cavalcade passes, the savages, wondering, threatening, inquiring, file by it. Suddenly a black chieftain appears in the entrance, with the Uraeus in one hand and the winged Beetle in the other. The Egyptians unveil and display Negroes and mulattoes clothed in the splendor of the Egyptian Court. The savages salaam; all greet him as Ra, the Negro. He mounts the throne and the cavalcade, led by posturing dancers and Ra, and followed by Egyptians and savages, pass in procession around to the right to the thunder of music and tomtoms. As they pass, Ra is crowned as Priest and King. While the Queen of Sheba and Candace of Ethiopia join the procession at intervals.

Slowly all pass out save fifty savages, who linger examining their gifts. The lights grow dim as Egyptian culture dies and the fifty savages compose themselves to sleep. As they sleep the light returns and the heralds proclaim

THE THIRD EPISODE, SAYING

"Hear ye, hear ye! All them that come to see the light and listen to the tale of the bravest and truest of the races of men, whose faces be black. Hear ye, hear ye, of the Third Gift of black men to this world—a Gift of Faith in Righteousness hoped for but unknown; men of the world, keep silence and hear ye this!" The banners change and read:

"The Third Gift of the Negro to the world, being a Gift of Faith. This episode tells how the Negro race spread the faith of Mohammed over half the world and built a new culture thereon."

There is a sound of battle. The savages leap to their feet. Mohammed and fifty followers whirl in and rushing to the right beat the savages back. Fifty Songhay enter and attack the Moham-medans. Fifty other Mohammedans enter and attack the Songhay. Turning, the Songhay bear the last group of Mohammedans back to the left where they clash with the savages. Moham-medan priests strive and exhort among the warriors. At each of the four corners of the temple a priest falls on his face and cries: "God is God! God is God! There is no God but God, and Mohammed is his prophet!" Four more join, others join until gradually all is changed from battle to the one universal cry: "God is God! God is God! There is no God but God, and Mohammed is his prophet!" In each corner, however, some Mohammedans hold slaves in shackles, secretly.

Mansa Musa appears at the entrance with entourage on horseback, followed by black Mohammedan priests and scholars. The procession passes around to the right with music and dancing, and passes out with Mohammedans and Songhay, leaving some Mohammedans and their slaves on the stage.

The herald proclaims

THE FOURTH EPISODE, SAYING

"Hear ye, hear ye! All them that know the sorrow of the world. Hear ye, hear ye, and listen to the tale of the humblest and the mightiest of the races of men whose faces be black. Hear ye, hear ye, and learn how this race did suffer of Pain, of Death and Slavery and yet of this Humiliation did not die. Men of the world, keep silence and hear ye this!" The banners change again and say:

"The Fourth Gift of the Negro to the world, being a Gift of Humiliation. This gift shows how men can bear even the Hell of Christian slavery and live."

The Mohammedans force their slaves forward as European traders enter. Other Negroes, with captives, enter. The Mohammedans take gold in barter. The Negroes refuse gold, but are seduced by beads and drink. Chains rattle. Christian missionaries enter, but the slave trade increases. The wail of the missionary grows fainter and fainter until all is a scene of carnage and captivity with whip and chain and only a frantic priest, staggering beneath a cross and crowned with bloody thorns, wanders to and fro in dumb despair.

There is silence. Then a confused moaning. Out of the moaning comes the slave song, "Nobody Knows the Trouble I've Seen," and with it and through the chained and bowed forms of the slaves as they pass out is done the Dance of Death and Pain.

The stage is cleared of all its folk. There is a pause, in which comes the Dance of the Ocean, showing the transplantation of the Negro race over seas.

Then the heralds proclaim

THE FIFTH EPISODE, SAYING

"Hear ye, hear ye! All them that strive and struggle. Hear ye, hear ye, and listen to the tale of the stoutest and the sturdiest of the races of men whose faces be black. Hear ye, hear ye, and learn how this race did rise out of slavery and the valley of the shadow of death. Men of the world, keep silence and hear ye this!" The banners change again and read:

> "The Fifth Gift of the Negro to the world, being a Gift of Struggle Toward Freedom. This picture tells of Alonzo, the Negro pilot of Columbus, of Stephen Dorantes who discovered New Mexico, of the brave Maroons and valiant Haytians, of Crispus Attucks, George Lisle and Nat Turner."

Twenty-five Indians enter, circling the Court right and left, stealthily and watchfully. As they sense the coming of the whites, they gather one side of the temple, watching.

Alonzo, the Negro, enters and after him Columbus and Spaniards, in mail, and one monk. They halt the other side of the temple and look about searchingly, pointing at the Indians. Slaves follow. One of the slaves, Stephen Dorantes, and the monk seek the Indians. The monk is killed and Stephen returns, circling the Court, tells his tale and dies. The Spaniards march on the Indians. Their slaves—the Maroons—revolt and march to the left and meet the Indians on the opposite side. The French, some of the mulattoes and Negroes, enter with more slaves. They march after the Spanish. Their slaves, helped by mulattoes and Toussaint, revolt and start back. The French follow the Spaniards, but the returning Haytians meet oncoming British. The Haytians fight their way through and take their place next to the Maroons. Still more slaves and white Americans follow the British. The British and Americans dispute. Attucks leads the Americans and the British are put to flight. Spanish, French and British, separated by dancing Indians, file around the Court and out, while Maroons, Haytians and slaves file around in the opposite direction and meet the Americans. As they pass the French, by guile induce Toussaint to go with them. There is a period of hesitation. Some slaves are freed, some Haytians resist aggression. George Lisle, a freed Negro, preaches the true religion as the masters listen. Peace ensues and the slaves sing at their tasks. Suddenly King Cotton arrives, followed by Greed, Vice, Luxury and Cruelty. The slave-holders are seduced. The old whips and chains appear. Nat Turner rebels and is killed. The slaves drop into despair and work silently and sullenly. The faint roll of tomtoms is heard.

The heralds proclaim

THE SIXTH EPISODE, SAYING

"Hear ye, hear ye! Citizens of New York, and learn of the deeds of eldest and strongest of the races of men whose faces be black. Hear ye, hear ye, of the Sixth and Greatest Gift of black men to the world, the Gift of Freedom for the workers. Men of New York, keep silence and hear ye this." The banners change and say:

> "The sixth and last episode, showing how the freedom of black slaves meant freedom for the world. In this episode shall be seen the work of Garrison and John Brown; of Abraham

Lincoln and Frederick Douglass, the marching of black soldiers to war and the hope that lies in little children."

The slaves work more and more dejectedly and drivers force them. Slave music comes. The tom-toms grow louder. The Veiled Woman appears with fire and iron. The slaves arise and begin to escape, passing through each other to and fro, confusedly. Benezet, Walker and Garrison enter, scattering their writings, and pass slowly to the right, threatened by slave drivers. John Brown enters, gesticulating. A knot of Negroes follow him. The planters seize him and erect a gallows, but the slaves seize his body and begin singing "John Brown's Body."

Frederick Douglass enters and passes to the right. Sojourner Truth enters and passes to the left. Sojourner Truth cries: "Frederick, is God dead?" Voices take up the cry, repeating: "Frederick, is God dead?" Douglass answers: "No, and therefore slavery must end in blood." The heralds repeat: "Slavery must end in blood."

The roll of drums is heard and the soldiers enter. First, a company in blue with Colonel Shaw on horseback.

A single voice sings "O Freedom." A soprano chorus takes it up.

The Boy Scouts march in.

Full brasses take up "O Freedom."

Little children enter, and among them symbolic figures of the Laborer, the Artisan, the Servant of Men, the Merchant, the Inventor, the Musician, the Actor, the Teacher, Law, Medicine and Ministry, the All-Mother, formerly the Veiled Woman, now unveiled in her chariot with her dancing brood, and the bust of Lincoln at her side.

With burst of music and blast of trumpets, the pageant ends and the heralds sing:

"Hear ye, hear ye, men of all the Americas, ye who have listened to the tale of the eldest and strongest of the races of mankind, whose faces be black. Hear ye, hear ye, and forget not the gift of black men to this world—the Iron Gift and Gift of Faith, the Pain of Humility and Sorrow Song of Pain, the Gift of Freedom and Laughter and the undying Gift of Hope. Men of America, break silence, for the play is done."

Then shall the banners announce:

"The play is done!"

Harriet Powers Pictorial Quilt

David Driskell, excerpt from the Introduction in Black Art Ancestral Legacy: the African Impulse in African-American Art, 1989[2]

Harriet Powers (October 29, 1837–January 1, 1910) was born to slaves near Athens, Georgia. Powers spent her life as a folk artist, specializing in nineteenth-century Southern quilting. Using the traditional applique technique, Powers' quilts recorded astronomical events, Bible stories, and local legends. In 1886, Powers began exhibiting her quilts, the first of which was shown at the Cotton Fair in Athens. When asked to sell the quilt, Powers immediately refused. Five years later, however, after experiencing financial difficulties, she sold her first quilt to Jennie Smith. The quilt was sold for $5, which is equivalent to $132 at the time this book was published. According to Smith, Powers orally described each square of her quilt after the purchase. Smith then arranged for it to be exhibited at the Cotton States Exposition in Atlanta in 1895. The Pictorial Quilt (Figure 12.1) was commissioned by a group of women at Atlanta University.

The quilt, along with Powers' descriptions, was given as a gift to a retiring trustee. Of the many quilts she made, only two have survived: Bible Quilt 1886 on display at the National Museum of American History in Washington, DC and Pictorial Quilt 1898 on display at the Museum of Fine Arts in Boston, Massachusetts.

Figure 12.1 Harriet Powers Pictorial Quilt, on display at the Museum of Fine Arts in Boston, Massachusetts

Note

1. Du Bois, W.E.B. (William Edward Burghardt), 1868–1963. The Star of Ethiopia: A pageant, 1914. W.E.B. Du Bois Papers (MS 312). Special Collections and University Archives, University of Massachusetts Amherst Libraries.
2. Driskell, David. (1989). Introduction, in Robert V. Rozelle, Alvia J. Wardlaw, & Maureen A. McKenna (eds), *Black Art, Ancestral Legacy: The African Impulse in African-American Art*. Dallas: Dallas Museum of Art.

LeRoi Jones

Amiri Baraka was born Everett LeRoi Jones on October 7, 1934, in Newark, New Jersey. Throughout his life, Baraka made a career of writing and activism spanning nearly fifty years through his poetry, drama, fiction, essays, and music criticism. Baraka's work and contributions to literature were recognized by fellowships from the Guggenheim Foundation and the National Endowment for the Arts, an award from the Rockefeller Foundation, and induction into the American Academy of Arts and Letters. During the 1960s, Baraka became an influential force in the Black arts movement as he encouraged the creation, embrace, and circulation of Black art. In 1963, Baraka published *Blues People: Negro Music in White America* as LeRoi Jones. *Blues People* serves as a seminal text of African American music and culture that considers the option of African American history being traced through the evolution of African American music. By chronicling African American music from slavery through the 1960s, Jones argues that "negro music" appealed to and influenced new America. Baraka critically examines the commodification of music as an entrée to understanding music as both performance and cultural expression. As he reflected on journey of Africans to America, Baraka notes that the blues were reflective of what Black people grew to be in America. Jones's personal connection to blues music and thoughts of that connection being extended to all African American people are personified through the timbre and desperation presented through blues music. These characteristics motivated Jones to study blues music and tie it to African American history. In 1999, "*Blues People*: Looking Both Ways," an essay authored by Baraka in a different work, revisits the influence of Africanisms on American culture rather than it being exclusively connected to African Americans. In this way, Baraka encourages the thought that the African presence and experience influenced all Americans, and such was the case for blues and jazz music. On January 9, 2014, Amiri Baraka died in Newark, New Jersey, after a lengthy battle with diabetes and complications following a recent surgery.

Introduction to Blues People

LeRoi Jones[1]

The Negro as slave is one thing. The Negro as American is quite another. But the *path* the slave took to "citizenship" is what I want to look at. And I make my analogy through the slave citizen's music—through the music that is most closely associated with him: blues and a later, but parallel development, jazz. And it seems to me that if the Negro represents, or is symbolic of, something in and about the nature of American culture, this certainly should be revealed by his characteristic music.

In other words, I am saying that if the music of the Negro in America, in all its permutations, is subjected to a socio-anthropological as well as musical scrutiny, something about the essential nature of the Negro's existence in this country ought to be revealed, as well as something about the essential nature of this country, *i.e.*, society as a whole.

Blues, had, and still has, a certain *weight* in the psyches of its inventors. What I am proposing is that the alteration or repositioning of this weight in those same psyches indicates changes in the Negro that are manifested externally. I am proposing that the weight of the blues for the slave, the completely disenfranchised individual, differs radically from the weight of that same music in the psyches of most contemporary American Negroes. I mean, we know certain definite things about the lives of the Negro slaves. We also, with even more certainty, know things about the lives of the contemporary American Negroes. The one peculiar referent to the drastic change in the Negro from slavery to "citizenship" is his music.

There are definite *stages* in the Negro's transmutation from African to American: or, at least, there are certain very apparent changes in the Negro's reactions to America from the time of his first importation as slave until the present that can, I think, be seen—and again, I insist that these changes are most graphic in his music. I have tried to scrutinize each one of these stages as closely as I could, with a musical as well as a sociological and anthropological emphasis.

If we take 1619, twelve years after the settling of Jamestown in 1607, as the date of the first importation of Negroes into this country to *stay* (not to be merely brought here for a time to do odd jobs, etc., and then be bumped off, as was very often the case), we have a good point in history to move from. First, we know that West Africans, who are the peoples most modern scholarship has cited as contributing almost 85 per cent of the slaves finally brought to the United States, did not sing blues. Undoubtedly, none of the African prisoners broke out into *St. James Infirmary* the minute the first of them was herded off the ship. We also know that the first African slaves, when they worked in those fields, if they sang or shouted at all, sang or shouted in some pure African dialect (either from the parent Bantu or Sudanic, with maybe even the Hamitic as a subbase, which would include Coptic, Berber, or Cushitic). But there are no records of 12-bar, AAB songs in those languages—at least none that would show a direct interest in social and agricultural problems in the Southern U.S. (although, it should be noted here, and I will go into it further in the chapter on Africanisms, the most salient characteristic of African, or at least West African, music is a type of song in which there is a leader and a chorus; the leading lines of the song sung by a single voice, the leader's, alternating with a refrain sung by the "chorus." It is easy enough to see the definite analogy between a kind of song in which there is a simple A-B response and a kind of song that could be developed out of it to be sung by one person, where the first line of the song is repeated twice (leader), followed by a third line (chorus), sometimes rhymed but usually dissimilar, and always a direct comment on the first two lines. And then we know of the patoistype languages and the other half-African languages that sprang up throughout the South, which must, after a time, have been what those various laments, chants, stories, etc., were told and sung in.

But what I am most anxious about here is the American Negro. When did he emerge? Out of what strange incunabula did the peculiar heritage and attitudes of the American Negro arise? I suppose it is technically correct to call any African who was brought here and had no chance of ever leaving, from that very minute when his residence and his life had been changed irrevocably, an American Negro. But it is imperative that we realize that the first slaves did not believe they would be here forever. Or even if they did, they thought of themselves as merely *captives*. This, America, was a foreign land. These people were foreigners, they spoke in a language which was not colonial American; and the only Western customs or mores of which they had any idea at all were that every morning at a certain time certain work had to be done and that they would probably be asked to do it.

And the point I want to make most evident here is that I cite the beginning of blues as one beginning of American Negroes. Or, let me say, the reaction and subsequent relation of the Negro's experience in this country in *his* English is one beginning of the Negro's *conscious* appearance on the American scene. If you are taken to Mongolia as a slave and work there seventy-five years and learn twenty words of Mongolian and live in a small house from which you leave only to work, I don't think we can call you a Mongolian. It is only when you begin to accept the idea that you *are* part of that country that you can be said to be a permanent resident. I mean, that until the time when you have sufficient ideas about this new country to begin making some lasting *moral* generalizations about it—relating your experience, in some lasting form, *in the language* of that country, with whatever subtleties and obliqueness you bring to it—you are merely a transient. There were no formal stories about the Negro's existence in America passed down in any pure African tongue. The stories, myths, moral examples, etc., given in African were *about* Africa. When America became important enough to the African to be passed on, in those *formal* renditions, to the young, those renditions were in some kind of Afro-American language.

And finally, when a man looked up in some anonymous field and shouted, "Oh, Ahm tired a dis mess,/Oh, yes, Ahm so tired a dis mess," you can be sure he was an American.

Afro-Christian Music and Religion

When the first slaves were brought to this country, there was no idea at all of converting them. Africans were thought of as beasts, and there was certainly no idea held among the whites that, somehow, these beasts would benefit by exposure to the Christian God. As late as the twentieth century there have been books "proving" the Negro's close relationship to lower animals that have been immensely popular in the South. The idea that perhaps slavery could be condoned as a method for converting heathens to the Christian God did not become popular until the latter part of the eighteenth century, and then only among a few "radical" Northern missionaries. There could be no soul-saving activities, N. N. Puckett points out in his book Folk Beliefs of the Southern Negro, where there was no soul.

But still Christianity was adopted by Negroes before the great attempts by missionaries and evangelists in the early part of the nineteenth century to convert them. The reasons for this grasping of the white man's religion by the North American Negro are fairly simple. First, his own religion was prohibited in this country. In some parts of the South, "conjuring" or use of "hoodoo" or "devil talk" was punishable by death or, at the very least, whipping. Also, the African has always had a traditional respect for his conqueror's gods. Not that they are always worshiped, but they are at least recognized as powerful and placed in the hierarchy of the conquered tribe's gods.

The growing "social awareness" of the slave can be mentioned as another reason for the African's swift embrace of the white man's God: social awareness in the sense that the African, or at least his progeny, soon realized that he was living in a white man's world. Not only was it an ancient African belief that the stronger tribe's gods were to be revered, but the African was also forced to realize that all the things he thought important were thought by the white man to be primitive nonsense. The constant contact between black and white in the United States must have produced in the black man a profound anxiety regarding the reasons for his status and the reasons for the white man's dominance. The African's belief in "stronger gods" assuaged or explained slavery for the African slave and was, perhaps, a partial explanation for his rapid adoption of pre-missionary Christianity. But for the American slave, Christianity was attractive simply because it was something the white man did that the black man could do also, and in the time of the missionaries, was encouraged to do. The house Negroes, who spent their lives finding new facets of the white culture that they could imitate, were the first to adopt Christianity. And they and their descendants, even today, practice the most European or American forms of Christianity. The various black Episcopal and Presbyterian churches of the North were invariably started by the black freedmen, who were usually the sons and daughters of "house niggers." The strange "melting pot" of the United States, where after a few decades the new African slaves were ridiculed by their "American" brothers because they were African! And this was for purely "social" reasons. That is, the slaves who had come to America only a few years earlier began to apply what they thought were the white man's standards to their own behavior as well as to that of their newly arrived brothers.

Sinner, what you gonna do When de World's on fi-er? Sinner, what you gonna do When de world's on fi-er? Sinner, what you gonna do When de world's on fi-er? O my Lawd.

Because the African came from an intensely religious culture, a society where religion was a daily, minute-to-minute concern, and not something relegated to a specious once-a-week reaffirmation, he had to find other methods of worshiping gods when his white captors declared that he could no longer worship in the old ways. (The first slaves thought of the white men as captors; it was later, after they had become Americans, that they began to think of these captors as masters and themselves as slaves, rather than captives.) The immediate reaction, of course, was to try to worship in secret. The more impressive rites had to be discarded unless they could be performed clandestinely; the daily rituals, however, continued. The common day-to-day stance of the African toward his gods could not be erased overnight. In fact, many of the "superstitions" of the Negroes that the whites thought "charming" were holdovers from African religions. Even today in many Southern rural areas, strange mixtures of voodoo, or other primarily African fetish religions, and Christianity exist. Among less educated, or less sophisticated, Negroes the particular significance of dreams, luck and lucky charms, roots and herbs, is directly attributable to African religious beliefs. Also, many aphorisms used by Negroes in strictly social situations spring from African religion.

For example, there was recently a rhythm & blues song that talked of "Spreading goober dust all around your bed/When you wake up you find your own self dead." To most whites (and indeed to most modern sophisticated city Negroes) the song was probably catchy but essentially unintelligible. But now in 1963, one hundred years after the Emancipation of slaves, there exists a song integrated somewhat into the mainstream of American society that refers directly to an African religious belief. (A goober is what a peanut is called by many Southern Negroes. The word itself comes from the African word gooba, which is a kind of African nut. In Africa the ground-up gooba was used to conjure with, and was thought to give one person power over another if the ground gooba ("goober dust") was spread around the victim's hut. In the South, peanut shells spread in front of someone's door supposedly cause something terrible to happen to him.)

"Never go to bed on an empty stomach," my grandmother has told me all my life. Perhaps the origins of this seemingly health-conscious aphorism have been forgotten even by her. But the Africans believed that evil spirits could steal your soul while you slept if your body was empty. "If the sun is shining and it is raining at the same time, the devil's beating his wife." "Sweeping out the house after dark is disrespectful." Both these aphorisms I heard when I was younger, and they are both essentially African. The latter refers to the African's practice of praying each night for the gods to protect him while he slept from evil spirits; it was thought that the benevolent gods would actually descend and sit in one's house. Sweeping at night, one might sweep the guardian out since he was invisible. The "gods" of the African eventually became "The Holy Ghos" of the American Negro.

And so to "outlaw" the African slave's religion completely was impossible, although the circumstance of slavery did relegate religious practice to a much smaller area of his life. But the African could not function as a human being without religion; he daily invoked the "conjure men," herb doctors and root healers, cult priests and sorcerers - the mystical forces he thought controlled the world. The sorcerer was consulted each day to find out the disposition of the gods toward a man and his activities, just as we dial our phones for the weather report.

The first attempts by Negroes to openly embrace the white Christ were rebuffed, sometimes cruelly, because of the Christian theologians' belief that Africans were beasts, literally, lower animals. "You would not give oxen the holy scripture." Also, on a slightly more humane level, it was thought by white Christians that if the Africans were given Christianity, there could be no real justification for enslaving them, since they would no longer be heathens or savages. In spite of this, the slaves did go off into the woods to hold some semblance of a Christian rite when they could. By the beginning of the nineteenth century, however, against the wishes of most of the planters and slave owners, attempts were made to convert the slaves because of the protests of the Quakers and other religious groups.

Fannie Kemble, in her journal of 1838 and 1839, reported: "You have heard, of course, many and contradictory statements as to the degree of religious instruction afforded to the Negroes of the South, and their opportunities of worship, etc. Until the late abolition movement, the spiritual interests of the slaves were about as little regarded as their physical necessities. The outcry which has been raised with threefold force within the last few years against the whole system has induced its upholders and defenders to adopt, as measures of personal extenuation, some appearance of religious instruction (such as it is), and some pretense at physical indulgences (such as they are), bestowed apparently voluntarily upon their dependents. At Darien a church is appropriated to the especial use of the slaves, who are almost all of them Baptists here; and a gentleman officiates it (of course, white) who, I understand, is very zealous in the cause of the spiritual well-being. He, like most Southern men, clergy or others, jump the present life in their charities to the slaves, and go on to furnish them with all requisite conveniences for the next." She added:

> Some of the planters are entirely inimical to any such proceedings and neither allow their Negroes to attend worship, or to congregate together for religious purposes. . . . On other plantations, again, the same rigid discipline is not observed; and some planters and overseers go even farther than toleration, and encourage these devotional exercises and professions of religion, having actually discovered that a man may become more faithful and trustworthy, even as a slave, who acknowledges the higher influences of Christianity.

The ambivalent attitude of the slave-holders toward the conversion of the slaves to Christianity is further illustrated by another of Miss Kemble's observations: ". . . this man is known to be a hard master; his Negro houses are sheds not fit to stable beasts in; his slaves are ragged, half-naked, and miserable; yet he is urgent for their religious comforts, and writes to Mr. Butler about 'their souls - their precious souls.'"

The Quakers and other religious groups began to realize that the only justification for slavery was that the slaves could be converted to Christianity, and the great missionary and evangelical movements of the nineteenth century began. Some of the churches, such as the Methodist and Baptist, began to send ministers among the slaves to convert them. Soon the grossest disparagement the "religious" Negro could make of another was that he or she was "a heathen." (When I spilled food on the table or otherwise acted with boyish slovenliness, my grandmother would always think to dress me down by calling me "a heathen.")

The emotionalism and evangelism of the Methodists and Baptists appealed much more to the slaves than any of the other denominations. Also, the Baptists, especially, allowed the Negroes to participate in the services a great deal and began early to "appoint" black ministers or deacons to conduct the services while the missionaries themselves went on to other plantations. And on the poorer plantation the lower-class white was more apt to be Baptist or Methodist than Episcopal or Presbyterian. Another, possibly more important, reason why the Negroes were drawn to the Baptist Church was the method of conversion. Total immersion in water, which is the way Baptists symbolize their conversion to the "true church" and the teachings of Christ, in imitation of Christ's immersion by Saint John "The Baptist," was perhaps particularly attractive to the early slaves because in most of the religions of West Africa the river spirits were thought to be among the most powerful of the deities, and the priests of the river cults were among the most powerful and influential men in African society.

The Christian slave became more of an American slave, or at least a more "Westernized" slave, than the one who tried to keep his older African traditions. The slave masters also learned early that the Africans who had begun to accept the Christian ethic or even some crude part of its dogma were less likely to run away or start rebellions or uprisings. Christianity, as it was first given to the slaves (as Miss Kemble pointed out), was to be used strictly as a code of conduct which would enable its devotees to participate in an afterlife; it was from its very inception among the black slaves, a slave ethic. It acted as a great pacifier and palliative, although it also produced a great inner strength among the devout and an almost inhuman indifference to pain. Christianity was to prepare the black man for his Maker, and the anthropomorphic "heben" where all his "sins and suffering would be washed away." One of the very reasons Christianity proved so popular was that it was the religion, according to older Biblical tradition, of an oppressed people. The struggles of the Jews and their long-sought "Promised Land" proved a strong analogy for the black slaves:

> Mary, don't you weep an' Marthie don't you moan, Mary, don't you weep an' Marthie don't you moan; Pharaoh's army got drown-ded, Oh Mary don't you weep. I thinks every day an' I wish I could Stan' on de rock whar Mose stood Oh, Pharaoh's army got drown-ded, Oh Mary don't you weep.

The Christianity of the slave represented a movement away from Africa. It was the beginning of Africa as "a foreign place." In the early days of slavery, Christianity's sole purpose was to propose a metaphysical resolution for the slave's natural yearnings for freedom, and as such, it literally made life easier for him. The secret African chants and songs were about Africa, and expressed the African slave's desire to return to the land of his birth. The Christian Negro's music became an expression of his desire to "cross Jordan" and "see his Lord." He no longer wished to return to Africa. (And one can see, perhaps, how "perfect" Christianity was in that sense. It took the slave's mind off Africa, or material freedom, and proposed that if the black man wished to escape the filthy paternalism and cruelty of slavery, he wait, at least, until he died, when he could be transported peacefully and majestically to the Promised Land.)

> Gonna shout trouble over When I get home, Gonna shout trouble over When I get home.

> No mo' prayin', no mo' dyin' When I get home. No mo' prayin' an' no mo' dyin' When I get home. Meet my father When I get home. Meet my father When I get home.

The religious imagery of the Negro's Christianity is full of references to the suffering and hopes of the oppressed Jews of Biblical times. Many of the Negro spirituals reflect this identification: Go Down, Moses, I'm Marching to Zion, Walk Into Jerusalem Just Like John, etc. "Crossing the river Jordan" meant not only death but also the entrance into the very real heaven and a release from an earthly bondage; it came to represent all the slave's yearnings to be freed from the inhuman yoke of slavery. But at the time, at least for the early black Christian, this freedom was one that could only be reached through death. The later secular music protested conditions here, in America. No longer was the great majority of slaves concerned with leaving this country (except, perhaps, the old folks who sat around and, I suppose, remembered). This was their country, and they became interested in merely living in it a little better and a little longer.

The early black Christian churches or the pre-church "praise houses" became the social focal points of Negro life. The relative autonomy of the developing Negro Christian religious gathering made it one of the only areas in the slave's life where he was relatively free of the white man's domination. (Aside from the more formally religious activities of the fledgling Negro churches, they served as the only centers where the slave community could hold strictly social functions.) The "praise nights," or "prayer meetings," were also the only times when the Negro felt he could express himself as freely and emotionally as possible. It is here that music becomes indispensable to any discussion of Afro-Christian religion.

"The spirit will not descend without song." This is an old African dictum that very necessarily was incorporated into Afro-Christian worship. The Negro church, whether Christian or "heathen," has always been a "church of emotion." In Africa, ritual dances and songs were integral parts of African religious observances, and the emotional frenzies that were usually concomitant with any African religious practice have been pretty well documented, though, I would suppose, rarely understood. This heritage of emotional religion was one of the strongest contributions that the African culture made to the Afro-American. And, of course, the tedious, repressive yoke of slavery must well have served to give the black slave a huge reservoir of emotional energy which could be used up in his religion.

"Spirit possession," as it is called in the African religions, was also intrinsic to Afro-Christianity. "Gettin' the spirit," "gettin' religion" or "gettin' happy" were indispensable features of the early American Negro church and, even today, of the non-middle-class and rural Negro churches. And always music was an important part of the total emotional configuration of the Negro church, acting in most cases as the catalyst for those worshipers who would suddenly "feel the spirit." "The spirit will not descend without song."

The first Afro-Christian music differed from the earlier work songs and essentially nonreligious shouts first of all in its subject matter and content. Secondly, the religious music became much more melodic and musical than the field hollers because it was sung rather than grunted or "hollered." (Though no aspect of Negro song is completely without the shout, if later, only as an element of style.) Also, this religious music was drawn from many sources, and represented, in its most mature stage, an amalgam of forms, styles, and influences.

Christianity was a Western form, but the actual practice of it by the American Negro was totally strange to the West. The American Negro's religious music developed quite similarly, taking its superficial forms (and instrumentation, in many cases) from European or American models, but there the imitation ended. The lyrics, rhythms, and even the harmonies were essentially of African derivation, subjected, of course, to the transformations that American life had brought into existence. The Negro's religious music was his original creation, and the spirituals themselves were probably the first completely native American music the slaves made. When I refer to the Negro's religious music, however, I mean not only the spiritual, which is used, I am aware, as a general catchall for all the nonsecular music made by the American black man, but I am referring as well to the church marches, ring and shuffle shouts, "sankeys," chants, camp or meetin' songs, and hymns or "ballits," that the Afro-Christian church produced.

But even as the masses of Negroes began to enter the Christian Church and get rid of their "heathenisms," Africa and its religious and secular traditions could not be completely shaken off. In fact, as Borneman points out: "The Methodist revival movement began to address itself directly to the slaves, but ended up not by converting the Africans to a Christian ritual, but by converting itself to an African ritual."

The more conscientious Christian ministers among the slaves sought to get rid of "all dem hedun ways," but it was difficult. For instance, the Christian Church saw dancing as an evil worldly excess, but dancing as an integral part of the African's life could not be displaced by the still white notes of the Wesleyan Hymnal. The "ring shouts" or "shuffle shouts" of the early Negro churches were attempts by the black Christians to have their cake and eat it: to maintain African tradition, however veiled or unconscious the attempt might be, yet embrace the new religion. Since dancing was irreligious and sinful, the Negro said that only "crossing the feet" constituted actual dancing. So the ring shout developed where the worshipers link arms and shuffle, at first slowly but then with increasing emotional display, around in a circle, singing hymns or chanting as they move. This shuffle, besides getting around the dogma of the stricter "white folks" Christianity also seems derived from African religious dances of exactly the same nature. "Rocking Daniel" dances and the "Flower Dance" were among the dances that the black Christians allowed themselves to retain. The so-called "sanctified" Protestant churches still retain some of these "steps" and "moo-mens" today. And indeed, the "sanctified" churches always remained closer to the African traditions than any of the other Afro-Christian sects. They have always included drums and sometimes tambourines in their ceremonies, something none of the other sects ever dared do.

A description of a typical Afro-Christian church service is found in H. E. Krehbiel's book. Krehbiel had excerpted it from the May 30, 1867, issue of *The Nation*:

> ... the benches are pushed back to the wall when the formal meeting is over, and old and young, men and women, sprucely dressed young men, grotesquely half-clad field hands - the women generally with gay handkerchiefs twisted about their heads and with short skirts - boys with tattered shirts and men's trousers, young girls bare-footed, all stand up in the middle of the floor, and when the 'sperichil' is struck up begin first walking and by and by shuffling around, one after the other, in a ring. The foot is hardly taken from the floor, and the progression is mainly due to a jerking, hitching motion which agitates the entire shouter and soon brings out streams of perspiration. Sometimes they dance silently, sometimes as they shuffle they sing the chorus of the spiritual, and sometimes the song itself is also sung by the dancers. But more frequently a band, composed of some of the best singers and of tired shouters, stand at the side of the room to 'base' the others, singing the body of the song and clapping their hands together or on the knees. Song and dance are alike extreme energetic, and often, when the shout lasts into the middle of the night, the monotonous thud, thud of feet prevents sleep within half a mile of the praise house.

The music that was produced by Negro Christianity was the result of diverse influences. First of all, there was that music which issued from pure African ritual sources and which was changed to fit the new religion—just as the ring shouts were transformed from pure African religious dances to pseudo-Christian religious observance, or the Dahomey river cult ceremonies were incorporated into the baptism ceremony. Early observers also pointed out that a great many of the first Negro Christian religious songs had been taken almost untouched from the great body of African religious music. This was especially true of the melodies of certain black Christian spirituals that could also be heard in some parts of Africa.

Maude Cuney-Hare, in her early book Negro Musicians and Their Music, cites the experience of a Bishop Fisher of Calcutta who traveled to Central Africa: "... in Rhodesia he had heard natives sing a melody so closely resembling Swing Low, Sweet Chariot that he felt that he had found it in its original form: moreover, the region near the great Victoria Falls have a custom from which the song arose. When one of their chiefs, in the old days, was about to die, he was placed in a great canoe together with trappings that marked his rank, and food for his journey. The canoe was set afloat in midstream headed toward the great Falls and the vast column of mist that rises from them. Meanwhile the tribe on the shore would sing its chant of farewell. The legend is that on one occasion the king was seen to rise in his canoe at the very brink of the Falls and enter a chariot that, descending from the mists, bore him aloft. This incident gave rise to the words 'Swing Low, Sweet Chariot,' and the song, brought to America by African slaves long ago, became anglicized and modified by their Christian faith."

It would be quite simple for an African melody that was known traditionally to most of the slaves to be used as a Christian song. All that would have to be done was change the words (which is also the only basic difference between a great many of the "devil music" songs and the most devout of the Christian religious songs. Just as many high school students put their own words to the tune Yankee Doodle Dandy, for whatever purpose, the converted slave had only to alter his lyrics to make the song "Christian"). Of course, the point here is that the slave had to be able to change the words, that is, he had to know enough of the language in which the new religion was spoken so that he could make up lyrics in that language. Christian songs in African tongues are extremely rare, for obvious reasons. (What is the word for God in any of the African dialects? The answer would be: Which god?)

Almost all parts of the early Negro Christian church service had to do in some way with music, which was also true of the African religions. And not only were African songs trans-formed into a kind of completely personal Christian liturgical music but African prayers and chants as well. The black minister of an early Christian church (as well as the Negro ministers of today's less sophisticated black churches) himself contributed the most musical and most emotional parts of the church service. The long, long, fantastically rhythmical sermons of the early Negro Baptist and Methodist preachers are well known. These men were singers, and they sang the word of this new God with such passion and belief, as well as skill, that the congrega-tion had to be moved. The traditional African call-and-response song shaped the form this kind of worship took on. The minister would begin slowly and softly, then build his sermon to an unbelievable frenzy with the staccato punctuation of his congregation's answers. "Have you got good religion?/Certainly, Lord," is the way one spiritual goes, modeled on the call-and-response, preacher-to-congregation type of song. When the preacher and the congregation reach their peaks, their music rivals any of the more formal Afro-American musics in intensity and beauty.

> Oh, my Lawd, God, what happened when Adam took de apple? (Amen, Amen). Yas, didn't de Lawd tell dat po' foolish sinner not to listen to that spiteful wo-man? (Amen, Amen). Yas, Lawd, Did he tell him or no? (Amen, Amen, Yas he told him, brother). And what did Adam do, huh? Yas, Lawd, after you told him not to, what did he do? (Amen, Amen, brother, preach, preach).

Another kind of song that the Negro church produced in America was one based on European or American religious (and sometimes secular) songs. In these songs the words often remained the same (with, of course, the natural variances of Negro speech). For instance, Puckett seemed puzzled by the use of the word fellom-city in Negro spirituals. The word, most old Negroes say, means some kind of peace, so I would think the word to be felicity. The melodies of many of the white Christian and European religious songs which the Negroes incorporated into their wor-ship remained the same, but the Negroes changed the rhythms and harmonies of these songs to suit themselves. The very fact that the Negroes sang these songs in their peculiar way, with not only the idiosyncratic American idiom of early Negro speech but the inflection, rhythm, and stress of that speech, also served to shape the borrowed songs to a strictly Negro idiom.

And usually, no matter how closely a Negro spiritual might resemble superficially one of the white hymns taken from sources like the Bay Psalm Book, the Wesleyan Hymnal, the Anglican Hymnal, or the Moody Hymnal, when the song was actually sung, there could be no mistake that it had been made over into an original Negro song. A very popular white Christian hymn like Climb Jacob's Ladder is completely changed when sung in the Negro church as Climin' Jacob's Ladda. Jesus, Lover of my Soul, a song out of the Sankey Hymnal, is changed by the Shouting Baptists of Trinidad into an unmistakably African song. And, as Herskovits noted, in a great many parts of the West Indies, all the Protestant pseudo-Christian religious songs are called "sankeys."

Rhythmic syncopation, polyphony, and shifted accents, as well as the altered timbral quali-ties and diverse vibrato effects of African music were all used by the Negro to transform most of the "white hymns" into Negro spirituals. The pentatonic scale of the white hymn underwent the same "aberrations" by which the early musicologists characterized African music. The same chords and notes in the scale would be flattened or diminished. And the meeting of the two

804 • THE NEW BLACKNESS

different musics, the white Christian hymn and the Negro spiritual using that hymn as its point of departure, also produced certain elements that were later used in completely secular music. The first instrumental voicings of New Orleans jazz seem to have come from the arrangement of the singing voices in the early Negro churches, as well as the models for the "riffs" and "breaks" of later jazz music. The Negro's religious music contained the same "rags," "blue notes" and "stop times" as were emphasized later and to a much greater extent in jazz.

Note

1. LeRoi Jones, *Blues People: Negro Music in White America and the Music the Developed From It* (1963).

Ed Bullins

Ed Bullins was born in Philadelphia, Pennsylvania, on July 2, 1935. Although Bullins is most known as a Black Arts Movement playwright, he also served as the minister of culture for the Black Panthers and won the New York Drama Critics' Circle Award and several Obie Awards. After witnessing "protest theater" in action while viewing Amiri Baraka's *Dutchman*, Bullins joined "Black House," the cultural center for the Black arts movement. Bullins considered art to be a form of cultural nationalism, and thusly believed that Black artists should not work with Whites. In his essay "Theatre of Reality," published in the *Negro Digest* in 1966, Bullins argues for the theatre of reality as an alternative for the Black actor and playwright. After acknowledging that "many times the black playwright finds himself in opposition to the black actor" and that "there are considerations that a novelist does not concern himself with but that a playwright is compelled to if the playwright is realistic and sincere about having his work produced," Bullins argues that there should be a theatre of reality. This imagined theater would produce "plays by Negros, concerning Negro characterization, and created for a general audience, not that special, almost exclusively White audience which patronizes Negro drama for obscure exotic reasons." For Bullins, the theatre of reality was the answer to the problems that Black playwrights and actors faced so often.

The Theater of Reality

Ed Bullins[1]

No one ... knows how to scream any more, and particularly actors ... no longer know how to cry out. Since they do nothing but talk and have forgotten they ever had a body in the theater, they have naturally also forgotten the use of their windpipes. Abnormally shrunk the windpipe is not even an organ but a monstrous abstraction that talks: actors ... no longer know how to do anything but talk.

Antonin Artaud, *The Theater and its Double*

IN THE contemporary American theater many times the black playwright finds himself in opposition to the black actor, principally when the actor manifests attitudes and behavior that the writer is engaged in altering.

There are considerations that a novelist does not concern himself with but that a playwright is compelled to if the playwright is realistic and sincere about having his work produced. The essential and most arbitrary element is humans: the producer, the director, the actors, the hypothetical audience, and sadly, the critic.

A generality that can be made is that the producer of stageplays is concerned with making money. In America, there are the Becks of the "Living Theater" in New York which the police shut down. They are currently touring in Europe because America resisted their dedication to pure and non-commercial theater. The Becks believe that producing plays which advance or keep vital dramatic art is a duty. They are so antitraditional as to have staged Ezra Pound's adaptation of classic Japanese *Noh theatre*, and in contemporary spirit, presenting Kenneth Brown's *The Brig*, a dramatic experience which resists labeling, not being quite a play nor an antiplay. The Becks, present production, *Frankenstein*, which opened in Europe is "experimental," which stretches understatement to its limits, but it may be the boldest attempt at staging Antonin Artaud's ideas for a *theater of cruelty* to date. The Becks' "Living Theater" is as diverse as art.

And there are too few young, dynamic people today like Peter Rachtman of the West Coast. Rachtman is one of the group that brought LeRoi Jones' powerful *Dutchman* and *The Toilet* to Los Angeles and San Francisco, and though profit-oriented, Rachtman is not discouraged from staging productions of quality though they be against the *status quo* and not meek and quite white "American" (if they are good box office). This is only to say that quality sells as does trash. Ideally, low-keyed quality plays can be produced successfully as can more sensational ones in good or poor taste, and this also implies that plays by or about Negroes have to be neither sensational, controversial nor banal. (Cinema has broken this ground with films such as *Lilies Of The Field* and *Nothing But A Man.*)

But whatever the play it should be honest. If honesty is controversial then that is the truth of drama. So it is for the black playwright to do the best he can at his job of writing and presenting his vision and not become prematurely emasculated by the prospect of not being produced only because of his race and the themes which come naturally from his cultural experience.

A black playwright must find his producer as one of any color must, and as the black novelist has to seek out a publisher, though the playwright may discover he has special handicaps in getting produced. For one, unlike the widening shelves of Negro novels, there have been only a small number of successfully produced Negro plays. That is, plays by Negroes, concerning Negro characterization, and created for the general audience, not that special, almost exclusively white audience which patronizes Negro drama for obscure exotic reasons.

There is hardly any precedent of success by which the Negro playwright can win his producer, and the producer, being commonly white, has the color-barrier as an intensifier of his suspicions that he is gambling on something into which he has minute insight. He worries that he can sell black novelty and innovation to a newly created audience. If there were any major black producers this factor might be reduced, but the situation appears to remain as it has been. The most relevant item in the playwright-producer relationship is cost. It may cost a producer 20 times more than a publisher to back black talent, and businessmen's ledgers are especially sensitive to two stains: red and black ink.

If there is a common prayer universally murmured by playwrights, one of its petitions is that their work get adequate direction. Adequate direction is usually more than the compulsion-driven playwright believes probable, and he feels inspired direction is entirely within the dimensions of miracle. When the playwright laments his past productions, the director is likely to be given a large share of the abuse, and the remainder goes to the aggregate components of the disaster. Of course, some playwrights can capably direct their own works, but this is rare; different aesthetic physics are at work in writing a play and manipulating the many elements that go into a staged play, and the writer is ordinarily too close to his "baby" to have the scope and objectivity needed to raise the work from the page and from within his imagination, so that it may be communicated completely to the audience. Happily for the novelist, he is the lord of the small universe he creates, and his fictional souls shuffle along in time to his whims and no other's.

The Negro playwright has a special problem in finding better than average direction: outside of the New York theater area there is an absence of capable black directors, and within New York the same statement possibly holds true. Why would a Negro playwright prefer a Negro director? It could be assumed by the writer that a director with like cultural experiences could better interpret the nuances and shading of meanings in the work, identifying somewhat with the characters, situations, and with the theme. If the reverse is true, if the playwright prefers *any* excellent direction to that of the average, then it is a problem that belongs to every playwright: to have his work interpreted skillfully, and when the playwright understands that the best direction is beyond the simple limits of interpretation, then the director's art and understanding of theater techniques can begin working, much to the benefit of the total production.

The total production stands very nearly upon the performances of the actors. Even Shakespeare has taken many a pratfall behind the ineptness of actors. For the playwright of color, finding qualified Negro actors for his cast is difficult, though there are numerous available bodies ready to stand before the lights and expose their teeth and overblown egos.

Of all his problems, the Negro playwright's greatest is the young "trained" actor and actress of his same race, not the lack of trained people. This training does not necessarily qualify these actors for many roles the black playwright has in mind. If a Negro playwright is to write effectively and honestly he must draw upon his experience. All Negroes do not come from the ghetto, naturally, but if the situations the playwright creates upon stage have characters he knows to have basis in truth, ordinarily these are black characters. It is very difficult for many Negro actors and actresses to identify with Negro characters from the masses, though they do well representing extremely middle class Negroes. The same may hold true for young white actors.

At auditions the black playwright might observe a black actress mouthing her lines like a white telephone operator or bouncing through a scene set in the black ghetto of South Philadelphia as if she were Doris Day aping the American version of the blue-eyed girl next door. Some male Negro actors appear horrified when asked to speak like Sonny Liston, and seem offended and say that they can not talk *that* way and will not even say *those* words. They mince out the exits leaving behind remarks like, "I thought an *actor* was needed." Sadly, the black playwright did not have it in him that day to create the modern American Othello or Cleopatra; he merely wrote from what he knew, so his contemporary play was left in need of just black actors, ones who were not afraid to *act* as black human beings.

A playwright's major problem as opposed to a novelist's is that each of his characters must be what he is; they all must stand tall. This must be brought out by the convincing performances of the actors. To be what the character is, then the actor must portray the character in an honest and natural manner. But today, it would not seem unlikely that a director would come before a Negro actor newly graduated from an American school of acting and spend hours with him saying, "Now, remember, in this part you are a Negro. You are black!" And the pity is that the actor would really have to sweat to get into his role; he would have to work diligently convincing himself that he was indeed Negro.

Often a characterization falls; the actor, the director or the playwright fails, collapsing the structure of the play's reality about their ears. A novelist has more range to ramble in than his characters' believability or their situations. He can even chat, philosophize and wisecrack with his readers. Characters in drama are resented by the audience for their not sticking to the point, maintaining the honesty of their motivations. With the Negro playwright it is the Negro actor who dramatizes the vital characters, and the actor must breath the truth of his own conviction in that character for his portrayal to be perfect.

But not all the blame rests with the black actor or his schooling. There are interracial, and a few entirely Negro, theater groups training black actors to do little other than the Greek classics, Shakespeare, Chekhov and Shaw, casting Negroes indiscriminately in every conceivable role, a sort of white characterization done in authentic black face. True, the experience for the actor is invaluable and should be a part of his training, but a hidden evil exists in the continuation or the strict adherence to this brand of liberality. It is a self-defeating device for the actor. The black actor is unintentionally made to say in essence that he can act too; he, a black man, can do the classic repertoire of the continent as can a white actor. That he can *act* and not only be stereotyped in butler roles set in the *ante bellum* South. Well, it should be known that he can act, especially by the actor. One of his number has won an Oscar, and others appear on nationwide TV, though it is questionable whether these are any criteria of adequate professional standards. Incidentally, these black actors play Negroes, not Creon.

Following the above type of reasoning is tantamount to the black author's wasting years telling his waiting readers that he can write, that he is concerned with the art of writing and nothing else, but getting almost no writing completed and in print, aside from his infrequent artistic manifestos sent out to indicate that he is still breathing. The fight by the black actor to prove that he can act is as much over as the black writer's fight to prove that he can write, and both should get to work at their crafts and be aware that Aristotle and his aesthetic dogmas are not of this time and never had been meant for the black artist anyway. There are new roles, new themes and new definitions being created and explored now, and the black actor and writer should become aware.

In approaching one of the "artistic" black theater groups, the Negro playwright's scripts may be taken and returned shortly and the playwright told that his work is too "experimental" or "obscene" if it uses too much of the Negro idiom of the ghetto.* The group's premise might be that when Negroes of flesh and blood are depicted on the stage, that this is verging upon revolution and is too drastic; it is far beyond the group's range of belief and comprehension. They can not become familiar with a real Negro on the stage. Or the playwright may be told that *they* do not bother with original scripts, that *they* do the classics or the work of proven Negro writers "like Langston Hughes," that is, the Negro writers who have made it somewhat with the white press and then are considered minor celebrities by the black bourgeoisie, then the artsy craftsy colored folk accept them as their own. When asked why *they* do not produce young black playwrights, the answer almost invariably is, "There are none, are there?" Of course there are none to their knowledge because of their refusal to look for or acknowledge any until the white critics deem it correct for them to. With this situation existing, entering little theater for the black playwright is more than likely not an asset to his career but a handicap, for he will seldom find other than the conventional, timid and intellectually lazy and backward bourgeois black masquerading as an artist.

The *theater of reality* should be mentioned now when speaking of the audience and the critic. The revolutionary nature of this theater is not of style and technique but of theme and character. Any theatrical style or method can be used separately or in combinations to reach the truth of the play. In this manner the play could begin naturalistically with a character in a realistic setting and progress through expressionism, surrealism, absurdity and back to realism, dramatizing the journey of the character through his own pysche to reach his loss of innocence, self-awareness or illumination. To reach what individually is called reality. The method is not the goal in this theater; the result must elicit the single response of "Yes!"

So it is not a call for a return to realism or naturalism that this theater calls for; it is the exposure of illusion through exploding myths and lies that are disguised as reality and truths. These myths, and especially those concerning the black man, clutter the heart of his existence, his humanity. Nor is this theater a plea for his humanity, time will not be wasted in silly issues.

This theater is not exclusively about Negroes nor for Negroes; its trend should only go counter to that force in Western society which dehumanizes, enslaves and defeats man at his best, whether this force originates in man's institutions or his bewildered psyche that has built a defense and power-structure that can not be much longer contained. This theater, in this century, may be viewed as against society, the American society in particular. By white critics it will undoubtedly be misnomered "protest literature," and, Yes, it will certainly expose some of the wrongs of the society. For this theater is against the hypocritical cant and morality of this sick society and demonstrates how sick the society is by exposing her sores, her warped humans. If this is social realism or protest then let it speak reality for all people, not only a temporarily deprived selfish middle-class.

Today, the bulk of the theater going audience is white. One problem for the Negro playwright is that part of the audience will resist the reality of his characters; they will refuse to identify with black characters in any way, even the middle-class Negro members of the audience will fight the characters if they come from the "submerged" elements of the culture. The characters of the new reality will be fought whether they are upon a stage or found in a book, and most of the inaccurate criticism of Negro works have had this kind of bias at its roots. The white critic is deceived by himself and his colleagues, and the university departments of literature, always

25 years behind, perpetuate and sustain these myths. One great boring myth is that black writers are collectively engaged in writing protest literature and can or will do little else. These same people should get hip to Chester Himes, a talent of major proportions, who has been around before a lot of them. This lie of *protest* has circulated so widely and convincingly that it has damaged most contemporary Negro writers; as passed over earlier, it may have destroyed the most talented black writer of today, but, perhaps the times will rescue him for his art.

And it is hokum: lately, two of the most authentic works of black protest literature have been the book *Black Like Me* and the documentary play *In White America*, and both have been authored by white men. But small knowledged English professors across the country, if they mention it at all, without having seen the production or having read the script, are branding LeRoi Jones' play, *The Toilet*, a protest play when it is simply a love story done in a melodramatic, naturalistic vein.

The writer can not worry about the audience; he knows there is a small hard-core audience for him and they will discover one another, and luckily the audience will grow to universal proportions. And the writer knows that there is only one critic, himself. All that a reviewer or a critic can do positively for a writer is to get him more audience appeal or get him more readers. If the critic fails to achieve this, then the writer should dismiss him. The black writer knows that the critics are white, and they are most certain not to understand his work or get its finer points, especially when the writer is not slanting his work to a middle-class white audience, and he is setting his own limitations and not relying upon the critics' judgments.

Honesty is what the writer should be after. The *theater of reality* is an attempt to return to man's honesty to himself, to his fellows and in his vision. It is indeed a theater of metaphysical yearnings. The playwright does this job by uncovering the reality of his art, his humanity, his existence as an intelligent and moral entity in the universe, and makes the entire universe an audience of this transformation of the psyche and spirit; this new revolution is of the mind and spirit. And the revolution seems to have begun, and if it has there are many facets to it. There are the doers, there are the theorists, and there are the chroniclers and story tellers. Each is working from within a framework of reality which can always be expanded, illuminated, and, hopefully, passed on.

Note

1. Ed Bullins, "Theatre of Reality," *Negro Digest*, 1966: 60–66.

Addison Gayle Jr.

Addison Gayle Jr. (1932–1991) devoted his life's work to establishing and circulating the necessity of a new Black aesthetic. He was not pleased with Eurocentric notions of literature and wanted Black art—namely, literature—to be valued. In his edited volume, *The Black Aesthetic* (1972), Gayle sought to make previous approaches to literary criticism and the argument for new theoretical lenses clear. In the introduction to that volume, Gayle argues that "unique art derived from unique cultural experiences mandates unique critical tools." This charge for a new approach to critical evaluation placed high value on the art that Blacks created. For the Black artist, "speaking honestly is a fundamental principle . . . he has given up the futile practice of speaking to whites, and has begun to speak to his brothers." For the Black critic, "the question . . . today is not how beautiful is a melody, a play, a poem, or a novel, but how much more beautiful has the poem, melody, play, or novel made the life of a single black man?" Gayle makes clear the voids of viewing Black literature from a White gaze. He, instead, encourages movement toward criticism that empowers and enlightens the Black artist and Black people.

The Black Aesthetic

Addison Gayle Jr.[1]

Introduction

A new note, discernible even to the most biased observer, was sounded in the art of black people during the nineteen fifties and sixties. "I will go on judging and elucidating novels and plays and poetry by Negroes according to what general powers I possess," writes Richard Gilman, "but the kind of Negro *writing* I have been talking about, the act of creation of the self in the face of the self's historic denial by our society, seems to me to be at this point beyond my right to intrude."

Some critics, less amenable to conversion than Gilman, would have us believe that only two elements separate the present-day black artist from his forerunner. One such element is anger! " . . . Negro writers are demonstrating the responsibility of the artist to the disciplines and traditions of art and literature . . . ," writes Herbert Hill; "simple protest and anger are not enough and rhetoric will not be useful in masking the inadequacies of literary craftsmanship." The other is black nationalism, which, according to Robert Bone, "for all its militancy is politically Utopian."

The element of black anger is neither new nor, as Herbert Hill would have us believe, passé. The black artist in the American society who creates without interjecting a note of anger is creating not as a black man, but as an American. For anger in black art is as old as the first utterances by black men on American soil:

> "If I had-a my way,
> I'd tear this building down
> Great God, then, if I had-a my way
> If I had-a my way, little children
> If I had-a my way,
> I'd tear this building down . . . . "

As old as Frances Ellen Watkins, who made one demand of her undertaker:

> "I ask no monument, proud and high
> To arrest the gaze of the passer-by,
> All that my yearning spirit craves
> Is bury me not in a land of slaves."

Nowhere does anger reach more intensive expression than in DuBois, who strikes a note that has found accord in the breast of contemporary black artists:

"I hate them, oh!
I hate them well,
I hate them, Christ!
As I hate hell!
If I were God,
I'd sound their knell
This day."

Neither is black nationalism a new element in black life or black art. In 1836, " . . . some of the delegates [at the National Negro Convention]," writes Philip S. Foner, "were convinced that Canadian colonization was still the most urgent business at hand. Others felt that it was necessary to concentrate upon building a better social order in the United States . . . . One group doubted the efficacy of associating with any set of white abolitionists, and advocated restricting the convention to Negro membership. Another, convinced of the inability to achieve equality for Negroes in existing institutions, favored continuing the establishment of separate schools and churches for the Negro people." This sentiment reaches dramatic form in the fiction of Martin Delaney, *Blake, or the Huts of America* (1859); Sutton Griggs, *Imperium in Imperio* (1899); and DuBois, *Dark Princess* (1928).

Again, animosity against the inept, sterile critiques of American academicians—so prevalent in black critical writings today—is not new. As early as 1900, Pauline Hopkins realized that art was " . . . of great value to any people as a preserver of manners and customs—religious, political, and social. It is a record of growth and development from generation to generation. No one will do this for us; we must ourselves develop the men and women who will faithfully portray the inmost thoughts and feelings of the Negro with all the fire and romance which lie dormant in our history . . . . " Twenty-two years later, William Pickens was more direct: "It is not simply that the white story teller will not do full justice to the humanity of the black race; *he cannot.*" William Stanley Braithwaite, an American critic in every essential, quotes from an article in the *Independent Magazine* (1925): "The white writer seems to stand baffled before the enigma, and so he expends all his energies on dialect and in general on the Negro's minstrel characteristics . . . . We shall have to look to the Negro himself to go all the way. It is quite likely that no white man can do it. *It is reasonable to suppose that his white psychology will get in the way.*" (Italics mine)

Nevertheless, there is a discernible element in black art today that is new, and Hoyt W. Fuller has come closest to pointing it out: "The Negro revolt is as palpable in letters as it is in the streets." Change revolt to war, and the characteristics that distinguish the old art from the new are readily apparent. The serious black artist of today is at war with the American society as few have been throughout American history. Too often, as Richard Wright noted, the black (artists) " . . . entered the court of American public opinion dressed in the knee pants of servility, curtsying to show that the Negro was not inferior, that he was human, and that he had a life comparable to other people." They waged war not against the society but against the societal laws and mores that barred *them* from equal membership. They were, in the main, anxious to become Americans, to share in the fruits of the country's economic system and to surrender their history and culture to a universal melting pot. They were men of another era who believed in the American dream more fervently than their white contemporaries. They saw the nation as a land of innocence, young enough to hold out promises of maturing into a nation of freedom, justice, and equality. The days of innocence have passed. The child has become the adult, and instead of improving with age, she has grown increasingly worse. Yesterday America was evil personified in her youth; today she is evil personified in adulthood.

The dimensions of the black artist's war against the society are highly visible. At the core of black art in the past was a vendetta against the South. The black novel, from William Wells Brown to Richard Wright, was concerned primarily with southern tyranny and injustice. Often the North escaped with no more than a rap on the knuckles. "Northern white people," wrote James Weldon Johnson in *The Autobiography of an Ex-Coloured Man* (1912), "love the Negro in a sort of abstract way, as a race; through a sense of justice, charity, and philanthropy, they will liberally assist in his elevation . . . ."

With the exception of writers such as Dunbar and Chesnutt, who viewed the black man's exodus from South to North as an exchange of one hell for another, black writers spoke of the North as the new Canaan, of northern whites as a different breed of man from their southern counterparts. Is it any wonder that black people, falling sway to increasing southern tyranny, began, in 1917, the exodus that swelled the urban areas of America in the sixties and seventies?

"I've seen them come dark/wondering/wide-eyed/dreaming/out of Penn Station . . . ," writes Langston Hughes, "but the trains are late. The gates open/but there're bars/at each gate." The bars were erected by northern, not southern, whites. Black people had run away from white terrorism in Savannah in 1904 and Atlanta in 1906, only to experience white terrorism in Ohio in 1904, Illinois in 1908, and New York in 1935. The evenhanded treatment of blacks North and South made little imprint upon Negro leaders who, then as now, were more willing to combat injustices down south than up north.

The task of pointing out northern duplicity was left to the black artist, and no writer was more effective in this undertaking than Richard Wright. When Wright placed Bigger Thomas and Mr. Dalton in a northern setting and pointed up the fact that Bigger's condition resulted from Dalton's hypocrisy, he opened a Pandora's box of problems for white liberals and Negro leaders, neither of whom could bring themselves to share his vision. Dalton is a white liberal philanthropist who, although donating money to "Negro uplift organizations," owns the slums in which Bigger Thomas is forced to live. His control of the young black man is more despotic than that of the southern plantation owner over blacks in the South: for him, the weapons of control are economic, social, and political.

He is more sagacious and dishonest than his southern counterpart; he has discovered a way to "keep the nigger in his place" without such aids as signs and restrictive covenants. He has constructed a cosmology that allows him to pose as a humanitarian on the one hand, while he sets about defining the black man's limitations on the other. His most cherished symbol of the black man is Uncle Tom; and he remains enamored of Nigger Jim, the black everyboy toward whom he feels paternalistic. Like Theodore Gross, he is able to share with Joel Chandler Harris " . . . the fears, laughter, and anger of the Negro"; and he is equally convinced with Gross that Harris " . . . contributed the most popular Negro characters to American fiction—Uncle Remus, Balaam, Ananias, and Mingo . . . "—characters whom he, too, believes to be representative of the race.

Thomas Nelson Page, Thomas Dixon, and Hinton Helper might create, for Southerners, the image of the black man as " . . . a degenerate, inferior, irresponsible, and bestial creature 'transformed by the exigency of war from a chattel to be bought and sold into a possible beast to be feared and guarded.' " Dalton, however, will not accept this image. Such portraits of black men disturb his humanitarian (read sexual) ideal of the black man. "In an effort to make Hell endurable," Robert Bone writes of James Baldwin, "Baldwin attempts to spiritualize his sexual rebellion. Subjectively, I have no doubt, he is convinced that he has found God. Not the white God of his black father, but a darker deity who dwells in the heart of carnal mystery . . . . The stranger the sex partner, the better the orgasm, for it violates a stronger taboo." Bone's inability to come to grips with the sexual aspects of Baldwin's novels, reveals more about Bone than it does about Baldwin.

At the least, it reveals a great deal about the Daltons of the North. In order to protect the Marys of the earth (Dalton's daughter in *Native Son*), they have defined the black man in the most negative terms possible. To the northern mind, Nigger Jim and Uncle Tom are opposite ends of the same pole; the young boy and the old man are both eunuchs, paternalistic wards who, one step removed from the jungle, are capable of limited, prescribed salvation. The inability of the Daltons to see the black man as other than an impotent sexual force accounts for much of the negative criticism by white writers about black literature; it also accounts for the sexually impotent black men who people the novels of William Styron and Norman Mailer.

The liberal ideology—both social and literary—of the northern Daltons has become the primary target of the Afro-American writer and critic. In the novels of John A. Williams, Sam Greenlee, Cecil Brown, and Ishmael Reed, the criticism of Don L. Lee, Ron Wellburn, LeRoi Jones, and Hoyt Fuller, to name but a few, the liberal shibboleths are called into question. The Daltons are brought before the bar of black public opinion and revealed for the modern-day plantation owners they are.

There is another, more important aspect to this war. The black artist of the past worked with the white public in mind. The guidelines by which he measured his production was its acceptance or rejection by white people. To be damned by a white critic and disavowed by a white public was reason enough to damn the artist in the eyes of his own people. The invisible censor, white power, hovered over him in the sanctuary of his private room—whether at the piano or the typewriter—and, like his black brothers, he debated about what he could say to the world without bringing censure upon himself. The mannerisms he had used to survive in the society outside, he now brought to his art; and, to paraphrase Richard Wright, he was forced to figure out how to sound each note and how to write down each word.

The result was usually an artistic creation filled with half-truths. His works were always seasoned with the proper amount of anger—an anger that dared not reach the explosive level of calling for total demolition of the American society—and condescension; condescension that meant he would assure his audience, at some point in the production, that he believed in the principles of Americanism. To return to Richard Wright, he was not " . . . ever expected to speak honestly about the problem. [He had to] wrap it up in myth, legend, morality, folklore, niceties, and plain lies."

Speaking honestly is a fundamental principle of today's black artist. He has given up the futile practice of speaking to whites, and has begun to speak to his brothers. Ofttimes, as in essays in this anthology, he points up the wide disparity between the pronouncements of liberal intellectuals and their actions. Yet his purpose is not to convert the liberals (one does not waste energy on the likes of Selden Rodman, Irving Howe, Theodore Gross, Louis Simpson, Herbert Hill, or Robert Bone), but instead to point out to black people the true extent of the control exercised upon them by the American society, in the hope that a process of de-Americanization will occur in every black community in the nation.

The problem of the de-Americanization of black people lies at the heart of the Black Aesthetic. "After the Egyptian and Indian, the Greek and Roman, the Teuton and Mongolian," wrote DuBois in 1903, "the Negro is a sort of seventh son, born with a veil, and gifted with second sight in this American world—a world which yields him no true self-consciousness, but only lets him see himself through the revelation of the other world. It is a peculiar sensation, this double consciousness, this sense of always looking at one's self through the eyes of others, of measuring one's soul by the tape of a world that looks on in amused contempt and pity. One ever feels his twoness—an American, a Negro; two souls, two thoughts, two unreconciled strivings; two warring ideals in one dark body, whose dogged strength alone keeps it from being torn asunder."

In 1961 the old master resolved the psychic tension in his own breast by leaving the country that had rewarded his endeavors with scorn and oppression. His denunciations of America and his exodus back to the land of his forefathers provide an appropriate symbol of the black man who de-Americanized himself.

His act proclaimed to black men the world over that the price for becoming an American was too high. It meant, at the least, to desert one's heritage and culture; at the most, to become part of all " . . . that has been instrumental in wanton destruction of life, degradation of dignity, and contempt for the human spirit." To be an American is to be opposed to humankind, against the dignity of the individual, and against the striving in man for compassion and tenderness: to be an American is to lose one's humanity.

What else is one to make of My Lai, Vietnam? A black soldier has been charged with joining his white compatriots in the murder of innocent Vietnamese women and children. How far has the Americanization of black men progressed when a southern black man stands beside white men and shoots down, not the enemies of his people, but the niggers of American construction?

To understand this incident and what must be done to correct it is to understand the Black Aesthetic. A critical methodology has no relevance to the black community unless it aids men in becoming better than they are. Such an element has been sorely lacking in the critical canons handed down from the academies by the Aristotelian Critics, the Practical Critics, the Formalistic Critics, and the New Critics. Each has this in common: it aims to evaluate the work of art in terms of *its* beauty and not in terms of the transformation from ugliness to beauty that the work of art demands from its audience.

The question for the black critic today is not how beautiful is a melody, a play, a poem, or a novel, but how much more beautiful has the poem, melody, play, or novel made the life of a single black man? How far has the work gone in transforming an American Negro into an African-American or black man? The Black Aesthetic, then, as conceived by this writer, is a corrective—a means of helping black people out of the polluted mainstream of Americanism, and offering logical, reasoned arguments as to why he should not desire to join the ranks of a Norman Mailer or a William Styron. To be an American writer is to be an American, and, for black people, there should no longer be honor attached to either position.

To paraphrase Saunders Redding, I have been enclothed with no authority to speak for others. Therefore, it is not my intention, in this introduction, to speak for the contributors to this anthology. Few of them may share my views; a great many may find them reprehensible. These are independent artists who demand the right to think for themselves and who, rightfully so, will resist the attempt by anyone—black or white—to articulate positions in their names.

Each has his own idea of the Black Aesthetic, of the function of the black artist in the American society and of the necessity for new and different critical approaches to the artistic endeavors of black artists. Few, I believe, would argue with my assertion that the black artist, due to his historical position in America at the present time, is engaged in a war with this nation that will determine the future of black art. Likewise, there are few among them—and here again this is only conjecture—who would disagree with the idea that unique experiences produce unique cultural artifacts, and that art is a product of such cultural experiences. To push this thesis to its logical conclusion, unique art derived from unique cultural experiences mandates unique critical tools for evaluation. Further than this, agreement need not go!

One final note: Less than a decade ago, anthologies on black writing were edited almost exclusively by whites. Today, there is a noticeable difference: the white academician edits an anthology and calls upon a black man to write the introduction. The editor then declares that his anthology "represents the best of black literature" or that he has chosen those works "which rank with the best in American artistic production."

This editor makes no such farcical and nonsensical claims. Represented in this anthology is not the best critical thought on the subject of the Black Aesthetic, but critical thought that is among the best. This anthology is not definitive and does not claim to be. The first of its kind to treat of this subject, it is meant as an incentive to young black critics to scan the pages of *The Black World* [*Negro Digest*], *Liberator Magazine, Soulbook, Journal of Negro Poetry, Amistad, Umbra*, and countless other black magazines, and anthologize the thousands of essays that no single anthology could possibly cover.

Many writers whose claim to recognition is equal to that of the other contributors and the editor have been left out of this anthology. This could not be helped. Perhaps it can be rectified. Instead of being content to write introduction for white editors, perhaps our serious black artists will edit anthologies themselves. If this is done, the present renaissance in black letters will escape the fate of its predecessor in the nineteen twenties, and endure. Then and only then will the revolution in black letters gain viability and continue right on!

Note

1. Excerpt from Addison Gayle Jr., "Introduction," in *The Black Aesthetic* (New York: Doubleday, 1971), pp. xv–xxiv.

Gwendolyn Brooks

Gwendolyn Brooks (June 7, 1917–December 3, 2000) was an American educator and poet. Brooks's career as an author began at the age of thirteen, when her first poem was published in a children's magazine and received more acclaim as years passed. Two decades later, in 1950, Brooks was awarded the Pulitzer Prize for Poetry for her second collection, *Annie Allen*, and she was the first African American to receive such an award. In her two-volume autobiographic text, *Report From Part One* (1972) and *Report From Part Two* (1996), Brooks explores her growth and development as an African American, a woman, and a poet. The second volume of the autobiography was completed while Brooks served as a poetry consultant to the Library of Congress; she was the first African American woman to do so.

Report From Part One: An Autobiography

Gwendolyn Brooks[1]

Although I do not know languages, I tried to involve my students with recommended translations of some French, German, Italian, and eastern literature, whether or not samples were included in our texts. Such inclusions were rarities indeed. I also involved them with black literature and Jewish literature, rarely touched upon by standard texts. (When I could, I brought black writers of my own acquaintance to visit, to speak, paying them myself.) At one school, the *prescribed* short story text, Short Story Masterpieces, edited by Robert Penn Warren and Albert Erskine, contained NO stories by blacks and only one story by a Jew—J. D. Salinger. "Our" poetry text, by Hieatt and Park, contained not one poem by a black.

. . . Such activities, I found, enabled *me* to enjoy a class—and when I enjoyed it, almost without exception so did my students.

Today's young people want IN, want to express themselves, to say what is on their minds.

They do not so much want "answers," for who, they stress, can solve for them?—they do not so much wish to discuss as to *speak*, simply. They want to be free to make, to create. If they are not allowed to create, they break. In a vacuum, breaking seems to them a form of creation.

More fervently now than ever before they want assurance that what they are doing in a school situation will strengthen or embroider their lot IMMEDIATELY. They want to feel that they are achieving or changing something on the spot.

The Field of the Fever. The Time of the Tall-Walkers

Everybody has to go to the bathroom.
That's good.
That's a great thing.

If by some quirk of fate blacks had to go to the bathroom and whites didn't I shudder to think of the genocidal horrors that would be visited on the blacks of the whole world. Here is what my little green *Webster's New World* has to say about a world-shaking word:

black (blak), adj. (A S *blaec*)
1. opposite to white: see color.
2. dark-complexioned. 3. Negro.
4. without light; dark. 5. dirty.
6. evil; wicked. 7. sad; dismal.
8. sullen. n.1. black pigment;

opposite of white. 2. dark clothing,
as for mourning. 3. a Negro. v.t.&v.i.,
to blacken.—black-out, to lose
consciousness.—blackly, adv:
—blackness, n.

Interestingly enough, we do not find that "white" is "opposite of black." That would "lift" black to the importance-level of white.

white (hwit), adj. (A S hwit).
1. having the color of pure snow
or milk. 2. of a light or pale
color. 3. pale; wan. 4. pure;
innocent. 5. having a light-
colored skin. n. 1. the color of
pure snow or milk. 2. a white
or light-colored thing, as the
albumen of an egg, the white
part of the eyeball, etc. 3. a
person with a light-colored skin;
Caucasian.—whiteness, n.

Until 1967 my own blackness did not confront me with a shrill spelling of itself. I knew that I was what most people were calling "a Negro;" I called myself that, although always the word fell awkwardly on a poet's ear; I had never liked the sound of it (Caucasian has an ugly sound, too, while the name Indian is beautiful to look at and to hear.) *And* I knew that people of my coloration and distinctive history had been bolted to trees and sliced or burned or shredded; knocked to the back of the line; provided with separate toilets, schools, neighborhoods; denied, when possible, voting rights; hounded, hooted at, or shunned, or patronizingly patted (often the patting-hand was, I knew, surreptitiously wiped after the Kindness, so that unspeakable contamination might be avoided.) America's social climate, it seemed, was trying to tell me something. It was trying to tell me something Websterian. Yet, although almost secretly, I had always felt that to be black was good. Sometimes, there would be an approximate whisper around me: *others* felt, it seemed, that to be black was good. The translation would have been something like "Hey—being black is *fun.*" Or something like "Hey—our folks have got stuff to be proud of!" Or something like "Hey—since we are so good why aren't we treated like the other 'Americans?' "

Suddenly there was New Black to meet. In the spring of 1967 I met some of it at the Fisk University Writers' Conference in Nashville. Coming from white white white South Dakota State College I arrived in Nashville, Tennessee, to give one more "reading." But blood-boiling surprise was in store for me. First, I was aware of a general energy, an electricity, in look, walk, speech, *gesture* of the young blackness I saw all about me. I had been "loved" at South Dakota State College. Here, I was coldly Respected. Here, the heroes included the novelist-director, John Killens, editors David Llorens and Hoyt Fuller, playwright Ron Milner, historians John Henrik Clarke and Lerone Bennett (and even poor Lerone was taken to task, by irate members of a no-nonsense young audience, for affiliating himself with *Ebony Magazine*, considered at that time a traitor for allowing skin-bleach advertisements in its pages, and for over-featuring light-skinned women). Imamu Amiri Baraka, then "LeRoi Jones", was expected. He arrived in the middle of my own offering, and when I called attention to his presence there was jubilee in Jubilee Hall.

All that day and night, Margaret Danner Cunningham—another Old Girl, another coldly Respected old Has-been—and an almost hysterical Gwendolyn B. walked about in amazement, listening, looking, learning. *What was going on!*

In my cartoon basket I keep a cartoon of a stout, dowager-hatted, dowager-furred Helen Hokinson woman. She is on parade in the world. She is a sign-carrier in the wild world. Her sign says "Will someone please tell me what is going on?" Well, although I cannot give a full-blooded answer to that potent question, I have been supplied—the sources are plural—with helpful materials: hints, friendly *and* inimical clues, approximations, statistics, "proofs" of one kind and another; from these I am trying to weave the coat that I shall wear. In 1967's Nashville, however, the somewhat dotty expression in the eyes of the cartoon-woman, the *agapeness*, were certainly mine. I was in some inscrutable and uncomfortable wonderland. I didn't know what to make of what surrounded me, of what with hot sureness began almost immediately to invade me. *I* had never been, before, in the general presence of such insouciance, such live firmness, such confident vigor, such determination to mold or carve something DEFINITE.

Up against the wall, white man! was the substance of the Baraka shout, at the evening reading he shared with fierce Ron Milner among intoxicating drum-beats, heady incense and organic underhumming. Up against the wall! And a pensive (until that moment) white man of thirty or thirty three abruptly shot himself into the heavy air, screaming "Yeah! *Yeah!* Up against the wall, Brother! KILL 'EM ALL! KILL 'EM *ALL!*"

I thought that was interesting.

There is indeed a new black today. He is different from any the world has known. He's a tall-walker. Almost firm. By many of his own *brothers* he is not understood. And he is understood by *no* white. Not the wise white; not the Schooled white; not the Kind white. Your *least* pre-requisite toward an understanding of the new black is an exceptional Doctorate which can be conferred only upon those with the proper properties of bitter birth and intrinsic sorrow. I know this is infuriating, especially to those professional Negro-understanders, some of them so *very* kind, with special portfolio, special savvy. But I cannot say anything other, because nothing other is the truth.

I—who have "gone the gamut" from an almost angry rejection of my dark skin by some of my brainwashed brothers and sisters to a surprised queenhood in the new black sun—am qualified to enter at least the kindergarten of new consciousness now. New consciousness and trudge-toward-progress.

I have hopes for myself.

African Fragment

Nairobi, Kenya.

Many many whites, sun-browned, wealthy, flying to the land of the black man.

When the whites on the plane speak of Africa they speak with an affected heartiness, with a glass possessiveness, with nervous bluster.

* * *

The first blacks I see in Africa enter the white man's big bird, quickly bob and dip about, cleaning out the trash.

* * *

Nairobi. I gulp down the Nairobi midnight air. I stride erectly from the plane to the airport. I tell myself, "I don't care what *any*body says; this is BLACKland—and I am *black*."

* * *

In my room, a wastebasket covered with "leopard" cloth. A "Renoir" on a wall. (White women. Pensive white women, plumply sitting.) There is a fat elephant on my key.

Note

1. Gwendolyn Brooks, *Report From Part One: An Autobiography* (Highland Park, MI: Broadside Press, 1972).

Toni Morrison

Toni Morrison was born Chloe Ardelia Wofford on February 18, 1931, in Lorain, Ohio. Morrison's historical and rhetorical prowess is personified through the language of her published novels, short stories, children's books, opera libretto, plays, essays, and literary criticism. As an author, novelist, editor, and professor, Morrison has contributed to American literature for many decades. As a result, she has received countless awards, including the Pulitzer Prize (1988), the American Book Award (1988), the Nobel Prize (1993), and the Presidential Medal of Freedom (2012). Toni Morrison's 1993 Nobel Prize Lecture begins with the story of an old blind woman who is approached by a group of young children. When the woman and the children meet, the children ask, "Is the bird we have in our hand living or dead?" The women replies, "I don't know whether the bird you are holding is dead or alive, but what I do know is that it is in your hands. It is in your hands." The old woman's acknowledgment of the presence of the bird, whether dead or alive, becomes the metaphor that shapes Morrison's speech. Throughout the speech, she focuses on the dying and living language that surrounds us. According to Morrison, the beauty of language lies in the act of allowing it to happen. As the dialogue between the children and the blind woman continue, the beauty of language in action is revealed through speaking, sharing, and storytelling. Together, the blind woman and the children use language to understand one another, learn from one another, and experience one another.

Nobel Lecture

Toni Morrison[1]

"Once upon a time there was an old woman. Blind but wise." Or was it an old man? A guru, perhaps. Or a griot soothing restless children. I have heard this story, or one exactly like it, in the lore of several cultures.

"Once upon a time there was an old woman. Blind. Wise."

In the version I know the woman is the daughter of slaves, black, American, and lives alone in a small house outside of town. Her reputation for wisdom is without peer and without question. Among her people she is both the law and its transgression. The honor she is paid and the awe in which she is held reach beyond her neighborhood to places far away; to the city where the intelligence of rural prophets is the source of much amusement.

One day the woman is visited by some young people who seem to be bent on disproving her clairvoyance and showing her up for the fraud they believe she is. Their plan is simple: they enter her house and ask the one question the answer to which rides solely on her difference from them, a difference they regard as a profound disability: her blindness. They stand before her, and one of them says, "Old woman, I hold in my hand a bird. Tell me whether it is living or dead."

She does not answer, and the question is repeated. "Is the bird I am holding living or dead?"

Still she doesn't answer. She is blind and cannot see her visitors, let alone what is in their hands. She does not know their color, gender or homeland. She only knows their motive.

The old woman's silence is so long, the young people have trouble holding their laughter.

Finally she speaks and her voice is soft but stern. "I don't know", she says. "I don't know whether the bird you are holding is dead or alive, but what I do know is that it is in your hands. It is in your hands."

Her answer can be taken to mean: if it is dead, you have either found it that way or you have killed it. If it is alive, you can still kill it. Whether it is to stay alive, it is your decision. Whatever the case, it is your responsibility.

For parading their power and her helplessness, the young visitors are reprimanded, told they are responsible not only for the act of mockery but also for the small bundle of life sacrificed to achieve its aims. The blind woman shifts attention away from assertions of power to the instrument through which that power is exercised.

Speculation on what (other than its own frail body) that bird-in-the-hand might signify has always been attractive to me, but especially so now thinking, as I have been, about the work I do that has brought me to this company. So I choose to read the bird as language and the woman as a practiced writer. She is worried about how the language she dreams in, given to her at birth, is handled, put into service, even withheld from her for certain nefarious purposes. Being a writer she thinks of language partly as a system, partly as a living thing over which one has control, but mostly as agency—as an act with consequences. So the question the children put to her: "Is it living or dead?" is not unreal because she thinks of language as susceptible to death, erasure; certainly imperiled and salvageable only by an effort of the will. She believes that if the bird in the hands of her visitors is dead the custodians are responsible for the corpse. For her a dead language is not only one no longer spoken or written, it is unyielding language content to admire its own paralysis. Like statist language, censored and censoring. Ruthless in its policing duties, it has no desire or purpose other than maintaining the free range of its own narcotic narcissism, its own exclusivity and dominance. However moribund, it is not without effect for it actively thwarts the intellect, stalls conscience, suppresses human potential. Unreceptive to interrogation, it cannot form or tolerate new ideas, shape other thoughts, tell another story, fill baffling silences. Official language smitheryed to sanction ignorance and preserve privilege is a suit of armor polished to shocking glitter, a husk from which the knight departed long ago. Yet there it is: dumb, predatory, sentimental. Exciting reverence in schoolchildren, providing shelter for despots, summoning false memories of stability, harmony among the public.

She is convinced that when language dies, out of carelessness, disuse, indifference and absence of esteem, or killed by fiat, not only she herself, but all users and makers are accountable for its demise. In her country children have bitten their tongues off and use bullets instead to iterate the voice of speechlessness, of disabled and disabling language, of language adults have abandoned altogether as a device for grappling with meaning, providing guidance, or expressing love. But she knows tongue-suicide is not only the choice of children. It is common among the infantile heads of state and power merchants whose evacuated language leaves them with no access to what is left of their human instincts for they speak only to those who obey, or in order to force obedience.

The systematic looting of language can be recognized by the tendency of its users to forgo its nuanced, complex, mid-wifery properties for menace and subjugation. Oppressive language does more than represent violence; it is violence; does more than represent the limits of knowledge; it limits knowledge. Whether it is obscuring state language or the faux-language of mindless media; whether it is the proud but calcified language of the academy or the commodity driven language of science; whether it is the malign language of law-without-ethics, or language designed for the estrangement of minorities, hiding its racist plunder in its literary cheek—it must be rejected, altered and exposed. It is the language that drinks blood, laps vulnerabilities, tucks its fascist boots under crinolines of respectability and patriotism as it moves relentlessly toward the bottom line and the bottomed-out mind. Sexist language, racist language, theistic language—all are typical of the policing languages of mastery, and cannot, do not permit new knowledge or encourage the mutual exchange of ideas.

The old woman is keenly aware that no intellectual mercenary, nor insatiable dictator, no paid-for politician or demagogue; no counterfeit journalist would be persuaded by her thoughts. There is and will be rousing language to keep citizens armed and arming; slaughtered and slaughtering in the malls, courthouses, post offices, playgrounds, bedrooms and boulevards; stirring, memorializing language to mask the pity and waste of needless death. There will be more diplomatic language to countenance rape, torture, assassination. There is and will be more seductive, mutant language designed to throttle women, to pack their throats like paté-producing geese with their own unsayable, transgressive words; there will be more of the language of surveillance disguised as research; of politics and history calculated to render the suffering of millions mute; language glamorized to thrill the dissatisfied and bereft into assaulting their neighbors; arrogant pseudo-empirical language crafted to lock creative people into cages of inferiority and hopelessness.

Underneath the eloquence, the glamor, the scholarly associations, however stirring or seductive, the heart of such language is languishing, or perhaps not beating at all—if the bird is already dead.

She has thought about what could have been the intellectual history of any discipline if it had not insisted upon, or been forced into, the waste of time and life that rationalizations for and representations of dominance required—lethal discourses of exclusion blocking access to cognition for both the excluder and the excluded.

The conventional wisdom of the Tower of Babel story is that the collapse was a misfortune. That it was the distraction, or the weight of many languages that precipitated the tower's failed architecture. That one monolithic language would have expedited the building and heaven would have been reached. Whose heaven, she wonders? And what kind? Perhaps the achievement of Paradise was premature, a little hasty if no one could take the time to understand other languages, other views, other narratives period. Had they, the heaven they imagined might have been found at their feet. Complicated, demanding, yes, but a view of heaven as life; not heaven as post-life.

She would not want to leave her young visitors with the impression that language should be forced to stay alive merely to be. The vitality of language lies in its ability to limn the actual, imagined and possible lives of its speakers, readers, writers. Although its poise is sometimes in displacing experience it is not a substitute for it. It arcs toward the place where meaning may lie. When a President of the United States thought about the graveyard his country had become, and said, "The world will little note nor long remember what we say here. But it will never forget what they did here," his simple words are exhilarating in their life-sustaining properties because they refused to encapsulate the reality of 600, 000 dead men in a cataclysmic race war. Refusing to monumentalize, disdaining the "final word", the precise "summing up", acknowledging their "poor power to add or detract", his words signal deference to the uncapturability of the life it mourns. It is the deference that moves her, that recognition that language can never live up to life once and for all. Nor should it. Language can never "pin down" slavery, genocide, war. Nor should it yearn for the arrogance to be able to do so. Its force, its felicity is in its reach toward the ineffable.

Be it grand or slender, burrowing, blasting, or refusing to sanctify; whether it laughs out loud or is a cry without an alphabet, the choice word, the chosen silence, unmolested language surges toward knowledge, not its destruction. But who does not know of literature banned because it is interrogative; discredited because it is critical; erased because alternate? And how many are outraged by the thought of a self-ravaged tongue?

Word-work is sublime, she thinks, because it is generative; it makes meaning that secures our difference, our human difference—the way in which we are like no other life.

We die. That may be the meaning of life. But we do language. That may be the measure of our lives.

"Once upon a time, . . . " visitors ask an old woman a question. Who are they, these children? What did they make of that encounter? What did they hear in those final words: "The bird is in your hands"? A sentence that gestures towards possibility or one that drops a latch? Perhaps what the children heard was "It's not my problem. I am old, female, black, blind. What wisdom I have now is in knowing I cannot help you. The future of language is yours."

They stand there. Suppose nothing was in their hands? Suppose the visit was only a ruse, a trick to get to be spoken to, taken seriously as they have not been before? A chance to interrupt, to violate the adult world, its miasma of discourse about them, for them, but never to them? Urgent questions are at stake, including the one they have asked: "Is the bird we hold living or dead?" Perhaps the question meant: "Could someone tell us what is life? What is death?" No trick at all; no silliness. A straightforward question worthy of the attention of a wise one. An old one. And if the old and wise who have lived life and faced death cannot describe either, who can?

But she does not; she keeps her secret; her good opinion of herself; her gnomic pronouncements; her art without commitment. She keeps her distance, enforces it and retreats into the singularity of isolation, in sophisticated, privileged space.

Nothing, no word follows her declaration of transfer. That silence is deep, deeper than the meaning available in the words she has spoken. It shivers, this silence, and the children, annoyed, fill it with language invented on the spot.

"Is there no speech," they ask her, "no words you can give us that helps us break through your dossier of failures? Through the education you have just given us that is no education at all because we are paying close attention to what you have done as well as to what you have said? To the barrier you have erected between generosity and wisdom?

"We have no bird in our hands, living or dead. We have only you and our important question. Is the nothing in our hands something you could not bear to contemplate, to even guess? Don't you remember being young when language was magic without meaning? When what you could say, could not mean? When the invisible was what imagination strove to see? When questions and demands for answers burned so brightly you trembled with fury at not knowing?

"Do we have to begin consciousness with a battle heroines and heroes like you have already fought and lost leaving us with nothing in our hands except what you have imagined is there? Your answer is artful, but its artfulness embarrasses us and ought to embarrass you. Your answer is indecent in its self-congratulation. A made-for-television script that makes no sense if there is nothing in our hands.

"Why didn't you reach out, touch us with your soft fingers, delay the sound bite, the lesson, until you knew who we were? Did you so despise our trick, our modus operandi you could not see that we were baffled about how to get your attention? We are young. Unripe. We have heard all our short lives that we have to be responsible. What could that possibly mean in the catastrophe this world has become; where, as a poet said, "nothing needs to be exposed since it is already barefaced." Our inheritance is an affront. You want us to have your old, blank eyes and see only cruelty and mediocrity. Do you think we are stupid enough to perjure ourselves again and again with the fiction of nationhood? How dare you talk to us of duty when we stand waist deep in the toxin of your past?

"You trivialize us and trivialize the bird that is not in our hands. Is there no context for our lives? No song, no literature, no poem full of vitamins, no history connected to experience that you can pass along to help us start strong? You are an adult. The old one, the wise one. Stop thinking about saving your face. Think of our lives and tell us your particularized world. Make up a story. Narrative is radical, creating us at the very moment it is being created. We will not blame you if your reach exceeds your grasp; if love so ignites your words they go down in flames and nothing is left but their scald. Or if, with the reticence of a surgeon's hands, your words suture only the places where blood might flow. We know you can never do it properly—once and for all. Passion is never enough; neither is skill. But try. For our sake and yours forget your name in the street; tell us what the world has been to you in the dark places and in the light. Don't tell us what to believe, what to fear. Show us belief's wide skirt and the stitch that unravels fear's caul. You, old woman, blessed with blindness, can speak the language that tells us what only language can: how to see without pictures. Language alone protects us from the scariness of things with no names. Language alone is meditation.

"Tell us what it is to be a woman so that we may know what it is to be a man. What moves at the margin. What it is to have no home in this place. To be set adrift from the one you knew. What it is to live at the edge of towns that cannot bear your company.

"Tell us about ships turned away from shorelines at Easter, placenta in a field. Tell us about a wagonload of slaves, how they sang so softly their breath was indistinguishable from the falling snow. How they knew from the hunch of the nearest shoulder that the next stop would be their last. How, with hands prayered in their sex, they thought of heat, then sun. Lifting their faces as though it was there for the taking. Turning as though there for the taking. They stop at an inn. The driver and his mate go in with the lamp leaving them humming in the dark. The horse's void steams into the snow beneath its hooves and its hiss and melt are the envy of the freezing slaves.

"The inn door opens: a girl and a boy step away from its light. They climb into the wagon bed. The boy will have a gun in three years, but now he carries a lamp and a jug of warm cider. They pass it from mouth to mouth. The girl offers bread, pieces of meat and something more: a glance into the eyes of the one she serves. One helping for each man, two for each woman. And a look. They look back. The next stop will be their last. But not this one. This one is warmed."

It's quiet again when the children finish speaking, until the woman breaks into the silence.

"Finally", she says, "I trust you now. I trust you with the bird that is not in your hands because you have truly caught it. Look. How lovely it is, this thing we have done—together."

Note

1. Toni Morrison, Pulitzer Prize Speech, Nobel Lecture, December 7, 1993. From *Nobel Lectures,* Literature 1991–1995, Editor Sture Allén, World Scientific Publishing Co., Singapore, 1997.

Faith Ringgold

Faith Ringgold is an artist, born on October 8, 1930, in Harlem, New York City. She is most known for her painted story quilts. Ringgold's quilts function as a meshing of art, craft, and storytelling that serve educational and activism purposes. Inspired largely by the fabric used at home by her fashion designer mother, Ringgold used the quilt as a space to share her perspective when female voices were not necessarily being heard and when no one would publish her auto-biography. As a result, much of Ringgold's work is permanently housed in collections in several museums—namely, the Solomon R. Guggenheim Museum, the Metropolitan Museum of Art, and the Museum of Modern Art. In addition to her extensive quilt collection, Ringgold has written and illustrated seventeen children's books, the first of which was *Tar Beach*. Ringgold's essay "The 1970s: Is There a Woman's Art?" was included in the collection *We Flew Over the Bridge: The Memoirs of Faith Ringgold* (1995). In "Woman's Art" Ringgold comments on the presence of women's art and Black art within the context of several movements—namely, the feminist movement and the women artist movement. Throughout her explanation, she explores thoughts of artists defining themselves through intersectional approaches. "The concept of making female images as opposed to male, and black images as opposed to white or abstract, was the crux of the issue" that Ringgold interrogated as she explored the question, "Is there a women's art, and if so, what is it?"

The 1970s: Is There a Woman's Art?

Faith Ringgold[1]

At the Art Workers' Coalition, some women had created Women Artists in Revolution (WAR) and they asked me to join and come to meetings, but I didn't have the time. I was too busy with Tom Lloyd and MOMA trying to get a wing for black artists, money allocated to buy black art-ists' works, and black trustees on the museum's board. Trying to get the black man a place in the white art establishment left me no time to consider women's rights. I had thought that my rights came with the black man's. But I was mistaken. Now what was I to do?

I first found out about the Women's Liberation Movement in 1967 from Flo Kennedy, the civil rights lawyer. I had called her to get some names of people to invite to my solo exhibition and she gave me those of Betty Friedan and Ti Grace Atkinson. They were the founding mem-bers of the National Organization for Women (NOW). Betty Friedan was the author of a most provocative book entitled *The Feminine Mystique*, which some felt made her the founder of the movement; and Ti Grace Atkinson, a feminist theorist, had been an art director in a Philadelphia museum. Flo suggested that both could be helpful to me, and further that I should arrange to meet them, join NOW, and get involved with the women's movement. I sent them all invitations to my 1967 show and attempted halfheartedly to reach the two women by phone with no suc-cess. Flo came to my opening with some women from NOW. They were all women's liberation-ists and I admired them that night for looking the part. They carried with them propaganda about the movement: notices of meetings, plans for feminist actions—all of which later came to be called "bra burnings" by the media.

It was not until 1970, however, that I got involved in the women's movement. In this year I became a feminist because I wanted to help my daughters, other women, and myself aspire to something more than a place behind a good man. The "Liberated" Biennale, the Whitney dem-onstrations, and the Flag Show were my first out-from-behind-the-men actions. In the 1960s I had rationalized that we were all fighting for the same issues and why shouldn't the men be in charge? I would be just the brains and the big mouth.

In the 1970s, being black and a feminist was equivalent to being a traitor to the cause of black people. "You seek to divide us," I was told. "Women's Lib is for white women. The black woman is too strong now—she's already liberated." I was constantly challenged: "You want to be liberated—from whom?" But the brothers' rap that was the most double-dealing was the cry that "the black woman's place is behind her man," when frequently white women occupied that position.

In May of 1970, Art Strike was formed out of the AWC. Its purpose, though not stated in quite this way, was to give superstar white male artists a platform for their protests against the war in Cambodia. Robert Morris, then called the "Prince of Peace," had issued an appeal for American artists to withdraw their work from the 1970 Venice Biennale. The purpose of this international exhibition was to display the work of contemporary artists of the "free" (white) world. Each nation chose and sent its own exhibit. In 1970, the Americans selected were Claes Oldenburg, Andy Warhol, Frank Stella, Robert Rauschenberg, Roy Lichtenstein, Jim Dine, and Robert Morris among others—all superstar white male artists.

Organized by Morris, the "Liberated" Venice Biennale was a protest against the war in Cambodia, and more generally against the American government's policies of racism, repression, sexism, and war. This protest exhibition was scheduled to open July 6, 1970, at the School of Visual Arts on West 23rd Street in New York City. I began to fantasize that, since the United States government had not presented in its original Venice selection an unbiased representation of the "fine" art of American artists, then we would now have the chance to rectify their short-sightedness. And, since there was a stated commitment among these powerful superstar white male artists concerning racism and sexism, surely there would be support for a *truly* liberated Venice Biennale. In fact, we could create an "open show," although it soon became sadly clear that that was hardly the intent of the organizers.

When I made this suggestion to the women artists preparing to install the show at the School of Visual Arts, they were aghast. "But there were no women in the original group that withdrew from Venice, and no blacks," they explained to me condescendingly. I explained: "That's because the committee which selected the artists for the Venice Biennale was racist and sexist, and we are not." Well, these women, many of whom had spoken to me at length about feminism and the women's movement, could see nothing politically wrong with presenting the show "as is"—with no women and no blacks. Even though it was the racist and sexist policies of the United States that were being protested, the goverment's prejudices were still dictating the show.

Art Strike took over the AWC, with Morris and the artist Poppy Johnson in charge. Michele was living at home now, attending City College and going to AWC meetings with me. She and I speedily formed an ad hoc group called Women Students and Artists for Black Art Liberation (WSABAL). We were persistent about liberating the "Liberated" Venice Biennale. We made it clear that WSABAL would demonstrate if the show did not include blacks and women. The white women at the AWC, including most of the WAR women, were against us. They didn't seem to understand the real meaning of the feminism they were espousing. Some "girlfriends" of the superstars were verbally abusive and physically threatening to us. We stood toe-to-toe at meetings in open confrontations. One woman became so irate at the prospect of having women and blacks included in the superstars' show that she screamed, "Don't you understand, we can't have that shit in this show!"

"We will demonstrate and close it down if it is not opened to include women and blacks," we responded forcefully. WSABAL was a small group composed of Tom Lloyd, Michele, and myself together with a couple of students from the School of Visual Arts who regularly attended AWC meetings. (The students had had a longstanding battle at the school over special funding for black students and demands for programs and black teachers.)

When we started to prepare a press release on our position, we needed to decide on how many blacks, women, and students should be included in the show. We wanted to prevent them from merely selecting a few token black male artists. "What percentage of women do you think we should demand to be in the show?" I asked Michele. She looked up from her reading and said abruptly and matter-of-factly, "Fifty percent." I was stunned. I had never heard anyone suggest that much equality for women. She was so young, not yet eighteen, and we had been through so much recently with Mexico and Barbara's tumultuous last year at high school. Maybe she was under a strain, maybe she just hadn't heard me right, or I hadn't heard her right. I asked again, "What percentage for the show . . . I mean of women?" This time I listened more closely. Michele looked up and, raising her voice, looked me dead in the eye. She repeated herself, "Fifty percent women, and fifty percent of those women have to be black and twenty-five percent have to be students." Well, the numbers game began. There were now all kinds of jokes over our percentage demands. The point, however, was made. We were talking here about real equality. After all, this was the way racism had worked all these years with percentages and quotas. Maybe we could now work it to our advantage.

All hell broke loose just before the show was to open. Brenda Miller, one of the women artists against the revised show, kidnapped the original show and took it to her loft in New York's Westbeth. (There was a secret plan to take the show to Washington, D.C., to open at the Corcoran Gallery, and the arrangements had been made with Walter Hopps, the director of the Corcoran.) But Morris, again in his role as Prince of Peace, got the show back in time for our opening. The liberated Liberated Venice Biennale was open to all who wanted to participate. The exhibition began on July 22, 1970, in the newly painted loft space of "Museum," the meeting place of AWC and Art Strike. The show consisted of more than fifty percent women and included more black artists, students, and political poster artists than any other "Biennale" before or since. However, some of the superstar artists and their dealers felt that the show was fraught with too much confusion and decided to withdraw. They included Claes Oldenburg, Richard Anuszkiewicz, Ernest Trova, Nicholas Krushenick, and Adja Yunkers. The ones remaining were Andy Warhol, Carl Andre, Frank Stella, Robert Rauschenberg, Roy Lichtenstein, Vincent Longo, Leonard Baskin, Jim Dine, Sam Francis, Robert Birmelin, Michael Mazur, Deen Meeker, Sal Romano, and, of course, Bob Morris.

Within a few weeks' time the show ended abruptly. As the story goes, one of the women artists enticed Bobby, the night watchman at Museum, into the back room under the ruse that they were going to make passionate love together—which, if you had known Bobby, you would know how funny that was. After she detained Bobby long enough for her women accomplices to get four works by the show's superstars out of the gallery, she released Bobby, leaving him "high," which he was all the time anyway, and "dry." The paintings were retrieved, again by Morris with the assistance of Carl Andre. They took the works back to Castelli and to the other galleries that had loaned them. The show was over. Security had been broken. And Bobby split.

In the fall of 1970 Poppy Johnson and Lucy Lippard formed an ad hoc women's group to protest the small percentage of women in all past Whitney Annuals. I was asked to join and I agreed. I was excited about the prospect of black women artists being included in the Whitney Annual. Our goal for the 1970 Annual was fifty percent women: Michele's equality percentage for women in the art world had caught on.

The corridors and galleries of the Whitney Museum became the focus of our attention. We went there often to deposit eggs. Unsuspecting male curatorial staff would pick up the eggs and experience the shock of having raw eggs slide down the pants of their fine tailor-made suits. I made hard-boiled eggs, painted them black, and wrote "50 percent" on them in red paint. I didn't want to waste food. They could eat my black eggs. Sanitary napkins followed. These upset the female staff as well as the men. Generally, everywhere the staff went they found loud and clear messages that women artists were on the Whitney's "case."

The Whitney Annual that year was to be a sculpture show. I was not making sculpture yet, and there were only a few black women sculptors in the country who were known. Elizabeth Catlett and Selma Burke were well-known figurative sculptors. Elizabeth Catlett was my all-time favorite but, because of the Whitney's well-known preference for abstract art, Catlett's prospects waned. Selma Burke was eliminated by a false report by one of the curators that she was dead. Instead, Betye Saar and Barbara Chase-Riboud were cited, whose work was more in line with the Whitney's taste. So they were the ones I unconditionally demanded to be in the show. Saar and Chase-Riboud became the first black women to be in the Whitney Annual; more to the point, they were the first black women ever to be exhibited at the Whitney Museum of American Art. The total percentage of women in the Whitney Annual in 1970 was twenty-three percent — as opposed to the previous years' averages of five to ten percent. This was better than ten percent, but it still wasn't fifty.

We decided to demonstrate during the opening to make that point. We had to get our demonstrators inside, since the opening was by invitation only, so we printed fake tickets and distributed them outside the museum on the night of the opening to anyone who wanted to demonstrate. A guard with an ultraviolet detector confiscated over a hundred forged tickets; nevertheless, we got in a lot of people. Once inside, we mingled with the crowd. Museum officials knew something was afoot as rumors began to spread that there was to be a demonstration that night. One of the trustees of the museum who was on our side, for whatever reason, was concerned that we would not be able to round up the women demonstrators, since everyone was all over the place, drinks in hand (the Whitney had free booze in those days), chatting and locating the art of friends (Louise Bourgeois was in the show) or talking to the other exhibiting artists. I assured him that we would be fine, and that everybody would know when and where the demonstration was happening, even though the show was spread out on the museum's three floors. What I didn't tell him was that we planned to blow police whistles to signal the start of our actions.

Although they supplied us with tickets to enter the museum, the white men in the show did not join our demonstration. (There were no black men there I could approach.) However, the fashionable Whitney art-going crowd was eager to witness our action. They had heard of "sit-ins" and now they were going to see one for themselves. At a predetermined time, Lucy Lippard and I began to blow our whistles. The women came toward the center of the main gallery on the second floor. We continued to blow. The people gathered around us and we formed a big circle sitting on the floor. Then we got up and walked around chanting, "Fifty percent women, fifty percent women." We pulled it off. The crowd was sympathetic, and the event satisfied our need to protest. The trustee I had spoken with seemed pleased that it happened.

Throughout the show we demonstrated every weekend, blowing our police whistles and singing off-key. Barbara and Michele, who were with me at these demonstrations, had suggested that we sing off-key intentionally. However astute their own ears (they are both musical, probably a talent inherited from Earl), intentional off-key singing was bearable to them, and natural to most of us. Barbara made up catchy tunes on the spot, and everybody joined in. "The Whitney is a helluva place, parlez-vous. The Whitney is a helluva place, parlez-vous. They're down on women and they're down on race, a honky donkey, parlez-vous." Flo Kennedy joined our line one Saturday and was quite at home, singing off-key and making music with police whistles.

The women artists' movement in New York was on its way. There was now a plethora of panels and statements being made concerning women's art and culture. Artists and other folk, both male and female, were beginning to demand explanations of the women's art movement. "Is there a women's art, and if so, what is it?" was the constant question posed to us. The concept of making female images as opposed to male, and black images as opposed to white or abstract, was the crux of the issue. "Who needs all this talk about black art and women's art?" some artists would say. "I'm just an artist who happens to be black or a woman." It was a real challenge to try to define oneself and one's art outside the narrow parameters of the mainstream art world. But we were doing this and it felt good.

Note

1. Faith Ringgold, *We Flew Over the Bridge: The Memoirs of Faith Ringgold* (Durham, NC: Duke University Press, 2005), pp. 175–180 (for artist statement and images).

Suzan-Lori Parks

Suzan-Lori Parks was born May 10, 1963 in Fort Knox, Kentucky, to a military family. She spent her early life living in a number of places, including being stationed in Germany for a period. She credits this diverse upbringing, as well as her undergraduate years at Mount Holyoke College, with influencing the accomplished writer she would ultimately become. She has received a number of notable awards. She is the first African American woman to receive the Pulitzer Prize for Drama. She received the MacArthur "Genius" Award and the Gish Prize for Excellence in the Arts. She has received a number of grants and fellowships, including from the National Endowment for the Arts, the Rockefeller Foundation, the Ford Foundation, the New York State Council on the Arts, and the New York Foundation for the Arts, and a Guggenheim Foundation Grant. The essay included in this section, written in spoken word style, is a think piece on the rhetorical work of black drama. By interrogating what a black play is, and for that matter what it is not, Parks helps the audience to know the purposes and diversity of black theater, and what audiences refer to as "the black play."

New Black Math

Suzan-Lori Parks

10 years after writing the essay "the equation for black people on stage" Im standing at the same crossroads asking the same questions. No sweat. Sometimes you can walk a hundred miles and end up in the same spot. The world ain't round for nothing, right? What is a black play? The definition is housed in the reality of two things that occurred recently and almost simultaneously: 26 August 05, playwright scholar poet-king August Wilson announces he is dying of cancer, and hurricane Katrina devastates the Gulf Coast. It feels like judgment day. What Im talking about today is the same and different. I was tidy back then. And now Im tidier. Tidier today like a tidal wave.

What is a black play?

A black play is angry.

A black play is fierce.

A black play is double voiced but rarely confused.

A black play got style.

A black play is of the people by the people and for the people.

A black play is smooth but not slick, heavy but not thick, cant be tamed, often does not comb its hair, wipes its mouth with the back of its black hand or with a linen napkin whichever is more readily available.

A black play is late.

A black play is RIGHT ON and RIGHT ON TIME.

A black play is deep.

A black play is armed/to the teeth.

A black play bows to god then rows the boat ashore.

A black play makes do if it got to/fights/screams/sings/dreams/WORKS IT/talks in code and tells it like it is ALL UP IN YA FACE.

A black play gives you five.

A black play is robust and alive.

A black play is in the house and looking *good*, too.

A black play is *bad* motherfucker.

A black play does not exist.

Every play is a black play.

SAY WHAT?

A black play is a white play when the lights go out.

A black play is a white play when you read between the lines.

A black play got its picture on the wall of your local post office.

A black play got its butt on death row for a crime it perhaps did not commit.

A black play got its black butt in the whitehouse, seated at the right hand of the man.

A black play keeps you up at night.

A black play is awake.

A black play gonna kick your ass.

A black play has genitals that people think about long after curtain comes down.

A black play is running for president.

A black play gotta get out the vote.

A black play is a leader, but seldom an elected official.

A black play as a child wondered why, if Jesse Owens won all them gold medals, then how come a black man couldn't beat a white man in a presidential race?

A black play is in the streets.

A black play aint no negro.

A black play is a nigger.

A black play is buck wild.

A black play is mixed.

A black play is on broadway, the great white way.

A black play is not on broadway, and furthermore, aint studying no broadway.

A black play is coming soon to a theatre near you.

A black play got a fro.

A black play know the know.

A black play go toe to toe, all the way out the do.

A black play gonna burn that m-f down, Monday-Friday and twice on the weekends.

A black play is chronic.

A black play takes into account that pollsters have found that black folks dont attend the theatres in numbers large enough to influence the selection of plays produced.

A black play is very intellectual.

A black play has studied, conducts discourse, and, on certain days of the week, can be found living in the big house of tradition.

A black play got a mission.

A black play dreams the impossible dream.

A black play is such things as dreams are made on.

A black play was the first black play ever to be written and will be the last black play standing.

A black play takes shape just outside the reaches of your white understanding, no matter what your color, baby.

A black play aint for you.

A black play aint about you.

A black play aint integrated and don't want to be.

A black play aint playing.

A black play knows that when audiences read it primarily through the rubric of "race relations," that those audiences are suffering from an acute attack of white narcissism. (If you have a need to see yourself reflected in things that are not directly about you, then you are one of the afflicted.)

A black play dont give a shit what you think.

A black play knows all about the black hole and the great hole of history and aint afraid of going there.

A black play sometimes puts its foot in its mouth, but, hell, a black play sometimes gots mouths to feed and shoe leather tastes like chicken when yr HONGRY.

A black play wants to know where HARRIET TUBMAN stay at?

A black play fights the power.

A black play wants to uplift the race.

A black play just might set the race back 10 years.

A black play is not political—that term don't even begin to approach its complexity, especially these days, dog.

A black play knows how to play the game.

A black play IZ.

A black play in the united states of america was ripped from the bosom of its motherland, caught by the man or sold down river by its brothers, crossed the atlantic in chains, had its gods smashed to bits and pieces, was handed Jesus as a pacifier (later, when Jesus wasn't working so good, welfare came into play), had its language ripped out its mouth, its family torn asunder— all this and more and a black play is still expected to play by the rules, is still expected to be interested in what the other deems interesting and valid and valued. HOW MUCH OF THAT SHIT CAN I BUY WITH FOODSTAMPS? Or, said another way: I PAY FIRST CLASS TAXES HOW COME I GET SECOND CLASS SERVICE? A black play aint playing your game, it might look like it's playing your game, but if it looks like that to you, then that just means you been played, honey.

A black play KNOWS what time it is.

A black play aint gonna give you the time of day.

A black play kicks a man when he's down, eats its own, has a faith in the system which is less a function of trust than confusion and fatigue, waits for the man to shape up his ship, in short makes all the mistakes of a great people fallen on hard times and working on getting they game back.

A black play is the feel good show of the century.

A black play is the blues.

A black play dont forget that in the 1980s mtv didnt want colored faces on its airwaves.

A black play dont forget the numerous hard times back in the olden days and the numerous hard times going on right now.

A black play keeps on keeping on.

A black play asks, where MARTIN and MALCOLM stay at?

A black play gets down.

A black play is old.

A black play is just getting started.

A black play asks, where MR. JAMES BALDWIN stay at?

A black play asks, where SATCHEL PAIGE and SON HOUSE and MEMPHIS MINNIE and GEORGE WASHINGTON CARVER and all them stay at?

A black play is often characterized by healthy doses of word play such as "snaps" and "yo Mamma" jokes.

A black play takes you to the bridge.

The Bridge

A black play by Suzan-Lori Parks

Characters: MOMMA, an older woman, and YO, her husband.

Setting: they sit atop their house which is under 20 feet of water. Helicopters from the National Guard in the near distance are about to perform a heroic rescue of our characters, but first:

YO: We just made the last payment on this house, too.
MOMMA: Yo, sometimes it be's that way sometimes.
YO: Everything we own is washed away.
MOMMA: Bank owned the house, then us.
YO: Now the flood owns everything, looks like.
MAMMA: You know it, Yo.
YO
MAMMA
(rest)
YO: How can you tell a nigger thats crazy from a nigger that aint crazy?
MAMMA: I don't know. How *can* you tell a nigger that's crazy from a nigger that aint crazy?
YO: The crazy nigger is the nigger that aint crazy.

Curtain

A black play is black.
   A black play is asked to explain itself.
   A black play is tempted to expose itself.
   The black play got a message.
   A black play knows the real deal.
   A black play is told that it is about race and a black play knows it's really about other shit.
   A black play knows that racerelations sell.
   A black play knows that racerelations are a holding cell.
   A black play is blacker than my new black cat, Houndog, named after Houndog Taylor, the blues guitarist, who is also a polydactyl brother.
   A black play is blacker than black.
   A black play is written by a black person.
   A black play has black actors.
   A black play is written by a white person and has white actors.
   A black play doesnt have anything to do with black people. Im saying *The Glass Menagerie* is a black play.
   SAY WHAT?
   EXCUSE ME?!?!
Cause the presence of the white suggests the presence of the black. Every play that is born of the united states of america is a black play because we all exist in the shadow of slavery. All of us. *The Iceman Cometh* is a black play. *Angels in America* is a black play and Kushner knows he's a brother. Its all black.

The Intermission

What in God's name are we gonna do to help our brothers and sisters get to the promised land in this lifetime? I know it's not fashionable to ask these questions. I know it's not fashionable to suggest that we have some housekeeping to do. I know it's uncool to suggest that we got to do something other than lay our problems on the doorstep of the man. I know it's unhip to confront our own trip but what should we do? Wait for the man to clean HIS house? Oh please.

   Sister on the Street: How did this essay about black theatre turn into a diatribe?
   Brother on the Corner (shouting from the sidelines): What you know about diatribe? You don'
      know what a diatribe is, yr just talking "diatribe" so she'll put you in her essay.

Sister on the Street: And me being in her essay's gonna be the end of your world? Sides, she's got a point. We gotta take more responsibility. We gotta quit waiting on the man. Tomorrow is always a new day dawning, but dont it often smell of the Same Old Shit?

Brother on the Corner: SOS! Im with you on that!

Sister on the Street: If you waiting on the man you gonna be waiting all your life.

Brother on the Corner: Plus in your next life too, dont forget about *karma* and shit.

Sister on the Street: People wanna be free but they spend their entire existence waiting on the man.

Brother on the Corner: Instead of breaking FREE and leading a whole lot of people to FREE-DOM with them.

Sister on the Street: Damn right.

Black Playwright: Either of you two got some change? My cellphone dont work around here and I need to use the payphone. Im putting in a call to Harriet Tubman. Im putting in a call to Nat Turner. Im calling up John Brown and Fredrick Douglass and Ms. Sojourner Truth. They are still here. Cause when they died they MULTIPLIED. Operator? We gotta crack the heart wide open cause when it healed up last time it healed up wrong, crack it open and reset it, heal it right. Crack the mind wide open cause when it healed up, our thoughts healed up wrong.

Brother on the Corner (rest): Do she know that pay phone don't work?

Sister on the Street: Yeah, she knows.

Black Playwright: Audiences still ask "what do black people think about such and such?" Black people think the world is fucked. Thats what black people think. Black people dont always use apostrophes neither. Black people took the rallying cry "burn baby burn" and turned it into the chorus of "Disco Inferno" and some of us danced all the way to the bank, thats what black people think. Black people know there is a war going on against our blackness and somehow we've been enlisted to fight on the front lines.

Brother on the Corner: Whats she talking about now?

Sister on the Street: A black play.

Brother on the Corner: Go ahead, girl.

End of Intermission

A black play fights the power.

A black play sometimes does not make it to the page or stage and consists of just some high-powered thoughts going on inside the bright blackness of yr head.

A black play is doctor heal-good cause theatre is a healing thing.

A black play gives us a role to play and, when someone steps into that role, the rest of us got someone like us to look at. Seeing yrself mirrored is a basic component of healthy psychological development. Im not talking about creating a series of model behaviors, but roles, like the roles in the passion play—you know what a passion play is—like when they reenact the journey of Christ on easter and the town gathers to watch an actor go through his moments as he carries his cross up the hill & c. So the black playwright gives us a role. Because it is in having a role that we have an opportunity to imaginatively participate. And it is through participation that we work out the demons.

A black play is a poem, like a life is a poem, like the bible is a poem, like the bhagavad-gita is a poem, a "song of god," "no effort is ever wasted," it says and "you have rights to your actions but not rights to the fruits of your actions," it says. The charioteer opens his mouth and shows us that he is the infinite.

A black play embraces the infinite.

A black play is . . . August Wilson. 2 Oct 2005: He died today.

A black play asks, where MR. AUGUST WILSON stay at?

A black play is not ignorant of history, but neither is the play history's slave.

A black play is tragic.

A black play is funny as hell.

A black play has contempt for the other. And love too.

A black play is currently studying how such a love and such a contempt can coexist in the same heart, in the same breath.

A black play plays well in countries where there are no "black" people—and yet, helps those in those countries to identify themselves as "black."

A black play employs the black not just as a subject, but as a platform, eye and telescope through which it intercourses with the cosmos.

A black play has at least one panther in it.

A black play recognizes the importance of the evidence of things unseen.

A black play is too much.

A black play can take you there.

A black play is simple.

A black play is COMPLICATED.

A black play is ALL THAT.

A black play is a piece of work.

A black play is worth the price of admission.

A black play is free.

PEACE

And

POWER

To the PEOPLE.

Section 12: Further Reading

Bearden, Romare and Harry Henderson, *A History of African-American Artists. From 1792 to the Present.* New York: Pantheon Books, 1993.

Copeland, Misty. *Life in Motion: An Unlikely Ballerina.* New York: Touchstone, 2014.

Dorsey, Thomas A. III and Alphonso Simpson. *Living the Life I Sing: Gospel Music from the Dorsey Era to the Millennium.* San Diego: Cognella, Inc., 2017.

Howard, Sheena and Ronald Jackson. *Black Comics: Politics of Race and Representation.* New York: Bloomsbury Academic, 2013.

Neal, Larry. "Black Art and Black Liberation." *Ebony Magazine, 24* (10): 54 (1969).

Southern, Eileen. *The Music of Black Americans: A History.* W. W. Norton & Company, 1997.

Section 12: Discussion Questions

1. What do you make of the repeated rhetorical move of enslaved rhetors to apologize for the limitations of their narratives and to offer an explanation for the questioning of their integrity?

2. In what ways do the pieces in this section project an argument about Black artistry? Locate and discuss concrete examples throughout the section.

3.   Metaphor is a common trope in African American rhetoric. Locate some uses in this section and offer an analysis for why this particular tool was employed and to what end.

4.   What do you understand the meaning behind Blues People to be, and how might that understanding be part of a larger argument about the lived experiences of Black people?

5.   Elaborate on Faith Ringgold's discussion of the intersectional dynamic of being a Black woman and an artist. Do you see evidence of this conversation in the work of other artists in this section? If so, locate examples.

INDEX

Page numbers for figures are in italics, and page numbers for tables are in bold.